Legacies of the International Criminal Tribunal for the Former Yugoslavia

Legacies of the International Criminal Tribunal for the Former Yugoslavia

A Multidisciplinary Approach

Edited by

CARSTEN STAHN

CARMEL AGIUS

SERGE BRAMMERTZ

COLLEEN ROHAN

Assistant Editor

RAFAEL BRAGA DA SILVA

OXFORD

UNIVERSITY PRESS

OXFORD
UNIVERSITY PRESS

Great Clarendon Street, Oxford, OX2 6DP,
United Kingdom

Oxford University Press is a department of the University of Oxford.
It furthers the University's objective of excellence in research, scholarship,
and education by publishing worldwide. Oxford is a registered trade mark of
Oxford University Press in the UK and in certain other countries

First Edition published in 2020
Impression: 1

Published in the United States of America by Oxford University Press
198 Madison Avenue, New York, NY 10016, United States of America

British Library Cataloguing in Publication Data
Data available

Library of Congress Control Number: 2019955605

ISBN 978–0–19–886295–6

Printed and bound by
CPI Group (UK) Ltd, Croydon, CR0 4YY

Foreword
By the UN SECRETARY-GENERAL

The creation of the International Criminal Tribunal for the former Yugoslavia in 1993 was a landmark development for justice for the people of the region. In creating the first-ever criminal Tribunal within the United Nations, the international community demonstrated a strong commitment to the principle that those responsible for perpetrating the most serious crimes of international concern should be held accountable for their actions.

The Tribunal went on to pioneer the creation of the contemporary architecture of international criminal justice, and has also inspired prosecutions and trials for international crimes at the domestic level. Moreover, it has pushed international expectations of accountability well beyond what was anticipated in 1993, transforming how we speak about and address situations in which serious international crimes are committed. We see this in the statements of Heads of State, in the work of journalists, and in public opinion. Impunity is no longer an option.

Ninety individuals, including senior political and military figures, were sentenced by the Tribunal for their crimes, including genocide, war crimes, and crimes against humanity. The Tribunal sat for more than 10,000 days of trial and heard testimony from nearly 5,000 people. Survivors and witnesses—men, women, and children who had experienced atrocious violence and tragic losses—refused to stay silent, and came to the Tribunal to tell their stories in court, to place their experiences on the record, and to see the perpetrators of crimes held accountable. It is because of the courage of these witnesses that the Tribunal leaves behind one of its most important legacies: the vast archival records documenting the horrors that occurred. These records ensure that the world will not forget that history cannot be rewritten and that the victims' voices will continue to resound down the decades.

Accepting the undeniable truth and facts of past tragedies is crucial for peace, truth, and reconciliation and for building a better future. This book is an important contribution to that goal, as well as a tribute to those who served the Tribunal, to whom we should all be deeply grateful.

António Guterres
New York
April 2020

Preface and Acknowledgements

The International Criminal Tribunal for the former Yugoslavia (ICTY) closed its operations on 31 December 2017, almost a quarter of a century after its creation. It was established while the conflict in the Balkans was ongoing. Its mandate covered the entire territory of the former Yugoslavia. The Tribunal was established to judge the responsibilities of individuals, not peoples. It had to 'learn by doing', establish working practices, and build a common institutional culture across Chambers, the Prosecution, Registry, and the Defence.

Looking back, the ICTY stands as a turning point in international criminal justice. It marked not only a test for the newly invigorated UN collective security system and cooperation among UN members, but has also started to shape the identity of the field relatively early. Many of the rulings of the first decade, such as *Tadić*, *Furundžija*, *Kunarac*, or *Galić*, have nowadays become 'classics' of international law. The fact that ICTY jurisprudence, procedures, and experiences are applied by other international courts and in domestic contexts, sometimes even beyond the criminal field, mark an important aspect of legacy.

However, legacies cannot be reduced to law. The Tribunal's experiences are much richer. They include not only criminal investigation, fair trials, and punishment, but less visible institutional practices, human interactions, and efforts to reach audiences. Many challenges continue beyond the lifespan of the Tribunal: maintaining peace, facilitating cross-community engagement with uncomfortable truths, combating stereotypes, preserving the dignity and well-being of witnesses, victims, and survivors, dealing with outstanding cases or enforcement of sentences, or strengthening accountability in the region more broadly.

As UN Secretary-General António Guterres noted at the ICTY closing ceremony in The Hague in December 2017, some acts of violence, such as destruction of the library in Sarajevo, may be viewed as a form of 'memoricide', that is, an attempt to 'erase the past'. The ICTY stands as a symbol to counter destruction of memory and the past. Through its records, archives, and testimonies, it keeps facts and events alive, and is at the same time transforming history. This dual perspective is reflected in the cover image of the book. It shows Vedran Smailović, the former principal cellist of the opera of Sarajevo (also known as the 'Cellist of Sarajevo'), playing on the ruins of the library, following its destruction during the siege of the city.

This volume is meant to stimulate ongoing conversation on the multiple dimensions of ICTY legacy, including approaches towards legacy itself. It includes accounts by insiders, who have shaped, lived, or experienced the work of the Tribunal, as well as external experts, who place practices in perspective or provide theoretical groundwork to understand legacies. It covers lesser well-known aspects of legacy, such as unexpected impacts on civil litigation, investigative lessons, defence and fair trial legacies, witness experiences, practices relating to interpretation and translation, judgement drafting, outreach or sentencing, as well as debates on societal reception and non-judicial legacies. The aim is not to glorify achievements or to pass definite judgement, but to invite further dialogue.

The idea for this book, and its multidisciplinary orientation, goes back to the ICTY Legacy Dialogues Conference, held in Sarajevo in June 2017. It approached legacy from different angles: normative or moral standpoints, operational and procedural dimensions, and historical and non-judicial perspectives. This approach is reflected in the contributions assembled here. They rely partly on discussions at the Sarajevo conference, the ICTY Legacy Dialogues, and the final ICTY symposium, hosted by the Grotius Centre for International Legal Studies in The Hague. They are complemented by additional scholarly voices who agreed to contribute.

We wish to thank all contributors for their collaboration, patience, and dedication to this project. Without their care, diligence, and openness to share experiences and fresh insights, this project would not have been possible.

Special thanks are owed to the members of the former ICTY Legacy Coordination Committee, including Chef de Cabinet Ana Cristina Rodriguez Pineda and Head of Communications Nenad Golčevski. Their work has laid the foundations for this volume. The publication process was supported by the exemplary assistance of our Assistant Editor, Rafael Braga da Silva, and the excellent editorial support of Leiden alumni, Hannah Wilson, Rita Maria Grajeda Diaz, and Justyna Niemczyk who served as interns at the Tribunal.

We wish to express our gratitude to the UN Secretary-General and the UN Office of Legal Affairs, including Legal Counsel Miguel de Serpa Soares and his team, for their warm support for this project and their commitment to the work of the ICTY and the International Residual Mechanism for Criminal Tribunals. Their voices add an invaluable UN perspective to ICTY experiences.

Finally, we would like to thank the wonderful team at OUP, including Merel Alstein and Jack McNichol, for making this book a reality, and photographer Kemal Hadžić, for allowing us to use the image of the 'Cellist of Sarajevo' for the cover.

We hope that this volume will provide novel insights and facilitate ongoing dialogue on the experiences and lessons of the ICTY in the years and decades to come.

The Editors
April 2020

Table of Contents

PART II LEGACY LENSES, THEORIZATIONS, AND NARRATIVES

PART III EXPRESSIVE PRACTICES, JUDICIAL RECORD, HISTORY, AND TRUTH

PART V CRIMINAL PROCEDURE, COURT MANAGEMENT, AND OUTREACH

PART VII IMPACT ON DOMESTIC LEGAL SYSTEMS

PART VIII SOCIETAL IMPACT, RECEPTION, AND GAPS

Table of Cases

ARBITRAL TRIBUNALS

DOMESTIC CASES

Australia

Bosnia and Herezgovina

Canada

EUROPEAN COURT OF HUMAN RIGHTS

EXTRAORDINARY CHAMBERS IN THE COURTS OF CAMBODIA

HUMAN RIGHTS CHAMBER FOR BOSNIA AND HERZEGOVINA

INTERNATIONAL COURT OF JUSTICE

INTERNATIONAL CRIMINAL COURT

INTERNATIONAL CRIMINAL TRIBUNAL FOR THE FORMER YUGOSLAVIA

Enver Hadžihasanović and Amir Kubura

Fatmir Limaj et al

Florence Hartmann

Gojko Janković and Radovan Stanković

Goran Jelisić

Goran Hadžić

Hazim Delić

Miroslav Kvočka et al

Mitar Rašević and Savo Todović

Mitar Vasiljević

Mladen Naletilić and Vinko Martinović

Mlado Radić

Momčilo Krajišnik

Momčilo Perišić

Momir Nikolić

Naser Orić

Nikola Šainović et al

Pavle Strugar

Predrag Banović

Radislav Krstić

Radomir Kovač

Radoslav Brđanin

Radovan Karadžić

Ramush Haradinaj et al

Ranko Češić

Stanislav Galić

Stevan Todorović

Stjepan Šešelj et al

Tihomir Blaškić

Vidoje Blagojević and Dragan Jokić

Vladimir Kovačević

Vlastimir Đorđević

Vojislav Šešelj

Vujadin Popović et al

Zeljko Mejakić et al

Zdravko Mucić et al

Zdravko Tolimir

Zlatko Aleksovski

Zoran Kupreškić et al

Zoran Žigić et al

INTERNATIONAL CRIMINAL TRIBUNAL FOR RWANDA

Augustin Ndindiliyimana et al

Clément Kayishema and Obed Ruzindana

Eliézer Niyitegeka

Ferdinand Nahimana et al

GAA

Table of Legislation

INTERNATIONAL INSTRUMENTS

Bilateral and Multilateral Agreement

General Treaties

European Parliament

Extraordinary Chambers in the Courts of Cambodia

International Court of Justice

International Criminal Court

International Criminal Tribunal for the Former Yugoslavia

NATIONAL INSTRUMENTS

Bosnia and Herzegovina

Canada

Croatia

France

Germany

Italy

Kosovo

Lebanon

United Kingdom

United States of America

List of Abbreviations

ABA	American Bar Association
ABiH	Bosnian Army
ADC	Association of Defence Counsel
AFP	*Agence France Press*
AIC	Akaike Information Criterion
AMT	American Military Tribunals
ARBiH	Army of the Republic of Bosnia and Herzegovina
ASEAN	Association of Southeast Asian Nations
ATS	Alien Tort Statute
BBC	British Broadcasting Corporation
BCS	Bosnian, Croatian, and Serb
BiH	Bosnia and Herzegovina
CBC	Canadian Broadcasting Corporation
CC	Criminal Code
CC BiH	Criminal Code of Bosnia and Herzegovina
CC SFRY	Criminal Code of the Socialist Federal Republic of Yugoslavia
CIU	Conference Interpretation Unit
CLSS	Conference and Language Service Section
CMSS	Court Management and Support Section
CPC	Criminal Procedure Code
DNA	Deoxyribonucleic acid
DVU	Document and Video Unit
ECCC	Extraordinary Chambers in the Courts of Cambodia
ECHR	European Convention on Human Rights and Fundamental Freedoms
ELSA	European Law Students Association
ETU	English Translation Unit
EU	European Union
EULEX	European Union Rule of Law Mission
EUROCLIO	Association of European History Teachers
FARC	Revolutionary Armed Forces of Colombia
FBiH	Federation of Bosnia and Herzegovina
FRY	Federal Republic of Yugoslavia
FTU	French Translation Unit
FYROM	Former Yugoslav Republic of Macedonia
HCHR-RS	Helsinki Committee for Human Rights in Republika Srpska
HDZ	Croatian Democratic Union
HLC	Humanitarian Law Center
HRW	Human Rights Watch
HVO	Bosnian Croat Army/Croatian Defence Council
ICC	International Criminal Court
ICCBA	International Criminal Court Bar Association
ICCPR	International Covenant on Civil and Political Rights

ICJ	International Court of Justice
ICL	International Criminal Law
ICMP	International Commission for Missing Persons
ICT	International Criminal Tribunal
ICTJ	International Center for Transitional Justice
ICTR	International Criminal Tribunal for Rwanda
ICTY	International Criminal Tribunal for the former Yugoslavia
IFOR	Implementation Force
IHL	International Humanitarian Law
IIIM	International, Impartial and Independent Mechanism
IMT	International Military Tribunal
IMTFE	International Military Tribunal for the Far East
IRMCT	International Residual Mechanism for Criminal Tribunals
JCE	Joint Criminal Enterprise
JNA	Yugoslav People's Army
KLA	Kosovo Liberation Army
KSC	Kosovo Specialist Chambers
LoPW	Law on Protection of Witnesses Under Threat and Vulnerable Witnesses
LoTC	Law on the Transfer of Cases
MICT	International Residual Mechanism for Criminal Tribunals
MNI	Minimum Number of individuals
mtDNA	mitochondria DNA
NATO	North Atlantic Treaty Organization
NCIS	Naval Criminal Investigations Service
NGO	Non-governmental Organization
NMT	Nuremberg Military Tribunal
NPR	National Public Radio
NSC	National Security Council
NWCS	National War Crimes Strategy
ODIHR	Office for Democratic Institutions and Human Rights
OED	Oxford English Dictionary
OHCHR	Office of the UN High Commissioner for Human Rights
OHR	Office of the High Representative
OLAD	Office for Legal Aid and Defence Matters
OSCE	Organization for Security and Co-operation in Europe
OTP	Office of the Prosecutor
PCR	Polymerase Chain Reaction
PHR	Physicians for Human Rights
PO BiH	Prosecutor's Office of BiH
PTG	Post-traumatic Growth
RAI	*Radio Televisione Italiana*
RBiH	Republic of Bosnia and Herzegovina
RFA	Requests for Assistance
RPE	Rules of Procedure and Evidence
RPF	Rwandan Patriotic Front
RS	Republika Srpska
SC	State Court
SCBiH	State court of Bosnia and Herzegovina
SCSL	Special Court for Sierra Leone
SDA	Party for Democratic Action

SDS	Serbian Democratic Party
SENSE	South East News Service Europe
SFRY	Socialist Federal Republic of Yugoslavia
SOP	Standard Operating Procedure
SPSC	Special Panel for Serious Crimes
STIF	European Union Special Investigative Task Force
STL	Special Tribunal for Lebanon
STR	Short Tandem Repeats
TJ	Transitional Justice
UN	United Nations
UNDP	United Nations Development Programme
UNICEF	United Nations Children's Fund
UNICRI	United Nations Interregional Crime and Justice Research Institute
UNITAD	United Nations Investigative Team to Promote Accountability for crimes committed by Da'esh
UNSC	United Nations Security Council
VRS	Bosnian Serb Army
VWS	Victims and Witness section
WA	Witness Assistants
WCPO	Office of the War Crimes Prosecutor
YIHR	Youth Initiative for Human Rights
YOP	Youth Outreach Project

List of Contributors

Carmel Agius is the current President of the International Residual Mechanism for Criminal Tribunals. He was the last President of the ICTY.

Marina Aksenova is a Professor of Comparative and International Criminal Law at IE University in Madrid.

Rosa Aloisi is an Associate Professor in the Department of Political Science, Trinity University.

Andy Aydın-Aitchison is Senior Lecturer in Criminology at the School of Law, University of Edinburgh, Scotland, where he teaches on the MSc Global Crime, Justice and Security. He holds a PhD from Cardiff University (2008). He is author of Making the Transition (Intersentia, 2011), a detailed account of police, court, and prison reforms in the context of the first ten years of post-war State building in Bosnia and Herzegovina.

Aldo Zammit Borda has a PhD from the Trinity College Dublin. He also is a Senior Lecturer in Public International Law, the Anglia Ruskin University, Cambridge.

Rafael Braga da Silva is an Attorney at Law. He holds a LL.M. from University for Peace and United Nations Interregional Criminal and Justice Research Institute (UNICRI). He also holds a LL.M. Adv. Studies in Public International Law *cum laude*, from the Grotius Centre for International Legal Studies, Leiden University.

Serge Brammertz is the current Chief Prosecutor of the International Residual Mechanism for Criminal Tribunals. Formerly, Chief Prosecutor of the International Criminal Tribunal for the former Yugoslavia.

Kei Hannah Brodersen is a PhD Candidate in the Department of Criminal Law and Criminology of the Faculty of Law in Maastricht University.

Janine Natalya Clark is a Professor of Gender, Transitional Justice and International Criminal Law at the Birmingham Law School.

Tatjana Dawson is the current Coordinator of the Responsible Behaviour Unit at the Artsen zonder Grenzen Nederland.

Margaret M. deGuzman is a James E. Beasley Professor of Law at Temple University Beasley School of Law. Professor deGuzman served as a law clerk in the Office of the Prosecutor of the International Criminal Tribunal for former Yugoslavia and as a legal adviser to the Republic of Senegal at the Rome Conference on the International Criminal Court. She has a PhD from the National University of Ireland's Irish Center for Human Rights, a JD from Yale Law School, an MALD from the Fletcher School of Law and Diplomacy, and a BSFS from Georgetown University's School of Foreign Service.

Viviane E. Dittrich is Deputy Director of the International Nuremberg Principles Academy. She is also Visiting Fellow at the Centre for International Studies at the London School of Economics and Political Science (LSE). Previously, she has been Honorary Research Associate at Royal Holloway, University of London, and Visiting Researcher at iCourts (Centre of Excellence for International Courts), University of Copenhagen. Dr Dittrich has published on the notion of legacy and legacy building at the international criminal tribunals. Drawing on extensive field research, her work comparatively investigates the ICTY, ICTR, SCSL, ECCC, ICC, and IMT (Nuremberg). After studies in France, England, and the US (Wellesley College) she received an MSc in International Relations from the LSE and a Master's degree from Sciences Po, Paris. She holds a PhD from the LSE.

Mark Drumbl is the Class of 1975 Alumni Professor at Washington & Lee University, School of Law, where he also serves as Director of the University's Transnational Law Institute. He has held visiting appointments at Oxford University, Université de Paris II (Panthéon-Assas), Vanderbilt University, University of Ottawa, Trinity College Dublin, University of Western Ontario, and University of Illinois College of Law, the University of Melbourne, and the University of Sydney.

Petar Finci is a Researcher in the International Committee of the Red Cross (ICRC). He worked as a Senior Information Assistant for the Outreach Office of the International Criminal Tribunal for the former Yugoslavia (ICTY). In this function he wrote and co-produced the film 'Sexual Violence and the Triumph of Justice'.

Audrey Fino is a lecturer at the University of Groningen, and a former Legal Officer in the Chambers of the International Criminal Tribunal for the former Yugoslavia (ICTY) and the United Nations Office of the High Commissioner for Human Rights.

Simone Gigliotti is a Senior Lecturer in Holocaust Studies, Department of History, Royal Holloway, University of London.

Ljiljana Hellman was born in Belgrade, Serbia. She holds a LL.M. in International Human Rights Law from the University of Essex, as well as a Masters Law Degree from the University of Belgrade. In the 1990s she worked as a Legal Analyst in the Belgrade-based NGO Humanitarian Law Center. After the fall of Milosević's regime she joined the OSCE Mission to Serbia as a Legal Adviser and Head of the War Crimes Unit. She was Balkans Project Manager at the Dutch NGO Impunity Watch and worked as a consultant for the OSCE/ODIHR and OSCE Mission in BiH. At the ICTY she worked as a Court Officer and Legal Officer. As of 2017 she works as the Head of Judicial Records and Court Operations Unit at the IRMCT. She has been a lecturer in various courses on international humanitarian law and author, co-author, and/or editor of many human rights reports and articles in the field of international law.

Barbora Holá is a Senior Researcher at the NSCR and Associate Professor at the Department of Criminal Law and Criminology at VU University of Amsterdam and co-director of CICJ.

Michael G. Karnavas is an American-trained lawyer qualified to appear before various international tribunals. Practising law for over thirty-five years, he has appeared before State and Federal Courts in the US, the ICTY, the ICTR, the ECCC, and the ICC and for over twenty-seven years he has taught trial advocacy skills to lawyers and law students, lectured extensively on international criminal law and procedure, authored trial advocacy practice manuals, articles and book chapters on international criminal law and procedure, and has been engaged in a variety of legal reform and development projects in Europe and Asia.

Kimi Lynn King is a Professor of Political Science in the College of Liberal Arts and Social Sciences at the University of Texas.

Jacqueline R. McAllister is an Assistant Professor of Political Science in the Kenyon College.

James Meernik is a Professor and the Coordinator of the Division of Social Sciences. He is also the Director of the Castleberry Peace Institute, University of Texas.

Jovana Mihajlović Trbovc is a political scientist dealing with political issues from the perspective of culture studies. Her research field is the politics of the past and public memory of the crimes which happened during the dissolution of Yugoslavia and during the Second World War. She is especially focused on the impact of the International Criminal Tribunal for the former Yugoslavia (ICTY) on the post-Yugoslav States, as well as the reproduction of the historical narratives in the school textbooks.

Christopher Mitchell is a barrister at Banco Chambers, Sydney. Formerly, he was a senior associate with Herbert Smith Freehills in Sydney, and an Associate Legal Officer with the ICTY OTP on Prosecutor v Popović et al, and Prosecutor v Radovan Karadžić. The views expressed herein are those of the author's alone and do not necessarily reflect the views of the International Criminal Court (in the case of Mr Vanderpuye), the International Criminal Tribunal for the former Yugoslavia or the United Nations in general.

Marko Divac Öberg is a Legal Officer in chambers at the Special Tribunal for Lebanon and, formerly, at the International Criminal Tribunal for the former Yugoslavia. Prior to that, he served as a legal adviser for human rights NGOs in Malawi and Palestine and as a law clerk at the International Court of Justice.

Victor Peskin is an Associate Professor at the School of Politics and Global Studies at the Arizona State University.

Amber Pierce is a PhD candidate at the Department of History, Royal Holloway, University of London.

Thomas Wayde Pittman is a former military trial judge (European Judicial Circuit) and retiree of the US Air Force Judge Advocate General's Corps. He served as a senior legal officer and, ultimately, as Head of Chambers at the International Criminal Tribunal for the former Yugoslavia. He also served as the Registrar's Chef de Cabinet at the Special Tribunal for Lebanon.

Adrian Plevin is a Legal Officer at the Special Tribunal for Lebanon. Formerly, he worked as an Associate Legal Officer at the International Criminal Tribunal for the former Yugoslavia.

Luigi Prosperi has a PhD from the Sapienza University of Rome. He was formerly an Associate Legal Officer at the Office of The Prosecutor in the International Criminal Tribunal for the former Yugoslavia

Colleen Rohan is an expert in criminal defence litigation in both domestic and international courts. She has represented members of the military and private clients in complex cases involving charges of genocide, murder, terrorism, war crimes, and crimes against humanity. In her domestic practice she specialized in death penalty cases, gang-related cases, international extradition, and post-conviction remedies.

Sandra Sahyouni is a Legal Officer at the Special Tribunal for Lebanon (STL).

Miguel de Serpa Soares is the Under-Secretary-General for Legal Affairs and United Nations Legal Counsel.

Ivor Sokolić is a Research Officer at the European Institute at the London School of Economics and Political Science. He works on the ERC-funded project 'Justice Interactions and Peacebuilding: From Static to Dynamic Discourses across National, Ethnic, Gender and Age Groups', which examines transitional justice processes across the former Yugoslavia. He holds a PhD from the UCL School of Slavonic and East European Studies and an MSc and BSc in European Politics from the Department of International Politics at the University of Wales, Aberystwyth.

Carsten Stahn is Professor of International Criminal Law and Global Justice and Programme Director of the Leiden University Grotius Centre for International Studies at The Hague, and Professor of Public International Law and International Criminal Justice at Queen's University Belfast. He has previously worked as Research Fellow at the Max Planck Institute for Comparative Public Law and International Law (2000–2003), as Legal Officer in Chambers of the International Criminal Court (2003–2007), and as Reader in Public International Law and International Criminal Justice at Swansea University. He obtained his PhD degree (summa cum laude) from Humboldt University Berlin after completing his First and Second State Exam in Law in Germany. He holds LL.M. degrees from New York University and Cologne/Paris I (Panthéon-Sorbonne).

Jennifer Trahan is a Clinical Professor, The Center for Global Affairs, NYU-SPS.

Kweku Vanderpuye is a Senior Trial Lawyer in the Office of the Prosecutor of the International Criminal Court. He served as a Trial Attorney with the Office of the Prosecutor (OTP) at the International Criminal Tribunal for the former Yugoslavia (ICTY) on Prosecutor v Popović et al, Prosecutor v Tolimir and Prosecutor v Mladić. Prior to this, he was a criminal defence lawyer in New York, including as a Supervising Attorney with The Legal Aid Society.

Iva Vukušić is a Visiting Research Fellow, War Studies Department, King's College London.

Joris van Wijk is Associate Professor at the Department of Criminal Law and Criminology at VU University of Amsterdam and co-director of the Center for International Criminal Justice (CICJ).

Introduction

Legacy as Dialogue—Reflecting on the ICTY Experience

Carsten Stahn

I.1 The Journey of the ICTY

'Borrowed robes, no seat, no courtroom, no prison, no budget, no computers, no staff and no rules. Widespread scepticism about the viability of the institution.'[1] This is how it started. The journey of the International Criminal Tribunal for the former Yugoslavia (ICTY) has been compared to a ship that has set sail and marked new frontiers. Unlike the International Criminal Court (ICC), the ICTY could not count on global civil society support to lobby for its emergence. It rather emerged as a result of the dedicated efforts of specific individuals, certain feelings of shame, and a unique geopolitical environment. It was an instrument to counter 'an erasing' of 'the past'.[2] At the beginning, there was a strong fear that the ship would never leave the dock. It has undertaken a remarkable journey, with both unexpected successes and challenges. It lasted for almost a quarter of a century—much longer than many had expected.

Throughout its almost two and half decades of existence, the Tribunal has undergone many changes. It was born in what many see now as a 'heroic' phase of international criminal justice. It faced many of the existential challenges of international criminal justice: selectivity; distance from crimes; victims and local communities; queries about identity, efficiency, and impact; and a complex interrelation with different types of politics. Despite its setbacks and imperfections, it is usually viewed as a relatively successful example of investigation and prosecution of international crimes. The ICTY can look back to strong record on arrest. It showed that powerful leaders, such as former Heads of State, Ministers, or Generals may face accountability for international crimes. It has contributed greatly to the clarification of facts and the establishment of the responsibility of individuals. As historians note:

> Without the ICTY's trials, we would not know so well what happened in Vukovar, Dubrovnik, Prijedor, Sarajevo, Srebrenica, Foča, Visegrad, Zvornik, Bijeljina, Mostar, Ahmići, Čelebići, Podujevo, Suva Reka, and many other places.[3]

[1] J Hocking, Opening Remarks, Legacy Conference, Sarajevo, Bosnia, and Herzegovina, 22 June 2017, available at <https://www.icty.org/x/file/Press/Statements%20and%20Speeches/Registrar/20170622-john-hocking-opening-remarks-sarajevo_en.pdf> accessed 21 October 2019.

[2] Secretary-General's remarks at Closing Ceremony for the International Criminal Tribunal for the Former Yugoslavia, 21 December 2017, available at <https://www.un.org/sg/en/content/sg/statement/2017-12-21/secretary-generals-remarks-closing-ceremony-international-criminal> accessed 21 October 2019.

[3] I Vukušić, 'Assessing the ICTY's Legacy' (*Justice Hub*, 26 July 2017) <https://justicehub.org/article/assessing-the-ictys-legacy//> accessed 21 October 2019.

Carsten Stahn, *Introduction* In: *Legacies of the International Criminal Tribunal for the Former Yugoslavia.* Edited by: Carsten Stahn, Carmel Agius, Serge Brammertz, Colleen Rohan, Oxford University Press (2020). © The Several Contributors
DOI: 10.1093/oso/9780198862956.003.0001

Some of the initial ambitions were over-enthusiastic. Even today, it cannot be taken for granted that principal perpetrators of international crimes will be held accountable. The ambition to ensure equality before the law and provide some sense of justice to victims is a monumental task. It arises anew in each atrocity context. The ICTY has shown that international criminal justice is possible. As former Registrar John Hocking has noted, this experience marks to some extent a point of no return: 'From here there is no turning back [. . .] accountability is not just an ideal . . . or a one-off.'[4]

The ICTY managed to stay its course due to different factors: focus, time, and institutional adjustment. The mandate allowed the Tribunal to focus in depth on the conflict in the former Yugoslavia. This distinguishes it from courts like the ICC, which has to move from one political context to another. The timeframe enabled the ICTY to benefit from changing geo-political conditions in the region and to gradually develop a pool of cases that build on each other in terms of law, narratives, and evidence.

The Tribunal itself was able to complete its mandate because it adjusted its own course during the journey. Institutionally, it has constantly re-invented itself, with different Prosecutors and prosecutorial strategies, changing jurisprudence, adjustments of rules and procedures, and developing outreach and Completion Strategies. A crucial factor for its success as a judicial institution was the support by EU and NATO in relation to arrest and compliance. Institutional factors, internal strategies and contributions of individuals are also part of the story.

I.2 The Need for Multi-disciplinary Perspectives

The ICTY is an institution with many faces. It is a court, an organization, and a social entity. It leaves a rich legal, institutional, and non-judicial legacy. Many of the classical juridical footprints of the work of the ICTY are covered in legal treatises or reflective volumes.[5] For example, the ICTY Manual on Developed Practices, which was developed as a part of the early legacy initiatives, contains a useful overview of experiences and practices.[6] However, the impact of the ICTY cannot be reduced to judgments, that is, convictions and acquittals, procedural experiences, or manuals. It needs to be regarded in a more holistic way. Many of its contributions are more subtle and complex. They are reflected in legal and societal discourse, testimonies, or institutional approaches.

Legacies are created through individual and collective narratives. They are constantly constructed and re-shaped. The notion of 'legacy' is often associated with a positive record or heritage, formed in the memory of others. But legacy can also be a form of power or control over the past or a technique to alter memory.[7] The ICTY has thus rightly itself looked at legacy through the lens of dialogue.[8] It has distinguished differentiated layers: broader

[4] See Hocking (n 1).

[5] See e.g. B Swart, A Zahar, and G Sluiter (eds), *The Legacy of the International Criminal Tribunal for the Former Yugoslavia* (OUP 2011); M Sterio and M Scharf (eds), *The Legacy of* Ad Hoc *Tribunals in International Criminal Law* (CUP 2019), R H Steinberg, *Assessing the Legacy of the ICTY* (Martinus Nijhoff 2011).

[6] See ICTY Manual on Developed Practices, Prepared in conjunction with UNICRI as part of a project to preserve the legacy of the ICTY (UNICRI Publisher 2009).

[7] As George Orwell has warned: 'Who controls the past controls the future. Who controls the present controls the past' in G Orwell, *1984* (Houghton Mifflin Harcourt 2017) 37.

[8] The ICTY Legacies Dialogue Conference framed a set of general recommendations. See Report of the International Tribunal for the Former Yugoslavia (1 August 2017) UN Doc A/72/266–S/2017/662, Annex (Outcome document of the Legacy Dialogues Conference of the International Tribunal for the Former Yugoslavia: Conclusions and recommendations).

normative contributions; operational legacies, including fair trial issues; participatory aspects; gender justice; and outreach from non-judicial legacies, such as historical legacy and impact on society.

Broadly speaking, legacies can be grouped around different sites of debate: (i) historic legacy, that is, the contribution of the ICTY to the framing of facts and events, including the value of the records in combating denial of crimes; (ii) investigative and experiential legacy, including approaches towards identifying evidence, experiences related to the delivery of testimony and access to justice; (iii) procedural legacies, including lessons learned from the management of proceedings, the treatment of parties and outreach; (iv) retribution and punishment; (v) normative legacies, that is, the impact of the work of the Tribunal on domestic legal systems; and (vi) ongoing debates over impact and societal reception. These discussions require insights from multiple disciplines and further empirical research.

I.3 Focus

This book addresses legacies from different observational standpoints. It encompasses voices from inside the Tribunal and external perspectives.

I.3.1 Challenges and Achievements—Internal Perspectives

The book starts at Part I with a set of reflections on legacy from 'inside', namely UN officials and practitioners. They trace achievements, challenges, and critiques from the perspective of different agents: Presidency, Prosecution, the Defence, and the UN Secretariat. These contributions set debates on legacy and ICTY performance into context in relation to other courts and tribunals, and the functioning of international criminal justice more generally.

Carmel Agius, the last President of the ICTY, revisits major contributions of the ICTY over twenty-four years. He argues that the Tribunal contributed to an 'ethos of accountability' while cautioning that adjudication alone is 'unlikely' to achieve 'reconciliation and resurrection of the rule of law'.

Serge Brammertz, the last Prosecutor of the Tribunal, examines the experiences of the ICTY and the International Residual Mechanism for Criminal Tribunals. He illustrates how the ICTY moved gradually from primacy to complementarity. He argues that the 'support to national justice sectors' in the former Yugoslavia counts among the most important legacies of the Tribunal.

Colleen Rohan explores the often-forgotten perspective of the Defence in relation to legacy. She traces the story of the naissance of the Association of Defence counsel. She argues that the role of the Association in relation to effective assistance to counsel and the efficient administration of justice paved the way for greater sensibility to structural challenges of the Defence function in international criminal justice.

UN Legal Counsel Miguel de Serpa Soares views the ICTY as an embodiment of a broader morality and responsibility and as a cornerstone of a broader UN system regarding accountability. He argues that in an 'ideal future', institutions such as the ICTY may 'not be necessary' and 'domestic jurisdiction will assume the main responsibility' for the prosecution of international crimes.

I.3.2 Theorizing Legal Legacies

Part II of the book moves from 'internal' to external perspectives. It engages with the broader way in which legacy is portrayed and theorized in international criminal justice. It analyses different legacy concepts, articulations and practices, use of narratives and metaphors as well as some unexpected effects of ICTY practice. It sheds a novel light on the complex identity of the ICTY, and the constant tension between normative aspiration, legal limitation, and societal expectation.

The opening chapter examines the transformation of the ICTY, its performative function, and the tension between core mandate and auxiliary functions. It traces different stages in the development of the Tribunal. It shows that the ICTY took an active role in shaping legal discourse, but was more reluctant to become engaged in societal discourse. Procedures were a means for the Tribunal to make itself heard and seen. However, the Tribunal lacked control over its own perception. The most visible legacy is the legal legacy, and the facts, stories, and narratives conveyed through proceedings. This may be explained partly by the nature of the Tribunal as a juridical institution.

Viviane E. Dittrich engages with ICTY legacy from an institutional perspective. She examines how the Tribunal developed a vision of legacy, how it professionalized this vision, and how it designed and implemented legacy projects in different phases of its institutional history, leading up to the International Residual Mechanism for Criminal Tribunals. She shows how legacy navigates between an institutional urge for self-preservation and self-redemption. According to her, legacies should be conceived as a cycle which involves legacy creation, consolidation, and contestation. The ICTY is thus a legacy leaver, while legacies are created, consolidated, and contested through diverse forms of social interaction.

Simone Gigliotti and Amber Pierce show how Prosecutors built legacies through narrative and rhetoric strategies, starting from post-Second World War practice to the ICTY. They trace the work and statements of three prosecutors: Telford Taylor (Nuremberg), Benjamin Ferencz (the *Einsatzgruppen* Trial of 1947–1948), and Serge Brammertz (Radovan Karadžić). They argue that legacy construction is tied to the idea of the Prosecutor as peace builder.

Mark Drumbl demonstrates some of the ICTY's unexpected footprints in domestic civil litigation, specifically private tort claims brought in the US under the Alien Tort Statute (ATS). He traces cases in which US federal judges adjudicating ATS disputes have relied upon ICTY cases and materials, and discusses how and for which purposes these materials—along with those of other international institutions—have been used. He identifies a fundamental dilemma in judicial legacy discourse. International jurisprudence—no different than any sources of law or precedent—may be misapplied, or wishfully applied, in national contexts. Debates within the domestic civil level inspired by the international migration tend not to percolate into the international realm.

I.3.3 Symbolic Meaning, Law, and History

Part III of the book explores virtues of symbolic expression used at the ICTY, as well as the controversial relationship between judicial record, history, and truth. The opening chapter by Marina Aksenova examines to what extent the ICTY produced normative change through expressivist and symbolic practices. Aksenova compares trials to quasi ritualistic events, drawing on Maurice Bloch's anthropological research on initiation rituals. She then analyses how judicial practices relied on expressivism and symbolism in relation to the definition of crimes, condemnation and stigmatization, and justification of punishment. She suggests that symbolic expression is necessary to convey authority beyond the mere formalism and rationality of criminal trials.

Luigi Prosperi and Aldo Zammit Borda examine the relationship of the ICTY to historical clarification, and risks arising from the use of judgments as historical record. ICTY Chambers haven taken different approaches. For instance, in *Krstić*, the Trial Chamber acknowledged that its task was to decide on the guilt or innocence of the accused within the boundaries of the indictment and it had to leave it 'to historians and social psychologists to plumb the depths of this episode of the Balkan conflict and to probe for deep-seated causes'. In other cases, however, judgments have been treated as authoritative historical record. The chapter argues that the identification of judicial truth has been one of the legacies of the ICTY. It claims that findings on distant or contextual historical events should be characterized as 'discursive beginnings for victims, local communities and future generations to engage with and debate the past beyond the courtroom'. It concludes that international tribunals should be open to admit alternative historical narratives when they establish historical facts or the contextual background of the crimes.

Andy Aydın-Aitchison explores the potential historical value of the evidence gathered, presented, and scrutinized in international criminal courts. He argues that trials have played an important, if not always unproblematic part in Holocaust historiography. He identifies how criminologists and others have started to make use of resources generated or collected by the ICTY and the International Criminal Tribunal for Rwanda (ICTR) to describe and analyse international crimes. The chapter argues that evidence and transcripts from international criminal courts do have great potential as a source of data for historical and social science analyses. But they need to be handled with care and with due attention to their limitations.

I.3.4 Experimental Legacies

Evidence and testimony are an important part of the experiential legacies of international criminal courts and tribunals. Part IV of the book addresses some of the lessons learned from ICTY practice, including remaining gaps and challenges.

Kweku Vanderpuye and Christopher Mitchell discuss legal issues associated with the collection, storage, and use of DNA evidence in international and national criminal trials, drawing on their experience in the Srebrenica cases. They show how DNA evidence was used to identify the number of victims in a mass grave, and links and patterns between a victim and one or more crime sites. They argue that the probative value of DNA evidence is maximized when it is used in conjunction with other forensic sciences (e.g. archaeology, pathology, and anthropology), and that reliance on all forensic sciences, not just DNA, is the most likely way of establishing a complete picture of the victim's identity, as well as the cause, manner, and circumstances of the victim's death.

Kimi Lynn King and James Meernik examine micro-level components shaping the witness experience. They develop a model of procedural justice to examine witness perceptions about the search for truth and justice, based on data from empirical study of witness experiences.[9] They show that fair treatment of defendants and witnesses by Prosecutors enhances the witness perceptions that their testimony has contributed to both truth and justice. They argue that testimonial challenges, such as delays in testifying, may undermine positive contributions. The chapter also demonstrates the critical importance of gender and ethnic identity. It claims that there are significant differences between male and female perceptions about testifying.

I.3.5 Judicial Practices and Outreach

Part V of the book turns to criminal procedure, court management, and outreach. In existing studies, much has been written on legal and procedural innovations of the ICTY. This book takes a slightly different angle. It examines lessons drawn from Court and Defence practices. It covers some areas that are rarely covered, such as Defence investigative ethics, judgment drafting, contempt cases against journalists, interpretation and translation, outreach and youth outreach.

The contribution by Michael G. Karnavas provides an insider perspective on Defence challenges in relation to international criminal litigation. Karnavas shows that the adversarial and hybrid procedural features of ICTY required Defence counsel to take a step back from their own system and adjust to new structures. He argues that the procedure devised by the Tribunal requires not only a certain set of litigation skills, but also imposes specific ethical duties on counsel. One of the novelties for counsel from inquisitorial systems is the ability to conduct an independent Defence investigation. The chapter examines particular lessons to be drawn from case preparation, witness interviewing, and Defence investigations. It concludes that many of these practices may also be of use for investigation and prosecution of crimes.

One of the lasting legacies of the ICTY are the many trial and appeal judgments that the tribunal rendered. The public pronouncements of the judgments are accompanied in each case by a statutorily-required 'reasoned opinion in writing'. Its length has varied from less than 100 pages to over 2,000 pages. Thomas Wayde Pittman and Marko Divac Öberg, who have served in Chambers, take a look at judgment drafting. They explain the structure of judicial production at the ICTY, as well as the requirements, different stages and methods of drafting trial and appeal judgments. They show that this process was a learning exercise. The interplay of different legal cultures at the ICTY complicated the drafting process and led to critiques relating to the readability and accessibility of judgments. Some judgments included detailed factual analysis of evidence in relation to crimes even in case of acquittals in order to mitigate frustrations by victims.

[9] See ICTY, *Echoes of Testimony; A Pilot Study into the Long-term Impact of Bearing Witness Before the ICTY* (ICTY 2016).

International criminal courts and tribunals enjoy a high degree of visibility and publicity. This may enhance their communication to a wide range of audiences, but also create vulnerabilities. Audrey Fino and Sandra Sahyouni deal with particular types of cases that are rarely discussed as part of legacy debates, namely contempt cases against journalists. International criminal tribunals are bound by human rights standards, including freedom of expression and freedom of the press. But the violation of protective measures for witnesses and victims or the disclosure of confidential information by journalists or media may constitute an offence against the administration of justice. It is contested to what extent such cases should be investigated or prosecuted by international tribunals themselves or domestic courts. The Statutes of the ad hoc tribunals did not contain an express power to deal with contempt cases. The chapter argues that such investigations and prosecutions may be necessary to uphold the integrity of proceedings. It shows that investigating and prosecuting journalists or media for contempt has caused criticism. It defends the view that the freedom of the press is not absolute and that the imposition of certain limits to reporting may be in line with domestic trends and human rights law.

Throughout its history, the ICTY held more than 10,000 days of trial. Ellen Elias-Bursać looks at a key aspect of ICTY proceedings that is often at the periphery, namely translating and interpreting. She tells the story of the set-up and conduct of language services at the ICTY. Language staff from the region initially faced suspicion inside the Tribunal and pressures in their home jurisdictions. The Tribunal adopted a Code of Ethics to deal with potential conflicts. The Code has framed standards for neutrality and accuracy which were crucial for Court practice. The chapter shows that language communication was ensured through a close relationship between Chambers, the Conferences and Language Section, and the Defence. Quality control of interpretation and translation was partially secured through members of Defence teams, rather than trial monitors used in Nuremberg or Tokyo. Particular problems arose in relation to defendants who decided to defend themselves and used interpretation and translation issues as part of their Defence strategy. For instance, Vojislav Šešelj sought to receive all court-related documents in Serbian and requested translation of the many books that he authored. Radovan Karadžić often read out documentary evidence to witnesses in Court, without securing translation first. This practice required witnesses to rely on in-Court-interpretation, based on the emphases favoured by Karadžić.

The following two contributions discuss outreach challenges. Petar Finci re-visits the merits and shortcomings of the ICTY's Outreach Programme. At the ICTY, outreach and a common approach to communication was only developed in 2010. Outreach was to some extent a reflection of the societal divisions that the ICTY encountered. In its early days, the Outreach Programme operated by trial and error, receiving mixed degrees of reception across countries in the region. The chapter argues that outreach may have been more successful if it had sent more realistic messages about the ICTY's goals and aspirations from the start, and if it had received greater support in institutional strategy (e.g. funding, field presence). The production of films and screening by the ICTY itself became an important instrument to reach comparatively large audiences.

Adrian Plevin examines strategies of youth outreach. Youth outreach has a strong link to transitional justice goals that are difficult to reach through trials alone (e.g. education, peaceful transformation). It was deliberately used in the last years of the ICTY in order to have a transformative effect for the future, namely to bring about 'positive change' in affected communities. It went beyond classical legacy strategies. It involved initiatives to stimulate an interest in justice, encourage reflection on the benefits and limits of punitive justice, challenge existing perception, and counter a culture of denial and intolerance. The chapter shows how the youth Outreach Programme went beyond public relations, targeted sensitive issues, and cooperated with educational institutions to promote 'fact-based education'. It argues that critical perspectives are important in order to promote history education reform and facilitate engagement with the ICTY's legacy.

I.3.6 Punishment and Sentencing

Punishment and sentencing in international criminal justice continue to divide opinion. International criminal courts and tribunals have been criticized for lack of sentencing coherence. Part VI examines merits and contradictions in ICTY sentencing practice. It also engages with dilemmas of post-conviction practice that are often overlooked in existing discourse.

Margaret M deGuzman discusses the sentencing practices of the ICTY. She shows that sentencing has in general been orientated towards global norms, rather than sentencing norms of the former Yugoslavia. The Statute obliged the ICTY to 'have recourse' to national practices. The Tribunal found that it was required to 'consult' national sentences, but was not bound to apply them. It developed its own sentencing methodology. In jurisprudence, retribution and deterrence became main sentencing rationales. Judges developed a principle of gradation, based on the criterion of gravity. The contribution argues that the ICTY's sentencing legacy lies in the fact that it promoted a process of building global sentencing norms that are reproduced in other contexts (e.g. the ICC). It claims that the 'relative lenience' of sentences may be defended by this objective.

The following contribution by Barbora Holá investigates to what extent ICTY sentencing differs from the practice of domestic courts in Bosnia and Herzegovina. It is often assumed that sentencing at the ICTY is inconsistent with domestic court practice. ICTY sentencing has been criticized for its leniency. The chapter challenges this claim. It shows that, contrary to public opinion, sentences given by the ICTY have been comparable to, or even more severe than, sentences in Bosnian domestic courts, including the State Court in Sarajevo. It derives this finding from empirical study of sentencing practice at the ICTY, the State Court, and Entity Courts. It explains this difference by the different nature of defendants (e.g. foot soldiers, lower-ranking individuals) prosecuted domestically and partly different sentencing goals.

The ICTY was one of the first international tribunals which had to establish sentencing agreements with States in order to enforce these sentences and to develop early release procedures. Joris van Wijk and Barbora Holá analyse post-conviction practices, namely what happened to ICTY defendants after conviction or acquittal. They argue that international practices are marked by contradictions. Sentences are enforced domestically. Defendants are spread out across jurisdictions. Enforcement practices pay limited attention to the sociology and specificities of atrocity crime. ICTY convicts are often treated as 'worst' categories of criminals in domestic enforcement practices, although they hardly pose any ongoing danger to society after imprisonment and removal from context. Rehabilitation is often cited as a factor for early release, but rarely verified and adjusted to the particularities of macro-criminality. The equal 'treatment of similarly situated prisoners' became in practice the main reason by the ICTY to allow early release. After return, some defendants were welcomed as war heroes in their home communities. Some acquitted defendants have faced risks of re-trial by domestic prosecutors. Existing problems suggest that post-conviction practices need refinement.

I.3.7 Impact on Domestic Legal Systems

The transformation of domestic legal systems was not one of the primary reasons for the establishment of the ICTY. But it has gradually grown into an important aspect of legacy. The ICTY recognized that domestic prosecutors and courts play a key role in shaping legal legacy. As John Hocking has noted:

> With the ICTY's voyage coming to an end, it is these courts, and significantly the courts in the region, that will continue to charter these new waters and push beyond the frontiers of the possible.[10]

However, this process is highly context-dependent. Legacy is not something that can be simply passed on. Part VII deals with key aspects and problems of the legal impact of the ICTY in the region. It shows that the success of rule of law reform and norm internalization is closely linked to justice narratives, institutional structures, and perceptions.

Ivor Sokolić examines the relationship between war narratives and legal reception in Croatia, based on fieldwork conducted in 2014 and 2015. He argues that the justice narrative sent through the ICTY proceedings conflicted with predominant war narratives in Croatia which sought to justify Croatian operations as self-defence against a larger Serbian aggressor. The chapter argues that the war narrative made it difficult for the justice narrative to gain ground. The ICTY was partly seen to be biased because it was attempting to equalize guilt. Acceptance and internalization of justice narratives is a long-term process.

Jennifer Trahan and Iva Vukušić demonstrate that adjudication in Bosnia and Herzegovina involved three interrelated levels: an international court (i.e. the ICTY); a hybrid court (i.e. the War Crimes Chamber of the State Court of Bosnia and Herzegovina in Sarajevo); and local cantonal and district courts. They argue that this model might deserve consideration in other contexts. The War Crimes Chamber enabled the Completion Strategy of the ICTY. One of its innovative features was its changing design. It started with a high degree of internationalization, but gradually 'localized' its own structures. Its activity was guided by criteria for prioritization of cases, in order to avoid backlog and focus on higher level and complex cases.

Tatjana Dawson and Ljiljana Hellman discuss the relationship between Serbia and the ICTY. The relationship to Serbia was marked by 'ups and downs'. The chapter argues that members of the legal profession in Serbia were generally open to cooperate with the ICTY, irrespective of the shifting political environment. It argues that the Completion Strategy modified the relationship. The drafting of the Law on Organisation and Competence of

[10] See Hocking (n 1).

Government Authorities in War Crimes Proceedings introduced specialized structures for investigation and prosecution in Serbia. This facilitated a growing number of domestic cases. Serbia included the concept of command responsibility in its domestic penal code, in order to remedy internal gaps.

Kei Hannah Brodersen analyses the ICTY's Impact on the Rights of Defendants in the Former Yugoslavia, based on two case studies: Bosnia and Herzegovina, and Serbia. She argues that the ICTY had only scarce effects on fairness of national war crimes proceedings or national criminal proceedings in general. The chapter shows that the ICTY was more successful in triggering normative change through socialization and persuasion in Bosnia based on a number of factors: the higher involvement of the Tribunal in the rebuilding of the Bosnian justice system, and lower rates of legitimacy in Serbia, not only amongst the Serbian population, but also amongst the country's political elite.

I.3.8 Societal Impact and Reception

The final part of the book, Part VIII, deals with some of the societal impacts of the ICTY, ongoing struggles over narratives, and domestic reception. It contrasts international ambitions with local experiences.

Jacqueline R. McAllister examines the impact of the ICTY on the peace process, including the way in which it influenced bargaining. She argues that the ICTY played a key role in facilitating negotiated settlements. It provided mediators with leverage to pressure Serb forces to speak with one voice. The Rules of the Road programme helped prevent a major post-Dayton crisis. The initial caution in indicting top leaders may have facilitated peace efforts.

Victor Peskin analyses to what extent the ICTY managed to transcend critiques of victor's justice, based on the Tribunal's battles with the Croatian government. He shows that the ICTY sought to distinguish itself from its predecessors through a principled commitment to investigate suspects from all sides. However, in practice, the Tribunal faced distinct challenges on prosecuting the 'winners of the Balkan wars'. The chapter claims that the ICTY Prosecution may have lost the battles in the Courtroom in relation to Croatian cases, but 'won the larger war over victor's justice'.

Jovana Mihajlović Trbovc explores to what extent ICTY trials have changed narratives about key elements of the 1992–95 war in public life in Bosnia and Herzegovina, such as Serbian responsibility, ethnic cleansing, and genocide based on newspaper articles on commemorative events. Her research challenges the assumption that there is direct nexus between establishment of facts and transformation of collective memory. The chapter argues that engagement with the past relates to societal attitudes rather than knowledge. ICTY judgments provided a frame around which public debates evolve. However, many of the ethnic and national divides that fuelled the conflict continue to be reflected in practices of memorialization.

Rosa Aloisi assesses the tensions between the truth recounted by the ICTY and the construction of the local collective memory through analysis of contemporary uses of sites of atrocities. The chapter argues that, while international justice offers some resolution to a post-war divided society, a full reconciliation is only possible when the communities come back together in acknowledging the occurrence of atrocities and the right of victims and survivors to places where they can mourn and remember. Criminal proceedings do not achieve reconciliation on their own, but provide at best a building block for reconciliation in the long term.

The closing chapter by Janine Natalya Clark sheds a new light on approaches towards reconciliation. She shows that ICTY trials had limited impact on inter-ethnic reconciliation, because they lacked the ability to transform the affective contexts related to commonly held beliefs. She questions whether facts alone provide a basis for reconciliation. According to her, greater emphasis should be placed on higher-level truths conveyed through judicial proceedings, which are easier to process. Such 'meta-truths' include insights about human suffering and immorality of behaviour. The chapter demonstrates that ICTY proceedings reflected such meta-truths in specific passages of judgments or guilty pleas by defendants. They mark a starting point for shared discursive spaces.

I.4 Continuing Dialogue

The book, as whole, suggests that the history of the ICTY is richer than imagined and continues to be written. Its story emerges not only through studies of the judicial record, archives, witness testimony, or reports by ICTY officials, but rather through ongoing discourse about legacy.

The value of the ICTY lies not only in its legal output and arrest record, or its impact or influence on other judicial entities (e.g. the ICC or domestic courts), but in its nature as an experiment of justice. The ICTY experience illustrates both the potential, as well as the inherent limitations and constraints of international criminal justice. It contributed to the shaping of international criminal justice as a juridical field and triggered new ways and methods to study and understand international justice. Lawyers tend to focus on prosecutorial or judicial practices. However, the main contribution is much larger. The ICTY generated critical discourse about some of the foundations and assumptions of the field and introduced novel ways of thinking about international justice as a normative project and its constituencies (e.g. the role of victims and affected communities). Legacy derives not only from its successes but also from its shortcomings or failures.

The ICTY will likely remain an object of study across fields in the future (e.g. politics, history, organizational theory, law, or sociology). It is important to engage not only with its visible record and performance, but to refine the ways, lenses, and methods through which it is studied. This may shed a differentiated light on its legacies. This book is a part of this journey. It traces some of its less obvious legacies and opens broader frames for discussion.

PART I
OPENING REFLECTIONS

1
The Last Testament of the ICTY

*Carmel Agius**

1.1 A Special Time

The closure of one of the most prominent, groundbreaking, and influential institutions of international criminal justice after twenty-five years of successful operation marks the end of an era for those of us who have been attached to the tribunal and for the affected communities in the former Yugoslavia. For the international community as a whole, it heralds the beginning of a new chapter in international criminal law.

I see this moment as a huge milestone for the discipline of international criminal law, not least because of the stark difference between the contemporary political climate and the one obtaining at the time when the International Criminal Tribunal for the former Yugoslavia (ICTY or Tribunal) first opened its doors. Before the Second World War ended, the notion of international criminal justice did not even exist in its present formulation.[1] War crimes were considered to be within the purview of domestic competence only; as a result, perpetrators were frequently seen as war heroes within their own territories.[2] It was the horror of the Holocaust which inspired the global community to question the absolute sovereignty of nations and demand international accountability for those responsible for war crimes and crimes against humanity.[3] The ICTY was similarly set up as a response to the grave abuses committed during the Yugoslav wars.

At both these times, there was an optimism associated with the creation of international courts: people were war-weary, and wanted very much to believe that these institutions would succeed in bringing justice to their perpetrators. It was this reason that led Richard Goldstone, the first[4] Chief Prosecutor of the ICTY, to conclude in 2005 that: '*international criminal justice ... has wide global acceptance*.'[5] However, the landscape has shifted since. States are withdrawing from the Rome Statute for the International Criminal Court (ICC),[6] there is 'tribunal fatigue' around existing institutions like the ICTY and the International Criminal Tribunal for Rwanda ('ICTR'),[7] and nationalistic tendencies are rising again,[8]

* Last President of the ICTY.

1 A Cassese, *International Criminal Law* (OUP 2003) 16.

2 R Goldstone, 'The Future of International Criminal Justice' (2005) 57 Maine Law Review 553, 556.

3 M C Bassiouni, 'From Versailles to Rwanda in Seventy-Five Years: The Need to Establish a Permanent International Criminal Court' (1997) 10 Harvard Human Rights Journal 11, 21.

4 I understand that Graham Blewitt acted as temporary prosecutor for a while before Mr Goldstone joined.

5 Goldstone (n 2) 556.

6 Fatou Bensouda, Assembly of State Parties, 2016.

7 C Stahn, 'Tribunals Are Dead, Long Live Tribunals: MICT, The Kosovo Specialist Chambers And The Turn To New Hybridity' (2016) <https://www.ejiltalk.org/tribunals-are-dead-long-live-tribunals-mict-the-kosovo-specialist-chambers-and-the-turn-to-new-hybridity/> accessed 1 May 2019.

8 C Pazzanese, 'In Europe, Nationalism Rising' (*Harvard Gazette*, 2017) <https://news.harvard.edu/gazette/story/2017/02/in-europe-nationalisms-rising/> accessed 13 May 2019; G Rachman, 'Trump, Putin, Xi And The

Carmel Agius, *The Last Testament of the ICTY* In: *Legacies of the International Criminal Tribunal for the Former Yugoslavia*. Edited by: Carsten Stahn, Carmel Agius, Serge Brammertz, Colleen Rohan, Oxford University Press (2020). © The Several Contributors
DOI: 10.1093/oso/9780198862956.003.0002

compelling States to privilege domestic sovereignty over other concerns. As a consequence, it may appear that the space for international criminal law, so painstakingly etched out over the course of the Nuremberg trials, the ICTY, the ICTR and other ad hoc tribunals, is shrinking.

Nevertheless, the message in this piece is one of hope: I am hopeful that the legacy of the ICTY can serve as a reminder to the international community that the ethos of accountability will remain as long as strong political will—at both the international and the domestic level—is channelled into successor judicial institutions. In the following pages, I discuss what these lessons are, and how they may apply in the current scenario.

1.2 The Backdrop of the ICTY

The creation of the ICTY was a bold, innovative, and unprecedented experiment. It was borne out of shock that such terrible events, such heinous crimes, could be happening again on European soil less than fifty years after the end of the Second World War, and out of a genuine political will to stop the conflict and bring the perpetrators to account.

It was established by the United Nations Security Council in the year 1993, while the Balkan wars were still underway, in order to address war crimes and crimes against humanity that were perpetrated in the territory of the former Yugoslavia during the start of the 1990s.[9] At the time, the creation of a tribunal such as the ICTY was an exceptional project, the likes of which were hitherto unexplored. It is interesting to note how this resulted in varied expectations from different spectators in the international community. Indeed, no one could have predicted how the ICTY would operate or progress, or foreseen all of the achievements and challenges that lay ahead. Many assumed that the ICTY was doomed from the get-go, and that it would fail to prosecute major perpetrators, while others opined that it would be able to prosecute only a handful of war criminals and wind down soon thereafter.

It is unsurprising that the ICTY commenced operations with little clarity on how the future would look—indeed, on how it would fulfil its challenging and arduous mandate. There was no single, binding handbook which governed all international courts; over the past twenty-four years, the ICTY has had to evolve its own procedural and jurisprudential approaches. Consequently, we have learned many invaluable lessons along the way. This is precisely why I have chosen to expound on the last testament of the ICTY, and the tortuous journey we have followed throughout the years of its existence.

As is commonly known now—owing in no small part to the testimonies delivered by so many courageous victims and witnesses before the ICTY—the conflicts in the Balkans arose as a result of rising tensions between different ethnicities in the region, culminating in declarations of independence by the constituent republics of the former Yugoslavia.

Rise Of Nostalgic Nationalism' (*Financial Times*, 2017) <https://www.ft.com/content/198efe76-ce8b-11e6-b8ce-b9c03770f8b1> accessed 13 May 2019.

[9] UNSC Res 827 (25 May 1993) UN Doc SRES/827 (1993).

The Yugoslav conflict was bloody and vicious; systematic detention and killing of military-aged men, extermination of entire families subscribing to certain religions, and rape and sexual slavery of women were commonly-used weapons of warfare. The international community responded with horror at this first major outbreak of armed conflict since the Second World War. This paved the way for a fast-emerging political will to both bring an end to the conflict and—equally importantly—make the perpetrators of the crimes answerable.

Thus motivated, the global community pushed for diplomatic negotiations with the leadership in the former Yugoslav republics. The Security Council publicly denounced the violence in the former Yugoslavia, calling for the creation of a Commission of Experts to review the evidence of grave breaches of the Geneva Conventions of 1949 and other violations of international humanitarian law committed in the territory of the former Yugoslavia.[10] Convinced that the perpetrators of the atrocities committed in the region ought to be brought to justice, the Security Council announced the establishment of an ad hoc international criminal tribunal to prosecute serious crimes committed during the Yugoslav wars.[11]

It is particularly significant that the report prepared by the Commission noted the '*victims' high expectations that this Commission will establish the truth and that the International Tribunal will provide justice*'.[12] It also referred to the need to '*emphasize the high expectation of justice conveyed by the parties to the conflict, as well as by victims, intergovernmental organizations, non-governmental organizations, the media and world public opinion*'.[13] Furthermore, a displaced person who had lost a son in the Yugoslav wars wrote in 1997: '*I would like to ask you to convict the war criminals . . . as swiftly as possible, so that the suffering mothers see justice done by the Tribunal as soon as possible.*'[14] These sentiments make it evident that the ICTY came into existence at a time where both—the international community and the affected persons—had great hopes for the future of international criminal justice. The world viewed the establishment of the ICTY with a powerful sense of optimism, that I believe was instrumental in imbuing the tribunal with a strong mandate to usher in accountability and the legal empowerment to fulfil that mandate, and an unwavering responsibility to live up to the expectations of its spectators and become a trailblazer for so many milestones of international criminal law.

At the same time, I absolutely have no doubt that not a single bystander at the time of the establishment of the ICTY—not even our most enthusiastic and zealous proponents—could have predicted that the tribunal would eventually succeed in trying all 161 persons indicted by it, including persons at the highest military and political levels; that the jurisprudence of the ICTY would contribute to the development of international humanitarian law and international criminal law in key ways; and that the success of the historic project that is the ICTY would serve as inspiration for other international criminal institutions that have since been created.

[10] UNSC Res 780 (6 October 1992) UN Doc S/RES/780 (1992).
[11] UNSC Res 827 (n 9).
[12] UNSC 'Letter date 24 May 1994 from the Secretary-General to the President of the Security Council' (27 May 1994) UN Doc S/1994/674.
[13] ibid.
[14] S K Ivkovic, 'Justice by the International Criminal Tribunal for the Former Yugoslavia' (2001) 37 Stanford Journal of International Law 255.

1.3 A Legacy that Lasts

For an international legal institution such as the ICTY, its success is marked not only by the immediate value of its decisions, but by the enduring contribution it makes to the corpus of existing or emergent law. Consequently, the ICTY has consistently worked to disseminate the information and knowledge collected over the past quarter-century, in the hope that national courts, other international courts, and civil society in the field of international justice may build on its achievements.

It is worth noting, at this point, some of the prominent areas where the ICTY has had the most powerful impact.

1.3.1 Forging a New Era of Accountability

It is undeniable that everyone associated with the Tribunal in any manner, including judges, prosecutors, defence counsel, legal officers, support staff at the Tribunal, and—most importantly—affected communities, including victims and witnesses, will have differing views on what constitutes the most important legacy that the ICTY will leave behind. Personally, as I have reiterated on several occasions, I believe that the ICTY's most fundamental legacy is its groundbreaking role in the fight against impunity. This may sound idealistic, but I truly believe that the work of the ICTY has *proven* to cynics in the outside world that it is not only desirable, but also eminently possible to hold perpetrators of the most heinous crimes accountable, and to bring them to justice, regardless of their position or level. The trials of Radovan Karadžić,[15] Ratko Mladić,[16] and Slobodan Milošević[17] have shown that the ICTY actively indicted high level players and was faithful to the task entrusted to it by the Security Council, namely to prosecute '*those most responsible*' for the crimes committed in the former Yugoslavia.

The ICTY has also proven that the nature of criminal responsibility attributable to persons in high positions of political and military power is best viewed through modes of liability such as aiding and abetting and joint criminal enterprise. In this regard, the Tribunal's significant contribution to the development and understanding of superior or command responsibility as a mode of liability must also be noted. It found, for instance, that a formal superior–subordinate relationship is not required for criminal liability to arise, but rather that the important threshold is that a person, whether a military, police or paramilitary commander, or a civilian leader such as a politician, exercised effective control.[18] The impact of the Tribunal's work is evident in the myriad references to its pronouncements by numerous organizations and institutions, from the International Committee of the Red Cross to other international courts, as well as in States' military manuals.[19]

[15] *Prosecutor v Karadžić* (Judgment) Case No IT-95-5/18-T (24 March 2016).

[16] *Prosecutor v Ratko Mladić* (Judgment) Case No ICTY-09-92-T (22 November 2017).

[17] See the case of *Prosecutor v Slobodan Milošević*. Case No IT-02-54.

[18] *Prosecutor v Delalić* et al (Judgment) Case No IT-96-21-A (20 February 2001) para 256.

[19] In addition to reference by organizations such as the International Committee of the Red Cross, international courts which have referred to the Tribunal's pronouncements in their own judgments and decisions include the International Court of Justice, the International Criminal Court, the Special Tribunal for Lebanon, the Extraordinary Chambers in the Courts of Cambodia, and the Special Court for Sierra Leone. In fact, the Statute of the Special Court for Sierra Leone provides in art 20(3) that the Judges of its Appeals Chamber 'shall be guided

In sum, these decisions have communicated a powerful message to persons across the globe: that crimes of serious concern to all of humankind, such as genocide, war crimes, and crimes against humanity, can in fact be tried in a court of law in today's time, and that no one—not even high ranking military officials, prime ministers, and presidents—can be immune from accountability.

1.3.2 Sexual Violence

I feel proud that one of the most historically and jurisprudentially significant achievements of the ICTY is its path-breaking role in bringing perpetrators of sexual crimes during conflict to justice.

The Tribunal's judgments have consistently brought to centre stage the legal protection afforded to the most vulnerable of any conflict, the victims. Among the most significant of these pronouncements are the findings that rape may be prosecuted as a grave breach of the Geneva Conventions and as a violation of the laws or customs of war,[20] that rape may constitute torture,[21] and that sexual enslavement can form enslavement as a crime against humanity.[22]

The ICTY's impact in this regard is undeniable: while sexual violence has been outlawed for more than a century,[23] no international tribunal had previously adjudicated on it in a satisfactory manner. The ICTY began investigating sexual crimes committed against women during the Yugoslav wars almost immediately after its establishment, clearly signalling its intent to consider matters of sexual violence as a matter of utmost concern and warranting absolute condemnation. Since its earliest cases, the ICTY dealt with allegations of sexual violence in the knowledge that such crimes are one of the very worst scourges of war and have a devastating effect on their victims.[24] It is therefore unsurprising that more than one-third of the persons found guilty by the ICTY have been convicted of crimes of sexual violence.[25]

It is my hope that other tribunals—national and international, existing and future—will continue building on this legacy and fighting for an end to impunity for sexual violence.

by the decisions of the Appeals Chamber of the International Tribunals for the former Yugoslavia and for Rwanda'. In military manuals, States often refer to the Tribunal's jurisprudence, see for instance the German Law of Armed Conflict Manual (ZDv 15/2, 2013), the United Kingdom Joint Service Manual of the Law of Armed Conflict (JSP 383, 2004), and the United States Department of Defence Law of War Manual (June 2015).

[20] *Prosecutor v Anto Furundžija* (Judgment) Case No IT-95-17/1-T (10 December 1998) para 172.

[21] *Prosecutor v Mucić* et al (Judgment) Case No IT-96-21-T (16 November 1998) paras 470–97.

[22] *Prosecutor v Kunarac* et al (Judgment) Case No IT-96-23 and 23/1 (22 February 2001) paras 539–43.

[23] See the Lieber Code. General Orders No 100: Instructions for the Government of Armies of the United States in the Field (24 April 1863) *reprinted in* 2 Francis Lieber, Contributions to Political Science 245, 247–74 (1881).

[24] Allegations of crimes of sexual violence have been heard in many cases before the Tribunal, including *Furundžija, Tadić, Mucić* et al, *Kupreškić* et al, *Blaškić, Kunarac* et al, *Kordić & Čerkez, Todorović, Krstić, Kvočka* et al, *Sikirica* et al, *Simić, Plavšić, Stakić, Češić, Brđanin, Blagojević & Jokić, Bralo, Rajić, Krajišnik, Martić, Haradinaj* et al, *Milutinović* et al, *Lukić and Lukić, Popović* et al, *Đorđević, Gotovina* et al, *Stanišić & Župljanin, Prlić* et al, *Stanišić & Simatović* and *Karadžić*.

[25] See 'In Numbers | International Criminal Tribunal For The Former Yugoslavia' (*ICTY*, 2016) <http://www.icty.org/en/features/crimes-sexual-violence/in-numbers> accessed 1 May 2019.

1.3.3 Protection of Victims and Witnesses

It is evident that the testimonies delivered by victims and witnesses constituted a necessary component of the fair and robust investigations and prosecution of crimes before the ICTY. Witnesses are instrumental in helping the Tribunal determine the underlying facts of the crimes with which the accused are charged, thereby facilitating the creation of a historical record of the events in the former Yugoslavia and the evaluation of the responsibility of the accused.

Most of the witnesses who choose to testify at the ICTY are either survivors of crimes themselves, or witnesses of brutalities, or family members of victims. For many such persons, describing the trauma suffered by them or their loved ones during the Yugoslav conflict is a challenging, painful exercise. In such a situation, it became imperative for the ICTY to offer enough support and protection to these witnesses to ensure that their dignity, safety, and psychological and mental health were safeguarded. Furthermore, as noted above, sexual violence was one among many atrocities prosecuted at the ICTY. Countless survivors of sexual assault mustered the courage to testify before the ICTY in order to bring perpetrators to justice. Given the power dynamics in sexual crimes—particularly in the highly charged environment of ethnic conflict—the need to promise to victims and witnesses protection, freedom from intimidation, and anonymity if necessary, became especially important. At the ICTY, I am proud to note that discretion and protection of victims and witnesses were never sacrificed at the altar of legal formalism.

The ICTY's Witness Support and Operations Unit and Witness Protection Unit (collectively referred to as VWS) was the first of its kind in the context of modern-day international criminal tribunals. During the ICTY's life span, the VWS provided assistance and support to approximately 5,500 witnesses called to appear before the Tribunal and to their accompanying support persons. As some witnesses testified on more than one occasion, this resulted in almost 8,500 visits to The Hague or video-link locations.

Almost two-thirds of the witnesses testified publicly without any in-court protective measures. However, when necessary to protect their security or privacy, the ICTY applied protective measures in accordance with the Tribunal's Rules of Procedure and Evidence. These included expunging the victim's or witness's name and other identifying information from the public record, assigning to him or her a pseudonym for the proceedings, modifying the victim's or witness' face or voice in televised proceedings, and conducting closed sessions.[26]

In addition to providing logistical and psycho-social support to witnesses, the ICTY also coordinated responses to address security threats to witnesses before, during, and after their testimony. Relocation was the most extreme response, with approximately 1 per cent of witnesses having been relocated. This required the Tribunal to cooperate closely with law enforcement agencies in The Netherlands, third States, as well as in the States of the former Yugoslavia.

A study conducted in 2012–2015 investigating the long-term impact of testifying on witnesses before the ICTY[27] found that the process of testifying is varied, complex, and

[26] International Criminal Tribunal for the former Yugoslavia, *Rules of Procedure and Evidence*, Rules 75 and 79 (adopted 12 November 1997, revised 30 September 2002, last amended 11 February 2005).

[27] International Criminal Tribunal for the former Yugoslavia, *Echoes of Testimonies: A Pilot Study into the Long-term Impact of Bearing Witness Before the ICTY* (UNT 2016).

different for each witness. Most of the participants had experienced severe emotional or physical trauma during the conflicts. The most frequently cited reasons for testifying were altruistic, namely to help the judges reach an accurate decision and to fulfil a moral duty to victims. The vast majority of the 300 witnesses interviewed stated that they felt fairly treated by the ICTY, regardless of whether they were called to testify for the Prosecution or the Defence, and that they felt like they had contributed personally to justice and truth telling.

1.3.4 Outreach

I am a firm proponent of the potential of sensitive and sustained dialogue to bring about agreement and understanding. This is precisely what the ICTY sought to achieve through its outreach programme, which offers the Tribunal an opportunity to work with the communities in the region and reflect on its work.[28] The outreach programme aims to ensure that despite the Tribunal's geographical distance from the locations of the atrocities, our judgments, trials, and appeals are accessible to the people of the region. Speaking before the General Assembly in 1999—the year that the outreach programme was first instituted—then President Gabrielle Kirk McDonald noted that the programme would focus on '*communicating with the peoples of the former Yugoslavia in the local languages, using innovative strategies to reach bar associations, other legal groups, universities and schools, media sources as well as the proverbial man and woman on the street*'.[29]

In 2017, I commented that the outreach programme, by functioning as a liaison between the tribunal and those who are most affected by the crimes committed in the former Yugoslavia, enabled countless people in the region to witness justice being done in the Hague and support justice being done at home. In addition, outreach also helped strengthen accountability efforts at international and national levels. As part of the outreach programme, the ICTY Office of the Prosecutor (OTP) regularly engaged with various local actors—including media outlets in the former Yugoslavia—not only to help foster acceptance of the Tribunal's work in the affected regions, but also to build local capacity to facilitate domestic prosecution of the crimes committed during the Yugoslav conflicts. I am optimistic that these efforts will be conducive towards developing measures to promote accountability at the domestic level. Furthermore, by ensuring that details, figures, and statistics are disseminated through an official mouthpiece—the ICTY itself—the outreach programme helped guard against the dangers of misinformation.

Another imaginative project developed by the ICTY outreach team is the Youth Outreach Programme, which seeks to harness the ability of young men and women in the former Yugoslavia—who may have been born after the conflicts subsided—to view their past with critical, objective insight, question entrenched narratives in their home countries, and assess the work of the ICTY in an impartial manner. Through this project, the ICTY connected with individuals who may be tomorrow's pacesetters in international criminal law—and indeed, for a field that demands as much compassion and empathy as it does

[28] International Criminal Tribunal for the former Yugoslavia, *Outreach: 15 Years of Outreach at the ICTY* (United Nations 2016) 1.

[29] International Criminal Tribunal for the former Yugoslavia, Press Release, Address to the United Nations General Assembly by Judge Gabrielle Kirk McDonald, President of the International Criminal Tribunal for the former Yugoslavia, 8 November 1999.

technical expertise, inspiring youth from post-conflict zones to think about international criminal justice can only be beneficial.

Further, although all the strategies described above are equally important in working towards reconciliation, the value of physical visits to the concerned regions by persons who represent the institution—such as legal officers, judges, and prosecutors—cannot be overstated. Not only do these visits communicate to affected communities that their histories and lives are important to the Tribunal, but real interactions with persons who suffered through the conflicts being adjudicated at the Tribunal help reaffirm our commitment to the cause, by putting faces to our abstract goals. It has now been seventeen years since I was appointed as a judge at the Tribunal. Only a few months subsequent to my appointment, I led the first ever on-site visit of judges to the region, beginning in Sarajevo. Since then, I have returned to Bosnia and Herzegovina and other parts of the former Yugoslavia, on countless occasions. However, my first experience in Sarajevo as a newly appointed judge of the ICTY will always be fresh in my mind as a humbling reminder of what we do, and why we do it.

For all these reasons, I strongly encourage all courts dealing with grave crimes of international concern to adopt robust outreach strategies. This will allow the significance of the work done by these chambers to be recognized, acknowledged, and understood by the witnesses and victims of the crimes.

1.3.5 Gender Parity

The success of an institution is heavily determined by its staff. It goes without saying that the ICTY enjoyed a multicultural work environment—it was not uncommon to walk down the corridor and hear three different languages been spoken—but its track record in terms of gender parity has also been exemplary. It achieved gender parity in 2009, and from 2008–2014 the rate of promotion for female staff was consistently greater than that of male staff.

The issue of gender equality has always been close to my heart. During the very first trial I presided over at the ICTY, the *Brđanin* case, I shared the bench with two outstanding women, Judge Taya from Japan and Judge Janu from Czech Republic, while Joanna Korner appeared as Counsel for the Prosecution under the erstwhile Chief Prosecutor, Carla Del Ponte. Since then, I have been fortunate to have continued working with many outstanding women in the field of international criminal law. In my own work, I have always appreciated the importance of being surrounded by persons from all walks of life, with diverse, interesting viewpoints, and I have actively hired and promoted talented women (as well as men) throughout the years. I believe that it is the responsibility of the highest levels to lead by example to ensure these goals are fulfilled. While selecting my staff, I strive to establish an environment that is both meritocratic and gender balanced, and I am proud to have achieved that at the Office of the President. Indeed, from my *Chef de Cabinet* to my legal officers, I am fortunate to be surrounded by a competent team that has always been predominantly composed of women.

Of course, gender equality in professional contexts requires not only equitable recruitment, but also equal opportunities to flourish and succeed at the workplace. At the ICTY, we channelled our energies towards cultivating a professional environment devoid of sexual harassment and abuse of authority. Further, recognizing the unsavoury fact that gender-neutral distribution of responsibilities in the domestic sphere is not yet a reality, the employees (women in particular) of the ICTY were invited to make use of our varied flexible working arrangements. Across all of the ICTY's organs, this practice was followed at all levels (including senior management) and has been encouraged from the top down.

At the same time, I recognize that there is a long way to go to achieve total gender parity—particularly at the very highest levels, including judges and principals at international courts. The ICTY has been fortunate to have had one of the most prolific war crimes prosecutors—Carla Del Ponte—at the helm of its OTP from 1999 to 2007. We witnessed a watershed moment in the history of gender parity in international justice, when all three ICTY principals were female.[30] Unfortunately, we do not have any women judges or principals at the ICTY at the end of our mandate, and I note that the cause of equal representation at the very highest levels across all international courts and tribunals requires much work still. To me, true gender parity can only be said to have been achieved when situations such as *Brđanin* become commonplace, rather than cause for celebration.

I am hopeful that other international institutions will build on the ICTY's example and continue to promote female talent at all levels. In terms of our impact on professional practices in international law, I believe this is one of the most significant legacies we will leave behind.

1.4 My Hopes for the Future

I truly believe that the ICTY was a pioneering instrument in replacing a culture of impunity with today's ethos of accountability. I am in the unique—and privileged—position of being the last president of this experimental, unpredictable, and ultimately, highly successful institution. This occasion of the closure of the ICTY is bittersweet to me for numerous reasons. First, I would like to unequivocally state how proud I am of all we have achieved over the past twenty-four years. Of course, given the unique historical circumstances that catalysed the ICTY's creation, much ink can be spilled about all we could have done differently. At the same time, I hope and believe that most will agree that there is a lot we have done right.

As in any field, however, we—practitioners of international criminal law—should be wary of resting on our laurels. The goal of global criminal justice is still quite a way off, and there is a lot of work yet to be done. I mean this in two different contexts: *first*, within the specific framework of the ICTY and the International Residual Mechanism for Criminal Tribunals (IRMCTs), there are still persons who ought to be indicted for their crimes in the former Yugoslavia. As always, these indictments and trials must be completed in conjunction with the implementation of appropriate, carefully oriented reconciliation and outreach plans in the concerned regions. It is my sincerest hope that the guideposts set up by the ICTY will continue to illuminate the way forward for justice in the republics of the former Yugoslavia.

Secondly, in a broader context, I firmly believe that the world as it stands today requires positive complementarity measures to be embraced by all countries. The cause of international criminal justice requires the global community to avow its commitment to

[30] Dorothee de Sampayo Garrido-Nijgh (Registrar, 1995–2000); Louise Arbour (Prosecutor, 1996–1999); Judge Gabrielle Kirk McDonald (President, 1997–1999).

principles of international law, peace, and security at all levels. Complementarity recognizes that international courts are last resorts, meant only to prosecute perpetrators of the gravest international crimes,[31] and that such courts should step in only where countries themselves are unable or unwilling genuinely to deliver justice.[32] Scholars[33] today advocate the adoption of 'positive' or 'proactive' complementarity measures, which extend further, encouraging the development of local capacity for international criminal investigation and prosecution. Trying perpetrators of mass atrocities at domestic and regional levels will be a step forward for both, the sovereign equality of States in the international community, and the protection of victims. I see a number of avenues through which this idea may be adopted into practice.

1.4.1 State Cooperation

In order for the mandate of the ICC to succeed, it is imperative that all the State parties observe its norms and ratify the Statute. It is also desirable for these countries to amend their domestic laws such that they reflect international criminal law principles. This would bolster criminal justice at local levels, allowing countries to prosecute crimes of international concern internally. In today's climate, it is important to emphasize that rather than militate against State sovereignty, such a practice is likely to reinforce sovereignty, by reducing the need for external intervention and adjudication.

Article 86 of the ICC Statute sets out the general obligation to cooperate, requiring States parties to '*cooperate fully*'[34] with the ICC in investigating and prosecuting crimes within the ICC's jurisdiction. In terms of the ICC Statute itself, this includes genocide, crimes against humanity, war crimes, and the crime of aggression. This *general* obligation to '*cooperate fully*' encompasses the responsibility of States to comply with requests made by the ICC to provide *specific* forms of assistance, such as the service of documents, provision of official documents, surrender of persons, and '*any other type of assistance which is not prohibited by the law of the requested State*'.[35]

On a case-to-case basis, third states not party to the ICC Statute may also be subject to various cooperation regimes. This becomes exceptionally important where crimes of international concern take place on territories of States that are not party to the ICC. For example, the United Nations Security Council noted in 2005 that '*the situation in Sudan continues to constitute a threat to international peace and security*'.[36] It referred the Darfur

[31] M Drumbl, 'Policy Through Complementarity: the Atrocity Trial as Justice' in C Stahn and M M El Zeidy (eds), *The International Criminal Court and Complementarity: From Theory to Practice* (CUP 2014) 210.

[32] O Bekou, 'Complementarity Principle' (*Oxford Bibliographies*, 2012) available at <https://www.oxfordbibliographies.com/view/document/obo-9780199796953/obo-9780199796953-0071.xml> accessed 13 October 2019.

[33] W W Burke-White, 'Proactive Complementarity: The International Criminal Court and National Courts in the Rome System of International Justice' (2008) 49 Harvard International Law Journal 53; See also L Carter, 'The Future of the International Criminal Court: Complementarity as a Strength or a Weakness?' (2013) 12 Washington University Global Studies Law Review 45; See also International Criminal Court, Report of the Bureau on Stocktaking: Complementarity to the 8th Session of the Assembly of States Parties, ICC Doc ICC-ASP/8/51 (2010) para 16.

[34] Art 86 of the Rome Statute of the International Criminal Court.

[35] Part IX of the Rome Statute of the International Criminal Court.

[36] UNSC Resolution 1591 (2005) UN Doc S/RES/1591 (2005).

crisis to the ICC, and urged Sudan—which is not party to the ICC Statute—and all other parties to the conflict to cooperate fully with the prosecution and investigation of the crimes that occurred in the context of the conflict.

While State sovereignty is an intrinsically important attribute, concerns regarding human life should, I believe, be paramount: in the above-mentioned conflict, before the Security Council's resolution, 200,000 refugees had fled to Chad from Darfur, while 1.65 million remained internally displaced within Darfur.[37] There are countless other crises currently ongoing in the world. At this juncture, States should be urged to enter into cooperation agreements with the ICC in order to facilitate efficient and impartial prosecution.

I also see immense potential in the establishment of hybrid courts and tribunals to enforce accountability at regional levels. 'Mixed' or hybrid courts combine domestic and international approaches while fulfilling their mandates to try crimes of international concern. Generally, such hybrid courts are created on an ad hoc basis to address location or time-bound situations. I find it important to make two observations concerning hybrid courts. *First*, I believe that the establishment of such institutions should be actively encouraged by the international community. These mixed courts can help allay States' anxieties regarding loss of domestic control over violent situations, as is feared in the case of the ICC.[38] By applying elements of domestic law—both substantive and procedural—to judicial proceedings, and employing local judges, prosecutors, and administrators, hybrid courts may be more easily acceptable in the present climate than their international counterparts.

Secondly, it is necessary to note that international cooperation remains indispensable even for hybrid courts. While the sponsor State plays a fundamental role in the administration and operation of the court, cooperation from other States continues to be essential, particularly in matters of extradition and arrest. If the court is located outside the concerned region—as was the case for the New York and Hague offices of the Special Court for Sierra Leone (SCSL) —inter-State assistance becomes all the more thorny and complicated.

1.4.2 Cooperation with Non-State Actors

Criminal courts—domestic, international, and hybrid—are only one probable mechanism. They are unlikely to bridge all gaps in accountability in all territories.[39] For example, there is no political impetus to create a tribunal to address gross human rights abuses in States like Afghanistan.[40] Cooperation with non-judicial actors like regional human rights commissions, non-governmental organizations, independent fact-finding bodies, and so on, in such situations can ensure that the question of accountability remains visible even where no courts are actively trying suspected perpetrators.

[37] 'Highlighting Insecurity In Sudan's Darfur, UN Urges Support For African Force—Chad' (*UN News*, 2004) <https://reliefweb.int/report/chad/highlighting-insecurity-sudans-darfur-un-urges-support-african-force> accessed 1 May 2019.

[38] C Wagner, 'Western Europe' in D M Mahone, C R Mohan and S Raghavan (eds), *The Oxford Handbook of Indian Foreign Policy* (OUP 2015) 502.

[39] P K Mendez, 'The New Wave of Hybrid Tribunals: A Sophisticated Approach to Enforcing International Humanitarian Law or an Idealistic Situation with Empty Promises?' (2009) 20 Criminal Law Forum 53.

[40] S Williams, *Hybrid and Internationalised Criminal Tribunals: Selected Jurisdictional Issues* (Hart Publishing 2012) 190.

Undeniably, justice is one of the basic prerequisites for achieving peace and reconciliation in post-conflict zones. This is particularly so given the indispensable role played by justice in bringing accountability to perpetrators and redress for victims. On its own, however, justice is insufficient to rebuild territories shattered by sectarian hatreds and violence. As noted by the International Center for Transitional Justice, atrocities and systematic abuses of human rights devastate entire societies, rendering their most essential institutions—both political and legal—fragile and unsound.[41]

Given the all-pervasive nature of the damage, mere adjudication is unlikely to deliver the kind of wholesale support required in post-conflict States to achieve reconciliation and resurrection of the rule of law. Such regions also need fruitful dialogues between the parties, strong commitment towards peace and understanding by the ruling leadership, and condemnation of denial of past atrocities. These hugely important functions cannot be played by international courts—our task is to prosecute, defend, and deliver justice. As my colleague Judge Fausto Pocar recently commented, the best thing a court can do is its own work.[42]

Accordingly, the international community must encourage and support non-governmental agencies, international organizations, academic institutions, and civil society actors that are working to facilitate reconstruction in post-conflict territories.

1.4.3 Capacity Building

The ICTY was never established with the intention to prosecute all persons suspected of having committed war crimes during the Yugoslav wars. It was intended to prosecute those 'most' responsible—that is, the leaders, spearheading the ethnic cleansing and genocidal missions within the territory of the former Yugoslavia—with the majority of the trials to be conducted within the region itself. Accordingly, the ICTY did not issue any new indictments after the year 2004, and instead focused a considerable portion of its energies towards transferring cases revolving around lower-level perpetrators to local judiciaries. In addition, we transmitted evidence that did not culminate in indictments to local courts, with the hope that it may be of some use.

Judicial systems of a territory torn apart by wars rooted in extremist ethnic and racial ideology necessarily require some overhauling. Recognizing this, the ICTY has lent assistance to lawyers, academics, and courts in the former Yugoslavia that are engaged in prosecuting crimes relevant to our work. In particular, we supported the creation of specialized chambers for investigating and adjudicating war crimes in the region, and helped with capacity building in existing functional chambers so that they could take on war crimes cases in addition to regular casework. We also ensured that legal professionals and witness support staff in the region were duly trained by personnel experienced with war crimes adjudication here at the Tribunal, so as to ensure that the highest standards of witness protection, rights

[41] 'What Is Transitional Justice?' (*International Center for Transitional Justice*, 2019) <https://www.ictj.org/about/transitional-justice> accessed 1 May 2019.

[42] This was mentioned at the symposium, though I am not sure which year it was that Judge Pocar made the statement.

of the accused, and evidentiary thresholds are applied while investigating and adjudicating crimes committed in the former Yugoslavia.

Looking ahead, I believe that other tribunals—and indeed, even other non-governmental and international organizations dealing with international criminal law—should emphasize capacity building in affected regions. At the Kampala Review Conference in 2010, States drew particular attention to the need to enlarge domestic competence to investigate and prosecute grave international crimes.[43] South Africa and Denmark observed the need for States to assist each other in combating impunity at its origin: the national level.[44] At the same time, while domestic competence to prosecute and investigate crimes within the jurisdiction of the ICC is unquestioned, States may lack adequate capacity to do so.[45] To ensure that this does not cause an accountability vacuum, international institutions must step in to assist States in building capacity to bridge these gaps.

This again ties back to the complementarity principle: only when States can individually prosecute war crimes and crimes against humanity at local or regional levels will the burden on international courts lessen. In order to ensure that international tribunals function only as last resorts, the global community should encourage the development of sound international criminal and humanitarian law practice at national levels. Effective national prosecutions and investigations are essential to achieve the cause of international criminal justice and end impunity in all territories.[46]

1.5 Conclusion

Despite its many achievements, the ICTY is mindful of the criticisms that have been levelled against its functioning. I will attempt to briefly address a few chief arguments here. It has been alleged that the ICTY operates with a pro-Western bias. I would like to highlight that not only is the ICTY staffed with persons from all nationalities at all levels, but in fact its trials and appeals are conducted in accordance with the most stringent judicial standards, and the prevalence of one ethnicity amongst the indictees is never intended as a judgement on the ethnic group itself. Indeed, in any identity-based conflict, perpetrators employ nationalistic ideologies and rhetoric in order to stoke passions and inculcate a culture of fear. Against this backdrop, Prosecutor Serge Brammertz's pronouncement at the heels of the *Mladic* Judgment is especially relevant: each perpetrator's guilt is his alone.[47]

Critics have also queried why the ICTY has cost so much, and the fact that the ICTY has operated for twenty-five years has come under attack from some quarters who argue that it ought to have wrapped up its decisions considerably sooner. Here, it must be acknowledged that the crimes tried at the ICTY—war crimes, crimes against humanity, genocide—are unique primarily because they are '*atrocity-related and linked to a longer history of conflict*'.[48]

[43] International Criminal Court, Review Conference of the Rome Statute (22 June 2010) No ICC RC/ST/CM/1.
[44] International Criminal Court, Review Conference of the Rome Statute Stocktaking of International Criminal Justice, *Taking stock of the principle of complementarity: bridging the impunity gap*, Annex V(c), No ICC 11-E-011110, 107.
[45] ibid.
[46] Burke-White (n 33).
[47] International Criminal Tribunal for the former Yugoslavia, Statement of Prosecutor Serge Brammertz in relation to the judgment in the case *Prosecutor v Ratko Mladić*, 22 November 2017.
[48] C Stahn, 'The Future of International Criminal Justice' (2009) 3 Hague Justice Journal / Journal Judiciaire De La Haye 257, 258.

As a result, the entire process of adjudication, including investigation, indictment, trial, prosecution, defence, and sentencing, is intricate and complex, more so than civil and criminal domestic cases in national jurisdictions. Added to this is the fact that most of the indictees before the ICTY were persons who historically held immense political, social, or military power—often all three. As a consequence, their arrest and subsequent trials necessitated immense logistical and administrative coordination on part of the Tribunal, and often on part of individual States as well. Other factors that have impacted case timelines include the health of the accused[49] and complexities associated with self-represented accused,[50] such as the need to reassign counsel.[51] Added to these circumstances, which were all beyond the control of the ICTY, was the challenge posed by continuous staff attrition over the past fifteen years. It is beyond doubt that the high turnover of staff, and in particular Chambers legal staff, affected the speed of the Tribunal's proceedings.

Further, when the Tribunal was formally established by the Security Council in 1993,[52] no formal consideration was given to its completion strategy and no precise time was determined for its conclusion, although it was evident that it was intended to function as an ad hoc institution and would be temporary in nature. Over the course of the following years, the international community sought to evaluate how tribunals like the ICTY and the ICTR could operate more efficiently.[53] The Group of Experts constituted for this purpose observed, inter alia, that '*the major objectives of the Security Council are in large part not fulfilled if only low-level figures rather than the civilian, military and paramilitary leaders who were allegedly responsible for the atrocities are brought ... for trial*' and that '*devoting huge resources to the prosecution of "small fry" while vindicating the wholly understandable and justified emotions of individuals and families victimized by atrocities would leave major goals largely unattained*'.[54] This emphasis on prosecuting only those most responsible for the crimes committed in the former Yugoslavia accorded with the erstwhile Prosecutor's statement that the foremost focus of the ICTY OTP ought to be on the investigation and trial of the leaders of the Federal Republic of Yugoslavia and the Republic of Serbia.[55]

To ensure that it did not utilize more time and resources than necessary or intended, ICTY has constantly worked in furtherance of this precise purpose: as early as 2001, Judge Claude Jorda, then President of the ICTY, spoke of the Tribunal's efforts to expedite its proceedings and focus its activity on cases concerning major leaders and high ranking

[49] See, for instance, UN Security Council, Eleventh Annual Report of the ICTY, UN Doc A/59/215-S/2004/627 (2004) para 124; and UN Security Council, Twelfth Annual Report of the ICTY, UN Doc A/60/267-S/2005/532 and A/60/267-S/2005/532/Corr1 (2005) para 82, in which it is noted that the case against Slobodan Milošević had been delayed on several occasions owing to the poor health of the accused; UN Security Council Completion Strategy Assessment, UN Doc S/2008/326 (2008) para 14, in which it is noted that the schedule in the *Delić* case was changed to sitting four days a week instead of five owing to the health of the accused; and UN Security Council Completion Strategy Assessment, UN Doc S/2009/252 (2009) para 16, in which it is noted that the commencement and progress of the *Stanišić and Simatović* trial had been significantly delayed due to the poor health of Jovica Stanišić.

[50] UN Security Council, Completion Strategy Report of 1 June 2010 (2010) UN Doc S/2010/270 (2010).

[51] UN Security Council, Completion Strategy Report of 13 November 2009 (2009) UN Doc S/2009/589 (2009).

[52] UN Security Council Resolution 827 (1993) UN Doc S/RES/827 (1993) para 2. See also UN Security Council Resolution 808 (1993) UN Doc S/RES/808 (1993).

[53] UN General Assembly Resolution 53/212 (18 December 1998) UN Doc A/RES/53/212 (1998).

[54] UN General Assembly, Financing the ICTY since 1991 (2000) UN Doc A/54/634-S/2000/597 (2000) para 96.

[55] See statement by Carla Del Ponte, Prosecutor of the International Criminal Tribunal for the former Yugoslavia on the investigation and prosecution of crimes committed in Kosovo, press release, 29 September 1999, <http://www.icty.org/en/press/statement-carla-del-ponte-prosecutor-international-criminal-tribunal-former-yugoslavia> accessed 13 October 2019.

officials.[56] The then Prosecutor similarly mentioned the potential transfer of certain cases of lesser importance to national jurisdictions in the former Yugoslavia, once those jurisdictions had built up their judicial capacities.[57] In 2002, the judges of the ICTY met to discuss a possible completion strategy, reviewing the report on the matter drafted by the President, Prosecutor, and the Registrar.[58] The joint report, which referred to the ICTY's completion strategy, was submitted to the Security Council. The Security Council welcomed the report, endorsing in particular the ICTY's proposed strategy for the transfer of cases involving intermediary and lower-level accused to competent national jurisdictions.[59]

These efforts demonstrate the ICTY's cognizance of its status as an ad hoc, temporary tribunal, and its conscientiousness and determination in formulating a workable process to expedite and conclude its own operations. Furthermore, the ICTY was not mandated to develop complex outreach strategies and try and achieve reconciliation in the affected regions. The fact is, however, that the ICTY progressed beyond the bare bones of these tasks, recognized the gravity of the matters within its jurisdiction, attempted to bring to justice more than a hundred persons alleged to have participated in the atrocities, and formulated outreach programmes to try and connect with the affected communities and gain acceptance for the Tribunal's painstaking work.

The sun has set on the ICTY, after a quarter of a century and completion of trials for all 161 of its indictees. Today's environment differs greatly from the time that the ICTY was established. Now, people are used to peace and stability, and are less amenable to sacrificing State sovereignty at the altar of international investigations. At the end of the twentieth century, the world was desperate to see perpetrators of mass atrocities brought to justice, investing fledgling institutions like the ICTY with immense optimism and expectation. I hope that we have done justice to these ideals.

At the time of the establishment of the ICTY, despite the knowledge that 'international criminal law' was an uncertain professional path, a substantial number of competent lawyers agreed to join this newborn institution. I can only conclude that these persons consented to what could be considered a major career gamble in those times, because they were cognizant of the historical significance of the task in their hands. These are the people who breathed life into an ad hoc tribunal whose path seemed unclear and daunting. I am very grateful to them, for I believe that they helped lay the foundation for the collaborative, optimistic culture that characterizes the ICTY today. The people who worked here were truly committed to the admirable mandate of the ICTY and were genuinely happy to work together to achieve that, without personal agendas. Today, faced with the threat of politicization, nationalism, and a floundering will to subject territories to international jurisdiction, the international community stands at a crossroads. While it deliberates the future of international criminal justice, this memory would serve it well: that at the heart of any successful judicial institution, there lie individual persons motivated to bring justice for unimaginable atrocities.

[56] UN Security Council, Agenda for the 4429th Meeting (2001) UN Doc S/PV.4429 (2001) 3–5.

[57] ibid 12.

[58] UN Security Council, Letter Date 17 June 2002 from the Secretary-General addressed to the President of the Security Council (2002) UN Doc S/2002/678 (2002) enclosure, para 6.

[59] UN Security Council, Statement by the President of the Security Council (23 July 2002) UN Doc S/PRST/2002/21 (2002).

Judge Antonio Cassese, who was the first president of both the ICTY and the Special Tribunal for Lebanon (STL), once observed that prior to the establishment of a tribunal, its circumstances tended to be more political than legal:[60] the rationales for creating that particular tribunal (and the failure to institute judicial mechanisms in other parts of the world); the mechanics of its proposed functioning; the negotiations surrounding its governing documentation. However, the atmosphere shifts once the tribunal is set up and begins functioning: prosecutors investigate, defence counsels assist accused persons, the judges convict or acquit. This is the first step towards reconciliation, albeit insufficient on its own.

The work of the ICTY, as well as other ad hoc tribunals like the ICTR, the STL, and the SCSL, has been instrumental in entrenching the expectation of accountability for international crimes. At this juncture, it is important for the international community to pledge to uphold this expectation, reinforce this culture of accountability, and refuse to backtrack into an age where impunity was the norm and justice an exception.

[60] R Bahnam, 'Hariri Tribunal Judge Antonio Cassese Talks To Asharq Al-Awsat' (*Special Tribunal for Lebanon*, 2009).

2

Making Complementarity a Reality

The Experiences of the ICTY and IRMCT Office of the Prosecutor

*Serge Brammertz**

2.1 Introduction

The International Criminal Tribunal for the former Yugoslavia (ICTY) recently completed its mandate with the delivery of its final judgments. For twenty-five years, the Office of the Prosecutor (OTP) fought to bring to justice those most responsible for the horrific atrocities committed during the conflicts in the countries of the former Yugoslavia. With all fugitives accounted for and ninety persons convicted, the OTP achieved credible results and a record of accountability unmatched by any other modern international criminal tribunal.

Upon its establishment, the ICTY was the archetype of international primacy, designed to remedy the failings of national accountability by replacing it with an international justice mechanism. Today, though, international courts are no longer seen as the primary, much less the only, mechanism to achieve justice for serious international crimes. While a coherent model is still in development, international justice is being increasingly nationalized. National courts are now understood to be an essential element of the solution, particularly in partnership with the international community.

Through the impetus of the ICTY Completion Strategy, the ICTY OTP moved away from primacy and towards the model of complementarity, prompting far more extensive engagement with national judiciaries in the countries of the former Yugoslavia. Distinct from complementarity as practised at the International Criminal Court (ICC), positive complementarity as practised by the ICTY OTP led to substantial improvements in the capacities of national judiciaries to process war crimes cases. Based on experiences and lessons learned, the OTP then pushed beyond notions of complementarity, by developing a new model of collaboration between international and national prosecutors, promoting more comprehensive justice.

This chapter explores the development over the last two decades in the ICTY OTP's relationships with national criminal justice. In this important area, the ICTY OTP has been part of a real-world laboratory for evolving theories and practices.

Section 2.2 begins by describing the shift at the ICTY from primacy to complementarity, illustrating how this concept was translated into law and providing examples of complementarity in practice. Section 2.3 discusses subsequent developments at the ICTY OTP that moved beyond the existing models of primacy and complementarity. The OTP's

* Current Chief Prosecutor of the International Residual Mechanism for Criminal Tribunals. Formerly, Chief Prosecutor of the International Criminal Tribunal for the former Yugoslavia.

Serge Brammertz, *Making Complementarity a Reality* In: *Legacies of the International Criminal Tribunal for the Former Yugoslavia*. Edited by: Carsten Stahn, Carmel Agius, Serge Brammertz, Colleen Rohan, Oxford University Press (2020).
DOI: 10.1093/oso/9780198862956.003.0003

contemporaneous activities with national prosecutors are described to indicate the contours of a new collaborative approach to international criminal justice. Finally, section 2.4 concludes by reflecting on the lessons from the ICTY OTP experiences that may help inform future accountability efforts and looks forward to the International Residual Mechanism for Criminal Tribunals (IRMCT) OTP and its continuation of what the ICTY began.

2.2 From Primacy to Complementarity at the ICTY

2.2.1 Challenges to Primacy in Practice

Investigations by the ICTY OTP formally began in 1994 in the midst of an ongoing conflict, and it was not until the end of 1995 that the Croatian and Bosnian hostilities ended. During the conflicts and for some years after, the OTP was only able to carry out limited investigations, primarily obtaining accounts of mass atrocities from witnesses. It did not receive the access it needed to obtain evidence, such as mapping crime scenes, exhuming mass graves, and interviewing potential insider witnesses. Cooperation from State and local authorities was needed to obtain access. Unfortunately, such cooperation was often not forthcoming.

During the investigation of crimes in the Republika Srpska, one of the two entities in Bosnia and Herzegovina (BiH), the OTP was repeatedly denied access by the authorities and advised by the international community not to enter the area due to security concerns, even after the conflict. It was not until late 1997 that the first search and seizure mission was conducted in Prijedor, where thousands of victims were brutally killed or detained in severe conditions in 1992. The situation was equally, if not more, difficult in Croatia and Serbia. It took ten years to get hold of documentation from the respective governments. Even with the legal authority of the Security Council through Chapter VII of the United Nations Charter, the OTP had to negotiate for access, in many instances with the same people who had been in power during the conflict.

Executing arrest warrants was also particularly problematic. The Dayton Peace Accords ended the conflict in BiH and established a peacekeeping mission. But while it required the States of the former Yugoslavia to cooperate with the ICTY, the peacekeeping forces were not under the same obligation. States that contributed peacekeepers were initially reluctant to arrest fugitives present in BiH who had been indicted by the ICTY. By 1997, only seven indictees were in custody, while more than fifty were at large.

Even once arrests finally began in BiH, rapidly increasing the number of accused in the ICTY's custody,[1] there continued to be significant problems with obtaining arrests in other States. The case of Ratko Mladić, former Commander of the Main Staff of the Bosnian Serb Army and one of the ICTY's most wanted fugitives, illustrates the problem. Mladić was indicted in 1995,[2] and an international warrant for his arrest was issued in 1996.[3] Until 2001, he was moving freely in Belgrade, fully aware that the government would not transfer him

[1] By mid-1998, there were already thirty indictees in the Tribunal's Detention Unit, almost four times as many as the year before.

[2] *Prosecutor v Mladić* (Initial Indictment) Case No IT-95-5-I (24 July 1995).

[3] *Prosecutor v Karadžić and Mladić*, (Review of Indictments Pursuant to Rule 61 of the Rules of Procedure and Evidence) Cases No IT-95-5-R61/IT-95-18-R61 (11 July 1996).

to The Hague. The difficulties arresting fugitives posed significant risks to the ICTY and the principle of primacy.[4]

At the same time, political frustrations arose within the Security Council. The international community started questioning when, if ever, the ICTY would complete its mandate. Projections that the ICTY's work would be completed in 2016 were already seen as too distant. These concerns were compounded by the overall negative public perception of the ICTY's legitimacy in the affected countries.

While the ICTY had been granted primacy under Article 9 of the ICTY Statute, that framework did not prove to be a sufficient solution to the challenges it was facing. More engagement was needed by the OTP with law enforcement, judicial and political authorities in the region. Over time, this approach, combined with pressure from the international community, resulted in obtaining the necessary access to evidence and the arrests of fugitives. Concurrently, post-conflict developments in the affected countries began creating the conditions necessary to envisage genuine prosecutions at the national level.[5] These developments were further supported by international diplomatic encouragement, in particular in the context of the European Union's negotiations on association and accession with Serbia, BiH, and Croatia.[6]

2.2.2 The Shift: The Completion Strategy

In 2001, Prosecutor Carla Del Ponte noted that the OTP estimated that there were approximately 8,000 individuals responsible for war crimes in the former Yugoslavia.[7] It was clear, particularly in light of the challenges that had already slowed its work, that the ICTY would not be able to process all these cases. This realization contributed to the development of the ICTY Completion Strategy. As ICTY President Claude Jorda suggested to the Security Council in November 2001, moving forward the ICTY 'should focus more on prosecuting crimes constituting the most serious breaches of international public law and order, primarily those committed by high-ranking military and political officials'.[8] This, however, would not result in impunity for the remaining cases, because it was envisaged that other cases against mid- and low-level suspects 'could, under certain conditions, be relocated; that is, tried by the courts of the States created out of the former Yugoslavia'.[9]

The Completion Strategy was formally submitted to the Security Council a year later.[10] In addition to identifying deadlines for the completion of its work, the ICTY recommended

[4] Then-President Cassese remarked, '[I]t was politically difficult to get rid of [the Tribunal]. However, one could paralyze it. A tribunal without defendants, without trials, would cost a fortune and produce nothing of value', P Hazan, *Justice in a Time of War* (Texas A&M University Press 2004) 69.

[5] See W Burke-White, 'The Domestic Influence of International Criminal Tribunals: The International Criminal Tribunal for the Former Yugoslavia and the Creation of the State Court of Bosnia & Herzegovina' (2008) 46 Columbia Journal of Transnational Law 279, 288; R Rastan, 'Complementarity: Contest or Collaboration?' in M Bergsmo (ed), *Complementarity and the Exercise of Universal Jurisdiction for Core International Crimes* (FICHL Publication Series 2010) 111.

[6] See I Rangelov, 'EU Conditionality and Transitional Justice in the Former Yugoslavia' (2006) 2 Croatian Yearbook of European Law and Policy 365, 365–75.

[7] UNSC, '4429th Meeting' (2001) UN Doc S/PV/4429, 31. See also International Criminal for the former Yugoslavia, Infographic: Investigations, available at <http://www.icty.org/sid/97> accessed 30 May 2018.

[8] UNSC (n 7) 5.

[9] ibid.

[10] International Criminal Tribunal for the Former Yugoslavia, 'Report on the judicial status of the International Criminal Tribunal for the former Yugoslavia and the prospects for referring certain cases to national courts, 17

that a number of cases involving lower and intermediate level accused be transferred to the State Court of BiH, which was then in the process of being established,[11] with the possibility to broaden the process to other countries if there were further developments.[12]

The ICTY indicated that there would need to be legal reforms at the ICTY to implement this proposal, and that the preferred solution was for the Security Council to amend the Statute. The ICTY further noted that significant changes would need to be made to the Rules to permit the referral process that was envisaged.[13]

The ICTY also indicated that significant legal reforms and capacity building would be needed in countries to which referrals would be considered. In particular, reforms were needed to ensure fair trial standards, equality of treatment, minimum conditions of detention, and the abolition of the death penalty. The ICTY further proposed a number of measures necessary to adapt national proceedings to the specific requirements of war crimes prosecutions, including integrating international judges in the national courts, training national judges on international criminal law, and making provision in national law for the protection of witnesses.[14]

In Resolutions 1503 and 1534, the Security Council endorsed the Completion Strategy as the best way to allow the ICTY to achieve its completion objectives. The Security Council further called on the donor community to support the establishment of a war crimes chamber in the State Court of Bosnia and Herzegovina.[15]

The Completion Strategy thus began shifting the ICTY from primacy to a potential model of complementarity, where national prosecutions of intermediate and low-level suspects would complement international prosecutions of high-level suspects in order to achieve more comprehensive accountability.[16] Such a division of labour represented a significant shift in attitudes at the ICTY. For the OTP, primacy was initially understood to be necessary for more successful prosecutions of senior-level suspects; referring cases, even against intermediate-level suspects, thus could be seen as creating a risk for the OTP's remaining trials. For the Chambers, primacy symbolized and contributed to significant trends perceived to be underway in international law, where international courts applying international law would be able to overcome barriers to justice raised by State sovereignty.

Yet in the face of a range of practical challenges, the ICTY was beginning to recognize the importance of national judiciaries. Admittedly, this process did not begin out of concern for increased national participation in post-conflict justice. Had the ICTY been able to secure the necessary cooperation from the outset and thus manage its caseload more expeditiously, it may have never found it necessary to look at national courts as potential partners. But the circumstances forced the ICTY to look beyond its courtrooms to ensure that accountability was achieved, and to propose a framework incorporating both international and national prosecutions.

June 2002', attached to a letter from the Secretary-General of the UN to the President of the Security Council (2002) UN Doc S/2002/678.

[11] ibid paras 63–68.
[12] ibid para 45.
[13] ibid paras 37–44.
[14] ibid paras 72–73.
[15] UNSC Res 1503 (28 August 2003) UN Doc S/RES/1503; UNSC Res 1534 (26 March 2004) UN Doc S/RES/1534. See also UNSC, 'Presidential Statement' (23 July 2002) UN Doc S/2002/PRST/21.
[16] UNSC (n 7) 5.

2.2.3 Positive Complementarity at the ICTY

2.2.3.1 *Reform at the ICTY*

Following the adoption of the Completion Strategy, Rule 11*bis* was significantly amended, changing it from a mechanism to regulate primacy to the means to begin implementing complementarity at the ICTY.[17] The amendments to Rule 11*bis* adopted on 30 December 2002 changed the title of the rule to 'Referral of the Indictment to Another Court'. To change the Rule from a deferral to a referral mechanism, Section (A) first expanded the eligible States to include the State where the crime was committed. Later, this was further amended to enable referral to any State 'having jurisdiction and being willing and adequately prepared to accept such a case'.

The procedure for referral was also significantly changed. Reflecting the procedure for deferral in Rule 9, only the Prosecutor could initiate the procedure under the initial version of Rule 11*bis*. The revised 11*bis* now also allowed the Trial Chamber to initiate a referral proceeding *proprio motu*.[18] In addition, the revised Rule 11*bis* for the first time required the Prosecutor to transfer 'appropriate' material to the State authorities, which had previously been entirely at the Prosecutor's discretion. Revisions were also made to clarify that the Trial Chamber could issue orders for the protection of witnesses or victims that would apply during the national proceedings.

The final significant amendments to Rule 11*bis* addressed the requirements for referral. First, the Trial Chamber was required to consider the criteria identified in the Completion Strategy, namely the gravity of the crimes charged and the level of responsibility of the accused. Second, the Trial Chamber was required to satisfy itself that the accused would receive a fair trial and would not face the death penalty.

It is remarkable that an international criminal tribunal endowed with primacy in its Statute was relatively easily able to transition to a complementarity model through amendments to its Rules alone. This is perhaps all the more surprising given the expansive interpretation of primacy that initially developed at the ICTY.

Moreover, there are many aspects of the legal regime for complementarity at the ICTY that commend it. The standards for referral are clear and relatively uncontroversial. If the accused is not among those most responsible, and the concerned State is willing and able to prosecute the case, the case would be appropriate for referral to national authorities. Referral motions did not create an adversarial relationship between the ICTY and national authorities. To the contrary, the ICTY was largely eager to refer cases, and so it was in the interests of both the ICTY and national authorities to establish the conditions for a fair trial based on the ICTY's indictment. Finally, referral at the ICTY involved strong evidentiary support to national authorities, who were not expected to independently investigate the cases with their own resources but would instead receive evidence gathered and analysed by the OTP.

[17] International Criminal Tribunal for the former Yugoslavia, *Rules of Procedure and Evidence*, Rule 11*bis* (adopted 12 November 1997, revised 30 September 2002, last amended 11 February 2005).

[18] Despite this revision, all referral motions have been filed by the OTP. See A Kontić and D Tolbert, 'The International Criminal Tribunal for the Former Yugoslavia ("ICTY") and the Transfer of Cases and Materials to National Judicial Authorities: Lessons in Complementarity' in C Stahn and M El Zeidy (eds), *The International Criminal Court and Complementarity: From Theory to Practice* (CUP 2011) 888.

While the legal reforms at the ICTY were one part of the work required to implement complementarity, the OTP would have a decisive role in ensuring that referred cases could be successfully prosecuted by national courts. Given the limited experience the national judiciaries had with complex war crimes cases, more needed to be done to prepare them to conduct these cases.

Accordingly, in 2004, the OTP established a small special unit—the 'Transition Team'—to coordinate the Office's cooperation efforts with national prosecutors from the former Yugoslavia. The Transition Team's mandate was to support domestic prosecutions, initially with respect to the 11*bis* cases, and later more generally. At its largest, this unit comprised three lawyers and thirteen support staff, including investigators, research assistants, language assistants, and document managers.

To support the 11*bis* cases, the Transition Team undertook activities in two primary areas. First, in addition to the indictment and supporting evidence, it collected and provided evidence not specifically required to prove the facts alleged in the indictment, but which would assist national prosecutors to better understand the case and its context, such as analyses of military organizations and crime patterns in other locations. In addition, the Transition Team shared OTP documents that provided additional information about the transferred case, such as motions for protective measures applicable to the witnesses in the transferred cases that provided further detail about the particular protection needs of those witnesses. These activities sought to provide national prosecutors with access to the OTP's institutional knowledge of the cases, not strictly necessary to prosecute the case but allowing national prosecutors to have a better understanding of its context.

Second, the Transition Team enabled direct communications between OTP staff and their national counterparts on case-specific issues. Through teleconferences and missions to the region arranged by the Transition Team, OTP prosecutors were able to answer to questions arising from 11*bis* cases and discuss critical matters such as the prosecutorial theory of the case, how the evidence transferred established the elements of the offences, possible defence arguments, and any particular strengths or weaknesses in the case. OTP members further prepared and discussed information on the witnesses, including credibility issues.

2.2.3.2 Reform in the Region: The Example of BiH

For the 11*bis* process to begin, legal reforms at the ICTY had to be matched by legal reforms in the countries of the region, particularly Bosnia and Herzegovina. In large measure, these legal reforms were spearheaded by the Office of the High Representative of Bosnia and Herzegovina (OHR), which worked together with Bosnian political and governmental authorities. ICTY representatives also participated in working groups and provided advice to the OHR.

In 2003, new criminal and criminal procedure codes were adopted at the national level to create an appropriate legal regime for the transferred proceedings. The 2003 Criminal Code of Bosnia and Herzegovina (CC BiH) represents a unique synergy of customary international law and treaty law applicable to international crimes with national law.[19] It

[19] Criminal Code of Bosnia and Herzegovina, Official Gazette of Bosnia and Herzegovina, 27 June 2003, No 3/03, 32/03, 37/03, 54/04, 61/04, 30/05, 53/06, 55/06, 32/07, 8/10. See Y Ronen, 'The Impact of the ICTY on Atrocity-Related Prosecutions in the Courts of Bosnia and Herzegovina' (2014) 113 Penn State Journal of Law & International Affairs 113, 148.

incorporates key elements from the 1949 Genocide Convention, the 1993 ICTY Statute, and the 1998 Rome Statute, as well as the 1977 Criminal Code of the Socialist Federal Republic of Yugoslavia (CC SFRY).

At the same time, the State Court of Bosnia and Herzegovina (Court of BiH) was established to apply the new criminal and criminal procedure codes and prosecute 11*bis* cases, as well as other complex crimes like corruption and organized crime. In 2005, a War Crimes Chamber was created within the Court of BiH, while a Special Department for War Crimes was created within the Prosecutor's Office of BiH (PO BiH). To ensure that the PO BiH and Court of BiH would be seen as independent and impartial in the adjudication of war crimes cases, an agreement was reached to further establish the Registry of the Court of BiH as an international component of the Court.[20] Through the Registry, the Court of BiH and the PO BiH temporarily became a hybrid tribunal composed of both international and national prosecutors and judges. International assistance was also provided through the Registry to defence counsel who would represent clients before the Court of BiH in war crimes cases.

To meet the specific needs of war crimes prosecutions, the Law on Protection of Witnesses Under Threat and Vulnerable Witnesses (LoPW) was adopted in 2003. Generally, the LoPW provides that the Court 'may order such witness protection measures provided for by this Law as it considers necessary'.[21] A wide range of protective measures are specifically addressed in the law, from using technical means to protect the identity of witnesses from the public, to allowing the testimony of witnesses whose identities are not known to the defence.

Finally, a Law on the Transfer of Cases (LoTC) was adopted in 2004.[22] It established the mechanisms necessary under domestic law for the 11*bis* procedure, the transfer of the accused, and the transfer of evidence. The LoTC provides that national prosecutors are required to submit a national indictment according to the facts and charges in the ICTY's indictment, amending the ICTY's indictment only to bring it in compliance with national procedure.[23] National prosecutors can, however, add new charges based on their investigations.[24]

The most significant features of the LoTC, however, are its provisions regarding evidence. Article 3 establishes a presumption that evidence gathered in accordance with the ICTY Statute and Rules is admissible, while also reiterating the fair trial protection of Article 6(3) of the ECHR. Perhaps most striking, Article 4 provides that adjudicated facts from ICTY judgments are admissible in BiH proceedings.

[20] Agreement between the High Representative for Bosnia and Herzegovina and Bosnia and Herzegovina on the Establishment of the Registry for Section I for War Crimes and Section II for Organized Crime, Economic Crime and Corruption of the Criminal and Appellate Divisions of the Court of Bosnia and Herzegovina and the Special Department for War Crimes, Organized Crime, Economic Crime and Corruption of the Prosecutor's Office of Bosnia, Official Gazette of Bosnia and Herzegovina—International Agreements, No 12/04, 1 December 2004.

[21] Law on Protection of Witnesses Under Threat and Vulnerable Witnesses, Official Gazette of Bosnia and Herzegovina, 24 January 2003, No 03/03, 2/03, 61/04, 55/05 ('LoPW').

[22] Law on the Transfer of Cases from the ICTY to the Prosecutor's Office of Bosnia and Herzegovina and the Use of Evidence Collected by ICTY in Proceedings before the Courts in Bosnia and Herzegovina, Official Gazette of Bosnia and Herzegovina, No 61/04, 46/06, 53/06, 76/06 ('LoTC').

[23] LoTC, art 2(1).

[24] LoTC, art 2(2).

2.2.3.3 *Complementarity in Practice*

The OTP filed its first 11*bis* motions in August 2004, and the last one in July 2007. In total, eight 11*bis* cases involving thirteen persons indicted by the ICTY were referred to courts in the former Yugoslavia. Of the eight, six were transferred to BiH, one to Croatia, and one to Serbia.[25] Seven of the eight cases were fully completed, while the eighth was suspended due to the inability of the accused to stand trial.

In assessing the 11*bis* proceedings as complementarity measures, it is immediately apparent that complementarity at the ICTY differed significantly from complementarity at the ICC. The ICC can only complement national courts to the extent that they are unwilling or unable to prosecute the case. At the ICTY, by contrast, complementarity began from the premise that national authorities could be assisted to prosecute cases by transferring to them cases that the ICTY OTP had already investigated. Both conceptually and legally, complementarity at the ICTY was a form of positive complementarity because it sought to change the *status quo* by increasing the number of national prosecutions concerning grave crimes.

From this perspective, the 11*bis* process provided eight more cases for national judiciaries to prosecute. In context, for example, between July 1997 and January 2005, national authorities in BiH tried ninety-four accused for war crimes.[26] Moreover, the crimes at issue in the six 11*bis* cases referred to BiH authorities were more complex and grave than their previous prosecutions. The impact of the ICTY's complementarity efforts was thus relatively significant in these terms alone. The 11*bis* proceedings also had important symbolic value. The referral of a case meant that international judges had concluded national law provided the necessary conditions for a fair and impartial trial. The fairness of the proceedings in practice was further regularly monitored by the Organization for Security and Co-operation in Europe (OSCE). National authorities thus had the opportunity to demonstrate to the international legal community that they were willing and able to fairly prosecute those suspected of serious crimes.[27]

Ultimately, however, the ICTY's complementarity efforts through the 11*bis* process should be assessed in terms of their broader impact on national prosecutions of war crimes in the relevant countries, particularly BiH.[28] If national courts only prosecuted the 11*bis* cases, or if the 11*bis* cases were *sui generis* proceedings in national courts, complementarity in practice would be very limited. National courts would support the ICTY by reducing its caseload, but the ICTY would have provided little support to national courts. In other words, in the context of the ICTY's initial primacy and the shift envisaged by the Completion Strategy, what is of interest is whether the 11*bis* proceedings promoted positive complementarity.

As a court with the core mandate of investigating and prosecuting crimes, the ICTY had limited scope for building the capacity of national courts. At the same time, however, its contributions could be particularly decisive because it had built its own capacity in specific

[25] International Criminal Tribunal for the Former Yugoslavia, Infographic: Transfer of Cases, available at <http://www.icty.org/en/cases/transfer-cases> accessed 30 May 2018.

[26] Kontić and Tolbert (n 18).

[27] Burke-White (n 5) 324; Ronen (n 19) 143.

[28] See A Chehtman, 'Developing Bosnia and Herzegovina's Capacity to Process War Crimes' (2011) 9 Journal of International Criminal Justice 547, 558–59; T Abdulhak, 'Building Sustainable Capacities—From an International Tribunal to a Domestic War Crimes Chamber for Bosnia and Herzegovina' (2009) 9 International Criminal Law Review 333, 337.

areas that could be invaluable to national courts and could not be provided by other actors. Specifically, from the perspective of practitioners, war crimes cases are unique in terms of the evidence required and the law to be applied, which in turn require new skills and knowledge. In its decade of work prior to the 11*bis* process, the ICTY had built strong capacity in both areas.

Each of the 11*bis* cases transferred to BiH presented challenging issues of law and fact for national prosecutors and judges. In a number of these proceedings, three issues in particular arose from legal reforms in BiH carried out to meet the ICTY's requirements for referral of cases: (i) the use of evidence gathered by the ICTY OTP and ICTY-adjudicated facts through the LoTC; (ii) the protection of vulnerable witnesses; and (iii) the application of international law defining international crimes.

One of the most striking technical aspects of the 11*bis* proceedings in BiH was that effectively all evidence, addressing both the crime base and the individual criminal responsibility of the accused, was gathered by a foreign authority, the OTP. A broad range of evidence was represented, including *viva voce* fact and expert witnesses who had previously given statements to the OTP and testified at the ICTY. The use of foreign evidence is often problematic in criminal proceedings, particularly if not gathered in strict accordance with the procedural regulations of the receiving State. Yet in the 11*bis* proceedings, the LoTC operated smoothly and a significant volume of ICTY evidence relevant to the charges against the accused was admitted.[29] The accused were similarly able to introduce ICTY evidence in their defence.[30]

The protection of vulnerable and threatened witnesses was another area in which the 11*bis* cases enabled important developments in the capacity of the PO BiH and Court of BiH to ensure the necessary production of evidence in war crimes proceedings. Prior to the commencement of the 11*bis* cases, there were significant concerns that practices regarding protection of witnesses in BiH were inadequate.[31] The adoption of the LoPW was a necessary step to improve the capacity of the Court of BiH to protect witnesses, but the law would need to be effectively applied in practice. This was complicated by the fact that nearly all witnesses in the 11*bis* proceedings had previously testified at the ICTY and been granted witness protection measures. The Court of BiH was thus required to apply the LoPW as national law while also adhering to protection measures previously ordered by the ICTY.[32]

Separate from evidentiary issues, the 11*bis* proceedings also significantly contributed to building the legal capacity of national authorities to process war crimes cases. This is evident in the application of international law defining genocide in the *Trbić* case. The *Trbić* case was the only 11*bis* case in which the accused was charged with genocide committed in Srebrenica in July 1995. The Court of BiH found that he was guilty of genocide for his

[29] The PO BiH was able to directly introduce nearly all evidence they received from the ICTY. Proposed evidence from the ICTY was only partially rejected in *Janković* and *Trbić*. See Court of Bosnia and Herzegovina, *Prosecutor's Office of Bosnia and Herzegovina v Janković*, Case No X-KR-05/161, First Instance Judgment, 16 February 2007 ('*Janković* First Instance Judgment') 20–26; Court of Bosnia and Herzegovina, *Prosecutor's Office of Bosnia and Herzegovina v Trbić*, Case No X-KR-07/386, First Instance Judgment, 29 April 2010 ('*Trbić* First Instance Judgment') 358–79.

[30] See Court of Bosnia and Herzegovina, *Prosecutor's Office of Bosnia and Herzegovina v Mejakić* et al, Case No X-KR/06/200, First Instance Judgment, 30 May 2008 (listing defence evidence, much of which originated with the ICTY, as evidenced by the 'ERN' numbers) 25–32.

[31] Human Rights Watch, 'Justice at Risk' (13 October 2004) 21.

[32] See Court of Bosnia and Herzegovina, *Prosecutor's Office of Bosnia and Herzegovina v Rašević and Todović*, Case No X-KR/06/275, First Instance Verdict, 28 February 2008, 36.

participation in a joint criminal enterprise, and he was sentenced to thirty years in prison.[33] As of the time of writing, this case still remains among the most significant genocide cases prosecuted at the Court of BiH, or any national court, in terms of the scope of the charges and the accused's military rank.[34]

A review of the Court of BiH's work thus suggests that the 11*bis* cases had valuable results in building the capacity of national prosecutors and judges.[35] The impact of the 11*bis* proceedings is in large measure attributable to three aspects. First, the 11*bis* process established clear targets that would need to be met for the referral of cases to be triggered, focusing on overarching structural issues—fair trial standards, independence and impartiality of the judiciary, and abolition of the death penalty—that were needed to create the necessary conditions for the criminal justice sector to operate. Second, as these cases were prepared by the OTP, they served as templates of international practices and standards for national prosecutors and judges unfamiliar with complex war crimes cases. These insights could then be applied to subsequent cases, thus domesticating international standards from the ICTY.[36] Third, national prosecutors and judges learned from the experience of adjudicating well-supported cases that raised challenging evidentiary and legal issues. Knowing that international prosecutors had been satisfied that there was sufficient evidence in support of the indictment, national prosecutors could focus their attention on the practice of war crimes cases, including how to lead witnesses, how to handle difficult procedural matters, and how to persuasively put forward a theory of the case.

2.3 Beyond Complementarity: Cooperation, Integration, and Capacity Building

2.3.1 The Challenge of Comprehensive Justice

The 11*bis* proceedings were important positive complementarity measures. Having successfully referred and supported these cases, the OTP would have been justified in concluding that the necessary tasks under the Completion Strategy had been completed and returning to an exclusive focus on its own work, the prosecution of those most responsible for the crimes.

However, the OTP was fully aware of the immense work remaining to be done to achieve more comprehensive justice for crimes committed during the conflicts in the former Yugoslavia. Because primacy had been the initial framework for the Office's activities, combined with a bottom-up prosecutorial strategy, extensive investigations had been undertaken covering thousands of crimes. With the adoption of the Completion Strategy, justice

[33] *Trbić* First Instance Judgment (n 29) paras 870–71.

[34] Milorad Trbić had initially been charged together with other senior—and mid-level VRS and MUP officials in the *Popović* et al case at the ICTY. The indictment that was referred to the Court of BiH charged Trbić with individual criminal responsibility as a member of a joint criminal enterprise for effectively all crimes committed in Srebrenica. The indictment alleged that Trbić was a member of a joint criminal enterprise with and shared the genocidal intent of senior VRS officials who were convicted for perpetrating genocide by the ICTY. See *Trbić* First Instance Judgment (n 29) para 276; *Prosecutor v Popović et al.* (Consolidated Amended Indictment) IT-05-88-PT (11 November 2005); *Prosecutor v Trbić* (Indictment) IT-05-88/1-PT (18 August 2006); *Prosecutor v Trbić* (Decision on Referral of Case under Rule 11*bis* with Confidential Annex) IT-08-88/1-PT (27 April 2007) para 6.

[35] See also: Burke-White (n 5) 345; Abdulhak (n 28) 335.

[36] Kontić and Tolbert (n 18) 888.

for these crimes depended on prosecutions by national courts, rather than the OTP. The OTP considered, however, that national ownership of further accountability efforts was not inconsistent with continued OTP involvement.

To give a sense of the scale of the issue, the National War Crimes Strategy (NWCS) for BiH, adopted in 2008, estimated that 1,285 investigations involving 5,895 known suspects were then underway, with another few hundred cases of known crimes for which no suspects had yet been identified. While not at the same scale, hundreds more war crimes cases remained to be investigated and prosecuted in other countries in the region, and third-party States were pursuing accountability for these crimes in their own domestic justice systems.

While there was increasing capacity in national criminal justice sectors, including as a result of the 11*bis* proceedings, the OTP concluded that it was best placed to undertake specific measures that would further strengthen national judiciaries. In particular, it possessed a resource essential to successful national war crimes prosecutions: its evidence collection. In addition, the OTP had developed trust and influence with key actors across sectors, including the international community, civil society, national legal practitioners, and national political authorities. With these advantages, the OTP was in the position to continue the process of transferring capacity from the ICTY to national courts that had begun with the 11*bis* proceedings.

Over the last decade, the OTP undertook a range of related programmes and informal activities, which certainly can be described as positive complementarity measures, as they have improved the capacities of national courts to prosecute war crimes cases. Equally, however, they represent a further shift at the ICTY beyond complementarity and towards a new model of international collaboration.

Both primacy and complementarity are often posed as a dichotomy: either there are international or national prosecutions of war crimes. The collaboration model developed by the OTP begins from a different perspective: a multiplicity of jurisdictions will necessarily be involved in post-conflict accountability. The challenge is not to decide whether cases will be allocated to one or another court, but rather how to harness the work of multiple courts in a more coherent way in order to achieve comprehensive justice.

In the collaborative model that developed for the former Yugoslavia, the OTP's role evolved to serve as a hub connecting the disparate activities of different courts. For many national prosecutors and judges, liaising with the Office to search its evidence collection, obtain materials, and develop a deeper understanding of the crimes has become a regular routine. By opening access to its evidence collection and in-house expertise, the OTP was able to significantly improve the efficiency of national war crimes prosecutions and ensure that additional value is achieved from the resources invested in obtaining that evidence and that expertise. Duplicative investigations are costly and pose significant risks to successful prosecutions.

In addition, the OTP worked to bring its partners into closer mutual relationships and has been able to forge more links between national judicial systems prosecuting these cases and with a variety of institutions, from international organizations like the United Nations to national prosecution services around the world. Likewise, the Office used its position of trust to improve interaction and resolve difficulties between civil society and national judiciaries.

Finally, the OTP increasingly engaged in monitoring and advisory functions, particularly with respect to regional war crimes prosecutions. These activities are distinct from the monitoring of 11*bis* cases undertaken by the OSCE, as the OTP did not seek to determine whether national cases meet criteria such as international fair trial standards. Rather, the OTP monitored whether there are areas to further improve efficiency and effectiveness, as well as identified challenges impeding successful prosecutions.

It should be noted that beyond the adoption of the Completion Strategy by the Security Council, the OTP was not specifically mandated to engage in efforts to develop a collaborative framework with national courts. As a result, the OTP has only been able to devote limited time and resources from within its existing capacities to engage in these efforts. Moreover, the OTP had to rely primarily on informal, rather than legal, authority, constraining the role it could play. Nonetheless, even with these limitations, the OTP was able to take significant steps towards realizing a model of collaboration for the prosecution of war crimes committed in the former Yugoslavia.

2.3.2 Access to Evidence

In the course of its investigations from 1994–2004, the OTP collected immense amounts of evidence on the crimes committed during the conflicts in the former Yugoslavia. While much of this evidence has been introduced in the OTP's cases, more has not, as it relates to crime scenes and suspects that have not figured prominently in cases at the ICTY. Evidence that has not been introduced in ICTY cases can only be accessed through the OTP, which must regulate access in order to protect confidential information.

The OTP's evidence collection totals more than ten million pages, including witness statements, documentary evidence, and expert reports on various subjects, and also includes thousands of hours of video and audio records, and a variety of physical evidence. All of this evidence has been logged and entered into fully searchable documentary databases, protected by security and confidentiality measures.

The OTP Transition Team was responsible for searching the OTP's databases in response to Requests for Assistance (RFA) and providing certified electronic copies to the requesting national judiciaries. As necessary, the Transition Team would consult with ICTY investigators and prosecutors familiar with the evidence or issues to target valuable evidence responsive to the RFA. The Transition Team could also inform the requesting party of the existence of relevant confidential material, and further request, on behalf of the requesting party, clearance from the ICTY judges to provide the material.[37] The OTP received and processed more than 5,500 RFAs.

The RFA process is functional, but cumbersome in the context of thousands of cases being investigated by a number of national prosecutors. Accordingly, the OTP further enabled remote access to its public databases by prosecution offices in the region, using secure encryption keys. This remote access system was built upon the Office's disclosure system, obviating the need to develop a new system. Through remote access, investigators and prosecutors in

[37] For example, Rule 70 material was provided to the OTP with strict confidentiality requirements and can only be disclosed to another party with express authorization from the provider. While the OTP cannot disclose such material without authorization, it could assist national authorities to request such authorization and liaise with the information provider. Similarly, national prosecutors could request access to statements given by protected witnesses. In such cases, the OTP could assist the requesting party to file a Rule 75(H) application for variation of protection measures to allow the requesting party access to protected information.

the region are able to conduct searches of the OTP's evidence collection themselves to identify relevant evidence for their investigations and generate leads. The Transition Team could then easily certify and provide official electronic records.

In 2009, the OTP decided to take a further step in enabling more effective access to its evidence collection by establishing the 'Liaison Prosecutors' project with funding provided by the European Union.[38] Under this project, the state-level prosecution offices from BiH, Croatia, and Serbia effectively seconded one prosecutor from each office to work together with the OTP's Transition Team. The liaison prosecutors enjoy three key benefits: they have unrestricted access to search the Office's non-confidential databases, allowing them to access more evidence than through the remote access system; they receive direct assistance from OTP staff in performing their searches, allowing them to better target relevant information and improve the effectiveness of their searches; and they can consult and liaise directly on site with OTP investigators and prosecutors with knowledge of the crimes being investigated.

The Liaison Prosecutor project achieved important results. Some liaison prosecutors conducted large numbers of searches for a number of cases, allowing their colleagues in their home offices to focus less on obtaining evidence and more on organising it for an effective case. Others focused on following developments in the ICTY's trials and appeals and updating their home office on new evidence that has been led and evidentiary issues that have arisen in proceedings. Still others focused their activities on specific, high priority cases for which evidence from the OTP is essential, allowing them to investigate the case from The Hague and take maximum advantage of the availability of OTP investigators and prosecutors.

The provision of access to the OTP's evidence collection is not only important for affected States, but also for third-party States that are conducting their own prosecutions or enforcing 'no safe haven' immigration policies. The OTP received large numbers of RFAs from countries outside the former Yugoslavia, including Australia, Canada, Germany, Sweden, and the US. The majority of these RFAs concerned immigration by refugees from the former Yugoslavia and were more in the nature of background checks. Later, prosecutors from third-party States dealing with either war crimes or immigration fraud cases sought access to OTP evidence in order to support their prosecutions. Similarly, OTP experts were called upon to assist investigations and prosecutions in third-party States.

2.3.3 Category II Cases

As a follow-up to the 11*bis* proceedings, the OTP initiated the Category II case programme. While the 11*bis* process was limited to cases that the OTP had indicted, there were a number of investigations underway involving intermediate-level suspects that would likely have led to an indictment if the Completion Strategy had not focused the OTP's remaining prosecutions on the most senior leaders. These 'Category II' cases were at various stages of

[38] See S Brammertz, 'The Legacy of the ICTY: Fair Trials and Cooperation with Local Courts' in R Steinberg (ed), *Assessing the Legacy of the ICTY* (Martinus Nijhoff 2011) 31; European Commission, Fact Sheet: Training War Crimes Prosecutors, Fighting Impunity in the former Yugoslav countries, available at <http://ec.europa.eu/enlargement/pdf/case-studies/2014/20140722_training_prosecutors_en.pdf> accessed 30 May 2018.

investigation, with some almost ready for indictment, while others required further investigations to determine whether an indictment would be appropriate. To ensure that these cases would be processed, the OTP in June 2005 began transmitting them to the appropriate national authority for further action.[39]

The Office monitored the progress of the Category II cases and reported the status of this work to the Security Council, among others.[40] The OTP also strongly insisted that the Category II cases be given high priority. This engagement generated results. By December 2015, the OTP of Bosnia and Herzegovina had taken prosecutorial decisions in all but one outstanding Category II case. Indictments have been confirmed and trial proceedings are ongoing.[41]

2.3.4 Regional Cooperation

One of the greatest challenges for national war crimes prosecutions in the former Yugoslavia, and indeed for collaboration as a model, is cooperation between national prosecution offices. When crimes, victims, and perpetrators cross borders, as can be expected in most post-conflict situations, transnational judicial cooperation is essential. In the countries of the former Yugoslavia, this problem is significantly exacerbated by a number of factors, including constitutional provisions and treaties precluding extradition, suspects who are nationals of more than one country, political distrust, and diverging legal systems. Cooperation between prosecution offices is the only way to address these situations.[42]

Accordingly, the OTP supported, through formal and informal channels, the development of mechanisms to strengthen regional cooperation.[43] In 2005, the prosecution services of Croatia and BiH signed the *Protocol on Agreement in Establishing Mutual Cooperation in Combating All Forms of Serious Crime*, followed by agreements between Serbia and Croatia and between Croatia and Montenegro concerning extradition. Specific agreements for war crimes prosecutions then began to be put in place in 2006, with the adoption of the *Agreement on Cooperation in the Prosecution of Perpetrators of*

[39] By the end of this programme in December 2009, the OTP had transferred seventeen files involving forty-three suspects to prosecution offices in BiH, Croatia, and Serbia.

[40] See 'Report of Serge Brammertz, Prosecutor of the International Criminal Tribunal for the former Yugoslavia, provided to the Security Council under paragraph 6 of Security Council resolution 1534 (2004)' (2016) UN Doc S/2016/454 paras 32–35 ('OTP May 2016 Completion Strategy Report'); 'Report of Serge Brammertz, Prosecutor of the International Criminal Tribunal for the former Yugoslavia, provided to the Security Council under paragraph 6 of Security Council resolution 1534 (2004)' (2015) UN Doc S/2015/342 para 46 ('OTP May 2015 Completion Strategy Report'); 'Report of Serge Brammertz, Prosecutor of the International Criminal Tribunal for the former Yugoslavia, provided to the Security Council under paragraph 6 of Security Council resolution 1534 (2004)' (2014) UN Doc S/2014/827 paras 43–46 ('OTP November 2014 Completion Strategy Report').

[41] ICTY, 'Assessment and Report of Judge Carmel Agius, President of the International Tribunal for the Former Yugoslavia, provided to the Security Council pursuant to paragraph 6 of UN Security Council Resolution 1534 (2004)' (2017) UN Doc S/2017/1001, 77–79.

[42] See OTP, 'Completion Strategy Report' (2016) para 28.

[43] See 'Report of Serge Brammertz, Prosecutor of the International Criminal Tribunal for the former Yugoslavia, provided to the Security Council under paragraph 6 of Security Council resolution 1534 (2004)' (2013) UN Doc S/2013/678 ('OTP November 2013 Completion Strategy Report') para 53; Report of Serge Brammertz, Prosecutor of the International Criminal Tribunal for the former Yugoslavia, provided to the Security Council under paragraph 6 of Security Council resolution 1534 (2004)' (2013) UN Doc S/2013/308 ('OTP May 2013 Completion Strategy Report') para 55.

War Crimes, Crimes against Humanity and Genocide between the prosecution services in Serbia and Croatia. Finally, in 2013, after strong participation by the OTP, the prosecution services of Serbia and BiH adopted the *Protocol of the Prosecutor's Office of Bosnia and Herzegovina and the Office of the War Crimes Prosecutor of the Republic of Serbia on Cooperation in Prosecution of Perpetrators of War Crimes, Crimes against Humanity and Genocide*. This was followed by similar protocols between other prosecutions services in the region.

Given that it is unlikely barriers to extradition will be removed, the protocols between prosecution offices focus on operational measures to transfer evidence from the national prosecutor that investigated the case to the national prosecutor who can obtain custody of the suspect. Without replacing agreements on mutual assistance in criminal matters, the protocols provide for a number of significant advancements in regional cooperation on war crimes cases. The respective prosecution services commit to exchange information on all pending cases so that parallel investigations can be identified. This commitment continues to apply as new suspects are identified. Perhaps most importantly, the protocols help to build trust by allowing both prosecution services to maintain the same case file, obviating concerns that the receiving office could simply close the investigation due to inability, unwillingness, or political pressure.

Over time, these protocols have been increasingly utilized to address the problem of cross-border fugitives. There have recently been a number of high-profile[44] and other cases that utilized the protocols, at least in part, building trust both among prosecutors and the general public in the regional cooperation process. The protocols have further created space for increasing informal regional coordination between prosecutors. Improved cooperation has already moved the accountability process forward in ways that could not have been foreseen even a decade ago.[45]

However, like agreements between the respective prosecution services, the protocols are imperfect because they do not have the same legal status as formal agreements between States. More broadly, protocols cannot fully address the essential issue of strategic coordination and cooperation between regional prosecution offices. Such regional and comprehensive strategic cooperation would involve, *inter alia*, identifying a common set of priorities for prosecutions, relating resources available at a regional level for those priorities, and establishing objective criteria to determine which prosecution service would be best placed to conduct investigations and prosecutions in particular cases.

In the context of the former Yugoslavia, such strategic cooperation would be difficult to achieve for a variety of reasons. Nonetheless, in future situations, an early focus on transnational cooperation between national prosecutors could yield valuable results. In this regard, it is important that legal reforms are implemented that not only improve cooperation between national and international authorities, but also ensure that mechanisms are in place to support cooperation between national prosecutors.

[44] See '15 Serbs are Arrested in Connection with 1993 Massacre' *New York Times* (5 December 2014); 'Serbia Arrests Seven Men over 1995 Srebrenica Massacre' *The Guardian* (18 March 2015).

[45] See Republic of Serbia Office of the War Crimes Prosecutor, Press Release, 'Fifteen Under Arrest on Suspicion of 1993 Seizure and Killing of 20 Passengers in Štrpci' 5 December 2014.

2.3.5 Monitoring and Advice

After the arrest of the OTP's last remaining fugitives in 2011 and following delays in processing the Category II cases, the Office increasingly devoted efforts to monitoring the status of war crimes prosecutions in the countries of the former Yugoslavia and providing advice on measures to further improve the efficiency and effectiveness of national prosecutions. The OTP then summarized its activities and assessments to the Security Council in its regular, biannual Completion Strategy reports.

The OTP consistently monitored and drew the attention of the international community to delays in the implementation of the BiH NWCS and other national war crimes strategies.[46] In addition, the Office identified technical and operational issues in national war crimes prosecutions.[47] The OTP also pointed to the need for appropriate resources and training.[48] Finally, the Office identified barriers to regional cooperation and encouraged prosecutors to better coordinate their activities.[49]

The OTP's increased role providing monitoring and advisory services for national justice efforts was welcomed by both international and national partners. Of course, other organizations, such as the OSCE, monitor national war crimes prosecutions and produce important analyses.[50] Nonetheless, the Office's practical expertise and extensive knowledge enabled it to identify issues that arose, understand what solutions were necessary to resolve them, and highlight the need for lasting, thorough engagement by international prosecutors with national prosecutions.

2.4 Conclusion

One of the most important legacies of the ICTY OTP is the support provided to national justice sectors in the countries of the former Yugoslavia. Sustained cooperation and coordination between the OTP and prosecutors throughout the former Yugoslavia in support of national investigations and prosecutions included numerous capacity building activities, the transfer of case files, and close cooperation on concrete investigations and prosecutions. Importantly, the ICTY OTP moved beyond complementarity towards a new model of international collaboration. The OTP's role evolved to serve as a hub connecting the disparate activities of different courts, helping harness the work of multiple courts in a more coherent way in order to achieve more comprehensive justice. Meaningful results were achieved, although much more still remains to be done.

[46] See OTP May 2016 Completion Strategy Report paras 33–35; OTP May 2015 Completion Strategy Report para 47; OTP November 2014 Completion Strategy Report paras 47–48; OTP May 2014 Completion Strategy Report paras 47–51.

[47] See OTP May 2016 Completion Strategy Report paras 34–35; OTP May 2015 Completion Strategy Report para 47; OTP November 2014 Completion Strategy Report paras 45, 48.

[48] See OTP May 2013 Completion Strategy Report paras 54, 69–72.

[49] See OTP May 2016 Completion Strategy Report paras 28–31; May 2015 OTP Completion Strategy Report paras 40–44; November 2014 OTP Completion Strategy Report paras 54–56; May 2014 OTP Completion Strategy Report paras 59–61.

[50] See Organization for Security and Co-operation in Europe, Combating Impunity for Conflict-Related Sexual Violence in Bosnia and Herzegovina: Progress and Challenges (2004–2014) 13 July 2015, available at <http://www.osce.org/bih/171906> last accessed 30 May 2018.

This experience has been an important lesson. The debate about positive complementarity and national justice for international crimes remains as relevant as ever, particularly in light of the key challenges facing the ICC.

Ultimately, the achievement of the ICTY's Completion Strategy will not be measured simply by the ICTY's closure, but rather by whether the countries of the former Yugoslavia build the rule of law and demonstrate that they can secure meaningful justice for the victims of serious crimes committed during the conflicts. Thus, as the Completion Strategy always foresaw, the completion of the ICTY's mandate is not the end of justice for war crimes, but the beginning of the next chapter. The work begun by the ICTY OTP must continue, to achieve more justice for more victims.

Further accountability for the crimes now depends fully on national judiciaries. It is clear that for this strategy to succeed, national counterparts will need as much—if not more—support than the ICTY received. The IRMCT, as a temporary institution with a reduced number of functions, can support the continued implementation of the Completion Strategy. The IRMCT OTP has identified the provision of assistance to national jurisdictions prosecuting crimes committed in the conflicts of the former Yugoslavia as a key priority. Chief prosecutors and national authorities have announced their desire to further strengthen cooperation with the Office and have requested its continued support and engagement, particularly assistance in meeting commitments established in national war crimes strategies. Building on the experience of and lessons learned by the OTP, the Mechanism's Office will prioritize best practices, including by responding to evidentiary, case-specific, and strategic requests for assistance, providing increased access to the Office's evidence collection, supporting national prosecutors in concrete cases, monitoring developments in accountability for national war crimes and supporting further capacity-building in the national criminal justice sector.

3

The ICTY and the Defence Legacy

The Association of Counsel Practising Before the ICTY

*Colleen Rohan**, **

'But the mere truth won't do. You must have a lawyer.'

Charles Dickens[1]

3.1 Introduction

The International Criminal Tribunal for the former Yugoslavia (ICTY) was established by the United Nations Security Council in 1993.[2] From the outset the ICTY showed itself to be a dynamic institution. An administrative and legal structure was created and put in place,[3] qualified staff were identified to immediately begin the work of the Chambers, Prosecution, and Registry, and investigations and prosecutions of the war crimes cases which fell within the Tribunal's jurisdiction were rapidly launched.[4]

There was, unfortunately, one large gap in this otherwise impressive performance. Despite the fact that the active participation of qualified counsel for the accused is a fundamental right of the accused under international law, essential to providing the accused with a fair trial, the defence as an institution was excluded from the structure of the Tribunal.[5] As a result, no provisions were made for recognizing and taking into consideration the defence perspective, concerns, or experience in the Tribunal's day-to-day work, even regarding matters which directly impacted the defence function, such as case funding, training, and access to office space. Defence counsel were left on their own, with little institutional support,

* Expert in criminal defence litigation in both domestic and international courts. She has represented members of the military and private clients in complex cases involving charges of genocide, murder, terrorism, war crimes, and crimes against humanity. In her domestic practice she specialized in death penalty cases, gang-related cases, international extradition, and post-conviction remedies.

** The author would like to thank founding ADC-ICTY President John Ackerman, and former ADC-ICTY President Gregor Guy-Smith for their insights and comments on the subject of this chapter.

1 Statement by Dr Allan Woodcourt to the wrongfully accused George Rouncewell in Charles Dickens *Bleak House*.

2 See UNSC Res 827 (25 May 1993) UN Doc UN/RES/827.

3 The first version of the Rules of Procedure and Evidence was drafted by tribunal judges and published by February 1994. They have been amended fifty times over the history of the ICTY to reflect changing circumstances and lessons learned from the ongoing litigation before the Tribunal.

4 The first trial at the ICTY began in May 1996 (*Prosecutor v Tadić* (Judgment) Case No ICTY-94-1 (26 January 2000)). As of that date, fourteen indictments had already been prepared in other cases involving fifty-seven accused, pre-trial proceedings were underway in three cases involving six accused, and in July 1996 the first guilty plea was accepted (*Prosecutor v Erdemović* (Sentencing Judgment) Case No ICTY-96-22 (29 November 1996)).

5 The Tribunal is comprised of three organs: the Chambers, the Prosecution, and the Registry. The defence function does not fall within any of those entities.

Colleen Rohan, *The ICTY and the Defence Legacy* In: *Legacies of the International Criminal Tribunal for the Former Yugoslavia*. Edited by: Carsten Stahn, Carmel Agius, Serge Brammertz, Colleen Rohan, Oxford University Press (2020). © The Several Contributors
DOI: 10.1093/oso/9780198862956.003.0004

to go about the task of defending accused in some of the most legally and factually complex cases that have arisen in criminal law.[6]

Nonetheless, as the mandate of the ICTY comes to a close, it is clear that there were significant improvements for the defence over the years of the Tribunal's operation. The increasing recognition of the need to include the defence, not just as counsel in court, but also in the daily life of the institution, positively and dramatically influenced the ability of counsel to competently and efficiently represent the accused. It also resulted in the Tribunal benefiting from the perspective and experience of the defence, for example, by agreeing to include defence counsel in those aspects of the operation of the Tribunal which directly affected defence responsibilities, such as on the Rules Committee, the ICTY Disciplinary Board and Panel, and in negotiations for legal aid for indigent accused and resources for defence teams.

This is not to say that all disagreements and conflicts between the defence and the other organs of the ICTY were positively resolved. There are a number of difficulties which have historically plagued the defence side of the courtroom in international criminal cases: insufficient case funding, inadequate or no access to important witnesses, increasing use of written statements which curtail the right to cross-examination, the overuse of closed, private sessions which may undermine the right to public trial, lack of cooperation from relevant government and police agencies, late disclosure from prosecutors, or the failure to timely disclose exculpatory evidence, to name a few. These are topics which have been addressed before and they will undoubtedly remain the subject of inquiry and controversy.[7]

The focus of this chapter, however, is on the reason for the improvements in the defence experience at the ICTY, as well as the quality of defence legal practice in the courtrooms. The primary reason and most enduring legacy of the defence on the eve of the closing of the ICTY is the establishment of the Association of Defence Counsel Practising Before the ICTY (ADC-ICTY), its official recognition by the ICTY, and the dedication and professionalism of its many members.[8]

[6] The Rules of Procedure and Evidence did include provisions explaining the qualifications counsel must have to serve as defence counsel at the ICTY and procedures for the appointment of counsel. ICTY RPE, Rule 44 [Appointment and Qualification of Counsel, January 1995]; Rule 45 [Assignment of Counsel, January 1995]; Rule 46 [Misconduct of Counsel, July 1997]. The ICTY also enacted a Directive on the Assignment of Counsel [August 1994] and a Code of Conduct for Defence Counsel [July 2002]. All of these rules have been substantively amended on numerous occasions, in particular Rules 44 and 45, which now contain significantly expanded and/or detailed requirements for the appointment and assignment of defence counsel.

[7] See M S Ellis, 'The Evolution of Defense Counsel Appearing Before the International Criminal Tribunal for the Former Yugoslavia' (2003) 37 New England Law Review 949; K Gibson, C Lussiaa-Berdou, 'Disclosure of Evidence' in K Khan, C Buisman, and C Gosnell (eds), *Principles of Evidence in International Criminal Justice* (Oxford Press 2010); K S Gallant, 'Politics, Theory and Institutions: Three Reasons Why International Criminal Defense is Hard and What Might Be Done About One of Them' (2003) 14(3) Criminal Law Forum 317; D Tolbert, 'The ICTY and Defense Counsel: A Troubled Relationship' (2003) 37(4) New England Law Review 975; J T Tuinstra, *Defense Counsel in International Criminal Law* (Asser Press 2009); J T Tuinstra, 'Defending the Defenders: The Role of Defence Counsel in International Criminal Trials' (2010) 8(2) Journal of International Criminal Justice 463; C C Jalloh and A BiBella, 'Equality of Arms in International Criminal Law' in W Schabas, Y McDermott, and N Hayes (eds), *The Ashgate Research Companion to International Criminal Law* (Ashgate 2013).

[8] The ADC over the years has had approximately 400 members coming from countries located all over the world. See comprehensive discussion of the creation of the ADC-ICTY in D Kennedy and I Dusterhoft, 'The Proper Role for International Defense Counsel Organizations' in C Rohan and G Zyberi (eds), *Defense Perspectives on International Criminal Justice* (Cambridge University Press 2017) 137–72.

Very little has been written about the ADC-ICTY to date.[9] Its benefit to the ICTY as a legal institution and its importance to individual defence counsel at the ICTY cannot be overstated. Among many other things, when the organization came into being it immediately created an institutional presence for the defence which was otherwise wholly lacking. As such it provided a much needed, organizational structure for the defence which enabled communication, discussion, and resolution of issues of collective concern to all defence counsel within the Tribunal. It also quickly became the source of much needed, consistent support and training for defence counsel, thereby improving the quality of defence practice and protecting the right of the accused to the adequate assistance of counsel.

Although the defence experience during the life of the ICTY is no doubt as varied as the hundreds of individual defence counsel who have travelled from their home jurisdictions to appear in ICTY courtrooms, their collective legacy is, without question, the creation and continuing existence of the ADC-ICTY.[10]

3.2 The Need for an Association of Defence Counsel at the ICTY

In the early years of the ICTY defence counsel, unlike staff in the three organs of the Tribunal, had no physical presence within the Tribunal building. Defence counsel came from all over the world. To represent an accused, defence counsel had to travel to the seat of the Tribunal in The Hague where the first order of business was to find a place to live. The Tribunal did not provide office space for defence counsel, so offices located outside the Tribunal needed to be set up as well.[11] Although the Office for Legal Aid and Defence Matters (OLAD) located within the ICTY Registry was available to assist counsel with some resources—such as making travel arrangements, finding translators, and filing case submissions—no other consistent institutional support existed for the defence.

There were also certain restrictions placed on the defence in the early days which appear to have served little to no purpose and were simply counterproductive. Defence counsel, for example, were not permitted to use the law library or eat in the cafeteria. Counsel were issued identification tags bordered in red which prevented their access to virtually all areas within the Tribunal building except for the common defence room and the courtrooms when counsel were expected to appear for trial. The doors in many areas of the Tribunal were festooned with signs warning that individuals with 'red passes' were not permitted entry. The Tribunal held public events from time to time and provided visitors to the ICTY with the opportunity to contact and speak with members of Tribunal staff. The defence, with extremely rare exceptions, were never asked to participate in these public functions.

[9] See D Kennedy and I Dusterhoft (n 8); and D Kennedy and I Dusterhoft, 'The Association of Defence Counsel Practicing Before the ICTY (ADC-ICTY)' *Manual on International Criminal Defence ADC-ICTY Developed Practices* (UNICRI, ADC-ICTY, ODIHR, OSCE 2011) 203–17.

[10] The ADC-ICTY has very recently changed its name, in light of the closing of the ICTY, to reflect its continued existence and a broadening of its membership. It is now known as the Association of Defence Counsel Practising Before the International Courts and Tribunals (ADC-ICT).

[11] There was one common room in the Tribunal for all defence counsel to share but it was universally deemed to be inadequate. It was not possible to conduct private meetings with witnesses or staff, for example, because the room was an open space with no private areas. There were not enough computers to equip all defence teams. Only one printer was available to be shared by all defence teams. Office supplies and other practical support was not provided.

Many, though not all, of these restrictions were lifted during the first decade of the ICTY's operation, however, defence counsel's sense of exclusion from the institution in which they were practising law was palpable. The ICTY, as an international legal institution, was meant to embrace and enforce the principle that the role and function of the defence was a necessary, indeed critical, aspect of its duty to ensure fair trials. The institutional cold shoulder to the defence as a group was often perceived—rightly or wrongly—as representing the opposite.

Defence counsel, like all of the other individuals working in the Tribunal, were the products of different legal backgrounds, ethical standards, and cultural norms. No system had been put in place, however, to address and remedy that circumstance so that counsel were conversant with the relevant standards of conduct applicable at the ICTY. Similarly, no consistent training was made available regarding the substantive or procedural aspects of the hybrid legal system employed at the ICTY. This led to the concern that some counsel, who qualified for appointment under ICTY Rules, were nonetheless potentially failing to provide the accused with competent representation.[12]

By 2002, the judges and defence counsel agreed that there was a need for the creation of a defence counsel association to assist in ensuring that a pool of qualified defence counsel would be available to handle the challenging, highly complex cases to be tried before the Tribunal. The creation of an association of counsel was also intended to enable defence counsel to make collective representations to the Tribunal on defence issues; a process seen as a necessary replacement for the hit-or-miss, inconsistent practice of individual defence counsel having to negotiate, separately and anew in each case, issues common to all defence teams such as funding and hiring of defence team staff.

The judges also considered it advisable to create such an association given the existence of the Code of Professional Conduct for Counsel Appearing before the International Tribunal. The judges expressed their concern that the ethical standards in the Code were understood and consistently honoured.[13] In fact, defence counsel were viewed with some suspicion within the Tribunal in the early years of the ICTY,[14] as issues had arisen with certain counsel regarding improper fee-splitting arrangements,[15] improper influencing of witnesses,[16] and revelation of confidential information.[17] Defence counsel as a group were, unfortunately, sometimes assessed through the lens of the improprieties of these few.

Defence counsel endorsed the need for a professional association on the same grounds as the judges, albeit from a different perspective. Counsel believed, based on experiences from

[12] See general discussion in C Rohan, 'Ethical Standards in International Criminal Law' in C Rohan and G Zyberi (eds), *Defense Perspectives on International Criminal Justice* (Cambridge University Press 2017) 41–74.

[13] ICTY, 'Code of Professional Conduct for Counsel Appearing before the International Tribunal' (2009) ICTY Doc IT/125 REV 3, Preamble.

[14] See generally D Tolbert (n 7); M S Ellis (n 7).

[15] See UN Secretary General, 'Report of the Office of Internal Oversight Services on the Investigation into Possible Fee-Splitting Arrangements Between Defence Counsel and Indigent Detainees at the International Criminal Tribunal for Rwanda and the International Tribunal for the Former Yugoslavia' (2001) UN Doc A/55/759.

[16] See ICTY, *Prosecutor v Tadić* (Judgment on Allegations of Contempt against Prior Counsel Milan Vujin) ICTY-94-1-A-R77 (31 January 2000) [witness tampering].

[17] See ICTY *Prosecutor v Zlatko Aleksovski* (Finding of Contempt of Trial Chamber I) ICTY-95-14/1-T (11 December 1998).

their domestic jurisdictions, that they should be given the opportunity to be self-governing, as well as the opportunity to assist their colleagues—through training and consultation—to avoid ethical mistakes and dilemmas.

Defence counsel also knew that no matter how experienced individual counsel were in the system of law utilized in their own countries, they were, at least upon their first arrival at the ICTY, often unfamiliar with the particular legal system utilized at the ICTY or with parts of it.[18]

The system of law adopted at the ICTY includes aspects of both the civil or continental legal system and the common law or adversarial legal system. The trials themselves, however, were to be conducted utilizing a primarily adversarial structure. Hence, each party to the case was entitled to conduct its own factual investigation of the charges prior to trial. During trial, each party was entitled to present witnesses as part of its case and to cross-examine witnesses presented by the opposing party.

This process required and presumed the active participation of defence counsel before, during, and after trial in appellate or post-conviction proceedings. In addition, all relevant international instruments regarding the rights of accused persons in criminal cases required that the accused is presumed innocent,[19] is entitled to a fair and public trial,[20] without undue delay,[21] is entitled to the assistance of legal counsel,[22] has the right to confront and cross-examine witnesses called against him or her at trial,[23] and has the right to 'adequate' time and facilities to prepare a defence.[24] The ICTY legal system recognized and sought to enforce these rights as fundamental to its obligation to provide fair trials, consistent with customary international law, as well its own Statute.

Although basic training in the substantive and procedural aspects of this hybrid system, as well as the courtroom skills pre-requisite to effectively defending an accused at trial was an obvious necessity, none was provided for defence counsel appearing in ICTY cases. That situation was exacerbated by the fact that defence counsel, unlike counsel for the Prosecution or Chambers, had no shared offices or other space in the Tribunal where institutional knowledge could be passed from one lawyer to the next in a supportive, professional manner. To the contrary, defence counsel were required, due to confidentiality considerations and potential conflicts of interest, to refrain from discussing many aspects of their individual cases with others.

[18] Newly arriving defence counsel were also unfamiliar with how to navigate the internal bureaucracy at the ICTY and how to use the various computer systems and databases available at the Tribunal. After the organization of the ADC-ICTY, training on these issues was provided by the association.

[19] ICTY Statute, art 21(3); ICTR Statute, art 20(3); ICC Statute, art 66; International Covenant for Civil and Political Rights (ICCPR), art 14(2); European Convention for the Protection of Human Rights and Fundamental Freedoms (ECHR), art 6(2).

[20] ICTY Statute, art 21(2); ICTR Statute, art 20(2); ICC Statute, art 67(1); ICCPR, art 14(1); ECHR, art 6(1).

[21] ICTY Statute, art 21(4); ICTR Statute, art 20(4); ICC Statute, art 67(1); ICCPR, art 14(3); ECHR, art 6(1) [trial must be 'within a reasonable time'].

[22] ICTY Statute, art 21(4)(b); ICTR Statute art 20(4)(b); ICC Statute 67(1)(b); ICCPR, art 14(3)(b); ECHR art 6(3)(c).

[23] ICTY Statute, art 21(4)(e); ICTR Statute, art 20(4)(e); ICC Statute, art 67(1)(e); ICCPR, art 14(3)(e); ECHR, art 6(3)(d).

[24] ICTY Statute, art 21(4)(b); ICTR Statute, art 20(4)(b); ICC Statute, art 67(1)(b); ICCPR, art 14(3)(b); ECHR, art 6(3)(b).

3.3 The Creation, Structure, and Activities of the Association of Defence Counsel Practising Before the ICTY

In light of the need to address the concerns raised by defence counsel and judges regarding the situation faced by the defence at the ICTY, a working group of four ICTY defence counsel, one member of the Dutch bar, and a representative from the ICTY Registry, was put together in 2002 to organize a defence association. That group drafted the constitution for the ADC-ICTY,[25] which was subsequently adopted by ICTY judges at their next plenary session.[26]

The ICTY Rules of Procedure and Evidence were subsequently amended to require that each defence counsel representing an accused before the Tribunal 'is a member in good standing of an association of counsel practising at the Tribunal recognized by the Registrar'.[27] The ICTY Registrar then officially recognized the ADC-ICTY as the association of counsel for the Tribunal.[28] Membership dues were established by the association as the primary means for financing the ADC-ICTY and its operation. 'Good standing' in an association of counsel, as defined in Rule 44(A)(iii) required, among other matters, that ADC-ICTY dues were kept up to date. As of this writing, the ADC-ICTY is the only independent association of defence counsel which has been officially recognized by an international criminal court.[29] It is also the only association with mandatory membership for counsel intending to represent an accused. Both factors—official recognition and mandatory membership—have played a major role in ensuring the ADC-ICTY was and continues to be a successful and effective association.

This official recognition was also crucial to the development of a positive relationship between the ADC-ICTY and the organs of the Tribunal. It made it clear that the ADC-ICTY was authorized to conduct business and engage in negotiations on behalf of its members. It legitimized the official standing of the association within the ICTY. It also reflected the Tribunal's affirmative support for the ADC-ICTY and its willingness to consult with it and work with it on those issues of concern to the defence and those issues which could affect the functioning of the defence at the Tribunal. Mandatory membership assured, for its part, that all defence counsel at the ICTY would have access to all benefits the ADC-ICTY was able to provide, including training.

In 2015 the ADC-ICTY was officially recognized by the Registrar for the Mechanism for International Criminal Tribunals (MICT) as the association representing defence counsel practising before the MICT. Rule 42(A)(iii) of the MICT Rules of Procedure and Evidence,

[25] The Constitution of the Association of Defence Counsel Practising Before the International Tribunal for the Prosecution of Persons Responsible for Serious Violations of International Humanitarian Law Committed in the Territory of the Former Yugoslavia since 1991 (The Hague, 23 October 2004) <https://www.adc-ict.org/documents> accessed 1 February 2018.

[26] The ADC is organized as a non-profit bar association under Dutch law. It is registered with Dutch authorities and, as such, is entirely independent from the ICTY itself.

[27] ICTY RPE (as amended), rule 44(A)(iii).

[28] UN General Assembly, 'Note by the Secretary General: Tenth Annual Report of the International Criminal Tribunal for the Prosecution of Persons Responsible for Serious Violations of International Humanitarian Law. Committed in the Territory of the former Yugoslavia since 1991' (2003) UN Doc A/58/297-S/2003/829, para 321.

[29] In 2016, an association of defence counsel was established at the International Criminal Court (International Criminal Court Bar Association, 'ICCBA'). To date, the ICC has welcomed the formation of the ICCBA but it has not yet officially recognized it by amendment to the rules or otherwise. Membership in the ICCBA is not compulsory in order to practise before the ICC. Membership in the ICCBA is also not required in order for individual counsel to represent an accused at the ICC.

like its predecessor at the ICTY, now provides that counsel must 'be a member in good standing of an association of counsel practicing before the Mechanism recognized by the Registrar'.[30]

The fact that the judges working with the MICT enacted this provision reflects the positive and mutually beneficial working relationship which developed between the ICTY and the ADC-ICTY over the lifetime of the ICTY, as well as the recognition of the value of such an organization to the efficient and fair functioning of the Tribunal itself. In fact, in an early decision from the MICT, its President held that no appeals remuneration policy for counsel representing indigent accused before the MICT would be permitted to go into effect unless and until the MICT Registrar had consulted with the ADC-ICTY, as that policy directly impacted on defence resources and functioning.[31]

The responsibilities, goals, and objectives of the ADC-ICTY, as delineated in its Constitution, illustrate the extent and value of the contributions such an organization can and does make to complex, multi-cultural institutions such as the ICTY.

As explained in its Constitution, the ADC-ICTY functions to support the efficiency and independence of defence counsel practising before the ICTY, to promote and ensure the proficiency and competence of counsel, to offer advice to the President, the judges and the Registrar in relation to modifications of the Rules of Procedure and Evidence and all Regulations, Practice Directives and Policies related to the work of defence counsel, and to oversee the performance and professional conduct of defence counsel.[32]

The ADC-ICTY fulfils these responsibilities through the activities of the various Constitutional committees which comprise the internal structure of the ADC-ICTY.[33]

The Executive Committee is the primary governing body of the ADC-ICTY. It is responsible for overseeing the day-to-day operations, activities, and management of the ADC-ICTY including finances, record keeping, maintaining membership lists, and assuring effective liaison with the organs of the Tribunal including the Registry and Chambers. Members of the Executive Committee are in most cases the individuals called upon to engage in negotiations with the Registry, OLAD, or other entities at the Tribunal regarding practical issues relating to defence counsel, such as legal aid policies. The Executive Committee is also responsible for overseeing communications with groups outside of the Tribunal including the media, NGO's, other professional organizations, and similar groups.

The Executive Committee nominates one member of the Disciplinary Council of the ADC-ICTY to represent the ADC-ICTY on the ICTY Disciplinary Panel and two ADC-ICTY members to represent the association on the ICTY Disciplinary Board, where they serve along with selected judges and members of the Registry.[34] This is one of the most important responsibilities for the ADC-ICTY as a whole. By serving on these internal ICTY disciplinary groups, the ADC-ICTY maintains an active role in proceedings involving

[30] IRMICT, Rules of Procedure and Evidence for the Mechanism for International Criminal Tribunals (2012) UN Doc MICT/1.

[31] *Augustin Ngirabatware v The Prosecutor* (Decision on Motion to Quash and Revise a Decision of the Registrar on Level of Complexity and Seeking Further Relief) MICT-12-29-A (26 February 2014).

[32] Constitution of the ADC-ICTY, art 2. Specific examples of these activities and their successful impact on the Tribunal as well as the defence function are discussed *infra*.

[33] Members of these committees are elected by democratic vote by the ADC-ICTY membership on a yearly basis. To be eligible to serve on a committee or to vote a member must be in good standing.

[34] ICTY Code of Professional Conduct for Counsel Appearing Before the International Tribunal. Art 40. The ICTY Disciplinary Panel and Disciplinary Board hear cases involving defence counsel facing complaints regarding alleged violations of ICTY ethical codes or other form of misconduct.

ethical complaints or other matters raised as to one of its members. It also represents the informed voice of defence counsel in the resolution of these complaints, and in that way, can assist in fairly adjudicating the merits of such complaints, while at the same time protecting the legitimate interests of the counsel or case at issue.

The ICTY requires that defence counsel meet certain minimum qualifications before he or she can be admitted to the list of counsel permitted to practise before the ICTY. The ADC-ICTY Membership Committee enforces these provisions; again, performing a valuable service to the ICTY itself as well as ADC-ICTY members.

Counsel who want to practise before the ICTY (as well as the MICT since 2015) are required to apply to the ADC-ICTY for membership. The ADC-ICTY Membership Committee reviews all such applications to assure compliance with the relevant ICTY or MICT requirements. If the Membership Committee determines that an applicant does not meet the required qualifications that decision will prevent that applicant from being admitted to the list of counsel for the ICTY which is maintained by the Registry.[35] Hence, the ADC has the ultimate responsibility to determine who is qualified for admission to the list of counsel and who is not; not the Registry. Any decision by the Membership Committee which is disputed can be appealed to the Executive Committee of the ADC-ICTY, whose decision will be final.[36]

The ADC-ICTY, in short, took on the responsibility to carry out the fundamentally important task of ensuring that counsel for the accused will be adequately qualified to provide the accused with competent representation. The Membership Committee has, from its inception, taken this role very seriously. Not all applicants to the ADC-ICTY were accepted. The same is now true for the MICT. The need for all applicants to fulfil all professional requirements has been vigorously enforced with observable, positive results as over time the quality and performance of defence counsel improved dramatically once these safeguards were identified, put in place, and fairly enforced. As is evident, this function of the ADC-ICTY, on its own, provided a significant, mutual benefit to defence counsel at the Tribunal and to the Tribunal itself.

As mentioned earlier, one of the challenges for defence counsel at the ICTY is the hybrid system of law adopted there which does not replicate any particular domestic legal system. That being the case, it was mandatory that defence counsel be provided with consistent, high quality training so that the rights of the accused are adequately protected at trial.

Given this obvious concern, the ADC-ICTY maintains a Training Committee which, like the gatekeeping function of the Membership Committee, has served over time to significantly enhance the quality of practice by the defence. This committee has the responsibility to design and implement advocacy training on substantive international criminal law for all ADC-ICTY members, whether assigned to a case or not, and to assist the Executive Committee in obtaining funding for such programmes.[37]

The ADC-ICTY has designed a number of different training programmes to fulfil its responsibility to provide its members with comprehensive training. In 2005, for example, the ADC-ICTY presented a three-day skills training programme in which all counsel, then assigned to cases, participated in practical exercises which required that they conduct direct

[35] Art 4, Constitution of the ADC-ICTY.
[36] Art 4(4), Constitution of the ADC-ICTY.
[37] Arts 20, 21, Constitution of the ADC-ICTY.

and cross-examinations and argue legal motions. In a show of institutional support for defence training, which has been ongoing since the establishment of the ADC-ICTY, the Registry, through OLAD, provided partial funding for this programme which was held in several conference rooms at a local hotel. OLAD also facilitated travel for the several defence counsel attending this training by coordinating monthly visits with clients to the same time frame as the training; a system which permitted counsel's travel expenses to be paid and assured that all affected counsel could attend.

The ADC-ICTY Constitution requires that the association meet once a year for a General Assembly in which association business is discussed and voted upon and during which elections are held for the various ADC-ICTY committees. The Training Committee, in conjunction with this yearly event, began in 2003 to present a half-day training session for all counsel who attend the General Assembly. The topics vary from year to year and have included review and analysis of ICTY jurisprudence, professional ethics, appeals and oral arguments on appeal, post-conviction issues, legal drafting, and orientation to the MICT including practical and jurisprudential issues. The experts conducting this training include members of the ADC-ICTY, as well as prosecutors, judges, and Registry staff from the ICTY and outside experts.[38] The training sessions also provide the opportunity for defence counsel to discuss their cases and share lessons learned from them with their defence colleagues; an extremely valuable interchange which could not occur in any organized fashion before the establishment of the ADC-ICTY.

The ADC-ICTY has provided training on the ICTY Code of Professional Conduct for Counsel on a number of occasions to ensure that all counsel have a clear understanding of the duties and obligations imposed upon them by that Code. This training maximizes counsels' ability to avoid ethical dilemmas or violations which could interfere with the effective representation of the accused or the conduct of proceedings. During the final years of the ICTY, the ADC-ICTY expanded this training to include non-lawyer members of defence teams, many of whom did not yet have a comprehensive understanding of all the ethical considerations which apply to their activities as non-lawyer members of legal teams. Over time, these trainings have attracted non-lawyer staff from the Registry, Chambers and Office of the Prosecutor (OTP); all of whom were welcomed by the ADC-ICTY to participate.

The structure of the ADC-ICTY includes a Disciplinary Council which is separate from the disciplinary mechanisms within the Tribunal itself.[39] The Disciplinary Council, unlike all other constitutional committees of the ADC, operates independently from the jurisdiction of the Executive Committee. It is responsible directly to the General Assembly of the ADC-ICTY; that is, all ADC members.[40] Its duties are to monitor the conduct of ADC-ICTY members,[41] adjudicate on any complaints filed as to the conduct of ADC-ICTY members, and to provide confidential advisory opinions on ethical matters when requested.

The existence of the Disciplinary Council has also been invaluable for ADC members and of direct assistance to the Tribunal. On several occasions during the operation of

[38] The ADC-ICTY has been fortunate in that outside experts—professors, scientists, authors, and staff from other international courts—have been enthusiastic about participating in these training sessions and willing to donate their time.

[39] Arts 15–19, Constitution of the ADC.

[40] Art 16, Constitution of the ADC.

[41] 'Monitoring' within the meaning of this provision does not mean some sort of ongoing oversight of counsel but rather the responsibility to remain aware of any counsel who has had a complaint filed against him or her through resolution of that process.

the Tribunal defence counsel, concerned about potential conflicts of interest, ethical dilemmas related to the accused or witnesses and other difficult issues, were able to consult with the Disciplinary Council, obtain the benefit of independent advice from members of the Council and/or obtain a written, confidential advisory opinion detailing the nature of the issue of concern to counsel and proposed solutions which are consistent with the requirements of the ethical Code. This kind of direct intervention and advice has served more than once to avoid future ethical problems or unintended misconduct on the part of counsel. It has also provided a needed protection for defence counsel whose behaviour has been challenged, when those challenges turn out to be unfounded. It has had an undeniably salutary effect on the administration of justice and the quality of the defence legal practice.

The ICTY has, in fact, availed itself of this assistance as well. During trial proceedings in a case involving multiple accused and multiple defence teams, one of the defence counsel was accused of professional misconduct based on his failure to disclose to the prosecution the identities of defence witnesses within a deadline promulgated by the Trial Chamber. The Trial Chamber contacted the ADC-ICTY and asked for an *amicus* brief on the question of whether counsel's behaviour was more than just a misinterpretation of the Chamber's order and had crossed the line and constituted unethical conduct.[42] The brief was duly filed and constituted part of the information available to an independent *amicus curiae*, who was thereafter appointed to investigate the matter.

The ADC-ICTY, in fact, maintains an Amicus Committee as a resource to the defence bar comprised of ADC-ICTY members willing to donate their time and experience by drafting *amicus curiae* briefs when the ADC-ICTY determines that such assistance will be of potential benefit to those requesting it and when doing so is consistent with the standards and goals of the ADC-ICTY Constitution.[43] It has provided such assistance on a number of varied topics at the ICTY and, in later years, at other courts such as the ICC, for example, in *Prosecutor v Hadžihasanović* (regarding the impact of the allocation of resources on an accused's right to a fair trial);[44] *Prosecutor v Brdjanin* (impact of potential expansion of the law relating to the application of joint criminal enterprise liability);[45] and *Prosecutor v Banda and Jerbo* (propriety of granting a stay of trial proceedings when the defence was precluded from conducting an independent pre-trial investigation).[46]

The ADC-ICTY now holds the unique position—based on its fifteen years of experience before an international criminal court—of having the institutional expertise to reliably provide this kind of expert assistance and insight on issues relating to the practice of international criminal law.

[42] *Prosecutor v Prlić* (Decision Subsequent to *Amicus Curiae* Report) ICTY IT-04-74-T (3 November 2009) [defence counsel was exonerated of misconduct allegations].

[43] Unlike the other committees mentioned here, the Amicus Committee is a creation of the Executive Committee, not the Constitution. It was created to provide the ADC-ICTY with a reliable way to address requests for *amicus* assistance made to the ADC-ICTY as the organization became better known in the international legal community.

[44] *Prosecutor v Hadžihasanović* (*Amicus* Brief of the Association of Defence Counsel—ICTY in Support of Joint Defence Oral Motion for Reconsideration of Decision on Urgent Motion for *Ex Parte* Oral Hearing on Allocation of Resources to the Defence and Consequences Thereof for the Rights of the Accused to a Fair Trial) IT-01-47-PT (14 July 2003).

[45] *Prosecutor v Brdjanin* (*Amicus Brief* of the Association of Defence Counsel—ICTY) IT-99-36-A (6 July 2005).

[46] *Prosecutor v Banda and Jerbo* (*Amicus Curiae* Brief of Association of Defence Counsel—ICTY on Defence Request for Temporary Stay of Proceedings) ICC-02/05-03/09 (20 February 2012).

The ADC-ICTY also maintains a Rules Committee created to take part in the ICTY Committee on the Rules of Procedure and Evidence. The ICTY Rules of Procedure and Evidence have frequently required amendment, as the procedures at the ICTY evolved, to codify lessons learned and developing experience in the litigation of cases. Prior to the creation of the ADC-ICTY, the ICTY Rules Committee had no procedure which permitted participation in the amendment process by the defence. ADC-ICTY Rules Committee members are now authorized to submit proposals for amendments to the ICTY Rules of Procedure and Evidence on behalf of the ADC-ICTY and to present the collective views of the defence on amendments proposed by others.[47]

The importance of the inclusion of the defence in this process is evident. It is a critical opportunity for the defence to have a direct voice in the development of and changes to the ICTY rules which govern the conduct of cases. Such developments often significantly affect the procedures at trial, substantive evidentiary rules, and the defence function. As noted by Kennedy and Dusterhoft:

> This participation is a vast improvement on the early years at the ICTY, when the Committee on Rules of Procedure and Evidence did not provide for any input from the defense community and, as a result, sometimes failed to take into account the impact of changes to the RPE on the defense function.[48]

In addition to the services provided by these substantive committees, ADC-ICTY members have participated on numerous occasions in negotiating improvements in the practice of law by the defence; some of which were fundamental to assuring that the accused has the time and facilities to prepare a defence; a right guaranteed under international law.

ADC-ICTY members, for example, negotiated additional office space for defence trial teams when, during a period when five or six cases were on trial at the ICTY at the same time, the defence common room in the Tribunal became essentially unworkable due to the daily congestion of several trial teams, all needing access to computers and printers at the same time. Similarly, a critical impasse arose regarding defence counsel access to disclosure materials during the pre-trial phase. The issue arose because defence counsel received significant portions of case disclosure through an electronic database which could only be accessed by use of computers located physically within the Tribunal. Defence counsel could not be physically present at the Tribunal during the pre-trial phase of their cases, however, because funding for assigned cases limited them to spending only a few days in The Hague each month. The impact of this glitch in the system was immediate and serious: counsel could not adequately prepare cases pre-trial, because they had no ongoing access to all relevant case disclosure.[49] The issue was solved when it was raised by the ADC-ICTY and, after

[47] The ICTY Committee on Rules of Procedure and Evidence is composed of at least three permanent judges and non-voting members from the defence and prosecution. See ICTY Practice Direction of Procedures for the Proposal, Consideration of and Publication of Amendments to the Rules of Procedure and Evidence of the International Tribunal (as amended) ICTY Doc IT/143/REV 2 (24 January 2002). Before the plenary of judges adopts a new rule, it is discussed at this committee.

[48] Kennedy and Dusterhoft (n 8) 156.

[49] The volume of disclosure in ICTY cases often exceeded millions of documents. It was not consistent with the accused's right to the time and facilities to prepare a defence to limit counsel's access to this mass of information, for pre-trial review, to a few days each month.

working with the Tribunal's technical services, secure 'remote keys' were negotiated which enabled counsel to access the system from their own computers.

There are many other examples. The lesson learned is that the accused rights to equality of arms, competent counsel, time and facilities to prepare a defence and other fair trial rights can only be reliably protected by an adequately resourced, well-informed defence, whose function is understood and respected by the international legal institutions.

The legacy of the defence experience at the ICTY is that it was a fundamental error to exclude any of the necessary actors in the legal process from participating in the institution's day-to-day functions and its legal community. The positive legacy, based on the experience of the ADC-ICTY, is that when the defence is recognized and included the quality of legal representation improves, communication within the institution is facilitated, and the efficient functioning of the legal proceedings as well as the effective protection of the rights of the accused is significantly enhanced.

3.4 Contributions of the ADC-ICTY to the Effective Assistance of Counsel, the Efficient Administration of Justice and to the Broader Legal Community

The ADC-ICTY contributions to the international legal community go beyond the four walls of the ICTY in a number of ways, not anticipated when the organization first came into existence.

In May of 2009 the ICTY published the 'ICTY Manual on Developed Practices',[50] as part of a broader project to promote and preserve the Tribunal's legacy.[51] The ICTY Manual is a useful publication. It describes the history of the Tribunal, its internal structure, and explains many of the legal principles utilized in the day-to-day activities of the Tribunal. At the time this Manual was drafted, the ADC-ICTY was asked to contribute a chapter describing the defence role and function at the ICTY and a chapter was prepared. The chapter was ultimately excluded, however, when the Prosecution objected to its inclusion.

These events turned out to be a cloud with a silver lining for the ADC-ICTY. The United Nations Interregional Crime and Justice Research Institute (UNICRI), which sponsored the ICTY Manual, decided on its own initiative and in cooperation with the ADC-ICTY, to sponsor a separate manual for the defence. Hence a practice-oriented manual, devoted entirely to the defence role and practice at the ICTY, written by experienced ADC-ICTY defence counsel, was published in 2011 as part of the War Crimes Justice Project involving the ADC-ICTY, UNICRI, and the OSCE Office of Democratic Institutions and Human Rights (ODIHR).[52]

The Defence Manual has been translated into Serbian, Croatian, Bosnian, and Albanian.[53] The ADC-ICTY is informed the Manual, anticipated to be used in the countries

[50] This Manual is available electronically at: <http://www.icty.org/x/file/About/Reports%20and%20P ublications/ICTY_Manual_on_Developed_Practices.pdf> accessed 1 February 2018.

[51] See ICTY, 'Publications' available at <http://www.icty.org/en/node/8127> accessed 1 February 2018.

[52] The ADC Manual is available electronically on the ADC-ICTY website: <https://www.adc-ict.org/documents/> accessed 2 February 2018; see also: C Rohan, 'The Defense in International Criminal Trials: Important Actor or Necessary Evil' in M Hieramente and P Schneider (eds), *The Defense in International Criminal Trials: Observations on the Role of the Defense at the ICTY, ICTR and ICC* (Nomos 2016) 17–28.

[53] The ADC has been informed that the Manual has also been translated into Spanish. Efforts are currently afoot to have it translated into French.

of the former Yugoslavia has, in fact, also been used to train lawyers in countries in Africa and South America. It is now included on the official website of the ICTY.[54] It represents a lasting legacy for the ADC-ICTY, as well as for the many ADC-ICTY lawyers who donated their time, skills, and considerable professionalism to making it a comprehensive, valuable contribution to the practice of international criminal law.[55]

Beginning in 2013, the ADC-ICTY broadened the scope of its yearly General Assembly meetings to include a one day conference to which the public as a whole is invited. These conferences have covered a very wide range of topics related to the practice of international criminal law including defence counsel ethics, current legal and other challenges facing the defence in the international criminal courts, and developments in international criminal law and international humanitarian law. Keynote speakers at the conferences have included members of the ICTY judiciary, distinguished practising criminal law counsel and, in 2017, the Registrar from the newly established Kosovo Specialist Chambers.

Hence the ADC, while expanding its membership and gaining increasing legitimacy within the ICTY, is also reaching out to the international community at large and, in the process, contributing to the public understanding of the nature of the defence function and the issues of concern to the defence—both positive and negative—within the international criminal courts.

The ADC-ICTY has also diversified its training activities. Beginning in 2006, it organized a Mock Trial to provide trial court skills training for students and young lawyers interested in the practice of international criminal law. ADC-ICTY members donated their time to provide a week of substantive lectures for participants, which culminated in a day-long trial during which participants could practise courtroom skills by examining witnesses and arguing legal motions in an actual courtroom setting. The Mock Trial was an instant success and benefitted greatly from the participation and support of the ICTY, which permitted use of one of its courtrooms for the exercise. Sitting ICTY judges volunteered their time to sit as the bench for the Mock Trial proceedings, providing a very realistic, challenging experience for Mock Trial participants. The programme, which is now put on yearly, has become extremely popular, drawing participants not only from interns and new lawyers working in the ICTY and other local international courts, but from law schools and law firms located in places like Germany, Australia, and the United Kingdom.[56]

Along the same lines, the ADC began a lecture series in 2014, also intended to provide substantive training for interns and young lawyers in the legal community. The series covers a number of practical subjects regarding the preparation and presentation of cases in the international criminal courts including drafting of submissions, drafting of appeals and oral arguments, direct and cross examination, pre-trial investigation, ethics, eye witness identification, and forensic evidence such as ballistics, handwriting, DNA, and legal standards relevant to the presentation of expert testimony.

[54] See ICTY (n 51).

[55] The Manual is also unique as it is oriented towards providing not only a description of the various skills involved in the preparation and presentation of a defence in international criminal proceedings, but also practice tips based on real cases. It includes a CD which contains numerous pleadings filed in ICTY cases as examples of how to draft substantive and procedural issues.

[56] ICTY audio-visual staff also donated their time for this programme since it began. They have sat through the Mock Trial proceedings to make sure all audio equipment in the courtroom was functioning and have recorded the proceedings for the participants, making them available in CD format for those who want them.

3.5 Conclusion

The ICTY is the flagship court among the post-Nuremberg international criminal courts. Almost all observers agree that it created an impressive body of jurisprudence and institutional experience which should provide guidance for any later international court, struggling to gain equal legitimacy within the confines of its jurisdiction and mandate.

The ADC-ICTY is also a flagship organization: the pioneer international association of defence counsel practising before the international criminal courts. It should be emphasized that none of the activities and contributions described in this chapter could have occurred but for the dedication and sense of community which developed within the membership of the ADC-ICTY as the organization grew and gained experience. ADC-ICTY members donated thousands of hours to these activities in addition to meeting the heavy responsibilities that go with representing an accused in an international war crimes case. They did so, despite differences in culture, language, and political ideology, by remaining focused on the sensibilities they shared as counsel for the accused: the need to create and maintain a highly qualified, well-informed, cohesive community of defence counsel as the most effective means of protecting the rights of the accused in international criminal cases.

4
The Moral Legacy of the ICTY

*Miguel de Serpa Soares**, **

4.1 Introduction

Years ago, in October 1999, the then Secretary-General, Mr. Kofi Annan, said in Sarajevo that the United Nations (UN) experience in Bosnia was one of the most difficult and painful in its history. 'No one regrets more than we the opportunities for achieving peace and justice that were missed. No one laments more than we the failure of the international community to take decisive action to halt the suffering and end a war that had produced so many victims'.[1] He added that 'we will never forget that Bosnia was as much a moral cause as a military conflict'[2] and that 'the tragedy of Srebrenica will haunt our history forever'.[3] We all remember that in the same year, the Secretary-General issued his report on the fall of Srebrenica, stressing that the international community as a whole had to accept 'its share of responsibility' for the ethnic cleansing campaign that culminated in the murder of some 7,000 unarmed civilians in Srebrenica.[4]

Morality and responsibility, these are two concepts that are intimately linked to the establishment of the International Criminal Tribunal for the former Yugoslavia (ICTY) in 1993. Indeed, before the acknowledgement of the responsibility of the international community by the Secretary-General in his 1999 Report, the Security Council established the International Tribunal for the former Yugoslavia,[5] which can be seen as the first measure addressing both the international community's moral duty and its responsibility to prosecute those responsible of serious violations of international law. With such a measure, the global community reaffirmed its commitment to addressing the impunity that had caused so much pain and sorrow. The moral responsibility of the international community to ensure accountability for the victims of crimes of this nature led to the development of an international accountability system (4.3), all which can be seen as emerging from the foundational work of the ICTY (4.2).

* Under-Secretary-General for Legal Affairs and United Nations Legal Counsel.

** The author wishes to acknowledge the assistance of Ms Ana Peyró Llopis, Principal Legal Officer in the Office of the Legal Counsel, with the research and preparation of this article.

[1] UN General Assembly, 'UN Bosnia experience one of most "difficult and painful" in its history says Secretary-General to Memorial Ceremony in Sarajevo' (11 October 1999) Press Release SG/SM/7168.

[2] ibid.

[3] ibid.

[4] UN General Assembly 'Report of the Secretary-General pursuant to General Assembly Resolution 53/35—The Fall of Srebrenica' (15 November 1999) UN Doc A/54/549, 111, para 501.

[5] UNSC Res 827 (25 May 1993) UN Doc S/RES/RES/827 (1993).

Miguel de Serpa Soares, *The Moral Legacy of the ICTY* In: *Legacies of the International Criminal Tribunal for the Former Yugoslavia.* Edited by: Carsten Stahn, Carmel Agius, Serge Brammertz, Colleen Rohan, Oxford University Press (2020). © The Several Contributors
DOI: 10.1093/oso/9780198862956.003.0005

4.2 The Foundational Work of the ICTY for an 'Age of Accountability'

The Security Council passed resolution 827 on 25 May 1993, formally establishing the ICTY,[6] the first ever criminal tribunal established by the UN and the first international criminal tribunal since the Nuremberg and Tokyo tribunals. In so doing, the Security Council noted that it was 'convinced'[7] that the establishment of the ICTY would contribute to the restoration and maintenance of peace, thereby acknowledging the existence of a close link between international criminal justice and the purposes of the UN. The creation of the ICTY was truly a groundbreaking moment. It had been close to fifty years since the Nuremberg and Tokyo War Crimes Trials were established. The 1948 Genocide Convention had entered into force in 1951, but no international criminal tribunal that would recognize individual criminal responsibility for such a crime had yet been established.

The creation of the ICTY demonstrated a new-found and serious commitment on the part of the international community that those responsible for perpetrating the most serious crimes of international concern should be held accountable for their actions. Since its establishment, all the 161 individuals indicted by the ICTY for serious violations of international humanitarian law have been accounted for and ninety individuals were sentenced for their crimes.

The landmark decisions of the ICTY established core legal concepts of international criminal law. One of the most important developments which emerged from the ICTY jurisprudence was the principle of individual criminal responsibility for international crimes, even with respect to acts of senior government officials. This is now a generally accepted principle which represents a significant and essential evolution in international criminal law that must be protected.

Moreover, the ICTY has been a pioneer in the creation of the contemporary architecture of international criminal justice and can rightly be considered to be the foundation of the global culture of accountability. The Tribunal has pushed international expectations of accountability beyond what was anticipated in 1993. Importantly, the ICTY has been instrumental in transforming the nature of the discourse around international justice and the starting point surrounding situations in which serious international crimes are committed.

This change in how we speak about these matters is evidenced by the now often repeated calls by the UN Security Council for the perpetrators of atrocities to be held accountable. It is seen in the statements of heads of State; in the work of journalists; and in expressions of public opinion. Accountability has taken root in our collective consciousness and calls to bring perpetrators to justice have become a recurring theme.

We are no longer willing to ignore these calls for justice. This is seen both at the international and the national level. Since the establishment of the ICTY, we have seen a flourishing of various entities established to ensure accountability: among others, the International Criminal Tribunal for Rwanda (ICTR), the Special Court for Sierra Leone (SCSL) and its Residual Court, the Extraordinary Chambers in the Courts of Cambodia, the

6 M S Soares, 'Special Editorial: An Age of Accountability' (2015) 13 Journal of International Criminal Justice 13 669.

7 UNSC Res 827 (n 5).

Special Tribunal for Lebanon (STL) and, of course, the International Criminal Court (ICC). Without the ICTY, and afterwards the ICTR, there might never have been a permanent ICC.

At the national level, the work of the ICTY inspired the establishment of the War Crimes Chamber in the State Court of Bosnia-Herzegovina, which has been working since 2005 to conduct war crimes trials according to international standards. The transfer of investigation files to national authorities, the referral of cases to the national courts, and the ongoing provision of evidence and assistance to enable them to prosecute the crimes that took place in the conflicts of the 1990s is a significant part of the ICTY's lasting regional legacy.

While these developments are to be praised, and the work of the ICTY sends a powerful message that impunity will not be tolerated, the cause of international criminal justice is a long-term undertaking, and we must remain attentive and resolute. With the support of the international community, and of course the UN, international criminal justice will continue to develop.

While the ICTY decisions have been instrumental in developing international criminal justice, both substantively and procedurally, most of them have also been a major step for the establishment of the truth about the war and the terrible atrocities that were committed—atrocities which affected generations of citizens, and which marked history. The future is not only the fight against impunity, the future is also truth and reconciliation.

The importance of establishing—when possible—the truth has often been noted in the context of reconciliation processes. But the scope of truth goes beyond as it is instrumental to the construction of the memories of the present and future generations. The Spanish writer Juan Goytisolo reported in 1993 the existence of a 'memoricide'.[8] He identified it as the insistence in erasing the past, an example of this being the destruction of cultural heritage, in particular noting the destruction of the Library of Sarajevo. The ICTY itself considered several cases with respect to the destruction of cultural property as the destruction of historic monuments and buildings was a strategic war objective. The ICTY jurisprudence led the way to establishing the criminalization of attacks against cultural property under international law. Notably, on 27 September 2016, the ICC found Mr Ahmad Al Faqi Al Mahdi guilty of the war crime of intentionally directing attacks against historic monuments and buildings dedicated to religion in Timbuktu, Mali.[9] This was the first case before the ICC to be exclusively focused on attacks on cultural property. While the applicable rules of the ICC and ICTY differ, the work of the ICTY opened the door and paved the way for consideration of this crime as the sole basis for establishing a war crime.

4.3 The Development of an International Accountability System

The ICTY has also been a precedent and an inspiration for the existing international accountability system. While tribunals such as the ICTR and the SCSL followed the model of the ICTY, other ad hoc criminal tribunals with some level of international participation or assistance were also created, such as the Extraordinary Chambers in the Courts of

[8] J Goytisolo, *Cuaderno de Sarajevo* (*El País*, 1993).

[9] On 27 September 2016, Trial Chamber VIII of the ICC found Mr Al Mahdi guilty, as a co-perpetrator, of the war crime of intentionally directing attacks against historic monuments and buildings dedicated to religion, including nine mausoleums and one mosque in Timbuktu, in June and July 2012. The decision was confirmed in appeals on 8 March 2018.

Cambodia, and others may still be created in the future. These could be along the lines of the new Kosovo Specialist Chambers and the Specialist Prosecutor's Office, established by a Kosovo domestic law to prosecute crimes which were the subject of criminal investigation by the Special Investigative Task Force or along the lines of the Hybrid Court for South Sudan, which is to be established further to the Agreement on the Resolution of the Conflict in South Sudan signed on 17 August 2015.[10]

The creation of this ICTY came at a time when there was a newfound and serious commitment on the part of the international community that those responsible for perpetrating the most serious crimes of international concern should be held accountable for their actions. In 1993, the establishment of international criminal tribunals was considered as the appropriate way to fight impunity for the most heinous crimes. Notably, since December 2016, a new trend is emerging with respect to criminal accountability mechanisms established by the UN. In contexts where it is difficult to foresee effective judicial accountability, there is an increasing appetite for, at a minimum, gathering and securing evidence in the meantime so that such evidence can be used in national, regional, or international courts that may in the future have jurisdiction over these crimes.

In December 2016, the General Assembly established an investigative mechanism for Syria to preserve and analyse evidence of violations of international humanitarian law and human rights violations, the International, Impartial and Independent Mechanism (IIIM).[11] The IIIM has two main tasks: (1) to collect, consolidate, preserve, and analyse evidence of violations of international humanitarian law and human rights violations and abuses committed in Syria; and (2) to prepare files in order to facilitate and expedite fair and independent criminal proceedings, in accordance with international law standards, in national, regional, or international courts or tribunals that have or may in the future have jurisdiction over these crimes, in accordance with international law.[12] The IIIM is not a court or tribunal with a jurisdiction attached, but it will support criminal prosecutions and apply criminal justice methodologies in its work, even if it cannot ultimately issue indictments or prosecute cases. The report to the General Assembly of 28 February 2018 notes that the IIIM model forges new approaches to international criminal justice, as accountability is now seen as a responsibility extending across multiple jurisdictions and involving coordination between national and international actors.[13]

A second example of this new trend in the field of international criminal accountability is the establishment of an investigative mechanism in Iraq. In September 2017, the Security Council requested the Secretary-General to establish an Investigative Team to support domestic efforts to hold ISIL (Da'esh) accountable, by collecting, preserving, and storing evidence in Iraq of acts that may amount to war crimes, crimes against humanity, and genocide committed by ISIL in Iraq.[14] The UN Investigative Team to Promote Accountability for

[10] Agreement on the Resolution of the Conflict in South Sudan, 17 August 2015, Chapter V: Transitional Justice, Accountability, Reconciliation and Healing, section 3, 43–45. The UN provided technical assistance with respect to the Hybrid Court for South Sudan, at the request of the Security Council, in particular on the foundational instruments of this Court.

[11] UN General Assembly, International, Impartial and Independent Mechanism to assist in the investigation and prosecution of persons responsible for the most serious crimes under international law committed in Syria since March 2011 (21 December 2016) UN Doc A/RES/71/248.

[12] ibid OP4.

[13] UN General Assembly, Report of the International, Impartial and Independent Mechanism to Assist in the Investigation and Prosecution of Persons Responsible for the Most Serious Crimes under International Law Committed in the Syrian Arab Republic since March 2011 (28 February 2018) UN Doc A/72/764, 6, para 12.

[14] UN Security Council, Res 2379 (21 September 2017), UN Doc S/RES/2379 (2017), OP2.

crimes committed by Da'esh (ISIL) (UNITAD) commenced its work on 20 August 2018[15] and has been deployed in Iraq.

More recently, on 27 September 2018, the Human Rights Council decided to establish an independent mechanism to collect, consolidate, preserve, and analyse evidence of the most serious international crimes and violations of international law in Myanmar since 2011 in order to facilitate and expedite fair and independent criminal proceedings.[16] It is worth noting that the mechanism could have direct access to victims and witnesses in Bangladesh. While the independent mechanism has no jurisdiction to prosecute the crimes at issue, the Pre-Trial Chamber of the ICC has ruled that the ICC may exercise jurisdiction over the deportation of the Rohingya people from Myanmar to Bangladesh.[17]

The establishment of these mechanisms demonstrates a significantly new approach that States have adopted in order to ensure some level of accountability for serious violations of international law where judicial accountability mechanisms may at the time not be an option. It is the expectation that these mechanisms will become instrumental to the success of eventual future criminal proceedings in domestic or international courts and it remains to be seen how the work of these mechanisms may be utilized by such courts. Importantly, these initiatives are not intended to delay the prosecution of such crimes where possible or undermine the work of the ICC when it has jurisdiction.

As seen with the ICTY, it is important to remember that accountability does not end with the completion of judicial proceedings, and any ad hoc tribunal, or any investigative mechanisms engaging with victims and gathering information, will likely give rise to entities that are necessary in order to discharge the residual functions arising from international criminal accountability. These functions include not only witness protection, but also the supervision of enforcement of sentences, petitions for early release, contempt cases, review of judgments and sentences, and management of archives.

States need to be aware that when they create any of these accountability structures, it is a long-term process and these structures will likely need to exist for a period of time that goes beyond the collection of evidence or the delivery of judgments. The failure to account for these long timelines can ultimately undermine the necessary financial support from States which tends to decline over long periods of time.

While reflecting on the legacy of the ICTY and on the future of the international accountability system, the international community could consider four specific areas to enhance the overall effectiveness of these criminal accountability mechanisms. One is of a financial nature while the others relate to efficiency and governance.

First, the ICTY benefitted from funding through assessed contributions of UN Member States. However, the length of the trials and the cost raised questions about the financing of these types of mechanisms and the possibility of improving efficiency. Several other institutions, established after the ICTY, have instead been financed through voluntary contributions from UN Member States. Finding resources to sustainably support these institutions remains a problem. Already today, as members of the international community consider

[15] UN Security Council, 'Letter dated 15 August 2018 from the Secretary-General addressed to the President of the Security Council' (17 August 2018), UN Doc S/2018/773.

[16] UN General Assembly, Resolution adopted by the Human Rights Council on 27 September 2018 (27 September 2018), UN Doc A/HRC/RES/39/2, OP22.

[17] On 6 September 2018, Pre-Trial Chamber I of the ICC decided that the Court may exercise jurisdiction over the alleged deportation of the Rohingya people from Myanmar to Bangladesh.

creating new institutions as the ones described above, funding for some of the existing hybrid institutions that are voluntarily funded has largely dried up, putting at risk the orderly conduct of the judicial process. Based on lessons learned, and in particular the experience of the International Residual Mechanism for Criminal Tribunals, consideration should be given in future tribunals to the possibility of appointing judges who would be paid on a 'when-employed' basis for functions that may not run continuously.

Second, the issue of the length of the proceedings is often identified as a concern with regard to the efficiency of international criminal justice. It appears that one reason that funding erodes over time is precisely because of the time required to obtain a judgment. Of course, the cases are complex and the proper administration of justice requires that issues be adequately investigated, proved, and judged. But there is no requirement that the decision in a criminal case stand as the definitive historical treatment of a particular incident, nor is it necessary that an accused be tried of all crimes that he or she may possibly have committed. There is an element of discretion that can be applied and should be evaluated.

Third, there is an opportunity for ad hoc international criminal tribunals and hybrid tribunals to further develop mechanisms of governance for their activities. Ideally, there should be a way of monitoring judicial productivity to ensure expeditious resolution of cases without endangering judicial independence, as happens in national systems. Comparable oversight should also exist for investigations and prosecutorial functions. In addition, there are increasing calls for judicial accountability and the need for mechanisms to respond to complaints that ensure procedural fairness and certainty for all involved when allegations of judicial misconduct arise.[18]

Last but not least, the treatment of victims needs to remain at the forefront of the work of these bodies. The very nature of the most serious violations of international law leaves a victim vulnerable and often in need of assistance. Victims of these crimes are, often for the very first time, involved in a criminal justice system which may require them to speak to police officers, investigators, lawyers, and judges and ultimately to testify in open court. Victims can find these processes confusing and overwhelming, particularly when they have an international component. Important progress has been made by different international and hybrid tribunals with respect to the treatment of victims. Many of them have witness and victim support sections responsible for providing various forms of crucial support to victims throughout the proceedings, including, but not limited to, expert psychological support and measures to ensure their protection.[19] A reflection needs to be undertaken to seek to ensure that victims continue to be recognized and treated with respect and dignity; that they are protected from any further victimization, intimidation, or further distress when they take part in the criminal justice process; that they receive appropriate support throughout the proceedings and that they have access to justice.

[18] For the International Residual Mechanism for criminal Tribunals, see MICT/14/Rev1, of 9 April 2018. This revision of the Code of Professional Conduct for the judges of the Mechanism sets out core judicial principles related to independence, integrity, confidentiality, and outside activities and establishes a complaints procedure. The judges of the Special Tribunal for Lebanon (STL) also adopted a code of professional conduct on 27 September 2016 (STL-CC-2016-04) and a complaints procedure was also established in the framework of the renewal of the contracts of the STL judges on 1 March 2018.

[19] Some Tribunals have established field offices, like the ICTR/Mechanism in Kigali, which provides essential support to victims and witnesses. The ICC also provides support to victims through its Trust Fund for Victims, which is mandated to secure reparations and appropriate forms of assistance for victims of serious crimes.

4.4 Conclusion

In an ideal future, institutions such as the ICTY will not be necessary and domestic jurisdictions will assume the main responsibility for the prosecution of international crimes, while offering guarantees to respect international standards. The important work of building domestic capacity in this regard continues to be necessary and the assistance of the international community in supporting nationally-owned efforts towards ensuring accountability for serious crimes under international law remains essential. The Special Criminal Court in the Central African Republic is an example of a domestic court (with certain hybrid features like foreign judges, a foreign prosecutor, and a foreign deputy registrar) steadily moving forward with its own investigations, cooperation with the ICC, judicial training, and outreach to constituencies. The UN peacekeeping mission deployed in that country (MINUSCA), together with the UN Development Programme (UNDP) and other UN departments and entities, have assisted the Central-African Government in the establishment of the Special Criminal Court.

In some contexts, however, domestic jurisdictions are simply not an option. Slavenka Drakulic, in her psychological essay on war criminals being tried in The Hague, *They would never hurt a fly*,[20] describes the strong emotions that the mere mention of the name of the city 'The Hague' provokes in Croatia, Serbia, and Bosnia and the little desire in these societies to uncover the truth.[21] Ms Drakulic concludes that, in the case of the crimes committed in the Balkans, '[j]ustice simply has to come from The Hague or it will not come at all—and all because we ourselves are not capable of washing our own dirty, bloody laundry'.[22] In these situations, as was the case in the Balkans, which led to the establishment of the ICTY, the international community will need to continue to be the driving force to ensure accountability and to provide justice to victims.

Legacy efforts are crucial in this regard, as they will remind the international community that the work to ensure respect for human rights and the rule of law continues, that the cause of justice endures, and that the hope to end impunity lives on. The ICTY leaves behind a powerful legacy of which we can all justly be proud.

[20] S Drakulic, *They Would Never Hurt a Fly* (Penguin Books 2005) 210.
[21] ibid 13.
[22] ibid 17.

PART II
LEGACY LENSES, THEORIZATIONS, AND NARRATIVES

5
The ICTY is Dead! Long Live the ICTY!
ICTY Legacies in Perspective

*Carsten Stahn**

5.1 Introduction

The International Criminal Tribunal for the former Yugoslavia (ICTY) has been a pioneering institution. Its 'lasting impact'[1] can be seen in a variety of fields: substantive law, procedure and working methods, technological innovation, memory, or more general contributions to the development of international criminal justice as a field. In scholarly discourse, it has become common to discuss these contributions under the umbrella of the term 'legacy', or better 'legacies'. However, 'legacy' is not something that we usually associate with courts. In a domestic setting, we rarely see such discussions. They speak to some extent to the exceptional nature of international criminal justice. Legacy policies are, in essence, an attempt to 'leave something useful behind'.[2] They mark to some extent a dialogue with the actual and imagined constituencies of international criminal law. Judges, Prosecutors, and defendants often speak to a broader epistemic community, audiences beyond the courtroom or future addresses, in an attempt to affirm 'something bigger'[3] than just the case at hand.

The ambition to leave a 'lasting legacy' is deeply rooted in the pedagogic rationale of international criminal proceedings. As historian Lawrence Douglas put it, mass atrocity trials are attempts to 'demonstrate the power of law to reintroduce order into a space evacuated of legal and moral sense'.[4] This sense was particularly visible after the Second World War. International criminal proceedings were always more than an attempt to secure punishment for perpetrators. This is captured in the famous words by Robert Jackson that the 'the record on which we judge these defendants today is the record on which history will judge us tomorrow'.[5]

* Professor of International Criminal Law and Global Justice and Programme Director of the Leiden University Grotius Centre for International Studies at The Hague, and Professor of Public International Law and International Criminal Justice at Queen's University Belfast.

[1] M P Scharf and M Sterio, 'Introduction' in M Sterio and M Scharf (eds) *The Legacy of* Ad Hoc *Tribunals in International Criminal Law: Assessing the ICTY's and the ICTR's Most Significant Legal Accomplishments* (CUP 2019) 3

[2] Report on the Special Court for Sierra Leone, Submitted by the Independent Expert Antonio Cassese, 12 December 2006, 61, para 276.

[3] F Mégret, 'Practices of Stigmatization' (2014) 76 Law and Contemporary Problems 286, 289.

[4] See L Douglas, *Memory of Judgment* (Yale University Press 2001) 3.

[5] ibid. Robert G. Storey, trial counsel at Nuremberg, put it even more radically: 'The purpose of the Nuremberg trial was not merely, or even principally, to convict the leaders of Nazi Germany [...]. Of far greater importance, it seemed to me from the outset, was the making of a record of the Hitler regime which would withstand the test of history'. See Holocaust Encyclopedia, Evidence from the Holocaust, <http://www.ushmm.org/wlc/en/article.php?ModuleId=10007147> accessed 10 October 2019.

Carsten Stahn, *The ICTY is Dead! Long Live the ICTY!* In: Legacies of the International Criminal Tribunal for the Former Yugoslavia.
Edited by: Carsten Stahn, Carmel Agius, Serge Brammertz, Colleen Rohan, Oxford University Press (2020). © The Several Contributors
DOI: 10.1093/oso/9780198862956.003.0006

The Nuremberg and Tokyo trials were partly attempts to re-educate society.[6] Law was used as an instrument to re-shape the foundations of society. This ambition was clearly visible in some of the first ICTY steps. Former ICTY President Antonio Cassese argued in his first annual report to the Security Council that the 'Tribunal will contribute to the peace process by creating conditions rendering a return to normality'.[7] He saw individual criminal responsibility as an instrument to counter feelings of collective guilt, which 'easily degenerates into resentment, hatred, and frustration and inevitably leads to further violence and new crimes'.[8] This argument is correct in principle. A tribunal cannot be expected to award a 'fair share' of guilt to each group of people. ICTY trials have made an important contribution by individualizing guilt. However, it often remained hard for affected communities not to see individual perpetrators as representatives of specific forms of collective evil. The framing of the ICTY as a project of reconciling ethnic division lacked societal grounding and support. It was assumed too easily that simply by doing its work, the ICTY would be able to break cognitive dissonance or integrate domestic societies.[9]

Today, there is broad consensus on the tribunal's importance, but also a more realistic picture of its limits. Realists claim that a tribunal cannot be expected to do more than the work of a court.[10] This greater sense of modesty is reflected in the ICTY's last reports. President Agius noted very frankly in the final annual report of the Tribunal to the International Tribunal to the Security Council and to the General Assembly:

> The denial of crimes and revisionism are both widespread throughout the region. Convicted war criminals are often glorified as heroes. The facts of the crimes are taught in classrooms around the world, but not in the countries where the crimes were committed.[11]

He has cautioned against viewing reconciliation as a legal goal. He said in his 2016 address at Srebrenica

> justice alone is not enough. Equally important are the processes of coming together; [. . .] acknowledging the past; grieving together; communicating with open hearts and minds; engaging in real dialogue; [all three ethnicities] have to want it, and have to work for it—at home, in schools, in places of worship, and of course, at government level.[12]

[6] See generally Y Totani, *The Tokyo War Crimes Trial: The Pursuit of Justice in the Wake of World War II* (Harvard University Press 2009); N Boister and R Cryer, *The Tokyo International Military Tribunal: A Reappraisal* (OUP 2008); M Futamura, *War Crimes Tribunals and Transitional Justice: The Tokyo Trial and the Nuremburg Legacy* (Routledge 2008).

[7] UNSC Report of the International Tribunal for the Prosecution of Persons Responsible for Serious Violations of International Humanitarian Law Committed in the Territory of the Former Yugoslavia Since 1991 (29 August 1994) UN Doc A/49/34/S/1994/1007 para 15.

[8] ibid para 16.

[9] See also Institute for Integrated Transitions, 'Changing the Narrative: The Role of Communications in Transitional Justice', 3.

[10] See K A Rodman, 'When Justice Leads, Does Politics Follow? The Realist Limits of Prosecutorial Agency in Marginalizing War Criminals' (2019) 17 Journal of International Criminal Justice 13.

[11] Report of the International Tribunal for the Former Yugoslavia (1 August 2017) UN Doc A/72/266–S/2017/662, para 51.

[12] Judge Agius, Address, CS/PR1667e, 11 July 2016, at <http://www.icty.org/x/file/Press/Statements%20and%20Speeches/President/160711_president_agius_srebrenica_en.pdf> accessed 9 October 2019.

The key difficulty for a tribunal is to find a midway between its narrow legal frame and its broader justice function. It needs be involved, but at the same time keep its distance. These two poles are in a constant tension. The ICTY experience is thus not necessarily a sign of institutional failure, but rather a reflection of the inherent tensions in international criminal justice.

5.2 Phases of the Tribunal

The ICTY was an 'experiment'. Its establishment was partly a reaction to feelings of neglect and shame by Western powers, which were bystanders to some of 'the largest crime on European soil since World War II'.[13] The establishment by the Security Council was a convenient alternative to military action[14] and a 'sign that the international community would not stand idly by and watch while barbaric acts were perpetrated'.[15]

Historically, the Tribunal went through different phases. Each of these phases has, to some extent, a legacy of its own. The Tribunal was created in what we now view as the 'heroic' age of international justice. Like other criminal institutions, the ICTY had teething problems. Initially, there was a feeling that the Tribunal would not get off the ground. Some feared that a failure of the ICTY 'would also mark the end of any international criminal justice'.[16] Relatively small cases broke the ice. The ICTY used a 'pyramid strategy',[17] through which it sought to gradually build cases against senior leaders through investigation and prosecution of mid- or low-level perpetrators. The *Tadić* case became the signature case. It is now a classic in many textbooks, perhaps even more than contemporary high-profile cases, although Duško Tadić was overall a relatively minor figure in the Yugoslav conflict. Whenever a student cannot give authority for an answer, *Tadić* is a safe fallback option.

The case had broader systemic significance. *Tadić*'s story formed the backbone of some of the most important legal moments in the development of international criminal justice: the famous 1995 Interlocutory Appeal on Jurisdiction,[18] which articulated the modern law on non-international armed conflict, or the legendary 1999 Appeals Judgment which reframed the test for the qualification of international armed conflicts ('overall control') and (re-) invented Joint Criminal Enterprise (JCE) beyond its post-Second World War context.[19] Most importantly, *Tadić* illustrated like hardly any other case the emancipation of international criminal justice in the United Nations system after 1945. Both ad hoc tribunals

[13] E Gordy, *Guilt, Responsibility and Denial: The Past at Stake in Post-Milosevic Serbia* (University of Pennsylvania Press 2013) 184.

[14] See G J Bass, *Stay the Hand of Vengeance: The Politics of War Crimes Tribunals* (Princeton University Press 2000) 207 ('an act of tokenism by the world community, which was largely unwilling to intervene in ex-Yugoslavia but did not mind creating an institution that would give the appearance of moral concern ... The Tribunal was built to flounder').

[15] ibid.

[16] A Cassese, (Interview, 2009) in H V Stuart and M Simons, (eds) *The Prosecutor and the Judge; Benjamin Ferencz and Antonio Cassese, Interviews and Writings* (Amsterdam University Press 2009) 46–89, 47–8.

[17] M Jarvis and K Vigneswaran, 'Challenges to Successful Outcomes in Sexual Violence Cases' in S Brammertz and M Jarvis (eds), *Prosecuting Conflict-Related Sexual Violence at the ICTY* (OUP 2016) 43.

[18] *Prosecutor v Dusko Tadić* (Appeals Chamber Decision) IT-94-1-AR72 (2 October 1995).

[19] See V Haan, 'The Development of the Concept of Joint Criminal Enterprise at the International Criminal Tribunal for the Former Yugoslavia' (2005) 5 International Criminal Law Review 167.

asserted their independence from their creator. Criminal adjudication was formally separated from the executive authority.

Then, the Tribunal faced the 'big fish versus small fish' dilemma. It was questionable whether the ICTY had enough power to go after the most responsible leaders. With growing arrests through international forces and political pressure, the tribunal was expected to try high-level defendants. It ran mega trials, like the Slobodan Milošević trial. This practice showed the complexity of cases, but also the risks of extensive charging and the limits of self-representation.[20] The ICTY became a laboratory for procedural adjustment and innovation. It sought to devise a system that is best suited to atrocity crimes. Initially, rules were largely drafted in analogy to domestic systems. But they had to adjust to the context of international criminal proceedings. One of the biggest successes of the procedural law is that it managed to identify certain weaknesses of a purely adversarial culture and to develop certain special rules for effective adjudication of international crimes. In some areas, such as sexual and gender-based violence, they are ahead of domestic systems.[21]

Over time, the tribunal almost became a victim of its success. Its caseload grew. This led to heightened expectations by affected communities, including victim groups. But it also posed capacity constraints. States soon became interested in downsizing. The tribunal solved this partly through the Completion Strategy. It had some positive spin-offs. It led to a 'rediscovery of complementarity', which has become crucial for other international criminal courts and tribunals as well. The Rules of the Road programme, outreach activities, and referral of cases to domestic entities brought the tribunal closer from The Hague to the region.

One of the common lessons from all tribunals is that mandates do not end with cases. The Completion Strategy resulted in a continuation strategy. Both the success of the ICTY and its weaknesses and failures inspired 'the creation of other courts and tribunals'.[22]

5.3 Messages of Normativity

The normative legacy of the ICTY is closely related to the messages that it sent about accountability, most notably the idea that law can respond to atrocity crime through criminal procedures and restore confidence in norms that have been violated. Its impact is not only linked to the quality of jurisprudence but the perception of the institution as an independent expression of justice in the eyes of the public.

One of the main achievements of the ICTY is that it brought the law out of the books. It marked more than a stepping stone for the broader project of creating a permanent international court. It provided a novel lens on crime construction, modes of liability, and criminal procedure. [23] It also manifested certain gaps in the legal architecture and a partly

[20] See Sterio and Scharf (eds) *The Legacy of* Ad Hoc *Tribunals in International Criminal Law: Assessing the ICTY's and the ICTR's Most Significant Legal Accomplishments* (n 1). See also H Abtahi and G Dawson, 'The Anatomy of the Milošević trial (2001–2006)' (2016) 1 Journal of International Criminal Justice 1.

[21] See S Brammertz and M Jarvis (eds), *Prosecuting Conflict-Related Sexual Violence at the ICTY* (OUP 2016).

[22] ibid.

[23] D Robinson and G MacNeil, 'The Tribunals and the Renaissance of International Criminal Law: Three Themes' (2016) 10 The American Journal of International Law 193.

autonomous approach to legal sources. Judge Meron gently spoke of the 'humanization of international humanitarian law'.[24]

The question of what constitutes 'good law' and 'bad law' remains in the eye of the beholder. It depends partially on the perspective. Defence, Prosecution, and victims have different perspectives. Certain constructions, such as individual criminal responsibility in non-international armed conflict, or the responsibility of civilian commanders gained quick acceptance. Other innovations, like JCE III, remained contested.[25] Some judgments were criticized. But the ICTY law undoubtedly provided a novel compass to re-think the foundations of international criminal justice.

Overall, the impact of the ICTY is not only grounded in individual legal acts or judgments but in the dialogue, communicative processes, or even disagreement generated through legal action. In the most general sense, ICTY practice has opened a novel discursive space between the ICTY, its speakers, and audiences. It has established a new lingual framework (Bosnian/Croatian/Serbian, i.e. 'BCS') and a common frame to speak about atrocity and put violations into words. The attempt to speak law beyond individual cases is a means to cope with some of the inherent limitations of international criminal justice, namely its physical detachment from local audiences,[26] its inherent selectivity, and its partly underdeveloped legal framework. The Hague has become to some extent a 'stage' for international criminal justice. Judgments carried a 'world-view' on specific facts, offences, or lines of responsibility that sought to counter domestic narratives.

The ICTY had a profound effect on the modern legal understanding of genocide.[27] Srebrenica has become a 'worldwide (…) Bosnian synonym for genocide', also becoming a model for other ICTY investigations and prosecutions.[28] The ICTY's main innovation lies in the fact that it adjusted the interpretation of genocide to different contexts, in particular killings and destruction carried out against parts of groups in limited geographic areas, such as enclaves and towns. It accepted that genocide is not a game of numbers. It ruled that destruction of a part of a group is sufficient if that part is 'emblematic' of the overall group. As Michelle Jarvis and Alan Tieger have noted, according to the ICTY experience,

> the question is not whether a particular set of crimes can be labelled in the abstract as 'genocide' but whether the individual accused person is responsible for genocidal acts committed with genocidal intent.[29]

In its first genocide conviction in relating to events in Srebrenica, namely the *Krstić* case, the ICTY accepted the argument that genocide may occur even when the exterminatory intent extends only to a limited geographic zone—something that has been called 'localized

[24] T Meron, 'The Humanization of Humanitarian Law' (2000) 94 American Journal of International Law 239.

[25] See L D Yanev, *Theories of Co-Perpetration in International Criminal Law* (Brill 2018) 40–2.

[26] See M Drumbl, 'Collective Violence and Individual Punishment: The Criminality of Mass Atrocity' (2005) 99 Northwestern University Law Review 539, 593.

[27] See, for example, M Jarvis and A Tieger, 'Applying the Genocide Convention at the ICTY: The Influence of Paradigms Past' (2016) 14 Journal of International Criminal Justice 857.

[28] J M Trbovc, 'On the Capacity of the ICTY to Shape Public Perception of the Bosnian War: Narratives of Genocide Inside and Outside of the Courtroom', Paper presented at the CEEISA-ISA 2016 Joint International Conference, available at <http://web.isanet.org/Web/Conferences/CEEISA-ISA-LBJ2016/Archive/92e2778c-77f1-46a5-951d-ebd41eed8f15.pdf> accessed 28 September 2019.

[29] Jarvis and Tieger (n 27) 869.

genocide'.[30] The ICJ has shown a rather wide degree of deference to ICTY case law in its genocide cases. It relied heavily on *Krstić* and found that the 'Court has no reason to depart from the Tribunal's determination that the necessary specific intent (*dolus specialis*) was established'.[31] The Srebrenica rulings closed a tragic cycle: the UN, the same organization that had failed 'victims' of the massacre in July 1995, came to provide some form of justice.

The message in relation to genocidal intent in relation to attacks in other municipalities has remained more ambiguous. The Prosecution sought to establish that genocide took place in all of Bosnia and Herzegovina. However, *Karadžić*[32] and *Mladić*[33] were acquitted for counts of genocide relating to other Bosnian municipalities, based on different reasons, such as the failure to establish specific genocidal intent or to destroy a substantial part of the group. This may fuel a perception that genocide only occurred in Srebrenica.

The overall record contains certain gaps and loopholes. The Tribunal never fully clarified the role of Serbia in relation to the events in Srebrenica. Serbs remained critical of the record because the ICTY acquitted leaders of the Kosovo Liberation Army like Ramush Haradinaj and Fatmir Limaj and overturned the convictions of Croatian generals Ante Gotovina and Mladen Markac for crimes committed during Operation Storm.

A second major innovation of the ICTY is that it adjusted the law to changing patterns of violence, including the role of non-State actors in the commission of crimes. This is reflected, inter alia, in the wide definition of armed conflict, which includes conflicts between armed groups,[34] the reading of the policy element of crimes against humanity, or the extension of torture or command responsibility to civilian structures.[35] The ICTY also adapted to changing means of warfare. It established, inter alia, that rape was used as a weapon of war in the municipality of Foča,[36] and that the shelling and sniping of Sarajevo constituted an act of terror against the civilian population.[37]

Through its jurisprudence, the ICTY tried not only to establish individual criminal responsibility but to contribute to the coherence of the international legal order. The Tribunal partly constituted the law that it enacted. In particular, it has taken an active stance on the development of international customary law.[38] It found that *opinio juris* may be more important than practice for the establishment of customary law in the humanitarian field and

[30] W A Schabas, 'Was Genocide Committed in Bosnia and Herzegovina? First Judgments of the International Criminal Tribunal for the Former Yugoslavia' (2001) 25 Fordham International Law Journal 23, 42.

[31] ICJ, *Application of the Convention on the Prevention and Punishment of the Crime of Genocide* (Bosnia and Herzegovina v Serbia and Montenegro), 26 February 2007, para 295.

[32] In *Karadžić*, the Trial Chamber decided that the actus reus of genocide was satisfied (*Prosecutor v Karadžić* (Judgment) IT-95-5/18-T (24 March 2016) para 2605), but not the specific intent, which could not be inferred from speeches, statements, or from the overall pattern of crimes (para 2625). The Appeals Chamber confirmed the acquittal, rejecting the Prosecution's appeal on this matter. *Prosecutor v Karadžić* (Judgment) MICT-13-55-A (20 March 2019) paras 712–46.

[33] The majority of the *Mladić* Trial Chamber found that the physical perpetrators of the killings in some of the municipalities did have the intention to destroy part of the Bosnian Muslim group as such (*Prosecutor v Mladić* (Judgment) IT-09-92-T (22 November 2017) paras 3456–526), but that such an intention did not cover a substantial part of it (ibid paras 3527–36).

[34] See *Prosecutor v Tadic* (Interlocutory Decision on Jurisdiction) IT-94-1-AR72 (2 October 1995).

[35] See *Prosecutor v Delalić* et al (Appeal Judgment) IT-96-21-A (20 February 2001).

[36] See *Prosecutor v Kunarac* et al (Judgment) IT-96-23 and IT-96-23/1-A (12 June 2002)

[37] See M Glasius, 'Terror, Terrorizing, Terrorism: Instilling Fear as a Crime in the Cases of Radovan Karadzic and Charles Taylor' in D. Zarkov and M. Glasius (eds), *Narratives of Justice In and Out of the Courtroom: Former Yugoslavia and Beyond* (Springer 2014) 45–61.

[38] See Y Tan, 'The Identification of Customary Rules in International Criminal Law' (2018) 34 Utrecht Journal of International and European Law 92.

grounded crimes in custom.[39] The reliance on customary law as a source was also a means to preserve its own legacy, namely to ensure that other courts follow its interpretations.

The ICC is both a result of, and a reaction to, the record of the ICTY. The very existence of the ICTY and the involvement of its personnel in treaty negotiations facilitated the establishment of the ICC.[40] The Rome Statute was directly influenced by the Statute and jurisprudence of the Tribunal, including many aspects of the definition of core crimes. Some have thus argued that the 'ad hoc's influence on the ICC may be their most important legacy'.[41] However, there is no linear line of progression. The Rome Statute deviated in key respects, by narrowing definitions (e.g. context elements of genocide and crimes against humanity, threshold of war crimes), filling gaps (e.g. sexual violence, protection of the environment), or changing methodologies (e.g. less flexibility towards judge-made law, more inquisitorial features, complementarity). Due to these differences, the ICC has formally rejected to consider ICTY jurisprudence as a directly applicable source of law. It adopted a different interpretation of modes of liability, through its focus on the control over the crime doctrine, rather than JCE. Notwithstanding this apparent separation between the ICTY and the ICC, the interpretation of crimes, modes of liability, defences, procedural law, or due process is filled with references to ICTY case law. The same use of ICTY practice by the ICC is seen in the issuance of policy papers by the ICC OTP, which draws upon the lessons learned by the ICTY OTP in several subjects, such as the prosecution of sexual and gender-based crimes.[42]

Maybe even more important than the law are the facts and the evidence that ICTY trials brought to light in judgments, transcript, and records. They mark the DNA of justice. They provide a basis to 'shrink the space of denial', as Diane Orentlicher put it in her report on the effects of the ICTY.[43]

5.4 Making Justice Heard and Seen

In a procedural sense, the ICTY reflected the idea that courts should not only do justice but also make it seen in a 'moral and historically unique sense'.[44] Procedures contained theatric and performative elements. They marked a performance of justice, they demonstrated that 'international criminal justice was possible'.[45] The number of individuals indicted was 161. Ninety individuals were sentenced for crimes.

Criminal proceedings were a means to influence public opinion, foster democratic debate, or inform future interpretation and meanings. The Tribunal relied on public

[39] See G Mettraux, *International Crimes and the* Ad Hoc *Tribunals* (OUP 2006).

[40] M Glasius, *The International Criminal Court: A Global Civil Society Achievement* (Routledge 2006) 51–53.

[41] See S Ford, 'The Impact of the Ad Hoc Tribunals on the International Criminal Court' in M Sterio and M Scharf (eds) *The Legacy of* Ad Hoc *Tribunals in International Criminal Law: Assessing the ICTY's and the ICTR's Most Significant Legal Accomplishments* (Introduction, CUP 2019) 307, 324.

[42] International Criminal Court, Office of the Prosecutor, 'Policy Paper on Sexual and Gender-Based Crimes (June 2014). See, in special, footnotes 2, 11, 21, 53, and 65.

[43] See D F Orentlicher, *Shrinking the Space of Denial: The Impact of the ICTY in Serbia* (OSJI 2008).

[44] S Felman, 'A Ghost in the House of Justice: Death and the Language of the Law' (2001) 13 Yale Journal of Law & the Humanities 241, 277–78; See also S Felman, *The Juridical Unconscious: Trials and Traumas in the Twentieth Century* (Harvard University Press 2002) 162. See D Meyerson, 'Why Should Justice Be Seen to Be Done?' (2015) 34 Criminal Justice Ethics 64; L Mulcahy, *Legal Architecture: Justice, Due Process and the Place of Law* (Glasshouse 2011); J Bosland and J Gill, 'The Principle of Open Justice and the Judicial Duty to Give Public Reasons' (2014) 38 Melbourne University Law Review 482.

[45] Ford (n 41) 324.

accessibility and visibility of trials to reinforce their impact. For instance, in the *Milošević* case, the OTP showed the Scorpions video not only for evidentiary purposes but rather to show the public what had happened.[46] At the time, much was already known of the fall of Srebrenica, especially through the work of ICTY investigators and other cases, such as *Nikolic* and *Obrenovic*.[47] The Prosecutor chose to show the nineteen minutes video, in order to make justice seen.[48] The video sent several messages: it shocked those present at trial, raising contentions from the Defence;[49] influenced other trials at the ICTY, the War Crimes Chamber, and also the ICJ;[50] and communicated to a wider audience, especially to the communities affected, that their pain was being seen and heard.[51]

A tipping point in strategy was the initiation of the outreach programme during the Presidency of Judge Gabrielle Kirk Mcdonald. The ICTY lacked control over how it was presented and perceived in the region. Outreach was set up to counter local manipulation, emphasize the impartiality and independence of the tribunal,[52] and re-gain control over its own image.[53] It reflected at the same time a turn of the tribunal towards its constituents, namely an 'engagement by the Tribunal's leadership in conducting local outreach and building a regional constituency to shift the false narratives about past atrocities'.[54] But it came at a point when existing divides were already deeply entrenched in domestic discourse and difficult to reverse.

The actual proceedings bear synergies with theatre and performance, involving a stage, actors, plots, and audiences.[55] They relied on drama, storytelling,[56] role-play, and social transformation. Trials did not only reconstruct what happened in the past but created a partially new reality through fact-finding, testimony, and adjudication. The performative features were reinforced by the largely adversarial nature of trial proceedings. Trials were a platform for competing narratives. The Prosecution sought to present defendants as rational human agents with criminal intent, while defendants themselves portrayed themselves partly as cogs in a machine, martyrs, or scapegoats of collective evil.[57] Procedural moves by one agent shaped the options available to the other actors—like in chess or a

[46] On the video, see I Vukušić, 'Nineteen Minutes of Horror: Insights from the Scorpions Execution Video' (2018) 12 Genocide Studies and Prevention 35.

[47] The cases files of *Prosecutor v Nikolic* and *Prosecutor v Obrenovic* are available at <http://www.icty.org/en/action/cases/4> accessed 12 September 2019.

[48] H Lennon, 'A Witness to Atrocity: Film as Evidence in International War Crimes' in T Haggith and J Newman (eds), *Holocaust and the Moving Image: Representations in Film and Television since 1933* (Thomson Press 2005) 67.

[49] ibid.

[50] International Court of Justice, Case Concerning the Application of the Convention on the Prevention and Punishment of the Crime of Genocide, 26 February 2007, available at <http://www.icj-cij.org/files/case-related/91/091-20070226-JUD-01-00-EN.pdf> accessed 12 September 2019.

[51] The video, after all, surfaced to the Prosecution Offices in Serbia and in The Hague after the coordinated effort of the NGO Humanitarian Law Center (HLC). See N Kandić, *Škorpioni od zločina do pravde* (Introduction,Humanitarian Law Center 2008) 7–8, referenced in Vukušić (n 46) 42.

[52] G K McDonald, 'Problems, Obstacles and Achievements of the ICTY' (2004) 2 Journal of International Criminal Justice 558, 569.

[53] D Tolbert, 'The International Criminal Tribunal for the Former Yugoslavia: Unforeseen Successes and Foreseeable Shortcomings' (2002) 26 The Fletcher Forum of World Affairs 7–19, 13.

[54] See Institute for Integrated Transitions, 'Changing the Narrative: The Role of Communications in Transitional Justice', 4.

[55] M Glasius and F Colona, 'The Yugoslavia Tribunal: the Moving Targets of a Legal Theatre' in D Abazović and M Velikonya (eds) *Post-Yugoslavia: New Cultural and Political Perspectives* (Palgrave 2014) 8–34.

[56] See P Brooks and P Gerwitz, *Law's Stories: Narratives and Rhetoric in the Law* (Yale Univeristy Press 1998).

[57] A Stolk, 'Sophisticated Beast? On the Construction of an "Ideal" Perpetrator in the Opening Statements of International Criminal Trials' (2018) 29 European Journal of International Law 677.

board game. Judges were deemed to act as umpires of narratives and counter-narratives,[58] based on the facts and evidence established at trial. However, judgments and opinions often contained their own forms and elements of storytelling. The 'truth' built was largely a 'procedural truth'.[59]

Criminal proceedings had a complex relationship with history. They framed historical discourse and were framed by it.[60] For some high-level defendants, trials were inherently connected to national history and their place in it. For instance, Karadžić presented himself 'as the defender of the Serbs as a historical victim', while the Prosecution emphasized his moral blame and legal responsibility 'for the ethnic crimes in Bosnia'.[61] Trials thus became a platform for communication with different and sometimes parallel audiences. They did not manage to overcome 'ethnic' divides regarding the adjudicated events, despite their establishment of facts.[62]

One important element of making justice seen and heard was to give a voice to victims. This process was mediated at the ICTY. Victims contributed to proceedings as witnesses, that is, as messengers for the parties of proceedings. Unlike in the ICC context, they were not autonomous actors, whose 'personal interests' are protected, but rather 'bounded' agents. This distinguished their intervention from more open formats of testimony and storytelling. Witnesses were not heard on their own sake, that is, to present their story, but rather to contribute to the case. The testimony was restricted to legally relevant information. The ICTY deserves credit for developing new rules and practices to facilitate testimony regarding sexual and gender-based crimes and avert traumas of secondary victimization through questioning in court. It relied inter alia on written statements, prior transcripts, and judicial notice in order to reduce examination and cross-examination of sexual violence victims. The testimony itself had partly a transformative effect. Findings of an institutional interview with 264 witnesses suggest that testifying was often a positive experience that may have some 'cathartic and satisfying elements'.[63]

One of the main challenges was to get others, in particular actors in the region, to listen. The overall record is marked by friction. The ICTY managed to fulfil its core mandate, namely to investigate and prosecute crimes, including senior military and political leaders, and to bring out facts and evidence. However, it failed to get domestic and local constituencies to engage in its work in an open and non-biased way:

> It did not provide a sense of justice for the vast majority of victims; it did not end the culture of impunity; it did not hold back the tide of revisionism; and it did not succeed in contributing to reconciliation.[64]

[58] See A B Houge, 'Narrative Expressivism: A Criminological Approach to the Expressive Function of International Criminal Justice' (2018) 19 Criminology & Criminal Justice 277.

[59] See K Ambos, 'International Criminal Procedure: "Adversarial", "Inquisitorial" or "Mixed"' (2003) 3 International Criminal Law Review 1.

[60] P M Wald, 'Foreword: War Tales and War Trials' (2008) 106 Michigan Law Review 901–22, 911.

[61] T Meijers and M Glasius, 'Expression of Justice or Political Trial? Discursive Battles in the Karadžić Case' (2013) 35 Human Rights Quarterly 720, 746.

[62] See J N Clark, *International Trials and Reconciliation: Assessing the Impact of the International Criminal Tribunal for the Former Yugoslavia* (Routledge 2014).

[63] ICTY, *Echoes of Testimonies—A Pilot Study into the Long-term Impact of Bearing Witness Before the ICTY* (UNT and ICTY 2016) 83.

[64] See Institute for Integrated Transitions, 'Changing the Narrative: The Role of Communications in Transitional Justice' 5.

The legacy remained partially centreed on witnesses and victims who contributed to proceedings, legal professionals, and international audiences. The experience of the tribunal suggests that the messages sent through trials, testimony, and judgment need to be connected more closely to its recipients, in order to be listened to. This may require more proactive engagement with local constituencies and media, rather than one-sided messaging, and closer integration of findings, testimonies, and archives into historical and human rights initiatives to counter denial and revisionism.[65]

5.5 Institutional Culture of the ICTY

In the network of international institutions, ICTY generally stands out in its professional culture. It formed a large community of professionals that shaped the making of international justice, its ethos, and its working methods. At the outset, those who joined the ICTY had to adjust to a system still in development and develop its own institutional culture, including the values, norms, practices, attitudes, and opinions that were acceptable in their workspace.[66] Over time the ICTY developed an institutional culture that branded its identity and ensured its adaptation and survival and contributed to the formation of a group of like-minded professionals. As Frédéric Mégret has noted, the ICTY may have shaped the image of a certain ideal type of 'the international criminal lawyer':

> strong on the technique but politically aware, rooted in history but with an eye on the *telos*; empathetic to victims but protective of defendants; savvy about states but accountable to 'Humanity', *etc.*[67]

The story of the Defence is a good illustration. The ICTY recognized that a fair and effective Defence serves not only the defendant but the interests of the criminal justice system as a whole. It essential for the integrity of proceedings and the process of truth-finding. Defence counsel are not only partisan agents, but to some extent officers of the court.

Defence counsel has set the institutional footprints for a better organization of Defence interests. A fundamental step was the creation of the Association of Defence Counsel, and the adoption of the Code of Professional Conduct for Counsel Appearing Before the International Tribunal.[68] In the courtroom, counsel fought many of the original battles that highlighted weaknesses in procedures or structural inequalities. Some defendants continued to regard the ICTY as a political tribunal. But it became clear that one cannot 'fight politics with politics' in the courtroom. Defendants had to engage with the legal case and the evidence. Defence attitudes shifted over time, also in light of interactions in the court, courtroom routine, as well as fairness and respect demonstrated towards the Defence.[69]

65 ibid 5.

66 M Hirshe, *An Invitation to the Sociology of International Law* (OUP 2015) 6; see also D Terris et al, *The International Judge: An Introduction to the Men and Women Who Decide the World's Cases* (Brandeis University Press 2007).

67 F Mégret, 'International Criminal Justice as a Juridical Field' (2016) 13 Penal Field 1, 41.

68 See generally C Rohan and G Zyberi, *Defense Perspectives on International Criminal Justice* (CUP 2017).

69 See F Mégret and M G Samson, 'Defiance, Defence, Repentance and What Lies Between' (2019) 17 Journal of International Criminal Justice 151, 155.

The ICTY has shaped a certain prosecutorial culture. The ICTY has shaped many of the modern techniques of investigation—and this before the rise of new technologies. The Srebrenica investigation stands out as an example. Forensic evidence and aerial footage managed to reconstruct how bodies were moved to secondary graves. The Tribunal has been praised for its success in securing arrest through cooperation with regional and international institutions. It has re-invented its prosecutorial strategies throughout the different life-cycles of the tribunal. The lessons are reflected in practice manuals and policy documents. ICTY practices cannot be transposed directly to other legal frameworks, since procedures and structures differ. However, they provide useful guidance to avoid mistakes of the past.

The working methods in Chambers are part of the legacy. The judicial output is a largely collective work. Issues, such as the drafting of judgments, and the analysis of evidence, are often surrounded by mystery since they are done in secret. Legal officers and judicial staff play an important role behind the scenes. They are, to some extent the 'kit' that keeps the judicial work together. They play multiple roles: they may be advisers, drafters, managers, psychologists, or mediators between judges. At trial, they have a key role in organizing evidence collected over years. Legacy is shaped by many by-products of judicial activity, such as compilations of jurisprudence, archival work, and education and training of domestic actors or manuals.[70]

ICTY institutional cultures are carried on through former staff members, professional networks, and movement of personnel across jurisdictions and institutions. Many ICTY staff members who have worked in the OTP, Chambers, or for the Defence have moved to other tribunals or embarked on careers in other areas, such as the rule of law or human rights (e.g. in NGOs, commission of inquiries, rule of law missions). Elena Baylis has referred to 'tribunal-hopping'.[71] Human beings thereby become the medium of the message. Such processes contribute to the transfer of legal know-how or sharing of working practices and institutional cultures. But they also have negative side-effects. They may create new social elites, exclude others from entering the field, foster certain inherent biases, or stifle innovation.

The more time advances, the more there is a risk that ICTY may be referred to as the 'golden rule'. It is a little bit like in Woody Allen's 'Midnight in Paris'. In the movie, the main character, Gil, travels back to the Paris of his dreams in the 1920s where he meets 'greats and goods' like Fitzgerald, Hemingway, Gertrude Stein, T. S. Eliot, Picasso, Dali, Cole Porter. Then he meets Adriana, who grew up as part of this generation. She is unimpressed with the 1920s. She is nostalgic for a different era: the Paris of the 1890s: *La Belle Epoque*. Legacy involves a similar dilemma. With new iterations of international criminal justice coming to existence, there is a risk that we remain stuck in the same loop that Gil and Adriana are: some nostalgia of, and belief in, the greatness of some prior historical era, which in turn eclipses the present.

5.6 Conclusions

Where does this leave us for the future? It is unlikely that many more international ad hoc tribunals will be established in coming years. They will remain an exception in institutional

[70] ICTY Manual on Developed Practices (UNICRI/ICTY 2008) available at <http://www.icty.org/x/file/About/Reports%20and%20Publications/ICTY_Manual_on_Developed_Practices.pdf> accessed 29 September 2019.

[71] E Baylis, 'Tribunal-Hopping with the Post-Conflict Justice Junkies' (2008) 10 Oregon Review of International Law 361.

terms. Like in the context of procedures, we are witnesses of a growing hybridization of justice, with new forms of creativity. Domestic justice is the future, with different shades of internationalization or regional impulses.

However, the legacies of the Tribunal are living ones. They continue to be shaped in judgments, domestic case law and practice, and societal discourse across countries, continents, and fields. Many of the most immediate impacts of the ICTY's legacy are reflected on the international plane. Local and societal perceptions are mixed. Transforming societal narratives requires more time. The most traceable effect in domestic structures is 'mostly legal and judicial'.[72] This outcome may be explained by the fact the ICTY is first and foremost a court. However, legal and judicial work does not simply speak for itself. One of the lessons of the ICTY experience is that international criminal courts need a communication strategy and better efforts to relate to their constituencies, in order to be heard and listened to.

The tribunal will live on in many ways: not only in history books and memories but through its working experiences, its lessons learned, and IRMCT practice. In this process, it is important not to embellish performance but to share experiences and to engage with critiques. Many of the contributions of the ICTY will need to be adjusted to different contexts. In this sense, one might say: the ICTY is dead, long live the ICTY.

[72] F Mégret, 'The Legacy of the ICTY as Seen Through Some of its Actors and Observers' (2011) 3 Göttingen Journal of International Law 1011, 1047.

6

Legacies in the Making at the ICTY

*Viviane E. Dittrich**

6.1 Introduction

Inasmuch as 'legacy talk' is ubiquitous in the study of international criminal justice now, it was not at all a decade ago when I embarked on the multi-year project on which this chapter draws. Although practitioners invoked the notion on a daily basis, in The Hague and elsewhere, scholars were slow to study it. Mine is no longer the only voice to make a case for studying—both conceptually and contextually—the social construction of legacy discourses and, ultimately, legacies. In this chapter, I recount how we got to where we are, and what is still amiss in the emergent scholarship on the legacies of the international criminal tribunals, especially in international legal approaches to it. More specifically, the chapter presents the contours of a more nuanced conceptualization of legacy.[1]

Talk about the completion and legacy of the international criminal tribunals has been all pervasive. The topic has been ubiquitous in the political and legal discourse on the ad hoc tribunals. Legacy has become a buzzword. This does not seem coincidental as the International Criminal Tribunals for the former Yugoslavia and for Rwanda (ICTY and ICTR)[2] were in the throes of their respective completion strategies, first formalized in 2003 and 2004,[3] transitioning to what has become known as a 'residual mechanism', their successor institution that continues the ongoing obligations or residual functions that will have to necessarily remain.[4] The ad hoc international criminal tribunals were increasingly scrutinized—legally, politically, and financially—in light of recurring criticisms of their cost, pace, legitimacy, and political relevance. At the turn of the millennium the finiteness of the tribunals came into sharper relief as a new awareness of their ad hoc, temporary

* Dr Viviane Dittrich is Deputy Director of the International Nuremberg Principles Academy. She is also Visiting Fellow at the Centre for International Studies at the London School of Economics and Political Science (LSE). Previously, she has been Honorary Research Associate at Royal Holloway, University of London, and Visiting Researcher at iCourts (Centre of Excellence for International Courts), University of Copenhagen. Dr Dittrich has published on the notion of legacy and legacy building at the international criminal tribunals. Drawing on extensive field research, her work comparatively investigates the ICTY, ICTR, SCSL, ECCC, ICC, and IMT (Nuremberg). After studies in France, England, and the US (Wellesley College) she received an MSc in International Relations from the LSE and a Master's degree from Sciences Po Paris. She holds a PhD from the LSE. Views expressed in this chapter do not necessarily reflect the views of the International Nuremberg Principles Academy.

1 This new conceptualization was originally elaborated in See V E Dittrich, 'Legacies in the Making: Assessing the Institutionalized Legacy Endeavour of the Special Court for Sierra Leone' in C C Jalloh (ed), *The Sierra Leone Special Court and its Legacy: The Impact for Africa and International Criminal Law* (CUP 2014). For a more comprehensive and the first book-length analysis, see V E Dittrich, *Present at the Completion: Creating Legacies at the International Criminal Tribunals*, book manuscript, January 2020.

2 For further analysis of the legal basis, authority, and operations of these tribunals, see W A Schabas, *The UN International Criminal Tribunals: The Former Yugoslavia, Rwanda, and Sierra Leone* (CUP 2006).

3 UN Docs S/RES/1503, 28 August 2003; S/RES/1534, 26 March 2004.

4 See UN Doc S/RES/1966, 22 December 2010, and International Residual Mechanism for Criminal Tribunals Statute.

Viviane E. Dittrich, *Legacies in the Making at the ICTY* In: *Legacies of the International Criminal Tribunal for the Former Yugoslavia*. Edited by: Carsten Stahn, Carmel Agius, Serge Brammertz, Colleen Rohan, Oxford University Press (2020).
DOI: 10.1093/oso/9780198862956.003.0007

nature emerged. This triggered heightened considerations of completion and closure. The Special Court for Sierra Leone (SCSL) was the first contemporary court to ceremonially close its doors in December 2013 and pioneered many legacy efforts.[5] Two years later, the ICTR closed in December 2015. Another two years later, the ICTY officially closed in December 2017.

This chapter explores the topic of legacy at the ICTY against the backdrop of theorizing the construction of legacies in lieu of assessing or measuring the effectiveness of the Tribunal per se or attempting an empirical assessment of the legacies of the ICTY or any particular legacy. The focus here is on the institutional perspective, the ICTY itself as legacy leaver and the institutional creation of legacies, not on the reception of the ICTY, nor its judgments or legacies as seen in the region. Such a wider perspective complements fine-grained legal analyses of particular topics concerning the ICTY's legal framework, procedures, and jurisprudence. The ICTY has been a ground breaking institution as the first contemporary international criminal tribunal. There is no shortage of assessments, appraisals, and re-appraisals by both proponents and critics of the Tribunal and international criminal justice. Much speculation about any possible or definitive legacy of the Tribunal and legacy previews abound. Scholarly literature is burgeoning.[6] The notion of legacy was prominently referred to at the final closing ceremony held on 21 December 2017, including by the UN Secretary General.[7]

The chapter is divided into three parts. First, in order to fully appreciate legacy formation and the spectrum of possible legacies it is necessary to unpack the notion of legacy and elucidate the social construction of legacies. This chapter highlights the importance of paying closer attention to the multifaceted social process of legacy formation and plural legacies in the making. Against this conceptual backdrop, the second part examines the institutional endeavour of legacy building at the ICTY, especially with a focus on the early developments. Through the prism of institutionalization, three separate yet interrelated dynamics are identified: developing a legacy vision, professionalizing legacy, and designing and implementing legacy projects. A particular focus is placed on the legacy conferences organized by the Tribunal itself. Finally, the dynamics of completion, closure, and continuation are explored. To this end, the emphasis is placed on elucidating the role of the Tribunal as temporary institution and legacy leaver. It is argued that while the Tribunal has completed its work in accordance with a Completion Strategy and formally closed its doors, the Tribunal lives on through its successor institution, the International Residual Mechanism for Criminal Tribunals, and its legacies.

[5] See V E Dittrich, 'Legacies in the Making: Assessing the Institutionalized Legacy Endeavour of the Special Court for Sierra Leone' in C C Jalloh (ed), *The Sierra Leone Special Court and its Legacy: The Impact for Africa and International Criminal Law* (CUP 2014); V E Dittrich, 'La Cour Spéciale Pour La Sierra Leone et La Portée de Son Héritage' (2014) 45 Études internationales 85.

[6] For book-length accounts with an explicit focus on the legacy of the ICTY see R H Steinberg, *Assessing the Legacy of the ICTY* (Martinus Nijhoff Publishers 2011); B Swart et al, *The Legacy of the International Criminal Tribunal for the Former Yugoslavia* (OUP 2011); J Gow, R Kerr, and Z Pajic, *Prosecuting War Crimes: Lessons and Legacies of the International Criminal Tribunal for the Former Yugoslavia* (Routledge 2013); M Sterio and M Scharf, *The Legacy of* Ad Hoc *Tribunals in International Criminal Law* (CUP 2019); Stahn et al, this volume.

[7] 'Secretary-General's Remarks at Closing Ceremony for the International Criminal Tribunal for the Former Yugoslavia (ICTY) [as Delivered]' (*UN*, 21 December 2017) <https://www.un.org/sg/en/content/sg/statement/2017-12-21/secretary-generals-remarks-closing-ceremony-international-criminal> accessed 15 April 2019.

6.2 Concept of Legacy

Legacies are a contest for influence over remembrance, a deliberate selective use of the past according to the demands of the present. The topic of legacy construction thus resonates with the politics of memory and creation of meaning. In this sense, given the social construction of legacies tribunals are to be studied as social actors.[8] International legal scholarship has produced invaluable insights into the *legal lives* of the tribunals but has sidelined their *social lives*.[9] To date, scant attention has been given to the multifaceted social process underpinning legacy formation, the tribunals as legacy leavers and the spectrum of their multiple legacies. Countering the dearth of attention given to the actual process of constructing legacies, this chapter sketches the contours of a framework on the legacy process placing the social construction of legacies at the centre of its analysis.[10] The relevance and poignancy of this new conceptual approach to legacy was evidenced by the readiness with which its core ideas were taken up directly.[11]

6.2.1 Language of Legacy

Leaving a legacy is not a novel idea or practice. Legacy building has ostensibly become a social and political expectation and responsibility mirrored in the ubiquitous question 'What will be your legacy?' This expectation has also increasingly become prominent for the tribunals both in terms of costs and expected deliverables. In anticipation of closure, we have witnessed a 'legacy turn' in the realm of the temporary international criminal tribunals.[12] This is in part because of the sheer expense of the tribunals and a fundamental realization by the international community that simply convicting a number of alleged perpetrators may not be sufficient to impact more broadly on post-conflict countries transitioning to societal stability, peace, and reconciliation.[13] Hence, pressure on the tribunals grew to demonstrate successes and lasting contributions 'outside the narrow confines of the courtroom'.[14] The awareness that international criminal tribunals should leave a lasting impact beyond prosecuting a select number of individuals is palpable. This ties into wider questions of aims of international criminal justice and assessment.[15] It could be argued that the consequences and impact of international criminal trials are increasingly scrutinized. Leaving a footprint,

[8] M R Madsen, 'Sociological Approaches to International Courts' [2014] The Oxford Handbook of International Adjudication.

[9] J Meierhenrich, 'The UN International Criminal Tribunals: The Former Yugoslavia, Rwanda and Sierra Leone by W A. Schabas' (2006) 102 American Journal of International Law 696.

[10] As originally articulated in Dittrich, 'Legacies in the Making: Assessing the Institutionalized Legacy Endeavour of the Special Court for Sierra Leone' (n 1).

[11] Cf. S Kendall and S M H Nouwen, 'Speaking of Legacy: Toward an Ethos of Modesty at the International Criminal Tribunal for Rwanda' (2016) 110 American Journal of International Law 212; C Stahn, 'Legacy in International Criminal Justice. Arcs of Global Justice' in Mt M deGuzman and D M Amann (eds) *Arcs of Global Justice* (OUP 2018).

[12] Dittrich, 'Legacies in the Making: Assessing the Institutionalized Legacy Endeavour of the Special Court for Sierra Leone' (n 1).

[13] V O Nmehielle and C C Jalloh, 'The Legacy of the Special Court for Sierra Leone' (2006) 30 Fletcher Forum of World Affairs 107.

[14] ibid 110–11.

[15] C Stahn, 'Between "Faith" and "Facts": By What Standards Should We Assess International Criminal Justice?' (2012) 25 Leiden Journal of International Law 251.

a sustainable footprint, after years or decades of activity is expected. The Independent Expert Report on the Special Court for Sierra Leone by Antonio Cassese formulated an imperative: 'This is the question of a tribunal's legacy: tribunals must leave something useful behind.'[16] But what this 'something useful' is remains disputed given different expectations, definitions, and constructions of legacy. A shared sense within and across tribunals as legacy leavers, becoming cognizant of wanting to leave a legacy, has emerged. This is also reflected in the gradual institutionalization of legacy exemplified below for the ICTY. The notion of legacy is also germane for the International Criminal Court (ICC) despite being a permanent institution.[17]

Legacy formation involves both retrospective and prospective, bestowing purpose and attributing meaning to the past, present, and future. In this sense, determining and constructing legacies implies an attribution of significance, grandeur, or gravitas to the respective legacy leaver. Vis-à-vis the spectre of organizational death, institutions facing closure have an immediate interest to engage in legacy building and by extension in 'immortality projects' or 'bids for immortality'.[18] Attempts to fabricate legacies and thus make activities and achievements intelligible are commonplace. The interplay between self-preservation and self-redemption also coloured legacy efforts at the tribunals. Over time legacies take on a specific role in terms of meaning making, image maintenance, and identity creation. The term legacies refers to the temporally evolving open-ended outcomes of retrospective and prospective processes involving multiple actors influencing the meaning and memory of events, narratives, and places. Legacies are not automatic or static, but rather the product of an ongoing constructive process. The dynamic and continuous re-interpretation of a legacy has also been pointed out by Mégret:

> A legacy is not something cast in stone for all times; rather it is an evolving intellectual relationship that we construct with an object receding in the past (to the point of it being strange to speak of legacy whilst the tribunal is still in activity), and that we are condemned to reinterpret on the basis of changing circumstances and assumptions.[19]

It is important to recognize the limits of controlling legacy formation and predetermining particular legacies. As has been astutely observed: 'one's legacy, in the sense of how one will be remembered, is largely out of one's own control. History renders the verdict, which will be re-evaluated over time.'[20] This indeed requires a sense of modesty as legacy leaver.[21]

No uniform or single definition of legacy seems to exist across the tribunals. The ICTY was the first tribunal to provide a definition of legacy:

[16] A Cassese, 'Report on the Special Court for Sierra Leone' para 76.

[17] V E Dittrich, 'Legacies of the International Criminal Court under Construction' (2013) Sicherheit und Frieden (S+F)/Security and Peace 197. . See also E Evenson and A Smith, 'Completion, Legacy, and Complementarity at the ICC' [2015] The Law and Practice of the International Criminal Court 1259.

[18] E Becker, *The Denial of Death* (The Free Press 1973); Z Bauman, *Mortality, Immortality and Other Life Strategies* (Stanford University Press 1992).

[19] F Mégret, 'The Legacy of the ICTY as Seen through Some of Its Actors and Observers' (2011) 3 Goettingen Journal of International Law 1011, 1014.

[20] R A Kane, 'From Generation to Generation: Thoughts on Legacy' (1996) 20 Generations 5.

[21] Kendall and Nouwen (n 11) 212–29.

'that which the Tribunal will hand down to successors and others', which 'includes, but is not limited to the findings of the Tribunal contained in its judgments, its contribution to the development of international law, the records and archives of the Tribunal, its contribution to the rule of law in the former Yugoslavia and its advancement of international justice'.[22]

An often-cited definition, introduced by the UN Office of the High Commissioner for Human Rights (OHCHR) policy tool *Maximizing the Legacy of Hybrid Courts*, defines legacy as the 'lasting impact on bolstering the rule of law ... by conducting effective trials to contribute to ending impunity, while also strengthening domestic judicial capacity'.[23] A number of publications have taken up this definition making it the most common definition used for hybrid courts. For instance, the SCSL explicitly adopted this definition in its 8th Annual Report in 2011.[24] It is also the most used definition in the Cambodian context given the involvement and activities of the OHCHR country office in Phnom Penh, yet the Extraordinary Chambers in the Courts of Cambodia (ECCC) as an institution has not officially provided a working definition. It seems, however, that the OHCHR definition is unnecessarily limited to a very narrow, albeit perhaps practical, conceptualization. It ultimately neglects to encapsulate the spectrum of possible legacies of a hybrid court or an international tribunal. Identifying what notion of legacy is used is crucial for effective communication and understanding, which becomes more complicated in a multi-lingual setting. When comparing the definitions, it appears more than one concept of legacy exists. At least two concepts can be discerned. A broad concept of legacy, which may include contributions to law, justice, peace, reconciliation, and societal dynamics, stands in contrast to a narrow notion solely covering the legal and judicial arena. Questions of purpose and interpretation of the legal, political, social, economic, or cultural components of international trials hereby take centre stage. The juxtaposition of what might be called a conservative definition and a broader definition has informed recent accounts.[25]

The ubiquity of talk about legacy and the general appeal as well as casual usage of the term warrants scrutiny. Three brief limitations of the current discourse will be noted. First, the term is often used in the singular, which seems problematic and misleading. It is argued that the common concept of legacy is too simplistic and one-dimensional which may bear a risk of distorting the overall ICTY legacy picture. It would be more accurate to speak of legacies, in the plural. The notion of multiple legacies,[26] instead of a single objective legacy,

[22] International Criminal Tribunal for the former Yugoslavia 'Assessing the Legacy of the ICTY' (*ICTY*) <http://www.icty.org/sid/10293> accessed 15 April 2019.

[23] Office of the High Commissioner for Human Rights OHCHR, 'Rule-of-Law Tools for Post-Conflict States: Maximizing the Legacy of Hybrid Courts' (2008) 4–5 <http://www.ohchr.org/Documents/Publications/HybridCourts.pdf> accessed 15 April 2019.

[24] Special Court for Sierra Leone SCSL, 'Eighth Annual Report of the President of the Special Court for Sierra Leone' (2010) <http://www.rscsl.org/Documents/AnRpt8.pdf> accessed 15 April 2019.

[25] See A Cole, 'What Is the International Criminal Court's Legacy?' (*The Guardian*, 16 July 2012) <http://www.theguardian.com/law/2012/jul/16/legacy-international-criminal-court> accessed 15 April 2019.

D Gozani, 'Beginning to Learn How to End: Lessons on Completion Strategies, Residual Mechanisms, and Legacy Considerations from Ad Hoc International Criminal Tribunals to the International Criminal Court' (2014) 36 Loyola of Los Angeles International and Comparative Law Review 331.

[26] Few publications use the plural, see K Campbell and S Wastell, 'Legacies of the International Criminal Tribunal for the Former Yugoslavia' (2008) <https://topslide.net/document/legacies-of-the-international-criminal-tribunal-for-the-former-yugoslavia> accessed 15 April 2019; Gow, Kerr, and Pajic (n 6); Stahn et al, this volume.

encapsulates a possible spectrum of legacies and recognises that multiple interpretations may coexist. This in turn raises the question of how these may be logically connected, complementary, competing, or even conflicting. Second, most often only marginal attention is paid to legacy leaving as a social constructive process. In the tribunal context a legacy is generally presented as a positive product of intent, deliberation, and planning. The underlying assumption is that any legacy is highly malleable by the legacy leaver, that is the Tribunal itself. Such an approach to legacy not only neglects the social dynamics of leaving a legacy, it also underestimates the crucial role of various stakeholders, including legacy recipients, while overestimating the legacy leaver's own influence and ability to control. Third, especially at the outset of the emerging discourse, 'legacy' has been used as an imprecise umbrella term. In early discussions there was some confusion between residual functions and legacy, including at the ICTY. One tribunal official pointedly observed, 'The discourse has improved. At the beginning everything was legacy, it was confusing and inaccurate.'[27] Although legacy may temporally overlap both with completion and residual or post-completion issues, it is important to clearly distinguish between these interrelated but separate processes. The success of any buzzword, such as the term legacy, calls for vigilance, especially where the focus is often exclusively on the positive aspects. What matters then are the processes of how legacies come into being and also remain in the making. It is to the social construction of legacies to which this chapter now turns.

6.2.2 Social Construction of Legacies

Legacy formation is ongoing, with no definitive starting point or end point. The multiplicity of actors results in a cacophony of voices and narratives which is an integral feature of legacy formation. There is certainly no monolithic perspective on legacy. A new framework placing the social construction of legacies at the centre has been developed, the contours of which shall be sketched here.[28] Legacy building pinpoints the productive power of legacy constructions. Indeed, understanding power is critical in this process. The construction of legacies is an inherently social process. Adopting a constructivist lens enables a 'focus on the role of ideas, norms, knowledge, culture and argument in politics, stressing in particular the role of collectively held "intersubjective" ideas and understandings of social life.'[29] Legacies as collective mental representations are an interesting example of the prevalence of creating intersubjective rather than idiosyncratic constructs of meaning. Similarly, the focus is less on their material reality and more on their value as 'social facts.'[30]

Legacies do not emerge in a singular, linear fashion as the construction of legacies is an inherently social process involving discussion, negotiation, and contestation. In light of the role and development of norms here a cyclical perspective is adopted to capture the continuous (re)construction of legacies.[31] The cycle of legacies has three phases: creation,

[27] Interview with ICTY official (The Hague, 1 July 2011).

[28] The below framework was originally articulated in Dittrich, 'Legacies in the Making: Assessing the Institutionalized Legacy Endeavour of the Special Court for Sierra Leone' (n 1).

[29] M Finnemore and K Sikkink, 'Taking Stock: The Constructivist Research Program in International Relations and Comparative Politics' (2001) 4 Annual Review of Political Science 391, 392.

[30] J R Searle and S Willis, *The Construction of Social Reality* (Simon and Schuster 1995).

[31] See norm circle in S Park and A Vetterlein, *Owning Development: Creating Policy Norms in the IMF and the World Bank* (CUP 2010) 20.

consolidation, and contestation. The cycle of legacies is best considered a heuristic device for examining how and why certain legacies or legacy constructions come to the fore. Such a perspective allows legacies to be examined at every stage in the cycle, thereby emphasizing a point often neglected: there is no definitive starting point or end point of legacy construction. While consolidation is an important dynamic, contestation is an equally critical part of the cycle of legacies. Legacies are neither static nor definitive, but subject to a process of ongoing interpretation, contestation, and evolution over time.

Multiple actors partake, deliberately or otherwise, in the process of legacy construction. The role of different actors has to date been given inadequate consideration. This oversight is problematic for two reasons. First, it turns a blind eye to the construction process of legacies and the interplay of intentionality and non-intentionality. A focus on the latter puts paid to the common assumption that legacies somehow simply happen or emerge organically. Legacies may not be rationally planned or controlled, rather are socially constructed. Second, such oversight ignores actor diversity. Not all actors are given equal weight, recognition, and standing by those both inside and outside of the legacy process. Legacies therefore may become sites of debate, contestation, and struggle. The developed framework distinguishes five ideal types of actors, indicative and reflective of the actor diversity: legacy leavers, producers, enforcers, recorders, and recipients.

The dyad between legator and legatee, that is leaver and recipient, frames the legacy process. Legacies are conventionally portrayed as transmitted, or often bestowed, from a leaver to the recipient(s). Such a simplification overlooks that their interaction is not solely unidirectional. Legacy leaving cannot be reduced to a simple sender–receiver model. Recipients can and do act upon legacies and are not solely passive recipients in the literal sense. Many leavers actively attempt to shape their legacies and how they want to be remembered. The institutionalization of legacy at the tribunals, including the ICTY, can be read in this regard. Active reception and (re)interpretation though shape their meaning and value anew. A plethora of stakeholders and consequently legacy recipients are to be recognized in the context of tribunals: victims, witnesses, defendants, tribunal staff, various professionals, civil society, the domestic justice systems and governments, other tribunals, the United Nations and international community. In the model presented here the legacy process remains dynamic, multifaceted, and ongoing given the actor interaction and continuous construction. The actor constellation may vary according to the respective stage in the legacy cycle, that is, creation, consolidation, or contestation.

All five types of actors engage in forms of legacy building as argued here. The question arises as to how much importance may be accorded to agency and deliberation in the process over time. Intentionality and the intentions of legacy actors is an important issue. It is crucial to appreciate the interplay between intended and unintended legacies, but, equally, between realized and unrealized legacies. The gap between intended meaning of legacies and their public or social meaning amongst different audiences is often overlooked. Finally, the politics of legacy construction deserve more attention than generally accorded, also in light of collective memory formation.[32] For our purposes here, given the scope of the chapter and volume overall, here the ICTY as a tribunal is considered as the institutional

[32] M Osiel, *Mass Atrocity, Collective Memory and the Law* (Transaction Publishers 1997).

legacy leaver. The chapter now turns to how the emerging legacy awareness within the ICTY was translated into institutional action and legacy strategizing.

6.3 Institutionalization of Legacy Building

Legacy building has become an institutional endeavour at the tribunals. It is argued that legacy building performs the function of a coping strategy vis-à-vis organizational demise that is aimed, first and foremost, at meaning making. The ICTY has embraced its role as legacy leaver and engaged in legacy building, that is, active 'deliberate legacy planning'.[33] Temporarily speaking, the ICTY did not pioneer legacy efforts; the SCSL has been shown to be a precursor pioneering many legacy developments and showcasing considerable institutional innovation by portraying itself early on as proactive and deliberate legacy leaver.[34] The ICTY showed innovation in refining the approach to some legacy projects including organizing so-called legacy conferences and engaging in dialogue on its own legacy, setting an example as a legacy leaver. The considerable efforts of the ICTY nonetheless show some reactivity and discontinuity over time, which is however not identical to a more resources-driven approach to legacy prevalent at the ECCC.[35]

Three main steps towards institutionalization of legacy are discernible. First, rhetorically, the Tribunal developed a legacy vision, which implies projection of self, here of an organization, into the future. Second, structurally, the Tribunal dedicated certain institutional posts to legacy. Third, practically speaking, designing and implementing legacy projects became an area of activity. These three processes did not necessarily occur consecutively in this order; however, for analytical purposes, they are considered in turn.

6.3.1 Developing a Legacy Vision

The ICTY started developing and articulating a legacy vision from 2007–2008 onward, nearly fifteen years into its existence. While the ICTY Annual Reports mentioned the term 'legacy issues' for the first time in 2004, talk about residual functions and a residual mechanism was officially largely subsumed under a discussion on legacy until 2008.[36] In particular when the Appeals Chamber Schedule Working Group under auspices of the ICTY Vice-President had to make major adjustments the topic of legacy became salient.[37] An important conceptual crystallization occurred with the redressing of the Completion Strategy by former ICTY President Pocar's 'continuation strategy' or 'strategy of continued legacy building'[38] as discussed in section 6.4.2. The explicit turn to legacy from 2007 can also be

[33] Nmehielle and Jalloh (n 13).

[34] Dittrich, 'Legacies in the Making: Assessing the Institutionalized Legacy Endeavour of the Special Court for Sierra Leone' (n 1).

[35] V E Dittrich, 'The Legacy of the Extraordinary Chambers in the Courts of Cambodia' in S M Meisenberg and I Stegmiller (eds), *The Extraordinary Chambers in the Courts of Cambodia: Assessing Their Contribution to International Criminal Law* (vol 6, Springer 2016).

[36] ICTY Annual Reports 2004–2008; Campbell and Wastell (n 26); F Pocar, *The ICTY's Completion Strategy: Continuing Justice in the Region* (CUP 2009).

[37] Interview with ICTY official (The Hague, 1 July 2011).

[38] Pocar (n 36).

read as a reaction to developments at the Tribunal. For instance, the most high-profile accused, Slobodan Milosević, died in custody in March 2006. Questions about the ICTY's legitimacy, *raison d'être*, and achievements were raised by outside observers, NGOs, and the media. Hence, the turn to legacy can be read as a response to existential questions posed by both international and domestic constituents.

Talk about a legacy vision became more prominent in 2010. The aim of holding the first legacy conference in 2010 was 'to make public the court's vision of its legacy and discuss it in open'.[39] Championing national ownership as leitmotiv of tribunal efforts former ICTY President Robinson explicitly refers to the Tribunal's 'legacy vision' and emphasises 'national ownership' as a key guiding concept.[40] The development of a legacy vision was portrayed as an inclusive process allowing for external input and evolution stating: 'through the exchange of ideas, we wanted to come to a fuller and richer vision of what the legacy should be'.[41] A certain normativity is clearly apparent. Moreover, in this process of developing a legacy vision, honesty, transparency, and critical assessment has been formally endorsed by ICTY President Robinson.[42] However, the vision was not fully publicized after the conference and how these pledges continued to play out in practice, until closure and especially beyond, remain to be fully seen. There is one strategic document on its legacy vision that is publicly available.[43] The report resembles a strategic legacy preview in which 'strategic considerations' are explicitly formulated. Therein it recognizes, inter alia, the importance of its core work, the preservation of its records, and the cooperation with states in the region of the former Yugoslavia as well as other UN agencies.[44] In the context of the first legacy conference in February 2010 a policy document described legacy as 'that which the Tribunal will hand down to successors and others', the broad definition referred to already.[45] This definition reveals an understanding of legacy as objectively measurable and transferable, that is, something that exists objectively and thus can be handed down.

The ICTY legacy vision was double. It is noticeable that legacy activities have encompassed both a regional and a global dimension despite an emphasis on national ownership. A key element of the ICTY's legacy strategy has been represented as a 'collegial partnership with the judiciaries in the former Yugoslavia'.[46] Indicia of this are for example the venues of the legacy conferences, held in The Hague and in the region respectively. Early legacy engagement was most visible and prominent under the leadership of President Pocar and President Robinson, later on the topic of legacy was no longer as explicitly championed until public engagement again surfaced and culminated in the ICTY Legacy Dialogues between 2016 and 2018 under President Agius. However, a focus on legacy was not the exclusive domain of the Office of the President.

39 Interview with former ICTY official (The Hague, 23 June 2011).

40 P L Robinson, 'National Ownership: The Key Concept of the Tribunal's Legacy Vision' in *Assessing the Legacy of the ICTY* (Brill Nijhoff 2011) 11.

41 ibid.

42 Robinson, 'National Ownership: The Key Concept of the Tribunal's Legacy Vision' (n 40).

43 P Robinson, 'Report of the President on the Assessing the Legacy of the ICTY Conference 2010' (2010) <http://www.icty.org/x/file/Press/Events/100427_legacyconference_pdt_report.pdf> accessed 15 April 2019.

44 ibid.

45 Steinberg, 'Assessing the Legacy of the ICTY' (n 6).

46 ICTY, 'Seventeenth Annual Report of the International Tribunal for the Prosecution of Persons Responsible for Serious Violations of International Humanitarian Law Committed in the Territory of the Former Yugoslavia since 1991' (2010) 3 <http://www.icty.org/x/file/About/Reports%20and%20Publications/AnnualReports/annual_report_2017_en.pdf> accessed 15 April 2019.

Thinking on long-term sustainability of efforts and impact emerged considerably earlier in the Office of the Prosecutor (OTP). This was due in part to the necessity for close contact between the OTP and prosecutorial offices in the region of the former Yugoslavia since the 1990s and in part due to foresight and a vision of cooperation and rule of law building in the region. International attention to building up legal systems in the region through a number of initiatives has coloured the legacy vision prevalent in the OTP which has a strong orientation towards the region of the former Yugoslavia. Origins of a more active engagement may be traced to the 'Rules of the Road' programme established by the Rome Agreement in February 1996. Examples of active engagement with a clear legacy dimension include the Liaison Prosecutor programme, cooperation practice, referral of cases, and reflections on lessons learned within the Office, for example, with regard to sexual and gender-based violence as elaborated in section 6.3.3.

The ICTY outlined a powerful, positive legacy vision and even provided legacy prognostications or legacy previews. Earlier discussions on goals and achievements can be seen as antecedents to legacy talk. The Tribunal reiterated narratives about how its work has served as impetus for numerous pioneering developments. For example, it has claimed that it 'has irreversibly changed the landscape of international humanitarian law and provided victims an opportunity to voice the horrors they witnessed and experienced'.[47] This also became reflected in the language in the annual reports submitted to the UN Secretary General and United Nations Security Council (UNSC). Numerous tribunal documents refer to 'legacy issues'. Speaking of 'issues', however, suggests that there are simply objective, technical matters to be dealt with accordingly. What is more, the issues are often discussed in apolitical and ahistorical terms.[48] Indeed, the fact alone of referring to 'issues' appears to shift the focus onto the mechanics of dealing with an 'issue' rather than the politics surrounding the topic itself. A mechanistic approach, however, eclipses questions of agency, deliberation, and power. The growing awareness of the importance of legacy and the desired external demonstration has resulted in the professionalization of legacy within the ICTY.

6.3.2 Professionalizing Legacy

The growing interest in legacy has become reflected structurally with the creation or renaming of posts at the Tribunal. An important step towards institutionalization was the creation of a professional post titled Legacy Officer in 2008, which acted as a legacy focal point within the Tribunal. The ICTY Office of the President took the lead on legacy. Then ICTY President Pocar created such a post in the Office of the President and deliberately recruited a staff member with extensive knowledge and work experience in the region and considerable outreach experience. This seems constructively aligned with the ICTY legacy vision placing the region into the centre not the periphery. After two years a legal officer in the Office of the President took up the position of Acting Legacy Officer. Another two years later, the chef de cabinet took over the title Acting Legacy Officer in 2012. In addition, in preparation of the legacy conferences held in 2010 and 2011 one staff member was given the

[47] 'About the ICTY' (*ICTY*) <https://www.icty.org/en/content/frontpage-intro-block> accessed 21 July 2015.
[48] See L Nader, 'The Words We Use: Justice, Human Rights, and the Sense of Injustice' [2010] Mirrors of Justice: Law and Power in the Post-Cold War Era 316.

title of Legacy Administrative Officer. In later years, the post was not kept in the budget of the Office of the President. In the final phase of the Tribunal prior to closure, a new Legacy Officer worked in the Communications Services.

One of the main objectives of the legacy work has been visibility on the engagement, centralization of efforts, and coordination across organs.[49] Certainly also fundraising has become part of the portfolio given that legacy was considered an extra budgetary activity. Contrary to the other tribunals, which all created legacy working groups or committees that were publicly acknowledged, the ICTY is the only tribunal that has not advertised the establishment of an explicit legacy working group or committee. Keeping in mind the trying environment of institutional downsizing, the eventual abolition of the legacy officer post as well as the absence of tribunal-wide formal committee prima facie may suggest an obvious deinstitutionalization or neglect of legacy. However, consultations on legacy have still taken place internally, mainly led by the Office of the President and the OTP.[50] In 2014, the OTP also advertised an internship position with an explicit focus on 'legacy' and considered hiring a legacy consultant.[51] The OTP also had its own legacy initiatives and projects as briefly sketched below.

The professionalization of legacy has led to the establishment of focal points for legacy within the Tribunal. It seems an appropriation of legacy, real or perceived, occurred across the tribunals by a particular section, which became seen as a hub of expertise and responsibility rather than that all staff members are involved and able to speak to the legacy of the Tribunal. Legacy building seems not to have been viewed by all as the spin-off of the quotidian judicial work of the tribunals but as a specific area of work carried out by specific staff members working on legacy within the Tribunal. The fundamental basis of the Tribunal's legacies is its core work, that is, investigations, trials, and judgments. This view was also held by staff within the Tribunal: 'Almost everything we do is legacy. The judicial work is our biggest legacy; it is not a special project, but our everyday work.'[52] As the tribunals were closing many judges and tribunal officials actually were approaching the end of their own professional careers. Thus, presenting the legacies of the tribunals was akin to reviewing their own *oeuvre* and lifetime achievements. In this sense, institutional legacy building intertwined with individual legacy building. In view of professionalizing legacy at the Tribunal, a major task was designing and implementing projects, including the organization of legacy conferences.

6.3.3 Designing and Implementing Legacy Projects

The proliferation of so-called legacy projects has further institutionalized legacy efforts across the tribunals. As legacy considerations became more concrete, the design of specific projects, so-called 'legacy projects', became fashionable amongst principals and section chiefs. Such projects reveal a certain legacy production. The ICTY has launched an array of different legacy projects, including projects aimed at recording its work, fostering dialogue

[49] Interviews with ICTY officials (The Hague, 29 June 2011, 30 June 2011).
[50] Interviews with ICTY officials (The Hague, 27 September 2012, 20 August 2013).
[51] Interview with ICTY official (The Hague, 14 May 2014).
[52] Interview with ICTY official (The Hague, 1 July 2011).

and rendering accessible and meaningful what the Tribunal hopes to preserve as its legacy. The early legacy projects have been characterized by partnerships with permanent institutions, allowing the ICTY to draw on expertise of other institutions and ensure a prompt implementation.[53] The ICTY successfully completed several legacy projects, which deserve brief mention here.

A first legacy project resulted in a comprehensive publication entitled *ICTY Manual on Developed Practices*. It was initiated by then President Pocar in 2008 and produced in partnership with the UN Interregional Crime and Justice Research Institute (UNICRI). The manual, collated and written by tribunal staff across organs, contains elaborate information on the procedures, proceedings, challenges, and innovations of the Tribunal.[54] The title was presented as a deliberate choice by Judge Robinson, under whose presidency the project came to fruition: 'It was a very conscious decision on the part of the Tribunal to use the expression "developed practices" and not "best practices" as there are no grounds to claim that the practices developed by the Tribunal are better than those of any court or legal system.'[55] However, there has not been consistency of this approach as the language of 'best practices' was used in tribunal documents in 2008.[56]

A second legacy project, developed together with the Office for Democratic Institutions and Human Rights (ODIHR) in 2008, envisaged an evaluation study of capacity building and a needs assessment of the local jurisdictions. The final project report was published in September 2009. Following the report recommendations, a major legacy project entitled the 'War Crimes Justice Project' was launched in partnership with ODIHR and UNICRI and funded by the EU, with an advertised budget of about $4.4 million. The project aimed to provide practical support to legal professionals in the region and transfer knowledge. A whole array of activities was envisaged under the framework, including, inter alia, an international humanitarian law-based e-learning portal, curricula, transcription of selected transcripts into Bosnian/Croatian/Serbian (BCS), and training sessions.[57] The project ended in October 2011.

Another legacy project with a clear regional focus was discussed early on during Pocar's presidency: the establishment of information centres in the region of the former Yugoslavia. The ambition was to establish such centres in different cities across the region of the former Yugoslavia, in Bosnia and Herzegovina, Croatia, and Serbia. While their feasibility for the region of the former Yugoslavia remained under discussion, the idea of information centres was pioneered by the ICTR in Rwanda years before. An ICTY mission was conducted to Rwanda in 2011.[58] After years of preparation and stalled negotiation, the first information centre on the ICTY opened in Sarajevo on 23 May 2018. According to the press release,

[53] See P L Robinson, 'Creating a Legacy That Supports Sustainable Rule of Law in the Region' in R H Steinberg (ed) *Assessing the Legacy of the ICTY* (Brill Nijhoff 2011).

[54] The manual does not contain an emphasis on defence activities. In response, within the framework of the War Crimes Justice Project funded by the EU the Association of Defence Counsel practising before the ICTY (ADC-ICTY) and UNICRI produced a Manual on International Criminal Defence (ADC-ICTY, 'Manual on International—ADC-ICTY Developed Practices' <http://www.icty.org/x/file/About/Reports%20and%20Publications/manual_developed_practices/ADC_ICTY_developed_practices_en.pdf> accessed 15 April 2019).

[55] Robinson, 'Creating a Legacy That Supports Sustainable Rule of Law in the Region' (n 53).

[56] See 'Tribunal And UNICRI Begin Project To Safeguard The Tribunal's Legacy' (*ICTY*, 23 April 2018) <http://www.icty.org/sid/9900/en> accessed 15 April 2019.

[57] See 'The War Crimes Justice Project' (*UNICRI*) <http://www.unicri.it/topics/international_criminal_law/war_crimes/>.

[58] Interview with ICTR official (The Hague, 28 June 2011).

legacy is portrayed as a centrepiece of activity: 'The Centre will ... promote the ICTY's legacy. The Centre's activities are envisioned to include the organization of a variety of public events, as well as assistance to external projects utilizing and reflecting on the legacy of the ICTY.'[59] It is not explicitly spelled out what the legacy is and what shape or form any promotion by the Centre might take. Mila Eminovic, Head of the ICTY Information Centre in Bosnia and Herzegovina, noted the historical significance: 'Sarajevo is the first city after Nuremberg which has the original courtroom of an international criminal tribunal and ... a possibility to witness its mandate.'[60] A decade on from the early discussions, the first and to date only information centre has been established in Sarajevo.

The ICTY outreach work can be viewed in light of the Tribunal's overall legacy engagement as outreach is a certain form of legacy promotion, a certain marketing and proactive legacy production. Like outreach, legacy work also is not funded by the Tribunal's core budget but has required extra budgetary funds. For example, antecedent outreach activities with a legacy focus worth highlighting here include the 'Bridging the Gap' conferences in Brčko, Foča, Konjic, Srebrenica, and Prijedor in 2004 and 2005. The conferences showed the interest of tribunal officials in dialogue and some clashes of perceptions regarding the Tribunal's role and work already crystallized in conference discussions at that time.[61] The ICTY Outreach Annual Reports published from 2011 represent a legacy recording exercise in addition to lessons learned manuals. The ICTY outreach programme produced a series of documentaries[62] on ICTY jurisprudence and key cases, which can be conceived as legacy recordings that were widely presented and distributed in The Hague and the former Yugoslavia. The outreach programme thus aimed to provide a 'visual legacy'.[63]

Moreover, the ICTY also initiated a legacy website development programme. During the eighteen-month grant period, funded by the Mott foundation, the aim was to provide a BCS translation. The ICTY website ultimately became available in English, French, BCS, Albanian, and Macedonian. Between 2008 and 2013 a number of other legacy projects were considered. For instance, the so-called Oral History Project resulted in thirty interviews of key tribunal personnel to record the early years of the ad hoc tribunals.[64] Other projects have been contemplated at the ICTY, for example, a so-called Virtual Tribunal, a version of a peace museum, and a victims' assistance initiative in the form of a Trust Fund. These projects however did not come to fruition, in part also due to lack of funding and capacity and shifting priorities.[65]

[59] International Residual Mechanism for Criminal Tribunals 'First Information Centre on ICTY in the Former Yugoslavia Opens in Sarajevo' (*IRMCT*, 23 May 2018) <http://www.irmct.org/en/news/first-information-centre-icty-former-yugoslavia-opens-sarajevo> accessed 15 April 2019.

[60] D Sito-Sucic, 'U.N. War Crimes Courtroom Displayed in Sarajevo to Preserve Tribunal's Legacy' (*Reuters*, 10 December 2018) <https://www.reuters.com/article/us-bosnia-tribunal-legacy/u-n-war-crimes-courtroom-displayed-in-sarajevo-to-preserve-tribunals-legacy-idUSKBN1O91OD> accessed 15 April 2019.

[61] See 'Bridging the Gap with Local Communities' (*ICTY*) <http://www.icty.org/sections/Outreach/BridgingtheGapwithlocalcommunities> accessed 21 July 2015.

[62] Documentaries include 'Sexual Violence and the Triumph of Justice' (2011), 'Crimes before the ICTY: Prijedor' (2013), 'Through their Eyes: Witnesses to Justice' and 'Crimes before the ICTY: Central Bosnia' (2015). See 'Documentaries' (*ICTY*) <https://www.icty.org/en/outreach/documentaries>.

[63] N Golčevski, 'Communicating Justice in Film: The Limitations of an Unlimited Field' in Sandra Ristovska and Monroe Price (eds) *Visual Imagery and Human Rights Practice* (Springer 2018).

[64] 'Ad Hoc Tribunals Oral History Project' (*International Center for Ethics, Justice and Public Life, Robert D. Farber University Archives & Special Collections Department, Brandeis University*) <http://bir.brandeis.edu/handle/10192/30830> accessed 15 April 2019.

[65] Interviews with ICTR and ICTY officials (The Hague, 28 June 2011, 30 June 2011, 1 July 2011).

The OTP continuously developed its own legacy activities, in close interaction with national prosecutors, and realized certain legacy projects. Based on its quotidian work and derived from necessity, over years also a system of assistance to national authorities was developed, so-called Liaison Prosecutors from the region joined the office in The Hague, and OTP staff were sent on loan to the region. Indeed, capacity building has been at the forefront of OTP legacy efforts. One example of a one-off legacy project concerns sexual and gender-based violence: what started out as a short lessons learned paper turned into a book-length volume edited by ICTY Prosecutor Serge Brammertz and Michelle Jarvis.[66] Another example is an event titled 'The Story of the ICTY Office of the Prosecutor (OTP): Starting from Scratch—What We've Learned from 20 Years of OTP Investigations and Prosecutions', which was held as part of the Legacy Dialogues with senior OTP staff in November 2017. The ICTY OTP also actively contributed to a joint legacy project that was initiated and implemented collaboratively across the tribunals: a *Compendium of Lessons Learned and Suggested Practices from the Offices of the Prosecutors*. The Compendium is a rich collection, however was intended as a working document to specifically assist prosecutors worldwide, hence its distribution has been limited.[67]

Overall, it may appear that the ICTY was active on legacy from 2008 and then did not follow up continuously. Yet it seems important to appreciate that identifying, preparing, and implementing projects involves considerable behind-the-scenes work, including work with donors and partners. Immediately prior to closure, at a time when legacy efforts could be anticipated to peak, the Tribunal indeed concentrated on organizing legacy conferences and high-level events. It seems that time and resources were dedicated to legacy work, albeit to varying levels, in parallel to the full-time continuation of court operations until the very end.

Legacy conferences can be considered important legacy projects. Compared to other tribunals, the ICTY has been the most active in terms of organizing conferences and engaging in public dialogue. Conferences have crystallized as particular public fora for legacy discourses The impressive number and level of organization that went into holding these conferences evidence the great interest and institutional efforts by the Tribunal as legator. Close to fifteen conferences specifically on the theme of legacy have been organized by or with the ICTY as outlined in Table 6.1.

In line with the two-fold legacy vision of the ICTY with a focus on regional and global legacies, conferences were organized by the Tribunal both in The Hague and in the region. Two main ICTY legacy conferences were held in The Hague in 2010[68] and 2011. The first conference was the focal point of the first Legacy Officer's term of office and the collaborative result of collective input from different sections. Following the two conferences held in The Hague, a series of three conferences was organized by the ICTY in the region, in Sarajevo, Zagreb, and Belgrade respectively, in 2011 and 2012. In the wake of the Gotovina and Markač Appeals Chamber judgment and reactions on the ground, however, an already planned and

[66] See S Brammertz and M Jarvis (eds), *Prosecuting Conflict-Related Sexual Violence at the ICTY* (OUP 2016).

[67] The compendium is available with member access at: 'International Association of Prosecutors' <https://www.iap-association.org> accessed 15 April 2019.

[68] Conference proceedings are available on Youtube, these represent important legacy recordings and have been published in a book format: Steinberg (n 6); ICTY, *ICTY Global Legacy* (Conference Proceedings of 15–16 November 2011, ICTY Outreach Programme 2012); ICTY, *Legacy of the ICTY in the Former Yugoslavia* (Conference Proceedings of 6 and 8 November 2012, ICTY Outreach Programme 2013).

Table 6.1 Conferences on 'legacy' organized by or with the ICTY (2009–2017)

Date	Title	Location	Organizer(s)
2009, June 15–16	Promoting the Legacy of International Tribunals: Regional Conference	Sarajevo, Bosnia, and Herzegovina	UNICRI in cooperation with ICTY
2010, Feb 23–24	Assessing the Legacy of the ICTY	The Hague, Netherlands	ICTY, Government of the Netherlands and the Sanela Diana Jenkins Human Rights Project at UCLA School of Law
2010, Dec 16	The Legacy of the International Criminal Tribunal for the former Yugoslavia and societies in the territory of the former Yugoslavia	Belgrade, Serbia	Belgrade Centre for Human Rights and Field Office Belgrade in cooperation with ICTY Outreach Programme
2011, Feb 24	The Legacy of the International Criminal Tribunal for the former Yugoslavia and societies in the territory of the former Yugoslavia	Zagreb, Croatia	Belgrade Centre for Human Rights in cooperation with Zagreb Law Faculty and the Croatian Society for European Criminal Law, with the support of ICTY Outreach Programme
2011, April 11	The Legacy of the International Criminal Tribunal for the former Yugoslavia and societies in the territory of the former Yugoslavia	Sarajevo, Bosnia and Herzegovina	Belgrade Centre for Human Rights in cooperation with ICTY Outreach Programme
2011, Nov 15–16	ICTY Global Legacy	The Hague, Netherlands	ICTY
2012, Nov 6	Legacy of the ICTY in the former Yugoslavia	Sarajevo, Bosnia and Herzegovina	ICTY
2012, Nov 8		Zagreb, Croatia	ICTY
2013, Nov 7–8	Building a Legacy: Lessons Learnt from the OTPs	Nuremberg, Germany	International Nuremberg Principles Academy
2013, Nov 26–27	ICTY Conference—Marking the Twentieth Anniversary of the Tribunal	Sarajevo, Bosnia and Herzegovina	ICTY Outreach Programme

(*Continued*)

Table 6.1 *Continued*

Date	Title	Location	Organizer(s)
2013, Nov 29	ADC-ICTY Legacy Conference	The Hague, Netherlands	ADC-ICTY
2016–2017	ICTY Legacy Dialogues	The Hague, Netherlands; Sarajevo, Bosnia and Herzegovina; Zagreb and Dubrovnik, Croatia; Belgrade, Serbia	ICTY
2017, May 5–6	The Legacy of the International Criminal Tribunal for the former Yugoslavia and the Nuremberg Principles	Nuremberg, Germany	International Nuremberg Principles Academy in collaboration with ICTY
2017, June 22–24	ICTY Legacy Dialogues Conference	Sarajevo, Bosnia and Herzegovina	ICTY

advertised legacy conference in Belgrade in November 2012 was cancelled at very short notice. This demonstrates that the preparation of the legacy conference had no bearing on the judicial calendar. Prior to closure, the Tribunal also organized a series of events in the region entitled ICTY Legacy Dialogues, culminating in a final legacy conference organized in Sarajevo in June 2017. While a detailed analysis of all conferences is beyond the scope of this chapter, certain purposes and dynamics of legacy conferences are briefly elucidated and snapshots of the early conferences and the final conferences are provided.

The purposes of legacy conferences have been manifold. Three aspects are particularly noted here: conferences offer a platform for self-presentation, provide a forum for dialogue and represent an opportunity for reflection and evaluation. First, legacy conferences have been seized as a key public platform for self-presentation and mediagenic presentation of legacies to a wider public. Such public moments were used as platform for presenting official accounts and for cementing certain legacy discourses and legacies. Talk about legacy has been used to market successes and as a public relations tool, which warrants more critical examination in light of what has been called a 'marketing culture of international criminal law'.[69] Unsurprisingly, tribunal officials have used conferences to present achievements and contributions in a certain light. In early conferences challenges often became camouflaged. In this sense, conferences resembled orchestrated events with a clear performative dimension. The performativity of legacy would deserve greater attention in this regard. Besides an apparent need to remember and to be remembered with a view to legitimization and meaning making, a sense of prerogative of interpretation emerged at the tribunals. Some tribunal officials even underscored an exclusive understanding of legacy. This is

[69] C Schwöbel, 'The Market and Marketing Culture of International Criminal Law' in C Schwöbel (ed) *Critical Approaches to International Criminal Law: An Introduction* (Routledge 2014) 264.

illustrative of an attempt of meaning making, which is poignant in light of the observation by James Boyd White that 'whatever it may purport to say what a judgment shall come to mean is a matter for the parties and their audience to address and decide'.[70] This pinpoints to the active reception of legacies and their continuous construction by legacy actors. As elaborated in the conceptual framework there is no prerogative for any single actor, including the legacy leaver, as a multiplicity of actors are involved in legacy constructions. This is an important dynamic in light of a recognition of a 'multiplicity of justice'[71] and intra-court as well as inter-court 'historical narrative pluralism'[72] that may arise. Any tendency to over-claim certain achievements or portray monocausal mechanisms appears rather myopic. A strong sense of prerogative of interpretation may result in a canonical representation of legacies.

Second, while affording tribunal actors with the opportunity for self-presentation and framing, legacy conferences have been framed as a forum for dialogue. The ultimate reception and construction of legacies take place in the public arena, hence conferences as public events are key moments of articulating and (re-)constructing legacies. For example, the first ICTY Legacy Conference, which took place in The Hague on 23–24 February 2010, issued an explicit open invitation for debate: 'The Tribunal wishes to hear the participants' ideas of the Tribunal's legacy' and 'The Tribunal welcomes all ideas and proposals in relation to the development of a comprehensive legacy vision and strategy'.[73] The 2010 and 2011 ICTY Legacy Conferences were the largest legacy conferences ever held by any tribunal, with approximately 350 participants each. During the final two years of the Tribunal, a concerted effort was undertaken by the Tribunal to engage with the wider public via an event series aptly labelled the 'ICTY Legacy Dialogues' from mid-2016 to the end of 2017. According to the Tribunal itself, 'the ICTY is seeking to ensure that its work and achievements remain accessible and meaningful, both for people in the region of the former Yugoslavia and worldwide'.[74] The title 'ICTY Legacy Dialogues' clearly indicates that a dialogical format was sought. Public debate was formally welcomed with actors in the region. It is noteworthy that the final conference in Sarajevo in June 2017 was accompanied by a public call for papers. The events in the Legacy Dialogues series included different formats, inter alia, the release of a report on witnesses and a documentary premiere, publication launch and other workshops. Towards the end of its legacy efforts, the different organs of the Tribunal and the Defence were invited to present in a four-part lecture series co-organized by the ICTY and the Grotius Centre for International Legal Studies of Leiden Law School.

Third, legacy conferences have also offered opportunities for reflection and evaluation. A central theme of conferences has been on 'lessons learned', with an increasing focus on legacy building.[75] Indeed, conferences also served as an arena for evaluative exercises and

[70] J B White, *Heracles' Bow: Essays on the Rhetoric and Poetics of the Law* (University of Wisconsin Press 1985) 185.

[71] K M Clarke and M Goodale, *Mirrors of Justice: Law and Power in the Post-Cold War Era* (CUP 2010) 1–27.

[72] B Sander, 'History on Trial: Historical Narrative Pluralism Within and Beyond International Criminal Courts' (2018) 67 International and Comparative Law Quarterly 547.

[73] ICTY, 'Seventeenth Annual Report of the International Tribunal for the Prosecution of Persons Responsible for Serious Violations of International Humanitarian Law Committed in the Territory of the Former Yugoslavia since 1991' (n 46) 11.

[74] 'ICTY Legacy Dialogues' (*ICTY*) <http://www.icty.org/en/features/icty-legacy-dialogues> accessed 15 April 2019.

[75] See V E Dittrich, 'Building a Legacy: Official Conference Report for International Nuremberg Principles Academy, Nuremberg' (2013) <http://www.conference-nuremberg.de/> accessed 15 April 2019; G Boas and G

a critical assessment to a certain extent. For example, a closer look at the title of the 2010 ICTY Legacy Conference 'Assessing the Legacy of the ICTY' is instructive. While the title 'suggests a dispassionate, scientific, positive, or empirical evaluation', it was observed by the editor of the resultant publication that 'this book is neither strictly dispassionate nor exclusively evaluative'.[76] To be sure, a practitioner conference may not share the same ambition as scholarship and rigorous empirical research, as evidence often remained anecdotal when certain legacies were asserted or proclaimed. While transparency and critical assessment are highlighted in theory, conferences organized or hosted by the tribunals as legacy leavers seem hardly the right setting for a rigorous methodologically sophisticated assessment of their work. Another example of public reflection and evaluation is a seminar organized by the International Nuremberg Principles Academy on the 'Legacy of the International Criminal Tribunal for the former Yugoslavia and the Nuremberg Principles' on 5–6 May 2017. The seminar, which included participation of all Principals, discussed the ICTY's legacy in terms of case law development, the prosecution of heads of States, defence strategies, and domestic jurisdiction. This conference was geared towards the global legacies of the Tribunal. This international focus was complemented by the final legacy conference that was held in Sarajevo, Bosnia and Herzegovina, on 22–24 June 2017. The conference was announced as a 'conference reflecting on the legacy of the ICTY and how others can build upon its achievements'. Between high-level opening and closing speeches the conference panels unfolded along the various types of ICTY legacy: normative, gender justice, non-judicial legacy, operational legacy, defence, witness protection, historical legacy, outreach. The conference programme reflected a recognition of the multiplicity of legacies and of the importance of judicial and non-judicial legacies, of global and regional legacies. Conferences have revealed the complex interplay between legacy creation, consolidation, and contestation, that is all phases of the cycle of legacies already presented.

The cacophony of voices and the multiplicity of actors and legacy discourses is a defining feature of legacy formation, and by extension of legacy conferences. A key question often neglected is whose voice is actually being heard at legacy conferences and, ultimately, recorded for posterity. Perceptions of the Tribunal have not been uniform across time and space.[77] Moreover, the literature on impact of the Tribunal paints a mixed picture.[78] The conferences organized by the Tribunal provided rare opportunities to actually hear the existent cacophony of voices, on the same day in the same place. Although potentially

Oosthuizen, 'Suggestions for Future Lessons-Learned Studies: The Experience of Other International and Hybrid Criminal Courts of Relevance to the International Criminal Court' [2010] International Criminal Law Societies. Prepared on behalf of International Criminal Law Services (ICLS).

[76] Steinberg (n 6) 3.

[77] On perceptions see S K Ivković and J Hagan, *Reclaiming Justice: The International Tribunal for the Former Yugoslavia and Local Courts* (OUP 2011); R Kerr, 'Lost in Translation? Perceptions of the ICTY in the Former Yugoslavia' in J Gow, R **Kerr**, and Z Pajić (eds), *Prosecuting War Crimes* (Routledge 2013), see https://www.taylorfrancis.com/books/e/9781315886244/chapters/10.4324/9781315886244-11>; D Saxon, 'Exporting Justice: Perceptions of the ICTY Among the Serbian, Croatian, and Muslim Communities in the Former Yugoslavia' (2005) *4 Journal of Human Rights* 559.

[78] See J D Meernik, A Nichols, and K L King, 'The Impact of International Tribunals and Domestic Trials on Peace and Human Rights after Civil War' (2010) *11 International Studies Perspectives* 309; D F Orentlicher, 'That Someone Guilty Be Punished: The Impact of the ICTY in Bosnia'; J N Clark, 'Judging the ICTY: Has It Achieved Its Objectives?' (2009) *9 Southeast European and Black Sea Studies* 123; M Klarin, 'The Impact of the ICTY Trials on Public Opinion in the Former Yugoslavia' (2009) *7 Journal of International Criminal Justice* 89.

dissonant or even disruptive for official self-presentation purposes by the tribunals, moments of tension, negotiation, or conflict represent important and necessary moments of legacy formation. Criticism and contestation of legacies is an inevitable part of legacy formation. It is noteworthy that tribunal officials engaged with scholars, practitioners, and civil society representatives in the different conference settings. Outside the tribunals there has been some discontent expressed by some about the content and format and participants of the conferences. Overall, inviting mainstream voices or the 'usual suspects' has been more common than including marginal or dissonant voices. By way of illustration, a moment of legacy contestation occurred during the 2010 ICTY Legacy Conference in the form of opposition from victim groups. This has been interpreted as a clear disconnect of two groups. In unusually direct language, then ICTY President Robinson addressed criticisms of failures head on openly noting: 'From the contributions made by victim groups, it is clear to me that there is a perception amongst victim communities that the Tribunal has failed to deliver all that was expected.'[79] Moreover, participants lamented that discussions on ICTY achievements and impact had overwhelmingly centred on Bosnia and Herzegovina. This was acknowledged: 'One issue that was noted in the conference as a failing was the absence of Kosovo, resulting from a variety of factors. […] many asked how the Tribunal could consider its legacy vision in the region without hearing the voice of Kosovo. The Tribunal shares the concern.'[80] The mere holding of the conference or absence of voices from the region at the 2011 ICTY Global Legacy Conference was also criticized. A small protest demonstration was staged in front of the World Forum, the conference venue just opposite the ICTY main building, on the first day of the conference on 15 November 2011. Such moments of contestation and clashing perceptions during conferences illustrate the multiplicity of voices on legacies of the tribunals, which reflect the multiplicity of actors involved in legacy constructions.[81] Conferences reveal particular accents on certain legacy dimensions and narratives. Some actors have not felt fully included in the conferences, although they are also legacy actors. Within the tribunals, certain actors or organs of the tribunals seem favoured to get the spotlight during legacy conferences, not least depending under whose aegis such conferences are organized. For example, the ICTY Global Legacy conference in 2011 was widely seen as a project of the Office of the President rather than of the Tribunal has a whole, with a particular focus on Chambers and the ICTY's jurisprudence. Another example is the perspective of the Defence. A defence legacy conference was organized by the ADC-ICTY in 2013 as response to the official ICTY legacy conferences in 2010/11 to highlight legacy contributions of the defence. As the Tribunal continued spinning legacy discourses the defence perspective was increasingly involved and visible in legacy activities, culminating in 'The Story of the Defence practising before the ICTY' being told as part of the ICTY Legacy Dialogues in 2017.

In sum, so-called legacy conferences afforded the Tribunal with a platform for self-presentation, a forum for dialogue, and an opportunity for reflection and evaluation.

[79] P Robinson, 'The Way Forward' in R H Steinberg (ed), *Assessing the Legacy of the ICTY* (Martinus Nijhoff Publishers 2011) 268.

[80] ibid 269.

[81] See S Vucetic, 'Oversell but Underperform? The Increasingly Troubled Legacy of the ICTY' (*CIPS*, 17 July 2013) <https://www.cips-cepi.ca/2013/07/17/oversell-but-underperform-the-increasingly-troubled-legacy-of-the-icty/> accessed 15 April 2019.

Conferences have been important public fora for legacy consolidation and legacy contestation. The result was a display of the inevitable cacophony of voices in legacy formation. In this sense, the multiplicity of actors and different voices, as evident at various conferences, has shaped the ongoing legacy building of the ICTY.

6.4 From Completion to Continuation

The lifespan of the ad hoc tribunals was explicitly linked to the completion of their mandates. As the debate on completion became more serious and nuanced while criticisms became prominent,[82] the international community showed increasing resolve to scrutinize more closely the efficiency and effectiveness of the tribunals. More attention was simultaneously paid to how and when the tribunals conclude their work, what will remain upon closure, what should remain, and how will and should the institutions be remembered. As the political pressure to close grew, three separate yet related issues appeared most prominent and pressing in light of the current political and legal considerations: completion of mandate, residual functions, and legacy. In view of the profound change of the institutional landscape and social dynamics,[83] only a brief sketch can be offered here with a focus on completion, and from completion to continuation as it pertains to legacy building.

6.4.1 Towards a Completion Strategy

What started as ad hoc references to the completion of judicial mandates soon was translated into full-fledged formalized completion *strategies*.[84] The ICTY developed what has been called a situational completion strategy. In contrast to global completion strategies which give consideration to completion issues *ex ante*, situational completion strategies solely consider such issues *in medias res*, that is after a tribunal has been created and had become fully operational.[85] Increasingly the focus turned to time lines for completion. The purpose was 'to make sure that the Tribunal concludes its mission successfully, in a timely way and in coordination with domestic legal systems in the former Yugoslavia'.[86] Alongside the language of closure and completion, the language of accomplishment or fulfilment of a 'mission' became pervasive in official documents. The first mention of conclusion of the judicial work appeared in the seventh ICTY Annual Report: 'In November 1999, the new President, the Judges, the Registrar and the Chamber Legal Support Service began to consider ways to permit the Tribunal to accomplish its mission more effectively and to deal with its greatly increased workload.'[87] Back in 2000, it was urged that the international

82 See R Zacklin, 'The Failings of Ad Hoc International Tribunals' (2004) 2 Journal of International Criminal Justice 541;.

83 M J Christensen, 'From Symbolic Surge to Closing Courts: The Transformation of International Criminal Justice and Its Professional Practices' (2015) 43 International Journal of Law, Crime and Justice 609.

84 The development of the completion strategies of the ICTY and the ICTR are intrinsically linked, however the focus here is on the ICTY.

85 K J Heller, 'Completion' in L Reydams, J Wouters, and C Ryngaert (eds), *International Prosecutors* (OUP 2012).

86 See 'Completion Strategy' (*ICTY*) <http://www.icty.org/sid/10016> accessed 15 April 2019.

87 ICTY, 'Seventh Annual Report of the International Tribunal for the Prosecution of Persons Responsible for Serious Violations of International Humanitarian Law Committed in the Territory of the Former Yugoslavia since

community 'should allow [...] the Tribunal to accomplish its mission'.[88] In an intriguing address to the UN General Assembly on 27 November 2001 the then ICTY President Claude Jorda referred to the completion of mission a remarkable eleven times.[89] Then ICTY President Jorda initiated planning and first timelines were drawn up.[90] In retrospect, former ICTY President Pocar emphasized, 'it would be wrong to suggest that the Security Council imposed the Completion Strategy upon the Tribunal. It was actually the ICTY that proposed this course of action, and it did so in a creative and courageous way'[91].

The actual decision to close was the result of lengthy discussions. As Schabas astutely observed, 'at the rate at which each tribunal has operated, there are enough suspects to keep them going for many decades. It would seem that ad hoc tribunals are almost by definition confronted with the difficulty of knowing when to stop'.[92] This 'difficulty of knowing when to stop' linked to the sheer number of criminal suspects was at the heart of the alleged tension between a political and legal imperative of when and how to close the tribunals and the deliberation involved. There was no blueprint or much guidance on closing an international organization, let alone a court. There seems to have been a mismatch between expectations of political actors, including States and the UNSC, and the Tribunal itself. Former ICTY President Patrick Robinson once remarked, 'It is a court of law, and as such it will always be prone to a certain degree of unforeseeability, which is a natural element in most kinds of judicial work, and particularly in trials as complicated as those at the Tribunal. The Tribunal cannot be wound up as though it were a bakery producing bread. It can only be wound up properly with appropriate sensitivity to the judicial character of its work'.[93]

The origins and unfolding of the completion strategies of the ad hoc tribunals can be traced in a series of formal letters, statements, and reports by the Tribunal Presidents, the Secretary General and the UNSC from 2000 to 2003.[94] The future closure of the Tribunal is mentioned for the first time in an official document on 12 May 2000 in a letter from then ICTY President Claude Jorda to the UN Secretary General.[95] Then a first report was presented to the UNSC in 2000.[96] In response to these letters and a letter from the Secretary General to the President of the UNSC dated 7 September 2000, the UNSC adopted Resolution 1329 on 5 December 2000, the first resolution calling 'to expedite the conclusion of their work at the earliest possible date'. The key decisions of Resolution 1329 concerned the establishment of a pool of *ad litem* judges in the ICTY, enlarged membership of the

1991' (2000) <http://www.icty.org/x/file/About/Reports%20and%20Publications/AnnualReports/annual_report_2000_en.pdf> accessed 15 April 2019.

[88] ibid.
[89] T W Pittman, 'The Road to the Establishment of the International Residual Mechanism for Criminal Tribunals: From Completion to Continuation' (2011) 9 Journal of International Criminal Justice 797.
[90] Interviews with ICTY officials and expert (The Hague, 24 August 2012, 1 October 2012, 12 April 2013).
[91] Pocar (n 36) 657.
[92] Schabas (n 2) 40.
[93] P Robinson, 'Address of Judge Patrick Robinson, President of the International Criminal Tribunal for the Former Yugoslavia, to the United Nations General Assembly' (8 October 2010) <http://www.icty.org/x/file/Press/Statements%20and%20Speeches/President/101008_pdt_robinson_un_ga_en.pdf> accessed 15 April 2019.
[94] For a detailed overview see ibid. See also D A Mundis, 'Completing the Mandates of the Ad Hoc International Criminal Tribunals: Lessons from the Nuremberg Process' (2004) 28 Fordham International Law Journal 591.
[95] See Pittman (n 89).
[96] UN A/55/382-S/2000/865 (14 September 2000). Current State of the International Tribunal for the Former Yugoslavia: Future Prospects and Reform Proposals, Report on the Operation of the International Tribunal for the Former Yugoslavia, Submitted by Judge Claude Jorda, President on behalf of the Judges of the Tribunal.

combined Appeals Chamber, election of two additional judges for the ICTR and a request to the Secretary General 'to submit to the Security Council, as soon as possible, a report containing an assessment and proposals regarding the date ending the temporal jurisdiction of the International Criminal Tribunal for the Former Yugoslavia'.[97] Three areas were highlighted in particular in the preamble: (1) reform measures, especially improvement of the Rules of Procedures and Evidence to speed up proceedings, (2) focus on civilian, military and paramilitary leaders in preference to minor actors and (3) suspension of indictments.

The first formalization of the ICTY Completion Strategy took shape in a 27-page report annexed to a letter from Judge Jorda to the UN Secretary General dated 10 June 2002.[98] The Completion Strategy conceived a three-stage process: (1) cessation of prosecutorial investigations by end of 2004; (2) closing of all first instance trial activities by end of 2008; and (3) all appellate proceedings by end of 2010. This provided the blueprint for a three-pronged approach. On 28 August 2003 the UNSC issued Resolution 1503 in which it urged the ICTR 'to formalize a detailed strategy, modelled on the ICTY Completion Strategy'[99] and importantly announced to no longer have a joint Prosecutor. The transfer of cases to national jurisdictions was an integral part of the strategy for both tribunals. UN Resolution 1534 issued a year later recalled that it 'urges each Tribunal to plan and act accordingly' and declares 'the Council's determination to review the situation [. . .] to ensure that the timeframes set out in the Completion Strategies and endorsed by resolution 1503 (2003) can be met'.[100]

Completion remained a moving target. Completion strategies have been repeatedly revised. The completion strategies set out timeframes for the judicial milestones necessary for the completion of the respective tribunal's mandate predicated on full cooperation and arrest of indictees. It soon became clear that the initial timelines of 2004, 2008, and 2010 for the ad hoc tribunals, as outlined in Resolutions 1503 and 1534, were too optimistic and stringent if considered deadlines rather than projected target dates. Given the complexity of trials, unforeseen circumstances and delays, and the late arrests of the two remaining fugitives, Mladić and Hadžić in May and July 2011 respectively, revisions have taken place on a regular basis. When the Appeals Chamber Schedule Working Group, working under the auspices of the Vice-President of the ICTY, had to make major adjustments and postponed dates for completion, the issue of legacy came into sharper relief.[101]

The genesis and articulation of the strategy can be viewed as reflecting the conflicting demands of expediency and the demands of justice. The Completion Strategy and derived procedural reforms to 'speed up' trials have been both welcomed in the light of fair trial rights, rights to a speedy trial, and due process. Critics have pointed to the incompatibility with an independent administration of justice. Expediency seems to have been a driver of the conceptualization and endorsement, in particular by the UNSC and the international

[97] UN S/RES/1329 (5 December 2000). Resolution 1329 (2000) adopted by the Security Council at its 4240th meeting.

[98] 'Report on the Judicial Status of the International Criminal Tribunal for the Former Yugoslavia and the Prospects for Referring Certain Cases to National Courts' (2002) <https://documents-dds-ny.un.org/doc/UNDOC/GEN/N02/434/47/IMG/N0243447.pdf> accessed 15 April 2019.

[99] UN S/RES/1503 (28 August 2003). Resolution 1503 (2003) adopted by the Security Council at its 4817th meeting, preamble.

[100] UN S/RES/1534 (26 March 2004). Resolution 1534 (2004) adopted by the Security Council at its 4935th meeting, preamble, arts 3 and 7.

[101] Interview with ICTY official (The Hague, 1 July 2011).

community. There has been continuous reference to completion 'at the earliest possible date'.[102] For example, judges have said they 'will not dance at the pace of the completion strategy' and have adamantly emphasized their independence.[103] Ultimately, it seems that political demands of expediency and efficiency may not over-ride core demands of justice. A UN press release from December 2009, dramatically titled 'Justice supersedes Completion Strategy Deadlines for International Criminal Tribunals in Security Council Debate' was released the same day.[104] It is not the intention here to engage in any discussion on the existence or absence of 'judicial effects', real or perceived, of the completion strategies.[105] The interplay of politics and law surrounding the completion strategies have been debated elsewhere, both by actors outside of the process and by actors on the inside.[106]

Winding down organizations and large-scale bureaucracies let alone judicial institutions such as the tribunals is a complex undertaking involving many political, legal, and administrative decisions. Against the backdrop of the shifting international political climate and increased scrutiny, the Tribunal developed a formal Completion Strategy which served as the road map with milestones and target dates for completion and, ultimately, closure. As completion and closure became more palpable, or in other words the spectre of organizational death loomed large, a turn to the future appeared—beyond completion.

6.4.2 Beyond a Completion Strategy

The completion of mandate and ensuing closure of the Tribunal was reinterpreted from within as a projection into the future. A forward-looking reinterpretation of completion in the light of continuation has been observed within the tribunals themselves. This is strongly linked to meaning making. For many, the spectre of organizational death did not necessarily represent 'the end'. For example, former ICTY Prosecutor Serge Brammertz highlighted how completion directly is linked to continuation of accountability efforts and cases taken

[102] UN S/RES/1329 (5 December 2000). Resolution 1329 (2000) adopted by the Security Council at its 4240th meeting, preamble.

[103] Interviews with ICTY and ICTR officials (The Hague, 27 September 2012, 20 September 2013).

[104] See United Nations Security Council, 'Justice Supersedes Completion Strategy Deadlines for International Criminal Tribunals in Security Council Debate, Following Briefings by Key Officials' (UN, 3 December 2009) <https://www.un.org/press/en/2009/sc9801.doc.htm> accessed 15 April 2019.

[105] See L D Johnson, 'Closing an International Criminal Tribunal While Maintaining International Human Rights Standards and Excluding Impunity' (2005) 99 American Journal of International Law 158; D A Mundis, 'The Judicial Effects of the "Completion Strategies" on the Ad Hoc International Criminal Tribunals' (2005) 99 American Journal of International Law 142; J Dieckmann and C Kerll, 'UN Ad Hoc Tribunals Under Time Pressure–Completion Strategy and Referral Practice of the ICTY and ICTR from the Perspective of the Defence' (2008) 8 International Criminal Law Review 87.

[106] See D Raab, 'Evaluating the ICTY and Its Completion Strategy: Efforts to Achieve Accountability for War Crimes and Their Tribunals' (2005) 3 Journal of International Criminal Justice 82; E Møse, 'The ICTR's Completion Strategy—Challenges and Possible Solutions' (2008) 6 Journal of International Criminal Justice 667; H Llewellyn, *The Security Council's Consideration of the Establishment of Residual Mechanisms for the International Criminal Tribunals* (CUP 2010); B B Landale and H Llewellyn, 'The International Residual Mechanism for Criminal Tribunals: The Beginning of the End for the ICTY and ICTR' (2011) 8 International Organizations Law Review 349; G McIntyre, 'The International Residual Mechanism and the Legacy of the International Criminal Tribunals for the Former Yugoslavia and Rwanda' (2011) 3 Goettingen Journal of International Law 923; G M Frisso, 'The Winding Down of The ICTY: The Impact of the Completion Strategy and The Residual Mechanism on Victims' (2011) 3 Goettingen Journal of International Law 1093.

up in the national judiciaries of the former Yugoslavia: 'So the completion of the Tribunal's mandate is not the end of war crimes justice, but the beginning of the next chapter.'[107]

An official reinterpretation or even rebranding of the Completion Strategy as 'continuation strategy', a 'strategy of continued legacy building', occurred over a decade ago in 2008 by then ICTY President Pocar.[108] Indeed, Pocar argued it is 'not so much a strategy to "complete" the work of the ICTY as it is a strategy designed to allow continuation by local actors of those activities that were initially "kicked off" by the ICTY under the mandate of the Security Council'.[109] The continuation of the ICTY's work by national jurisdictions has been seen as natural since it involves 'returning cases to where they belong'.[110] Rule 11*bis* cases have played a fundamental role in legacy formation. The courts in the region handling thousands of cases, especially the War Crimes Chamber in Bosnia and Herzegovina and in Serbia, have been continuing important work and playing a key role in legacy formation. Judicial law reforms in the region have been connected to the Completion Strategy of the Tribunal, which will continue to have an impact after closure.[111] Completion and continuation are not mutually exclusive. Hence, the question whether it is or should be called either a completion or a continuation strategy perhaps poses the wrong question. While the Tribunal in question completed its work, the work is being carried forward and continued by other courts and its successor organization as the Tribunal as legacy leaver ceased to exist and passed on the baton to other legacy actors.

While the ad hoc tribunals may have disappeared institutionally speaking as formal organizations upon completion of mandate and closure, it is argued here they continue to live on. The tribunals may have ceased to exist in the formal, juridical register, yet they certainly live on in the social and mental register. The final closure of the tribunals coincides with their formal, legal death at the end of their lifespan. However, they persist institutionally speaking. Two forms of institutional persistence of the tribunals are identified here: residual mechanisms and legacies. The actual successor organizations provide the tribunals with a symbolic continued existence given that these organizations were designed to carry out 'residual' functions of the tribunals. With the creation of the residual mechanisms, organizational death has been reinterpreted as a transition rather than as an endpoint. This has been emphasized by staff members of the tribunals as the following utterances show: 'afterlife would be the residual mechanism'[112] or 'afterlife, yes, hopefully not a reincarnation'.[113] One observer also suggested the ICTY 'will continue in a sort of un-death' through the Mechanism.[114] It has been noted the Mechanism represents nothing less than the 'UN's newest international criminal tribunal'[115]—even if it may appear miniature in comparison to its antecedents, the ICTY and ICTR. Former ICTY President and MICT President

[107] <https://www.icty.org/x/file/Press/Statements%20and%20Speeches/Prosecutor/170512-remarks-by-the-prosecutor.pdf>.

[108] See F Pocar, 'Completion or Continuation Strategy? Appraising Problems and Possible Developments in Building the Legacy of the ICTY' (2008) 6 Journal of International Criminal Justice 655.

[109] See ibid 661.

[110] See ibid.

[111] See ibid.

[112] Interviews with ICTR and ICTY officials (The Hague, 21 June 2011, 28 June 2011, 1 July 2011).

[113] Interview with ICTY official (The Hague, 1 July 2011).

[114] M Milanović, 'The Impact of the ICTY on the Former Yugoslavia: An Anticipatory Postmortem' (2016) 110 American Journal of International Law 233.

[115] Pittman (n 89) 797.

Theodor Meron has argued that the Mechanism represents a new model of an international criminal tribunal.[116]

The acknowledgement of post-completion or post-closure issues relating to the functioning and completion of mandate of the tribunals eventually led to a major institutional development: the creation of new organizations, so-called residual mechanisms. The work of a judicial institution continues well after its last case has been tried. Post-closure obligations include judicial and prosecutorial activities and residual functions. A significant number of experts were consulted[117] and prepared expert meetings and provided input. Debates concerned the nature and design as well as location of any residual mechanism but also the role played by the UNSC. In 2009, the UN Secretary-General identified eight residual functions: trial of fugitives, trial of contempt cases, protection of witnesses, review of judgments, referral of cases to national jurisdictions, supervision of enforcements of sentences, assistance to national authorities, and management of the archive.[118] The planning phase for residual mechanisms also generated some speculative and critical scholarship on the topic.[119] In order to ensure that the closure did not result in impunity the trial of remaining fugitives was considered as a primary residual function. In this regard, former ICTY President Robinson underlined, 'It would be a lasting stain on the legacy of the Tribunal if these accused were to remain untried by the Tribunal and would send the wrong message with respect to the international community's commitment to the former Yugoslavia.'[120] Following the arrests of Ratko Mladić and Goran Hadžić, on 26 May 2011 and on 20 July 2011 respectively, the ICTY had no more fugitives. Other residual functions however remained prominent. Three interrelated aspects need to be considered: how best to preserve, secure, and make the archives accessible. Certainly, the archives represent a most important tangible legacy of the ICTY also in light of the politics of memory.[121]

The International Residual Mechanism for Criminal Tribunals (hereinafter Mechanism) was established in the logic of closing the ad hoc tribunals while continuing necessary functions. On 22 December 2010 with a vote of fourteen to none, with one abstention (Russian Federation), the UNSC adopted Resolution 1966 establishing the Mechanism.[122] It was

[116] See T Meron, The Mechanism: A New Model of International Criminal Tribunal, UN Audiovisual Library of International Law, https://legal.un.org/avl/ls/Meron_CLP_video_2.html

[117] See C Aptel, 'Closing the U.N. International Criminal Tribunal for Rwanda: Completion Strategy and Residual Issues' (2008) 14 New England Journal of International and Comparative Law 169; G Oosthuizen and R Schaeffer, 'Complete Justice: Residual Functions and Potential Residual Mechanisms of the ICTY, ICTR and SCSL' (2008) 3 Hague Justice Journal 48; C Reiger, 'Where to from Here for International Tribunals? Considering Legacy and Residual Issues' [2009] International Center for Transitional Justice Briefing; V Oosterveld, *International Law and the Closure of the International and Hybrid Criminal Tribunals* (CUP 2010).

[118] United Nations Security Council, 'Report of the Secretary-General on the Administrative and Budgetary Aspects of the Options for Possible Locations For the Archives of the International Tribunal for the Former Yugoslavia and the International Criminal Tribunal for Rwanda and the Seat of the Residual Mechanism(s) for the Tribunals' (2009) S/2009/258 <https://www.securitycouncilreport.org/atf/cf/%7B65BFCF9B-6D27-4E9C-8CD3-CF6E4FF96FF9%7D/Tribunals%20S%202009%20258.pdf> accessed 15 April 2019.

[119] See C Denis, 'Critical Overview of the "Residual Functions" of the Mechanism and Its Date of Commencement (Including Transitional Arrangements)' (2011) 9 Journal of International Criminal Justice 819; Oosthuizen and Schaeffer (n 117); G Acquaviva, 'Was a Residual Mechanism for International Criminal Tribunals Really Necessary?' (2011) 9 Journal of International Criminal Justice 789.

[120] UN S/2006/898 (16 November 2006). Letter dated 15 November 2006 from the President of the International Tribunal for the Prosecution of Persons Responsible for Serious Violations of International Humanitarian Law.

[121] See various chapters on the ICTY archives in Part III in Steinberg (n 6); K Campbell, 'The Laws of Memory: The ICTY, the Archive, and Transitional Justice' (2013) 22 Social & Legal Studies 247.

[122] UN S/RES/1966 (22 December 2010). Resolution 1966 (2010) adopted by the Security Council at its 6463rd Meeting.

designed to have two branches, one for the ICTY in The Hague which started functioning on 1 July 2013 and one for the ICTR in Arusha which started functioning on 1 July 2012. Given that the Mechanism has so-called 'continuing' and 'ad hoc' functions, it represents an organization of 'variable geometry'.[123] It also bears noting that the Mechanism focuses on core judicial functions of a tribunal,[124] and is not endowed with an explicit competence and mandate in the field of outreach or legacy. This hints at the fact that the Mechanism, just like the completion strategies, appeared caught in design between short-term financial and political considerations of expediency and long-term considerations of justice and effectiveness. Although wide consultations took place between tribunal officials and UN officials in New York about institutional design, the Mechanism has been perceived by some tribunal officials as a 'creation of the Office of Legal Affairs'.[125] UNSC Resolution 1966 makes plain the UNSC vision: 'the international residual mechanism should be a small, temporary and efficient structure, whose functions and size will diminish over time, with a small number of staff commensurate with its reduced functions'.[126] In order to ensure such a structure and to leverage the organizational competence and institutional knowledge of tribunal staff, the practice of 'double-hatting' became a central feature of the transition process. This refers to the process of staff members working in two roles, in this case for two connected but separate organizations, that is, for the ICTY and the Mechanism.

Similar to the term Completion Strategy, the term Residual Mechanism also fails to impart a sense of continuation at first glance. The use of the adjective 'residual' lamentably fails, as has been observed, to 'convey the sense that these are core ongoing obligations, chiefly of the international community, some of which will concern life-or-death matters and fundamental human rights'.[127] Indeed, one commentator noted, it is 'somewhat unfortunate, that the new Mechanism perpetuates, even in its own name, the expression "residual mechanism", based on the assumption that the functions which remain once trials and appeals have concluded are merely of a "residual" nature'.[128] The actual term 'residual mechanism' has proven a contested term by those working inside the tribunals. While the pervasive use of the seemingly more elegant and pronounceable acronym 'MICT' standing for 'Mechanism for International Criminal Tribunals' has slipped past the attention of, or rather been tolerated by the UNSC and Informal Working Group on International Tribunals and UN Office of Legal Affairs, since 2018 the official name appears on all official documentation.[129] The official name of the Mechanism was an important part of the lengthy negotiations in New York prior to UNSC Resolution 1966 and hence is likely to have sticking power in policy circles.[130]

The Tribunal is also seen to live on through its legacies. Legacy building has emerged as a strategy with a view to institutional persistence. A heightened concern about legacy and about how the closure will affect the impact and image of the respective tribunal was

[123] Interview with ICTY official (The Hague, 13 May 2014).

[124] See Pittman (n 89).

[125] Interviews with ICTY and ICTR officials (The Hague, 25 September 2012; Arusha, 20 September 2013).

[126] UN S/RES/1966 (22 December 2010). Resolution 1966 (2010) adopted by the Security Council at its 6463rd Meeting.

[127] Oosthuizen and Schaeffer (n 117) 50; G Acquaviva, '"Best before Date Shown": Residual Mechanisms at the ICTY' in A H J Swart, A Zahar, and G Sluiter (eds), *The Legacy of the International Criminal Tribunal for the Former Yugoslavia* (OUP 2011).

[128] Acquaviva (n 119) 796.

[129] See website https://www.irmct.org/en

[130] Interviews with UN officials (New York, 17 April 2013, 19 April 2013).

detectable. Legacy formation is ongoing during the lifespan of the Tribunal and during the completion process. Within the tribunals attempts at controlling the legacies left behind have be observed, which has beentranslated into restriction, real or perceived, of speaking about legacy work. Legacy building already occurs throughout the lifetime of the legacy leaver. The ongoing work and lifetime achievements are embued with meaning all along, even if the creation of meaning has been intensified prior to closure. Extending Klarin's typology of 'four battles' (for survival, for respect, for hearts and minds, and for time)[131] mapped onto the ICTY's first ten years of existence, a fifth and final stage of tribunal development was proposed: a 'battle for its legacy'.[132] Rather than adhering to the view of legacy building as final stage in a tribunal's development, here it is emphasized that legacy building, which in a sense may resemble a contest over the influence of remembrance in light of the politics of memory, encompasses or accompanies all other battles rather than presenting a battle that follows temporally speaking. Thus, a non-linear conceptualization of legacy is proposed to capture the ongoing dynamics as the legacies of the ICTY remain in the making. The term battle however captures well the confrontation given interpretations of legacies that may be conflicting or contradictory. Understanding the role of international dynamics and domestic political and legal developments in the region, and the role of particular actors including other courts, political elites and policy makers, the media, affected communities and the acquitted and convicted persons,[133] as well as tribunal officials and epistemic communities is critical in order to fully place legacy formation into context. This is, however, beyond the scope of this chapter.

No tribunal alone can build its own definitive legacy as collective interaction and multiplicity of voices are part and parcel of the construction of legacies, both inside andoutside the tribunals. The dyad of legacy leaver and recipient(s) already introduces an in-built dialogical constellation. No legacy leaver can unilaterally fully plan or control legacies. It has been emphasized that 'legacy does not arise simply from 'the policies and actions of the tribunals themselves'; indeed, 'effective legacy must be a result not just of the policies and actions of the tribunals themselves but of a multiplicity of actors that seek to ensure that the tribunals have a lasting impact'.[134] While recognizing the multiplicity of actors, the underlying assumption of a homogeneity and convergence of actor interests and legacy visions is problematic. The diversity of actors and social dynamics involved in legacy construction has hitherto been largely overlooked. Prior to the closure of the tribunals, and beyond their closure, their legacies already have become sites of discussions and struggles over the tribunals' definitive meaning for the post-conflict country or region and international criminal justice.[135] Borrowing from Antonio Cassese, in its role as legator the Tribunal also 'remains very much like a giant without arms and legs',[136] requiring the support of other legacy actors

[131] M Klarin, 'The Tribunal's Four Battles' (2004) 2 Journal of International Criminal Justice 546.

[132] R Kerr, 'Introduction: Trials and Tribulations at the ICTY' in J Gow, R Kerr, and Z Pajić (eds), *Prosecuting War Crimes: Lessons and Legacies of the International Criminal Tribunal for the Former Yugoslavia* (Routledge 2013) 1.

[133] See special issue on 'war criminals coming home', e.g. B Hola and O Simic, 'ICTY Celebrities: War Criminals Coming Home'; M A Drumbl, 'Epilogue: Homecoming Kings, Queens, Jesters, and Nobodies' (2018) 28 International Criminal Justice Review 438.

[134] Reiger (n 117) 4.

[135] This section builds on material articulated in Dittrich, 'Legacies in the Making: Assessing the Institutionalized Legacy Endeavour of the Special Court for Sierra Leone' (n 1).

[136] A Cassese, 'On the Current Trends Towards Criminal Prosecution and Punishment of Breaches of International Humanitarian Law' (1998) 9 European Journal of International Law 2, 13.

to fulfil its legacy vision. Ultimately, paraphrasing Wendt, legacy is what tribunals make of it; but also, what all other actors make of it, too. In order to appreciate the possible spectrum of legacies it is important to consider multiple disciplines and standpoints. This present volume is an example of a legacy recording, conscious of the plurality of views and containing different voices and multiple perspectives.

The ongoing construction of legacies continues well after the legacy leaver has ceased to exist, that is, the Tribunal has closed. On the occasion of the closing ceremony of the ICTY on 21 December 2017, the UN Secretary General emphasized the importance of legacy and noted that while the Tribunal is closing its doors, much remains to be done: 'Just as the whole international community, including the United Nations, has had to acknowledge their share of responsibility for the massacre, so must the various communities of the former Yugoslavia build on the legacy of the Tribunal and deepen their efforts towards trust and full reconciliation.' on the UN Secretary General continued in French and formulated an appeal in light of legacy:

> C'est pour cette raison que la cérémonie organisée aujourd'hui sur le thème de l'héritage, ou encore legs, a tant de profondeur. Le mot latin legatus signifie à l'origine 'ambassadeur' ou 'envoyé'. Il nous appartient désormais de rester les ambassadeurs de la mémoire et de faire savoir que les tragédies comme celles qui se sont produites en ex-Yougoslavie ne doivent jamais être oubliées. Nous tous devons aussi être des ambassadeurs des droits de l'homme, de l'état de droit et de la justice.[137]

Here, the UN Secretary-General picks up the central idea of the legacy concept presented here above highlighting that actors play a central role in legacy formation and that all actors may become legacy actors, whether deliberate or otherwise, partaking in memory formation and the contest for influence over remembrance.

In sum, the topic of completion and closure has come to define the organizational developments at the tribunals in various ways. The Mechanism is formally presented as tasked with 'maintaining the legacy of both institutions'.[138] The Mechanism acts as a guardian of the legacy of the ICTY and ICTR. The responsibility for legacy building and legacy preservation was thus shifted from the ad hoc tribunals as legacy leavers to the Mechanism. The latter has taken up the role of legacy recipient, but also legacy producer, enforcer, recorder, and, ultimately, legacy leaver. The interplay of completion and continuation, and organizational continuity and discontinuity, has been identified here as a shaping factor of the organizational development of the ad hoc tribunals and of the process of meaning making and legacy formation.

6.5 Conclusions

The official closure of the Tribunal was a crystallization point for legacy discourses and assessments. The significance of legacies intimately entwines with the attribution of meaning

[137] 'Secretary-General's Remarks at Closing Ceremony for the International Criminal Tribunal for the Former Yugoslavia (ICTY) [as Delivered]' (*UN*, 21 December 2017) <https://www.un.org/sg/en/content/sg/statement/2017-12-21/secretary-generals-remarks-closing-ceremony-international-criminal> accessed 15 April 2019.

[138] See 'About the IRMCT' (*IRMCT*) <http://www.irmct.org/en/about> accessed 15 April 2019.

to the past, present, and future. The interplay of remembering and forgetting shapes legacy discourses and ultimately legacy formation. Legacy building is aimed at self-legitimization and meaning making in light of the politics of memory. Indeed, legacy creation often begins with thinking about what a legacy leaver wishes to leave behind. The Tribunal became engaged not only with successful completion of mandate at a fixed point in time but also, and importantly, with institutional persistence of an indefinite duration. Two forms of institutional persistence of the Tribunal were identified here: the Residual Mechanism and legacies. The findings draw attention to the fact that legacy formation has been ongoing since before the Tribunal completed its work and turned to legacy building as an institutional endeavour. The notion of plural legacies advocated here recognizes the multiplicity of meanings and variety of contributions as viewed by different and multiple actors. It has been shown that it would seem erroneous to assume a monolithic perspective on legacy, both inside and outside the Tribunal. A new conceptualization of legacy has been forwarded, emphasizing the retrospective as well as prospective multi-dimensionality of social processes to maintain or influence meaning making and memory formation. Greater awareness of the constructed nature of legacies enables us to paint a more nuanced picture than currently exists. Legacies have been constructed during the lifetime of the Tribunal and their reception and reconfiguration will last well beyond. The ICTY legacies remain in the making.

Legacy building has become an institutional endeavour at the ICTY, which became fuelled by an institutional urgency of meaning making transcending organizational death. While the Tribunal may be viewed as institutional legacy leaver, it bears emphasizing that the Tribunal is not a unitary actor in this regard. Legacy efforts cut across all organs of the Tribunal. Particular individuals in specific positions left their mark on the legacy activities of the Tribunal. This chapter has captured how legacies of the Tribunal have been constructed from within the institution itself. Through the prism of institutionalization of legacy this chapter traced how the concept of legacy took hold at the Tribunal rhetorically, structurally, and practically in three steps: developing a legacy vision, professionalizing legacy, and developing legacy projects. The chapter explored how the proliferation of tribunal-driven legacy projects and efforts of documentation, memorialization, and legacy building has shaped and continues to shape the actual legacy process. The legacy conferences served multiple purposes simultaneously: a platform for self-presentation and presentation of the Tribunal's developing legacy vision, a forum for dialogue and an opportunity for reflection and evaluation. Demands for legacy have been formulated increasingly and the Tribunal attempted to respond and to meet and manage expectations. A more nuanced understanding of the notion and construction of legacies enriches the wider understanding of the ICTY and its legacies. Tangible and intangible legacies, judicial and non-judicial legacies, have been created, consolidated, and contested with a view to meaning making. Discussions, utterances, and recordings, including books such as the present volume, are an integral part of what Bassiouni called the 'intellectual ferment'[139] when referring to the Nuremberg legacy and contribute to the ongoing legacy formation of the tribunals.

[139] M C Bassiouni, 'The "Nuremberg Legacy"' in G Mettraux (ed), *Perspectives on the Nuremberg Trial* (OUP 2008) 596.

7

The Narrative Legacies of Exceptional Crime

The Prosecutor as a Peacebuilder

Simone Gigliotti and Amber Pierce***

The debate over prosecuting war crimes, genocide, and crimes against humanity continues to be scrutinized in the shadow of the International Military Tribunal (IMT) at Nuremberg's Palace of Justice in 1945–1946. This trial and the United States Nuremberg Military Tribunal (NMT) which prosecuted twelve subsequent proceedings between 1946 and 1949 were landmarks in the development of international law and justice. Central to this debate is the legal legacy of the judgments reached in the IMT, NMT, and subsequent international criminal courts, and the role that the prosecutor plays within these narrative frameworks. With the closure of the International Criminal Tribunal for the former, this debate has never been more pertinent with cases against once key political figures such as Radovan Karadžić (under the prosecution of Serge Brammertz), continuing to emphasize the centrality of individual criminal responsibility (Article 7(1) of the Statute of the Tribunal) and hence enabling human rights law and jurisprudence to develop beyond its post-Second World War findings.

Critical to the understanding of exceptional crimes, individual responsibility for them, and their normative legacies for domestic and international law, is the role and rhetorical lead of the prosecutor. Not simply an interpreter of the law, prosecutors are also curators of historical fact, data, and judgments, required to demystify complex narratives of criminal wrongdoing while balancing sensitivity of oral representation through opening statements and evidence selection. In addition, prosecutors inhabit a larger societal function as proponents of peacebuilding and moral orientation. Scholars have long documented the contested and conflicting legacies of war crimes trials as sources of discursive performance, historical truth, and pedagogical instruction.

This chapter contributes to the discussion on the legacies of Nuremberg by focusing on prosecutors at the trials, and their post-trial interventions in public life. It examines the evolution and efficacy of the prosecutor as an author of an anti-genocide narrative, focusing on the statements and peace-building rhetoric of Telford Taylor at NMT and Serge Brammertz at the ICTY. It examines how they portrayed perpetrators' exceptional crimes as narratives about war, dictatorship and peace building, and the efficacy of the law as a moral instrument of accountability and crime prevention in transitional and post-conflict societies.

* Simone Gigliotti, Senior Lecturer in Holocaust Studies, Department of History, Royal Holloway, University of London.

** Amber Pierce, PhD Student, Department of History, Royal Holloway, University of London.

Simone Gigliotti and Amber Pierce, *The Narrative Legacies of Exceptional Crime* In: *Legacies of the International Criminal Tribunal for the Former Yugoslavia*. Edited by: Carsten Stahn, Carmel Agius, Serge Brammertz, Colleen Rohan, Oxford University Press (2020).
 DOI: 10.1093/oso/9780198862956.003.0008

7.1 Trial Rhetoric and Truth-Telling: Conflict and Reconciliation

This chapter's focus on prosecution rhetoric is part of an emerging emphasis on the efficacy of international criminal justice as an instrument of accountability, self-examination, and crime prevention in transitional and post-conflict societies. This literature is ever increasing and interdisciplinary, with the IMT continuing to serve as a key legal and political event for re-assessment. Janine Natalya Clark, for example, in her chapter in this volume, examines the relationship between meta-normative truths and factual truths, suggesting that the former concept that encompasses moral wrongs has a greater degree of influence in society's acceptance of the factual truths of a regime or perpetrator's criminality. Her argument about the narrative potential of trials find earlier echo in discussions of the broad-ranging narrative-making functions of international criminal justice. Prosecutors' statements in international forums are rhetorical evidence of political moralities at work, as noted in Mark Osiel's analysis, and defence of, the 'liberal show trial'.[1] Osiel notes that the 'orchestration of criminal trials for pedagogic purposes—such as the transformation of a society's collective memory—is not inherently misguided or morally indefensible . . . Liberal show trials are ones self-consciously designed to show the merits of liberal morality and to do so in ways consistent with its very requirements'.[2] Yet the universalizing ambition of liberal show trials conducted at the international level in transitional societies is organically flawed since there is, according to Harmen Van der Welt, no shared vision or truth about the narrative of a 'dark past' which is acceptable to perpetrators, victims, and bystanders.[3]

Discussions about which truths will prevail and disappear in constructions of the dark past in legal settings, and the purpose of trials in relation to civic courage and dialogue, also feature in assessments of the trial setting of the courtroom as the scene for a 'discursive battle' between justice and political morality. Tim Meijers and Marlies Glasius, for example, apply the notion of 'expressivism' to the ability of courts to 'send messages' as a key feature in rethinking the relationship between normative legitimacy, support, and utility of international trials, as based on their assessment of the case of Radovan Karadžić at the International Criminal Tribunal for the former Yugoslavia.[4] Marlies Glasius develops this concept further in relation to legal expressivism and messaging based on her readings of the proceedings against Charles Taylor before the Special Court for Sierra Leone (SCSL) and the reception of messaging by opinion leaders in Monrovia. The notion of messaging, she contends, 'is an account of *how* and *why* international criminal trials may be expected to contribute to ending impunity, reconciliation, peace, or prevention. In doing so, it takes inspiration from the theory of expressivism. This is a normative legal theory that does provide an account of the "how" and "why". It considers law as a form of messaging to populations about what constitutes desirable and undesirable behaviour'.[5] This foregoing assessment

[1] See M J Osiel, *Mass Atrocity, Collective Memory and the Law* (Transaction Publishers 1999) 65. See also his chapter, M J Osiel, 'In Defense Of Liberal Show Trials-Nuremberg and Beyond' in G Mettraux (ed), *Perspectives on the Nuremberg Trial* (Oxford University Press 2008) 704–28.

[2] See Osiel (n 1) 65.

[3] H van der Wilt, 'Crimes Against Humanity: A Category *Hors Concours* in (International Criminal Law)' in B van Beers, L Corrias, and W G Wernerp (eds), *Humanity Across International Law and Biolaw* (Cambridge University Press 2014) 38.

[4] See T Meijers and M Glasius, 'Expression of Justice or Political Trial? Discursive Battles in the Karadzic Case' (2013) 35 Human Rights Quarterly 720.

[5] M Glasius, '"It Sends a Message": Liberian Leaders' Responses to the Trial of Charles Taylor' (2015) 13 Journal of International Criminal Justice 419, 419.

suggests that messaging is a rhetorical innovation of the IMT and NMT from 1945 to 1949. Although they were not the only criminal justice mechanisms in operation during the early post-war period, the shared ambition of these tribunals' lead prosecutors to envision a peace-building and transnational morality, induce social consensus about the wartime past in Germany, and its perpetrators and victims, and to rebuild civil society under transitional political and legal frameworks are ongoing, if not contested and ultimately culturally productive, concerns of international criminal justice, as noted by Clark, Osiel, and Glasius, among other scholars.

7.2 Nuremberg Legacies: The IMT

The 1945–1946 IMT in Nuremberg, Germany, was a landmark international forum for the punishment of the major war criminals of the Nazi State. The lead US prosecutor, Robert Jackson, introduced the trial with a now-iconic statement which set the tone for a tribunal that is now widely regarded as both precedent-setting in terms of the Nuremberg Charter and international law, and also problematic in its political and didactic aspirations: 'The wrongs which we seek to condemn and punish have been so calculated, so malignant, and so devastating, that civilization cannot tolerate their being ignored, because it cannot survive their being repeated.'[6] Jackson's opening speech cast the perpetrators' behaviour in terms that foregrounded decades of scholarship about the pathology of top-level Nazi perpetrators—their greed, destructive impulses, enslavement practices, and extermination programmes. The ensuing trial proceedings not only provided an enduring empirical record but also a moral companion for future use to pursue individuals, organizations, and States accused of crimes against peace, war crimes, and crimes against humanity. As Jackson put it, Allied prosecutors, 'must never forget that the record on which we judge these defendants today is the record on which history will judge us tomorrow'.[7] The portrayal of their dictatorship of torment over Europe, Asia, and global populations merited a broad moral coalition from the terrorized and eventually victorious Allied nations. This transnational mandate of Allied participation in the prosecution of the remaining (or indictable) high-ranking Nazi leadership was part of a broader prosecutorial fervour on the part of the US and Allied governments after the Second World War that was replicated with the International Military Tribunal for the Far East (IMTFE) from 1945 to 1948.

The IMT and the NMT contributed to the development of international legal precedent that formed the basis of the International Criminal Tribunal for the former Yugoslavia (ICTY), the International Criminal Tribunal for Rwanda (ICTR), and the International Criminal Court (ICC).[8] The IMT comprised prosecutors representing the victorious Allied

[6] Justice Jackson. *Trial of the Major War Criminals Before the International Military Tribunal* [Nuremberg 14 November 1945—1 October 1946] Volume 2 (21 November 1945) 98–99.

[7] R H Jackson: Biography (last updated: 15 February 2012) <https://www.roberthjackson.org/article/robert-h-jackson-biography/> accessed 29 November 2016; Justice Jackson, *Trial of the Major War Criminals before The International Military Tribunal* [Nuremberg 14 November 1945—1 October 1946] Volume 2 (21 November 1945) 101.

[8] D Bloxham, *Genocide on Trial: War Crimes Trials and the Formation of Holocaust History and Memory* (Oxford University Press 2001) 1–2. For a contrasting view of Nuremberg as a legal 'diversion' in human rights progress, see A D Moses, 'Raphael Lemkin, Culture, and the Concept of Genocide' in D Bloxham and A. D Moses (eds), *The Oxford Handbook of Genocide Studies* (Oxford University Press 2010) 36.

powers: Sir Hartley Shawcross (United Kingdom), François de Menthon (France), Roman Rudenko (Union of Soviet Socialist Republics), and the lead US prosecutor, Robert Jackson. The Nuremberg prosecutors founded one fundamental legal human rights term and set in motion the acceptance of another. Firstly, 'crimes against humanity' came to be defined as 'murder, extermination, enslavement, deportation, and other inhumane acts committed against any civilian population, before or during the war; or persecutions on political, racial or religious grounds'.[9] Though the 1998 Rome Statute amended the definition of the act, Nuremberg also affirmed that the charge of crimes against humanity does not require proof of evidence, compared to the charge of genocide which requires the specific 'intent to destroy, in whole or in part, a national, ethnical, racial or religious group'.[10] In comparison, while crimes against humanity is deemed to be part of *jus cogens*, the highest standing order in international legal norms, Raphael Lemkin's term 'genocide' suffered numerous shortcomings at the hands of the Allied prosecutors.[11] Shawcross reasoned 'the individual must transcend the state', given the State-sponsored nature of genocide stipulated in Article IX of the United Nations Convention on the Prevention and Punishment of the Crime of Genocide (1948), and the fact that crime of genocide was not limited to wartime. It is not surprising, therefore, that the Allied prosecutors did not fully endorse an act that risked undermining the authority of member regimes, as the charge of 'genocide' did.[12]

Thus, while the legacy of Nuremberg can be critiqued on this omission, doing so merely on that basis risks relegating the jurisprudence that the 'glamour' of the IMT, as Kim Priemel and Alexa Stiller described it, has displaced, namely that of the NMT (or Nuremberg subsequent proceedings) and the IMTFE.[13] Furthermore, the application of the Nuremberg legacy to the IMT in 1945–1946 and also in purely legal terms is limited in that it downplays the synergistic or collaborative conversations that occur between the law and its fortification and challenge in public culture, and indeed minimizes attention to prosecutors' impact beyond the law. This activity includes becoming a spokesperson or peace-builder at large who cautions against unheeded lessons in post-conflict and post-genocide societies where the law has been the principal instrument of attempted democratization and reconciliation.

[9] *Trial of the Major War Criminals Before the International Military Tribunal* (Nuremberg 14 November 1945—1 October 1946) Volume 1. Art 6(c).

[10] Rome Statute of the International Criminal Court 1998, Part 2: art 7; Yale Genocide Studies Program, 'Definition: Crimes Against Humanity' <http://gsp.yale.edu/themes/crimes-against-humanity> accessed 31 October 2016; *Convention on the Prevention and Punishment of the Crime of Genocide.* Approved and Proposed for Signature and Ratification or Accession by General Assembly Resolution 260 A (III) of 9 December 1948. Entry into Force: 12 January 1951, In Accordance With art XIII <http://www.ohchr.org/EN/ProfessionalInterest/Pages/CrimeOfGenocide.aspx> accessed 14 March 2017.

[11] M Cherif Bassiouni, 'International Crimes: *Jus Cogens and Obligatio Erga Omnes*' (1997) 59 (4) Law and Contemporary Problems 68–74, 63–74; R Lemkin, *Axis Rule in Occupied Europe* (Rumford Press 1944) xi.

For the shortcomings of the term 'genocide' and the Convention on the Prevention and Punishment of the Crime of Genocide, see L Kuper, 'Theoretical Issues Relating to Genocide' in G J Andreopoulos (ed), *Genocide: Conceptual and Historical Dimensions* (University of Pennsylvania Press 1994) 43; W A Schabas, 'The Law and Genocide' in D Bloxham and A D Moses (eds), *The Oxford Handbook of Genocide Studies* (Oxford University Press 2010) 125–6; G Sluga, *Internationalism in the Age of Nationalism* (University of Pennsylvania Press 2013) 9.

[12] J Tirman, 'How the World Came to Define Genocide and Crimes Against Humanity' (*The Washington Post*, 22 July 2016) <https://www.washingtonpost.com> accessed 5 December 2016; Kuper, 'Theoretical Issues Relating to Genocide' 36; P Sands, *East West Street: On the Origins of Genocide and Crimes Against Humanity* (Weidenfeld & Nicolson 2016) 349; H Lauterpacht, *An International Bill of the Rights of Man* (first published 1945, Oxford University Press 2013) 49; M Koskenniemi, 'Hersh Lauterpacht and the Development of International Criminal Law' (2004) 2 Journal of International Criminal Justice 810, 813; W A Schabas, *Genocide in International Law: The Crime of Crimes* (Cambridge University Press 2000) 418.

[13] See Kim C Priemel and Alexa Stiller, 'Nuremberg's Narratives: Revising the Legacy of the 'Subsequent Trials' in K C Priemel and A Stiller (eds), *Reassessing the Nuremberg Military Tribunals* (Berghahn Books 2012) 2.

The efforts of forging peace-building narratives from intellectual immersion in the bureaucratic and violent perpetrator of criminal wrongdoing can be found in prosecutors' peace-building ambitions, specifically those of Telford Taylor and most recently Serge Brammertz at the ICTY.

7.3 A Displaced Legacy: Law, Lore, and the Trials of the NMT

Studies of the IMT legacy include those of M. Cherif Bassiouni who has distinguished between its moral-ethical and legal dimensions. The moral-ethical dimension, he noted back in 1986, has been 'intellectual ferment' in scholarly studies, legal doctrine, and jurisprudence, a visibility that has also migrated to speeches, educational materials, and aspirational governance standards of humanitarian and other non-government organizations.[14] It is this moral-ethical legacy which, to him, has promoted the influence of the Nuremberg legacy on legal developments. The uses of IMT jurisprudence or rather of its prosecutors' often-unfulfilled ambitions to foreground enduring didactically sustainable narratives have been insightfully examined by Donald Bloxham and Lawrence Douglas. Notions of judicial memory, presence, and ostensible absence (of Jewish witnesses and a specific focus on the Holocaust) and the narrative construction of international law featured as themes of their studies. For Douglas, the IMT's influence as 'lore' has accrued through a globally-embedded pedagogy: 'Law students around the globe now dutifully study the so-called "Nuremberg Principles," the norms of international law, which insist, among other things, that "acts of state" and "superior orders" supply no defense against the charge of perpetrating international crimes.'[15]

Documents amassed at the IMT and studied by scholars contributed to that 'lore'. For example, the IMT supplied the evidentiary basis of early histories of the Third Reich and the Nazi State, including Raul Hilberg's still-influential *The Destruction of the European Jews*, among many others.[16] The 'lore' of the IMT to which Douglas refers also related to the IMT as a criminal depiction of the high-ranking Nazi leadership and its one-sidedness which denied Jewish witnesses a voice on the stand, and by design, diffused the ethnic specificity of the persecution of Jews as genocide, and downplayed Raphael Lemkin's activism to have it included on the general indictment.[17]

This perspective, however, is difficult to sustain faced with an ever-growing body of research that embeds the invaluable contributions of Jewish lawyers such as Jacob Robinson, advocates, research assistants, and organizations including the World Jewish Congress and the Institute of Jewish Affairs into the IMT's preparation and trial proceedings.[18] To be sure,

[14] M C Bassiouni, R A Falk, and Y Onuma, 'Nuremberg: Forty Years After' (1986) 80 Proceedings of the Annual Meeting (American Society of International Law) 59, 60.

[15] See L Douglas, 'From IMT to NMT: The Emergence of a Jurisprudence of Atrocity' in K C Priemel and A Stiller (eds), *Reassessing the Nuremberg Military Tribunals* (Berghahn Books 2012) 277.

[16] See K Priemel and A Stiller (eds), *Reassessing the Nuremberg Military Tribunals* (Berghahn Books 2012).

[17] The pathway towards the prosecution of genocide at specific NMT trials has been documented elsewhere, such as the NMT Einsatzgruppen trial of 1947. See H Earl, 'Prosecuting Genocide Before the Genocide Convention: Raphael Lemkin and the Nuremberg Trials, 1945–1949' (2013) 15 (3) Journal of Genocide Research 317.

[18] On the contributions of Jewish political activism and individuals, see J Loeffler, *Rooted Cosmopolitans: Jews and Human Rights in the Twentieth Century* (Yale University Press 2018). His work is preceded by that of M R Marrus, 'A Jewish Lobby at Nuremberg: Jacob Robinson and the Institute of Jewish Affairs, 1945–1946' (February 2006) 27 (4) Cardozo Law Review 1651; L Jockusch, 'Justice at Nuremberg? Jewish Responses to Nazi War-Crime

it was these individuals and organizations which understood and surmised that the criminal intent of genocide was central to the war, and yet its assessment at the IMT as a crime against humanity, as a subset of other crimes, deferred its introduction until the NMT under prosecutors such as Benjamin Ferencz.[19] As Laura Jockusch notes, the 'Final Solution', 'was a crime unprecedented and specific not in terms of the quantity of its victims but rather as judged by the substance of the murder's ideological motivation, geographical scope, and method. Yet for all the consideration accorded the persecution and extermination of the Jews, it was treated as a subsidiary event at the IMT'.[20]

The Jewish 'Nuremberg' arguably materialized with the trial of Adolf Eichmann in Jerusalem in 1961, and produced a ubiquitous literature about the memory of the Holocaust in Israel, the emergence of the survivor as legal witness, produced a distinct body of witness testimony at Holocaust trials, and ongoing studies about the jurisdictional legitimacy of the trial itself.[21]

Discussions about the extremity of criminal actions, as reflected in intent and individual responsibility, feature in the scholarship about the NMT, which to some extent, provides a functionalist narrative on the decades old debate in Holocaust historiography about causality, method, structure, and agency. These trials have been the subject of numerous recent books (some of which were based on PhD dissertations),[22] and feature in recent scholarship which attempts to analyse the continuities between the IMT and NMT in addition to the international criminal law which mandated the latter tribunal's. Contributors to Kim Priemel and Alexa Stiller's recent compilation, *Reassessing the Nuremberg Military Tribunals*, advance important arguments about the NMT's legacy in historiographical and jurisprudential terms. The NMT, as Priemel and Stiller note in their introduction to the volume, 'aspired to nothing less than indicting the entire Nazi state and analysing its workings in an authoritative way. Structures rather than individuals and institutional representatives rather than easily identifiable villains, were to be publicly prosecuted, literally for everyone to see'.[23] The NMTs indictments of 177 defendants from Nazi society's professional

Trials in Allied-Occupied Germany' (2012) 19 Jewish Social Studies 107; J A Bush, 'Nuremberg and Beyond: Jacob Robinson, International Lawyer' (2016–2017) 39 Loyola Los Angeles International and Comparative Law Review 259.

[19] See Earl (n 17) and H Earl, 'Legacies of the Nuremberg SS-Einsatzgruppen Trial after 70 Years' (2016–2017) 39 Loyola Los Angeles International and Comparative Law Review 95.

[20] Jockusch (n 18) 133.

[21] On this topic (in recent order), see B Stangneth, *Eichmann before Jerusalem: The Unexamined Life of a Mass Murderer* (Knopf 2014); Forum on 'The Eichmann Trial Fifty Years On' (2011) 29 German History 265–82; H Safrian, *Eichmann's Men* (Cambridge University Press 2009); D Cesarani, *Eichmann: His Life and Crimes* (Vintage Books 2004); H Yablonka, *The State of Israel vs. Adolf Eichmann* (Schocken 2004); J Robinson, *And the Crooked Shall be Made Straight: The Eichmann Trial, the Jewish Catastrophe, and Hannah Arendt's Narrative* (Macmillan 1965); H Arendt, *Eichmann in Jerusalem* (first published 1962, Penguin Books 1994). For Eichmann before Jerusalem, see L Jockusch, 'Justice at Nuremberg? Jewish Responses to Nazi War-Crime Trials in Allied-Occupied Germany' (2012) 19 Jewish Social Studies 107, 133; S Felman, 'Theaters of Justice: Arendt in Jerusalem, the Eichmann Trial, and the Redefinition of Legal Meaning in the Wake of the Holocaust' (2001) 27 Critical Inquiry 201; H Yablonka and M Tlamim, 'The Development of Holocaust Consciousness in Israel: The Nuremberg, Kapos, Kastner, and Eichmann Trials' (Fall 2003) 8(3) Israel Studies 1 (translated from the Hebrew by Ora Cummings with David Herman); I Zertal, *Israel's Holocaust and the Politics of Nationhood* (Cambridge University Press 2005).

[22] For a broad overview, see P Heberer and J Matthäus (eds), *Atrocities on Trial: Historical Perspectives on the Politics of Prosecuting War Crimes* (University of Nebraska Press in association with the United States Holocaust Memorial Museum 2008), and specifically V Hébert, *Hitler's Generals On Trial: The Last War Crimes Tribunal At Nuremberg* (University Press of Kansas 2010).

[23] Priemel and Stiller (n 16) 2. See also K C Priemel, *The Betrayal: The Nuremberg Trials and German Divergence* (Oxford University Press 2016).

and military elites included doctors, judges, prosecutors, government ministers, SS officers, and military leaders. These proceedings reflected the transnational landscape of criminal collusion and yet their relative subordination in terms of legacy to the IMT merits review.

Douglas and other contributors to *Reassessing the Nuremberg Military Tribunals* attest that the NMT's prosecutorial vision embedded a disturbing behavioural and sociological expression to the IMT's legacy of individual criminal responsibility under international law. Taylor's repeated statements in various proceedings at the NMT, which will be examined shortly, detailed the depravity, inhumanity, and civilizational decline of Germany under Nazi dictatorship. His opening statements and presentation of evidence portrayed the everyday impacts of conspiratorial collusion in the Nazi State through practices of slave labour, extermination, deportation, medical experiments, transnational displacements, and untold sufferings. The NMT narrative was thus customized to the crimes under investigation, building a 'jurisprudence of atrocity'[24] that continues in contemporary prosecutions of defendants at the ICTY and ICTR.[25] Heller argued that 'the NMTs might not have given birth to international criminal law, but they clearly nurtured it into adolescence'.[26] He commends the IMT's legal innovation of introducing crimes against peace, crimes against humanity, and the crime of criminal membership. But, he argues, 'there is remarkably little criminal law in the IMT judgment: nothing on evidence and procedure; almost nothing on modes of participation, defenses, or sentencing. Even the discussion of the crimes themselves is relatively cursory and unsystematic'.[27] It was the NMT proceeding against Otto Ohlendorf (Case Number 9), under the young American-Jewish prosecutor Benjamin Ferencz, which argued for the genocidal specificity of the 'Final Solution' against the Jews, using self-authored *Einsatzgruppen* reports to establish the criminal and genocidal intent of its commanders.[28] Ferencz applied Raphael Lemkin's definition of genocide to the case at hand, asking the judges to adopt an anthropological perspective when assessing the *Einsatzgruppen's* intent to define and destroy the Jews as an ethnic group:

> Proof of a million murders will not be the most significant aspect of this case. We charge more than murder, for we cannot shut our eyes to a fact ominous and full of foreboding for all of mankind. Not since men abandoned tribal loyalties has any state challenged the right of whole peoples to exist. And not since medieval times have governments marked men for death because of race or faith. Now comes this recrudescence—this Nazi doctrine of a master race—an arrogance blended from tribal conceit and a boundless contempt for man himself. It is an idea whose toleration endangers all men. It is, as we have charged, a crime against humanity.[29]

The IMT and NMT lay further claims to non-legal legacies that build on Bassiouni's observation about the moral-ethical imprint in studies of the internationalizing of criminal law and the humanizing of law itself. Studies by scholars of European history, the Holocaust,

[24] Douglas (n 15) 281.

[25] For an overview of how NMT jurisprudence was applied in the ICTY, see K J Heller, *The Nuremberg Military Tribunals and The Origins of International Criminal Law* (Oxford University Press 2011) 369.

[26] ibid 402.

[27] ibid 3.

[28] Earl (n 17) 317.

[29] See Trials of War Criminals Before the Nuernberg Military Tribunals Under Control Council Law No 10 [October 1946—April 1949] Volume IV: The Einsatzgruppen Case/The RuSHA Case 31–32.

and genocide have examined the origins of human rights,[30] debates about the efficacy of the definition of genocide and its difficult prosecutorial pathway through the IMT, NMT, and current tribunals,[31] and through to the surge of the biographical approach.[32] As Jonathan Bush notes, the publication of biographies of Nazi-era criminals at the time and which continue to this day, was mirrored in autobiographies, memoirs, and personal reports of trial participants or attendees, whether journalists, psychologists, and translators.[33] Yet, absent from these conscious self-assessments are critical appraisals of the key legal protagonists at the trials. Indeed an analysis of the 'prosecutor' in terms of office, legacy, and impact is very minimal in scholarship of the conflated yet distinct IMT and NMT legacies. The historiographical and sociological value of 61,000 documents that Allied investigators compiled and submitted for official registration was generally understated by US prosecutor Robert Kempner in his closing statement at the Ministries trial when he reported that: 'These contemporaneous records constitute the unerasable, self-written history book concerning those men who for so long clung together for better or worse, for richer or poorer, in Hitler's Third Reich, until their ill-fated union began to crack in the last months of the Nazi era in the face of common defeat and the impending wreck of their booty-laden ship of state'.[34] These rhetorical flourishes were part and parcel of prosecutors' narrative staging of Germany's decline and corruption.

To be sure, the documentary proof of crime presented at the NMT proceedings was bookended by characterizations of an individual's moral choice, ongoing historicization of dictatorial regimes, civilizational 'best' behaviour, and appeals to philosophical reason. Taylor's apprenticeship was with Robert Jackson at the IMT, as one of his senior deputies. His presentations of cases at the NMT invoked several of Jackson's legendary speeches on several occasions, particularly the opening statement.[35] Yet Taylor was not only a prosecutor for the US, he was also a highly visible public 'peace-builder' of foreign policy in post-war Germany. Hecontinued the legacy of Jackson, and interpreted the parameters of criminal law to adjudicate accountability, democratization anxieties, and the moral 're-education' of a traumatized if not largely indifferent and resistant German populace to such measures. Heller notes that although Taylor rejected including a specifically 'Jewish case' in the NMT trials, the opening statements and judgments in numerous proceedings are suffused with

[30] From a very large field, see M Duranti, *The Conservative Human Rights Revolution* (Oxford University Press 2017); Sands (n 12); S Moyn, *The Last Utopia: Human Rights in History* (Harvard University Press 2012); M Mazower, *Governing the World: The History of an Idea* (Penguin Press 2012); A F Vrdoljak, 'Human Rights and Genocide: The Work of Lauterpacht and Lemkin in Modern International Law' (2010) 20 The European Journal of International Law 1163.

[31] See D M Crowe, *War Crimes, Genocide, and Justice: A Global History* (Palgrave Macmillan 2014); C Card and A T Marsoobian (eds), *Genocide's Aftermath: Responsibility and Repair* (Blackwell 2007); H Ball, *Prosecuting War Crimes and Genocide: The Twentieth-Century Experience* (University Press of Kansas 1999).

[32] See Bush (n 17). See also V R Berghahn and S Lässig (eds), *Biography Between Structure and Agency: Central European Lives in International Historiography* (Berghahn Book 2008), chapters 9, 10, and 11 deal specifically with Nazi perpetrators.

[33] Examples of these publications include: T Townsend, *Mission at Nuremberg: An American Army Chaplain and The Trial of the Nazis* (William Morrow 2014); R W Sonnenfeldt, *Witness to Nuremberg* (Arcade Publishing 2006); L Goldensohn, *The Nuremberg Interviews: An American Psychiatrist's Conversations with the Defendants and Witnesses* (Random House 2005); and R West, *A Train of Powder* (Viking Press 1955).

[34] R Kempner, Trials of War Criminals Before the Nuremberg Military Tribunals Under Control Council Law No 10 [October 1946—April 1949] Volume XIV: Ministries Case 2.

[35] 'The wrongs which we seek to condemn and punish have been so calculated, so malignant, and so devastating, that civilization cannot tolerate their being ignored, because it cannot survive their being repeated.' *Trial of the Major War Criminals Before the International Military Tribunal* [Nuremberg 14 November 1945—1 October 1946] Volume 2 (21 November 1945) 98–102.

detailed narratives of the Holocaust: 'the creation and administration of the concentration camps in *Pohl*; the construction of Auschwitz III-Monowitz in *Farben*; the 'resettlement' of Jews in occupied territory and the systematic theft of their property in *RuSHA*; the extermination of Jews in the Soviet Union in *Einsatzgruppen*; the use of Jewish slave labor by German industry in *Krupp*; the implementation of the Nuremberg Laws in *Ministries*'.[36]

The NMT's ambition was more than punitive and judicial. Taylor recognized that the trial preparations and proceedings needed informed research, and robust critical analysis, if their legacy was to be secured and perpetuated not just in Germany, but also as a transnational legal and storytelling precedent. In an interview in 1952, he asked, should Nuremberg 'be done as a play, a novel, a history? I don't want just another book on the legal side, for Nuremberg was far more than that. It became a sort of institution, set in the environment of a changing Germany'.[37] Taylor's uncertainty over how to narrate the legacy of atrocity in meaningful ways was not unusual in the post-war period. Such struggles also met novelists, historians, and philosophers of the Holocaust. Which medium was most compelling to tell the story of the NMT's chief Nazi perpetrators and the horror that they and their institutions wrought? Such struggles stayed with Taylor. One of his most acclaimed works, *The Anatomy of the Nuremberg Trials* incorrectly suggests a sweeping assessment of the thirteen trials of the IMT and NMT. Rather, it lays out the inner architecture of the IMT, profiles of its defendants and a sober assessment of achievements and failings. References to his role at the NMT are limited to a paragraph where he mentions ongoing war crimes trials at the Palace of Justice and the increase in influence of Soviet satellites in the context of the Cold War.[38] At the time of his death, his companion piece to *The Anatomy of the Nuremberg Trials* remained unfinished.[39] Reviewing his numerous opening statements at the NMT, therefore, can provide the reader with an impassioned guide to the themes of this unfinished 'public history' of war and its insecure peace. They also outline the minimum foundations for an effective post-dictatorship transition which were, for the most part, implemented, though not altogether effectively, in occupied and West Germany.

7.4 Giving Atrocity a Usable Narrative

A deep critical reading of Taylor's presentation of the cases against the leadership and industries of the Nazi State at the NMT is beyond this chapter. Instead, a number of his opening statements from various cases will be introduced to provide a pathway intothe rhetorical flair of prosecutors at the NMT and demonstration of messaging, taking the cue from Glasius' notion of expressivism. This approach also has some alignment to Sofia Stolk's analysis of opening statements at the IMT, the SCSL, and the ICC.[40] Stolk suggests that the cross-trial focus reveals a 'recurrent, self-justifying narrative where both rootedness in history and a break with the past are key to singing the tribunal into existence as a crucial

[36] Heller (n 25) 1–8.

[37] L Nichols, 'Talk with Telford Taylor' The New York Times Book Review (14 December 1952) VII: 14. As Quoted in: Bush (n 18) 259.

[38] T Taylor, *Anatomy of the Nuremberg Trials: A Personal Memoir* (Alfred A. Knopf, Inc. 1992) 640.

[39] Bush (n 18) 259.

[40] See S Stolk, 'The Record on Which History Will Judge Us Tomorrow' (2015) 28 Leiden Journal of International Law (Auto-History in the Opening Statements of International Criminal Trials) 993, 993.

mechanism in the transition from chaos to peace'.[41] Central to her argument is the notion of 'auto-history' where prosecutors engaged in justifying the legitimacy of trials through the invocation of a tribunal's *own* history. She asserts that the'scrutiny of such 'auto-histories" as a specific form of history-telling illuminates an overlooked dimension of trials as fora for writing history'.[42] The meta-historical ambitions of prosecutors certainly utilise Stolk's notion of internal referencing.Taylor and many others have done similar in relation to phrases from Jackson's opening statement at the IMT, but they are not the only narrative reference point or point of recall. As will be argued, Taylor's various opening statements can be read as vignettes of an early 'public history' of the narrative grapple with Nazi atrocities in the very terms introduced earlier. Which narrative form or genre was amenable, or sufficiently flexible, to accommodate order, intention, and catastrophe in this traumatic public history, not to mention the one that was largely under-disclosed as it related to the persecution of Jewish victims? A play, a novel, or something else altogether? As we will see, Taylor presented the geographies of, and motivation for, exceptional crime as a hybrid narrative that was customized to the cases at hand to express the operational 'behemoth' sitting in the Palace of Justice. The vignettes which express this early public history would come to feature in historiography of the Nazi regime and the Holocaust several decades later. As its curator and spokesperson, this narrative was specific in its assignation of individual criminal responsibility and yet necessarily contextualized in the structural foundations of political, moral, and social disorder which gave such extensive and offensive wrongdoing its normative face.

Scholars introduced earlier including Lawrence Douglas and Kevin Jon Heller have analysed the documentary ambition and didactic challenges of Holocaust trials, to educate 'still-skeptical publics about Nazi atrocities'.[43] These elements were evident in Taylor's opening statement in the Medical Case (Karl Brandt et al, Case 1). The opening statement was Taylor's introduction to his 'public history' of exceptional crime and introduced the use of metaphors to narrate illegality. Nazi society, its victims, perpetrators, industries, and collaborators all featured in it. Taylor inferred that ordinary Germans were the Nazis' first victims: 'mere punishment of the defendants, or even of thousands of others equally guilty, can never redress the terrible injuries which the Nazis visited on these unfortunate peoples'.[44] He reserved, as did many other litigators, scholars, educators, and psychologists in the early post-war period in Europe, special attention to war-damaged children and the dystopian future that awaited them. How would they perceive the rights and wrongs that war wrought? 'Will they attribute it to the overwhelming weight of numbers and resources that was eventually leagued against them? Will they point to the ingenuity of enemy scientists? Will they perhaps blame their plight on strategic and military blunders by their generals?'[45] Taylor also re-appropriated the popular Nazi propaganda metaphors of disease and disability to explain the state of the German nation and the will of the US to unearth its devastating global impact: 'A nation which deliberately infects itself with poison will inevitably sicken and die. These defendants and others turned Germany into an infernal combination of a lunatic asylum and a charnel house'.[46]

[41] ibid.
[42] ibid.
[43] See Heller (n 25) 36998.
[44] T Taylor, 'Opening Statement for the United States of America' Trial 1—Medical Case. Paper 1 (12 September 1946) 27 <http://digitalcommons.law.uga.edu/nmt1/1> accessed 4 July 2017.
[45] ibid 28.
[46] ibid 29.

The use of customized metaphors continued in the Justice Case (Josef Altstetter et al, Case 3) and extended into the legal organization of political governance. Noting the unusual nature of the case, Taylor noted the law's ugly transformation into 'brutish tyranny',[47] and contextualized the antiquity of the crime (despotism, conquest, pillage, and slaughter), with the modernity of its method.[48] Vital to Taylor's opening statement was the insistence that the Justice Case was more than retribution. Taylor insisted that the case was visibly demonstrative in that it must return to Germany a 're-consecrated' temple of justice. A return to the rule of law through invoking the physical metaphor of the 'temple of justice' which birthed and litigated German jurisprudence was vital to the democratization of post-war Germany.

Taylor's opening statements in further cases included warnings and musings about dictatorship, greed, wealth, and poverty (Case 5, Friedrich Flick et al,), and responses to ongoing criticisms about the justness of the trials in post-war Germany, itself under Allied occupation and subjected to ongoing denazification policies. The Farben case (Carl Krauch et al, Case 6), saw Taylor's narrative drift into Dante's *Inferno*, which was also the inspiration for Primo Levi's metaphorical reflections about Auschwitz.[49] References to darkness, decline, and a dystopian nightmare provided a rather theatrical and sensationalist tone:

> The world around us bears not the slightest resemblance to the Elysian Fields. The face of this continent is hideously scarred and its voice is a bitter snarl; everywhere man's works lie in ruins, and the standard of human existence is purgatorial. The first half of this century has been a black era; most of its years have been years of war, or of open menace, or of painful aftermath, and he who seeks today to witness oppression, violence, or warfare need not choose his direction too carefully nor travel very far. Shall it be said, then, that all of us, including these defend ants, are but the children of a poisoned span? And does the guilt for the wrack and torment of these times defy apportionment?[50]

Hell's compatriot figure was the corpse. In the Hostage Case (Case 7, Wilhelm List et al) Taylor reminded the judges to remember 'the corpse' that is indelibly associated with the Allied liberation of Jewish victims at Nazi concentration camps as the reason for why the criminals' activities are on trial.[51] The victims of genocide could not be re-victimized by abandoning the pursuit of justice, as Taylor put it: 'We cannot restore the moral fabric of Europe by laying a shroud over unshriven and unburied corpses.'[52]

[47] T Taylor, 'Opening Statement for the United States of America' Trial 3—Judges Case. Paper 4 (5 March 1947) 31 <http://digitalcommons.law.uga.edu/nmt3/4> accessed 4 July 2017: 'The root of the accusation here is that those men, leaders of the German judicial system, consciously and deliberately suppressed the law, engaged in an unholy masquerade of brutish tyranny disguised as justice, and converted the German judicial system to an engine of despotism, conquest, pillage, and slaughter.'

[48] ibid.

[49] See P Levi, *If This Is a Man/The Truce* (Stuart Woolf tr, Abacus 2014); P Balakian, 'Poetry in Hell: Primo Levi and Dante at Auschwitz' (January/February 2008) 37 The American Poetry 3.

[50] T Taylor, 'Opening Statement for the United States of America' Trial 6—I.G. Farben Case. Paper 6 (27 April 1947) 99 <http://digitalcommons.law.uga.edu/nmt6/6> accessed 4 July 2017.

[51] T Taylor, 'Closing Statement on Behalf of the Prosecution' Trial 7—Hostage Case. Paper 3 [3 February 1948] <http://digitalcommons.law.uga.edu/nmt7/3> accessed 4 July 2017: 'But Germany is not the only devastated and stricken land, and for every crime there is not only a criminal but a victim. In the minds of many peoples are memories so mordant that they cannot be forgotten. If the course of justice is stayed, these sores will only fester the longer and spread the wider. We cannot restore the moral fabric of Europe by laying a shroud over unshriven and unburied corpses.'

[52] ibid.

Taylor diversified his narrative strategies to encompass spatial history. The opening statement in the Ministries Case (Ernst von Weizsaecker et al, Case 11) saw him focus on the precinct of Wilhelmstrasse in Berlin and contrast it with urban governance locations in London and Paris, asking the judges to visualize the gathering of conspirators in Wilhelmstrasse and their destruction of democratic governance in the German Reichstag. This case, as with the IG Farben case and the Krupp cases (Alfried Krupp et al, Case 10), targeted German industrialists and provided extensive documentary material about sub camps, forced labour, and a philosophy of power which facilitated widespread plunder and military conquest.

There were several legacies of narrating these exceptional crimes, as briefly outlined through a selection of Taylor's opening statements at the NMT. The first was an early public history of what has now emerged as the moderate-functionalist position in Holocaust historiography.[53] The second was a self-conscious curatorship of the agents and inefficiencies of Nazi dictatorship, its enablers, opportunists, and profiteers. Thirdly, Taylor's anxiety about how 'best' to tell the story of Nuremberg was indicative of the time—just as Jewish scholars, survivors, and philosophers agonized over language and extremity, so too did Taylor in relation to the narrative of widespread criminal wrongdoing that overflowed the courtroom of defendants, witnesses, and legal representatives at the NMT. The documentary evidence of excess illegality and inhumanity required hybrid narrative forms. He acknowledged the challenges to the dissemination of the documentary proceedings in reports from May and August 1949 (the latter was the most comprehensive).[54] The reports detailed incompetence at various levels, especially in terms of the non-availability of the proceedings to German schools and universities, and recommendations for their use as storytelling sources for peace building and democratization. Yet, the context and mood were somewhat against Taylor. He bemoaned what he perceived as the 'passing' of the NMT into insignificance, and 'truths' of German history contained in the documents presented therein. The presence of dictatorships in post-war Europe continued to stalk his writing: 'If Germany again falls victim to this delusion, it will be because the lesson of Nuremberg has not, even yet, sunk in; for the Nuremberg record provides, above all, an eloquent demonstration of the terrible handicaps under which any nation, burdened by dictatorship, labors.'[55]

The perception that the credibility of the IMT and NMTs were diminished as biased examples of victors' justice did not deter Taylor's commitment to their potential peacebuilding legacy. Devin Pendas notes that the NMT's ambition for didactic influence, by providing new documentary evidence of the Nazi state, was premature in Germany's post-war occupation context. The trials 'led to neither a historical appreciation for the "deep bite" of Nazism on German society, nor, in the western zones, to a sustainable and far reaching German jurisprudence of crimes against humanity'.[56] The Germans' changing attitude towards the NMT's jurisprudence of atrocity was thus deferred or delayed until West Germans

[53] See R Bessel, 'Functionalists vs. Intentionalists: The Debate Twenty Years on or Whatever Happened to Functionalism and Intentionalism?' (February 2003) 26 (1) German Studies Review 15.

[54] T Taylor, 'The Nuremberg War Crimes Trials: An Appraisal' (May 1949) 23 (3) Proceedings of the Academy of Political Science (The United States and the Atlantic Community) 19, 29, and *Final report to the Secretary of the Army on The Nuernberg War Crimes Trials under Control Council Law No. 10* (Telford Taylor, Brigadier General, USA, Chief of Counsel for War Crimes), 15 August 1949. See link: https://www.loc.gov/rr/frd/Military_Law/pdf/NT_final-report.pdf accessed 29 January 2020.

[55] ibid Taylor, 'The Nuremberg War Crimes Trials: An Appraisal' (May 1949), 30.

[56] D O Pendas, 'The Fate of Nuremberg: The Legacy and Impact of the Subsequent Nuremberg Trials in Postwar Germany' in Priemel and Stiller (eds), *Reassessing the Nuremberg Military Tribunals* (Bergahn Books 1949) 268.

confronted the legacy of the Nazi State and Nuremberg anew through the Eichmann trial, the Frankfurt Auschwitz trial, the Vietnam War, and in public culture of memorials, films, and television. The narrative legacies of the prosecutor as a narrator and public historian of criminal wrongdoing and advocate of justice for Jewish and non-Jewish victims was re-purposed in new judicial and national settings that inherited the legal and didactic aspirations of the IMT and NMT and also their respective jurisprudential biases and burdens.

7.5 Prosecutors at the ICTY: The Case of Radovan Karadžić

Since its establishment, the ICTY (the Chief Prosecutor of whom was Serge Brammertz having assumed duties on 1 January 2008) has indicted 161 persons for serious violations of humanitarian law committed on the territory of the former Yugoslavia between 1991 and 2001.[57] Proceedings against 161 accused have been concluded, with 90 individuals sentenced. Whilst these figures within their own context are impressive in achieving justice for the genocide victims in the former Yugoslavia, arguably it was only until the arrest and trial of Radovan Karadžić that the ICTY's legal legacy came to fruition. As a founding member and President of the Serbian Democratic Party amongst other titles, on 24 March 2016, Karadžić became the highest-ranking political leader from the Srebrenica genocide to be found guilty of war crimes and crimes against humanity, having murdered close to 8,000 Bosnian Muslim men and boys in Srebrenica in 1995.[58] As stipulated in his amended indictment, whilst Karadžić was originally charged with sixteen counts of human rights violations (nine of which were charges of genocide, crimes against humanity, and crimes that were perpetrated against the civilian population and against places of worship throughout the territory of the Republic of Bosnia and Herzegovina), it was the emphasis the prosecution team, made up of Alan Tieger and Hildegard Uertz-Retzlaff, placed on Article 7(1) of the Statute of the Tribunal that marked this case as a turning point in international criminal tribunals.[59] According to Article 7(1): 'A person who planned, instigated, ordered, committed

[57] A legal professional, serving for more than a decade in senior positions charged with investigating and prosecuting grave international crimes, Serge Brammertz assumed his duties as Chief Prosecutor of the International Criminal Tribunal for the former Yugoslavia on 1 January 2008. He was reappointed by the Security Council on 14 September 2011. On 29 February 2016, he was appointed by the United Nations Security Council to serve as Prosecutor of the Mechanism for International Criminal Tribunals, a position he continued to hold while performing his functions at the Tribunal. Prior to his role as Chief Prosecutor, in January 2006 United Nations Secretary-General Kofi Annan appointed him as Commissioner of the United Nations International Independent Investigation Commission into the assassination of former Lebanese Prime Minister Rafik Hariri, a post he held until the end of 2007. Previously, in September 2003 he was elected by the Assembly of State Parties as the first Deputy Prosecutor of the International Criminal Court. In that capacity, he was in charge of establishing the Investigations Division of the Office of the Prosecutor, and initiated the first ICC investigations in Uganda, the Democratic Republic of Congo and Darfur. For more on Brammertz, see his profile: United Nations International Criminal Tribunal for the former Yugoslavia, 'Serge Brammertz: The Prosecutor' <http://www.icty.org/en/about/office-of-the-prosecutor/the-prosecutor> accessed 19 May 2017.

[58] Radovan Karadžić was President of the Serbian Democratic Party (SDS) until his resignation on 19 July 1996, Chairman of the National Security Council of the so-called Serbian Republic of Bosnia and Herzegovina (later Republika Srpska—'RS'), President of the three-member Presidency of RS from its creation on 12 May 1992, until 17 December 1992, and thereafter sole President of RS and Supreme Commander of its armed forces until July 1996.

IT-95-5/18 *The Prosecutor of the ICTY v Radovan Karadzic, Ratko Mladic*. Case Information Sheet. [July 24, 1995] UN, ICTY. IT-95-5-I.

[59] Indictment (24 July 24 1995) IT-95-5-I; *The Prosecutor v Radovan Karadžić* IT-95-5/18-PT (19 October 2009) 3; Radovan Karadžić. Case Information Sheet; Press Release Statement on The Arrest of Radovan Karadžić (The Hague) [21 July 2008] UN, ICTY.

or otherwise aided and abetted in the planning, preparation or execution of a crime ... shall be individually responsible for the crime.'[60] Whilst this article is in line with the argument against the defence of superior orders that was first presented in Nuremberg, whereby the defendants claimed since they had been following orders they could not be held criminally responsible for their actions, throughout Karadžić's trial, the prosecution presented Article 7(1) within the totality of the assumed genocidal criminal operations committed alongside the need for victim justice.[61]

Certainly, whilst the prosecutors at Nuremberg had presented themselves as the forerunners of justice against their defendants, it was not until the Eichmann trial that the concept of 'victim rights' became established in international criminal court.[62] Such a legacy from Eichmann lead prosecutor Gideon Hausner, and the subsequent importance of the verdict of the trial for the victims, can be clearly traced throughout Karadžić's trial. From Brammertz's press statement following Karadžić's arrest, to the opening statement of the prosecution ('for those survivors, there's been no recovery, no restoration of lives that have not and cannot be restored ... their ongoing tragedy ... is part of the lasting legacy of the accused's crime'), the victim narrative shaped the trial and thus its impact within international law.[63] Indeed, in the closing statement of the prosecution, Tieger claimed:

> Thus, the prosecution seeks no expansion or broadening of the law on genocide; we seek only the application of the Statute and the jurisprudence of this Tribunal, which are intended to provide a measure of justice for communities that have been targeted for destruction and a measure of protection for those that might in future.[64]

Interestingly, whilst the sentencing of Karadžić affirmed individual criminal responsibility alongside the victim narrative, the judgment also harked back to the legal debate at Nuremberg between the hierarchy of the terms crimes against humanity and genocide. Whilst the wider media consider genocide to be the 'ultimate crime', in Karadžić's case the appeals chamber established that 'there is no hierarchy of crimes', concluding that they were unable to identify or infer genocidal intent beyond reasonable doubt.[65] Though coinciding with the opinion of legal scholars, such a verdict unsurprisingly could be seen to many

[60] Updated Statute of the International Criminal Tribunal for the Former Yugoslavia. UN, International Tribunal for the Prosecution of Persons Responsible for Serious Violations of International Humanitarian Law Committed in the Territory of Former Yugoslavia 1991 (September 2009) art 7(1).

[61] For the founding work on the importance of individual criminal responsibility, see Lauterpacht (n 12) 49; M Koskenniemi, 'Hersch Lauterpacht and the Development of International Criminal Law' (2004) 2 Journal of International Criminal Justice 814. Lauterpacht's view of individual criminal responsibility as a quintessential part of international law continues to be shared by a whole generation of international lawyers, shown most recently in the discussions held over superior order in the 2016 International Nuremberg Principles Academy Annual Forum.

[62] Forum on 'The Eichmann Trial Fifty Years On' (n 21).

[63] Brammertz claimed that 'this is a very important day for the victims who have waited for this arrest for over a decade'. Press Release Statement on The Arrest of Radovan Karadžić (The Hague) [21 July 2008] UN, ICTY; Prosecution Opening Statement. ICTY (2 November 2009) 665.18–666.9 <http://www.icty.org/x/cases/karadzic/trans/en/091102IT.htm> accessed 25 May 2017.

[64] Importantly, throughout the closing statement, the ICTY prosecution referenced the crime of genocide in line with Lemkin's original definition, a clear difference to the line of argument presented by the prosecution in Nuremberg. Prosecution Closing Statement. ICTY (29 September 2014) 47586.7–47586.19 <http://www.icty.org/x/cases/karadzic/trans/en/140929ED.htm> accessed 27 May 2017.

[65] *Prosecutor v Radovan Karadžić* [24 March 2016] IT-95-5/18-T. Volume IV, V 2524; Tribunal Press Release, 'Tribunal Convicts Radovan Karadžić for Crimes in Bosnia and Herzegovina' (*The Hague*, 24 March 2016) <http://www.icty.org/en/press/tribunal-convicts-radovan-karadzic-for-crimes-in-bosnia-and-herzegovina> accessed 21 May 2017.

victims as justice cut short. Whilst Karadžić was rightly convicted, his sentence of forty years imprisonment without the legal proof that genocide was committed highlights a gulf between the public and legal understanding of what criminal 'justice' really is.[66]

For Brammertz: 'As prosecutors, our job has been to shine a light on what has been hidden and establish facts based on the evidence we have gathered. I remain hopeful that this work, while not perfect, can help contribute to reconciliation and a more peaceful future.'[67] Undeniably the arrest and judgment against Karadžić has demonstrated that justice can be achieved in parts and, at least within the legal sphere, each trial enables anti-genocide and human rights law to evolve beyond what it was prior to the tribunal's establishment.[68] Moreover, with increasing numbers of victims, survivors, and their families agreeing to testify and contribute to the justice process, we are potentially being presented with a new, more productive age of cooperation between the prosecutor as peace-builder alongside the victim as testifier.[69] However, the limitations of Karadžić's conviction of genocide again raise the question of the ability of ad hoc international criminal tribunals to successfully target genocide. Indeed, justice and the role of the prosecutor does not end in the courtroom. There are several critical issues that need to be addressed as a result of the shortcomings of the prosecutors since Nuremberg, extending from victim compensation to denial of crimes committed.[70]

7.6 Pursuit of Reconciliation

With the closure of the ICTY, there is an urgency to create a usable historic and legal legacy. The Tribunal acknowledges that the public perception of its work and role is rarely positive, and in response has taken steps to improve its image through the Tribunal's Legacy Project SENSE (South East News Service Europe), providing coverage of the work of the ICTY and ICC by focusing on the victim narrative, descriptions of their ordeal, and documentary footage.[71]

Nonetheless, since 1995 there has been a surge in domestic prosecution of international crimes so as to bring real justice to those who have suffered at the hands of war criminals.[72] The most infamous of these courts, belonging to the ICTR, is another example of where an international criminal tribunal, despite its positive legacy outside of its region, has failed to address the grass roots justice the people desire. As a result of its inability to address the broad scope of crimes committed, bring to justice the considerable number of perpetrators, and promote the country's need for reconciliation, Rwanda's *gacaca* courts ('justice on the

[66] For debates over genocide and crimes against humanity by legal scholars, see Schabas (n 12) 418; H Lauterpacht, *The Function of Law in the International Community* (first published 1933, The Lawbook Exchange, Ltd 2000) 3–4; Lauterpacht (n 12) 49.

[67] S Brammertz, 'Prosecuting Genocide: The ICTY and the Future of International Criminal Justice' (Sarajevo, 11 June 2015) <http://www.icty.org/x/file/Press/Statements%20and%20Speeches/Prosecutor/150611_prosecutor_brammertz_sarajevo_en.pdf> accessed 23 May 2017.

[68] S Brammertz, 'Srebrenica: Remembering and Honoring the Victims of Genocide' (New York, 1 July 2015) <http://www.icty.org/x/file/Press/Statements%20and%20Speeches/Prosecutor/150701_prosecutor_brammertz_un_ny_srebrenica_en.pdf> accessed 23 May 2017.

[69] Brammertz (n 67).

[70] ibid.

[71] M Klarin, 'Building the ICTY Legacy for Local Communities' in R H Steinberg (ed), *Assessing the Legacy of the ICTY* (Martinus Nijhoff Publishers 2011) 111.

[72] SENSE Tribunal, 'About SENSE' <http://www.sense-agency.com/home/home.4.html> accessed 14 June 2017; Klarin (n 71) 112–113; M S Ellis, 'Coming to Terms with its Past—Serbia's New Court for the Prosecution of War Crimes' (2004) 22 (2) Berkeley Journal of International Law 165, 165.

grass') emerged as an attempt to alleviate strain on the tribunal's legal system in a response to the backlog of untried genocide cases and begin a process of reconstructing the damaged social fabric.[73] Whilst Gacaca Law may advocate the objectives of reconciliation and restorative justice, the selective reading of the *gacaca's* legal statute demonstrated in the *gacaca* courts themselves have given way to much speculation over their pursuit of reconciliation. Criticism has included claims that the *gacaca* courts represent fraud justice (disturbingly distinguishing between genocide and war crimes committed during the same era and only trying those accused of genocide), as well as views that within a post-genocide legal, military, and political context, the courts have prolonged the trauma of the victims involved generating a regressive path of reconciliation.[74] Given such views, the shortcomings of the ICTR has arguably led to a flawed domestic risk that has ultimately contributed to the insecurity of all Rwandan citizens in the future since *gacaca* courts pursue inequitable justice, accentuates the ethnic divide, and can be interpreted as revenge.[75]

Domestic human rights courts have not been confined to the jurisdiction of the ICTR. Regarding the ICTY, the Tribunal was never intended to be the sole measure to end impunity for these crimes, and thus its lasting legacy will depend on how local judiciaries continue the prosecution of perpetrators.[76] As a result, domestic War Crimes Chambers have been established across the former Yugoslavia with support from the US government and the ICTY. One example is the Serbian War Crimes Chamber instituted in 2003.[77] Prior to July 2003, only a small number of individuals had been prosecuted and tried for war crimes in Serbia. However, the Serbian War Crimes Prosecutor's Office has since issued a number of indictments, including those transferred from the ICTY's Office of the Prosecutor, for crimes committed in Zvornik, Bosnia and Herzegovina in 1992.[78] Yet despite apparent progress, the War Crimes Chambers, much like the *gacaca* courts, are encountering unique challenges. Arguably, the most pressing is that despite an estimated thirty-two to thirty-five cases being in the investigative or pre-trial stage, overall, the number of prosecutions remains low and the political will necessary to support the trials remains problematic due to a lack of cooperation between Bosnia and Herzegovina, Croatia, and Serbia.[79] Furthermore, the uncertainties around the prosecutor's ability to charge on the basis of command responsibility (despite the legacy of Nuremberg's ruling against the superior orders defence) mean

[73] After decades of violence between the two ethnic groups, the Hutu and Tutsi, in Rwanda, violence peaked in 1994 with the genocide of Tutsis, during which the Hutu majority slaughtered 800,000 Tutsi and moderate Hutus, leaving the country with 120,000 accused *génocidaires* awaiting trial. C J Le Mon, 'Rwanda's Troubled Gacaca Courts' (Winter, 2007) 14 (2) Human Rights Brief 1; A Corey and S F Joireman, 'Retributive Justice: The Gacaca Courts in Rwanda' (2004) 103 African Affairs 73, 73; P Clark, *The Gacaca Courts, Post-Genocide Justice and Reconciliation in Rwanda: Justice Without Lawyers* (Cambridge University Press 2010) 3.

[74] For works condemning the Gacaca courts as fraud justice, see A Wierzynska, 'Consolidating Democracy Through Transitional Justice: Rwanda's Gacaca Courts' [2004] New York University Law Review 1934; Clark (n 73) 342–43. For works in reference to the Gacaca courts as generating prolonged trauma, see Clark (n 73) 19–25; J Sarkin, 'The Tension Between Justice and Reconciliation in Rwanda: Politics, Human Rights, Due Process and The Role of The Gacaca Courts in Dealing with the Genocide' (October 2001) 45 (2) School of Oriental and African Studies 143; K Brounéus, 'Truth-Telling as Talking Cure? Insecurity and Retraumatization in the Rwandan Gacaca Courts' (2008) 39 (1) Security Dialogue 55

[75] Clark (n 73) 345–55; Corey and Joireman (n 73) 73–89.

[76] Human Rights Watch, 'Unfinished Business: Serbia's War Crimes Chamber' (June 2007) <https://www.hrw.org/legacy/backgrounder/eca/serbia0607/1.htm#_ftn1> accessed 14 June 2017; United Nations, International Criminal Tribunal for the former Yugoslavia, 'Development of the Local Judiciaries' <http://www.icty.org/en/outreach/capacity-building/development-local-judiciaries> accessed 14 June 2017; Klarin (n 71) 112.

[77] Human Rights Watch (n 76); Ellis (n 72) 189; ICTY (n 75).

[78] ICTY (n 76). For up-to-date cases in pretrial or investigative stage, see Human Rights Watch (n 76).

[79] ibid.

that without adequate support, funding, and a broader awareness by the public to understand the effort made by the War Crimes Prosecutor's Office (even with the role of SENSE), there is a limit to how successful the War Crimes Chamber can be in prosecuting those responsible for atrocities.[80]

Subsequently, as Carla Del Ponte said in March 2005, the creation of domestic courts demonstrates that 'the public is only interested . . . in politically, not judicially, defined truth' concluding that 'international justice is cheap'.[81] In the case of the ICTY, and similarly the ICTR, their creation was part of a larger political international intervention to reverse the polarizing effects that war and genocide had within these politically divided nation States, and an attempt to construct a new political community and national identity.[82] Therefore, whilst the judicial and legal achievements of the ICTY are significant, ultimately this is a Tribunal that was set up to benefit the citizens of the former Yugoslavia. Thus, in order, to comprehensively assess the Tribunal's legacy, it is essential to examine the impact that it is having on the ground.[83] A comparison between the stance of the ICTY towards reconciliation in 2010 and 2015 does demonstrate some progress, particularly within the international sphere in recognizing their responsibility in remembering the Srebrenica genocide.[84] However, within the public discourse a very different picture remains, illustrated through the 2010 'Pillar of Shame' project which spelt out the letters 'UN' using 16,744 shoes, representing the numbers of the victims of Srebrenica, to highlight the UN's ineffectiveness in preventing the Srebrenica genocide. Furthermore, in 2015, denial and speculation still surrounded the genocide, firstly with supporters for Karadžić preaching his innocence, and secondly with Milorad Dodik, the President of Republika Srpska, declaring Srebrenica as 'the biggest sham of the twentieth century'.[85] Given such toxic politics, it is not surprising that the surviving victims and their families are still seeking justice through an underfunded system with only the hope of reconciliation guiding them though. Until its closure in December 2017, the ICTY faced many problems addressing the rights, grievances, and fears of the communities whilst tackling their legal requirement to gain judicial acceptance for the binding element of these prosecutions.[86]

7.7 Conclusion

What types of usable narratives of atrocity, peace, and reconciliation do prosecutors build from their years of intellectual and practical experience of dealing with war criminals? What

[80] ibid.

[81] R M Hayden, 'What's Reconciliation Got to do With It? The International Criminal Tribunal for the Former Yugoslavia (ICTY) as Antiwar Profiteer' (2011) 5 (3) Journal of Intervention and Statebuilding 313, 314.

[82] M Humphrey, 'International Intervention, Justice and National Reconciliation: The Role of the ICTY and ICTR in Bosnia and Rwanda' (2003) 2 (4) Journal of Human Rights 502–04.

[83] H McRobie, 'What Stands in the Way of Bosnia Reconciliation' (*The Guardian*, 21 June 2010) <https://www.theguardian.com/commentisfree/2010/jun/21/bosnia-still-waits-reconciliation> accessed 6 June 2017; J N Clark, 'The ICTY and the Challenges of Reconciliation in the Former Yugoslavia' (*E-International Relations*, 23 January 2012) <http://www.e-ir.info/2012/01/23/the-icty-and-the-challenges-of-reconciliation-in-the-former-yugoslavia/> accessed 6 June 2017.

[84] R Hodzic, 'Twenty Years Since Srebrenica: No Reconciliation, We're Still at War' (*International Center for Transitional Justice*, 29 June 2015) <https://www.ictj.org/news> accessed 20 June 2017.

[85] McRobie (n 83); Hodzic (n 84).

[86] Humphrey (n 82) 504.

is the legacy of such narratives? This chapter's goal was to bring nuance to the definition of the Nuremberg legacy, following M. Cherif Bassiouni's discussion of the moral-ethical sphere which must remain core to discussions of the cultural legacy and public work of prosecutors beyond the courtroom or in discussions of their impact. It introduced a selection of Telford Taylor's rhetorical propensities at the NMT which curated the impact of the Nazi State that still remained a threat to post-war Germans and their capacity to appreciate the value of bringing a tyrannical dictatorship to account in a post-conflict and peace-aspiring society. Furthermore, it examined Serge Brammertz's efforts to prosecute war criminals in the context of national jurisdiction and genocide denial in the region of the ICTY.

Pro-Nazi sentiments and antisemitism persisted after the war in Germany (occupied, West and East) and in other parts of Europe, but the West's prosecutorial preoccupation with Nazi war criminals waned as the civilizational clash turned to Communism and the spread of dictatorships in Europe and around the world. Taylor's post-war commentary, interviews, and academic writing saw him continue to advocate for justice and the rule of law, however inconvenient and controversial.[87] So, too, has Brammertz. Serbia and the ICTY are now engaged in a war of 'truth' between the political leaders and the public. The resistance to an honest discussion of a genocidal past in Serbia and taking social responsibility for what has been legally sanctioned and recognized at the ICTY is now widespread. Serbia's education minister is threatening to ban textbooks about the Srebrenica genocide and the siege of Sarajevo. These are a few examples of the trend to rewrite or reject unpalatable genocidal pasts that are occurring not just in Serbia, but also in Poland, Hungary, Turkey, and other countries that are actively promoting exclusionary ultra-nationalist politics and dogma. The emergence of the concept of alternative truths, and the valorization of denial of genocidal intention and State-level culpability, and ultra-nationalism, can be attributed to many factors, and tribunals of a national and international variety cannot be the only mechanism to adjudicate and prosecute their inflammatory impacts.[88]

Commenting on the upward trend to revise Serbia's past and the work of trials to reverse that trend, Brammertz optimistically remarked recently that for a 'peaceful future, there must be shared agreement on the recent past'.[89] Doubtless Telford Taylor would have agreed. Both men validated the law's limited transformative impact when used in isolation from other narrative, preventative, and legally binding instruments of justice.

[87] Taylor's activism and writings about Vietnam saw him investigated by the Central Intelligence Agency for alleged communist sympathies. See the (basically unreadable) National Security Archive file as part of the CIA file on Adolf Eichmann <http://nsarchive.gwu.edu/NSAEBB/NSAEBB150/box14_do_file_vol1/doc22.pdf> and Richard Breitman, 'Introductory Entry' Nazi War Crimes Interagency Working Group (IWG), IWG Declassified Records, Records of the Central Intelligence Agency (RG263), National Archives, College Park, MD, USA <https://www.archives.gov/iwg/declassified-records/rg-263-cia-records/rg-263-report.html> accessed 1 July 2017.

[88] On this topic, see T Meron, 'Reflections on the Prosecution of War Crimes by International Tribunals' (July 2006) 100 (3) The American Journal of International Law 551.

[89] E M Lederer, 'Prosecutor: Denial of Yugoslav and Rwanda War Crimes Widespread' (*The Spokesman Review*, 7 June 2017) <http://www.spokesman.com/stories/2017/jun/07/prosecutor-denial-of-yugoslav-and-rwanda-war-crime/> accessed 8 June 2017.

8

Meandering Jurisprudence and Unanticipated Legacies

The ICTY's Reach into Domestic Civil Litigation

Mark Drumbl[*, **]

This chapter examines the ICTY's jurisprudential footprint—its legacy in law. Particularly, it illustrates how footprints and legacies may be unanticipated. We expect international criminal law to infuse the register of domestic criminal law, whether formally through incorporation of treaty and custom or informally through experience and analogy. And, reciprocally, we expect domestic criminal law to inform international criminal law, whether formally through the development of general principles of law or, once again, informally, through experience and analogy. Circulation thereby arises within the curricular sphere of penal responsibility.

Despite the above, the chapter documents the ICTY's footprints as they have wandered into domestic private law and tort litigation. It does so through an assessment of the presence of ICTY materials and case law in domestic civil litigation in the US for gross human rights abuses, specifically in judgments rendered in Alien Tort Statute (ATS)[1] claims brought in US federal courts. The ATS allows victims of human rights abuses to file tort-based lawsuits for violations of the laws of nations (a phrase taken to mean customary international law).

US judges of general jurisdiction who cite ICTY work product to determine the rule of application in an ATS dispute, equally frequently refer to the case law and materials of other institutions, notably the International Criminal Tribunal for Rwanda (ICTR), International Criminal Court (ICC), International Military Tribunals (IMT), and American Military Tribunals (AMT). This chapter delves into the citations made by US federal judges of general jurisdiction to ICTY cases and materials in ATS cases. Among all the international criminal tribunals, the ICTY is cited most often in these cases and, hence, occupies a *primus inter pares* place. This chapter updates ICTY citations, extracts them from the more general data-set elsewhere considered,[2] and places them within the framework of other references made by US judges when adjudicating on ATS matters. However, this journey is much more animated than merely observing and coding citations: it is a journey suffused with richly

* Class of 1975 Alumni Professor at Washington & Lee University, School of Law, where he also serves as Director of the University's Transnational Law Institute. He has held visiting appointments at Oxford University, Université de Paris II (Panthéon-Assas), Vanderbilt University, University of Ottawa, Trinity College Dublin, University of Western Ontario, and University of Illinois College of Law, the University of Melbourne, and the University of Sydney.

** This chapter draws from and in parts updates and expands the author's article: M A Drumbl, 'Extracurricular International Criminal Law' (2016) 16 International Criminal Law Review 412.

1 28 USC § 1350 (2012). The ATS is also known as the Alien Tort Claims Act (ATCA) or Alien Tort Act (ATA).

2 M A Drumbl, 'Extracurricular International Criminal Law' (2016) 16 International Criminal Law Review 412.

Mark Drumbl, *Meandering Jurisprudence and Unanticipated Legacies* In: *Legacies of the International Criminal Tribunal for the Former Yugoslavia*. Edited by: Carsten Stahn, Carmel Agius, Serge Brammertz, Colleen Rohan, Oxford University Press (2020). © The Several Contributors DOI: 10.1093/oso/9780198862956.003.0009

normative and theoretical hues on a variety of themes, including transnational legal migrations, comparative judicial method, and the (ir)relevance of jurisprudential categories.

The experiences of US courts of general jurisdiction as 'receivers' or 'ignorers' of international criminal law are instructive in terms of striking an appropriate relationship between national courts and international law. Should national courts serve as dispassionate law enforcers, as translators of law, as nihilistic deniers of law, or as engaged law creators? Should international judges be mindful of the, at times unforeseen, afterlife of the jurisprudence they create? While international criminal lawyers may welcome the broad diffusion of international norms, including from the criminal to civil context in a rich array of venues, concerns emerge as to whether the content of the norms will fragment and, thereby, weaken international law's purported universality.

In light of the sharply limited capacity of international criminal courts and tribunals, domestic tort claims as avenues for redress for systematic human rights abuses will likely grow in number. The experiences of US courts of general jurisdiction as 'receivers' of international criminal law reveal broader patterns of transnational legal migration that will become increasingly relevant. There is much to learn from these circulatory practices. ATS litigation also constitutes a 'Petri dish' of sorts which shows how and in what fashion customary international law emerges and, more importantly, is seen to emerge.

8.1 Giving Atrocity a Usable Narrative

The ATS dates from the First Congress (1789). It is a succinct instrument that reads as follows:

> The district courts shall have original jurisdiction of any civil action by an alien for a tort only, committed in violation of the law of nations or a treaty of the United States.[3]

The ATS thereby dispenses with the contextual requirement that claimants must allege that customary international law forms an actionable part of the general common law of the jurisdiction in which the claim is brought.[4] To be clear, and unlike other jurisdictions (such as Canada), the question whether customary international law forms part of US federal common law remains an unsettled matter. The ATS obviates these nettlesome conversations by providing a statutory remedy that embeds a cause of action for conduct that violates customary international law.[5]

[3] ibid.

[4] In Canada, see *Araya v Nevsun Resources Ltd* (2016) BCSC 1856 (Supreme Court of British Columbia) (citing inter alia the ICTY Furundzija judgment in this regard); *Bouzari v Islamic Republic of Iran* [2004] OJ No 2800 (Ontario Court of Appeal) paras 63–66; *R v Hape* [2007] 2 SCR 292 (Supreme Court of Canada) para 39 ('prohibitive rules of customary international law should be incorporated into domestic law in the absence of conflicting legislation').

[5] On the other hand, the fact that the ATS provides a statutory grant for judges to apply customary international law displaces conversations as to whether customary international law forms part of the federal common law and, as such, whether it may be directly applicable. In this regard, the ATS offers an easy answer. If the ATS were repealed, however, then human rights activists would lose this access point without having embedded customary international law within the frame of the generally applicable federal common law. That said, it remains unclear whether trends among US judges over the past century would suggest any likelihood that judges would in fact find customary international law to be directly applicable in US Federal Court in this fashion.

The ATS lay largely dormant for two centuries. Beginning in 1980 with the Second Circuit Court of Appeals' judgment in the Filártiga litigation, however, plaintiffs turned to the ATS to pursue redress in US courts for atrocity crimes committed elsewhere.[6] A first wave of litigation targeted individual tortfeasors (natural persons) as direct principle perpetrators. A second wave then arose, which targeted corporate defendants (legal persons) on theories of aiding and abetting abuses committed by natural persons as direct perpetrators.

Plaintiffs face a number of growing hurdles in bringing an ATS claim. First, to demonstrate that the wrongful behaviour constitutes a violation of the 'law of nations'. US courts have generally equated the laws of nations with customary international law. In its 2004 opinion in the *Sosa* case, the US Supreme Court ruled that, while the identification of substantive causes of action under the ATS should proceed cautiously, the statutory remedy is not to be limited only to those violations of the laws of nations acknowledged in 1789.[7] Rather, the remedy covers violations extant today that bear comparable universality and specificity to those that had been recognized in 1789. Courts are to invigilate this process of trans-historical analysis. Actionable contemporary norms must be of sufficiently definite, obligatory, mutual, and universal character. Although the 'law of nations' is taken by US courts to mean customary international law, the importation of these latter criteria further qualifies the traditional understanding of its elements.[8]

Second, plaintiffs must navigate jurisdictional questions about the reach of US courts. In the 2013 Kiobel case, the US Supreme Court curtailed the scope of ATS claims by requiring proof of a compelling nexus with the US:

> [E]ven where the claims touch and concern the territory of the United States, they must do so with sufficient force to displace the presumption against extraterritorial application. Corporations are often present in many countries, and it would reach too far to say that mere corporate presence suffices.[9]

Among the goals of the presumption against extraterritoriality is to 'avoid the international discord that can result when US law is applied to conduct in foreign countries'.[10] An ATS case can no longer proceed if the asserted wrongful conduct has entirely occurred outside of the US; nor can a case proceed if the conduct relevant to the focus of the ATS complaint occurred in a foreign state.[11] A defendant's US citizenship, while relevant, is not on its own

[6] *Filártiga v Peña-Irala*, 630 F 2d 876 (2d Cir 1980) (involving a civil claim by two Paraguayan citizen parents against a Paraguayan police officer who tortured and killed their son in Paraguay; the family initiated the claim after both parties had emigrated to the US).

[7] *Sosa v Alvarez-Machain*, 542 US 692 (2004).

[8] While customary international law constitutes the rule of decision to determine a substantive violation of the ATS, another debate has erupted in ATS jurisprudence: whether customary international law or domestic US law ought to serve as the rule of decision in determining the modes by which an alleged tortfeasor becomes implicated in the tortious conduct. Overall, the tendency appears to be that customary international law should govern this latter determination as well.

[9] *Kiobel v Royal Dutch Petroleum Co*, 133 S Ct 1659, 1669 (2013). The facts of Kiobel involved Nigerian citizens, albeit long-time legal residents of the US on asylum grounds, who pleaded that Dutch, British, and Nigerian oil exploration and extraction corporations aided and abetted the Nigerian government in committing systemic human rights violations during the 1990s. All nine Supreme Court judges dismissed the case, holding that the factual context was too remote from the US to justify allowing the claim to continue.

[10] *RJR Nabisco Inc v European Community*, 136 S Ct 2090 (2016) at 2100.

[11] *Adhikari v Kellogg Brown & Root Incorporated*, 845 F3d 184 (5th Cir 2017).

dispositive to satisfy the requirement that the litigation sufficiently touches and concerns the US. Claims would continue, however, where the underlying conduct (including manufacture, financing, managing, or developing) occurs in the US, where the conduct was intended to impact the US, and possibly where the US may be harbouring an alleged wrongdoer.[12] In 2016 a District Court in Washington State rebutted the presumption against extraterritoriality when the defendant psychologists were US citizens, ran a company located in the US that assisted with interrogations at CIA detention sites outside the country, devised interrogation programmes and allegedly executed contracts in the US.[13] Also in 2016, in a case involving a different statute (the Racketeer Influence and Corrupt Organizations Act), the US Supreme Court backpedalled a bit from the crispness of Kiobel in rebutting the presumption of extraterritoriality.[14]

Third, foreign corporations may no longer be sued as defendants in ATS litigation. In April 2018, the United States Supreme Court ruled as much in a case called *Jesner v Arab Bank*, by flatly holding the inappropriateness of extending ATS liability to foreign corporations.

Finally, plaintiffs must skirt other obstacles as well. These include the political affairs doctrine, availability of immunities, and exhaustion of local remedies. US judges may invoke each and all of these to determine a matter not to be properly justiciable. Governmental and political entities, notably the US State Department, may express firm opinions regarding ongoing litigation—for example, how it interfaces with international comity—and may actively share that opinion with the deciding judges. To be clear, ATS verdicts are infrequently enforced. Victims rarely collect and individual defendants often are impecunious or outside the jurisdiction. At times, cases are settled and compensation will pass hands as part of that settlement.

In sum, and notwithstanding considerable constriction, the ATS persists. Over several decades of implementation and interpretation, ATS litigation has generated a trove of jurisprudence that determines the content of customary international law. The ATS retains key aspects of penal law, in that the tort claim hinges upon finding a breach of a customary international criminal norm. On the other hand, ATS litigation departs from penal proceedings when it comes to venue (civil litigation at the national level), remedy (monetary damages), burden of proof (balance of probabilities), goals (compensation rather than incarceration), standing (private plaintiffs), and management (national judges in courts of general jurisdiction).

ATS litigation, moreover, triggers expressive effects. It ventilates obscured tragedies and empowers victims who initiate claims. ATS litigation also educates the public. The judgment of the Second Circuit Court of Appeals in *Kadić v Karadžić*, for example, widely disseminated the horrors of Bosnian rape camps and endemic gender-based violence at a time when the ICTY was still in its infancy.[15] The Kadić judgment also identified—as early as the mid-1990s—the plausibility that genocide took place in Bosnia.

[12] Following *Kiobel*, an array of US Circuit Courts of Appeal have considered the application of 'touch and concern' to ATS cases. Discussed in M A Drumbl (n 2) 417–21.

[13] *Salim v Mitchell*, 183 F Supp 3d 1121 (2016) (ED WA).

[14] *RJR Nabisco* (n 10).

[15] *Kadić v Karadžić*, 70 F 3d 232 (2d Cir 1995).

8.2 ICTY Materials in ATS Litigation: Research Method and Findings

The ICTY case law and materials are taken to mean: (1) judicial decisions of both the ICTY Trial Chambers and the Appeals Chamber; and (2) the ICTY Statute itself. A search of US federal judgments was initiated through the *WestlawNext* database platform in the summer of 2013.[16] This search generated an opening sample baseline of federal judgments. Judgments decided since 2013 were subsequently integrated into the analysis, albeit on a piecemeal basis, in an effort to qualitatively assess the case law. A second database search was undertaken in the summer of 2015 to consolidate the findings.[17] For this specific chapter, the author undertook a third search in March 2017.[18]

ICTY case law and materials appear only in a modest number of ATS cases. But these citations are neither sporadic nor intermittent, nor are they thoughtless. Which ICTY materials receive the most attention? The ICTY Statute is frequently cited. References are also made to a number of cases. Moreover, when it comes to case citation, a fairly scattershot approach is taken. They are broadly dispersed and not clustered into one or two cases alone. The earlier decisions of the ICTY get more traction, but this appears simply to be because of a matter of time and being a forerunner.

Inconsistent treatment of the same putative rule arises among the differing judicial circuits. The federal courts in the US are organized regionally into 'Circuits' (there are eleven numbered Circuits plus the DC Circuit). This fragmentation among Circuits may vex outside readers, but it actually is somewhat uneventful within the US federal system, insofar as the different Circuits can proceed in their own directions. In situations of serious Circuit splits, however, the US Supreme Court steps in to resolve such *différends*. That said, this variability among judges and Circuits with regard to content and meaning might pose a *sui generis* set of challenges when it comes to international law as a rule of decision, particularly in light of international law's universalizing aspirations and the importance of predictable State consent (as delivered by the federal government). This variability may be problematic when it occurs *within* a national jurisdiction; as it may be problematic when it occurs as *among* different national jurisdictions. In both instances, courts, either within or among national systems, may seek to create international law rather than simply apply international law. Such juridical tendencies earned the scorn of Lord Hoffman in the *Jones v Saudi Arabia* case, which involved a claim of torture brought in the United Kingdom and the applicability *inter se* of immunities to international crimes. In discussing jurisprudence from Italy that dismissed immunities as a lower-order value, Lord Hoffman warned:

> It is not for a national court to 'develop' international law by unilaterally adopting a version of that law which, however desirable, forward-looking and reflective of values it may be, is simply not accepted by other states.[19]

[16] Cody Phillips undertook this search. For much greater detail on the research methodology, see M A Drumbl (n 2).

[17] Annie Cox undertook this search.

[18] This subsequent search identified no additional ICTY citations in the period extending from February 2016 to March 2017.

[19] *Jones v Saudi Arabia* [2006] UKHL 26 para 63 (appeal taken from [2004] EWCA Civ 1394). Sovereign immunity questions continue to be adjudicated in the Italian courts. See *Simoncioni v Germany* Judgment No 238/2014 (Decision No) ILDC 2237 (IT 2014).

Beyond these preliminaries, what are the key findings from the ATS data-set? Five central takeaways can be identified.

8.2.1 Judges Loop ICTY Materials with References to the Work Product of the ICTR, SCSL, IMT, ICC, and AMT

The case law and materials of the ICTY and ICTR overall tend to be cited by US judges in complementary, and often perfunctory, string fashion to support the same substantive legal rule. This methodology suggests that US federal courts view the ICTR and ICTY outputs as confirmatory of each other or, perhaps, that they determine the existence of a substantive legal rule of customary international law when the jurisprudence of the two ad hoc tribunals is aligned.[20] Ordinarily, however, the palpable practice is to more prominently feature the ICTY's work.[21]

US federal courts also cite the Rome Statute and the 'Nuremberg' proceedings (both the IMT and the AMT). On rare occasion, the Special Court for Sierra Leone (SCSL) and the ICJ also surface.[22] Within the text of ATS opinions, the Nuremberg-era sources typically precede discussion of the materials from the contemporary international tribunals. US courts thereby approach the development and crystallization of a customary norm somewhat longitudinally. On the other hand, at times a perceived lack of clarity or continuity in the international jurisprudence militates in favour of US courts' finding that a norm lacks the requisite definiteness and universality. This triggers a fascinating question, to wit, whether the 'progressive development' of the law may paradoxically undermine the existence of a customary rule in the first place. 'Progressive development' may not build law by accretion but, instead, may dissolve the very existence of law, as consistency matters. Hence, do international judges have a responsibility to 'develop' the law modestly in order to preserve its binding nature? What about dissenting judgments? Too vivid a dissent, perhaps, similarly may intimate that a customary rule is no longer clear or definite. In a sense, the pursuit of progressive perfection may risk becoming the enemy of the good.

US courts cite the Rome Statute despite the obvious reality that the US is not a party thereto and, under President Bush, had in fact renounced its signature on the treaty.[23] References to the Rome Statute are often made to consolidate, buttress, or support interpretations of the laws of nations grounded in citations to the ad hoc tribunals and Nuremberg-era institutions. References to the Rome Statute, however, also arise in contexts of dissonance and fragmentation, typically with regard to the requirements for aiding and abetting liability where the approach of the Rome Statute may be contrasted to that attributed to the ICTR and ICTY. Whereas the Rome Statute's approach is seen as propounding a specific intent requirement for aiding and abetting, ICTR and ICTY materials tend to be understood to

[20] *Khulumani v Barclay Nat'l Bank Ltd*, 504 F 3d 254, 278 n14 (2d Cir 2007) (Katzmann J, concurring).

[21] The ICTY also is given particular gravitas. See ibid 254, 279 (Katzmann J, concurring, citing Brownlie in support of the proposition that '[t]he ICTY has been specifically recognized as having provided "a number of significant findings on issues of law"' and also citing Cassese to make a similarly pioneering point).

[22] See *Doe v Nestle*, 748 F Supp 2d 1057, 1068–69, 1083, 1126 (CD CA 2010), rev'd in part and vacated in part, 766 F 3d 1013 (9th Cir 2014).

[23] *Khulumani* (n 20) (Katzmann J, concurring, applying the finding of the ICTY Trial Chamber in Furundzija that the Rome Statute may be taken 'as constituting an authoritative expression of the legal views of a great number of states').

support a knowledge requirement. So, for example, in *Doe VIII*, the Ninth Circuit Court of Appeals held that the ad hoc tribunals 'have declared the knowledge standard suffices under customary international law'.[24] In this context, the Circuit Court in *Doe VIII* relied primarily on the work of the ICTY.[25]

The entangled nature of these citations suggests that US judges perceive international courts and tribunals as constituting some form of system, though also acknowledge dissonance within that system.

8.2.2 Judges Take ICTY Materials as Evidence of the Existence and Content of a Rule of Customary International Law

A district court in the District of Columbia described the ICTY (and ICTR) as 'authoritative' on the subject of interpreting customary international law.[26] A decade earlier, another district court judge had held:

> United States courts that have been required to describe elements of the 'law of nations' or other international law concepts have frequently turned to the decisions of the International Criminal Tribunals for the Former Yugoslavia and Rwanda, and have, with apparently only one exception, approved of such decisions.[27]

US federal courts appear to consider the case law and materials of international criminal courts and tribunals alternately as *sources* of international law,[28] or as *evidence* of customary international law.[29] Although these materials help identify and legitimate a rule of decision, this vacillation among US judges generates some doctrinal confusion. Furthermore, those courts that view these materials as sources hedge as to whether these are primary or subsidiary sources pursuant to Article 38 of the Statute of the International Court of Justice. The most representative way to describe the approach of US federal judges, however, is that they turn to ICTY case law and materials as authoritative evidence of the existence and content of a customary rule (in other words, of the state of customary international law). In her 2005 opinion on the motion for judgment on the pleadings in *Presbyterian Church*, Judge Cote also emphasized the following indicia of the jurisprudential value of the ICTY and

[24] *Doe VIII v Exxon Mobil Corp*, 654 F 3d 11, 30–31, 36 (D C Cir 2011); see also ibid 34 ('The knowledge standard appears to conform with the standard for aiding and abetting liability in many other countries, including France, Germany, England, Canada, Australia, and Switzerland').

[25] ibid 34.

[26] *Doe v Exxon Mobil*, 2015 WL 5042118, 7 (DDC) (noting also that '[t]he decisions of the International Military Tribunal at Nuremberg and the other post-World War II Nuremberg tribunals also provide authoritative guidance about the content of customary international law').

[27] *Presbyterian Church of Sudan v Talisman Energy Inc*, 226 FRD 456, 478 n 21 (SDNY 2005). cf *Mehinovic v Vuckovic*, 198 F Supp 2d 1322, 1344 (ND GA 2002) (noting that the statutes and opinions of the ad hoc tribunals are 'particularly relevant').

[28] See *Doe VIII* (2011) (n 24); *Doe* (2014) (n 22) 1020.

[29] See *Presbyterian Church v Talisman*, 374 F Supp 2d 331, 338 (SD NY 2005) (Judge Cote holding that: 'Although the Tribunals do not create *new rules* of customary international law, they occupy a special role in enunciating the current content of customary international law norms. ICTY and ICTR opinions typically engage in nuanced and exhaustive surveys of international legal sources, and as such, they are exceedingly useful as persuasive evidence of the content of customary international law norms'); see also *Almog v Arab Bank*, 471 F Supp 2d 257, 287 (ED NY 2007).

ICTR Statutes: (1) their creation by Security Council resolution, which are binding upon all member states; (2) the imperative nature of their prosecutorial mandates; and (3) their purpose to 'adjudicate violations of customary international law'.[30]

8.2.3 Confirmatory, but also Juris-generative or Juris-nihilist

For the most part, references to ICTY materials in domestic ATS litigation primarily reinforce or confirm the existence of certain substantive rules of customary international law. At times, however, these references are juris-generative in that they establish new law, applicable directly at the national level, which may in fact be more progressive than the extant rules as generally understood. For example, *Lively* references ICTY judgments (and other international sources) to support the proposition that an orchestrated campaign of intimidation of LGBTI persons constitutes persecution as a crime against humanity.[31] Specific mention was made of the Naletilić and Martinović Trial Judgment as supporting the proposition that 'international courts have interpreted the identity of the group requirement broadly to encompass persecution of a discrete identity', and of the *Tadić* Trial Judgment to help ground the ruling that 'customary international law does not in general limit the type of group that may be targeted for persecution'. In other instances, however, judges assertively turn to international materials so as to conclude that a particular rule does not exist as custom. In sum, then, the recourse to international materials may serve purposes that are activist and, in this sense, may constitute yet another device that common law judges deploy in attaining the outcomes that they simply wish to obtain. ICTY materials, therefore, become both juris-generative, as well as juris-nihilist (or juris-eliminationist).

The fact that many ATS cases are initially adjudicated on motions to dismiss or summary judgment motions—in which the facts are taken in the most favourable fashion for the plaintiffs and the legal standard of pleading is one of plausibility[32]—may encourage a slightly more elastic view of the content of customary international law.[33]

8.2.4 Which Rules?

References to the ICTY materials are diverse but cluster around three substantive areas: (1) aiding and abetting as a mode of liability; (2) the definition and legal elements of genocide and crimes against humanity; and (3) corporate liability. This section discusses each area

[30] *Presbyterian Church* (n 29) 338. Judge Cote also viewed decisions of the Nuremberg tribunals in this fashion. ibid 336 n 10–11. *Quaere* whether it is appropriate for her to do so in light of the fact that these tribunals were established in very different fashion than the ICTY or ICTR. Judge Cote felt similarly about the ICC. ibid 339. As regards the ICC, she noted: 'The objections raised by the United States [to the Rome Statute] centered on the *procedures* contained in the final draft ... not the *substance* of the international legal rules contained therein.'

[31] *Sexual Minorities of Uganda v Lively*, 960 F Supp 304, 310 (D MA 2013) ('[M]any authorities implicitly support the principle that widespread, systematic persecution of individuals based on their sexual orientation and gender identity constitutes a crime against humanity that violates international norms').

[32] See *Ashcroft v Iqbal*, 556 US 662, 678 (2009) ('To survive a motion to dismiss, a complaint must contain sufficient factual matter, accepted as true, to "state a claim to relief that is plausible on its face"'). In reviewing a motion to dismiss, the court must accept as true all factual allegations in the complaint and draw all reasonable inferences in favour of the party that resists the motion.

[33] Many ATS judgments also arise on motions for leave to amend existing complaints.

in turn. ICTY materials are invoked both by plaintiffs, as well as defendants. On this note, ICTY (and international) cases and materials do not necessarily serve only to expand the law but, instead, may serve to narrow it down—this is particularly the case when it comes to the question of corporate liability under the ATS. Interestingly, ICTY cases also have been introduced into evidence to 'provide a comprehensive review of the background of the [Balkans] conflict'[34] and, in this regard, the value of the ICTY's work is not only jurisprudential, but also historical, as an authentic and authoritative narrative source of what 'happened'.

8.2.4.1 Aiding and Abetting

Establishing the availability and parameters of aiding and abetting liability under customary international law became particularly salient to ATS litigation once plaintiffs targeted corporations as defendants insofar as corporations could only be accessorily linked to the wrongdoing. ICTY materials inform judicial conversations about the existence of aiding and abetting liability under customary international law[35] and, secondly, help delineate the required elements of such liability (i.e. addressing whether a defendant need act only with knowledge of the criminal goals or must purposefully intend to facilitate those goals). The existence of aiding and abetting liability is settled in ATS jurisprudence. Considerable fractiousness, however, emerges regarding the elements that a plaintiff must establish both in pleading and subsequently at trial. This fractiousness reflects the reality, as these questions are not neatly resolved in and among the enabling instruments and practices of the various international criminal courts and tribunals.

The *actus reus* of aiding and abetting requires proof of providing assistance or other forms of support to the commission of a crime. This assistance must be substantial. Controversy arises, however, over whether international law imposes the additional requirement that assistance must be specifically directed towards the commission of the crime. In 2014, the ICTY resolved quarrels regarding proof of specific direction in Šainović when, overturning its own antecedent case law, the ICTY Appeals Chamber ruled in favour of rejecting the specific direction requirement as part of the *actus reus* in contexts where the defendant is remote from the crimes.[36] In December 2015, the Šainović approach was affirmed by the ICTY Appeals Chamber in its judgment in Stanisić and Simatović. The ICTY's departure from the specific direction requirement has nonetheless not defused this controversy

[34] *Mehinovic* (n 27) 1329. See also ibid 1344: 'The United States has explicitly endorsed the approach of the ICTY Statute and the convening of the Tribunal'.

[35] See *Khulumani* (n 20) (per curiam). In his concurring opinion, Judge Katzmann relied heavily on ICTY materials, holding that 'the provision of aiding and abetting liability in the ICTY statute reflects a determination by both the Secretary-General and the Security Council […] that such liability is firmly established in customary international law'). ibid 274 (see also ibid at 275 in which ICTY case law is discussed: 'The [ICTY] … conducted a probing and thoughtful analysis of international law sources in its early decisions to confirm that aiding and abetting liability is recognized in customary international law'). Judge Hall instead relied on federal common law. ibid 284–92. See also: *Doe v Nestle* (n 22) ('Aiding and abetting liability is prominent in the Nuremberg Tribunals, the International Criminal Tribunals for the Former Yugoslavia and Rwanda, and the Statute of the International Criminal Court'); *Presbyterian Church v Talisman*, 453 F Supp 2d 633, 666–68 (SD NY 2006).

[36] *Prosecutor v Šainović* (Judgment) ICTY-05-87-A (23 January 2014) paras 1617–25. In this case, the ICTY Appeals Chamber explicitly rejected the position on specific direction in the *actus reus* that had been adopted in the earlier and controversial Perišić case (*Prosecutor v Perišić* (Judgment) ICTY-04-81-A (28 February 2013)). Relatedly, the Appeals Chamber of the Special Court for Sierra Leone also decided not to pursue the specific direction requirement in the Taylor case. (See *Prosecutor v Taylor* (Appeals Judgment) SCSL-03-01-A (26 September 2013) para 486.) Because of the framing of the appeal by the defence, however, much of the discussion of specific direction in the *Taylor* appeals judgment took place within the elements of the *mens rea*. ibid paras 471–81.

within ATS adjudication. While noting the rejection of the specific direction test by the SCSL and some ICTY judgments (though not the repudiation of the test in Šainović), the Ninth Circuit nonetheless refused to formally relax the specific direction requirement for domestic purposes.[37] The District of Columbia Circuit, on the other hand, remains unyielding in its view that specific direction is not an element of aiding and abetting liability under customary international law.[38]

The standard for *mens rea* in aiding and abetting triggers additional debate, notably, whether knowledge alone, given proof of the substantial effect of the defendant's acts upon the commission of the crime, suffices or whether purpose must be shown. US judges are split when it comes to the knowledge or purpose element. Some rely on knowledge alone.[39] These judges, for example on the District of Columbia Circuit, have invoked ICTY materials.[40] The jurisprudence of the ad hoc tribunals is generally taken to affirm a knowledge standard. Other US judges, however, require the higher bar of intentionality. On this note, in the Second Circuit the appropriate test is whether the defendants acted with the purpose to aid and abet the violations of customary international law committed by someone else.[41] The Fourth Circuit, after conducting a detailed review of international materials, approaches the question similarly.[42] As discussed in detail *infra*, judges who prefer this option look beyond the ad hoc tribunals for support, and incline towards the Rome Statute as an authoritative source. The Ninth Circuit for its part has declined to formally establish whether a purpose or knowledge standard applies to aiding and abetting ATS claims.[43] That said, within the Ninth Circuit, in January 2017 a US District Court in the Northern District of California interpreted persuasive authority as 'point[ing] strongly toward purpose as the governing *mens rea* standard'.[44]

8.2.4.2 Existence of Genocide and Crimes Against Humanity Under Customary International Law and Identification of Elements Thereof

US judges consult ICTY materials in support of the prohibition of genocide and crimes against humanity as customary international law and, as a secondary matter, to clarify key elements thereof.[45] A number of these citations was used to determine that crimes against

[37] *Doe v Exxon Mobil Corp*, 69 F Supp 3d 75 (D C Cir 2014).

[38] *Doe v Exxon* (n 26) 10.

[39] See *Romero v Drummond*, 552 F 3d 1303 (11th Cir 2008); *Sinaltrainal v Coca-Cola Co*, 578 F 3d 1252 (11th Cir 2009).

[40] *Doe* VIII (2011) (n 24); *Doe* (2014) (n 22) 1023. Assessing the US case-law, Manuel Ventura argues that purpose does not reflect customary international law. M J Ventura, 'Farewell "Specific Direction": Aiding and Abetting War Crimes and Crimes Against Humanity in Perišić, Taylor, Šainović et al., and US Alien Tort Statute Jurisprudence' in S C-Maslen (ed), *The War Report: Armed Conflict in 2013* (Oxford University Press 2014) 511–53, 513.

[41] *Mastafa v Chevron Corp*, 770 F 3d 170, 191–92 (2d Cir 2014). In the Second Circuit, the 'mens rea standard for aiding and abetting liability in ATS actions is purpose rather than knowledge alone' (noting also 'the lack of a sufficient international consensus' for imposing individual liability for persons 'who knowingly (but not purposefully) aid and abet a violation of international law').

[42] *Aziz v Alcolac Inc*, 658 F 3d 388 (4th Cir 2011).

[43] *Doe* (2014) (n 22) 1023–24. The Ninth Circuit found sufficiently plausible evidence to satisfy the more 'stringent' purpose standard in this case and hence allowed the proceedings to continue without needing to resolve the legal question.

[44] *Brill v Chevron Corp*, 2017 WL 76894 (ND CA, 2017).

[45] See *Krishanti v Rajaratnam*, No 2.09-cv-05395, 2010 WL 3429592 8 (D NJ 26 August 2010); *Almog* (n 29) 275 (citing the Tadić trial judgment in support of the proposition that '[t]o be a crime against humanity, the emphasis must not be on the individual but rather on the collective—the individual is victimized not because of his or her individual attributes but because of membership in a targeted civilian population'); *Bowoto v Chevron Corporation*, No C 99-02506 SI, 2007 WL 2349343 (ND CA) (citing the Limaj trial judgment in support of the meaning of

humanity are proscribed by customary international law.[46] An impulse may arise to cite the ICTY (and the ICTR and Rome Statute) because of the absence of a comprehensive treaty prohibiting crimes against humanity, unlike the case of genocide. These judicial references intimate that the work of international criminal courts and tribunals can fill gaps when treaty law is unavailable to constitute first-best evidence of a rule of customary international law.

ICTY sources also help elucidate the elements of these crimes. They have clarified the definition of genocide and of the requisite level of specific intent,[47] as well as the substantiality requirement.[48] Furthermore, they have legitimized the inference of genocidal intent from facts and circumstances,[49] and have been invoked to assess the level of knowledge of an accused to establish liability for crimes against humanity.[50] The materials are also used to define elements of persecution as a crime against humanity, including the purposive finding of protected groups in the *Lively* trial judgment discussed earlier. When the US judges adjudicating ATS claims have faced the challenge of identifying whether a food or medical blockade constitutes a crime against humanity, they relied on the ICTY decisions as well. In *Sarei v Rio Tinto*, the Ninth Circuit had held that such a blockade could not constitute a crime against humanity:

> The ICTR and the ICTY do not refer to deprivation of food and medicine. [...] The ICTY requires the 'intent to kill on a massive scale.' *Prosecutor v Brdjanin*, Case No. IT-99-36-A, 477 (Int'l Crim. Trib. for the Former Yugoslavia Apr. 3, 2007).
>
> [...] Plaintiffs' claim for crimes against humanity can come within the statutes only if the blockade constitutes 'other inhumane acts.' A food and medical blockade may well be an 'other inhumane act[ ]' constituting a crime against humanity. The International Law Commission has recognized that the statutes could not list every possible crime against humanity, stating that 'it was impossible to establish an exhaustive list of the inhumane acts which might constitute crimes against humanity.' *Prosecutor v Kupreskic*, et al., IT-95-16-T, Judgment, 565 n. 828 (Jan. 14, 2000) (quoting Report of the International Law Commission on the Work of its Forty-Eighth Session, 6 May-26 July 1996, UNGAOR 51st Sess. Supp. No. 10 (A/51/10) (Crimes Against the Peace and Security of Mankind), 17).
>
> To meet the [...] test, however, the blockade must be a violation of a recognized specific norm. The statutes do not create such a norm. There is no source of recognized international law that yet identifies a food and medical blockade as an 'other inhumane act[ ]' or otherwise qualifies it as a crime against humanity.[51]

'widespread' and 'systematic', the Blaskić appeals judgment in support of the meaning of 'systematic', and the Tadić, Kunarac, Kupreskić cases to clarify the meaning of 'population', and the Galić case to clarify the determination of crimes against humanity generally).

46 See *Doe v Rafael Saravia*, 348 F Supp 2d 1112, 1115 (ED CA 2004).
47 *Abagninin v AMVAC Chem Corp*, 545 F 3d 733, 739 (9th Cir 2008).
48 *Doe v Qi*, 349 F Supp 2d 1258, 1307 (ND CA 2004).
49 *Presbyterian Church* (n 29) 456, 479.
50 *Mehinovic* (n 27) 1322, 1352–54.
51 *Sarei v Rio Tinto*, 671 F 3d 736, 767–68 (9th Cir 2011) *vacated*, 133 S Ct 1995 (2013) to follow Kiobel, remanded to 722 F 3d 1109 (9th Cir 2013). On remand, the initial district court opinion to dismiss with prejudice was affirmed. A vacated opinion should have no precedential effect but Doe (2014) explicitly re-affirmed the analysis of the vacated 2011 Sarei opinion on the topic of corporate liability. The Sarei litigation involved a claim brought by residents of Papua New Guinea against an international mining company.

US courts have also turned to ICTY materials where a non-State actor is alleged to commit crimes against humanity, in particular, regarding the question whether the non-State actor must exercise a level of de facto control over territory in order to be held responsible. US judges similarly relied on Tribunal's work when examining the policy requirement for crimes against humanity.[52] In *Krishanthi v Rajaratnam*, a district court found that the LTTE (Sri Lanka) met this burden for the purposes of plausibility pleading. The Ninth Circuit turned to the Limaj Trial Judgment to rule that '[d]e facto control thus requires control similar to that of a State or government, such as erecting checkpoints on main roads, increasing examples of command and control, developing civilian structures, and holding a substantial percentage of territory'.[53] Whether the de facto control requirement firmly exists as an element of the plan, or policy aspect of crimes against humanity under customary international law, remains unclear.

Finally, ICTY materials have been deployed to elucidate grave breaches and aspects of war crimes[54] and command responsibility.[55]

8.2.4.3 Corporate Liability

ICTY materials have been interpreted as germane to the sinuous (and finally resolved) question whether corporations can be found criminally liable under international criminal law and, hence, by analogy to the question whether they may incur civil liability for violations of the laws of nations. While ICTY materials are seen as helpful to these debates, judges have along this journey drawn strikingly different inferences from them.

The District of Columbia Circuit in *Doe VIII v Exxon* (2011),[56] and the Seventh Circuit in Flomo (2011),[57] each has held that corporations can be sued under the ATS. The Doe VIII litigation, staccato in nature because of appeals, reversals, *vacaturs*, and remands, continues: in July 2015, the district court allowed some of the ATS claims to continue because they displaced the presumption against extraterritoriality and because the law in the D.C. Circuit is clear that corporations can be sued under the ATS.[58] In Doe VIII, Judge Kavanaugh dissented in the Circuit Court of Appeals. He opined that the ATS did not reach corporate actors.[59] To buttress his conclusion, he referenced the ICTY as only having jurisdiction over natural persons. In this regard, the establishment of international tribunals to punish individuals may paradoxically crimp the ability of the law to reach entities or

[52] See *Abagninin* (n 47) (interpreting the Tadić Trial Judgment as indicating that 'the traditional conception ... was that a policy must be present and must be that of a state', but noting that '[t]his conception was expanded [in Tadić] to include non-State entities which, although not part of the legitimate government, have de facto control over a defined territory').

[53] ibid.

[54] *Mehinovic* (n 27) 1322.

[55] *Doe v Qi* (n 48) 1258, 1307.

[56] *Doe VIII* (n 24) 57 ('Given that the law of every jurisdiction in the United States and of every civilized nation, and the law of numerous international treaties, provide that corporations are responsible for their torts, it would create a bizarre anomaly to immunize corporations from liability for the conduct of their agents').

[57] *Flomo v Firestone National Rubber Company*, 643 F 3d 1013, 1019 (7th Cir 2011).

[58] *Doe v Exxon* (n 26). Although the 2011 Circuit Court of Appeals opinion in *Doe VIII* has been vacated, the reasons for *vacatur* and the course of subsequent proceedings in the litigation reaffirm the legal analysis of the Court of Appeals on the critical points of jurisdiction, corporations as defendants, methodological recourse to international materials, and aiding and abetting liability.

[59] *Doe VIII* (n 24) 83–84 (Kavanaugh, J., dissenting); see also *Khulumani* (n 20) 254, 321–26 (2d Cir, 2007) (opinion of Judge Korman, relying on several international sources to express considerable scepticism regarding the existence of corporate liability under customary international law).

collectivities. The expansion of a system of international law that individualizes guilt may narrow the range of appropriate defendants.

On the other hand, other judges turned to the same set of ICTY materials and reached an opposite conclusion. For example, Judge Cote, in dismissing the motion for judgment on the pleadings in Presbyterian Church, held:

> [That] the ICTY and ICTR Statutes do not provide for corporate criminal liability for genocide and other atrocities carries very little weight as those Statutes were devised in the context of ethnic and tribal warfare where atrocities committed by private individuals, not corporations, loomed large. Such an argument is akin to claiming that a rule governing the law of the sea has not reached the status of customary international law because a number of landlocked States have not accepted it.[60]

That said, and to be very clear, Judge Cote's view was even at the time no longer good law in her own court, the Second Circuit. In 2010, the Second Circuit ruled that corporations may not be held liable for violations of international law under the ATS.[61] This 2010 ruling arose in the Kiobel litigation that eventually went to the Supreme Court. While it was widely anticipated at the time that the Supreme Court would decide Kiobel on the question whether corporations can be sued under the ATS, in part because of splits among lower courts, the Supreme Court subsequently ordered the case to be newly briefed and approached it from the unanticipated perspective of extraterritoriality and jurisdiction. The Supreme Court's opinion in Kiobel did not address corporate liability. Interestingly, in the 2014 Mastafa case, the Second Circuit did not seize the opportunity to dismiss the complaint because of the corporate nature of the two defendants.[62] One District Court judge has interpreted the US Supreme Court's mention in Kiobel that 'mere corporate presence' cannot overcome the presumption against extraterritoriality as implicitly indicating the existence of corporate liability.

In September 2014, in *Doe v Nestle*, the Ninth Circuit ruled that there is no categorical rule of corporate immunity or liability under the ATS. In this regard, the Ninth Circuit explicitly reaffirmed the corporate liability analysis it had previously reached pre-Kiobel in *Sarei v Rio Tinto*.[63] This analysis requires a court's attention, in each claim, to international law and determination of whether corporations are subject to the norms underlying that specific claim.[64] Claims in the *Doe v Nestle* litigation—brought by former child slaves forced to harvest cocoa in Côte d'Ivoire—involved allegations that defendant corporations aided and abetted child slavery by providing assistance to the Ivorian farmers. The Ninth Circuit Court of Appeals held that the prohibition against slavery was universal and could be asserted against the corporate defendants. The Ninth Circuit had previously held in Sarei that

[60] *Presbyterian Church* (n 29) 331, 336 (motion for judgment on the pleadings); see also ibid 336 n 10 ('Indeed, for the purposes of this case, the value of the ICTY and ICTR Statutes, as well as the decisions of their Tribunals and ATS cases addressing similar subject matter . . . is that they confirm that customary international law prohibiting violations of *jus cogens* norms such as genocide applies to private actors *in addition to* state actors').

[61] *Kiobel* (n 9) 111, 120 (relying on the lack of corporate liability in international tribunals as evidence of customary international law disfavoring corporate liability).

[62] *Mastafa* (n 41).

[63] *Doe* (2014) (n 22) 1021–22 (affirming the three principles about corporate liability: no categorical immunity, liability under the ATS is independent of international norms of enforcement, and universal norms can provide the basis for an ATS claim against a corporation) (citing Sarei (n 51)).

[64] ibid 1022 ('First, the analysis proceeds norm-by-norm').

the norms against genocide and against war crimes were applicable to corporations.[65] In Sarei, in fact, the Ninth Circuit had held that a norm could form the basis for an ATS claim even in the absence of a decision from an international tribunal enforcing that norm against a corporation. Returning to the *Doe v Nestle* litigation, the Ninth Circuit held that 'corporate liability under an ATS claim does not depend on the existence of international precedent enforcing legal norms against corporations'.[66] Of significance is that the Ninth Circuit in *Doe* buttressed its finding with reference to Article 5(c) of the ICTY Statute. The Ninth Circuit noted that, pursuant to the ICTY Statute, the condemnation of 'persons responsible' for enslavement of civilian populations was 'broadly phrased', which it took as evidence that 'the prohibition against slavery applied to state actors and non-state actors alike, and there are no rules exempting acts of enslavement carried out on behalf of a corporation'.[67]

In 2018, the US Supreme Court, as mentioned earlier, finally and definitively ruled that the ATS does not permit corporate liability in the case of foreign corporations. So ends this saga.[68]

8.2.5 Nothing More (or Less) than Simple Legal Realism?

A review of ATS jurisprudence reveals the existence of varied approaches of US judges to customary international law. Some tread cautiously with regard to its content, while others proceed quite audaciously. Another group ignores international law entirely, even when called upon to enforce the ATS which requires application of the law of nations. US federal judges are, therefore, attitudinally diverse. This contradicts the general image of the US as monolithically shying away from purposive interpretations of international legal norms. US courts, and thus US judges of general jurisdiction, engage, and remain engaged with, nettlesome questions central to the practice of international criminal law. They approach the subject matter creatively, and give life to international authorities in unexpected ways unforeseen to international criminal lawyers.

On the other hand, all this diversity may suggest little more than judicial opportunism, and the deployment of citations to legitimate preferred a priori outcomes. In this regard, the availability of international sources and materials may simply constitute another arrow in the indeterminate quiver of the common law method.

8.3 Theoretical Questions

This chapter identifies cases in which US federal judges adjudicating ATS disputes have relied upon ICTY cases and materials, and discusses how and for which purposes these materials—along with those of other international institutions—have been received. The research is best described as rudimentary and qualitative: elemental tabulations. These

65 *Sarei* (n 51) (finding no bar to genocide liability under the ATS for corporations).

66 *Doe* (2014) (n 22) 1021 (noting also that 'the absence of decisions finding corporations liable does not imply that corporate liability is a legal impossibility under international law' and 'that the lack of decisions holding corporations liable could be explained by strategic considerations').

67 ibid 1022.

68 *Jesner v Arab Bank*, 138 S Ct 1386 (3 April 2018).

modest research findings nonetheless evoke a fascinating story of legal transplant, migration, digestion, legacy, and professionalism—on this latter point, the relationship of national judges with international law.

This chapter identifies a new usage of the ICTY's work product. What to make of it? On the one hand, these migrations facilitate wider awareness, recognition, and internalization of international criminal law. It is not assured, however, that the content of the law thusly diffused is accurately appreciated by national judges, or is even capable of predictable appreciation, thereby imperilling international law's general aspirations of doctrinal consistency, universalism, and legitimacy. International jurisprudence—no different than any sources of law or precedent—may be misapplied, or wishfully applied, in national contexts. International judgments involving the specifics of a conflict or of a state with which national judges may have little familiarity may be particularly susceptible to error in terms of subsequent extracurricular application.

The turn by US judges to international materials in ATS litigation represents an example of what Anthea Roberts identifies as 'comparative international law', that is, the reality that national courts are more than just international law enforcers, but may also serve as international law creators, and that national variations in the judicialized domestication of international law is a subject worthy of study.[69] At times, moreover, the US experience in ATS litigation is that certain judges ignore international law entirely, and determine the content of the 'laws of nations' by reference to US law only, or US incorporation of international law alone.

International law, as shaped and created by national courts and, therefore, possibly divergent in certain areas, is, according to Roberts, a reality that ought to be central to any discussion of international law's sources. On this note, perhaps Lord Hoffman's admonition of national courts as international law creators is ill-placed. While the *Lively* court may be chastised for creating a new rule of international law, it may simply be unwise to expect a national court to exercise greater restraint in applying customary international law than national constitutional or human rights law. Acting in such a fashion might excessively prioritize the place of legislatures and executives in the process of incorporating international law. Drawing from the work of Karen Knop, who posits national courts as translators of norms rather than mere enforcers of norms, Roberts observes that 'even if national courts attempt to faithfully enforce international law, its domestication requires them to simultaneously assert their own legal language'.[70]

As among courts of various states, then, questions arise as to 'what extent national courts engage in strategic interpretation' of customary international law, rather than interpretation 'based on prevailing practice and *opinio juris*'.[71] Within the courts of a specific State, divergent understandings among national judges as to the substantive content of international law may reflect the most prosaic insights of legal realism. That is, the availability of international law may simply accord judges another tool or device to achieve what they already

[69] A Roberts, 'Comparative International Law? The Role of National Courts in Creating and Enforcing International Law' (2011) 60 International and Comparative Law Quarterly 57, 60. Comparative international law studies how actors in different national and regional systems interpret, understand, and apply international law.

[70] ibid 74, 76 ('The repeated application of international law by the national courts of particular countries may, over time, lead to distinct dialects developing that exist somewhere between international and national law, and between law enforcement and creation').

[71] P H Verdier and M Versteeg, 'International Law in National Legal Systems: An Empirical Investigation' (2015) 109 American Journal of International Law 514, 533, 531.

wish to achieve within the often fraught indeterminacy and selectivity of judicial method, in particular, in common law jurisdictions.

The purposes of tort law may differ so significantly from those of criminal law, either in general or specifically in the case of massive human rights violations, that movement from one realm to the other should best be viewed cautiously. Extracurricular application could therefore be dissuaded. International criminal tribunals, on this note, might *ex ante* preempt such movement by declaring that their work product ought to have limited reach. Judges on international tribunals might thereby disclaim the possibility that their national counterparts operating in courts of general jurisdiction pick up their work product and apply it to private law disputes.

ATS litigation, nonetheless, opens up questions as to the relationships between tort law and criminal law in transitional justice generally. Interestingly, in the Khulumani litigation (which concerned claims brought by South Africans that multinational corporations should be liable for aiding and abetting the *apartheid* regime), Judge Katzmann, citing the Furundzija Trial Chamber judgment, held that 'the ICTY has recognized the propriety of civil remedies for violations of international criminal law in certain circumstances', specifically referencing torture.[72]

8.4 Conclusion: A Call for Greater Endogeneity

Manuel Ventura notes that defense teams at the ICTY and SCSL have relied on ATS cases in arguing for an enhanced purpose requirement for aiding and abetting liability. Ventura laments, however, that when the SCSL and ICTY judges came to visit, and then revisit, the specific direction requirement, they failed to appreciate the pertinent analyses of US courts.[73] He suggests that the debate over the *mens rea* requirements that plague ATS litigation is a 'mirror image' to the debates over the requirements of the *actus reus* in cases of remoteness of the accused; yet, the international tribunals have failed to learn from the robust conversations that have occurred within the ATS context.[74] Interestingly, national courts in different jurisdictions that may—on occasion—be called upon to adjudicate civil liability for international crimes may reference ATS cases. The British Columbia Supreme Court, for example, cited ATS cases in preliminary proceedings on a contemporary slavery claim against a corporate defendant.[75]

Hence, while international norms may have extracurricular application in this specific instance at the domestic civil level, and national courts may reference each other *inter se* even among different jurisdictions, debates within the domestic civil level inspired by the international migration tend not to percolate into the international realm. A lack of endogeneity arises. As Ventura aptly notes, while US courts 'are cognizant of the discussions and debates in ICL,' even in extracurricular contexts, 'international lawyers should also be similarly aware that there is more to ICL than the four corners of The Hague'.[76] This

[72] *Khulumani* (n 20) 270.

[73] Ventura (n 40) 546 ('There was no substantive engagement or analysis' of the reasoning in *Doe VIII* or Presbyterian Church).

[74] ibid 512.

[75] *Araya* (n 4) paras 473–75.

[76] Ventura (n 40) 548.

admonition is pertinent. International law happens in many places far removed from its venerated centres. A new wave of scholarship is emerging which explores the diverse historical hinterland of international criminal law and hence epistemologically pluralizes the roots from which we as international lawyers imagine our own discipline to grow.[77] As a profession, we would do well to embrace the diverse and disconnected venues—and the clever yet on occasion clumsy ways—in which international law is manufactured, often by *bricolage*. Fetishizing the reified, and often languid, vortices of the high-profile international tribunals belies the vivacity and eclecticism of the places that make, apply, and chide international law.

[77] K Heller and G Simpson (eds), *The Hidden Histories of War Crimes Trials* (Oxford University Press 2013); M A Drumbl, 'Stepping Beyond Nuremberg's Halo: The Legacy of the Supreme National Tribunal of Poland' (2015) 13(5) Journal of International Criminal Justice 903, 932.

PART III

EXPRESSIVE PRACTICES, JUDICIAL RECORD, HISTORY, AND TRUTH

9

Symbolic Expression at the International Criminal Tribunal for the Former Yugoslavia

Marina Aksenova[*, **]

9.1 Introduction

To understand the origins of the International Criminal Tribunal for the former Yugoslavia (ICTY), it is worth comparing the wording of the three UN Security Council resolutions leading to its creation. The first one established the Commission of Experts to analyse information pertaining to the violations of international humanitarian law on the territory of the former Yugoslavia ('Commission').[1] In October 1992, over a year after the atrocities had erupted, the Security Council expressed 'grave alarm' at continuing reports about widespread crimes in the region, in particular mass killings and 'ethnic cleansing'. The wording of the rest of the document was rather restrained and technical, focusing on States' obligation to comply with international humanitarian law and calling on them to compile information on infringements with a view to submitting it to the newly established investigative body.

The Commission of Experts issued its interim report less than five months later.[2] Having considered it, the Security Council used stronger language to express, once again, 'grave alarm over continuing reports of widespread violations', and to stress the need to put an end to those crimes and bring to justice persons responsible for them. Thus, just a few days following the interim report, the UN Security Council members swiftly decided on the establishment of the Tribunal to further those aims. The new institution was also called to contribute to loftier goals, such as the restoration and maintenance of peace.[3] Finally, resolution 827 establishing the Tribunal in May 1993 under Chapter VII of the UN Charter adopted even more aspirational language, adding it to the pragmatic discussion of the future Tribunal's operation. This document listed specific crimes committed on the territory of the former Yugoslavia, including organized and systematic detention and rape of women,

* Professor of Comparative and International Criminal Law at IE University in Madrid, marina.aksenova@ie.edu.

** I would like to thank Matias Means and Jed Odermatt for their patience and help with this project. I am also grateful to the Institute of Advanced Studies of the Central European University for providing the funding and access to the premises of the OSA Vera and Donald Blinken Open Society Archives in Budapest. This support was essential for the successful completion of this chapter.

1 UN Security Council Resolution 780 (6 October 1992), UN Doc S/RES/780 (1992).

2 UN Security Council, 'Letter dated 9 February 1993 from the Secretary-General addressed to the President of the Security Council, transmitting the interim report of the Commission of Experts established pursuant to resolution 780 (1992) to provide the Secretary-General with its conclusions on the evidence of grave breaches of the Geneva Conventions and other violations of international humanitarian law committed in the territory of the former Yugoslavia' (10 February 1993), UN Doc S/25274.

3 UN SC Resolution 808 (22 February 1993), UN Doc S/RES/808 (1993).

Marina Aksenova, *Symbolic Expression at the International Criminal Tribunal for the Former Yugoslavia* In: *Legacies of the International Criminal Tribunal for the Former Yugoslavia*. Edited by: Carsten Stahn, Carmel Agius, Serge Brammertz, Colleen Rohan, Oxford University Press (2020). © The Several Contributors DOI: 10.1093/oso/9780198862956.003.0010

and emphasized the belief of the Council members that the new tribunal 'will contribute to ensuring that such violations are *halted and effectively redressed*'.[4]

There are two angles of looking at the increase in the intensity of language in these resolutions. From the linguistic point of view, one may observe enhanced performativity of the statements made by the Security Council. John Austin in his seminal work 'How to Do Things with Words' explained that some utterances are not descriptive but rather operational, or, as he calls them, 'performative'.[5] Their function is to 'do' rather than to reflect what is. How does one determine whether a statement is indeed performative? What is important is that the words must be uttered in accordance with the established procedure by persons vested with certain authority.[6] For instance, declaration 'I do' may amount to an act of getting married if uttered in the context of a wedding ceremony by the one who is getting married. The intent of the party pronouncing the statement does not attest to its performativity as such but rather it indicates whether it is a 'happy statement', meaning it is aligned with subsequent action.[7] It is clear from the language of the resolutions that all of the conditions were present to make the statements of the Security Council operational, and the alarming tone attested to the strength of the intention of the parties to take some action about the unfolding atrocities in the Balkans.

The second angle for explaining the language in the resolutions is that of symbolic power. It is through the invocation of the juridical power of law that the Security Council attempted to do something about the ongoing crimes.[8] The decision of the stakeholders to direct their outrage through the channel of law was not coincidental for legal avenue was the one which was most available at that point in time. It was clear that something needed to be done at an international level, and, as a result, the tribunal was instituted on behalf of the community of nations with one overarching aim: condemnation of evil deemed universal. The language of the Security Council resolutions demonstrates an intensifying worldwide concern over offences committed in the course of the Balkan war. In other words, the time was right to bring those matters to the attention of the tribunal mandated to conduct prosecutions in the name of universal values. In this sense, the overarching purpose of the ICTY was symbolic—to uphold the value of human dignity through the ritual of criminal prosecutions in the light of the inability of local actors to prevent further escalation of atrocities.[9] Symbolic power was deployed to attain the symbolic objective.

This all-encompassing objective subsumes all other goals mentioned in the resolutions and, later on, in the Tribunal's jurisprudence. The Tribunal was created to be a unifying cohesive force upholding the universal value of human dignity through 'claiming, naming and blaming'.[10] David Luban describes the process of honouring human dignity as a way of allowing someone to tell their story, insisting that it is told and assuming it is told in good faith.[11] The Tribunal was meant to do just that. In this regard, it can be counterpoised with

[4] UN SC Resolution 827 (25 May 1993), UN Doc S/RES/827 (1993), emphasis added.

[5] J L Austin, *How to Do Things with Words* (Oxford University Press 1962).

[6] ibid 26.

[7] ibid 39–40.

[8] P Bourdieu, 'The Force of Law: Toward a Sociology of the Juridical Field' (1987) 38 Hastings Law Journal 814, 823.

[9] For more on symbolism of international criminal law see M Aksenova, 'Symbolism as a Constraint on International Criminal Law' (2017) 30 Leiden Journal of International Law 475–99.

[10] D Luban, *Legal Ethics and Human Dignity* (Cambridge University Press 2007) 147.

[11] ibid 88.

the divisive rhetoric stirring ethnic tensions that led to the escalation of violence. A documentary the *Death of Yugoslavia* shows how in 1987, youthful Slobodan Milošević—at that time number two in the Serbian Communist Party—addressed a crowd of rioting Serbs in Kosovo with the words 'no one should dare to beat you again'. The narrator in the documentary holds this moment as a point of no return in the Balkan conflict.[12] It could very well be this speech deepened regional ethnic divisions, driving people further away from each other. The work of the ICTY could be seen as countering the split created by violence by appealing to a common ground—shared humanity.

This chapter relies on two theoretical frameworks to demonstrate the way in which the ICTY expressed itself in a symbolic way: the theory of discourse analysis developed by Michel Foucault[13] and an anthropological exploration of the symbolic nature of rituals across different societies by Maurice Bloch.[14] Section 9.2 of this chapter explains the applicability of both theories to the present discussion. The discourse analysis brings to light symbolic expression as the underlying objective of the ICTY by focusing on the *content of its output*. In contrast, Bloch's explanation of symbolic significance of rituals in connecting individuals to institutional structures transcending their consciousness is helpful in identifying the *structure* within which this content is generated. The following sections briefly deal with various ways in which the symbolic expression manifested itself at the ICTY: through the process of its establishment (9.3), its institutional design (9.4), rhetoric in the judgments (9.5), and, finally, through the way in which the ICTY frames its achievements (9.6).

9.2 Theoretical Framework

Foucault's approach referred to as 'the discourse analysis' allows conceptualizing the world not as sequences of historical occurrences, each with a distinct point of beginning and end, but rather as a more fluid set of social practices reflected in dominant discourse and often shaped by it. This theory is helpful in explaining the normative shift that took place through the UN Security Council resolutions. Discourse holds a script about what to do and not to do reflective of these practices. Statements within the discourse are 'signposts' describing specific events. The question central to Foucault's theory is not so much what any particular statement means in isolation but rather how is it that one particular statement appeared rather than another.[15] The answer to this question usually extends beyond the statements themselves to the intention of the speaking subject, their conscious and subconscious activity, intended meaning and context in which the statement occurred.[16] Here, one can trace a direct link to the theory of performative speech, which heavily relies on the context in which the utterances are made and the intention of the speaker for determining both the nature of the statement (whether it is operational or not) and its subsequent effect (whether the subject intends to follow through with subsequent action).[17]

[12] Documentary 'The Death of Yugoslavia', part 1, available at https://www.youtube.com/watch?v=vDADy9b2IBM accessed 5 February 2020.

[13] M Foucault, *Archeology of Knowledge* (Taylor & Francis 1969).

[14] M Bloch, *Prey into Hunter: The Politics of Religious Experience* (Cambridge University Press 1992).

[15] ibid 26–27.

[16] ibid.

[17] Austin (n 5).

The statement therefore is always an event in itself reaching beyond language and meaning.[18] The incision that the statement makes on the body of dominant discourse carries the potential of altering social practices. Documents leading to the creation of the ICTY as well as its output in the form of judgments and decisions can be seen as a sequence of statements generated by the overarching symbolic purpose of the tribunal. By adopting certain vocabulary when speaking about mass atrocities, the tribunal promoted change in the way the world perceives political violence. Labelling certain events as 'genocide' or 'crimes against humanity' had an effect extending beyond mere legal qualification of a specific instance of atrocity. What it did essentially was decry, denounce, and outlaw this kind of human activity.

How does this viewpoint square with Judith Shklar's brilliant essay on the limits of legalism, where she points out that 'the remote past cannot be legally tried and remote future cannot be controlled'?[19] Admittedly, this quote refers specifically to the charge of the crime of aggression, which took prominence at the Nuremberg and Tokyo trials but had limited impact on the future development of international law until now. Shklar's concern was that legalistic approach to war and peace does not have much deterrent effect in a world without common interest in peace.[20] If the common foundation is missing, law alone cannot fix the problem by prospectively outlawing certain conduct. One may object that criminalizing aggressive war at Nuremberg and Tokyo, while not bringing about the immediate results, did percolate into the future by ultimately resulting in the inclusion of the crime of aggression into the Rome Statute of the International Criminal Court.[21] In the same manner, the statements of the ICTY resulted in criminalization and stigmatization of other types of atrocious conduct. This activity, while referring to the specific acts in the past, had a clear effect on the future. This effect was both legal in a sense of forming the body of case law to support the subsequent development of the discipline of international criminal law and practical for such rhetoric by the ICTY simultaneously raised the threshold of permissible conduct in the time of hostilities.

One can say that not only the content but also the form of tribunal's expression is highly symbolic. It is the ritual of criminal trial that transforms legal pronouncements into 'events' in Foucauldian sense. The ritual designed to strengthen the authority of the act of legal interpretation, such as reading of the judgment in the courtroom, deserves the study as much as the legal act itself.[22]

The format of an international criminal trial provides the necessary context to alleviate juridical language to the level where its impact extends beyond some specific factual scenario. As Rosa Aloisi and James Meernik eloquently argue in their book 'Judgment Day', international judges act as 'social entrepreneurs' by invoking powerful emotive rhetoric. They invest their judicial capital in promoting moral authority of the norms they are upholding. This way, they remedy deficiencies left by application of domestic punishment rationales, such as retribution, that are often insufficient to 'speak' to the pain suffered by victims.[23] The framework of a trial is essential for the successful execution of this task.

[18] Bloch (n 14) 28.
[19] J Shklar, *Legalism* (Harvard University Press 1964) 171.
[20] ibid 187.
[21] Art 8*bis* of the Rome Statute of the International Criminal Court.
[22] Bourdieu (n 8) 828.
[23] R Aloisi and J Meernik, *Judgment Day: Judicial Decision Making at the International Criminal Tribunals* (Cambridge University Press 2017) 115–18.

The context of social relationships helps to understand the significance of any symbolic action,[24] including that of a criminal trial. This point leads to the second—anthropological—framework inspiring analysis in this article.

Maurice Bloch—a well-known anthropologist—made his scientific contribution by observing quasi-universality of the minimal religious structures across different societies.[25] In his seminal work *Prey into Hunter*, Bloch studied various rituals performed by different cultures and concluded that irreducible common structures underlie all of these rituals. Bloch explained this common core by the urge, found in most societies, to overcome the dichotomy between the transience of human life and the permanence of institutions. Rituals are ways to extend human existence beyond the natural biological process of birth, growth, and death.[26] Abner Cohen, another anthropology scholar, shared a somewhat similar understanding of this function of symbolic action. He noted that men resort to symbolic action to establish identity and to develop solutions to profound unresolvable questions, such as life and death, good and evil.[27]Accepting that an overarching purpose of international criminal law is upholding the value of human life and dignity in times of political chaos, necessarily leads to the conclusion that certain symbolic action is required to transmit this message to a wider community. International criminal trials are thus perfect examples of symbolic action tackling perennial issues of human existence. Their innate structure closely resembles that of other symbolic rituals practised by various societies.

It is instructive to explore in more detail one of the rituals discussed by Maurice Bloch in his work *Prey into Hunter*. Take, for example, the initiation ritual practised by Orokaiva—an indigenous people of Papua New Guinea. Bloch describes how in Orokaiva tradition, like in many others, initiation signifies the beginning of life as a full moral person. This progression consists of two parts: first, a person's transition from a 'homegrown native vitality' to 'transcendental', and, secondly, return to real life after having incorporated features defying impermanence of an individual life. The ritual accompanying this journey serves as a symbolic representation of such transformation.

The ritual consists of several stages. First, children who are being initiated are chased by a group of threatening outsiders wearing feather masks. The strangers are actually adults from the village playing the part of spirits. Children in their native vitality play the part of pigs, thus the whole process resembles a hunt. After the hunt, the initiates enter the symbolic period of 'death' when they are taken to the huts outside of the village; they are not permitted to eat normal food, wash, or speak out loud. In this period the children learn various secrets about the world of spirits. After some time in seclusion, 'rebirth' happens. The children return to the village as transformed individuals—partially human and partially spirit. They come back as hunters and end the ritual with a symbolic slaughter of pigs, followed by victorious consumption of meat.[28]

Bloch explains how by going through this process, children conquer their native vitality (of pigs) and replace it by an external or consumed vitality. They symbolically transform themselves from 'prey' into 'hunter'. The whole process is therefore that of empowerment

[24] A Cohen, *Two-Dimensional Man: An Essay on the Anthropology of Power and Symbolism in Complex Society* (Routledge 1977) 4.
[25] Bloch (n 14) 3.
[26] ibid 4.
[27] Cohen (n 24) 13–14.
[28] Bloch (n 14) 8–23.

and maturity. The initiated extend their existence beyond the constrains of a single life by joining the transcendental. Yet they still return to the present as changed morally mature individuals.[29] Essential to Bloch's analysis is the idea of 'rebounding violence'. In the first part of the ritual, transcendental uses violence to drive out native vitality through an external drama: elders-spirits are hunting children-pigs. Violence then returns at the end when vitality is re-introduced from external sources—the consumption of the meat of killed pigs. After having experienced transcendental, it is through an act of violence that individual takes control of his human finite nature. The whole ritual process can therefore be understood as a transformation occurring through 'rebounding violence' constructed at the public and at the experiential level.[30] The end result is building human association with permanent institutional structures.

There is more in common between Orokaiva initiation rituals and international criminal trials than meets the eye. International criminal trials are modern representations of rebounding violence, where law is the embodiment of violence. Authority of law ultimately rests on violence actual or symbolic for, as Derrida pointed out, there is no law without force. The crucial element of law is thus its enforceability, which exists only when actual sanctions are threatened in case of non-compliance.[31] The choice to address crimes occurring in the Balkans through criminal prosecutions can be seen as a deliberate decision by the international community to exercise measured violence on its behalf. The purpose was to expunge the offenders of commonly shared values through quasi-ritualistic performance of a criminal trial. The promise of violence was reflected in the process of capturing the suspects to be tried by the tribunal, the threat of criminal sanctions, as well as the legal basis supporting the creation of the ICTY—Chapter VII of the UN Charter, historically used to justify forcible measures.

Pursuant to the tribunal's constitutive documents, the first element of rebounding violence was indicting and apprehending individuals accused of bearing responsibility for mass atrocities. Because of the novelty of the whole enterprise, this first stage posed certain challenges. For the most of its first two years of operation, the ICTY had no defendants in custody even though it had issued more than thirty public indictments. Louise Arbour, former Chief Prosecutor at the ICTY, even called for the creation of a specialized military force tasked with enforcing arrest warrants issued by the Tribunal precisely due to the difficulties with executing arrests of individuals, especially at the beginning of the ICTY's operation.[32] The lack of convincing enforcement machinery also affected the way in which the tribunal defined the powers of the Prosecution. Judge Nieto-Navia stressed in *Tadić* that the Prosecution must be allowed to appeal acquittals because while it prosecutes '*on behalf of the international community*, it is not supported by a governmental apparatus with abundant resources.'[33]

The criminal trial itself is an intermediate transformative process whereby guilt or innocence of the accused is established. It is the 'external drama' of assigning individual

[29] ibid 19.

[30] ibid 5–6.

[31] J Derrida, 'Force of Law: The "Mystical Foundation of Authority"' in D Cornell, M Rosenfeld, and D Carlson (eds), *Deconstruction and the Possibility of Justice* (Routledge 1992).

[32] L Arbour, 'International Tribunals for Serious Violations of International Humanitarian Law in the Former Yugoslavia and Rwanda' (2000–2001) 46 McGill Law Journal 195.

[33] *Prosecutor v Tadić Duško* (Judgment) Case No IT-94-1-A (15 July 1999), Declaration of Judge Nieto-Navia, para 10, emphasis added.

blame for collective wrongdoing. It takes place in public but has experiential dimension too. Its purpose is to extrapolate 'evil' and restore the value of human life affected by the conflict. In addition to that, the context of a criminal trial allows stories to be told and verified by independent 'outside' mediators, who are international judges. It is not coincidental that the ICTY lists as one of its achievements establishing beyond a reasonable doubt crucial facts related to crimes committed in the former Yugoslavia.[34] Finally, violence returns through sentencing of those found guilty of mass atrocities. In this instance, condemnation of evil occurs on behalf of an external force—the international community—and, arguably, goes beyond the specific individual found guilty of an international crime. Connection to permanent values endorsed by the Tribunal—is thereby ascertained.

The following sections of the chapter take a more practical approach to interpreting the ICTY's overarching symbolic objective. They look at different ways through which the Tribunal manifested its concern for human dignity and served as a symbolic space for the expression of this concern. The two theoretical frameworks discussed already serve as an inspiration for the following analysis. The purpose is not, however, to neatly fit the theories with the realities of the Tribunal's operation but rather to link the discussion of the ICTY's legacy to a wider theoretical base. The language used by the Commission and the Tribunal deserves particular attention in the context of the theory of discourse analysis. It is not just the plain meaning of words that matters but also the context in which these words were uttered and the impact they had on the formation of the modern body of international criminal law. A lot of the pronouncements by the Commission and the ICTY became 'events' in the Foucauldian sense of the word, setting the trend and creating a certain narrative, based on which the world viewed the atrocities committed in the Balkans and the response of an international community to these atrocities.

9.3 Establishment

The origins of the ICTY could be traced back to the establishment of the investigative body tasked with collecting information pertaining to violations of international humanitarian law happening on the territory of the former Yugoslavia.[35] The work of the Commission is significant in understanding the nature of symbolic expression of the ICTY for it established a necessary connection between the facts and the law, thereby preparing ground for the Tribunal's operation. Cherif Bassiouni, who served as the head of the Commission of Experts, explained that the Commission worked on three tracks: (1) developing a database of received information and its analysis; (2) conducting on-site investigations; and (3) relying on certain governments to conduct investigations on its behalf.[36]

The Commission was not originally set up with the specific mandate of collecting evidence for future prosecutions; this prospect was however envisaged by several members of the Security Council at the time of its creation. Resolutions 808 and 827 establishing

[34] UN ICTY Website, Achievements, available at <http://www.icty.org/en/about/tribunal/achievements> accessed 13 May 2019.

[35] UN SC Resolution 780 (6 October 1992), UN Doc S/RES/780 (1992).

[36] M C Bassiouni, 'The United Nations Commission of Experts Established Pursuant to Security Council Resolution 780' (1994) 88 American Journal of International Law 794–95.

the ICTY refer to the Commission's interim report, but the degree of its influence on policy-makers' final choice to set up the Tribunal is unknown.[37] What is certain is that the Commission's meticulous assembly of information, its liaisons with multiple governments and non-governmental organizations,[38] and its engagement with volunteer experts during its on site investigations[39] all led to the climate conducive of the creation of the criminal tribunal.[40]

In its work, the Commission identified a number of legal avenues to be further developed by the Tribunal, thereby solidifying its contribution to the development of international law. For example, the Commission consistently held the view that irrespective of the qualification of the conflict or parts thereof as one of an international or non-international character, there was sufficient legal basis to cover all violations committed on the territory of the former Yugoslavia.[41] This position was later upheld by the ICTY in the *Tadić* decision on jurisdiction.[42] In line with identified key issues, the final report contained a number of thematic annexes, including 'Ethnic Cleansing',[43] 'The Battle and Siege of Sarajevo',[44] and 'Rape and Other Forms of Sexual Assault'.[45] Examination of these annexes in their draft and final form reveals an incredible amount of work undertaken by the Commission and its members.

For instance, Annex VI was dedicated to the battle and siege of Sarajevo. It covered historical, ethnographic, and cultural aspects of the city before proceeding to the discussion of factual circumstances of the siege, which led to the deaths of nearly ten thousand people at the time of the drafting of the annex. Part of this document provides a detailed chronology of events, including a calculation of daily civilian casualties over an extended period of time submitted by the BiH Institute for Public Health.[46] Such visualization of the daily loss of human life carried a strong emotional message. The same section of the annex also contained a daily chronology of sniping activity in or around Sarajevo compiled on the basis of press reports. For example, on 5 August 1992, Reuters reported a mortar attack on an apartment complex next to the Holiday Inn, which killed one person and wounded four others. These descriptions conferred on the reader the notion of terror occurring in the city during the siege.

Annex IX entitled 'Rape and Other Forms of Sexual Assault' was part of the Commission's study pursuing a threefold objective: (1) to identify specific individual cases, patterns, and policies; (2) to establish foundations in fact for allegations of rape and sexual assault in this

[37] Bassiouni (n 36) 790–91.

[38] The list of non-governmental organizations from the territory of the former Yugoslavia and other countries is appended to the Final Report of the Commission of Experts. It included organizations with diverse focus, such as the Danish Helsinki Committee, Consorzio Italiano di Solidarieta', Centre for Croat Unions, Bosnia Action Committee, German Caritas, American Refugee Committee, Amnesty International, and many others. See UN Security Council, 'Letter Date 24 May 1994 from the Secretary-General to the President of the Security Council' (27 May 1994), UN Doc S/1994/674/Annex I.C.

[39] Bassiouni (n 36).

[40] Bassiouni notes that the Commission collected 64,000 pages of documents submitted by various sources. See Bassiouni (n 36) 795.

[41] ibid 795.

[42] *Prosecutor v Tadić* (Decision on the Defence Motion for Interlocutory Appeal on Jurisdiction) Case No IT-94-1-AR72 (2 October 1995).

[43] UN Security Council, 'Final Report of the Commission of Experts Established Pursuant to Security Council Resolution 780 (1992) dated 27 May 1994 ('Final Report'), UN Doc S/1994/674, paras 110–28.

[44] ibid paras 183–94.

[45] ibid paras 232–53.

[46] Final Report (n 43), Annex VI, 8.

conflict, and more particularly their use as an instrument of war; and (3) to serve as a basis for eventual prosecution by the ICTY for rape and sexual assault cases.[47] Bassiouni noted that this rape investigation was the first one of its kind conducted in time of war.[48] The expectation was therefore that the ICTY would give 'this particularly heinous crime its utmost attention',[49] which the Tribunal did.

The Commission cooperated with a variety of sources of information, including a few governments. Table 9.1 contains several excerpts from the official submissions of the Federal Republic of Yugoslavia (FRY) in 1991–1994. These files were attached to the final report of the Commission of Experts and are currently stored at the OSA Vera and Donald Blinken Open Society Archives in Budapest, Hungary.[50] Highlighted statements are examples of how language was used by one of the parties to the Balkan conflict to set the discourse in a certain direction.

One observes several trends by analysing the tone of this correspondence. First, there was a general and, what appears to be genuine, support for a lasting peace. United Nations efforts in this regard were welcomed. Secondly, FRY's highest officials in theory condemned the practice of ethnic cleansing irrespective of where and against which people it was pursued. In practice, they primarily recognized victimization of one group and not all others. For example, the Report of the Government of the FRY submitted to the Commission of Experts on 10 November 1992 contained a number of eyewitness reports supplied by Yugoslav and foreign reporters. These reports were categorized according to the types of grave breaches of the Geneva Conventions. The section 'wilful killing of civilians' included the description of forty-two incidents accompanied by the brief indication of victim and possible perpetrator. Only one out of forty-two incidents was attributed to the Territorial Defence force of the Serbian Republic. The rest were assigned either to the Croatian or 'Moslem'[51] forces, or both.[52] Finally, there was strong distrust of international efforts to challenge the dominant victimization narrative.

Based on all of the information submitted to it in the course of its work, the Commission of Experts eventually concluded in its final report that there existed significant evidence of violations of international humanitarian law, which was duly passed to the newly established tribunal. Experts observed that the crimes committed were 'particularly brutal and ferocious in their execution'.[53] Increasingly strong language was reserved for the discussion of the degree of victimization:[54]

> The Commission is *shocked* by the high level of victimization and the manner in which these crimes were committed, as are the populations of all the parties to the conflict. The difference is that each side sees only its own victimization, and not what their side has done to others.

[47] Final Report (n 43), Annex IX, 6.
[48] Bassiouni (n 36) 798.
[49] ibid 799.
[50] Available at <http://www.osaarchivum.org/> accessed 13 May 2019.
[51] Term used in the correspondence.
[52] Report of the Government of the FRY submitted to the Commission of Experts established pursuant to Security Council Resolution 780 (1992), No 7/11 Press Release, identical to report communicated under cover S/24779, 10 November 1992 ('Report of the Government of 10 November 1992').
[53] Final Report (n 43), paras 310–11.
[54] ibid para 319, emphasis added.

Table 9.1 Official Submissions of the Federal Republic of Yugoslavia (FRY) attached to the final report of the Commission of Experts (excerpts from 1992)

Date	Type of document	Citation
7 August 1992	Letter from the President of the FRY Dobrica Cosic to the Secretary General[a]	'With reference to *unfounded allegations* of the existence of concentration camps on the territory of the Federal Republic of Yugoslavia, I should like to propose the setting up of an international commission of prominent international figures, preferably former concentration camp inmates, like, for example, Mr. Elie Wiesel, with the task of examining the plausibility of the claims that such 'concentration camps' are in existence in Bosnia and Herzegovina, Croatia and the Federal Republic of Yugoslavia . . . '
24 October 1992	Letter from the President of the FRY Dobrica Cosic to the Co-Chairmen of the International Conference on the former Yugoslavia[b]	'According to my information and reports of the United Nations Protection Force (UNPROFOR) and the European Community Monitoring Mission (ECM) the Yugoslav Army *very correctly and without a single incident* withdrew its forces from the territory of the Republic of Croatia on 20 October 1992. However, immediately after the withdrawal [. . .], members of the Army of the Republic of Croatia caused an incident and opened fire on the territory of Eastern Herzegovina (Bosnia and Herzegovina).'
10 November 1992	Report of the Government of the FRY submitted to the Commission of Experts[c]	'The Government of the Federal Republic of Yugoslavia *supports the establishment of the Commission of Experts* to collate, examine and analyze information relating to grave breaches of the Geneva Conventions and other violations of international law.' 'Over half a million of refugees fleeing the war and terror in Croatia and Bosnia and Herzegovina have *found shelter in the FR of Yugoslavia*'
23 November 1992	Statement by the Government of the FRY in connection with some parts of the second report on the situation of human rights in the territory of the FRY prepared by Mr Tadeus Mazowiecki, Special Rapporteur of the Commission on Human Rights[d]	'The Government has *unequivocally, absolutely and with overwhelming public support condemned and rejected the policy of so-called 'ethnic cleansing'* irrespective of where and against which people it is being pursued.' 'In the view of the Federal Government there is *no proof for the claim* about planned 'erosion of Albanian culture.' 'The impression one has from the report of Mr. Mazowiecki is that the Special Rapporteur puts an equation mark between the situation in Kosovo and Metohija and the one in Vojvodina, which is absolutely not true.'
27 November 1992	Letter to Mr Fritz Kalshoven, Chairman Commission of Experts to supplement Report of the Government of 10 November 1992[e]	Enclosed 'Memorandum of the Government of Yugoslavia on *the crime of genocide in Croatia* and the vandalizing of Memorial Of Jasenovac'. '*The aggression of the Croatian Republic* against the Republic of Srpska is obvious . . . '

Table 9.1 *Continued*

Date	Type of document	Citation
10 December 1992	Letter from Dr Momcilo Grubac, Minister for Human Rights and the Rights of Minorities of the Federal Republic of Yugoslavia addressed to the Secretary General[f]	'In connection with the report on the situation of human rights in the territory of the former Yugoslavia, submitted by the Special Rapporteur, Mr. Tadeusz Mazowiecki, on 17 November 1992 [. . .], I would like to draw your attention to the following.' 'The Government of the Federal Republic of Yugoslavia fully supports the activities of the United Nations* aimed at improving the situation of human rights and humanitarian law in the territories of the former Socialist Federal Republic of Yugoslavia still affected by the armed conflict . . . ' 'In that context, the Government of the Federal Republic of Yugoslavia considers that full and consistent compliance with the following principles is essential . . . *condemnation and cessation of the policy and practice of ethnic cleansing* by whomever it is committed and wherever it occurred.' '*The basic and primary goal is to achieve lasting peace* in Bosnia and Herzegovina' 'Regarding those sections of Mr. Mazowiecki report dealing with the situation in the Federal Republic of Yugoslavia, particularly in Kosovo and Metohija, Vojvodina and those parts of the country designated "Sandzak", *there are a number of inaccuracies not reflecting true state of affairs*.'

[a]Document number A/46/956, emphasis here and in all the subsequent paragraphs added.

[b]Document number A/47/577.

[c]Report of the Government of the FRY submitted to the Commission of Experts established pursuant to Security Council Resolution 780 (1992), No 7/11 Press Release, identical to report communicated under cover S/24779, 10 November 1992 ('Report of the Government of 10 November 1992').

[d]Document No A/47/712.

[e]Document No 1309/92 (handwritten).

[f]Document No A/47/781.

The final report concluded by emphasizing 'the high expectation of justice conveyed by the parties to the conflict, as well as by victims, intergovernmental organizations, non-governmental organizations, the media and world public opinion,' and 'popular expectations of a new world order based on the international rule of law' that would require 'no less than effective and permanent institutions of international justice'.[55] Using the terminology of Aloisi and Meernik, the Commission of experts, along with the judges who were engaged at a later stage, acted in their role as 'entrepreneurs'.[56] The experts used their position of authority to draw attention to the appalling nature of crimes committed in the former Yugoslavia and to garnish support for further action.

[55] ibid para 320.
[56] Aloisi and Meernik (n 23) 115.

9.4 Institutional Design

Law can be conceptualized as an institutionalized form of the life of people.[57] The social significance of the symbolism of ritual sheds light on the nature and process of this institutionalization.[58] There are features in the architecture of the ICTY highlighting its position as an institution of universal condemnation of evil. Some elements in particular are conducive of symbolic expression of this overarching objective. These features are the form of the institution, its authority derived from consensus, expediency of its creation, and its continuity in time.

The ICTY was created as a court—an institutional form of confrontation and contestation most likely to produce the strongest outcome in terms of condemnation. Polarity, inherent in a criminal trial, allowed to single out those most responsible and attain a certain measure of atonement through the imposition of punishment.

The failure of the international community to take effective measures to halt atrocities in the former Yugoslavia from the outset created enormous pressure for an effective and quick response. This collective impetus crystallized at the level of international community and materialized through the legal avenue. Creation of an international tribunal was arguably the most suitable solution at that time for it directed the accumulated will and outrage of multiple stakeholders in a highly contained and seemingly manageable manner to the court tasked with adjudicating on the issues high on the agenda. The power was invested in the 'juridical capital'.[59] From an anthropological viewpoint, the choice of criminal proceedings opened the door to the legitimate exercise of violence (through the enforcement of arrest warrants and the execution of sentences) necessary to effectuate transition desired by many interested parties.

Matheson and Scheffer noted that the proponents of international prosecution were genuinely appalled by the atrocities being committed.[60] The hopes ran high: to hold the major perpetrators of atrocity crimes accountable, while, at the same time, deterring repetition of such offences and giving victims a sense of justice and to encourage reconciliation.[61] The international community moved quickly with the creation of the court. On 10 February 1993, the Commission of Experts filed its interim report, five days later members of the Security Council reached an agreement on the need for an international court and on 22 February, the Security Council unanimously decided that such a court would be created.[62] Furthermore, on 3 May 1993, the Secretary General produced a report containing a draft statute of the Tribunal, which was unanimously adopted by the Security Council on 25 May 1993 without any amendments to avoid possible delays.[63]

Matheson and Scheffer observed that it was far from certain at the outset that using Chapter VII authority to create a criminal tribunal and to impose penalties on individuals would be acceptable to the international community as a whole.[64] The report of the

57 R M Unger, The Universal History of Legal Thought, work in progress, available at <http://www.robertounger.com/en/wp-content/uploads/2017/01/the-universal-history-of-legal-thought.pdf>, accessed on 3 May 2019.

58 Bloch (n 14) 10.

59 Bourdieu (n 8) 823.

60 M J Matheson and D Scheffer, 'Symposium on the International Criminal Tribunals for the Former Yugoslavia and Rwanda: The Creation of the Tribunals' (2016) 110 American Journal of International Law 173.

61 ibid.

62 Matheson and Scheffer (n 66) 175.

63 Bassiouni (n 36) 792; ibid 176.

64 Matheson and Scheffer (n 66) 179.

Secretary General containing the draft statute of the Tribunal indicated that in the ordinary course of events a treaty would underlie the establishment of such a tribunal, but in the present circumstances creation by the Security Council was legally justified and more effective.[65] This move was only possible due to an overwhelming international consensus reached at the point of the ICTY's conception.

Temporal jurisdiction of the Tribunal started in 1991 and continued indefinitely into the future, leaving it up to the Security Council to decide on the appropriate time to complete its mandate.[66] Nineteen years later, on 22 December 2010, the Security Council created the Mechanism for International Criminal Tribunal (MICT)—a residual body for both the ICTY and the International Criminal Tribunal for Rwanda (ICTR), formally bringing the ICTY's operation to the stage of completion.[67] Despite limited temporal scope of the Tribunal, one cannot help but notice continuity in its work: the Commission of Experts in the final report stressed the importance of the precedent of creating an ad hoc tribunal for the future establishment of a permanent body vested with similar functions. Such an institution—the International Criminal Court—was in fact created a few years later. At the other end of the existence of the ICTY, the MICT inherited most of its functions, perpetuating its operation and values into the future.[68]

9.5 Rhetoric in the ICTY Judgments

Symbolic expression at the ICTY is most evident in its output, which primarily consists of judgments and decisions. The nature of rhetoric employed by the tribunal gives an insight into how the symbolic objective of international criminal justice is integrated in its legal reasoning.[69] According to Derrida, to be just the decision of a judge must not only follow the rule of law but must also *assume* it.[70] Facts of the case are always unique; therefore, adherence to the doctrine of precedent has its reasonable limits. Assuming responsibility for a case at an international criminal tribunal, like the ICTY, involves assuming responsibility for delivering justice and a measure of accountability to individual victims and to humanity as a whole. One of the main challenges is for the message of condemnation to be universally understood and accepted.[71]

How does one assess the level of incorporation of the symbolic objective in the reasoning of judges at the ICTY? The study of Aloisi and Meernik, in which they measured judicial expressivism through rhetoric, adopted qualitative approach to expressive statements.[72]

[65] UN Security Council, 'Report of the Secretary General Pursuant to Paragraph 2 of Security Council Resolution 808 (1993)', UN Doc S/25704 (3 May 1993), paras 18–30.

[66] ibid para 62.

[67] UN Security Council Resolution 1966 (22 December 2010), UN Doc S/RES/1966 (2010).

[68] G Acquaviva, '"Best Before Date Shown": Residual Mechanisms at the ICTY' in B Swart, A Zahar, and G Slutter (eds) *The Legacy of the International Criminal Tribunal for the Former Yugoslavia* (Oxford University Press 2011).

[69] See also Sofia Stolk's work on the purposeful use of grand words in the opening statements in international trials. S Stolk, '"The Record on Which History Will Judge Us Tomorrow": Auto-History in the Opening Statements of International Criminal Trials' (2015) 28 Leiden Journal of International Law 993.

[70] Derrida (n 31) 251, emphasis added.

[71] P Bourdieu, *Language and Symbolic Power* (Polity 1991) 55.

[72] Aloisi and Meernik (n 23) 130.

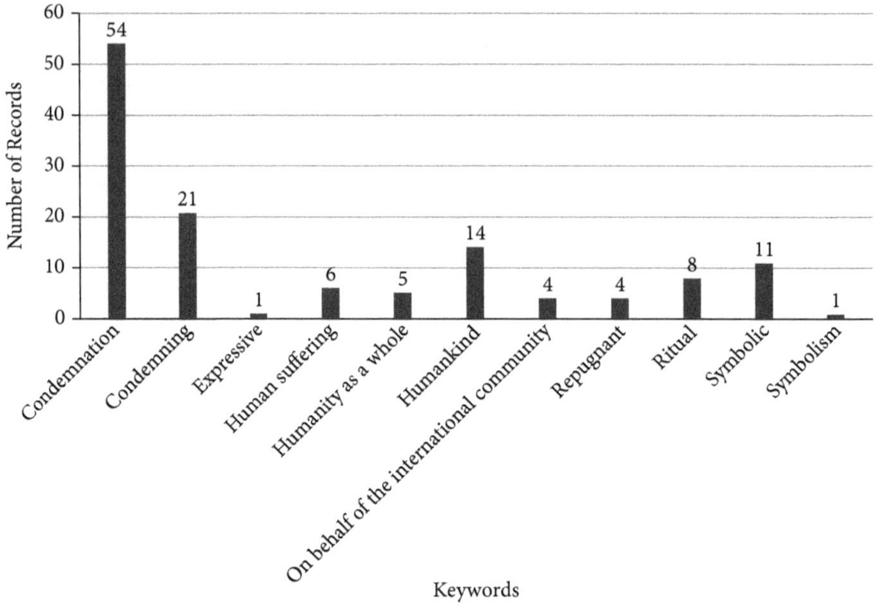

Figure 9.1 Keywords in the ICTY judgments (number of times mentioned)

They chose to focus on the context in which these statements appeared. When it came to the selection of the relevant passages, the authors selected those that the judges 'owned'. This was done by the search of key indicators such as 'The Trial Chamber finds . . . '.[73] The mini-analysis in this section is likewise qualitative but concentrates rather on the utterances themselves.

Certain keywords evaluated within their context may prove to be a good indicator of the degree of incorporation of the symbolic objective in judicial reasoning. The words selected for this article to describe an overarching goal of international criminal justice as a forum for the universal of condemnation of evil are the following: *condemnation, condemning, expressive, human suffering, humanity as a whole, humankind, on behalf of international community, repugnant, ritual, symbolic, symbolism*.[74] The list is clearly not exhaustive and is intended to demonstrate how (if at all) emotive expressions as to the nature of exercise at stake find their way into judicial reasoning and for what purpose. Figure 9.1 reveals the frequency of occurrence of these keywords in the judgments of the ICTY from the beginning of its work and until the end of 2015.

As one can see from the graph, the keywords show up in the documents relatively few times given that the ICTY Trial and Appeal Chambers together issued over one hundred judgments, some running over one thousand pages. This result exemplifies judges' reluctance to become too emotionally involved in their legal reasoning. It is clear that taking an emotive stand on the matter goes to the outer limits of judicial activity, which is characterized by rationalization.[75] It involves discharging of some of the judicial capital and stepping

[73] ibid.
[74] In the following citations these words are italicized.
[75] Bourdieu (n 8) 817.

outside of a purely legal role in assuming moral authority.[76] The reluctance of judges to engage with moral authority could thus be explained in part by concerns of stretching the boundaries of the principle of legality, which places limits on the exercise of judicial creativity. The principle of judicial impartiality and independence also plays a role in keeping the language of the judgments restrained and neutral. Finally, many judges before joining the ICTY had been trained and practised as professional judges in their national jurisdictions, where the possibilities for expressivism are even more limited.

However, these few instances of keywords appearing in the judgments do provide sufficient context for understanding the nature of symbolic expression at the ICTY. One can identify four general themes within which the keywords appeared: sentencing, definition of crimes, indication of association with the international community, and, finally, explaining the nature of judicial function. Within each of these broad categories keywords formed integral parts of statements reflective of dominant social practices at the time of the creation of the ICTY and in the following years. Each statement did not merely serve the purposes of addressing circumstances of an individual case but shaped the discourse within the field in general. The nature of legal practice ensured that the statements were replicated in subsequent judgments, and, some of them, such as those defining new offences, served as 'events' bringing new prohibited conduct to the plane of international criminal justice.

9.5.1 Sentencing

As one can see from the graph in Figure 9.1, the word 'condemnation' returned the most results during the search. Half of the results for this term related to sentencing practice and this is not a coincidence. The imposition of punishment is arguably the most emotional part of any criminal justice process. Émile Durkheim called it 'a passionate reaction graduated in its intensity'.[77] It is through punishment that the society affected by the crime expresses its condemnation. This practice is particularly aggressive and exclusionary, yet it produces solidarity around the values that are restored.[78] In the case of international criminal law, the community united around certain values is international. The following citation from *Aleksovski* is sometimes cited in support of the expressive (or using the terminology of this chapter 'symbolic') function of international criminal law:[79]

> Accordingly, a sentence of the International Tribunal should make plain the *condemnation* of the international community of the behaviour in question and show that the international community was not ready to tolerate serious violations of international humanitarian law and human rights.[80]

[76] See also Aloisi and Meernik (n 23) 129.

[77] E Durkheim, *The Division of Labour in Society* (Palgrave MacMillan 1984) 48.

[78] G H Mead, 'The Psychology of Punitive Justice' (1918) 23 American Journal of Sociology 577.

[79] H van der Wilt, 'Joint Criminal Enterprise: Possibilities and Limitations' (2007) 5 Journal of International Criminal Justice 99, fn 39; M Damaška, 'What is the Point of International Criminal Justice?' (2008) 83 Chicago-Kent Law Review 329.

[80] *Prosecutor v Aleksovski* (Appeals Judgment) Case No IT-95-14/1-A (24 March 2000) para 185. See also *Prosecutor v Kunarac* et al ('Foča') (Judgment) Case No IT-96-23-T and IT-96-23/1-T (22 February 2001) para 841.

Returning to the idea of rebounding violence discussed in section 9.1 of this chapter, punishment is the second 'leg' of violence inherent in the ritual of an international criminal trial. Punishment is there to indicate symbolic transformation that occurred between the moment of bringing the accused into the ICTY custody (and thereby establishing control over the person) and the moment of declaring their guilt or innocence, and the imposition of penalty in the former case. Drawing parallels with Orokaiva initiation, it is the act of sentencing that establishes a connection between an individual act of offending and universal values that it hurts. It is through this form of condemnation that society extrapolates 'evil' and re-affirms those values. In this situation, society is understood as humanity as a whole:

> One of the purposes of punishment for a crime against humanity lies precisely in stigmatising criminal conduct which has infringed a value fundamental not merely to a given society, but to *humanity as a whole*.[81]

The Statute of the ICTY provides minimum guidance on sentencing, allowing for wide judicial discretion.[82] Article 24 of the ICTY Statute only suggests that in imposing the sentences, the Trial Chambers should consider such factors as the gravity of the offence and the individual circumstances of the convicted person, as well as mitigating and aggravating circumstances. In this context, it is interesting that the term 'symbolic' was used in conjunction with the word 'sentence':

> The Prosecution further states that it does not seek a '*symbolic* sentence'; that it does not adopt any political position, let alone an 'overtly political stance'; that it is not the product of any frustration nor is its position dependent on the status of any other accused; and that it seeks only an appropriate sentence for the crimes for which the Trial Chamber found Momčilo Krajišnik responsible, based on the gravity of those crimes and his role in them.[83]

It was thus stressed that the sentence to be rendered by the tribunal would not be 'symbolic'. It is clear that the meaning of the term 'symbolic' used in the preceding paragraph is nearly opposite to the one adopted in this chapter. Its purpose in the preceding paragraph is to underline the retributive element of the sentences rendered by the tribunal rather than to stress the overarching mission of the court. This example is a good illustration of the importance of context in understanding the legacy of the ICTY.

Save for some notable exceptions—such as the definition, and then the restatement of the goals of international criminal justice—the phrasing of Article 24 of the ICTY Statute, which is generic, has not been expanded upon much beyond this point in the case law of the ICTY.[84] As early as 1996, the *Erdemović* Trial Chamber of the ICTY adopted 'retribution, or "just deserts", as legitimate grounds for pronouncing a sentence for crimes against humanity, the punishment having to be proportional to the gravity of the crime and the moral guilt of the convicted'.[85] Retribution thus places most weight on the principle of

[81] *Prosecutor v Erdemović* ('Pilica Farm') (Sentencing Judgment) Case No IT-96-22-T (29 November 1996) para 64.
[82] A Cassese, *International Criminal Law* (Oxford University Press 2008) 51.
[83] *Prosecutor v Krajišnik* (Appeals Chamber Judgment) Case No IT-00-39-A (17 March 2009) para 770.
[84] M Aksenova, *Complicity in International Criminal Law* (Hart 2016) 210.
[85] *Prosecutor v Erdemović* (n 87).

proportionality—the sentence must be proportionate to the gravity of criminal conduct.[86] The idea of condemnation surfaces a number of times in the context of retributive rationale:

> As a form of retribution, the sentence serves as *condemnation* by the international community of the crimes committed and should not be misunderstood as a means of expressing revenge or vengeance.[87]
>
> In light of the purposes of the Tribunal and international humanitarian law generally, the Trial Chamber understands retribution to be the expression of *condemnation* and outrage of the international community at such grave violations of, and disregard for, fundamental human rights at a time that people may be at their most vulnerable, namely during armed conflict.[88]
>
> Recourse to the gravity of the offence, with considerations for the role of the accused in the commission of the offence and the impact of the offence on victims, should help guide a trial chamber in its determination of what sentence is necessary to reflect the indignation and *condemnation* of the international community for the crimes committed.[89]

In addition to the gravity of the offence, the judges consider mitigating and aggravating circumstances. Instruments of the ICTY and the ICTR did not include the list of such circumstances, deliberately leaving them to the discretion of the judges.[90] In the *Jelisić* case, judges took the following aggravating factors into account; 'the *repugnant*, bestial and sadistic nature of Goran Jelisić's behaviour', '[h]is cool-blooded commission of murders', and his enthusiastic participation in the crimes.[91] In *Ojdanić*, the Chamber acknowledged that the accused 'took some measures to reduce *human suffering* during the conflict', but chose to place minimal weight on this as a mitigating factor.[92] By contrast, in *Plavšić*, the accused pleaded guilty and invoked her awareness of the suffering she caused as evidence of remorse:

> She continued by saying that in their fear, especially those for whom the Second World War was more than a memory, the leadership violated the basic duty to restrain itself and to respect the human dignity of others: '[t]he knowledge that I am responsible for such *human suffering* and for soiling the character of my people will always be with me'.[93]

Appealing his twenty-year sentence for murder, rape, and unlawful confinement and inhuman treatment of Bosnian Muslim civilians, Miroslav Bralo argued for lesser condemnation due to

[86] A von Hirsch, 'Proportionate Punishment: A Desert Perspective' in A von Hirsch, A Ashworth and J Roberts (eds) *Principled Sentencing* (Hart Publishing 2009) 117

[87] *Prosecutor v Stanišić & Župljanin* ('Bosnia and Herzegovina') (Trial Judgment) Case No IT-08-91-T (27 March 2013) para 890; see also *Prosecutor v Krajišnik* (Appeals Chamber Judgment) Case No IT-00-39-A (17 March 2009) para 759; *Prosecutor v Šainović* et al (Judgment) Case No IT-05-87-T (26 February 2009) para 316; *Prosecutor v Delić* (Judgment) Case No IT-04-83-T (15 September 2008) para 559.

[88] *Prosecutor v Blagojević & Jokić* (Judgment) Case No IT-02-60-T (18 January 2005) para 818; *Prosecutor v Obrenović* ('Srebrenica'), (Judgment) Case No IT-02-60/2-S (10 December 2003) para 50; *Prosecution v Nikolić, Momir* ('Srebrenica') (Judgment) Case No IT-02-60/1-S (2 December 2003) para 86.

[89] *Prosecutor v Blagojević & Jokić* para 819.

[90] *Prosecutor v Obrenović* (Sentencing Judgment) ICTY Case No IT-02-60/2 (10 December 2003) para 91.

[91] *Prosecutor v Jelisić* (Appeals Judgment) Case No IT-95-10-A (5 July 2001) para 86.

[92] *Prosecutor v Šainović* et al (Judgment) Case No IT-05-87-T (26 February 2009) para 1187.

[93] *Prosecutor v Plavšić* ('Bosnia and Herzegovina') (Judgment) Case No IT-00-39-S and IT-00-40/1-S (27 February 2003) para 72.

societal breakdown in the Vitez municipality in Bosnia and Herzegovina. He asserted that 'participation of numerous local people in the attack, all acting under unlawful orders, revealed the extent of the breakdown of societal and moral norms in this area in April 1993 and that, while this approach does not condone the atrocities committed, "extreme circumstances" and a "climate of fear and uncertainty" warrant a lesser degree of condemnation of the individual perpetrator'.[94] This argument was rejected by the Appeal's Chamber on the ground that large sections of the population across Bosnia and Herzegovina were subjected to the same pressure and yet did not respond in the same manner as Bralo.[95] The Appeals Chamber concluded by restating the formula adopted by the Trial Chamber that the principle of retribution 'amounts to an expression of *condemnation* by the international community at the *horrific* nature of the crimes committed, and must therefore be proportionate to his specific conduct'.[96]

9.5.2 Definition of Crimes

One of the biggest achievements of the ICTY is developing the body of international criminal law. Robinson and MacNeil in their evaluation of the legacy of the ICTY, noted that the tribunal's impact on substantive international criminal law is overall positive: 'our assessment is that the Tribunals have performed admirably and even unexpectedly well'.[97] Arguably, it is the symbolic mission of the ICTY that created impetus for defining and refining offences, many of which only existed in the schematic form at the time of the Tribunal's creation. The Tribunal's mission could be said to have added weight to the existing customary international law. Applying the framework of discourse analysis to the definition of substantive offences by the ICTY, one can conclude that the work of the Tribunal contributed to crystallization and solidification of many prohibitions. From the standpoint of performative speech, judicial utterances were operational, they set standards of conduct.

For example, one of the early judgments in *Čelebići* solidified the prohibition of inhumane treatment by observing that '[o]n the strength of this almost universal *condemnation* of the practice of inhuman treatment, it can be said that its prohibition is a norm of customary international law'.[98] Likewise, the *Stakić* Appeals Chamber noted the proliferation of international instruments *condemning* forcible transfer and held that the notion of forcible transfer had therefore clearly been accepted as conduct criminalized as early as 1992.[99]

Both the ICTY and the ICTR played crucial roles in modernizing the law on sexual violence in the field of international criminal justice.[100] The International Military Tribunal in Nuremberg as well as the Geneva Conventions did not deal with this crime directly. The International Military Tribunal for the Far East in Tokyo discussed the rape of Nanking but

[94] *Prosecutor v Bralo* (Judgment on Sentencing Appeal) Case No IT-95-17-A (2 April 2007) para 12.
[95] ibid para 13.
[96] ibid para 82, emphasis added; *Prosecutor v Bralo* (Sentencing Judgment) Case No IT-95-17-S (7 December 2015) para 22.
[97] D Robinson and G MacNeil, 'The Tribunals and the Renaissance of International Criminal Law: Three Themes'(2016) 10 The American Journal of International Law 193.
[98] *Prosecutor v Mucić* et al ('Čelebići Camp') (Judgment) Case No IT-96-21-T (16 November 1998) para 517.
[99] *Prosecutor v Stakić* (Appeal Judgment) Case No IT-97-24 (22 March 2006) para 317; *Prosecutor v Tolimir* ('Srebrenica') (Trial Judgment) Case No IT-05-88/2-T (12 December 2012) para 803.
[100] Robinson and MacNeil (n 103) 201.

its analysis was largely factual and did not dwell on the legal components of the category of sexual offences.[101] As a result, the Statute of the ICTY did not expressly mention rape as a war crime, but only as a crime against humanity.[102] The Commission of Experts duly identified the gap and raised awareness of this problem through its pilot study of rape. The tribunals carried on work commenced by the Commission and recognized rape as a war crime, a crime against humanity, and an integral part of torture and genocide:

> The Trial Chamber emphasises once again that international humanitarian law, along with basic principles of humanity, require that individuals who are detained during an armed conflict must be treated humanely, and that the rape and torture of a woman in this context is a most heinous crime requiring unequivocal *condemnation*.[103]
>
> In other words, the nature of the crime and the forms that it takes, as well as the intensity of international *condemnation* of torture, suggest that in the case of torture all those who in some degree participate in the crime and in particular take part in the pursuance of one of its underlying purposes, are equally liable.[104]
>
> The fact of being made the subject of abuse of this nature also causes a psychological trauma that results, on the one hand, from having been humiliated and victimised, and on the other, from suffering the *condemnation* of the members of their community if they report what has been done to them.[105]

The ICTY judges also used particularly emotive language when discussing the category of crimes against humanity. Unlike war crimes and genocide, this group of offences has not been codified in a treaty, leaving its legal basis somewhat unclear. Customary international law provided sufficient proof to satisfy the basic requirements of the principle of legality but also left space for further development of the essence of this category of offences as an attack on humanity as a whole. Arguably, pronouncements by the ICTY presented below reflect not only the sentiment pertaining to crimes against humanity but also, more generally, the feelings towards the offences prosecuted by the tribunal:

> This follows from the requirement that crimes against humanity be committed on a widespread or systematic scale, the quantity of the crimes having a qualitative impact on the nature of the offence which is seen as a crime against more than just the victims themselves but against *humanity as a whole*.[106]
>
> The Trial Chamber further recalls the finding of the Appeals Chamber in relation to crimes against humanity generally, [b]ecause of their heinousness and magnitude [crimes against humanity] constitute egregious attacks on human dignity, on the very notion of humaneness. They consequently affect, or should affect, each and every member of *[human] kind*, whatever his or her nationality, ethnic group and location.[107]

[101] *The Tokyo War Crimes Trial*, vol 22, at 49,605.
[102] ibid.
[103] *Prosecutor v Bralo* (Sentencing Judgment) Case No IT-95-17-S (7 December 2015) para 33.
[104] *Prosecutor v Furundžija* ('Lašva Valley') (Judgment) Case No IT-95-17/1-T (10 December 1998) para 254.
[105] *Prosecutor v Mucić* et al ('Čelebići Camp') (Judgment) Case No IT-96-21-T (16 November 1998) para 484.
[106] *Prosecutor v Tadić* ('Prijedor') (Judgment) Case No IT-94-1-T, (7 May 1997) para 73.
[107] *Prosecutor v Obrenović* ('Srebrenica') (Judgment) Case No IT-02-60/2-S (10 December 2003) para 65; *Prosecution v Nikolić, Momir* ('Srebrenica') (Judgment) Case No IT-02-60/1-S (2 December 2003) para 105.

> With regard to a crime against humanity, the Trial Chamber considers that the life of the accused and that of the victim are not fully equivalent. As opposed to ordinary law, the violation here is no longer directed at the physical welfare of the victim alone but at *humanity as a whole*.[108]

There is no formal hierarchy of the gravity of the offences in the ICTY Statute. The judges nonetheless reserved particularly strong language for genocide. Radoslav Krstić became the first person convicted of genocide at the ICTY. *Krstić* therefore delivers a powerful message of condemnation of this crime pointing to its particular heinousness: '[a]mong the grievous crimes this Tribunal has the duty to punish, the crime of genocide is singled out for special *condemnation* and opprobrium'.[109] Its particular gravity also justified the imposition of stricter *mens rea* requirements: [t]his knowledge on his part alone cannot support an inference of genocidal intent. Genocide is one of the worst crimes known to *humankind*, and its gravity is reflected in the stringent requirement of specific intent.[110]

9.5.3 Association with the International Community

The words 'condemnation' and 'condemning' were often used to signify international reprobation of certain acts and events. Such contextual deployment of these terms points in the direction of universality of values promoted by the tribunal. As mentioned in section 9.1 of this chapter, the existence of an external observer—the public—is essential for the occurrence of the ritual, which is both a public and an experiential event. The ritual of a traditional criminal trial requires the existence of a certain society that shares values violated by the offence. It is through prosecution that this society channels its outrage against the offender and restores the values that were hurt.[111] In case of the ICTY, the society appalled by the violations is the entirety of the humankind. The rhetoric of the Tribunal is thus underlining its association with a wider international community. This is essential to bring 'public' to the stage and stress the Tribunal's mission of upholding values on behalf of a broader international community:

> This finding is strengthened by the Trial Chamber's fundamental conviction that the Security Council, in persistently *condemning* the widespread violations of international humanitarian law committed throughout the conflict in Bosnia and Herzegovina and, indeed, in establishing the International Tribunal to prosecute and punish such violations, did not consider that the protection of the whole corpus of international humanitarian law could be denied to particular groups of individuals on the basis of the provisions of domestic citizenship legislation.[112]

[108] *Prosecutor v Erdemović* ('Pilica Farm') (Sentencing Judgment) Case No IT-96-22-T (29 November 1996) para 19.

[109] *Prosecutor v Krstić* (Appeals Judgment) Case No IT-98-33-A (19 April 2004) para 36.

[110] ibid para 134; *Prosecutor v Šainović* et al (Appeals Judgment) Case No IT-05-87-A (23 January 2014) Declaration of Judge Liu, Footnote 32; *Prosecutor v Tolimir* ('Srebrenica') (Judgment) Case No IT-05-88/2-T (12 December 2012) para 1172.

[111] Durkheim (n 83).

[112] *Prosecutor v Mucić* et al ('Čelebići Camp') (Judgment) Case No IT-96-21-T (16 November 1998) para 275,

The UN Security Council passed Resolution 1345 on 21 March, *condemning* the violence and welcoming the involvement of various international bodies in addressing the crisis. International organizations became involved in monitoring, and preventing further violence.[113]

Following the attack, the UNSC adopted Resolution 913 on 22 April 1994 which '*condemn[ed]* in the strongest possible terms the Bosnian Serb forces for their continued offensive against the safe area of Goražde, which has resulted in the death of numerous civilians and tremendous *human suffering*'.[114]

9.5.4 Nature of Judicial Function

The keywords serving as pointers in the present discussion about the nature of symbolic expression at the ICTY came up in dissenting and separate opinions. The rhetoric in these opinions naturally reflects judges' personal understanding of their role and limits of their function within the ICTY.[115] It is interesting to contrast these findings with the views expressed during an interview: when asked about the tribunal's objectives, two ICTY presidents—judges Fausto Pocar and Theodor Meron—replied in ways that reflected their conservative understanding of judicial function. Fausto Pocar stated: 'I would take it that the ICTY was entrusted with prosecuting and holding trials for the main perpetrators ... and that's the only task. [...] Although the Security Council may have had other goals, such as fostering 'peace, stability and reconciliation, the tribunal itself cannot act as though it has a "political mandate" '. Judge Theodor Meron expressed a similar sentiment. In his view, 'the primary goal of an international tribunal is to do justice and punish atrocities'.[116] The examination of the discourse in the separate and dissenting opinions of these judges yields similar conclusions as to their self-awareness as judges. It is quite clear that the judges are not merely deducing conclusions applicable to the case based on the law, but also enjoy some autonomy in discharging their judicial capital in accordance with their inner convictions.[117]

The word 'condemnation' appears in two important separate and dissenting opinions appended to the appeal judgment in *Galić*. This case dealt with responsibility of Stanislav Galić, the commander of the Bosnian Serb troops stationed around Sarajevo, for ordering attacks on the city over the course of twenty-three months during the siege of the city. Mr Galić was initially sentenced by the Trial Chamber to twenty years of imprisonment for his role in the atrocities. The Prosecution appealed this sentence as failing to adequately reflect the gravity of crimes at stake. The Appeals Chamber upheld the Prosecutor's appeal, finding that the Trial Chamber abused its discretion in imposing such a lenient sentence. As a result, the sentence of Mr Galić was increased to life imprisonment.[118] Four out five judges from the bench submitted separate or dissenting opinions. Judges Meron and Pocar argued

[113] *Prosecutor v Boškoski & Tarčulovski* (Judgment) Case No IT-04-82-T (10 July 2008) para 214.

[114] *Prosecutor v Perišić* (Judgment) Case No IT-04-81-T (6 September 2011) para 1532.

[115] The term coined by Aloisi and Meernik 'judicial entrepreneurs' is most fitting to describe this aspect of judicial activity. See Aloisi and Meernik (n 23) 115.

[116] D Orentlicher, *Shrinking the Space for Denial: The Impact of the ICTY in Serbia* (Open Society Institute 2008) 53.

[117] See Bourdieu (n 8) 826.

[118] *Prosecutor v Galić* (Appeals Judgment) Case No IT-98-29-A (30 November 2006) para 456.

against the increase, while judges Shahabuddeen and Schomburg expressed their support for a harsher penalty.

Judge Pocar agreed with the majority that the Trial Chamber committed a discernible error in the exercise of its discretion by sentencing Mr Galić to twenty years of imprisonment. Such outcome is 'unreasonable and unjust' when 'as a result of Mr. Galić's conduct over the course of 23 months, '[i]nhabitants of Sarajevo—men, women, children and elderly persons—were terrorized and hundreds of civilians were killed and thousands wounded during daily activities such as attending funerals, tending vegetable plots, fetching water, shopping, going to hospital, commuting within the city, or while at home'.[119] At the same time, Judge Pocar insisted that the International Covenant on Civil and Political Rights guarantees in Article 14(5) the right of appeal, which could only be secured by remitting the case back to the Trial Chamber.[120] He ultimately supported due process guarantees for the convicted person, while acknowledging the gravity of conduct at stake—this position aligned with his personal view of the Tribunal's main and only task of prosecuting main perpetrators.

Judge Meron also disagreed with the increase but on different grounds. He argued that an increase is justified 'only if one of two conditions is met: either the sentence is clearly out of proportion with sentences we have given in similar situations, or the sentence is otherwise so low that it demonstrably shocks the conscience'.[121] He further held that neither condition was satisfied in the present case, as a twenty-year long sentence is hardly 'a two-and-a-half-year slap-on-the-wrist' and is longer than most sentences imposed by the ICTY.[122] He concluded:

> The majority's decision to increase Galić's sentence to life imprisonment may satisfy our sense of *condemnation*. But this increase disserves the principles of procedural fairness on which our legitimacy rests. As the highest body in our court system, we are not readily accountable to any other authority and thus have a particular obligation to use our power sparingly.[123]

In contrast, Judge Shahabuddeen, expressed a different view when it comes to the role of condemnation and powers of the Appeals Chamber. He argued in his separate opinion in *Galić* that '[i]t is the function of this Court to have regard to the victims and the consequences on the victims. It is the function of this Court to reflect the public *condemnation* for offences of this kind'.[124] While Judges Meron and Shahabuddeen may not necessarily disagree on the specific purposes of sentencing, they clearly approach the idea of public condemnation from a different angle. Judge Meron is more pragmatic, keeping in mind narrow constraints of the principle of legality, while Judge Shahabuddeen stresses the overarching objective of the ICTY to denounce the worst atrocities.

[119] ibid Partially dissenting opinion of Judge Pocar, para 1.
[120] ibid para 3.
[121] *Prosecutor v Galić* (Appeals Judgment) Case No IT-98-29-A (30 November 2006), Separate and partially dissenting opinion of Judge Meron, para 6.
[122] ibid para 10.
[123] ibid para 13.
[124] ibid Separate Opinion of Judge Shahabuddeen, para 33.

9.6 Formulation of Successes (and Failures)

This last section of the chapter deals with the remaining important avenue through which the ICTY manifests its symbolic power. Judge Pocar modestly praised the ICTY and ICTR in *Mrkšić* as 'examples of best practice for the *prosecution* of international crimes'.[125] The tribunal itself (as an institution) was more generous with the assessment of its work. The ICTY website offers a more extensive list of its achievements, including holding leaders accountable, bringing justice to victims and giving them voice, establishing crucial facts relating to the conflict, developing international law, and strengthening the rule of law, thereby contributing to reconciliation.[126] While some successes, such as developing international law are indisputable,[127] others are open for discussion. The claim of this chapter as to the overarching symbolic objective of the ICTY invites enhanced scrutiny of its possible contribution to reconciliation. The idea of reconciliation resonates with the purpose of any symbolic ritual to denote a break with the past by facilitating the 'rite of passage' from one state to another. In case of an international criminal trial, the transition would be towards collective healing by virtue of putting to rest old battles and tensions that had led to violence in the first place. This new state occurs as a result of a criminal process, which provides space for hearing and assessing conflicting narratives.

Despite the desire of the ICTY to create a shared narrative, Marko Milanovic observed that it is far from clear that the tribunal's judgments have contributed to forging a historical record that is accepted by all parties to the conflict.[128] The divisions date back in time. For instance, correspondence from the FRY Government from 1992 appended to the report of the Commission of Experts evidenced 'denialism' about crimes committed by members of one's own ethnic group.[129] Expectations of international community were such however that the creation of the ICTY would produce a common narrative for the region, leading to healing and reconciliation. [130] This expectation aligns with the nature of a symbolic ritual as having the unifying power to bring members of the community together over certain shared beliefs.

Relatively recent opinion polls however suggest that a common narrative in the Balkans is still an aspiration as most ethnic groups carry on believing their group was the subject of most victimization, while rejecting or mitigating the responsibility for committing offences against members of other ethnic groups.[131] Talking about specific crimes, longitudinal polling in Serbia between 2004 and 2011 produced relatively consistent results that only around half of the population in Serbia believed the Srebrenica massacre happened,

[125] *Prosecutor v Mrkšić-Šljivančanin* (Appeals Judgment) Case No IT-95-13/1-A (5 May 2009) Partially dissenting opinion of Judge Pocar, para 11, emphasis added.

[126] See <http://www.icty.org/en/about/tribunal/achievements> accessed 5 February 2020.

[127] See Robinson and MacNeil (n 103); M Milanović, 'The Impact of the ICTY on the Former Yugoslavia: an Anticipatory Postmortem' (2016) 110 American Journal of International Law 233; K Askin, 'Reflections on Some of the Most Significant Achievements of the ICTY' (2002–2003) 37 New England Law Review.

[128] Milanović, ibid 256.

[129] Table 9.1 of this chapter.

[130] Refik Hodzic pointed to the failure of outreach in this regard as he noted that media and the ICTY outreach did not sufficiently target the Serb community to challenge prevalent denialism, R Hodžić, 'Living the Legacy of Mass Atrocities. Victim's Perspectives on War Crimes Trials' (2010) 113 8 Journal of International Criminal Justice 126.

[131] Milanovic (n 133) 243–46. See for detailed surveys: <http://www.bgcentar.org.rs/bgcentar/eng-lat/citizens-perceptions-of-human-rights-law-and-practice/stavovi-prema-ratnim-zlocinima-haskom-tribunalu-domacem-pravosudu-za-ratne-zlocine/> accessed 15 April 2019.

and only around one third considered it to be a crime.[132] In contrast, in Bosnia an overwhelming 99.5 per cent of the population believed it to be true and 95.7 per cent considered the Srebrenica massacre to be a crime.[133] Milanovic explained this paradox, in part, by the nature of human decision making, which is not fully rational, with emotions and cognitive biases often overtaking the whole process.[134]

The projection of the ICTY's symbolic power therefore depended in large part on the acceptance of its findings by the local audience and not only on its endorsement by the international community.[135] Perceived legitimacy of the ICTY stems not so much from the outreach and the Tribunal's engineering but from identification of large parts of population with indictees.[136] Biases come into play when people feel that their social identity is collectively threatened by, for instance, the indictments issued against members of one's own group.[137] A way to mitigate this cognitive dissonance between regional and international dominant narratives in the Balkans was by placing the blame on the external force—the ICTY.[138] Opinion polls suggest that in 2011 only 22 per cent of the Serbian population considered the establishment of the ICTY necessary, while 65 per cent said it was unnecessary.[139] An even larger proportion of the population—73 per cent—believed the ICTY to have a different attitude towards people indicted for war crimes depending on their nationality.[140]

It is for this reason, the assumption that uncovering truth leads to reconciliation is far from certain, at least in the short term, as each party tends to continue relying on its own biases.[141] The Tribunal is unable to address fully this problem stemming from the nature of the human psyche.[142] Indeed, one big challenge of a ritual of an international criminal trial is its emotional and intellectual inaccessibility to local communities.[143] Trials in general and international criminal trials in particular restrain the emotional component out of respect for the objectivity of law. Bourdieu rightfully observes that what distinguishes modern legal rituals from all other types of rituals is their rational nature.[144] The paradox of a trial is that adjudication involves the exercise of personal, moral, and legal authority, but it is done in a

[132] Milanović (n 133) 247.

[133] ibid 248. These results exclude data from the ethnically mostly Serb Republika Srpska.

[134] M Milanovic, 'Establishing the Facts about Mass Atrocities: Accounting for the Failure of the ICTY to Persuade Target Audiences' (2016) 47 Georgetown Journal of International Law 1321.

[135] See M Tripkovic, 'Not in our name! Visions of Community in International Criminal Justice' in M Aksenova, E Van Sliedregt and S Parmentier (eds) *Breaking the Cycle of Mass Atrocities: Criminological and Socio-Legal Approaches to International Criminal Law* (Hart 2019).

[136] S Ford, 'A Social Psychology Model of the Perceived Legitimacy of International Criminal Courts: Implications for the Success of Transitional Justice Mechanisms' (2012) 45 Vanderbilt Journal of Transnational Law 405, 411.

[137] ibid 423.

[138] ibid 428.

[139] Ipsos Stategic Marketing Report: Attitudes towards war crimes, the ICTY and the national judiciary, OSCE, 30 October 2011.

[140] ibid 45. Mirko Klarin noted, along the same vein, that only 8 per cent of Serbs believed cooperation with the ICTY is important. M Klarin, 'The Impact of the ICTY Trials on Public Opinion in the Former Yugoslavia' (2009) 7 Journal of International Criminal Justice 89.

[141] ibid.

[142] M Milanovic, 'Establishing the Facts about Mass Atrocities: Accounting for the Failure of the ICTY to Persuade Target Audiences'(2016) 47 Georgetown Journal of International Law 1321.

[143] K King and J Meernik, 'Assessing the Impact of the International Criminal Tribunal for the Former Yugoslavia: Balancing International and Local Interests While Doing Justice' in B Swart, A Zahar, and G Slutter (eds) *The Legacy of the International Criminal Tribunal for the Former Yugoslavia* (Oxford University Press 2011) 13.

[144] Bourdieu (n 8) 828.

highly formalized way and with express reference to the body of law not to impede the logical appearance of the system.

It is arguably the 'weak' aspect of the ritual of condemning evil using the means of criminal law. The nature of law is such that it requires rationality and does not account for individual and collective biases, often driven by emotions and preconceived ideas that go beyond the scope of the case at issue. Yet the international community, including the Tribunal itself, measures its achievements not only in terms of the number of prosecutions and convictions, but also in terms of its impact on transitional justice, reconciliation, and victims. This approach is largely dictated by the symbolic purpose of the ICTY and the expectations of universal justice vested on the tribunal. It is very possible however that a long-term effect of the ICTY's operation will resonate fully with the deep-seated beliefs challenged by its prosecutions

9.7 Conclusion

This chapter has explored symbolic expression at the ICTY. It is argued that the tribunal manifests its mission of administering justice on behalf of humanity as whole through the way in which it was created, its institutional design, its adopted judicial rhetoric, and, finally, the manner in which its successes and failures are formulated. Law imposes inevitable constraints on attaining the overarching purpose of condemning evil. As one can see from the analysis of judicial rhetoric, there is only limited space available for the expression of emotions. Such a mismatch between the aim of universal condemnation and available legal instruments makes it essential to resort to quasi-ritualistic performance to establish the necessary connection between specific cases and the general sentiment of outrage. Traditional rituals employ violence—real or symbolic—to signify transition from one state of being to another, from individual to transcendental. In the context of international criminal law, violence takes the form of enforcement of arrest warrants and, later on, the imposition of penalties. It is through this process that the 'evil' is formally isolated and condemned, thus allowing for an opening to move forward with reconciliation and healing.

10
A Partial View of History
ICTY Judgments as 'Judicial Truths'

Luigi Prosperi and Aldo Zammit Borda**, ****

10.1 Introduction

The judgments of the International Criminal Tribunal for the former Yugoslavia (ICTY) have been influential and widely cited for their factual findings and large bodies of evidence on the conflict in the former Yugoslavia.[1] While these findings were made in the context of the Tribunal's mandate to determine the criminal responsibility of the accused, there is little doubt that they have also contributed to the historical narrative of the conflict in the region.[2] Writing in relation to international criminal tribunals more generally, one commentator has noted:

> The modern international criminal tribunals, for the former Yugoslavia, Rwanda, and Sierra Leone, were established to address major conflicts in different parts of the world. Each has now generated an enormous volume of case law. The tribunals have held many dozens of major trials. In most of these, there have been important debates about the historical dimensions of the situation being considered.[3]

By providing 'detailed and well-substantiated records of particular incidents and events',[4] the ICTY has provided a body of evidence that is invaluable for historians, and so in that sense, the legacy of this Tribunal and its contribution towards a better understanding of the

* PhD, Sapienza University of Rome; formerly Associate Legal Officer at the Office of The Prosecutor, International Criminal Tribunal for the former Yugoslavia. [prosperil@luiss.it]
** PhD, Trinity College Dublin; Senior Lecturer in Public International Law, Anglia Ruskin University, Cambridge. [aldo.zammitborda@anglia.ac.uk]
*** The Authors would like to thank Bill Tomljanovich and Moshe Hirsch for their invaluable comments on a first version of this contribution. They would also like to thank Jessica Caiazzo and Monika Zakrzewska for their research assistance. All errors are the authors' own.

1 They have been cited, inter alia, by the International Court of Justice, the European Court of Human Rights, the Human Rights Chamber for Bosnia and Herzegovina and the European Parliament. See Application of the Convention on the Prevention and Punishment of the Crime of Genocide (*Bosnia and Herzegovina v Serbia and Montenegro*) (Judgment) [2007] ICJ Rep 191, 43, para 223; *Mehida Mustafić-Mujić et al v the Netherlands* App no 49037/15 (ECtHR, 30 August 2016), para 87; *Ferida Selimović et al v the Republika Srpska* ('The Srebrenica Cases') (Decision on Admissibility and Merits) Human Rights Chamber for Bosnia and Herzegovina CH/01/8365 (7 March 2003) paras 15–28; and European Parliament resolution 2015/2747(RSP) of 9 July 2015 on the Srebrenica Commemoration [2017] OJ C265.

2 See S P Ramet, 'Martyr in His Own Mind: The Trial and Tribulations of Slobodan Milošević' (2004) 5 Totalitarian Movements and Political Religions 112, 114.

3 W A Schabas, *Unimaginable Atrocities: Justice, Politics, and Rights at the War Crimes Tribunals* (Oxford University Press 2012) 158.

4 UN Secretary General, *The Rule of Law and Transitional Justice in Conflict and Post-conflict Societies* (23 August 2004) UN Doc S/2004/616, paras 38–39.

Luigi Prosperi and Aldo Zammit Borda, *A Partial View of History* In: *Legacies of the International Criminal Tribunal for the Former Yugoslavia*. Edited by: Carsten Stahn, Carmel Agius, Serge Brammertz, Colleen Rohan, Oxford University Press (2020). © The Several Contributors DOI: 10.1093/oso/9780198862956.003.0011

history of the region will last long after the trials have completed.[5] This, however, raises the question of the role of international criminal trials in writing historical narratives of events surrounding atrocity crimes, a question which 'has been largely overlooked' in the legal literature.[6] With some notable exceptions,[7] the questions of the appropriate role of history in international criminal trials has received little academic attention.[8]

This chapter begins by providing an overview of the three main phases in the ICTY's use of history. It then considers three schools of thought around the question of the role of international criminal trials in writing historical accounts, namely, those who argue that it is not for courts to write history; those who argue that historical discussions are inevitable in criminal trials; and those who argue that, aside from being inevitable, such discussions are desirable. Section 10.3 then explores the converging and diverging methods and aims of law and history, and section 10.4 discusses the impact of the changing rules on admissibility of evidence on history writing. Section 10.5 goes on to consider two practical examples of how such rules may impact on the historical narrative written by international criminal trials. In these two cases, information deemed not detrimental to the parties' case was admitted at trial. Such information included references to the involvement of third parties in the commission of crimes which were eventually referenced in the judgments. The chapter concludes that the relationship between international criminal trials and history writing is a dynamic, contingent, and complex one. However, one cautionary tale arises from the analysis, namely, that to expect the ICTY—and international criminal tribunals in general—to write detailed historical narratives of the conflicts they are called to assess is possibly to overburden them.

10.2 Approaches to History at the ICTY

Before discussing the ICTY's approaches to history, it has to be recognized that approaches to history and historiography are contested. As one writer put it, 'there appears to be no consensus regarding what precisely is meant by the "truth" and the "historical record" produced by international criminal tribunals'.[9] Section 10.3 will outline some of the differences between the methods and aims of law and history, differences which have led some authors to consider that historical truth 'is different from legal truth'.[10] Moreover, within the discipline

[5] R A Wilson, *Writing History in International Criminal Trials* (Cambridge University Press 2011) 18. For example, a well-known instance of historians making use of criminal trial records to develop a historical narrative is Arendt's *Eichmann in Jerusalem*, which soberly details the horror of the mass deportations and killings of Europe's Jews, and is based primarily on the trial transcripts and exhibits admitted in evidence during the trial: see F Gaynor, 'Uneasy Partners—Evidence, Truth and History in International Trials' (2012) 10 Journal of International Criminal Justice 1257, 1258.

[6] F Conrad, 'Writing History in International Criminal Trials. By Richard Ashby Wilson' (2012) 44 New York University Journal of International Law and Politics 999, 1042.

[7] R J Evans, 'History, Memory, and the Law: The Historian as Expert Witness' (2002) 41 History and Theory 326–45 and Wilson (n 5). This chapter builds on the research undertaken by Evans and Wilson and we owe a debt of gratitude to these authors.

[8] Conrad (n 6) 1045. This question is related to the broader Human Rights and transitional justice questions of victims' right to the truth: see D Groome, 'The Right to Truth in the Fight against Impunity' (2011) 29 Berkeley Journal of International Law 175, 176.

[9] Gaynor (n 5) 1263.

[10] B de Graaf, 'The Difference between Legal Proof and Historical Evidence: The Trial of Slobodan Milosevic and the Case of Srebrenica' (2006) 14 European Review 499, 5s05. See also S Stolk, '"The Record on Which History Will Judge Us Tomorrow": Auto-History in the Opening Statements of International Criminal Trials' (2015) 28 Leiden Journal of International Law 993, 995.

of history itself, there are debates around what is meant by writing history and, especially, around the possibility of arriving at some kind of historical truth.[11] There are also important distinctions between history in a scientific sense, whose 'foremost collective purpose is to achieve an understanding of the complex life and changes of past human societies',[12] and memory, which is 'constructed in the present and is influenced by contemporary society and its particular features'.[13] While we do not have the space to directly engage in these debates, we will limit ourselves to noting that there may be different views over the meaning of 'history', used extensively in the discussion below.

The role of history at the ICTY has fluctuated significantly over the course of the Tribunal's lifespan. Wilson identified three main phases in its use of history: (1) the production of background information, asserting only a weak causality to the charges in the *Tadić* case; (2) the elaboration of monumental history and ambitious claims about causality in the *Milošević* case; and finally (3) a focus on micro-histories of events surrounding particular crimes in the *Brđanin* case.

The *Tadić* judgment started with an extended history of the Balkans.[14] Wilson noted that;

> [t]he *Tadić* Trial Judgment wrote the historical run-up to the conflict in Bosnia as the backdrop to a tragic play. Yet nowhere does the language of *Tadić* suggest that historical events brought about the 1991–1995 conflict in Bosnia. The judgment's historical narrative does not lead inexorably toward ethnic cleansing and war, as other outcomes were possible.[15]

This historical narrative bore only a weak, if any, causal relationship with the accused's crimes, and its primary purpose was to provide context for the international judges and other parties, who were not directly familiar with the region. However, this historical background was not value-neutral. It functioned as a cognitive framework to understand the ensuing actions which would inevitably favour certain interpretations over others.[16] In *Tadić*, for instance, the background information set out by the Chamber tended to contradict Serb nationalist explanations of the conflict, which accorded 'great significance to incidents that occurred in 1941 or even in 1389'.[17] Wilson noted that, in subsequent cases, lawyers quickly recognized the importance of this background historical context and used it strategically to construct a framework that organized scattered acts, statements, and events, in a narrative that best suited their arguments.[18]

In *Milošević*, the accused was charged, inter alia, with war crimes and the crime of genocide. However, there was no direct documentary evidence of an order for genocide, and the prosecution conceded that 'there is little direct evidence to that precise effect, such as a

[11] For more information, see M Stuart-Fox, 'Two Views of the History of Histography and the Nature of History' (2007) 4 History Australia 44.1. See also C B McCullagh, 'What Do Historians Argue About?' (2004) 43 History and Theory 18, 18–19.

[12] P Zagorin, 'Rejoinder to a Postmodernist' (2000) 39 History and Theory 201, 209.

[13] M Hirsch, 'The Role of International Tribunals in the Development of Historical Narratives' (2018) 20 Journal of the History of International Law 391, 397.

[14] *Prosecutor v Duško Tadić* (Judgment) ICTY-94-1 (7 May 1997) paras 53–126 ('*Tadić Judgment*').

[15] Wilson (n 5) 74.

[16] M Koskenniemi, 'Between Impunity and Show Trials' in J A Frowein and R Wolfrum (eds), *Max Planck Yearbook of United Nations Law* (vol 6, Kluwer 2002) 1, 16–17.

[17] Wilson (n 5) 76.

[18] ibid 77.

specific order to commit genocide signed by the accused or a confession by him'.[19] The prosecution, thus, had to prove *dolus specialis* through inferential and circumstantial evidence. It submitted that:

> the Trial Chamber must look at all the facts and circumstances proved in the Prosecution case and that 'if a sufficient number of circumstances can be objectively identified that together demonstrate a coherent series of actions on the part of the Accused, a reasonable tribunal of fact would be entitled to draw the necessary inference that the Accused did intend the destruction of part of the Bosnian Muslim group'.[20]

An important element of the prosecution's thesis, in this regard, was based on historical arguments, namely that special intent to commit genocide was not accidental but the culmination of a century-old ideological programme to carve a Greater Serbia.[21] Wilson referred to this case as 'the high-water mark of historical debate at the ICTY. Here, we see the greatest role for a grand, sweeping metanarrative of history that led inexorably to the alleged crimes of the accused'.[22] On his part, the accused denounced what he saw as historical reductionism and attacked various aspects of the historical narrative set out by the prosecution.[23] In this trial, the narrative of Greater Serbia collided head-on with the self-determination stories of the seceding populations.[24] It is considered that the clash of narratives in *Milošević* had undertones of the struggle, in memory politics, over whose memories will be preserved and institutionalized to represent a nation's past, and whose memories will be repressed and forgotten.[25]

After *Milošević*, a third, more indirect and complex relationship developed between history and criminal intent at the ICTY.[26] The judges' growing emphasis on the factual circumstances of the crime militated against broad contextual and interpretative forms of evidence. Wilson noted that, '[c]oinciding as they did with the added imperatives of the ICTY's completion strategy, these jurisprudential developments reduced the incentives for prosecutors to integrate contextual and historical expert witnesses into their cases ... '.[27] Instead, the prosecution's focus needed to be narrowed to the point that it barely ventured outside the immediate circumstances of the actual crimes. An example of the new model was an expert report from the *Brđanin* trial focusing on the existence of local Bosnian Serb governing structures, rather than their interpretation or origins.[28] This approach could be referred to as microhistory. However, it is debatable whether it is history at all. The *Brđanin* report did not deal with remote events or their longitudinal development; it addressed how

[19] *Prosecutor v Slobodan Milošević* (Decision on Motion for Judgment of Acquittal) ICTY-02-54 (16 June 2004) para 121.
[20] ibid.
[21] It should be emphasized that historical arguments were not the *only* component of the prosecution's case, which also included important oral and documentary evidences. See Ramet (n 2) 133.
[22] Wilson (n 5) 98.
[23] *Prosecutor v Slobodan Milošević* (Public Transcript of Hearing) ICTY-02-54-T (24 July 2003) 24866–9. See also Koskenniemi (n 16) 1.
[24] ibid 12.
[25] M Palmberger, 'Making and Breaking Boundaries: Memory Discourses and Memory Politics in Bosnia and Herzegovina' in M Bufon (ed), *The Western Balkans—A European Challenge* (Založba Annales 2006) 525, 526–28.
[26] Wilson (n 5) 111.
[27] ibid 120.
[28] ibid 124.

the Serbian crisis staffs operated at the time of the crimes—it served, therefore, as a contextualization of the crimes themselves.[29]

The above overview of the changing role of history in the jurisprudence of the ICTY presents a complex dynamic and demonstrates that the relationship between judging international crimes and writing a history of an armed conflict 'cannot be characterized by either harmonious accord or inherent contradiction'.[30] The ambivalence over the appropriate role of writing history in international criminal trials is reflected in the wider scholarship, a subject which is considered next. Three main schools of thought may be identified here: (1) those who argue that it is not for courts to write history; (2) those who argue that historical discussions are inevitable in criminal trials; and (3) those who argue that, aside from being inevitable, such discussions are indeed desirable.

10.2.1 It is Not for the Court to Write History

In *Krstić*, the Trial Chamber acknowledged that its task was to decide on the guilt or innocence of the accused within the boundaries of the indictment, and it had to leave it 'to historians and social psychologist to plumb the depths of this episode of the Balkan conflict and to probe for deep-seated causes'.[31] This view has been echoed by courts in the domestic sphere, too. For instance, the Lausanne District Police Court, in considering the charge of genocide denial with respect to the defendant Perinçek, held 'it is not for the Court to write history'.[32]

Arguments from both law and sociology have been proffered in support of this position. In the legal field, liberal legalism holds that the sole function of a criminal trial is to decide on the criminal responsibility of the accused. For instance, the ICTY was established 'for the *sole* purpose of prosecuting persons responsible for serious violations of international humanitarian law committed in the territory of the former Yugoslavia . . . ',[33] and there was no explicit mandate to narrate the history of the armed conflict.[34] Thus, liberal legalism would posit that the Tribunal should not attempt 'to answer the broader questions of why a conflict occurred between certain peoples in a particular place and time, nor should it pass judgment on competing historical interpretations'.[35]

Another argument from the socio-legal field concerns the quality of the history written by courts. In view of a range of factors, including jurisdictional limits, evidentiary thresholds, special categories of crimes, as well as other considerations, international criminal tribunals will invariably only ever be able to consider a limited number of crimes from any given conflict.[36] As such, they may only ever hope to produce a partial historical account of

[29] T W Waters, 'Book Review of Writing History in International Criminal Trials by Richard Ashby Wilson' (2012) 35 Political and Legal Anthropology Review 347, 347–50.
[30] Wilson (n 5) 13.
[31] *Prosecutor v Radislav Krstić* (Judgment) ICTY-98-33 (2 August 2001) para 2.
[32] Cited in *Perinçek v Switzerland* App no 27510/08 (ECtHR, 15 October 2015) para 22.
[33] UNSC Res 827 (25 May 1993) UN Doc S/RES/827, para 2 (emphasis added).
[34] See section 10.4.
[35] Wilson (n 5) 3.
[36] See Koskenniemi (n 16) 10.

a conflict.[37] Moreover, some have emphasized the divergences in the methods and aims of law and history.[38] As a result of these differences, Wilson notes that:

> international tribunals can get the history of a country badly wrong when trying genocide cases as a result of their quest for certainty and fixity in defining ethnic groups. There always exists the possibility, and even the likelihood, that history is being oversimplified and misused in an international trial; that the prosecution's conception of nationalist history is overly deterministic, or that the defense's contextualization of the crimes bolsters a *tu quoque* defense in an effort to mitigate punishment.[39]

In a significant study, focusing on the question of whether it was desirable for non-criminal international tribunals to be employed in constructing collective memories, Hirsch considered three sociological perspectives: structural-functional, symbolic-interactionist, and social conflict. He found that from two of these perspectives, it was not desirable for international courts to participate in constructing collective memory. From the perspective of symbolic interactionism, '[i]n light of the extreme socio-cultural diversity in the global community, it is doubtful whether meaningful collective memories can be formed by global tribunals (often detached from the relevant local communities)'.[40] Furthermore, from a social conflict perspective, Hirsch noted that '[i]n light of tribunals' susceptibility to the development of historical narratives promoted by powerful actors, the social conflict perspective generally embraces a mistrustful attitude towards the involvement of tribunals in this sphere'.[41] Although Hirsch's comments relate to the role of courts in collective memory, they are to some extent also applicable to the writing of history.

10.2.2 Historical Discussions as Legally Relevant

Speaking in connection with the International Criminal Tribunal for Rwanda, its former President, Navanethem Pillay, held that the need for evidence on Rwandan history and culture in relation to certain trials was inevitable because it was legally relevant.[42] Pillay held that:

> [w]e judges agreed that you can't avoid this question of history of Rwanda, otherwise it's just one ethnic group killing another ethnic group with no reason why. History is necessary for an understanding of why the conflict occurred.[43]

From this view, therefore, the need for historical narratives reflects the nature of international criminal trials and the relative unfamiliarity of international judges with the

[37] ibid 11–12. In this context, the author notes: 'One of the few uncontroversial merits of truth commissions vis-a-vis criminal justice has been stated to lie in the way the former are able to canvass much more widely and deeply the criminality under scrutiny and thus to offer more opportunities for closure, healing and reconciliation.'
[38] See section 10.3.
[39] Wilson (n 5) 17.
[40] Hirsch (n 13) 408.
[41] ibid 413.
[42] Wilson (n 5) 20.
[43] ibid 72.

history and culture of the region in which the alleged crimes were committed.[44] Peskin argued that, given their relative autonomy from nation-States and the special nature of the crimes they adjudicate, historical discussions of armed conflicts were a necessary part of such trials.[45] He held that '[w]hether we like it or not, historical discussions are here to stay at international tribunals'.[46] Moreover, from a structural-functional perspective, Hirsch noted that 'the formation and spreading of unifying international memories that are likely to enhance international social integration'.[47]

Historical discussions are particularly pertinent to those categories of crimes, such as genocide and persecution, that require proof of discriminatory intent. For instance, the crime of genocide requires proof of *dolus specialis* on the part of the accused, in that, the accused must have acted with intent to destroy, in whole or in part, a protected group, as such. Thus, particularly in the absence of specific documentation evidencing such intent, the prosecution case may be assisted if the prosecution can connect violent methods with political and historical objectives which were held by the accused.[48] In such cases, recourse to historical discussion is inevitable because it is legally relevant to elaborate the *mens rea* requirements. Similar considerations may apply to other categories of crimes, such as crimes against humanity, which need to be 'widespread and systematic', implying a close examination of both the historical and social settings in which those crimes occurred.[49]

10.2.3 Courts Uniquely Capable of Documenting Complex Wartime Narratives

Some have argued that, in view of the structures, powers, and procedures of international tribunals, not least their painstakingly sifting through large bodies of evidence, they are particularly well-suited to engage in reliable historical discussions.[50] Peskin noted that, for many observers, international criminal tribunals were uniquely capable of documenting complex wartime histories rigorously and impartially, and by doing so could help lay the foundations for nation-building and national reconciliation. International criminal tribunals are regarded as the most authoritative truth finders at the top of a hierarchy of officially produced knowledge in which the reports of United Nations commissions and expert groups occupied the next rung down.[51]

In an address to the UN General Assembly in the early years of the ICTY, Antonio Cassese, the Tribunal's first President, held that the institution was creating 'a historical record of what occurred during the conflict thereby preventing historical revisionism'.[52]

[44] Koskenniemi notes that the need for historical contextualization may not arise in domestic trials, even when the crimes were exceptionally shocking, as there would normally be 'little doubt about how to understand the relevant acts in their historical context' (Koskenniemi (n 16) 12).

[45] V Peskin, 'Seeing Like a Court: Documenting Histories of Armed Conflict through the Lens of Judging International Crimes' (2013) 35 Human Rights Quarterly 769, 771.

[46] ibid.

[47] Hirsch (n 13) 406.

[48] Wilson (n 5) 21.

[49] ibid.

[50] Groome (n 8) 176, 187.

[51] Peskin (n 45) 770.

[52] Address of Antonio Cassese, President of the International Criminal Tribunal for the Former Yugoslavia, to the General Assembly of the United Nations, 4 November 1997—as quoted by M Karnavas, 'Gathering Evidence in

Subsequently, Cassese made the point that ensuring the history of atrocities was not forgotten was important not only for those who survive: '[f]orgetting means that victims are murdered twice: first, when they are exterminated physically, and thereafter when they are forgotten'.[53]

In her report to the UN Security Council and the General Assembly, the former President of the ICTY, Judge Gabrielle Kirk McDonald placed emphasis on the Tribunal's history-writing role. While acknowledging that the ICTY's primary purpose was the prosecution of persons responsible for serious violations of international humanitarian law, she held: '[i]n addition, through its judicial proceedings the Tribunal establishes a historical record which provides the basis for the long-term reconciliation and reconstruction of the region'.[54] McDonald held further that '[i]n creating a historical record, the Tribunal has a significant contribution to make to the creation of conditions conducive to an objective assessment of the events of this decade ...'.[55]

Some have gone so far as to argue that, in cases of conflicts involving mass atrocities, because punishing a few individuals could never come close to measuring up to such crimes, establishing historical narratives of the events should be one of the most important functions of international criminal tribunals, possibly more so than punishing the perpetrators.[56] Such historical accounts were necessary to enable the commencement of the healing process for the victims and for didactic purposes, 'for teaching younger generations of the dangers involved in particular policies'.[57]

As may be seen from the above, therefore, there is considerable disagreement over the appropriate role of writing history in international criminal trials, and recognition that this is a complex and contingent question. This ambivalence may, in part, stem from the diverging methods and aims of law and history, a subject which is explored next.

10.3 The Methods and Aims of Law and History

The aversion of some historians towards courts as writers of historical accounts, built upon a perceived distinction of simplified judgements of the law on one hand and complex contextualization and interpretation of history on the other, is not always well-grounded.[58] This is because the adversarial settings of courts, allowing for rigorous examination of competing arguments, as well as detailed scrutiny of extensive evidence, may contribute to creating 'a

International Criminal Trials—The View of the Defence Lawyer' in M Bohlander and C May (eds), *International Criminal Justice: A Critical Analysis of Institutions and Procedures* (May Publishers 2007) 77.

53 A Cassese, *International Criminal Law* (OUP 2003) 5.

54 UN General Assembly 'Fifth Annual Report of the International Tribunal for the Prosecution of Persons Responsible for Serious Violations of International Humanitarian Law Committed in the Territory of the Former Yugoslavia since 1991' (7 August 1998) UN Doc A/53/219, para 202.

55 ibid para 286.

56 Koskenniemi (n 16) 2–3.

57 ibid 4–5.

58 F F Oerskov, 'The Truth, the Whole Truth and Nothing but The Truth: The Historian, The Court, and The David Irving Trial' (2016) Historiography: Themes in Its History and Approaches to Its Theory 4 <https://www.academia.edu/25720564/The_Truth_the_Whole_Truth_and_Nothing_but_the_Truth_The_Historian_the_Court_and_the_David_Irving_Trial> accessed May 2019.

firm baseline of understanding' of events.[59] It is considered that there is much common ground in the aims and methods of law and history, and the two are not necessarily irreconcilable. The starting point for this discussion, therefore, is that overstressing the points of divergence could serve to forestall a deeper appreciation of how they are effectively combined in international criminal trials.[60]

Moreover, Hirsch observed that, in the marketplace of memory, in writing historical narratives of conflicts, tribunals would be competing against other agents of memory, including diverse State and non-State actors such as political parties, historians, the mass media, and NGOs.[61] With this in mind, the real question should be: in a context where other agents of memory, some of which would be far less reliable than tribunals, would be more than ready to step in, would it be desirable that international tribunals would not be active in this field?

Nevertheless, there are important differences between legal and historical approaches. Law's epistemology is positivist and realist, demanding definite and verifiable evidence. In determining criminal responsibility, courts often endorse one narrative of events above all others. History, on the other hand, is more pluralistic and interpretative, and may integrate the elements of competing accounts. Wilson notes that '[h]istorians often recognize that historical truths are provisional and that their evidence and conclusions are not always verifiable or free of ambiguity'.[62] On the one hand, historians would consider it pretentious to say they were searching for 'the Truth'.[63] On the other, with the exception of some radical postmodernists, most historians would demand some level of accuracy of historical claims. As one historian put it:

> we continue to appraise all knowledge-claims for their degree of truth; and to require good arguments, conformity to logic, sound evidence, objectivity, reasons that can withstand criticism, and, in general, rational support and justification for beliefs and propositions about the world and the human past . . . [64]

In this context, although early ICTY judgments made grand claims about discovering the truth as 'a cornerstone of the rule of law and a fundamental step on the way to reconciliation',[65] later judgments presented more qualified claims, noting that 'the "truth" can never be fully established or satisfied'.[66] Therefore, it would appear that there is some level of convergence between law and history in this area.

However, there are also differences, including in relation to rules on the admissibility of evidence[67] and standards of proof, as well as questions of agency and causation. In determining criminal responsibility, criminal courts seek linear connections between actions and focus on the role of individual agency and subjective intentions. History, on the other

[59] Wilson (n 5) 220. However, some have argued that 'institutional incentives and legal strategies can lead to the pursuit of incomplete and inaccurate histories' (see Peskin (n 45) 778).
[60] Wilson (n 5) 218.
[61] Hirsch (n 13) 394.
[62] Wilson (n 5) 7.
[63] Zagorin (n 12) 209.
[64] ibid 207.
[65] *Prosecutor v Dražen Erdemović* (Sentencing Judgment) ICTY-96-22 (5 March 1998) para 21.
[66] See *Prosecutor v Momir Nikolić* (Sentencing Judgment) ICTY-02-60/1 (2 December 2003) para 60, referring to *Prosecutor v Vidoje Blagojević* et al (Guidelines on the Standards Governing the Admission of Evidence) ICTY-02-60 (23 April 2003).
[67] Discussed in section 10.4.

hand, recognizes multiple layers of causality and intentions, recognizing that 'the meaning of historical events often exceeds the intentions or actions of particular individuals and can be grasped only by attention to structural causes'.[68] While lawyers are therefore more likely to reduce the historical context in order to isolate particular events and attribute criminal responsibility, historians generally espouse a more multi-layered outlook, which is based on the view that 'any single human act is embedded in an intricate matrix of causal relations,'[69] and which may also accommodate incoherence and serendipity.[70]

Another significant divergence concerns taxonomy and conventions. Law comprises several special categories and conventions (such as temporal prescription) which require criminal courts to perceive historical events through specific and idiosyncratic lenses, which may be different from the lenses used in history and other social sciences. For instance, with respect to the legal definition of genocide under the 1948 Genocide Convention, which is the prevailing definition in law and has been accepted by the ICTY,[71] one historian wondered 'to what extent is it legitimate to adopt an international legal norm resulting from a political compromise between states as a basis for historical, sociological or anthropological inquiry?'[72]

While international criminal tribunals suffer from some significant limitations regarding the development of historical narratives, they are not necessarily less reliable or effective than other agents of memory. Hirsch observes that in many cases, when compared with other agents of memory (e.g., the mass media, national governmental bodies, or historians), international criminal proceedings 'tend to mitigate inequalities and often provide more opportunities to additional parties to present their evidence'.[73]

Moreover, international tribunals often enjoy enhanced legitimacy and attract widespread attention.[74] On balance, therefore, it may indeed be desirable for international criminal tribunals to contribute towards the writing of historical narratives of conflicts. However, an important factor which has to be taken into consideration when assessing their narratives is the specific lenses which frame their approach. With respect to the ICTY, one factor by which the Tribunal's approach was influenced was the changing rules of admissibility of evidence, a subject which is considered next.

10.4 The Impact of the Rules on Admissibility of Evidence on History Writing

As noted above, the UN Security Council resolution establishing the ICTY did not explicitly accord the Tribunal a history-writing function. Nonetheless, despite the lack of references to such a function in the Statute, it may be argued that through the attribution of

[68] Koskenniemi (n 16) 13–14.
[69] Wilson (n 5) 217.
[70] T Pollmann, 'Coherence and Ambiguity in History' (2000) 39 History and Theory 167; and W M Reddy, 'The Logic of Action: Indeterminacy, Emotion, and Historical Narrative' (2001) 40 History and Theory 10, 11.
[71] This definition of genocide was reflected verbatim in the Rome Statute of the International Criminal Court.
[72] J Sémelin, *Purify and Destroy: The Political Uses of Massacre and Genocide* (Hurst 2013) 321. Indeed, at 311 *et seq*. the author points to significant divergences over the definition of genocide in the social sciences.
[73] Hirsch (n 13) 417.
[74] See N Rajkovic, 'On "Bad Law" and "Good Politics": The Politics of the ICJ Genocide Case and Its Interpretation' (2008) 21 Leiden Journal of International Law 885, 893.

primacy over national jurisdictions (Article 9) in relation to the prosecution of the conducts which 'prima facie' could have been qualified as crimes under Articles 2 to 5, the Tribunal has also been conferred a primary role over the *narrative* of the related events. On the procedural level, the Statute stipulates that—provided that it determined that a prima facie case existed—the prosecution has to prepare indictments containing concise statements of the facts and crimes charged (Article 18, para 4), while the Trial Chambers have a legal duty to ensure that the trial is fair and expeditious (Article 20, para 1).

Section 2 discussed the three main phases in the ICTY's approach to history writing. Significantly, these phases were broadly reflected in three subsequent amendments to the Rules of Procedure and Evidence ('RPE' or 'Rules').[75]

In fact, considering that the crimes charged rested on a particular personal disposition of the accused towards the victims (specially in relation to persecution), in the first trial held before the Tribunal (*Tadić*) the Prosecution sought the admission of evidence consisting in comprehensive accounts of the history of the Balkans through the testimony of expert witnesses. Having deemed those accounts as 'relevant evidence' with 'probative value' (in compliance with Rule 89(C) of the Rules), the Trial Chamber dedicated several hearings to the direct and cross-examination of such experts.[76] As a result, *Tadić* Trial Judgment conveyed a long history of the Balkans, summarized in seventy-three paragraphs under the header 'The context of the conflict' (see Section 2).[77]

This was possible because at the time the *Tadić* trial was held, the rules on the admissibility of evidence were informed by the adversarial model. According to Rule 85(A), for instance, the parties chose the respective expert witnesses, determined the subject of their testimony, provided them with the materials on which they had to testify, and prepared them for direct and cross-examination. Under such a system, the parties were allowed to 'shop for favorable expert testimony', select one that would be 'compatible with their position and "theory of the case"', and give him/her the materials which more likely would confirm it.[78]

In 1998, some inquisitorial features were introduced to the RPE, respectively allowing the judges to limit the number of witnesses called by the parties to provide testimony about the same issue (new Rules 73*bis* and 73*ter*), and the parties to get written statements of expert witnesses admitted into evidence without calling the witness to testify in person, if the other party did not request to cross-examine him/her (new Rule 94*bis*).[79]

A second amendment, adopted in December 2000, permitted the admission into a case of written statements—including in the form of reports relating to the relevant historical, political, or military background, unless the other party sought to prove the evidence unreliable or prejudicial or requested cross-examination, or the judges deemed the cross-examination appropriate (new Rule 92*bis*).[80] In December 2002, by amending Rule 94*bis*,

[75] International Criminal Tribunal for the former Yugoslavia, Rules of Procedure and Evidence (entered into force 14 March 1994) UN Doc IT/32.

[76] In particular Dr James Gow, Lecturer of the Department of War Studies at King's College (London), called as Prosecution witness, was examined for three and a half days.

[77] See *Tadić Judgment* (n 14).

[78] See K Turkovic, 'Historians in Search for Truth about Conflicts in the Territory of Former Yugoslavia as Expert Witnesses in front of the ICTY' (2004) 36 Časopis za suvremenu povijest (Journal of Contemporary History) 41, 51.

[79] International Criminal Tribunal for the former Yugoslavia, Rules of Procedure and Evidence (entered into force 14 March 1994) UN Doc IT/32/Rev13 (adopted 9–10 July 1998).

[80] International Criminal Tribunal for the former Yugoslavia, Rules of Procedure and Evidence (entered into force 14 March 1994) UN Doc IT/32/Rev19 (adopted 1 and 13 December 2000).

the opposing party was attributed the faculty to challenge the expert's qualifications, or the relevance of (parts of) his/her report.[81]

Finally, a significant shift in the prosecutorial strategy would result from the 'post-*Milošević*' decision to adopt a strict crime-based approach and limit the scope of those reports,[82] which was also advisable in light of the duty to expedite the proceedings, as sanctioned by the UN Security Council in the Resolution 1503/2003.

These successive amendments to the RPE—and particularly the new Rule 92*bis*, with respect to the admission at trial of written statements relating to historical background, as long as they are not challenged by the parties—could have a direct impact on the quality of historical information admitted at trial.

An analogous criticism may be moved in relation to 'adjudicated facts': the decision to amend Rule 94[83] in order to allow a trial chamber to take judicial notice of facts or documentary evidence 'validated' in a previous judgment certainly promotes judicial economy, but at the same time significantly affects the quality of the historical accounts provided by the tribunal.

In fact, in both circumstances the parties will focus their resources on challenging documents containing historical information of direct relevance to aspects of their case.

Once again, the *Milošević* trial represents a watershed in the tribunal's history. More than any other case, it was exemplary of the impact the inherent tension between history writing and determining the criminal responsibility of the accused may have on a trial. This tension is reflected in the apparently explanatory warning given by the Chief Prosecutor Carla Del Ponte during the Prosecution's opening statement, that 'it is Slobodan Milošević's personal responsibility which the Prosecution intends to demonstrate for the crimes ascribed to him, nothing but that, but all of that'.[84]

Due to the accused's position (as President of Serbia and of the Federal Republic of Yugoslavia) and the implications of the modes by which the Prosecution intended to attach liability to him (the participation to three different joint criminal enterprises (JCE), in relation to the conflicts in Kosovo, Croatia, and Bosnia respectively), and also in light of the decision to join three indictments in one single trial,[85] in order to prove *all of* Milošević's personal criminal responsibility vis-à-vis conducts occurring between 1991 and 1999, the

[81] International Criminal Tribunal for the former Yugoslavia, Rules of Procedure and Evidence (entered into force 14 March 1994) UN Doc IT/32/Rev26 (adopted 12 December 2002).

[82] As recalled by one Prosecution expert witness, reports would focus on the circumstances immediately surrounding the alleged crimes, dealing with individual towns or regions where the accused conducted their deeds and seeking to explicate the political culture in which the perpetrator came to wield power (see R Donia, 'Encountering the Past: History at the Yugoslav War Crimes Tribunal' (2004) 11 The Journal of the International Institute <http://quod.lib.umich.edu/j/jii/4750978.0011.201/--encountering-the-past-history-at-the-yugoslav-war-crimes?rg n=main;view=fulltext> accessed May 2019).

[83] A Letter (B) was introduced by an amendment adopted in July 1998 (n 64), and interpreted as conferring the Trial Chamber a discretionary power to narrow the issues at trial, under the condition, among other things, that those facts were relevant to the case, had been settled by an Appeals Chamber, and didn't go to the accused's act, conduct, or mental state see, *ex plurimis: Z. Kupreškić* et al *Case* (Decision on the Motions of Drago Josipović, Zoran Kupreškić, and Vlatko Kupreškić to admit additional evidence pursuant to Rule 115 and for judicial notice taken pursuant to rule 94(B)) ICTY-95-16 (8 May 2001) para 6; and *Prlić* et al *Case* (Decision on Motion for Judicial Notice of Adjudicated Facts Pursuant to Rule 94(B)) ICTY-04-74 (14 March 2006) para 12.

[84] *Prosecutor v Slobodan Milošević* (Public Transcript of Hearing) ICTY-02-54-T (12 February 2002) 11.

[85] As recalled by Carla Del Ponte, the Prosecution's strategy was 'to join the three indictments, relying on a JCE theory whose unifying element was a plan to establish a Greater Serbia' (C Del Ponte, 'Difficulties for the Participants—Indictment Correct, Trial Impossible' in T W Waters (ed), *The Milošević Trial—an Autopsy* (OUP 2013) 138).

Prosecution was required to present a comprehensive narrative of the disintegration of Yugoslavia—or, as noted by Wilson, a 'monumental history' of the conflict.[86] In fact, Del Ponte's proclamation that the Tribunal 'will write only one chapter, the most bloody one'[87] of such history not only collided with the implied duty to historically contextualize Milošević's actions, but also—and most of all—with Milošević's *right* to challenge the Prosecutor's version and to present his own narrative. A corollary to this right was that he would be allowed to challenge the Prosecution's narrative by arguing that the trial had the aim of asserting the collective responsibility of Serbia, and that his role would thus be 'to defend, not merely himself, but the whole nation'.[88] Moreover, Milošević's plan would benefit from the Court's decision to allow him to represent himself at trial.[89] As emphatically put by Veton Surroi, 'for Milošević, what was happening was not a trial; it was a panel on history [...], in which his role would be defined as the guardian of the Serbian historic truth'.[90]

In the end, according to Carla Del Ponte '[t]he main factor contributing to the trial's length was the Rules of Procedure and Evidence'.[91] In her view, to prevent this from happening, the Court should have not only placed significant restrictions on the time and scope of the Defence case, but also on the subject matter of proposed witness testimony—a choice that the judges would later make *on the basis* of the lessons learned during the *Milošević* trial.[92] However, considering that the Appeals Chamber held that to introduce such restrictions only on the Defence case would violate the principle of basic proportionality enshrined in Article 21 of the Statute, the only viable option for a Chamber would be to implement an aggressive case management plan with respect to the Prosecution case.[93]

This even-handed approach of the ICTY was necessary in order to prevent what Koskenniemi[94] has described as 'show trials', namely trials which silence the accused and seek to convey unambiguous historical truths to their audience. The price to pay in safeguarding the trial's legitimacy consists in granting that judges will construct facts out of what the parties are able to bring forward (in compliance with the procedural techniques informing the admission of evidence). In other words: in order for the trial to be fair, the accused must be entitled to challenge the Prosecution's version of the truth.

86 Wilson (n 5) 86.

87 *Milošević Trial Transcript* (n 84) 10.

88 T W Waters, 'The Trial—IT-02-54, *Prosecutor v Milošević*' (n 85) 58.

89 ibid 67–69 (arguing that even if this strategy may have negatively affected his chances of being acquitted, he gained a unique opportunity 'of influencing his legacy and politics in Serbia'). In the same spirit, see C Del Ponte (n 85) 146, arguing that Milošević 'did not even bother to mount a proper defense', and instead 'chose to present a political defense, to speak directly to his constituents in Serbia, to exploit each trial day ... as an opportunity for political diatribe'.

90 V Surroi, 'Conversations with Milošević—Two Meetings, Bloody Hands', in W Waters (ed), *The Milošević Trial—an Autopsy* (OUP 2013) 225–26.

91 Del Ponte (n 85) 140.

92 Waters ('Biopsy—The Legacies of Milošević', in Waters (n 85) 489) argued that '[t]he tighter grip shown by judges in more recent trials of prominent accused is in part a practice directly drawn from the lessons of Milošević, in part as a consequence of changed rules ... that themselves derive from the experience of that trial', and that 'the pressure to shorten trials ... derives principally from the recognition of how long the *Milošević* trial was ...'.

93 See G Boas, *The Milošević trial: Lessons for the Conduct of Complex International Criminal Proceedings* (CUP 2007) 194–95—referring to the Appeals Chamber's decision in *Orić* (*Orić* case (Interlocutory Decision on Length of Defence Case) ICTY-03-68 (20 July 2005) paras 5–7). On the other hand, Carla Del Ponte argued that '[a] tribunal's trial chamber should refrain from unilaterally shrinking complex leadership cases' (C Del Ponte and C Sudetic, *Madame Prosecutor—Confrontations with Humanity's Worst Criminals and the Culture of Impunity* (Other Press 2009) 376).

94 Koskenniemi (n 16) 33–35.

Irrespective of the approach adopted in the rules on the admission of evidence, a critical choice seems to rest with the Prosecution: that is to determine, by broadening or narrowing the scope of an indictment, how much history—and how much *competing* history—would be allowed into the trial.[95]

As a result, it must be acknowledged that especially due to the recognition of equality of arms between the parties, international criminal trials are not primarily concerned with writing a comprehensive historical narrative of conflicts, since the judges are at best in a position to provide a balanced, but nevertheless partial truth—a truth which is very much framed within a tribunal's specific lens and the Parties' narratives, and which will be addressed below as *judicial truth*.[96]

10.5 The Involvement of Third Parties: 'Contextual' Allegations as Quasi-criminal Responsibility?

The new architecture on the admission of evidence, together with other factors including resource limitations of the parties, could tend to allow for less rigorous scrutiny and acceptance of statements not affecting the accused's position. As discussed below, the information deemed irrelevant or not detrimental to the latter's case, including that related to the involvement of third parties in the commission of crimes, has been admitted at trial—and eventually referred to in the judgments. Moreover, and even more worryingly, two prominent corollaries to the right to a fair trial—the right to defend oneself from accusations and the right to confront witnesses—have only been applied in relation to living persons.

The findings related to an accused standing trial in a separate case are barred from being admitted against him/her under Rule 94, since the only option available to the Prosecution is the joining of investigations or trials (Rules 48 and 82). On the other hand, ICTY basic documents do not afford much protection to the deceased,[97] either in terms of limits to the

[95] However, for the enormous documentary record produced by the Prosecution with regard to Milošević Trial 'can provide historians with access to materials they might never have been able to assemble,' it can be considered as 'a gift to historiography' (Waters (n 88) 73—in the same spirit, see also F Bieber, 'Do Historians Need a Verdict?' in W Waters (ed), *The Milošević Trial—an Autopsy* (OUP 2013) 352). Furthermore, since ICTY support in the Balkans was often based on the assumption that once a record was established by the tribunal, it would be difficult for local societies not to acknowledge the truth—that atrocities were committed—this acknowledgment may also facilitate reconciliation (see D F Orentlicher, 'That Someone Guilty Be Punished—The Impact of the ICTY in Bosnia' *International Centre for Transitional Justice* and *Open Society Justice Initiative* (2010) 42–43, 89–100 <https://www.ictj.org/sites/default/files/ICTJ-FormerYugoslavia-Someone-Guilty-2010-English.pdf> accessed May 2019). As highlighted by Carla Del Ponte (Del Ponte and Sudetic (n 93) 371–72), the Tribunal's record, 'if historians, writers, and journalists do their jobs effectively, will make it difficult for future demagogues in Croatia, Serbia, Bosnia and Herzegovina, Macedonia, and Kosovo to foment interethnic hysteria,' because '[t]hanks to the tribunal's work, no one group in the lands of the former Yugoslavia ... can proclaim itself a victim and nothing else'. In fact, the evidence gathered during the trial may have 'an effect on how future generations understand the region's history and how the conflicts came to pass' ('Weighing the evidence—Lessons from the Slobodan Milosevic trial' (*Human Rights Watch*, December 2006) 1 <https://www.hrw.org/sites/default/files/reports/milosevic1206webwcover.pdf> accessed May 2019.

[96] In this regard, it has also been noted that when the statements of historians who appear as expert witnesses are challenged, the Trial Chamber may decide to resolve the issue 'by adopting appropriately neutral language' (*Tadić Judgement* (n 14) para 54). In such circumstances, the judges may in fact prefer to 'sort through the contradictory opinions of competing experts' by 'removing the weight of such evidence' or even by 'removing expert evidence from consideration altogether' (see A Appazov, *Expert Evidence and International Criminal Justice* (Springer 2016) 7).

[97] According to Rule 54 the Trial Chamber has to terminate proceedings in case of the death of the accused (see *Prosecutor v Hadzić* (Order Terminating the Proceedings) ICTY-04-75 (22 July 2016)). *A fortiori*, a person deceased before the initiation of the investigation can't be qualified as suspect (and be granted the suspect's rights).

admissibility of evidence or by granting a standing to a counsel/representative. The only instrument available is the request to appear as *amicus curiae*, which a Trial Chamber can grant (to a person, an organization, or a State) 'if it considers it desirable for the proper determination of the case' (Rule 74).

Two cases may provide a clearer understanding of the implications of this legal shortcoming. In the *Prlić* case, the Trial Chamber dismissed a request for leave to appear as *amicus curiae* filed by the Government of the Republic of Croatia—wishing to clarify issues related to 'the participation of the political and military leaders in the joint criminal enterprise' alleged in the indictment, including the then President Franjo Tuđman—because such submissions 'shall be limited to questions of law', whereas the points raised by Croatia went 'far beyond the scope of the indictment', and the appearance of the State 'would not be in the interests of justice'.[98]

Due to the political impact of the subsequent reference to President Tuđman as a member of the JCE in *Prlić* Trial Judgment,[99] in 2016 the Croatian Government filed a new request for leave to appear as *amicus curiae* at the appeals phase. In dismissing the request, the Appeals Chamber emphasized that 'findings of criminal responsibility made in a case before the Tribunal are binding only on the accused in a specific case', and that the Trial Chamber 'made no explicit findings concerning [the] ... participation in the JCE' and thus did not find Tuđman guilty of any crime, since in light of the presumption of innocence the findings 'regarding the mere existence and membership of the JCE do not ... constitute findings of criminal responsibility of any persons who were not charged and convicted in the case' and 'on the part of the state of Croatia'.[100]

On the other hand, factual findings made in *Karadžić* Trial Judgment[101] were invoked by the Serbian Government in the days following its issuance as constituting a legal finding on Slobodan Milošević's—and the then Serbian Government's—non-involvement in the genocidal campaign conducted around Srebrenica in 1995.[102] The heated reactions spurred by these statements forced ICTY Prosecutor Serge Brammertz to step in and highlight that '[t]he only person on trial in Karadžić's case was Karadžić', and 'while Milošević did not face final judgement in the courtroom, the facts and evidence [discussed during his own trial] remain'.[103]

These two examples show that, as a consequence of the new architecture on the admission of evidence, even though historical information introduced at trial may not be directly objectionable to the parties in the case, such information is far from neutral and could have an impact on the historical narrative. In these two cases, historical and political discussions took centre stage, and a different organ of the Tribunal had to recall that in accordance

[98] *Prosecutor v Prlić* et al (Decision on Request by the Government of the Republic of Croatia for Leave to Appear as *Amicus Curiae*) ICTY-04-74 (11 October 2006) paras 4–5.

[99] See 'Hague Judges Jail Bosnian Croat Leaders, Condemn Tudjman' (*Deutsche Welle*, 29 May 2013) <http://www.dw.com/en/hague-judges-jail-bosnian-croat-leaders-condemn-tudjman/a-16846447> accessed May 2019.

[100] *Prosecutor v Prlić* et al (Decision on Application by the Republic of Croatia for Leave to Appear as *Amicus Curiae* and to Submit *Amicus Curiae* Brief) ICTY-04-74 (18 July 2016) para 9.

[101] Inter alia, the Trial Chamber found that '[b]y May 1995, it appeared to international representatives that the split between Slobodan Milošević and the Accused was complete' (*Prosecutor v Karadžić* (Public Redacted Version of Judgment Issued on 24 March 2016) ICTY-95-5/18 (24 March 2016) para 3296).

[102] S Dragojlo, 'Milosevic's Old Allies Celebrate His "Innocence"' (*BIRN*, 16 August 2016) <http://www.balkaninsight.com/en/article/milosevic-s-old-allies-celebrate-his-innocence--08-16-2016> accessed May 2019.

[103] S Brammertz, 'Slobodan Milosevic is No hero' (*Al Jazeera*, 24 August 2016) <http://www.aljazeera.com/indepth/opinion/2016/08/slobodan-milosevic-hero-160823124808287.html> accessed May 2019.

with a basic corollary to the principle of legality—the presumption of innocence—the above-mentioned findings have no impact on the criminal liability of persons who were not charged in the specific case.

In conclusion, problematic as it may be, in some cases international criminal tribunals will be required to engage in assessing historical events also in relation to un-indicted or deceased individuals. However, it will rest with the judges and outreach programmes to clarify that those findings cannot be equated with the determinations on the criminal responsibility of the third parties involved. Such historical assessments shall therefore be regarded 'as one piece of the puzzle in reconstructing particular events'.[104]

10.6 Conclusion

Through its case law, and detailed and well-substantiated records of particular incidents and events, the ICTY has provided a body of evidence that is invaluable for historians. Its contribution towards a better understanding of the history of the region will last long after the trials have completed. This chapter has argued that the evolution of the relationship between criminal adjudication and the writing of historical narratives at the ICTY represents one of the most important lessons for future tribunals.

Absent of a clear demarcation of its mandate in relation to history writing, the Tribunal's organs found themselves embroiled in deliberations concerning the historical context of the crimes. In fact, early on, the Prosecution intended its mandate to prosecute the gravest crimes committed during the conflict as implying a duty to convey 'grand narratives' of the events (irrespective of the weak causal relationship with the charges).

In the following years, and especially after the proceedings against Slobodan Milošević collapsed, the prosecution adopted a narrower crime-based approach. In the same period, the UN Security Council imposed upon the ICTY the so-called 'Completion Strategy': in order to meet the request to expedite proceedings, among other things the Tribunal had to substantially amend the rules on the admission of evidence, reducing the role of lengthy historical analyses and historian expert witnesses.

As a result, later judgments generally contain historical information which had been deemed directly linked to the charges. Moreover, the judges adopted a more neutral approach, to the point that they would ignore expert evidence when confronted with contradictory narratives which were challenged by the parties. Having, on the other hand, subjected the historical information not objected by the parties to a lesser level of scrutiny, they have been forced to clarify that the judgments have no impact on those persons who had not been charged.

As a matter of fact, the ICTY has been an extraordinary recipient of documents and evidence of substantial historical value. As recalled in the Fifth Annual Report on its activities, not only did the Tribunal contribute to developing a historical narrative of the conflict, but it also disseminated information widely, through its outreach programme, within the former Yugoslavia, thus empowering people and enabling them to challenge and change the culture which had led to the conflict.[105]

[104] Bieber (n 95) 355.

[105] Fifth Annual Report (n 54) paras 296–97.

However, to argue that this Tribunal—and international criminal tribunals in general—are in the position to provide an 'authoritative' and definitive account of historical events connected to the conduct they are called to assess is to overburden them. First of all, because—as demonstrated in this chapter—such a conclusion could only be reached by overlooking the essential difference between the methods and parameters respectively informing the quest for historical and judicial truths. And most of all, because no trier of fact is in the position to provide an authoritative account of events, for a criminal tribunal approaches history from its own specific lens, and is bound by procedural norms imposing conditions on the admissibility of evidence.[106] It is ultimately primarily concerned with information related to the criminal responsibility of the accused. As underlined by Florian Bieber, '[e]ven if a Court were understood to produce "definitive histories of conflicts[,]" ... the judicial process inherently focuses on determining the guilt of an individual', and thus the historical record it produces 'is inherently a by-product, not its purpose'.[107]

One of the most significant legacies of the ICTY is, in fact, the acknowledgement that what international criminal tribunals are able to provide is a *judicial* truth, consisting in a version of the events based upon the evidences tendered and deemed admissible and credible in accordance with the rules and the context of the trial.[108] Instead of being treated as authoritative narratives, international criminal tribunals' findings on distant or contextual historical events, as well as those related to third parties should better be characterized as 'a discursive beginning for the examination of particular episodes of mass violence'.[109] Accordingly, as suggested by Hirsch, when international tribunals are bound to establish historical facts in order to grasp the contextual background of the crimes, it seems desirable that tribunals:

> acknowledge that the particular historical narrative presented in their judgment is provisional, and based on the specific legal context and facts available to them (and not rule out the development of alternative historical accounts in different contexts).[110]

In conclusion, since as pointed out by the Trial Chamber, (international) criminal tribunals are not the arbiters of historical facts,[111] recalling an observation made by Hannah Arendt in relation to the *Eichmann* trial in Jerusalem, it is now as then necessary to keep in mind that 'even the noblest of ulterior purposes ... can only detract from law's main business: to weigh the charges ..., to render judgement, and to mete out punishment'.[112]

[106] In this regard, Sander underlines that 'rather than the result of neutral acts of deduction, judicial narratives inevitably depend on the choices made by the multiplicity of actors who interact within international criminal proceedings', including 'the ability of the prosecution and defence teams to access evidence, prosecutorial charging policies, the procedural and evidential framework relied upon to admit, scrutinize and evaluate evidence, and the interpretation of substantive legal categories' (B Sander, 'History On Trial: Historical Narrative Pluralism Within And Beyond International Criminal Courts' (2018) 67 International and Comparative Law Quarterly 547, 574).

[107] Bieber (n 95) 350.

[108] ibid 351.

[109] Sander (n 106) 575.

[110] Hirsch (n 13) 411.

[111] *Prosecutor v Dragan Nikolić Case* (Sentencing Judgment) ICTY-94-2 (18 December 2003) para 122.

[112] See H Arendt, *Eichmann in Jerusalem. A Report on the Banality of Evil* (Viking 1965) 253.

11

Handle with Care

ICTY, Juridical By-products, and Criminological Analyses

*Andy Aydın-Aitchison**, **

This chapter starts with claims made for the potential historical value of the evidence gathered, presented, and scrutinized in international criminal courts. Human Rights Watch claimed of the ICTY that 'future generations will use the evidence to understand the region's history',[1] while Mullins identified records from the International Criminal Tribunal for Rwanda (ICTR) as a source of 'thick' description[2]. Earlier trials have played an important, if not always unproblematic, part in Holocaust historiography.[3] Recently, criminologists and others have started to make use of resources generated or collected by the ICTY and ICTR to describe and analyse international crimes.[4] Methodological aspects of these studies are not always fully or explicitly developed and so we must reflect on how we can make scholarly use of ICTY material, on the challenges and limitations of the source material, on the kinds of questions that material is best suited to answering, and on how to build as robust a set of findings as possible. This chapter argues that while evidence and transcripts from international criminal courts have great potential as a source of data for analyses in criminology, and by extension other social sciences and historical research, they need to be handled with care, recognizing gaps, regional specificity, and the need to assess validity. The chapter compares judicial and scholarly approaches, examines access and transparency, issues around the construction of a body of evidence in the trial process and matters relating to witnesses. There are many reasons to take the ICTY as a 'best case scenario' of international judicial

* Senior Lecturer in Criminology at the School of Law, University of Edinburgh, Scotland, where he teaches on the MSc Global Crime, Justice and Security. He holds a PhD from Cardiff University (2008). He is author of Making the Transition (Intersentia, 2011), a detailed account of police, court, and prison reforms in the context of the first ten years of post-war State-building in Bosnia and Herzegovina. His current research focuses on making use of testimony and evidence from the International Criminal Tribunal for the former Yugoslavia to answer criminological questions.

** Versions of this chapter were presented at the ICTY Legacy Dialogue, Sarajevo, June 2017 and 17th European Society of Criminology conference, Cardiff, September 2017. I am grateful to colleagues for questions and comments on those and other occasions that have helped shape the final version. Particular thanks go to Ellie Bates, Edina Bećirević, Kirsten Campbell, Mark Drumbl, Agata Fijalkowski, and Carsten Stahn. The full panel in which the paper featured in Sarajevo is available at: <https://www.youtube.com/watch?v=TtHjUGDNykM>.

1 Human Rights Watch, *Weighing the Evidence: Lessons from the Slobodan Milošević Trial* (HRW 2006) 14.

2 C W Mullins, '"We are Going to Rape You and Taste Tutsi Women": Rape During the 1994 Rwandan Genocide' (2009) 49 British Journal of Criminology 719, 720.

3 V N Dadrian, 'The Turkish Military Tribunal's Prosecution of the Authors of the Armenian Genocide: Four Major Court-martial Series' (1997) 11 Holocaust and Genocide Studies 28; D Bloxham, *Genocide on Trial: War Crime Trials and the Formation of Holocaust History and Memory* (OUP 2010).

4 D A Komar, 'Variables Influencing Victim Selection in Genocide' (2008) 53 Journal of Forensic Sciences 172; Mullins (n 2); S Klusemann, 'Massacres as Process: A Micro-sociological Theory of Internal Patterns of Mass Atrocities' (2012) 9 European Journal of Criminology 468; S Tanner and M Mulone, 'Private Security and Armed Conflict: a Case Study of the Scorpions During the Mass Killings in Former Yugoslavia' (2013) 53 British Journal of Criminology 41.

Andy Aydın-Aitchison, *Handle with Care* In: *Legacies of the International Criminal Tribunal for the Former Yugoslavia.* Edited by: Carsten Stahn, Carmel Agius, Serge Brammertz, Colleen Rohan, Oxford University Press (2020). © The Several Contributors
DOI: 10.1093/oso/9780198862956.003.0012

sources as data, and I examine two different approaches taken to using the court's output in criminological research. They make a strong case for using the ICTY as part of scholarly efforts to make sense of the violent disintegration of State and society in Yugoslavia.

11.1 Background

Human Rights Watch have claimed of the ICTY that 'future generations will use the evidence to understand the region's history',[5] while another author identified ICTR records as a source of 'thick' description.[6] Based on a reading of historiographical material, accounts of court processes and a detailed examination of two empirical studies, I argue that while evidence and transcripts from international criminal courts have great potential as a source of data for historical and social science analyses, they need to be handled with care and with due attention to their limits of coverage. Moreover, the demands of a robust and methodologically sound analysis of data situated in the context of its creation need to be met. The paper compares judicial and scholarly approaches, examines access and transparency, as well as issues around the construction of a body of evidence in the trial process; and finally, matters relating to witnesses. As there are variations across trial venues, I ultimately focus on the ICTY as a 'best case scenario' and examine two different approaches to using the court's output.[7] The paper provides a foundation for further rigorous criminological, social-scientific, and historical research making use of ICTY records.

A number of research papers use judgments, testimony, and evidence from international courts as data to varying degrees. The Nuremberg tribunals and other post-Second World War trials play an important, if not always unproblematic, part in Holocaust historiography.[8] Earlier judicial proceedings, although providing less primary source material, have been used to develop analyses of the Armenian genocide, the intent of the Ittihadists, and the organized implementation of killings.[9] Recently, criminologists and others have started to make use of resources generated or collected by the ICTY and ICTR to describe and analyse international crimes.[10] A number of papers in the *Journal of Genocide Research* have utilized the ICTY sources, providing analyses of ethnic boundary maintenance,[11] cognitive dissonance,[12] and heterogeneity and individual inconsistency among perpetrators.[13] These papers offer original and significant development of frameworks for understanding genocide and other atrocity crimes, but do not make explicit their approach to ICTY material

5 Human Rights Watch (n 1) 14.

6 Mullins (n 2) 720.

7 E Bećirević, *Genocide on the Drina River* (Yale University Press 2013); A Aitchison, 'Police and Persecution in the Bosnian Krajina: Democratisation, Deprofessionalisation and Militarisation' (2016) 14 Criminal Justice Issues 1.

8 C Gerlach, 'The Eichmann Interrogations in Holocaust Historiography' (2001) 15 Holocaust and Genocide Studies 428; E Haberer, 'History and Justice: Paradigms of the Prosecution of Nazi Crimes' (2005) 19 Holocaust and Genocide Studies 487; Bloxham (n 3).

9 Dadrian (n 3).

10 Komar (n 4); Mullins (n 2); Klusemann (n 4); Tanner and Mulone (n 4).

11 C Carmichael, 'Violence and Ethnic Boundary Maintenance in Bosnia in the 1990s' (2006) 8 Journal of Genocide Research 283.

12 B Lieberman, 'Nationalist Narratives, Violence Between Neighbours and Ethnic Cleansing in Bosnia and Hercegovina: A Case of Cognitive Dissonance' (2006) 8 Journal of Genocide Research 295.

13 J N Clark, 'Genocide, War Crimes and the Conflict in Bosnia: Understanding the Perpetrators' (2009) 11 Journal of Genocide Research 421.

and its historical by-products.[14] It is time to reflect on how we can make scholarly use of ICTY's work, the challenges and limitations of the source material, the kinds of questions it is best suited to answer, and on how to build as robust a set of findings as possible. In order to do this, I first review material on making use of juridical decisions in the study of atrocity. I proceed to discuss two different approaches taken in recent research, focusing on their relative merits and the scope for improvement.[15]

11.2 Juridical By-products: Issues with Testimony and Evidence

11.2.1 The Judicial and Academic Approaches

Certain common features between the judicial and scholarly approach suggest courts' outputs can be treated as data for analysis. Certainly, in more positivist approaches, a focus on facts, proof, and the 'detailed reconstruction of events' points towards commonalities in orientation of courts and scholars.[16] The commonalities might be somewhat stretched, and rely on a superficial reading of the judicial and scholarly enterprises. Wilson contrasts a positivist legal approach with the pluralism of historical research resting on continual interrogation, reinterpretation, and academic discussion.[17] History's judgement, unlike that of the court, is never final. Nonetheless, the underlying commonality in methods can point to testimony and evidence as data. Eltringham draws the comparison between the 'coercive and enticed remembering' that takes place in the courtroom and in oral history,[18] and the common aims around producing a 'coherent narrative', capable of explaining and interpreting, as opposed to merely recording events.[19] Thus, even if the scholarly endeavour is a more long-term and indefinite project than the act of judging, there is a case for drawing on courts' diverse outputs.

11.2.2 Access and Backstage Activity

The level of access to material will vary according to different jurisdictions and different periods. Browning, in his research on a police reserve battalion, gained access to original interrogation material,[20] whereas Lyons noted, in reference to her experience working at the ICTR, that even defence counsel would not have access to the questions asked in an initial prosecution interview, only the resulting statement.[21] When reviewing testimony, an analyst has no access to the coaching and preparation that takes place 'backstage',[22] and so

[14] I follow Eltringham in using the term by-product noting that the records are not the primary objective of tribunals. N Eltringham, '"We are Not a Truth Commission": Fragmented Narratives and the Historical Record at the International Criminal Tribunal for Rwanda' (2009) 11 Journal of Genocide Research 55, 57.

[15] Bećirević (n 7); Aitchison (n 7).

[16] C A Nielsen, 'Can We Salvage a History of the former Yugoslav Conflicts from the Milošević Trial' in T Waters (ed), *The Milošević Trial: an Autopsy* (OUP 2014) 326, 331; see also Haberer (n 8) 489.

[17] R Wilson, *Writing History in International Criminal Trials* (CUP 2011) 7.

[18] Eltringham (n 14) 55.

[19] ibid 59.

[20] C Browning, *Ordinary Men: Reserve Police Battalion 101 and the Final Solution in Poland* (Penguin 2001) xv.

[21] B Lyons, 'Enough is Enough: the Illegitimacy of International Criminal Convictions' (2011) 13 Journal of Genocide Research 287, 289.

[22] Eltringham (n 14) 62.

is missing some of the key contextual information around the process through which the testimony (as data) is produced. Further, in order to protect witnesses and to facilitate the court's own access to sensitive material, large parts of hearings may be conducted away from the public and with redactions from the publicly available record. For example, across the seventy-nine sessions in the main trial phase of *Tadić,* five were completely closed, and a further thirty-two involved varying degrees of redaction.[23] Other cases may not reach completion, although in cases such as *Milošević*, where an interim *98bis* judgment was given,[24] researchers seeking some comfort in judicial confirmation of evidence can still find it to a degree.[25] Nonetheless, a researcher is most likely presented with an incomplete set of records arising from a process that is not open to his or her scrutiny, a fact compounded by prosecutorial selection which precedes judicial proceedings.

11.2.3 Partisanship and Control

The issue of access shows that researchers utilizing court documents have little or no control over what material they receive. Equally, and as opposed to researchers generating their own primary data through interviews, they have no control over the conditions under which it is produced. What goes on record is the product of a series of purposeful decisions taken by the key actors in the trial process. The selection of lines of investigations, documents, and witnesses is a partisan process, involving multiple actors with differing rationales, and only ever producing a partial record.[26] In the adversarial system, it is in the interests of prosecutors to put forward only the strongest, most robust, and most easily corroborated evidence. Likewise, defence strategies focus on disrupting the narratives put forward by the prosecutor. It is not just the selection of witnesses and documents, but the control of witnesses in court through examination and cross-examination that dictates what goes on record. The outcome may be 'directed rediscription' or 'dialogical collaboration',[27] but like other forms of secondary data, it is one where a researcher must accept the direction chosen by another. The international tribunals may not go as far as inquisitorial systems in focusing on 'continuous forensic examination', but judges in the ICTR and ICTY are, nonetheless, more

[23] *Prosecutor v Duško Tadić* (Judgment) ICTY No IT-94-0 (26 January 2000); it is worth noting that what is redacted will be structured in particular ways that can limit the presence of particular voices in the testimony. Kirsten Campbell, present at the ICTY Dialogue in Sarajevo (**), 1 hr 20 min ff, noted that witnesses regarding sexual violence were often those whose very sensitive testimony would be redacted. Her earlier work notes the under-representation of women, and their disproportionate concentration in giving evidence on gender-related crimes. Combined with the redaction, this serves to marginalize women's experience of the war as a feature of the available testimony records. See K Campbell, 'The Gender of Transitional Justice: Law, Sexual Violence and the International Criminal Tribunal for the former Yugoslavia' (2007) 1 International Journal of Transitional Justice 411.

[24] *Prosecutor v Slobodan Milošević*, (Decision on Motion for Judgment of Acquittal), ICTY IT-02-54 (16 June 2004).

[25] Nielsen (n 16).

[26] Browning (n 20) xvi; Eltringham (n 14) 58. Procedural protections, which will vary from system to system, will mitigate this through disclosure rules to some extent making the prosecution material, including potentially exculpatory or mitigating material, available to the defence. See *Rules of Procedure and Evidence* (ICTY 8 July 2015) rules 66 and 68. The point was raised at the Sarajevo ICTY Legacy Dialogue (**), particularly by H van der Wilt (22 min ff) and M A Drumbl (1 hr 17 min ff), both in terms of the fragmentation resulting from a series of mini-narratives produced by the court and the unevenness and historical distortion implied by the limited number of atrocities that are internationally judicialized. On the gendering of this selection process, see Campbell (n 23).

[27] Eltringham (n 14) 61.

active in the trial process.[28] Yet, given the different backgrounds of judges, this active approach is not consistent across trials and the chamber still seeks to place boundaries around what is heard and probed in court, rather than seeking out the 'whole story'.[29] A somewhat terse comment directed from the bench at counsel in *Vasiljević* captures this:

> What is its relevance? We are not here to write a history of what happened throughout the whole of Bosnia.[30]

Eltringham quotes an officer of the chamber in the ICTY, stating that researchers need to start with the judgment *before* going to documents.[31] The point being made relates to credibility; equally though, carefully reviewing the indictment, opening statements, and judgment at some point in the analytical process gives the researcher a stronger sense on the boundaries placed around a hearing and the limits of the resulting data. In looking at examples of research utilizing the ICTY documentation, the paper will return to the question of at which stage these particular documents are best consulted.

11.2.4 Forgetting, Misrepresentation, and Perjury by Witness

Aside from the aims and strategies of prosecution and defence teams and the approach of judges, testimony is shaped by witnesses who may forget, misrepresent, or directly perjure themselves in trials. In international tribunals, there are often lengthy gaps between the events and the trial. The trial of Hissène Habré at the Extraordinary African Chambers commenced roughly twenty-five years after his rule came to an end. Even the earliest ICTY trials heard evidence three to four years after the events in question (see *Tadić*). This represents a challenge in terms of memory, and post-hoc interpretation of events through frameworks shaped by what has happened subsequently. It also allows witnesses, who wish to pursue particular outcomes, to spend time developing a narrative.[32] Browning, while speaking for the 'frankness' of his own sources, also recognized that testimony could be 'exculpatory, alibi-laden and mendacious' and that there were various reasons for this, including repression, forgetting, and lying for fear of judicial consequences. [33]

Nancy Combs provides an extensive review of problems based on three international judicial bodies covering Rwanda (ICTR), Sierra Leone (SCSL), and East Timor (SPSC).[34] A number of problems, when taken together, lead her to express grave concern over the reliability of testimony in these courts, a concern echoed by ICTR defence attorney Beth Lyons.[35] The problems comprise a package of issues around communication, including the use of complex compound questions and the educational level of witnesses.[36] Anders'

[28] K P Apuuli, 'Procedural Due Process and the Prosecution of Genocide Suspects in Rwanda' (2009) 11 Journal of Genocide Research 11, 13 and 16.

[29] Wilson (n 17) 8, quoting Geertz.

[30] *Prosecutor v Vasiljević* (Transcripts) IT-98-32 (20 November 2001) 2866, lines 15–16.

[31] Eltringham (n 14) 69, fn 124.

[32] Gerlach (n 8) 431, on Eichmann.

[33] Browning (n 20) xv-xvi; also, Nielsen (n 16) 338.

[34] N Combs, *Fact-finding without the Facts: the Uncertain Evidentiary Foundations of International Criminal Convictions* (CUP 2010).

[35] Combs (n 34) 4; Lyons (n 21).

[36] Combs (n 34) 21, 48.

analysis of the Joseph Marzah testimony at the SCSL adds to this the problems of translation across linguistic and cultural barriers.[37] Other challenges arise from various incentives which are offered to witnesses,[38] and the lack of funding and skills available to defence teams.[39] This is compounded by deficiency of documentary corroboration, placing a heavy reliance on witnesses, but giving a thin basis to assess competing accounts.[40] The value of documents is emphasized by Wienorka who notes that they are not subject to brow-beating in cross examination or to forgetting.[41] This lack of documentation is assessed as an 'open door' to those wishing, for whatever reason, to present false testimony.[42] Although Combs sees the ICTY as a special case compared to her three study sites, her proposal to review each witness as an individual, and to account for their interest structures including self-protection, personal animosity, and financial structures is equally relevant when working with the Tribunal's records.[43]

11.2.5 Research Ethics

By utilizing existing sources *in the first instance*, research can be conducted without the necessity of harming potential respondents who experienced horrific and traumatic events. The kind of difficulties this could create are evident in the courtroom discussion of the impact of giving evidence on protected witness BT12.[44] Yet at the same time, by stopping at the testimony of the ICTY, one risks replicating the exclusion of witnesses that is inevitable on account of the limited aims and resources of the ICTY, and arising from the strategic considerations of prosecutors and defence counsel. As such, while this paper presents a strong case for starting with the available ICTY sources, a commitment to providing voice to the witnesses of atrocity suggests that using the ICTY as an initial foundation and as a sensitizing process before approaching witnesses should be a precursor to the wider efforts to interview and quote those who saw events first hand. This combination is evident in the work of Bećirević, and should inform the collective endeavour of analysing the events in Bosnia and Herzegovina and the other former Yugoslav republics.

11.2.6 ICTY: A 'Best Case' Research Tool Among International Courts?

The preceding review of research literature highlights many challenges in overcoming the limitations arising from using a by-product of a structured process geared towards testing legal, as opposed to historical, claims. If not a flawless data source, the ICTY represents a best-case among international courts. Combs set it to one side in her thorough critical

[37] G Anders, 'Testifying About "Uncivilized Events": Problematic Representations of Africa in the Trial against Charles Taylor' (2011) 24 Leiden Journal of International Law 937, 940ff.
[38] Combs (n 34) 136.
[39] ibid 94, 146.
[40] ibid 12, 167.
[41] A Wienorka, 'The Witness in History' (2006) 27 Poetics Today 385, 389.
[42] Combs (n 34) 101.
[43] ibid 5, 130 ff.
[44] See *Prosecutor v Brđanin* (Transcripts) IT-99-36 (12 April 2002) discussion from 4209 forwards; for more on the traumatic and theraputic dimensions of testimony, see R Hodžić, 'Living the Legacy of Mass Atrocities: Victims' Perspectives on War Crimes Trials' (2010) 8 Journal of International Criminal Justice 125.

analysis of international tribunals. Among other reasons, she saw fewer problems arising from 'educational, cultural and linguistic' difference between witnesses and court officials.[45] Added to this is the level of documentation available in the ICTY,[46] which helps to address some of Combs' concerns around proper scrutiny and corroboration of oral testimony. Nonetheless, care is still required when handling ICTY resources as data, including witness-by-witness scrutiny of interest structures and quality of exchanges in court, attention to judicial evaluations of reliability, and analytical judgments taken across any data set of evidence and testimony as a whole. As will be seen, with cases running to the tens of thousands of pages of transcripts, and thousands of pieces of evidence, this is no small task. While Browning described his sources as 'vivid and detailed',[47] the transcripts from the ICTY often record lengthy and mundane exchanges, and legal argument frequently breaks the flow of witness testimony. In the following section, I review the approaches taken in two works,[48] explore how these approaches shape their contributions to historical and criminological research, and identify areas for future development.

11.3 Two Scholarly Approaches to ICTY as a Data Source

The chapter now turns to two published works, reviewing the purpose of those works and the supporting empirical material they draw from the ICTY archives. Edina Bećirević's monograph *Genocide on the Drina River*, in particular its fourth chapter, is an engagement with evidence on seven eastern Bosnian Municipalities. She argues that the jurisprudence of the ICTY[49] and the ICJ[50] failed to correctly recognize genocide when positive findings of genocide were limited temporally and spatially to the events in Srebrenica in July 1995.[51] My shorter publication, 'Police and Persecution in the Bosnian Krajina', focuses on northwest Bosnia, particularly the municipalities of Banja Luka, Ključ, Prijedor, and Sanski Most, and is part of a larger project on police participation in war crimes during conflicts in the former Yugoslavia.[52] The papers represent two different enterprises, respectively categorization and explanation, but both rest on a common foundation of empirical description based in part on evidence drawn from the ICTY. The approach to the ICTY differs in the two pieces of research. While I begin with court transcripts and testimony, Bećirević works with the judgment which provides a guide to relevant testimony and witnesses for follow-up interviews. As will be seen, this fits with the different purposes of the two researchers.

45 Hodžić (n 44) 5.
46 Nielsen (n 16) 328.
47 Browning (n 20) 210.
48 Bećirević (n 7); Aitchison (n 7).
49 This has been reinforced with the judgment of Radovan Karadžić (under appeal), subsequent to Bećirević' book. *Prosecutor v Karadžić* (Public Redacted Version of Judgement) IT-95-5 (24 March 2016).
50 *Application of the Convention on the Prevention and Punishment of the Crime of Genocide (Bosnia and Herzegovina v Serbia and Montenegro)*, Judgment, (ICJ Reports 2007) 43.
51 Bećirević (n 7) 81 to 143; the municipalities concerned are Zvornik, Vlasenica, Bratunac, Rogatica, Foča, Višegrad, and Srebrenica.
52 Aitchison (n 7); for details of the wider project, see A Aitchison, 'Exploring Police Activities During Armed Conflict: Bosnia and Herzegovina, Croatia, Kosovo and Macedonia' (9th European Society of Criminology conference, Ljubljana, September 2009) <https://www.academia.edu/1663236/Exploring_police_activities_during_armed_conflict_Bosnia_and_Herzegovina_Croatia_Kosovo_and_Macedonia_Ljubljana_2009_> accessed 20 March 2018.

11.3.1 Genocide on the Drina River

Bećirević's empirical analysis provides a richly sourced account of events in the seven eastern municipalities.[53] Of the 315 footnotes in Chapter 4, around three quarters provide an empirical foundation, with remaining footnotes supporting general background, conceptualization and providing a comparative framework which puts events in eastern Bosnia in the context of a wider set of genocidal violence including that against European Jews, the Ottoman Armenians, and Rwandan Tutsi.[54] Of footnotes concerning empirical evidence, 110 make direct reference to the tribunal, covering ten cases and more general references to material found in the ICTY archive.[55] Collectively, these footnotes provide evidence on the immediate background in the municipalities and the unfolding events, participants, and outcomes (eighty), and on connections between these events and government policy and the statements of leading protagonists (thirty). Table 11.1 provides a breakdown of what Bećirević cites, showing that she draws on different phases of proceedings, but predominantly on the main trial and judgment stages. Testimony is drawn both from direct citation of transcripts and from witnesses cited in judgments. In the latter case, the citations are included as testimony, rather than as the core part of the judgment.

In keeping with her aim of using undisputed ICTY documentation,[56] the vast bulk of sources are agreed facts and evidence presented in open court. Thus, they are subject to examination and cross-examination and constitute adjudicated points. A small number of citations draw on indictments across three cases: *Nikolić* (concerning Vlasenica); *Deronjić* (Bratunac); and *Lukić and Lukić* (Višegrad). Regarding *Nikolić*, three notes point to details in the first amended indictment regarding police ultimatums to Muslims in Vlasenica,[57]

Table 11.1 Breakdown of ICTY sources used by Bećirević: type of source

Phase	Source	Number
Pre-trial	Indictment	9
	Agreed facts	6
Main trial	Exhibits and documents	35
	Testimony	25
	Other proceedings	1
Judgment	Main and sentencing	34
Total		110

[53] Bećirević (n 7) 81 to 143.
[54] See Bećirević (n 7) at 86, fn 24–28.
[55] Those cases are *Prosecutor v Deronjić* IT-02-61 (ICTY 2004); *Karadžić* (n 49); *Prosecutor v Kunarac* IT-96-23 and IT-96-23/1 (ICTY 2001); *Prosecutor v Lukić and Lukić* IT-98-32 (ICTY 2009); *Milošević* (n 24); *Prosecutor v Dragan Nikolić* IT-94-2 (ICTY 2003); *Prosecutor v Orić* IT-03-68 (ICTY 2006); *Prosecutor v Todović and Rašević* IT-97-25 (ICTY 2005); *Prosecutor v Vasiljević* (n 30); *and Prosecutor v Zelenović* IT-96-23/1 (ICTY 2007). Further evidence is drawn from *Todović and Rašević* X-KRŽ-06/275 after its transfer to the Court of Bosnia and Herzegovina (SBiH 2008), and from a further case, *Paunović* X-KR-05/16 (SBiH 2006). These cases would also involve material held in ICTY archives.
[56] Bećirević (n 7) xi; also at 80 for the focus on testimony and supporting documentation.
[57] Bećirević (n 7) 97 fn 82, citing *Prosecutor v Nikolić* (n 55) First Amended Indictment 12 February 1999, para 3.

subsequent interrogations involving beatings and killings,[58] and the ultimate decimation of the Muslim population arising from flight, detention, and murder.[59] While these are general factual claims made by the prosecutor in an early indictment, they can be found in the third and final indictment.[60] This is a far more detailed and individualized account of Nikolić's actions at the Susica detention camp between June and September 1992. While the focus is predominantly on those individual actions,[61] the wider context remains central to proving crimes which are defined as part of a widespread and systematic attack,[62] and it is presented as part of the additional factual basis of the indictment. This, in turn, provided the basis of a guilty plea, made in open court on 18 December 2003, including the admission of 'all factual details' in the indictment.[63] Again, in *Deronjić*, a guilty plea was entered, meaning that the full presentation of evidence in the chamber was circumvented, but the facts as presented in the indictment phase and in an additional factual statement were admitted and considered by the judges.[64] In the case of the final indictment cited, all claims can be cross-referenced to testimony and adjudicated facts presented in the factual section of the judgment.[65]

A further breakdown of citations of ICTY sources, provided in Table 11.2, is useful for highlighting the uneven potential of court by-products as data. In certain municipalities, Bećirević is able to draw extensively on ICTY sources, and in three cases more than half of her citations point to the output of the court. At the other end of the scale, in Rogatica, only one footnote out of twenty draws on the ICTY. This is reflective of differences in coverage of each municipality in ICTY prosecutions, further explored in Table 11.3.

Table 11.3 is the product of a review of forty-four ICTY indictments covering Bosnia in which proceedings have been completed to the point of a judgment in the first chamber. The cases cover a total of eighty-two accused, and range from identifying crimes in only one municipality through to as many as thirty. Based on this review, charges relate to Sarajevo (comprised of ten municipalities) and fifty-three of Bosnia's remaining ninety-nine pre-war municipalities. The areas most strongly represented are Eastern Bosnia (Bratunac, Srebrenica, Vlasenica, Višegrad, and Zvornik), Sarajevo, the Krajina region (particularly Banja Luka, Ključ, Prijedor, and Sanski Most), Central Bosnia (Vareš, Vitez, Zenica), Sarajevo, and Foča. This means that there are significant pockets of interest from a research perspective that are not covered by the Bosnian cases at ICTY, notably the municipalities around Bihac in the far north west of the country, referred to as 'Bosnia's forgotten battlefield'[66] and areas of Serb majority population that came under the control of Croat

[58] *Prosecutor v Nikolić* (n 55) First Amended Indictment para 5.

[59] ibid para 6.

[60] *Prosecutor v Nikolić* (n 55) Third Amended Indictment 31 October 2003, paras 39, 41, and 42 respectively.

[61] ibid paras 3–35.

[62] ibid para 36.

[63] *Prosecutor v Nikolić* (n 55) Sentencing Judgment 18 December 2003, para 3.

[64] *Prosecutor v Deronjić* (n 55). Bećirević (n 7), cites the Second Amended Indictment of 30 September 2003 at 102–06, fn 98, 100, 113, 122, and 123 corresponding to paragraphs 1, 18–20, and 22–26 of the indictment and showing Deronjić's position in the SDS, detailing the disarmament of Muslims, and accounting for actions of the JNA, Territorial Defence, and Police with specific reference to Glogova village. In the Sentencing Judgment of 30 March 2004 the admission of the facts of the indictment is found in para 3.

[65] Bećirević (n 7) 126, fn 235, citing *Prosecutor v Lukić and Lukić* (n 55) 2nd Amended Indictment 27 February 2006, particularly para 28. The relevant findings can be found in the Judgment of 20 July 2009, para 49, backed by testimony and adjudicated facts in fn 127, 128, and 131.

[66] B O'Shea, *Bosnia's Forgotten Battlefield: Bihac* (History Press 2012).

Table 11.2 Breakdown of ICTY sources used by Bećirević: municipality

Municipality	Number of sources	As % of all citations of evidence for municipality
Foča	23	79
Bratunac	22	59
Višegrad	19	54
Srebrenica	17	40
Zvornik	13	38
Vlasenica	7	36
Rogatica	1	5
Non-specific	8	–
Total	110	–

Table 11.3 Municipalities identified in review of 44 ICTY indictments

Number of cases	Municipalities
>5	8 + Sarajevo: Bratunac, Foča, Prijedor, Sarajevo (10 municipalities), Srebrenica, Vlasenica, Višegrad, Vitez, Zvornik
4	9: Banja Luka, Bosanki Samac, Brčko, Busovača, Ključ, Sanski Most, Vareš, Zenica, Žepče
3	8: Bijeljina, Bosanski Novi, Donji Vakuf, Jablanica, Kotor Varoš, Mostar, Prozor, Teslić
2	16: Bileća, Bosanski Krupa, Bosanski Petrovac, Celinac, Doboj, Gačko, Kalinovik, Nevesinje, Novi Travnik, Prnjavor, Rogatica, Sipovo, Skender Vakuf, Sokolac, Travnik, Zavidovici
1	12: Bugojno, Čajniče, Čapljina, Goražde, Gornji Vakuf, Kakanj, Kiseljak, Konjic, Maglaj, Odžak, Rudo, Stolac

authorities in Drvar, Glamoc, and Grahovo.[67] It may be that some of this may be addressed by extending the use of court output beyond ICTY, for example to the Court of Bosnia and Herzegovina, but that goes beyond the focus of this chapter. The uneven distribution presents a challenge for the researcher, but more significantly a risk that in taking a lead from available legal sources the broader research enterprise presents a skewed picture of events.[68]

So far, the analysis of Bećirević's chapter shows that she is able to draw extensively on ICTY material, but that this is limited by the reach of prosecutions across different municipalities. Aside from the observation that some municipalities are sparsely covered and

[67] A review of information from OSCE on cases against 234 accused, heard in various courts in Bosnia, shows that by May 2014, five cases concerning Glamoc and Drvar had been heard at the Cantonal Court in Livno, the Supreme Court of the Federation of Bosnia and Herzegovina, and the Court of Bosnia and Herzegovina.

[68] Bloxham (n 3) examines the role of the Nuremberg tribunals in shaping the subsequent historical debate on the Holocaust, at times 'muddying the waters', 2.

others not at all, a closer reading of one of her case studies identifies where she has drawn upon other supporting material, and how an approach that goes beyond indictments and judgments might yield further results. For example, Višegrad, with slightly more than half the evidence cited drawn from the ICTY, is used as a municipality where Bećirević challenges the lack of any finding of genocide. Bećirević is critical of the court, noting that neither indictment nor judgment identifies a 'pervasive' atmosphere of killing and death, with highly visible killings of Bosniaks on the town's historic bridge, on the streets, and through burning groups alive in homes.[69] This underlines the different orientations of the court, producing a judicial account focused on responsibility for specific events, and the thicker description sought in qualitative social science.[70]

Bećirević goes beyond the ICTY sources, in this case the *Vasiljević* judgment and *Lukić* indictment, to draw on a UN report, published survivor testimony, contemporary reportage, and her own interviews.[71] To some extent, it is fair to say that, by focusing on individual guilt linked to specific proven incidents, notably the killing of five men and attempted killing of two others on the banks of the Drina river, and the killing of at least fifty-nine people in a fire on Pionirska Street, the written judgment in *Vasiljević* does not focus in detail on the wider atmosphere. Nonetheless, on account of the specific requirements of crimes categorized as violations of laws of war[72] or as crimes against humanity,[73] the court does consider the broader background, and events in Višegrad and the surrounding area. This includes eyewitness evidence of arbitrary killing and posthumous evidence of large scale killings of mixed groups with no military clothing or equipment found with human remains.[74] Eight witnesses are cited regarding the disappearances in the town.[75] Extensive testimony is mentioned in the judgment regarding the bodies recovered from the Drina river between May and July, suggesting hundreds were killed, and indicating the mutilated state of the bodies recovered.[76] Regarding the public nature of violence the court cites the testimony of Zivorad Savić, who identified the sight of bodies on the river banks and blood on the bridge, the town's most prominent landmark.[77] In *Vasiljević* the court concludes that hundreds were killed arbitrarily,[78] and likewise in *Lukić and Lukić* although the focus of the judgment is on a set of discrete incidents in which the accused are implicated, the wider context of lootings, arson, beatings, abduction, rape, and murder, as well as the extent of killing is covered with reference to supporting evidence heard in court.[79] This suggests that a detailed reading of the testimony underpinning the judgment can yield further evidence of value in building a descriptive historical account of events. This will be picked up in the following section.

[69] Bećirević (n 7) 127.
[70] The point is made by Mirjan Damaška, that individualization, and the neglect of collective responsibility, is a 'distortion of historical reality' M R Damaška, 'What is the Point of International Criminal Justice' (2008) 83 Chicago-Kent Law Review 329, 332–33 including fn 5 and 6.
[71] Bećirević (n 7) 127–29, fn 238–42, 244, and 249.
[72] *Prosecutor v Vasiljević* (n 30) judgment, paras 24–27 on art 3 of the ICTY statute.
[73] ibid paras 28–38 on art 5 of the ICTY statute.
[74] ibid para 51, fn 93, particularly pathologist John Clark on close range killing with high velocity weapons.
[75] ibid para 51, fn 94.
[76] ibid para 52, fn 95, particularly citations of Mevsud Poljo and protected witnesses VG21 and VG79.
[77] ibid.
[78] ibid para 56.
[79] *Prosecutor v Lukić and Lukić* (n 55) paras 46, 50–52, and 65.

The final seven footnotes are a good indication of the added value of Bećirević's approach, and while there may be issues with using her broader conclusions from these to provide a specifically legal critique of judgements on individual criminal cases of genocide, they do go further in assisting our thinking about genocide in terms of societal responsibility.[80] In setting up her framework, Bećirević draws on Stanton's eight stages of genocide, which is completed with a final stage of *denial*.[81] She returns to this in her penultimate chapter.[82] The final footnotes in the material on Višegrad handle the *post-hoc* denial of crimes subsequent to the end of the conflict. She draws on her own interview material with a doctor accused of denying treatment to Bosniaks, an anonymous Serb from the town, and on the writing of *Guardian* journalist Ed Vulliamy, himself a witness in several ICTY trials. This presents a picture of individual and collective denial in the town, combining dismissal of knowledge, silence, lack of regret, and harassment of those who might threaten the silence.[83] For parties to the trial, this broader social process of denial offers little basis for inferences on individual intent and culpability, but it speaks strongly to more social science oriented concepts of genocide.

Ultimately, Bećirević's careful empirical analysis, starting with ICTY output but going beyond this through primary data collection, shows the value and certain limitations of working with court output. While coverage of Bosnia and Herzegovina is uneven, the court does offer a wealth of data on particular regions within the country. Pushing that material as far as it can go, further than Bećirević has gone here, provides not just a sense of discrete incidents, but some of the wider context that allows analysts to make claims about policies and systems that can support categorization of a series of events as genocide, even where that runs counter to the court's own judgment. The further primary data collection conducted by Bećirević shows that historical and social research can make an important contribution by reaching beyond an individualized interpretation of responsibility for genocide to a strongly conceptualized and socially situated understanding of the phenomenon. This, in turn, supports either a critique of the court and the law, or a limiting of ambition in relation to the law: the first is to say that the legal form cannot adequately represent and identify the category of genocide as it has developed in the social sciences; the second is to say that the judge and the social researcher serve different functions and that each has their own system of meaning in which genocide is interpreted. It should be no surprise that these two systems support different conclusions based on the same evidence.

11.3.2 Police and Persecution in the Bosnian Krajina

In my own work, I have taken a different approach to Bećirević, starting with testimony and evidence rather than with the indictment and judgment.[84] This has implications on the possible breadth of the research because of the sheer volume of material involved; Rudof's

[80] On societal, as opposed to individual and State responsibility, see J Subotić, 'Expanding the Scope of Post-Conflict Justice: Individual, State and Societal Responsibility for Mass Atrocity' (2011) 48 Journal of Peace Research 157.
[81] Bećirević (n 7) 14–15.
[82] ibid 144–79.
[83] ibid 130–31, fn 256–62.
[84] Aitchison (n 7).

cautionary note on the *time* required in going through testimony is especially relevant here.[85] However, it avoids the possibility that judges, addressing questions of guilt and innocence in relation to particular crimes, overlook material of direct relevance to researchers' own questions. The work in question is a relatively narrow study of the role of the police in atrocity crimes in the Krajina region in Northern Bosnia, asking how and why they came to participate in widespread and extreme ethnically-targeted violence. The research draws directly on only two cases, *Brđanin*, and *Stanišić and Župljanin*,[86] selected to combine local, regional, and central levels of authority, and police and political officials. Even this narrowing involved the reading and coding of around 52,000 pages of testimony, covering over 600 court sessions and the testimony of over 400 witnesses, and more than 3,000 exhibits ranging from individual photos to extensive government documents and transcripts of parliamentary proceedings.[87] The extent of the dataset necessitated the use of qualitative analysis software (NVivo) to manage the process of coding and analysis. The output is based on the testimony of fifty-six named and nine protected witnesses who were not identified in open court. Additionally, twenty-seven exhibits[88] were utilized, supporting a description of police participation in violence,[89] as well as an explanation which looks at processes of democratization, politicization, deprofessionalization, and militarization.[90] These are located in the context of particular historical legacies from the Yugoslav period, including the relationship between State and party under communist rule, the ethnic key in making appointments, and principles of All People's Defence.[91]

The two sections which present empirical material describe and explain the police role in wartime violence, include 127 references, of which 113 provide evidence as opposed to argument, framing or background. Of these, only one draws on material beyond the ICTY archive,[92] one is drawn from an ICTY judgment and one from arguments presented by parties to the trial.[93] The remaining 110, summarised in Table 11.4, relate directly to the records of testimony or exhibits from the two cases studied. With multiple references in the footnotes, this amounts to reference to 199 points in the archival record. The footnotes are

Table 11.4 Breakdown of ICTY sources used by Aitchison

Case	Footnotes	Form of evidence	Footnotes
Brđanin	65	Testimony	88
Stanišić & Župljanin	33	Exhibit	10
Both	12	Both	12
Total	110	Total	110

[85] J W Rudof, 'Research Use of Holocaust Testimonies' (2006) 27 Poetics Today 451, 460, but more generally throughout her article on the investment of effort required.

[86] *Prosecutor v Brđanin* (n 44); *Prosecutor v Stanišić and Župljanin* (Judgment) IT-08-91 (27 March 2013).

[87] At the time of writing, the full set of more than 4,300 exhibits in *Stanišić and Župljanin* had not yet been released on the public database maintained by the ICTY, and so this reflects only those called in *Brđanin*.

[88] Aitchison (n 7) 3–4.

[89] ibid 4–10.

[90] ibid s 5, at 10–15.

[91] For the substantive detail, see ibid., 11 and 13–14.

[92] ibid 7, fn 45, referring to evidence of killings at Omarska detention camp beyond those covered in judgments.

[93] ibid respectively at 10, fn 66, referring to the judgment in *Prosecutor v Mrđa* (Judgement) IT-02-59 (31 March 2004), and 10 fn 72.

broken down by case and by form of evidence referred to in Table 11.4. What is evident from this is the weight that the paper is placing on the output of the court and, in particular.

A further exploration of the descriptive section shows the extent of reliance on court archives. Section 4 describes the police contribution to creating a hostile environment for non-Serbs, through participating in killings, civilian detention facilities, and various forms of harassment. The purpose is to document police presence, their cooperation with other organized forces and civilian political structures and their actions. The example of Section 4.1 deals specifically with detention camps in which large numbers of civilians were detained and in particular identifies denigration, physical and sexual violence, and killings.[94] In outlining the overall police role in relation to camps, I draw on eye-witness testimony regarding who acted as camp guards, and what uniforms they wore; on documents from Bosnian Serb authorities; and testimony from Bosniaks who sought to negotiate over access to, and release of those in the camps. For specific police actions in the camps, testimony of victims, witnesses to killings and Bosnian Serb officials is cited. This includes a Bosnian Serb politician recognizing that sexual violence took place at the temporary facility at the Kotor Varoš saw mill, and a State Security official's account of guards shooting at inmates in the Omarsksa camp. In total, in these two paragraphs, seventeen named and three protected witnesses provide a robust overall sense of the camp environment and the contribution of the police.

Two further phases of scrutiny, not undertaken in the analysis of the Karjina material, would make these descriptive findings more robust. First, in the process of coding transcripts and then revisiting texts and sources through those codes, each point of reference is removed from the context of the individual witness' testimony as a whole. When returning to coded text, reading immediately surrounding text provides important contextualization. Where reliance is placed on a particular sub-section of testimony in the analysis phase, re-reading the individual witness testimony *as a whole* can support a broader assessment of consistency and quality of evidence. Second, by going straight to testimony without referring to the judgment (in direct contradiction to Eltringham's source's advice), a researcher misses the potentially helpful assessment of judges with regard to witness reliability. In a separate ongoing analysis of *Tadić*, the judgment identifies witnesses whose testimony is only relied on in part because of inconsistencies with others,[95] or because of discrepancies in evidence emerging through cross-examination.[96] These judicial cautions need not dictate the way in which a researcher handles the material, but are useful flags for points where further care and attention is valuable in using the court's by-products. In the case of witness L, the entire testimony had to be disregarded after disavowal by the prosecution, once the cross-examination revealed the evidence to be false. The careful witness-by-witness scrutiny and use of the judgment in this way takes seriously Combs' concerns about the quality of evidence, and the need to account for witnesses' interest structures. Here, one more stage is useful in the analysis and writing process: examining the totality of witnesses and testimony supporting any one point, to act as a check on potential distortion by witnesses acting in line with personal or political interests. In the example given in the preceding paragraph, six of the twenty witnesses held leadership posts at various levels of the Party

[94] ibid 6–7.
[95] *Prosecutor v Tadić* (n 23) at para 430, regarding Mehmedalija Huskić.
[96] ibid at para 224, regarding Elvir Grożdanović.

for Democratic Action (SDA), the largest Bosniak party, and the dominant party in the Sarajevo government during the war. Again, this need not rule out use of their testimony, but acts as a flag for considering whether political interests may influence their evidence, and calls for further attention to corroboration from other sources.

While the emphasis in the final section of the Krajina paper is on explanation rather than description, this still rests on a foundation of evidence of the factors called upon to explain the institutional participation in the violence described in Section 4. Where this is about democratization processes preceding the war, the paper is more reliant on published sources outside the ICTY to provide the necessary background.[97] The sections outlining politicization and deprofessionalization (5.2) and militarization (5.3) again draw extensively on testimony and other evidence from the two ICTY cases. Section 5.2 advances the argument that continuity of a strong link between party and State, and principles of ethnic representation in the distribution of leadership positions combined with transitional lustration and multi-party democracy were dominated by ethnically-based parties. This provides the context for appointments based on ethnicity and political allegiance without regard for qualifications and experience. After the division of the Ministry of Interior in the Spring of 1992, this led to a largely Serb police force strongly tied to the Serb Democratic Party (SDS) in the Krajina region. The section includes twenty-three separate references covering forty-five points of testimony from twenty-seven witnesses and two exhibits. The witnesses come from both prosecution (nineteen) and defence (eight) phases of the trials, and include fourteen police officers (ten Bosnian Serb, four Bosniak) and six politicians, including those from both SDA and SDS, the dominant parties in the Krajina following the 1990 elections. It is worth noting that this balance between Bosnian Serb and Bosniak witnesses is more characteristic of *Stanišić and Župljanin*, a case heard from 2009 onwards, as opposed to *Brđanin*, where prosecution opened in 2002. The distance from events and the political changes in Bosnia and Herzegovina may have created opportunities for a more diverse set of witnesses to be heard. While the balance of witnesses does not overcome the partiality inherent in processes of selecting particular incidents to provide evidence of particular crimes under the ICTY statute, it nonetheless provides a certain degree of balance and robustness in developing an account that answers a relatively narrowly defined research question. So long as a researcher makes reference to indictments, transcripts relating to procedural considerations and the judgments in building up his or her understanding of the selection process, and keeps in mind the limitations this places on the research questions that can be asked of testimony, as well as the need for scrutiny of the quality of the evidence identified above, the ICTY provides a rich seam of data for scholars of the war, and in particular for criminologists with a focus on the role of institutions in atrocity crimes.

11.4 Conclusions

The chapter has identified a number of issues in utilizing the resources of international criminal trials to support historical and social science analyses, particularly those arising from the boundaries around what evidence is brought forward and the potential quality of

[97] Aitchison (n 7) 11 (s 5.1).

that evidence. By exploring, in some detail, two examples of scholarship that draw on the ICTY, selected as a 'best-case' for robust evidence, the paper has identified strong potential for continued engagement with court records. In the first instance, where scholars are asking questions that seek to revisit issues subject to court judgment, indictments and judgments are the logical starting point for analysis. The review of Bećirević shows the wider value of extending beyond the judgment with primary data collection, but the analysis of her work also highlights that further valuable material can be mined from a more detailed reading of the testimony supporting the judgment.

This does not limit a researcher to simply replicating the conclusions of judges, as is evident in Buss' reappraisal of sections of the Krstić judgment concerning patriarchal social structures in Srebrenica,[98] and it is not surprising that judicial and social science interpretations of the same material may differ, given diverging conceptual frameworks. Weaving together ICTY and other sources supports criminological and historical conclusions that reach beyond the remit of judges in a criminal procedure. Taking an alternative approach which prioritizes testimony as an entry point for analysis again shows the potential of ICTY sources, in this case to support description and subsequent explanation in relation to defined research questions. Case selection can be guided by high-level summaries available through the ICTY, but a further sense of limitations of the material in general and of specific testimony as data should be informed by a review of indictments and judgments. Nonetheless, given identified gaps in the Tribunal's coverage, it can only ever be one part of scholarly efforts to make sense of the violent disintegration of State and society in Yugoslavia.

[98] D E Buss, 'Knowing Women: Translating Patriarchy in International Criminal Law' (2014) 23 Social and Legal Studies 73.

PART IV

EVIDENCE, WITNESS TESTIMONY, AND WITNESS EXPERIENCES

12

Lessons Learned from the Use of DNA Evidence in Srebrenica-related Trials at the ICTY

Kweku Vanderpuye and Christopher Mitchell***

12.1 Introduction

On the late afternoon of 11 July 1995, the Bosnian Muslim-held town of Srebrenica fell to Bosnian Serb forces after a three-year siege. In the following days, Bosnian Serb forces executed as many as 7,826 Bosnian Muslim men and boys who surrendered or were captured after the fall of the town.[1] Six main execution sites were used,[2] with thousands of victims buried in five primary mass graves.[3] Scores of smaller-scale executions and burials also occurred during this period.[4]

On 10 August 1995, the United Nations Security Council was presented with aerial imagery of suspected mass graves in the Srebrenica region.[5] In response,[6] Bosnian Serb forces disinterred the five main primary mass graves in a clandestine operation. The victims' disarticulated and mangled remains were then scattered among more than thirty remote secondary grave sites.[7] This was the complex forensic picture confronting international investigators and forensic science experts when they first gained access to the region in 1996.

By March 2009, seventy-three Srebrenica-related graves had been identified and all but one exhumed:[8] thirty-one primary graves, thirty-seven secondary graves and five whose designation is unknown.[9] Since then, new graves have been discovered and exhumed.[10] The

* Kweku Vanderpuye (JD, University of California, Hastings) is a Senior Trial Lawyer in the Office of the Prosecutor of the International Criminal Court. He served as a Trial Attorney with the Office of the Prosecutor (OTP) at the International Criminal Tribunal for the Former Yugoslavia (ICTY) on *Prosecutor v Popović* et al, *Prosecutor v Tolimir* and *Prosecutor v Mladić*. Prior to this, he was a criminal defence lawyer in New York, including as a Supervising Attorney with The Legal Aid Society.

** Christopher Mitchell (BA, LLB (Hons)) is a barrister at Banco Chambers, Sydney. Formerly, he was a senior associate with Herbert Smith Freehills in Sydney, and an Associate Legal Officer with the ICTY OTP on *Prosecutor v Popović* et al, and *Prosecutor v Radovan Karadžić*. The views expressed herein are those of the authors alone and do not necessarily reflect the views of the International Criminal Court (in the case of Mr Vanderpuye), the International Criminal Tribunal for the former Yugoslavia or the United Nations in general.

1 *Prosecutor v Vujadin Popović* et al (Judgment) ICTY-05-88-T (10 June 2010) para 664.

2 Kravica Warehouse, Orahovac, Petkovci Dam, Kozluk, Branjevo Military Farm, and the Pilica Dom.

3 Glogova (associated with the Kravica Warehouse), Orahovac, Petkovci Dam, Kozluk, and Branjevo Military Farm (which also contains the remains of victims from the Pilica Dom executions).

4 *Prosecutor v Radovan Karadžić* (Judgment, Section C (Srebrenica Component) ICTY-95-5/18-T (24 March 2016); *Karadžić* Exhibit 4772, Update to the Summary of Forensic Evidence—Exhumation of the Graves and Surface Remains Recoveries Related to Srebrenica, January 2012, Prepared by Dušan Janc, ICTY-OTP Investigator, 13 January 2012 (Janc Report).

5 *Karadžić* Trial Judgment (n 4) para 5450.

6 ibid para 5514.

7 ibid paras 5503–14.

8 *Popović* Trial Judgment (n 1) para 608.

9 ibid.

10 Janc Report (n 4).

Kweku Vanderpuye and Christopher Mitchell, *Lessons Learned from the Use of DNA Evidence in Srebrenica-related Trials at the ICTY* In: *Legacies of the International Criminal Tribunal for the Former Yugoslavia*. Edited by: Carsten Stahn, Carmel Agius, Serge Brammertz, Colleen Rohan, Oxford University Press (2020). © The Several Contributors DOI: 10.1093/oso/9780198862956.003.0013

ongoing task of locating and exhuming these graves, and identifying and reassociating the victims' remains, has been described as the world's greatest forensic puzzle.[11] It was solved through two decades of investigative and forensic work including archaeology, anthropology, pathology, and DNA analysis.

The potential importance of DNA analysis in establishing not only a legal, but an historical, record and accounting of the number and identities of victims of mass atrocity crimes is clear.[12] Its significance is often crucial, especially given the highly charged nature of these cases. Similarly, the effective presentation of DNA evidence in complex and lengthy international proceedings comes with challenges to which novel and pragmatic solutions are required, forged, and from which lessons and best practices may be derived.

To this extent, the chapter considers salient issues arising in the context of the International Criminal Tribunal for the former Yugoslavia's (ICTY) Srebrenica-related trials. Section 12.2 provides a basic overview of DNA analysis, profiling, and matching. Section 12.3 analyses the use of DNA evidence in *Prosecutor v Vujadin Popović* et al (*Popović*) and *Prosecutor v Radovan Karadžić* (*Karadžić*). Section 12.4 addresses five particular procedural and evidentiary issues from these trials which may be relevant to other complex cases involving large numbers of victims and mass graves. Finally, section 12.5 summarizes ten lessons learned from the DNA-related litigation in these cases, with a view to assisting others in using, or challenging (as the case may be), similar evidence in future proceedings.

12.2 An Overview of DNA

12.2.1 What is DNA?

Deoxyribonucleic acid (DNA) comprises the genetic material that makes every person unique with one exception: identical twins.[13] Most DNA is found in cell nuclei in the form of chromosomes (nuclear DNA). Organisms inherit half of their nuclear DNA from their male parent and half from their female parent. A small amount of DNA is also found in cell structures known as mitochondria (mtDNA), inherited matrilineally.[14]

DNA was first observed in 1869 by Swiss chemist Freidrich Miescher who, at the time, was studying proteins in the nuclei of white blood cells obtained from pus-covered bandages.[15] In 1944, scientists discovered that DNA was the vehicle by which hereditary traits

11 C Jennings, *Bosnia's Million Bones: Solving the World's Greatest Forensic Puzzle* (St Martin's Press 2013).

12 See *Prosecutor v Ratko Mladić* (Judgment) ICTY-09-92-T (22 November 2017) inter alia paras 3007, 3042 (noting previously adjudicated facts concerning, and the Chamber's determination of, the number of Srebrenica-related victims).

13 Standard DNA testing cannot distinguish between identical twins, but ultra-deep next generation sequencing may be able to; see J Weber-Lehmann, E Schilling, G Gradl, D C Richter, J Wiehle, and B Rolf, 'Finding the Needle in the Haystack: Differentiating "Identical" Twins in Paternity Testing and Forensics by Ultra-deep Next Generation Sequencing' (2014) 9 Forensic Science International: Genetics, 42.

14 M Smith, *DNA Evidence in the Australian Legal System*, LexisNexis Butterworths Australia, First Edition, 2016, paras 1.23–1.34; US National Library of Medicine <https://www.nlm.nih.gov> accessed 7 December 2017.

15 L Pray, 'Discovery of DNA Structure and Function: Watson and Crick' (2008) 1(100) Nature Education 1 < https://www.semanticscholar.org/paper/Discovery-of-DNA-Structure-and-Function%3A-Watson-and-Pray/9788c917dae2445fbd8ceacba2110ed60b6c72a7 > accessed 21 February 2020.

are transmitted between generations.[16] In 1953, the structure of DNA was first identified as the now familiar three-dimensional double helix.[17]

12.2.2 DNA Profiling

In the mid-1980s, two discoveries led to the development of DNA profiling as it is known today. *First*, in 1984, English geneticist Alec Jeffreys observed that human DNA contained repetitive sequences known as microsatellites or short tandem repeats (STR). The number of repeats in an STR marker is highly variable between individuals, making STR analysis an effective method of identification.[18] *Second*, in 1985, a method of DNA amplification known as polymerase chain reaction (PCR) was created.[19] PCR amplification allows small amounts of DNA to be replicated or copied, producing larger amounts for analysis. The technique revolutionized forensic DNA profiling because it made possible the analyses of trace amounts of DNA which might otherwise have previously been insufficient.[20]

Presently, nuclear STR testing is the most common method of DNA profiling.[21] It involves analysing the number of repeat sequences and unique combinations of alleles (genetic variations) in STR markers. The first step of this process involves identifying and amplifying (through PCR) relevant STR markers. The resulting DNA fragments are then separated by a process called electrophoresis, and the results (that is, the numbers of repeating sequences and unique allele combinations in each fragment) plotted on a graph called an electropherogram. The raw data represented in the electropherogram is used to derive a DNA profile, which can then be compared with other DNA profiles to determine whether there is a match.[22]

In addition to nuclear STR testing, three other DNA profiling methods are used in certain circumstances. *First*, mtDNA profiling can distinguish between male and female DNA, as well as assist in identifying an individual through their maternal lineage.[23] MtDNA testing is particularly useful where the biological sample is old or severely degraded. In these circumstances, it may be impossible to extract any nuclear DNA because each cell contains only a single unit. However, because multiple copies of mtDNA are present in each cell, successful extractions may still be possible.[24] *Second*, Y chromosome testing can distinguish between male and female DNA and identify a person through their paternal lineage.[25] *Third*, low copy DNA analysis can be used

[16] O Avery, 'Studies on the Chemical Nature of the Substance Inducing Transformation of Pneumococcal Types' (1944) 79 Journal of Experimental Medicine 137.

[17] J D Watson and F Crick, 'Structure for Deoxyribose Nucleic Acid' (1953) 171 Nature 737.

[18] Smith (n 14) para 1.11.

[19] K Mullis, 'The Unusual Origin of the Polymerase Chain Reaction' (1990) 262 Scientific American 56.

[20] Smith (n 14) para 1.9.

[21] See ICMP, 'DNA Reports Guide' (16 December 2010) <https://www.icmp.int/wp-content/uploads/2015/04/icmp-fsd-dna-50-2-doc.pdf> accessed 28 February 2018.

[22] ibid; Smith (n 14) paras 1.51–1.53 and figure 1.5.

[23] MtDNA is identical between maternal relatives, and therefore cannot distinguish between individuals with common maternal lineage (e.g. mtDNA in siblings with the same mother will be identical). Nonetheless, establishing familial links through mtDNA can be used to exclude a match, or where a DNA sample could only have come from one family group member (e.g. if only one member of a family has been reported missing, the discovery of a body with a positive mtDNA match to other family members may indicate that the body is that of the missing family member).

[24] Smith (n 14) paras 1.56–1.57.

[25] ibid para 1.55.

when the biological sample is particularly small (i.e. a single cell). However, DNA analysis using this method is more susceptible to legal challenges, given the greater potential for contamination of a single cell.[26]

12.2.3 DNA Matching

Two DNA samples that do not match can generally be regarded as proof that the two samples came from different people (barring a technical or procedural error in the testing process).[27] However, a match between two samples does not definitively prove that the samples came from the same person. For this reason, matches are expressed in terms of a 'probability' that the compared samples come from the same person.

To calculate the probability of a match, a DNA profile must be analysed against sample profiles from a given population. Population samples are used to calculate the frequency with which certain genetic characteristics appear in a specific population.[28] Thus, the larger the population sample, the greater the reliability of estimating the frequency of a given DNA profile within it, and the greater the probability that relevant samples, when matched, come from the same person.[29]

Where STR testing is the profiling method used, the number of STR markers analysed is also relevant to determining the probability of a match. In short, the more STR markers analysed, the greater the potential for differentiation among the tested samples and thus, the higher the probability that matching profiles come from the same person. For example, the US Combined DNA Index System (a national DNA database maintained by the Federal Bureau of Investigation), requires twenty core STR markers to be tested for a known offender's profile to be submitted to the database.[30] Fewer than twenty, but a minimum of eight, STR markers are required for profiles collected in other circumstances to be submitted to the database.[31]

12.2.4 The First Uses of DNA Evidence in National Proceedings

DNA matching was first used in national legal proceedings in the English case *R v Pitchfork*.[32] In 1983, a schoolgirl called Lynda Mann was raped and murdered in Leicestershire. The police subsequently sought blood and saliva samples from thousands of men in the area. The perpetrator, Colin Pitchfork, was not initially identified through this process because he persuaded a friend to provide a sample in his stead. However, Pitchfork's friend subsequently told the story to another person and Pitchfork

[26] ibid para 1.54.
[27] ibid para 1.62.
[28] ibid Chapter 3.
[29] ibid paras 1.62–1.78.
[30] Until 31 December 2016, thirteen core STR markers were used. See Frequently Asked Questions on CODIS and NDIS, FBI <https://www.fbi.gov/services/laboratory/biometric-analysis/codis/codis-and-ndis-fact-sheet> accessed 27 February 2018.
[31] ibid. The precise number of STR markers required depends on the type of specimen submitted.
[32] *R v Pitchfork* [2009] EWCA Crim 963; Smith (n 14) para 1.13.

was arrested. Pitchfork's DNA linked him with Lynda Mann's murder, another murder, and two other sexual assaults.[33]

DNA was accepted for the first time by a US court in 1988.[34] The following year, in the New York case of *People v Castro*,[35] evidence of DNA profiling (using an early form known as the RFLP method) was subject to a comprehensive challenge under the *Frye-Middleton* rule, which required that novel scientific evidence be 'generally accepted as reliable' to be admissible.[36] Although admissible under the *Frye-Middleton* test, the court excluded the evidence because the laboratory in question failed to follow appropriate control procedures.

The first significant uses of DNA evidence in Australia occurred in the 1989 and 1992 cases *R v Tran*[37] and *R v Lucas*.[38] In both cases, the DNA test results were excluded because the prejudicial effect of the evidence was found to outweigh its probative value. Since those early cases, Australian courts have taken a similar approach to the US. For example, in 2001, an Australian court held an extensive three-month *voir dire* into the reliability of the STR testing method, holding that it was sufficiently reliable if appropriate control procedures were followed.[39]

12.3 DNA Evidence in Srebrenica-related Trials at the ICTY

12.3.1 The Srebrenica Forensic Project

From 1996 to 2001, the ICTY's Office of the Prosecutor (OTP) was responsible for the examination of Srebrenica-related mass graves.[40] In that period, the forensic work focused on the identification, exhumation, and examination of the graves' contents by experts in archaeology, anthropology, pathology, ballistics, soil, pollen, and textiles.[41]

The identification of human remains started in 1996, when a joint OTP/Physicians for Human Rights (PHR) team exhumed mass graves at Branjevo Farm, Cerska, Nova Kasaba, and Lazete.[42] PHR and the International Committee for the Red Cross identified forty-four individuals, primarily through clothing and personal belongings found on the bodies.[43] That year, the OTP also engaged the US Naval Criminal Investigations Service (NCIS) to process the Pilica Dom and Kravica Warehouse execution sites. The NCIS collected 234 representative hair, blood, and tissue samples from the Pilica Dom;

[33] *Pitchfork* (n 32); Smith (n 14) para 1.13.

[34] *Andrews v State* 533 So 2d 851 (1988); Smith (n 14) para 1.15.

[35] *People v Castro* 545 NY Sid 985 (1989); S Patton, 'DNA Fingerprinting: the Castro Case' (1990) Harvard Journal of Law & Technology 223.

[36] *Frye v United States*, 293 F 1013, 1014 (DC Cir 1923); *People v Middleton*, 54 NY 2d 42, 49 (1981).

[37] *R v Tran* (1990) 50 A Crim R 233.

[38] *R v Lucas* (1992) 55 A Crim R 361.

[39] *R v Karger* [2001] SASC 64, upheld in *R v Karger* [2002] SASC 294.

[40] *Popović* Exhibit P02993, Summary of forensic evidence by Dean Manning, 27 November 2007, 1.

[41] The authors note, in particular, the work of Professor Richard Wright, Dr William Haglund, Fredy Peccerelli, Jose Baraybar, Dr Christopher Lawrence, and Dr John Clark and their respective teams; Dr Anthony Brown; Jean-Rene Ruez, Dean Manning, Dusan Janc, Helge Brunborg, and Ewa Tabeau; the US Naval Criminal Investigation Service, the US Bureau of Alcohol, Tobacco, Firearms and Explosives, and the Nederlands Forensisch Instituut.

[42] *Popović* Exhibit P00649 (Summary of Execution Points and Mass Graves by Manning), Annex A.

[43] ibid. Nine of these identifications were subsequently re-identified by the ICMP: see *Karadžić* Exhibit P04772.

166 of which contained human DNA.[44] The NCIS also collected 149 representative hair, blood, and tissue samples from the Kravica Warehouse, of which 142 contained human DNA.[45]

However, the identification of Srebrenica-related victims through DNA matching did not start in earnest until much later. In 2001, the ICTY handed over responsibility for examining the known graves and identifying new graves to the Government of Bosnia and Herzegovina.[46] This task has since been undertaken by the Bosnian Government in cooperation with the International Commission for Missing Persons (ICMP).[47]

12.3.2 The ICMP

The ICMP opened its DNA laboratory in 2001 and received ISO 17025 accreditation in 2007.[48] Since 2001, it has identified thousands of human remains exhumed from Srebrenica-related mass graves by matching DNA samples from the remains against DNA samples provided by relatives.[49]

The ICMP uses STR testing as its primary method of DNA profiling,[50] with mtDNA and TJ-chromosome analysis used when necessary to resolve or finalize certain DNA matches.[51] The ICMP's DNA programme, which involves genetic kinship analysis of complex cases,[52] normally targets sixteen STR markers.[53]

The ICMP's matching process works as follows. Newly-derived DNA profiles are analysed via computer against ICMP's DNA profile database. The database contains DNA profiles from more than 85,000 relatives of persons reported missing across the former Yugoslavia, and more than 24,000 DNA samples taken from human remains exhumed from graves across the former Yugoslavia (not only Srebrenica-related graves).[54] This analysis identifies any genetic patterns consistent with a familial relationship. If such a pattern is identified, a statistical probability calculation is performed with the minimum match requirement in most cases being 99.95 per cent.[55]

44 *Karadžić* Exhibit P04772 2.

45 ibid 5.

46 *Popović* Exhibit P02993 (n 40) para 1.

47 *Karadžić* Exhibit P04644 (ICMP Methodology Report) para 1 (noting the ICMP's status as a non-governmental organization established in 1996 to assist 'the political and technical co-operation of governments and other authorities in locating and identifying persons missing as a result of armed conflicts').

48 ISO 17025, a standard developed by the International Organization for Standardization for laboratories, is one of the most important accreditation programmes establishing the general requirements for competence to carrying out tests and/or calibrations. See ISO/IEC 17025:2005 General requirements for the competence of testing and calibration laboratories <https://www.iso.org/standard/39883.html> accessed 27 December 2017. The accreditation was granted by the accreditation body DACH (Deutsche Akkreditierungsstelle Chemie). See *Karadžić* Exhibit P04644 (ICMP Methodology Report) (n 47) para 28.

49 See ICMP, 'Over 7,000 Srebrenica Victims have now been recovered' <https://www.icmp.int/press-releases/over-7000-srebrenica-victims-recovered/> accessed 21 February 2020.

50 Evidence of Thomas Parsons, *Popović* T 20869.

51 See ICMP, 'Standing Capacity' <https://www.icmp.int/what-we-do/technical-assistance/standing-capacity/> accessed 27 December 2017; see also ICMP, 'DNA-Led Human Identification' <https://www.icmp.int/news/dna-led-human-identification/> accessed 27 February 2018.

52 ibid.

53 ICMP DNA Reports Guide (n 21).

54 *Karadžić* Exhibit P04644 (ICMP Methodology Report) (n 47) para 3.

55 Evidence of Thomas Parsons, *Popović* T 20876–77.

12.3.3 The *Popović* Case

The trial judgment in the seven-accused *Popović* case was delivered on 10 June 2010. Vujadin Popović and Ljubisa Beara were convicted of genocide and sentenced to life imprisonment. Drago Nikolic was convicted of aiding and abetting genocide and sentenced to thirty-five years' imprisonment. Radivoje Miletic, Ljubomir Borovcanin, Vinko Pandurevic, and Milan Gvero were convicted of crimes against humanity and/or war crimes and received sentences ranging between five and nineteen years' imprisonment. These convictions and sentences were substantially upheld on appeal.[56]

Popović marked the first occasion that the OTP had sought to adduce the ICMP's DNA evidence in a Srebrenica-related trial. It did so for three purposes. *First*, it was necessary to identify the Srebrenica victims.[57] *Second*, by identifying the unique DNA profile of each body or body part recovered from a Srebrenica-related mass grave, the DNA evidence provided an accurate account of the number of victims within each grave and prevented double-counting of victims whose fragmented remains appeared in multiple graves.[58] Previously, the OTP had relied purely on anthropological analysis to establish the minimum number of individuals (MNI) within and across the graves,[59] but the ICMP data was more accurate.[60] This aspect of the DNA evidence was particularly important in light of the reburial operation, whereby the remains of many victims were scattered across multiple secondary and even tertiary graves. *Third*, the DNA evidence was capable of establishing links between primary and secondary graves where remains of a single individual were recovered from two or more graves.[61]

The OTP-led expert evidence from Dr Thomas Parsons, the ICMP's Director of Forensic Sciences,[62] and tendered through him the relevant ICMP standard operating procedures (SOPs) and DNA match data for Srebrenica.[63] This data showed that as of November 2007 the ICMP had obtained DNA samples from the relatives of 7,772 individuals reported missing in July 1995; DNA profiles from 8,445 sets of remains found on the surface and in Srebrenica-related graves, representing 5,280 unique DNA profiles; and had matched 5,055 of these unique profiles with the DNA of family members.[64]

Dr Parsons testified that in the rare instances where an ICMP identification might be erroneous, additional investigation was undertaken. He further set out three reasons explaining why additional investigation might be necessary: (a) as a consequence of a kinship-based analysis, where a victim had additional relatives who had not been reported missing, a match report may be issued for the wrong relative, since no other missing relative would have been known; (b) mislabelling of a DNA sample prior to arriving at the

[56] *Prosecutor v Popović* et al (Appeal Judgment) ICTY-05-88-A (20 January 2015).

[57] *Popović* Trial Judgment (n 1) para 664.

[58] ibid paras 654, 664.

[59] The anthropological method of calculating the MNI in a mass grave involves selecting a unique bone (i.e. a bone that only appears once in each human, such as the left femur), then counting how many times that unique bone appears in the grave.

[60] *Popović* Exhibit P02993 (n 40) 2.

[61] *Popović* Trial Judgment (n 1) paras 653, 654, 663.

[62] *Popović* T 20866–0925.

[63] *Popović* Exhibit P04494 (confidential).

[64] ibid *Popović* Trial Judgment (n 1) para 639. Dr Parsons also relied on the ICMP data to estimate that the total number of persons buried in the Srebrenica-related graves was 8,100. This evidence did not directly relate to the science of DNA matching, or the ICMP's processes, and will not be addressed further here.

ICMP; and (c) switching of a sample or label during the testing process.[65] Notably, the November 2007 data showed only eight cases requiring further investigation due to apparent inconsistencies.[66]

The defence called two experts in response: Dr Debra Komar and Dr Oliver Stojkovic. Dr Komar raised three main challenges: (a) some of the ICMP's 'matches' could not distinguish between two or more putative individuals, giving rise to a risk of duplication; (b) the use of DNA to calculate the MNI in a grave was problematic while the exhumation of graves was ongoing; and (c) DNA profiling is not sufficient evidence of identity of itself, and such conclusions should only be made in conjunction with anthropological review.[67] For his part, Dr Stojkovic raised two issues: (a) 4,000 of the ICMP matches had occurred before the ICMP had received international accreditation; and (b) he was unable to assess the reliability of the ICMP data as the relevant electropherograms were not provided to him.[68]

The Trial Chamber did not accept these arguments.[69] Specifically, it rejected Dr Komar's methodology for eliminating supposed 'duplicate' matches,[70] and accepted DNA as an accurate means of determining MNI.[71] It also held that Dr Komar's concern that DNA analysis should be complemented by anthropological examination was addressed by Dr Parson's evidence that the ICMP undertook additional investigation where appropriate.[72] In addition, it held that ICMP's 2007 accreditation was an expression of approval of its work, rather than a factor undermining its work prior to that date.[73]

In relation to the issue of electropherograms, the Trial Chamber noted that Dr Stojkovic had been provided with a set of electropherograms relating to tests done on remains recovered from a discrete grave site at Bisina;[74] which he analysed and conceded that they fell within the ICMP's acceptable range for reporting matches.[75] The Trial Chamber thus held that Dr Stojkovic's analysis 'serves only to strengthen the conclusion that the DNA analysis conducted by the ICMP is reliable. There is no basis to conclude that further disclosure [of additional electropherograms] would have led to a different conclusion in this case'.[76]

The Trial Chamber ultimately concluded that the ICMP data was reliable,[77] and relied on it for all three purposes submitted by the OTP. The Trial Chamber's findings relating to the reliability of the DNA evidence and its rejection of the defence experts' challenges were subsequently upheld on appeal.[78]

[65] Evidence of Thomas Parsons, *Popović* T 33404; *Popović* Exhibit P04526 (confidential).
[66] *Popović* Exhibit P04526 (confidential).
[67] *Popović* Exhibit 2D00534; *Popović* T 23872–4051. Dr Komar also gave evidence in relation to non-DNA-related forensic science evidence. Those aspects of her evidence are not addressed here.
[68] *Popović* Exhibit 1D1069; *Popović* T 22974–3028.
[69] *Popović* Trial Judgment (n 1) paras 642–49.
[70] ibid para 642.
[71] ibid para 654, 664.
[72] ibid para 643–44.
[73] ibid para 643.
[74] ibid para 647–48.
[75] ibid para 648.
[76] ibid para 649.
[77] ibid para 664.
[78] *Popović* Appeals Judgment (n 56) paras 287–91; 317–28.

12.3.4 The *Karadžić* Case

The *Karadžić* trial judgment was delivered on 24 March 2016. Dr Karadžić was sentenced to life in prison upon his convictions for genocide, crimes against humanity, and war crimes in relation to Srebrenica, as well as crimes against humanity and war crimes in relation to crimes committed in other Bosnian municipalities throughout the war. The matter is currently on appeal.

The OTP sought to adduce the ICMP's Srebrenica-related DNA data for the same three purposes as was done in *Popović*. The OTP again led Dr Parsons' expert evidence, tendering through him the relevant ICMP SOPs and match data for Srebrenica through March 2012.[79] That data showed that by then the ICMP had obtained 6,772 unique DNA profiles and had matched 6,606 of them with the DNA of family members.[80] Some of this data was tendered confidentially, but later made public by the Trial Chamber either in whole or as redacted, over objections of the OTP and the ICMP.[81]

From the outset, Dr Karadžić made clear his intention to challenge the DNA evidence by commissioning an independent audit or re-analysis of the ICMP data. At the 17 August 2009 pre-trial conference,[82] Dr Karadžić sought disclosure of the entire ICMP database for the purposes of analysing a representative sample of some 300 Srebrenica-related cases.[83] This gave rise to two issues. *First*, many relatives of missing persons who had provided blood samples to the ICMP (blood donors) had not expressly consented to the use of their genetic data in criminal proceedings.[84] *Second*, the size of the database meant that obtaining consents or waivers from the blood donors would take a substantial amount of time. Ultimately, it was agreed that Dr Karadžić would not receive the entire database, but would randomly select 300 cases, and the ICMP would provide the case files once consent had been obtained from the 1,200-odd relevant blood donors.[85]

At this pre-trial conference, the Presiding Judge made two further observations of relevance to other cases. *First*, if a method by which the defence could test DNA evidence could not be agreed among the parties, and the Trial Chamber considered there to be 'some potential unfairness in the use of material which could not be checked', it would take steps to resolve the issue.[86] While these steps were not elaborated on, it is likely that the Presiding Judge meant that the Trial Chamber might limit or exclude the evidence. *Second*, where the contemplated testing involved substantial public resources, the importance of the DNA evidence to the case was to be considered when authorizing their use.[87] Thus, the relative proportionality was a relevant factor. For example, if DNA was not the sole evidence on which

[79] *Karadžić* T 26547–674.

[80] ibid T 26585.

[81] *Prosecutor v Radovan Karadžić* (Decision on the Accused's Motion to Unseal ICMP Exhibits) IT-95-5/18-T (25 April 2012); and *Prosecutor v Radovan Karadžić* (Decision on Prosecution's Motion for Partial Reconsideration or Clarification of the Chamber's Decision on the Accused's Motion to Unseal ICMP Exhibits) IT-95-5/18-T (5 September 2012).

[82] *Karadžić* T 110–61.

[83] ibid T 112.

[84] ibid T 117.

[85] ibid T 119; *Karadžić* Trial Judgment (n 4) para 5566. Some 1,200 donor consents were required because each case file (or match) involves the blood samples of as many as three or four relatives.

[86] *Karadžić* T 118.

[87] ibid T 121.

the OTP relied, this may properly influence a determination as to the appropriate size of the representative sample to be tested.[88]

On 19 March 2010, the Trial Chamber ordered Dr Karadžić to 'immediately complete his selection of 300 cases for further DNA analysis'.[89] In early 2012, Dr Karadžić provided the ICMP with a request for 295 randomly selected and five specifically identified case samples.[90] The ICMP subsequently provided 286 case files, but was unable to obtain consents for the remaining fourteen cases.[91] Dr Karadžić then sought an order from the Trial Chamber compelling the ICMP's production of the fourteen cases.[92] In dismissing the request, the Trial Chamber found that 286 cases was a sufficiently large sample, Dr Karadžić could also select fourteen replacement cases, and there was no basis to believe that the cases where consent could not obtained were the most likely to involve fraud.[93]

On 11 March 2013, Dr Karadžić filed a motion seeking to exclude the DNA evidence, arguing that he was unable to test it in a 'scientifically valid way'. He submitted that its admission would thus violate his fair trial rights, and that the ICMP's position on consent meant there was no way to obtain a truly random sample.[94] However, the Trial Chamber dismissed the motion because the issues raised had already been decided, and Dr Karadžić had been afforded an adequate opportunity to test the DNA evidence.[95]

In the end, Dr Karadžić chose not to present expert evidence challenging ICMP's methodology or results.[96] The Trial Chamber accepted the reliability of the ICMP data[97] and indeed, relied on it for all three purposes submitted by the OTP.

12.4 Analysis

There is an extensive body of jurisprudence and other material from around the world analysing scientific, procedural, and legal issues associated with the use of DNA evidence.[98] It is beyond the scope of this chapter to engage with all those issues, although many equally apply to the *Popović* and *Karadžić* cases. The following analysis instead focuses on five aspects of the DNA evidence in *Popović* and *Karadžić* which are likely to be of particular relevance to other mass atrocity cases involving large numbers of victims and mass graves.

[88] ibid T 120–21.

[89] *Prosecutor v Radovan Karadžić* (Order on Selection of Cases for DNA Analysis) IT-95-5/18-T (29 March 2010) See also *Prosecutor v Radovan Karadžić* (Decision in Relation to Selection of Cases for DNA Analysis) IT-95-5/18-T (23 September 2011).

[90] *Prosecutor v Radovan Karadžić* (Interim Order on the Accused's Motion for Binding Order to the International Commission for Missing Persons) IT-95-5/18-T (19 July 2012).

[91] *Prosecutor v Radovan Karadžić* (Decision on the Accused's Motion for Binding Order to the International Commission for Missing Persons) IT-95-5/18-T (4 March 2013).

[92] ibid.

[93] ibid paras 26–29.

[94] *Prosecutor v Radovan Karadžić*, (Motion to Exclude DNA Evidence) IT-95-5/18-T, Defence (11 March 2013).

[95] *Prosecutor v Radovan Karadžić* (Decision on Motion to Exclude DNA Evidence) IT-95-5/18-T (16 April 2013).

[96] *Karadžić* Trial Judgment (n 4) para 5567.

[97] *Karadžić* Trial Judgment (n 4) para 5568.

[98] See the cases and materials discussed in Smith (n 14) and M Lynch et al, *Truth Machine: The Contentious History of DNA Fingerprinting* (First Edition, University of Chicago Press 2008).

12.4.1 The Multiple Purposes of DNA Evidence

Identifying the victims of a mass atrocity such as Srebrenica is of critical importance for the victims' families, the truth-seeking function of international courts and tribunals, and often to the prosecution or defence of individual cases. *Popović* and *Karadžić* show how DNA evidence can be relevant for two additional purposes beyond victim identification; that is, the calculation of MNI and establishment of links between crime sites.

Establishing an accurate count of victims is important where their number may be relevant to proof of an offence (for example, genocide or extermination as a crime against humanity).[99] It may also assist in establishing an accurate case theory and historical record. For example, witnesses may give materially different estimates of the number of victims killed and buried at a particular location or locations. An accurate assessment of MNI in the grave(s) will remove this uncertainty and, importantly, inform investigative and analytical steps. For instance, it may provide an indication of the logistics involved in a killing or burial operation, such as the number of transport vehicles that would have been required, the time it would have taken to carry out these acts, or the amount of ammunition needed to do so.

Proving DNA links between two or more crime sites is also important to establishing an accurate prosecutorial case theory and the historical record. For example, if the same unique DNA profile is recovered from a known execution site and a mass grave site, it is a reasonable inference that the individual was killed at that execution site, then buried in the primary grave. If large numbers of unique DNA profiles follow the same pattern, the inference becomes stronger. This is precisely how some of the connections between the Srebrenica primary, secondary, and tertiary graves were established, together with other linkage evidence including soil, pollen, ballistics, blindfolds, ligatures, and glass connections between the graves.[100]

12.4.2 The Complexities of Related Victims

The Srebrenica victims included many immediate family groups; fathers and sons, brothers, cousins, grandfathers and grandsons, uncles and nephews. As a result, many of the ICMP blood donors were not immediate relatives of the deceased. The presence of multiple related victims gives rise to two potential limits on the use of DNA evidence, which may be of relevance to other mass atrocity cases.

The first limit is that the nature of the relationship between the victim and the blood donors may affect the strength of a positive identification of a given individual. For example, assume that the remains of four brothers are exhumed from a mass grave and matched with DNA from a paternal grandfather and maternal grandmother. In these circumstances, STR testing should be able to derive a unique DNA profile for each brother, and establish that they are all related to the blood donors and to each other. However, in the

[99] There is no minimum number of victims for the crimes of genocide and extermination as a crime against humanity. However, the number of victims may still be relevant to establishing whether a 'substantial' part of the protected group was targeted (for genocide) or the 'large number of victims' or 'massive scale' of the killings (for extermination). See *Popović* Trial Judgment (n 1) paras 607, 800, and 831–33.

[100] *Popović* Trial Judgment (n 1) para 655.

context of a kinship-based analysis, it is impossible to determine which unique profile belonged to which brother, whereas this might be possible with more immediate relatives as blood donors. Any such limitation in the evidence should be explained to the relevant court or tribunal to avoid it being misinterpreted as a scientific deficiency, procedural fault, or methodological error in double counting.[101]

The second limit may arise if mtDNA analysis, rather than STR testing, is the profiling method used. As noted above, family members with a common maternal lineage have identical mtDNA, meaning that those relatives' remains cannot be distinguished by mtDNA alone. In these circumstances, an MNI calculation using mtDNA profiles is likely to be lower than the true number because each unique profile will only be counted once. In addition, mtDNA may not, in and of itself, be able to establish definitive links between different crime sites in some circumstances. For example, if two siblings are killed at different locations and buried in different graves, mtDNA samples would be unable to distinguish which victim was killed at which site. It is therefore important to ensure that the type of DNA profiling used properly supports the purpose for which the evidence is being adduced, and attends to the evidentiary circumstances of the case.

12.4.3 Procedural Reliability and Co-mingled Remains

Procedural error is the area in which DNA evidence is most open to legal challenge. This has been the case in national courts since DNA was first admitted.[102] It is no different in international courts; in *Popović* and *Karadžić*, the admissibility of DNA evidence ultimately turned on the court's satisfaction with the propriety and reliability of the DNA profiling and matching procedures.[103]

The following factors were considered relevant to the propriety and reliability of the DNA evidence in *Popović* and *Karadžić*, and are likely to be similarly relevant to other cases involving DNA evidence. *First*, whether the DNA laboratory is accredited, and if so, to what standard. *Second*, what, if any, SOPs are place at the DNA laboratory to prevent or detect any irregularities in the profiling or matching processes. In this respect, the *Popović* Trial Chamber noted Dr Parsons' evidence that the ICMP had detected irregularities in only eight out of thousands of Srebrenica-related cases, and undertook additional investigation once those irregularities were detected.[104] *Third*, what oversight procedures are in place to ensure that the SOPs are adhered to and the integrity of the data is maintained.

A further issue addressed in *Popović*, and also likely to be relevant in other cases involving mass graves, is the potential for co-mingled remains to result in an erroneous identification.[105] This issue arises when a set of remains thought to belong to a single individual includes the co-mingled remains of another. In these circumstances, a misidentification can arise if a DNA profile determined for 'body A' was in fact derived from a co-mingled bone belonging to 'body B'.

[101] Defence witness Dr Komar made the double-counting argument in *Popović*, and the Trial Chamber rejected it. See *Popović* Trial Judgment (n 1) paras 643–44.
[102] See *People v Castro* (n 35); *R v Karger* [2001] (n 39), upheld in *R v Karger* [2002] (n 39).
[103] *Karadžić* Trial Judgment (n 4) para 5568.
[104] *Popović* Trial Judgment (n 1) paras 643–44.
[105] ibid.

To address the issue of potential co-mingling, the anthropological examination of remains, and the creation of an overall 'biological profile' of a given individual, should remain an important part of the identification process. This process involves a physical examination of the remains to ensure that the sex, age, and stature of all aspects of the remains are consistent with the DNA results. There are at least three cases at the ICMP where the biological profile created by the ICMP showed that the DNA-sampled bone came from an individual different than the person identified through other means.[106] In two cases, the DNA data suggested an individual of a different age than indicated by the physical examination of the associated remains. In a third, the DNA suggested that the victim was male, but the anthropological analysis indicated female. In all three cases, the remains were re-tested and co-mingling was identified.[107]

12.4.4 Defence Re-analysis of DNA Matches

The defence challenge to the DNA evidence in *Karadžić* involved the intersection of three competing interests: the defence's right to re-analyse the DNA evidence, the use of public resources in that re-analysis, and the ICMP's contractual obligation to keep the genetic data of blood donors confidential.

As the Presiding Judge during the *Karadžić* pre-trial proceedings suggested, if the OTP sought to rely on DNA evidence which the defence could not check, and the Trial Chamber considered there to be some unfairness in the use of that evidence, the evidence may have been excluded.[108] A key issue in any case of this kind will therefore be the determination of what constitutes 'adequate checking' for purposes of satisfying procedural fairness.

Not unexpectedly, adequate checking does not mean that a party is entitled to re-analyse all samples in all cases. For example, if the case involved thirty victims and DNA evidence was central to the prosecution's case, the re-analysis of all thirty cases may be deemed necessary and appropriate, irrespective of whether public funding was to be used (that is, the resources of the court or tribunal in question). For larger numbers of victims (in the hundreds or thousands), a representative sample is more likely to be deemed adequate, providing that the sample size is sufficient to obtain a scientifically significant and reliable result. The precise numbers of the representative sample will turn on the numbers of victims involved, whether the re-analysis will utilize public funding and the centrality of DNA to the case. Where DNA is not central to the case, a smaller sample may be considered sufficient to safeguard a party's procedural rights, again providing that the sample size is sufficient to obtain a reliable result.

An additional relevant factor arises where blood donors do not consent to the disclosure of their confidential genetic data. In these circumstances, there are two potential means by which an adequate sample can still be obtained. *First*, the parties can adopt (or the court can order) a method of random sampling which automatically substitutes in another DNA case

[106] L Yazedjian et al, *The Importance of Using Traditional Anthropological Methods in a DNA-Led Identification System*, paper presented at the Annual Meeting of the American Academy of Forensic Sciences, New Orleans, Louisiana, 2005.

[107] ibid.

[108] *Karadžić* T 118.

file if one cannot be used due to the absence of consent.[109] *Second*, the court could order the production of the samples, irrespectively. However, this may alienate victims' groups and reduce DNA laboratory cooperation in future cases, which may have a collateral effect of impeding post-conflict justice and accountability efforts in the affected region. There may also be an issue of whether the court has the relevant power. At the ICTY, the issue of the ICMP's compellability was not finally decided.[110] Similar issues may arise with other courts such as the International Criminal Court, the Special Tribunal for Lebanon, or the Special Court for Sierra Leone (particularly, where the DNA laboratory is not within a territory wherein those courts have jurisdictional primacy), or national courts in which the DNA laboratory is located outside their jurisdiction.

12.4.5 A Holistic Approach to Forensic Evidence

The Srebrenica mass graves are an incredibly complex source of evidence, in large part due to the numerous victims, the number and remote location of the grave sites, the degraded and co-mingled condition of the victims' remains and contents of the graves, and the complicated interrelationship of the graves due to the sweeping reburial operation. The DNA evidence is an important part of untangling this complexity, but it should not be viewed in isolation; nor can it provide all the answers. *Popović* and *Karadžić* affirm the importance of adopting a holistic approach to establishing a victim's individual identity and the cause, manner, timing, and circumstances of their death.[111] Two examples are illustrative.

There is no question that the Srebrenica-related DNA evidence constitutes the primary evidence upon which the victims' identities have been established. Nevertheless, anthropology, pathology, and the analysis of grave artefacts continue to play a role in this process, particularly given the risk of co-mingled remains, and the complications caused by multiple victims from the same family. *Popović* also makes clear that the role of these other forensic disciplines, particularly anthropology, in detecting errors in the identification process, has bearing on the reliability and therefore admissibility of DNA evidence,[112] which itself forms *a part* of that process.

More broadly, *Popović* and *Karadžić* involved a range of scientific issues relating to the time, date, cause, manner, and circumstances of the Srebrenica victims' deaths to which the DNA evidence could not speak directly, or at all. For example, in *Karadžić*, the defence argued that the Srebrenica-related graves contained the bodies of persons killed in unrelated events and buried at different times.[113] In dismissing these arguments, the Trial Chamber relied principally on expert evidence from archaeologists and pathologists.[114] The OTP and

[109] In *Karadžić*, only fourteen of 300 cases were withheld by the ICMP due to absence of consent, and the Trial Chamber specifically noted that the adoption of such a method would have overcome the deficit. See *Karadžić*, Decision on the Accused's Motion for Binding Order to the International Commission for Missing Persons (n 91) paras 26–29.

[110] *Karadžić*, Decision on the Accused's Motion for Binding Order to the International Commission for Missing Persons (n 91).

[111] See *Karadžić* Trial Judgment (n 4) para 539.

[112] *Popović* Trial Judgment (n 1) paras 643–44.

[113] *Karadžić* Trial Judgment (n 4) paras 5531–39; testimony of Dusan Dunjic, *Karadžić* T 41747; 41761–63; 41793–94.

[114] *Karadžić* Trial Judgment (n 4) paras 5531–43; testimony of Dr Richard Wright, *Karadžić* T 22307, 22313; testimony of Dr Christopher Lawrence, *Karadžić* T 22482; testimony of Fredy Peccerelli, *Karadžić* T 22741; testimony of Dr William Haglund, *Karadžić* T 23913–14.

defence also agreed that cause and manner of death of many of the Srebrenica victims could not be determined purely by forensic science evidence due to the substantial damage to the remains and the high degree of decomposition.[115] Cause and manner of death for these victims was ultimately determined by the Trial Chamber, based principally on a combination of expert evidence from pathologists and surrounding factual evidence.[116]

The benefits of a holistic approach also extend beyond matters of proof and admissibility, to case presentation. In cases like Srebrenica which involve large numbers of victims, it can assist the court to use one or two representative examples to illustrate the exhumation, autopsy, and identification processes from start to finish. The identification of Srebrenica victim Mesa Efendic was one such example used in a Srebrenica-related trial at the ICTY.[117] Mr Efendic's detention by Bosnian Serb forces on 13 July 1995 at Potocari (near Srebrenica) was captured on film. At the time, he was wearing dark coloured trousers, a light-coloured shirt, and a short-sleeved red vest. He was subsequently reported missing. In 1998, a body was exhumed from the Kozluk mass grave and given the designation 'KK543B'. The exhumation and autopsy reports and photographs show that body KK543B was found in the Kozluk grave dressed in dark-coloured trousers, a light-coloured shirt, and a red vest. Years later, the ICMP's DNA analysis identified body KK543B as that of Mr Efendic. This example—made poignantly clear through the images of Mr Efendic's red vest on film, in the grave, and on the autopsy table—left no doubt as to the reliability and probative value of all the forensic sciences involved in the identification process.

12.5 Lessons Learned

The *Popović* and *Karadžić* cases exemplify the important role of DNA evidence in the investigation and litigation of cases involving mass atrocities, as well as the complications to that evidence caused by mass interments and multiple related victims. These cases also highlight two key admissibility issues relevant to DNA evidence: the reliability of the DNA profiling and matching procedures employed, and the procedural fair trial implications in respect of the opportunity to adequately check such evidence. We hope that the above discussion assists others in the investigation and litigation of similar issues in the future.

To conclude, we summarize below ten key 'lessons learned' from the DNA-related litigation in *Popović* and *Karadžić*, which may be helpful in utilizing or challenging similar evidence effectively in future cases.

1. The parties should seek to engage as early as possible to determine whether and how to address issues related to challenges to DNA evidence, including whether all matches or a representative sample will be examined or tested, and whether there are any relevant confidentiality issues attending to such evidence requiring the obtaining of donors' consents and/or waivers;

[115] *Karadžić* Trial Judgment (n 4) para 5546.
[116] *Karadžić* Trial Judgment (n 4) paras 5546–57.
[117] The relevant evidence is summarized in *Prosecutor v Tolimir* (Judgment) ICTY-05-88/2, T 7695–706.

2. If a party's re-analysis of a representative sample of DNA matches is pursued, consider using a method of random sampling which automatically substitutes another case in when a given case cannot be used due to privacy considerations;
3. The most appropriate approach to presenting DNA evidence at trial will depend on the significance of the evidence and the extent to which it is contested. Different approaches may include: (a) a comprehensive analysis of both the science of DNA profiling and each step in the identification process; (b) a simple approach focusing principally on the identification of the victims in that case; (c) a middle ground which educates the court on the basics while avoiding extensive scientific or technical detail;
4. Consider calling an overview witness such as the head of the DNA laboratory, who can explain the basics of DNA testing, establish the reliability of the testing procedures applied and authenticate the test results. If a specific DNA match is contested, evidence from the technician involved may also be necessary;
5. The reliability of the relevant DNA profiling and matching techniques must be established in all cases. Relevant SOPs should be explained and tendered. Evidence should also be adduced of laboratory certification and the applicable accreditation standards, the training and proficiency testing of technicians, and what oversight processes and procedures are in place for detecting and correcting any procedural errors;
6. Explain any complicating factors relating to the collecting of the samples, for example, whether there is any risk of co-mingling, or the presence of multiple related victims, and how those factors have been addressed in the evidence;
7. Explain any unusual aspects or limitations on the testing process, for example, whether low copy DNA analysis was used, whether the sample population database is small, or whether the number of STR markers used was low;
8. When presenting the case, consider using one or more examples to step through the DNA profiling and matching process from the point of sample collection through to the issuance of a match report;
9. Ensure that the purpose for which the DNA evidence is relied on is supported by the profiling method involved. This may be a consideration where mtDNA profiling is used and there are multiple maternally-related victims;
10. A holistic approach to the use of forensic evidence is preferable. This is particularly the case if the evidence goes beyond victim identification and into issues of cause, manner, timing, or other circumstances of death.

13

Whither Thou Truth and Justice

Witness Perceptions About their Contributions to the ICTY

Kimi Lynn King and James Meernik***

13.1 Introduction

The witnesses who appear before international war crimes tribunals are the most critical stakeholders in the search for truth and justice. The exponential growth in transitional justice mechanisms has led practitioners and scholars to seek a better understanding about the experiences of those who provide the historical record and tell their story about their country's violent conflict. Any tribunal, when assessing its legacy, should closely examine the witness experience from the perspective of the witnesses themselves and what they think about the contributions their testimony made to the discovery of truth and the provision of justice. Witnesses testify to tell the narrative of war, and the experience reflects that complexity for those personally involved and it also has ramifications for those who carry out the tribunal's mandate. If witnesses are not fully integrated into the testimonial process and equipped to provide accurate and useful testimony, or if the tribunal does not support and show concern for witness well-being—it is questionable whether any tribunal can say it has furthered the quest for truth and accomplished justice.

What does it mean for a witness to contribute to truth and justice? What are the factors that play into whether witnesses feel as though they have contributed to that mission? This chapter explores the witness experience at the International Criminal Tribunal for the former Yugoslavia (ICTY) by looking at data from a recent study to evaluate in depth the impact of testifying on witnesses *during the time of testifying*. Borrowing from theories of procedural justice, we use a logistic regression model to evaluate what contributes to witness perceptions about the search for truth and justice in order to better understand not only the legacy of the ICTY as an institution, but to also better understand the role of witnesses and their legacy.[1]

We detail below one theoretical approach to the testimonial process, emphasizing fairness and social identity in the testimonial treatment and the challenges witnesses face when testifying. We specify eight hypotheses and provide an analysis for each. As the results reveal, we find that fair treatment of defendants and witnesses by the prosecuting attorneys and a lack of bias regarding ethnicity are significantly correlated to witness perceptions that

* Professor of Political Science in the College of Liberal Arts and Social Sciences at the University of Texas.
** Professor; Coordinator of the Division of Social Sciences; Director of the Castleberry Peace Institute, University of Texas.

[1] Data examines witness experiences during the war, during the testimonial process, and in the post-testimonial phase. K King et al, 'Echoes of Testimonies: A Pilot Study into the Long-Term Impact of Bearing Witness Before the ICTY' (*ICTY, UNT*, 2016) <http://bit.ly/2ICTY-Echoes> accessed 09 August 2018.

Kimi Lynn King and James Meernik, *Whither Thou Truth and Justice* In: *Legacies of the International Criminal Tribunal for the Former Yugoslavia*. Edited by: Carsten Stahn, Carmel Agius, Serge Brammertz, Colleen Rohan, Oxford University Press (2020). © The Several Contributors DOI: 10.1093/oso/9780198862956.003.0014

their testimony has contributed to both truth and justice. As for stressors that occur for witnesses during the time of testimony (e.g. translation problems, trial delays and postponements, being away from home, concerns about consequences of testifying, physical, and psychological issues), only witnesses who experienced delays and postponements were significantly less likely to believe they had contributed to justice (the results were insignificant for truth). Witnesses who believed that support from the Victims and Witnesses Section (VWS) minimized stressors associated with testifying were significantly more likely to think that they had contributed to justice. Finally, there are also ethnic differences that emerge. Bosnian Croats, and Serbs are *less likely* to feel that they have contributed, but Bosniaks and Albanians are *more likely* to think they contributed to justice. Out of all the aforementioned groups, only Bosnian Croats are *less likely* to perceive they have contributed to the truth. We conclude with what the findings say about what it means to 'bear' witness and what this means for the legacy of the ICTY.

13.2 The Witness Experience

The impact of tribunals on witnesses begins at the moment contact is made between the individual and the ICTY. Ultimately, the witnesses' knowledge about what happened during the wars in the former Yugoslavia culminates in testifying at the Tribunal, but the impact of this process may continue long after the witness has returned home.[2] The scholarly debate has been lively regarding whether tribunals, as well as other transitional justice institutions, do more harm than good, with theories tending to focus at the micro-level context of the witness experience inside the institution where it occurs. This is especially important given the impact that testifying can have on witnesses' psychological well-being.[3] While testifying may provide closure for traumatic events for some individuals,[4] it is also possible that the process of testifying itself may have negative consequences.[5]

These negative consequences may also manifest in witness perceptions about whether the ICTY has done more harm than good when it comes to truth, justice, and reconciliation.[6] Those affected by the wars also have beliefs about the events that occurred and an understanding about what truth and justice mean.[7] Coupled with the fact that people are

[2] E Stover, *The Witnesses: War Crimes and the Promise of Justice in The Hague* (University of Pennsylvania Press 2005); S Stepakoff et al, 'Self-reported Psychosocial Consequences of Testifying in a War Crimes Tribunal in Sierra Leone' (2015) 4 International Perspectives in Psychology: Research, Practice, Consultation 161; S Stepakoff et al, 'The Experience of Testifying in a War-Crimes Tribunal in Sierra Leone' (2015) 21 Peace and Conflict: Journal of Peace Psychology 445; King et al (n 1).

[3] S Bandes, 'Victims, "Closure", and the Sociology of Emotion' (2009) 72 Law and Contemporary Problems 1; N Henry, 'Witness to Rape: The Limits and Potential of International War Crimes Trials for Victims of Wartime Sexual Violence' (2009) 1 International Journal of Transitional Justice 114; N Henry, 'The Impossibility of Bearing Witness: Wartime Rape and the Promise of Justice' (2010) 16 Violence Against Women 1098; J Herman, 'The Mental Health of Crime Victims: Impact of Legal Intervention' (2003) 16 Journal of Trauma Stress 159; N Henry, *War and Rape: Law, Memory, and Justice* (Routledge 2011).

[4] K Moghalu, 'Reconciling Fractured Societies: An African Perspective on the Role of Judicial Prosecutions' in R Thakur and P Malcontent (eds), *From Sovereign Impunity to International Accountability: The Search for Justice in a World of States* (United Nations University Press 2004); Stover (n 2).

[5] Bandes (n 3).

[6] M Martins and J Bronsther, 'Stay the Hand of Justice? Evaluating Claims that War Crimes Trials Do More Harm than Good' (2017) 146 Daedalus 83; J Clark, *International Trials and Reconciliation: Assessing the Impact of the International Criminal Tribunal for the Former Yugoslavia* (Routledge 2014).

[7] S Ford, 'A Social Psychology Model of the Perceived Legitimacy of International Criminal Courts: Implications for the Success of Transitional Justice Systems' (2012) 2 Vanderbilt Journal of Transnational Law 405; M Klarin, 'The

more likely to accord legitimacy and provide support to a judicial system if they believe they have some voice, influence, or impact over the institutional process and outcomes[8], understanding what witnesses believe about their contributions may increase our understanding about strengthening transitional justice mechanisms.

Rather than focus on witness perceptions about whether the ICTY as an institution has established the truth and contributed to justice, as has been done elsewhere[9], we take a more nuanced view of the micro-level approach by examining whether witnesses believe *they personally have contributed to truth and justice* by having testified at the ICTY. We recognize that the witnesses have individual and social identities affiliated with groups who appear before the Tribunal, and our focus on the relationship between tribunals and stakeholders adds another piece of the procedural and restorative justice puzzle which examines the 'consequences of human rights violations'. If witnesses believe they have contributed, it may validate their experience, and ultimately enhance the ICTY's legacy[10] and foster reconciliation in the region.[11]

13.3 Truth and Justice

At every stage of the transitional justice process the concepts of truth and justice are interwoven, and for transitional justice measures to matter, they must overcome challenges to legitimacy.[12] Judicial mechanisms associated with transitional justice are expected to implement truth (the discovery of what happened and the establishment of the historical record) and justice (determinations about responsibility, guilt, and punishment), and they are also expected to balance the rights of the witnesses and defendants.[13] What 'justice' or

Impact of the ICTY Trials on Public Opinion in the Former Yugoslavia' (2009) 7 Journal of International Criminal Justice 89; J Meernik, 'Explaining Public Opinion on International Criminal Justice' (2015) 7 European Political Science Review 567; D Orentlicher, *Shrinking the Space for Denial: The Impact of the ICTY in Serbia* (Open Society Initiative 2008); J Subotić, *Hijacked Justice: Dealing with the Past in the Balkans* (Cornell University Press 2009).

[8] J Doak, 'Enriching Trial Justice for Crime Victims in Common Law Systems: Lessons from Transitional Environments' (2015) 21 International Review of Victimology 139; T Tyler, *Why People Obey the Law* (Yale University Press 1990); T Tyler and J Darley, 'Building a Law-Abiding Society: Taking Public Views About Morality and the Legitimacy of Legal Authorities into Account When Formulating Substantive Law' (2000) 28 Hofstra Law Review 707.

[9] K King and J Meernik, *The Witness Experience: Testimony at the ICTY and Its Impact* (Cambridge University Press 2017); Clark (n 6); Stover (n 2); E Stover and H Weinstein, *My Neighbor, My Enemy: Justice and Community in the Aftermath of Mass Atrocity* (Cambridge University Press 2004).

[10] R David, 'What We Know About Transitional Justice: Survey and Experimental Evidence' (2017) 38 Political Psychology 151, 154; K Clamp, 'Clearing the Conceptual Haze: Restorative Justice Concepts in Transitional Settings' in K Clamp (ed), *Restorative Justice in Transitional Settings* (Routledge 2016) 16, 20; W Lambourne, 'Transitional Justice and Peacebuilding after Mass Violence' (2009) 3 International Journal of Transitional Justice 28; Doak (n 8).

[11] Stover (n 2); Stover and Weinstein (n 9); M Biro et al, 'Attitudes Toward Justice and Social Reconstruction in Bosnia and Herzegovina' in E Stover and H Weinstein (eds), *My Neighbor, My Enemy: Justice and Community in the Aftermath of Mass Atrocity* (Cambridge University Press 2004). We do not assess here whether there are causal relationships or the impact on reconciliation, but prior work suggests that ethnocentrism contributes to undermining reconciliation; Clark (n 6).

[12] David (n 10); J Selimovic, 'Perpetrators and Victims: Local Responses to the International Criminal Tribunal for the former Yugoslavia' (2010) 57 Focaal 50; N Roht-Arriaza and J Mariezcurrena, *Transitional Justice in the Twenty-First Century: Beyond Truth versus Justice* (Cambridge University Press 2006); W Lambourne, 'Transitional Justice and Peacebuilding after Mass Violence' (2009) 3 International Journal of Transitional Justice 28.

[13] A Trotter, 'Witness Intimidation in International Trials: Balancing the Need for Protection Against the Rights of the Accused' (2013) 44 George Washington International Law Review 521; H Haider and T Welch, 'The

'truth' mean for these stakeholders helps inform debates about *if* tribunals matter, and also *why* and *how* they matter.[14] As one former judge noted, without war crimes witnesses there can be no trials.[15] We now turn to our theory and development of hypotheses about specific factors we think will have an impact on how witnesses assess their contributions to truth and justice.

Identity. Witnesses called to testify have both individual and social identities they bring to the adjudication process,[16] that frame their interpretation about the nature of truth and justice being dispensed and their role in the process. The context of witness identities matters because individuals form opinions about how institutions *should respond* to violations, and also about how institutions *actually do respond* to such violations. It is here that personal and social identity theories overlap—personal identity assists in explaining unique characteristics about the witness experience—especially during the time of testimony, while social identity is connected to explanations stemming from bias, prejudice, and intergroup conflicts[17] which may have more enduring effects on perceptions of truth and justice.

> Personal identity encompasses idiosyncratic characteristics, such as abilities, physical and psychological traits, and interests, whereas social identity encompasses salient classifications that describe a social group or aggregate, such as gender or nation.[18]

We suggest, both personal and social identities shape witness beliefs about their contributions to truth and justice.[19] On a personal level, the burden of bearing witness is distinctive and individualized. Each person faces challenges—physical, psychological, or logistical—they must overcome. These individuals have social identities, as representatives of a group, whether it is their gender, national affiliation, or ethnic identity,[20] and this too has consequences for witnesses and how they interpret their contributions to truth and justice.

Fairness. Like identity, witness perceptions about fair treatment from all of the calling parties relates to procedural justice—people are more likely to accept judicial outcomes if they believe the process was fair.[21] A corollary following from this, is that witnesses may

Protection of Witnesses in Bosnian War Crimes Trials: A Fair Balance Between the Interest of the Victims and the Right of the Accused?' (2008) 20 The Denning Law Journal 55.

[14] David (n 10); Stepakoff et al, 'Self-reported Psychosocial Consequences' (n 2); Stepakoff et al, 'The Experience of Testifying' (n 2); Orentlicher (n 7); Stover and Weinstein (n 9).

[15] P Wald, 'Dealing with Witnesses in War Crimes Trials: Lessons from Yugoslavia Tribunal' (2002) 5 Yale Human Rights & Development Law Journal 1.

[16] David (n 10); T Tyler, 'Social Justice: Outcome and Procedure' (2000) 35 International Journal of Psychology 117; M A Hogg et al, 'A Tale of Two Theories: A Critical Comparison of Identity Theory with Social Identity Theory' (1995) 58 Social Psychology Quarterly 255; H Tajfel, 'Introduction' in H Tajfel (ed), *Social Identity and Intergroup Relations* (Cambridge University Press 1982).

[17] L Huddy, 'Contrasting Theoretical Approaches to Intergroup Relations' (2004) 25 Political Psychology 947; L Huddy, 'Context and Meaning in Social Identity Theory: A Response to Oakes' (2002) 23 Political Psychology 825.

[18] R David, 'International Criminal Tribunals and the Perception of Justice: The Effect of the ICTY in Croatia' (2014) 8 International Journal of Transitional Justice 476, 480.

[19] ibid 11–12; David (n 10).

[20] Huddy, 'Contrasting Theoretical Approaches to Intergroup Relations (n 17); Huddy, 'Context and Meaning in Social Identity Theory' (n 17); Tajfel (n 16).

[21] Tyler (n 16).

also think that any unfair treatment may be related to their identity or affiliation. When witnesses testify, threats to personal identity—unfairness, psychological, or physical distress—may contribute to witnesses feeling marginalized.[22] Impartiality and being treated equally with dignity and respect[23] can contribute to positive perceptions about policy actors and justice regardless of identity[24] because procedural justice speaks to fairness, impartiality, and procedural equity during the testimonial process.[25]

Concerns about fair treatment of in-groups versus out-groups are dominant in the evaluation of transitional justice, because the search for truth and justice should include fair treatment to *all* witnesses and defendants,[26] regardless of ethnicity or national origin.[27] This perception of in-group and out-group status has an impact on and can influence perceptions of truth, justice, and the justice cascade.[28] To the extent that ICTY policy actors (prosecution, defence, and the judges) provide fair treatment to all those who are hailed before the Tribunal, additional legitimacy may be accorded to the institution if individuals feel that they have contributed.[29] In that sense, the present study departs from other research because we do not examine whether witnesses think that the ICTY has been fair as an institution (macro-level), but instead evaluate whether fair treatment contributes to witness perceptions about truth and justice (micro-level) because perceptions of personal and social identity are intertwined.[30]

Because social and ethnic identities, along with personal perceptions, are interrelated, injustice or maltreatment against one is an attack upon all. Being protective of one's own group means that witnesses may resist information that is critical of their own in-group,[31] even as they may be conversely more attentive to treatment of the out-group by the institution. It is not whether the institution has shown bias towards one group, it is whether all groups are treated fairly which shapes individual perceptions. With that in mind, we now turn to how personal identities (e.g. role orientation, fair treatment of defendants and witnesses) and individual challenges (e.g. logistical, physical, or psychological stress) shape perceptions about truth and justice.

It is not just fair treatment and identity that are important during the testimonial process, but also the extent to which they have had to overcome threats to their physical and personal well-being.[32] Travel, delays at trial, and even the actual in-court testimony can

[22] S Cody and A Koenig, *Bearing Witness at the International Criminal Court: An Interview Survey of 109 Witnesses* (University of California: Berkeley, Human Rights Center 2014); Stover (n 2); Stover and Weinstein (n 9).

[23] S Blader and T Tyler, 'A Four-Component Model of Procedural Justice: Defining the Meaning of a "Fair" Process' (2003) 29 Personality & Social Psychology Bulletin 747; Tyler (n 16).

[24] L Mazerolle et al, 'Shaping Citizen Perceptions of Police Legitimacy: A Randomized Field Trial of Procedural Justice' (2013) 51 Criminology 33.

[25] Tyler (n 16); Blader and Tyler (n 23).

[26] D Kravetz, 'The Protection of Victims in War Crimes Trials' in T Bonacker and C Safferling (eds), *Victims of International Crimes: An Interdisciplinary Discourse* (TMC Asser Press 2013) 149–63.

[27] Clark (n 6).

[28] D Corkalo et al, 'Neighbors Again? Intercommunity Relations After Ethnic Cleansing' in E Stover and Ha Weinstein (eds), *My Neighbor, My Enemy: Justice and Community in the Aftermath of Mass Atrocity* (Cambridge University Press 2004); K Sikkink, *The Justice Cascade: How Human Rights Prosecutions Are Changing World Politics* (WW Norton 2011).

[29] S Stepakoff et al, 'Why Testify? Witnesses' Motivations for Giving Evidence in a War Crimes Tribunal in Sierra' (2014) 8 International Journal of Transitional Justice 426.

[30] Huddy, 'Contrasting Theoretical Approaches to Intergroup Relations' (n 17); Huddy, 'Context and Meaning in Social Identity Theory' (n 17); Hogg et al (n 16).

[31] Ford (n 7) 423.

[32] King et al (n 1) 82–87.

be highly stressful if witnesses have physical or human security concerns.[33] Testifying in a multi-lingual environment in a foreign court is difficult,[34] and physical and emotional reactions during testifying can add to distress, and can alter impressions witnesses have about their participation in the court proceedings.[35] Conversely, certain factors may alleviate such stress such as support from VWS or support to help with the testimonial process. Thus, both the stress of testifying and the alleviation of that stress may also play a role in how witnesses perceive the testimonial experience.

We suggest that these factors are important for better understanding what it means for witnesses to believe they have contributed to truth and justice, and set out below exploratory factors that influence witness perceptions.

13.4 Testimonial Process and Witness Support

13.4.1 Calling Party

The Office of the Prosecutor (OTP) and the Association of Defence Counsel (ADC) practising before the ICTY are the counsel responsible for conducting the questioning of the witnesses. As primary policy actors, with whom witnesses have the most frequent contact, their role orientations and treatment of witnesses matter. Depending on who the calling party is (prosecution or defence), perceptions about fair treatment are associated with *both* and this may have an impact on whether witnesses feel they have meaningfully contributed.[36] Even if a witness perceives that the calling party treated her fairly, a negative experience with the opposing counsel may undermine feelings of truth and justice.[37]

Hypothesis 1: Witnesses who believe they were personally treated fairly by the prosecution and/or the defence are more likely to perceive they have contributed to truth and justice.

It is not just the fair treatment of the witness as an individual, but also fair treatment by the OTP and Defence towards *all* persons—across *all* groups—that may matter as well.[38] Individual witnesses are part of the collective group of witnesses who have been called, and their perceptions about how *all* witnesses, not just those with whom they identify as in-group or out-group, are treated may be linked to feelings of having contributed. Likewise, individuals are called to bear witness either for or against the defendant(s). Presumably, the

[33] Cody et al (n 22).

[34] E Elias-Bursac, 'Shaping International Justice: The Role of Translation and Interpreting at the ICTY in The Hague' (2012) 7 Translation and Interpreting Studies 34.

[35] King and Meernik (n 9); King et al (n 1).

[36] Stepakoff et al (n 29); M Karnavas, 'The Rights of the Accused' (*ADC-ICTY Legacy Conference Proceedings* 29 November 2013) <http://michaelgkarnavas.net/files/ICTYLegacyConference_Karnavas.pdf> accessed 09 August 2018; S Vasiliev, 'The Role and Legal Status of the Prosecutor in International Criminal Trials' (2010) <http://dx.doi.org/10.2139/ssrn.1715465> accessed 09 August 2018.

[37] Blader and Tyler (n 23); Tyler (n 16).

[38] We note that fair treatment by the judges (also policy actors) is also important for witness beliefs about fairness. Wald (n 15). There were only four witnesses called by Chambers and all four of these were also called by OTP. Overwhelmingly (93.3 per cent) witnesses believe they were fairly treated by Chambers. King et al (n 1) 99. We also note that statistical models examining fair treatment by the VWS are also impossible to run, because again the vast majority of witnesses (95.3 per cent) believe they were treated fairly by VWS. Instead we measure VWS performance by whether witnesses felt VWS support was important for reducing stress during the time of testimony *infra*.

ICTY—as a neutral and impartial arbiter—provides fair treatment towards all regardless of calling party, ethnic status, or national origin.[39] Witnesses have views about individual and collective (social) identities,[40] however, it is important to consider not only how *witnesses or defendants of one's own ethnicity* are treated, but to also measure how *witnesses or defendants* *not of one's own ethnicity* are treated for the interests of truth and justice to be served.[41]

Hypothesis 2: Witnesses who believe other witnesses were treated fairly by the ICTY are more likely to perceive they have contributed to truth and justice.

Hypothesis 3: Witnesses who believe defendants were treated fairly by the ICTY are more likely to perceive they have contributed to truth and justice.

13.4.2 Logistical Difficulties and Challenges to Well-being

Witnesses may encounter challenging obstacles along the path to testifying and there are important commonalities that witnesses have indicated make testifying more difficult.[42] Travelling to a foreign court to face questions in an unfamiliar environment means being away from home, family, and friends.[43] Even after arriving, there are postponements and delays of testimony.[44] Once on the stand, a witness may find it difficult to focus if he or she is concerned about the consequences of testifying, such as the impact of testimony on family, security concerns, and what might happen when the witness returns home.[45] The trial process is slow, especially because of simultaneous language translation (Bosnian, Croatian, Serbian; French, and English).[46] Language barriers between the Defence, OTP, and Chambers mean that the process is even slower still because questions and statements must be translated to and from a witness' native language.[47] Finally, witnesses have both physical and emotional reactions during testifying, and this can vary according to the war-time trauma, symptoms, overall well-being, and witness resilience.[48]

These reactions range from emotional distress to panic attacks and anxiety, to physical manifestations of distress such as trouble breathing, heart palpitations, headaches, and crying.[49]

[39] Wald (n 15); Karnavas (n 36).

[40] Huddy, 'Contrasting Theoretical Approaches to Intergroup Relations' (n 17); Huddy, 'Context and Meaning in Social Identity Theory' (n 17).

[41] Wald (n 15). We also contend (*infra*) that feelings of ethnic identity as part of the in-group or out-group of parties to the Yugoslav conflict also matter, but these are separate and apart from fair treatment of witnesses and defendants identified as Bosniak, Bosnian Serb, Bosnian Croat, Croat, Serb, and Kosovar Albanian, and other.

[42] King et al (n 1) 82–87.

[43] Stover (n 2); Stepakoff et al (n 29).

[44] King et al (n 1) 85.

[45] Cody et al (n 22).

[46] Elias-Bursac (n 34).

[47] Witnesses in a multi-lingual environment face unique difficulties because they must slow their speech down for simultaneous interpretation and then listen closely to questions that may be difficult to follow because of the complicated way in which it may be presented. J Karton, 'Lost in Translation: International Criminal Tribunals and the Legal Implications of Interpreted Testimony' (2008) 4 Vanderbilt Journal of Transnational Law 1. This process has subjected the ICTY to criticisms about translation and interpretation. Elias-Bursac (n 34).

[48] K King and J Meernik, 'The Burden of Bearing Witness: The Impact of Testifying at War Crimes Tribunals' (2017) Journal of Conflict Resolution <https://doi.org/10.1177/0022002717736567> accessed 21 December 2017; Stepakoff et al, 'Self-reported Psychosocial Consequences' (n 2); Stepakoff et al, 'The Experience of Testifying' (n 2).

[49] King et al (n 1) 81.

Witnesses who experience these obstacles maybe review their testimony through a more critical lens when it comes to shaping their views about the witness experience.

Hypothesis 4: Witnesses who experienced testimonial challenges during the time of testimony are less likely to perceive they have contributed to truth and justice.

Just as witnesses may experience threats to physical and psychological well-being, witnesses may rely on external sources of support to alleviate the stress of testifying. To address the needs of witnesses during this process, witnesses may seek support from the VWS or other non-VWS support to help navigate testifying. VWS provides support for all witnesses called to appear—Chambers, Prosecution, and Defence, and the unit is typically the first point of contact between witnesses and remains with them through the testimonial phase including follow-up. Witness Assistants (WA) provide twenty-four-hour support for all witnesses and accompanying support for dependent persons.[50] Once the trial begins, the WAs are the *only* contact the witness has because of legal restrictions.[51] The mission of the VWS is to minimize the psychological, emotional, and physical distress that witnesses may experience coming to a foreign court, in a distant land, to testify about traumatic events. Witnesses may also seek support from those close to them such as family, friends, or even other witnesses to help better deal with testifying.[52] This witness support is also essential for facilitating the ICTY's proceedings, and to the extent that the witness experience is marred by difficulties, it may have an impact on how witnesses perceive their involvement.[53]

Hypothesis 5: Witnesses who indicated that support by the VWS helped to alleviate physical and psychological issues during the testimonial process are more likely to perceive they have contributed to truth and justice.

Hypothesis 6: Witnesses who relied on support from others including family, friends, or others to help alleviate physical and psychological issues during the testimonial process are more likely to perceive they have contributed to truth and justice.

The above elements are part of an individual witness' experience during the testimonial process, but witnesses also have social identities as part of a collective group that includes gender and ethnicity. Thus, we also incorporate social identities related to the witness experience into our examination, and it is to those factors we now turn.

[50] ibid 15. An accompanying or support person may come with a witness based on a VWS assessment of witness needs. A witness may also be accompanied by a dependent person (typically a primary caretaker and no alternative person to attend the dependent during the duration of the testimony. Approximately 13 per cent of ICTY witnesses travelled to The Hague with an accompanying person or dependent. The VWS reviews witnesses for vulnerability including witness age, psychological condition, risk of re-traumatization, health condition or disability requiring intensive daily support, or any other particular witness circumstances requiring specific support.

[51] Under ICTY Rules of Procedure and Evidence (Rule 90), witnesses swear a declaration at the start of their testimony that there will be no communication with the OTP or the Defence team until completion of testimony, unless otherwise instructed by the Chamber. While they can talk to the VWS staff, they cannot discuss the content of their testimony with VWS staff either.

[52] This group includes any person(s) other than VWS support including spouses, family, friends, co-workers, religious personnel, or legal counsel. In sum, any other person who can help the witness understand the process.

[53] Cody et al (n 22); Stepakoff et al (n 29); Stover (n 2).

13.5 Social Identity (Gender and Ethnicity)

The legitimacy of transitional justice mechanisms depends on perceptions of their fairness towards all.[54] Whether the ICTY has fulfilled its objectives of minimizing prejudice depends on which objectives and norms are being assessed and which groups are being queried.[55] The ICTY has been accused of marginalizing female witnesses (especially women who have endured sexual violence)[56] and lacking neutrality towards different ethnic groups.[57]

These disparate views based on gender and ethnic social identities have implications for procedural and reparatory justice because if women and different ethnic groups feel they are not integrated into the institution's goal of seeking truth and justice, it may cast a shadow on the ICTY's legacy.[58] Gender-based violence, frequently accepted and tolerated at the community level even when a country is not at war, continues on during the war and carries over into post-conflict society[59] and views about transitional justice.[60] Targeting persons based on gender and ethnicity reinforces perceptions about social identities—ethnic and sexual violence (typically, but not solely related to females)[61] is common among soldiers who carry out violence in conflict zones.[62] Ethnic women, seen as the enemy by other persons who are *not* of their ethnicity are singled out for abuse and enslavement, while their men and boys are eliminated during massacres. Rape as a war weapon has multiple purposes allowing males to dehumanize the population, to interfere with reproductive and familial capacities, to establish ethnic conquest; and to give soldiers the 'spoils' of war.[63] Thus, women have a distinctive role as witnesses before tribunals, and their experience varies from men.

Like gender identity, ethnic identity also may contribute to perceptions of truth and justice. The Yugoslav wars were the result of partisan leadership advocating ethnic homogeneity, and favouritism for one's ethnic in-group and derogation of another ethnic out-group.[64] Scholars have typically found that Bosniaks and Kosovar Albanians have the

[54] David (n 18).

[55] David (n 10).

[56] J Mertus, 'When Adding Women Matters: Women's Participation in the International Criminal Tribunal for the Former Yugoslavia' (2008) 38 Seton Hall Law Review 1297 <http://scholarship.shu.edu/shlr/vol38/iss4/4> accessed August 2018.

[57] D Arzt, 'Views on the Ground: The Local Perception of International Criminal Tribunals in the Former Yugoslavia and Sierra Leone' (2006) 603 The Annals of the American Academy of Political and Social Science 226; J Clark, 'From Negative to Positive Peace: The Case of Bosnia and Hercegovina' (2009) 8 Journal of Human Rights 360–84; Ford (n 7); J Hagan and S Ivković, 'War Crimes, Democracy, and the Rule of Law in Belgrade, the Former Yugoslavia, and Beyond' (2006) 605 The Annuals of the American Academy 130; Klarin (n 7); J Meernik, 'The International Criminal Court and the Deterrence of Human Rights Atrocities' (2015) 17 Civil Wars 318; L Nettelfield, *Courting Democracy in Bosnia and Herzegovina* (Cambridge University Press, 2010); Orentlicher (n 7); Subotić (n 7); United Nations Development Programme, *Human Development Report* (Oxford University Press 1994).

[58] David (n 10); Clark (n 6).

[59] V Hudson et al, *Sex and World Peace* (Columbia University Press 2014).

[60] N Henry, 'Theorizing Wartime Rape: Deconstructing Gender, Sexuality, and Violence' (2016) 30 Gender & Society 44–56; F Aoláin, 'Women, Security, and the Patriarchy of Internationalized Transitional Justice' (2009) 31 Human Rights Quarterly 1055.

[61] Increasingly the international community recognizes that male sexual violence during war is more common than thought. Sexual taboos about masculinity limit our understanding about sexual violence against men. Arguably transitional justice mechanisms have marginalized the issue. See P Schulz, 'Transitional Justice for Male Victims of Conflict-Related Sexual and Gender-Based Violence?' (2016) International Journal of Rule of Law, Transitional Justice and Human Rights <https://ssrn.com/abstract=2839320> accessed 10 August 2018.

[62] Henry (n 60).

[63] C MacKinnon, 'Rape, Genocide and Women's Human Rights' in A Stiglmayer (ed), *Mass Rape: The War Against Women in Bosnia-Herzegovina* (University of Nebraska Press 1994).

[64] Clark (n 6); Stover (n 2); Stover and Weinstein (n 9); Ford (n 7); Klarin (n 7).

highest levels of support for the ICTY with Croats and Serbs lagging behind.[65] Most of those indicted and convicted by the ICTY have been Bosnian Serbs and native Serbs who are critical of the Tribunal for failing to recognize their 'defensive' struggle against hostile Islamic and Croatian forces.[66] While Bosniaks have generally been supportive of the ICTY, they too have found fault with the Tribunal when it fails to convict or punish severely persons in other ethnic groups.[67] These perceptions of ethnic bias may be shaped or reinforced by the media or elites, but regardless, culpability and victimization are usually leveled at the out-group.[68] Thus, witness ethnic identities may have an impact on how they view whether they have contributed to truth and justice.

Hypothesis 7: Women who testify before the ICTY are less likely to perceive they have contributed to truth and justice.

Hypothesis 8: Ethnic identification correlates with whether witnesses perceive they have contributed to truth and justice.

With these points in mind, we now turn to an empirical analysis of hypotheses and whether each has an impact on witness' perceptions about their contributions to truth and justice.

13.6 Data and Model

The ICTY called over 4,700 witnesses to testify during its existence; and a survey using a quota and random sample of 300 witnesses who testified between 1999–2012 from Bosnia-Herzegovina, Croatia, Serbia, and Kosovo is used for our analysis. The sample includes a representative group of witnesses as presented (Figure 13.1) with 84.3 per cent (n=253) males and 15.7 per cent (n=47) females[69] (slightly higher than the overall at the ICTY where approximately 13 per cent of all witnesses have been women).

Turning to the question of whether witnesses feel they have contributed, large majorities of witnesses (strongly) agreed that their testimony contributed to the discovery of truth (71 per cent) and justice (67 per cent). Only small percentages (strongly) disagreed that

[65] Arzt (n 57); A Jakobsson-Hatay, 'Peacebuilding and Reconciliation in Bosnia and Herzegovina, Kosovo and Macedonia 1995–2004' (*Swedish Emergency Management Agency*, 2005); Meernik (n 7); Nettelfield (n 57); V Peskin, 'Beyond Victor's Justice? The Challenge of Prosecuting the Winners at the International Criminal Tribunals for the Former Yugoslavia and Rwanda' (2005) 4 Journal of Human Rights 213–31; V Peskin, *International Justice in Rwanda and the Balkans: Virtual Trials and the Struggle for State Cooperation* (Cambridge University Press 2008).

[66] S K Ivković and J Hagan, *Reclaiming Justice* (Oxford University Press 2011); Stover (n 2).

[67] This is ethnic in-group, out-group narrative is reflected in findings that 90 per cent of Bosniaks, 74 per cent of Kosovar Albanians, 60 per cent of Croatians, and one-third of Serbs agreed or strongly agreed that they supported the ICTY. Meernik (n 7). Inter-group tension is also reflected in surveys where 40 per cent believe that the ICTY was created to 'put the blame for war sufferings on the Serbs' and 73 per cent believe that the ICTY has different attitudes towards groups depending on their ethnicity. OSCE and Ipsos, 'Attitudes Toward War Crimes Issues, ICTY and the National Judiciary' (*OSCE*, 2011) 16, 22 <https://www.osce.org/serbia/90422?download=true> accessed 10 August 2018.

[68] Ford (n 7); Klarin (n 7).

[69] King et al (n 1) 36. The sample includes 253 men (84.3 per cent) and forty-seven women (15.7 per cent) with eighty-one (27 per cent) persons identifying as Croat; seventy-eight (26 per cent) Bosniak; ninety-five (31.7 per cent) Serb, twenty-five (8.3 per cent) Albanian, and the remainder identified another ethnicity or not at all. Ages range from 28–94 years old (average age 59 years old). Interviewees testified in forty-one different trials involving ninety defendants with two-thirds of the witnesses appearing only once. Almost two-thirds of the interviewees appeared for the OTP with the remaining one-third appeared for Defence (seventeen witnesses appeared for both while four Chambers witnesses also appeared for OTP). The cooperation rate for participating was 56.8 per cent.

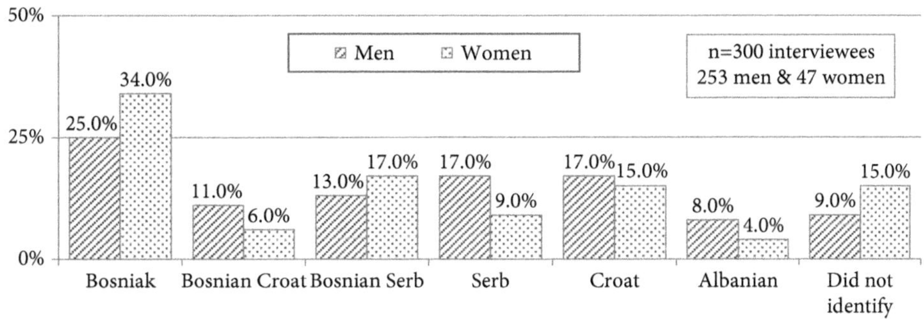

Figure 13.1 Percentages of men and women according to witness ethnic self-identification

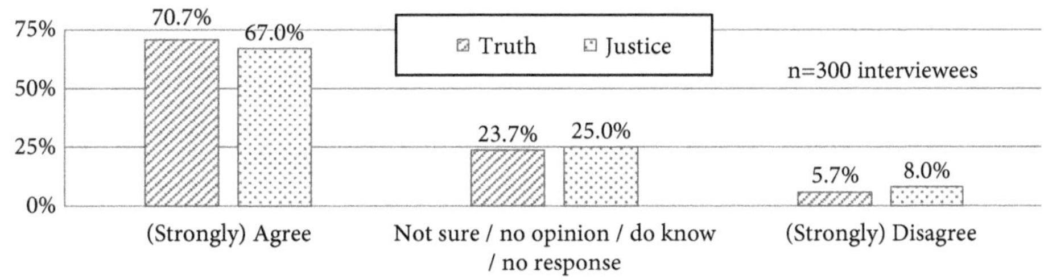

Figure 13.2 Percentage of witnesses and contributions to truth and justice

they did not contribute to truth and justice (6 per cent and 8 per cent, respectively) (Figure 13.2), while even larger percentages of witnesses were more likely to not know how they feel. Long-term prospects for the advancement of international and transitional justice are connected to feelings of efficaciousness, to the legitimacy of transitional justice mechanisms,[70] and to increasing the chances for post-conflict reconciliation.[71] So if witnesses are unsure about their contributions, it may undermine the prospects for maintaining the peace.

The results in Table 13.1 (Truth) and Table 13.2 (Justice) rely on logistic regression appropriate when the dependent variable is a dichotomous choice (whether the witness agrees/ strongly agrees that he or she contributed to truth or justice at the ICTY). Witnesses who testify multiple times face additional challenges, thus we used cluster observations into three distinct categories to reflect the underlying data structure and the witness experience itself. In the survey sample, there are witnesses who testified once (n=195), twice (n=72), and three or more times (n=33).[72] Clustering more accurately measures different 'groups' of

[70] Kravetz (n 26).
[71] Clark (n 6).
[72] Testimonial fatigue occurs when witnesses who make repeat appearances before judicial bodies experience an adverse impact on their physical and mental well-being. The Echoes of Voices study found that 15 per cent of repeat witnesses experienced fewer physical reactions and less emotional distress when they appeared in later trials (data not shown), while 8 per cent of witnesses said their symptoms increased when they later testified. King et al (n 1) 84. Similarly, more complex models of witness fatigue and resilience finds that persons who testify multiple times may actually have a more positive view about the ICTY as it relates to how they feel about their own personal testimony. King and Meernik (n 48). Cluster-correlated data arise frequently in the social sciences. Clustering on one particular factor which has underlying significance allows for better measurement because it measures the standard errors within units (e.g. persons who testified only once) and compares them to other clusters (e.g. those persons who testified twice, or three or more times).

Table 13.1 My testimony contributed to the discovery of the truth about the wars about here

My testimony contributed to the discovery of the truth about the wars	Odds Ratio	Robust Standard Error	Z	P>|z|	Sig.	Marginal effects
OTP was fair to me	1.71	0.38	2.46	0.01	**	10.0%
Defence was fair to me	1.54	0.50	1.34	0.18		7.8%
Witnesses (not) of my ethnicity treated fairly	1.57	0.24	2.93	0.00	**	7.7%
Defendants (not) of my ethnicity treated fairly	1.75	0.55	1.79	0.07		9.6%
Delays, re-scheduling, postponement	1.01	0.40	0.01	0.99		0.1%
Being away from home	0.99	0.39	−0.02	0.99		−0.1%
Physical problems while testifying	1.76	1.05	0.94	0.35		8.9%
Translation issues	0.54	0.19	−1.74	0.08		−11.7%
Anxiety†	1.70	0.37	2.45	0.01	**	8.8%
Consequences of testifying†	2.60	1.06	2.35	0.02	*	13.2%
VWS support	1.10	0.05	1.98	0.05	*	1.7%
Other support	1.46	0.56	0.99	0.32		6.5%
Female	0.65	0.38	−0.75	0.46		−8.1%
Bosniak	2.07	1.13	1.34	0.18		11.3%
Bosnian Croat	0.47	0.06	−5.67	0.00	**	−14.9%
Bosnian Serb	0.62	0.14	−2.11	0.04	*	−9.1%
Croat	1.34	0.82	0.48	0.64		4.7%
Serb	0.46	0.22	−1.60	0.11		−15.2%
Albanian	3.94	3.28	1.65	0.10		16.4%
Constant	0.36	0.22	−1.71	0.09		
n=295						

Clustered on number of appearances * $p < 0.05$ ** $p < 0.01$

Goodness-of-fit statistics-Truth	
Log-likelihood-Model	−138.092
Intercept-only	−178.036
McFadden	0.224
McFadden (adjusted)	0.213
Cox-Snell/ML	0.237
Cragg-Uhler/Nagelkerke	0.338
AIC	280.184
Pseudo-R^2	0.224

† Correlations were significant, but not in the direction hypothesized.

Table 13.2 My testimony contributed to justice about here

My testimony contributed to justice	**Odds Ratio**	**Robust Standard Error**	**Z**	**P>|z|**	**Sig.**	**Marginal effects**
OTP was fair to me	2.79	0.93	3.09	0.00	**	21.5%
Defence was fair to me	1.92	0.94	1.33	0.18		12.8%
Witnesses (not) of my ethnicity treated fairly	1.37	0.09	5.11	0.00	**	5.8%
Defendants (not) of my ethnicity treated fairly	2.10	0.57	2.74	0.01	**	13.7%
Delays, re-scheduling, postponement	0.45	0.11	−3.29	0.00	**	−16.1%
Being away from home	1.69	0.70	1.26	0.21		8.7%
Physical problems while testifying	1.46	0.75	0.73	0.46		6.8%
Translation issues	0.58	0.15	−2.10	0.04	*	−11.1%
Anxiety†	1.65	0.12	7.08	0.00	**	8.9%
Consequences of testifying	1.48	0.52	1.11	0.27		6.6%
VWS support	1.80	0.29	3.69	0.00	**	10.7%
Other support	1.16	0.12	1.49	0.14		2.8%
Female	0.35	0.13	−2.76	0.01	**	−22.5%
Bosniak	3.45	1.45	2.95	0.00	**	19.4%
Bosnian Croat	0.31	0.13	−2.77	0.01	**	−25.6%
Bosnian Serb	0.76	0.25	−0.84	0.40		−5.2%
Croat	1.29	0.23	1.39	0.17		4.4%
Serb	0.45	0.07	−5.45	0.00	**	−16.8%
Albanian	3.53	2.13	2.09	0.04	*	17.0%
Constant	0.22	0.10	−3.19	0.00		
n=295						

Clustered on number of appearances * $p < 0.05$ ** $p < 0.01$

Goodness-of-fit statistics-Justice	
Log-likelihood-Model	−134.176
Intercept-only	−186.113
McFadden	0.279
McFadden (adjusted)	0.268
Cox-Snell/ML	0.297
Cragg-Uhler/Nagelkerke	0.414
AIC	272.352
Pseudo-R^2	0.279

† Correlations were significant, but not in the direction hypothesized.

witnesses based on a common characteristic—repeat appearances at the ICTY. The results indicate that the overall goodness of fit tests as reflected in both the McFadden (and adjusted McFadden) score are in the range social scientists look for (between 0.2 and 0.4), and the Pseudo-R^2 of Truth (0.224) and Justice (0.279) indicates the factors in the model explain approximately 22.4 per cent and 27.9 per cent of what correlates with witnesses perceiving they have contributed to truth or justice.

Comparing the two models of truth and justice, the model measuring witness perceptions about contributing to justice has a better fit according to the Akaike Information Criterion (AIC) score which measures the quality of statistical models (lower values of AIC tend to indicate a better 'fit' for the model). The justice model more accurately predicts the outcome of whether witnesses believe they have contributed to 'providing justice' as compared to whether witnesses believe they have contributed to the 'discovery of the truth about the wars in the former Yugoslavia'. Turning to the individual models, seven of the variables for the truth model reach statistical significance (four are significant at the * $p < 0.05$ level while three are ** $p < 0.01$), while twelve of the variables for the justice model achieve significance (two are significant at the * $p < 0.05$ level and ten achieve the higher level of significance ** $p < 0.01$).

13.6.1 Fair Treatment

The findings show that witnesses are more likely to be affected by their perceptions of fair treatment by the prosecution rather than by the defence.[73] Witnesses who believe 'OTP was fair to me' are 10 per cent more likely to believe they have contributed to truth and 21.5 per cent *more* likely to believe they have contributed to justice (Tables 13.1 and 13.2—marginal effects).[74] Of all the independent variables in the model, witnesses are most likely to (strongly) agree that the OTP was fair to them, while there is less agreement (especially by women) on whether the Defence was fair (Figure 13.3).

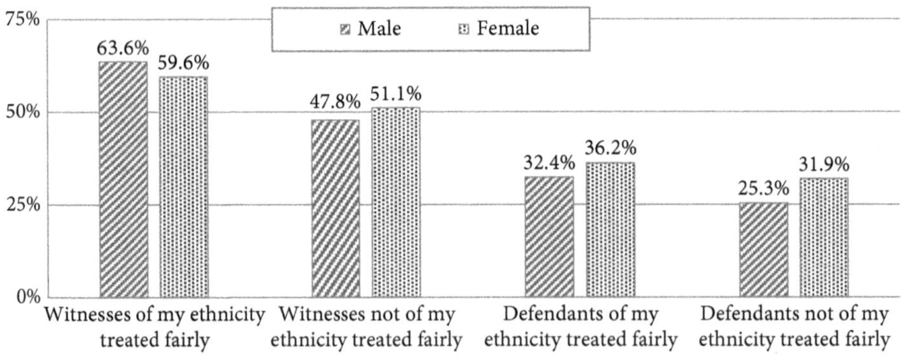

Figure 13.3 Fair treatment by OTP and Defence

[73] J Ciorciari and A Heindel, 'Victim Testimony in International and Hybrid Criminal Courts: Narrative Opportunities, Challenges, and Fair Trial Demands' (2016) 56 Virginia Journal of International Law 265.

[74] The marginal effect measures how the outcome (dependent variable—whether the witnesses think their testimony contributed to truth or justice) is affected by changes in the explanatory (independent) variables. This allows us to assess the magnitude of the impact of any given variable because it measures the impact of a one unit change in the independent variable on the dependent variable of interest.

This serves as an important comparison point to other studies of OTP witnesses that have found fair treatment by the prosecution contributed to positive feelings about the ICTY and a willingness to testify again if needed.[75] These findings may not be indicative of all victims from the Yugoslav wars in general (witnesses are only one subset of all those affected by the conflict). General population and victims' surveys have found that those having survived the conflict can be more critical towards the ICTY's treatment of witnesses.[76] Moreover, certain types of trials (such as those involving sexual violence or high profile defendants) pose obstacles regarding fair treatment of witnesses when facing the need to balance the right to fair trial for defendants.[77] Here, however, we find support for the proposition that witnesses are more likely to believe they have contributed if they have been treated fairly. In contrast to the role of the OTP, the results are not statistically significant in either model for fair treatment by Defence.

Why the difference between OTP and Defence counsel? Perhaps OTP has professional advantages to ensure fairness because it has a vastly different organizational structure compared to Defence. As one of the three constituent organs at the ICTY—staffing is more stable, and more safeguards exist to ensure professional conduct with the United Nations bureaucracy providing accountability and oversight.[78] Critically the OTP has greater resources at its disposal that may give a strategic advantage to leveraging professional development of staff,[79] especially compared to Defence.[80] This in turn may lead to the standardization of protocols and additional training for OTP, regarding the treatment of witnesses and may have consequences for witnesses feeling that they have been treated more fairly. The results here are not conclusive by any means, but further research should examine whether OTP has strategic institutional advantages that may translate into witness perceptions about the process and what it means for truth and justice.

The above speaks to fair treatment of the individual witness, but does the fair treatment of other witnesses and defendants contribute to witness feelings of truth and justice? To measure this, we used a scale from 0–2 measuring whether interviewees (strongly) agreed witnesses with the same ethnicity (and not of the same ethnicity) were treated fairly.[81] This allows us to analyse whether witness treatment or defendant treatment (regardless of ethnicity) correlates with witness feelings about having contributed. The results indicate that

[75] Stover (n 2) 103.

[76] D Mendeloff, 'Truth-Seeking, Truth-Telling, and Postconflict Peacebuilding: Curb the Enthusiasm?' (2004) 6 International Studies Review 355; D Mendeloff, 'Trauma and Vengeance: Assessing the Psychological and Emotional Effects of Post-Conflict Justice' (2009) 31 Human Rights Quarterly 592; M B Dembour and E Haslam, 'Silencing hearings? Victim-Witnesses at War Crimes Trials' (2004) 15 European Journal of International Law 151.

[77] Ciorciari and Heindel (n 73); G Mischkowski and G Mlinarevic, 'The Trouble with Rape Trials—Views of Witnesses, Prosecutors and Judges on Prosecuting Sexualised Violence During the War in the Former Yugoslavia' (*Medica Mondiale*, 2009) <http://bit.ly/2oJD6xn> accessed 10 August 2018; M Staggs-Kelsall and S Stepakoff, 'When We Wanted to Talk about Rape: Silencing Sexual Violence at the Special Court for Sierra Leone' (2007) 1 International Journal of Transitional Justice 355.

[78] L Reydams et al (eds), *International Prosecutors* (Oxford University Press 2012); N Combs, 'Legitimizing International Criminal Justice: The Importance of Process Control' (2012) 33 Michigan Journal of International Law 321.

[79] M Wierda and A Triolo, 'Resources' in L Reydams et al (eds), *International Prosecutors* (Oxford University Press 2012); G Townsend, 'Structure and Management' in L Reydams et al (eds), *International Prosecutors* (Oxford University Press 2012).

[80] See C Rohan and G Zyberi, *Defense Perspectives on International Criminal Justice* (Cambridge University Press 2017); C Sriram et al, *War, Conflict and Human Rights: Theory and Practice* (Routledge 2017).

[81] Coded 0 if they thought *neither* witnesses of their own or other ethnicities were treated fairly, 1 if they thought *either* their own ethnicity *or* the other ethnicities were treated fairly, and 2 if they thought *both* witnesses of their own ethnicity and the other ethnicities were treated fairly. The same scale applied to treatment of defendants.

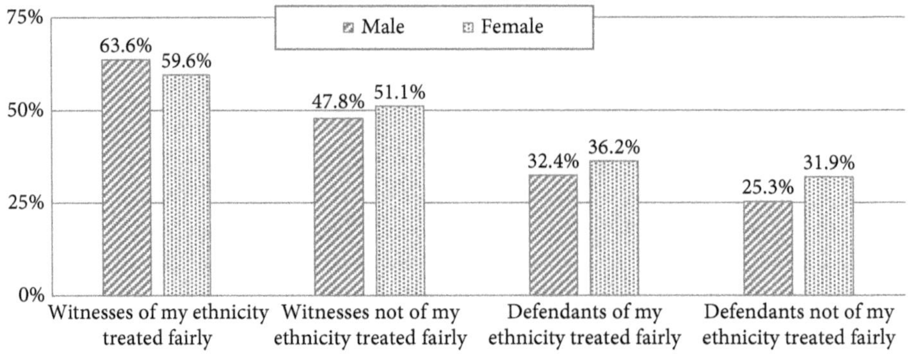

Figure 13.4 Percentage who (strongly) agree witnesses/defendants treated fairly

witnesses believe their in-group was treated fairly, but are not as likely to believe that witnesses from other ethnic groups were treated fairly. This analysis holds for views of defendant fair treatment as well. Witnesses are more likely to indicate that defendants from other ethnic groups were less likely to be treated fairly. This finding may hinge on how witnesses interpret the meaning of 'fairness' or alternately, witnesses' willingness to speak about fairness vis-à-vis other groups, and how such groups were treated by the tribunal. A second interpretation of the results is that witnesses may perceive that persons of their own ethnicity were not treated favourably enough as compared to others (hence it is 'less fair') while others not of their own ethnicity were treated 'more favourably' (thus it is also 'less fair' because favouritism was involved). Still, there is yet a third interpretation because in general witnesses are less likely to believe that witnesses not of their own ethnicity, as well as defendants of any ethnicity were less likely to be treated fairly. This is a distinct possibility given the data trend in Figure 13.4 which graphically illustrates decreasing levels of fair treatment. Witnesses may not feel as though they can speak for the fair treatment of others because of social distance. Witnesses may be more comfortable identifying with other witnesses even if those other witnesses are not of their own identity. Or they may be able to reach judgement even about defendants because at least their ethnic identities are similar. For defendants who are not of the witness' identity, the witness can neither identify with the role of the defendant nor with his ethnic identity. Thus, these results illustrate that there is still much that we do not fully understand about witness perceptions and fairness at the ICTY, and what it means for its legacy.

We hypothesized that witness perceptions about whether witnesses and defendants were treated fairly increased the likelihood that an individual felt that they had contributed to truth and justice, and there is empirical support for this proposition in both models. The results are highly significant with witnesses being 7.7 per cent (Truth) and 5.8 per cent (Justice) more likely to believe they have contributed when they perceive witnesses were treated fairly. Similarly, perceptions of fair treatment of the defendant also correlate with witness perceptions. Witnesses are 9.6 per cent (Truth) and 13.7 per cent (Justice) more likely to believe they have contributed if other defendants were treated fairly in the witness' estimation. The findings contribute to the debate about personal and social identity as it relates to ethnicity and perceptions about in-group and out-group fair treatment.[82]

[82] Ford (n 7); David (n 18).

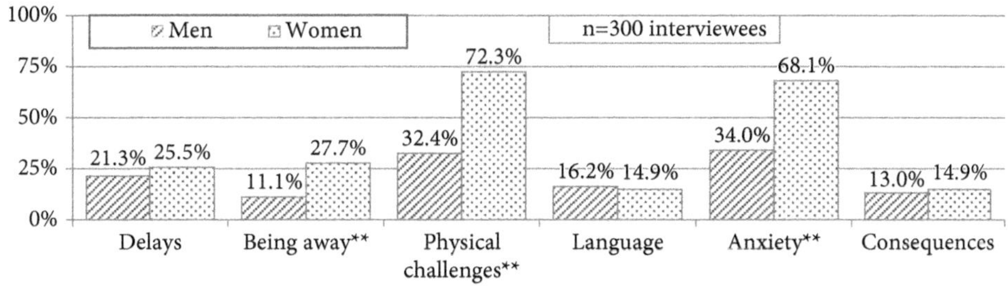

Figure 13.5 Factors in the testimonial process
** $p < 0.01$

These findings have implications for individual witnesses and also for the development of the international and transitional legal regimes, as well as for the ICTY's legacy. When individuals believe that the process is fair, that the legal officers are unbiased, and that judicial institutions are neutral in their application of the law, there can be 'greater overall satisfaction with the legal experience and more positive affect with respect to an encounter with the justice system'.[83] All judicial systems need legitimacy if their rules are to be respected and enforced,[84] and the ICTY is no different. Fair treatment of witnesses, defendants, and other stakeholders (e.g. other victims, those affected by the wars) means that if people experience personally that decision-makers and authorities are acting fairly, this may enhance legitimacy of the legal regime, ultimately establishing deference to decisions made by the authority.[85]

13.6.2 Testimonial Challenges

Beyond fair treatment, the testimonial process itself presents multiple challenges and potential obstacles in the search for truth and justice. Delays, being away from home, physical reactions during testimony, translation issues, anxiety, and concerns about the consequences of testifying are among the most common for witnesses (Figure 13.5).[86] Before analysing the impact of each factor in our model, we ran difference of means test between men and women. Women are significantly more likely to note the challenges of being away, to express physical difficulties, and to acknowledge anxiety during the time of testimony. While the bivariate analysis (Figure 13.4) indicates that women are more likely to indicate that both delays and being away are stressors, only being away is significant for women (with over one in four raising that as a concern, while slightly more than one in ten men mention it as a stressor).

Issues concerning delays, anxiety, and the consequences of testifying are statistically significant in the 'truth' model, while delays, translation issues, and anxiety are statistically significant in the 'justice' model. Perhaps the wisdom of William Penn (1693) 'to

[83] A Lind and T Tyler, *The Social Psychology of Procedural Justice* (Springer 1998).
[84] T Franck, *The Power of Legitimacy among Nations: Fairness in International Law and Institutions* (Oxford University Press 1990).
[85] Combs (n 78) 372; Tyler and Darley (n 8); Tyler (n 16); Lind and Tyler (n 83).
[86] King et al (n 1).

delay justice is injustice' is most applicable here. Witnesses are 16.1 per cent *less* likely to believe they have contributed to justice if they have experienced delays in their testimony, but the effect does not hold up for truth. It has been argued that lengthy, complex war crimes trials may further the cause of justice, but witnesses most certainly do not perceive it as such.[87] While delays undermine justice, being away does not have the same effect (it is statistically insignificant in both models). Still there are significant differences for women who are away from home as compared to men, and thus we still need to dig deeper into how witnesses view their roles in contributing to justice.[88]

Witnesses can encounter any number of physical reactions to appearing before a tribunal, which can have deleterious effects, and the results indicate that women are significantly affected by these challenges. In Figure 13.4, the greatest disparity between men and women is in the category involving persons who[89] experience physical issues while testifying, with women experiencing much higher rates in the top four categories: heart palpitations (49 per cent), crying (32 per cent), dry mouth (30 per cent), and shortness of breath (17 per cent) (results not shown). While the results in the bivariate analysis are significant for gender, the effect is insignificant in both models, most likely because the inclusion of gender (female) in the model explains much of the variation in physical challenges. Like other research, we find that physical challenges for witnesses may be particularly acute at the time of testimony, and especially so for women.

Once on the stand, it is not just physical challenges that can distract a witness from feeling focused. Language barriers and becoming acclimated to simultaneous translation may make it more difficult. This is the one indicator where women (14.9 per cent) have less challenges than men (16.2 per cent), although the results are insignificant for the gender comparison when we conducted a t-test (results not shown). In the full models, however, language issues are statistically significant for justice, but not for truth. Of note is that for both models, challenges related to translation decreased the probability that witnesses believed they contributed to justice and truth supporting other findings that translation challenges make it difficult for court personnel, and also produce adverse consequences for the witnesses.[90]

Undoubtedly, some of the greatest challenges witnesses face relate to the anxiety that comes with testifying and the concerns related to the consequences of testifying—especially for those who have to testify about traumatic experiences or who may worry about what will happen to them because they testified.[91] We posited that witnesses who expressed higher levels of anxiety and concerns about the consequences of testifying would be less likely to think that they had contributed to justice. The results indicate that the effect is not as we hypothesized.

[87] A Whiting, 'In International Criminal Prosecutions, Justice Delayed Can Be Justice Delivered' (2009) 50 Harvard International Law Journal 323.

[88] Stover (n 2).

[89] E Stover et al, 'Confronting Duch: Civil Party Participation in Case 001 at the Extraordinary Chambers in the Courts of Cambodia' (2011) 93 International Review of the Red Cross 503; R McNally, *Remembering Trauma* (Harvard University Press 2003); Stepakoff et al, 'The Experience of Testifying' (n 2); Staggs-Kelsall and Stepakoff (n 77).

[90] Elias-Bursac (n 34); J Karton, 'Alfred E. Neuman' (2008) 41 Vanderbilt Journal of Transnational Law 11; D Buss, 'Knowing Women: Translating Patriarchy in International Criminal Law' (2014) 23 Social and Legal Studies 73.

[91] Stover (n 2); Stepakoff et al, 'Self-reported Psychosocial Consequences of Testifying' (n 2).

Emotional distress, having panic attacks, or experiencing anxiety tend to undermine witness well-being[92] and may harm some witnesses.[93] Here the differences between men and women are stark, with almost twice as many women as men indicating that anxiety made testifying more difficult.[94] Perhaps women are more willing to disclose their feelings about anxiety, have higher levels of anxiety for socio-cultural reasons, or face multiple challenges because of trauma and living in post-conflict societies—all of these factors tend to contribute to increased levels of anxiety.[95] Regardless, it points to a need by those working with witnesses to be aware of the unique needs women face in terms of both physical and psychological challenges during the time of testimony.[96]

Overall, when anxiety is considered across the range of factors related to whether witnesses perceive they have contributed to justice, the results are positive and highly significant—witnesses who experienced anxiety during the testimonial process were *more* likely to believe they had contributed to truth (8.8 per cent) and justice (8.9 per cent). What might account for this? Other research on post-traumatic growth (PTG) and psychological adjustment after trauma has found individuals' ability to cope in the face of trauma can contribute to adaptation and resilience which is associated with PTG.[97] Anxiety, while debilitating for many individuals, may also lead to an enhancement of external coping mechanisms for others, and contribute to one's resilience.[98] It may also be that witnesses who had higher levels of anxiety while testifying feel they have a greater investment in having testified, and this anxiety is also part of their more positive view of the process.[99] The findings once again show that the witness experience is complex and their adjustment in the face of that experience needs much more research if we are to better understand the intricate nature of what it means to testify.

The results from witness concerns about the consequences of being called to testify including threats to human security[100] or uncertainties about socio-economic well-being are also illuminating and speak to the impact of negative external events on internal coping.[101]

[92] Bandes (n 3); Henry, 'Witness to Rape' (n 3); Henry, 'The Impossibility of Bearing Witness' (n 3); Herman (n 3).

[93] K Brounéus, 'The Trauma of Truth Telling: Effects of Witnessing in the Rwandan Gacaca Courts on Psychological Health' (2010) 54 Journal of Conflict Resolution 408; Mendeloff, 'Trauma and Vengeance' (n 76); Dembour and Haslam (n 76).

[94] U Funkeson et al, 'Witnesses to Genocide: Experiences of Witnessing in the Rwandan Gacaca Courts' (2011) 17 Peace and Conflict: Journal of Peace Psychology 367.

[95] M Seguin and B Roberts, 'Coping Strategies Among Conflict-Affected Adults in Low- and Middle-Income Countries: A Systematic Literature Review' (2017) 12 Global Public Health 811; B Roberts and J Browne, 'A Systematic Review of Factors Influencing the Psychological Health of Conflict-Affected Populations in Low- and Middle-Income Countries' (2011) 6 Global Public Health 814; C McLean and E Anderson, 'Brave Men and Timid Women? A Review of the Gender Differences in Fear and Anxiety' (2009) 29 Clinical Psychology Review 496.

[96] Stepakoff et al, 'Self-reported Psychosocial Consequences' (n 2).

[97] L Blackie et al, 'Post-Traumatic Growth as Positive Personality Change: Developing a Measure to Assess Within-Person Variability' (2016) 69 Journal of Research in Personality 22; D Winter et al, *Trauma, Survival and Resilience in War Zones: The Psychological Impact of the War in Sierra Leone and Beyond* (Routledge 2016); S Joseph and L Butler, 'Positive Changes Following Adversity' (2010) 21 PTSD Research Quarterly 1–3.

[98] S Priebe et al, 'Course of Post-Traumatic Stress Disorder Following War in the Balkans: 1-year Follow-Up Study' (2013) 43 Psychological Medicine 1837; D Ajdukovic et al, 'Recovery from Posttraumatic Stress Symptoms: A Qualitative Study of Attributions in Survivors of War' (*PLOS One*, 2013) <http://journals.plos.org/plosone/article?id=10.1371/journal.pone.0070579> accessed 10 August 2018; Herman (n 3).

[99] King and Meernik (n 48); Stepakoff and others, 'The Experience of Testifying' (n 2).

[100] M Bates, 'Balancing Act: The Rights of the Accused and Witness Protection Measures' (2014) 17 Trinity College Law Review 143; Trotter (n 13).

[101] D Spini et al, 'Towards a Community Approach of the Aftermath of War in the Former Yugoslavia: Collective Experiences, Social Practices, and Representations' in D Spini et al (eds) *War, Community, and Social*

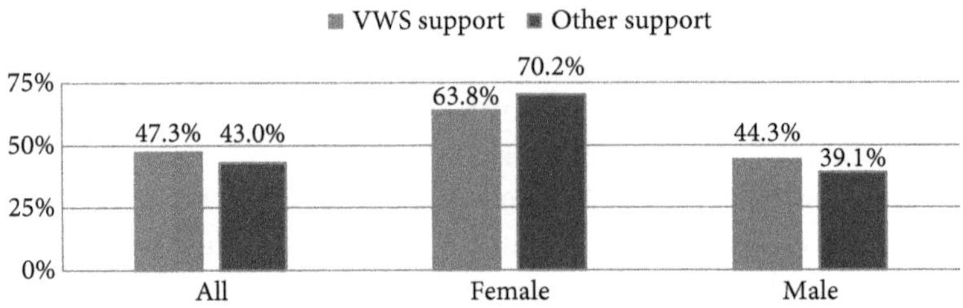

Figure 13.6 Support from VWS and others for handling stress of testifying

We hypothesized that during the time of testifying, these security and socio-economic concerns may interfere with the witnesses' ability to focus on the testimonial process and may undermine how witnesses feel about testifying.[102] When it comes to considerations about the consequences of testifying, however, the results here are statistically insignificant between men and women (Figure 13.4) and in the model regarding contributing to justice (Table 13.2). Strikingly, witnesses are actually 13.2 per cent *more* likely to believe they have contributed to the truth if they are concerned about the consequences of testifying (significant $p > 0.05$). Perhaps witnesses, aware of the potential impact that testifying may have on their lives, believe that their testimony is even *more* important for the truth to be told as a recognition of what they go through as a result of speaking out. Their testimony is a direct reflection of telling their story so that the truth be known.

In the face of the above stressors, witnesses also have mechanisms to deal with testimonial challenges. As the results in Figures 13.6 and 13.7 indicate, VWS support, support from others, as well as the use of an internal strategy to help them cope,[103] are the most frequently used approaches for dealing with physical and emotional stressors associated with testifying. Women are significantly more likely than men to rely on VWS support, but both VWS support and support from others are important for both men and women for adjusting to the testimonial process. Like other needs assessments of witnesses, who testify about war crimes, witnesses indicate that there is a need for institutional as well as familial and community support during and following the testimonial process,[104] and this is especially true for women. Self-reliance on internal strategies is second only to VWS and other support for women, and it ranks first for men (with relying on an internal strategy being second). In terms of the next most frequent indicators for reducing stress, witnesses specified that having an adjustment to their schedule or speaking with someone who could help them better understand the process helped. Of the remainder, distractions or increasingly relying

Change: Collective Experiences in the Former Yugoslavia (Springer 2013); E Hutchison and R Bleiker, 'Emotional Reconciliation: Reconstituting Identity and Community after Trauma' (2008) 11 European Journal of Social Theory 385.

102 Stepakoff et al, 'The Experience of Testifying' (n 2).

103 An internal strategy means that the witness relies on internal self-reliance mechanisms including: thinking this has to be done; reminding oneself that he or she has survived worse than this; writing thoughts down; concentrating on immediate tasks; taking it one day at a time; focusing on achievements; using humour; avoiding difficult situations; keeping thoughts to themselves; relying on religious beliefs; and remembering the victims.

104 Stepakoff et al, 'Self-Reported Psychosocial Consequences' (n 2); Stepakoff et al, 'The Experience of Testifying' (n 2); D Popović and others, 'A Situation and Needs Assessment of the Cantonal/District Prosecutor's Offices and Courts in the Field of Witness/Victim Support and Protection in War Crimes in BiH' (*UNDP BiH*, 2010) <http://bit.ly/UNDPBiHcourts> accessed 10 August 2018.

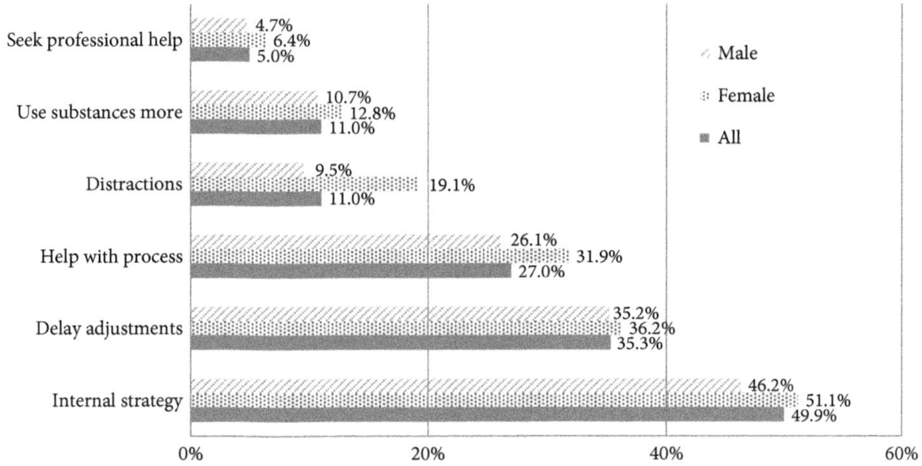

Figure 13.7 Other strategies for handling stress of testifying[a]

[a] From lowest to highest overall, Figure 13.6 aggregates specific categories of methods for reducing stressors associated with testifying—broken down by gender percentages. Seeking professional help included seeing a doctor or having therapy. Increased substance usage included alcohol, drugs (prescription and illicit), tobacco, and caffeine. Distractions included recreational activities, being in a new environment, and taking excursions. Help with the process includes speaking with someone to help better understand the process and being more comfortable with the process. Being able to adjust delays associated with testifying included having a rest period, limiting or increasing the length of the stay, and postponing the appearance altogether.

on substances (e.g. tobacco, alcohol) are used less frequently. Of concern is that few witnesses seek professional help, which echoes other findings that even in the post-testimonial phase witnesses are less likely to get assistance for their psychological well-being. These provide clear indicators of what assists witnesses with reducing stress during the time of testimony and should be incorporated into future best practices for assisting witnesses.

Turning now to gender and ethnicity, the findings here are consistent with other work finding that gender and ethnicity are critical demographics for explaining perceptions about the ICTY.[105] While women are 22.5 per cent *less* likely than men to feel they have contributed to justice, the same cannot be said of the truth (although statistically insignificant, women are still 8 per cent *less* likely to feel they have contributed). Consistent with other qualitative findings about transitional justice, there seems to be a side to truth and justice which may marginalize women,[106] but the insignificance makes the results here inconclusive.

As for ethnicity, there is very little new here that has not been addressed fully by the extant literature. Ethnicity matters. Bosniak/Muslim respondents are *more* likely to believe they have contributed to both truth (11.3 per cent) and justice (19.4 per cent), but the results are significant only for the latter. Bosnian Croats are significantly *less* likely to believe they have contributed to truth (−4.9 per cent) and justice (−25.4 per cent), while Bosnian Serbs are only significantly *less* likely to believe they have contributed to the truth (−15.4 per cent) and the

[105] K Ivković and J Hagan, 'Pursuit of Justice and the Victims of War in Bosnia and Herzegovina: An Exploratory Study' (2016) 65 Crime, Law and Social Change 1.

[106] Buss, 'Knowing Women' (n 90); A Björkdahl and J Selimovic, 'Gendered Justice Gaps in Bosnia–Herzegovina' (2014) 15 Human Rights Review 201.

results are insignificant for justice. The results are not significant for Croats in either model, and only for Serbs in the justice model (although we note that Serbs were also less likely to think they contributed to the truth). Albanian perceptions are almost the reverse mirror image of Serb beliefs about contributions as they are *more* likely to believe they have contributed to truth (16.4 per cent) and justice (17 per cent). These results are expected given that a majority of research about the ICTY has found similarities when it comes to ethnicity-based perceptions about truth and justice in the former Yugoslavia.[107]

13.7 Conclusions

There are five critical takeaways from the findings of this research. First, fair treatment by the prosecution towards witnesses themselves, as well as other witnesses and defendants, regardless of ethnicity correlates positively with witnesses' assessments of their contributions to justice, and somewhat to truth (fair treatment by the Defence and towards defendants were not statistically significant). Second, the testimonial challenges, specifically delays in testifying, may undermine perceptions of positive contributions to truth and justice. Nonetheless, the possibility exists that such obstacles may also contribute to positive feelings some witnesses have about testifying. Logistical technicalities, such as delays and difficulties with translation may undermine witness perceptions of justice. Counterintuitively, those who indicated higher levels of anxiety about testifying, or noted they were concerned about the consequences of testifying, were *more* likely to believe they contributed to justice. Third, support by VWS is important for reducing stressors associated with testifying, more so than seeking support from family and extended social networks. Fourth, women are much less likely than men to feel that they have contributed to justice. Given the small numbers of women who appeared before the ICTY overall (approximately 13 per cent of all witnesses), this raises further need to look more closely at the impact of testifying on women because their needs are unique compared to men. Fifth, ethnicity continues to be a dominant feature in witness perceptions about the ICTY. The results are substantially similar to other research finding that Bosniaks and Albanians are more likely to feel they have contributed; Bosnian Croats and Serbs are less likely to think they have contributed to justice; and Bosnian Croats and Bosnian Serbs indicate that they are less likely to feel as though they have contributed to justice.

Clearly the impact of testifying needs more analysis to untangle the knot of how challenges during testifying may serve to detract or enhance from the witness experience if we are to understand the impact of transitional justice mechanisms. If these stakeholders do not believe that they have participated in a meaningful manner, the institution's legitimacy and perhaps its legacy are called into question.[108] Given the critical importance of gender and ethnic identity in shaping the nature of the conflict and cases before the ICTY and influencing witness perceptions of fairness and personal efficacy, the positive impact of the ICTY on political developments in the former Yugoslavia may rest in part on convincing various groups of the ICTY's lack of bias and fairness. The present research adds to the debate surrounding the impact of the ICTY on witnesses and it has implications for the

[107] King and Meernik (n 48); Ivković and Hagan (n 66); Ivković and Hagan (n 106); Stover (n 2).
[108] Stover (n 2).

ICTY's legacy by demonstrating that identity and fairness issues matter a great deal in personal assessments of the witnesses' contributions to truth and justice. Ensuring a positive legacy for the ICTY may well depend on the extent to which it can convince the witnesses and other stakeholders that the ICTY is fair towards all. While much work has focused on the institution's contribution to truth and justice about the wars in the former Yugoslavia,[109] more work is still needed to explain the connections between witness contributions to The Hague Tribunal's mission and the larger impact this has on the ability of the ICTY to contribute to peace and reconciliation in the region.[110]

One of the most important opportunities for further inquiry involves closer examination of what 'fairness' and 'fair treatment' mean for witnesses in the testimonial process. Given that most witnesses will have little information on which to formulate judgements regarding how fairly other witnesses and the defendants are treated, what sorts of factors explain their views? To what extent does ethnicity affect such judgements? Do outcomes matter more than process in witness evaluations of fairness? Many unresolved theoretical issues surrounding the role of gender and justice remain. Women are a relatively small percentage of those actually testifying, but there are significant differences between male and female perceptions about testifying. What is it about the experience that is gender distinctive, and why is it that women feel greater levels of stress and less likely to feel they have contributed to truth, and justice in particular? It is the ultimate determination about these questions of truth and justice that contribute to the legacy of the ICTY, and may also be at the heart about truth and justice for witnesses and the region itself.

[109] David (n 10).
[110] Clark (n 6).

PART V

CRIMINAL PROCEDURE, COURT MANAGEMENT, AND OUTREACH

14

Defence Investigative Ethics

Practical Lessons from the ICTY's Legacy for Counsel Practising in the Region

Michael G. Karnavas[*, **]

14.1 Introduction

The International Criminal Tribunal for the former Yugoslavia (ICTY) was created by the United Nations Security Council to deal with mass atrocities (genocide, war crimes, and crimes against humanity) committed during the conflicts resulting from the break-up of the former Yugoslavia. It was the first international tribunal of its kind since the Nuremberg and Tokyo International Military Tribunals (IMTs). Its mission was to bring to justice persons responsible for serious violations of international humanitarian law committed in the territory of the former Yugoslavia, and to contribute to the restoration and maintenance of peace.[1] It was also expected to contribute to the development of international law and procedure—much as the IMTs had done.[2]

The ICTY has generally lived up to its expectations: it has been the model court from which all other ad hoc international(ised) tribunals, courts and some national courts have benefited. Though not without legitimate criticisms (e.g. the dubious claim that joint criminal enterprise, commonly referred to as JCE—a mode of liability concocted by the *Tadić* Appeal Chamber[3]—existed under customary international law),[4] its legacy is far reaching

* Michael G Karnavas is an American-trained lawyer qualified to appear before various international tribunals. Practising law for over thirty-seven years, he has appeared before State and Federal Courts in the US, the ICTY, the ICTR, the ECCC, the ICC, and the IRMICT and for nearly thirty years he has taught trial advocacy skills to lawyers and law students, lectured extensively on international criminal law and procedure, authored trial advocacy practice manuals, articles and book chapters on international criminal law and procedure, and has been engaged in a variety of legal reform and development projects in Europe and Asia.

** The author is profoundly indebted to Suzana Tomanović, his Co-Counsel at the ICTY in the Blagojević and Prlić cases and his most senior legal assistant at the Brčko Law Revision Commission, for helping him grasp some of the peskiest nuances of the civil law system, for her invaluable contributions to the legal reforms carried out in the Brčko District, Bosnia and Herzegovina (BiH) (most notably, revising the criminal procedure by eliminating the functions of the investigative judge and adding adversarial modalities), and for her unvarnished professional advice for the past twenty years.

1 United Nations Security Council, Resolution 827 (25 May 1993) UN Doc S/RES/827 (1993) 1–2.

2 Most notable are the Nuremberg Principles—a set of guidelines for determining what constitutes war crimes—drafted by the United Nations International Law Commission in 1950, codifying the jurisprudence of the International Military Tribunals and the subsequent trials under Control Council Law No 10, Punishment of Persons Guilty of War Crimes, Crimes Against Peace and Against Humanity, 20 December 1945, 3 Official Gazette Control Council for Germany 50–55 (1946).

3 *Prosecutor v Tadić* (Judgment) IT-94-1-A (15 July 1999) paras 220–28.

4 Much has been written about JCE, but for an insider's confession debunking the claim that JCE represented customary international law, see M Shahabuddeen, 'Judicial Creativity and Joint Criminal Enterprise' in S Darcy and J Powderly (eds), *Judicial Creativity at the International Criminal Tribunals* (Oxford University Press 2010) 188. His own words are as revealing as his penned decisions and opinions are disingenuous: 'Joint criminal enterprise has roots in the common law and co-perpetratorship has roots in the civil law. Neither, considered with the problem of intent, can claim the status of customary international law. It is recognized that universality of support

Michael G. Karnavas, *Defence Investigative Ethics* In: *Legacies of the International Criminal Tribunal for the Former Yugoslavia*. Edited by: Carsten Stahn, Carmel Agius, Serge Brammertz, Colleen Rohan, Oxford University Press (2020). © The Several Contributors
DOI: 10.1093/oso/9780198862956.003.0015

in just about every aspect of international and national criminal justice. From court administration to complex trial management, victim and witness protection, innovative e-court systems, criminal procedure, best practices on investigating and gathering evidence, professional standards, outreach, promoting human rights and the end of impunity for mass human rights violations, and war crimes through fair trials for those accused, the ICTY footprint is indelibly visible in all international(ised) tribunals and courts that have followed.

The ICTY adopted a hybrid procedure. Improvising from the IMTs—the only available international criminal procedures that were tried and tested at that time—the ICTY judges crafted Rules of Procedure and Evidence (RPE) that heavily leaned on the adversarial side (at least initially).[5] Civil law modalities were also infused in the RPE, especially concerning evidentiary matters. With no investigating judge, the prosecution was responsible for conducting the investigation, virtually unsupervised and with no stimulative measures for ensuring that exculpatory evidence was searched for and collected.[6]

As in the common law systems,[7] in the ICTY's party-driven system, each party was responsible for its own case and for presenting its case at trial. Unlike the civil law systems, there was no common dossier (case file); each party was required to investigate and gather its own evidence. While the prosecution was required to provide the defence with all gathered material relevant to the case and not subject to any disclosure restrictions,[8] the defence was only required to provide the prosecution and the court the material it intended to use at trial—a decision invariably made at the conclusion of the prosecutor's case-in-chief.[9] While

is not needed for the development of customary international law; generality approaching universality will do, depending on the particular situation. But in this case such generality of support is lacking: each of the two theories is supported by a considerable part of the world. That is not consistent with either theory being regarded as customary international law.' For the reference to this being 'an error', see 202–03: 'The writer has referred to an error of the Tribunal, to which he was a party; it concerns the question whether joint criminal enterprise was customary international law insofar as it permits of a conviction without proof of intent. In this respect, two rival theories—joint criminal enterprise and co-perpetratorship—hold sway in major parts of the world, but not generally; neither is therefore entitled to be regarded as customary international law. Excepting judicial creativity, there is no basis on which they could apply in this case.'

5 Discussing a shift in the trial practice of the ICTY, see D A Mundis, 'From "Common Law" Towards "Civil Law": The Evolution of the ICTY Rules of Procedure and Evidence' (2001) 14 Leiden Journal of International Law 367.

6 Remarkably for those coming from civil law systems, at the ICTY there is no obligation on the prosecution to search for exculpatory material. Unless the prosecution happens to come across exculpatory evidence, the prosecution does not need to make efforts to search for such evidence. Rules of Procedure and Evidence of the ICTY, IT/32/Rev 50, 8 July 2015, Rule 68 provides that 'the Prosecutor shall, as soon as practicable, disclose to the Defence any material which in the actual knowledge of the Prosecutor may suggest the innocence or mitigate the guilt of the accused or affect the credibility of the Prosecution case' (ICTY RPE).

7 I use the plural 'systems' because there is no such thing as *the* common law system or *the* civil law system. Each system has its own nuances and distinctions. As Kai Ambos observed, unfortunately, many common law lawyers sometimes write about civil law systems exclusively relying on common law sources, taking the French model as the only civil law model, and failing to at least distinguish the German prosecutorial model. See K Ambos, 'International Criminal Procedure: "Adversarial", "Inquisitorial" or Mixed?' (2003) 3 International Criminal Law Review 1, 3–4. The civil law systems can roughly be divided into two major models, the French model (with the investigating judge) and the German model, where the prosecutor charges and investigates, though even between each of these models there can be significant differences. There are also, what I would refer to as the hybrid civil law systems, as in Italy, BiH, Macedonia, and elsewhere, where adversarial modalities have been added to the proceedings, allowing the defence to gather evidence, initiate the questioning of witnesses and cross-examine opposing witnesses with leading questions, and even placing the burden of proof beyond a reasonable doubt on the prosecution.

8 See ICTY RPE Rules 66(C), 68(iii)–(iv), and 70(B)–(F).

9 At the ICTY, the defence need only disclose the evidence gathered that it intends to introduce at trial, and need only disclose the material after the prosecution rests its case-in-chief and after the outcome of any Rule 98*bis*

these practical considerations are axiomatic in common law systems, they are not appreciated in many civil law systems. In civil law systems, evidence is gathered by the investigating judge or the prosecution. The defence is forbidden to investigate, meet with witnesses, or gather physical evidence,[10] and the concept of moving for a judgement of acquittal (also referred to as a directed verdict or a no case to answer motion) made at the conclusion of the presentation of the prosecution's case-in-chief[11] does not exist.

Initially, the ICTY procedure proved challenging to defence counsel from the former Yugoslavia (and from other civil law states).[12] Coming from a rather passive, judge-controlled system, they were unfamiliar with investigating, gathering evidence, developing a theory of the case, proofing witnesses to testify, conducting cross-examination, making and meeting cogent objections to preserve the trial record for appeal, and so on.[13]

These new adversarial modalities and responsibilities also came with new ethical considerations. For instance, how does one conduct a witness interview without tainting the source of the evidence—the witness' memory? What should one do when coming across

motion for a judgment of acquittal. See ICTY RPE Rule 67. Having to disclose its evidence during the prosecution's case-in-chief would enable the prosecution to present rebuttal evidence. This would place the defence at a great disadvantage of commencing trial without fully knowing the extent of the prosecution's evidence.

[10] For example, see French Criminal Procedure Code (amended as of 2016), arts 70, 114–19 (duties of investigating judge); arts 81(9), 82–1(1) (defence counsels' right to make investigative requests), available at <http://www.legifrance.gouv.fr> accessed 8 May 2019; German Criminal Procedure Code (amended as of 2014), art 170(1) (no investigating judge; investigations are carried by the public prosecutor); arts 239, 240 (defence right to make investigative requests, examine witnesses) available at <http://www.gesetze-im-internet.de> accessed 8 May 2019.

[11] See ICTY RPE Rule 98*bis*. Generally, the Trial Chamber would evaluate the prosecution evidence presented in its case-in-chief on a *prima facie* basis—taking the evidence at its highest without questioning its credibility and reliability 'unless incapable of belief'. The standard of proof at the judgment of acquittal stage is evidence capable of supporting a conviction. In other words, the prosecution was merely required to present enough evidence capable of supporting a conviction beyond a reasonable doubt—whether a 'reasonable trier of fact' *could* (as opposed to *would*) convict based on the evidence before it. In December 2004 the Rule was amended to mean that the Trial Chamber would enter a judgment of acquittal on any count if it found no evidence capable of supporting a conviction. This effectively lowered the Trial Chamber's standard of review of the evidence in favour of the prosecution. See e.g., *Prosecutor* v. *Jelisić* (Judgment) IT-95-10-A (5 July 2001) paras 26–7, 55.

[12] As former Chief Judge of the US Court of Appeals for the District of Columbia Circuit and former ICTY Judge Patricia Wald remarked in 2001, '[u]nderstandably, the bulk of defense counsel are Balkan-trained lawyers and are typically not experienced at cross-examination. Some are quick learners, but others are painfully awkward and unfocused on just what they are trying to accomplish. They sometimes argue with or even criticize the witnesses. They also go off on tangents that are not always relevant to the case. The Tribunal is now operating training courses for appointed lawyers, but, candidly, it is not easy to acculturate lawyers in a wholly new legal system in a few days of lectures or even simulated exercises. As an American judge, I frankly find many ICTY defense cross-examinations painfully unhelpful to my own judgment'. Judge P M Wald, 'The International Criminal Tribunal for the Former Yugoslavia Comes of Age: Some Observations on Day-To-Day Dilemmas of an International Court' (2001) 5 Journal of Law & Policy 87, 104. Discussing similar criticisms, see M Ellis, 'The Evolution of Defense Counsel Appearing Before the International Criminal Tribunal for the Former Yugoslavia' (2003) 37 New England Law Review 949, 954–63. See also D Tolbert, 'The ICTY and Defence Counsel: A Troubled Relationship' (2002–2003) 37 New England Law Review 975 discussing issues of fee-splitting, lack of training, problems with the choice and qualification of counsel, discipline, and the role of the bar association in resolving these problems.

[13] This excerpt from the status conference serves as another example of the mis-appreciation of certain adversarial modalities by some defence counsel not trained in adversarial proceedings:

> [Counsel]: [Interpretation] Your Honour, we didn't believe that it was up to us to organise this. We thought that the Trial Chamber would give instructions to an expert here in The Hague.
> [JUDGE]: Not at all. You raised the issue about the signature. It's for you to establish, if you wish to, that there's at least a reasonable doubt that it, that it is not her signature. I don't know whether I expressed the onus properly there, but you know what I mean. You raised the issue about the signature, the one that she denied having made. You want to now show that it was her signature. If you want to show it, you have to prove it. It's not up to the Trial Chamber to work it out for you.
> *Prosecutor v Kunarac* (Transcript) IT-96-23&23/1 (21 September 2000) 6050, ll 16–25, 6051, ll 1–2.

physical evidence that is incriminating? What are acceptable practices in securing a witness' testimony, such as compensating a witness for any expenses or offering them the equivalent of any wages lost while meeting with them or when they come to The Hague to give evidence? How should one ethically prepare a witness to give evidence at trial? How does one plea bargain? And so on.

The ICTY adopted the Code of Professional Conduct for Counsel Appearing before the International Tribunal,[14] but like most national codes of conduct, it provided only general principles with scant details[15] to guide defence counsel through many of the new challenges that were likely to be confronted throughout the course of the adversarial proceedings.[16] With no detailed commentary or practical guidance, [17] these codes remain unsettled or non-expressive on the more nuanced issues, which defence counsel invariably encounter.[18] For instance, what if a client insists on giving false evidence? What if it becomes known to defence counsel that a defence witness provided false, or misleading, or even mistaken evidence that benefits the client? Even a sufficiently detailed code of conduct cannot prescribe a course of action for every eventuality. Inevitably, there are circumstances when the answer

[14] Code of Professional Conduct for Counsel Appearing before the International Tribunal, IT/125 REV 3, as amended on 22 July 2009 (ICTY Code of Conduct).

[15] For instance, art 11 of the ICTY Code of Conduct outlines in a broad conceptual fashion defence counsel's duty of due diligence: 'Counsel shall represent a client diligently and promptly in order to protect the client's best interests. Unless the representation is terminated or withdrawn, counsel shall carry through to conclusion all matters undertaken for a client within the scope of his legal representation.'

[16] In common law/adversarial systems, codes of conduct are generally drafted as concrete legal rules and may be accompanied by extensive commentary providing detailed advice and situational examples as to how counsel should resolve discrete ethical dilemmas in practice. Contrastingly, in civil law systems, codes of conduct are generally drafted as broad-brush principles intended to guide counsel in exercising professional discretion. Principally, most of the modern codes of conduct combine these two drafting styles, with some provisions drafted as concrete legal rules that restrict or regulate counsel's conduct in specific scenarios, while others are merely aspirational and intended to guide counsel's professional discretion. See MC Daly, 'The Dichotomy between Standards and Rules: A New Way of Understanding the Differences in Perceptions of Lawyer Codes of Conduct by U.S. and Foreign Lawyers' (1999) 32 Vanderbilt Journal of Transnational Law 1117, 1122. This can be problematic for counsel seeking guidance concerning their ethical duties and professional responsibilities in situations where even experience may be insufficient to provide ready and unambiguous answers.

[17] The American Bar Association (ABA) Model Rules of Professional Conduct is a good example of a code with a detailed commentary providing practical advice and situational examples as to how a lawyer should resolve particular ethical dilemmas. For instance, in relation to the duty of diligence, among other things, the commentary specifies: 'Perhaps no professional shortcoming is more widely resented than procrastination. A client's interests often can be adversely affected by the passage of time or the change of conditions; in extreme instances, as when a lawyer overlooks a statute of limitations, the client's legal position may be destroyed. Even when the client's interests are not affected in substance, unreasonable delay can cause a client needless anxiety and undermine confidence in the lawyer's trustworthiness. A lawyer's duty to act with reasonable promptness, however, does not preclude the lawyer from agreeing to a reasonable request for a postponement that will not prejudice the lawyer's client.' ABA Model Rules, Rule 1.3, cmt 3, available at <http://www.americanbar.org/groups/professional_responsibility/publications/model_rules_of_professional_conduct/rule_1_3_diligence/comment_on_rule_1_3.html> accessed 8 May 2019. The ABA is a voluntary but powerful bar association. The Model Rules of Professional Conduct promulgated by the ABA have been incorporated into the ethics rules of most States.

[18] When providing clear and definitive rules governing counsel behaviour, codes of conduct purportedly legislate, whereas when guidance is 'emphasize[d] over legislation, rules become less absolute and less enforceable.' See FC Zacharias, 'The Quest for a Perfect Code' (1998) 11 Georgetown Journal of Legal Ethics 787, 789. Generally, codes of conduct commonly provide scant guidance on how to resolve dilemmas commonly confronted by counsel, which inevitably leads to inconclusiveness. Devising rules for every ethical eventuality is unrealistic, since possible scenarios are infinite. See HL Feldman, 'Codes and Virtues: Can Good Lawyers Be Good Ethical Deliberators?' (1996) 69 Southern California Law Review 885, 889. For general issues confronting defence counsel appearing before international(ised) criminal tribunals and courts due to the absence of a bar to provide guidance and protection, see K Gibson, J R W D Jones, M G Karnavas, and M Taylor, 'Regulation of the International Bar: The Particular Challenges for Defence Counsel at the International Criminal Courts and Tribunals' in W A Schabas and S Murphy (eds), *Research Handbook on International Courts and Tribunals* (Edward Elgar Publishing Cheltenham 2017) 407–49.

to a challenging ethical question is not readily available. And then, of course, there is the issue of defence counsel's understanding of the code through the prism of his or her national code and where certain terms of art may take on a different meaning.[19]

Appreciatively, with training, seminars, exchanges of knowledge among colleagues from disparate systems, and from experience that comes only from hands-on involvement in a case, defence counsel from the former Yugoslavia and from other civil law/non-adversarial systems, over time acquired the new skills relevant to the adversarial modalities as well as an abiding appreciation of the ethical duties and constraints attendant to the ICTY hybrid criminal procedure.

As the ICTY was trailblazing in setting the standard on international criminal law and procedure, states that emerged from the former Yugoslavia underwent post-conflict transitional justice legal reforms. Significant changes to their criminal procedures were being made, most prominently in Bosnia and Herzegovina (BiH). These changes involved efforts to transition their criminal procedures from pure civil law to hybrid procedures with adversarial modalities akin to those adopted by the ICTY. Serendipitously, the skills and knowledge acquired by defence counsel while practising at the ICTY would become directly transferable to their national practice.

14.1.1 Legal reform of emerging states from former Yugoslavia

The former Yugoslavia had a developed criminal justice system based on the French civil law model, with the investigating judge in charge of conducting investigations on instructions by the prosecutor. By all accounts, the criminal justice system functioned reasonably well, with each organ or party in the criminal justice chain knowing its respective obligations and the parameters of its remit. But even well-developed criminal procedures can become sclerotic and out-dated. Post-conflict transitional justice reforms occasionally provide opportune possibilities for ushering in innovative reforms—especially as in the case of BiH. In light of the General Framework Agreement for Peace in Bosnia and Herzegovina (usually referred to as the Dayton Peace Agreement), BiH came under the administrative supervision (more like governance) of the Office of the High Representative ('OHR'),[20] thus making it possible to introduce reforms (not always prudent) which under normal circumstances would meet strong headwinds and a lack of political will.

The need for improving the criminal justice system, and even eliminating the investigating judge, was appreciated. What remained an open question was to what extent should reforms be made. The answer, of course, would need to factor in the ability to absorb and implement any reforms, which to a large extent, would depend on available training and resources to ensure that all those in the criminal justice chain would appreciate the essence and application of any modalities adopted from non-civil law criminal procedures.

[19] For more on defence counsel's ethical obligations see M G Karnavas, 'Defence Counsel Ethics, the ICC Code of Conduct and Establishing a Bar Association for ICC List Counsel' (2016) 16 International Criminal Law Review 1048, 1048–16, 1048–01. For an overview of the applicable codes of conduct for international(ised) criminal tribunals and courts see Michael G Karnavas, 'Codes of Conduct for Counsel in International Criminal Proceedings' in Hélène Ruiz Fabri (ed), *Max Planck Encyclopedia of International Procedural Law* (OUP, entry forthcoming 2020).

[20] The Office of the High Representative (OHR) was established as an ad hoc international institution to oversee the implementation of civilian aspects of the Dayton Peace Agreement which ended the war in BiH, negotiated in Dayton, Ohio, and signed in Paris on 14 December 1995. <http://www.ohr.int/?lang=en> accessed 8 May 2019.

Then came the Final Award of the Arbitral Tribunal for Dispute Over Inter-Entity Boundary in the Brčko Area.[21] It called for the Brčko area of BiH to be established as a district autonomous from the Republika Srpska and the Federation of BiH—the two entities of BiH.[22] The Final Award provided for a law revision commission 'with the responsibility for proposing modifications of exiting law to produce a uniform system of laws throughout the District'.[23] Accordingly, the Brčko Law Revision Commission was established, providing it with an exquisite opportunity to make significant innovative changes to the existing criminal procedure of BiH,[24] albeit only in so far as they applied to the newly created Brčko District. Ultimately, the Brčko District criminal procedure would serve as the basis for the revised criminal procedure for BiH, incorporating virtually all adversarial modalities and other innovative measures.[25]

The innovative measures introduced in the Brčko criminal procedure called for eliminating the investigative judge, introducing adversarial party-driven procedures, establishing the agency for legal aid, reforming and monitoring police activities, and reforming the court administration.[26] Similar measures have been adopted in some of the states that emerged from the breakup of the former Yugoslavia, namely, the Republic of North Macedonia,[27] Serbia,[28] Montenegro,[29] and Kosovo.[30] Croatia was also planning

[21] Pursuant to the Dayton Peace Agreement, BiH was officially divided into two Entities—the Republika Srpska and the Federation. Control over the Brčko Area could not be resolved during the peace negotiations at Dayton. Rather than holding up or forgoing the possibility of reaching a peace agreement, the parties agreed to have the Brčko Area dispute resolved through binding arbitration. See General Framework Agreement for Peace in Bosnia and Herzegovina, 14 December 1995, 35 ILM 75 (1996).

[22] The Final Award called the Brčko area to be established as an autonomous district deriving its powers from the Republika Srpska and the Federation which would hold the entire area Brčko area in 'condominium' after delegating all of their powers of governance to 'a new institution, a multi-ethnic democratic government to be known as the Brčko District of BiH'. The Final Award vested the international Supervisor with powers considerable powers, and specifically called for the Supervisor to establish a law revision commission to propose modifications of the then existing laws in order to produce a uniform system of laws. See Arbitration for the Brčko Area (Fed Bosn & Herz v Rep Srpska), Final Award, paras 9, 11, 61 (1999), 38 ILM 534 (1999) (The Final Award).

[23] The Final Award, Annex, paras 5–6. For a detailed account of the reform process, see M G Karnavas, 'Creating the Legal Framework of the Brčko District of Bosnia and Herzegovina: A Model for the Region and other Post-conflict Countries' (2003) 97 American Journal of International Law 111, 131. See also OHR-North Office of the High Representative, Brčko Law Revision Commission Chairman's Final Report, 31 December 2001.

[24] The degree and depth of legal and administrative reforms in the Brčko District would not have been possible without Deputy High Representative and Supervisor of Brčko (1997–2000) US Ambassador Robert William Farrand's support and audacity for bold, innovative, reforms. See generally, Robert William Farrand, *Reconstruction and Peace Building in the Balkans: The Brcko Experience* (Rowman & Littlefield Publishers 2011). See also 'BRCKO Law Revision Commission Chairman's Final Report' (31 December 2001) <https://www.esiweb.org/pdf/bridges/bosnia/BLRC_ChairmansRep.pdf≥ accessed 8 May 2019.

[25] Criminal Procedure Code of Bosnia and Herzegovina, Official Gazette of BiH No 72/13, 2013 ('BiH CPC'), unofficial translation available at <https://www.legislationline.org/documents/section/criminal-codes/country/40/Belgium/show> accessed 8 May 2019.

[26] Law on Criminal Procedure of the Brcko District of Bosnia and Herzegovina, Official Gazette of the Brcko District of BiH No. 10/03, <http://www.tuzilastvobih.gov.ba/files/docs/zakoni/ZKP_BD/ZKP_BD_10_03_eng.pdf≥, accessed 8 May 2019.

[27] Criminal Procedure Code of the Republic of North Macedonia, Official Gazette No 150 2010 (Macedonia CPC). Unofficial translation available at <https://www.legislationline.org/documents/section/criminal-codes/country/31/Netherlands/show> accessed 8 May 2019.

[28] Criminal Procedure Code of Serbia, Official Gazette of the Republic of Serbia, No 72/2011, 2011, (Serbia CPC). Unofficial translation available at <https://www.legislationline.org/documents/section/criminal-codes/country/5/Russian%20Federation/show> accessed 8 May 2019.

[29] Criminal Procedure Code of Montenegro, Official Gazette of Montenegro, No 35/15, 2015, (Montenegro CPC). Unofficial translation available at <https://www.legislationline.org/documents/section/criminal-codes/country/57/Mongolia/show > accessed 8 May 2019.

[30] Criminal Procedure Code of Kosovo, Law No 04/L-123, approved by the Kosovo Assembly on 13 December 2012, effective 1 January 2013 (Kosovo CPC) Official translation available at <http://www.kuvendikosoves.org/?cid=2,191,980> accessed 8 May 2019. In a recent Review of the Implementation of the New Kosovo CPC, the

to eliminate the investigative judge,[31] although the new Criminal Procedure Code (CPC) prescribes the participation of investigators and investigative judges in certain cases.[32]

Recognizing the novel challenges resulting from the adoption of party-driven adversarial modalities into their criminal procedures, prompted these states to embrace a wide range of training for defence counsel on such basic advocacy skills such as how to ethically conduct investigations, the art and science of cross-examination, plea-bargaining,[33] as well as more substantive matters such as evidentiary principles and ethics. This training provided by the national bars in partnership with non-government organizations such as the American Bar Association[34] and international organizations such as the Organization for Security and Co-operation in Europe[35] proved invaluable. By transitioning into hybrid criminal procedures, it was not just a matter of all those involved (judges, prosecutors, defence counsel, judicial police, and inspectors) adjusting to their new role and learning the skills that went with the new procedures, but of also understanding the fundamental principles behind the new modalities and the purposes they intend to serve.

Organization for Security and Co-operation in Europe (OSCE) observed that the shift envisioned in the new Kosovo CPC to a primarily adversarial procedure is not seen in practice. The new Kosovo CPC was published only three days before it came into effect, giving no time to provide extensive training on how to apply the new code. See OSCE Mission in Kosovo, Review of the Implementation of the New Criminal Procedure Code of Kosovo, 1 June 2016, Executive Summary, p 4. Similar problems with the implementation of the new criminal procedures were encountered in other countries in the region. See *New Trends in Serbian Criminal Procedure Law and Regional Perspectives (Normative and Practical Aspects)* (Ana Petrović and Ivan Jovanović eds, OSCE Mission to Serbia, 3 September 2012).

[31] The 2003 *Operational Plan for the Implementation of the Justice Reform* stated: 'The new Law on criminal proceedings is being prepared. One of the novelties in this law shall be the termination of investigation as a part of criminal proceedings done by the court.' Operational Plan for the Implementation of the Justice Reform, Republic of Croatia, Ministry of Justice, Local and Self Government, Zagreb, June 2003, p 6.

[32] The Criminal Procedure Code of the Republic of Croatia (Croatia CPC) was amended by the Croatian Parliament in 2014. Under the new Croatia CPC, the State Attorney is in charge of investigation with investigative judge holding him or her in check. The accused and his or her defence team may conduct an investigation when there are criminal proceedings against the accused; however, to collect evidence and interview witnesses, the accused and/or his or her defence team are required to make investigative requests to the State Attorney and the investigative judge. See Criminal Procedure Code of Croatia, Official Gazette No 152/08, 76/09, 80/11, 121/11, 91/12, 143/12, 56/13,145/13, 152/14, 2014, arts 213, 213a, 213b, 213c.

[33] Plea bargaining is generally considered an anathema in civil law systems, where truth in pleading is essential. Sentence bargaining, however, is perfectly acceptable, as long as the accused pleads to all the crimes established by the evidence and acknowledged through his or her admissions. See J I Turner, 'Plea Bargaining and International Criminal Justice' (2007) 48 University of the Pacific Law Review 219, 224–26. The ICTY has opted for the civil law approach, which I characterize as 'truth in pleading and sentencing'. One has to plead to what the evidence shows are proved crimes, and agree to a sentence reflective of the crimes and attendant mitigating factors. A watershed moment in plea bargaining for the ad hoc tribunals was in the *Erdemović case*. At his initial appearance in 1996, Erdemović entered a guilty plea to the first count of the indictment (crimes against humanity) and was sentenced to ten years of imprisonment. On appeal, the Appeals Chamber considered *proprio motu* the validity of his plea, granting the opportunity to plead anew, finding that Erdemović's guilty plea was not informed. In 1998, Erdemović changed his plea to guilty with respect to the second count (murder as a violation of the laws or customs of war). His sentence was reduced to five years. See *Prosecutor v Erdemović* (Judgment) IT-96-22-A (7 October 1997) paras 3–4; *Prosecutor v Erdemović* (Transcript) IT-96-22 (14 January 1998) 22, ll 3–20.

[34] For American Bar Association projects in BiH, Croatia, Kosovo, Macedonia, Montenegro and Serbia, see Balkans Regional Rule of Law Network Program, at <http://www.americanbar.org/advocacy/rule_of_law/where_we_work/europe_eurasia/regional_balkans.html> accessed 8 May 2019.

[35] In assisting the legal reform, OSCE missions in BiH, Kosovo, Montenegro, Serbia, and Skopje (Macedonia) organize and facilitate trainings on the new criminal procedure. For more information on the OSCE rule of law activities in the region, see <http://www.osce.org/rule-of-law> accessed 8 May 2019.

14.1.2 The ICTY and its legacy

Auspiciously, the procedure adopted by the ICTY proved to be highly relevant in the criminal procedure reform efforts of some of the states that emerged from the former Yugoslavia. Considering the similarities between the ICTY procedure and the adversarial modalities adopted by these states, defence counsel practising in these jurisdictions and before the newly established Kosovo Specialist Chambers (KSC)[36] can draw copious lessons from the ICTY legacy.

In all adversarial procedures (pure common law or party-driven hybrid), defence counsels' ability to impact the trial proceedings to a large extent depends on the fruits of a targeted, purposeful, and diligent investigation, which in no small measure will inform the theory of the case and attendant strategies and tactics. Thus, defence counsel in the states where adversarial modalities akin to those of the ICTY have been adopted—as defence counsel at the ICTY—are required to locate witnesses and gather evidence, identify a theory of the case, have witnesses summoned to give evidence, prepare (proof) their witnesses to give evidence, and so on. Of course, the right and obligation to investigate also comes with a host of responsibilities and ethical dilemmas. These responsibilities and the requisite attendant skills in meeting them are generally novel for many defence counsel trained in civil law systems, where conducting investigations is the sole remit of the investigating judge or prosecution. Failure to appreciate these inescapable responsibilities or to acquire the needed skills in ethically meeting them can result in ineffective legal representation and/or professional misconduct.

Unquestionably, the ICTY experience—its legacy—has much to offer, complimenting the training already provided (and ongoing). Over the years, through its directives, jurisprudence, and practice, the ICTY has been an incubator for best practices on investigating, gathering evidence, witness preparation and proofing, professional ethics and more. These best practices are just as applicable in ordinary courts as they are in the specialized courts or chambers handling war crimes cases, such as the War Crimes Section of the State Court of BiH[37] and the KSC. But even if not directly applicable, they are useful in thinking through investigative challenges and ethical dilemmas.

In this chapter I will discuss the fundamentals of defence investigations in trials with adversarial modalities and the ethical pitfalls defence counsel might encounter, and offer

[36] The Kosovo Specialist Chambers is an internationalized set of chambers within the Kosovo judiciary established to try crimes against humanity, war crimes, and other crimes under Kosovo law committed by persons of Kosovo/Yugoslav citizenship or against persons of Kosovo/Yugoslav citizenship between 1 January 1998 and 31 December 2000 in the territory of Kosovo. See Law on Specialist Chambers and Specialist Prosecutor's Office, Law No 05/L-053, 3 August 2015, arts 6–9, 13–15. The Kosovo Specialist Chambers (KSC) retains many of the civil law attributes and review mechanisms associated with the criminal procedure of the former Yugoslavia, though in many ways it is also kindred to the ICTY, having also incorporated modalities from other international(ised) tribunals and courts. For a brief analysis of the KSC see my blog series on the KSC: Michael G Karnavas, 'Kosovo Specialist Chambers, Part 1: Its Statute and Rules of Procedure and Evidence in a nutshell' (24 May 2017) <http://michaelgkarnavas.net/blog/2017/05/24/kosovo-specialist-chambers-part-1/>; 'Kosovo Specialist Chambers, Part 2: Fundamentals of the KSC Statute' (1 June 2017) <http://michaelgkarnavas.net/blog/2017/06/01/ksc-statute-fundamentals/> 'Kosovo Specialist Chambers, Part 3: Peculiar Features of the Statute' (5 June 2016) <http://michaelgkarnavas.net/blog/2017/06/05/ksc-part-3-peculiar-features/> accessed 8 May 2019.

[37] The State Court of BiH was established in 2002. In 2004 it formed a war crimes section (The War Crimes Chamber). The amended law entered into force on 6 January 2005 and the War Crimes Section has since been trying accused charged with genocide, crimes against humanity, and war crimes. Law on the Court of Bosnia and Herzegovina, Official Gazette of Bosnia and Herzegovina, 49/09, May 2009. The ICTY has transferred six cases to the State Court of BiH pursuant to Rule 11*bis*.

practical advice. Since defence counsels' specific professional duties and responsibilities to a large extent depend on the procedure that applies, and considering the ICTY's party-driven adversarial system, for contextual purposes, I will first provide a cursory overview of the adversarial procedure and professional obligations of zealousness and due diligence central to defence ethics in common law / adversarial hybrid systems. I will then discuss the fundamentals of case preparation and analysis, for further context and better appreciation of the pre-trial and investigation activities expected of defence counsel in mounting a robust defence in adversarial proceedings. Finally, I will discuss the practical aspects of investigating and gathering evidence, and will offer some best practices and tips, which, if followed, should keep the expectedly zealous defence counsel well within the accepted ethical boundaries.

14.2 Brief Overview of the Trial Procedure with Adversarial Modalities

Essential to understanding what is expected of defence counsel is an appreciation of the court's procedure—not just the *what*, but the *how* and the *why*. Indeed, the court's procedure informs defence counsel of their ethical and professional responsibilities.

Under the court-led criminal procedure of the former Yugoslavia, defence counsel were active during the investigative stage only to the extent that they could make investigative requests to the investigating judge; they were not permitted to investigate and gather evidence.[38] Moreover, during the trial proceedings defence counsel were relatively passive. The trial judge was in total control of the proceedings, carrying the burden, if you will, of being intimately convinced from the adduced evidence of having come as close to the truth as possible. This burden is vastly different from that of the prosecution's in common law (and hybrid adversarial) proceedings where the prosecution exclusively carries the burden of proving beyond a reasonable doubt the alleged charges.

The trial judges in civil law systems determine which witnesses will give *viva voce* testimony[39] and what documentary evidence will be admitted and considered, exhaustively question the witnesses, address all legal issues, and attempt to find the truth.[40] If a witness or the accused departs from his or her previous testimony, it is up to the presiding judge to apprise him or her of the departure, clarify the reasons for the new or different testimony, and, if necessary, read the prior testimony to the witness or the accused.[41] The prosecution and

[38] Criminal Procedure Code of the Socialist Federal Republic of Yugoslavia, Official Gazette of the SFRY 4/77, 36/77, 14/85, 26/86, Translations on Eastern Europe Political, Sociological, and Military Affairs, US Joint Publications Research Service No 1410, 10 August 1977 (SFRY CPC). Art 322 of the SFRY CPC provides that the parties may request that new facts be investigated and new evidence obtained up until the end of the trial, and may also present again those motions which the presiding judge or panel has already rejected. SFRY CPC, art 282(3): 'The presiding judge of the panel may order that new evidence be taken for the trial even if there is no motion by the [parties].'

[39] ibid art 281: 'Witnesses and experts proposed by the prosecutor in the indictment or accusation and by the accused in the traverse of the indictment shall also be summoned to the trial except for those whose examination in the trial is not required in the judgment of the presiding judge of the panel.'

[40] ibid art 292(2): 'It is the duty of a presiding judge to see that the subject matter is fully examined, that the truth is found, and that everything be eliminated which prolongs the proceeding, but does not serve to clarify the matter.' As the Latin adage goes, which some civil law judges enjoy reciting to the parties, '*Dabo mihi facta, dabo tibi ius*'—'Give me the fact[s], I'll give you the law.'

[41] ibid arts 317(3), 328.

defence counsel can question witnesses, but only through non-leading questions (leading questions—those that suggest the answers—are prohibited),[42] and generally to merely supplement the exhaustive questioning performed by the judges who, to emphasize, are entrusted with the responsibility to get as close to the material truth as possible.[43] Notably, a failure to draw out a relevant line of questioning or to raise any legal issues would have no consequences for the appeal. In other words, unlike in common law/adversarial proceedings, the failure to make a record and preserve errors for appeal did not bar the appellate court from conducting its own assessment. This civil law feature seemingly remains in the hybrid procedures with adversarial modalities adopted in BiH, Serbia, North Macedonia, Montenegro, Croatia, and Kosovo. Nonetheless, with the absence of the investigating judge and with the prosecution taking on an adversarial role and not compelled to investigate for exculpatory evidence (as expected of the prosecution in civil law systems such as Germany where there is no investigating judge),[44] defence counsel must be proactive, and play a significant role throughout the proceedings.

During the pre-trial stage, defence counsel must investigate and collect evidence,[45] whereas during the trial stage, they are responsible for presenting their case through cross-examining adverse witnesses,[46] calling their own witnesses, and seeking to admit evidence.[47] Thus, as defence counsel at the ICTY, defence counsel of the former Yugoslavia cannot—as in the past—passively observe the proceedings during the pre-trial stage as the now-defunct investigating judge carried out (purportedly) an impartial investigation,

[42] ibid art 232: 'In the interrogation of witnesses it is prohibited to use deception or to put leading questions.' Art 324: 'The provisions which apply to questioning witnesses and experts in the preliminary examinations shall be appropriately applied to their questioning in the trial.'

[43] ibid art 327(1): 'When the presiding judge completes the questioning of a witness or expert, the members of the panel may put questions to the witness or expert directly. The prosecutor, accused, defense counsel, injured party, legal representative, attorney and experts may put questions directly to witnesses and experts with permission of the presiding judge.' ibid art 292(2): 'It is the duty of a presiding judge to see that ... the truth is found.'

[44] In Germany, investigations of serious offences are carried out by the public prosecutor, who has broad powers to interrogate suspects, summons and interrogate witnesses, including experts. There is an investigating judge, whose function is limited to granting warrants for coercive measures upon application from the public prosecutor, including arrest, pre-trial detention, search, seizure, or surveillance of telecommunication warrants. Similar to France, under Section 160(2) of the German Code of Criminal Procedure, the public prosecutor in Germany has an obligation to search for both incriminating and exculpatory evidence, supposedly making the public prosecution office 'the most objective authority in the world.' Shawn Marie Boyne, 'The German Prosecution Service: Guardians of the Law?' 6 (Springer, 2014). The idea of the prosecution being a neutral part of the legal system is still upheld in Germany, in theory. Many of my German colleagues beg to differ with this rather bold statement; it appears that almost everyone agrees that the idea that the public prosecutor office is the embodiment of neutrality, detachment and objectivity in carrying out its mandate is no more—if it ever were. In practice, things are much more adversarial than they should be. Some recent critical studies of the German prosecution practices have argued that prosecutors have abandoned the role of objective decision-makers. According to Eberhard Siegismund, Deputy Director General in the Judicial System Division, Federal Ministry of Justice, 'the public prosecution office is, however, not infrequently said, as the "cavalry of the law," to demonstrate a certain "dashing spirit" and is thus thought to be blind in its enthusiasm for prosecution.' Eberhard Siegismund, 'The Public Prosecution office in Germany: Legal Status, Functions and Organization', UNAFEI Annual Report for 2001 and Resource Material Series No 60, pp 58–76, 59 (2003).

[45] BiH CPC, art 50(1); Serbia CPC, art 68(9); Macedonia CPC, arts 70, 78, 306; Croatia CPC, arts 64(8), 64(9). Kosovo CPC provides that the parties may apply to the State prosecutor to investigate and collect certain evidence. See Kosovo CPC, art 216. Similarly, in Montenegro, the investigation is led by the prosecution. Montenegro CPC, art 275.

[46] BiH CPC, art 262; Serbia CPC, arts 68(10), 89(2), 99; Macedonia CPC, arts 70, 384; Montenegro CPC, arts 114, 347; Croatia CPC, art 420; Kosovo CPC, arts 9(2), 332, 334.

[47] BiH CPC, art 261(1); Serbia CPC, art 68; Macedonia CPC, art 70; Montenegro CPC, art 4; Croatia CPC, art 64(9), 64(10); Kosovo CPC, art 9.

searching for inculpatory as well as exculpatory evidence with equal zeal. They must investigate and gather evidence in support of their case.

14.3 Ethical Duty of Zealousness and Due Diligence

The procedural differences between the civil law and the common law or hybrid adversarial systems have a direct effect on the role played by defence counsel and their professional and ethical obligations.

In civil law inquisitorial systems, the defence plays a subsidiary role. Their participation in investigation is limited and mediated through the supervision of the independent investigative organ-assisting the independent and impartial enquirer (investigative judge or magistrate, depending on the system) to collect and evaluate the conflicting views of the prosecution and the accused in getting to the truth.[48]

In common law or hybrid adversarial systems, defence counsel are independent actors required to zealously advocate for their client's interests. Their overarching, if not exclusive, obligation is to zealously represent their clients. To a large extent this is done by being due diligent in every aspect of their functions and duties, such as conducting a thorough investigation to search for evidence, making all necessary written and oral submissions related to the law and facts, addressing all relevant evidentiary objections in a timely and coherent fashion, thoroughly preparing for the examination of all prosecution witnesses, securing expert testimony when necessary and preparing an effective and credible (plausible) defence through defence witnesses and documentary evidence. Failure on the part of defence counsel to do any of the above when considered reasonable and necessary for ensuring effective legal representation could result in an ethical breach—not to mention ineffective assistance of counsel and a denial of the client's fair trial rights.

Zealousness and diligence are overarching duties central to and connected with defence counsels' other ethical duties of independence, loyalty, confidentiality, lack of conflict of interests, and communication.[49] A zealous defence requires defence counsel to attack the prosecutor's evidence to the extent possible. Defence counsel are ethically bound to challenge the prosecutor's evidence forcefully and effectively, including challenging evidence that may appear or even be known to be sound—as long as it is done within the acceptable bounds of the criminal procedure and ethical constraints set out by the applicable codes of conduct.[50]

48 For a cogent analysis of the different roles played by defence counsel in inquisitorial and adversarial systems, see J Hodgson, 'The Role of the Criminal Defence Lawyer in an Inquisitorial Procedure: Legal and Ethical Constraints' (2006) 9 Legal Ethics 125, 134 observing that in civil law systems, defence counsel 'is not cast as primary actor in the process, but rather functions as an auxiliary to the *magistrate*' who supervises the pre-trial investigation and is seen to be the more neutral representative of the wider public interest. See also M G Karnavas, 'Making Sense of the Standard & Burden of Proof in Hybrid Courts: Reflections on the Common Law & Civil Law Approaches to Proof', (27 April 2016) <http://michaelgkarnavas.net/blog/2016/04/27/making-sense-burden-of-proof/> accessed 16 February 2020.

49 See eg, 'International Criminal Tribunal for the former Yugoslavia Code of Conduct for Counsel appearing before the International Tribunal' (adopted 12 June 1997, revised 6 August 2009), IT/125 Rev 3, art 3; *International Criminal Court Code of Professional Conduct for Counsel* (adopted 2 December 2005) ICC-ASP/4/Res/1, art 5

50 Analysing defence counsel's duty to zealously represent their clients, see M G Karnavas, 'Defence Counsel Ethics, the ICC Code of Conduct and Establishing a Bar Association for ICC List Counsel' (2016) 16 International Criminal Law Review 1048. See also M H Freedman, 'In Praise of Overzealous Representation—Lying To Judges, Deceiving Third Parties, And Other Ethical Conduct' (2006) 34 Hofstra Law Review 771, discussing several

Defence counsel are not required to pursue the true account of the facts of the case or to promote a dispassionate application of the law to the facts. They are not expected to balance the competing interests of all affected persons, such as the victims and civil parties. Quite to the contrary, defence counsel must exclusively pursue their client's interests. They have an obligation to remain detached as they zealously exploit every conceivable opening and press every conceivable advantage that may benefit their client, short of knowingly presenting false evidence or making false representations to the court.[51] These obligations are necessary to ensure that trials are fair. A conviction without this sort of robust defence is likely to be unreliable. All the more reason why it is absolutely necessary for defence counsel to vigorously and nonjudgmentally test the evidence, and in doing so, assist the judge in determining the facts. Importantly, however, defence counsel cannot be effective by simply relying on the evidence gathered by the prosecution; they must conduct their own investigation to search for and gather evidence that may be useful in undermining the prosecution's case and/or underpinning their own case. In other words, trial activities in adversarial proceedings are dependent on pre-trial case preparation, intrinsic of which is the collection of evidence through investigation—an indispensable task for mounting credible defences, which, save for the evidence gathered through defence counsel's investigative efforts, would otherwise be unavailable to the accused. A decision not to investigate would assuredly result to a failure of due diligence (an ethical breach),[52] and could even result to ineffective assistance of counsel (a legal breach of the client's fair trial rights). Of course, the extent to which the defence is able to investigate is determined by the applicable Statute and RPE of the tribunal or court in which the case will be tried. Although there may be some procedural commonalities among the international criminal tribunals, the applicable Statute and RPE, as well as any guiding jurisprudence, dictate the defence's investigative maneuverability: whether it is actually permitted to search for and interview witnesses, access archives, collect documentary evidence, etc.[53]

hypotheticals in which a defence counsel can ethically make a false statement to third parties and judges in negotiations, or ethically engage in conduct involving dishonesty, fraud, deceit, or misrepresentation in sting operations.

[51] See M H Freedman, 'Getting Honest About Client Perjury' (2008) 21 Georgetown Journal of Legal Ethics 133; M H Freedman, 'Professional Responsibility of the Criminal Defense Lawyer: The Three Hardest Questions' (1966) 64 Michigan Law Review 146. For instance, zealousness may require defence counsel to impeach a witness or adduce evidence from a witness where defence counsel has a particular opinion as to the veracity of the evidence. To do otherwise would deny the court the opportunity to have the evidence tested so that it may have some confidence in its credibility assessments. For a different point of view, see J I Turner, 'Legal Ethics in International Criminal Defense' (2010) 10 Chicago Journal of International Law 685, 697 arguing that in international criminal proceedings defence counsel should refrain from impeaching a truthful witness to avoid muddling the record.

[52] The duty of diligence is not always explicitly stated, but is implied in various rules requiring promptness, competence, zeal, commitment, dedication, and workload management. *See supra* note 21 regarding Defence counsel's duty of diligence.

[53] For example, the Extraordinary Chambers in the Courts of Cambodia ('ECCC'), a domestic Cambodian court with international assistance, is based on the French civil law system and is inquisitorial by nature. The Co-Investigating Judges at the ECCCC are responsible for conducting investigations and the Defence may not 'conduct any investigative action, including questioning [a witness]'. Agreement Between the United Nations and the Royal Government of Cambodia Concerning the Prosecution Under Cambodian Law of Crimes Committed During the Period of Democratic Kampuchea, 6 June 2003, art 5(1); Law on the Establishment of Extraordinary Chambers in the Courts of Cambodia for the Prosecution of Crimes Committed During the Period of Democratic Kampuchea, with inclusion of amendments as promulgated on 27 October 2004, NS/RKM/1004/006, art 23 new; *Case of MEAS Muth*, 003/07-09-2009-ECCC-OCIJ, (Decision on MEAS Muth's Request for the Co-Investigating Judges to Clarify Whether the Defence May Contact Individuals Including) [REDACTED], 4 December 2015, D173/2.3, para 15.

While it may not always be possible to collect evidence to exonerate the accused or to mitigate the case against him or her, it is essential to search for and gather relevant evidence for raising reasonable doubt or presenting alternative plausible explanations—especially where adverse inferences can be drawn from circumstantial evidence.[54] Indeed, defence counsel's ability to make an impact during the trial proceedings depends on the efforts made, strategies chosen, and results achieved in tactically executing pre-trial activities with purpose, vision, and diligence—all of which to some degree depend on the admissible evidence defence counsel have at their disposal.

In exercising their ethical and professional duties of zealousness and due diligence, defence counsel must locate witnesses and gather evidence, identify a theory of the case, have witnesses summoned to give evidence, prepare (proof) their witnesses to give evidence, and engage witnesses at trial: to confront prosecution witnesses by cross-examining them with leading questions (preferably) to draw out the weaknesses of the prosecution's case, and directly examine defence witnesses to advance the theory of the case. Defence counsel are also expected to raise evidentiary objections and make oral and written submissions to address all legal issues to perfect the *record*[55] for appeal. Put differently, defence counsel must identify their destination, and the possible means and routes available to get to that destination, taking adequate preparatory measures to meet any challenges likely to be encountered in getting to that destination. Ultimately, part and parcel of defence counsel's due diligence obligations throughout the pre-trial and trial stages is to establish a trial record from which defence counsel will not only argue their case at the end of the trial, but from which they can attempt to resuscitate on appeal. The consequences of not having a trial record with properly preserved errors could be devastating[56] —unless such errors can be raised on appeal or addressed by the appeal judges *proprio motu*, which is generally permissible in civil law systems.[57] In the adversarial system, failure to make the record strips the client of a chance to overturn a conviction or preserve an acquittal.[58]

[54] Unlike in civil law systems, where the judges are expected to issue the verdict based on their inner convictions, in adversarial proceedings the burden of proof in establishing the accused's guilt is placed on the prosecution. As such, the duty of defence counsel is to put the prosecution to proof. The *trier of fact* (jury or judge) is not required actively to seek the truth; it need only decide whether the evidence produced during the proceedings substantiates the charges and proves beyond a reasonable doubt the accused's guilt. For an excellent, albeit dated research and analysis of US jurisprudence in relation to the burden of proof practices, see G P Fletcher, 'Two Kinds of Legal Rules: A Comparative Study of Burden-of-Persuasion Practices in Criminal Cases' (1968) 77 Yale Law Journal 880–935.

[55] The record is the documentation of everything that happened during the proceedings, from the investigation all the way until the final judgment. It is the official collection of all the pleadings, exhibits, orders and word for word testimony that took place during the trial. To a large extent it is dependent on the search for evidence, making and meeting objections during proceedings and the motion practice.

[56] As put by the United States Court of Appeal for the Second Circuit in *Jones v. Vacco*, 126 F. 3d 408 (2d Cir 1997), 'God may know but the record must show.'

[57] The Supreme Court Chamber of the ECCC exercised its authority to raise issues of law *ex proprio motu* irrespective of whether such issues were raised before the lower Chambers. See Case of *KAING Guek Eav*, 001/18-07-2007-ECCC/SC, Appeal Judgment, 3 February 2012, F28, para 15.

[58] *Delalić et al* serves as a good example. Judge Karibi-Whyte was accused of sleeping during substantial portions of the trial proceedings. Counsel for Esad Landžo (one of the Accused) did not formally raise this issue before the Trial Chamber but filed this issue as a ground of appeal. Counsel for Landžo explained the failure to raise this issue during trial proceedings by stating that she had approached 'this sensitive issue in the most diplomatic way possible.' [para 641] The record had not been made when necessary—i.e. during the trial proceedings when the facts effectively occurred and the legal issue arose. The Appeals Chamber held that 'the matter must be raised with the court at the time the problem is perceived in order to enable the problem to be remedied.' See *Prosecutor v Delalić et al.* (Judgment) IT-96-21-A (20 February 2001) paras 620–23, 628, 641–47.

14.4 Case Preparation

All trial activities are dependent on pre-trial case preparation. Aside from mastering the facts of the case and applicable law, there is a need to search for and gather evidence in order to strengthen, to the extent possible, the defence case for trial—even if merely to raise reasonable doubt or present alternative plausible explanations—especially where adverse inferences can be drawn from circumstantial evidence.[59] The objective of pre-trial case preparation is to identify and develop a theory of the case, for no case in adversarial proceedings can be properly tried without a *theory of the case*. It does not matter whether the proceedings are based on the adversarial system, the civil law system, or a hybrid system. The theory of the case is nothing more than a logical persuasive story of what happened from the defence perspective—i.e. the 'reason', 'justification', or 'explanation' as to why the defence should prevail at trial. The theory of the case must be logically and consistently developed so that, upon examination of the evidence and testimony from all the witnesses, the Trial Chamber can rationally render a judgment in favor of the defence. The theory of the case is dependent on the charges, the facts, the applicable law, the possible defences (if any), the potential witnesses, the admissible documentary evidence, and any plausible alternative explanations that negate the alleged charges or diminish the accused's responsibility. Once the theory of the case is identified, all actions taken thereafter—from pre-trial to the end of trial must, single-mindedly be in furtherance of it.

The theory of the case will generally emerge once the defence has had an opportunity to dissect the prosecution's evidence, analyse the disclosure material, conduct its own investigation (where permitted) and meet with the client and potential witnesses (where permitted), and take instructions from the client/accused. Defence counsel must select *the* most persuasive (and therefore *the* most plausible) theory of the case before preparing and presenting *that* theory of the case to the Trial Chamber. All ensuing strategic decisions, as well as some tactical ones, are dependent on the selected theory of the case. Thus, in developing the strategy for and during the trial stage, defence counsel should consider the significance of each witness to the case, the points each witness is likely to establish on direct or cross-examination (and why), how these points may impact or advance the defence's theory of the case, what significance is likely to be attached to any accompanying documents or testimonial evidence and what, if any, plausible options are available in dealing with the Prosecution's strategic approach to its case. Tactical decisions will follow.[60]

14.4.1 Learning the Case

The best place to start learning your case is with the charging document (arrest warrant or indictment) and accompanying disclosure material. Defence counsel must read the charging document thoroughly to understand the events as perceived by the respective parties

[59] ibid, see text in footnote 54, G P Fletcher, 'Two Kinds of Legal Rules: A Comparative Study of Burden-of-Persuasion Practices in Criminal Cases' (1968) 77 Yale Law Journal 880–935.

[60] See Gregor G Smith, 'Theory of the Case' in Colleen Rohan and Gentian Zyberi (eds) *Defense Perspectives on International Criminal Justice* (Cambridge University Press 2017) (discussing the importance and development of the theory of the case).

and to identify the role each witness will play during the litigation process. Defence counsel should begin by:

- Breaking down the charging document by separating the background information from the facts;
- Reading the supporting material, reviewing any exhibits or documentary evidence cited in the charging document, and visiting the crime scene;
- Having a clear understanding of the available facts (which will assist in identifying any apparent or potential issues that will need to be addressed during the pre-trial stage); and
- Listing facts that are good and bad, including wishful facts you hope to develop through investigation.

After mastering the facts, the next step is to review the law—objectively. It is essential to have a clear understanding of the operative law. The objective for defence counsel is to have a basic understanding of the applicable law before discussing the legal and factual issues with the client and other members of the defence team. Incrementally, a list of potential issues will emerge which defence counsel will intuitively recognize as relevant to the case. Defence counsel should:

- List all legal arguments or defences that appear relevant;
- List all the elements of each charge to focus on what must be proved by the prosecution and, accordingly, what must be challenged and disputed by the defence; and
- List all potential issues that may be relevant to the case.

14.4.2 Brainstorming the Theory of the Case

Brainstorming the theory of the case is the process of dissecting the facts and applicable law and the distillation of the case to its essentials. Here are some tips to keep in mind when brainstorming:

- **Start with the law.** Without a clear understanding of the applicable law, it is impossible to appraise the facts. Start by listing the elements of each charge in the charging document and any available defences. This becomes the checklist for evaluating the available facts and determining the need for legal motions, investigative tasks, consultation with expert witnesses, etc.
- **Consider what facts the prosecution will be relying on.** Examine carefully each witness statement and consider whether the witness's account of the facts is biased, prejudiced, or unreliable (hearsay).[61] Can the facts in the charging document be disproved

[61] The ICTY Appeals Chamber defined hearsay evidence as an out of court statement tendered 'to establish the truth of what that person says'. See *Prosecutor v Aleksovski*, (Decision on Prosecutor's Appeal on Admissibility of Evidence) IT-95-14/1-AR-73 (16 February 1999) ('*Aleksovski* Admissibility Decision'), para 14. While hearsay evidence is admissible at the ICC, Chambers take a 'cautious approach in assessing evidence originating from hearsay . . . assessing the weight to be accorded to it, taking into account the context and conditions in which such evidence was obtained, and with due consideration of the impossibility of questioning the information source in court'. *Prosecutor v Bemba* (Trial Judgment) ICC-01/05-01/08 (21 March 2016) para 238. The ICC Appeals

and how? Are there any possible explanations to damaging facts? All facts that are beyond change—i.e. facts that cannot be disputed or where an alternative explanation cannot be provided—must be analysed clinically: what possible inferences and conclusions can be drawn? Ultimately, the goal is to piece the facts together to establish reasonable doubt. The context may be important, since certain facts when considered in isolation may be misleading.

- **List possible legal defences together with anticipated attacks for each legal theory.** Select the best possible theory of the case. Unless defence counsel can articulate clearly and concisely what the case is all about, they do not know their theory of the case.
- **Identify investigative tasks.** Identifying the investigative tasks of a case is part and parcel of the process of developing a theory of the case. Defence counsel should identify what further investigations need to be done from the client's instructions and the evidence gathered. Potential theories and approaches will emerge, which in turn will help to narrow down and focus the investigative efforts. Ultimately, the theory of the defence case will emerge. All actions thereafter—during or outside of the court proceedings—will dictate the course of action to be taken by defence counsel.
- **Draft a general analysis.** When brainstorming the case, defence counsel should draft a general analysis to facilitate discussions with team members, including:
  - Anticipated legal issues;
  - Possible theories of the defence case;
  - Defence counsel's impressions of the complaining witnesses or client;
  - Need for experts;
  - Inconsistencies within the documents; and
  - A general list of possible investigative assignments.

At the conclusion of the brainstorming, the defence theory should be developed as soon as possible. The theory will enable defence counsel to focus investigative activities accordingly. Every investigative step should be in line with and advance the defence's theory. Suffice it to say, the prosecution will be doing the same: attempting to identify the possible defence theories and looking for ways to dissect and destroy them.

14.5 Effective Use of Investigators

Anyone employed by defence counsel to investigate acts on behalf of defence counsel must conduct themselves professionally and ethically, as their conduct directly implicates defence counsel.[62] Thus, before hiring an investigator, his or her background, professional

Chamber held that "the fact that evidence is hearsay does not necessarily deprive it of probative value, but does indicate that the weight or probative value afforded to it may be less 'although even this will depend upon the infinitely variable circumstances which surround hearsay evidence'. *Prosecutor v Ngudjolo* (Appeal Judgment) ICC-01/04-02/12 (27 February 2015) para 226, quoting *Aleksovski* Admissibility Decision, para 15.

[62] See ICTY Code Conduct, art 34, stating that 'Counsel shall be responsible for the conduct of other members of his team who provide services for counsel.'

qualifications, and experience must be checked. This is an integral part of defence counsel's due diligence obligations.[63]

It is important to find an investigator who is capable and willing to provide an accurate, comprehensive, and objective analysis. The concept of a private investigator may be foreign in some jurisdictions. Using lawyers as investigators may seem reasonable, however, if investigating is not part of the legal culture, their legal background is not helpful. Former investigating judges, police inspectors, and detectives may be ideal candidates because of their established set of skills.

In selecting an investigator, the preferred skills, qualifications, and qualities may depend on the type and nature of the case. For instance, in dealing with military events, it may be necessary to search and gather coded or specially drafted documents. A former military analyst, who knows how to locate these documents, how to analyse their content, and who to contact for more information and verification, will be invaluable.

In some cases, it may be important to consider and appreciate linguistic or cultural nuances. In complex cases, several investigators and analysts may be necessary, each focusing on his or her respective area of expertise. Realistically, the investigative team should be selected based on the specific needs of the case. Thus, defence counsel must know their case and appreciate the issues involved before hiring investigators.

Defence counsel are responsible for providing guidance to and supervising the work of investigators, and thus are well advised to draft an agreement for the investigator to sign, bearing in mind three points:

- The investigator will need explicit guidance on what to do, what to look for, and what the relevant issues are;
- The investigator will need explicit guidance on how to properly collect evidence to avoid any foundational challenges or problems with the chain of custody during the trial; and
- The investigator will need explicit guidance on how to ethically carry out the assigned tasks.

No assumptions should be made that an investigator will know exactly what to do. Investigators should be instructed that when in doubt, they must contact defence counsel for further instructions before taking action. Defence counsel are ultimately responsible for actions taken by investigators acting on their instructions.

[63] Due diligence is a defence counsel's duty to do anything and everything to ensure that all fair trial rights are fully accorded to the client, including making legal challenges through written and oral submissions, checking the veracity and accuracy of evidence that may be used against the client, objecting to the admissibility of evidence, confronting witnesses, consulting with experts when necessary and relevant, and so on. *Prosecutor v Tadić* (Decision on Appellant's Motion for the Extension of the Time-Limit and Admission of Additional Evidence) IT-94-1 (15 October 1998) para 47: 'Due diligence is a necessary quality of counsel who defend accused persons before the International Tribunal .... As stated above, the requirement of due diligence includes the appropriate use of all mechanisms of protection and compulsion available under the Statute and the Rules of the International Tribunal to bring evidence on behalf of an accused before the Trial Chamber.' The ICTY Appeals Chamber in *Krstić* added that defence counsel must also bring 'any difficulties in relation to obtaining evidence on behalf of the accused ... to the attention of the Trial Chamber'. *Prosecutor v Krstić* (Decision on Application for Subpoenas) IT-98-33-A (1 July 2003) paras 5, 9–14.

14.5.1 Investigative Memorandum

Before going over the case with the investigator, defence counsel should draft a memorandum outlining the charges, facts, witnesses, possible defences, strengths and weaknesses of the case, and any other information that might be useful for the investigator. Defence counsel must ensure that investigators, at a minimum, are familiar with the documents in the file, have a general sense of the theory of the case, and appreciate who may be potential witnesses, the weaknesses and strengths of the case, and the general efforts required of them to get the case ready for trial. Since the investigator cannot be expected to know all the intricacies of the substantive criminal law and procedure, it is useful to list in the memorandum the elements of each crime charged. This will allow the investigator to know and appreciate what the prosecution will need to prove and, conversely, what the defence needs to challenge.

14.5.2 Brainstorming the Case with the Investigator

Discussing the case with the investigator is one of the most important aspects of pre-trial case preparation in search for and developing the theory of the case.

After reviewing the memorandum and any selected documents provided to the investigator, the investigator should be sufficiently prepared to bring to the brainstorming session his or her knowledge and experience, with case-specific ideas and suggestions. By going over the documents and discussing the possible theories of the case, the investigator can assist defence counsel by identifying the factual issues requiring resolution, providing impressions of the strengths and weaknesses of the case, listing and prioritizing the investigative tasks, and, above all, acting as a sounding board by drawing out the prosecution's points of view.

In sum, defence counsel and the investigator must focus on the irreconcilable aspects of the case which must be addressed and explained at trial. This will inform defence counsel about what must be investigated, what to prioritize, whether experts may be needed, and to what extent the resources available for investigative tasks will suffice to carry out what is absolutely necessary and reasonable to ensure that the client is afforded all of his statutorily (and constitutional) fair trial rights, commonly reflected in Articles 14 and 15 of the International Covenant on Civil and Political Rights.[64]

14.6 Collection of Evidence

It is important to handle, process, and store evidence with extreme caution. During the trial proceedings the prosecution may challenge how evidence was collected. It is good practice to have detailed instructions for the investigators designed to preserve *the chain of custody*—an uninterrupted detailed record documenting the handling of a piece of evidence

[64] International Covenant on Civil and Political Rights, arts 14 and 15 <https://www.ohchr.org/en/professionalinterest/pages/ccpr.aspx> accessed 13 February 2020; see also M G Karnavas 'ADC-ICTY Legacy Conference – The Rights of the Accused' <http://michaelgkarnavas.net/files/ICTYLegacyConference_Karnavas.pdf> accessed 13 February 2020.

and showing that it has been unaltered. The moment a piece of evidence is collected, the chain of custody commences. The chain of custody is necessary for laying the foundation for accepting the evidence at trial:[65]

- *Relevance*—the evidence has a tendency to make the existence of a fact or consequence more probable or less probable than without the evidence;[66]
- *Authenticity*—the matter or thing in question is exactly what it is claimed to be. For example: the knife, the gun, the video, amongst other things;[67] and
- *Reliability*—the evidence is in the same condition as when it was used or located; that is, it was not tampered with or altered, or based on (un)corroborated hearsay.[68]

Part of the investigative process may involve the collection of physical evidence, so it is important to appreciate the need to exercise extreme caution when handling such evidence. Depending on the case, physical evidence may come in all different shapes and forms, and may come from different sources. A host of ethical issues may arise when coming across and handling physical evidence. Consequently, it is important for investigators to have detailed instructions on what to do or not to do when dealing with physical evidence.

14.6.1 Crime Scene Evidence

The most delicate evidence comes from a crime scene. Since part of the investigative process is to visit the relevant areas where any incidents or crimes may have occurred, it is not out of the ordinary to occasionally come across a piece of evidence that may have been left behind, unnoticed by the police investigators or authorized officials. In such an eventuality, any tampering with such evidence would amount to a serious breach of ethics and may even constitute a crime.

The question that begs answering is what to do once confronted with such evidence? The simple answer is: *it depends*. The first thing to do, irrespective of whether a decision is made to collect the evidence or simply leave it, is to photograph it at its exact location as found. If a decision is made to pick the evidence up and examine it, the evidence may be compromised, especially if it contains fibres or fingerprints that may be useful. As such, care must be taken when lifting evidence. It is prudent to wear rubber gloves to avoid compromising the evidence and to avoid any potential health risks from handling it. If a decision is made to

[65] The ICTY generally applies the 'principle of free evaluation of evidence'. ICTY RPE, Rule 89. This principle favours the admissibility of evidence and provides that it should be evaluated in a light most favourable to the accused. *Prosecutor v Stakić* (Provisional Order on the Standards Governing the Admission of Evidence and Identification) IT-97-24-PT (25 February 2002) p. 4. The basic test for the admissibility of evidence is that it be relevant and probative, though in assessing the evidence and ascribing what weight, if any, to give to it, authenticity and reliability play a major role. If the probative value of the evidence is substantially outweighed by the need to ensure a fair trial, then it should not be admitted. One example for excluding evidence in furtherance of promoting a fair trial is where evidence is obtained by methods which cast substantial doubt on its reliability or if its admission is antithetical to, and would seriously damage, the integrity of the proceedings (eg torture-tainted evidence). ICTY RPE, Rule 95.

[66] ICTY RPE, Rule 89(C).

[67] ibid Rule 89(E).

[68] *Prosecutor v Aleksovski,* (Decision on Prosecutor's Appeal on Admissibility of Evidence) IT-95-14/1-AR73 (16 February 1999) para 15, stating that Rule 89(C) gives the Trial Chamber broad discretion to admit relevant hearsay evidence, but that the evidence must be shown to be reliable.

collect the evidence, it would be useful to have a clean container (plastic baggies and paper bags depending on the evidence) to collect it. Before making such decisions, it is necessary to ask what, if anything, will be done with the evidence. In other words, will it be independently tested (assuming that such testing is permissible), or will it be turned over to police investigators.

Collecting evidence to destroy it or to hide it is impermissible, illegal, and unethical. It is defence counsels' responsibility to advise and instruct their investigators in advance as to what, if anything, should be done with such evidence. The better practice is that defence counsel instruct investigators to refrain from doing anything before contacting defence counsel for further instructions. This message should periodically be drilled into anyone working on the defence team, but especially for investigators. If instructions are not followed, it is incumbent on defence counsel to act immediately. Depending on the circumstances, defence counsel may need to inform the prosecution and the court, that the investigator has compromised the integrity of the physical evidence or has tampered with the witnesses.

Mistakes can be cured and even forgiven; cover-ups cannot and will not be forgiven. Ethical lapses can turn defence counsel into an accessory to a crime, resulting in serious consequences. No case or client is worth risking defence counsels' reputation, integrity, and above all, their license to practice law.

14.6.2 Documentary Evidence

During the course of the investigation it may be necessary to gather documentary evidence either from official archives or private individuals. Since some of this evidence may be useful to introduce at trial, it is vital to ensure that defence counsel can demonstrate that the documents are relevant, authentic, and reliable. Since it may be necessary to demonstrate the origin and authenticity of the document, it is important to keep in mind that the custodian of the document may need to give evidence or submit some sort of proof as to the authenticity, condition, and origin of the document. As such, investigators must keep track of where and from whom documentary evidence has been obtained, whether revealing the source of the documents would present a problem, whether the custodian would object to having his or her name associated with the documents and would be willing to give sworn evidence as to how he or she came into possession of the documents.

Defence counsel should always be mindful of confidentiality and the protection of sources. For example, in *Prlić* et al at the ICTY, the Prlić Defence was provided with certain documents to be used during the trial proceedings with the understanding that the sources of the documents would remain confidential. Having a professional obligation not to reveal those sources—because to have done otherwise could have undermined the integrity of the Prlić Defence and could have sent a chilling message to future sources—the Prlić Defence did not disclose the identity of the sources to the Trial Chamber.[69]

[69] *Prosecutor v Prlić* et al, (Jadranko Prlić's Motion for Protective Measures of Certain Documents & Additional Classification of Certain Subjects Included in the Motion for Admission of Documentary Evidence) IT-04-74-T (4 January 2009) para 1.

In *Prlić* et al., the Trial Chamber decided there was insufficient information to justify and grant protective measures to these sources, and that the Prlić Defence never should have promised anonymity to the sources. In an oral decision, the Trial Chamber asked Counsel for Prlić to explain why the witnesses refused to reveal that they provided certain documents, prompting a refusal to reveal the sources of the documents without their consent.[70] This led to the Trial Chamber having the ICTY Registrar appoint an *Amicus Curiae* (independent counsel) to determine whether the repeated refusal by Prlić's Counsel to disclose the sources of the documents constituted professional misconduct.

The *Amicus Curiae* found that 'the sum of the circumstances does not permit us to establish the determining facts that indicate that the Defence Counsel acted to "willfully and knowingly interfere with the administration of justice" by failing to identify the sources of the documents requested for admission by way of a written motion'.[71] The *Amicus Curiae* reasoned that 'the importance of sources in the context of an investigation, as the latter seeks to collect prosecution evidence against a person being investigated or defence evidence for an accused, is fundamentally the same. The bond of trust that rests on the respect of a commitment of confidentiality and non-disclosure of the identity is essential'.[72] Ultimately, the Trial Chamber dropped its investigation.[73]

While defence counsel can enter into confidentiality agreements with sources, much like journalists do in their investigative reporting,[74] consequences can flow. The major consequence of using confidentiality agreements is the loss of evidence. The trial chamber is entitled to know the provenance of material used as evidence and the refusal to give up a source can result in the material not being admitted into the record. Counsel, as part of their ethical duties, must inform the client of this consequence. If the client insists on using the material, of course, the source needs to be made aware and given an opportunity to consider whether to risk being exposed.

14.7 Interviewing Witnesses

The manner of conducting interviews is vitally important for the case. Each legal system has its own peculiarities regulating the taking of statements and interviewing some categories of witnesses, such as traumatized witnesses or victims. Defence counsel must be acquainted with the procedures and practices, and must convey them to their investigators.

70 *Prosecutor v Prlić* et al (Order Appointing an Amicus Curiae) IT-04-74-T (3 July 2009) p. 4.

71 *Prosecutor v Prlić* et al (Legal Opinion—*Amicus Curiae* Response to the Chamber's Questions Following the Order Appointing an *Amicus Curiae* of 25 August 2009) IT-04-74-T (6 October 2009) para 90.

72 ibid para 84.

73 *Prosecutor v Prlić* et al (Decision Subsequent to *Amicus Curiae* Report) IT-04-74-T (3 November 2009).

74 See Testimony of Judith Miller, Senior Writer for the New York Times, before the Senate Judiciary Committee of the US Senate (19 October 2005) <https://www.judiciary.senate.gov/imo/media/doc/miller_testimony_10_19_05.pdf> accessed 16 February 2020: 'Confidential sources are the life's blood of journalism. Without them, whether they are in government, large or small companies, or in non-profit organizations, people like me would be out of business. As I painfully learned while covering intelligence estimates of Saddam Hussein's weapons of mass destruction, we are only as good as our sources. If they are wrong, we will be wrong. And a source's confidence that we will not divulge their identity is crucial to his or her readiness to come to us with allegations of fraud or abuse or other wrongdoing, or even a dissenting view about government policy or business practices that the American public may need to know.'

It is imperative to recognize that a witness is under no obligation to cooperate with defence counsel, to speak or answer questions, to provide a statement, or to hand over any physical evidence. Not only is it counterproductive to try to compel an unwilling witness to cooperate, it could lead to a perception that the witness is being harassed or coerced.

If a witness whom defence counsel intends to interview is represented by another counsel, defence counsel must notify the witness' counsel before approaching and interviewing the witness. Counsel for the represented witness can advise his or her client of the right to refuse to cooperate, however, it is up to the witness to make that decision. It is good practice to invite counsel for the witness to be present during the interview.

When interviewing prosecution witnesses, defence counsel must avoid giving an impression that they are trying to elicit a particular answer by asking leading questions or confronting witnesses with alternative accounts. The safest practice—which applies when interviewing all witnesses—is to avoid posing leading questions or putting alternative accounts.

If there is evidence available that could assist the witness' memory, it may be appropriate to clarify or refresh the witness' memory. This should only be done when what is used to clarify or refresh the witness' memory is something that the witness has generated or has previously seen.

Telling witnesses the theory of the defence case should be avoided. By telling witnesses the potential theories, the interviewer runs the risk of influencing the witnesses, or at least giving that impression. This could have serious consequences: witnesses could mistakenly assume they are being pressured to tailor their statement to fit the defence theory. It could also contaminate the source of the evidence: the independent memory of the witnesses. This would raise the spectre of witness tampering—another grave ethical breach to be avoided.

One method to use in nudging a potential witness to cooperate is to first approach a friend or acquaintance of the witness and see if he or she could assist with setting up a first informal meeting with the potential witness. Using third parties can be useful in explaining to potential witnesses the basis of the interest in having them answer a few questions. Having these third parties present during the first meeting may be helpful in ensuring that the ice is broken and that the meeting does not go beyond providing some general explanations. It also helps to have a friendly face present who can vouch for the nature of the meeting in the event there is any question as to the tone and tenor of the discussion. There is one cautionary caveat: it is never good practice to interview a witness in the presence of a third party or other witnesses.

The best approach in dealing with any witness is to inform him or her of the overall objective: to assist the accused in the preparation of the defence case. To avoid any ethical dilemmas, the best practice is to:

- Never suggest to a witness what the answer to a question should be;
- Never tell a witness what he or she should say or testify;
- Never tell a witness to destroy evidence;
- Never tell a witness not to cooperate with the prosecution;
- Never threaten a witness either directly or indirectly;
- Never misrepresent to a witness your identity or function;
- Never misrepresent facts to a witness;

- Always remind a witness that you are only interested in the truth; and
- Always be courteous and respectful to a witness.

A good practice is to assume that the information being provided may not be entirely accurate or even true. Even if persuaded that the witness is providing an accurate account, diligence requires double-checking the witness' account against other reliable evidence.

After interviewing witnesses, it is good practice to have a debriefing session as soon as possible. During these debriefing sessions, defence counsel and investigators should assess the interviews, noting their impressions and any other vital information, such as whether there is a need for a follow-up, whether the documents were received, whether names of other potential witnesses were provided, and so on. Impressions from the interview must be kept separately from the investigative report or witness statement. Such work product needs to be kept separate and should never be disclosed to the prosecution. Also, all information from witnesses is confidential, so it must be treated with care and stored in a secure environment.

Defence counsels' duty to zealously represent clients is tempered by the ethical constraints generally spelled out in the codes of conduct, and defence counsels' overarching duties to the court in ensuring the integrity of the proceedings. At the ICTY, there are examples where defence counsel have breached their ethical obligations and duties to the Court when handling witness evidence.

In *Tadić*, the ICTY Appeals Chamber (ruling in the first instance) found that defence counsel Milan Vujin, acted 'dishonestly and improperly' by coaching and bribing witnesses into providing false and inaccurate evidence.[75] The Appeals Chamber found that Mr Vujin:

- Instructed witnesses preparing to make statements to his co-counsel to lie;
- Nodded his head to indicate to witnesses during their interviews when to say 'yes' and when to say 'no';
- Intimidated witnesses in a manner which dissuaded them from telling the truth;
- Knowingly instructed a witness to make false statements to the tribunal; and
- Paid money to a person giving a statement when pleased with the information provided.[76]

The Appeals Chamber remarked that while such 'conduct on the part of the counsel [was] intended ... to assist in winning the case for the client whom counsel represents,' counsel's conduct 'ha[d] been *against* the interest of his client' and 'even worse, particularly when the client is in custody and relies so heavily upon his counsel for assistance ... [such] conduct strikes at the very heart of the criminal justice system'.[77] The conviction was upheld on appeal, with the Appeals Chamber ordering that the Registry would have discretion to refer the matter to Mr Vujin's national bar.[78] Mr Vujin was given a fine and removed from the ICTY list of defence counsel.

In *Lukić and Lukić*, Jelena Rašić, a member of the defence team, plead guilty to bribing a potential witness, Mr Tabaković, by asking him to sign a pre-prepared witness statement

[75] *Prosecutor v Tadić* (Judgment on Allegations of Contempt Against Prior Counsel, Milan Vujin) IT-94-1-A-R77 (31 January 2000) para 167.
[76] ibid paras 131–59.
[77] ibid para 167 (italics in original).
[78] *Prosecutor v Tadić* (Appeal Judgment on Allegations of Contempt Against Prior Counsel, Milan Vujin) IT-94-1-A-R77 (27 February 2001) p 7.

in exchange for €1,000 and by offering him additional money to testify on behalf of her client.[79] Ms Rašić also admitted that she gave Mr Tabaković two pre-prepared statements, the details of the creators of which were left blank, to be signed by two other potential witnesses in exchange for €1,000. Mr Tabaković's statement and the other two statements were later revised and updated, and disclosed to the prosecution.[80] The Trial Chamber sentenced Ms Rašić to twelve months of imprisonment, deducting seventy-eight days already spent in detention and suspending the remaining eight months of the sentence, on the condition that Ms Rašić would not commit any crime during the next two years.[81] The Appeals Chamber upheld the sentence.[82]

14.8 Taking Notes and Statements

Unless absolutely required, it is never a good idea for defence counsel to take a statement or to tape-record an interview without knowing in advance what the witness will say, to protect the defence case.

It is not advisable to take detailed notes during the first meeting. Best to have an informal conversation to determine if the witness is friendly, useful, informative, and to determine the likely content of their evidence. Taking notes in subsequent meetings with the witness is useful in preparing a statement or an interview summary, or can be used to brief other investigation team members. Such notes are considered work product and are not subject to being disclosed to the prosecution.[83] The better practice is to have a separate team member take notes while the interviewer concentrates on asking questions (having a conversation) with the witness.

Only after hearing the witness' account, and only if it is helpful to the case, should a decision be made on whether to make a written statement. Deciding whether to memorialize a witness' statement or whether to abandon a witness is not always readily apparent. It may be that the witness has some useful information, but also has damaging information which is far too harmful to use in the defence case. If the harmful information outweighs the useful information, taking a written statement is not recommended. Since there is no obligation to inform the prosecution of any information gathered through investigation that is to the client's disfavour, there is no profit in taking a statement or tape-recording an interview which may inadvertently fall into the hands of the prosecution. It is good practice, when possible, to double-check the information against other witnesses and other documentary evidence before taking a statement.

When taking a statement, the better practice is to keep the statement short, concrete, and relevant; less is more. Simple and short sentences without adjectives and adverbs work best. A good statement describes (as opposed to tells) what the witness saw, heard, and perceived, hopefully enabling the reader or listener to vicariously experience the witness' account. No liberties should be taken when drafting a statement and the embellishment of facts is

[79] *Prosecutor v Rašić* (Written Reasons for Oral Sentencing Judgment, delivered orally on 7 February 2012 and filed on 6 March 2012) IT-98-3211-R77.2, para 11.

[80] ibid paras 12–13.

[81] ibid para 31.

[82] *Prosecutor v Rašić* (Judgment) IT-98-32/1-R77.2-A (16 November 2012).

[83] Documents prepared by defence counsel in the course of litigation are protected under the related doctrine of 'work product'. This doctrine protects reports, memoranda, and other internal documents from disclosure. See Rule 70(A) of the ICTY RPE.

inappropriate and unethical. Witnesses called to give evidence will be held accountable to what was previously memorialized as being a *true, accurate, and a complete* statement. And if the interviewer caused a misrepresentation in the witness' statement provided during the interview, serious consequences could follow, with defence counsel being ultimately responsible.

14.9 Reimbursing Witnesses for Costs Related to Interviews and Testifying

There should be no dilemma as to whether defence counsel can pay witnesses for their testimony. Suborning perjury by bribing witnesses to give false testimony amounts to knowingly and intentionally breaching ethical obligations and gives rise to criminal charges.

Defence counsel may reimburse witnesses for their reasonable travel costs. A witness who incurs financial losses or expenses (such as taking time off work or having to pay for accommodation and food) as a result of the interview should be reimbursed, provided the expenses are reasonable and necessary.

It is prudent to always keep the receipts and to document any reimbursement to clearly specify what the payment was for. Defence counsel must make it clear to the witness that the payment is not being made for the substance of the testimony, but is made solely to compensate the witness for the money lost. No promises should be made to reward or give an impression that the payment is made for the substance of the testimony.

14.10 Working with Expert Witnesses

A witness with special knowledge, training, or experience whose purpose is to assist the trial judges in understanding the evidence or determining a fact in issue is generally considered an 'expert witness'. An expert witness is 'a person whom by virtue of some specialized knowledge, skills or training can assist the trier of fact to understand or determine an issue in dispute'.[84] Expert witnesses are called to proffer an opinion on a fact or issue as a means of assisting the fact finder (the judge). Normally, they are only necessary to assist with technical, scientific, or other information that is ordinarily outside the judges' knowledge and experience.[85] Expert witnesses are prohibited from rendering an opinion as to the ultimate legal issue, that is, on the issue of guilt or innocence.[86] They are also generally prohibited from rendering an opinion on a legal issue.[87]

[84] *Prosecutor v Galić* (Decision Concerning the Expert Witness Ewa Tabeau and Richard Philipps) IT-98-29-T (3 July 2002) p 2; *Prosecutor v Brđanin* (Decision on Prosecution's Submission of Statement of Expert Witness Ewan Brown) IT-99-36-T (3 June 2003) p 4; *Prosecutor v Strugar* (Decision on Defence Motions to Oppose Expert Reports Pursuant to Rule 94*bis*) IT-01-42-PT (13 January 2006) para 37; *Prosecutor v Milošević* (Decision on Admission of Expert Report of Robert Donia) IT-15-98-29/1-T (15 December 2007) para 7

[85] *Prosecutor v Delalić* (Decision on the Motion by the Prosecution to Allow the Investigators to Follow the Trial During the Testimonies of the Witnesses) (20 March 1997) para 10.

[86] *Prosecutor v Hadžihasanović,* (Decision on Report of Prosecution Expert Klaus Reinhardt) IT-01-47-T (11 February 2004) p 3. '[A]n expert witness may not be authorized to offer his opinion on the criminal liability of the accused, a matter which falls within the sole jurisdiction of the Chamber at the close of the trial[.]' See also *Prosecutor v Kordić and Čerkez* (Transcript) IT-95-14-2-T (28 January 2000) p 13278, ll 16–25, p 13279, ll 1–12.

[87] While experts are generally prohibited from rendering an opinion on a legal issue, experts at the ICTY have been permitted to testify about issues related to, for example, the constitutional framework, interpretation of

Before a person can be certified as an expert (in some national courts there are lists of certified experts from which to select), he or she must have the requisite expertise and ability to perform independent expert evaluations, and should be willing to give an opinion in a rational, objective, and timely manner. Irrespective of the fact that the expert is court-certified and has an impeccable or erudite educational and professional background, defence counsel should not overestimate the 'objectivity' or 'quality' of the expert witness' opinions or findings.

As with lay witnesses, it is unethical to attempt to influence the content of the expert report, for instance, by limiting the material and providing limited facts for the expert's analysis, or worse yet, suggesting a desired result. It is unethical to make experts part of the defence team by letting them sit through the defence briefing or brainstorming sessions. It is also unethical to prepare a report in advance and have an expert sign on to it when he or she was not the author.

Experts should be properly qualified to address the subject matter, and must provide their opinion impartially and transparently by clearly explaining the facts they relied on and the methods used in arriving at their conclusions. If the expert's report is not helpful to the defence or otherwise does not satisfy defence counsel, the best practice is not to use that report, as opposed to searching for an expert who can produce a report tailored to a desired result.

Defence counsel may pay expert witnesses for their work, but the amount must be reasonable and commensurate with their services. Any financial incentives offered to influence the expert's conclusions or report are unethical.

14.11 Witness Proofing

If the witness is expected to testify, it is prudent to proof the witness in advance as to what the expected questions will be during the courtroom proceedings. Generally, 'proofing' refers to 'a meeting ... between a party to the proceedings and a witness, usually shortly before the witness is to testify in court, the purpose of which is to prepare and familiarize the witness with courtroom procedures and to review their evidence'.[88]

While defence counsel aim to meet their obligation to adequately prepare a witness for testimony, they should be careful not to cross the line into witness coaching. Witness proofing is effective when done properly. It entails:

- Familiarizing the witnesses with what happens in court, the witnesses' function, their basic rights such as the right not to answer questions if they are self-incriminating, the role of the parties and judges, and maybe even a walk through the courtroom; and

laws, and regulations that existed at the time and place of conflicts, and the procedural dimensions of the legal system relevant to the events. See *Prosecutor v Blaškić*, IT-95-14-T (Transcript) 297–358. Expert witness Dr Zoran Pajic testified on the constitutional framework of BiH from 30 June 1997 until 3 July 1997. See also *Prosecutor v Hadžihasanović* (Decision on Report of Prosecution Expert Klaus Reinhardt) IT-01-47-T (11 February 2004) pp 3–4. General Klaus Reinhardt, commander of German troops within NATO forces stationed in BiH, was permitted to express his opinion on the issue of subordination, a matter of military law.

[88] *Prosecutor v Haradinaj* et al (Decision on Defence Request for Audio-Recording of Prosecution Witnesses Proofing Sessions) IT-04-84-D (23 May 2007) para 8, citing *Prosecutor v Milutinović* (Decision on Ojdanić Motion to prohibit Witness Proofing) IT-05-87 (12 December 2006).

- Going over the witness' testimony, including any documents that are likely to be shown to the witness from which questions may be asked, and giving the witness an opportunity to refresh his or her memory of statements he or she may have given in the past.

The familiarization aspect of witness proofing has been separated into a distinct category of witness preparation. It is considered an essential function. At the ICTY, the familiarization process has been viewed as part and parcel of the general functions carried out by the Victims and Witnesses Section.[89]

The preparation or 'proofing' aspect is generally performed by defence counsel, though it is useful if the investigator is aware of the technique and, if possible, is present during the proofing session. It is important to understand that this process is not for the purpose of 'coaching' a witness as to what he or she should say. That would be unethical. Generally, during the proofing session the witness should be informed of how the questioning process occurs, the questions he or she can expect to hear, the general order of the questions, and the documents on which he or she is expected to comment. The better practice recommended to defence counsel is to:

- Review the statements together with the witness and question the witness on inconsistencies in his or her prior statements;
- Explain the topics that the calling party intends to cover in direct examination;
- Explain the topics on which the witness may be questioned during cross-examination;
- Explain to the witness that he or she may be questioned in court on matters other than those upon which investigators previously questioned the witness;
- Show the witness potential exhibits and ask him or her to comment on them for the purpose of determining the utility of using the exhibits in court;
- Explain the role of the various participants in the courtroom;
- Inform the witness about appropriate witness behaviour, including the need to speak slowly and concisely; and
- Subject to the restrictions below, answer any questions the witness may have, including about what to expect in court.

It is prohibited to:

- Seek to influence the substance of the witness' answers, either directly or indirectly, for instance, by informing the witness of the type of evidence that would assist the calling

[89] Unlike at the ICTY, at the International Criminal Court (ICC) the issue of witness proofing is controversial, with some chambers allowing both witness familiarization and preparation, and others allowing witness familiarization by the Victims and Witnesses Unit only, and prohibiting proofing by the calling party. Generally, the argument goes that proofing has been used to coach witnesses to tailor their evidence, thus obstructing or perverting the course of justice. Concerning the inconsistencies in approach to proofing at the ICC, and other tribunals, see Witnesses Before the International Criminal Court, An International Bar Association International Criminal Court Programme Report on the ICC's Efforts and Challenges to Protect, Support and Ensure the Rights of Witnesses, July 2013, pp 21–26, <http://www.ibanet.org/ICC_ICL_Programme/Reports.aspx>. The issue of whether proofing is acceptable at the ICC is not without academic debate. Advocating against the practice of witness proofing, see W Jordash,'The Practice of "Witness Proofing" in International Criminal Tribunals: Why the International Criminal Court Should Prohibit the Practice' (2009) 22 Leiden Journal of International Law 501; K Ambos, '"Witness Proofing"' Before the ICC: Neither Legally Admissible nor Necessary' in C Stahn and G Sluiter (eds) *The Emerging Practice Of The International Criminal Court* (Brill 2009) 599. For an opposing view, see R Karemaker, B D Taylor, and T W Pittman, 'Witness Proofing in International Criminal Tribunals: A Critical Analysis of Widening Procedural Divergence' (2008) 21 Leiden Journal of International Law 683.

party's case, suggesting whether the witness' answers are right, or leading the witness in an inappropriate way;

- Train the witness on questions and answers expected during the witness' in-court testimony so that the witness memorizes those questions and answers; and
- Inform the witness of the evidence of other witnesses (including oral testimony and prior recorded statements).

14.12 Investigating During the Trial and Beyond

Although most of the investigation by the defence should have been performed during the pre-trial stage, much will remain to be done as the trial begins. Usually the investigation at the trial stage is focused on background checks of witnesses, double-checking what witnesses may have represented in statements, verifying the veracity of any information that the witnesses reveal in court that was not previously known, and, of course, searching for witnesses and documentary evidence for the defence case. While the defence may have identified the core of its witnesses and documentary evidence for its case, because of the organic nature of the trial there may be a need to further investigate and fine-tune the anticipated defence case.

The defence case will depend on what the prosecution credibly established during its case-in-chief. The final decision on whether and to what extent to put on a defence case (to call witnesses) will be made after the prosecution has rested its case. Whether to put on a case is also influenced by what other co-accused are anticipated to do, as well as any risks associated with allowing the prosecution to put on additional evidence through cross-examination of the defence witnesses or to call additional witnesses in rebuttal. There is no sense in opening a door for more or overlooked incriminating evidence by putting on a case that does not effectively advance the defence's theory of the case. It is not just about strategy and tactics, but also about having sufficient information to make an informed decision. Hence, the investigation never ceases from the moment the defence gets into the case until the trial is over, and sometimes it carries on even beyond.[90]

14.13 Conclusion

The reform of the criminal procedures in some of the states that emerged from the former Yugoslavia provides for party-driven procedures, transitioning from civil law procedures to a more hybrid system with adversarial modalities. These new procedures require defence counsel to be much more engaged both at the pre-trial and trial stages of the proceedings. Defence counsel are now responsible for conducting their own investigations in search for evidence. This requires a new skill set and solid understanding of the ethical considerations

[90] ICTY RPE Rule 115—consistent with the practice before other international(ised) criminal tribunals—permited a party to present additional evidence to the Appeals Chamber during the appeal stage. If the Appeals Chamber found: (1) that the additional evidence was not available at trial; (2) that the additional evidence is relevant and credible; and (3) that it could have been a decisive factor in reaching the decision at trial, the Appeals Chamber would consider the additional evidence and any rebuttal material along with the evidence already on record.

guiding defence investigations and the gathering of evidence. Many lessons and best practices can be drawn from the ICTY legacy, considering the similarities between the ICTY procedure and the legal reforms adopted by these states. And for defence counsel who practised at the ICTY, they will find that the adversarial skills they acquired and experience gained are directly transferable to their national practice.

Throughout the investigation process defence counsel are likely to come across various obstacles. Difficulties in finding witnesses, documents, and obstruction by the prosecution or State authorities require defence counsel to resort to the most efficient ways of overcoming these obstacles, while remaining within the ethical boundaries prescribed by the code of conduct. Summing up some practical considerations discussed, defence counsel when undertaking investigations are advised to:

- Prepare the case by learning the facts and the law, analysing the indictment and evidence disclosed by the prosecution;
- Choose investigators based on the specifics of the case;
- Develop a theory of the case as early as practicable and focus investigative activities accordingly. Every investigative step should advance the defence theory;
- Give explicit instructions and training to defence team members, especially investigators, on acceptable ethical boundaries of investigation and gathering of evidence;
- Consider evidentiary principles and rules as to the admissibility of evidence to avoid, to the extent possible, the exclusion of evidence gathered; and
- Identify as early as possible contacts and potential sources of information and proceed transparently and methodically in collecting information.

The success (or failure) of defence counsel rests on preparation and a clear understanding of what is required and what is prohibited. With proper planning and adherence to the practical and ethical considerations discussed in this chapter, defence counsel will be able to diligently conduct investigations, an essential element in providing zealous representation to the client. There is also the issue of having adequate resources, especially for investigating the case, which, inexorably, includes doing due diligence on the evidence gathered by the prosecution (how reliable and exact is it) plus gathering evidence in support of the defence case.

Unless the accused is sufficiently wealthy and is prepared to generously fund his or her defence, generally, court-assigned defence counsel are inherently disadvantaged from an *equality of arms*[91] perspective. By the time defence counsel get involved in a case and come into possession of all the disclosure material, the prosecution has been investigating, meeting with witnesses, and fine-tuning its case. Understandably, the prosecution is given greater resources and access to witnesses and evidence given their functions and responsibilities.

For defence counsel to effectively and ethically investigate a case, resources (proportionate to those available to the prosecution, as opposed to the same amount) are required to employ competent investigators. 'Even a competent lawyer may not be able to mount an

[91] '[E]quality of arms obligates a judicial body to ensure that neither party is put at a disadvantage when presenting its case.' *Prosecutor v Tadić* (Judgment) IT-94-1-A (15 July 1999) paras 48, 50 (discussing principles laid down by the European Court of Human Rights and by the Human Rights Committee). While art 21 of the

adequate defence against the state, with all its resources, if he has next to nothing for investigation and effectively works for starvation wages.'[92]

Regrettably, almost without exception, the states which emerged from the former Yugoslavia which adopted adversarial modalities in their procedures, afford indigent accused only legal representation, without providing any funds for investigative purposes.[93] As a consequence, either no meaningful investigative action is taken, or the accused (if not in custody) or their family assist in investigating, or defence counsel personally does the investigation (and runs the risk of being a witness or being accused of tampering with the evidence) or defence counsel pays for investigative services from the meagre legal fees provided for his or her legal services.

Unquestionably, there are serious ethical pitfalls in having the accused or their family conduct the investigation, particularly given their potential lack of objectivity. Yet, the alternative of not doing an investigation is not an acceptable option; failing to be due diligent is unethical[94] and could also amount to ineffective legal assistance of counsel. To require defence counsel pay for the investigation when already under-compensated is iniquitous and untenable. Defence counsel assigned to represent an indigent accused-whose liberty depends, in part, on the afforded quality of legal representation, intrinsic of which is the investigative process of searching for witnesses, verifying the accuracy of the prosecution evidence, and the collection of physical and documentary evidence-should not be compelled with the Hobson's choice of either financing the investigation or forgoing it and thus being in breach of his ethical responsibilities. To rectify this clear imbalance and violation

ICTY Statute and art 20 of the ICTR Statute provide that '[a]ll persons shall be equal before the International Tribunal', the Appeals Chamber explained that the principle of equality of arms does not require material equality between the parties in terms of financial or human resources. *Prosecutor v Nahimana* et al (Judgment) ICTR-99-52-A (28 November 2007) para 220; *Prosecutor v Kayishema & Ruzindana* (Judgment) ICTR-95-1-A, para 69. As the Appeals Chamber explained, equality of arms is not to be interpreted to mean that the defence is 'entitled to precisely the same amount of time or the same number of witnesses as the Prosecution'. *Prosecutor v Orić* (Interlocutory Decision on Length of Defence Case) IT-03-68-AR73.2 (20 July 2005) para 7. It is a principle of basic proportionality, rather than strict mathematical equality, that governs the resources allocated to the two sides (*Prosecutor v Orić*).

[92] Anthony Lewis, *The Silencing of Gideons Trumpet*, N.Y. Times, 20 April 2003, Section 6, p 53, available at <https://www.nytimes.com/2003/04/20/magazine/the-silencing-of-gideon-s-trumpet.html> accessed on 8 May 2019.

[93] Based on my discussions with lawyers from BiH, Serbia, Macedonia, Croatia, and Kosovo, they all complain of not having investigative funds allocated to them when court-appointed to represent indigent clients, even in very serious cases, including cases where war crimes and crimes against humanity and genocide are alleged.

[94] The duty of diligence is not always explicitly stated, but is implied in various rules requiring promptness, competence, zeal, commitment, dedication, and workload management. For example, see Bar Association of Republika Srpska, Lawyers Ethics Code of The Bar Association of Republic of Srpska, 12 March 2005, art 3: 'A lawyer always has to act in the best interest of his client, has to place that interest even above his personal interest and interest of his colleagues.' (Unofficial translation.) Bar Association of the Federation of BiH, Code of Professional Ethic for Attorneys in Federation of BiH, 14 December 2002. Chapter 2, para 1: 'An attorney must devote to his client all his skills and conscientiousness by providing legal aid with no delay or halt.' (Unofficial translation.) Bar Association of Serbia, Code of Professional Ethic of Attorneys-At-Law, 11 February 2012, art 7.2: 'Conscientiousness of an attorney-at-law shall encompass careful, diligent, resolved and timely representation.' (Unofficial translation.) Code of Professional Ethics of The Attorneys, Attorney's Professional Associates and Attorney's Trainees of the Chamber of Attorneys of the Republic of Macedonia, English translation by OSCE Mission to Skopje Rule of Law Unit/Judicial Reform Division, 4 August 2015, art 5: 'The lawyer is obliged to represent and defend his/her client conscientiously, using all necessary means which are permitted by the Law or by other regulations.' Croatian Bar Association, Attorney's Code of Ethics, 19 June 1999, para 41: 'An attorney shall exercise all his or her professional skill and conscientiousness to represent a client and render his or her legal assistance without delay or hesitation.' (Unofficial translation.) Kosovo Bar Association, Lawyers Code of Professional Ethics, 1 December 2012, art 22: 'A lawyer should not cause his client unnecessary expenses. A lawyer gives advice and defends his/her client with dignity and honesty. He regularly informs the client with the subject of his case.' (Unofficial translation.)

of the principle of equality of arms, the state authorities need to provide reasonable funds for necessary investigations in cases where the accused is represented by court appointed defence counsel.

In promoting the fruits of its legacy to the states of the former Yugoslavia (and elsewhere), the ICTY/IRMCT must not only generously share and help pass on its best practices and lessons learned, but it *must* also engage the powers that be in these states in discussions on the importance of adequately funding the defence representing indigent suspects and accused, and the need to find a solution to the current inequality of arms gap: the lack of and refusal to provide investigative resources for indigent suspects and accused who can no longer rely on the investigative judges to conduct a thorough and balanced investigation.

If the ICTY legacy has taught anything to those unfamiliar with adversarial proceedings concerning the rights of the accused and effective legal representation, it is that no case can properly be prepared and tried without investigative efforts that are both targeted and ethically conducted. This is a legacy lesson worth promoting.

15

Judgments and Judgment Drafting

*Thomas Wayde Pittman** *and Marko Divac Öberg***

15.1 Judgments

15.1.1 Types and Bases of Judgments

When the International Criminal Tribunal for the former Yugoslavia delivered judgment in its final trial in the case of *Prosecutor v Mladić*,[1] and final appeal in the case of *Prosecutor v Prlić* et al,[2] the occasions marked the Tribunal's forty-fifthth trial judgment[3] and fortieth

* Thomas Wayde Pittman is a former military trial judge (European Judicial Circuit) and retiree of the US Air Force Judge Advocate General's Corps. He served as a senior legal officer and, ultimately, as Head of Chambers at the International Criminal Tribunal for the former Yugoslavia. He also served as the Registrar's Chef de Cabinet at the Special Tribunal for Lebanon.

** Marko Divac Öberg is a Legal Officer in chambers at the Special Tribunal for Lebanon and, formerly, at the International Criminal Tribunal for the former Yugoslavia. Prior to that, he served as a legal adviser for human rights NGOs in Malawi and Palestine and as a law clerk at the International Court of Justice.

[1] *Prosecutor v Mladić* (Judgment) Case No IT-09-92-T (22 November 2017).

[2] *Prosecutor v Prlić* et al (Judgment) Case No IT-04-74-A (29 November 2017).

[3] *Prosecutor v Tadić* (Judgment) Case No IT-94-1-T (7 May 1997); *Prosecutor v Mucić* et al (Judgment) Case No IT-96-21-T (16 November 1998); *Prosecutor v Furundžija*, Case No IT-95-17/1-T (10 December 1998); *Prosecutor v Aleksovski* (Judgment) Case No IT-95-14/1-T (25 June 1999); *Prosecutor v Jelisić* (Judgment) Case No IT-95-10-T (14 December 1999); *Prosecutor v Kupreškić* et al (Judgment) Case No IT-95-16-T (14 January 2000); *Prosecutor v Blaškić* (Judgment) Case No IT-95-14-T (3 March 2000); *Prosecutor v Kunarac* et al (Judgment) Case No IT-96-23-T (22 February 2001); *Prosecutor v Kordić and Čerkez* (Judgment) Case No IT-95-14/2-T (26 February 2001); *Prosecutor v Krstić* (Judgment) Case No IT-98-33-T (2 August 2001); *Prosecutor v Kvočka* et al (Judgment) Case No IT-98-30/1-T (2 November 2001); *Prosecutor v Krnolejac* (Judgment) Case No IT-97-25-T (15 March 2002); *Prosecutor v Vasiljević* (Judgment) Case No IT-98-32-T (29 November 2002); *Prosecutor v Naletilić and Martinović* (Judgment) Case No IT-98-34-T (31 March 2003); *Prosecutor v Stakić* (Judgment) Case No IT-97-24-T (31 July 2003); *Prosecutor v Simić* et al (Judgment) Case No IT-95-9-T (17 October 2003); *Prosecutor v Galić* (Judgment) Case No IT-98-29-T (5 December 2003); *Prosecutor v Brđanin* (Judgment) Case No IT-99-36-T (1 September 2004); *Prosecutor v Blagojević and Jokić* (Judgment) Case No IT-02-60-T (17 January 2005); *Prosecutor v Strugar* (Judgment) Case No IT-01-42-T (31 January 2005); *Prosecutor v Halilović* (Judgment) Case No IT-01-48-T (16 November 2005); *Prosecutor v Limaj* et al (Judgment) Case No IT-03-66-T (30 November 2005); *Prosecutor v Hadžihasanović and Kubura* (Judgment) Case No IT-01-47-T (15 March 2006); *Prosecutor v Orić* (Judgment) Case No IT-03-68-T (30 June 2006); *Prosecutor v Krajišnik* (Judgment) Case No IT-00-39-T (27 September 2006); *Prosecutor v Martić* (Judgment) Case No IT-95-11-T (12 June 2007); *Prosecutor v Mrkšić* et al (Judgment) Case No IT-95-13/1-T (27 September 2007); *Prosecutor v Milošević* (Judgment) Case No IT-98-29/1–T (12 December 2007); *Prosecutor v Haradinaj* et al (Judgment) Case No IT-04-84-T (3 April 2008); *Prosecutor v Boškoski and Tarčulovski* (Judgment) Case No IT-04-82-T (10 July 2008); *Prosecutor v Delić* (Judgment) Case No IT-04-83-T (15 September 2008); *Prosecutor v Milutinović* et al (Judgment) Case No IT-05-87-T (26 February 2009); *Prosecutor v Lukić and Lukić* (Judgment) Case No IT-98-32/1-T (20 July 2009); *Prosecutor v Popović* et al (Judgment) Case No IT-05-88-T (10 June 2010); *Prosecutor v Đorđević* (Judgment) Case No IT-05-87/1-T (23 February 2011); *Prosecutor v Gotovina* et al (Judgment) Case No IT-06-90-T (15 April 2011); *Prosecutor v Perišić* (Judgment) Case No IT-04-81-T (6 September 2011); *Prosecutor v Haradinaj* et al (Judgment) Case No IT-04-84*bis*-T (29 November 2012); *Prosecutor v Tolimir* (Judgment) Case No IT-05-88/2-T (12 December 2012); *Prosecutor v Stanišić and Župljanin* (Judgment) Case No IT-08-91-T (27 March 2013); *Prosecutor v Prlić* et al (Judgment) Case No IT-04-74-T (29 May 2013); *Prosecutor v Stanišić and Simatović* (Judgment) Case No IT-03-69-T (30 May 2013); *Prosecutor v Karadžić* (Judgment) Case No IT-95-5/18-T (24 March 2016); *Prosecutor v Šešelj* (Judgment) Case No IT-03-67-T (31 March 2016); *Prosecutor v Mladić* (Judgment) Case No IT-09-92-T (22 November 2017).

Thomas Wayde Pittman and Marko Divac Öberg, *Judgments and Judgment Drafting* In: *Legacies of the International Criminal Tribunal for the Former Yugoslavia*. Edited by: Carsten Stahn, Carmel Agius, Serge Brammertz, Colleen Rohan, Oxford University Press (2020).
 DOI: 10.1093/oso/9780198862956.003.0016

appeal judgment[4] since its creation over twenty-three years earlier.[5] These totals exclude other types of judgments such as sentencing judgments following guilty pleas (twenty-one)[6] and appeals therefrom (nine),[7] contempt judgments (twenty-two)[8] and appeals

4 *Prosecutor v Erdemović* (Judgment) Case No IT-96-22-A (7 October 1997); *Prosecutor v Tadić* (Judgment) Case No IT-94-1-A (15 July 1999); *Prosecutor v Aleksovski* (Judgment) Case No IT-95-14/1-A (24 March 2000); *Prosecutor v Furundžija*, Case No IT-95-17/1-A (21 July 2000); *Prosecutor v Mucić* et al (Judgment) Case No IT-96-21-A (20 February 2001); *Prosecutor v Jelisić* (Judgment) Case No IT-95-10-A (5 July 2001); *Prosecutor v Kupreškić* et al (Judgment) Case No IT-95-16-A (23 October 2001); *Prosecutor v Kunarac* et al (Judgment) Case No IT-96-23-A/1 (12 June 2002); *Prosecutor v Krnolejac* (Judgment) Case No IT-97-25-A (17 September 2003); *Prosecutor v Vasiljević* (Judgment) Case No IT-98-32-A (25 February 2004); *Prosecutor v Krstić* (Judgment) Case No IT-98-33-A (19 April 2004); *Prosecutor v Blaškić* (Judgment) Case No IT-95-14-A (29 July 2004); *Prosecutor v Kordić and Čerkez* (Judgment) Case No IT-95-14/2-A (17 December 2004); *Prosecutor v Kvočka* et al (Judgment) Case No IT-98-30/1-A (28 February 2005); *Prosecutor v Stakić* (Judgment) Case No IT-97-24-A (22 March 2006); *Prosecutor v Naletilić and Martinović* (Judgment) Case No IT-98-34-A (3 May 2006); *Prosecutor v Simić* (Judgment) Case No IT-95-9-A (28 November 2006); *Prosecutor v Galić* (Judgment) Case No IT-98-29-A (30 November 2006); *Prosecutor v Brđanin* (Judgment) Case No IT-99-36-A (3 April 2007); *Prosecutor v Blagojević and Jokić* (Judgment) Case No IT-02-60-A (9 May 2007); *Prosecutor v Limaj* et al (Judgment) Case No IT-03-66-A (27 September 2007); *Prosecutor v Halilović* (Judgment) Case No IT-01-48-A (16 October 2007); *Prosecutor v Hadžihasanović and Kubura* (Judgment) Case No IT-01-47-A (22 April 2008); *Prosecutor v Orić* (Judgment) Case No IT-03-68-A (3 July 2008); *Prosecutor v Strugar* (Judgment) Case No IT-01-42-A (17 July 2008); *Prosecutor v Martić* (Judgment) Case No IT-95-11-T (12 June 2007); *Prosecutor v Krajišnik* (Judgment) Case No IT-00-39-A (17 March 2009); *Prosecutor v Mrkšić and Šljivančanin* (Judgment) Case No IT-95-13/1-A (5 May 2009); *Prosecutor v Milošević* (Judgment) Case No IT-98-29/1-A (12 November 2009); *Prosecutor v Boškoski and Tarčulovski* (Judgment) Case No IT-04-82-A (19 May 2010); *Prosecutor v Haradinaj* et al (Judgment) Case No IT-04-84-A (19 July 2010); *Prosecutor v Gotovina and Markač* (Judgment) Case No IT-06-90-A (16 November 2012); *Prosecutor v Lukić and Lukić* (Judgment) Case No IT-98-32/1-A (4 December 2012); *Prosecutor v Perišić* (Judgment) Case No IT-04-81-A (28 February 2013); *Prosecutor v Šainović* et al (Judgment) Case No IT-05-87-A (23 January 2014); *Prosecutor v Đorđević* (Judgment) Case No IT-05-87/1-A (27 January 2014); *Prosecutor v Popović* et al (Judgment) Case No IT-05-88-A (30 January 2015); *Prosecutor v Tolimir* (Judgment) Case No IT-05-88/2-A (8 April 2015); *Prosecutor v Stanišić and Simatović* (Judgment) Case No IT-03-69-A (9 December 2015); *Prosecutor v Stanišić and Župljanin* (Judgment) Case No IT-08-91-A (30 June 2016); *Prosecutor v Prlić* et al (Judgment) Case No IT-04-74-A (29 November 2017).

5 UN Security Council Resolution 808, UN Doc S/RES/808 (1993); UN SC Resolution 827 (25 May 1993), UN Doc S/RES/827 (1993).

6 *Prosecutor v Erdemović* (Sentencing Judgment) Case No IT-96-22-T (29 November 1996); *Prosecutor v Tadić* (Sentencing Judgment) Case No IT-94-1-T (14 July 1997); *Prosecutor v Erdemović* (Sentencing Judgment) Case No IT-96-22-T*bis* (5 March 1998); *Prosecutor v Tadić* (Sentencing Judgment) Case No IT-99-22-T*bis*-R117 (11 November 1999); *Prosecutor v Todorović* (Sentencing Judgment) Case No IT-35-9/1-S (31 July 2001); *Prosecutor v Mucić, Delić and Landžo* (Sentencing Judgment) Case No IT-96-21-T*bis*-R117 (9 October 2001); *Prosecutor v Sikirica, Došen and Kolundžija* (Sentencing Judgment) Case No IT-95-8-S (13 November 2001); *Prosecutor v Simić* (Sentencing Judgment) Case No IT-95-9/2-S (17 October 2002); *Prosecutor v Plavšić* (Sentencing Judgment) Case No IT-39 and 40/1-S (27 February 2003); *Prosecutor v Banović* (Sentencing Judgment) Case No IT-02-65/1-S (28 October 2003); *Prosecutor v Nikolić* (Sentencing Judgment) Case No IT-02-60/1-S (2 December 2003); *Prosecutor v Obrenović* (Sentencing Judgment) Case No IT-01-43 (10 December 2003); *Prosecutor v Nikolić* (Sentencing Judgment) Case No IT-94-2-S (18 December 2003); *Prosecutor v Češić* (Sentencing Judgment) Case No IT-95-10/1-S (11 March 2004); *Prosecutor v Jokić* (Sentencing Judgment) Case No IT-01-42/1-S (18 March 2004); *Prosecutor v Deronjić* (Sentencing Judgment) Case No IT-02-61-S (30 March 2004); *Prosecutor v Mrđa* (Sentencing Judgment) Case No IT-02-59-S (31 March 2004); *Prosecutor v Babić* (Sentencing Judgment) Case No IT-03-72-S (29 June 2004); *Prosecutor v Bralo* (Sentencing Judgment) Case No IT-95-17-S (7 December 2005); *Prosecutor v Rajić* (Sentencing Judgment) Case No IT-95-12-S (8 May 2006); *Prosecutor v Zelenović* (Sentencing Judgment) Case No IT-96-23/2-S (4 April 2007).

7 *Prosecutor v Tadić* (Judgment) Case No IT-94-1-A and IT-94-1-A*bis* (26 January 2000); *Prosecutor v Mucić, Delić and Landžo* (Judgment) Case No IT-96-21-A*bis* (8 April 2003); *Prosecutor v Nikolić* (Judgment) Case No IT-94-2-A (4 February 2005); *Prosecutor v Babić* (Judgment) Case No IT-03-72-A (18 July 2005); *Prosecutor v Deronjić* (Judgment) Case No IT-02-61-A (20 July 2005); *Prosecutor v Jokić* (Judgment) Case No IT-01-42/1-A (30 August 2005); *Prosecutor v Nikolić* (Judgment) Case No IT-02-60/1-A (8 March 2006); *Prosecutor v Bralo* (Judgment) Case No IT-95-17-A (2 April 2007); *Prosecutor v Zelenović* (Judgment) Case No IT-96-23/2-A (31 October 2007).

8 *Prosecutor v Aleksovski* (Contempt Judgment) (Nobilo), Case No IT-95-14/1-T (11 December 1998); *Prosecutor v Tadić* (Contempt Judgment) (Vujin), IT-94-1-A-R77 (31 January 2000); *Prosecutor v Simić* et al (Contempt Judgment) (Avramović and Simić), Case No IT-95-9-R77 (30 June 2000); *Prosecutor v Tolimir* (Contempt Judgment) (Pećanac), Case No IT-05-88/2-R77.2 (9 December 2001); *Prosecutor v Milošević* (Contempt Judgment) (Bulatović), Case No IT-02-54-R77.4 (13 May 2005); *Prosecutor v Limaj* et al (Contempt Judgment) (Beqaj), Case No IT-03-66-R77 (27 May 2005); *Prosecutor v Blaškić* (Contempt Judgment) (Marijačić and Rebić), Case No IT-95-14-R77.2 (12 March 2006); *Prosecutor v Blaškić* (Contempt Judgment) (Jović), Case No IT-95-14 and 14/2-R77

therefrom (ten),[9] and review judgments (one).[10] The various types of judgments find their basis in the Tribunal's Statute and Rules of Procedure and Evidence.

The statutory basis for judgments derives primarily from Article 23 of the ICTY Statute. Simply titled 'Judgement', Article 23 contains two subparagraphs which refer only to trial judgments.

1. The Trial Chambers shall pronounce judgements and impose sentences and penalties on persons convicted of serious violations of international humanitarian law.
2. The judgement shall be rendered by a majority of the judges of the Trial Chamber, and shall be delivered by the Trial Chamber in public. It shall be accompanied by a reasoned opinion in writing, to which separate or dissenting opinions may be appended.

From the first subparagraph, it is not entirely clear whether judgments were envisioned to be mandatory in the absence of a conviction, but it has been the consistent practice since the first case in which an accused was acquitted on all counts of an indictment.[11] What is undeniably explicit from both subparagraphs is that judgments are required to be 'pronounce[d]', 'rendered' and 'delivered', however these words are defined or may overlap. Furthermore, while it appears that a written reasoned opinion is a document distinct from, and accompanying, a judgment, the practice has been that the judgment and the written reasoned opinion are one and the same. We will return to these latter two points in a later discussion.

Article 23 follows the common law approach of allowing individual judges of a Chamber to express their separate or dissenting opinions. In practice, judges have availed themselves of this right in almost every judgment. Most often, a separate opinion is one that concurs

(30 August 2006); *Prosecutor v Blaškić* (Contempt Judgment) (Margetić), Case No IT-95-14-R77.6 (7 February 2007); *Prosecutor v Haradinaj* et al (Contempt Judgment) (Haxhiu), Case No IT-04-84-R77.5 (24 July 2008); *Prosecutor v Šešelj* (Contempt Judgment) (Petković), Case No IT-03-67-R77.1-I (11 September 2008); *Prosecutor v Haradinaj* et al (Contempt Judgment) (Haraqija and Morina), Case No IT-04-84-R77.4 (17 December 2008); *Prosecutor v Popović* et al (Contempt Judgment) (Jokić), Case No IT-05-88-R77.1 (27 March 2009); *Prosecutor v Šešelj* (Contempt Judgment), Case No IT-03-67-R77.2 (24 July 2009); *Prosecutor v Milošević* (Contempt Judgment) (Hartmann), Case No IT-02-54-R77.5, (14 September 2009); *Prosecutor v Lukić and Lukić* (Contempt Judgment) (Tabaković), Case No IT-98-32/1-R77.1 (18 March 2010); *Prosecutor v Haradinaj* et al (Contempt Judgment) (Kabashi), Case No IT-04-84-R77.1 (16 September 2011); *Prosecutor v Šešelj* (Contempt Judgment), Case No IT-03-67-R77.3 (31 October 2011); *Prosecutor v Karadžić* (Contempt Judgment) (Tupajić), Case No IT-95-5/18-R77.2 (24 February 2012); *Prosecutor v Lukić and Lukić* (Contempt Judgment) (Rasić), Case No IT-98-32/1-R77.2 (6 March 2012); *Prosecutor v Šešelj* (Contempt Judgment), Case No. IT-03-67-R77.4 (28 June 2012); *Prosecutor v Karadžić* (Contempt Judgment) (Krstić), Case No IT-95-5/18-R77.3 (18 July 2013).

[9] *Prosecutor v Tadić* (Judgment) (Vujin), Case No IT-94-1-A-R77 (27 February 2001); *Prosecutor v Aleksovski* (Judgment) (Nobilo), Case No IT-95-14/1-AR77 (30 May 2001); *Prosecutor v Blaškić* (Judgment) (Marijačić and Rebić), Case No IT-95-14-R77.2-A (27 September 2006); *Prosecutor v Blaškić* (Judgment) (Jović), Case No IT-95-14 and 14/2-R77-A (15 March 2007); *Prosecutor v Popović* et al (Judgment) (Jokić), Case No IT-05-88-R77.1-A (25 June 2009); *Prosecutor v Haradinaj* et al (Judgment) (Haraqija and Morina), Case No IT-04-84-R77.4-A (23 July 2009); *Prosecutor v Šešelj* (Judgment) Case No IT-03-67-R77.2-A (19 May 2010); *Prosecutor v Milošević* (Judgment) (Hartmann), Case No IT-02-54-R77.5-A (19 July 2011); *Prosecutor v Šešelj* (Judgment) Case No IT-03-67-R77.3-A (28 November 2012); *Prosecutor v Šešelj* (Judgment) Case No IT-03-67-R77.4-A (30 May 2013).

[10] *Prosecutor v Šljivančanin*, Review Judgment, Case No IT-95-13/1-R.1 (8 December 2010).

[11] Zejnil Delalić was acquitted at trial of all twelve counts for which he was charged, *Prosecutor v Mucić* et al (Judgment) Case No IT-96-21-T (16 November 1998); and his acquittals were affirmed on appeal, *Prosecutor v Mucić* et al (Judgment) Case No IT-96-21-A (20 February 2001). For a single-accused example, Sefer Halilović was acquitted at trial on the sole count of the indictment, and the acquittal was affirmed on appeal. Both the trial and appeal required written judgments: *Prosecutor v Halilović* (Judgment) Case No IT-01-48-T (16 November 2005), and *Prosecutor v Halilović* (Judgment) Case No IT-01-48-A (16 October 2007).

in the end result of the majority's reasoning for any given factual or legal finding or conclusion, but not necessarily with the reasoning itself. Dissenting opinions are often expressed with respect to only a part of the judgment. Judgments by majority have the same binding effect as unanimous judgments.[12] Further, there is no jury and all fact-finding is done by the judges.[13] It would indeed be difficult to envisage a jury system in international criminal law, given the length and complexity of the trials. The public nature of judgments does not preclude them from containing confidential parts.[14]

Article 25 of the ICTY Statute governs appellate proceedings, and provides that:

1. The Appeals Chamber shall hear appeals from persons convicted by the Trial Chambers or from the Prosecutor on the following grounds: (a) an error on a question of law invalidating the decision; or (b) an error of fact which has occasioned a miscarriage of justice.
2. The Appeals Chamber may affirm, reverse or revise the decisions taken by the Trial Chambers.

Article 25 does not explicitly refer to a 'judgement' on appeal, but rather to the Appeals Chamber's authority to affirm, reverse, or revise certain erroneous legal and factual decisions of the Trial Chambers. What form this affirmation, reversal, or revision takes was left open by the Statute, and could conceivably have been termed an 'opinion' in the tradition of, for example, the highest appellate body of the US—the US Supreme Court—which pronounces principal or majority 'opinions' as opposed to judgments.[15] However, the judges of the ICTY, on the basis of their power to adopt rules of procedure and evidence for the conduct of, inter alia, appeal proceedings,[16] chose to clarify that the Appeals Chamber pronounces a 'judgement' on appeal, using language similar to Article 23 of the Statute.[17] Consequently, the affirmation, reversal, or revision of Trial Chambers' decisions has been referred to as a judgment since the first completed case on appeal.[18]

[12] *Prosecutor v Prlić* et al (Decision on Jadranko Prlić's Consolidated Interlocutory Appeal against the Trial Chamber's Orders of 6 and 9 October 2008 on Admission of Evidence) Case No IT-04-74-A (12 January 2009) para 27.

[13] *Prosecutor v Blagojević* et al (Decision) Case Nos. IT-02-60-AR73, IT-02-60-AR73.2, IT-02-60-AR73.3 (8 April 2003) para 22.

[14] *In the Case against Vojislav Šešelj* (Judgment) IT-03-67-R77.2-A (19 May 2010) para 32.

[15] See <https://www.supremecourt.gov/opinions/opinions.aspx> accessed 1 May 2019.

[16] Art 15 (Rules of Procedure and Evidence) of the ICTY Statute:

> The judges of the International Tribunal shall adopt rules of procedure and evidence for the conduct of the pre-trial phase of the proceedings, trials and appeals, the admission of evidence, the protection of victims and witnesses and other appropriate matters.

[17] Rule 117 (Judgment on Appeal) of the ICTY Rules of Procedure and Evidence:

> (A) The Appeals Chamber shall pronounce judgement on the basis of the record on appeal together with such additional evidence as has been presented to it.
> (B) The judgement shall be rendered by a majority of the Judges. It shall be accompanied or followed as soon as possible by a reasoned opinion in writing, to which separate or dissenting opinions may be appended.
> (C) In appropriate circumstances the Appeals Chamber may order that the accused be retried according to law.
> (D) The judgement shall be pronounced in public, on a date of which notice shall have been given to the parties and counsel and at which they shall be entitled to be present.

[18] *Prosecutor v Erdemović* (Judgment) Case No IT-96-22-A (7 October 1997).

Article 26 of the ICTY Statute governs review proceedings, which are to address the review of a judgment in light of certain newly discovered facts. It provides:

> Where a new fact has been discovered which was not known at the time of the proceedings before the Trial Chambers or the Appeals Chamber and which could have been a decisive factor in reaching the decision, the convicted person or the Prosecutor may submit to the International Tribunal an application for review of the judgement.

Since the only explicit reference in the ICTY Statute to a 'judgement' concerns the pronouncement of a Trial Chamber under Article 23, it would appear on its face that the 'judgement' to be reviewed is the trial judgment. However, the Rules of Procedure and Evidence governing review proceedings refer to an additional discovery criterion which aids in clarifying that the judgment to be reviewed can be either a trial or appeal judgment. Rule 119(A) in part sets forth:

> Where a new fact has been discovered which was not known to the moving party at the time of the proceedings before a Trial Chamber or the Appeals Chamber, and could not have been discovered through the exercise of due diligence, the defence or, within one year after the final judgement has been pronounced, the Prosecutor, may make a motion to that Chamber for review of the judgement [. . .].

The reference to 'that' Chamber—to which a motion for review may be made—indicates the Chamber before which the new fact was unknown or not discoverable at the time through due diligence, whether it be in proceedings before a Trial Chamber or the Appeals Chamber. Furthermore, Rule 120 provides that review of the judgment and pronouncement of a 'further' judgment is required where the new fact 'if proved, could have been a decisive factor in reaching a decision'.[19] In the *Šljivančanin* Review Judgment, the Appeals Chamber relied on Article 26 and Rules 119 and 120 in pronouncing a further appellate judgment.[20]

Continuing with the regulatory basis for the types of judgments, Rule 100 refers specifically to the pronouncement of sentence in a judgment following conviction on a guilty plea. The practice of the ICTY Trial Chambers has been to combine the Rule 62*bis* criteria for entering a finding of guilt on the basis of a plea[21] with the pronouncement of sentence in one reasoned opinion in writing, referred to as a Sentencing Judgment.[22]

Another rules-based category of judgments is found in Rule 98*bis*, which provides for a Judgment of Acquittal:

> At the close of the Prosecutor's case, the Chamber shall, by oral decision and after hearing the oral submissions of the parties, enter a judgement of acquittal on any count if there is no evidence capable of supporting a conviction.

[19] The test was restated as 'if proved, could fundamentally alter the balance of the evidence related to the case' in *Prosecutor v Šljivančanin* (Decision with Respect to Veselin Šljivančanin's Application for Review) Case No IT-95-13/1-R.1 (14 July 2010) 3.

[20] *Prosecutor v Šljivančanin* (Review Judgment) Case No IT-95-13/1-R.1 (8 December 2010) para 12.

[21] Rule 62*bis* permits Trial Chamber to enter a finding of guilt where it is satisfied that the plea is voluntary, informed, unequivocal, and that a sufficient factual basis exists for the crime and the accused's participation in it.

[22] See (n 6).

The word 'shall' suggests that the Chamber must render such a judgment—if there is no evidence capable of supporting a conviction—even if the Defence does not request it. However, that is not how the provision has been interpreted in practice. For instance, in the *Haradinaj* et al case, the Defence neither requested a judgment of acquittal nor put on a Defence case. The Trial Chamber proceeded to issue the trial judgment, acquitting two out of the three accused.[23]

The requirement of an oral decision is the result of an 8 December 2004 amendment to the Rule which had in its previous form permitted a Trial Chamber to enter a judgment of acquittal for any offence charged in the indictment after the close of the Prosecutor's case, either on motion of an accused or *proprio motu*, if it found insufficient evidence to sustain a conviction on the charge. The rationale for the amendment specifying the use of an oral decision was the result of a growing practice of Trial Chambers to address the sufficiency of the evidence in writing, which effectively grew away from the notion of a directed verdict and into a quasi 'pre-Judgement'. This was best exemplified by the 140-page Rule 98*bis* decision in the case of *Prosecutor v Slobodan Milošević*.[24] This practice consumed precious resources and was abandoned as part of an effort to speed up trials.

A final type of judgment utilized by the ICTY arose in the context of the crime of contempt of the Tribunal under Rule 77, which is defined by the Rule as the knowing and wilful interference with the Tribunal's administration of justice.[25] Although the Rule refers to a 'decision' rather than a judgment,[26] in practice the decision is in the form of, and captioned as, a judgment.[27] The Rule permits a first-instance contempt judgment to be oral,[28] yet all of the twenty-two first-instance judgments were written.

15.1.2 Pronouncement of Judgments

Rule 98*ter* of the Rules includes two subparagraphs containing language that derives from Article 23 of the ICTY Statute and which mandate that the judgment shall be both pronounced in public and accompanied or followed by a reasoned opinion in writing.

> (A) 'The judgement shall be pronounced in public, on a date of which notice shall have been given to the parties and counsel and at which they shall be entitled to be present, subject to the provisions of Rule 102 (B).'
>
> ...
>
> (C) 'The judgement shall be rendered by a majority of the Judges. It shall be accompanied or followed as soon as possible by a reasoned opinion in writing, to which separate or dissenting opinions may be appended.'

As a matter of terminology, it would appear from the plain language of the Statute and Rules that the 'judgement' is what is pronounced in public; in other words, what is read in open

23 *Prosecutor v Haradinaj* et al (Judgment) Case No IT-04-84-T (3 April 2008) paras 6, 502–04, app A, para 25.
24 *Prosecutor v Milošević* (Decision on Motion for Judgment of Acquittal) Case No IT-02-54-T (16 June 2004).
25 Rule 77(A) of the Rules.
26 For example, Rule 77(J) refers to a 'decision rendered by a Trial Chamber under this Rule'.
27 See (n 8).
28 Rule 77(J) and (K) of the Rules.

court. However, what is read in open court is a prepared judgment summary that includes the disposition of, or verdict on, the counts in the indictment. Indeed, standard language at the delivery of the judgment includes: 'What I will now read out is a summary of the Chamber's findings. This summary does not constitute a part of the judgement. Only the official judgement which will be made available at the close of this hearing is authoritative.'[29] Given the length of some of the trial and appeal judgments, discussed further, use of summaries was a wise practice.

Both Article 23 of the Statute and Rule 98*ter* of the Rules refer to the judgment being 'accompanied' by a reasoned opinion in writing. In practice, the judgment itself is in a written form and encompasses the reasoned opinion. Indeed, Rule 98*ter* (D) refers to the requirement of serving a 'copy of the judgement' on the accused, which would not be possible if the judgment were not in writing. Furthermore, while it would appear from the plain language of the Statute and Rules that the 'reasoned opinion' is a written document which accompanies or follows the judgment, the document containing the reasoned opinion is in fact always captioned 'Judgement'.

15.1.3 Reasoned Opinion Requirement of Judgments

The reasoned opinion requirement is not universal, but is largely drawn from the civil legal system.[30] According to the Appeals Chamber, the right of an accused under Article 23 of the Statute to a reasoned opinion is an aspect of the fair trial requirement embodied in Articles 20 and 21 of the Statute.[31] The case law that has developed under the European Convention on Human Rights establishes that a reasoned opinion is a component of the fair hearing requirement, but that 'the extent to which this duty ... applies may vary according to the nature of the decision' and 'can only be determined in the light of the circumstances of the case'. The European Court of Human Rights has held that a 'tribunal' is not obliged to give a detailed answer to every argument.[32] This is a good thing, because the requirement for a reasoned opinion has a direct and obvious correlation to the length of a judgment. If trial chambers had to address every argument, whatever its merits, their judgments would be even longer and the trials less expeditious.

The Appeals Chamber expanded upon the reasoned opinion requirement in the *Prosecutor v Kvočka* et al case, in a seminal and much-cited paragraph:

> The Appeals Chamber recalls that every accused has the right to a reasoned opinion under Article 23 of the Statute and Rule 98*ter*(C) of the Rules. However, this requirement relates to the Trial Chamber's Judgement; the Trial Chamber is not under the obligation to justify its findings in relation to every submission made during the trial. The Appeals Chamber

[29] T 17543, *Prosecutor v Šešelj* (Judgment) Case No IT-03-67-T (31 March 2016).

[30] In the practice of the US, reasoned opinions in writing are generally not required in criminal trials. A trial judgment may be no more than a verdict on or disposition of the charges in the indictment.

[31] Art 20(1) provides that 'The Trial Chambers shall ensure that a trial is fair and expeditious and that proceedings are conducted in accordance with the rules of procedure and evidence, with full respect for the rights of the accused and due regard for the protection of victims and witnesses'. Art 21(2) provides that 'In the determination of charges against him, the accused shall be entitled to a fair and public hearing [...]'.

[32] *Prosecutor v Furundžija*, Case No IT-95-17/1-A (21 July 2000) para 69 (internal citations omitted) with further references.

> recalls that it is in the discretion of the Trial Chamber as to which legal arguments to address. With regard to the factual findings, the Trial Chamber is required only to make findings of those facts which are essential to the determination of guilt on a particular count. It is not necessary to refer to the testimony of every witness or every piece of evidence on the trial record. It is to be presumed that the Trial Chamber evaluated all the evidence presented to it, as long as there is no indication that the Trial Chamber completely disregarded any particular piece of evidence. There may be an indication of disregard when evidence which is clearly relevant to the findings is not addressed by the Trial Chamber's reasoning, but not every inconsistency which the Trial Chamber failed to discuss renders its opinion defective. Considering the fact that minor inconsistencies commonly occur in witness testimony without rendering it unreliable, it is within the discretion of the Trial Chamber to evaluate it and to consider whether the evidence as a whole is credible, without explaining its decision in every detail. If the Trial Chamber did not refer to the evidence given by a witness, even if it is in contradiction to the Trial Chamber's finding, it is to be presumed that the Trial Chamber assessed and weighed the evidence, but found that the evidence did not prevent it from arriving at its actual findings. It is therefore not possible to draw any inferences about the quality of a judgement from the length of particular parts of a judgement in relation to other judgements or parts of the same judgement.[33]

The Trial Chamber's reasoned opinion must be based on the entire body of evidence:

> The task of a trier of fact is that of assessing all the relevant evidence presented with a holistic approach; this is all the more necessary in cases as complex as the ones before the International Tribunal. According to the Statute and the Rules, a trier of fact should render a reasoned opinion on the basis of the entire body of evidence and without applying the standard of proof 'beyond reasonable doubt' with a piecemeal approach.[34]

With respect to the standard of review, the Appeals Chamber has held that it is necessary for any appellant claiming an error of law on the basis of the lack of a reasoned opinion to identify the specific issues, factual findings, or arguments that the appellant submits the trial chamber omitted to address and to explain why this omission invalidates the decision.[35] The following are guidelines provided to the Trial Chambers:

> With regard to factual findings, a Trial Chamber is required only to make findings on those facts which are essential to the determination of guilt on a particular count. It is not necessary to refer to the testimony of every witness or every piece of evidence on the trial record. In short, a Trial Chamber should limit itself to indicating in a clear and articulate, yet concise manner, which, among the wealth of jurisprudence available on a given issue and the myriad of facts that emerged at trial, are the legal and factual findings on the basis of which it reached the decision either to convict or acquit an individual. A reasoned opinion consistent with the guidelines provided here allows for a useful exercise of the

[33] *Prosecutor v Kvočka* et al (Judgment) Case No IT-98-30/1-A (28 February 2005) para 23 (internal references omitted).
[34] *Prosecutor v Halilović* (Judgment) Case No IT-01-48-A (16 October 2007) para 128.
[35] *Prosecutor v Stanišić and Župljanin* (Judgment) Case No IT-08-91-A (30 June 2016) para 18.

right of appeal by the Parties and enables the Appeals Chamber to understand and review the Trial Chamber's findings as well as its evaluation of the evidence.[36]

In the case of *Prosecutor v Perišić*, the Appeals Chamber held that in certain circumstances, insufficient analysis of evidence on the record can amount to a failure to provide a reasoned opinion.[37] Furthermore, an analysis limited to a select segment of the relevant evidentiary record is not necessarily sufficient to constitute a reasoned opinion.[38]

The Appeals Chamber has described how the reasoned opinion requirement applies on appeal:

> The rationale of a judgement of the Appeals Chamber must be clearly explained. There is a significant difference from the standard of reasoning before a Trial Chamber. Article 25 of the Statute does not require the Appeals Chamber to provide a reasoned opinion such as that required of the Trial Chamber. Only Rule 117(B) of the Rules calls for a 'reasoned opinion in writing.' The purpose of a reasoned opinion under Rule 117(B) of the Rules is not to provide access to all the deliberations of the Appeals Chamber in order to enable a review of its ultimate findings and conclusions. The Appeals Chamber must indicate with sufficient clarity the grounds on which a decision has been based. However, this obligation cannot be understood as requiring a detailed response to every argument.[39]

This statement does not suggest that there is any difference in terms of practical impact between the reasoned opinion requirement at trial and on appeal.

15.1.4 Length of Judgments

In view of the reasoned opinion requirement, it should come as no surprise that ICTY trial judgments have routinely amassed several hundred pages, and five have exceeded 1,000 pages.[40] Judgments are authorized to be filed in either the English or French language, and are typically translated into the other language, as well as into the language of the accused.[41] The longest English language trial judgment resulted from the case of *Prosecutor v Karadžić*, and totalled 2,590 pages.[42] The longest trial judgment in the French language, and longest overall, from the case of *Prosecutor v Prlić* et al, amounted to 'a 2,629-pages-long document divided into six volumes, including four annexes and partially dissenting or separate

[36] *Prosecutor v Hadžihasanović and Kubura* (Judgment) Case No IT-01-47-A (22 April 2008) para 13 (internal citations omitted).

[37] *Prosecutor v Perišić* (Judgment) Case No IT-04-81-A (28 February 2013) para 92.

[38] ibid para 95.

[39] *Prosecutor v Kunarac* et al (Judgment) Case No IT-96-23-A/1 (12 June 2002) para 42.

[40] *Prosecutor v Prlić* et al (Judgment) Case No IT-04-74-T (29 May 2013); *Prosecutor v Karadžić* (Judgment) Case No IT-95-5/18-T (24 March 2016); *Prosecutor v Mladić* (Judgment) Case No IT-09-92-T (22 November 2017); *Prosecutor v Milutinović* et al (Judgment) Case No IT-05-87-T (26 February 2009); *Prosecutor v Stanišić and Župljanin* (Judgment) Case No IT-08-91-T (27 March 2013).

[41] Rule 3(A) of the Rules: 'The working languages of the Tribunal shall be English and French'; Rule 98*ter*(D) of the Rules: 'A copy of the judgement and of the Judges' opinions in a language which the accused understands shall as soon as possible be served on the accused if in custody. Copies thereof in that language and in the language in which they were delivered shall also as soon as possible be provided to counsel for the accused.'

[42] *Prosecutor v Karadžić* (Judgment) Case No IT-95-5/18-T (24 March 2016).

opinions'.[43] Such was the enormity of the *Prlić* et al trial judgment that one defence counsel addressed the Chamber at the Appeals Hearing as follows:

> Your Honour, this wasn't a short judgment. We have six volumes. It's very difficult to bring it to court. The majority is 1800 pages. It dwarfs even 'War and Peace' at 1200 and some pages.[44]

Of course, the reasoned opinion requirement is not the only cause for such extraordinary lengths of the trial judgments. Judge and former President Theodor Meron has remarked: 'At the most basic level, the criminal cases tried before the Tribunals are unprecedented in scope and scale, and involve crimes almost never prosecuted on a national level, such as genocide'[45] and which 'can often involve dozens of crime sites, thousands of victims, and enormous volumes of written material'.[46] The *Prlić* et al Trial Chamber, for example, noted that '[d]uring the proceedings . . . the Chamber admitted approximately 10,000 exhibits into evidence and heard 145 Prosecution witnesses, seven of whom were expert witnesses, as well as 61 Defence witnesses, seven of whom were expert witnesses'.[47] One practical result of such voluminous evidence, however, is that a trial chamber's effort to provide an *appeal-proof* reasoned opinion in a highly complex case is quite likely to result in an equally voluminous judgment.

Nor are trial judgments the only lengthy judgments—the Appeal Judgment in the case of *Prosecutor v Šainović* et al weighed in at 810 pages,[48] and in the case of *Prosecutor v Popović* et al, the tally was 716 pages.[49] The judgment in the Tribunal's final case on appeal, *Prosecutor v Prlić* et al, was 1,450 pages in length.[50] Even cases concerning the administration of justice are complex—the longest contempt trial judgment was sixty pages,[51] and the longest contempt appeal judgment was fifty-four pages in length.[52]

15.1.5 Finality of Judgments

With lengthy proceedings and judgments comes the risk that accused and convicted persons may not outlive the trial or appeal, especially where the person was already a senior political or military leader at the time of the alleged commission of the crimes charged in the indictment. In discussing lengths of judgments, the judgment in the trial of Slobodan Milošević was omitted because his untimely death on 11 March 2006—after four years of trial but before a judgment was pronounced—had the legal effect of terminating all proceedings.[53] This is true notwithstanding that

[43] T 52979, *Prosecutor v Prlić* et al (Judgment Summary) Case No IT-04-74-T (29 May 2013).
[44] T 274, *Prosecutor v Prlić* et al (Appeal Hearing) Case No IT-04-74-A (21 March 2017).
[45] T Meron, *The Making of International Criminal Justice: The View from the Bench: Selected Speeches* (OUP 2011) 280.
[46] ibid 283.
[47] T 52978-52979, *Prosecutor v Prlić* et al (Judgment Summary) Case No IT-04-74-T (29 May 2013).
[48] *Prosecutor v Šainović* et al (Judgment) Case No IT-05-87-A (23 January 2014).
[49] *Prosecutor v Popović* et al (Judgment) Case No IT-05-88-A (30 January 2015).
[50] *Prosecutor v Prlić* et al (Judgment) Case No IT-04-74-A (29 November 2017).
[51] *Prosecutor v Tadić* (Contempt Judgment) (Vujin), IT-94-1-A-R77 (31 January 2000).
[52] *Prosecutor v Milošević* (Judgment) (Hartmann), Case No IT-02-54-R77.5-A (19 July 2011).
[53] *Prosecutor v Milošević* (Order Terminating the Proceedings) Case No IT-02-54-T (14 March 2006).

> [b]y 24 November 2005 this 'whale' of a trial had produced 46,639 pages of transcript and 2,256 separate written filings amounting to 63,775 pages. The prosecution had introduced 930 exhibits, amounting to 85,526 pages, as well as 117 videos.[54]

What of the case where a convicted person dies while appeal is pending on a completed trial judgment? This happened twice, first in the case of *Prosecutor v Delić*[55] and again in the case of *Prosecutor v Popović* et al.[56] In *Delić*, the accused, Rasim Delić, was convicted at trial of violations of the laws and customs of war (detainee maltreatment) on the basis of superior responsibility, with the Presiding Judge dissenting from the verdict. Delić appealed and the Appeal Hearing had taken place when after nineteen months of proceedings, he died.[57] The Appeals Chamber had little difficulty in finding 'as a matter of principle' that the appellate proceedings should be terminated for lack of jurisdiction over the person.[58] The question of how to regard the trial judgment was novel, and one in which common and civil law jurisdictions each had different approaches and no general principle or prevalent approach could be discerned.[59] Ultimately, the Appeals Chamber rejected the approach wherein a conviction at trial is vacated by death of an appellant, and unanimously followed the approach considering such a trial judgment to be final in law, with the pivotal reasoning resting on the absence of a presumption of innocence in appeal proceedings before the Tribunal.[60] The Appeals Chamber relied conclusively on the *Delić* reasoning in the *Popović* et al appeal when one of the appellants, Milan Gvero, died before a judgment could be pronounced, thereby terminating all proceedings and considering the Trial Judgment final in relation to Gvero.[61]

15.2 Judgment Drafting

While judgments are arguably the most visible, tangible, and important features of the legal legacy of the Tribunal, the process of formulating the judgments is probably the least known and understood among all the various processes which have contributed to the making of international justice at the ICTY. It is naturally acknowledged that formulating a judgment goes hand-in-hand with judicial deliberations on the evidence presented in court of crimes, criminal responsibility, and the factors which affect sentencing. The secrecy of deliberative decision-making is unquestioned; it is a necessary guarantee of judicial independence and integrity. However, to the extent that the processes of judgment formulation—the nuts-and-bolts of drafting if you will—can be shared publicly without undermining in any respect the substantive deliberations of a case, then it ought to be done in the interests of identifying

[54] G Boas, *The Milošević Trial: Lessons for the Conduct of Complex International Criminal Proceedings* (CUP 2007) xii. In the absence of a *Milošević* trial judgment, an excellent guide otherwise to the complete proceedings exists in the form of a research article, H Abtahi and G Dawson, 'The Anatomy of the Milošević Trial (2001-2006)' (2016) 1 Journal of International Humanitarian Action 1

[55] *Prosecutor v Delić* (Judgment) Case No IT-04-83-T (15 September 2008).

[56] *Prosecutor v Popović* et al (Judgment) Case No IT-05-88-T (10 June 2010).

[57] *Prosecutor v Delić* (Decision on the Outcome of Proceedings) Case No IT-04-83-A (29 June 2010) paras 1–5.

[58] ibid 6–8.

[59] ibid paras 9–13.

[60] ibid paras 14–15.

[61] *Prosecutor v Popović* et al (Decision Terminating Appellate Proceedings in Relation to Milan Gvero) Case No IT-05-88-A (7 March 2013).

the various achievements, challenges, best practices, and lessons learned over the course of more than two decades.

15.2.1 Who Drafts the Judgments?

Judgments are drafted by lawyers assigned to the Chambers Legal Support Section of the Registry, one of the three organs of the Tribunal. However, the drafts are produced, revised, and finalized at the instruction and under the oversight of the judges assigned to a particular Chamber, or bench. This is the briefest of replies to the question 'who drafts the judgments?' What follows is a deservedly much more detailed reply.

Chambers is made up entirely of judges (including the President), and their responsibility is to adjudicate cases brought by the Prosecutor (and other matters uniquely before the Office of the President). The Chambers Legal Support Section lies within the Registry's Judicial Support Division, and it employs the lawyers and administrative staff who support the judges (including the President). In practical terms, Chambers (the judges, who are not United Nations staff members) and the Chambers Legal Support Section (the lawyers and administrative support staff, who are United Nations staff members) are collectively known within the Tribunal as 'Chambers'. Chambers is led by the President, who coordinates the work of Chambers and supervises the activities of the Registrar, among other functions.[62] The President is assisted by a Head of Chambers, who manages the assignment of resources of Chambers and supervises all of the lawyers.[63] Chambers is organized into three Trial Chambers (I, II, and III) and an Appeals Chamber. The President acts as Presiding Judge of the Appeals Chamber and each Trial Chamber has a Presiding Judge. So far, so good. The organization gets a bit more difficult to grasp when you consider that within the Appeals Chamber there is a bench of five judges assigned for each case on appeal (and each bench is called 'the Appeals Chamber'), and within each of the three Trial Chambers there is a bench of three judges assigned for each case at trial (and each bench is called 'the Trial Chamber'). It gets even tougher to grasp when you consider that Chambers at its peak from about 2005 to 2011 had numerous cases still in the pre-trial stage (each assigned to its own 'Pre-trial' Chamber) and other unique judicial bodies active, for example, the Referral Bench and Joinder Bench.

What is the significance of the organization of Chambers to the topic of judgment drafting? The primary significance is that, in addition to each judge having an individual lawyer assigned (specifically to support that judge in any or all of his or her assigned cases), there is also a drafting team of lawyers assigned to support each bench of judges. At trial, the practice has been for the lawyers assigned to specific judges to meld into the drafting team(s) for cases to which the judge is assigned, whereas on appeal the lawyers assigned to specific judges rarely form part of the drafting team. The rationale for the distinction is twofold. First, judges are rarely assigned to more than one trial bench at a time, and certainly no more than two, because with most trials operating on an almost daily basis with court sessions lasting at least half a day, there would be no time for any more. In such circumstances,

62 Art 14 of the ICTY Statute; Rule 19 of the Rules.
63 Rule 33*ter* of the Rules. ICTY public website: The Head of Chambers acts as the principal legal adviser on legal issues arising across the Chambers.

it made more sense to have each trial judge's lawyer assist the drafting team keep up with the pace of daily sessions. Judges on appeal can be assigned to several cases at any given time because court sessions are very infrequent on appeal. In these circumstances, the judges are better served having their own lawyer provide individual support across the spectrum of multiple cases rather than focusing attention on only one by joining that case's drafting team. The second rationale relates to deliberations. Chambers lawyers are typically present for all deliberations (with sentence determination being the one uniform exception), but the support needed for trial deliberations is less because the bench is always on the same schedule and the evidence is fresher in the judges' minds. On appeal, the judges must deliberate on several ongoing cases at different stages of progress and according to a schedule in which milestone events (the briefing of appeals and the appeal hearing) might be separated by a year or more, and in which written deliberations have certain advantages—all reasons which justify the full-time support of a lawyer to stay organized.

One key practice to note is that while Chambers lawyers have privileged confidential relationships with the judges, it is generally limited according to assignment. Chambers lawyers are usually assigned to either trial support or appellate support, but not both at the same time. Further, assignment to a drafting team limits one's confidential relationship to the judges of that trial bench. For example, a Chambers lawyer assigned to the drafting team for Trial A will hold confidences with the judges on the bench of Trial A, but not Trials B, C, or D to which the lawyer is not assigned. The rationale is based on the 'need to know' principle, and the common sense view that it is easier to ensure confidentiality where fewer people have access to deliberative information. The confidential relationship exists in order to facilitate the secrecy of deliberations and decision-making, and therefore a Chambers lawyer who is not assigned to a particular drafting team has no need to know of that team's deliberations or to hold confidences with its judges. This restriction forms a core part of all Chambers working methodology. Electronic folders, where draft judgments are stored, are organized according to cases and accessible only by members of the drafting team assigned to a case. On the other hand, once a judgment (or order or decision) has been filed, even if it is filed in a confidential form, it is accessible by any Chambers lawyer in the Tribunal's electronic research judicial database since it is then jurisprudence on which another bench may wish to rely.

Chambers lawyers fill positions within the Chambers Legal Support Section ranging from the United Nations P-1 to P-5 level with the Head of Chambers at the D-1 level. The President's *Chef de Cabinet*[64] and the senior legal officers supervising Appeals Chamber staff and each of the three Trial Chambers are at the P-5 level. The backbone of the Section are the P-2 associate legal officers and P-3 legal officers who generally serve as full-time drafters or as judge-assigned lawyers, while P-4 legal officers and the P-5 senior legal officers perform most of the reviewing functions before team drafts are presented to the judges for consideration. The background of most Chambers lawyers is education and/or experience in public international law with a focus on international criminal law, international humanitarian law, and/or international human rights law. Some enter Chambers

[64] ICTY public website: The President of the Tribunal also appoints a Chef de Cabinet and Deputy Chef de Cabinet, as well as a Head of Chambers. The Chef de Cabinet acts as the President's adviser and operational focal person on all United Nations, diplomatic, political and administrative matters. The Deputy Chef de Cabinet assists the Chef de Cabinet in planning, organizing, and coordinating activities within the Office of the President.

with only domestic criminal law experience or judicial clerking experience. In the latter years of the Tribunal, more lawyers entered with prior experience at an international criminal tribunal. Although the lawyers come from around the globe, there is a healthy percentage of lawyers whose native language is English, and to a lesser extent, French. This is because all judicial orders, decisions, and judgments must be filed in one of the two working languages of the Tribunal, yet only a small percentage of the judges have English or French as their native language. Several Chambers lawyers are fluent in both official languages.

15.2.2 Responsibilities and Role of the Legal Support Staff

While the focus on the legal support staff for this chapter is on their role in judgment drafting, there are a number of underlying responsibilities on which the judgment drafting support is built. The ICTY public website provides this description:

> The Registry employs numerous legal staff who assist the judges by conducting research on various issues in international criminal law, international human rights law and international humanitarian law.
>
> In addition, legal staff help the judges in preparing and managing cases as well as processing evidence and documents submitted during trial. They also participate in the drafting of legal memoranda, decisions, and judgements. The judges and legal officers are also assisted by legal interns who are required to be, at a minimum, in their final year of law studies.

Judge Theodor Meron, in describing the judicial decision-making process within the Appeals Chamber in particular, compared the responsibilities of the legal support staff to national law clerks:

> Generally, a team of legal staff considers the issues that arise with respect to particular motions or appeals and provides judges with helpful briefing papers and notes to assist in their decision-making. This assistance is essentially the same as that provided by judicial clerks in the United States, but involves a larger number of staff, reflecting the complexity and scale of the cases before the Tribunals, which can involve dozens of crime sites, thousands of victims, and enormous volumes of written materials.[65]

From a recruitment standpoint, the following responsibilities were routinely included in vacancy announcements for associate legal officers in Chambers:

> Conduct legal research on a diverse range of assigned issues in criminal law, international law, international humanitarian law and other area(s) of specialization using multiple research sources; select relevant material, analyse information and present findings for internal review in either written or oral form;

[65] Meron (n 45) 283.

> On behalf of the Judges, assist in the preparation of legal opinions and advice, draft background memoranda, decisions and judgments of the Tribunal;
>
> . . .
>
> Assist the Judges in the processing of evidence and documents submitted during trial;

The Appeals Chamber assessed the role of legal support staff for the judges in the case of *Prosecutor v Mladić*, after defence counsel for Mladić filed a motion for a fair trial or mistrial arguing that legal support staff for the trial chamber in the *Karadžić* trial—which had a 'virtually identical' indictment—could not impartially support the trial chamber in the *Mladić* trial, as '[t]his overlap of duties places Legal officers in a position to influence the Judges' analysis of the evidence, which ultimately compromises the right of an Accused to be presumed innocent'.[66] The Trial Chamber rejected the argument, and the Defence appealed. The Appeals Chamber held:

9. The Appeals Chamber recalls that legal officers assisting Judges at the Tribunal are not subject to the same standards of impartiality as the Judges of the Tribunal, and that judicial decision-making is the sole purview of the Judges. Legal officers merely provide assistance to the Judges in legal research and preparing draft decisions, judgements, opinions, and orders in conformity with the instructions given to them by the Judges.
10. Notwithstanding the above, in some cases, a prospective staff member's statements or activities may be so problematic as to either impugn the perceived impartiality of the Judges or the appearance thereof, or, even if this were not the case, the Tribunal's fundamental guarantees of fair trial. In this respect, the Appeals Chamber recalls in particular, that an unacceptable appearance of bias exists, *inter alia*, where the circumstances would lead a reasonable observer, properly informed, to reasonably apprehend bias.

. . .

29. Turning to Mladić's submissions that the Trial Chamber erred in determining that bias of the Impugned Staff would not affect his right to be presumed innocent and implicitly acknowledged that a lack of impartiality of staff would be acceptable, the Appeals Chamber considers that Mladić misunderstands the applicable law and the relevant findings of the Trial Chamber.
30. The Appeals Chamber is of the view that the Trial Chamber correctly recalled that the Impugned Staff provides assistance to the Judges while the decision-making remains entirely in the Judges' purview and that neither the Rules of Procedure and Evidence of the Tribunal nor the related jurisprudence provide for the disqualification of the Impugned Staff. In doing so, the Trial Chamber did not acknowledge that a lack of impartiality of staff was acceptable, as Mladić suggests. Rather, the Trial Chamber considered that Mladić's submissions were based on the incorrect assumption that legal officers assisting Judges are subject to the same standards of impartiality as the Judges of the Tribunal, and that Mladić's submission was therefore ill-founded and irrelevant. Moreover, the Appeals Chamber observes that the Trial Chamber did not limit itself to assess the

[66] *Prosecutor v Ratko Mladić* (Motion for a Fair Trial and the Presumption of Innocence or, in the Alternative, a Mistrial) Case No IT-09-92-T (19 May 2016) paras 10–13, 24.

> question whether the standard of judicial impartiality was applicable to staff members but specifically examined the role of Impugned Staff in the Judges' decision-making process. Having considered the tasks allocated to the Impugned Staff in the present case, the Trial Chamber concluded that the assistance the Impugned Staff provides does not influence the decision-making ability of the Judges. Recalling that legal officers merely provide assistance to the Judges in legal research and preparing draft decisions, judgements, opinions, and orders in conformity with the instructions given to them by the Judges and that the judicial decision-making is the sole purview of the Judges, the Appeals Chamber sees no error in the Trial Chamber's approach. Mladić's argument that the Impugned Staff may have reached conclusions on the evidence tendered in the *Karadžić* case and may rely on these conclusions in the present matter merely shows disagreement with the Trial Chamber's assessment but falls short of demonstrating any error in the Trial Chamber's conclusion that Mladić's fair trial rights were not violated.[67]

In sum, legal support staff assist in drafting judgments but all decision-making authority remains with the judges.

15.2.3 How are the Judgments Drafted

The major division between the methodologies of judgment drafting in Chambers lies between drafting trial judgments and drafting appeal judgments.

Preparing a trial judgment begins almost immediately after a case has been assigned to a specific bench for trial.[68] Depending upon the number of accused to be tried, the Head of Chambers assigns a number of drafters to assist the bench, and the Trial Chamber's senior legal officer appoints a team leader from among the drafters. The minimum size for a team—assisting in a single-accused trial with relatively few charges in the indictment—is typically five, comprised of one P-3 or P-4 legal officer and four P-2 associate legal officers. The team leader's first task is to prepare for the case management responsibilities by reading the indictment and the pre-trial briefs of the parties, and ensuring that all pre-trial decisions and orders and all pending motions are identified and summarized for the bench. The team leader also makes an internal timeline for the case based on the number of witnesses to be called by each party and the number of hours granted for case presentation. Next, the team leader will use the indictment and the briefs to prepare a skeletal outline for the trial judgment which the drafting team will adjust and develop over time as evidence is adduced at trial, and as the parties' strategies and themes become clear.

The outline serves as a table of contents for the trial judgment, and usual chapter headings might include:

- introduction to the accused and the charges in the indictment;
- general considerations regarding evaluation of the evidence;
- general overview of the armed conflict and politico-military structure;

[67] *Prosecutor v Mladić* (Decision on Interlocutory Appeal Against Decision on Defence Motion for a Fair Trial and the Presumption of Innocence) Case No IT-09-92-AR73.6 (27 Feb 2017) (internal citations omitted).

[68] See *Prosecutor v Krajišnik* (Judgment) Case No IT-00-39-A (17 March 2009) para 134.

- jurisdictional basis;
- applicable law on the substantive crimes charged in the indictment;
- evidence of crimes at specific crime locations (often called the 'crime base' evidence);
- applicable law on the form(s) of individual criminal responsibility charged in the indictment;
- evidence of the accused's responsibility, and any defences;
- factual and legal findings and conclusions, and the disposition (or verdict);
- law and evidence related to sentencing, if required; and,
- glossary and procedural background of the case as annexes.

Certain drafting tasks can begin at once.[69] For example, the applicable law on the crimes and forms of responsibility charged in the indictment does not need to await the introduction of evidence before being drafted. If there are aspects of the law which the parties have highlighted in their pre-trial briefs, the drafting team can begin at once to research them thoroughly. If there are any agreed facts or judicially noticed facts, these can be entered into the outline. In short, the drafting team takes the opportunity early to set into writing anything relatively concrete or undisputed, knowing that the draft can always be modified if circumstances require.

Once trial begins, the bench is assisted in its court sessions by a member of the drafting team who sits at the table in front of and below the Presiding Judge. This legal officer wears a robe and follows the proceedings on a computer monitor that displays a real-time transcript of the proceedings. The team leader may also sit in court or follow the proceedings from his or her office. As the evidence is adduced, the legal officer compartmentalizes it according to the prepared outline for later review and analysis. There have been technological developments which have made this function much easier, but the essential task is to organize the evidence admitted at trial in such a way that all evidence on a certain point—including credibility and reliability of the evidence—is collated, whether introduced through one or numerous witnesses (including any called by defence) or whether elicited through direct or cross-examination. This is what is usually meant by processing of evidence. It is similar to what the parties do in marshalling the facts in their closing briefs and arguments, but without the component of persuasion. The role of Chambers staff is not to guide the bench to a certain decision, but rather to make certain that all contested evidence is reckoned and that no necessary decisions are overlooked. In trials lasting more than one year, perhaps several years, this is a job requiring lawyers who understand the trial process, and who are highly organized and vigilant. To avoid unnecessary delays, it is important to continue processing the evidence throughout the trial.

When all evidence has been received, the judges retire to their chambers to deliberate in private.[70] It is after closing arguments from the parties are heard that deliberations begin in earnest and the draft trial judgment begins to take shape as judicial decisions are made.

69 Assessment and Report of Judge Carmel Agius, President ofthe International Tribunal for the Former Yugoslavia, provided to the Security Council pursuant to para six of Security Council resolution 1534 (2004) (18 May 2017 to 29 November 2017), S/2017/1001, ('Final Completion Strategy Report'), para 77: 'Work processes within Chambers have, since very early in the Tribunal's existence, included commencing the drafting of judgments at an early stage during trials. This means that analysis of evidence is conducted as soon as the evidence is received by the Trial Chamber. Similarly, drafting of appeal judgments begins very early during the appeal proceedings.'

70 Rules 29 and 87(A) of the Rules.

Trial judgments are typically drafted in the following order. First, the Trial Chamber will check that the requirements for exercising its jurisdiction are met. If so, it will address the crimes alleged in the indictment. It will make factual findings on each charge, based on the relevant collated evidence. Once the factual conclusions are drawn, the judges apply the law and make legal findings on whether or not the alleged crimes are proven beyond a reasonable doubt. If any alleged crimes have been proven, the Trial Chamber will turn its attention to the alleged responsibility of the accused. Once again, it will begin by making factual findings based on the evidence. Then it will apply the law on the relevant modes of liability charged in the indictment and determine whether or not the criminal responsibility of the accused has been proven beyond a reasonable doubt. The Trial Chamber must decide separately on each charge of the indictment, and separately on the charges against each accused.[71] If the Trial Chamber finds any of the accused guilty, it will proceed to convict and sentence them, determining the length of each prison sentence.[72] Otherwise, it acquits them.

When drafting the judgment, the Trial Chamber must be vigilant to stay within certain parameters. First, all findings must be circumscribed by what is alleged in the indictment. Second, the findings must be based only on what was admitted into evidence. Third, the Trial Chamber must apply the right standard of proof. According to the Appeals Chamber, all factual findings underlying the elements of the crime or the form of responsibility alleged, as well as all those indispensable for a conviction, must be made beyond reasonable doubt.[73] Other findings do not need to meet this high standard of proof. The Trial Chamber is also guided by the final briefs of the parties. However, trial chambers have not considered themselves bound to remain within the confines of the arguments presented by the parties.

In assessing the evidence, the judges weigh each piece of evidence in light of the totality of the evidence to determine its probative value.[74] The Appeals Chamber has held that a trial chamber has a broad discretion to consider all relevant factors in determining the weight to attach to the evidence of any given witness.[75] Relevant factors include the credibility of the evidence, any inconsistencies within it, the existence of corroborating or contradictory evidence, whether the evidence is hearsay and could be tested in cross-examination, whether it emanates from an accomplice to the accused, and whether the Prosecution's case is based on direct or circumstantial evidence. A Trial Chamber can reasonably accept certain parts of a witness' testimony and reject others.[76]

It is important to have a good system of quality control in place for judgment drafting. Otherwise, the trial chamber may find itself overlooking important evidence, misinterpreting the evidence, failing to provide sufficient evidentiary support for its findings, forgetting to make important findings, or contradicting itself. Such mistakes may expose the trial judgment to being reversed on appeal. In one case, the Appeals Chamber noted that the presentation of a vast amount of detailed evidence had apparently hindered the Trial Chamber from focusing on the evidence underlying the crimes charged, and that in most cases it had not made specific explicit factual findings with regard to each element

71 Rule 87(B) of the Rules.
72 Rule 87(C) of the Rules.
73 *Prosecutor v Halilović* (Judgment) Case No IT-01-48-A (16 October 2007) paras 122–23.
74 *Prosecutor v Limaj* et al (Judgment) Case No IT-03-66-A (27 September 2007) para 153.
75 *Prosecutor v Lukić and Lukić* (Judgment) Case No IT-98-32/1-A (4 December 2012) para 112.
76 *Prosecutor v Boškoski and Tarčulovski* (Judgment) Case No IT-04-82-A (19 May 2010) para 59.

of the crimes.[77] The Appeals Chamber reversed a substantial number of the Trial Chamber's findings.

The drafting of judgments on appeal is a very different matter. Whereas the trial chamber's findings are based on the evidence, as a rule the Appeals Chamber's findings are based on the trial chamber's findings. At trial the accused are presumed innocent and the burden is on the Prosecution to prove their case beyond a reasonable doubt; on appeal it is the trial judgment that is 'presumed innocent', in the sense that the burden is on the appellants to show that the Trial Chamber erred. While the Trial Chamber must base its findings on the entire body of evidence, on appeal the Appeals Chamber will in principle consider only the arguments advanced by the parties and the factual support to which they refer.

According to Article 25 of the Statute, convicted persons and the Prosecutor have standing to appeal a trial judgment, based either on an error of law invalidating the decision or an error of fact which has occasioned a miscarriage of justice. The Appeals Chamber does not operate as a second Trial Chamber conducting a trial *de novo*.[78] The consistent practice of the Appeals Chamber in its later years has been to set out the standard of appellate review in each appeal judgment.[79] The standard is rather complicated, but its three most essential aspects are errors of fact, errors of law, and defective arguments.

The appellant must meet a high burden to demonstrate an error of fact. Indeed, the Appeals Chamber will only substitute its own finding for that of the trial chamber when no reasonable trier of fact could have reached the original decision. Further, only an error of fact which has occasioned a miscarriage of justice will cause the Appeals Chamber to overturn a decision by the trial chamber.[80] The Appeals Chamber has explained the reason for this high burden as follows:

> Pursuant to the jurisprudence of the Tribunal, the task of hearing, assessing and weighing the evidence presented at trial is left primarily to the Trial Chamber. Thus, the Appeals Chamber must give a margin of deference to a finding of fact reached by a Trial Chamber. Only where the evidence relied on by the Trial Chamber could not have been accepted by any reasonable tribunal of fact or where the evaluation of the evidence is 'wholly erroneous' may the Appeals Chamber substitute its own finding for that of the Trial Chamber. It must be borne in mind that two judges, both acting reasonably, can come to different conclusions on the basis of the same evidence.[81]

The situation is different with regard to alleged errors of law. Trial Chambers are no better placed than the Appeals Chamber to know the law. In fact, the Appeals Chamber has a greater responsibility in this regard, since its decisions of law are binding upon the trial chambers.[82] Consequently, the Appeals Chamber reviews the Trial Chamber's findings of law to determine whether or not they are correct.[83] In other words, the appellant's burden is

[77] *Prosecutor v Kordić and Čerkez* (Judgment) Case No IT-95-14/2-A (17 December 2004) paras 383–84.
[78] ibid para 21; *Prosecutor v Limaj* et al (Judgment) Case No IT-03-66-A (27 September 2007) para 135.
[79] See *Prosecutor v Prlić* et al (Judgment) Case No IT-04-74-A (29 November 2017) paras 18–25.
[80] ibid paras 18, 21.
[81] *Prosecutor v Kupreškić* et al (Judgment) Case No IT-95-16-A (23 October 2001) para 30 (internal references omitted).
[82] *Prosecutor v Aleksovski* (Judgment) Case No IT-95-14/1-A (24 March 2000) para 113.
[83] See *Prosecutor v Prlić* et al (Judgment) Case No IT-04-74-A (29 November 2017) para 20.

not particularly high, as he or she must merely convince the Appeals Chamber that the Trial Chamber got the law wrong.[84]

Finally, the Appeals Chamber has repeatedly held that it will not consider a party's submissions in detail when they are obscure, contradictory, vague, or suffer from other formal and obvious insufficiencies.[85] In practice, the Appeals Chamber has dismissed many arguments on that basis. It has also routinely listed the types of deficient submissions on appeal which need not be considered on the merits:

> (1) arguments that fail to identify the challenged factual findings, that misrepresent the factual findings or the evidence, or that ignore other relevant factual findings; (2) mere assertions that the trial chamber must have failed to consider relevant evidence, without showing that no reasonable trier of fact, based on the evidence, could have reached the same conclusion as the trial chamber; (3) challenges to factual findings on which a conviction does not rely, and arguments that are clearly irrelevant, that lend support to, or that are not inconsistent with the challenged finding; (4) arguments that challenge a trial chamber's reliance or failure to rely on one piece of evidence, without explaining why the conviction should not stand on the basis of the remaining evidence; (5) arguments contrary to common sense; (6) challenges to factual findings where the relevance of the factual finding is unclear and has not been explained by the appealing party; (7) mere repetition of arguments that were unsuccessful at trial without any demonstration that their rejection by the trial chamber constituted an error warranting the intervention of the Appeals Chamber; (8) allegations based on material not on record; (9) mere assertions unsupported by any evidence, undeveloped assertions, or failure to articulate an error; and (10) mere assertions that the trial chamber failed to give sufficient weight to evidence or failed to interpret evidence in a particular manner.[86]

The practice of appeal proceedings developed towards the following model. First, one or more parties file an appeal against the trial judgment. The opposing party then files a response, most often followed by a reply from the appellant. Once the case is fully briefed, the Presiding Judge and his or her legal officers examine the arguments of the parties and prepare a so-called 'preparatory document'. The Presiding Judge sends it to the other judges assigned to the case so as to fully inform them about the appeal and assist them at the appeal hearing and during deliberations. With the assistance of the preparatory document, the judges identify any pertinent questions to put to the parties in advance of the appeal hearing. At this hearing the parties supplement their written arguments with oral arguments and respond to the Appeals Chamber's questions. Judges may ask the parties additional questions and the convicted appellants may choose to make a brief address to the Appeals Chamber at the end of the hearing.

After the appeal hearing, the judges retire to their chambers to deliberate. Based on the outcome of the deliberations, the legal officers convert the preparatory document into a first draft judgment, while incorporating the new information from the appeal hearing. They draw the judges' attention to difficult issues requiring particular attention, in the form

[84] ibid paras 18–19.
[85] ibid para 24.
[86] ibid para 25.

of notes to the judges or possible alternative approaches presented as 'options'. Similarly, the judges would be alerted in case there was no clear majority on a particular issue. The Presiding Judge oversees this process and circulates the first draft judgment to the judges. The judges request edits to the draft judgment, which the legal officers implement before circulating the second draft judgment. This process continues until all judges are satisfied with the judgment or have opted to write separate opinions on specific matters. Occasionally, where necessary, the Appeals Chamber holds additional evidentiary hearings or requests supplementary written submissions from the parties. Once all issues are settled, the Appeals Chamber schedules a public hearing at which it pronounces the appeal judgment, in summary form.

15.3 Impact of Judgments

One should not entirely separate the legal and technical aspects of judgments and judgment drafting from the reception of judgments after they enter the public domain. Once a judgment has been signed by the judges, filed with the Registry and summarily announced in open court, hard copies are distributed to the parties and an electronic version is uploaded onto the Tribunal's public website for immediate access. Barring some unforeseen typographical error or other reason requiring a corrigendum, the judgment thereafter speaks for itself. Judges are loath to publicly comment on their judgments, and the media office typically issues a very straightforward description of the judgment that can be fairly characterized as a capsule version of the summary read in court. It is left to practitioners, scholars, journalists, politicians, members of the general public, and those most affected by the judgment (the accused and the victims of criminality) to draw meaning from the judgment. Those in or allied with the legal profession usually care most about whether the judgment contains some new legal development and whether the analysis throughout the judgment is sound and reliable. The general public, and especially victims and witnesses, care almost exclusively about the verdict.

A joint pilot study by the ICTY Victims and Witnesses Section and researchers and the University of North Texas Castleberry Peace Institute addressed the perceptions of ICTY judgments with a representative sample of 300 witnesses who had given testimony before the Tribunal. With respect to a witness's perception of the effectiveness of his or her testimony, most witnesses were 'pleased when their contribution is acknowledged by the Tribunal and when they see that their testimony is relied upon in the final judgement'.[87] Yet in exploring positive and negative appraisals of testimony experience, the category least cited as positive included the satisfaction of witnesses with the judgments and sentences, and the second most negative impact factor related to dissatisfaction with judgments and sentences. The witnesses 'expressed their unhappiness about judgments in cases, particularly regarding whether they provided justice, met expectations, and allocated proper punishment'.[88] Later questioning of the witnesses revealed that they found sentences to be too lenient or too harsh, but also inconsistent; and had concerns with the fairness of acquittals

[87] University of North Texas and ICTY Victims and Witnesses Section, *Echoes of testimonies*: A Pilot Study into the long-term impact of bearing witness before the ICTY, Revised October 2016, 103.
[88] ibid 107–08.

and reversal of convictions.[89] This illustrates the difficulty in measuring the quality, or success, of a judgment based on how it is received by the members of the public, even those most affected by it.

Over the course of time, the authors of the present chapter observed that judges expended more effort in the judgments to make detailed factual findings as to the evidence of an underlying crime for which the accused would nonetheless be acquitted for a failure of the evidence to prove individual criminal responsibility. This was done for several reasons, but one was undoubtedly to ameliorate the inevitable disappointment to victims of the underlying crime. It was important to communicate that the Chamber by acquitting an accused was not saying that no crime occurred. This is one of the rare occasions where a judgment might be seen in part as addressing a particular audience other than the parties.

Looking at judgments at the regional level brings us to the question frequently asked in the final year of the Tribunal's existence—whether it has fulfilled its purpose of contributing to the restoration and maintenance of peace.[90] Measuring such impact is inherently difficult. Judge and former ICTY President Gabrielle Kirk McDonald addressed reconciliation in her message on the occasion of the Final ICTY Symposium: 'Not only did the Tribunal assign culpability, its judgements also made broader factual and legal findings based on evidence, tested by the rigors of trial, that constitute a historical record of what transpired. When the climate in the region is right, and with the availability of other tools of transitional justice, these judgements can be utilized in a reconciliation process, should the people of the region embrace it.'[91] Certainly, though, it remains for the people to embrace the judgments. According to one scholar, Marko Milanović, who analysed a series of public opinion surveys in order to address the impact of the ICTY on the attitudes of the peoples of the former Yugoslavia, the ICTY 'failed to persuade the relevant populations that the findings in its judgments are true'.[92] He is especially critical of the length of the judgments, characterizing them as 'excessively long' and arguing that 'ordinary individuals will not make up their mind on the ICTY, or on specific crimes addressed by the ICTY, by reading the many thousands of pages of the ICTY's judgements'.[93] Nevertheless, ICTY judgments may succeed on other fronts. For instance, the Conference of the ICTY Legacy Dialogues earlier included among its expert recommendations in order to assist national and regional courts that 'ICTY judgements should, where possible, be integrated into the jurisprudence

[89] ibid 114.

[90] UN SC Resolution 827 (1993) 'International Criminal tribunal for the former Yugoslavia (ICTY)' (25 May 1993) S/RES/827.

[91] Tribunal Statement—Message by Judge Gabrielle Kirk McDonald on the Occasion of the Final ICTY Symposium, The Hague, 18 December 2017. See also Final Completion Strategy Report, para 61. 'Relevant in this context also is the Tribunal's fact-finding work and its role in establishing an historical record in respect of the conflicts of the 1990s. While not part of its official mandate, its contributions in this respect are noteworthy. Not only has the Tribunal established beyond reasonable doubt countless facts in relation to crimes that were once subject to dispute, every trial and appeal judgment of the Tribunal has set out facts regarding, for example, the relevant historical background and political developments, the modus operandi of military, police and paramilitary forces, and the acts and conduct of the accused and persons subordinate to them. In addition to the evidence presented in court, admissions of guilt from a number of accused have also greatly contributed to the establishment of the facts. The Tribunal's creation of an historical record is a key part of its legacy that will stand the test of time and continue to assist in combating denial and revisionism in the region of the former Yugoslavia.'

[92] M Milanović, 'The Impact of the ICTY on the Former Yugoslavia: An Anticipatory Post-Mortem' (2016) 110 American Journal of International Law 233, 235, 258.

[93] M Milanović, 'Establishing the Facts About Mass Atrocities: Accounting for the Failure of the ICTY to Persuade Target Audiences' (2016) 46 *Georgetown Journal of International Law* 1321, 1333, 1343.

of national jurisdictions in the former Yugoslavia'.[94] One safe conclusion is that the impact of ICTY judgments is yet to be felt in full.

15.4 Conclusion

Judgment drafting at the ICTY has also led to critical self-reflection. Notably, Judge Patricia Wald (ICTY judge 1999–2001 and former Chief Judge of the Court of Appeals for the DC Circuit) offered a sharp critique of trial judgment drafting:[95]

> Because ICTY trials are long and fact specific and because legal assistants are often assigned to the Chambers as a whole, with only one junior legal assistant assigned to any individual judge, the task of initially drafting the Chambers' judgments, to a very considerable degree, is not infrequently delegated to the pool of legal assistants who commonly are selected by the Presiding Judge or the senior legal officers. Reading some of the several-hundred-pages-long, format-stylized judgements of the ICTY, one can guess that many of the judgments are the work of a committee rather than an individual judge or judges.
>
> I also have the impression that the purpose of a judgment may vary within legal cultures. In my U.S. experience the emphasis is on telling the parties and the public why the judges came to a particular result in light of relevant facts and law. In the culture of some of my colleagues, the format appears to be more ritualistic, requiring a formal recitation of what the parties argued; what the abstract legal theory is; what the factual findings of the court are; and then, finally and not always predictably, the ultimate result.
>
> There seems to be less premium on making transparent the judges' reasoning as to how the law applies to the facts, except where dissenting or concurring judges file separate statements. In my opinion, there is less emphasis on style and readability. For these reasons ICTY judgements sometimes seem stilted, bureaucratic, and insufficiently reasoned, making them largely inaccessible to the reader and frustrating to the press and even legal scholars who try to analyze them.

Gideon Boas, ICTY senior legal officer (1998–2006) assigned to the Slobodan Milošević trial, echoed the views of Judge Patricia Wald:[96]

> As former ICTY Judge Wald has acknowledged, the chamber's legal staff performs the bulk of the research, and typically drafts large portions of the trial judgement. The legal officers' drafts are, of course, subject to approval, revision, and rejection by the judges. The degree of judicial involvement in the drafting varies by judge and according to the importance each judge gives to a given issue or portion of the discussion.

[94] ICTY Legacy Dialogues, Outcome of the ICTY Legacy Dialogues Conference: Conclusions and Recommendations, 22–24 June 2017, Sarajevo, Bosnia, and Herzegovina, 3.

[95] P Wald, 'The International Criminal Tribunal for the Former Yugoslavia Comes of Age: Some Observations on Day-To-Day Dilemmas of an International Court' (2001) 5 Washington University Journal of Law & Policy 87, 93–94.

[96] G Boas et al, *International Criminal Procedure, International Criminal Law Practitioner* (Vol III, CUP 2011) 292, fn 241, and 418–19, fn 244.

> Judge Wald's words are still true today, and the other tribunals have perpetuated the cumbersome drafting style begun in the ICTY's first case. Chambers expend considerable energy ticking off the boxes of the established ritual. They often describe the facts witness by witness, municipality by municipality, and dedicate large swathes of the judgement to recounting the parties' arguments before finally turning to what is often a cursory analysis of the law and application of the facts to that law.
>
> The exercise frequently involves a perfunctory comparative survey of national law on a given subject. Among the many stylistic habits that lend an air of stiltedness to judgements (and other decisions) are the judges' routine reference to themselves in the third person as 'the Trial Chamber', instead of the much simpler 'we', and their tendency to preface many sentences with an unnecessary 'The Trial Chamber notes that' instead of simply stating the proposition. In addition, many judges make frequent use of Latin, and refer to the accused formalistically by first and last name in every sentence. See, e.g., *Halilović* Trial Judgement, supra note 22 (repeatedly using the full given and surname of each witness and other person discussed in the judgement, including the accused Sefer Halilović). Some trial chambers see the need to preface the accused's name, on each instance, with 'Mr.', 'Ms.', 'Gen.', 'Col.', and the like. Much of this stylistic awkwardness seems to stem from a belief by some judges and legal staff that inaccessible language is still stylistically valued in legal writing in the English language. On this issue generally, see Bryan A. Garner, *Legal Writing in Plain English* (2001).

As acknowledged by these authors, part of the criticism comes down to an opposition between legal cultures. The ICTY was a laboratory in combining different national legal cultures into a new coherent whole. The outcome was not immune to criticism. For instance, the judgments could no doubt have been shorter and easier to read. Nevertheless, there are some legitimate explanations for this. For instance, ICTY Trial Chambers had to ensure a fair and expeditious trial[97] and uphold the right of the accused to be tried without undue delay.[98] This led them to try to minimize the time between the close of evidence and the moment of issuing the trial judgment, even if it meant less time spent on polishing and perfecting it. Another factor affecting readability was the choice made in many trial judgments to first set out all relevant evidence and then to draw conclusions on that basis, rather than going straight to factual findings. Though more cumbersome, this approach provided more transparency in the Trial Chamber's reasoning, facilitated its internal quality control, and showed the Appeals Chamber that all relevant evidence had been considered.

It is also worth noting that the judgment drafting practices at the ICTY evolved over time. Internal efforts were made to learn from past experiences, develop judgment drafting manuals, and provide training in judgment drafting. Overall, increasing emphasis was placed on explaining how the judges came to a certain conclusion. Compare for instance the Appeals Chamber's treatment of the controversial 'specific direction' requirement in the law on aiding and abetting, set out in a single paragraph in the *Tadić* judgment (1999) and spanning thirty-three densely footnoted paragraphs in the *Šainović* et al judgment (2014).[99]

[97] Art 20(1) of the ICTY Statute.

[98] Art 21(4)(c) of the ICTY Statute.

[99] *Prosecutor v Tadić* (Judgment) Case No IT-94-1-A, (15 July 1999) para 229; *Prosecutor v Šainović* et al (Judgment) Case No IT-05-87-A (23 January 2014) paras 1617–50.

As a result of such efforts, there was a clear overall trend towards improved judgment drafting during the life of the ICTY, and internal criticism of the sort exemplified above was largely absent in the final decade. Hopefully, present and future international criminal courts and tribunals may learn from the successes and shortcomings of judgment drafting at the ICTY. Perhaps the present chapter may make a modest contribution in that regard.

16

Muzzling the Press

When Does the Law Justify Reporting Restrictions? Contempt Cases Against Journalists at the ICTY and Beyond

Audrey Fino and Sandra Sahyouni**, ****

16.1 Introduction

'Publicity is the very soul of justice', the English philosopher Jeremy Bentham once wrote.[1] This and other maxims are a frequent leitmotiv to modern discourses on the need to ensure open and public trials as a means to deter abuses. Far from being shallow pronouncements, they illustrate how publicity has come to be considered one of the lynchpins of a fair trial, so intimately intertwined with it in the public consciousness as to be virtually indissociable.

In practice, however, the publicity of trials has limited capacity without other aids. The doors to a courtroom can be opened and a trial made accessible, but this only takes on effective meaning when those who can attend are also able to disseminate the details of judicial proceedings beyond the courtroom, to those who cannot. The necessary interplay between publicity and *publicizing* explains the significant role the press has assumed in concretizing the principle of a public trial, so much so that the press is now seen as being an extension of a courtroom's public gallery.[2] Given this dynamic, it was perhaps inevitable that a court's authority to limit the publicity of trials, and by extension, sanction those who contravene those limits, could be viewed as an infringement on the freedom of the press.

Constraints on freedom of the press have been most striking at international criminal tribunals, where violations of court-ordered measures have led to several landmark, yet contentious prosecutions of journalists for contempt of court, with the International Criminal Tribunal for the former Yugoslavia (ICTY), as the grandfather

* Audrey Fino is a lecturer at the University of Groningen, and a former Legal Officer in the Chambers of the International Criminal Tribunal for the former Yugoslavia (ICTY) and the United Nations Office of the High Commissioner for Human Rights.

** Sandra Sahyouni is a Legal Officer at the Special Tribunal for Lebanon (STL).

*** The views expressed herein are solely those of the authors and not of the ICTY, the United Nations, or the STL. The authors thank Edel Regan, Gabriella Carpentieri, and Thomas Wayde Pittman for their valuable assistance and support, and Hala El Amine and Miša Zgonec-Rozej for their comments on earlier drafts.

[1] J Bentham, 'Bentham's Draught for the Organization of the Judicial Establishments, Compared with that of the National Assembly, with a Commentary on the same' in J Bowring (ed), *The Works of Jeremy Bentham* (vol 4, Simpkin, Marshall & Co 1863) 316.

[2] *R. v Burrell* (Reasons for refusing the Crown's application for reporting restrictions on aspects of the complainant's evidence) [2004] Central Criminal Court, 17 December 2004, para 25; *MacDougall v Knight* [1889] 14 AC 194, para 200.

Audrey Fino and Sandra Sahyouni, *Muzzling the Press* In: *Legacies of the International Criminal Tribunal for the Former Yugoslavia.* Edited by: Carsten Stahn, Carmel Agius, Serge Brammertz, Colleen Rohan, Oxford University Press (2020). © The Several Contributors
DOI: 10.1093/oso/9780198862956.003.0017

of modern international criminal tribunals, paving the way. Despite developing the law on this issue, however, its prosecutions of journalists generated befuddlement, and at times controversy.

But to what extent is the controversy justified? In most jurisdictions, the right to freedom of expression, and by extension the freedom of the press, is not absolute, and subject to overriding societal priorities, such as national security, public order, and public morals.[3] In the context of criminal proceedings, the right to a public trial can be curtailed if it would more adequately serve the interests of justice than publicity. Informed by a comparative look at laws and jurisprudence drawn from select common law and civil law jurisdictions, as well as those of the ICTY and the array of modern international criminal tribunals, this chapter posits that measures to restrict reporting in international criminal procedure are in fact fully in line with domestic trends and international human rights law. By extension, and despite the polemics it may cause, the ability of international criminal tribunals to hold in contempt those who violate such reporting restrictions also mirrors the powers conferred upon judges in domestic jurisdictions to sanction similar violations, whether by virtue of the common law, or on the basis of statutory provisions prohibiting the reporting of certain aspects of the judicial process. In short, the ability of international criminal tribunals to restrict the publicizing of certain information—for example, when it endangers vulnerable persons—and to subsequently punish it if it does occur, is unexceptional when considered in tandem with the ability of domestic courts to do the same.

This chapter begins by providing an overview of the facts leading to the contempt cases brought against journalists at the ICTY, International Criminal Tribunal for Rwanda (ICTR), and Special Tribunal for Lebanon (STL), exposing the criticism and controversy that the cases have sparked in the public domain, but also, to some extent, in the legal community. As these types of contempt cases often involve an underlying offence, namely the violation of a judicial order granting protective measures to victims and witnesses or an order of non-disclosure of confidential information, the chapter continues by discussing the law governing such orders—*i.e.* the law on reporting restrictions—both domestically and internationally in the context of freedom of the press. In doing so, the legal frameworks in place in the UK, Canada, France, and Italy are used as comparative reference points.[4] Finally, the last section of the chapter analyses the actual law of contempt at international tribunals. In particular, it reviews the reasoning in the contempt judgments issued by the ICTY and the STL, with the four chosen domestic jurisdictions providing helpful reference points. On the basis of this discussion, the chapter hopes to demonstrate that criticisms against international tribunals unfairly overlook similar legal frameworks and practices domestically, and that the law of contempt at the ICTY and the STL is in line with human rights law.

[3] One jurisdiction that comes to mind as evading this trend is of course the US. However, even its Supreme Court, despite upholding the primacy of the First Amendment to its Constitution on free expression and acknowledging the special role of the press under it, has held that there are cases where it is justifiable to limit or exclude the press. See *Bridges v California*, 314 US 252, 263 (1941); *Marshall v U.S.*, 360, US 310 (1959); *Estes v Texas*, 381 US 532 (1965); *Sheppard v Maxwell*, 384 US 333 (1966).

[4] These jurisdictions were chosen, not only based on the authors' familiarity with them, but also because they offer a representative sample of legal trends in both common and civil law systems.

16.2 Factual Overview and Public Reactions to Prosecutions of Journalists at the International Tribunal

Of the larger number of contempt cases that have taken place at the international tribunals, a total of seven have involved journalists, five being at the ICTY and two at the STL.[5] This number includes only those prosecutions that have been brought to conclusion, that is, with a final judgment being handed, whether of acquittal or guilt. In addition to these, on at least two occasions, notably at the ICTR, allegations of contempt have been brought before or by judges against the media, without however making it past this stage.

It is notable that contempt trials, while they are procedurally conducted as separate trials in their own right, typically unfold within the context of other judicial proceedings, and can be considered, in a way, their by-product. In order for anyone to be accused of interfering with the administration of justice, justice must necessarily be in the process of being administered, have been administered, or about to be administered. This will become apparent in the overview presented below, which places the contemptuous offences in the context of the broader judicial proceedings to which they are intrinsically linked.

16.2.1 The ICTY

The first contempt cases against journalists to ever be brought to trial in the modern era of the international criminal tribunals were against two Croatian journalists and an editor in the broader context of the *Blaškić* trial at the ICTY.[6] Tihomir Blaškić was a former colonel in the Croatian Defence Council (HVO) and was in command of the HVO troops in Central Bosnia between 1993–1994 when war crimes were committed there against Bosnian Muslims.[7] Not only was this one of the first ICTY cases against a Croat in 1996—and by then, Blaškić had been promoted to general of the army of the Republic of Croatia[8]—but,

[5] At the ECCC, the investigating judges sought to prosecute Voice of America (Khmer) after it allegedly published confidential information. However, bar a few media releases, there is no further information publicly available on the ECCC's website: ECCC '*Statement from the Co-Investigating Judges Regarding Contempt of Court Proceedings Against Voice of America*' (31 August 2011) <https://www.eccc.gov.kh/en/articles/statement-co-investigating-judges-regarding-contempt-court-proceedings-against-voice> accessed February 2018; ECCC 'The Court Report (September 2011)' <https://www.eccc.gov.kh/en/publication/court-report-september-2011> accessed February 2018.

The SCSL has had six contempt cases, though none involved the press: *Independent Counsel v Samura* (Judgment in Contempt Proceedings) SCSL-2005-01 (26 October 2005); *Independent Counsel v Brima* et al (Sentencing Judgment in Contempt Proceedings) SCSL-2005-02 and SCSL-2005-03 (21 September 2005); *Prosecutor v Senessie* (Sentencing Judgment) SCSL-2011-01-T (12 July 2012); *Independent Counsel v Bangura* et al (Judgment in Contempt Proceedings) SCSL-2011-02-T (25 September 2012); *In the Matter of Contempt Proceedings Arising from the Case of Prosecutor v Taylor* (Judgment in Contempt Proceedings) SCSL-12-01-T (19 October 2012); *Independent Counsel v Taylor* (Judgment in Contempt Proceedings) SCSL-12-02-T (25 January 2013). The ICC has had one contempt case so far, for the offence of corruptly influencing defence witnesses and presenting their false evidence to the court under art 70 of the ICC statute: *Prosecutor v Bemba* et al (Public Redacted Judgment on the appeals of Mr Jean-Pierre Bemba Gombo, Mr Aimé Kilolo Musamba, Mr Jean-Jacques Mangenda Kabongo, Mr Fidèle Babala Wandu, and Mr Narcisse Arido against the decision of Trial Chamber VII entitled 'Judgment pursuant to Article 74 of the Statute') ICC-01/05-01/13 (8 March 2018).

[6] *Prosecutor v Ivica Marijačić and Markica Rebić* IT-95-14-R77.2; *Prosecutor v Josip Jović* IT-95-14 and IT-95-14/2-R77; *Prosecutor v Domagoj Margetić* IT-95-14-R77.6; *Prosecutor v Tihomir Blaškić* IT-95-14-T.

[7] *Prosecutor v Tihomir Blaškić* (Appeal Judgment) Case No IT-95-14-A (29 July 2004).

[8] *Prosecutor v Tihomir Blaškić* (Judgment) IT-95-14-T (3 March 2000) para 2 and fn 2.

given the nationalistic bend of the government in Croatia at the time, any news related to this case was bound to make headlines.

It is, therefore, not surprising that in November and December 2000, the Croatian daily newspaper *Slobodna Dalmacija* published excerpts of statements by a protected witness, including his identity.[9] The witness was none other than Stipe Mesić, who had gone on to become President of Croatia. Mesić had been granted protective measures as a prosecution witness and given testimony before the ICTY in closed session in the *Blaškić* case.[10] Every few days, over a period of one month, the newspaper printed excerpts of statements he had given to the prosecution, as well as of transcripts of non-public court hearings concerning his testimony.[11] In spite of an order by the relevant trial chamber on 1 December 2000 to cease and desist the publications, refrain from publishing confidential information regarding any protected witness generally, and a warning that ignoring this order would expose the authors and those responsible for any publication to contempt of the tribunal, publication continued.[12]

Faced with the newspaper's continued failure to abide by the court's order, the prosecution charged *Slobodna Dalmacija*'s editor-in-chief, Josip Jović, with contempt of the tribunal under Rule 77(A) and Rule 77(A)(ii) of the Rules of Procedure and Evidence (Rules) of the ICTY, which refer specifically to the ICTY's power to punish anyone who 'discloses information relating to those proceedings in knowing violation of an order of a Chamber'.[13] Jović was charged with intentionally violating the orders of the tribunal and as such interfering with the administration of justice.[14]

A similar event transpired in November 2004, when the Croatian newspaper *Hrvatski List* published an article by Ivica Marijačić, the newspaper's editor-in-chief.[15] The article revealed the identity of a protected witness who had testified in the *Blaškić* case in December 1997, and excerpts of a statement the witness had given to the prosecution prior to his testimony.[16] The article, which also mentioned that the witness had testified in non-public proceedings before the ICTY,[17] was printed next to an interview with Markica Rebić, formerly the head of the Croatian Security Information Service, an intelligence branch of the Croatian government, who was said to be the source.[18]

The ICTY prosecutor filed an indictment against both Marijačić and Rebić, charging them with contempt of the tribunal punishable under Rule 77(A)(ii) of the Rules for knowingly and wilfully interfering with the administration of justice, by publishing the identity

[9] *Prosecutor v Josip Jović* (First Amended Indictment) IT-95-14 and IT-95-14/2-R77 (19 May 2006) para 4; *Prosecutor v Josip Jović* (Judgment) IT-95-14 and IT-95-14/2-R77 (30 August 2006) (Jović Trial Judgment) paras 1–2, 4.

[10] Jović Trial Judgment (n 9) paras 1–2. The Appeals Chamber lifted the protective measures applicable to Mesić on 24 January 2006. Jović Trial Judgment, para 8.

[11] First Amended Indictment (n 9) para 4; Jović Trial Judgment (n 9) paras 3–7.

[12] First Amended Indictment (n 9) paras 5–12; Jović Trial Judgment (n 9) paras 4–6.

[13] First Amended Indictment (n 9) paras 13–14; Jović Trial Judgment (n 9) para 10.

[14] First Amended Indictment (n 9) paras 13–14; Jović Trial Judgment (n 9) para 15.

[15] *Prosecutor v Ivica Marijačić and Markica Rebić* (Third Amended Indictment) IT-95-14-R77.2 (14 October 2005) paras 1, 5.

[16] Third Amended Indictment (n 15) paras 3–7; *Prosecutor v Ivica Marijačić and Markica Rebić* (Judgment) IT-95-14-R77.2 (10 March 2006) (Marijačić and Rebić Trial Judgment) paras 1, 7.

[17] Third Amended Indictment (n 15); Marijačić and Rebić Trial Judgment (n 16) paras 1, 7.

[18] Rebić was not a journalist. Third Amended Indictment (n 15) paras 5, 7, 9; Marijačić and Rebić Trial Judgment (n 16) paras 1, 7.

of the protected witness, his statement, and the fact that he had testified in non-public proceedings.[19]

The intrigue around the *Blaškić* case came to a head in July 2006 when a freelance journalist from Zagreb, Domagoj Margetić,[20] authored an article about protected witnesses, acknowledging that their identities were protected, and published the complete witness list of the *Blaškić* case on his website.[21] A few days later, the article was published on another website with a hyperlink to the witness list on Margetić's own website.[22] Around this time, Margetić also published two more articles on his website, revealing the identity of two of the protected witnesses in the *Blaškić* case, as well as the date of their testimonies and the fact that they had testified in closed session.[23] These second and third articles were also published on other websites which hyperlinked to Margetić's own website.[24] On 28 July 2006, the ICTY issued an order to Margetić to immediately cease and desist from publishing the identities of protected witnesses and to remove the witness list from his website.[25] On 1 August 2006, the web host ceased operation of the website.[26]

Margetić was charged with contempt of the tribunal under Rule 77(A) of the Rules for knowingly and wilfully interfering with its administration of justice when he published, for nearly a month, the witness list and related articles on his website.[27] The indictment further alleged that by exposing this protected material to a wider audience—through its publication and dissemination by other internet web users and by hyper-linking to the protected information—Margetić committed contempt under Rule 77(A)(iv) of the Rules by interfering with witnesses.[28]

The fourth ICTY contempt case against the media took place in 2005 in connection with the prosecution of the Kosovar Albanians Ramush Haradinaj, Idriz Balaj, and Lahi Brahimaj.[29] When he was indicted, Haradinaj was about to become the prime minister of Kosovo and he was the first high-ranking Kosovar politician to be charged by the ICTY. During the Kosovo war in 1998, he was a commander of the Kosovo Liberation Army (KLA).[30] Balaj and Brahimaj were both members of the KLA, and Balaj was also commander of the Black Eagles, a special unit of the KLA.[31] All three men were charged with crimes committed by KLA forces under their command in 1998 against Serb, Kosovar Roma/Egyptian civilians, and Kosovar Albanian civilians perceived to be collaborating

[19] Third Amended Indictment (n 15) paras 10–12; Marijačić and Rebić Trial Judgment (n 16) paras 3–4, 7–8.

[20] Domagoj Margetić had been previously charged with contempt for having published protected information regarding a witness from the *Blaškić* case in the newspaper *Novo Hrvatsko Slovo*. *Prosecutor v Stjepan Šešelj, Domagoj Margetić, Marijan Križić* IT-95-14-R77.5. The prosecutor withdrew the indictment in that case before the trial started. *Prosecutor v Stjepan Šešelj, Domagoj Margetić and Marijan Križić* (Decision on the Prosecution Motion to Withdraw the Indictment) IT-95-14-R77.5 (20 June 2006).

[21] *Prosecutor v Domagoj Margetić* (Indictment) IT-95-14-R77.6 (30 August 2006) paras 3–4; *Prosecutor v Domagoj Margetić* (Judgment on Allegations of Contempt) IT-95-14-R77.6 (7 February 2007) (Margetić Trial Judgment) paras 1–2.

[22] Indictment (n 21) para 6; Margetić Trial Judgment (n 21) para 3.

[23] Indictment (n 21) paras 5, 7; Margetić Trial Judgment (n 21) para 4.

[24] Margetić Trial Judgment (n 21) para 4.

[25] Indictment (n 21) para 8; Margetić Trial Judgment (n 21) para 5.

[26] Indictment (n 21) para 9; Margetić Trial Judgment (n 21) para 5.

[27] Indictment (n 21) paras 12–13, 15; Margetić Trial Judgment (n 21) para 9–10.

[28] Indictment (n 21) paras14–15; Margetić Trial Judgment (n 21) para 12.

[29] *Prosecutor v Ramush Haradinaj, Idriz Balaj, and Lahi Brahimaj* (Judgment) IT-04-84-T (3 April 2008) (Haradinaj et al Trial Judgment).

[30] *Prosecutor v Ramush Haradinaj, Idriz Balaj, and Lahi Brahimaj* (Fourth Amended Indictment) IT-04-84-T (16 October 2007) (Haradinaj et al Indictment) paras 2, 4–7.

[31] Haradinaj et al Indictment (n 30) paras 9, 12.

with Serb forces in the Dukagjin area of Kosovo.[32] The trial was marred by witness intimidation and fear,[33] and set against a background of deep political unrest in Kosovo, which was seeking independence from Serbia.

With political tensions around the case running high, in December 2007, during the trial, Baton Haxhiu, the editor of a Kosovar newspaper, published the name of a protected witness from the case.[34] The article further referred to the protected witness'ssupposed place of residence and mentioned that his name 'was found on the list of witnesses who were to testify under full confidentiality against Ramush Haradinaj's group'.[35] Haxhiu was charged on 27 June 2008 under Rule 77(A)(ii) of the Rules for writing and publishing an article in a newspaper which revealed the identity of a protected witness who had appeared in the *Haradinaj* et al trial.[36] According to the indictment, Haxhiu knowingly and wilfully interfered with the administration of justice in knowing violation of orders by a trial chamber of the tribunal.[37]

The fifth case at the ICTY is in many ways distinct from the ones that came before it. Formerly a correspondent for the French newspaper *Le Monde*, Florence Hartmann had been employed as spokesperson for the office of the prosecutor of the ICTY from 2000 to 2006.[38] In September 2007, she authored a book entitled *Paix et Châtiment*,[39] which disclosed information related to two confidential decisions of the appeals chamber in the *Slobodan Milošević* case, including the content and purported effect of these decisions, as well as a specific reference to their confidential nature.[40] On 21 January 2008, she wrote an article entitled 'Vital Genocide Documents Concealed', published by the Bosnian Institute, a UK-registered charity aiming to provide education and information on the history and culture of Bosnia-Herzegovina. The article disclosed information relating to the same two confidential decisions she had discussed in her book.[41]

The Amended Order in Lieu of Indictment charged Hartmann with contempt punishable under Rule 77(A)(ii) of the Rules.[42] She was indicted for knowingly and wilfully interfering with the administration of justice by disclosing confidential information in knowing violation of two decisions of the appeals chamber filed in the *Slobodan Milošević* case.[43]

[32] ibid paras 14, 24.

[33] Haradinaj et al Trial Judgment (n 29) paras 22–25, 28; *Prosecutor v Ramush Haradinaj, Idriz Balaj, and Lahi Brahimaj* (Judgment) IT-04-84-A (19 July 2010) paras 48–49. Haradinaj and Balaj were acquitted on retrial. *Prosecutor v Ramush Haradinaj, Idriz Balaj, and Lahi Brahimaj* (Public Judgment with Confidential Annex) IT-04-84*bis*-T (29 November 2012).

[34] The newspaper article was redacted in the indictment. *Prosecutor v Baton Haxhiu* (Order Lifting Confidentiality of the Indictment) IT-04-84-R77.5 (20 May 2008) (Public Redacted Indictment) paras 1–2; *Prosecutor v Baton Haxhiu* (Judgment on Allegations of Contempt) IT-04-84-R77.5 (24 July 2008) (Haxhiu Trial Judgment) para17.

[35] Haxhiu Trial Judgment (n 34) paras 3, 17 and fn 10.

[36] Public Redacted Indictment (n 34); Haxhiu Trial Judgment (n 34) para 3.

[37] Public Redacted Indictment (n 34); Haxhiu Trial Judgment (n 34) para 3.

[38] In the case against *Florence Hartmann* (Amended Order in Lieu of an Indictment on Contempt and Annex to Order in Lieu of an Indictment) IT-02-54-R77.5 (27 October 2008) ((Amended Order) and (Annex) respectively) para 1, 4; in the case against *Florence Hartmann* (Judgment on Allegations of Contempt) IT-02-54-R77.5 (14 September 2009) (Hartmann Trial Judgment) para 1.

[39] Amended Order (n 38) para 1; Annex (n 38) para 2; Hartmann Trial Judgment (n 38) paras 2–3.

[40] Amended Order (n 38) para 1; Annex (n 38) paras 1–2; Hartmann Trial Judgment (n 38) paras 2–3; *Prosecutor v Slobodan Milošević*. IT-02-54-T. The two decisions of the Appeals Chamber ordered to be filed confidentially in the *Slobodan Milošević* case were (a) a decision on the request for review of the Trial Chamber's oral decision of 18 July 2005 (IT-02-54-R108*bis*.2), filed on 20 September 2005; and (b) a decision on the request for review of the Trial Chamber's decision of 6 December 2005 (IT-02-54-AR108*bis*.3), filed on 6 April 2006.

[41] Amended Order (n 38) para1; Annex (n 38) para 3; Hartmann Trial Judgment (n 38) para 4.

[42] Annex (n 38) para 5.

[43] ibid para 5; Hartmann Trial Judgment (n 38) paras 3–4.

The case generated a great deal of public interest and controversy. Article 19, a non-governmental human rights organization that monitors threats to freedom of expression, not only called Hartmann's case 'troubling', but filed an *amicus* brief in the proceedings.[44] Its submissions included a discussion of international and national legal standards regarding freedom of expression and set out some ways in which domestic jurisdictions addressed freedom of expression in the context of contempt of court.[45] To this day, the case is the target of critical commentary. An article in the British newspaper *The Guardian*, not mincing its words, called it '[a]mong the more outrageous farces along the tribunal's long and winding road'.[46]

16.2.2 The STL

The STL is unique amongst the international tribunals for having been established to try those accused of a single crime: the terrorist attack which killed the former Lebanese Prime Minister Rafik Hariri and others on 14 February 2005—though it also has jurisdiction on other attacks if these are considered connected.[47] As a result of this singular focus and given the absence, until very recently, of other cases to deflect and dilute the public's attention, the institution was particularly exposed to scrutiny. This was exacerbated by the pace of its prosecutorial work, which saw a six-year gap between the crime and the filing of an indictment in the main case under the STL's jurisdiction,[48] and a further three years between the filing of the indictment and the opening of trial on 16 January 2014.[49]

It is amidst a climate of intense speculation and cynicism within Lebanon, fuelled by this long wait for results, that the events which led to the STL's two contempt prosecutions took place. Following the now familiar pattern seen at the ICTY, both cases concerned the revelation of the identities of alleged witnesses. The offences occurred six months apart, in 2012 and 2013, and built on the general curiosity about the evidence upon which the prosecution might rely to prove its case in *Prosecutor v Ayyash* et al.

In the first of the two STL contempt cases, an *amicus curiae* prosecutor recommended charges against the Lebanese television network *Al Jadeed* TV and its deputy head of news and political programmes, Karma Al Khayat. The accused had broadcast a series of reports titled 'Tribunal Witnesses' in August 2012, in which eleven purported confidential

44 Article 19 'ICTY: Hartmann case troubling' (10 October 2011) <https://www.refworld.org/docid/4e9437ce2.html> accessed February 2018. In the case against *Florence Hartmann* (*Amicus Curiae* Brief on Behalf of Article 19) IT-02-54-R77.5 (18 February 2010).

45 In the case against *Florence Hartmann* (*Amicus Curiae* Brief on Behalf of Article 19) IT-02-54-R77.5 (18 February 2010).

46 E Vuliamy, 'Ratko Mladić Will Die in Jail. But Go to Bosnia: You'll See He Won' (*The Guardian*, 22 November 2017) <https://www.theguardian.com/commentisfree/2017/nov/22/ratko-mladic-bosnia-camps-mass-murder-torture-rape-serbian?CMP=share_btn_wa> accessed February 2018.

47 Art 1 of the STL's Statute; Rules 11 and 12 of the STL's Rules. Three cases were found to be 'connected' to the Hariri case by the pre-trial judge: *Prosecutor v Ayyash* (Public redacted version of 'Decision on the Prosecutor's connected case submission of 30 June 2011' of 5 August 2011) STL-18-10/I/PTJ (16 September 2019). In 2019, the pre-trial judge confirmed an indictment in relation to these connected cases: *Prosecutor v. Ayyash* (Public redacted version of the 'Decision on the 13 June 2019 version of the indictment and the documents filed pursuant to the decision of 15 May 2019', dated 19 June 2019) STL-18-10/I/PTJ (16 September 2019).

48 *Prosecutor v Ayyash* et al (Decision Relating to the Examination of the Indictment of 10 June 2011 Issued against Mr Salim Jamil Ayyash, Mr Mustafa Amine Badreddine, Mr Hussein Hassan Oneissi, and Mr Assad Hassan Sabra) STL-11-01/I (28 June 2011) para 5.

49 *Prosecutor v Ayyash* et al (Scheduling Order) STL-11-01/PT/TC (10 December 2013).

witnesses in the *Ayyash* et al case, were approached by journalists of the network using hidden cameras and asked about their involvement with the STL.[50] The reports were broadcast over a number of days, and then uploaded on the network's website, YouTube channel, and Facebook page.[51] The day after the first broadcast, the STL began undertaking a number of measures to stop the dissemination, starting with a notice of cease and desist emailed to Khayat and culminating with an order from the pre-trial judge for the immediate removal of any confidential information or material allegedly related to witnesses from *Al Jadeed*'s websites and any other public platforms.[52] Finally, on 31 January 2014, Khayat and *Al Jadeed* TV were charged with knowingly and wilfully interfering with the administration of justice, first by 'broadcasting and/or publishing information on purported confidential witnesses, thereby undermining the public confidence in the STL's ability to protect the confidentiality of information about, or provided by, witnesses or potential witnesses', and second by failing to remove the information from *Al Jadeed* TV's public platforms, thereby violating the pre-trial judge's order.[53]

In the second contempt case, Ibrahim Al Amin, the editor-in-chief of the Lebanese newspaper *Al Akhbar*, was alleged to have co-authored and published two articles, on 15 and 19 January 2013, identifying and publishing the photographs of thirty-two so-called 'confidential' witnesses. The first article, 'STL Leaks: The Prosecution's Surprise Witnesses' was followed days later by one titled 'The STL List: Why We Published'. Both articles were also made available on the newspaper's website.[54] On 31 January 2014, Al Amin and *Al Akhbar* were charged with knowingly and wilfully interfering with the administration of justice.[55]

The case against Al Amin and *Al Akhbar* drew comparatively less attention than the first, largely because, save for an aborted participation at the initial appearance, both refused to engage in the proceedings; they elected to remain silent during the proceedings and refused to appoint counsel.[56] Al Khayat, in contrast, appointed seasoned counsel and seized the opportunity at the opening of her trial to make an impassioned statement in court about freedom of the press.[57] Her case was widely covered in both the local and international press, the reporting often revealing a sympathetic slant to her plight and juxtaposing the case against the slow pace of the *Ayyash* et al trial and its un-apprehended accused. [58]

[50] In the case against *New TV S.A.L Karma Mohamed Thasin Al Khayat* (Redacted Version of Decision in Proceedings for Contempt with Orders in Lieu of an Indictment) STL-14-05/I/CJ/ (31 January 2014) paras 36, 38. The Order in Lieu of Indictment was later amended to correct the name of the corporate accused.

[51] In the case against *Al Jadeed [Co] S.A.L./New T.V. S.A.L. (NTV) Karma Mohamed Tahsin Al Khayat* (Public Redacted Version of Judgment) STL-14-05/T/CJ (18 September 2015) (Al Jadeed Judgment) paras 51, 74, 130–40; in the case against *Al Jadeed [Co.] S.A.L./New T.V. S.A.L. (N.T.V.) Karma Mohamed Tahsin Al Khayat* (Public Redacted Version of Judgment on Appeal) STL-14-05/A/AP (8 March 2016) (Al Jadeed Appeal Judgment) paras 124–53.

[52] Al Jadeed Judgment (n 51) paras 9–10.

[53] ibid para 5.

[54] In the case against *Akhbar Beirut S.A.L. and Ibrahim Mohamed Al Amin* (Redacted Version of Decision in Proceedings for Contempt with Orders in Lieu of an Indictment) STL-14-06/I/CJ (31 January 2014) paras 51, 54.

[55] ibid Disposition.

[56] Specifically, Mr Al Amin, appearing on his behalf and that of Al Akhbar S.A.L, walked out of the hearing: in the case against *Akhbar Beirut S.A.L. and Ibrahim Mohamed Al Amin* (Transcript) STL-14-06/I/CJ (29 May 2014) 13–14.

[57] In the case against *Al Jadeed [Co.] S.A.L./New T.V. S.A.L. (N.T.V.) Karma Mohamed Tahsin Al Khayat* (Transcript) (20 April 2015) 48–55.

[58] O Bowcott, 'Trial of Lebanese Broadcaster Charged with Contempt of Court Opens in Hague' (*The Guardian*, 16 April 2015) <https://www.theguardian.com/world/2015/apr/13/hezbollah-suspect-at-large-journalists-in-dock-at-hague-un-tribunal> accessed February 2018; BBC, 'Lebanese Journalist on Trial for Contempt at Hague' (*BBC News*, 6 April 2015) <http://www.bbc.co.uk/news/world-middle-east-32331559> accessed February 2018; A Taylor, 'The U.N.'s Tribunal in Lebanon has Cost Millions and Made No Arrests. Now the Journalists are on Trial'

Civil society also sounded in on the debate, echoing the accused's arguments on freedom of speech and the press. When the defence filed a preliminary motion challenging the STL's jurisdiction to try a legal person—which was a first in international criminal justice—the judge invited *amicus* briefs on the issue. Eighteen briefs were received, most from past and present political figures in Lebanon, academics, and various professional associations.[59] Nearly all ignored the narrow legal issue before the judge, contending instead that the STL had no jurisdiction over contempt and that freedom of the press should override other considerations.[60]

16.2.3 The ICTR

The ICTY's sister tribunal saw two contempt prosecutions brought to a procedural conclusion during its lifespan, though neither were against journalists.[61] On two occasions, however, a party attempted to bring charges of contempt against the media, unsuccessfully. The first attempt unfolded during the *Bagosora* et al trial, which concerned four senior military officers charged notably with genocide, crimes against humanity, and war crimes.[62] The prosecution became aware that Thierry Cruvellier, a journalist for the French agency *Diplomatie Judiciaire*, had mentioned the identity and profession of a would-be prosecution witness in an article published on the agency's website.[63] After unsuccessfully requesting Cruvellier to remove the article from the internet, the prosecution filed a motion *ex parte* before the trial chamber, arguing that he had violated standing protective measures and was therefore in contempt of court.[64] The chamber concluded, however, that based on the information in the motion, the witness was not actually covered by any protective measures.[65] Moreover, it pointed out that some of the information allegedly publicized by Cruvellier had already been mentioned in the prosecution's pre-trial brief, which was a public document, and that the witness, when he had been contacted by Cruvellier, had not appeared particularly concerned about protecting his anonymity.[66] On this basis, the chamber dismissed the motion.[67]

Some years later, a Radio Rwanda journalist, Jean Gatare, faced a similar situation in another case. The defence for Augustin Ndindiliyimana, a Rwandan general charged with

(*The Washington Post*, 7 April 2015) <https://www.washingtonpost.com/news/worldviews/wp/2015/04/07/the-u-n-s-tribunal-in-lebanon-has-cost-millions-and-made-no-arrests-now-the-journalists-are-on-trial/?utm_term=.a88944fb7d3e> accessed February 2018; R Fisk, 'Ten Years Later, and we Still Don't Know Who Assassinated Lebanon's Leader. So Why is the Court Tasked with the Inquiry Going After a Journalist?' (*The Independent*, 12 April 2015) <http://www.independent.co.uk/voices/comment/ten-years-later-and-we-still-don-t-know-who-assassinated-lebanons-leader-10171414.html> accessed February 2018.

[59] In the case against *New TV S.A.L. Karma Mohamed Tahsin Al Khayat* (Decision on motion challenging jurisdiction and on request for leave to amend order in lieu of an indictment) STL-14-05/PT/CJ (24 July 2014) para 18.

[60] ibid paras 14–22.

[61] *Prosecutor v GAA* (Judgment and sentence) ICTR-07-90-R77-I (4 December 2007); *Prosecutor v Léonidas Nshogoza* (Judgment) ICTR-07-91-A (15 March 2010).

[62] *Prosecutor v Bagosora* et al (Judgment and sentence) ICTR-98-41-T (18 December 2008) para 2.

[63] *Prosecutor v Bagosora* et al (Decision on the Prosecution motion *ex parte* in the matter of violation of the Trial Chamber's witness protection orders, and contempt of court) ICTR-98-41-T (5 July 2002).

[64] ibid paras 1–3.

[65] ibid paras 13–19.

[66] ibid para 20.

[67] ibid para 21.

genocide, claimed Gatare had published the names of two protected witnesses who had agreed to testify for the defence, in violation of a judicial order.[68] The defence made a number of related arguments, not least of which that Gatare's publication seriously undermined Ndindiliyimana's ability to defend himself because potential defence witnesses were now reluctant to testify.[69] The trial chamber concluded that no contempt had been committed.[70] It attributed the blame roundly to all the actors in the courtroom for not being more diligent in mentioning the names and pseudonyms of protected witnesses and the details of their testimony.[71] The chamber also made it a point to mention that some of that sensitive information had in fact been revealed in open court by defence counsel himself, before being picked up by Radio Rwanda and redacted from the court record.[72]

Drawing on both his and Gatare's experiences before the ICTR, Cruvellier penned a report for the non-governmental organization Reports Without Borders in the wake of the contempt proceedings against the Croatian journalists at the ICTY.[73] He denounced the procedural laws, arguing that in his case, the filing of the prosecution motion *ex parte* was 'contrary to the most elementary rules of due process'.[74] While he acknowledged the judges' gatekeeping role against frivolous or unsubstantiated claims of contempt, he was nevertheless highly critical of both the ICTY and ICTR for allowing such cases to even come to light. Cruvellier qualified the allegations made against him by the prosecution, and against Gatare by the defence, as a 'disturbing illustration of the dangers of arbitrariness and perversion when journalists are accused of violating orders issued by these courts'.[75]

Cruvellier's pessimistic assessment of the law on contempt and his forewarning of its potential for abuse is emblematic of the reactions the cases surveyed above have often elicited in the press. This is perhaps unsurprising, for two main reasons. First, the media is arguably the entity that is the most directly impacted by reporting restrictions other than the person to whom they may be granted, since the measures typically do not conceal identities of witnesses or other information from the accused, but rather from the public at large. By definition, such restrictions constrain the press's ability to carry out its role as the public purveyor of information. It is therefore natural that the larger the constraint on its voice, the more forcefully it feels and articulates its frustration at not being able to use it.

Second, and more relevantly for the purposes of this chapter, the media's focus on what it portrays as the unfettered authority of international criminal tribunals to hold journalists in contempt is out of context, and as a result, distorted. It overlooks the fact that legislation and judicial power have been developed at the domestic level for the same purpose and with the same design. To demonstrate this relationship, the next section of this chapter will analyse reporting restrictions at the international tribunals side-by-side with their procedural equivalent in domestic jurisdictions. This will provide the backdrop to the subsequent section of the chapter, which will examine the law on contempt itself and what happens

[68] *Prosecutor v Ndindiliyamana* et al (Decision on request for certification of appeal from the decision of Trial Chamber dated 13 June 2004 (sic) dismissing applicant's request for a citation for contempt of the journalist Gatare of Radio Rwanda for publishing the names of protected witnesses) ICTR-2000-56-T (1 July 2005).

[69] ibid, paras 1–6.

[70] ibid, para 20.

[71] ibid, para 21.

[72] ibid, para 17.

[73] T Cruvellier, 'Why Journalists Should be Worried by the Rwanda Tribunal Precedents' (*Reports Without Borders*, 10 July 2006) <https://rsf.org/sites/default/files/rapport_gb.pdf> accessed February 2018.

[74] ibid.

[75] ibid.

when reporting restrictions are violated by the media. In doing so, it hopes to answer the question of whether, and if so to what extent, Cruvellier's criticism is legitimate.

16.3 The Legal Basis for Restricting Reporting of Judicial Proceedings

16.3.1 In Human Rights Law

The starting point for any discussion on the media's role in reporting judicial proceedings is to underline that Bentham's dictum on the publicity of trials embodies the general rule. It is, as such, enshrined in most major international and regional human rights instruments.

The Universal Declaration of Human Rights, considered by many to be the foundation of the modern human rights framework, provides at its Article 10 that everyone is entitled in full equality to a fair and public hearing by an independent and impartial tribunal, in both civil and criminal matters.[76] The right to a public trial is further reiterated at its Article 11, which deals specifically with penal offences. Article 10 of the Universal Declaration is by and large reproduced at Article 14(1) of the International Covenant on Civil and Political Rights (ICCPR),[77] which provides that everyone is entitled to a fair and public hearing by a competent, independent, and impartial tribunal. Both the Universal Declaration and the ICCPR are phrased in a way that juxtaposes publicity with fairness and identifies the two as distinct elements, rather than one being a component of the other. The dichotomy is explained by the fact that, contrary to a fair trial, a public trial is not an end in and of itself in the context of human rights.[78] It is instead a means to assess whether the components that render a trial fair are present. By being subjected to society's watchful eye, the reasoning goes, a court is much less likely to engage in abuses.[79]

In laying out the general principle on the publicity of trials, regional human rights instruments reprise the language from the ICCPR. The American Convention on Human Rights[80] and the European Convention on Human Rights[81]—which are the two oldest regional human rights treaties and the ones with the most extensive body of jurisprudence—as well

[76] Universal Declaration of Human Rights (adopted 10 December 1948) UNGA Res 127 A (III) (Universal Declaration). On the status of the Universal Declaration in public international law, see *Legal Consequences for States of the Continued Presence of South Africa in Namibia (South West Africa) Notwithstanding Security Council Resolution 276* (1970) (Advisory Opinion) [1971] ICJ Rep 16, para 57; *United States v Iran* (Judgment of 24 May) [1980] ICJ Rep 3, para 42; H Hannum, 'The Status of the Universal Declaration of Human Rights in National and International Law' (1995–1996) 25 Georgia Journal of International and Comparative Law 287; N S Rodley, 'Human Rights and Humanitarian Intervention: The Case Law of the World Court' (1989) 38 International and Comparative Law Quarterly 326, 333.

[77] International Covenant on Civil and Political Rights (adopted 16 December 1966, entered into force 23 March 1976) 999 UNTS 171 (ICCPR).

[78] B McLachlin, 'Courts, Transparency and Public Confidence—To the Better Administration of Justice' (2003) 8 Deakin Law Review 1, 11.

[79] *Attorney-General v Leveller Magazine* Ltd, [1979] AC 440, para 450; J J Spigelman, 'Seen to be Done: The Principle of Open Justice—Part II' (2000) 74 Australian Law Journal 378, 378; A Barak, 'Foreword: A Judge on Judging: The Role of a Supreme Court in a Democracy' (2002) 116 Harvard Law Review 19, 162.

[80] American Convention on Human Rights (adopted on 22 November 1969, entered into force July 1978) 1144 UNTS 123 (American Convention) art 8(5).

[81] European Convention for the Protection of Human Rights and Fundamental Freedoms, as amended by Protocols Nos 11 and 14 (entered into force on 4 November 1950) ETS 5 (European Convention) art 6(1).

the Association of Southeast Asian Nations (ASEAN) Declaration on Human Rights[82] and the Arab Charter on Human Rights,[83] which are more recent offshoots, all explicitly state that judicial proceedings shall be public in criminal matters. The African Charter of Human and Peoples' Rights is unique in making no mention of publicity at its provision on the right to fair trial.[84] Despite this textual lacuna—or perhaps, because of it—the African Commission on Human and Peoples' Rights has nevertheless made it clear that the right to a fair trial also includes the right to a public hearing.[85]

None of these texts, however, make the right to a public trial absolute and non-derogable. The Universal Declaration allows for the exercise of rights and freedoms to be subjected to legal limitations so long as they are for the purpose of 'securing due recognition and respect for the rights and freedoms of others and of meeting the just requirements of morality, public order and the general welfare in a democratic society'.[86]

The ICCPR contains a detailed limitation to the right to a public trial:

> […] The press and the public may be excluded from all or part of a trial for reasons of morals, public order (ordre public) or national security in a democratic society, or when the interest of the private lives of the parties so requires, or to the extent strictly necessary in the opinion of the court in special circumstances where publicity would prejudice the interest of justice; but any judgement rendered in a criminal case or in a suit at law shall be made public except where the interest of juvenile persons otherwise requires or the proceedings concern matrimonial disputes or the guardianship of children.[87]

The publicity of a trial can also be limited under the ICCPR because of the 'special duties and responsibilities' that accompany freedom of expression.[88] Article 19(3) on the right to freedom of expression specifies that it may be subject to certain restrictions, on condition that these are provided by law, and necessary for the respect of the rights and reputations of others, the protection of national security, public order, public health, or morals. In commenting on this provision, the ICCPR's monitoring body, the Human Rights Committee, has stated that the restrictions must be appropriate to achieve their protective function, proportionate to the interest to be protected, and the least intrusive option available.[89]

[82] ASEAN Human Rights Declaration (Adopted on 18 November 2012) art 20(1). The ASEAN Declaration is not a binding treaty as such: see C S Renshaw, 'The ASEAN Human Rights Declaration 2012' (2013) 13 Human Rights Law Review 557.

[83] Arab Charter on Human Rights (Adopted 22 May 2004, entered into force 15 March 2008) (2005) 12 International Human Rights Report 893 (Arab Charter) art 13(2).

[84] The African Charter of Human and Peoples' Rights (Adopted 27 June 1981, entered into force 21 October 1981) (1982) 21 ILM 58, art 7. It should be noted that both the ASEAN Human Rights Declaration and the Arab Charter have been criticized for not meeting international norms on human rights: UN News Centre, 'Arab rights charter deviates from international standards, says UN official' (30 January 2008) <http://www.un.org/apps/news/story.asp?NewsID=25447#.WepIa0x7FBw> accessed February 2018; Human Rights Watch, 'Civil society denounces adoption of flawed ASEAN Human Rights Declaration' (19 November 2012) <https://www.hrw.org/news/2012/11/19/civil-society-denounces-adoption-flawed-asean-human-rights-declaration> accessed February 2018.

[85] Principles and Guidelines on the Right to a Fair Trial and Legal Assistance in Africa (2003) DOC/OS (XXX)247, (A) (3); Amnesty International 'A Guide to the African Charter on Human and Peoples' Rights' (2006) <https://www.amnesty.org/download/Documents/76000/ior630052006en.pdf> accessed February 2018.

[86] Universal Declaration art 29(2).

[87] ICCPR art 14(1).

[88] ICCPR art 19(3).

[89] UN Human Rights Committee 'General Comment No 34' (12 September 2011) CCPR/C/GC/34 paras 22, 34.

The European Convention very closely mirrors the ICCPR's formulation of the right to a public trial, though it also includes the interests of juveniles amongst the grounds on the basis of which the press and public can be excluded from judicial hearings:

> Judgment shall be pronounced publicly but the press and public may be excluded from all or part of the trial in the interests of morals, public order or national security in a democratic society, where the interests of juveniles or the protection of the private life of the parties so require, or to the extent strictly necessary in the opinion of the court in special circumstances where publicity would prejudice the interests of justice.[90]

Similarly to the ICCPR, the European Convention's provision on the right to a public trial should, for completeness sake, be read side-by-side with its provision on freedom of expression.[91] In the same way that trial publicity is subjected to limitations, the European Convention conditions the right to freedom of expression (including the freedom to impart information), to 'special duties and responsibilities'.

The other regional instruments equally subject the right to a public trial and the freedom of expression to other overriding interests, but with some nuances. Although the ASEAN Human Rights Declaration does not qualify the right to a fair trial in any way, it contains a general provision stating that rights and freedoms can be curtailed if provided by law and solely for the purpose of securing due recognition for the human rights and fundamental freedoms of others, and to meet the requirements of national security, public order, health, public safety, public morality, and the 'general welfare of the peoples in a democratic society'.[92]

The American Convention on Human Rights and the Arab Charter stand somewhat apart from their counterparts by subjecting the publicity of criminal trials only to the interests of justice, rather than broader societal interests.[93] In this sense, they create what is arguably the narrowest exception to publicity amongst both the regional and international human rights instruments. Again, however, as with the other human rights instruments, this is counterbalanced by the provision limiting the right to freedom of expression in wording that is nearly identical to Article 19(3) of the ICCPR.[94]

16.3.2 Domestic Jurisdictions

The bases on which the international human rights instruments allow limitations to the publicity of a trial have been conjugated at the domestic level in a variety of ways. With respect to the rights of the accused, it has meant that journalists can be restricted from reporting on aspects of a trial if doing so would undermine the presumption of innocence. In Canada for instance, at the stage of deciding on an accused's interim release, the prosecutor or the accused may request a judge to order that certain matters not be published for a specific period.[95] The temporal scope of the reporting ban or restriction issued under this

90 European Convention art 6(1).
91 European Convention art 19(2)—(3).
92 ASEAN Human Rights Declaration art 8.
93 American Convention art 8(5); Arab Charter art 13(2).
94 American Convention art 13(2); Arab Charter art 32(2).
95 Criminal Code, RSC, 1985, c C-46 (Canadian Criminal Code) s 517.

provision is noteworthy: it must essentially remain in force until the proceedings against the accused come to a close. This is summed up quite aptly in a guidebook designed to explain the Canadian justice system to journalists: 'Once the need to protect the right to a fair trial evaporates, the media can report everything said at the hearing.'[96] In addition, where the law grants a judge the discretion to order a publication ban, the Canadian Supreme Court has held that a test of necessity applies. Specifically, a publication ban should only be ordered when it is necessary to prevent real and substantial risk to the fairness of a trial, and because the salutary effects of the publication ban outweigh the deleterious effects to the free expression of those affected by the ban.[97]

Similar legislation to protect the presumption of innocence exists in France and Italy, where the law governing the freedom of the press forbids the dissemination of images of anyone in handcuffs or other types of restraints if that person has not yet been found guilty.[98] More fundamentally of course, these civil law jurisdictions have as a cornerstone to their criminal justice system '*le secret de l'instruction*', the principle according to which the investigation led by the *juge d'instruction* (the investigating magistrate) must remain secret, notably in order to protect the rights of the accused to a fair trial.[99] In a case concerning the publication of secret judicial documents by a Swiss journalist, the European Court of Human Rights observed that the disclosure of information protected by the '*secret de l'instruction*' was punishable in thirty Council of Europe States.[100]

Notwithstanding the fact that protecting the rights of the accused also serves the broader interests of society, legislation in various domestic jurisdictions also imposes limits on the publicity of trials with the goal of protecting the rights of persons other than the accused, the most salient example being the protection of vulnerable persons, such as victims of serious crimes and minors. A State's sense of responsibility towards vulnerable persons permeates both criminal and civil proceedings. It is the reason, for instance, that in family law cases, where divorce proceedings and child custody battles often risk exposing children to the media's glare, the names of minors and their parents remain confidential. The protection of such identifying information often does not even need to reach judicial consideration to come into play; it is laid down as a rule by law, in what is known as an 'automatic' reporting restriction.[101]

As to criminal proceedings, the United Kingdom, for instance, gives victims of sexual offences lifetime anonymity.[102] At the stage where only an allegation of a sexual offence is made, the name and address of the victim cannot be published if they can lead to the victim's identification. Where a suspect has formally been accused of committing a sexual offence, however, the prohibition is categorical and broad: nothing that is likely to lead members of the public to identify the victim can be published during his or her lifetime.[103] Somewhat less forceful, Canadian criminal law makes reporting restrictions for sexual

[96] Canadian Judicial Council, *The Canadian Justice System and the Media* (Ottawa 2007) 24.

[97] *Dagenais v Canadian Broadcasting Corporation* [1994] 3 RCS 835, 875, 878.

[98] Loi du 29 juillet 1881 sur la liberté de la presse (last modified 29 January 2017) art 35 *ter*; Codice di procedura penale art 114 (6)(bis).

[99] Codice di procedura penale art 114 (1)-(2), 329.

[100] *Bédat v Switzerland* (2016) ECHR 313, 80–81.

[101] Children Act 1989 (UK), s 97; Child and Family Services Act, RSO 1990, c C-11 (Canada), sub-s 45 (8); Loi du 29 juillet 1881 sur la liberté de la presse, art 39 *bis*; Cass No 6338/1994. Referring to *DPR* fn 448, art 13, 22 September 1988 (Italy).

[102] Sexual Offences (Amendment) Act 1992 (UK) s 1.

[103] ibid.

offences automatic, but only once it is requested from the victim.[104] French law is equally protective of victims of sexual crimes.[105]

In addition to protections afforded to victims, the identities of witnesses can also be protected from the public during criminal proceedings, whether because the witnesses are vulnerable, or because their anonymity is part and parcel of what allows them to conduct their work, as is the case with law enforcement officers and informants.[106] Moreover, the Canadian Criminal Code allows judges to order that any information that could identify a witness not be disclosed in the course of the proceedings if it is in the interests of the proper administration of justice, taking into account factors such as the right to a fair and public hearing, the existence of effective alternatives, and society's interest in encouraging the reporting of offences and the participation of victims and witnesses in the criminal justice process.[107]

It is worth specifying that forbidding the media from publishing information is not necessarily tantamount to barring them from the courtroom. In fact, the two are quite distinct, as the law can restrict reporting without limiting access to a courtroom, and vice versa.[108] Implicit in allowing access while forbidding publicization, is an assumption (and trust) that journalists, despite being privy to information, will refrain from disseminating it knowing that doing so is against the law. Judges often remind the public of this obligation orally in court, or with a notice prefacing their judgments.[109] On a more substantial level, 'exclusion orders' limiting access to a courtroom often fulfil a more immediate and short-termed purpose than reporting restrictions, namely to reduce the intimidating nature of the setting, particularly when vulnerable persons are testifying.[110]

This review of domestic legislation is representative rather than exhaustive. It illustrates nevertheless that in jurisdictions of distinct legal traditions, despite procedural nuances, the exceptions on the basis of which the publicity of trials can be limited are similar, if not identical. It is interesting to observe that there is a decent level of awareness of this legal landscape within journalistic communities. Large media outlets have detailed guidelines for both their employees and the public, explaining the legal context within which they operate. As an example, the United Kingdom's British Broadcasting Corporation (BBC) and Channel 4 networks have handbooks and editorial guidelines on their websites outlining the parameters of reporting on legal proceedings.[111] The Canadian Broadcasting Corporation (CBC)'s website on Journalistic Standards and Practices similarly declares:

[104] Canadian Criminal Code, s 486.4.

[105] Loi du 29 juillet 1881 sur la liberté de la presse (n 98) art 39 *quinquies*.

[106] Serious Organised Crime and Police Act 2005 (UK), s 75; Canadian Criminal Code (n 95) s 486.4, 486.5, 486.31; Loi du 29 juillet 1881 sur la liberté de la presse (n 98) art 39 *sexies*.

[107] Canadian Criminal Code (n 95) s 486.31.

[108] See Serious Organised Crime and Police Act 2005 (UK), s 75 (2) (a) (b); Codice di procedura penale art 473(2)

[109] In Canada: *Children's Aid Society of the Region of Peel v F.* (K.J.) [2009] ONCJ 252 (CanLII); *R v J.S.D.* [2014] BCCA 284 (CanLII); *R v Waterhouse* [2017] BCSC 999 (CanLII); *R v Mastop* [2013] BCCA 494 (CanLII); *Carlson v CBD* [2013] SKQB 351; *R v El Aitki* [2011] QCCQ 914; Barnes (Re) [2016] CanLII 35043 (NL SCTD). In the United Kingdom: Re R (Closed Material Procedure: Special Advocates: Funding) [2017] EWHC 1793 (Fam); *B v D* [2017] EWCOP 15; *Appleton v Gallagher* [2015] EWHC 2689 (Fam).

[110] Children and Young Persons Act 1933 (UK) s 37; Code de procédure pénale, art 306, 306–1; Codice di procedura penale, art 472(3*bis*); *R v Burrell* (n 2) para 38. Exclusion orders have declined in recent years in Canada because of the increased use of videotaping and shielding screens during the testimony of vulnerable persons: Canadian Judicial Council *The Canadian Justice System and the Media* (n 96) 22.

[111] BBC, Editorial Guidelines <http://www.bbc.co.uk/editorialguidelines/guidelines/law> accessed February 2018; Channel 4, Producers Handbook <http://www.channel4.com/producers-handbook/media-law/contempt-and-reporting-legal-proceedings> accessed February 2018.

> We take care not to compromise the proper course of ongoing or potential legal proceedings and to take into account the presumption of innocence enjoyed by every person accused of a crime.
>
> In many situations the law imposes restrictions such as publication bans, sealing of documents and closed-door proceedings. Such orders are sometimes automatic or sometimes issued in the course of a proceeding. Reporters have a duty to inform themselves of the existence and nature of these orders and to understand their scope.[112]

The CBC even undertakes not to disclose any information that would identify a victim, witness, or accused 'by deduction' if a publication ban is in place.[113]

In France, the news agency *Agence France Press* (AFP) calls for its journalists to be cognizant of the legal definition of minors before interviewing or filming children and to make themselves aware of any legislation governing the media coverage of minors whether they are victims, authors of, or witnesses to a crime.[114] Lastly, in Italy, the Order of Journalists has guidelines on the responsibilities of journalists when reporting on, for instance, minors and other vulnerable individuals, and information surrounding criminal proceedings.[115] *Radio Televisione Italiana* (RAI), the Italian state media corporation, has a Code of Ethics for its employees outlining the same responsibilities.[116]

16.3.3 At the ICTY

The right to a public trial, as well as the related string of exceptions, has been reprised by the international criminal tribunals. As one ICTY trial chamber stated, '[o]ver and above the reasons that public proceedings facilitate public knowledge and understanding and may have a general deterrent effect, the public should have the opportunity to assess the fairness of the proceedings. Justice should not only be done, it should be seen to be done'.[117] While the accused at the ICTY were entitled to a fair and public hearing, this could be restricted on a number of grounds [118]

Rule 79(A) of the ICTY Rules covered these grounds. Thus, a trial chamber could order that the press and the public be excluded from all or part of the proceedings for reasons of: public order or morality; the safety, security, or non-disclosure of the identity of a victim or witness; or the protection of the interests of justice.[119]

[112] CBC, Reporting to Canadians, Journalistic Standards and Practices <https://cbc.radio-canada.ca/en/vision/governance/journalistic-standards-and-practices> accessed February 2018.

[113] ibid.

[114] Charte AFP des bonne pratiques éditoriales et déontologiques (22 juin 2016) 10 <https://www.afp.com/sites/default/files/paragraphrich/201704/22_juin_2016_charte_deontologique.pdf> accessed February 2018. The major French news outlets do not otherwise appear to have editorial guidelines like those of the CBC, BBC, and Channel 4, at least not publicly available.

[115] Testo unico dei doveri del giornalista (19 February 2016) art 5–6 <http://www.odg.it/content/testo-unico-dei-doveri-del-giornalista> accessed February 2018.

[116] RAI Codice Etico 8 <http://www.rai.it/dl/doc/1507016930316_CODICE%20ETICO%20cda%2027%20luglio%202017_Eng.pdf> accessed February 2018.

[117] *Prosecutor v Kunarac* et al (Order on Defence Motion pursuant to Rule 79) IT-96-23-T (22 March 2000) para 5; see also *Prosecutor v Karadžić* (Decision on Prosecution's Motion for Protective Measure for Witness KDZ487) IT-95-5/18-T (24 November 2009) para 18.

[118] ICTY Statute, art 20(4), 21(2) 22; ICTY Rule 78.

[119] ICTY Rule 79.

Furthermore, the ICTY Rules allowed the prosecutor to be relieved of the obligation to disclose information not only to the public, but even to the defence, if such disclosure affected the prosecution's further or ongoing investigations,[120] was contrary to the public interest, for any other reasons, or affected the security interests of any State.[121] The Rules referred to an exhaustive list of exceptions to a public trial. It is, however, testimony to the fact that restricted access to information surrounding a trial was an exception, that the ICTY Rules required chambers to publicly reason any decision to order such a restriction.[122]

The protection of vulnerable victims and witnesses was most often the reason why the public and the press were excluded from attending or reporting on ICTY proceedings. At the pre-trial stage, the protective measure usually took the form of delayed disclosure to the defence (and to the public at large) of the identity of the prosecution witnesses and the likely subject of their testimony at trial.[123] In exceptional circumstances, it was permissible to delay disclosure until such time as the preparation of the defence would not be adversely affected.[124] Disclosure of the identity of witnesses was at times even delayed until after the trial commenced.[125] During the trial itself, however, an order of confidentiality given by a chamber, as envisaged in Rules 69 and 75 of the ICTY Rules, was the most common way to protect victims and witnesses. Rule 69(A) held that in exceptional circumstances, either party could request the non-disclosure of the identity of a victim or witness who was in danger or at risk until such person was brought under the protection of the tribunal. Rule 75 listed the measures that could be taken, even *proprio motu* by the chamber, as long as they were consistent with the rights of the accused. These were:

(i) measures to prevent disclosure to the public or the media of the identity or whereabouts of a victim or a witness, or of persons related to or associated with a victim or witness by such means as:
   (a) expunging names and identifying information from the Tribunal's public records;
   (b) non-disclosure to the public of any records identifying the victim or witness;
   (c) giving of testimony through image—or voice—altering devices or closed circuit television; and
   (d) assignment of a pseudonym;
(ii) closed sessions, in accordance with Rule 79;
(iii) appropriate measures to facilitate the testimony of vulnerable victims and witnesses, such as one-way closed circuit television.

Good cause had to be shown for protective measures to be granted.[126] The ordering of closed session was the most extreme protective measure that could be taken.[127] It meant

[120] ICTY Rule 66(C).

[121] ICTY Rules 66(C), 68(iv).

[122] For instance, the appeals chamber held that a trial chamber had erred by holding a hearing in closed session without prior notice to the public. This did not however amount to a miscarriage of justice or prejudice to the accused Jokić. *Contempt proceedings against Jokić* (Judgment on Allegations of Contempt) IT-05-88-R77.1-A (3 July 2009) para 26.

[123] ICTY Rule 69.

[124] ibid.

[125] See e.g. *Prosecutor v Šešelj* (Decision on Vojislav Šešelj's Appeal against the Trial Chamber's Oral Decision of 7 November 2007) IT-03-67-AR73.6 (24 January 2008) para 15; *Prosecutor v Karadžić* (Decision on Accused's Sixty-Sixth Disclosure Violation Motion) IT-95-5/18-T (8 February 2012) para 17.

[126] *Prosecutor v Brđanin & Talić* (Decision on Motion by Prosecution for Protective Measures) IT-99-36-PT (3 July 2000) para 53.

[127] *Prosecutor v Milošević* (Decision on Prosecution Motion for Trial Related Protective Measures for Witnesses (Croatia)) IT-02-54-T (30 July 2002) para 6.

that the audio and video broadcast of the court proceedings was suspended and blinds were lowered in the courtroom so that members of the press and public sitting in the public gallery would not be able to see or hear any part of the proceedings.[128] The transcript of a closed session was marked as such, and was not made available to the public.[129] A private session was similar in nature to a closed session but was generally used for short periods during proceedings.[130] When a chamber ordered a private session, the audio and video broadcast was suspended, but the blinds in the courtroom were not lowered; therefore those sitting in the public gallery were able to see the proceedings, though they were unable to hear anything being said.[131] Those parts of the proceedings that were conducted in private session were redacted from the public version of the transcript.[132] A public hearing could be turned into a private session at any time if the need arose.

ICTY jurisprudence required that there be an objective risk to the security or welfare of a witness or his or her family for protective measures to be granted.[133] The more extreme the protection sought, the more onerous the obligation upon the party requesting it to establish the risk involved.[134] The minimum measure required to protect the witness' legitimate fears was normally taken.[135]

Protective orders were also necessary to protect the right to privacy of victims and witnesses in cases of violent crime, such as sexual assault. Rules 75(A) and 79(A)(ii) of the Rules were broad enough to cover such cases. Moreover, protective measures were also necessary to protect not only victims and witnesses but also their families from serious threats, for instance, in situations where the victims or potential witnesses, by giving testimony before the ICTY, were perceived by their community as collaborating with the enemy.[136] Despite the end of the conflict, this protection was vital in the cases heard before the ICTY, where ethnic divisions, if not tensions, persisted.

Another established practice of the ICTY was to issue redacted versions of judicial documents, when the latter contained information which, if disclosed, could cause prejudice, concerns about safety, or serious embarrassment to a party or a witness.[137]

[128] *Marijačić & Rebić* Trial Judgment (n 16) para 24.

[129] ibid.

[130] ibid.

[131] ibid.

[132] ibid.

[133] *Prosecutor v Milutinović* et al (Decision on Lazarević Motion for Protective Measures for Witness SD3) IT-05-87-T (28 November 2007) para 3.

[134] *Prosecutor v Milošević* (n 127) para 5; *Prosecutor v Milošević* (Decision on Prosecution's Motion for Protective Measures) IT-98-29/1-T (12 February 2007) 11; *Prosecutor v Milutinović* et al (Decision on Lazarević Motion for Protective Measures for Witness SD3) IT-05-87-T (28 November 2007) 3.

[135] *Prosecutor v Milošević* (Decision on Prosecution's Motion for Protective Measures) IT-98-29/1-T (12 February 2007) para 11; *Prosecutor v Milošević* (n 127) para 5. Closed session was granted, for example, in the case of a prosecution Muslim witness who lived in a community with violent Serb nationalist elements, where it was shown that there could be repercussions from supporters of the Serb accused. The fact that the accused's case had a higher profile than the previous case in which the witness had testified in public session was also a consideration in favour of closed session. *Prosecutor v Popovic* et al (Decision on Urgent Prosecution Motion for Additional Protective Measures for Witness KDZ084) IT-05-88-A and IT-95-5/18-T (10 May 2012) para 3.

[136] Furthermore, information relating to the genetic material of alleged victims, including the genetic material of family members, was kept confidential under Rule 75 in order to protect their privacy. *Prosecutor v Karadžić*, (Decision on the Accused's Motion to Unseal ICMP Exhibits) IT-95-5/18-T (25 April 2012) para 9.

[137] *Prosecutor v Popovic* et al (Judgment) IT-05-88-A (30 January 2015) para 1957.

The practice also extended to judgments.[138] As such, the public redacted version of a judgment sufficiently allowed for public scrutiny of the judgment in order to safeguard the right to a fair trial.[139]

In the broader context of large-scale atrocities and armed conflict, national security interests were of particular relevance to international criminal proceedings. Absent its own police force, the prosecution, in its role of investigating international crimes, was therefore heavily dependent on intelligence and sensitive information provided by States and international organizations. Disclosure of maps, aerial photographs (of mass graves sites, for instance), and intercepted communications or other contemporaneous evidence, in the form of internal reports or communications, at times shed light on the context of an armed conflict, and the linkage evidence needed for effective prosecution of high-level political and military leaders. Because of national State security interests, States or organizations would consequently only be forthcoming with information on condition of confidentiality.[140] This was regulated by Rule 70 of the ICTY Rules, on the basis of which the identity of the sources of the information could be redacted, as well as contacts with intelligence agencies of other countries.[141] States have nonetheless not been allowed to use Rule 70 'as a blanket right to withhold, for security purposes, documents necessary for trial from being disclosed' for use as evidence, as this would defeat the very purpose of the ICTY.[142] Indeed, such an interpretation of Rule 70 would conflict with a State's obligation under Article 29 to co-operate with the ICTY.[143]

As to the 'public order' as a reason to limit publicity of some aspects of a trial,[144] the Hartmann Appeal Judgment held that the protection of public order in Article 19(3) of the ICCPR was intended to 'include the prohibition of the procurement and dissemination of confidential information'.[145] The broader notion of the protection of the public order has also been understood to include the narrower one of the prevention of disorder or crime.[146] ICTY's Judge Shahabuddeen once noted that the term 'public order' has been interpreted to include restrictions necessary for the protection of the 'essential elements of

[138] ibid.

[139] ibid para 1958.

[140] *Prosecutor v Milošević* (Public Version of the Confidential Decision on the Interpretation and Application of Rule 70) IT-02-54-AR108*bis* and AR73.3 (23 October 2002) para 19.

[141] *Prosecutor v Stanišić & Simatović* (Decision on the Republic of Serbia's Request for Protective Measures for Four Documents) IT-03-69-T (12 April 2012) paras 12–14; *Prosecutor v Stanišić & Simatović* (Decision on the Republic of Serbia's Request for Protective Measures for Three Witnesses) IT-03-69-T (17 April 2012) paras 22, 25; *Prosecutor v Stanišić & Simatović* (Decision on the Republic of Serbia's Request for Protective Measures in Relation to Defence Documents) IT-03-69-T (18 July 2012) para 23; See also ICTY Rule 54*bis*.

[142] *Prosecutor v Milutinović* et al (Decision on Request of United States of America for Review) IT-05-87-AR108bis.2 (12 May 2006) para 38 and fn 91.

[143] *Prosecutor v Milutinović* et al (n 142). The disclosure of the means and methods used by security services twenty years earlier did not damage a State's national security interests. *Prosecutor v Stanišić & Simatović* (Decision on the Serbia's Request for Protective Measures in Relation to Defence Documents) IT-03-69-T (18 July 2012) paras 22—25. While protective measures were granted for documents containing the name of current State security operatives, documents containing the names of former operatives were not redacted. *Prosecutor v Stanišić & Simatović* (Decision on the Republic of Serbia's Request for Protective Measures for Three Witnesses) IT-03-69-T (17 April 2012) para 21; *Prosecutor v Mladić* (Decision on Republic of Serbia's Motion for Protective Measures) IT-09-92-T (15 July 2014) paras 14–15.

[144] ICTY Rule 79(A)(i); see text to n 119 in s 16.3. The Legal Basis for Restricting Reporting of Judicial Proceedings, sub-s 16.3.3. At the ICTY.

[145] In the case against *Florence Hartmann* (Judgment) IT-02-54-R77.5-A (19 July 2011) (Hartmann Appeal Judgment) para 160.

[146] See ECHR art 10(2); see also ICTY Rule 66(c).

the administration of justice'.[147] Arguably, the latter would also be covered by the 'interests of justice',[148] a useful catch-all term.

Even though the ICTY Rules incorporated the notion of 'public interest', absent in Articles 14(1) and 19(3) of the ICCPR,[149] they did not expand the range of exceptions to a public trial permitted under human rights law. This is because these exceptions, as described above, have been interpreted restrictively.[150]

16.3.4 Beyond the ICTY

The extent of the ICTY's impact on international criminal law is evident from the legal texts of the other international criminal tribunals, which have to a large degree been modelled on those of the ICTY. The ICTR, Special Court for Sierra Leone (SCSL), and STL have reproduced Article 21(2) of the ICTY's statute and similarly subject the accused's right to a public hearing to measures ordered by the chamber for the protection of victims and witnesses.[151] In addition, the ICTY's Rules on delayed disclosure, open and closed hearings, and measures to protect victims and witnesses, and confidential information are closely mirrored in the Rules of the ICTR, SCSL, and STL.[152]

It is interesting to note that an inconsistency between Article 21(2) of the ICTY's statute and Rule 75 of its Rules has been carried over at the ICTR, SCSL, and STL. Specifically, the statute for each of those institutions expresses the right of the accused to a public trial as being subject to the need to protect victims and witnesses. In contrast, the Rules of each institution reverses the formula, by stating that judges can order measures for the privacy and protection of victims and witnesses, provided that those measures are consistent with the rights of the accused.[153] The case law on the subject, however, relies on the language found in the relevant Rule, as opposed to the statutory provision.[154]

Although the Extraordinary Chambers in the Courts of Cambodia (ECCC) and the ICC statutes' general provisions on the publicity of trials depart from those of the other

[147] *Prosecutor v Brđanin & Talić* (Decision on Interlocutory Appeal) IT-99-36-AR73.9 (11 December 2002) Separate Opinion of Judge Shahabuddeen para 8.

[148] ICTY Rule 79(A)(iii); see text to n 119 in s 16.3. The Legal Basis for Restricting Reporting of Judicial Proceedings, sub-s 16.3.3. At the ICTY.

[149] See text to nn 77, 87–89 in s 16.3. The Legal Basis for Restricting Reporting of Judicial Proceedings, sub-s 16.3.1. In Human Rights Law.

[150] In any event, some of these notions may be redundant in an international criminal tribunal environment—what public morality should an international tribunal be required to safeguard?

[151] ICTR Statute, art 19 (4), 20(2)-21; SCSL Statute, art 17 (2); STL Statute, art 16(2).

[152] cf ICTY Rules 66, 69, 70, 75, 78–79 and ICTR Rules 66, 69, 70, 75, 78–79; STL RPE, Rules 115–18, 133, 136, 137; SCSL Rules 69, 70, 75, 78–79; ICC Statute art 54 (3), 72–73 and ICC Rules 76, 81, 82, 86–88.

[153] cf ICTY Statute, art 21(2) and ICTY Rule 75(A); ICTR Statute, art 20(2)-21 and ICTR Rule 75(A); SCSL Statute, art 17(2) and SCSL Rule 75(A); STL Statute, art 16(2) and STL Rule 133(A).

[154] *Prosecutor v Milošević* (n 127) para 4: 'The hierarchy between these interests is clearly reflected in Article 20 of the Statute, which provides expressly that the rights of the accused take precedence over the protection of the victims, as they are to be given "full respect", while the protection of victims is to be given "due regard".' The chamber overlooked art 21(2) of the statute, which explicitly subjects the accused's right to a fair and public hearing to the protection of victims and witnesses; *Prosecutor v Karadžić* (Decision on Prosecution's motion for delayed disclosure for KDZ456, KDZ493, KDZ531, and KDZ532, and variation of protective measures for KDZ489) IT-95-5/18-PT (5 June 2009) para 1; *Prosecutor v Ayyash* et al (Consolidated decision on the Prosecution Motions for Protective Measures regarding Ten Witnesses) STL-11-01/T/TC (2 July 2014) para 6: 'The Trial Chamber will grant protective measures case-by-case, on the basis of persuasive evidence for each application, and only when it is satisfied that the protective measures will not prejudice the rights of the Accused to a fair trial.'

international criminal tribunals,[155] the influence of the ICTY is noticeable. For one, the ECCC reproduces the ICTY statute's Article 20(4) on the court's duty to provide for the protection of victims and witnesses through measures including the conduct of *in camera* proceedings.[156] Although it does not explicitly condition a fair and public hearing on the protection of victims and witnesses in the manner that the ICTY, ICTR, SCSL, and STL statutes do, it articulates the principle of trial fairness and expeditiousness 'with full respect for the rights of the accused and for the protection of victims and witnesses', effectively placing the protection of victims and witnesses on equal footing with the rights of the accused.[157]

The ICC statute departs the most from the statutes of other tribunals in how it legislates the exception to public trials. This variation is largely textual, however, rather than an alteration of the principle. For one, it enshrines the judicial authority to limit a trial's publicity at its Article 68, which governs the protection of victims and witnesses, whereas the statutes of other tribunals place that limitation in their provision on the rights of the accused. This conveys clearly that the rights of the accused must be balanced by the safety concerns of victims and witnesses. It also allows the ICC to legislate the protection of victims and witnesses in far greater detail than do the other tribunals in their statutes, a level of detail which would be incongruous in a provision on the rights of the accused.

The ICC statute also details certain procedural aspects of the law on reporting restrictions which other tribunals have instead placed in their Rules, such as the advisory role of the Victims and Witnesses Unit[158] and a State's ability to request an order for non-disclosure of its information.[159] Most significantly, Article 68 lays down an automatic restriction to publicity for victims of sexual violence or children who are victims or witnesses. It is unique amongst the international tribunals for reversing the presumption in this manner, since protective measures and orders for non-disclosure of information are normally granted at other international tribunals upon request, but always on the basis of judicial discretion.[160] Interestingly, Rule 87 of the ICC's Rules appears to reverse the statute's presumption back to bring it more in line with the procedure at the other international criminal tribunals, by making judges' decision to order protective measures a discretionary rather than an automatic one.[161] Despite this inconsistency, however, the normal practice at the ICC is for protective measures to be granted upon request from the party calling a witness.[162]

This survey of domestic and international trends demonstrates that both national and international jurisdictions apply comparable principles when it comes to reporting restrictions. With the array of measures available at international tribunals to restrict reporting, and the extent to which the measures' integrity depends upon the compliance of not only the participants in the judicial process, but also those outside it, it is crucial to have an

[155] Law on the establishment of the extraordinary chambers in the courts of Cambodia for the prosecution of crimes committed during the period of Democratic Kampuchea, art 34 new; ICC Statute, art 7.

[156] Law on the establishment of the extraordinary chambers in the courts of Cambodia for the prosecution of crimes committed during the period of Democratic Kampuchea, art 33 new.

[157] ibid.

[158] ICC Statute art 68(4); W A Schabas, *The International Criminal Court: A Commentary on the Rome Statute* (OUP 2013) 822–24.

[159] ICC Statute art 68(6).

[160] ICC Statute art 68 (2); Schabas (n 158) 825–26. See also Kosovo Specialist Chambers (KSC)'s Rule 80(4)(e) of its Rules.

[161] ICC Rule 87 (1).

[162] *Prosecutor v Lubanga* (Decision on the prosecution's oral request regarding applications for protective measures) ICC-01/04-01/06-1547 (9 December 2008) para 6.

enforceable sanctioning system. This is where the power to hold in contempt of court those who violate its orders comes into play.

16.4 The Law of Contempt

Given the politically charged nature of their work, it was perhaps inevitable that the international tribunals would eventually come to face the situation of having their orders flouted. The sanctioning mechanism they resorted to in these situations was the offence of contempt of court.

16.4.1 Domestic Jurisdictions

Contempt of court, is of course, in its purest sense, a common law concept. It developed in English law on the premise that judges are invested with the power to maintain law and order in the courtroom as an inherent and essential component of their judicial function.[163] This power extends beyond the courtroom and includes the authority to prevent the judicial process from being obstructed, namely by punishing non-compliance with court orders.[164] In common law countries, although courts continue to be able to exercise this inherent authority, some forms of contempt have more recently come to be codified in legislation. The United Kingdom's *Contempt of Court Act 1981* creates, specifically in relation to publications, a strict liability rule for interference with the course of justice regardless of the intent to do so.[165]

Canada's law on contempt, evolved as it is from English law, is now similarly based both in the unwritten common law and in legislation.[166] The Canadian Supreme Court has held that proof of criminal contempt rests on proving that the accused defied a court order in a public way (the *actus reus*), with intent, knowledge, or recklessness as to the fact that the public disobedience will tend to depreciate the authority of the court (the *mens rea*).[167]

More broadly, and moving away from the common law nomenclature of contempt, the Canadian Criminal Code and other Canadian legislation consider violations of reporting restrictions to be offences that can result in sanctions. Even when they are not labelled contempt as such, these types of violations attack the core authority of a court by resisting or frustrating its administration of justice. Sanctions for violating reporting restrictions in Canada include fines of up to CA$10,000, imprisonment for up to three years, or a combination of both.[168] Fines and prison sentences are not the only consequence of publication ban

[163] G Sluiter et al (eds), *International Criminal Procedure: Principles and Rules* (OUP 2013) 764.

[164] I H Jacob, 'The Inherent Jurisdiction of the Court' (1970) 23 Current Legal Problems 23, 27–28; *AG v Punch Limited* et al [2002] UKHL 50; *AG v Times Newspapers Ltd* [1992] 1 AC 191.

[165] *Contempt of Court Act 1981*, ss 1 and 2. The strict liability rule applies only to publications which create a substantial risk that the course of justice will be seriously impeded or prejudiced, and if proceedings are active at the time of the interference. The threshold of 'substantial risk' is a high one. The publication must namely add sufficiently to the existing risk of prejudice to the proceedings to create a substantial risk: *R v Burrell* (n 2); *AG v Express Newspapers* [2004] EWHC 2859 (Admin); *Chief Constable of Greater Manchester v Channel 5 Broadcast Ltd* [2005] EWCA Civ 739.

[166] Canadian Criminal Code, s 9, 484; *R v Publications Photo-Police Incorporé* [1990] 1 SCR 851; *AG v Québécor Média Inc*, 2011 QCCQ 15413, 35, 43.

[167] *United Nurses of Alberta v Alberta* (Attorney General) 1992 1 SCR 910 25.

[168] Child and Family Services Act, R.S.O. 1990, c C-11, s 85 (3); Canadian Criminal Code, s 517 (2), s 787 (1).

violations, as courts can also order that the violating material be withdrawn from the public domain. In an age of quick-spreading information, however, courts have nevertheless pondered the fairness of punishing media outlets who fail to comply with orders to pull information from the public domain, when the information in question has meanwhile been picked up and further disseminated through news aggregation websites.[169]

Even in jurisdictions where the notion of contempt does not exist per se, conduct that undermines judicial authority is sanctioned in other ways. In France, many of the forms of conduct which the common law treats as criminal contempt constitute an offence under the French Criminal Code or Code of Criminal Procedure, such as disobeying an order to appear or produce documents before the court, giving false testimony and interfering with witnesses.[170] To prevent publication bans from being meaningless, the French law on freedom of the press imposes fines when information that by law cannot be published finds its way in the media. These range from €3,750 to €18,000 for publishing the following: the details of an indictment before it is read in a public hearing; information enabling the identification of minors who have left their guardians, committed suicide, or were victims of a crime; information allowing the identification of victims of sexual crimes; the identities of police, military, personnel from the ministry of defence, or certain kinds of customs agents; and details of hearings and court records on family law matters.[171] These sanctions are in addition to damages that can be awarded if the publication of information or images, for instance of victims of crimes, are considered an intrusion into their or their families' private lives.[172]

A similar offence against the administration of justice is found in the Italian Criminal Code.[173] Its Article 684 provides that whoever publishes, in whole or in part, even in summary form or for information purposes only, judicial acts or documents from criminal proceedings the publication of which is prohibited by law, is punishable by imprisonment of up to thirty days or with a fine from €51 to €258. The prohibition against publication under Italian law covers any medium as long as the publication is directed at an indeterminate number of persons.[174] The Italian Court of Cassation has held that it is irrelevant to the existence of this offence that the information had already been disseminated by anothers.[175] The reasoning behind this was that this subsequent publication increased the dissemination of the judicial act which should not have been publicized.[176]

16.4.2 The ICTY and ICTR

There is no mention in either of the ad hoc tribunals' statutes of a power to deal with contempt. The ICTY appeals chamber has held, however, that the tribunal possesses an inherent

169 *R v The Canadian Broadcasting Corporation* [2017] ABQB 329.

170 Code pénal, art 434-11, 434-13, 434-14, 434-1, 434-15-1; M Chesterman, 'Contempt: In the Common Law, But Not the Civil Law' (1997) 46 International and Comparative Law Quarterly521, 521.

171 Loi du 29 juillet 1981 sur la liberté de presse, art 38, 39, 39 *bis*, 39 *quinquies*, 39 *sexies*.

172 Affaire Société de Conception de Presse et d'Édition c France [2016] ECHR 216; *Hachette Filipacchi Associates v France* [2007] ECHR 5567.

173 Codice di Procedura Penale art 684.

174 Codice di Procedura Penale art 114.

175 Cass No 7674/1984; Cass No 473/2013.

176 Cass No 7674/1984; Cass No 473/2013.

jurisdiction, deriving from its judicial function, to ensure that the exercise of its jurisdiction, expressly given to it by the statute, is not frustrated, and that its basic judicial functions are safeguarded.[177]

The appeals chamber, called to address this issue early on in the ICTY's life, cautioned that 'care must be taken not to treat the considerable amount of elaboration which has occurred in relation to Rule 77 over the years as if it has produced a statutory form of offence enacted by the judges of the Tribunal'.[178] It reasoned that judges' power to adopt rules of procedure and evidence did not entail a power to create rules which prohibited new offences. It was a power to adopt rules for the conduct of matters falling within both the inherent jurisdiction of the tribunal, and its statutory jurisdiction.[179] It considered that the content of these inherent powers could be discerned from the usual sources of international law.[180]

The inherent power of the ad hoc tribunals as international criminal courts to hold in contempt those who 'knowingly and wilfully interfere with its administration of justice' thus encompasses conduct that would necessarily fall within the general concept of contempt—'conduct which tends to obstruct, prejudice or abuse the administration of justice'.[181] At both the ICTY and the ICTR, this includes, though is not limited to, disclosing information relating to tribunal proceedings in knowing violation of an order of a chamber.[182] In addition, inciting and aiding and abetting contempt is also punishable under Rule 77(B) of the Rules.[183] The maximum penalty for contempt at the ICTY is a term of imprisonment not exceeding seven years, or a fine not exceeding €100,000, or both.[184] The ICTR has lighter penalties, with terms of imprisonment not exceeding five years, or a fine not exceeding US$10,000, or both.[185]

A violation of a court order as such constitutes an interference with the tribunal's administration of justice.[186] No additional proof of harm to its administration of justice is required.[187] In other words, once a court order is violated (*actus reus*), there need be no further inquiry into the actual interference that took place, nor whether there was a real risk to the administration of justice, because the violation in itself was an interference with the administration of justice.[188] As a corollary, the fact that information disclosed by an accused

[177] *Prosecutor v Tadić* (Judgment on Allegations of Contempt against Prior Counsel, Milan Vujin) IT-94-1-A-R77 (31 January 2000) (Vujin Contempt Judgment) paras 13–18, referring to eg *Northern Cameroons Case (Cameroon v United Kingdom)* [1963] ICJ Rep 29; *Nuclear Tests Case (Australia v France)* [1974] ICJ Rep 259–60, para 23; *Prosecutor v Aleksovski* (Judgment on Appeal by Anto Nobilo Against Finding of Contempt) IT-95-14/1-AR77 (30 May 2001) paras 30, 36; *Prosecutor v Beqaj* (Judgment on Contempt Allegations) IT-03-66-T-R77 (27 May 2005) (Beqaj Contempt Judgment) para 9; *Prosecutor v Marijačić & Rebić* (Appeal Judgment) IT-95-14-R77.2.A (27 September 2006) (*Marijačić* et al Appeal Judgment).

[178] Vujin Contempt Judgment (n 177) para 24.

[179] ibid paras 24–25.

[180] ibid paras13–18 and fn 11, 24, 28; Beqaj Contempt Judgment (n 177) para 9.

[181] ICTY Rule 77(A); ICTR Rule 77(A); Vujin Contempt Judgment (n 177) paras 25–26. The 'Practice Direction on Procedure for the Investigation and Prosecution of Contempt Before the International Tribunal' was issued on 6 May 2004, IT/227.

[182] ICTY Rule 77(A)(ii); ICTR Rule 77(A)(ii).

[183] *Prosecutor v Marijačić & Rebić* (Decision on Prosecution's Motions to Amend the Indictment) IT-95-14-R77.2 (7 October 2005) para 39. There is an automatic right of appeal in contempt cases. ICTY Rule 77(J)-(K).

[184] ICTY Rule 77(G). See also ICTY Rule 77(I)-77*bis*.

[185] ICTY Rule 77(G). See also ICTR Rule 77(I).

[186] *Prosecutor v Jović* (Judgment) IT-95-14 and IT-95-14/2-R77-A (15 March 2007) (Jović Appeal Judgment) para 30; Marijačić et al Appeal Judgment (n 177) para 44; Hartmann Appeal Judgment (n 145) para 107.

[187] Jović Appeal Judgment (n 186) para 30; Hartmann Appeal Judgment (n 145) para 107.

[188] Hartmann Appeal Judgment (n 145) para 107.

in contempt proceedings was already in the public domain is not a defence in cases of violations of judicial orders of non-disclosure, including protective measures.[189] The *mens rea* requirement for a violation of Rule 77(A)(ii) of the Rules is knowledge that the disclosure in question is in violation of a chamber's order.[190] The appeals chamber has also held that individuals, including journalists, cannot decide to publish information covered by confidentiality on the basis of their own assessment of the public interest in that information.[191]

As to the discrete issue of contempt and journalists, the Hartmann Appeal Judgment addressed Hartmann's right to freedom of expression as a journalist quite extensively.[192] The appeals chamber held that there is no strong presumption of unrestricted publicity in criminal proceedings on matters that a chamber had ruled should remain confidential.[193] Recalling the Jović Appeal Judgment on the disclosure of testimony given in closed session, it held that the effect of a closed session was similar, in that it was intended 'to exclude the public, including members of the press, from the proceedings and to prevent them from coming into possession of the protected information being discussed therein. In such cases, the presumption of public proceedings under article 20(4) of the Statute does not apply'.[194]

In so ruling, the appeals chamber unequivocally held that there was no inconsistency with freedom of expression principles enshrined in the ICCPR.[195] Noting that Article 21 of the ICTY statute mirrored Article 14 of the ICCPR, the appeals chamber recalled that the Human Rights Committee interpreted Article 14(1) of the ICCPR to require that courts' judgments be made public, with 'certain strictly defined exceptions'.[196] Guided by the standard set out under Article 19 of the ICCPR, and its *travaux préparatoires*, the appeals chamber considered that Hartmann's freedom of expression was legitimately restricted as it was not only provided by law, but also proportionately necessary to protect against the dissemination of confidential information.[197]

The appeals chamber further noted that the trial chamber had correctly assessed that the effect of Hartmann's disclosure of confidential information decreased the likelihood that States would co-operate with the ICTY in the future, thereby undermining its ability to exercise its jurisdiction to prosecute and punish serious violations of humanitarian law.[198]

[189] Jović Appeal Judgment (n 186) para 30; Marijačić et al Appeal Judgment (n 177) para 45; Hartmann Appeal Judgment (n 145) paras 91–92.

[190] Jović Appeal Judgment (n 186) para 27.

[191] Marijačić et al Trial Judgment (n 16) para 39; *Prosecutor v Haxhiu* (Judgment on Allegations of Contempt) IT-04-84-R77.5 (24 July 2008) para 28. See also Hartmann Appeal Judgment (n 145) para 113. The ICTR appeals chamber has also relied on the jurisprudence of the ICTY in its contempt cases. This is hardly surprising given that at the time, many judges sat on the appeals chamber of both ad hoc tribunals. See *Léonidas Nshogora v Prosecutor* (Judgment) ICTR-07-91-A (15 March 2010) paras 56, 65; *Eliézer Niyitegeka v Prosecutor* (Decision on Motion for Clarification) ICTR-96-14-R75 (20 June 2008) para 11.

[192] Hartmann Appeal Judgment (n 145) paras158–65.

[193] ibid para 158.

[194] ibid para 158 referring to Jović Appeal Judgment (n 186) 21.

[195] Hartmann Appeal Judgment (n 145) paras 160–61 The appeals chamber also noted that it was not bound by the findings of regional or international courts including the ECtHR jurisprudence. Hartmann Appeal Judgment (n 145) para 159.

[196] Hartmann Appeal Judgment (n 145) para160.

[197] ibid para 161 The appeals chamber considered that the two appeal decisions in the case of *Prosecutor v Slobodan Milošević* that Hartmann disclosed, contained restrictions on the freedom of expression that were 'provided by law'. This was because they were filed confidentially under measures granted pursuant to Rule 54 *bis* of the Rules. Furthermore, the appeals chamber held that restricting Hartmann's freedom of expression in this manner was both proportionate and necessary because it protected the 'public order' by guarding against the dissemination of confidential information. These restrictions were therefore within the ambit of art 19(3) of the ICCPR. Hartmann Appeal Judgment (n 145) para161.

[198] Hartmann Appeal Judgment (n 145) para 162.

In this context, prosecuting an individual for contempt was proportionate to the effect Hartmann's actions had on the ICTY's ability to administer international criminal justice.[199]

16.4.3 Beyond the Ad Hoc Tribunals

Of the STL's two contempt cases, the most mediatized one, against *Al Jadeed* and Al Khayat, was overturned on appeal (essentially for procedural reasons to do with proper service of court documents to the accused).[200] This means the STL has only ever issued one conviction for contempt, which was in the case against *Al Akhbar* and its editor-in-chief Al Amin, a conviction which was not appealed.

Putting aside the outcomes, the evidentiary thresholds applied by the STL in the two cases were consonant with each other, and relied on the precedents that had broken ground at the ICTY with regards to the elements of the crime of contempt. The trial judge, who was the same in both cases, held that any conduct charged under Rule 60*bis(A)* of the STL's Rules must, if proven, amount to a knowing and wilful interference with the administration of justice.[201] One charge that had been brought against the accused in both cases (knowingly and wilfully interfering with the administration of justice by publishing information about purported confidential witnesses) did not entail the violation of a judicial order.[202] The judge noted that the disclosure of information on purported confidential witnesses in the absence of a judicial order does not necessarily interfere with the administration of justice, though it could do so, if certain effects and a culpable state of mind are proved.[203] He therefore concluded that the prosecution had to establish that the accused deliberately published information on purported confidential witnesses, and in doing so, knew that their conduct was objectively likely to undermine public confidence in the STL's ability to protect the confidentiality of information about witnesses or potential witnesses.[204] In essence, this meant that the publication of information could be punished on the basis that it interferes with the administration of justice, even where no judicial order actually prohibited the publication per se.

In the *Al Jadeed* case, however, a second charge had also been brought against the accused, one that specifically involved the violation of a judicial order, namely the one issued by the pre-trial judge ordering the removal of the witness information from the public domain, which the STL's Registry had repeatedly attempted to serve upon the accused.[205] Relying upon what he considered to be the ICTY's clear jurisprudence, the judge reasoned that if the publication of witness information was in violation of a court order, the very act of that publication would amount to an interference with the administration of justice, so long as the accused had knowledge that the disclosure was in violation of an order.[206] The judge was convinced the prosecution had relieved itself of its burden of proof and convicted one of the accused, Al Khayat, on that basis. The issue of whether the two accused were

199 ibid.
200 Al Jadeed Appeal Judgment (n 51) paras 156–73.
201 ibid para 38.
202 ibid para 37.
203 ibid para 40.
204 ibid para 50.
205 ibid para 51.
206 ibid paras 45, 54.

aware of the existence of the pre-trial judge's order (in other words whether it had been properly served on them) became a contentious issue, and one on the basis of which the appeal panel ultimately overturned Al Khayat's conviction.[207]

No discussion of contempt at the international criminal jurisdictions would be complete without pointing out the extent to which the ICC's legal framework stands apart from those of the ICTY and the other international criminal tribunals. The ICC statute corrects one fundamental lacuna that the ICTY and its counterparts had to grapple with early on: the absence of any explicit jurisdiction in their statutes to hold someone in contempt. The ICC statute, in contrast, has two provisions dealing with offences against the administration of justice and misconduct before the court: Articles 70 and 71.[208] This foresight contains its own shortcomings, however, as it is unclear which of these two provisions, if any, would form the basis for prosecuting those who publish confidential information in violation of judicial orders.

Article 70 covers conduct that is fundamentally egregious to the administration of justice, such as false testimony, forged evidence, witness interference, and corrupting court officials. But it makes no mention of violations of judicial orders or unlawful disclosures. Moreover, it lists the offences exhaustively, not leaving any room for conduct that is not explicitly mentioned in the provision. It certainly does not contain a *chapeau* in the way the Rules of the other tribunals do to cover interference with the administration of justice in a general way.[209]

Article 71 of the ICC statute covers misconduct that is of a less serious nature than that listed at Article 70 and that occurs 'before' the court, in other words, that takes place in the courtroom.[210] As a result, the provision would not cover the publication or broadcasting of confidential information, particularly if it had been done by third parties who would not under normal circumstances even be in the courtroom—such as journalists. In any event, Article 71, read together with Rule 171 of the ICC's Rules, provides sufficient indication that the situations it intends to cover are where the offender is physically in the courtroom, and for offences of a less serious nature than those covered at Article 70.

It is therefore anyone's guess how the ICC will handle violations of judicial orders, including those granting protective measures. Perhaps, as some have speculated, the reason for this apparent omission in the ICC statute is so that the ICC can refer such matters to States Parties on the basis of the principle of complementarity.[211] Complementarity, however, requires the existence of a crime in the ICC statute, which is obviously not the case when it comes to violations of judicial orders. Alternatively, these concerns could be nothing more than a red herring if judges invoke regulation 29 of the Regulations of the Court,[212] which stipulates:

> 1. In the event of non-compliance by a participant with the provisions of any regulation, or with an order of a Chamber made hereunder, the Chamber may issue any order that is deemed necessary in the interests of justice.

207 ibid paras 156–73.
208 ICC Statute, art 70–71.
209 Sluiter et al (n 163) 755.
210 ICC Statute art 71(1) states: 'The Court may sanction persons *present before it* who commit misconduct, including disruption of its proceedings or deliberate refusal to comply with its directions […].' (Emphasis added.)
211 Sluiter et al (n 163) 755.
212 W A Schabas, *An Introduction to the International Criminal Court* (CUP 2014) 156.

2. This provision is without prejudice to the inherent powers of the Chamber.

Relying on a legal text that is even lower in the hierarchy of norms than the Rules, however, would no doubt trigger a controversy comparable to the one the ICTY faced when it invoked the doctrine of inherent jurisdiction for its first contempt case. Moreover, the provision only appears to apply to persons who are participating in the proceedings, like the parties and the legal representatives of victims. Time will tell.

Like the ICC, the International Residual Mechanism for Criminal Tribunals (IRMCT), the successor of the ICTR and ICTY, has been given the power to prosecute cases of contempt under Article 4 of its founding statute, thus clearly ensuring this power is a statutory one, and no longer relying on customary international law as the ICTY had done. The IRMCT's jurisdiction covers not only knowing and wilful interference with the administration of justice or false testimony before the IRMCT itself, but also before the ICTY and ICTR.[213] On the other hand, Rule 90 of its Rules replicates, almost verbatim, that of the ICTY. It also echoes the respective rules on publicity of trials and its limitations in the case of judicial orders of non-disclosure, including protective measures granted by a chamber.[214] Nonetheless, it is incumbent on the IRMCT to consider referring such cases to the authorities of a State, taking into account the interests of justice and expediency.[215] Whether this requirement will affect the number and kind of contempt cases the IRMCT itself will prosecute remains to be seen.

Interestingly, the newly set-up Kosovo Specialist Chambers (KSC) has jurisdiction over crimes against humanity and war crimes, as well as over offences against the administration of justice—some similar to contempt cases—which are recognized under the Kosovo Criminal Code.[216] As a derivative of Kosovar law, the constituent Law on the Kosovo Specialist Chambers and Specialist Prosecutor's Office (KSC Law) also conceives of certain restrictions to an accused's right to a public trial.[217] It further provides for a penalty in cases of non-compliance with non-disclosure orders.[218]

213 UNSC Res 1966 (22 December 2010) UN Doc S/Res/1966 1(4).

214 IRMCT Rules 55, 71(C), 73(D), 75, 86, 92–93. There have been some contempt-related decisions by the IRMCT but no contempt judgments have been rendered as yet. See e.g. *Prosecutor v Maximilien Turinabo* et al and *Prosecutor v Augustin Ngirabatware* (Decision on Prosecution Motion for Joinder of the Ngirabatware and Turinabo et al Contempt Cases) MICT-18-116-PT and MICT-19-121-PT (10 December 2019).

215 UNSC Res 1966 (22 December 2010) UN Doc S/Res/1966 1(4), 6.

216 Law on Ratification of the International Agreement between the Republic of Kosovo and the European Union on the European Union Rule of Law Mission in Kosovo, Law No 04/L-274; Law on Specialist Chambers and Specialist Prosecutor's Office, Law No 05/L-053 (KSC Law) art 6, 15(2) refer to ch XXXII, arts 384–86, 388, 390–407, ch XXXIII, arts 409–11, 415, 417, 419, 421, and ch XXXIV, arts 423–24 of the Kosovo Criminal Code 2012, Law 04/L-082.

217 KSC Law (n 216), art 21(2) stipulates the right to 'a fair and public hearing, subject to Article 23 of this Law and any measures ordered by the Specialist Chambers for the protection of victims and witnesses'. The Rules before the KSC, also provide for restrictions to a public trial for reasons of public order, security, national security interest of Kosovo or a third State, non-disclosure of the identity of a witness or a victim participating in the proceedings, or in the interests of justice. KSC Rule 120. See also KSC Rules 80, 82–84, 105, 108, 111. Rule 80 of the KSC Rules goes further than the ICTY Rules in that it allows, 'in exceptional circumstances and subject to any necessary safeguards' for the possibility of total anonymity of a witness. KSC Rules 80(4)(e)(ii), 147; *KSC Constitutional Court (Judgment on the Referral of the Rules of Procedure and Evidence Adopted by Plenary on 17 March 2017 to the Specialist Chamber of the Constitutional Court Pursuant to Article 19(5) of Law No 05/L-053 on Specialist Chambers and Specialist Prosecutor's Office)* KSC-CC-PR-2017-01 (26 April 2017) paras 132–40. KSC Rule 77(4)(e) referred to therein is the revised KSC Rule 80(4)(e). See KSC-BD-03/Rev1/2017.

218 KSC Rules 65, 165.

The KSC Law also explicitly provides for customary international law as a source of law, and indicates that in determining the customary international law applicable at the time of the alleged crimes, the panels of the KSC may resort to subsidiary sources, such as the jurisprudence of the international ad hoc tribunals, the ICC, and other criminal courts.[219] It will be interesting to see how this is interpreted by the panels, and whether the ICTY's jurisprudence on contempt of court in general, and by journalists in particular, will be adopted as customary international law by the panels, or whether it will be merely considered instructive, if at all.

16.5 Conclusion

Orders for protective measures and the non-disclosure of information in international criminal trials are very closely linked to the increased level of visibility of these trials in comparison to most domestic ones,[220] as a result of the crimes under their jurisdiction. This high visibility goes hand-in-hand with sophisticated outreach and public information strategies that are rarely found in domestic jurisdictions, including the live streaming of proceedings online, exposure through actively managed Facebook, Twitter, LinkedIn, and Flickr accounts and the posting of videos on YouTube channels. This is in addition to more traditional methods of educating the public and affected communities, which the ICTY had notably done by allowing access to the public gallery, regularly issuing press releases, holding weekly press conferences, and managing a multitude of educational campaigns throughout the years. The downside of such high visibility, however, is the increased exposure to the media and the public at large of the witnesses who testify, the victims whose harrowing experiences are described at length, and politically sensitive intelligence gathered by States and other entities.

Despite these unique aspects, however, restrictions on the publicity of international criminal trials follow rules no different than those at the domestic level. That these restrictions are more striking than they would normally be in domestic jurisdictions is, ironically, only a sign of how much more visible international criminal trials are.

Despite a relatively widespread recognition of these unique realities, international tribunals' prosecution of journalists for contempt has not been spared the occasional criticism within the legal community itself. Even supporters of international justice find the ICTY's forays into prosecuting and punishing contempt of court, a waste of time and resources. Some argue that the international criminal tribunals should leave the investigation and prosecution of contempt cases and any offences against the administration of justice to national courts.[221] How this would be feasible in practice, let alone effective, is unclear, particularly considering the difficulties encountered at times in securing States' co-operation with international tribunals.

219 KSC Law, art 3(2)-(3).

220 See generally D Stepniak, *Audio-visual Coverage of Courts* (Cambridge University Press 2009). Loi sur la liberté de presse, art 38 ter; Contempt of Court Act 1981, s 9; Criminal Justice Act 1925, s 41; *R. v Pilarinos* 2001 BCSC 1332 (CanLII) 40–42; Ontario Court of Justice Act, s 136; *R. v Squires* (1989) 69 C.R. (3d) 337 (Ont Dist Ct).

221 W A Schabas, 'The Yugoslavia Tribunal also Engages in Debt Collection' (25 March 2016) <http://humanrightsdoctorate.blogspot.nl/2016/03/the-yugoslavia-tribunal-also-engages-in.html> accessed February 2018.

Current international practice seems to indicate that the opposite view has nevertheless established itself. Indeed, there is no longer anything exceptional in the international criminal tribunals' ability to prosecute and punish violations of protective measures and orders of non-disclosure as part of their power to ensure the proper administration of justice and ultimately the rule of law. Absent such a power, these institutions would be unable to uphold the integrity of their own proceedings. In any event, and as demonstrated, these limitations are wholly in line with human rights law and the practice in various domestic jurisdictions.

At the end of the day, as is so often the case in criminal justice, judges need to undertake a balancing act on a case-by-case basis between equally important but at times competing interests. The right of the accused to a public trial, that of the public to be informed of criminal proceedings and the role of the press to act as the bridge between the two, have to be weighed against other legitimate rights and interests, namely, the safety and security of witnesses and victims, their right to privacy, the security concerns of States and international organizations, public order, and the interests of justice. Despite the relative clarity of the law, however, the sensitivity and importance of the issues are such that the controversy will most likely persist.

17

Translating and Interpreting at the ICTY

Lessons Learned

*Ellen Elias-Bursać**

17.1 Introduction

In international war crimes trials, witnesses testify through an interpreter about translated documents tendered as evidence; attorneys argue through an interpreter about both the translated documents and the interpreting; and judges adjudicate on interpreted testimony and translated evidence. It is then fully visible in every one of the more than 10,000 days of trial at the International Criminal Tribunal for the former Yugoslavia (ICTY), that the translators and interpreters have played an active role in shaping international justice.

Francesca Gaiba[1] and Kayoko Takeda[2] laid the groundwork for analysis of the challenges facing the set-up and conduct of language services in war crimes courts. They highlight challenges such as recruitment and training, staff bias, trauma, the technological innovations of equipping a booth for simultaneous interpreting, the monitoring of translation and interpreting quality, and the editing of transcripts.

In the course of its twenty-four years of managing the translation and interpreting at the ICTY, the Conference and Language Service Section (CLSS) faced many challenges as they provided language-related services to the Office of the Prosecutor (OTP), defence counsel, Registry, and Chambers. The long tenure of the ICTY and the extent of its mandate to try 161 indictees in over 100 trials, the length of the trials, the number and nature of the languages spoken by the defendants and witnesses, the technological innovations introduced to the courtrooms; all these created challenges and opportunities that went beyond those faced by the language services in Tokyo (lasting thirty months and trying twenty-eight indictees) and Nuremberg (lasting eleven months and trying twenty-two indictees). This chapter will consider an array of these challenges, ranging from practical matters, such as the correction of errors, to organizational questions of how to staff the booth and translation services of an ad hoc war crimes tribunal, to procedural matters, such as whether the ICTY languages staff could be compelled to testify before the court.

CLSS included the Conference Interpretation Unit (CIU), the French Translation Unit (FTU), and the English Translation Unit (ETU), as well as a terminology unit. The CIU

* Former Reviser/translator at the ICTY and author of E Elias-Bursać, *Translating Evidence and Interpreting Testimony at a War Crimes Tribunal: Working in a Tug-of-War* (Palgrave-Macmillan 2015).

1 Gaiba has published studies of interpreting at the International Military Tribunal (1945–6), known as the Nuremberg trial. See F Gaiba, *The Origins of Simultaneous Interpretation: The Nuremberg Trial* (University of Ottawa Press 1998).

2 Kayoko Takeda has written studies on interpreting at the International Military Tribunal for the Far East (1946–8), also known as the Tokyo trials. See K Takeda, *Interpreting the Tokyo War Crimes Tribunal: A Sociopolitical Analysis* (University of Ottawa Press 2010).

Ellen Elias-Bursać, *Translating and Interpreting at the ICTY* In: *Legacies of the International Criminal Tribunal for the Former Yugoslavia.* Edited by: Carsten Stahn, Carmel Agius, Serge Brammertz, Colleen Rohan, Oxford University Press (2020). © The Several Contributors
DOI: 10.1093/oso/9780198862956.003.0018

provided simultaneous interpreters for the booth and consecutive interpreters for meetings and depositions; the FTU translated ICTY documents and Tribunal communications from English into French. The ETU translated those same ICTY documents from French into English, and from English and French into Bosnian, Croatian, Serbian, Albanian, and Macedonian; as well as translating most of the documentary evidence presented in the courtroom from these languages into English.

I worked in the ETU of CLSS for six years as a translator and reviser, going through documentary evidence that had been translated from Bosnian, Croatian, and Serbian originals into English by CLSS translators. This experience and research into nine trials: *Tadić, Furundžija, Kunarac* et al, *Halilović, Slobodan Milošević, Šešelj, Krstić, Gotovina* et al, and *Karadžić*, provided the basis for a monograph[3] and two articles[4] analysing how translation and interpreting have shaped ICTY procedures and jurisprudence. From these studies I draw the data and examples used in this chapter. The research was conducted by searching through the trial transcripts available to the public on the ICTY website, using keywords such as translator, translation, translating, CLSS, and so forth to identify the discussions that went on during the proceedings about these subjects.

17.2 Challenges Facing CLSS

The reality faced by those who set up CLSS[5] in the 1990s was that the availability of experienced translators and interpreters working out of Bosnian, Croatian, Serbian, Albanian, and Macedonian into English and French, the working languages of the Tribunal, was significantly less than the number needed. CLSS had to furnish the courtroom booths with a full roster of interpreters, and form language units to supply the proceedings with English-language translations of documentary evidence, at the same time as it had to provide all the ICTY institutional documents, such as the *Statute, Rules of Procedure and Evidence*, indictments, judgments, and all official submissions and motions, in both working languages (English and French), as well as the languages of the defendants and witnesses in each trial. They therefore had to recruit native speakers from the former Yugoslavia who were able to work into English or French, as their second language. While interpreting or translating into a language other than one's native language is not common professional practice, languages of limited diffusion such as those spoken by the defendants and witnesses at the ICTY almost always require it.

This situation compelled the language services to set up training, cross-training, and secondment practices. These opportunities for staff ultimately proved to be essential for retaining translators and interpreters and for honing their skills. Everyone who worked there

[3] E Elias-Bursać, *Translating Evidence and Interpreting Testimony at a War Crimes Tribunal: Working in a Tug-of-War* (Palgrave-Macmillan 2015).

[4] E Elias-Bursać, 'Shaping International Justice: The Role of Translation and Interpreting at the ICTY in The Hague' (2012) 7 Translation and Interpreting Studies 34; E Elias-Bursać, 'Pushing Back: Witnesses and Translation in the Radovan Karadžić Trial' (2016) Getuigen tussen geschiedenis in herinnering 123 and 98.

[5] M Draženović-Carrieri, 'BCS—A Practical Approach' in R Lučić (ed), *Lexical Norm and National Language: Lexicography and Language Policy in South-Slavic Languages after 1989* (Verlag Otto Sagner 2003); J Pavetić, 'Interview with Greiss Lecturer Marijana Nikolić' (2012) 21 SlavFile: Newsletter of the Slavic Languages Division 6–7, 9.

knew the ICTY was an ad hoc institution so their position was not permanent. Some sixty translators and interpreters responded to a survey I was allowed to conduct when I was writing my book. The respondents spoke of the importance to them of the cross-training programme. Their comments suggest that the variety provided by working both as an interpreter and a translator made their work experience at the ICTY more engaging and provided them with skills they could apply in later jobs.[6]

Having language services staffed largely from the region, some of them having been through the war themselves, others having fled the country to avoid the war, yet others whose lives were hardly touched by the war, meant a host of security concerns for the Tribunal administration. The assumption prevailed that translators and interpreters from Croatia, Bosnia and Herzegovina, Serbia, and other parts of the former Yugoslavia brought with them a certain amount of vulnerability for the institution. Most of the CLSS language staff had family still living in the region. If family members were pressured, the staff might be coerced into subverting the integrity of the Tribunal, or the staff members themselves might hold personal biases about the war. This assumption is present in all war-related translation institutions.[7] As Mona Baker writes, 'Wartime translators and interpreters are variously narrated as trustworthy and reliable, or as a (potential) threat to security.'[8] Mirko Klarin, however, disputes this:

> Such suspicion was a pity, because it hindered the Prosecutors, investigators and analysts who had come from all over the world from bridging the cultural gap that divided them from this remote area that was under their jurisdiction ... [9]

There is scant information available to substantiate the suspicions that language staff from the region did, indeed, jeopardize ICTY security. In his book on the arrests of Tribunal indictees, Julian Borger mentions a single case of an interpreter who infiltrated the language services.

> Her true status only became apparent after she left The Hague, when she resurfaced as a senior diplomat in a Croatian mission abroad, an extraordinary career progression for a translator who had supposedly been a private citizen. An ICTY investigator also had her hotel room broken into while she was visiting Zagreb and ten disks of evidence collected on the Medak Pocket killings were stolen.[10]

While this single incident does not prove or disprove the trustworthiness of the more than 500 CLSS language staff and the hundreds of translators and interpreters who worked on contract over the life of the Tribunal, the fact that other such stories haven't been aired in

[6] Elias-Bursać (n 3) 99–100.

[7] L Askew, 'A Perceived Neutrality: An Englishwoman's Reflections on Working as an Interpreter for Suspect and Witness Interviews at the International War Crimes Tribunal for the former Yugoslavia' in C Andrew and S Tobia (eds), *Interrogation in War and Conflict: A Comparative and Interdisciplinary Analysis* (Routledge 2014); C S Namakula, 'Language Rights in the Minimum Guarantees of Fair Criminal Trial' (2012) 19 The International Journal of Speech, Language and the Law 80.

[8] M Baker, 'Interpreters and Translators in the War Zone: Narrated and Narrators' (2010) 16 The Translator 209.

[9] M Klarin, 'The Tribunal's Four Battles' (2004) 2 Journal of International Criminal Justice 552.

[10] J Borger, *The Butcher's Trail: How the Search for Balkan War Criminals Became the World's Most Successful Manhunt* (Other Press 2016) 105–06.

public suggests that this was a rarer occurrence than the founders of the Tribunal had feared it might be.

Not only did language staff from the region have to face suspicion from their colleagues at the Tribunal, but they were also faced with hostile attitudes about the Tribunal voiced by friends and family from the region, where the institution was frequently reviled by domestic media. To the question posed in a language services survey of how CLSS language staff responded to critiques of the Tribunal, 75 per cent of the respondents said they found they often had to explain the ICTY, defend it, or justify it.[11]

17.3 The Code of Ethics

These and other issues facing the language services in the early years of the Tribunal prompted the publishing of a code of ethics articulating the role of language staff in the work of the courtroom in 1999, six years after it began its work. The *Code* dictates the standards of conduct, requiring language staff to behave in a courteous, polite, and dignified manner, to uphold professional integrity and dignity by preventing personal or other interest from interfering with the discharge of their duties, and by adhering reliably to appointments and deadlines. The *Code of Ethics* obliged translators and interpreters to maintain confidentiality even to the point of exercising discretion after the expiration or termination of the interpreter's or translator's employment, to maintain impartiality and disclose any conflict of interest, to uphold competence and accuracy in their work.[12]

This last, the stricture to convey 'with the greatest fidelity and accuracy, and with complete neutrality, the wording used by the persons they interpret or translate',[13] was the most controversial and oft-cited of the points raised in the *Code of Ethics*. The definition of what 'fidelity and accuracy' meant in the context of the work of the Tribunal, evolved over time.

In order to ensure the accuracy of the translations and interpreting, procedures were set in place for querying, commenting on, or criticizing a translation or interpreting choice. A party complaining of a perceived error was instructed to submit an internal memorandum to CLSS requesting that the translation or transcript be checked. If an error was indeed confirmed, CLSS would correct either the translation or the transcript accordingly. There are hundreds of such memoranda available to the public in the ICTY Court Records database. There will always be errors in translations and interpreting, and these mechanisms for correction were essential to the integrity of the proceedings.

Philip Hepburn, head of the ICTY ETU for many years, questioned the use of the term 'fidelity':

> The rigid insistence of the Code of Ethics on complete fidelity to the original and even word-for-word translation undoubtedly stems from an outdated view of translation as a purely technical process in which the translator is expected merely to 'transfer' what is on

[11] Elias-Bursać (n 3) 32–46.

[12] *The Code of Ethics for Interpreters and Translators Employed by the International Criminal Tribunal for the Former Yugoslavia*, ICTY IT/144 (8 March 1999). <http://www.icty.org/x/file/Legal%20Library/Miscellaneous/it144_codeofethicsinterpreters_en.pdf> accessed 13 October 2017.

[13] ibid art 10.

the page and leave the more difficult task of interpreting its meaning and significance to the clients, in this case lawyers and judges.[14]

Indeed, Hepburn's view echoes the CLSS response to a motion raised by the defence counsel of *Milutinović* et al who requested 'verbatim' transcripts and interpreting in 2007. In their internal memorandum requesting verification of portions of the transcript record, Sreten Lukić's defence team asserted:

> For purposes of preserving a proper record of these proceedings, and more importantly, for purposes of preparing cross examination, it is essential for the transcript and record of proceedings, as much as possible, [to] provide an accurate, verbatim record of the sworn testimony of witnesses. Without such a record, the integrity of these proceedings is called into question.[15]

The Registry's reply is a succinct statement on the position of the CLSS CIU on the question of the accuracy standard for interpreters, by contrasting it to translating:

> The language service provided by the Registry during court proceedings at the Tribunal is interpretation and not translation. Interpretation is used for oral communication, whereas translation deals with transcription of the written word (…). Simultaneous interpretation is the rendition of the speech in the target language as it is being delivered in the source language. Since interpreters, unlike translators, have to deal with fleeting messages in real time, synthesizing and editing are not only legitimate interpretation techniques but they are necessary to make it possible … [T]he Registry notes that the level of accuracy and completeness of simultaneous interpretation services provided for hearings meets the highest standards expected of the profession.[16]

Despite this unambiguous statement from the conference interpreters, however, Radovan Karadžić submitted a motion in 2013 for a full review of the transcripts of the testimony by all Bosnian, Croatian, and Serb (BCS) speakers to testify in his trial, based on a day in court for which he claimed he had noted serious interpreting errors. CLSS investigated the claim by comparing the audio recordings for that day of court with transcripts, and ascertained that the interpreting had been well over 90 per cent accurate:

> (…) the level of accuracy of simultaneous interpretation in the Tribunal is much higher than that of simultaneous interpretation in the private sector or that required by the courts in some domestic jurisdictions. Indeed, the very same transcript the Accused submits contains a large number of errors is in fact 98.4 per cent accurate. Accordingly, the Chamber is not convinced that errors in interpretation of the proceedings at the Tribunal and in this particular case are as commonplace or as serious the Accused makes them out to be.[17]

[14] P Hepburn, 'The Translation of Evidence at the ICTY: A Ground-Breaking Institution' (2012) 7 Translation and Interpreting Studies 62.

[15] *Prosecutor v Milan Mulutinović* et al (Decision on Lukić Motion to Compel Registry to Provide Verbatim Transcripts of Proceedings) ICTY-IT-05-87-T (27 September 2007) para 1.

[16] ibid para 2.

[17] *Prosecutor v Radovan Karadžić* (Decision on the Accused's Motion for Revision of Trial Transcripts) ICTY-IT-95-5/18-T (3 July 2013) para 7.

The CLSS statement quoted above distinguishes the accuracy standard maintained by interpreters from that maintained by translators. Internal memoranda such as those described above were also submitted when the wording of the translation of an evidentiary document was disputed. Everyone in the courtroom had before them on their monitors both the original document and its translation; when they felt they had identified an error in a translated document they were encouraged to bring their request for a correction to the attention of CLSS. If CLSS agreed that the correction was warranted, they would reissue the translation.

While this was done whenever the error was deemed so serious that it impeded understanding the probative value of the translated evidence, there was potential for confusion for investigators researching documents for future trials if they came across the two translations (the erroneous one and the amended one) of the same document circulating within the ICTY evidence collection.

Another way that two versions of a translated document might enter the ICTY document system was through duplicate submissions. The documents which arrived at the Tribunal as potential evidence came from many different sources. Occasionally a document would slip through in several copies and be given to different translators to translate. Such duplicate translations were sometimes noticed by the translators and revisers but there were instances when several versions of the same document would be tendered. The *ICTY Manual* notes that '... the existence of duplicates can cause confusion, place unnecessary demands on translation, and [they] are extremely difficult to remove from the system'.[18] Duplicates were also a wasteful expense and their timely identification was a significant source of savings. In 2011, '[t]he Office of Document Management received 69,731 pages of translation requests of which 16,231 were identified as duplicate pages, resulting in a saving of approximately $1,313,253'.[19]

17.4 The Languages Services Survey

When surveyed about what they would consider the most rewarding aspect of their ICTY job, a number of the CLSS staff said that this was working with victims and helping witnesses make their voices heard. Others saw their Tribunal post as a valuable opportunity for professional development and a chance to have one's translations revised by professionals and benefit from work with experienced interpreters. Yet others mentioned their appreciation of the collegiality and teamwork, while a few spoke frankly of the appeal of the excellent salary.[20]

In response to the question of what was most challenging, some language staff mentioned the challenges of mastering the terminology for evidentiary material, legal and military language. Others spoke of the pressing deadlines; interpreting for the

[18] ICTY-UNICRI, 'ICTY Manual on Developed Practices' (United Nations Interregional Crime and Justice Research Institute, 2009) <https://www.icty.org/x/file/About/Reports%20and%20Publications/ICTY_Manual_on_Developed_Practices.pdf> accessed 5 February 2020.

[19] UNGA-UNSC 'Nineteenth annual report of the International Tribunal for the Prosecution of Persons Responsible for Serious Violations of International Humanitarian Law Committed in the Territory of the Former Yugoslavia since 1991' (1 August 2012) UN Doc A/67/214-S/2012/592 <http://www.icty.org/x/file/About/Reports%20and%20Publications/AnnualReports/annual_report_2012_en.pdf> accessed 13 October 2017.

[20] Elias-Bursać (n 3) 35–39.

courtroom where everything that is said is for the record; the monotony of the routine, and the tedium of the subject matter. Several described the disturbing subject matter of the trials, testimonies, and documents, interpreting for war criminals, dealing with a topic that for most of the translator's friends and relatives was a thing of the past, and facing the fact that behind long lists of victims, names on paper were real people who used to have more or less ordinary lives. Yet others felt betrayed by some of the Tribunal judgments.[21]

Despite the vulnerability of their position and the disturbing nature of the work, 90 per cent of the respondents said they were glad to have worked at the ICTY.

The survey also provided evidence of how decisive for ICTY translators and interpreters was the role of the Staff Welfare Office. Psychologist Kevin Cullen, helped many to deal with traumatic reactions to the disturbing material they were interpreting and translating.[22] The contrast is unambiguous between comments from language staffers who came to work at the ICTY before the Staff Welfare Office was set up and those who were hired after it was in place. When asked what advice they would offer to a translator or interpreter considering similar work, one interpreter described the harrowing experience of working at the ICTY in the early years without the support of a counsellor. This person wrote: 'I was extremely surprised and shocked that there was NO professional psychological support on offer'. Another said: '... one of the major failings of the ICTY is its general neglect of the potentially traumatic experience of working in great and prolonged detail with often very graphic and painful descriptions of incidents that occurred during the war.'[23]

In striking contrast, language staff who began working at the ICTY after the Welfare Office had been set up, refer to these services as an expected and reliable source of support, as with this comment: 'The job deals with those accused of war crimes and crimes against humanity. The ICTY has support systems in place for those who wish to request emotional or psychological counselling.' This contrast underscores the vital importance of counselling support for language staff who work with victims of a war and on documents detailing atrocities.[24]

17.5 Translation and Interpreting in the Courtroom

As the arrests and trials began in the mid-1990s, setting the pace for providing documentary evidence in translation to the courtroom for the growing number of trials proved a major challenge for CLSS. The parties to *Tadić*, the first trial, tendered 465 exhibits, but later trials relied increasingly on documentary evidence. In *Karadžić,* a trial that ran for four years near to the end of the work of the Tribunal, the parties tendered 11,481 exhibits with some 40,000 pages of documents. The 2009 Annual Report states

[21] Elias-Bursać (n 3) 40–44.

[22] See also Elias-Bursać (n 3) 42; N S Nicholson, 'Interpreting at the International Criminal Tribunal for the Former Yugoslavia (ICTY): Linguistic and Cultural Challenges' in H Tonkin and M Frank (eds), *The Translator as Mediator of Cultures* (John Benjamins 2010) 46.

[23] Elias-Bursač (n 3) 48.

[24] See also R Morris, 'The Gum Syndrome: Predicaments in Court Reporting' (1999) Forensic Linguistics 6; S Berk-Seligson, *The Bilingual Courtroom: Court Interpreters in the Judicial Process with a New Chapter* (University of Chicago Press 2002).

that the CLSS translation units translated 70,000 pages that year.[25] At this point CLSS numbered some seventy-five translators and seventy-five interpreters, or roughly 10 per cent of the overall ICTY staff.

At times seven to ten trials were running concurrently, as was the case between 2004 and 2014, and therefore the greatest challenge for the translation units was prioritizing, in conjunction with Chambers and the parties, the pace for translating evidence. CLSS quickly became a bottleneck.

In a Registry document circulated within the Tribunal in 2006, the priorities for translation from Bosnian, Croatian, and Serbian or Macedonian or Albanian into English are set forth as follows:

- Correspondence from the former Yugoslavia to Registry/President or Chambers (I)
- Medical reports, short communications from detainees (I)
- Urgent documents to be tendered as evidence for witnesses who are due to appear within the next few days (Only short documents or extracts can be accepted for urgent translation) (I)
- Urgent documents needed to meet Rules of Procedure and Evidence deadlines or specifically mandated by an order of the Chamber (I)
- Self-represented Accused's filings to the Court, Bureau or President (I)
- Other documents needed to meet Rules of Procedure and Evidence deadlines or specifically mandated by an order of the Chamber (II)
- Documents to be tendered as evidence in ongoing trials (II)
- Documents to be tendered as evidence in forthcoming trials for which a start date has been set (III)
- Documents to be tendered as evidence in trials for which no start date has been set (IV)[26]

This list offers a glimpse into the hierarchy of tasks the language services juggled, particularly in the peak years of proceedings. As the bulk of Prosecution evidence had to be translated before discovery, coordination and prioritizing became essential and were, at times, a stumbling block to the smooth roll-out of trial after trial. For instance, in the *Šainović* et al appeals judgment, defendant Sreten Lukić based his appeal on the difficulties he had experienced in gaining access to CLSS so documents could be translated for his defence. The appeals chamber in *Šainović* et al found that the trial chamber had

> ... effectively limited Sreten Lukić's access to the translation resources of the Tribunal by setting deadlines within which CLSS was unable to complete all of Lukić's outstanding requests for translation due to its capacity constraints' (...) but the appeals chamber also found that Lukić had 'failed to demonstrate that the Trial Chamber's error resulted in prejudice to him'.[27]

[25] UNGA-UNSC 'Sixteenth annual report of the International Tribunal for the Prosecution of Persons Responsible for Serious Violations of International Humanitarian Law Committed in the Territory of the Former Yugoslavia since 1991' (31 July 2009) UN Doc A/64/205-S/2009/394 <http://www.icty.org/x/file/About/Reports%20and%20Publications/AnnualReports/annual_report_2009_en.pdf> accessed 13 October 2017.

[26] *Registry Policy Governing Translation Services Provided by the Registry* (International Criminal Tribunal for the Former Yugoslavia 2006) 5.

[27] *Prosecutor v Šainović* et al (Appeals Chamber Judgment) ICTY-IT-05-87-A (23 January 2014) para 120.

In response to the problems they were encountering with the CLSS bottleneck, the OTP decided to set up their own translation service, the Document and Video Unit (DVU), in 2002. DVU translations were initially defined as support documents to aid OTP researchers and attorneys prepare indictments and trials. Only CLSS translations were to be tendered as evidence because, unlike the DVU translations, at first, the CLSS translations had been fully revised and were ready for the scrutiny of the courtroom. Furthermore, at first, DVU translators were hired on three-month contracts as administrative, rather than professional, staff. Over time, however, the DVU formed teams of translators who were able to develop a consistent terminology, and a team of revisers was assembled as quality supervisors. At this stage the rule of thumb became that a translation from a source other than CLSS would be submitted to CLSS for re-translation only if it were disputed by one of the parties or a witness. Uncontested non-CLSS translations were, therefore, allowed in as evidence in the Tribunal's last trials. While the formation of the DVU relieved some of the pressures within the OTP for access to translation services, the fact that they provided another source of translated documentary evidence did mean that the documents scrutinized in the courtroom came from a variety of translation services, including CLSS translators, DVU translators, and external contract translators. This resulted, on occasion, in terminological inconsistencies and disputes.

An important distinction between CLSS and the DVU was that CLSS was a part of Registry and hence served the whole Tribunal, while the DVU was a part of the OTP and therefore produced translations which were intended to serve the prosecution in trials. In contrast, CLSS provided translating and interpreting services for the prosecutors, the defence counsel, Registry, and the judges. Once a trial had begun and the evidence translated for the OTP had been disclosed to the defence, the ETU would shift its main focus to translating for the needs of the defence counsel as they prepared for their half of the trial. This meant that when the Tribunal was at its peak of activity, CLSS was largely devoted to translating documentary evidence for the defence in the ongoing trials.

17.6 Monitoring Quality

The fact that CLSS was part of Registry was a feature of ICTY organization that set it apart from the Nuremberg and Tokyo trials. In both of those institutions the OTP was tasked with setting up the language services. The ICTY Registry-based service was a key step forward towards equality of arms. The OTP and the defence counsel therefore shared the CLSS resources of knowledge and expertise.

> The Defence must be placed on an equal procedural footing with the Prosecution for the principle of equality of arms to be respected. The Tribunal has a duty to provide administrative and logistical support to the Defence because the Defence is not an organ of the Tribunal, and the seat of the Tribunal is far away from the crime scene, as well as from counsel's place of residence and support network. (. . .). The defence should be able to directly contact sections of the Tribunal relevant to their work such as [the Court Management and Support Section] CMSS, CLSS, Security, and Chambers. These direct contacts increase

efficiency and help integrate the defence who were kept at a distance and isolated during the earlier years.[28]

The fact that CLSS was part of Registry also meant that the Chambers were free to consult with CLSS interpreters and translators on matters of language. And CLSS was the Tribunal-wide arbiter for language-based disputes.

The ICTY also introduced a new system for quality control of translation and interpreting. The Nuremberg and Tokyo trials used monitors to control quality in proceedings where interpreting was required.[29] In contrast, defence counsellors were tasked at the ICTY with monitoring the quality of interpreting and translation. While this was not spelled out in the Rules of Procedure and Evidence, it became standard practice, recognized by the parties.[30]

In this regard, Mark Harmon, a prosecutor in the Krstić case, remarked, 'I'm indebted to my colleagues from the defence. They speak the language; they are able to notice certain errors that have appeared in translations in exhibits that have been tendered by the Prosecutor's Office'.[31] The defence attorney Predrag Milovančević raised a similar point: '... my job as defence counsel is to monitor how words are being interpreted'.[32]

The efforts to monitor quality were vastly aided by a key technological innovation. The on-site, real-time court record of the English stream of all that was said, either originally in English or as interpreted by the English booth, scrolled by with only a few minutes of delay on the monitors in front of each courtroom participant. This facilitated on-the-spot discussion of and dispute over language-related issues and made it easier for attorneys, indictees, judges, and other courtroom staff to spot and remark on inaccuracies in the translation and interpreting. Hence guaranteeing a more accurate transcript.[33]

This, in turn, eased the correction process described in section 17.3. The fact that the judges were able to adjudicate based on a corrected transcript meant there were far fewer glaring linguistic misunderstandings than there would have been had such an accurate transcript not have been available.

17.7 Visibility

The language staff were visible and recognized every day in ICTY proceedings, in contrast to the usual behind-the-scenes role for translators and interpreters. Attorneys often made a point of recognizing them.

> MR. SAXON: (...) Your Honours, before we begin our formal submissions today, the Prosecution would like to take a moment to express its gratitude to, first of all, the interpreters and other members of CLSS who have laboured to ensure that the courtroom

[28] ICTY Manual (n 18) 211.

[29] Monitors are still used at the (relatively small number of) trials held before the International Court of Justice in The Hague in which witnesses testify in languages other than English and French.

[30] These and the other quotes are taken from transcripts published on the ICTY website which are available to the public and have not been revised or altered.

[31] *Prosecutor v Krstić* (transcripts) ICTY-IT-98-33 (28 July 2000) 5876.

[32] *Prosecutor v Martić* (transcripts) ICTY-IT-95-11 (21 September 2006) 8774–75.

[33] Hepburn (n 14) 58.

> interpretation and the translation of documents in this case have been accurate and comprehensive.[34]
>
> We thank CLSS for their unstinting efforts and support. As I said on previous occasions, the interpreters have one of the most difficult jobs in this Tribunal, and I think you will all agree with me that within this case they have been extremely patient, forthcoming, and efficient.[35]

When a witness or attorney spoke too quickly, the interpreting would fast become unintelligible, leaving the transcript garbled, and the judges unable to follow the proceedings. Whenever this happened, the judges intervened to slow the pace and ensure the legibility of the transcript:

JUDGE ANTONETTI: [Interpretation] Just a minute. You're going too fast. Our interpreters are very vigilant, very competent, but you are going too fast.[36]

JUDGE ORIE: Mr. Barkovic, I will read to you a portion of your evidence, of which we're not fully certain that it's completely or accurately translated. I must add to this that your speed of speech creates these kinds of problems and [it is] not the lack of competence of our interpreters or transcribers.[37]

These interventions on the behalf of the interpreters sometimes allowed judges and attorneys to interject a moment of levity:

MR. JONES: (. . .)-- I'm sorry, I'll go slowly for the stenographer, who's giving me dirty looks.[38]

JUDGE ORIE: Mr. Russo, if you'd take a breath now and then, the interpreters can do the same.[39]

MR. KUZMANOVIC: Your Honour, I apologise, and I apologise to the interpreters for my speed. I will do my best to calm down.

JUDGE ORIE: MR. . . . Mr. Kuzmanovic, if I give a sign to calm down, if you start apologising, then that has to be translated as well.[40]

Having worked in the translation units, I can state that the respect, status,[41] and visibility accorded to translators and interpreters at the ICTY, did much to alleviate the difficulties inherent in working on documents and testimony about atrocities. There were, however, instances, when interpreters and translators were scapegoated.

VOJISLAV ŠEŠELJ: [Interpretation] Mr. President, that explanation is not complete. The interpreters working here are people with very limited -- a limited general knowledge level and they can't understand many things. They would have to be more proficient

[34] *Prosecutor v Ljube Boškoski and Johan Tarčulovski* (transcripts) ICTY-IT-04-82 (6 May 2008) 10974.
[35] *Prosecutor v Popović* et al (transcripts) ICTY-IT-05-88 (15 September 2009) 38414.
[36] *Prosecutor v Šešelj* (transcripts) ICTY-IT-03-67 (12 March 2008) 4778.
[37] *Prosecutor v Gotovina* et al (transcripts) ICTY-06-90 (13 July 2009) 20182.
[38] *Prosecutor v Orić* (transcripts) ICTY-IT-03-68 (1 December 2004) 2325.
[39] *Prosecutor v Gotovina* et al (transcripts) ICTY-06-90 (3 September 2008) 7886.
[40] ibid 7829.
[41] Many of the interpreters were in P4 positions, enjoying the same status as the attorneys (other than the P5 senior trial attorney who was in charge of a trial) working for the Prosecution.

> in military terminology. In military terminology, 'rank,' in military Yugoslav terminology, 'rank' and 'title' could never be synonyms. (. . .) Now those translators of yours don't seem to have any general education, quite obviously, and then they make these extremely big and significant mistakes.[42]

17.8 Terminology

Although all the documentary evidence was translated at first into both French and English, it became clear, as the number of trials grew, that the cost of translating the hundreds of thousands of pages of evidence required into both languages would be prohibitive. This led the Francophone judges to agree to adjudicate based on English-language translations of evidence. Hence the FTU translated into French only ICTY documents such as indictments, judgments, and internal communications.

The bulk of the translation of evidence, therefore, fell to the ETU. Philip Hepburn, ETU head for many years, offers a comprehensive description of the kinds of documents the ETU translated:

> The evidentiary material therefore includes not only many thousands of statements from people who lived through the horrors of prison camps, forced expulsions, mass executions, deliberate targeting of civilians and gang rape, but also laws, decrees and other dry extracts from federal, republican and municipal official gazettes. In between come judgements, indictments, and similar documents emanating from local courts, legal commentaries, military rulebooks, organizational manuals, technical instructions, autopsies, and other medical reports, expert reports on every conceivable subject, thousands upon thousands of the daily situation reports prepared by brigades, divisions, and corps of every army, military orders, pay lists and inventories of hardware, police and intelligence reports, parliamentary transcripts, minutes of local party meetings, newspaper reports, book extracts, handwritten personal diaries, official logs, telephone intercepts, invoices, receipts, delivery notes, birth and death certificates, and all kinds of correspondence.[43]

There were several terms which arose in case after case. For instance, the meaning of the military term *asanacija*, translated by CLSS as 'restoration of the terrain' and 'sanitary and hygienic measures', was frequently queried by the OTP in the trials pertaining to the massacres that had taken place in Srebrenica. The term refers to actions undertaken by a military team in the aftermath of a battle, and entails the removal of carcasses and dead bodies, the repair and opening of traffic arteries and waterways, and whatever else necessary to allow the civilian population to return. In military documents tendered in the Srebrenica trials, however, the term arises instead in the context, as the Prosecution demonstrated, of the mass clandestine burial of the bodies of thousands of massacred men and boys. The OTP was successful in its use of discussions about how to translate this term to elicit information about the massacres the term was designed to hide.[44]

[42] *Prosecutor v Šešelj* (transcripts) ICTY-IT-03-67 (28 February 2008) 4275.
[43] Hepburn (n 14) 58–59.
[44] Elias-Bursać, *Shaping International Justice* (n 4); Elias-Bursać (n 3) 181–93.

Another military term, this one raised by defence counsel in many trials, was the word *rukovodjenje*. In a civilian, business context the word is translated as 'management', while in a military context it refers to one of the responsibilities held by a commander, usually given as 'control' in English, as in the phrase 'command and control'. In case after case, defendants advocated for translating the term *rukovodjenje* as 'management', in their attempt to diminish their responsibility for the atrocities committed on the defendant's watch.[45] The discussion used up so much courtroom time over the years that before the trial of Ratko Mladić began,[46] a committee met which included representatives of the OTP, defence counsel, and CLSS, and together they drew up a *Lexicon of Military Terms*[47] which dictates how controversial terms such as *rukovodjenje* are to be translated and interpreted, with the desired effect of reducing these courtroom disputes.

17.9 Annotation

Chambers informed CLSS in the early years of the Tribunal that translators should refrain from annotating translations. Any dispute over wording, they explained, should be raised by one of the parties or a witness in the courtroom, rather than by a translator in a document. Expansions of abbreviations were allowed as was the occasional addition of 'as printed' or 'as written' following a word or phrase which, for reasons of legibility, spelling errors, or ambiguous wording, had been unclear in the original.

There was, however, an exception to this rule: the annotation of derogatory terms for ethnic groups. Several pejorative epithets came up frequently in documents in reference to enemy forces. The words 'Chetnik' and 'Ustasha' were frequently used to refer pejoratively to Serbs and Croats, respectively, but as these are defined in the Oxford English Dictionary (OED) that was used by the ETU as its referential standard. They were treated as English-language words and were not italicized or annotated. But words such as *balija* and *šiptar* are not listed as English-language or even foreign words by the OED. In order to preserve for the judges the tenor of the document,[48] CLSS did annotate these terms. The term *balija* would be annotated as 'derogatory for Bosnian Muslim' the first time it appeared in a document, and subsequently given in its original form, *balija*, italicized, throughout the text. For *balija* the characterization of 'derogatory' was not disputed. Both witnesses and defendants who testified agreed that the term is pejorative. In *Brđanin* the fact that the defendant had often used pejorative language was ultimately recognized to be part of his criminal activity; had the ETU not annotated the pejorative language in this evidence, the Chamber would not have had evidence of the defendant's derogatory usage.

Witnesses and defendants were not uniformly in agreement, however, regarding the characterization of the word *šiptar* as pejorative for Kosovar Albanians. The fact that CLSS translations regularly annotated *šiptar* as 'derogatory for Albanian' provoked such dispute among witnesses that the Chambers of the Kosovo trials requested that CLSS change the wording in hopes of reducing the amount of courtroom time spent disputing this

[45] Elias-Bursać (n 3) 208–14.
[46] *Mladić* was the last trial to be heard before the ICTY.
[47] *Lexicon of Military Terms*, 16 January 2013. (Provided to the author by the OTP)
[48] C Del Ponte, 'Investigation and Prosecution of Large-Scale Crimes at the International Level: The Experience of the ICTY' (2006) 4 Journal of International Criminal Justice 553.

annotation. CLSS finally agreed to a compromise: the first time the word *šiptar* appeared in a text it was given as *šiptar* 'Albanian'. Thereafter it would appear throughout the translation as *šiptar*,[49] allowing the judges to see that the author of the document had chosen to use the word *šiptar* instead of the more neutral terms of 'Albanian' or 'Kosovar Albanian'.

These are just a few of the language-related disputes which arose during ICTY trials, offered as illustration of the strategies developed by CLSS to deal with controversial terminology and of the ways that translation and interpreting issues were discussed in the courtroom.

17.10 Translators Testifying

Another issue arose pertaining to ICTY translators and interpreters for which a protocol was developed in the course of the work of the Tribunal: the question of whether CLSS and other ICTY translators and interpreters could be called to testify. The first time this arose was in *Tadić*, the first ICTY trial. A name had been partially obscured in a document due to a faulty typewriter ribbon. The name was impressed on the document page without ink. The CLSS translator, however, was able to discern the name and to include it in the translation. The OTP summoned her to court in order to ascertain the credibility of her judgement call.[50]

The second instance, also at the behest of the OTP, was when an interpreter was summoned to describe in detail a telephone conversation, during which he had interpreted between a suspect and an ICTY investigator.[51]

In a third instance, the defence counsel was the party seeking to subpoena a CLSS interpreter, requiring that she testify about her work interpreting a deposition between an ICTY indictee and an attorney for the Prosecution at which no defence counsel had been present.[52] This summons prompted the Chamber to issue an *obiter dictum* entitled 'The Position of the Interpreter'.[53] The Chamber based their general statement on the principle that: 'the stream of justice should be kept pure and undefiled from extraneous factors or fear or prejudice arising from the transaction between the parties'.[54] In other words, the *obiter dictum* issued by the Mucić Chamber was designed to protect language staff as judicial functionaries from intimidation and pressure, and stipulated that they should be shielded from testifying before the Tribunal.

17.11 Trials of Self-represented Accused

The most challenging work for the language services was for the trials of the self-represented accused, *Milošević, Šešelj, Tolimir, Karadžić*, and the *Krajišnik* appeal. While the parties

[49] Elias-Bursać (n 3) 149–60.
[50] *Prosecutor v Tadić* (transcripts) ICTY-IT-94-1 (05 June 1996) 1840–41.
[51] *Prosecutor v Dokmanović* (transcripts) ICTY-IT-95-13a (08 September 1997) 93–99.
[52] *Prosecutor v Mucić* et al (transcripts) ICTY-IT-96-21 (20 February 2001).
[53] *Prosecutor v Mucić* et al (Trial Chamber Decision) ICTY-IT-96-21-T (8 July 1997) 17–20.
[54] S Muller, 'Immunities of ICTY Staff Members, Assets and Archives Before the ICTY' in R May et al (eds), *Essays on ICTY Procedure and Evidence: In Honour of Gabrielle Kirk McDonald* (Brill 2000) 444.

employed various translation-based strategies in all ICTY trials, the self-represented accused relied on a particularly broad array of translation-related strategies with which to pursue their defence.

The Chamber in *Šešelj* acquiesced to Vojislav Šešelj's motion that his mastery of English be considered inadequate, to allow him to conduct his trial in Serbian, in accordance with Rule 3 (B) of the *Rules of Procedure and Evidence* which states 'An accused shall have the right to use his or her own language'.[55] This meant that all internal communications between the defendant and the Chamber, OTP, and Registry were translated by the ICTY language units. This was in contrast to most ICTY trials in which the defence counsellors were required to demonstrate their ability to communicate in English or French with all parts of the ICTY. Over the nine years during which *Šešelj* was underway, from 2003 to 2012, this commitment absorbed a significant portion of the unit's translator-hours.

Before Šešelj turned himself in in 2003 he declared that he was coming to The Hague to undermine the work of the Tribunal. Apparently, he soon saw that the translation units were a bottleneck in the best of circumstances and pursued an aggressive strategy of pushing the language services to the very limit of what they could handle. Once Šešelj had been granted the dispensation to conduct his trial in Serbian, he proceeded to employ a series of translation-related strategies in his defence, the most prominent being his oft-repeated demand to receive all court-related documents in Serbian. The tone of the following quote illustrates his defiant attitude towards the Tribunal and his derisive use of the demand to have all documents translated into Serbian as a way to obstruct the work of the Tribunal.

> ŠEŠELJ: The Trial Chamber can also decide that I receive all documents in the Chinese language; theoretically that is possible but it is undoable. (. . .) I fully commiserate with the suffering of the registry in terms of translation. If they have 30 translators, let them employ 300 translators. It is not really my problem. It's not something that has to do with me and that I have to resolve it; it's the problem of this Court. If you do not have enough translators, if you have 30, then employ 300. If 300 is not enough, make it a thousand.[56]

Šešelj also employed other procedural strategies, such as requesting that the eighty books he had authored be translated into English by CLSS. It was CLSS policy, however, not to translate entire books. If a party wished to quote from a book they could select the section and have that translated; if they preferred to have the entire book translated they could find an external translator to translate the book on contract and pay for it out of their own budget, rather than tying up CLSS with the request.

Šešelj also requested translations of transcripts from trials at the Rwandan Tribunal which included charges of hate speech (as did his trial), as well as translation into Serbian of the transcripts of several ICTY trials conducted in Albanian. While none of these requests exceeded his rights as a defendant, they tested the limits of the resources of the CLSS translation units. The Rwandan transcripts were ultimately translated at the expense of Šešelj's defence budget by translators outside of CLSS.

[55] ICTY Rules of Procedure and Evidence, ICTY Doc IT/32/Rev50 (2015). <http://www.icty.org/en/documents/rules-procedure-evidence> accessed 13 October 2017.

[56] *Prosecutor v Šešelj* (transcripts) ICTY-IT-03-67 (2 May 2007) 1065–66.

Radovan Karadžić was required by the Tribunal to conduct his defence in English. In the course of the forty-one months of his trial he developed an array of translation-related strategies to this end. A key strategy of Karadžić's was, in fact, the absence of translation. More often than not, he presented documentary evidence to a witness without having arranged to have the document translated beforehand. He'd then read the document aloud, the interpreters in the booth would provide an on-site interpretation, and the witness would be expected to discuss the document based only on what he or she had been able to catch from the interpretation. When faced with this in the courtroom witnesses protested:

- WITNESS: Dr. Karadzic, I'd like [you to] show me the document if you could that says this. I'm kind of stuck here just following your words and the translation of your words. I'd sure prefer to be looking at a document.[57]
- WITNESS: Well, I could answer your question if I had a translation into English of the text.[58]
- WITNESS: (...) I can't comment further. Unless it's translated, I won't comment.[59]
- WITNESS: The way you present it here, I don't accept it, because you're translating from English a document which I don't have before me.[60]

While the Chamber cautioned Karadžić repeatedly to make arrangements to secure translations of the evidence he brought to court, he ignored their cautions, complaining that the pace of his trial was devastating for his health and he couldn't take the time to arrange for translations. His strategy of reading documents in the courtroom also gave Karadžić the opportunity to place emphasis wherever he chose. In fact, many of the documents he dealt with in this fashion had already been translated for earlier trials and were readily available in the ICTY translation database. Attorneys for the OTP often ran a quick search mid-session and retrieved the translation from the database. Karadžić appears to have come to expect them to do so. On one occasion he said:

> THE ACCUSED: [Interpretation] If there is a translation, it would be useful to have it, for the sake of the other participants, so we don't need to waste time reading aloud, for the sake of the interpreters.[61]

Another of his strategies was to follow the transcript closely on his monitor and interrupt the proceedings whenever he found something to complain about. My research into *Karadžić* transcripts found more than 170 such interventions. Fifty-seven of these complaints interrupted the prosecutor mid-examination. These interruptions allowed him not only to dominate but to interrupt the other party's examination of witnesses. They also allowed him to reduce what had been a discussion about wartime atrocities to a dispute over terminology.

Judge Kwon frequently reminded Karadžić to submit any language-related concerns to CLSS in an internal memorandum. A search among the court records, however, would seem to indicate that very few such submissions were ultimately made to CLSS from the

[57] *Prosecutor v Karadžić* (transcripts) ICTY-IT-95-5/18 (2 June 2010) 3254.
[58] *Prosecutor v Karadžić* (transcripts) ICTY-IT-95-5/18 (29 June 2010) 4308.
[59] *Prosecutor v Karadžić* (transcripts) ICTY-IT-95-5/18 (15 September 2010) 6879.
[60] *Prosecutor v Karadžić* (transcripts) ICTY-IT-95-5/18 (4 November 2010) 9105.
[61] *Prosecutor v Karadžić* (transcripts) ICTY-IT-95-5/18 (12 October 2010) 7767.

accused requesting a change in the wording of a translation. This suggests that his terminological disputes were seldom germane to the trial.

17.12 Jurisprudence

The ultimate test of whether misunderstandings, mistranslations, and other language matters interfered with the administration of justice is the credence these issues are accorded in ICTY judgments.

Hepburn writes of the 'impossibility of providing a perfect "faithful" translation that conveys every nuance of the meaning of the original' and describes this as a 'major, but by no means insurmountable obstacle to the use of translated materials at the ICTY'. His reasoning is that the parties can always refer to the originals in their discussions, and treat the translations as 'provisional'.[62]

As a result of this provisional character, and the fact that the parties, Chambers, and witnesses could follow the English-language transcript on their monitors with a delay of only a few minutes, questions of translation and interpreting were raised several times a day in almost every one of the more than 10,000 trial sessions held during the ICTY's tenure as a court.

Over 85 per cent of the trial judgments and more than half of the appeals judgments have either paragraphs or footnotes, or, in several cases, whole sections, referring to language matters that had an impact on the trial. These mentions focus largely on errors, disputes over terminology, interpreter testimony, procedural issues. The mentions of errors in trial judgments refer for the most part to issues of lesser gravity, such as the misspelling of names and words.

The preponderance of procedural matters over linguistic errors in appeals would suggest that most appellants for the defence do not perceive the raising of language errors as an opportunity for overturning or mitigating a conviction. In only one instance—an interpreting error in the *Momir Nikolić* sentencing appeal—did the error have an impact on the outcome of the trial. In their closing arguments, the defence counsel drew a comparison between the crimes to which Biljana Plavšić pleaded guilty and the crimes to which M Nikolić pleaded guilty. The comparison was interpreted as follows: 'In the persecution campaign in the Plavšić case, at least 50,000 persons were killed, while in the campaign in the Nikolić case **only 7,000 persons were killed**.'[63] The defence protested that they had said 'around 7,000', not 'only 7,000'. CLSS checked the wording and agreed to change the transcript to read 'around 7,000', and the appeal was upheld and accorded weight in the appeal judgment.[64]

The fact that this is the only instance of a language-related appeal influencing a judgment is more eloquent than any other as to the success of CLSS in providing testimony and documentary evidence through interpreting and translation which facilitated communication, withstood scrutiny, and allowed the ICTY trials to run.

[62] Hepburn (n 14) 62–63.

[63] *Prosecutor v Momir Nikolić* (Judgment on Sentencing Appeal) ICTY-2006-IT-60/1 (08 March 2006) fn 177 (Emphasis added).

[64] Elias-Bursac (n 3) 134–35.

17.13 Conclusion

The challenges and innovations addressed in this chapter include the recruitment of language staff, their training and psychological support, the technology of making the English-language court record available in real time to all courtroom participants, the development of the Code of Ethics, the evolution of a standard of accuracy in both translation and interpreting, the mechanisms available for requesting a correction, the careful planning necessary to provide language services to several concurrent trials, the terminological challenges of translating a wide range of documents, the question of how much to annotate translations and how to translate derogatory ethnic terms, and the challenges posed by the translation strategies employed by self-represented accused.

In building on the precedents of the language services employed by the Nuremberg and Tokyo trials, the ICTY innovated in a number of ways. Separate language services were set up by Registry (CLSS) and the OTP (the DVU), and while at first this arrangement created some confusion, with conflicting terminology and standards, in time the two services improved their coordination. Having observed the parallel development of CLSS and the DVU, the International Criminal Court set up both a Registry and an OTP translation service from the start.[65]

The relationship between Chambers and CLSS, and the defence counsel and CLSS, made possible by the fact that the language services were part of Registry and served the entire Tribunal and both parties, lies at the heart of the success in communication at the Tribunal. The translators and interpreters of the ICTY, in their work interpreting testimony and translating evidence, have demonstrated that the complexities and nuances of testimony on war crimes can indeed be understood by a panel of judges from other countries, and the judges, based on their understanding of the language of the testimony and evidence, are able to adjudicate on the war crimes with insight thanks to the work of the language services.

[65] A Tomić and A B Montoliu, 'Translation at the International Criminal Court' (2013) 1 New Trends in Translation Studies 221.

18
Was it Worth it?
A Look into the Results of the ICTY's Outreach Programme

Petar Finci[*,**]

18.1 Introduction

In hindsight, it seems obvious: an institution established to 'contribute towards the restoration and maintenance of peace'[1] in a given area would probably have executed that part of its mandate more efficiently were it to engage the local population in a meaningful dialogue about its mission, goals, and due processes. The matter becomes less clear when this political mission is imposed upon an international criminal court, designed to adjudicate cases of individual criminal responsibility for crimes committed in the said area, but ill-prepared to intervene in transitional justice processes and post-conflict recovery.

In 1993, when the International Criminal Tribunal for the former Yugoslavia (henceforth, the ICTY or the Tribunal) was established, there was little experience to build upon from its immediate predecessors, the International Military Tribunals (IMT) in Nuremberg and Tokyo. Indeed, even the term 'transitional justice' itself was only in its infancy. While certain efforts were made by the Allies to introduce the German public to the work of the IMT, they were carried out as part of the occupying forces' strategy to de-Nazify the Germans and were not carried out by the IMT itself. In addition, these efforts all but ceased by 1949 with the beginning of the Cold War.[2]

When the ICTY began the process of creating an operational judicial institution from 1994 onward, it was immediately recognized that the media had taken a 'keen interest in the activities of the Tribunal' and the necessary infrastructure and staff were put in place to satisfy the need of the public for information.[3] As Olga Kavran points out, this was a

* Researcher in the International Committee of the Red Cross (ICRC). He worked as a Senior Information Assistant for the Outreach Office of the International Criminal Tribunal for the former Yugoslavia (ICTY). In this function he wrote and co-produced eight films about the work of the ICTY.
** The author would like to thank Olga Kavran, David Tolbert, and Refik Hodžić for their insight and information, as well as Dr Carsten Stahn for his comments on early drafts of this chapter.

1 UN SC Resolution 827 (1993) 'International Criminal Tribunal for the former Yugoslavia (ICTY)' (25 May 1993) S/RES/827.

2 Illustrative is the story about the film produced about the IMT by the American Office of Strategic Services in 1948. By the time *Nuremberg: Its Lessons for Today* was completed, the memory of the trial itself was slowly being replaced by more urgent issues, notably the blockade of Berlin by the Russians and the beginning of the Cold War. Also, rebuilding Germany was taking precedent over the post-war goal of re-educating Germans. After the film was finished, it had a short run in German theatres and some tens of thousands of people saw it. It was subsequently shelved and only restored in 2014. See C Delage, *Caught on Camera: Film in the Courtroom from the Nuremberg Trials to the Trials of the Khmer Rouge* (University of Pennsylvania Press 2013).

3 ICTY 'Report of the International Tribunal for the Prosecution of Persons Responsible for Serious Violations of International Humanitarian Law Committed in the Territory of the Former Yugoslavia since 1991' UNGA 49th Session (29 August 1994) UN Doc A/49/342 para 125.

Petar Finci, *Was it Worth it?* In: *Legacies of the International Criminal Tribunal for the Former Yugoslavia*. Edited by: Carsten Stahn, Carmel Agius, Serge Brammertz, Colleen Rohan, Oxford University Press (2020). © The Several Contributors
DOI: 10.1093/oso/9780198862956.003.0019

remarkable foresight, because 'no national court at the time had a public information department'.[4] A part of this infrastructure was a live-feed from ICTY's courtrooms to the media, which was established from the very first trial onwards and which enabled the first concentrated efforts by a media outlet to communicate the work of the Tribunal to the people in the former Yugoslavia (The American news organization Internews recorded the video feed and produced *The Hague Diaries* TV programme, which from 1996 to 1998 was the primary source of video coverage of the ICTY in the former Yugoslavia).[5] However, while some efforts were made by external agencies to provide information specifically to the people in the former Yugoslavia, there was almost a complete lack of official information about the work of the ICTY in any of the languages of the affected region.

Some years into the ICTY's existence, it was recognized that the public information framework that was established to serve the media in two official languages, English and French, largely failed to have any impact in the former Yugoslavia. Rather, the lack of official information provided an opportunity for actors to present the work of the Tribunal in line with their political interests. David Tolbert remembers: 'The Tribunal was subject to [a] great deal of misinformation and we needed to at least get our voice out there, describe what we were doing.'[6] If the ICTY was, in the words of its first President, Antonio Cassese, to be a tool 'for promoting reconciliation and restoring true peace', there was a real need to establish a more robust communications strategy.[7]

18.2 Establishment and Financing

The story of the creation of what was to become the first Outreach Programme by an international criminal court is by now fairly well known. Shortly after becoming the President of the ICTY in November of 1997, Judge Gabrielle Kirk McDonald learned that many people in the former Yugoslavia had reservations regarding the Tribunal's findings regarding the camps for civilians in the area of Prijedor, Bosnia and Herzegovina (BiH). This led her to send a fact-finding mission to the former Yugoslavia in November of 1998, which conducted over a hundred interviews in Croatia and BiH with local and international governmental and non-governmental representatives, lawyers, judges, activists, and international institutions. The mission report found that many in the former Yugoslavia considered the

4 Olga Kavran, Personal Interview (August 2017). Kavran was one of the first employees in the ICTY's Outreach Programme, where she worked from early 2000 to late 2006 as Deputy Coordinator. Today, she is the Head of Outreach in the Special Tribunal for Lebanon.

5 See Internews Network final report 'Building Blocks of Peace; Creating an Infrastructure of Free, Democratic and Tolerant Electronic Media in Bosnia-Herzegovina' (August 2000) 56 <http://pdf.usaid.gov/pdf_docs/Pdabs451.pdf> accessed February 2018.

6 David Tolbert, Personal Interview (July 2017). Among his various positions in the ICTY, Tolbert was Chef de Cabinet of Gabrielle Kirk McDonald at the time the Outreach Programme was being conceived. At the time of writing, he was President of the International Center for Transitional Justice.

7 ICTY 'Report of the International Tribunal for the Prosecution of Persons Responsible for Serious Violations of International Humanitarian Law Committed in the Territory of the Former Yugoslavia since 1991' UNGA 49th Session (29 August 1994) UN Doc A/49/342 para 16. The mention of reconciliation in this report opened a long and ongoing discussion on the mandate of international criminal courts and their possible role in contributing to transitional justice in territories where crimes prosecuted by the courts occurred. At the ICTY itself, contributing to reconciliation in the former Yugoslavia was initially proclaimed as one of the desired goals of the work of the ICTY and in particular its Outreach Programme, but was quietly abandoned over the years in favour of a more narrow interpretation of the Tribunal's mandate.

Tribunal to be 'depersonalised, distant and unresponsive, too narrow in its focus and too legalistic in its outlook'.[8]

Even at this stage, and despite the support of the then ICTY President, the establishment of a specialized programme for communication with the people in the former Yugoslavia was not without challenges. For one, the ICTY's Office of the Prosecutor (OTP) were 'unhappy with the process and the report and they objected very strongly', because 'they thought they were establishing relationships on the ground and that that was their job'.[9] A compromise was found by placing the newly established Programme in Registry rather than under the auspices of the Office of the President, so that, in the words of David Tolbert, the Prosecution would not feel 'that their territory was being invaded'.[10] While the OTP eventually supported the Outreach Programme in many of its activities, a more substantial opposition to the concept of a judicial institution engaging in this type of matter remained throughout the existence of the Programme. As Kavran puts it: 'We always had this problem of having to convince some of the decision makers within the institution that certain things need to be done, why it's important to do them, why it's important to communicate, to explain, to reach out, to address misconceptions. It was always an uphill battle.'[11]

Crucially for the future of the ICTY's Outreach Programme, some of this opposition came from those who decided to finance the Programme. The initial funding for the Outreach Programme was provided by voluntary contributions by governments and Non-governmental Organizations (NGOs).[12] Judging from an incomplete record, the ICTY management had intended to include the Outreach Programme in its regular budget and took steps to that effect in 2000. The ICTY Annual Report to the UN Security Council (7th August 2000) states: '[i]t is proposed that the Outreach Programme should be made part of the main Tribunal budget for 2001'.[13] However, when the UN Secretary General submitted his report on financing of the ICTY to the UN General Assembly on 24 October 2000, the proposal to include the Outreach Programme in the ICTY's regular budget was not included.[14] The report was, however, accompanied with a footnote explaining that 'the delayed submission of the document is attributable to the extensive consultations that had to be carried out between the Headquarters and the International Tribunal for the former Yugoslavia prior to finalization of the budget proposals'.[15] It would appear that the idea to finance the fledgling Outreach Programme from the regular ICTY budget fell through the cracks during the said extensive consultations.

[8] Outreach Programme, Registry, ICTY 'Outreach: 15 Years of Outreach at the ICTY' (2016) 2 <http://www.icty.org/x/file/Outreach/15-years-of-outreach/outreach-15_en_light.pdf> accessed February 2018. Judge Gabrielle Kirk McDonald retold the story about the establishment of the Outreach Programme. Somewhat contrary to the spirit of transparency and outreach, the report of the fact-finding mission is classified.

[9] David Tolbert, Personal Interview (July 2017).

[10] ibid.

[11] Olga Kavran, Personal Interview (August 2017).

[12] ICTY 'Seventh annual report of the International Tribunal for the Prosecution of Persons Responsible for Serious Violations of International Humanitarian Law Committed in the Territory of the Former Yugoslavia since 1991' UNGA 55th Session (7 August 2000) UN Doc A/55/273 para 218 <http://www.icty.org/x/file/About/Reports%20and%20Publications/AnnualReports/annual_report_2000_en.pdf> accessed 10 May 2018.

[13] ibid para 219.

[14] Report of the Secretary-General 'Financing of the International Tribunal for the Prosecution of Persons Responsible for Serious Violations of International Humanitarian Law Committed in the Territory of the Former Yugoslavia since 1991 (24 October 2000) UN Doc A/55/517' <http://www.un.org/ga/search/view_doc.asp?symbol=A/55/517> accessed February 2018.

[15] ibid 1.

The reasons for this were not officially given.[16] The message, on the other hand, was received and understood. The proposal to include the Outreach Programme in the ICTY's regular budget was not repeated, not even in 2003, when the UN Security Council encouraged 'the ICTY and ICTR Presidents, Prosecutors, and Registrars to develop and improve their outreach programmes',[17] in an apparent recognition of the role these programmes may play in the tribunals' completion strategies. For the rest of its existence, the financing of the ICTY's Outreach Programme depended on voluntary contributions.[18]

This created a complicated situation with regards to strategic planning and implementation of activities, as well as reporting and evaluation of success indicators. Namely, while the Outreach Programme was formally part of the ICTY's Registry, it adapted its planning, activities, and reporting by necessity to requirements of a range of donors, in particular the European Commission.[19] As a result, as Kavran recalls, a significant amount of time was spent by the head of Outreach on preparing the fundraising documentation, from proposals to interim reports to final narrative and financial reports.

Secondly, the main grant of the European Commission largely covered the operational costs of staff and travel of the Outreach Programme, but not the organization of activities, for which the funds had to be sought elsewhere.[20] This had an impact on the Outreach's ability to choose its activities independently, because it relied on establishing partnerships with a range of organizations and institutions in order to maintain presence in the public sphere in the former Yugoslavia. Thirdly, since the Outreach Programme already had contractual obligations to external organizations, little effort was invested within the ICTY

[16] The UN General Assembly did on 16 January 2001 adopt a Resolution in which it endorsed 'the recommendation of the Advisory Committee that judicial activities of the International Tribunal for the former Yugoslavia should have priority over public relations activities and attendance to external meetings' (See GA Resolution 55/225 (16 January 2001) para 7 <http://www.un.org/ga/search/view_doc.asp?symbol=A/RES/55/225> accessed August 2017). But, the Advisory Committee on Administrative and Budgetary Questions clearly commented on travel costs of the ICTY judges and not on the public relations overall. See Report of the Advisory Committee on Administrative and Budgetary Questions 'Financing of the International Tribunal for the Prosecution of Persons Responsible for Serious Violations of International Humanitarian Law Committed in the Territory of the Former Yugoslavia since 1991; Proposed Requirements for 2001' (22 November 2000) UN Doc A/55/642 <http://www.un.org/ga/search/view_doc.asp?symbol=A/55/642> accessed February 2018.

[17] See UN SC Resolution 1503 (28 August 2003) UN Doc S/RES/1503(2003) <http://www.icty.org/x/file/Legal%20Library/Statute/statute_1503_2003_en.pdf> accessed February 2018.

[18] The story of Outreach Programme's funding contrasts with another of the ICTY's project aimed at cooperation with the local actors. According to the ICTY website, the Rules of the Road procedure, established under the Rome Agreement of 18 February 1996, regulated the arrest and indictment of alleged perpetrators of war crimes by national authorities. As part of the Tribunal's contribution to the re-establishment of peace and security in the region, the ICTY prosecutor agreed to provide an independent review of all local war crimes cases. If a person was already indicted by the OTP, he could be arrested by the national police. If the national police wished to make an arrest where there was no prior indictment, they had to send their evidence to the OTP. Under the Rome Agreement, decisions of the OTP became binding on local prosecutors. Like the Outreach Programme, Rules of the Road began as an externally funded project. However, unlike the Outreach Programme, Rules of the Road was included into the regular budget some two years into its existence. David Tolbert made an educated guess in a conversation that the Rules of the Road produced results that were 'possible to measure', which made it more attractive in the eyes of UN member states that decided on budgetary issues.

[19] For a list of donors and contributions see Outreach Programme, Registry, ICTY 'Outreach: 15 Years of Outreach at the ICTY' (2016) 90 <http://www.icty.org/x/file/Outreach/15-years-of-outreach/outreach-15_en_light.pdf> accessed February 2018.

[20] The first Outreach Programme's report to the European Commission, covering the period from October 1999 to December 2002 lists this issue as one of the problems in implementation of activities: 'As the Outreach Programme primarily funds itself through voluntary donations a certain amount of time and effort is exerted to generate other external funding for specific activities and projects. This is not a problem in of itself however it does take time away from activities that would otherwise be spent on improving two-way communication between the Tribunal and the population in the region of the former Yugoslavia.'

to define clear strategic goals of the Programme and, consequently, there were almost no mechanisms established to measure the impact of the activities on target audiences.

There were other factors that significantly influenced the ability of the Outreach Programme to engage its primary audiences: the 1999 war in Kosovo and NATO air strikes in Kosovo and Serbia, which caused the ICTY's field office in Belgrade to close down until mid-2001; changes in internal policies, which impacted the field representatives' right to speak directly to the media in their respective countries; and relatively frequent changes in Outreach management, with every manager bringing their own understanding of the Programme's goals, with direct consequences for the volume and type of activities. However, these are all common enough challenges in an organization dealing with transitional justice processes in a post-conflict society. What made the issues faced by the ICTY's Outreach Programme different was the fact that it officially formed a part of a large international organization, but was treated as an NGO both within its mother institution and outside it.[21]

Technically speaking, part of Outreach's funding did come from the ICTY through use of facilities and services, such as the office space, IT equipment, IT support, and the use of vehicles in the field, as well as management of staff-related administration. In addition, some Outreach-related activities were performed by staff paid from the regular ICTY budget, notably the translation of the ICTY's web page content into Bosnian/Croatian/Serbian (BCS) and, partly, Macedonian and Albanian. Furthermore, the Outreach representatives in the former Yugoslavia were renamed into Registry Liaison Officers in 2005 and subsequently paid from the regular ICTY budget. The Outreach Programme also relied on the ICTY graphic designer for design of its informational materials, and part of the documentary production duties were performed by an ICTY staff member.

While the UN evidently covered part of the expenses of the ICTY's Outreach Programme, it is worth noting that it also collected part of the funds Outreach was spending on activities in the form of a 'project management fee'. The UN charges 13 per cent administrative overhead for any activity organized by its funded programmes, including those funded from external sources, such as the Outreach Programme. One of the ways to work around this additional cost, in the early days of the Programme, was to arrange for direct financing of a given activity by the donor to the implementing partner in the field, with the Outreach Programme acting as a sort of guarantor to both sides.

18.3 Planning and Reporting Activities

The Outreach Programme was the first of its kind, therefore a key question in its early stages was what is outreach and what does it include? David Tolbert remembers:

> I think we had sort of a general goal of countering the propaganda against the Tribunal. There was a lot of false information that we were torturing people in the D[etention] U[unit]. So, part of it was to counter these false narratives and the propaganda about

[21] Olga Kavran, Personal Interview (August 2017). Kavran recalls the early days: 'At the beginning we kind of felt as if we were an NGO. We had the worst of all worlds. On one hand, we were treated like an NGO and not really a part of the institution, while on the other we were subject to all the different institutional constraints, because we were operating within the framework of the UN.'

> the Tribunal. And, on the other hand, I guess in a more positive way, was to try to show the victims how the Tribunal was working towards the recognition of victims and their suffering.[22]

Part of the confusion resulted from the term 'outreach' itself, which was largely unknown outside of North America and, indeed, had never been successfully translated in to the languages of the former Yugoslavia.

The Outreach Programme was dedicated to explaining the work of the Tribunal to the people in the former Yugoslavia and 'addressing the effects of misconceptions and misinformation'.[23] In its 1999 Annual Report to the UN General Assembly, the ICTY reported that the Outreach Programme would engage its target audiences in the following ways:

> development of local networks; distribution of materials; creation of additional media-monitoring and analysis capacity; regular press events; establishment of video links between the Tribunal and the region; coordination of visits to and from the Tribunal; representation in appropriate forums and relevant international organization activities; and presentations to educational institutions and other audiences.[24]

Executing this mandate presented the founding team with a plethora of issues. At the time, as Kavran recalls, 'there was no one who was speaking on behalf of the Tribunal in any capacity in the local languages',[25] so the first task was to translate available information and distribute it to journalists in the countries of the former Yugoslavia. Refik Hodžić concurs that 'the media, journalists and their professional associations were probably the most important target group'. Another major target group, according to Hodžić, were legal experts from the former Yugoslavia, because 'it was considered that they were the natural allies, who would, once they understood what the Tribunal was doing, spread the word in influential circles'.[26] Establishing contacts in the field with NGOs and victims' associations was another area of early activity, as was providing live streaming of the ICTY trials.

However, much like the ICTY itself, once established, the Outreach Programme was largely left to its own devices. There was little, if any, effort to define clear goals or success criteria. Kavran notes that in the informational 'void' that the Outreach Programme entered, production of any official information in the local languages could have been considered a worthwhile goal.[27] The fact remains that, whatever modicum of success the Outreach

[22] David Tolbert, Personal Interview (July 2017).

[23] ICTY, 'Report of the International Tribunal for the Prosecution of Persons Responsible for Serious Violations of International Humanitarian Law Committed in the Territory of the Former Yugoslavia Since 1991' (25 August 1999) UN Doc A/54/187 para 150 <http://www.icty.org/x/file/About/Reports%20and%20Publications/AnnualReports/annual_report_1999_en.pdf> accessed February 2018.

[24] ibid para 151.

[25] Olga Kavran, Personal Interview (August 2017).

[26] Refik Hodžić, Personal Interview (July 2017). Hodžić worked in the Outreach office in The Hague from 2000 until 2002, when he moved to Sarajevo, BiH, to the position of the Outreach Coordinator there. At the time of writing, he was Director of Communications in the International Centre for Transitional Justice. The interview with Hodžić was translated from Bosnian by the author.

[27] Olga Kavran, Personal Interview (August 2017).

Programme achieved in its early years, it was more a result of imaginative use of resources and contacts by its early staff than any concentrated institutional effort.[28]

Significantly more attention was given to the reporting of activities. From its first, founding conference in 1998 to the legacy-related activities in 2017, the Outreach Programme kept a record of its activities, including; the place and type of activity, the targeted audience and, occasionally, the number of participants. This information was distributed internally, used when reporting to donors and was eventually made available online, on the ICTY website.[29] Unfortunately, the records do not encompass all of the Outreach Programme's activities over the years. For example, the significant effort invested in the creation, in 2002, and maintenance of the ICTY webpage in languages of the former Yugoslavia, in particular BCS is mentioned only occasionally in the record of activities. On the other hand, it features prominently in the project reports to the European Commission.[30] The situation was somewhat different with the Outreach contribution to the ICTY social media efforts from 2010 onwards, because by that time the decision was made to publish an annual Outreach Programme report, which included a short report on both web and social media, alongside other, more traditional activities.[31]

In addition, the format of reporting has been somewhat inconsistent. For example, some activities were listed as a single activity, even though they took place regularly throughout a given year.[32] Additionally, the number of participants was reported so sporadically in the early years as to render an attempt to make comparisons over the years impossible. This changed from 2011 onwards, as mechanisms were put in place to track and report the number of beneficiaries of Outreach's activities, in particular in regards to the Youth Outreach project. Therefore, it is only possible to compare the statistics annually from 2011 onwards, but not, for example, the period 2005–2010 with 2011–2016.

However, the information made available in these reports makes it possible to analyse some aspects of the Outreach Programme over the years; such as the percentage of events organized by Outreach as compared to the events organized by partners. Another aspect is the geographical distribution of the Outreach activities, both in terms of the targeted audience and in terms of where the events took place. Finally, while many events fall into more than one category, it is possible to identify some general trends regarding the spread of activities targeting broad professional categories (students, judiciary, NGOs, grass-roots, media).

Chronologically, the following research divides the sixteen years of Outreach Programme (at the time of writing) into three periods, as follows: 1999–2004, 2005–2010, and 2011–2016. The end of the first period coincides with the end of OTP's investigations. The second period covers the years up to the adoption of the first official institution-wide Outreach

[28] Refik Hodžić, Personal Interview (July 2017). Hodžić stated: 'I do not remember any strategic meetings across the organisation, with the OTP, Chambers and Registry, at which we would discuss what was the strategy and what were the desired outcomes.'

[29] ICTY Outreach Activities Archive: http://www.icty.org/en/outreach/activities-archive.

[30] Even though the activity itself was reported to the donor, the Outreach reported until 2008 that the number of people benefitting from its web pages in BCS was 'difficult to estimate'. With the introduction of the new website in 2008, the reporting became much more specific in terms of individual visitors and page-views.

[31] ICTY Outreach Annual Reports: <http://www.icty.org/en/outreach/outreach-annual-reports> accessed February 2018.

[32] For example, in 2004, the Outreach Programme published a weekly column in *Balkan* newspaper, which is reported as one activity. ICTY, 'Tribunal Columns in "Balkan" Newspaper' (2004) <http://www.icty.org/en/outreach/activities-archive/2004> accessed February 2018.

strategy in 2010. The third period covers the activities implemented as part of the first and the subsequent strategies to promote and document the ICTY's legacy in the wake of its imminent closure.[33]

18.4 The Early Years: 1999–2004

Following the establishment of the Outreach Programme in 1999, the ICTY's Registry made a decision to add a Registry component to the already existing field offices operated by the ICTY's OTP in Belgrade, Priština, Sarajevo, and Zagreb. The main role of the newly established Registry offices in the field was to support the activities of the Outreach Programme. One senior staff, the Outreach Coordinator, and one assistant were the focal points in their respective countries for all enquiries related to the work of the ICTY, as well as for all activities of the Outreach Programme. The establishment of the Outreach presence in the former Yugoslavia was a key step, which enabled the Programme to engage directly with the local population and attempt to bridge the geographical gap between the Tribunal and the people most affected by its work.[34] The Outreach Programme reported 257 activities in this formative period. A large majority took place in the countries of the former Yugoslavia (74.3 per cent) with the rest taking place in The Hague (24.5 per cent) or elsewhere.

Due to the fact that the Outreach Programme was established on the eve of discussions about the Tribunal's completion strategy, this period saw substantial effort invested in establishing contacts between the ICTY and the local judiciaries, with the aim of aiding the capacity building of the local courts to deal with large cases involving international crimes. Most of the activities concentrated on BiH, Serbia, and Croatia. Nearly 27 per cent of activities reported in this period fall into work with judiciary. This is closely followed by the work with students (24 per cent), again mostly from Serbia, Croatia, and BiH. As we will see, these two groups were, for a significant portion of Outreach's existence, the most targeted by outreach efforts, with NGOs, media, and grass-root communities receiving considerably less attention.[35]

In terms of audiences, Serbians were the most targeted by Outreach activities in this period, with close to 37 per cent, followed by Bosnians (19.4 per cent), and Croatians (17.8 per cent). This is an interesting fact, given that there were almost no activities in Serbia in the wake of the NATO bombing of Serbia in 1999 and until well into 2001, when the ICTY field office was reopened in Belgrade. However, following the arrest and transfer of Slobodan Milošević to the Tribunal in 2001, there was a surge of civil sector activities related to transitional justice in Serbia, which strongly influenced the number of Outreach activities.

Some 68 per cent of all activities reported by Outreach in this period were organized by partners, with 21.5 per cent jointly organized by the Outreach Programme and its partners and only 10.5 per cent organized by the Outreach Programme alone.

[33] The final year of the Outreach Programme, 2017, was not included in this analysis.

[34] The field offices in Pristina and Zagreb were closed at the end of 2012.

[35] Again, this should be qualified by reference to incomplete data: for example, 2004 saw three Bridging the Gap conferences that addressed grassroots communities in BiH. In the Outreach reporting pattern, this counts as three activities. However, the conferences were covered by the media, they resulted in documentary productions that aired on television stations in BiH, booklets were produced from the conference transcripts and distributed at Outreach events for years after the events.

18.5 2005–2010

The Outreach Programme reported 449 activities in this period, an increase of more than 43 per cent compared to the previous period. Like in the previous period, nearly three quarters (73 per cent) took place in the countries of the former Yugoslavia, with around 24 per cent of activities organized in The Hague and the remaining 3 per cent elsewhere.

The trend of targeting mostly students and the judicial officials in the former Yugoslavia continued in this period, with activities involving students comprising 30 per cent of activities, and judiciary closely following at 23 per cent. The significant change in this period is related to the beginning of the Outreach-organized high-school lectures in Kosovo, which amounted to more than 53 per cent of all student-related activities. The students from Serbia were targeted in 21.5 per cent of activities, with the remaining percentage divided among students from other countries.

In terms of judiciary, this period was characterized by the establishment of the War Crimes Chamber in Serbia in 2003 and the Court of Bosnia and Herzegovina in 2004, which strongly influenced the Outreach efforts to contribute to the ICTY's efforts at capacity building of the newly established courts. Consequently, 45 per cent of activities aimed at judiciary concentrated on BiH and 26.5 per cent on Serbia, with the rest divided between Croatia, Macedonia, and Kosovo.

In regards to audiences, BiH took the first place from Serbia, largely due to the strong focus on judiciary mentioned above. Some 31 per cent of all activities targeted groups from BiH, followed by 23 per cent from Serbia, close to 19 per cent from Kosovo, some 14 per cent of mixed groups and 9 per cent from Croatia, with both Macedonia and Slovenia represented in less than 5 per cent.

Another significant shift in this period relates to the ratio of activities organized by Outreach alone, jointly with partners to activities, or organized by partners alone, with Outreach representatives taking part. Some 48.5 per cent of all activities reported were organized by partners, a decrease of nearly 30 per cent compared to the previous period. Outreach participated in organization of 28.5 per cent of activities and itself organized nearly 23 per cent of activities, an increase of more than 100 per cent. This clearly indicates that the Outreach Programme reached maturity in this period and began relying much more on its acquired experience in organizing activities.

18.6 Outreach Legacy Activities: 2001 to End

It was not until some ten years into the Outreach's existence that the ICTY adopted an institution-wide approach to communications, which led to the adoption of an Outreach strategy in 2010. This document, written by the then Head of Outreach, Nerma Jelačić, and adopted as a policy document by the ICTY principals from all three organs, envisaged the Outreach Programme's activities for the remaining years of its work as an attempt to document and communicate the key achievements of the ICTY and so contribute to the ongoing dialogue about the legacy of this institution and its importance to the people in the former Yugoslavia. Two major projects envisaged in the Strategy were consistently implemented during the legacy period, the Youth Outreach and the documentary production, while others, such as the second series of Bridging the Gap conferences or seminars for parliamentarians, were never implemented.

The final period of Outreach activity reported 526 activities, an increase of 15 per cent. More than 84 per cent of activities took place in the former Yugoslavia, 13 per cent in The Hague and the rest elsewhere. Since one of the main components of the Outreach strategy was youth work, it is not surprising that 60 per cent of all activities targeted this group. One of the major changes in this period relates to a drastic fall in the number of activities targeting judiciary, with not even 9 per cent of activities focusing on this group. Importantly, 73 per cent of judiciary activity took place in a single year, 2011, within the large War Crimes Justice Project co-organized by the ICTY, OSCE/ODIHR and UNICRI, with funding from the European Union.[36] In the years following this project, the Outreach work with the judiciary all but ceased. Some of the focus was instead transferred to the support the Outreach Programme provided in organizing the ICTY legacy conferences in 2010, 2011, 2012, 2013, and 2017,[37] the planning of and negotiations related to information centres in the countries in the former Yugoslavia, as well as an attempt to create a repository of ICTY's legacy in film and video form.

Another significant change in Outreach activities was the shift in target audiences. Namely, Serbian groups accounted for only about 12 per cent of all, which was a nearly 100 per cent decrease compared to the previous period and almost 350 per cent decrease compared to the early days. The main reason for this was the refusal of Serbian authorities to permit the Outreach representatives to engage with one of the primary target groups in this period, high-school students, following the ICTY Appeals Chamber acquittal of Croatian generals in 2012.[38] Bosnian groups comprise 36 per cent of the total during this period, followed by 16.5 per cent of Croatians, 15.5 per cent of mixed groups, and 11 per cent of Kosovo groups. This period also saw a continuation of a trend towards an increase of activities organized by Outreach, with more than 53 per cent (mostly educational) activities falling into this category. Some 30 per cent of activities were organized by partners and the rest were organized in cooperation with partners.

18.7 Summary of Activities

Overall, the Outreach Programme reported 1,232 activities from 1999 to 2016. Consistently with the numbers shown per individual periods, some 79 per cent of all activities took place in the countries of the former Yugoslavia and about 19 per cent took place in The Hague. Nearly 42 per cent of activities targeted students, with this number boosted by several rounds of high-school and university presentations in the final years.[39] This was

[36] See ICTY 'Capacity Building' <http://www.icty.org/en/outreach/capacity-building> accessed February 2018.

[37] See ICTY 'Legacy Conferences' <http://www.icty.org/en/features/legacy-conferences> accessed February 2018.

[38] S Kranjc, 'Hague Appeal Tribunal Frees Jailed Croatian Officers' (*Reuters*, 16 November 2012) <http://www.reuters.com/article/uk-warcrimes-gotovina-acquittal-idUKBRE8AF0MS20121116> accessed February 2018: the Serbian authorities announced their decision to 'scale back' the cooperation with the ICTY to 'technical level', which did not include any facilitation of Outreach activities.

[39] Outreach Programme, Registry, ICTY 'Outreach: 15 Years of Outreach at the ICTY' (2016) 85 <http://www.icty.org/x/file/Outreach/15-years-of-outreach/outreach-15_en_light.pdf> accessed March 2017: the Youth Outreach Project reached 8,900 high-school and university students and 200 educators.

followed by 17.5 per cent of activities targeting judicial officials from the former Yugoslavia. Interestingly, more than 14 per cent of activities reported by the Outreach Programme do not fall into any of the main categories listed above (students, judiciary, media, grass-roots, NGO) and either target mixed audiences or could be classified as activities outside of the main scope of Outreach's work.[40] Some 10 per cent of activities targeted media outlets directly, either through education of journalists and editors, or through activities designed to be carried by media (i.e. TV screenings of Outreach produced films).[41] The activities specifically targeting local communities and NGOs stands at 7.8 per cent and 7.4 per cent respectively. Again, these numbers do not include activities that may have involved the local communities, but did not specifically target them, such as film screenings, or activities co-organized with local NGOs, which had a different target group.

Regardless of periodical fluctuations, with respect to targeted audiences, citizens of BiH were the most represented group, with almost 31 per cent of all Outreach activities aimed at them. Despite the relatively poor showing in the final years of Outreach, the Serbians follow with 21.5 per cent, while the mixed groups take the third place with 14.7 per cent of activities. The Croatians were targeted in 14 per cent of the activities, Kosovars in nearly 13 per cent, while Macedonians, Montenegrins, and Slovenians together amount to 6 per cent of Outreach activities. Nearly 45 per cent of all activities reported by the Outreach Programme were organized by partners, with Outreach representatives being invited to take part. Some 33 per cent of the activities were organized by the Outreach Programme itself and the rest were organized jointly.

The available reports offer a cursory glance into the financing of the Outreach activities. In some reports, the sponsorship of the activity is clearly stated, while in others in can be reasonably inferred. However, even though the available information is not sufficient for establishing exact numbers, the general trend throughout the seventeen years of the Outreach Programme indicates the near total dependence on external sources of funding for implementation of activities. Up to 80 per cent of activities reported by Outreach were sponsored by partners. Despite this, the Outreach Programme established during its legacy period a major project that did not require additional funding, which illustrated the possibilities of low-budget targeting of key constituencies: the documentary production.[42]

18.8 The Documentary Production

The Outreach Strategy from 2010 envisaged utilization of the facts established by the ICTY, the materials accumulated during investigations and trials, the witness testimonies and the

[40] Some examples of side-activities reported by Outreach may include video-link presentations with the University of Iowa (ICTY 'Video-conference with Iowa University (31 October 2008) <http://www.icty.org/en/outreach/activities-archive/2008> accessed February 2018); visits by US cadets to the regional office in Sarajevo (ICTY 'US Cadets visiting ICTY Office in Sarajevo' (16 July 2015) <http://www.icty.org/en/outreach/activities/us-cadets-visiting-icty-office-sarajevo> accessed February 2018); a visit of Lithuanian journalists to The Hague (ICTY 'Visit of Lithuanian Journalists' (11 June 2008) <http://www.icty.org/en/outreach/activities-archive/2008> accessed February 2018).

[41] This number does not include coverage of Outreach-related events in various media outlets.

[42] The production budgets of Outreach's feature length documentary films were as a rule lower than €15,000 per film, which included the travel costs for shooting on locations, the DVD printing costs and promotional costs, but not the salaries of staff involved in the production, which were financed from the Outreach and the ICTY budget, respectively.

trial recordings to create informational and educational materials for use in the final years of the Tribunal's existence and beyond. One of the key results of this idea was the Outreach programme's documentary production project, which has existed since 2010.

This was not the first time that an international court used its video record in promotional and educational activities. The US Army produced an ill-fated film following the IMT in Nuremberg,[43] and the Russian Army made their own version of the film on the Nuremberg trials. Indeed, the ICTY itself produced a documentary film titled *Justice at work* in 2001, telling the story of the institution's establishment and mandate. However, the documentary project of the Outreach Programme from 2010 onward was the first ever attempt by a judicial institution to use film to present and explain its work, investigations, and prosecutions of cases, as well as the resulting jurisprudence, in its own words. The reasoning behind this type of film production was that it was:

> of the utmost importance that such content is produced internally, with the Tribunal maintaining editorial control and focus on the content. This would ensure that sufficient attention is given to the facts and the legal process that lead to their establishment, rather than often irrelevant, politically-coloured information dominating the media coverage of ICTY cases.[44]

From 2010 to 2016, The Outreach Programme produced six long and fifteen short films, with some of the topics and content overlapping between the long and the short films. All of the films were produced both in English and at least one of the languages of the former Yugoslavia, with some translated into French or other languages. The promotional efforts were mostly focused on the long films, because they were perceived to have a longer lasting educational value, while the short films were mostly used on the Tribunal's social media networks. Consequently, the Outreach organized, alone or with partners, more than thirty screenings of the long films in the former Yugoslavia and additional ones in The Hague. In addition to this, the films were offered to TV stations in the region, where more than twenty TV stations broadcast some or all of them, and some more than once. All of the longer films were also screened on UN TV.

Following the promotional rounds, DVD copies were distributed to thousands of recipients in the former Yugoslavia and around the world, especially targeting academia and NGOs. Unfortunately, the subsequent use of the distributed films was not regularly reported back to the Outreach Programme. While it is known from anecdotal evidence that the films are used in classrooms from Argentina to Croatia to South Africa, the exact numbers are impossible to establish at this time.

It is much easier to extract numbers related to the final channel of distribution, the internet. The Outreach Programme promoted the films through the ICTY's web page and social media, all of which offer a possibility to track the number of views for individual clips. The six long films available online received more than 60,000 views in different languages, while the fifteen short films were viewed more than 370,000 times.[45] In terms of

[43] See (n 2).
[44] ICTY Outreach Strategy Document (June 2010) 8.
[45] Last checked in December 2016.

total numbers of beneficiaries, the documentary project was by far the most successful undertaking of the ICTY's Outreach Programme.

Of course, the numbers alone do not measure impact, in particular on the key target audiences. It should be noted that, with some exceptions, the number of viewers was higher for English versions than those in languages of the former Yugoslavia. For one, albeit drastic example, the short film on Srebrenica was viewed 160,000 times in English compared to about 12,000 in Bosnian.[46] On the other hand, the documentary production proved to be a cheap instrument for reaching comparatively large audiences. Already now, with the ICTY hearings completed, the Outreach productions are increasingly the first point of contact with the ICTY for young people from around the world who visit the Tribunal or seek information online. It is reasonable to expect that they will continue to be used for information and education long after the ICTY closed down in 2017.

18.9 Conclusions and Lessons Learned

As noted above, throughout Outreach's history, little effort was invested into measuring impact on target audiences.[47] The above analysed reports, as well as the reports to the European Commission, offer occasional references to responses from the audiences to Outreach activities, almost all of them being commendations. In fairness to the Outreach Programme, it should be noted that in order to measure the impact of its many and varied activities in different countries in the former Yugoslavia, it would have needed to employ services of researchers and support staff that were far beyond its budgetary capabilities. Nonetheless, with more strategic thinking invested in the importance of measuring impact, the budgetary constraints could have been overcome, as the Outreach Programme itself demonstrated.

In the later stage of its work, the Outreach Programme established a partnership with Castleberry Peace Institute of the University of North Texas (UNT), which was handed the questionnaires from the Youth Outreach presentations and will publish an analysis of the students' responses to the lectures and presentations in due course. Given the amount of interest generated by the outreach activities of international courts in the academic community, partners for similar collaborations should not be difficult to find. This example may provide useful guidance for the current and future outreach programmes and their efforts to measure their impact in a more systematic manner.

Additional difficulty in measuring the impact of the Outreach Programme is the fact that its activities did not take place in a vacuum. It would be nearly impossible to separate the impact created by the Outreach Programme from the impact of the ICTY's judicial work on the public opinion in the former Yugoslavia. It has already been noted that local

[46] In fairness, it should be said that Outreach's long films have a much more balanced ratio of English and BCS audiences.

[47] Notable exceptions are the study visits to the Tribunal of groups of students, jurists, or journalists that were held over several days and that included at their end a standardized questionnaire with questions related to organization of the visit and impact the presentations had on the knowledge of the participants. Similar questionnaires, albeit more focused on the impact of the presentation on knowledge and perception, were handed out to high-school and university students as part of the Youth Outreach project from 2010 onwards.

perceptions of judicial results, such as acquittals and short prison sentences, strongly influenced the public opinion in the affected communities, in particular victim communities.[48] One example for this was a strong reaction of both the human rights activists and Bosnian Muslim victim representatives during the 2013 ICTY Anniversary Conference in Sarajevo. A group of young Bosnian activists used the media presence before the beginning of the conference programme to have their protest recorded while holding a placard with the words 'RIP Justice'. The victim representatives, on the other hand, turned their backs for the duration of the key-note speech to the speaker, the then ICTY President Theodor Meron.[49] Despite these protests against what was perceived as institutionalized injustice, both protesting groups made it very clear in personal communication that their appreciation of the Outreach Programme continued unabated. The main reason for this was the often expressed feeling that, despite the differences in opinion regarding outcomes of some cases, the information from the ICTY remained essential to these, and other, groups in the former Yugoslavia and the Outreach Programme was a major facilitator of making it available in local languages. This dichotomy introduces perhaps the most important lesson learned in the course of the ICTY's outreach efforts—that of managed expectations.

The Outreach Programme operated in political environments in which political actors were, more often than not, invested in undermining the work of the ICTY and interpreting its decisions and judgments in line with their own agendas of national homogenization. As Hodžić rightly points out:

> We could have invested huge money in outreach, could have had a PR capacity, a capacity to do whatever we wanted, but it still could not have replaced the mechanisms available to Milošević and Tuđman, consisting of media, academia, religious community, which had real power.[50]

This was one of the key reasons why contributing to reconciliation, which was one of the early proclaimed goals of outreach activity, was quietly dropped from the list of desired outcomes along the way. Another reason was a progressive understanding that an international court of law was not the best equipped to deal with political and societal issues such as reconciliation. Consequently, the ICTY officials over the years gradually attempted to distance themselves from this goal.[51] It is possible, as Hodžić points out, that the Outreach

[48] See D Orentlicher, 'That Someone Guilty Be Punished: The Impact of the ICTY in Bosnia' *New York: Open Society Institute* (2010) and M Hellman, 'Challenges and Limitations of Outreach: From The ICTY to The ICC' in C De Vos, S Kendall, and C Stahn (eds) *Contested Justice: The Politics and Practice of International Criminal Court Interventions* (Cambridge University Press 2015).

[49] Both groups were protesting the ICTY Appeals Chamber acquittal of Serbian general Momčilo Perišić, who was accused of crimes committed in BiH by the Bosnian Serb Army with the support of Serbian military, of which he was the head during the relevant period. Perišić's acquittal was widely perceived in BiH as a decisive, if not final, setback in an attempt to establish responsibility of Serbian official structures for crimes committed in BiH.

[50] Refik Hodžić, Personal Interview (July 2017).

[51] See the welcoming remarks of the ICTY's last President, Judge Carmel Agius, at the opening of the 2017 Legacy Conference in Sarajevo: 'However, often the criticisms reflect a misunderstanding of the nature and purpose of the Tribunal, which is a court of law with a limited mandate. The Tribunal was not mandated to achieve reconciliation in the region, for example, and it was never meant to bring to justice all of those responsible for the crimes committed during the war. The task given to it by the Security Council was to try "those most responsible" for these crimes and "thus contribute to the restoration and maintenance of peace in the region."' ICTY 'Opening Address at the Final ICTY Legacy Conference in Sarajevo 22 June 2017' <http://www.icty.org/x/file/

Programme would have had more impact had the message been more clear and realistic from the beginning—the court will establish facts and adjudicate its cases, but the responsibility of using these facts for reconciliation lies with the local politicians.[52] Similarly, local authorities have the responsibility for creating favourable circumstances for prosecution of lower-level perpetrators in local courts and informing their respective constituencies about the process. The outreach efforts of the international courts following in the steps of the ICTY will benefit from making this separation of responsibilities clear to their target audiences from the very beginning.

While it is impossible to say what the public perception of the ICTY would be in the former Yugoslavia were it not for the Outreach Programme, it may be safely assumed that most of the official information about the ICTY reached the former Yugoslavia through the Outreach Programme's efforts.[53] It can also be safely predicted that the materials that the Outreach Programme created during its legacy period will remain the major source of ICTY-created information about, not only its own work in the former Yugoslavia, but also elsewhere. Given that the total cost of the Outreach Programme amounted to around 0.5 per cent of the total ICTY's budget,[54] the answer to the question 'was it worth it?' is a resounding 'yes'.

However, looking forward, the question should probably be: 'Could it have been better?' The answer is, again, unambiguous. Like its mother organization, the ICTY's Outreach Programme was an experiment in the newly emerging world of international criminal justice. In the early days, with little preceding experience to rely on, the Outreach Programme started from humble beginnings and with poorly defined goals. As the analysis of the reported activities above shows, it managed to become increasingly more independent from outside organizational, if not financial help over the years and to find increasingly focused and meaningful ways to engage its target audiences. Yet, taking into account the size of the target audience and the sustained efforts in the former Yugoslavia to counter the ICTY's findings with nationalist rhetoric, the Outreach Programme was throughout its history both understaffed and underfunded.

This lesson has been picked up by some of the international courts that came after the ICTY, some of which included outreach efforts in their regular budgets and defined goals that are clear and measurable.[55] As Kavran concludes, 'outreach is an obligation and should be treated as such'.[56] What this means in practice is that outreach efforts should

Press/Statements%20and%20Speeches/President/170624-welcoming-remarks-president-carmel-agius.pdf> accessed February 2018.

[52] Refik Hodžić, Personal Interview (July 2017).

[53] For example, even the press releases issued by the ICTY were translated into BCS by Outreach staff before being sent to the media outlets in the former Yugoslavia. Before the Outreach Programme was established, the press releases were issued in English and French only.

[54] At the estimated $2 billion. See UN Tribune, 'Croatia Pres. Protests to UNSC Over ICTY Release of Seselj' (12 February 2014)< http://untribune.com/tag/icty/> accessed February 2018.

[55] For ICC Outreach Strategy see ICC, 'Strategic Plan for Outreach of the International Criminal Court' (*Assembly of States Parties 5th Session*, 29 September 2006) ICC-ASP/5/12 <https://www.icc-cpi.int/NR/rdonlyres/FB4C75CF-FD15-4B06-B1E3-E22618FB404C/185051/ICCASP512_English1.pdf> accessed February 2018.

It is worth noting that the Special Tribunal for Lebanon is the only international/internationalized court to date to include the Outreach Programme in its Rules of Procedure and Evidence (Rule 52) Special Tribunal for Lebanon, Rules of Proecdure and Evidence, Rule 52 (2017) <https://www.stl-tsl.org/images/RPE/RPE_EN_April_2017.pdf> accessed February 2018.

[56] Olga Kavran, Personal Interview (August 2017).

be included in the institutional strategic thinking from the very beginning, should be financed and supported by their mother institution and should, where possible, establish an early and extensive field presence. Together with establishment of clear goals and reporting mechanisms, this approach may help to make international courts and their outreach programmes into a much more meaningful contribution to wider transitional justice mechanisms.

19

The Legacy of Youth Outreach at the International Criminal Tribunal for the Former Yugoslavia

*Adrian Plevin**

19.1 Introduction

Since the launch of the International Criminal Tribunal for the Former Yugoslavia's (ICTY or Tribunal) Outreach Programme in late 1999 until the Tribunal's closure, thousands of students were welcomed to the institution's headquarters in The Hague for behind-the-scenes views of its operations. Groups of visiting students learned about the complexities of conducting international criminal proceedings, engaged in question-and-answer sessions with judges and ICTY personnel, viewed documentaries, and absorbed key facts about the Tribunal's principal achievements. From the relative isolation of The Hague, far from communities most affected by the events that informed the ICTY's judicial work, there were limits to one's ability to fully comprehend the institution's sphere of influence in the former Yugoslavia and to fully contextualize its work. The experience is very different amongst the communities that bore the brunt of the conflict and still bear the scars of its aftermath.

My brief involvement in the Outreach Programme's Youth Outreach Project (YOP), delivering outreach presentations to university students in Zagreb and Skopje, left lasting impressions of the Tribunal's influence in the region of the former Yugoslavia and, in particular, its contributions to perceptions of the recent past. As an institution 'intended to contribute to the restoration of international peace and security',[1] outreach generally—and youth outreach in particular—played a key role in communicating the ICTY's own narrative of its work to audiences in the countries of the former Yugoslavia and in The Hague. While the Outreach Programme has been the subject of critical and comparative analysis,[2] neither youth-specific programming nor the YOP itself have been specifically addressed in the literature.

As the years since the conflict occurred continue to pass and a generation not born into conflict comes of age, youth outreach in the region of the former Yugoslavia becomes an area worthy of focused attention. Just as outreach became increasingly important for

* Legal Officer at the Special Tribunal for Lebanon. Formerly, he worked as an Associate Legal Officer at the International Criminal Tribunal for the Former Yugoslavia.

[1] G Kirk McDonald, 'Sixth Annual Report of the International Tribunal for the Prosecution of Persons Responsible for Serious Violations of International Humanitarian Law Committed in the Territory of the former Yugoslavia since 1991' UN Doc A/54/187 (2 August 1999) para 146.

[2] For example, N H Pentelovitch, 'Seeing Justice Done: The Importance of Prioritizing Outreach Efforts at International Criminal Tribunals' (2007) 39 Georgetown Journal of International Law 445; J N Clark, 'International War Crimes Tribunals and the Challenge of Outreach' (2009) 9 International Criminal Law Review 99.

Adrian Plevin, *The Legacy of Youth Outreach at the International Criminal Tribunal for the Former Yugoslavia* In: *Legacies of the International Criminal Tribunal for the Former Yugoslavia*. Edited by: Carsten Stahn, Carmel Agius, Serge Brammertz, Colleen Rohan, Oxford University Press (2020). © The Several Contributors DOI: 10.1093/oso/9780198862956.003.0020

maintaining the relationship between the ICTY and the region of the former Yugoslavia in the final years of the ICTY's mandate,[3] now more than ever after the ICTY's closure, there is a pressing need to give attention to future strategies for youth outreach, in the region in particular. To limit this paper to exploration of the YOP, however, would be to misrepresent the rich history of youth-focused outreach programming at the ICTY. With the Tribunal's closure as its catalyst, this contribution examines the development of the ICTY's youth outreach programming, explores its significance and examines possible initiatives for the future of youth outreach as a tool for supporting wider peace-building initiatives. It is informed, in part, by personal experiences and reflections on involvement in the final stages of the YOP.

19.2 Youth Outreach at the ICTY

Established in 1999—at the initiative of then ICTY President Gabrielle Kirk McDonald—to address the spread of misinformation in the communities most affected by the Tribunal's work,[4] the Outreach Programme later grew to encompass a broad range of activities and to become a key component of the ICTY's public relations strategy.[5] Faced with a widespread prevalence of negative perceptions of the Tribunal in the former Yugoslavia, Kirk McDonald identified the need to counter the frequent politicization of the ICTY's work and combat the spread of misinformation.[6] The impetus for outreach was more than the desire to take ownership of the narratives of the ICTY in the region: from the Tribunal's perspective, it was a practical necessity. Negative perceptions of the ICTY and its work were exploited by regional authorities to justify a lack of cooperation with the Tribunal, immediately hampering the work of the Office of the Prosecutor and also damaging efforts to improve relations between the various affected communities in the former Yugoslavia.[7]

Since its establishment, the ICTY's Outreach Office pioneered a host of outreach activities aimed at a diverse range of audiences. These served as the inspiration for outreach programmes at other international institutions, including the International Criminal Tribunal for Rwanda (ICTR), the Extraordinary Chambers in the Courts of Cambodia (ECCC), Special Court for Sierra Leone (SCSL), the Special Tribunal for Lebanon (STL), and the International Criminal Court (ICC).[8] Activities directed towards youth have formed a central component of the ICTY's Outreach Programme since its inception. This culminated, in

[3] ICTY, 'Outreach Programme' <http://www.icty.org/en/outreach/outreach-programme> accessed 20 May 2018.

[4] G Tortora, R Pejić-Sremac, J E Adwan, and N Golčevski (eds), 'Outreach: 15 Years of Outreach at the ICTY' (ICTY, 2016) 9; Kirk McDonald (n 1) paras 3, 146–48; S Darehshori, 'Lessons for Outreach from the Ad Hoc Tribunals, the Special Court for Sierra Leone, and the International Criminal Court' (2007) 14 New England Journal of International & Comparative Law 299, 301.

[5] Falling under the banner of the Immediate Office of the Registrar, the work of the ICTY Outreach Office complemented that of the Public Information Office whose tasks included: maintenance of the bank of materials accessible via the Tribunal's website, issuing press releases, responding to media requests, and monitoring regional media. See ICTY, 'Organisational Chart', <http://www.icty.org/en/about/tribunal/organisational-chart> accessed 20 May 2018.

[6] Kirk McDonald (n 1) para 146; Darehshori (n 4) 301.

[7] Kirk McDonald (n 1) 146.

[8] On the outreach activities of other international criminal justice institutions see Darehshori (n 4); Pentelovitch (n 2); Clark (n 2); R Kerr and J Lincoln, *The Special Court for Sierra Leone—Outreach, Legacy and Impact* (Kings College London 2008).

December 2011, with the establishment of the YOP. In the years that have followed, thousands of high-school, undergraduate, and postgraduate students across the region participated in the project through its various iterations at Headquarters and in the region.[9] The nature of activities directed towards youth—high-school and university students, young professionals and youth organizations—since the Outreach Programme's inception, are explored further.

19.2.1 The Development of Youth Outreach

The ICTY has 'placed young people's potential to bring about positive change in their communities at the heart of its work' from the very beginning of the Outreach Programme.[10] The earliest such example occurred shortly after the Outreach Programme's launch in November 1999, when the ICTY welcomed visiting students from the University of Sarajevo to its Headquarters in The Hague—the first non-judicial visit of its kind.[11] The week-long study visit included three days of presentations, in turn comprised of meetings with judges as well as officials from the Office of the Prosecutor, and opportunities to learn about unique features of the Tribunal, such as its work with witnesses and the Detention Unit. The two remaining days were dedicated to allowing the students to follow trial proceedings in the courtroom.[12] At the outset of the Programme, study visits were considered the 'main tool' to connect the ICTY with the region and, consequently, became a staple component of the Outreach Programme.[13] The week-long format was quickly abandoned, however, and replaced by shorter, tailor-made presentations. At the same time, the ICTY welcomed an increasingly diverse range of audiences from outside the former Yugoslavia, as well as those from within the region itself. Visits from the region were supported by civil society groups, such as the European Law Students Association (ELSA), whose Slovenian chapter were amongst the first civil society organizations to facilitate student visits to the ICTY.[14] Such support was necessary, as visits to Headquarters involved significant logistical and financial burdens for participants coming from outside The Netherlands. As a result, this form of outreach was limited in its capacity to provide access to information to audiences from the former Yugoslavia. These limitations were acknowledged soon after the Outreach Programme commenced, as the ICTY recognized the need to engage youth in the region could not be achieved through visits to Headquarters alone.

The first youth outreach event inside the region of the former Yugoslavia took the form of a presentation delivered by the ICTY's Outreach representative in 2000, at a roundtable discussion at the Faculty of Law of the University of Osijek, Croatia.[15] Such presentations eventually became the mainstay of youth outreach programming in the region. However, programming also diversified over the following years, as the Outreach Programme grew

[9] Tortora (n 4) 9.

[10] ibid.

[11] ICTY, 'Outreach Archives 1999' <http://www.icty.org/en/outreach/activities-archive/1999> accessed 20 May 2018.

[12] ibid.

[13] Tortora (n 4) 9.

[14] ICTY, 'Outreach Archives 2002' <http://www.icty.org/en/outreach/activities-archive/2002> accessed 20 May 2018.

[15] ibid.

to encompass broader audiences both within and outside of the former Yugoslavia. In 2000 alone, Outreach representatives and other ICTY personnel participated in human rights schools, and law students were interviewed for the ICTY outreach documentary *Justice at Work*, which concerned the creation of the Tribunal, and was later screened in Outreach presentations. Meanwhile, the first-ever working visit of ICTY judges to Croatia, since the Tribunal's establishment, provided students from the Faculty of Law at the University of Zagreb the opportunity to participate in a public forum to discuss the Tribunal's mandate and work.[16] These activities occurred alongside conferences and symposia, the production and screening of Outreach documentaries exploring aspects of the ICTY's case work, the dissemination of ICTY-related literature and case materials to university libraries, and student visits to the ICTY's field offices in the former Yugoslavia. This growth in youth-orientated activity was made possible thanks to the support of various universities, NGOs and civil society organizations, government departments, and international organizations that played a key role by partnering with the Outreach Office and assisting in programme development.

Initially, youth outreach in the region was directed almost exclusively towards university students as the majority of youth-orientated outreach consisted of presentations delivered to law faculties from across the region. Efforts were soon made, however, to engage students of a broader range of disciplines and address the ICTY's work from a wider range of perspectives: journalism, political sciences, security studies, human rights, peace and justice, and even geography. Laudably, even in its early years, the Outreach Programme never shied from public criticism of the ICTY and its work. To the contrary, Outreach personnel have deliberately and actively engaged with critics. In 2002, for example, the Outreach Office in the Federal Republic of Yugoslavia (FRY) in conjunction with the Belgrade Open School, organized a public debate between the FRY Outreach representative and Professor Kosta Čavoški, a well-known ICTY critic.[17]

As the Outreach Programme matured, the breadth of youth beneficiaries also expanded. By 2003, high-school students were also specifically targeted as beneficiaries, for the first time.[18] Organized in conjunction with the Kosovo Ministry of Education in 2006,[19] the rollout of high-school presentations witnessed the dramatic expansion of the numbers of youth reached through outreach.[20] The presentations, which were incorporated into the civic education syllabus, aimed to introduce students to the creation of the ICTY, its structure and functions, the nature of its work, and expectations for after the Tribunal's closure.[21] This expansion in the age range of youth outreach beneficiaries revealed an important trend: in its early years, outreach in the region was directed at audiences who lived through the conflicts. As the Outreach Programme expanded, however, its emphasis shifted towards the next generations,[22] in recognition of the fact that '[w]hilst many ... youth did not live

16 ibid.

17 ICTY 2002 (n 14).

18 ICTY, 'Outreach Archives 2003' <http://www.icty.org/en/outreach/activities-archive/2003> accessed 20 May 2018.

19 The designation 'Kosovo' is used without prejudice to positions on status, in line with UN Security Council Resolution 1244, UN Doc S/RES/1244 (1999).

20 ICTY, 'Outreach Archives 2006' <http://www.icty.org/en/outreach/activities-archive/2006> accessed 20 May 2018.

21 ibid.

22 See N Golčevski (ed), 'The Tribunal and the Next Generation' (*ICTY*, 2015) <http://www.icty.org/x/file/Outreach/reaching_out/education_youth_brochure_2014_en_web.pdf> accessed 20 May 2018.

through the events that devastated the Balkans in the 1990s, these young people will shape the way their nations deal with the legacy of the conflict in the years to come'.[23]

With the launch of the Young Justice Advocates programme in 2007, youth outreach expanded to incorporate capacity-building activities. Organized by the ICTY Serbia Outreach representative in conjunction with Belgrade-based NGO Youth Initiative for Human Rights (YIHR), the programme provided both training on the substance of the ICTY's work and on the methodology of conducting further workshops with high-school students.[24] This typically week-long 'training for trainers' model raised awareness amongst participants of the most contentious issues arising from the Tribunal's work, familiarized them with ICTY materials and provided the opportunity to take part in practical exercises speaking on various topics related to the ICTY.[25] The programme has been heralded as having a profound impact upon participants, 'inspiring them to launch workshops and activities across the country where they spread awareness about the Tribunal's work to thousands of young people'.[26]

Just as the ICTY's communication strategy embraced the use of contemporary technologies to communicate with global audiences,[27] the Outreach Programme also sought to deploy new technologies where possible. Video-conferencing was first used in 2008 to stream outreach presentations to students from the University of Iowa. Though its subsequent use has been modest, video-conferencing has enabled students outside of The Netherlands to engage with outreach activities conducted from the ICTY's Headquarters.[28] In 2009, it was expanded into the former Yugoslavia for the first time, when the ICTY Chambers and the Registry Spokesperson in The Hague met with political science and journalism students in Zagreb over video-conference link.

One of the more intensive opportunities for youth engagement was provided through the Regional Internship Programme which first launched in 2007. The Programme, organized in conjunction with the YIHR, engaged over thirty students during the five years of its operation. It incorporated, for selected candidates from across the region, five-month internships at the ICTY's Headquarters followed by three-month internships in the region—either with a national war crimes court, a national prosecutor's office, or with local organizations working on issues related to war crimes—together with follow-up activities organized by YIHR, such as promoting their work, experience and critical reflections to peers.[29] It was envisaged that the programme would enable the interns to gain practical experience and contribute 'directly to building the capacity of new generations in Serbia to try war crimes cases'.[30] Though its form and substance have varied according to the opportunities and audiences available, youth-orientated outreach programming was quickly established as a means of providing educational opportunities to youth, both inside and outside the region and elsewhere.

[23] Tortora (n 4) 9.
[24] ICTY, 'Outreach Activities 2007' <http://www.icty.org/en/outreach/activities-archive/2007> accessed 20 May 2018.
[25] ICTY, 'Outreach Archives 2008' <http://www.icty.org/en/outreach/activities-archive/2008> accessed 20 May 2018.
[26] Tortora (n 4) 16.
[27] UNICRI, *ICTY Manual on Developed Practices Manual* (UNICRI Publisher 2009) 190.
[28] ICTY, 2008 (n 25).
[29] Tortora (n 4) 14.
[30] ICTY, 2008 (n 25).

19.2.2 The Youth Outreach Project

In 2010, the ICTY adopted a new outreach strategy with the dual aims of reaching all sections of society in the former Yugoslavia, on the one hand, and promoting the ICTY's role in ending impunity and stimulating the process of dealing with the past, on the other.[31] It was in the context of this new strategy that efforts to rethink approaches to engaging youth in the region stemmed the development of the YOP in 2011.[32] The YOP itself consisted of two principle goals. The first was quantitative: to dramatically increase the number of young people targeted by ICTY outreach. The second was qualitative: 'to improve the understanding the ICTY's work and mandate amongst the high school aged population (16–18 year-olds) and university students in Bosnia and Herzegovina, Kosovo, Croatia, Serbia (Former Yugoslav Republic of Macedonia (FYROM)) and Montenegro'.[33] It pursued this qualitative goal by attempting to: (i) provide an overview of the Tribunal's findings on crimes committed and the responsibility of individuals from the cases of most interest to specific audiences, through individual ICTY speakers who tailored presentations to relevant regions and local communities; (ii) stimulate an interest in justice, accountability, and the ICTY's contributions to both, amongst youth in the former Yugoslavia; (iii) encourage reflection on the benefits and limitations of punitive justice as well as other mechanisms of transitional justice through discussion and debate; (iv) test the perceptions of young people in relation to the conflicts that took place in the former Yugoslavia; (v) provide additional information and tools for dealing with the legacy of conflicts that occurred in the region;[34] (vi) contribute to the dismantling of the culture of denial and intolerance by generating reflection amongst young people about the crimes committed in the recent past and ways to avoid future repetitions, by identifying crimes as deplorable, regardless of the ethnicity of the perpetrator or victim;[35] and (vii) create conditions for the continued and sustainable education of youth in the former Yugoslavia about the work of the ICTY and issues arising from the conflicts in the region.[36] For university students in particular, additional objectives were pursued, namely, increasing knowledge about international criminal law and humanitarian law and their practical implementation at the ICTY, through academic presentations across the universities;[37] and furthering the professional development of students.[38] Initially, it was only possible to deliver the project in a limited form in high-schools in Bosnia and Herzegovina. In 2012 however, thanks to financial support provided by the Government of Finland, the roll-out of the project was extended across Croatia, FYROM, Kosovo, Montenegro, and Serbia, and also broadened to include university students as originally envisaged.[39]

The refocusing of priorities following the adoption of the 2010 Outreach Strategy led the YOP to reach larger numbers of youth and children. Youth-orientated programming itself

[31] N Jelačić (ed), *ICTY Annual Outreach Report 2011* (ICTY 2012) 3, 5.
[32] Tortora (n 4).
[33] ICTY Outreach Office *(Draft) Report for a Project: Year 2011–2012* (ICTY 2013) 4 (on file with the author).
[34] ibid 4–6.
[35] ICTY Outreach Office, *(Draft) Report for a Project: Year 2012–2013 Report* (ICTY 2014) 4 (on file with the author); ICTY Outreach Office, *(Draft) Report for a Project: Year 2013–2014* (ICTY 2015) 4 (on file with the author).
[36] ICTY, Draft Report 2015 (n 35) 4.
[37] ICTY, Draft Report 2014 (n 35) 6; ICTY, Draft Report 2015 (n 35) 4.
[38] ICTY, Draft Report 2014 (n 35) 6.
[39] Tortora (n 4) 9.

largely followed on from the models experimented with in the Outreach Programme's earlier years. However, the most significant component of the YOP was the delivery of a series of presentations discussing the work of the ICTY, and how it has contributed to bringing those responsible for atrocities committed to justice, while promoting dialogue with high-school and university students about these issues.[40] Such presentations typically provided students with an overview of the Tribunal's establishment, structure, and influence on international responses to mass atrocity crimes,[41] as well as highlighting the core international crimes under the Tribunal's mandate (genocide, crimes against humanity, and war crimes) and exploring the ICTY's contributions to international criminal law and humanitarian law. Some presentations examined thematic contributions of ICTY prosecutions to accounting for the crimes of the recent past, such as forcible displacement and sexual crimes. Though always tailored appropriately to particular audiences,[42] presentations tended to be deliberately legalistic. Antonija Krstulović Dragičević PhD, a lecturer at the University of Split Faculty of Law, described this as 'the greatest benefit of these lectures' for her students, remarking that it provided them 'insight into the work of the international criminal tribunals from the perspective of the legal profession, devoid of the political context through which the public frequently receives information and which creates perceptions about the adjudication in the international criminal context'.[43] Here was a conscious effort by those administering the Outreach Programme to avoid reinforcing wartime divisions or victimization along ethnic lines, whilst providing an accurate and transparent account of the Tribunal's approaches to criminal accountability.

Although the Outreach Office curated the content of lectures so as to avoid politicizing the Tribunal's judicial work, it never shied away from addressing controversy where it arose. Outreach personnel worked to identify potentially sensitive topics and to appropriately brief staff involved in outreach delivery to be able to respond. For example, before travelling to the region, ICTY staff were comprehensively briefed on relevant aspects of the current political climate at their destination, were provided with insight into local attitudes towards the Tribunal, and were prepared with knowledge of the specific cases relevant to the geographical area of their destination. ICTY staff were also apprised of the anticipated relevance of recent or high-profile cases or judicial developments to their audiences, the attitudes of local media, and of any political controversy surrounding or related to the Tribunal or its work that might have been encountered in some form during a visit. This information was supplemented by the detailed feedback provided by other ICTY staff who had visited the same localities on previous occasions. Such feedback would note the types of questions asked by previous audiences, their attitudes and level of pre-existing understanding, and areas of particular interest or controversy. The data gathered became instructive for maximizing the engagement. For instance, in the FYROM, one outreach lecturer concluded, after conducting two visits to the same three universities, that 'presenting highly sensitive

[40] Jelačić (n 31) 7; ICTY, Draft Report 2013 (n 33) 4.

[41] On the concept of mass atrocity crimes, see G Evans, *The Responsibility to Protect* (Brookings 2009) 11–30.

[42] The content of presentations on international crimes to undergraduate students in the region of the former Yugoslavia addressed the same issues as presentations delivered, for example, to the legal community at Eurojust in The Hague, although varying in depth, complexity, and presentation style.

[43] Golčevski (n 22) 8.

issues associated with the ICTY in that country ensured a high degree of attention from the students'[44]—information which would shape future visits to the FYROM.

More informally, presentations were often fine-tuned thanks to useful assistance provided by partners on the ground. My own experience—both in Zagreb and Skopje—was of being greeted by academic staff ahead of delivering lectures. Having the opportunity to talk candidly about their impressions of their own students' capacities, experiences of the conflict and post-conflict society, depth of legal, historical, and institutional knowledge, level of political engagement and impressions, as well as existing attitudes and biases towards the ICTY and its work, and even anticipated levels of comfort with my presentation style (including my Australian accent) were all invaluable for making last-minute adjustments to presentations, to ensure that lectures were tailored suitably, in substance and form, to maximize students' engagement.

In addition to the presentations in the region, the YOP oversaw the delivery of a number of other activities. The Outreach Office continued to facilitate study visits to the ICTY's headquarters. The thousands of study visits that took place since the launch of the Outreach Programme in late 1999 saw more than 105,000 students and professionals visit ICTY headquarters in some 4,200 group visits to the end of 2015,[45] with that number added to in 2016 and 2017. Essay writing competitions were organized in 2013 and 2014, providing the more than 200 high-school students who participated with the opportunity to critically reflect upon the role of international criminal trials.[46] In 2012, the YOP expanded the range of its beneficiaries beyond youth—to include school-aged children—when Outreach representatives in Bosnia and Herzegovina participated in the ninth *Sarajevo Kid's Festival*, in a programme that combined entertainment and education.[47] At the same festival in 2013 and 2014, some 200 children aged seven to fourteen were invited to specially-tailored educational workshops where they were shown age-appropriate material of war time events and ICTY proceedings, before being encouraged to express their thoughts on the significance of international criminal justice through drawings.[48]

Incorporating visions of the ICTY's legacy into its programming, the Outreach Office also utilized the YOP to initiate a number of projects designed at building the capacity of local actors to ensure continuing education of young people about the ICTY's legacy following the institution's closure. This programming included: (i) the implementation, in 2014, of a pilot workshop to train high-school teachers to enable them to independently deliver regular presentations on the ICTY's work and contributions to international justice; (ii) visits by university lecturers from across the region to The Hague to gain first-hand insight into the Tribunal's work and discuss the avenues for the integration of ICTY jurisprudence into curricular; and; (iii) partnerships with regional NGOs, independently selected by the ICTY as suitable candidates for delivering future youth outreach presentations.[49] The training of a select group of teachers was made possible with the assistance of partners

[44] ICTY, Draft Report 2013 (n 33) 5. In FYROM, the issue of amnesties for alleged war criminals, adopted by the Parliament, was particularly divisive. ibid.

[45] ibid 15.

[46] Golčevski (n 22) 2.

[47] ICTY, 'Bridges of trust and friendship: working to ensure a peaceful future for the Balkans' <http://www.icty.org/en/outreach/activities/bridges-trust-and-friendship-working-ensure-peaceful-future-balkans> accessed 20 May 2018.

[48] Golčevski (n 22) 2.

[49] ibid 3.

active in the region, such as the NGO Helsinki Committee for Human Rights in *Republika Srpska* (HCHR-RS), who were provided substantive training about the ICTY's role and work, in addition to practical training concerning the youth outreach delivery, designed to supplement the teachers' existing teaching material on transitional justice.[50]

This capacity-building work was supported by the wealth of multi-purpose informational material provided about the ICTY and its achievements, much of which has been updated regularly and maintained on the Tribunal's website.[51] This includes, handouts explaining terminology commonly used in relation to the Tribunal's work, thematic outreach documentaries,[52] the *Bridging the Gap* outreach presentation series, which was subsequently compiled in to a five-part documentary series,[53] an interactive map containing information on crimes investigated by the Tribunal,[54] infographics, excerpts of witness testimony, case summaries,[55] and of course, databases of judicial proceedings and important decisions. To further assist in building the capacity of local actors to the delivery of youth outreach independently, electronic copies of presentations were provided to teachers or academic staff as a teaching resource.[56] In 2013–2014, the Outreach Office commenced the development of a digital multimedia educational toolkit containing information about the ICTY, including facts about the crimes established during judicial proceedings, to serve as a source of 'ready-made instructional materials for educators [at] all levels in the countries of the former Yugoslavia'.[57] The work of finding a suitable platform for the dissemination and maintenance of the toolkit appears to remain ongoing.[58]

The assistance of local partners was instrumental in facilitating the expansion of the YOP and to ensuring future youth outreach initiatives continue in the region. Principally, coordination with and the approval of the Ministries of Education, across the region, has been essential to enabling the Outreach Office the access required to rollout the YOP. The level of success in attaining this support, however, varied significantly from country to country, with the unfortunate consequence of limiting the opportunities for youth outreach and adding substantially to the administrative and logistical burden of the Outreach Office in coordinating the YOP.[59] At the same time, support from the NGO community has also been critically important. For instance, the teacher training initiatives, undertaken in partnership with the HCHR-RS, are expected to facilitate the delivery of continued implementation of the YOP through lectures to high-school students, via HCHR-RS members, as the organization possesses the relevant certification to conduct lectures in high-schools.[60] During 2012–2013, cooperation was initiated with the international NGO 'EUROCLIO—Association of European History Teachers', resulting in the development of plans for a multi-media history textbook to be written by history teachers from across the region of the

[50] ICTY, Draft Report 2015 (n 35) 6.
[51] ibid.
[52] ICTY, Draft Report 2013 (n 33) 6.
[53] ICTY, 'Bridging the Gap with local communities' <http://www.icty.org/en/outreach/bridging-the-gap-with-local-communities> accessed 20 May 2018.
[54] ICTY, 'Interactive Map' <http://www.icty.org/sid/10913> accessed 20 May 2018.
[55] IRMCT, 'ICTY Remembers: The Srebrenica Genocide 1995–2015' <https://www.irmct.org/specials/srebrenica20/> accessed 7 February 2020.
[56] ICTY, Draft Report 2013 (n 33) 6.
[57] ICTY, Draft Report 2015 (n 35) 6.
[58] ibid.
[59] For example, ICTY, Draft Report 2013 (n 33) 1–3, 7.
[60] ibid 7.

former Yugoslavia, about the crimes which occurred throughout the conflict, and based on ICTY archival material.[61] It is envisaged that the teachers involved in the production of the textbook will then be able to provide training in its subject matter to their colleagues, further contributing to the legacy of the YOP across the region.[62]

19.3 Youth Outreach and Transitional Justice

19.3.1 The Role of Youth Outreach

International criminal justice institutions such as the ad hoc tribunals, the ICC, and hybrid tribunals are one of the principal initiatives for implementing transitional justice agendas in post-conflict societies.[63] According to the International Center for Transitional Justice (ICTJ), transitional justice 'refers to the ways countries emerging from periods of conflict and repression address large scale or systematic human rights violations so numerous and so serious that the normal justice system will not be able to provide an adequate response'.[64] The Secretary-General of the United Nations defines transitional justice as consisting 'of both judicial and non-judicial processes and mechanisms, including prosecution initiatives, facilitating initiatives in respect of the right to truth, delivering reparations, institutional reform and national consultations'.[65] All the while, transitional justice is essentially concerned with promoting opportunities for reconciliation, peace, and democracy.[66] As Vinck and Pham observe, outreach plays a central role in any transitional justice process.[67] As such, the intersect between transitional justice and youth outreach is deserving of specific consideration.

Legalists would espouse that, in terms of peace building, a key benefit of institutions like the ICTY, as a response to mass atrocity crimes, is the institutionalization and moderation of desires for revenge that might otherwise perpetuate the outbreak of future conflicts.[68] International criminal prosecutions help clarify the historical record,[69] or even change the

[61] ibid 6.

[62] ibid.

[63] OHCHR, *Rule of Law Tools for Post-Conflict States, Maximizing the Legacy of Hybrid Courts* (OHCHR 2008) 3. For a comprehensive analysis of the topic of international criminal justice institutions and transitional justice topic see L Vinjamuri and J Snyder, 'Advocacy and Scholarship in the Study of International War Crime Tribunals and Transitional Justice' (2004) 7 Annual Review of Political Science 345.

[64] ICTJ 'What is Transitional Justice?' <https://www.ictj.org/about/transitional-justice> accessed 20 May 2018.

[65] UN Secretary-General, 'Guidance Note of the Secretary-General: United Nations Approach to Transitional Justice' (March 2010) <https://www.un.org/ruleoflaw/files/TJ_Guidance_Note_March_2010FINAL.pdf> accessed 20 May 2018.

[66] J H R DeMeritt, 'Transitional Justice: Prospects for Post-War Peace and Human Rights' in T D Mason and S McLaughlin Mitchell (eds), *What Do We Know About Civil Wars?* (Rowman & Littlefield 2016) 180.

[67] P Vinck and P N Pham, 'Outreach Evaluation: The International Criminal Court in the Central African Republic' (2010) 4 International Journal of Transitional Justice 2. See generally E Cole and K Murphy, 'History Education Reform, Transitional Justice and Transformation of Identities' in P Arthur (ed) *Identities in Transition: Challenges for Transitional Justice in Divided Societies* (CUP 2011).

[68] G Bass, *Staying the Hand of Vengeance* (PUP 2000) 304; R Teitel, 'The Law and Politics of Contemporary Transitional Justice' (2005) 38 Cornell International Law Journal 837, 847–48. See Vinjamuri and Snyder (n 63) 345.

[69] Bass (n 68) 286–304; J V H Holtermann, '"One of the Challenges that Can Plausibly Be Raised Against Them"? On the Role of Truth in Debates about the Legitimacy of International Criminal Tribunals' in N Hayashi, C M Bailliet, and J Nicholson (eds), *The Legitimacy of International Criminal Tribunals* (CUP 2017) 2010; M Ignatieff, 'Articles of Faith' [1996] Index on Censorship 25, 113.

behaviour of post-conflict States towards favouring the influence of legal traditions by articulating and encouraging compliance with legal norms.[70] They are a form of retributive transitional justice mechanism—intended to hold individual perpetrators to account—with the ancillary aims of deterring future crimes, strengthening the rule of law, and instilling victims with a sense of justice.[71] Pragmatists, however, would note the limit of the peace-building capacity of criminal trials to prevent future conflict from arising.[72] For example, some observers are critical of the deterrent effect international prosecutions have had, particularly in the former Yugoslavia.[73] Trials, moreover, are neither a means of unambiguously bridging divides between former adversaries nor a failsafe method of shifting the blame for atrocities from ethnic groups viewed in their entirety, to those individuals found to be criminally responsible.[74] The utility of outreach, in this respect, is that it has a distinct and supplementary function as a form of restorative (or non-retributive) transitional justice.[75] As Baroni observes, '[i]f the Tribunal is at all to fulfill its objectives of promoting security, reconciliation and strengthen the rule of law in the former Yugoslavia, the work of the Court needs to reach directly the ordinary citizens of the region who are the ultimate peace-builders'.[76] Outreach is thus a tool that enables international criminal justice institutions to complement the role of criminal prosecutions, in part, to address the shortcomings of punitive mechanisms in achieving the aims of transitional justice.

To understand the role of youth outreach in transitional justice it is useful to recall the aims of outreach activities. In former President Kirk McDonald's words, the Outreach Programme was intended 'to enable the Tribunal to better inform the people of the former Yugoslavia of its work in the local languages and to combat distortion of the Tribunal's record'.[77] Similar aspirations exist for outreach at other international criminal justice institutions. The ICC Outreach Unit defines its task as 'aim[ing] to cultivate a level of awareness and understanding of the ICC's mandate and mode of operations, promote access to and understanding of judicial proceedings, and foster realistic expectations about the Court's work';[78] the Public Affairs Section responsible for outreach at the ECCC 'strives to reach out to Cambodians to inform about the progress of the court and to win their support';[79] outreach activities at the SCSL 'aim[ed] to promote understanding of the [Special Court]

[70] See M Minow, *Between Vengeance and Forgiveness; Facing History after Genocide and Mass Violence* (Beacon 1998) 50; T Meron, *Law Crimes War Comes of Age: Essays* (OUP 1998) 304; G Bass, 'Milošević in The Hague' (2003) 82 (3) Foreign Affairs 95.

[71] DeMeritt (n 66) 4–5.

[72] See P Akhavan, 'Beyond Impunity: Can International Criminal Justice Prevent Future Atrocities?' (2001) 95 American Journal of International Law 7; Bass (n 68) 283.

[73] Vinjamuri and Snyder (n 63) 352. See V Hussain, 'Sustaining Judicial Rescues: The Role of Outreach and Capacity-Building Efforts in War Crimes Tribunals' (2005) 45 Virginia Journal of International Law 547, 581; A A Shvey, 'Striving for Accountability in the Former Yugoslavia' in J E Stromseth (ed), *Accountability for Atrocities: National and International Responses* (Transnational Publishers 2003) 70.

[74] Vinjamuri and Snyder (n 63) 352.

[75] DeMeritt (n 66) 4–5; See Cole and Murphy (n 67) 35. Other forms of non-retributive transitional justice, such as truth commissions, reparations, and memory projects, are intended to offer victims compensation, or reparation for crimes, or to contribute to the lasting preservation of memories. DeMeritt (n 66) 5. DeMeritt also points to a third category of transitional justice processes and institutions—*retributive and non-retributive* mechanisms—which would include amnesties, purges, exile, or lustrations, intended to impose punishment for wartime abuses while also providing 'a psychological break with the past'. ibid 6.

[76] F Baroni, 'The International Criminal Tribunal for the Former Yugoslavia and its Mission to Restore Peace' (2000) 12 Pace International Law Review 233, 247.

[77] ECCC, 'Outreach' <https://www.eccc.gov.kh/en/tags/outreach> accessed 01 July 2018.

[78] ICC Outreach Unit, *Outreach Report 2010* (ICC 2010) 8.

[79] ECCC (n 77).

and respect for human rights and the rule of law in Sierra Leone, to disseminate information and encourage dialogue, to foster two-way communication [...] and to facilitate the participation of all Sierra Leone nationals in the judicial processes';[80] and the Outreach and Legacy Unit of the STL defines its primary goal as 'bring[ing] the tribunal's work closer to the Lebanese people'.[81]

These aims, like the range of youth outreach activities conducted by the ICTY, demonstrate that outreach is an inherently broad-scale exercise. Experience demonstrates that its substance is multi-disciplinary—engaging audiences on technical issues in fields as diverse as law, history, journalism, and geography, targeting audiences of all ages and composition with various proximity to the subject conflict, and being intrinsically linked to peace-building and transitional justice initiatives. All the while, its content is informed by the mandate, functions, and achievements of the international criminal justice institution it serves. While youth outreach overlaps with the public relations functions of these institutions, the former essentially remains an educational exercise. In the case of the ICTY, where the vast majority of youth outreach activities were conducted in the form of lectures and presentations to schools and universities, this exercise has, at least in part, demonstrated its suitability for integration into the regular curricula.

19.3.2 Youth Outreach Legacy

The definition of legacy, in the context of the ICTY, has been inspired by that adopted for the first legacy conference held in The Hague, in 2010. In the lead up to that conference, legacy was defined broadly as 'that which the Tribunal will hand down to successors and others'.[82] This includes 'findings of the Tribunal contained in its judgements, its contribution to the development of international law, the records and archives of the Tribunal, its contribution to the rule of law in the former Yugoslavia and its advancement of international justice'.[83] Similarly, the Office of the United Nations High Commissioner for Human Rights (OHCHR), refers to the legacy of (hybrid) international criminal justice institutions as the 'lasting impact on bolstering the rule of law in a particular society, by conducting effective trials to contribute to ending impunity, while also strengthening domestic judicial capacity'.[84] What then, is the role that youth outreach can play in contributing to the ICTY's legacy?

It was an inescapable reality for the ICTY as it faced its closure that the narratives of its jurisprudence, achievements, and impact in the region trended towards historical rather than contemporary relevance. The subject matter of youth outreach lectures in the ICTY's final years likewise tended towards helping students understand and examine recent historical events, rather than serving more direct aims, such as laying the foundations for fostering cooperation with the Tribunal, as was intended of the Outreach Programme

[80] Kerr and Lincoln (n 8) 11.

[81] STL, 'Outreach—Communicating the mission' <https://www.stl-tsl.org/en/about-the-stl/structure-of-the-stl/registry-stl/outreach> accessed 20 May 2018.

[82] ICTY, 'Assessing the Legacy of the ICTY' <http://www.icty.org/sq/node/9200> accessed 20 May 2018.

[83] ibid.

[84] OHCHR, *Rule of Law Tools for Post-Conflict States, Maximizing the Legacy of Hybrid Courts*, HR/PUB/08/2 (OHCHR 2008) 4–5.

upon its inception. This subtle shift never detracted from the legacy value of youth outreach, however. Rather, it served to emphasize it. As Cole and Murphy note:

> history education […] can play an important role in the transformation and historical narratives that are associated with many of the processes of [restorative] justice and moral repair. These include public apology, broadly understood to include acknowledgement and the presentation of a narrative comprehensible to the victims, recognition of victims and their narratives, hither to often silenced or disbarred through prejudice and stereotyping; public deliberation of the meaning of the past; message of political and social-non repetition . . . .[85]

The contributions of youth outreach to this transformation of historical narratives are both practical and substantive.[86] In terms of the former, tailored youth outreach programming, responsive and accountable to its beneficiaries, can help to consolidate trust between international justice institutions and the communities they serve and hope to inform. In terms of the latter, youth outreach provides a means for spreading the information communities require to engage with justice processes.[87] Perhaps the greatest prospect for youth outreach, however, is its potential to contribute towards pragmatic peace-building efforts. It was this understanding that underpinned the YOP, insofar as it was recognized that:

> fact-based education of the next generation about the recent violent past is crucial for building a lasting peace and stability. For this reason the Tribunal sought to reach out directly to students in the region with a factual overview of its judgements relating to crimes committed during the conflicts. In this way, participants were encouraged to think critically about the way in which the conflicts have been narrated to them in the past, and better equipped to form their own opinions on both the history and future of their communities.[88]

A niche role for the legacy of this fact-based youth outreach lies in strengthening the ICTY's contributions to the content of history education in the former Yugoslavia. Speaking of the positive reaction of his students and the deep impact that outreach presentations had upon them, teacher Islam Zulović from the Sarajevo Fifth Grammar School remarked that the content of youth outreach lectures 'should be included in the regular curriculum'.[89] But the impetus for focusing on history education reform is not merely anecdotal. It underlines the need to address, what Cole and Murphy (and others), term as the 'legacy of violence: zero-sum identities'. Zero-sum identities, prevalent still in the former Yugoslavia, can be thought of as highly polarized group-identities that threaten prospects of reconciliation, whereby individuals in post-conflict societies tend to primarily identify themselves as members of (polarized) groups forged during the conflict.[90] In the context of the former Yugoslavia,

[85] Cole and Murphy (n 67) 334.

[86] C Ramírez-Barat, *Engaging Children and Youth in Transitional Justice Processes: Guidance for Outreach Programmes* (ICTJ 2012) 4.

[87] ibid.

[88] Golčevski (n 22) iv.

[89] ibid 8.

[90] Cole and Murphy (n 67) 338. See also D Bar-Tal, 'Collective Memory of Physical Violence: It's Contributions to the Culture of Violence' in E Cairns and M Roe (eds), *The Role of Memory in Ethnic Conflict* (Palgrave Macmillan 2003) 77–93.

these identities are evidenced through the ethnic divisions that became synonymous with the various warring parties, protagonists, and victims of the conflict, and which still dominate social and political discourse in the region. Individuals' attachments to these polarizing identities, however, are more likely the *result* of the conflict than the cause of it.[91] As Ahkavan notes, conflicts in the region 'were not expressions of spontaneous blood lust or inevitable historical cataclysms' but 'resulted from the deliberate incitement of ethnic hatred and violence by which ruthless demagogues and warlords elevated themselves to positions of absolute power'.[92] After conflict has ended, the challenge for those seeking to promote reconciliation and build lasting peace is that political and social narratives—including historical narratives—are prone to repeating, exacerbating, and doubling-down on these zero-sum identities.[93] Reform of history education curricula, while far broader than the ambit of youth outreach, presents an opportunity to redefine these narratives and explore alternate identities within post-conflict societies, and is thus key to the success of reconciliation and peace-building efforts.[94]

There are obvious limitations to what youth outreach can hope to achieve in this respect after the ICTY's closure, but its potential is palpable. One possible opportunity to deconstruct existing identity structures is to continue the delivery of youth outreach activities that address the conflict in the region in a manner that deliberately avoids focusing upon zero-sum identities. Such targeting need not be complicated given the similarity of crime-bases across the region. Examples might include focusing outreach material on thematic crimes, such as forcible removal and detention that were replicated and perpetrated against various ethnic-groups across the region, or classes of victims—women, children, and the elderly—to foster empathetic responses that bridge ethnic/national divides. This work began already in the form of thematic ICTY documentaries such as *Justice at Work, Through Their Eyes: Witnesses to Justice* and *Sexual Violence and the Triumph of Justice* as well as the collections of victim testimony[95] and statements of guilt compiled on the ICTY's website.[96]

19.4 Recommendations

Irrespective of what may be said for the ameliorative effect of the ICTY's legacy, it is an unfortunate and inescapable reality that the rhetoric of conflict remains present in many areas of the former Yugoslavia.[97] As well as being a hindrance to reconciliation efforts, this rhetoric also hampers the possibility of wide-scale engagement with, and objective and balanced analysis of, the ICTY, its work and of course, its legacy.[98] The ICTY's mandate, achievements, and jurisprudence addressed only limited aspects of the conflict in the former Yugoslavia and did so exclusively through a framework focused on international

91 Cole and Murphy (n 67) 338.
92 Akhavan (n 72) 7.
93 See C Kauffman, 'Possible and Impossible Solutions to Ethnic Wars' (1996) 20 International Security 136.
94 Cole and Murphy (n 67) 334–68.
95 ICTY, 'The Voice of Victims' <http://www.icty.org/en/features/voice-of-the-victims> accessed 20 May 2018.
96 ICTY, 'Statements of Guilt' available at <http://www.icty.org/en/features/statements-guilt> accessed 20 May 2018.
97 K Wu, 'Experiences that Count: A Comparative Study of the ICTY and SCSL in Shaping the Image of Justice' (2013) 9 Utrecht Law Review 60, 62; E Cole, 'Shortcomings of ICTY Outreach in Bosnia-Herzegovina: A Case Study' (2013) 3 The Owl 10.
98 Wu (n 97).

criminal justice. Youth outreach, as a component of history education, however, provides the opportunity to contribute to reinforcing peace-building strategies in a manner that criminal trials alone cannot.

The ICTY's Outreach Strategy, including the implementation of the YOP, made significant headway in identifying the niche role of youth outreach in contributing to transitional justice in the former Yugoslavia by supplementing educational initiatives to address the region's recent past. In the twilight period of the ICTY's mandate, the institution was forced to come to terms with a decreasing role in shaping the future of youth outreach in the region. Limits on the time and resources at its disposal, and the practical realities associated with the downsizing of the institution resulted in the necessary diversion of energy to the task of closing, particularly in its final months. This section explores both the role taken by the ICTY in its final phases to shape the future of youth outreach and a non-exhaustive list of proposals for those interested in continuing the ICTY's pioneering work, following its closure.

19.4.1 The ICTY's Role in Shaping the Legacy of Youth Outreach

In the early days of the Outreach Programme, critics stressed the need for greater visibility of outreach work.[99] This visibility was subsequently achieved, in part, through the continued efforts of the Outreach Office to grow the Outreach Programme and through collaboration with local partners ranging from civil society to international organizations to Ministries of Education throughout the region. Visibility is equally important looking forward, as new actors will be required to fill the void left by the ICTY and become custodians not only of youth outreach, but of the Tribunal's legacy.

As Werby and Werby observe, 'any outreach effort needs to make choices: who to reach, how to reach them, and what to say'.[100] Until its closure, it was still the ICTY that was best placed to identify both short- and long-term aspirations for youth outreach programming in the region—even if it would not continue to play a role in realizing such aims. As the creator of the longest-standing Outreach programme of any international criminal justice institution, the ICTY's efforts to consolidate lessons learned and its own perspectives on recommendations for the future, and to disseminate them, were particularly crucial. Some significant headway was made in this respect. Initiatives such as the publication *Outreach: 15 Years of Outreach at the ICTY* made important contributions to this exercise by providing an overview of lessons learned, existing challenges, and the way forward.[101] In addition, much work was undertaken to ensure that youth outreach continues past the ICTY's closure. In the final annual report, submitted to the UN Security Council, President Carmel Agius made several recommendations regarding the future of the ICTY's Outreach Programme, emphasizing the importance of a strong field presence, two-way communications, and the availability of appropriate funding. The report also recommended that

[99] K Cibelli and T Guberek, *"Justice Unknown, Justice Unsatisfied?" Bosnian NGOs Speak about the International Criminal Tribunal of the Former Yugoslavia* (Education and Public Inquiry and International Citizenship at Tufts University 2000) 21.

[100] C Werby and O Werby, 'Practical Strategies for Youth Outreach' (*ICC, ICC Forum—Invited Experts on Outreach Question*) <http://iccforum.com/outreach> accessed 20 May 2018.

[101] See Totora (n 4) 81–84.

information about the work and legacy of the Tribunal continue to be accessible in official and local languages through the establishment of information centres and that '[o]ne of the key target groups of the ICTY's legacy should be youth'.[102] However, no further detail was developed.[103] Whether the Security Council, or the UN more generally, move to pursue these recommendations remains to be seen. But, in the absence of a clear vision of the future of youth outreach emanating from the ICTY itself, the atmosphere is ripe for the UN to develop its own vision for the future of youth outreach aimed at preserving the legacy of its pioneering international criminal justice institution. This vision should be clearly articulated as early as possible and should: (i) identify an overarching strategy for protecting the legacy of the ICTY through future youth outreach, including specific objectives to build upon the YOP's achievements; (ii) identify, insofar as possible, estimates of resources required to implement such future youth outreach strategies; and (iii) develop guidelines and toolkits for coordinating and evaluating youth outreach strategies, to be shared publicly or with partner organizations internationally and in the region, as appropriate.[104]

This future vision of youth outreach could build upon information readily available to the ICTY Outreach Office through its own project analyses regarding the implementation of the YOP and should, insofar as possible, incorporate feedback from partners, critics, and collaborators, whilst giving appropriate consideration to the desires of youth in the region. The overarching vision should be publicized on the Tribunal's legacy website, which should provide comprehensive access to those supporting materials that may help future custodians of youth outreach work towards realizing the Tribunal's vision.

19.4.2 Recommendations for Academia

There is a palpable need for further research on the role and effectiveness of outreach generally, and youth outreach in particular, as a mechanism of transitional justice. Despite being essentially an educational activity, outreach programming has evolved from public relations exercises. Youth outreach programming has benefitted from the input of the lawyers—judges, prosecutors, and others—with particular insight of the work and achievements of various aspects of the Tribunal's work. Feedback from teachers, university staff, and students in the region has also been incorporated into tailoring outreach activities. There is room, however, for greater exploration of youth outreach programming from the perspective of educational theories and by experts in educational design. Additionally, Cole and Murphy's foray into the role of history education reform as a means of promoting reconciliation in post-conflict societies, points to the need for further analysis of the specific role and contributions of youth outreach programming as a mechanism of transitional justice.[105] Questions to be explored include: whether the youth outreach delivered by external actors is more or less effective than fully integrating the same material into the regular curricular;

[102] C Agius, *Twenty-fourth and final annual report of the International Tribunal for the Prosecution of Persons Responsible for Serious Violations of International Humanitarian Law Committed in the Territory of the Former Yugoslavia since 1991*, UN Doc A/72/266 (1 August 2017) 25.

[103] cf C Agius, *Assessment and Report of Judge Carmel Agius, President of the International Tribunal for the Former Yugoslavia, provided to the Security Council pursuant to paragraph 6 of Security Council resolution 1534 (2004)*, UN Doc A/72/266 (29 November 2017) paras 189–99.

[104] cf Pentelovitch (n 2) 113–15.

[105] Cole and Murphy (n 67) 334–68.

what format and subject matter are most effective for engaging audiences of different ages in the subject matter of the ICTY's work and achievements; and how frequently youth outreach programmes ought to be incorporated into syllabi.

19.4.3 Recommendations for the International Community at Large

The Tribunal was first and foremost a criminal court. The period leading to its closure naturally required the ICTY to invest its remaining resources in ensuring that the winding down of its operations, the finalization of its judicial mandate, the archiving of records, the liquidation of assets, the departure of personnel, and the necessary handover to the Residual Mechanism for International Criminal Tribunals (MICT) was as smooth and efficient as possible. As former President Patrick Robinson noted, at the conclusion of the first legacy conference in 2010, there was a need for the Tribunal to 'focus on its key expertise and make use of the possibility of cooperating with other actors who are best positioned to assist it'.[106] That statement remains true following the ICTY's closure. The preservation, delivery, and maintenance of effective youth outreach as a means of ensuring the Tribunal's legacy is now totally dependent upon the support of States, international organizations, other than the ICTY, governments within the region, and civil society.

As foreshadowed already, perhaps the most significant contribution that can be made to ensuring the ICTY's legacy through future youth outreach in the region is by encouraging history education reform. The ICTY has produced a wealth of archives and tailor-made educational material, based on established facts, that could be incorporated or introduced into regular curricula in schools, high-schools, and universities across the region of the former Yugoslavia. Considering the resistance experienced to date and the logistical difficulties of delivering any youth outreach outside of regional centres, the support of Ministries of Education throughout the region will be critical. Interested States should be encouraged to use diplomatic channels to stress the importance of incorporating fact-based discussion of international trials into regular education programmes. History education reform, however, need not exclude criticism of the Tribunal or its legacy. To the contrary, the YOP has demonstrated that embracing discourse around critical perspectives is crucial to promoting engagement with the ICTY's legacy and work.

There is room too, for new partnerships in achieving these aims. For instance, the United Nations Children's Fund (UNICEF)—which is both active in the region and prioritizes children's rights-based approaches to its programming—may be a useful partner in pursuing the agenda of history education reform. International organizations should therefore be encouraged to explore avenues for utilizing their existing relationships and credibility, to add history education reform to agendas in the region. Likewise, States and civil society should encourage Ministries of Education, throughout the region, to engage in dialogue with relevant actors as to how best to incorporate factual information about the ICTY and its work into regular history education, in a manner that contributes to reconciliation efforts rather than reinforcing existing divides.

[106] P L Robinson, 'Report of the President on the Conference Assessing the Legacy of the ICTY' (ICTY, 27 April 2010) para 11(iv).

With the ICTY closed, it is imperative that the MICT assume oversight of the Tribunal's legacy, including its outreach work, in the absence of any formal effort by the UN Security Council to vest this work elsewhere. To achieve this aim, the MICT will require sufficient financial and human resources to help oversee the coordination, development, and the rollout of a lasting and impactful vision for youth outreach. This will necessarily include adopting appropriate follow-up channels and methods of evaluation, until the sustainability of the youth outreach in the former Yugoslavia can be guaranteed.[107]

Finally, while existing initiatives such as the educational toolkit and EUROCLIO textbook should be encouraged and supported with appropriate resources, there is also room for the development, by educators in the region, of new narratives of the conflict and the ICTY. Those willing to explore the recent past through perspectives that cut across, rather than reinforce, zero-sum identities should be particularly favoured and prioritized. Such narratives could be based in the ICTY's archives and jurisprudence and utilize the existing tools and material available for youth outreach. But those involved in developing both the substance and form of future youth outreach activities should, wherever possible, prioritize the role of the region's youth, as the future custodians of the Tribunal's legacy, in shaping the future outreach in the former Yugoslavia.

[107] Cibelli and Guberek (n 99) 24.

PART VI

PUNISHMENT, SENTENCING, AND BEYOND

20
Punishing for Humanity
The Sentencing Legacy of the ICTY

*Margaret M. deGuzman**

20.1 Introduction

When the ICTY's judges started sentencing defendants they had a choice to make: should they follow the sentencing practices of the former Yugoslavia or chart their own course? They mostly chose the latter. Although they took national sentencing practices into account, they declined to be bound by them and, indeed, diverged from them in many cases. Instead, they undertook to create global sentencing norms—norms that are now being applied at the International Criminal Court (ICC) and other supranational institutions.

The choice to build global norms rather than rely on national norms was not an obvious one. The International Criminal Tribunal for the former Yugoslavia's (ICTY) Statute provided little guidance about how the judges ought to arrive at sentences, apart from the requirement that they 'have recourse to the general practice regarding prison sentences in the courts of the former Yugoslavia'. The ICTY judges could easily have interpreted this ambiguous provision to require them to follow the sentencing practices of the former Yugoslavia whenever practicable. They could have sought to ascertain and implement the applicable legal rules in the former Yugoslavia and to emulate the ways in which national judges interpreted and applied those rules. Although some aspects of national sentencing practices would have to be modified to account for the different substantive law the ICTY applied, the ICTY judges could have essentially adopted the sentencing practices national courts use for serious crimes such as murder, rape, and torture.

If the judges had viewed the ICTY as essentially a stand-in for the collapsed national courts, it seems likely they would have chosen that path. Although the Tribunal was 'international' in the sense that it was created under and applied international law and was comprised of international personnel, the judges could have conceived their role as giving voice to the temporarily voiceless national courts. Instead, the ICTY's judges, like most ICTY personnel and the international community more generally, conceived of the Tribunal as a global institution with an important role in giving voice to the global community. As a result, the judges gave limited attention to national sentencing practices, focusing instead on forging global sentencing norms. Some scholars criticize this choice, arguing the Tribunal

* James E. Beasley Professor of Law at Temple University Beasley School of Law. Professor deGuzman served as a law clerk in the Office of the Prosecutor of the International Criminal Tribunal for former Yugoslavia and as a legal adviser to the Republic of Senegal at the Rome Conference on the International Criminal Court. She has a PhD from the National University of Ireland's Irish Center for Human Rights, a JD from Yale Law School, an MALD from the Fletcher School of Law and Diplomacy, and a BSFS from Georgetown University's School of Foreign Service.

Margaret M. deGuzman, *Punishing for Humanity* In: *Legacies of the International Criminal Tribunal for the Former Yugoslavia*. Edited by: Carsten Stahn, Carmel Agius, Serge Brammertz, Colleen Rohan, Oxford University Press (2020). © The Several Contributors
DOI: 10.1093/oso/9780198862956.003.0021

was insufficiently attentive to defendants' right to prior notice of applicable penalties.[1] Although some defendants may have suffered more punishment than they would have under applicable national law, it is far from clear that this was unfair.[2] Moreover, the ICTY's choice to develop global norms enabled it to build a global sentencing legacy for other international courts to follow. This chapter begins by explaining how the ICTY came to focus on building global sentencing norms, before briefly exploring some of the norms that emerged from the ICTY's sentencing practice. The conclusion highlights the impact of this legacy on the sentencing practices of other courts.

20.2 Privileging Global Norms

The ICTY's Statute provided the judges with little indication of how they should determine sentences. In addition to requiring the judges to 'have recourse' to national sentencing practices, the Statute's short 'penalties' provision limited punishment to imprisonment and instructed judges to 'take into account such factors as the gravity of offence and the individual circumstances of the convicted person'.[3] A provision on '[e]nforcement of sentences' stipulated that imprisonment would be served in the prisons of States that agree to accept convicted persons; and another on '[p]ardon or commutation of sentences' asserted that when a convicted person is eligible for pardon or commutation under the laws of the state where the person is imprisoned, the State must notify the Tribunal, and the Tribunal's President, after consulting the judges, would decide the matter 'on the basis of the interests of justice and the general principles of law'.[4] Finally, the Tribunal's Rules of Procedure and Evidence specified that, in addition to the factors listed in the Statute, the judges must take into account 'such factors as' aggravating and mitigating circumstances, including 'substantial cooperation with the Prosecutor'.[5]

These provisions reflect a mix of national and supranational norms. On the one hand, the judges must 'take account' of national sentencing norms in the former Yugoslavia; on the other, the Statute itself conflicts with those norms by allowing lengthy prison sentences, including life imprisonment, and by disallowing the death penalty. The relevant rules in the former Yugoslavia limited courts to imposing a maximum of fifteen years in prison, a death sentence, or in death-eligible or aggravated cases, up to twenty years in prison.[6] The ICTY Statute further deviated from the laws of the former Yugoslavia by providing that the national laws of the place of imprisonment—not the former Yugoslavia—determined whether and when a convicted person was eligible for pardon or commutation, and it was the Tribunal's President who decided whether to grant such relief, not based on national law but on 'the interests of justice and the general principles of law'—ideas that resonated

[1] See S Dana, 'Beyond Retroactivity to Realizing Justice: A Theory on the Principle of Legality in International Criminal Law Sentencing' (2009) 99 Journal of Criminal Law and Criminology 857, 887–905.

[2] See W A Schabas, 'Sentencing by International Tribunals: A Human Rights Approach' (1997) 7 Duke Journal of Comparative and International Law 461, 468–83 (arguing the possibility of serious penalties for international crimes is foreseeable).

[3] Statute of the International Criminal Tribunal for the former Yugoslavia (adopted 25 May 1993 UNGA Res 827) art 24.

[4] ibid arts 27–28.

[5] Rules of Procedure and Evidence of the ICTY (adopted on 11 February 1994) 101.

[6] Criminal Code of The Socialist Federal Republic of Yugoslavia (1977) Official Gazette of the Socialist Federal Republic of Yugoslavia (SFRY) no 44/1977, ch XVI.

in international law.[7] Finally, while the Statute comported with the law of the former Yugoslavia in requiring judges to consider aggravating and mitigating circumstance, unlike that law, it specified that cooperation with the Prosecutor may be considered in mitigation.[8]

The decision to interpret 'have recourse' to mean 'consult' rather than 'apply', came in the ICTY's first sentencing judgment in the *Erdemović* case.[9] The Trial Chamber began by noting that the Criminal Code of the former Yugoslavia included war crimes and genocide, but not crimes against humanity, the crimes to which Erdemović had pled guilty.[10] For those crimes which the Chamber deemed similar to crimes against humanity, the penalty in the Code was five to fifteen years, or twenty for aggravated or death-eligible cases. [11] The Trial Chamber drew from these provisions the 'principle' 'that the code reserves its most severe penalties for crimes, including genocide, which are of a similar nature to crimes against humanity'.[12] The Trial Chamber interpreted the ICTY Statute to also require an examination of the relevant national case law,[13] but it found no decisions involving cases it considered similar to the one before the Tribunal. More generally, the Chamber asserted that it was unable to obtain sufficient information about national cases to take them into consideration in determining sentence length.[14] The Chamber concluded: 'in light of the limited number of decisions available, the Trial Chamber cannot draw significant conclusions as to the sentencing practices for crimes against humanity in the former Yugoslavia'.[15] The Chamber then engaged in a rather confused discussion of *nullum crimen sine lege* and *nulla poena sine lege*, wherein it seemed to conflate these distinct principles,[16] before concluding:

> Given the absence of meaningful national judicial precedents and the legal and practical obstacles to a strict application of the reference to the general practice regarding prison sentences in the courts of the former Yugoslavia, the Trial Chamber considers that the reference to this practice can be used for guidance, but is not binding ... Whenever possible, the International Tribunal will review the relevant legal practices of the former Yugoslavia *but will not be bound in any way by those practices in the penalties it establishes and the sentences it imposes* for the crimes falling within its jurisdiction.[17]

Having reached the conclusion that it was not bound to follow the sentencing practices of the former Yugoslavia, the Trial Chamber went on to elaborate its own views on various sentencing principles, including that 'when crimes against humanity are involved, the issue of the existence of any aggravating circumstances does not warrant consideration'.[18] In its discussion of various potentially applicable factors, such as the relevance of the fact

[7] cf Rome Statute of the International Criminal Court (signed 17 July 1998) 2187 UNTS 38544 art 38.

[8] J Leinwand, 'Punishing Horrific Crime: Reconciling International Prosecution with National Sentencing Practices' (2009) 40 columbia Human Rights Law Review 799, 819–20 (citingS K Ivković, 'Justice by the International Criminal Tribunal for the Former Yugoslavia' (2001) 37 stanford Journal of International Law 255, 288).

[9] *Prosecutor v Erdemović* (Trial Chamber Sentencing Judgment) IT-96-22-T (29 November 1996) para 33.

[10] ibid para 34.

[11] ibid paras 34–35.

[12] ibid para 35.

[13] ibid para 37.

[14] ibid.

[15] ibid.

[16] Dana (n 1) 890–91.

[17] *Prosecutor v Erdemović* (n 9) paras 39–40 (emphasis added).

[18] ibid para 45.

that Erdemović was following superior orders, the Chamber failed to interrogate the law of the former Yugoslavia, turning instead to international precedent, in particular to the Nuremberg judgment.[19]

In elaborating the 'purposes and functions of the penalty', the *Erdemović* Trial Chamber looked first to international sources and then to national systems generally before mentioning the purposes elaborated in the Criminal Code of the former Yugoslavia.[20] The Chamber justified this lack of emphasis on the purposes in the Criminal Code of the former Yugoslavia in part by reference to the extraordinary nature of the crimes the ICTY adjudicated. According to the Chamber, caution should be exercised in applying the purposes of national criminal law because national courts 'punish all sorts of offences, usually ordinary crimes'.[21] Thus, although it mentioned purposes elaborated in some cases from the former Yugoslavia, it did not seem to give them great weight.[22] After asserting that the courts of the former Yugoslavia emphasized the preventive role, the Trial Chamber adopted both deterrence and retribution as guiding principles for sentencing at the Tribunal.[23] With regard to the expressive function of punishment, the Chamber focused not on expressing norms to the victims and perpetrators of the crimes, but rather on the international community's norm expression:

> On the basis of the above, the International Tribunal sees public reprobation and stigmatisation *by the international community*, which would thereby express its indignation over heinous crimes and denounce the perpetrators, as one of the essential functions of a prison sentence for a crime against humanity.[24]

The ICTY's first sentencing judgment thus forged a new path: sentences would largely be determined on the basis of the judges' views about how best to effectuate global condemnation and inflict just punishment. When they considered such factors as Erdemović's remorse, cooperation with the prosecutor, and 'factors relating to personality', they made no attempt to examine relevant norms in national courts. Although the sentence the Trial Chamber ultimately awarded Erdemović—ten years in prison—conformed with the relevant rules in the Criminal Code of the former Yugoslavia, the Chamber did not link the sentence to those rules.[25]

Subsequent trial chambers generally followed the approach taken in *Erdemović*. Although they began their decisions by acknowledging their obligation to 'take account' of the sentencing practices of the former Yugoslavia and sometimes included a discussion of relevant practices, they also asserted their ultimate discretion. In *Blaškić*, the Trial Chamber held that the sentencing practices of the former Yugoslavia were 'indicative and not binding',[26] and the *Kupreškić* Chamber affirmed it was not bound to follow those

[19] ibid para 45.
[20] ibid paras 59–61.
[21] ibid para 62.
[22] ibid para 63.
[23] ibid para 64 ('In the light of this review of international and national precedents relating to crimes against humanity (or crimes of the same nature), the Trial Chamber deems most important the concepts of deterrence and retribution').
[24] ibid para 65 (emphasis added).
[25] *Prosecutor v Erdemović* (Trial Chamber Sentencing Judgment) IT-96-22-T*bis* (5 March 1998) para 23.
[26] *Prosecutor v Blaškić* (Trial Chamber Judgment) IT-95-14-T (3 March 2000) para 759. See also *Prosecutor v Aleksovski* (Trial Chamber Judgment) IT-95-14/1-T (25 June 1999) para 242 (stating that the sentencing practices of the former Yugoslavia 'may be used merely as a guide'); *Prosecutor v Erdemović* (n 9) para 40 ('Whenever

practices.[27] Some chambers took more serious notice of the sentencing norms of the former Yugoslavia. For instance, in the *Furundžija* case, the Trial Chamber adopted sentencing factors, many of which were contained in the Yugoslavian Penal Code.[28] However, their application of those principles did not draw seriously on the practice of the courts of the former Yugoslavia.[29] Scholars who have studied the ICTY's sentencing practice have mostly concluded that the Tribunal did not give significant weight to the sentencing practices of the former Yugoslavia in reaching sentencing decisions.[30] As Barbora Holá notes, most decisions simply list sentencing factors 'with no detailed discussion as to their particular effect on sentence severity'.[31]

Some ICTY sentencing judgments are explicit about their goal of promoting global sentencing norms. The Trial Chamber in the *Obrenović* case stated:

> As the Tribunal is applying international law, it must have due regard for the impact of its application of internationally recognised norms and principles on the global level. Thus, a trial chamber must consider its obligations to the individual accused in light of its responsibility to ensure that it is upholding the purposes and principles of international criminal law.[32]

Likewise, the *Kupreškić* Trial Chamber asserted that part of the purpose of sentencing at the ICTY was 'to strengthen the resolve of all involved not to allow crimes against international humanitarian law to be committed as well as to create trust in and respect for the developing system of international criminal justice'.[33]

Another way in which the ICTY judges expressed their intention to promote international objectives was in their interpretation of the goal of retribution. Many of the Trial

possible, the International Tribunal will review the relevant legal practices of the former Yugoslavia but will not be bound in any way by those practices in the penalties it establishes and the sentences it imposes for the crimes falling within its jurisdiction').

27 *Prosecutor v Zoran Kupreškić* (Trial Chamber Judgment) IT-95-16-T (14 January 2000) para 840.

28 *Prosecutor v Furundžija* (Trial Chamber Judgment) IT-95-17/1-T (10 December 1998) para 285. See also S Glickman, 'Victims' Justice: Legitimizing the Sentencing Regime of the International Criminal Court' (2004) 43 Columbia Journal of Transnational Law 229, 254–55.

29 *Prosecutor v Furundžija* (n 28) paras 292–96 (out of a page and a half discussion of sentencing factors, only two paragraphs address the practice in the former Yugoslavia). See also *Prosecutor v Miodrag Jokić* (Trial Chamber Sentencing Judgment) IT-01-42/1-S (18 March 2004) paras 104–11 (acknowledging that the SFRY laws are important for sentencing, but not including them in the discussion of aggravating and mitigating factors); *Prosecutor v Galić* (Trial Chamber Judgment and Opinion) IT-98-29-T (5 December 2003) paras 762–68 (the two-page discussion of the defendant's sentence does not explain whether or how the SFRY sentencing laws were being applied).

30 See B Holá, C Bijleveld, and A Smeulers, 'Consistency of International Sentencing: ICTY and ICTR Case Study' (2012) 9 European Journal of Criminology 539, 541 ('Reference to local practice has been construed restrictively by the tribunals, and judges cite applicable domestic provisions mostly as a formality'); K Ambos, *Treatise on International Criminal Law, Vol 2: The Crimes and Sentencing* (OUP 2014) 282 (asserting that international tribunals merely pay 'lip service' to domestic sentencing practices).

31 B Holá, 'Consistency and Pluralism of International Sentencing: An Empirical Assessment of the ICTY and ICTR Practice' in E van Sliedregt and S Vasiliev (eds), *Pluralism in International Criminal Law* (OUP 2014) 197; But see Y Shany, 'Seeking Domestic Help: The Role of Domestic Criminal Law in Legitimizing the Work of International Criminal Tribunals' (2013) 11 Journal of International Criminal Justice 5, 21 ('In actuality, the ICTY's sentencing judgments have tended to afford some consideration to the scale of penalties in the Penal Code of the Socialist Federal Republic of Yugoslavia (SFRY), and have employed, by and large, the sentencing-related method of analysis recognized in the former Yugoslavia').

32 *Prosecutor v Obrenović* (Trial Chamber Sentencing Judgment) IT-02-60/2-S (10 December 2003) para 47.

33 *Prosecutor v Zoran Kupreškić* (n 27) para 848.

Chambers noted retribution as an important goal of sentencing at the ICTY. Retribution is typically considered a deontological goal with no requirement of positive consequences in the world beyond the convicted person receiving their 'just deserts'. The judges of the ICTY, however, took what might be termed an expressive view of retribution, claiming that the purpose of retribution is, in the words of the *Aleksovski* Appeals Chamber, 'not fulfilling a desire for revenge but . . . duly *expressing the outrage of the international community* at these crimes'.[34]

The ICTY's global norms orientation in sentencing is also evident in the absence of any statutory rule or other norm allowing convicted persons to appeal their sentences on the grounds they violated the sentencing practices of the former Yugoslavia. The ICTY shared an Appeals Chamber with the International Criminal Tribunal for Rwanda, which, in itself, probably made it less likely to base its review on norms of the former Yugoslavia. The Appeals Chamber was generally reluctant to entertain appeals claims based on comparisons to other cases. To the extent it considered such claims, the comparisons were to other international cases, not cases from the former Yugoslavia.[35]

Although the judges paid limited attention to the sentencing norms of the former Yugoslavia, the sentences they imposed did not diverge widely from those typically imposed in the courts of the former Yugoslavia. As Barbora Holá's chapter in this volume demonstrates, the sentences are fairly vertically consistent.[36] The ICTY judges imposed life sentences in a few cases, but most ICTY sentences were in the fifteen to twenty-year range permitted in the Criminal Code of the former Yugoslavia.[37] Although the provisions of the Criminal Code may have had some influence on these outcomes,[38] the judges' general orientation toward global norm creation suggests they chose sentences they viewed as comporting with widely accepted sentencing practices around the world and with international human rights law.[39] The next section elaborates on some of the global sentencing norms that emerged from the ICTY's sentencing practice.

20.3 Global Sentencing Norms

The ICTY operated on a fairly blank slate as it sought to craft global sentencing norms for international crimes. The International Military Tribunals at Nuremberg and Tokyo had sentenced a small number of convicted persons for such crimes, putting some of them to death and imposing life sentences on many others.[40] Moreover, the judgments those

[34] *Prosecutor v Aleksovski* (Appeals Chamber Judgment) IT-95-14/1-A (24 March 2000) para 185 (emphasis added).

[35] J J Clark, 'Zero to Life: Sentencing Appeals at the International Criminal Tribunals for the Former Yugoslavia and Rwanda' (2008) 96 Georgetown Law Journal 1685, 1698–99.

[36] See B Holá, Chapter 21 in this book. See also Leinwand (n 8) 815 (stating that the ICTY generally showed reluctance to depart from the twenty-year maximum sentence under the former Yugoslavia's criminal code).

[37] See S Beresford, 'Unshackling the Paper Tiger: The Sentencing Practices of the ad hoc International Criminal Tribunals for the Former Yugoslavia and Rwanda' (2001) 1 International Criminal Law Review 33, 49.

[38] Shany (n 31) 21.

[39] For a discussion of the importance of human rights law in international sentencing see M M deGuzman, 'Harsh Justice for International Crimes?' (2014) 39 Yale Journal of International Law 1, 28.

[40] M Futamura, *War Crimes Tribunals and Transitional Justice: The Tokyo Trial and the Nuremburg Legacy* (Taylor & Francis e-Library 2007) 154, Table A.4 (indicating that twenty-five defendants were sentenced at the Tokyo Trial, of which sixteen received life sentences and seven were sentenced to be hanged); K J Heller, *The Nuremberg Military Tribunals and the Origins of International Criminal Law* (OUP 2011) 314–22 (noting that of

Tribunals rendered provided little in the way of justification,[41] nor did they elaborate in detail on the purposes they sought to effectuate through sentencing.[42]

What then are some of the 'global sentencing norms' the ICTY helped forge? Although it is too soon to build a definitive list, and any such list will change over time in any event, this section discusses a few of the sentencing norms the ICTY generated that are likely to continue to influence future international courts and tribunals. Indeed, as the concluding section shows, some of these norms have already been used by other such institutions, and even by national courts adjudicating international crimes.

20.3.1 (Mostly) Rejecting Harsh Punishment

The ICTY's sentences tended to be rather lenient compared to sentences in many national contexts.[43] Some commentators have criticized the Tribunal for this relative leniency.[44] But a strong argument can be made that the ICTY's judges accurately identified the preferences of the 'international community'—or at least many of its members—when it declined generally to inflict very long prison sentences. When representatives of most of the world's States negotiated the Rome Statute of the International Criminal Court (ICC), they too rejected very long prison sentences. The Rome Statute limits terms of imprisonment to a maximum of thirty years, except in extraordinary cases when a life sentence in permitted.[45] Moreover, some of the drafters of the Rome Statute viewed life sentences as too severe, and this perspective contributed to the inclusion in the Statute of a provision allowing for early release.[46] The ICTY's sentences both reflected and helped to craft this evolving norm of relative leniency. Out of eighty-two final sentences, only five were life sentences, the median term was fifteen years, and the average was 15.54.[47] The ICTY held that early release could

the original sentences handed down at the Nuremberg Trials, nineteen defendants received life sentences and twenty-five were sentenced to death).

[41] A M Danner, 'Constructing a Hierarchy of Crimes in International Criminal Law Sentencing' (2001) 87 Virginia Law Review 415, 418 ('The judgments from the Nuremberg and Tokyo Tribunals span thousands of pages, but their sentences were given in terse one line declarations, with little or no explanation of the bases for the distinctions between the various sentences imposed on the defendants'); M A Drumbl, *Atrocity, Punishment, and International Law* (CUP 2007) 50; Heller (n 40) 313–14.

[42] See *Prosecutor v Erdemović* (n 9) para 59 ('The only precedents in international criminal law relevant for the International Tribunal—the judgements of the International Military Tribunals at Nuremberg and Tokyo—do not expressly state the purposes sought in imposing sentences for war crimes or crimes against humanity').

[43] M B Harmon and F Gaynor, 'Ordinary Sentences for Extraordinary Crimes' (2007) 5 Journal of International Criminal Justice 683, 686.

[44] See A N Keller, 'Punishment for Violations of International Criminal Law: An Analysis of Sentencing of the ICTY and ICTR' (2001) 12 Indiana International and Comparative Law Review 53, 63; J Ohlin, 'Proportional Sentences at the ICTY' in B Swart, A Zahar, and G Sluiter (eds), *The Legacy of the International Criminal Tribunal for the Former Yugoslavia* (OUP 2011).

[45] Rome Statute of the International Criminal Court (signed 17 July 1998) 2187 UNTS 38544 art 77(1). The inclusion of life sentences in the Rome Statute has been criticized as contrary to evolving human rights norms. See E Gumboh, 'The Penalty of Life Imprisonment Under International Criminal Law' (2011) 11 African Human Rights Journal 75, 92.

[46] See 'Final Act of the UN Diplomatic Conference of Plenipotentiaries on the Establishment of an International Criminal Court' (17 July 1998) UN DOC A/CONF183/13 (Vol III) 62 fn 203 (noting that the addition of a provision requiring mandatory consideration of early release arose in part to meet concerns delegations raised about the severity of life sentences or lengthy imprisonment).

[47] M A Drumbl, 'And Where the Offence is, Let the Great Axe Fall: Sentencing under International Criminal Law' in P Kastner (ed), *International Law in Context* (Routledge 2018) 309; see also J W Doherty and R H Steinberg, 'Punishment and Policy in International Criminal Sentencing: An Empirical Study' (2016) 110 American Journal

be granted after a convicted person had served two thirds of the sentence, even when the sentence is life imprisonment.[48] Although the norms of the former Yugoslavia may have contributed to these outcomes as discussed above, the judges' general focus on global objectives suggests they intended the sentences they imposed to reflect global norms.

20.3.2 Adopting (Mostly) Consequentialist Purposes of Punishment

Another area where the ICTY developed norms is in identifying the purposes of punishment. Although the sentencing judgments were not uniform in their discussions of goals, most asserted that the two principal purposes are deterrence and retribution.[49] These two goals were given roughly equal importance. According to the Appeals Chamber: '[Deterrence] "must not be accorded undue prominence in the overall assessment of the sentences to be imposed on persons convicted by the International Tribunal". An equally important factor is retribution'.[50] The judgments gave significantly less weight, if any, to other standard purposes of punishment, such as rehabilitation, incapacitation, and restoration.[51]

Notably, the judges were not clear about whether they intended a deontological or consequentialist form of retribution. Retribution is usually understood as the view that people ought to be punished according to their 'just deserts' simply because that is the right thing to do. Many theories exist to justify the infliction of retributive punishment, including, for instance, that punishment exacts appropriate revenge[52] or reaffirms the moral worth of crime victims.[53] Most of these theories reflect the belief that retribution is a deontological good; no positive consequences of punishment are necessary to justify its imposition. This theory is often contrasted with consequentialist theories such as deterrence and rehabilitation, which look to one or more socially desirable outcomes to justify punishment. A third category of justifications is expressive rationales. These assert that punishment is justified when, and to the extent, it expresses appropriate moral and social norms, such as condemnation of criminal conduct.[54] Some expressive theories are deontological—the expression is

of International Law 49, 73–74; A Smeulers, B Holá, and T van den Berg, 'Sixty-Five Years of International Criminal Justice: The Facts and Figures' in D L Rothe, J D Meernik, and T Ingadóttir (eds), *The Realities of International Criminal Justice* (Martinus Nijhoff 2013) 22–23.

[48] *Prosecutor v Galić* (Reasons for the President's Decision to Deny the Early Release of Stanislav Galić And Decision on Prosecution Motion) MICT-14-83-ES (23 June 2015) para 27.

[49] *Prosecutor v Aleksovski* (n 34) para 185 ('The Appeals Chamber accepts the general importance of deterrence as a consideration in sentencing for international crimes ... [a]n equally important factor is retribution').

[50] ibid.

[51] See *Prosecutor v Delalić* et al (Appeals Chamber Judgment) IT-96-21-A (20 February 2001) para 806 ('[A]lthough rehabilitation ... should be considered as a relevant factor, it is not one which should be given undue weight').

[52] R Posner, 'Retribution and Related Concepts of Punishment' (1980) 9 Journal of Legal Studies 71, 82.

[53] H Morris, 'Persons and Punishment' (1968) 2 Monist 475, 476–79 ('Justice—that is punishing such individuals—restores the equilibrium of benefits and burdens by taking from the individual what he owes, that is, exacting the debt'); J Murphy and J Hampton, *Forgiveness and Mercy* (CUP 1988) 125–26 ('[R]etributive punishment is the defeat of the wrongdoer at the hands of the victim ... that symbolizes the correct relative value of wrongdoer and victim [and] is a symbol that is conceptually required to reaffirm a victim's equal worth in the face of a challenge to it').

[54] R A Duff, *Trials and Punishments* (CUP 1986) 267 ('Punishment aims to express to [the criminal] the condemnation which her crime warrants').

considered good in itself, and others are consequentialist—expression is valuable because it produces beneficial consequences in the world.[55]

The ICTY judges adopted what might be termed an expressive approach to retribution. The Appeals Chamber stated: '[Retribution] is not to be understood as fulfilling a desire for revenge but as duly *expressing the outrage of the international community* at these crimes'.[56] Similarly, the *Bralo* Trial Chamber described retribution as 'the concept that whatever sentence is imposed on a convicted person amounts to an expression of condemnation by the international community at the horrific nature of the crimes committed, and must therefore be proportionate to his specific conduct'.[57] Such statements leave open the question whether expressing the outrage of the international community is an important good in itself or is instead as a means of crime prevention. In some judgments, however, retribution is framed as part of the broader preventive goals of the Tribunal, giving it a consequentialist feel. For instance, the *Nikolić* Trial Chamber asserted:

> In light of the purposes of the Tribunal and international humanitarian law generally, retribution is better understood as the expression of condemnation and outrage of *the international community* at such grave violations of, and disregard for, fundamental human rights at a time that people may be at their most vulnerable, namely during armed conflict. It is also recognition of the harm and suffering caused to the *victims*.[58]

Given that the goals of the Tribunal and of international humanitarian law centre around prevention, this framing of retribution as part of that broader mission rings consequentialist. Although this utilitarian understanding of retribution does not comport with the most common usages of the term,[59] it likely reflects emerging global values. While no global consensus on the purposes of punishment exists, global human rights norms support an approach that, unlike standard retributivist theories, balances considerations of desert with other values including, in particular, the human dignity of the defendant.[60]

20.3.3 Centring Gravity

The ICTY's sentencing judgments reveal the centrality of the concept of gravity to sentencing at the Tribunal. According to the Appeals Chamber, the gravity of the offense is 'the

[55] V Tadros, *The Ends of Harm: The Moral Foundations of Criminal Law* (OUP 2011) 27 (describing the 'communicative' function of punishment as having either intrinsic or instrumental value).

[56] *Prosecutor v Aleksovski* (n 34) para 185 (emphasis added).

[57] *Prosecutor v Bralo* (Trial Chamber Sentencing Judgment) IT-95-17-S (7 December 2005) para 22. See also *Prosecutor v Tolimir* (Trial Chamber Judgment) IT-05-88/2-T (12 December 2012) para 1209 ('Retribution is not to be understood as a desire for revenge but as an expression of the outrage of the international community towards these crimes').

[58] *Prosecutor v Nikolić* (Trial Chamber Judgment) IT-02-60/1 (2 December 2003) para 86 (emphasis added).

[59] As Ralph Henham writes, 'denunciation does not imply communicative aspirations', R Henham, 'Philosophical Issues in International Sentencing' (2003) 1 Journal of International Criminal Justice 64, 76.

[60] See D Koller, 'The Faith of The International Criminal Lawyer' (2008) 40 New York University Journal of International Law and Politics 1019, 1026 ('[A]rguments from retribution are fundamentally inconsistent with the basic dictates of international human rights law that underlie international criminal law'); M Tonry, 'Punishment and Human Dignity: Sentencing Principles for Twenty-First Century America' (2018) 47 Crime and Justice 119 (arguing that the focus of many US scholars on retribution is out of step with punishment theory in other western countries).

primary consideration when imposing a sentence and is the "litmus test" for determining the appropriate sentence'.[61] Although, as I have written elsewhere, gravity determinations tend to be quite subjective,[62] some studies have shown that ICTY sentences reflect a relatively consistent approach to the concept. According to Barbora Holá et al, ICTY sentences demonstrate 'a clear gradation of severity based on the protected interest violated by the defendant's conduct' with offenses against life attracting the highest sentences, offenses against human integrity garnering the second highest, and offenses against property the least severe.[63] Additionally, crimes committed with discriminatory motives tend to be treated as more serious and receive more punishment than non-discriminatory crimes.[64]

The importance of gravity for sentencing purposes is often linked to the need to reflect the offender's culpability appropriately.[65] Although the ICTY rejected the idea that a formal hierarchy of seriousness exists among international crimes,[66] the Tribunal's sentencing practice tends to reflect such a gradation, with sentences for genocide often exceeding those for crimes against humanity, which in turn exceed those for war crimes.[67] Additional factors that contribute to the gravity assessment include victim vulnerability, particularly for crimes involving women and children,[68] and 'the scale and brutality of the crimes; the convicted person's position of authority and the overall impact of the crime upon the victims and their relatives'.[69]

The abuse of a position of leadership is a particularly important gravity factor. ICTY judges frequently cited leadership role as a basis to increase or reduce sentences.[70] It is not the position of authority in itself that affects sentences, but rather the use the leader made of that position.[71] For instance, in the *Babić* case, the Trial Chamber found that the accused used his position as a regional political leader to further criminal conduct, including by making 'inflammatory speeches during public events and in the media which prepared the ground for the Serb population to accept that their goals could be achieved through acts of persecution ...'.[72] The Appeals Chamber affirmed that this was appropriately counted in aggravation.[73] The judges also sometimes took low position into account in mitigation.[74] Barbora Holá has called this a 'principle of gradation' that 'mandates judges to consider a relative significance of a defendant in the broader context of the conflict as such'.[75]

[61] *Prosecutor v Nikolić* (Judgment on Sentencing Appeal) IT-02-60/1-A (8 March 2006) para 11.
[62] M M deGuzman, 'How Serious are International Crimes? The Gravity Problem in International Criminal Law' (2012) 51 Columbia Journal of Transnational Law 18.
[63] B Holá, A Smeulers, and C Bijleveld, 'International Sentencing Facts and Figures: Sentencing Practice at the ICTY and ICTR' (2011) 9 Journal of International Criminal Justice 411, 426.
[64] ibid 424; *Prosecutor v Nikolić* (n 58) para 105. See also *Prosecutor v Blaškić* (n 26) para 785.
[65] See *Prosecutor v Delalić* et al (n 51) para 430.
[66] *Prosecutor v Tadić* (Judgment in Sentencing Appeals) IT-94-1-A (26 January 2000) para 69.
[67] S D'Ascoli, *Sentencing in International Criminal Law* (Hart Publishing 2011) 225; Doherty and Steinberg (n 47) 56; Holá et al (n 63) 422.
[68] *Prosecutor v Kunarac* et al (Trial Chamber Judgment) IT-96-23-T and IT-96-23/1-T (22 February 2001) para 858; *Prosecutor v Blaškić* (n 26) para 786.
[69] *Prosecutor v Tolimir* (n 57) para 1215.
[70] *Prosecutor v Blagojević* (Appeals Chamber Judgment) IT-02-60-A (9 May 2007) para 324.
[71] *Prosecutor v Hadžihasanović and Kubura* (Appeals Chamber Judgment) IT-01-47-A (22 April 2008) para 320.
[72] *Prosecutor v Milan Babić* (Judgment on Sentencing Appeal) IT-03-72-A (18 July 2005) para 81.
[73] ibid.
[74] *Prosecutor v Tadić* (n 66) para 56; *Prosecutor v Limaj* (Trial Chamber Judgment) IT-03-66-T (30 November 2005) para 732 (considering in mitigation the fact that the defendant had no leadership role).
[75] B Holá, 'Sentencing at the ICTY: Doing Justice to Complex Realities of International Crimes?' (2017) 4 Humanity <http://humanityjournal.org/wp-content/uploads/2017/07/02.-Hola-Sentencing-at-the-ICTY.pdf> accessed 16 May 2018.

Procedurally, the Appeals Chamber held that gravity must be considered in conjunction with other factors, including aggravating and mitigating circumstances, rather than in isolation, in order to identify a sentence appropriate to both the circumstances of the accused and the gravity of the crime.[76] Additionally, the judges must be careful not to double count factors as contributing to both a crime's gravity and as aggravating circumstances. As the Appeals Chamber explained in the *Krajišnik* case:

> [W]hile a Trial Chamber should strive to distinguish between the gravity of the criminal conduct and the aggravating circumstances, it might be difficult or artificial to separate the two in some cases. For instance, in the present case, Krajišnik's contribution to the crimes of the JCE is precisely his abuse of his powers and public positions; this element arguably concerns both the 'gravity of the criminal conduct' and the 'aggravating circumstances'. What is important is to avoid double-counting (i.e. no factor should be taken into account twice in sentencing)....[77]

Although these gravity norms were not always consistently interpreted or applied,[78] they constitute an important part of the ICTY's sentencing legacy.

20.3.4 Broad Judicial Discretion

The ICTY established a norm of broad judicial discretion with respect to the factors considered in sentencing. According to the Appeals Chamber: '[I]t is established practice that trial courts exercise a broad discretion in the factors they may consider on sentence'.[79] As such, the judges adopted a liberal approach to the evidence admissible for sentencing purposes. Quoting the Supreme Court of the US, the Appeals Chamber asserted that 'modern concepts individualising punishment have made it all the more necessary that a sentencing judge not be denied an opportunity to obtain pertinent information by a requirement of rigid adherence to restrictive rules of evidence properly applicable to the trial'.[80] The judges also held that it was within their discretion to determine the weight to be given to particular mitigating circumstances.[81] They assessed relevant factors holistically, weighing aggravating and mitigating circumstances along with the gravity of the crime and the role of the accused.[82]

The judges' determination that they had broad discretion in sentencing led them to consider a wide array of factors to be relevant. With respect to mitigation, the ICTY Statute and

[76] *Prosecutor v Šainović* et al (Appeals Chamber Judgment) IT-05-87-A (23 January 2014) para 1837.

[77] *Prosecutor v Krajišnik* (Appeals Chamber Judgment) IT-00-39-A (17 March 2009) para 787.

[78] B Holá, 'International Sentencing: A Game of Russian Roulette or Consistent Practice?' (Uitgeverij BoxPress, 2012) 55 ('The distinction among factors relevant to evaluate "the basic" gravity of the offence and aggravating factors is not clear-cut and the jurisprudence in this respect is inconsistent: The same factors are in some cases discussed within the assessment of the gravity of the offence, yet in other cases these factors are deemed to aggravate the sentence').

[79] *Prosecutor v Delalić* et al (n 51) para 787.

[80] ibid.

[81] ibid para 777.

[82] *Prosecutor v Jokić* (Appeals Chamber Judgment on Sentencing Appeal) IT-01-42/1-A (30 August 2005) para 67.

Rules of Procedure and Evidence listed only two factors: superior orders[83] and substantial cooperation with the Prosecutor.[84] Yet the judges identified many other factors they considered relevant to mitigation.[85] For instance, in the *Hadžihasanović* case, the Appeals Chamber affirmed the Trial Chamber's decision to take account of the offender's intelligence and good education as mitigating factors.[86] In *Tadić*, the absence of a criminal record was cited,[87] and in numerous cases, the judges took the defendants' good deeds into account.[88]

A particularly important norm the ICTY helped establish is that mitigation is available in exchange for a guilty plea and for cooperating with the Prosecutor. The rationale for mitigation for cooperation at the global level is broader than that in many national contexts. At the national level, mitigation for cooperation is generally conceived as a way to incentivize accused persons to provide evidence against other accused persons. The norm the ICTY promulgated, on the other hand, rewards cooperation in significant part for its ability to contribute to reconciliation among communities affected by conflict. As the Trial Chamber explained in the *Nikolić* case:

> The Trial Chamber finds that, in contrast to national legal systems where the reasons for mitigating a punishment on the basis of a guilty plea are of a more pragmatic nature, the rationale behind the mitigating effect of a guilty plea in this Tribunal is much broader, including the fact that the accused contributes to establishing the truth about the conflict in the former Yugoslavia and contributes to reconciliation in the affected communities. The Trial Chamber recalls that the Tribunal has the task to contribute to the 'restoration and maintenance of peace' and to ensure that serious violations of international humanitarian law are 'halted and effectively redressed'.[89]

In the *Jokić* case, the Trial Chamber found that the defendant's plea 'has the potential to strengthen the foundations for reconciliation between the peoples of the former Yugoslavia and for the restoration of a lasting peace in the region'.[90]

Surrender to the Tribunal[91] and expressions of remorse and sympathy for the victims were also considered in mitigation. Such remorse was sometimes counted even in the absence of an admission of guilt, as long as the defendant accepted 'some measure of moral blameworthiness for personal wrongdoing'.[92] Even sympathy or compassion for the victims

[83] Statute of the International Criminal Tribunal for the former Yugoslavia (adopted 25 May 1993 UNGA Res 827) art 7(4).

[84] Rules of Procedure and Evidence of the ICTY (adopted 11 February 1994) 101(b)(ii).

[85] *Prosecutor v Tolimir* (n 57) para 1228 ('Mitigating circumstances that have been identified in the jurisprudence of the Tribunal include cooperation with the Prosecution; the admission of guilt or a guilty plea; the expression of sincere remorse; sympathy, compassion or sorrow for the victims of the crimes; voluntary surrender; good behaviour while in detention; the personal and family circumstances of the convicted person; the post-conflict conduct of the convicted person; the duress under which he acted; indirect or limited participation in the commission of the crime; diminished mental responsibility; age; assistance to victims; fully complying with certain obligations, such as the terms and conditions of provisional release; and preventing others from committing crimes. Ill-health of the convicted person is to be considered as a mitigating factor only in exceptional cases').

[86] *Prosecutor v Hadžihasanović and Kubura* (n 71) para 329.

[87] *Prosecutor v Tadić* (Trial Chamber Sentencing Judgment) IT-94-1-T (14 July 1997) para 63.

[88] J Galbraith, 'The Good Deeds of International Criminal Defendants' (2012) 25 Leiden Journal of International Law 799, 806–09 (discussing cases in which good deeds were treated as mitigating factors).

[89] *Prosecutor v Dragan Nikolić* (Trial Chamber Sentencing Judgment) IT-94-2-S (18 December 2003) para 233.

[90] *Prosecutor v Miodrag Jokić* (Trial Chamber Sentencing Judgment) IT-01-42/1-S (18 March 2004) para 77.

[91] ibid para 73.

[92] *Prosecutor v Strugar* (Appeals Chamber Judgment) IT-01-42-A (17 July 2008) paras 365–66.

without remorse was considered a mitigating factor.[93] Personal circumstances were also considered in some cases, including: 'the advanced age of an accused, his good behaviour whilst at the United Nations Detention Unit, his full compliance with the terms and conditions imposed upon him during provisional release, and his family situation'.[94] Finally, post-conflict conduct was sometimes counted in mitigation. For instance, in the *Blagojević* case, the defendant was given credit for his 'active engagement in planning, managing, and organizing a system of de-mining in the army of the Republika Srpska',[95] and Biljana Plavšić, former co-president of the Serbian Republic of Bosnia and Herzegovina, received credit for contributing to peace in the region by ensuring acceptance of the Dayton Agreement.[96]

With respect to aggravating circumstances, the ICTY Statute and Rules of Procedure and Evidence provided no examples but left it entirely to the judges' discretion what would be counted. As noted above, the abuse of a position of trust was an important aggravating circumstance in some cases. Other factors included 'prolonged and systematic involvement in criminal conduct',[97] and obstruction of justice.[98] The Appeals Chamber counted 'verbal abuse' as an aggravating factor in the *Vasiljević* case.[99] Victim vulnerability also aggravated the sentence in some cases.[100] Finally, motive could be counted in aggravation or mitigation. As the Trial Chamber in the *Delalić* case explained:

> For instance, where the accused is found to have committed the offence charged with cold, calculated premeditation, suggestive of revenge against the individual victim or group to which the victim belongs, such circumstances necessitate the imposition of aggravated punishment. On the other hand, if the accused is found to have committed the offence charged reluctantly and under the influence of group pressure and, in addition, demonstrated compassion towards the victim or the group to which the victim belongs, these are certainly mitigating factors which the Trial Chamber will take into consideration in the determination of the appropriate sentence.[101]

In sum, the ICTY established norms of broad judicial discretion in sentencing and identified a wide array of factors to be taken into account holistically in allocating punishment.

20.4 Conclusion

The ICTY's judges chose to forge new global norms rather than adhere to, or even be strongly guided by, the sentencing norms of the former Yugoslavia. The ICTY Statute itself diverged from national norms in some respects, in particular by rejecting the death penalty, but also required the judges to consult national practices in determining sentences. The judges interpreted this requirement loosely, reserving to themselves a wide discretion that

93 ibid.
94 *Prosecutor v Miodrag Jokić* (Trial Chamber Sentencing Judgment) IT-01-42/1-S (18 March 2004) para 100.
95 *Prosecutor v Blagojević and Jokić* (Appeals Chamber Judgment) IT-02-60-A (9 May 2007) para 328.
96 *Prosecutor v Plavšić* (Sentencing Judgment) T-00-39&40/1-S (27 February 2003) para 94.
97 *Prosecutor v Popović* (Appeals Chamber Judgment) IT-05-88-A (30 January 2015) para 2038.
98 ibid para 2046.
99 *Prosecutor v Vasiljević* (Appeals Chamber Judgment) IT-98-32-A (25 February 2004) para 161.
100 *Prosecutor v Deronjić* (Judgment on Sentencing Appeal) IT-02-61-A (20 July 2005) para 127.
101 *Prosecutor v Delalić* (Trial Chamber Judgment) IT-96-21-T (16 November 1998) para 1235.

enabled them to identify a range of global sentencing objectives and factors to apply in pursuit of those objectives.

As a result of this global focus, ICTY sentencing jurisprudence has contributed significantly to the process of building global sentencing norms. The sentencing norms created at the ICTY have already had a substantial influence on other tribunals, including, most importantly, the ICC. The sentencing provisions of the Rome Statute and the ICC Rules of Procedure draw significantly on the norms developed at the ICTY. The ICC's judges have followed ICTY jurisprudence, for instance, in holding that the gravity of the offense 'is a principal consideration in imposing a sentence'.[102] Like the ICTY judges, ICC judges have emphasized their discretion to determine relevant factors in the gravity analysis as well as aggravating circumstances.[103] ICC judges have cited ICTY judgments liberally in support of their gravity analyses,[104] and for their holding that gravity factors cannot be double counted as aggravating factors.[105] Other ICTY holdings cited in ICC sentencing judgments include that admission of guilt can be a mitigating circumstance,[106] that efforts to promote peace and reconciliation can be counted in mitigation,[107] and that statements of remorse can affect sentencing.[108]

Other international tribunals have also relied on the ICTY's sentencing jurisprudence. In the *Taylor* case, the Special Court for Sierra Leone cited several ICTY decisions in support of its gravity analysis.[109] In sentencing a defendant for contempt, a judge of the Special Tribunal for Lebanon noted:

> I am also guided by the well-established sentencing practice of the International Criminal Tribunal for the former Yugoslavia ('ICTY') in contempt matters. I agree with the ICTY's case-law that the most important factors in determining the appropriate penalty in a contempt case are the gravity of the conduct and the need to deter repetition and similar conduct by others.[110]

Even the State courts of Bosnia and Herzegovina have relied on ICTY jurisprudence regarding the relevance of various sentencing factors.[111] In sum, the ICTY's efforts to forge global sentencing norms have helped to build a foundation that other international courts, and perhaps some national courts, are likely to follow for the foreseeable future.

[102] *Prosecutor v Bemba* (Decision on Sentence pursuant to Article 76 of the Statute) ICC-01/05-01/08 (21 June 2016) para 15.

[103] ibid.

[104] ibid fns 43–48.

[105] *Prosecutor v Lubanga* (Decision on Sentence pursuant to Article 76 of the Statute) ICC-01/04-01/06 (10 July 2012) para 35.

[106] *Prosecutor v Al-Mahdi* (Judgment and Sentence) ICC-01/12-01/15 (27 September 2016) para 100.

[107] *Prosecutor v Katanga* (Decision on Sentence pursuant to Article 76 of the Statute) ICC-01/04-01/07 (23 May 2014) para 91 (citing *Prosecutor v Blagojević and Jokić* (Trial Chamber Judgment) IT-02-60-T (17 January 2005) paras 858–60).

[108] ibid para 117 (citing *Prosecutor v Dragan Nikolić* (Sentencing Judgment) IT-94-2-S (18 December 2003) para 242).

[109] *Prosecutor v Taylor* (Sentencing Judgment) SCSL-03-01-T (30 May 2012) paras 19–20, fns 27–36.

[110] *Prosecutor v Akhbar Beirut SAL* (Reasons for Sentencing Judgment) STL-14-06/S/CJ (5 September 2016) para 15.

[111] Y Ronen, *Bosnia and Herzegovina: The Interaction Between the ICTY and Domestic Courts in Adjudicating International Crimes* (DOMAC 2011) 54–56.

21
Vertical Inconsistency of International Sentencing? The ICTY and Domestic Courts in Bosnia and Herzegovina

Barbora Holá[*, **]

... whether you are a princess or a prostitute, whether you are the President of the United States or the President of Liberia, the law is above you. That should be the guiding principle. That is the essence, we submit, of the rule of law. Whether that, however, currently is the case is a matter of debate.[1]

21.1 Introduction

The law is above all. And everyone is equal before the law. At least in theory, the principles of equality before the law, fair trial, equality of punishment and its impact on convicts and prisoners count among the fundamental human rights. Amongst others, they require punishment to be 'proportionate' to the crime committed and sentences to be 'consistent'. Ideally, similar offenders convicted of comparable crimes committed under similar circumstances should be punished similarly.[2] However, as with any other ideal, realization of this seemingly noble goal is complex, difficult, and challenging, even within a single legal system.[3] Consistency of punishment becomes even more complex where perpetrators of the same international crimes, committed within the same conflict, are prosecuted by different courts. These courts are governed by different laws and apply different punishment goals, principles, and factors. In such circumstances, disparities can easily emerge, even if legally justifiable within each particular legal system. Perpetrators suspected of international crimes committed during the Balkan wars in the 1990s have been prosecuted not only at

* Senior Researcher at the NSCR and Associate Professor at the Department of Criminal Law and Criminology at VU University of Amsterdam and co-director of CICJ.

** This research was funded by the Dutch Organization for Scientific Research (NWO). The author would like to thank Almir Maljevic, Mirza Buljubasic, Ademir Durakovic, Ljubisa Mandic, and the OSCE for research assistance during field work and data gathering.

1 C Griffiths in *Prosecutor v Charles Taylor* (Transcript of Hearing) SCSL-2003-01-T (9 March 2011) 49389.

2 S D'Ascoli, *Sentencing in International Criminal Law. The UN* Ad Hoc *Tribunals and Future Perspectives for the ICC* (Hart Publishing 2011) 30.

3 This chapter, however, shies away from any assessment of desirability of consistency of punishment/sentencing for international crimes within a legal system or across different ones, nor assumes any legal standards in this respect. It approaches sentencing and punishment as an empirical legal phenomenon and uses 'consistency of punishment/sentencing' in a descriptive sense, not as a normative criterion or a legal principle. The aim of the chapter is not to argue 'for' or 'against' consistency of punishment in international criminal justice, it analyses the empirical reality of sentencing.

Barbora Holá, *Vertical Inconsistency of International Sentencing? The ICTY and Domestic Courts in Bosnia and Herzegovina* In: *Legacies of the International Criminal Tribunal for the Former Yugoslavia.* Edited by: Carsten Stahn, Carmel Agius, Serge Brammertz, Colleen Rohan, Oxford University Press (2020). © The Several Contributors DOI: 10.1093/oso/9780198862956.003.0022

the United Nations International Criminal Tribunal for the former Yugoslavia (ICTY), but also, and predominantly, by courts in the successor countries of the former Yugoslavia, including Bosnia and Herzegovina (Bosnia, BiH).[4] Both legal scholars and the general public assume—on the basis of mainly anecdotal evidence—that sentencing of international crimes at the ICTY and at domestic courts has been widely divergent.[5] As the so-called 'most responsible' are tried, convicted, and sentenced by the ICTY, their apparently more lenient sentences easily fuel ideas of those most responsible getting off the lightest. Indeed, victims of international crimes have consistently criticized the ICTY sentences as extremely lenient.[6] Public surveys conducted in Bosnia, Serbia, or Croatia time and again demonstrate public disillusionment with the ICTY and its punishment practices.[7] The public imagination of harsh punishment for these 'most serious of crimes' clearly does not square with the Tribunals' practices, which are considered insufficient, sometimes even insulting to victims—a mockery of justice, or simply biased.

This perceived dichotomy between the 'national' and the 'international' raises the question how the Tribunal's sentencing practices really compare to those of domestic courts dealing with the similar instances of war crimes, crimes against humanity, and genocide? Is it indeed the case that those prosecuted at the international level are better off? So far, no systematic empirical inquiry of sentencing of perpetrators of international crimes committed during the Bosnian war has been conducted. This chapter intends to start closing this gap. It presents initial findings of an empirical study carried out over the past four years. Based on original data, the chapter analyses and contrasts punishment laws and practices concerning international crimes at the ICTY and at Bosnian domestic courts.

The chapter starts with a description of the development of a three-tiered system of post-war prosecutions and punishment. Between 1993 and 2017, the ICTY has focused progressively on a select group of what it considered the most responsible suspects. Locally, however, the BiH courts tried and prosecuted the majority of persons. In 2005, the initially internationalized State Court (SC) in Sarajevo started to exercise its jurisdiction over international crimes and was to try the most complex cases of war crimes. The local courts of the constitutive entities and self-governing Brčko district (in total sixteen) were to deal with the remaining cases. The courts operating within these three levels of justice are independent of each other and no hierarchical relationship exists among them. As will be demonstrated below, each of them have applied different sets of laws with different legal regulations applicable to sentencing of perpetrators of international crimes. Section 21.3 turns attention to these different punishment laws. It shows that, on a general level, all three

[4] Criminal courts in other European countries, such as Denmark, Germany, Norway, or Sweden have also prosecuted perpetrators of international crimes committed during the wars in Bosnia.

[5] cf L A Barria and S D Roper, 'Judicial Capacity Building in Bosnia and Herzegovina: Understanding Legal Reform Beyond the Completion Strategy of the ICTY' (2008) 9 Human Rights Review 317, 326; F de Sanctis, 'Reconciling Justice and Legality, A Quest for Fair Punishment in Cases on Bosnian Atrocity Crimes' (2014) 12 Journal of International Criminal Justice 847, 859–60.

[6] cf L J Nettlefield, *Courting Democracy in Bosnia and Herzegovina, The Hague's Tribunal Impact in Post-War State* (Cambridge University Press 2013) 25.

[7] cf M Milanovic, 'The Impact of the ICTY on the Former Yugoslavia: An Anticipatory Postmortem' (2016) 110 American Journal of International Law 233; S K Ivkovich and J Hagan, *Reclaiming Justice—The International Criminal Tribunal for the Former Yugoslavia and Local Courts* (Oxford University Press 2011); R Hodzic, 'Living the Legacy of Mass Atrocity, Victims' Perspectives on War Crimes Trials' (2010) 8 Journal of International Criminal Justice 113, 121–22; J N Clark, 'The Limits of Retributive Justice, Findings of an Empirical Study in Bosnia and Herzegovina' (2009) 7 Journal of International Criminal Justice 463, 471; M Klarin, 'The Impact of the ICTY Trials on Public Opinion in the Former Yugoslavia' (2009) 7 Journal of International Criminal Justice 89, 90.

sets of laws are comparable and provide judges with a large margin of discretion to mould a sentence to reflect particularities of an individual case. There is no strict guidance, nor strict mandatory sentences stipulated in the laws. Judges at all three levels of justice are given a relatively large discretion when it comes to fitting the sentence to the crime. Sentencing practices and severity of sentencing outcomes handed out at the three levels of courts are compared and contrasted in Section 21.4. The analysis demonstrates that in contrast to the popular belief, sentences handed out at the ICTY have been on an aggregate level comparable, or more severe compared to those handed out by the Bosnian domestic courts. In particular, the ICTY sentences are comparable in severity to those handed out by the State Court in Sarajevo. Both these courts, however, delivered much more severe sentences compared to the Bosnian entity courts, which tried a majority of defendants. Reasons behind the identified sentence severity gap are largely attributable to (i) a very different population of cases prosecuted; and (ii) different sentencing goals prioritized at different levels of courts. Consequently, Section 21.5 discusses that judges at different levels of courts seem to have spotlighted different sentencing goals and, consequently, put emphasis on different considerations in sentencing. In other words, the 'banality of offender' versus 'atrocity of crime' dilemma, which is present in almost each and every case of punishing perpetrators of international crimes, was resolved differently at the ICTY and at the Bosnian courts, in particular at the entities level.

21.2 Three-tiered System of Prosecutions of International Crimes in Bosnia

In the early 1990s, 'unimaginable' atrocities were committed on the European soil yet again. Large-scale massacres, mass rapes, torture, unlawful detentions in concentration camps, and mass deportations of hundreds of thousands of innocent civilians are the tragic images of ethnic cleansing that came to represent the dissolution of the Socialist Federal Republic of Yugoslavia (SFRY). The July 1995 genocide in Srebrenica committed by the Bosnian Serb forces against Bosnian Muslim civilians right before the war ended, represents a tragic culmination of the violent conflict. It is estimated that between 95,940[8] and 104,732[9] people were killed during the armed conflict in Bosnia and Herzegovina alone. Around 12,000–50,000 women were raped,[10] and around 31,500 persons are still missing more than twenty years after the end of war.[11] Atrocities were committed by all parties to the conflict, be it (Bosnian) Serbs, (Bosnian) Croats, or Bosniaks,[12] and many individuals in one way or another were involved in violence. The exact number of perpetrators might never be known, but given the large scale and systematic character of atrocities and the fact that the war lasted for almost four years, one can assume that the number of perpetrators is high, amounting

[8] M Tokača, *Bosnian Book of Death I, II, III & IV* (Research Documentation Centre Sarajevo 2012).

[9] J Zwierzchowski, E Tabeau, 'The 1992–95 War in Bosnia and Herzegovina: Census-Based Multiple System Estimation of Casualties' (Global Costs of Conflict Research Workshop, Berlin, February 2010).

[10] D Crowe, *War Crimes, Genocide, and Justice: A Global History* (Palgrave Macmillan 2014) 343.

[11] J Sarkin, L Nettelfield, M Matthews, and R Kosalka, *Missing Persons from the Armed Conflicts of the 1990s: A Stocktaking* (International Commission on Missing Persons 2014).

[12] Relative to other ethnicities, Bosnian Serbs, however, are generally believed to have been responsible for international crimes committed on a much larger scale (see UN, *Final Report of the Commission of Experts Established Pursuant to Security Council Resolution 780* (1992)).

to thousands.[13] The calls for accountability and justice gained momentum early on in the war. Two years before the Srebrenica massacre, in 1993, the ICTY was established by the United Nations to 'put an end to such crimes [...] and to bring to justice the persons who are responsible for them'.[14] As the first international criminal tribunal set up after the end of the Cold War, operating in a very complex and challenging political environment, the ICTY had a slow start. It took three years before it became fully operational and had the first suspects in the dock. The ICTY, however, surprised many and after the initial struggles it developed into a well-functioning international institution. Nevertheless, given the limited resources of the court, it soon became very clear that the ICTY would only touch 'the tip of the iceberg' and be able to prosecute only a handful of suspects.[15]

In order to bring as many perpetrators as possible to account, domestic courts were required to complement and eventually take over the prosecutions. Since the early 2000s, courts in Bosnia and Herzegovina started to step in. Slowly, but surely. The Law 29/00 of Court of Bosnia and Herzegovina was adopted in 2000. Two years later, the State Court of Bosnia and Herzegovina (SC) was established. In 2004, its War Crime Division was set up and started its activities in 2005 as an internationalized institution combining domestic and international prosecutors, judges, and other staff members.[16] Before 2005, war crimes cases had been brought to trial only very sporadically in front of the pre-existing entity courts around Bosnia.[17] After the judicial sector reform in 2003/2004, five district courts in Republika Srpska (RS), ten cantonal courts in Federation of Bosnia and Herzegovina (FBiH), and the Brčko basic court all had jurisdiction to try war crimes.[18] The SC was to deal with the most complex cases of war crimes, while less complex cases were to be tried at entity courts. According to the 2008 War Crimes Strategy,[19] complexity of a case was defined by several criteria including gravity of offence (determined by a legal qualification of a criminal offence, form, and severity of certain acts), capacity and role of offenders (taking

[13] J N Clark, 'The State Court of Bosnia and Hercegovina: A Path to Reconciliation?' (2010) 13 Contemporary Justice Review 371, 376. According to Clark, (gu)estimates of a number of suspected war criminals range from 10,750 to 16,000 possible suspects at different times (citing the Bosnian State Prosecutor Office in B Ivanišević, *The War Crimes Chamber in Bosnia and Hercegovina: From Hybrid to Domestic Court* (International Centre for Transitional Justice 2008) 9) to less than 6,000 (citing an interview with Mirsad Tokača, Research Documentation Centre in Sarajevo). The recent Council of Europe Report states that there are still around 5,000 war crimes suspects to be processed by the authorities in BiH (N Muiznieks, *Report Following the Visit to Bosnia and Herzegovina from 12 to 16 June 2017* (CommDH 2017) 28) para 15).

[14] UNSC Res 827 (25 May 1993) UN Doc S/RES/RES/827, Preamble.

[15] Progressively over the course of its existence, the ICTY limited its focus on senior leaders and those deemed to be the most responsible. See UN Security Council, Res 1503 (28 August 2003), UN Doc S/RES/1503 (2003).

[16] As of 2012, the SC has been staffed only by domestic judges, prosecutors, and other personnel and preceding this year, the international staff was gradually phased out from the institution.

[17] It was reported that there were only fifty-five convictions for war crimes (thirty-one in Federation of BH and twenty-four in Republika Srpska) before 2008 (Council of Ministers of Bosnia and Herzegovina, *National Strategy for War Crimes Processing* (29 December 2008)). On the scarce domestic prosecutions prior to 2005, see D Schwendiman, 'Prosecuting Atrocity Crimes In National Courts: Looking Back On 2009 In Bosnia And Herzegovina' (2010) 8 Northwestern University Journal of International Human Rights 269; W Burke-White, 'Domestic Influence of International Criminal Tribunals: The International Criminal Tribunal for the Former Yugoslavia and the Creation of the State Court of Bosnia-Herzegovina' (2007) 46 The Columbia Journal of Transnational Law 279.

[18] The appeals can be lodged to the Supreme (RS and FBH) or Apellate (Brčko) courts. There is no hierarchical relationship between the entity courts and the SC and criminal justice systems within each entity and on the State level is independent of each other and do not interact (only in some specified instances, e.g. transfer of less sensitive/complex cases from the State court to an entity court), especially when it comes to decision making.

[19] *War Crimes Strategy 2008* (n 17). The Strategy aimed to provide a systematic approach to solving the problem of the large number of outstanding war crimes cases. It presented a comprehensive strategy for prosecutions and trials of war crimes and defined time frames for their processing.

into account a position of authority of an offender, public function and also form and degree of participation in the offence), and other factors such as connection to other cases, interests of victims, or consequences for a local community.

Consequently, courts at three levels of criminal justice have been trying and sentencing perpetrators of international crimes committed during the conflict in BiH. The trials were held: (i) at an international level by the ICTY; (ii) at domestic/internationalized level by the SC; and (iii) at domestic/local level by the entity courts in two constitutive entities of Bosnia: Republika Srpska and Federation of BiH, and one self-governing Brčko District. Not only are these systems of courts independent of each other and no hierarchical relationship exists among them, but also each of them applies different sets of laws with different legal regulation applicable to sentencing of perpetrators of international crimes. This, at least theoretically, creates an environment where similar perpetrators, who committed similar crimes within the same conflict, can be subjected to widely different punishment, depending on what court tries their case. Whether that indeed was the case in practice is discussed in subsequent paragraphs. The next section compares the three legal frameworks applicable to sentencing.

21.3 Sentencing Legal Frameworks

The ICTY is governed by its 1993 Statute (ICTY Statute)[20] and the Rules of Procedure and Evidence (RPE).[21] Two sets of laws have been applied by domestic courts in Bosnia: the 1976 Criminal Code of the Socialist Federal Republic of Yugoslavia (SFRY CC),[22] and following the 2003 reform of judiciary, the 2003 Criminal Code of Bosnia and Herzegovina (BiH CC).[23] At face value, the legal provisions on punishment provided for in these different laws regarding sentencing principles, sentencing factors, and sentencing ranges vary. Indeed, commentators often raised concerns regarding the varying legal frameworks and consistency of sentencing practices in Bosnia.[24] This section will demonstrate that all three sets of laws are actually surprisingly comparable and, more importantly, all provide judges with a large margin of discretion to mould a sentence to reflect particularities of an individual case. There is no strict guidance nor are severe, mandatory sentences stipulated in the laws. Judges at all three levels of justice are given a relatively large discretion when it comes to fitting the punishment to the crime.

The ICTY Statute together with the RPE provide only very general guidelines on sentencing. There are no sentencing goals stipulated, no detailed set of relevant sentencing factors nor sentence ranges for individual crimes. The law vests judges with large discretion when

[20] Statute of the International Criminal Tribunal for the Former Yugoslavia adopted 25 May 1993 by the UN SC Resolution 827/1993.

[21] Rules of Procedure and Evidence of the International Criminal Tribunal for the former Yugoslavia, UN Doc IT/32/Rev 37 (1994).

[22] The 1976 SFRY Criminal Code adopted by the Federal Assembly on 28 September 1976 and in force since 1 July 1977.

[23] The 2003 Criminal Code of Bosnia and Herzegovina adopted by the Parliamentary assembly of Bosnia and Herzegovina on 27 June 2003 and published in the official Gazette 37/03, as amended by Law 8/10.

[24] cf Barria and Roper (n 5) 326; de Sanctis (n 5) 859; Y Ronen, 'The Impact of the ICTY on Atrocity-Related Prosecutions in the Courts of Bosnia and Herzegovina' (2014) 3 Penn State Journal of Law & International Affairs 113, 145–46; O Martin-Ortega, 'Prosecuting War Crimes at Home: Lessons from the War Crimes Chamber in the State Court of Bosnia and Herzegovina' (2012) 12 International Criminal Law Review 589, 607.

determining a sentence. According to the ICTY positive law, the sentence shall be limited to imprisonment and the maximum term is life imprisonment.[25] There is no sentencing tariff setting minimum and maximum penalties for individual crimes. The judges are also instructed, if applicable, to order the restitution of property unlawfully acquired by criminal conduct to its legal owner.[26] This remedy, however, has never been used in the ICTY jurisprudence. The factors that judges shall take into account in the sentencing determination include 'such factors as the gravity of the offence and the individual circumstances of the convicted person'.[27] What is actually meant by the 'gravity of crime' or which 'individual circumstances' are relevant is unclear. Furthermore, when determining the terms of imprisonment, judges shall have recourse to the local courts' practices regarding prison sentences.[28] Rule 101 clarifies the regulation of the sentence determination only to a very limited extent. It instructs judges to take into account any aggravating and/or mitigating circumstances when determining the sentence. However, no list of aggravating and mitigating factors is provided. Only two potential mitigating factors are explicitly mentioned: 'superior orders'[29] and 'substantial cooperation with the Prosecutor'.[30] Effectively, judges are left to determine on a case-by-case basis almost all aspects of a sentence, including sentence severity, which could theoretically range from one day to life imprisonment. That is the case also with sentencing goals, principles, and factors relevant for sentence determination and justifying a concrete sentence.

Despite this broad manoeuvring space for sentence determination, the ICTY judges have developed a relatively consistent approach to sentencing in case law over time.[31] Concerning the goals pursued by punishment, the positive law is silent. Throughout the case law, especially at the initial stages of the ICTY, different purposes of punishment were emphasized in different cases. ICTY judges were also not consistent in their proclamations as to what the primary aim was.[32] Over time, however, the sentencing ambitions became more realistic and coherent, and deterrence and retribution have been considered as the primary goals of sentencing.[33] The third most frequently cited sentencing objective is offender rehabilitation which, however, according to judges, should be not given undue weight because of the seriousness of international crimes.[34]

[25] Art 24 ICTY Statute, Rule 101 RPE.

[26] Art 24(3) ICTY Statute.

[27] Art 24(2) ICTY Statute.

[28] Art 24(1) ICTY Statute. This provision was inserted in the Statute in particular out of concerns stemming from the *nulla poena sine lege* principle and prohibition of retroactive punishment. See W Schabas, 'Perverse Effects of Nulla Poena Principle: National Practice and the Ad Hoc Tribunals' (2000) 11 European Journal of International Law 521, 522. This provision has been construed by judges restrictively, holding that it does not render an obligation to follow the domestic Yugoslavian practice. The SFRY sentencing practice is, however, one of the factors judges should take into account. If a sentence departs from limits set in this practice, reasons must be given for such a departure. See *Prosecutor v Dragan Nikolic* (Appeals Judgment) Case No IT-94-2-A (4 February 2005) para 69.

[29] Art 7(4) ICTY Statute.

[30] Rule 101 RPE.

[31] cf B Holá, *International Sentencing—'Game of Russian Roulette' or Consistent Practice?* (BOXPress 2012); D'Ascoli (n 2).

[32] cf M A Drumbl, *Atrocity, Punishment and International Law* (Cambridge University Press 2007) 65; B Holá, 'Sentencing of International Crimes at the ICTY and ICTR: Consistency of Sentencing Case Law' (2012) 4 Amsterdam Law Forum 3, 6–7.

[33] cf *Prosecutor v Karadzic* (Judgment) Case No IT-95-5/18-T (24 March 2016) para 6025; *Prosecutor v Popovic* et al (Judgment) Case No IT-04-74-T (29 May 2013) para 1275; *Prosecutor v Milutinovic* et al (Judgment) Case No IT-05-87-T (26 February 2009) para 1144.

[34] *Karadzic* (n 33) para 6025; *Milutinovic* (n 33) para 1146; *Prosecutor v Deronjic* (Judgment on Sentencing Appeal) Case No IT-02-61-A (20 July 2005) para 136. In a handful of cases, however, judges seem to ascribe

In line with the emphasis put on retribution, 'the starting point' of sentence determination, 'the litmus test' for sentence severity and 'the factor of paramount importance' according to the ICTY judges is the gravity of the offence.[35] In this respect, the principles of proportionality, totality, and gradation are the governing criteria: a penalty is to reflect the totality of the crimes committed by a person,[36] and be proportionate to the gravity of his or her crimes,[37] while taking into account his or her position in the overall conflict and role in the particular crimes.[38] For the purposes of sentencing, gravity is determined *in concreto* by examining the particular circumstances of the case.[39] In most cases, the concept of gravity was interpreted as encompassing two main aspects: (i) harm assessment, that is, the magnitude of harm caused by the offender and represented by, for example, the cruelty, nature, and circumstances of the crime, the number of victims and their vulnerability, or the impact of the criminal conduct on victims, their relatives and targeted communities; and (ii) culpability assessment—the form and degree of the accused's participation in the crime, including his position of authority.[40]

After evaluating the gravity of crimes, ICTY judges further individualize sentences by assessing aggravating and mitigating circumstances. Over the years, the Tribunal accepted a wide range of factors in aggravation/mitigation of a sentence.[41] Only those circumstances directly related to the charged offences and to the offenders when they committed the offence can be accepted in aggravation.[42] Aggravating factors accepted by the ICTY judges most often relate to a degree of harm caused by an offender (such as particular cruelty, brutality of crimes, a number or suffering of victims); his degree of guilt (such as abuse of superior position, enthusiastic participation, zeal, encouragement, and leading role in crimes) and motive (such as revenge, enrichment, discrimination). Conversely, mitigating factors do not need to relate directly to the offences,[43] and judges typically discuss the offender's personal circumstances, including but not limited to his or her character, family circumstances, or behaviour prior to the conflict; circumstances related to a degree of harm (assistance to victims, measures to reduce suffering); degree of guilt (low position in the overall hierarchy or limited role in crime); post-crime conduct of a defendant (remorse, promotion of peace, expression of sympathy to victims); or proceedings-related behaviour (guilty plea, voluntary surrender, or cooperation with Prosecution).[44] The most common aggravating

more importance to rehabilitation. cf *Prosecutor v Jokic* (Sentencing Judgment) Case No IT-01-42/1-S (18 March 2004) para 36, *Prosecutor v Obrenovic* (Sentencing Judgment) Case No IT-02-60/2-S (10 December 2003) para 53.

[35] cf *Prosecutor v Aleksovski* (Appeals Judgment) Case No IT-95-14/1-A (24 March 2000) para 182; *Prosecutor v Mucic* et al,(Appeals Judgment) Case No IT-96-21-A (20 February 2001) para 731; *Prosecutor v Limaj* et al (Judgment) Case No IT-03-66-T (30 November 2005) para 724.

[36] Rule 87(C) RPE; cf *Popovic* et al (n 33) para 1281.

[37] cf *Prosecutor v Deronjic* (Judgment) Case No IT-02-61-T (30 March 2004) para 154.

[38] *Prosecutor v Tadic* (Judgment in Sentencing Appeals) Case No IT-94-1A (26 January 2000) paras 55–58.

[39] The ICTY have rejected the notion of abstract hierarchy between individual categories of international crimes. Crimes against humanity, for example, are not considered inherently more serious than war crimes. cf *Karadzic* (n 33) para 6033 and included references. For a more elaborate discussion of the concept of gravity, see Holá (n 31) 47–56.

[40] cf *Prosecutor v Stanisic and Zupljanin* (Appeals Judgment) Case No IT-08-91-A (30 June 2016) para 1106; *Karadzic* (n 33) para 6031.

[41] For a complete list, see Holá (n 31) 77–82.

[42] *Karadzic* (n 33) para 6035; *Popovic* et al (n 33) para 1285.

[43] cf *Popovic* et al (n 33) para 1285; *Prosecutor v Kunarac, Kovac, and Vukovic* (Judgment) Case No IT-96-23 and 23/1-T (22 February 2001) para 911.

[44] cf Holá (n 31) 59–72. Compare also an illustrative list of mitigating and aggravating factors enumerated by judges in *Karadzic* (n 33) paras 6035, 6036.

factor cited by ICTY judges is 'the abuse of a position of authority, leadership, influence, or trust', while 'family circumstances' is cited most frequently in mitigation.[45] Whether a certain factor constitutes a mitigating or aggravating circumstance depends largely on the particular circumstances of each case.[46]

Consequently, despite the loose guidance provided in the Statute and RPE, in the ICTY sentencing case law, judges seem to have developed and followed a similar 'algorithm' when determining sentences. Sentence severity at the ICTY seems to be primarily determined by factors relating to the gravity of the crime (by applying the principles of proportionality, totality, and gradation) and assessing harm caused by the offence and culpability of the offender. The sentence is then adjusted and individualized by taking into account aggravating and mitigating factors ('principle of individualization'), which have included a broad range of factors, most frequently further reflecting the degree of harm, degree of guilt and personal circumstances of the offender.[47]

The legal framework applicable to prosecution and sentencing of international crimes in Bosnia has undergone significant changes since the conflict ended. Which laws are to be applied to the crimes committed during the 1990s conflict still remains contested and debated.[48] In 2003, the 1976 Socialist Criminal Code (SFRY CC) was replaced by the Criminal Code of Bosnia and Herzegovina (BiH CC), which, among many other amendments, introduced the category of crimes against humanity to the Bosnian criminal law,[49] or new modes of liability such as superior responsibility.[50] The 2003 BiH CC was drafted to reflect developments in international criminal law and jurisprudence.[51] According to Schwendiman, these changes were modelled mainly on the Statute of the International Criminal Court and considered essential before the ICTY could begin to transfer some of its cases to the Bosnian courts under the Rule 11*bis*.[52]

Since provisions relating to principles and factors relevant to punishment seem to be very similar under both criminal codes, the 1976 SFRY CC and 2003 BiH CC will be discussed together. Under both criminal codes, sentences applicable to international crimes are limited to incarceration. The main difference between the two laws relates to the sentence ranges applicable to international crimes. Under the 1976 CC, war crimes and genocide could be subjected to sentences ranging from five years to twenty years imprisonment.[53] Under the 2003 CC, the minimum imprisonment sentence applicable to war crimes, crimes

[45] B Holá, A Smeulers, and C Bijleveld, 'International Sentencing Fact and Figures: Sentencing Practice at the ICTY and ICTR' (2011) 9 Journal of International Criminal Justice 411, 433, 435.

[46] *Popovic* et al (n 33) para 1289; *Stanisic, Zupljanin* (n 40) para 1124.

[47] For much more detailed discussion of sentencing approach of the ICTY judges and problematic aspects therein from the standpoint of consistency, such as confounding of factors related to the gravity assessment with aggravating factors, see Holá (n 31) 26–76.

[48] See de Sanctis (n 5) 856–64, discussing divergent jurisprudence and implementation of the principle of legality in Bosnia preceding and following the ECtHR decision in Maktouf and Damjanovic (Judgment, *Maktouf and Damjanovic v Bosnia and Herzegovina*, Applications Nos 2312/08, 34179/08, 18 July 2013).

[49] Art 172 BiH CC.

[50] Art 180 (2) BiH CC.

[51] cf Martin-Ortega (n 24) 607.

[52] Schwendiman (n 17) 276.

[53] Arts 141–44 SFRY CC. These provisions stipulate death penalty as a maximum applicable sentence. Since the death penalty was abolished in Bosnia in 1998, the maximum sentence applicable to international crimes under the SFRY CC is twenty years imprisonment (art 38(2)). For certain specified acts, such as membership in a group organized for a purpose of committing international crimes (art 145(2)); unlawful killing of an enemy during an armed conflict (art 146(1)); or destruction of cultural and historical monuments (art 151), the minimum sentence is not less than one year.

against humanity, and genocide is generally ten years,[54] while the maximum sentence is a long-term imprisonment (i.e. imprisonment for a term of twenty-one to forty-five years) reserved 'for the gravest forms of serious criminal offences perpetrated with intent'.[55]

Articles 5 and 33 of the 1976 SFRY CC and Articles 6 and 39 of the BiH CC provide for purposes of criminal sanction and of punishment. Despite differences in the exact wording of these articles, the enumerated sentencing goals overlap and include retribution,[56] general and specific deterrence,[57] protection of society and victims,[58] offender rehabilitation,[59] and expressivism.[60] Article 2(2) of the 2003 BiH CC (and similarly Article 2 SFRY CC) stipulates the principle of necessity of criminalization and criminal sanctions, which should be proportionate 'with the degree and nature of the danger against personal liberties, human rights and other basic values'.

More detailed regulation of general sentencing principles and factors for meting out punishments is provided for in Article 41 SFRY CC and Article 38 BiH CC. For each particular offence a severity of punishment is limited by the sentence ranges stipulated by the law. While having in mind the purposes of punishment, judges are instructed 'to take into account all the circumstances bearing on the magnitude of punishment', be it in mitigation or in aggravation. The laws provide a demonstrative list of categories of factors that might be used in aggravation or mitigation of a sentence within the legally provided ranges (depending on the circumstances of a particular case). In particular, both criminal codes guide judges to take into account the following: 'the degree of guilt, the motives of perpetrating the offence, the degree of danger or injury to the protected object, the circumstances in which offence was perpetrated, the past conduct of the perpetrator, his personal situation and his conduct after the perpetration of the criminal offence, as well as other circumstances related to the personality of the perpetrator'.[61] These categories of relevant sentencing factors are not exhaustive or mandatory (judges are not obliged to consider each category in each and every case). It is also notable that they to a large extent resemble factors used at the ICTY to determine gravity of crimes (harm and culpability of offender), and to individualize sentences, as described above. In the actual sentencing practices (considering the cases collected for the purposes of this study) the most frequent factors referred to in aggravation of a sentence across all Bosnian courts include cruelty of attack; multiplicity or status of victims (minors/elderly); multiplicity of offences committed by an offender or his persistence in criminal conduct; impact of crimes on victims/survivors; abuse of position of

[54] Similar to the SFRY CC, for certain specified types of criminal behaviour, such as membership in a group organized for the purpose of perpetrating international crimes (art 176(2)); calling on or instigating perpetration of international crimes (art 176(4)); unlawful killing of an enemy during an armed conflict (art 177 (1)); unlawful appropriation of belongings from the killed or wounded on battlefield in a cruel manner (art 178(2)); destruction of cultural, historical, and religious monuments (art 183(1)) and certain other acts specified in the 2003 BiH CC the minimum sentence is lower (one year) with the maximum ten years imprisonment. A limited number of crimes is subjected to even lower statutory minimum and maximum sentence of six months and five years (such as unlawful appropriation of belongings from the killed or wounded on battlefield (art 178(1)); violating the protection granted to bearers of flags of truce (art 181); unjustified delay in repatriation of prisoners of war (art 182); or misuse of international symbols (art 184 (2)).

[55] Art 42b BiH CC.

[56] Arts 2, 5(2) SFRY CC; arts 2, 39a BiH CC.

[57] Art 33(1)(2) SFRY CC; art 6a, 39b, c BiH CC.

[58] Art 5(2), 33(3) SFRY CC; art 6a, b BiH CC.

[59] Art 33 (1) SFRY CC; art 6a, 39b BiH CC.

[60] Art 33 (3) SFRY CC; art 39d BiH CC.

[61] Art 41(1) SFRY CC; art 48(1) BiH CC.

trust; prior crimes of offender; or discriminatory motive. Conversely, factors such as family circumstances; conduct during trial; time lapse between a trial and the crimes (this factor is particularly frequent at the entity-level courts); the fact that offender committed no prior crimes; young age during the crimes; chaotic situation of war; assistance to victims; or current circumstances of the offender, such as health or economic situation; or his guilty plea and cooperation with Prosecution (the SC) are the most frequently cited in mitigation of sentences. A special set of considerations is provided for in the laws in case of sentencing recidivists. Judges should pay a special attention to whether the offences are of a similar type, perpetrated from the same motive, and to the time lapse between the previous conviction/release from prison and the new offence.[62]

The laws also provide Bosnian judges with the possibility to hand out a sentence below the statutory minimum in case 'the court determines the existence of highly extenuating circumstances, which indicate that the purpose of punishment can be attained by a lesser punishment'.[63] In such cases, the criminal codes provide limits to a possible sentence reduction. For cases of international crimes, where the minimum sentences are generally set to five years (SFRY CC), or ten years (BiH CC), the minimum reduced sentence could be one year and five years, respectively.[64] As will be discussed, this provision seems to have been used relatively frequently in case of war crimes perpetrators, in particular by the entity-level courts. Both criminal codes also contain provisions allowing judges to reduce sentences under specific circumstances.[65] Additionally, some provisions regulating specific types of international crimes contain guidelines for mitigation or aggravation of sentences, if certain conditions are fulfilled. For example, Article 145 SFRY CC/176 BiH CC criminalizing organization of a group of people with the purpose of committing international crimes provides for a possibility of sentence reduction for a member of such group, who exposes the group without having perpetrated an offence in its ranks. Furthermore, Article 180 of the BiH CC provides that acting upon superior orders 'may be considered in mitigation of punishment if the court determines that justice so requires'. In a number of instances, the Criminal Codes provide for a possibility of aggravated sentence in case a particular act is committed in cruel manners, following the base motives, or when there is multiplicity of victims.[66] The 2003 judicial reforms also introduced a new set of criminal procedural rules, and the new 2003 Criminal Procedure Code governing the proceedings at the SC included the possibility of a guilty plea and provided the Prosecutors with an option to propose a sentence below the statutory minimum, in case a defendant pleads guilty.[67]

Clearly, sentencing laws in Bosnia and Herzegovina applicable to international crimes are much more detailed and structured compared to the ICTY Statute. However, this brief

[62] Art 41(2) SFRY CC; art 48(2) BiH CC.

[63] Art 42(1) SFRY CC; art 49b BiH CC.

[64] Art 43 SFRY CC; art 50 BiH CC.

[65] cf art 9(3) SFRY CC/art 24(3) BiH CC excessive self-defence; art 10(3) SFRY CC/art 25(3) CC BiH acts resulting from negligently caused danger causing extreme necessity; art 25a(2) CC BiH offences committed under the influence of resistible force or a threat; art 19(2) SFRY CC/art 26(2), 27 CC BiH attempt; art 23(2) SFRY CC/art 30(2) CC BiH incitement when the crime has not materialized; art 24(1) SFRY CC/art 31 CC BiH aiding and abetting; art 12(2) SFRY CC/art 34(2) CC BiH diminished mental capacity.

[66] cf 146 SFRY CC/177 BiH CC unlawful killing or wounding of the enemy in cruel or insidious way, out of greed or from other base motives or if more persons have been killed; art 147 SFRY CC/178 BiH CC marauding, where marauding in a cruel manner is met with a higher sentence.

[67] Art 231 Criminal Procedure Code adopted by the Parliamentary Assembly of Bosnia and Herzegovina on 1 March 2003 and published in the official Gazette 36/03, as amended by Law 72/13.

overview indicates that in essence sentencing goals, principles, and factors stipulated in the Bosnian positive laws resemble those developed in the ICTY case law. There are differences in particular aspects and details, but on a general level, arguably, the legal frameworks are largely comparable. Retribution, deterrence, and rehabilitation are to guide judges as general goals of sentencing. In Bosnia, additional sentencing goals such as protection of society or expressivism are provided for in law, while at the ICTY, in some cases, judges also emphasized different sentencing aims such as reconciliation, expressivism, protection of society and others. Factors related to the assessment of harm caused by the offence (in Bosnia phrased in laws as 'degree of danger and injury of the protected object' and 'circumstances, in which the offence was perpetrated'), of the offender's culpability ('degree of guilt', 'motives') and of his personal circumstances prior to, parallel with, and following the offence, are stipulated as relevant sentencing considerations by the Bosnian criminal codes and being used by judges to determine sentences in particular cases at the ICTY and in Bosnia. Furthermore, despite more detailed legal regulation of sentencing in Bosnia, Bosnian judges have also, similar to the ICTY, been provided with relatively extensive discretionary powers when it comes to the determination of punishment in individual cases. The sentencing ranges provided for in the Bosnian criminal codes are broad (five–twenty years imprisonment under the 1976 SFRY CC and ten–forty-five years under the BiH CC) and the laws give judges large space to navigate within and beyond the provided margins. Except for a limited number of exceptions, Bosnian judges are not instructed on how to weigh factors they consider relevant to sentence determination in individual cases. The following section discusses how this broad discretion has materialized in practice of the ICTY, the Bosnian SC, and entity courts, and compares and contrasts sentence severity across the three levels of courts in their actual sentencing practices.

21.4 Sentencing Practice

In order to contrast the severity of sentencing outcomes across the three levels of justice, this section uses an original, empirical database on sentencing practices at the ICTY and at Bosnian courts. The database includes data on all judgments finalized on trial or appeal by the ICTY as of November 2017, which were collected from its website and coded. All final judgments rendered by courts in Bosnia (i.e. by the SC and by all sixteen entity courts) in the period after the war ended in 1995 until January 2016, which have been archived by the Organization for Security and Cooperation in Europe (OSCE) in its war crimes trials monitoring capacity, were collected and coded. The data gathering in Bosnia was conducted by local researchers during the fieldwork in Sarajevo, which lasted from January 2015 until June 2016.[68]

Descriptive statistics based on final sentencing outcomes, such as averages and frequencies, is used to contrast and discuss sentence severity at the three levels of justice for different categories of cases.[69] The chapter, first, contrasts sentencing outcomes across the

[68] Code book used during the field work and the SPSS database are available with the author.

[69] Since the discussion is based on descriptive statistics, no generalizable or causal claims when it comes to consistencies or inconsistencies of sentencing practices can be made. In order to assess consistency of sentencing across the courts conclusively, one would need to model sentencing decision-making using a multi-level, multivariate regression and control for as many as possible legal factors (and extra-legal factors, such as gender or ethnicity of defendants and decision-makers), that could theoretically affect sentence decision-making. Presented

three levels of courts on an aggregate level for all cases included in the database. Thereafter, in order to get better insights and shed further light on differences in punishment practices, sentence severity is compared based on: (i) a category of crime defendants were convicted of, that is, genocide, crimes against humanity, and war crimes; and (ii) a position of authority a defendant occupied during the conflict. Before doing so, however, the next two paragraphs provide a general overview of the collected cases for each (i) the ICTY; (ii) the SC; and (iii) the entity courts.

As of 1 November 2017, the ICTY indicted 161 persons and finalized proceedings for 150 accused: eighty-two were convicted, eighteen acquitted, thirteen referred to national jurisdiction, and thirty-seven saw their indictments withdrawn or deceased before the verdict. The conviction rate at the ICTY, computed as a proportion of convictions from all cases, which were tried and ended by a final conviction or acquittal (i.e. 100 individuals), is 82 per cent. The trial judgment against Ratko Mladić was delivered on 22 November 2017 and Mladić was sentenced to life in prison. In addition, the appeals judgment in the *Prlić* et al case involving six accused was rendered on 29 November 2017 and for a large part, the ICTY Appeals Chamber affirmed their convictions and sentences.[70] These two cases were the final pending cases before the ICTY, which closed its doors at the end of 2017. The Mechanism for International Criminal Tribunals (MICT) is taking over the residual functions of the Tribunal, including the appeals of three individuals; Radovan Karadžić, Vojislav Šešelj, and Mladić, and retrial of two other defendants (Stanišić and Simatović).

The database of international crimes cases decided by the Bosnian courts consists of data on 568 defendants, against whom a final judgment was handed out as of January 2016 by Bosnian courts. The earliest cases stem from September 1995. Out of these, 238 defendants were tried by the SC and 330 by the entity courts (177 individuals were tried by cantonal courts in FBiH; 128 individuals by district courts in RS; and twenty-five individuals by the basic court in Brčko). The SC convicted 177 defendants, sixty were acquitted and one case dismissed (conviction rate: 74.6 per cent). The entity courts convicted 235 individuals, acquitted ninety and in the case of five individuals included in the database, the case was dismissed or adjourned (conviction rates per entity: FBiH: 78.6 per cent; RS: 62.7 per cent; Brčko: 76 per cent). The next sections compare and contrast sentencing practices for convicted defendants across the three systems of courts. Therefore, the sample consists of a total of eighty-two individuals convicted at the ICTY, and 177 and 235 defendants convicted at the SC and at the entity courts, respectively.

The average sentence handed out by the ICTY is 15.6 years imprisonment. In addition, the ICTY convicted five individuals to the maximum sentence of life imprisonment.[71] The

results, however, are the first systematic and the most comprehensive empirical comparison of international and Bosnian domestic punishment practices and in this sense, represent one of the first attempts to bring empirical data to discussions. See also OSCE, 'Delivering Justice in Bosnia and Herzegovina: An Overview of War Crimes Processing from 2005 to 2010' (*OSCE*, 2011) <http://www.osce.org/bih/108103?download=true > accessed 9 November 2017; Y Ronen, 'Bosnia and Herzegovina: The Interaction Between the ICTY and Domestic Courts in Adjudicating International Crimes' (*DOMAC Report*, 2011) <https://en.ru.is/media/domac/Domac8-2011-YR.pdf> accessed 9 November 2017.

70 The case of *Prlic* et al is not included in the reported statistics.

71 See the ICTY cases of *Galic* (IT-98-29), *Milan Lukic* (IT-98-32/1), *Tolimir* (IT-05-88/2), *Popovic* (n 33), and *Beara* (IT-05-88). In addition, Ratko Mladic received a life sentence on trial. His case is currently pending at the MICT. And after the completion of the chapter, *Karadzic*'s (n 33) forty-year sentence was also increased to life imprisonment on appeal.

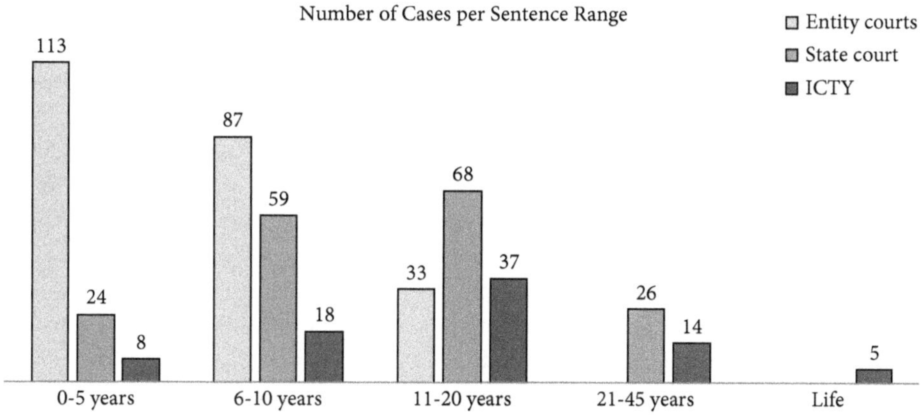

Figure 21.1 Number of cases per sentence range per level of courts

SC has a slightly lower average sentence of 12.9 years, while the average sentence handed out by the entity courts is only 6.1 years. Figure 21.1 further breaks down cases according to sentence severity and depicts number of cases divided per sentence range. As discussed already, the ICTY Statute does not stipulate sentence ranges for individual crimes, while Bosnian criminal codes provide for minimum sentences and maximum sentences for international crimes. Consequently, cases were divided into five categories according to a sentence range: zero–five years (five years imprisonment is a statutory minimum under the 1976 SFRY CC), six–ten years (ten years imprisonment is a statutory minimum under the 2003 BiH CC), eleven–twenty years (twenty years being the statutory maximum under the 1976 SFRY CC), twenty-one–forty-five years (i.e. long-term imprisonment (statutory maximum) under the 2003 BiH CC) and life imprisonment, which is a maximum sentence available to the ICTY judges. Interestingly, in practice the entity courts almost exclusively rely on 1976 SFRY CC when sentencing perpetrators of war crimes, while the SC seems to apply the 2003 BiH CC more frequently (in only 35 per cent of collected cases judges relied on the 1976 SFRY CC).[72]

Surprisingly, taking into consideration the fact that international crimes are labelled as 'the most serious crimes of international concern' the vast majority of sentences handed out at all levels of courts is below twenty years of imprisonment (100 per cent at entity courts; 85.3 per cent at the SC; 76.8 per cent at the ICTY). Only a very limited number of individuals are punished to sentences at the upper range of the severity scale above twenty years of imprisonment at the SC and at the ICTY. What is even more surprising is that almost half of the defendants at the entity courts and the SC (47.9 per cent at the entity courts; 42.3 per cent at the SC) are sentenced below the statutory minima provided for international crimes by the criminal codes applied in these cases. Per laws judges are permitted to hand out sentences below the stipulated ranges, in case they consider that sentencing goals will be achieved with a reduced sentence, when exceptional mitigation exists.[73] This possibility

[72] These differences relate to discussions and conflicting interpretations and application of the principle of legality and *lex mitior* principle, which as noted above (n 48) are still ongoing, controversial, and unresolved in Bosnia. It is beyond the scope of this chapter to discuss complexities of this legal issue, however, more detailed discussion can be found in de Sanctis (n 5).

[73] See art 42(1) SFRY CC; art 49b BiH CC.

is employed by Bosnian judges surprisingly often when punishing international crimes. In these cases, judges often use a mix of personal circumstances of a defendant, such as his family situation, current socio-economic circumstances or health considerations, and the fact that he has not committed any crimes before and since the war (time lapse), as exceptional mitigation to reduce sentences below the prescribed minimum. Despite the fact that offences in such cases are often very serious instances of killing, sexual violence, or maltreatment of victims, these individual circumstances of defendants combined with the fact that they, at the time of a verdict, do not seem to constitute any danger to the society, seem to balance out seriousness of committed crimes.

When the distribution of cases according to sentence severity is compared across the three levels of courts, it appears that cases decided at the SC and the ICTY follow a similar (relatively normal) distribution with the most frequent category of sentences between eleven and twenty years being at the middle of the spectrum (38.4 per cent at the SC; 45.1 per cent at the ICTY) and a lower number of sentences falling at both tails, being it more lenient or more severe. Though the distribution of sentences at the SC is more skewed towards more lenient sentences below ten years of imprisonment (47 per cent of all sentences at the SC fall below ten years, while at the ICTY it is 31 per cent). In contrast, the vast majority of sentences handed out by the entity courts (84.7 per cent) falls below ten years of imprisonment. Taking into account the average sentences at each of the levels, these very general statistics already indicate that while the sentence severity distribution across the totality of cases seems to be relatively comparable at the ICTY and the SC (with the SC leaning more towards the lower part of the spectrum), the entity courts seem to be much less punitive.

However, in order to understand this difference, one needs to see what type of cases and what type of defendants are tried by each level of courts. Consequently, average sentences (in years) at each level of courts according to the category of crimes a defendant was convicted of are depicted in Table 21.1.

Table 21.1 demonstrates that there are significant differences among the types of cases tried by each level of courts. The entity courts convicted defendants exclusively of war crimes (100 per cent), which is also the most frequent category of conviction at the State

Table 21.1 Average Sentences (in years) per Category of Crimes per Level of Courts*

	WC	CAH	GEN	CAH + WC	GEN+CAH+WC
ICTY	9.4 (18)	12.04 (21)	NA	19.6** (36)	35*** (2)
State Court	8.5 (82)	16.1 (78)	20.8 (13)	18.0 (2)	NA
Entity Courts	6.1 (233)	NA	NA	NA	NA

*The numbers in brackets depict the number of cases within each category.

** Two individuals falling under this category, Stanislav Galic and Milan Lukic, were convicted to life imprisonment. Since life imprisonment is an indeterminate sentence with no numerical value, this sentence was not included in the statistics.

*** Three individuals falling under this category, Zdravko Tolimir, Ljubisa Beara, and Vujadin Popovic, were convicted to life imprisonment and consequently, not included in the statistics.

Court (46.3 per cent) followed by crimes against humanity (44 per cent). The ICTY rendered most convictions for a combination of war crimes and crimes against humanity (43.9 per cent). Thirteen individuals (7.3 per cent) were convicted of genocide at the State Court and five individuals at the ICTY (in combination with war crimes and crimes against humanity) (6 per cent). In all these cases genocide convictions were related to offences committed during the take-over of the Srebrenica enclave. No other crimes committed during the Bosnian war were classified as genocide by any of the courts.

The reasons for a different composition of convictions at each level of courts might be multiple and can range from: (i) more pragmatic considerations (it is arguably easier to prosecute someone for war crimes compared to crimes against humanity or genocide, given the evidentiary hurdles of proving contextual elements of crimes against humanity or genocide, combined with a lack of experience with and reluctance to charge these complex cases of international crimes at the State level and entity-level courts);[74] (ii) to those related to applicable laws (the 1976 SFRY CC, which is applied at the entity courts, does not provide for crimes against humanity); and finally (iii) to those more speculative ones (such as a different understanding or conceptualization of the conflict by Prosecutors; since classification of atrocities as crimes against humanity might imply a top-down, systematic, planned campaign organized by State authorities, while war crimes can be relatively isolated incidents committed by 'rogue' soldiers at each side of the 'civil war').

Despite the fact that under all applicable laws, sentence ranges are identical for all categories of crimes, that is, genocide, crimes against humanity, and war crimes have the same statutory minima and maxima.[75] Table 21.1 demonstrates that in practice sentences are gradated depending on a category of convicted crimes. Genocide, as the crime of crimes, seems to be subjected to the most severe sentences, followed by crimes against humanity, and war crimes seems to be sentenced the least.[76] At both, the ICTY and the State Court, which dealt with all the crime categories, average sentences are rank ordered depending on the category of crimes.[77] Consequently, as the entity courts dealt exclusively with war crimes, the different composition of cases can help explain differences in punishment severity levels between the different courts.

In order to examine sentencing outcomes even further, the final results present average sentences per each level of courts divided by a position/a level of authority a defendant exercised during the conflict. Arguably a position of a defendant in the overall political or military hierarchy of a State or an organization can have consequences not only for prosecutions,[78] but also for assessment of their level of culpability for the purposes of sentencing. Individuals with authority over others and possibilities to influence behaviour of their followers are generally considered more culpable for systematic, organized criminality such as

[74] cf J Korner, 'Processing of War Crimes at the State Level in Bosnia and Herzegovina' (*OSCE*, 2016) <http://www.osce.org/bih/247221?download=true> accessed 8 November 2017.

[75] Note, however, that these minimum and maximum sentences differ per law as discussed already.

[76] For an overview of scholarly debates regarding comparison of gravity *in abstracto* among individual categories of international crimes for the purposes of sentencing cf Holá et al (n 43) 415, 421–23.

[77] The question remains, however, whether the heavier sentences for genocide or crimes against humanity are related solely to the fact that cases were characterized as genocide or crimes against humanity and this characterization in itself attracts a heavier sentence (related to gravity *in abstracto*), or whether these cases are sentenced harsher because they are indeed the very worst cases with the greatest number of death and harm caused (related to gravity *in concreto*).

[78] It is arguably much more complex to link 'desktop' defendants to crimes committed on the ground without a 'smoking gun' evidence and direct links to the committed crimes.

Table 21.2 Average Sentences (in years) per Position of Defendants per Level of Courts*

	No authority	Low-ranking	Middle-ranking	High-ranking
ICTY	14.6 (13)	14.1** (33)	17.2*** (21)	17.7**** (15)
State Court	12.6 (129)	13.5 (45)	19.7 (3)	NA
Entity Courts	6.0 (213)	5.9 (16)	NA	NA

*The numbers in brackets depict the number of cases within each category.

** One low-ranking individual was convicted to life imprisonment and is not included in the statistics.

***One middle-ranking individual was sentenced to life.

**** Three high-ranking individuals were sentenced to life imprisonment.

international crimes. At the ICTY, for example, the principle of gradation has been developed and applied by judges to the question of punishment, to reflect the relative significance of a defendant in the overall conflict, and 'abuse of position of authority' has been cited as the most frequent aggravating factor. In Bosnia, according to the 2008 War Crimes Strategy, a position of defendant and a level of authority is one of the criteria to determine complexity for the purposes of distribution of war crimes cases among the State Court and the entity courts. Table 21.2 depicts average sentences per level of courts depending on a position of defendant and their level of authority in military, police, paramilitary units, territorial defense, or political institutions during the war.[79]

Before comparing punishment severity, the distribution of cases divided by a position of defendant across the three levels of courts is discussed. Similar to a category of convicted crimes, there are significant differences across the courts. These differences in composition of convicted defendants, based on their level of authority, certainly shed further light on the variation in sentence severity across the courts. The vast majority of those convicted by the SC (129 individuals; 72.9 per cent) and entity courts (213 individuals; 93.2 per cent) had no authority at all, or were low-ranking (forty-five individuals; 25.4 per cent at the SC; sixteen individuals; 6.8 per cent at entity courts). Only three defendants tried at the SC were classified as middle-ranking, and none as high-ranking. There were no high-ranking or middle-ranking defendants convicted by the entity courts. At the ICTY the picture is more diverse. Especially at the beginning of its functioning, the ICTY tried many individuals without any authority (thirteen individuals; 15.9 per cent) and lower-ranking individuals, who constitute the dominant group convicted by the ICTY (thirty-three individuals; 40.2 per cent). After the ICTY adopted the Completion Strategy in 2003, it centred its focus only on those

[79] Four categories of defendants based on a level of authority were distinguished: (1) High—top military and political leaders, who had the authority to decide on the form and implementation of State-wide policies and military campaigns; (2) Middle—intermediate level of military and political officials and leaders, who implemented and executed policies decided upon by the top-level authorities. They were accountable to their superiors, but also had authority over others, e.g. regional political leader, higher-ranking military commanders, heads of executive units within the State bureaucratic apparatus; (3) Low—low level individuals with limited but still some authority over others such as camp commanders, shift leaders, local army commanders, and local politicians; and (4) No authority—rank and file soldiers, camp guards, random individuals etc. who exercised no authority over others.

considered most responsible, while cases of lower-ranking perpetrators were transferred to the domestic courts. Consequently, 25.6 per cent of those tried were classified as middle-ranking (twenty-one individuals) and 18.3 per cent as top-level State officials (fifteen individuals). There might be many reasons for the large prevalence of cases of lower-ranking defendants and foot soldiers at the Bosnian courts. Legally, it is a complex undertaking to link higher-ranking defendants to crimes committed on the ground and Prosecutors might have been hesitant to attempt to do so, either for a lack of experience or a lack of evidence.[80] Also, given the political climate in Bosnia, one can also speculate the extent to which domestic Prosecutors might have been reluctant to issue indictments against the former States' officials and power-holders, who might still have significant political and social capital in the current society.

When it comes to sentence severity, the average sentences do not indicate clear-cut differences across the categories. The lower-ranking defendants tried at the entity courts (and convicted of war crimes) were subjected to the most lenient sentences. Similarly, at the State Court, lower-ranking defendants (coded as those with no or low authority) were subjected to significantly less severe sentences (average of 12.6 years of imprisonment for those with no authority and 13.5 years of imprisonment for low-ranking individuals) compared to the three middle-ranking defendants (average of 19.7). Similar patterns are detectable at the ICTY with a slightly lesser difference between the lower-ranking defendants (individuals with no authority were on average sentenced to 14.6 years imprisonment and low-ranking defendants to 14.1 years imprisonment) and those who occupied positions with a higher level of authority (middle-ranking defendants got on average 17.2 years imprisonment while high-ranking ones were on average subjected to 17.7 years of imprisonment). What is also notable is that average sentences categorized per position of a defendant are, again, relatively comparable at the SC and at the ICTY.

As the above demonstrates, on an aggregate level, the ICTY sentences seem to have been more severe compared to the Bosnian courts, especially at the entity courts level. However, since population of defendants, based on their level of authority, and population of cases based on a category of crimes prosecuted at each level of courts is clearly so divergent, it is difficult to compare the punitiveness across the courts.[81] The entity-level courts have dealt only with individuals without any or only limited levels of authority over others, who were convicted exclusively of isolated incidents of war crimes. This, in itself, can provide an indication of why the sentences handed out at the entity courts are much more lenient compared to the ICTY, but also the State Court. If punishment levels are compared in cases with similar characteristics (lower-ranking defendants convicted exclusively of war crimes), the differences in sentence severity are not so startling. At the SC, such cases led to on average 8.5 years imprisonment (based on eighty-two cases) and at the ICTY the average sentence is higher and amounts to 11.5 years of imprisonment (eight cases). Therefore, and keeping in mind the limited number of cases, limitations of descriptive statistics and the fact that the

[80] cf Korner (n 74). The only high-ranking individual tried at the State Court, Momcilo Mandic, a former Minister of Justice at the RS Government was acquitted as Prosecution did not present sufficient evidence to prove a common intent or link him to the crimes on the ground. *Prosecutor of Bosnia and Herzegovina v Mandic*, State Court of Bosnia and Herzegovina, Judgment, Case No X-KR-05/58, 18 July 2007.

[81] Given the fact that the chapter is based on descriptive statistics, it is impossible to make any conclusive claims regarding consistency or inconsistency of sentencing across the different levels of courts. However, presented results provide the first empirically based and systematic comparisons of sentence severity and can serve as an indication of sentencing patterns.

comparison categories are still relatively general (and do not control, for example, for underlying acts of conviction, number of victims, modes of liability and other factors possibly relevant for sentence determination), the ICTY still seems to have been more punitive (the average is almost double the average of entity-level courts).

21.5 'Atrocity of Crime' versus 'Banality of Offender' Dilemma in Punishing International Crimes

Contrary to what many assume, the punishment practices at the Bosnian courts, in particular at the entities level, have actually been much less severe than at the ICTY. Reasons for differences of punishment are related not only to different legal frameworks with different sentencing ranges stipulated for international crimes, but above all to the widely different composition of cases. In Bosnia, the vast majority of those brought to justice were foot soldiers or low-ranking individuals prosecuted and punished for isolated incidents of war crimes. This can provide at least a partial explanation for comparably more lenient punishment practices. Many of these offenders were convicted for the most serious crimes, such as (multiple) killings, torture, or sexual violence, which would, under normal circumstances, probably entail severe punishment. Surprisingly, however, Bosnian judges seem to have reduced punishment stipulated for international crimes below the statutory minimum relatively often. In many cases judges considered that goals of punishment, in the sense of individual deterrence, protection of society, and offender rehabilitation, would be attained even by a reduced sentence. A personal situation of an offender, his family circumstances and otherwise law-obedient behaviour outside of the context of the war, combined with the fact that a significant amount of time has often passed since the war, were used as 'exceptional mitigation' of punishment. In this sense, judges seem to have prioritized 'banality of an offender' over 'atrocity of crimes' they have committed, when deciding on punishment.

At the ICTY this balancing act[82] seems to have been resolved differently. The ICTY judges, following predominantly a retributive logic, tasked to condemn the atrocities and express 'the outrage of the international community', prioritized the seriousness of crimes as the main factor in meting out punishment. The main and most important consideration for determining sentence severity, according to the ICTY judges, was the gravity of crimes, usually elaborately discussed in sentencing judgments. Almost all defendants judged at the ICTY were portrayed in their defense submissions as perfect, conscientious, and tolerant citizens, prior to and after their involvement in atrocities. On the balance of probabilities, ICTY judges accepted these 'facts' as mitigation. Most often, however, they swept them under the carpet 'given the extreme cruelty of crimes' or 'sheer brutality of the offences'. The good character of an accused, a prior history of tolerance, and crime-free behaviour were

[82] International crimes often entail very serious offences committed during extraordinary circumstances of war, political, or societal upheaval. Under such circumstances, many otherwise law obedient, well-socialized, exemplary soldiers, citizens, politicians get involved in atrocities and commit international crimes. This in itself, for the purposes of punishment, creates a dilemma on how to balance 'atrocious character of crimes' versus 'banality of offenders'. Crimes are extremely serious and in retributive sense deserve the most severe punishment; while perpetrators are under normal circumstances unlikely to re-offend. Through the lenses of individual deterrence, protection of society, or offender rehabilitation, as applied to ordinary offenders, they would, therefore, not deserve the most severe sentences.

usually given no or only very limited weight in sentencing. Consequently, the atrocity of crime versus the banality of offender dilemma seems to have been resolved differently by the ICTY and by the Bosnian judges, in particular at the entity courts. Permissive character of sentencing laws at all three levels of justice does not a priori dictate which goals and factors are to be prioritized. It is within the discretion of judges to determine the punishment best fitting the circumstances of the crime and the offender. Judges at the ICTY and at the Bosnian courts seem to have put emphasis on different sets of punishment goals, which in turn determined the relative weight given to the gravity of crimes and to the personal circumstances of offenders as relevant factors when sentencing. This differential balance can, in turn, offer another explanation for differences in punishment levels among the three systems of courts.

21.6 Conclusion

In Bosnia, the consequences of the past wars are still very much present. Individual, societal, political, and juridical accounting with the past is far from being closed. The ICTY has indisputably contributed significantly to the legal and judicial dealing with the past. The three-tiered system of prosecution and punishment of perpetrators of international crimes implemented in Bosnia and Herzegovina following the wars in the early 1990s was praised as a possible model for the future interaction between the international and the domestic justice systems after atrocities. As any other reckoning with the past atrocities, however, it was also fiercely criticized, especially by victims' organizations, local political leadership, or survivors themselves, be it justifiably, or less so. The analysis of this chapter can be seen as one of the first attempts to bring empirical data to often impressionistic, politically, but also emotionally charged discussions regarding post-war criminal justice in Bosnia. Much more empirical and theoretical research is needed to disentangle and compare prosecutions and sentencing of perpetrators of international crimes in the former Yugoslavia and to assess the legacies of the juridical dealing with the past. The comparative overview of sentencing laws and practices presented in this chapter can be seen as the first, modest step in that direction. It demonstrates that, contrary to public perceptions and imaginations, sentences handed out at the ICTY have been, on an aggregate level, comparable or more severe, relative to those handed out by the Bosnian domestic courts. Reasons behind the identified sentence severity gap are arguably largely attributable to: (i) a very different population of cases prosecuted at the ICTY and at domestic courts; and (ii) different sentencing goals prioritized at different levels of courts. It is, however, a different question whether any of these sentences can ever be (considered) adequate. Punishing international crimes is always an extremely complex task involving balancing different goals and interests, weighing a multiplicity of factors and 'translating' the unimaginable suffering, cruelty of atrocities, and offender's culpability into a simplistic metric of a number of years in prison. Arguably, no criminal punishment, no matter how severe or how well legally justified and consistent with other cases at other courts, would ever be adequate and measure up to the anguish and destruction caused by international crimes.

22

When Justice is Done

The ICTY and the Post-trial Phase

Joris van Wijk and Barbora Holá***

Until 30 September 2017, the International Criminal Tribunal for the former Yugoslavia (ICTY) has convicted eighty-two individuals with a final judgment and acquitted eighteen individuals of all charges. Of these sentenced individuals five (6.1 per cent) serve a life sentence, the majority of these have been sentenced to determinate sentences which range from two to forty years. The average determinate sentence is 15.6 years. Based on our previous work[1] this chapter focuses on the 'post-trial phase' at the ICTY and discusses what happens to ICTY defendants after being convicted or acquitted.

The first part will provide an overview of 'post-conviction challenges', and discuss the many dilemmas that the ICTY, States which enforce ICTY sentences, and the sentenced individuals themselves have faced. Special attention is given to the designation of an enforcement state and the conditions under which international prisoners serve their sentences. This part will also discuss early release practices at the ICTY, focusing on factors that are considered in granting early release and problematizing whether and to what extent individuals can, upon release, be considered rehabilitated.

In turn, the second part discusses 'post acquittal challenges', focusing in particular on the possibility and occurrence of subsequent prosecutions in domestic courts, following an acquittal at the ICTY. The conclusion assesses the ICTY's legacy when it comes to post-conviction issues. The data presented are based on an analysis of case law, academic literature, interviews with relevant stakeholders and, if academic sources were not available, newspapers and online sources.

* Associate Professor at the Department of Criminal Law and Criminology at VU University of Amsterdam and co-director of the Center for International Criminal Justice (CICJ).

** Senior Researcher at the NSCR and Associate Professor at the Department of Criminal Law and Criminology at VU University of Amsterdam and co-director of CICJ.

[1] This chapter is a compilation of content which has previously been published in the following contributions: B Holá and J van Wijk, 'Life After Conviction; an Empirical Analysis' (2014) 12 Journal of International Criminal Justice 109; J Kelder, B Holá and J van Wijk, 'Rehabilitation and Early Release of Perpetrators of International Crimes: A Case Study of ICTY and ICTR' (2014) 14 International Criminal Law Review 1177; B Holá, J Kelder, and J van Wijk, 'Effectiveness of International Criminal Tribunals: Empirical Assessment of Rehabilitation as Sentencing Goal' in C Bailliet and N Hayashi (eds), *Legitimacy and Effectiveness of International Criminal Tribunals* (Hart Publishing 2017); B Holá and J van Wijk, 'Acquittals in International Criminal Justice: Pyrrhic Victories?' (2017) 30 Leiden Journal of International Law 24. The results presented in this chapter are part of the larger research project 'When Justice is Done'. For more details see <http://www.whenjusticeisdone.org> accessed 1 March 2020.

Joris van Wijk and Barbora Holá, *When Justice is Done* In: *Legacies of the International Criminal Tribunal for the Former Yugoslavia.* Edited by: Carsten Stahn, Carmel Agius, Serge Brammertz, Colleen Rohan, Oxford University Press (2020). © The Several Contributors
DOI: 10.1093/oso/9780198862956.003.0023

22.1 Post-conviction Challenges

The drafters of the ICTY Statute almost entirely neglected issues regarding the enforcement of sentences. As one commentator noted 'the contrast between the meticulous regulation of the prosecution and trial, and the nearly total neglect of regulation for the execution of sentences could hardly have been more glaring'.[2] The following section examines the most pertinent post-conviction challenges encountered at the ICTY relating to (i) designation of an enforcement state where a prisoner will serve his/her sentence; (ii) conditions of incarceration; (iii) early release; and (iv) post-release.

22.1.1 Designation of Enforcement States

According to Article 27 of the ICTY Statute a convicted individual is to serve his/her sentence in a State designated from a list of States willing to enforce the Tribunal's sentences. The imprisonment is governed by the laws of the State enforcing the sentence and subjected to the supervision of the Tribunal.[3] The very limited regulation of the enforcement of sentences in the Statute is complemented by the Rules of Procedure in Evidence (RPE). Rules 103 and 104 of the RPE, however, do not add much more clarity and simply reiterate the regulation contained in the Statute. The President of the Tribunal is responsible for designation of the enforcement State. The transfer to the designated State shall be effected as soon as possible after the final verdict and, pending the transfer, the convicted person remains in the detention unit of the respective tribunal.[4]

Consequently, the ICTY has relied on a decentralized network of States to implement the custodial sanctions. The system is based on the double-consent of individual States: first, a state must enter into a general sentence enforcement agreement with the ICTY whereby it expresses its willingness to enforce sentences in the future and second, the States that concluded such agreements are to give consent to accept individual convicts on an ad hoc basis. The designation of an enforcement State is further elaborated upon in the Practice Directions, policy papers issued by the Presidents of the Tribunals.[5] On an ad hoc basis, after a final verdict, the Registrar approaches selected States that entered into enforcement agreements to indicate their preparedness to do so in the particular case.

The ICTY Practice Directions contains general criteria which should be considered when deciding which State(s) to approach: (i) the national laws regarding pardon and

[2] S Karstedt, 'Life After Punishment for Nazi War Criminals: Reputation, Careers and Normative Climate in Post-war Germany' in S Farrall et al (eds), *Contemporary Perspectives on Life After Punishment* (Routledge 2011) 240–76, 243.

[3] Due to the time-consuming nature of international criminal proceedings, many of the released in practice served a considerable part or the whole of their sentence prior to their conviction in the UN detention centre. Consequently, the UN detention centre can 'de facto' also be regarded an integral part of the sentencing enforcement system.

[4] Rules of Procedure and Evidence of the International Criminal Tribunal for the former Yugoslavia (RPE) IT/32 (1994) Rule 103.

[5] ICTY Practice Direction on the Procedure for the International Tribunal's Designation of the State in which a Convicted Person is to Serve his/her Sentence of Imprisonment IT/137/Rev1 (1 September 2009); ICTR Practice Direction On The Procedure For Designation Of The State In Which A Convicted Person Is To Serve His/Her Sentence Of Imprisonment [As revised and amended on 23 September 2008] (September 2008); Special Court of Sierra Leone Practice Direction for Designation of State for Enforcement of Sentence (10 July 2009).

commutation of sentences, maximum sentence available and other consideration relating to the ability of the state to enforce a particular sentence; (ii) equitable distribution of convicted persons among all the States; and (iii) other relevant considerations.[6] If the approached State expresses its willingness to accept the convict, the proposal is made to the President to designate it as the enforcement State in that particular case.

Convicted persons have no right to be heard in this respect. They may inform the President of their preferences but these can be disregarded, without motivation.[7] In the decision-making process, the President generally has a wide discretion but is asked to consider several factors, such as; whether the convicted person is expected to serve as a witness in further proceedings, whether the person will be relocated as a witness following the sentence, and any medical or psychological reports, linguistic skills, general conditions of imprisonment and rules governing security and liberty in the State concerned.[8] Particular attention should be paid to the proximity of the convicted person's relatives.

Also, in the Manual on Developed Practices, the ICTY emphasizes that the Tribunal should pay special attention to geographical distance between the enforcement State and the former Yugoslavia, in order to enable family and friends to visit the prisoners.[9] In practice, however, many convicts have been sent to countries far away from their homes and relatives. For example, when the ICTY's first convict, Erdemović, was about to serve his sentence, the ICTY entered into enforcement agreements with Norway, Finland, and Italy. Since Italy is geographically closest to the former Yugoslavia, one would have expected Erdemović to be imprisoned there. He, however, was sent to Norway.[10]

In practice, it is not entirely clear what considerations have been taken into account when approaching and designating an enforcement State since the majority of decisions and communications between the Tribunal and individual states are confidential. According to one of our interviewees, who worked at the ICTY Office for Legal Aid and Defence Matters (OLAD), the most important consideration is how many ICTY prisoners the country already has.[11] This criterion is also emphasized in the ICTY Manual on Developed Practices—the ICTY strives to ensure an even burden-sharing among enforcement States in terms of the number of convicted persons transferred and the length of the sentences imposed.[12] Since many of the ICTY convicts do not speak any language, other than their own, the linguistic skills of a person are not the decisive criterion.[13]

Finding an enforcement State is often a very burdensome process involving 'a lot of diplomacy'.[14] This is also demonstrated by the fact that it has taken on average ten months at the ICTY, after the final verdict is issued, to transfer a convict to an enforcement country.[15]

[6] ICTY Practice Direction (n 5) para 3 (a)–(c).

[7] *Order withdrawing confidential Status of 31 May 2006 Decision on Request of Zoran Žigić* IT-98-30/1-ES (1 October 2008); interview with a legal adviser of Haradin Bala, (27 and 30 May 2013) where he indicated that Bala wanted to go to Italy but ended up in France. Transcripts of all interviews are on file with authors.

[8] ICTY Practice Direction (n 5) para 4.

[9] *ICTY Manual on Developed Practices*, prepared in conjunction with UNICRI as part of a project to preserve the legacy of the ICTY (Turin: UNICRI Publisher 2009) 152.

[10] M M Penrose, 'Lest We Fail: The Importance of Enforcement in International Criminal Law' (1999–2000) 15 American University International Law Review 322, 367.

[11] Interview with a former Intern at Office for Legal Aid and Defence Matters (OLAD) ICTY (The Hague, The Netherlands, 10 April 2013).

[12] M M Penrose, 'Spandau Revisited: The Question of Detention for International War Crimes' (1999–2000) 16 New York Law School Journal of Human Rights 553, 554.

[13] Interview with a former OLAD Intern (n 11).

[14] ibid.

[15] Data as of September 2017.

Another employee of the OLAD unit at the ICTY, however, claimed that out of human rights considerations factors such as proximity of family members, presence of people able to speak to a prisoner in a language he understands, and security level of a potential prison are all relevant factors when approaching States with the request to enforce a particular sentence.[16] All in all, the ICTY has concluded general enforcement agreements with sixteen different European countries and a number of ad hoc enforcement agreements with Germany. The ICTY's prisoners have been scattered across thirteen countries and no country has held more than seven convicts.[17]

22.1.2 Imprisonment Regimes

As demonstrated above, the ICTY convicts have been serving their sentences in different European countries and consequently, have experienced widely different prison regimes, as prison systems differ considerably within Europe.[18] On the one hand, prison conditions of the Scandinavian countries are known to be very favourable and prisoner-friendly. Norway, for example, exemplifies what is referred to as Scandinavian 'exceptionalism' in penal policies.[19] It has a low level of imprisonment, small prisons, a low occupancy rate, with a single cell for each prisoner and a progressive system focused on rehabilitation. On the other hand, countries such as Italy or France are characterized by the overcrowded prisons, shared prison cells and a lesser focus on rehabilitation and progressive reintegration of prisoners.[20]

Not only are there differences between individual European countries regarding the general prison systems, but prison conditions also vary within the countries themselves and even within prison units, within the same prison, depending on the security level. Whether an international prisoner is placed in a high security prison, protective custody, regular prison, or an open prison has great consequences for their daily life and influences the execution of his/her sentence to a considerable extent. The Statute and RPE are virtually silent regarding the type of prisons international convicts shall be sent to. This determination lies with domestic authorities and arguably differs per State and per convict.

According to a former employee of the ICTY OLAD the majority of international prisoners are placed in high security prisons, but 'that is where things go wrong'.[21] Due to the character of international crimes, international convicts are often classified as 'the worst criminals' by domestic authorities. In practice, however, many of them are former politicians or military/State officials, who according to our respondent, pose no danger to society. Therefore, 'there is practically no need to place them in high security facilities'.[22]

Our interviews with national prison authorities, however, suggest that at least some countries take a slightly more nuanced approach. This seems particularly to be the case

[16] Interview with a former Legal Officer at the OLAD ICTY (The Hague, The Netherlands, 7 June 2013).

[17] Twenty-three ICTY convicts served their entire sentence in the UNDU in The Hague.

[18] A M van Kalmthout, F B A M Hofstee-van der Meulen, and F Dunkel (eds) *Foreigners in European Prisons* (Wolf Legal Publishers, 2007) 9.

[19] J Pratt, 'Scandinavian Exceptionalism in an Era of Penal Excess' (2007) 48 British Journal of Criminology 119.

[20] cf B Moody 'Italy's overcrowded prisons close to collapse' (*Reuters*, 12 June 2013) <http://www.reuters.com/article/2013/06/12/us-italy-prisons-idUSBRE95B0IF20130612> accessed January 2018; T John, 'Inside the Heart of French Prisons' (*Time*, 28 February 2017) <http://time.com/4681612/french-prisons/> accessed January 2018.

[21] Interview OLAD ICTY (n 16).

[22] ibid.

after they have had some experience in detaining international prisoners. In Norway, for example, international convicts are indeed placed in high security prisons, but not necessarily in maximum security units with the strictest regime.[23] Each transferred person is subjected to an individual security and health assessment and depending on a number of criteria a decision is made. Such criteria includes: his/her risk of fleeing, safety concerns in regards to the potential risk from other inmates (religion and ethnicity of other inmates is taken into account), and health considerations (such as the need for specialized health care).[24]

Erdemović, as the first international convict, was placed in a high security prison with a strict security regime because '[a]t the time Norway didn't know what to expect'.[25] Over time, however, it turned out that international prisoners are usually 'exemplary prisoners' with a very low risk of escape compared to other categories of inmates, such as organized criminals.[26] As noted by a representative of the Norwegian Ministry of Justice '[from] [o]ur past experiences with the ICTY convicts [we] learned that they don't cause many problems in detention and that they don't pose a real risk to escape'.[27] Over time, therefore, international convicts were placed in high security prisons but with more lenient security regimes.[28] This decision, according to our respondents, caused no problems: 'They behaved very [well] ... obviously there are individual differences, but some of them actually behaved quite like they would do in the military. If a prison officer would come in uniform, they would straighten up and stand up right.'[29]

In contrast in Sweden, as a matter of standard operating procedure all international convicts are initially placed in 'protective custody units'(small units of six to twelve inmates with a strict security regime). Typically, persons staying in these units have requested a stay there because they are being or feel threatened, for example because they talked to the police, or have debts with other prisoners. The international convicts are, in a way, an exception in these units, because they are automatically placed in protective custody for security reasons.[30] Conversely, in Finland, Hazim Delić was transferred to an open prison—a facility without any walls.[31]

ICTY prisoners are typically integrated into domestic prison populations and national prison authorities do not distinguish between international convicts and other inmates.[32] International prisoners are treated as any other foreign prisoners, in the domestic context, which leads to differences in their treatment compared to the 'ordinary' domestic prisoners. Prison authorities have to account for cultural and linguistic differences, while

23 Interview with a representative of the Correctional Services Department, Ministry of Justice, Norway (5 June 2013).

24 Interview with former counsellor at National Directorate of the Correctional Services Department, Ministry of Justice, Norway (4 June 2013).

25 ibid.

26 ibid.

27 Interview with Correctional Services Department, Norway (n 23).

28 ibid.

29 Interview with Correctional Services Department, Norway (n 23).

30 Interview with a representative of National Security Unit, Prison and Probation Service, Sweden (18 June 2013).

31 *Order Issuing a Public Redacted Version of Decision on Hazim Delić's Motion for Commutation of Sentence* IT-96-21-ES (15 July 2008) para 7. The President notes that Delić was transferred to Satakunta prison, which is, according to the official website of the Finnish Criminal Sanctions Agency, an open institution.

32 Interview, National Security Unit (n 30); interview with a representative of Directrice Penitentiaire D'Insertion et de Probation, Ministry of Justice, France (20 May 2013); interview with a defence lawyer of Goran Jelisić, Italy (June 2013); interview with a representative of the Danish Prison and Probation Service, Denmark (13 May 2013).

distance from their countries of origin substantially limits the possibility of family visits.[33] For example, Bala was never visited by his family while imprisoned in France for four and a half years and his defence lawyer states that the main reason for this lies in practical obstacles such as the costs of travelling and housing and the visa requirements for Kosovars in France.[34] The interviewed prison officials from Norway also underlined the extra costs of family visits for the international prisoners.[35] For this reason 'the national treatment of international prisoners', is at times modified. When international prisoners are visited by their families in Norway or France, for example, special arrangements are made regarding visiting hours. Visiting hours are adjusted so that the prisoners can spend as much time as possible with their family within the limited timeframe the family spends in the country of imprisonment.[36]

Furthermore, in many countries, such as Sweden or Norway, a progressive system of incarceration is adopted whereby national prisoners will move, throughout their imprisonment, to lower security level prison facilities with more lenient regimes and less significant limitations on an inmates' freedom. The more 'progressed' in the system, an inmate is, the higher the possibility of leave is in order to gradually reintegrate the offender into society. This system is, however, not implemented in case of foreign prisoners in general, and international prisoners in particular.[37] The prison authorities try to minimize the potentially negative impact of these policies on international prisoners by adopting specifically tailored measures in order to alleviate their possible frustrations: 'We asked ourselves how we could give [one of the international prisoners] something as a compensation for the lack of family contact and the limitations he faced in leaving prison. So he could take a coffee outside, get some physical activity.'[38]

One of the ways to cater for this was to provide the prisoner with relatively more escorted leaves from prison. This started with a closely monitored visit to the local town, gradually leading to several trips a month which included cycling, Nordic skiing, watching football matches, or making a two-day hike in the mountains. Not all international prisoners are, however, provided with such options. With respect to leaves, our data suggests that the approach across countries and prisons differs considerably. Countries typically deny requests to leave the country of imprisonment and go home—even when faced with tragic personal circumstances.[39] Besides this, quite varying leave policies have been applied. In Sweden, international prisoners do not have the possibility to go on unaccompanied leaves. 'They can, together with prison staff, three to four times a year go on leave for a maximum period of four to six hours.'[40] In contrast, in Norway:

> The Hague people can go on leave. This is not directly after their arrival. But if they behave well, they too are allowed to go on leave. In principle, detainees have the right to a

[33] Interview Directrice Penitentiaire D'Insertion et de Probation (n 32).

[34] Interview with a legal adviser for Haradin Bala (n 7).

[35] Interview with a representative of Norwegian prison II, Norway (14 June 2013).

[36] Interviews (n 32).

[37] Interview with a representative of Norwegian prison III, Norway (27 June 2013); Interview National Security Unit (n 30).

[38] Interview with a representative of Norwegian prison IV, Norway (24 July 2013).

[39] The French district court, for example, denied a prisoner's request to attend the funeral of his mother: interview with legal adviser of Haradin Bala (n 7).

[40] Interview National Security Unit (n 30).

> maximum of 18 days per year. If they have children or special needs, this can be upgraded to 30 days. Inmates can for example request to visit a friend, or stay a weekend over with family members. The prison officers can set conditions that they for example are not allowed to leave a certain area.[41]

One of the prisoners in Norway who got acquainted with a Serbian family living in the vicinity of his prison was, for example, allowed to spend some weekends at their place.[42]

One of the most interesting questions regarding imprisonment of international criminals is their rehabilitation. Rehabilitation is often cited as one of the goals of international sentencing and it is particularly emphasized when considering early release. As discussed already, international prisoners are (with slight modifications) simply incorporated into domestic prison populations and subjected to the same rehabilitation programmes as ordinary domestic criminals.[43] As one of the respondents noted: 'For us, it is important to treat them like anybody else who committed a serious crime.'[44] There are, however, several problems with this approach: (i) as discussed, international prisoners are usually kept in high security establishments and do not progress through the system to lower security regimes. Rehabilitation programmes in many countries are adjusted to the progressive nature of incarceration and a larger variety of rehabilitative activities are available in lower security prisons; (ii) rehabilitative programmes are usually offered in a language of the country where a prison is located. This can be a major problem for many international prisoners who simply do not speak the language and consequently, do not have access to the offered rehabilitation activities; and above all (iii) it might be questionable to what extent rehabilitation programmes developed for ordinary criminals are suitable for international prisoners who committed their crimes under very specific circumstances and are by many criminologists regarded as a different type of criminal, compared to ordinary rapists or murderers.[45] They are nonetheless all placed in normal domestic correctional facilities amongst perpetrators of conventional crimes. The question here is to what extent domestic prison officers and therapists are instructed to, and are capable of, safeguarding the Tribunals' ambitious goal of rehabilitating these offenders. The director of a small prison in northern Norway mentioned that the ICTY never directly, or via the Ministry, instructed prison authorities to work on rehabilitation. She also questioned if her prison actually had the expertise to deal with these matters, arguing that it was unusual to have inmates who committed such levels of violence.

> For normal crimes we had programmes. Programmes like 'breaking drug abuse' or 'breaking violence'. Many prisoners go to these programmes, they talk in group sessions or individually about the crime. (. . .) But what competence do we have to deal with them [the ICTY convicts] (. . .) To think about a programme for war criminals is out of reach (. . .) We are not educated in these matters.[46]

[41] Interview Norwegian Prison II (n 35).

[42] Interview with a representative of Norwegian prison III (n 37).

[43] Interview with a former representative of Norwegian prison I, Norway (2 July 2013); Interview with a lawyer at the Judicial Unit of the Criminal Sanctions Agency, Ministry of Justice, Finland (5 August 2013); interviews (n 32); interview Norwegian Prison II (n 35).

[44] Interview Correctional Services Department (n 23).

[45] A L Smeulers, *In opdracht van de staat: Gezagsgetrouwe criminelen en internationale misdrijven* (Prisma Print 2012); M A Drumbl, *Atrocity, Punishment and International Law* (Cambridge University Press 2007).

[46] Interview Norwegian prison IV (n 38).

22.1.3 Early Release

Similar to conditions of imprisonment, the commutation of sentences and pardons are, according to the ICTY Statute, governed by the law of the enforcement State. Article 28 of the ICTY Statute states that if an imprisoned individual is eligible for commutation of sentence, according to the domestic law of the State of enforcement, the State shall notify the Tribunal. The President of the Tribunal then decides if an early release of the individual is warranted, taking into account 'the interests of justice' and 'general principles of law'.[47] Consequently, on the face of it, the eligibility for early release differs depending on the laws of the enforcement State. The Tribunal, however, retains a supervisory power in this respect and an international prisoner should not be released without the approval of the President. The four factors the President considers when making such decisions are provided for in Rule 125 of the ICTY RPE: (i) the gravity of crimes; (ii) the treatment of similarly situated prisoners; (iii) prisoner's demonstration of rehabilitation; and (iv) any substantial cooperation with the Prosecutor.

In actual early release practice, the 'gravity of the crimes' criterion has rarely played much of a role. In none of the decisions has the President mentioned a crime to be of a relatively low gravity suggesting that this would positively impact the early release decision making. Neither has gravity of the crimes been the only decisive factor *not* to release someone. The 'treatment of similarly situated prisoners' criterion, on the other hand, seems to be a very decisive criterion for granting early release. Although domestic laws, regarding the early release are very divergent,[48] over the years 'an unwritten rule' developed that international prisoners qualify for release only after having served two-thirds of their sentences. This two-thirds threshold was applied due to the fact that in the majority of enforcement countries prisoners are eligible for early release after serving two-thirds of their sentence. With regard to the fourth criterion, 'substantial cooperation with the Prosecutor' the President in some instances refused to take into account cooperation prior to conviction since it was already taken into account in mitigation of sentence.[49] In some cases cooperation of the accused during trial is considered when granting early release,[50] while a guilty plea in the trial phase can also be qualified as such.[51] After conviction, it seems that there must be some active engagement by a prisoner with the Prosecution, such as testimony in other trials, in order to be taken into account in favour of the early release. The mere availability of the convict to testify is not to be considered as a form of cooperation. When the Prosecution does not ask for cooperation, the willingness to cooperate is treated as a neutral factor.[52]

[47] Art 28 ICTY Statute (1993). A similar regulation is contained in the ICTR (art 27) and SCSL (art 23) Statutes. Also see Rules 123, 124 ICTY RPE; Rules 124,125 ICTR RPE; and Rules 123, 124 SCSL RPE.

[48] For example, in France and Finland, under specified circumstances, convicts are eligible for early release after serving 1/2 of their sentence. In contrast in Belgium, Denmark, Sweden, or Norway the necessary period to be served is 2/3 and in Spain generally 3/4 of an imposed sentence.

[49] *Decision of the President on Commutation of Sentence of Mlado Radić*, IT-98-30/1-ES (22 June 2007) para 15.

[50] cf *Public Redacted Decision of President on Early Release of Dragan Obrenović*, IT-02-60/2-ES (21 September 2011) para 28; *Public Redacted Version of Decision of the President on the Early Release of Omar Serushago*, MICT-12-28-ES (13 December 2012) para 30; *Decision on the Early Release Request of Juvenal Rugambarara*, ICTR-00-59 (8 February 2012) para 10.

[51] *Public Redacted Version on Decision of the President on Sentence Remission of Goran Jelisić*, IT-95-10-ES (28 May 2013) paras 31, 32.

[52] *Decision of the President on the Application for Pardon or Commutation of Sentence of Drago Josipović*, IT-95-16-ES (30 January 2006) para 10; *Public and Redacted Version of the 27 March 2013 Decision of the President on Early Release of Radomir Kovač* IT-96-23&23/1-ES (3 July 2013) para 30; *Decision of the President on Commutation of Sentence of Predrag Banović*, IT-02-65/1-ES (10 March 2006) paras 5, 14; however, in the decision of 3 September

22.1.4 Measuring Rehabilitation

The way in which the President has in actual practice been assessing the third factor in the context of early release— 'the prisoner's demonstration of rehabilitation'—could best be described as flawed. The President is vested with large discretionary powers regarding how to interpret the concept of rehabilitation and what factors to consider relevant 'to demonstrate rehabilitation'. Given that rehabilitating perpetrators of ordinary crimes incarcerated in their home countries is already challenging, one would expect that rehabilitating 'enemies of mankind' in foreign prisons would be even more difficult.[53] In this regard it is problematic that our analysis of early release decisions demonstrates that Presidents' interpretation of rehabilitation is by no means straightforward. Instead of using a clear definition and clear assessment criteria, the President relies on a seemingly coincidental, ad hoc list of numerous factors which relate to (i) the convict's period in prison; (ii) his/her future prospects; (iii) his/her reflection on crimes; and (iv) his/her personal characteristics.

The vast majority of early release decisions, but not all, discuss various factors related to the *period in prison* as demonstrating a prisoner's rehabilitation. In these instances, terms such as 'exemplary behaviour', 'good conduct', and a 'model prisoner', were used.[54] In some decisions, conduct in prison was the only indicator of rehabilitation. Other factors that relate to the period in prison are the extent to which the prisoner: interacted with fellow inmates; participated in training or rehabilitation programmes; tried to learn the local language; was deemed to have 'changed for the better'; got promoted to, or behaved well in, a more lenient prison regime; and demonstrated a positive attitude towards other nationalities in prison. The second group of factors relates to the *future perspectives* of the prisoner. The most important factor in this respect is whether prisoners have good family relations. If they do, they are regarded as being more likely to return to a stable family and lead a normal, crime-free life. The prisoner's relationship with his/her home country, as well as his/her career prospects, is also deemed relevant. The explicitly expressed intention not to reoffend in the future was also regularly taken into account. Additionally, the Tribunal pays attention to the question of how the prisoner *reflects upon his/her crimes*. In this regard, the President seems to distinguish between acceptance of responsibility and showing remorse, but without making a clear conceptual differentiation and without attaching any consequences to the difference between both types of reflection.[55] In the majority of cases, where this factor was mentioned, the prisoner was considered to have reflected upon his/her deeds, and either accepted responsibility, or shown remorse, or both. In some decisions,

2008 actually granting early release to Banović, the President weighed his willingness to cooperate in favour of his request for early release (para 14).

[53] The ICTY Trial Chamber in its first ever judgment in the Erdemović case recognized that cultural and linguistic difficulties of being imprisoned in far-off third countries may also impact ICTY prisoners (*Prosecutor v Erdemović* (Trial Chamber Judgment) IT-96-22-T (29 November 1996) para 75), but the Tribunal has not since undertaken any actions to mitigate possible problems. Consequently, as already referred to, international prisoners have limited access to rehabilitative programmes in general, let alone treatment, which is specifically tailored towards the specific crimes they committed.

[54] Specific references to decisions in relation to the factors mentioned in this paragraph can be found in Kelder, Holá, and Wijk (n 1).

[55] For a much more elaborate discussion on acceptance of responsibility and remorse at ICTY, see B Holá, J van Wijk, F Constantini and A Korhonnen, 'Does Remorse Count? ICTY Convicts' Reflections on Their Crimes in Early Release Decisions' (2018) 28 International Criminal Justice Review 349.

however, the President concluded that the prisoner had not taken in the meaning of his/her sentence; had not sufficiently reflected upon his/her crimes; had failed to accept responsibility; or had shown no remorse, or denied committing any crime. This finding, however, seems not to have any repercussions on the evaluation of the level of prisoner's rehabilitation by the President. Finally, though to a lesser extent, the tribunals consider the *personal characteristics of a prisoner*, such as mental health (psychiatric illness or absence thereof), personality traits, conduct prior to the perpetration of crimes, and age.

Although the President does not use a clear definition of rehabilitation, the discussion above suggests that, to a certain extent, early release decisions do operationalize rehabilitation in a rather systematic way. The factors taken into account by the Presidents to a large extent reflect rehabilitation as operationalized in many domestic jurisdictions with respect to ordinary crimes, focusing on (i) rehabilitation processes in prison, such as vocational training and programmes, behaviour in prison, and reflection on crimes; and (ii) reintegration prospects of the prisoner, such as his/her family ties and prospects of employment. As such, it seems that the tribunals rely on a rather 'traditional' concept of rehabilitation. This might be caused by the fact that the President is largely dependent on the information provided to him/her by the national prison authorities enforcing the Tribunals' sentences and that, consequently, any discussion of rehabilitation is based largely on this information. Arguably, domestic prison authorities, while evaluating the eligibility of international prisoners for early release and preparing their submissions to the Tribunal, rely on their 'standard operating procedures' and apply the same format and tools to international prisoners as their domestic/ordinary counterparts.

The ICTY President had, until 2017, only in three instances (Dragoljub Kunarac in 2017, Haradin Bala in 2013, and Mlađo Radić in 2013) *postponed* the early release of an international prisoner after having served two-thirds of his sentence based on a negative assessment of his level of rehabilitation. Radić's release, for example, was blocked arguing that the prisoner's rehabilitation 'has been impeded by his inability to come to terms with his environment' and:

> there is little to no evidence of actual rehabilitation other than his response to the material provided by him in which he expresses his regret for the suffering of the victims. Based upon the foregoing, I consider [...] demonstration of rehabilitation to be a neutral factor in my assessment of his suitability for early release.[56]

Reiterating that the Tribunal's practice of granting early release after having served two-thirds of a sentence is not an entitlement, the President decided that the request for early release should be denied for the time being, and that the prisoner should be granted early release almost one and a half years later than he was supposed to, on the basis of the two-thirds criterion.[57] This means that, apart from these three individuals, *all other convicts* granted early released at the ICTY by 2017 had been found sufficiently rehabilitated after having served two-thirds of their sentences.

[56] *Decision of President on Application for Pardon or Commutation of Sentence of Mlađo Radić*, IT-98-30/1-ES ICTY (9 January 2013) para 26.

[57] Why the President believes Radić to be better rehabilitated on 31 December 2012 is not explained. No conditions were set.

When assessing the level of rehabilitation, the President seems to do little to critically evaluate the sources, which are submitted to demonstrate prisoners' rehabilitation. The fact that the Tribunal is not actively involved in the enforcement of sentences means that the President relies heavily on information provided by third parties. According to Article 3(b) of the ICTY Practice Direction on the Procedure for the Determination of Applications for Pardon, Commutation of Sentence and Early Release, the Registry shall, in reaction to an early release request, ask for:

> reports and observations from the relevant authorities in the enforcement State as to the behaviour of the convicted person during his or her period of incarceration and [. . .] any psychiatric or psychological evaluations prepared on the mental condition of the convicted person during the period of incarceration.[58]

Although enforcement States have not been given any guidance on how to rehabilitate international prisoners, the President typically trusts their reports and follows their advice in relation to the prisoners' level of rehabilitation. The Norwegian authorities, for example, addressed Obrenović's custodial behaviour by stating that he had not breached any rules or regulations during his detention. The President was informed by a letter that Obrenović reliably served as a kitchen assistant for several years 'taking full responsibility for his duties and fulfilling his obligations very accurately'. Based on the information provided, the President was of the view that 'Mr. Obrenović's good behavior while serving his sentence demonstrates some rehabilitation and weighs in favour of his early release'.[59] How Obrenović's accurate fulfilment of obligations in the kitchen actually assists in rehabilitating this former military officer convicted of persecuting hundreds of civilians remains unclear. Typically, the President does not question such issues.

ICTY's early release decisions paint a picture of a rather lenient President who generally trusts the information provided by either the authorities of the enforcement State or the convict him or herself. It raises questions as to the extent to which this trust is justified. For obvious reasons, convicts have 'vested' interests in demonstrating rehabilitation. But the same can, to some extent, be said about the enforcement States. They bear the costs of incarcerating convicts who are generally not to be reintegrated in their societies and are to be relocated or repatriated. How positive would they be in the assessment of international prisoners' behaviour and levels of rehabilitation if they were to reintegrate in their own societies?

22.1.5 Post Release

In domestic criminal proceedings, after being released early, individuals are usually subjected to reintegration programmes, stipulated conditions, and supervision of a parole

[58] Practice Direction on the Procedure for the Determination of Applications for Pardon, Commutation of Sentence and Early Release of Persons Convicted by the International Tribunal, ICTY, IT/146/Rev3 (16 September 2010). Similar provisions are contained in the SCSL Practice Direction for Designation of Sate for Enforcement of Sentence (10 July 2006) art 5 (C), (D).

[59] *Public Redacted Version of Decision of President of Early Release of Dragan Obrenović* ICTY, IT-02-60/2-ES, ICTY (21 September 2011) para 23.

officer. In contrast, at the ICTY there is no institutional oversight, and a general lack of information regarding the lives of the former prisoners. Early release at the ICTY is equivalent to unconditional pardon in domestic penal systems. Released individuals are not subjected to any conditions, there is no possibility for them to be called upon to serve the remainder of their sentence,[60] and no assistance is provided regarding their reintegration into society. However, there are indications that the return of international prisoners to society and their post-release life is not entirely problem-free.

In general, the fate of released international prisoners is to a large extent determined by the way in which the conflict ended in their respective countries, their political or societal status, and the living circumstances of their family members. The former Yugoslavia disintegrated into various successor countries, largely reflecting the ethnic lines of former fighting groups. The ICTY's Serb prisoners are thus free to return to Serbia, Croats to Croatia, and Bosniacs to Bosnia. The most prominent ones are at times welcomed as war heroes in their respective countries and may continue to publicly justify their crimes, often to the dismay of victim groups. Some return to their communities, live with their families, and again become active in municipal politics, while others cannot find jobs, feel rejected by society, have lost their pension entitlements and fight to make a living.[61]

A related and perhaps even more complicating element is that ICTY-released prisoners often return to deeply divided societies which are—even years after the atrocities have taken place—still dealing with the legacy of a destructive war and genocide. The President's assessment of prisoners' rehabilitation efforts and future reintegration opportunities are, however, only focused on the convicts' individual position. This leads to various, quite fundamental, questions: can the individual rehabilitation process of international perpetrators in a Swedish or Spanish vacuum be successful without reflecting on the society (s) he is to return to? Does it accurately address the collective nature of the crimes (s)he committed, the destruction of social fabric (s)he was part of, and the still profound ethnic or religious divisions in the society (s)he may (or may not) return to? And how does it relate to the Tribunal's other sentencing goals of retribution and reconciliation? One only has to review the post release statements of Biljana Plavšić or Veselin Šljivančanin to understand the possibly detrimental consequences of the Tribunal's limited take on rehabilitation for the reconciliation processes in the former Yugoslavia. After being released both denied having committed any crimes and argued they would act in the same manner again.[62] For released individuals making such statements is of course not forbidden. At the same time such statements for obvious reasons outrage victim groups, tear open old wounds and possibly create instability in an already fragile region. In the absence of specialized rehabilitation programmes, which seriously address the nature of international crimes, profoundly confront perpetrators with the shortcomings and effects of destructive nationalist or ethnic ideologies, and make them reflect on the consequences of their crimes, it comes as no surprise that some of the perpetrators continue to justify their crimes and adhere to the same world view as during the conflict.

[60] J H Chui, 'Early Release in International Criminal Law' (2014) 123 The Yale Law Journal 1785.

[61] Holá and van Wijk (2014) (n 1) 129–30.

[62] J Subotić, 'The Cruelty of False Remorse: Biljana Plavšić at The Hague' (2012) 36 Southeastern Europe 39–59, 50; Č 'Šljivančanin: Išao bih u Vukovar' (*PTC*, 22 November 2012) <http://www.rts.rs/page/stories/sr/story/125/Dru%C5%A1tvo/1216416/%C5%A0ljivan%C4%8D anin%3A+I%C5%A1ao+bih+u+Vukovar.html> accessed January 2018; O Simic, '"I Would Do the Same Again": In Conversation with Biljana Plavšić' (2018) International Criminal Justice Review 317–32.

The experiences at the ICTY remind us that if international criminal justice initiatives are serious about successfully rehabilitating its convicts and reintegrating them in post-conflict regions, they may consider re-conceptualizing the traditional notion of rehabilitation and tailor it to the specifics of international crimes, their perpetrators, and the societies they come from. Using the conventional concept of rehabilitation, as the ICTY has done, may in this regard not suffice. Instead, we suggest putting more emphasis on the promotion of 'healing damaged relationships', an element which has historically been at the heart of modern penal systems, but in more recent years became largely overshadowed by the 'what works approach' and the focus on less re-offending. The development of such a new concept and related rehabilitation activities is complex and needs much more research and analysis. But as a start, one could think of making more serious efforts to actively 'de-ideologise' perpetrators, confront them with the impact of their crimes by, for example, organizing mediation sessions with victims or by setting certain specific conditions upon release. As Subotić writes it may be incredibly difficult and unlikely to change the perspectives of these individuals.[63] But that in itself is no argument not to try. It is similarly difficult to hold the most responsible perpetrators of international crimes accountable, to deter future perpetrators from committing such crimes, and to provide justice to victims. The goals of international criminal justice are by definition set high.

22.2 Post-acquittal Challenges

Persons acquitted by international criminal tribunals typically spent a long time in detention, often during a period in which their country of origin has massively changed. This is no exception for ICTY convicts. This means that they, upon release, may encounter difficulties after returning back to society and face challenges in finding a house or a job and reuniting with family members, with no avenue to acquire compensation for their economic and personal losses. Zejnil Delalić, for instance, claims that the almost two years he spent in pre-trial detention at the ICTY resulted in the collapse of his business.[64] Another recurring issue is the negative stigma, which might stem from having been tried. Former Bosnian Croat Army (HVO) member Mirjan Kupreškić, for example, returned to his Bosnian hometown Vitez and claims that some townspeople still view him as a war criminal.[65] Former captain in the Serbian-dominated Yugoslav People's Army (JNA) Miroslav Radić voices similar complaints. Acquitted in 2007, he complained in a 2008 article that the world still sees him as a member of the notorious 'Vukovar Three' and that his two children continue to carry this burden.[66] Sefer Halilović filed a lawsuit against a political opponent for being called a 'war criminal' in 2013.[67]

[63] J Subotić, ibid 40–41.

[64] J D Michels, 'Compensating Acquitted Defendants for Detention before International Criminal Courts' (2010) 8 Journal of International Criminal Justice 407.

[65] According to the Sarajevo-based Center for Investigative Reporting 'Bosniak neighbors in Vitez remember those years he spent in a cell (...) and see the 41-year-old Bosnian Croat still as a war criminal; one who had a good lawyer'. See The Center for Investigative Reporting in Sarajevo (CIN) 'Defence and prosecution: a tale of two side' (11 July 2005) <http://www.cin.ba/en/na-razlicitim-stranama-istog-zlocina/> accessed January 2018.

[66] G Otašević, 'Miroslav Radić tuzi Srbiju' (*Politika*, 2 November 2008) <http://www.politika.rs/rubrike/Drustvo/Miroslav-Radic-tuzi-Srbiju.lt.html> accessed January 2018.

[67] Fena, 'Sefer Halilović podnio tužbu protiv Radmanovića' (*Bošnjaci.net*,14 February 2013) <http://bosnjaci.net/prilog.php?pid=48222> accessed 6 February 2018.

At the same time it should be noted that in particular, in the former Yugoslavia, a smooth transition to post-trial life certainly is possible, not in the least because the Tribunal's findings on the lack of individual criminal responsibility of a defendant is often perceived as evidence of 'collective vindication', which challenges general feelings of 'collective stigma'.[68] Because of these perceptions some more prominent acquitted persons have arguably even benefitted from their trials and the subsequent acquittals. Most illustrative in this regard is perhaps the acquittal of the former Croatian army general Ante Gotovina. After his acquittal in 2012 an estimated 100,000 enchanted Croats waited to see the government plane, which transported him home, touch down on Croatian soil. As already noted by others,[69] the Croatian government and many citizens had regarded his trial as nothing less but an attack to discredit the young republic of Croatia. Between 2006 and 2012, the Croatian State spent millions of euros on his legal support.[70] In the eyes of many Croats, Gotovina's acquittal heralded the dismissal of the '*Stigma Hrvatska*' (Croatian stigma).[71] In fact, virtually all other republics of the former Yugoslavia have their own acquitted heroes who after a warm welcome—at least initially—reintegrated without many challenges.[72]

A serious challenge that all ICTY-acquitted individuals however have in common is the fact that they have been, or in the future may be, confronted with subsequent prosecutions by other international or domestic prosecutors. Indeed, various ICTY acquitted have been sought for additional prosecutions in the countries of their former adversaries. For example, Croatia issued a request to extradite Miroslav Radić from Serbia,[73] while Serbia requested Bosnia to extradite Naser Orić,[74] which also led to his arrest by Switzerland in 2014.[75] Although the criminal investigation of Fatmir Limaj, which Serbia's War Crimes Prosecutor publicly announced,[76] never made it into an extradition request he was arrested in 2011 pursuant to an order by the District Court of Pristina, operating under the European Union Rule of Law (EULEX) Mission.[77] Despite Kosovar Ramush Haradinaj

[68] R Williams, 'The Fog of War Crimes Prosecution; the ICTY Appeals Chamber Acquits Perišić' (*TerraNullius*, 1 March 2013) <http://terra0nullius.wordpress.com/2013/03/01/the-fog-of-war-crimes-prosecution-the-icty-appeals-chamber-acquits-perisic/> accessed January 2018.

[69] See J Clark, 'Courting Controversy; The ICTY's Acquittal of Croatian Generals Gotovina and Markač' (2013) 11 Journal of International Criminal Justice 399, 418.

[70] 'Croatia's Hague Spending on Ante Gotovina Revealed' (*Croatiaweek*, 23 December 2013) <http://www.croatiaweek.com/croatias-hague-spending-on-ante-gotovina-revealed/> accessed January 2018.

[71] J Hopkin, 'Croatia Starts to Hope Again, as a "War Crime" Stigma is Lifted' (*The Guardian*, 20 November 2012) <http://www.theguardian.com/commentisfree/2012/nov/20/croatia-war-crime-stigma-lifted> accessed January 2018.

[72] For more details, see Holá and van Wijk (2014) (n 1).

[73] Agence France Presse, 'Croatia Charges Serb Whom UN Court Freed' (27 November 2007) <https://listserv.buffalo.edu/cgi-bin/wa?A2=JUSTWATCH-L;53aa9fb9.0711> accessed January 2018.

[74] M Ristic and D Dzidic, 'Serbia Probes Bosnian Army Commander Naser Orić' (*Balkan Investigative Reporting Network*, 29 January 2014) <http://www.balkaninsight.com/en/article/serbia-investigates-bosniak-commander-naser-oric> accessed January 2018.

[75] Balkan Investigative Reporting Network, 'Bosnian Army Wartime Commander Naser Orić Arrested' (10 June 2015) <http://www.balkaninsight.com/en/article/bosnian-army-wartime-commander-naser-oric-arrested?utm_source=feedburner&utm_medium=twitter&utm_campaign=Feed%3A+LatestHeadlinesFromBosniaAndHerzegovina+%28Bosnia+and+Herzegovina%3A+Latest+Headlines%29> accessed January 2018.

[76] Information online available at <https://trialinternational.org/latest-post/fatmir-limaj/ > accessed 30 January 2020.

[77] In May 2012, the EULEX Court acquitted him on all charges. This verdict was annulled by Kosovo's Supreme Court in November 2012, while the ordered retrial, again, resulted in an acquittal in September 2013. EULEX, 'Defendants in Klecka case acquitted' (17 September 2013) <http://www.eulex-kosovo.eu/en/pressreleases/0485.php> accessed 15 April 2015.

having been tried, acquitted, retried and acquitted at the ICTY,[78] he too is probably well aware that investigators of the recently established Kosovo Specialist Prosecutor's Office are digging into his past in order to link him to an organ smuggling ring, which was allegedly active during the 1998 Kosovo conflict. Already in 2014, a European Union Special Investigative Task Force (STIF) report mentioned that individuals at the most senior levels of the Kosovar Liberation Army could face prosecution for conducting 'a campaign of persecution'.[79]

From a strictly legal perspective, follow-up prosecutions often do not violate the 'double jeopardy' or *ne bis in idem* principle which holds that no one shall be tried or punished again for an offence for which he has already been convicted or acquitted.[80] *Ne bis in idem* is a concept based on fairness to the accused and a desire for finality in criminal cases.[81] In the context of this discussion, where international and domestic criminal courts are working side by side prosecuting international crimes, the so-called 'downward vertical effects' of the principle, that is, whether or not domestic prosecution can take place *after* a final decision by an international criminal tribunal, is of particular interest.[82] Carter extensively studied this issue and concludes that it is accepted that subsequent State prosecution for the same crime and the same underlying conduct is possible only on the basis of new evidence.[83]

In reality, however, it is not inconceivable that new evidence related to the same conduct is identified by domestic prosecutors. They are, compared to their international counterparts, usually better equipped in terms of their institutional capacity and proximity to crime scenes and domestic archives, to ask for cooperation of their own State authorities. Their general embedding in the domestic criminal justice systems provides them with easier access to potential evidence. In addition, subsequent prosecutions may also relate to additional international crimes, which were committed during the same violent conflict or persecutory campaign, and were left outside of the scope of the international prosecution. Limited jurisdiction, limited resources, and the sheer scale of the atrocities often do not allow international prosecutors to consider all possible criminal behaviour of defendants. For that reason and in order to secure convictions, they often purposefully limit their investigations in terms of temporal and spatial scope. Illustrative in this regard is that when the Prosecutor of the Serbian War Crimes Chamber said that he was looking into crimes committed by Fatmir Limaj, he also added that the crimes he was investigating had not been included in the ICTY indictment.[84]

Moreover, given the often politically-charged context of the transitional period after atrocities and a potential desire of former warring parties to 'settle accounts' by other means, persons acquitted by international criminal tribunals can face subsequent prosecutions in

[78] *Prosecutor v Ramush Haradinaj, Idriz Balaj, and Lahi Brahimaj* (Public Judgment) IT-04-84bis-T (29 November 2012).

[79] D Bilefsky and S Sengupta, 'Senior Guerrilla Leaders Tied to Acts of Persecution After Civil War' *The New York Times* (30 July 2014) A8.

[80] See art 14 (7) of the International Covenant on Civil and Political Rights (ICCPR) (adopted 16 December 1966, entered into force 23 March 1976) 99 UNTS 171.

[81] L E Carter, 'Complementarity and the International Criminal Court: The Role of Ne Bis in Idem' (2010) 8 Santa Clara Journal of International Law 165.

[82] ibid 165, 172.

[83] ibid 180–84.

[84] Trial Watch Fatimir Limaj (2017) <https://trialinternational.org/latest-post/fatmir-limaj/> accessed January 2018.

domestic courts of their former adversaries, which are often subject to highly politicized confrontations. When Bosnian war hero Naser Orić was acquitted, thousands of Bosniak fans received him at Sarajevo Airport.[85] Serbia's National Council for Cooperation with the ICTY in response issued a statement that the verdict 'cannot contribute to either achieving justice and truth nor to regional reconciliation'.[86] Serbia's War Prosecutor's arrest warrant, which followed suit in 2014, caused significant tensions in the already uneasy relationship between Serbia and Bosnia. While Orić argued that the Serbs 'hope to find a way to balance the crimes committed in 1992–1995', Bosnian President Izetbegović added that Serbia 'should reconsider its actions towards Bosnian civilians' if it 'hopes to become an EU member'.[87] The fact that Serbia and Bosnia do not have an extradition agreement for war crimes[88] only strengthens the belief that the arrest warrant could be seen as a politically motivated move by the Serbian prosecutor to 'make things even' among the former warring parties, especially given the fact that Serbs typically perceive the ICTY as Serb-biased.[89]

Following a strictly legal line of reasoning, one could argue that as long as fundamental legal principles relating to fairness, presumption of innocence, and *ne bis in idem* principle are taken into account, successive prosecutions of suspected war criminals or génocidaires are not problematic. Given the heinous nature of the crimes committed and the fight against impunity, the international community tries to take every necessary step to hold alleged perpetrators accountable. At the same time, the situation leads to some thorny political and normative questions. The experiences of ICTY-acquitted individuals suggest that it is perfectly possible that an acquittal by an international criminal tribunal may be shortly after followed by an extradition request from a domestic prosecutor. This leads to fundamental questions, which current practitioners in international criminal justice need to reflect upon: is it problematic if domestic prosecutors fervently 'complement' the job of international prosecutors? Should we accept internationally-funded domestic war crimes prosecutors using their position and resources in prosecuting individuals, who have already been acquitted by international criminal tribunals? Also, might such prosecutions be politically motivated?

22.3 Conclusion

This chapter discussed the 'post-trial phase' at the ICTY, focusing on the question what happens to ICTY defendants after being convicted or acquitted. It illustrates that the setup of the sentence enforcement system at the ICTY is not transparent, is conceptually underdeveloped, and leads to inequalities in the treatment of international prisoners. The prisoners are sent to various countries around Europe and it is not clear what considerations,

85 S Olivera, 'Bringing "Justice" Home? Bosnians, War Criminals and the Interaction between the Cosmopolitan and the local' (2011) 12 German Law Journal 1388, 1392.

86 Ristic (n 74).

87 'Serbia to Prosecute Bosnian War Hero Naser Orić' (*World Bulletin*, 31 January 2014) <http://www.worldbulletin.net/news/127979/serbia-to-prosecute-bosnian-war-hero-naser-oric> accessed January 2018.

88 Ristic (n 74).

89 Orić was eventually arrested in Switzerland and extradited to Bosnia. In October 2017 the Bosnian state court acquitted him of killing three Serb prisoners of war in the Bratunac and Srebrenica area. A Muslimovic, 'Srebrenica Commander Naser Orić Acquitted of War Crimes' (*Balkan Transitional Justice*, 9 October 2017) <http://www.balkaninsight.com/en/article/naser-oric-srebrenica-commander-war-crimes-trial-verdict-10-06-2017> accessed February 2018.

except for political factors, are taken into account when deciding on the enforcement country. They are scattered in different prisons across and within various countries and subjected to largely differing prison conditions. In general, ICTY convicts are integrated into domestic inmates' populations and typically serve their time in units with serious offenders of ordinary crimes like murderers, child molesters, or drug traffickers. They follow similar daily routines and are offered existing rehabilitation programmes. One might question whether rehabilitating *génocidaires* and war criminals in the same way as ordinary delinquents makes much sense given the specific character of international crimes and their perpetrators. Despite being usually convicted of very serious crimes, the international criminals committed their crimes under very specific (ideological, social, individual) circumstances and arguably differ from ordinary criminals. We would argue this should be duly reflected in designing their rehabilitation programmes. The vast majority of international prisoners are deemed to be rehabilitated from international crimes when they attended work activities or language courses and behaved well in the respective prisons. Therefore, they are released after having served two-thirds of their sentences. ICTY practice demonstrates that the concept of rehabilitation from international crimes and its assessment and implementation in practice is far from clearly developed and would benefit from further conceptualization and reassessment. After their release, the prisoners simply disappear from the radar of the international community (unless they enter witness protection programmes and cooperate with the tribunals) and there is no supervision of their conduct or any attention paid to their activities. Some go back to their countries of origin and return to the political posts they held prior to or during the periods when crimes were committed.

As to the acquittals, the chapter illustrates what an ambivalent message such a decision actually conveys. Whereas a conviction confirms that atrocities have been committed and a responsible person has been held accountable, an acquittal means that the court has *not* established that the accused is responsible for the crimes he has been charged with, but this does *not* mean that no crimes have been committed, *nor* that the acquitted person is innocent. While former ICTY President Meron once argued that acquittals show the health of the international criminal justice system,[90] this chapter brings into question to what extent the negative repercussions some acquitted individuals experience after their release, does not also show the chronic ailment of that very system. Some ICTY acquitted may have 'benefitted' from their status as a former defendant, but a considerable number are confronted with serious problems. They arguably continue to carry the stigma of being tried by an international criminal tribunal. Given the large-scale character of international crimes and the typically very limited focus of international prosecutions, they—similar to the ones who are convicted—can in principle be confronted with new prosecutions any time and anywhere, either by regular or specialized domestic war crimes prosecutors. Due to the complexity of the cases and the gravity of the crimes, defendants have often spent very lengthy periods in detention with no avenue to acquire compensation for their economic and personal losses. Given all of the above, for many an acquittal by an international criminal tribunal can mean winning a pyrrhic victory.

[90] See BBC HARDtalk (16 March 2013) <http://www.bbc.co.uk/programmes/p015gwb1> accessed 6 February 2018.

To conclude, the ICTY has been confronted with a number of practical and fundamental challenges with regards to the post-trial phase. The inequalities and the lack of a principled approach towards the regulation and practical implementation of enforcement of international sentences and the way in which acquitted individuals continue to bear the consequences of once having been prosecuted by the Tribunal have clear repercussions for the Tribunal's legacy and should be taken into account when drafting new policies in the field of international criminal justice.

PART VII

IMPACT ON DOMESTIC LEGAL SYSTEMS

23
Narratives of Justice and War in Croatia

Ivor Sokolić[*,**]

23.1 Introduction

The field of transitional justice struggles to explain why the expressivist messages of trials often fail to reach or influence domestic audiences. Human rights norms, related to the transitional justice process, seem to work in some instances, while not in others. This chapter investigates this dynamic through the case study of Croatia and the 1991–1995 conflict, nationally referred to as the 'Homeland War'. It is defined by the interaction between two key narratives: a justice narrative, promoted by domestic and international war crimes trials; and, an emotional, everyday war narrative. The chapter deals with the question of why human rights norms become distorted or undermined when they reach local publics?

In Croatia, there is a pervasive, nearly universal among ethnic Croats, notion that Croatia was a victim of Serbian aggression. According to this narrative, Croatia led a war of self-defence, with the aim of not only saving the Croatian state but preventing the destruction of the Croatian nation. At the same time, a justice narrative is also present in Croatia, one based on the norms of transitional justice. Actors who wish to promote one or the other have similar expressivist goals, those of building a narrative, authenticating it as the truth, and passing it on to the society in question. The official war narrative and the justice narrative exist in the same space and interact with each other; at times coming into conflict and undermining each other, at other times affirming each other and becoming aligned.

The strength of the war narrative in Croatia and the distrust of the International Criminal Tribunal for the former Yugoslavia (ICTY) and domestic judiciary have resulted in a stymied development of the rule of law and understandings of law in Croatia. This has allowed for a tolerance for certain crimes to exist, such as revenge crimes, crimes of passion, or killings of Serb civilians. This chapter outlines the nature of such attitudes and attempts to answer why this is. Overall, respondents revealed a tolerance for deviance in the context of war crimes committed by Croats. Various factors of the dominant war narrative, such as the unorganized and unprepared defence, were seen as a mitigating circumstance to such war crimes. These crimes were often defined in relation to Serbian crimes, which were seen as a part of a planned aggression. Transitional justice institutions had to operate in the context of localized complexities and normative expectations in attempting to instil a rule of law

* Dr Ivor Sokolić is a Research Officer at the European Institute at the London School of Economics and Political Science. He works on the ERC funded project 'Justice Interactions and Peacebuilding: From Static to Dynamic Discourses across National, Ethnic, Gender and Age Groups', which examines transitional justice processes across the former Yugoslavia. He holds a PhD from the UCL School of Slavonic and East European Studies and an MSc and BSc in European Politics from the Department of International Politics at the University of Wales, Aberystwyth.

** An earlier version of this chapter was published in I Sokolić, *International Courts and Mass Atrocity: Narratives of War and Justice in Croatia* (Palgrave MacMillan 2019).

Ivor Sokolić, *Narratives of Justice and War in Croatia* In: *Legacies of the International Criminal Tribunal for the Former Yugoslavia*. Edited by: Carsten Stahn, Carmel Agius, Serge Brammertz, Colleen Rohan, Oxford University Press (2020). © The Several Contributors
DOI: 10.1093/oso/9780198862956.003.0024

norm in the public. Respondents across the board regarded all domestic and international institutions, including legal ones, as corrupt and inefficient. Consequently, they were dissatisfied with and distrustful of them, and therefore, felt powerless in an unresponsive system where justice was imposed from above.

Localized folk theories of law also played a large role in the legal reasoning of study respondents. This allowed for an apologetic attitude towards certain crimes, based on an understanding of the law that was not legally consistent but was consistent with emotional and political narratives. This means that in Croatian society the dominant war narrative plays a large role in shaping attitudes towards law. Finally, factual inaccuracies often served the purpose of justifying respondents' narratives. This vindicated Croatian crimes, or at least lowered them to the level of common crimes, rather than war crimes. Croatian war crimes were unexceptional crimes in war (to be punished more leniently), while Serb crimes were exceptional war crimes (to be punished more harshly). Moreover, the definition of 'civilian' differed between Serbs and Croats, in that Serbs were not viewed as civilians. Despite the ICTY and, especially recently, domestic courts providing legally sound judgments and strongly adhering to legal justice over political justice, concurrent understandings of law have not been achieved.

23.2 Trial as Theatre—Transitional Justice, Expressivism, and Norms

This chapter echoes the findings from much of the recent transitional justice scholarship studying the former Yugoslav States.[1] This assumes that law's key goals of deterrence and retribution should not receive the same amount of attention in transitional situations, when prosecutions should be evaluated on their pedagogical potential.[2] When such trials are effective as public shows, they can lead to a shift towards more liberal values. These aims also work in unison with the more traditional aims of deterrence and retribution. Domestic and conventional criminal courts also have expressivist aims in their work and court decisions hold a greater significance than most other occurrences.[3] Even retribution has been argued to be a form of expressivism.[4] The ICTY trial chambers did sometimes state expressivist goals in verdicts, such as to strengthen social solidarity and incubate moral consensus in the public, despite causing a high degree of controversy amongst lawyers, who often rejected

[1] E Gordy, *Guilt, Responsibility, and Denial: The Past at Stake in Post-Milošević Serbia* (University of Pennsylvania Press 2014); L J Nettelfield, *Courting Democracy in Bosnia and Herzegovina: The Hague Tribunal's Impact in a Postwar State* (Cambridge University Press 2010); J Obradović-Wochnik, *Ethnic Conflict and War Crimes in the Balkans: The Narratives of Denial in Post-conflict Serbia* (I.B. Tauris 2013); M Ostojić, *Between Justice and Stability: The Politics of War Crimes Prosecutions in Post-Milošević Serbia* (Ashgate 2014); V Pavlaković, 'Fulfilling the Thousand-year-old Dream: Strategies of Symbolic Nation-building in Croatia' in P Kolstø (ed), *Strategies of Symbolic Nation-building in South Eastern Europe* (Ashgate 2014); J Subotić, *Hijacked Justice: Dealing with the Past in the Balkans* (Cornell University Press 2009).

[2] M Osiel, *Mass Atrocity, Collective Memory and the Law* (Transaction Publishers 1998).

[3] E S Anderson, E Pildes, and R H Pildes, 'Expressive Theories of Law: A General Restatement' [2000] University of Pennsylvania Law Review 1503; P Brooks and P Gewirtz, *Law's Stories: Narrative and Rhetoric in the Law* (Yale University Press 1996); J Feinberg, *Doing and Deserving: Essays in the Theory of Responsibility* (Princeton University Press 1970).

[4] J Hampton, 'Moral Education Theory of Punishment' [1984] Philosophy and Public Affairs 208.

any kind of goals that were not narrowly legal.[5] Trials aimed to draw a line for the future and achieve a sense of legitimacy in the transition.[6]

The discord between retribution, deterrence, and expressivism arises from the application of traditional criminal law, developed to address conventional deviance to mass atrocity, which is a unique phenomenon. Despite the acknowledgement of this by most scholars and practitioners, methods of punishment and sentencing for such crimes remain surprisingly ordinary when compared to Western legal systems.[7] Courts often prove to be insensitive to the nuances of affected societies, especially with regards to reconciliation.[8] For example, disregard of local political nuances in Serbia alienated transitional authorities and threatened the legitimacy and stability of domestic institutions.[9] Transitional justice efforts are, therefore, most likely to succeed if they act in accordance with the domestic political situation.

Drumbl concludes that domestic or international tribunals designed for the purpose of punishment for war crimes struggle to achieve the aims of retribution and deterrence, while greater success (although still limited) is achieved in pursuing expressivist goals.[10] Expressivist goals are not held in the same high regard by courts and practitioners as retribution or deterrence, but such aspects of trials can have a strong messaging effect and can help affirm the value of law in society.[11] This can lead to a level of pedagogical performativity that can be hard to reproduce via any other legal mechanism.

Expressivist messages of courts may lead to norm change through norm 'cascades' or 'spill-over' from one level of society to another.[12] As norms of criminal accountability for war crimes and other violations of international humanitarian and human rights law begin to cascade, the notion of individual responsibility should also gain international momentum. Local actors in affected States, not only advocates in advanced liberal democracies, should increasingly blame atrocities on individuals (i.e. specific leaders), rather than collectives (i.e. whole communities or ethnicities). It remains, however, debatable how norms gain social force in a situation when the institutional and social requirements for the rule of law are absent. The difficulty in accounting for this scenario arises from the potential absence of norm leaders or a lack of willingness in the population to accept a norm. Subotić and Lamont have questioned the universal validity of these models by focusing on the former Yugoslav States.[13] Subotić argues that domestic norm believers are required to take the lead in norm change and in many States these are absent or lack the authority to influence social change, while States may still display institutional markers of compliance. Lamont agrees with this and points out that most Latin American analyses studied NGOs that were initially composed of direct relatives of victims. The Krajina Serb community, for example, was almost completely ejected from Croatia in 1995, which may help to explain

[5] See *Prosecutor v Kordić and Čerkez* (Appeals Chamber Judgment) ICTY-IT-95-14/2-A (17 December 2004).

[6] R G Teitel, 'The Law and Politics of Contemporary Transitional Justice' [2005] Cornell International Law Journal 837, 845.

[7] M A Drumbl, *Atrocity, Punishment and International Law* (Cambridge University Press 2007).

[8] M Osiel, *Making Sense of Mass Atrocity* (Cambridge University Press 2009).

[9] Ostojić (n 1).

[10] Drumbl (n 7).

[11] *Prosecutor v Kordić and Čerkez* (n 5).

[12] M Finnemore and K Sikkink, 'International Norm Dynamics and Political Change' [1998] International Organization 887; T Risse, S C Ropp, and K Sikkink, *The Power of Human Rights: International Norms and Domestic Change* (Cambridge University Press 1999).

[13] C K Lamont, *International Criminal Justice and the Politics of Compliance* (Ashgate 2010); Subotić (n 1).

the relative absence of local NGO pressure since the victims of human rights abuses were no longer members of the domestic political community. International pressure on States does not enter a domestic political vacuum; rather, it always interacts with domestic political conditions to guide strategies of compliance. Relevant factors for this are domestic demand from below, veto players (also known as spoilers), and competing coalitions.[14]

Norms in the study are defined as collective expectations for the proper behaviour, values, and perceptions of actors with a given identity.[15] Under this theory, norms can either define identities or prescribe behaviour, or they can do both. This chapter views norms as historical and social constructions. Norms of behaviour are also intrinsically connected to identity narratives, which form the basis for actors' behavioural choices.[16] Norms are not isolated variables, instead they are connected to narratives that individuals or communities use to relate to the world around them.[17] They also constitute actions, since action only 'becomes meaningful in the process of narrating a constitute story of the self'.[18] Narratives, therefore, are norms and by studying societal narratives this study simultaneously delves into societal norms.

23.3 Focus Groups in a Post-conflict Society

This analysis of Croatia provides a critical and exemplifying single case study. It is critical, since it tests and elucidates existing theories.[19] It is exemplifying, since it captures the circumstances of an everyday situation.[20] It is a mixture of the two, since many instances of transitional justice exist across the globe, but each is also highly unique. In other words, the case study provides more description of the process in this instance; it uses established theories to explain a single case and it also tries to develop theory and identify new variables worth pursuing in future research, although it is far from an outlier case.[21] Finally, the case study is both internally and externally valid. It makes conclusions about the Croatian case, but it also says something about transitional justice that may be applicable to other cases.

The primary method of data collection was focus groups, dyads when it was not possible to organize focus groups, and follow-up interviews. Focus groups were chosen since they can best gather data on the complex interactional dynamics that lead individuals to share some truths, withhold others, and build alternate versions of reality in a group.[22] They do not 'force' opinions on individuals (such as surveys may do) and they strongly reflect the independence of human opinion by further removing the interviewer from the study (by encouraging the group to discuss amongst themselves, rather than directly with the

[14] Subotić (n 1).

[15] P J Katzenstein, *The Culture of National Security: Norms and Identity in World Politics* (Columbia University Press 1996).

[16] A Wendt, *Social Theory of International Politics* (Cambridge University Press 1999) 366.

[17] C O Meyer 'Convergence Towards a European Strategies Culture? A Constructivist Framework for Explaining Changing Norms' [2005] European Journal of International Relations 523.

[18] C S Browning, *Constructivism, Narrative and Foreign Policy Analysis: A Case Study of Finland* (Peter Lang 2008) 11.

[19] A Bryman, *Social Research Methods* (Oxford University Press 2016) 62.

[20] Bryman (n 19); R K Yin, *Case Study Research: Design and Methods* (Sage 2009) 48.

[21] A L George and A Bennett, *Case Studies and Theory Development in the Social Sciences* (MIT Press 2005) 75.

[22] J A Hollander 'The Social Contexts of Focus Groups' [2004] Journal of Contemporary Ethnography 602.

moderator) and by focusing on social context, where opinion tends to be created, thereby increasing external validity.[23]

In terms of the nature of the topic, focus groups are good at tackling abstract concepts and investigating issues that could be illuminated by the display of social norms.[24] Moreover, anthropological research has shown that publics that have recently witnessed violence or atrocity (even if from a distance) may hold coping practices that are taken-for-granted in society.[25] Focus groups are adept at exploring taken-for-granted concepts since, more so than any other interview method, they permit spontaneous expression of ideas by participants by allowing individuals to employ the language that they are used to using to discuss an issue to an extent that is difficult to replicate in a more structured and formal interview. Essentially, the approach shows not only how individuals feel but also why they feel that way and how they construct narratives.

The method is useful in the case of Croatia and transitional justice since it is effective in gaining trust when interviewing ex-combatants, whose trust can be hard to attain and who often attempt to provide narratives that fit with their ideas of what the researcher is looking for.[26] When constructed with the appropriate care and run properly, they also become effective in discussing sensitive issues. Moreover, this spontaneity adds to reliability since respondents are not able to coordinate their answers in advance, as they may do in surveys or individual interviews with a similar number of participants.[27] Follow-up interviews were used to verify responses and to speak to individuals that were quiet in the groups.[28]

Eleven focus groups and two dyads were conducted, involving a total of fifty-two participants. They consisted of middle- and high-school history teachers, members of smaller war veterans' associations and pensioners in Zagreb, Sisak, Zadar, and a non-urban location for each segment. Each group consisted only of individuals from the target segment in a specific location. Teachers were targeted because they are central to the process of teaching young people narratives. Pensioners were targeted because they are a highly politicized and large grouping, which had lived through Yugoslavia, the Homeland War, the Tuđman regime, and the post-Tuđman period. Members of war veterans' associations were chosen because they are an influential and vocal part of Croatian civil society. The aim was to target veterans' groups that are not consistently being quoted in the newspapers, since their opinions are readily available.

Zagreb was used as it is the political and cultural centre of the country. Sisak was selected because it was on the frontline and a domestic war crimes trial dealt with crimes committed in the city. Zadar was used since it is in a different region of Croatia than Sisak and was also directly affected by the war. Moreover, the region is known as a hotbed for Croatian right

[23] J Söderström, 'Ex-combatants at the Polls: Exploring Focus Groups and Electoral Meaning' [2011] Anthropology Matters 1, 4,

[24] J Lewis, 'Design Issues' in J Ritchie and J Lewis (eds), *Qualitative Research Practice: A Guide for Social Science Students and Researchers* (Sage 2003) 60.

[25] It is questionable how 'recent' the conflicts in the former Yugoslavia are, as nearly twenty years has passed since they ended. Obradović-Wochnik (n 1) has shown that the public in Serbia similarly continues to speak as if past is still continuing, as if the wars are not over.

[26] M Christensen and M Utas, 'Mercenaries of Democracy: The "Politricks" of Remobilized Combatants in the 2007 General Elections, Sierra Leone' [2008] African Affairs 515; I Sokolić, 'Researching Norms, Narratives and Transitional Justice: Focus Group Methodology in Post-Conflict Croatia' [2016] Nationalities Papers 932; Söderström (n 23).

[27] Söderström (n 23) 4.

[28] For more details on focus groups in the post-conflict setting, see Sokolić (n 26).

wing, often nationalist, politics. The non-urban locations were close to the three chosen cities, rather than in completely different parts of Croatia.

The transcripts were analysed using narrative analysis. This approach was suited to the qualitative, single case, and constructivist nature of the study, since it focuses on identifying the key narrative (or story) that is being told by participants, it looks at how this narrative is constructed, what the intention of the participant is, what the nature of the audience is, and what the meaning of the narrative is.[29] The focus of analysis is on 'how do people make sense of what happened' rather than 'what actually happened'.[30] Narrative analysis is, therefore, well suited to gaining an insight into how individuals construct the world around them. In qualitative analysis, it focuses on the stories that individuals employ to account for events and it has effectively been used to retell traumatic and major life events.[31] This means that narrative analysis is both a data collection and a data analysis technique. It is an approach to analysing the data generated from focus groups, but the focus group themselves form a part of the narrative analysis since they are used to stimulate the telling of narratives to be analysed.[32]

23.4 Defence and Victimhood—The Dominant War Narrative

The Croatian war narrative is concerned with the belief that the war was defensive; that it was an attempt to create a democratic Croatian state, which the Croatian people expressed a desire for through a referendum; that a distinction must be made between the Greater Serbian aggressor and the victim; that the most recent war memory must be kept alive; and, that war heroes must be protected. This narrative is nearly universally accepted among ethnic Croats and was central to the nation-building process in the State.[33] It forms a founding myth that helps the society explain its origins and define what it stands for.[34] The war narrative is composed of six core components, apparent in all transcripts. These are: self-defence; survival and struggle, epitomized by the unprepared and unarmed fledgling State; Serbia and Serbs as the aggressor; Yugoslavia as a broken State; victimization, built around several focal points, such as Vukovar and Dubrovnik; and, the notion that the war is not over. To some individuals, the war and the struggle for independence remain central to their lives.

The war narrative is inscribed by parliament in institutionalized form through the Declaration on the Homeland War (*Deklaracija o Domovinskom Ratu*) and the Declaration on Operation Storm (*Deklaracija o Oluji*). Croatia's first post-Tuđman government was initially willing to actively cooperate with the ICTY, but due to a public backlash and the threat of certain facets of the war being criminalized, they issued the Declaration on the Homeland War in 2000, the same year they came to power. The Declaration puts in the official State writing a single interpretation of the past, regardless of whether or not it is correct. It paints Croatia as exclusively a victim of international 'Greater Serbian' aggression; it puts

[29] C K Riessman, *Narrative Analysis* (Sage 1993).
[30] Bryman (n 19) 589.
[31] Riessman (n 29).
[32] Bryman (n 19) 590.
[33] Pavlaković (n 1).
[34] M Eliade, *Myth and Reality* (Allen & Unwin 1963).

the whole blame for the start of the conflict on Serbia (and none on the Tuđman regime); it ignores that there were elements of civil war (despite this still being an academically debated issue); and, it denies any official Croatian involvement in Bosnia, despite ICTY rulings contradicting this.[35] Moreover, it binds all citizens, media, and public bodies to follow these points and elevates them to the status of core values of the Croatian State and people (*narod*).

It also includes contradictions that were reflected in focus group discussions. For example, it refers specifically to *individual* war crimes, a common manner of describing alleged Croatian war crimes, whilst also referring to crimes committed in *aggression*, which are seen as planned and committed by Serbia, Serbs, and the Yugoslav National Army as a group.[36] In comparison to the memory and narrative surrounding the Second World War, the Homeland War provides a much stronger foundation on which to build consensus and, subsequently, a nation State.[37] Certain topics on the Homeland War continue to be debated, both publicly and academically, however, there exists a national consensus that the Declaration and most of the themes outlined represent the truth. For example, the very term 'Homeland War' is loaded, but is now used across nearly all Croatian society, media, and politics to refer to the conflict.[38]

Operation Storm had the potential to undermine the notion of Croatian defence since it was an aggressive military occupation to retake lands (at times this is also how it is justified as being defensive, because its aim was to *re*take *lost* lands). The Declaration on Operation Storm was issued in 2006 in order to pre-empt an ICTY verdict that might criminalize the military operation. Unlike its earlier counterpart, it does not focus on the core values of the Croatian State, but instead it attempts to define the nature and events of the operation. It cites key facts, actors, dates, and goals, much like a historical document, although it is not academic in nature, since it does not use sources or define terms.[39] It was less influential than the Declaration on the Homeland War, although it also aimed to create an official version of events during the 1990s.[40] It presents a change of tack from its earlier counterpart, since it no longer focused so much on defence (it is more focused on response to aggression), but instead it focuses on cooperation with Bosnia, as well as allies in the West, thereby countering any arguments over Croatian aggression in the neighbouring state.

23.5 Courts and the Justice Narrative

The justice narrative is composed of the stories that transitional justice institutions in Croatia and in The Hague try to impart on the Croatian public. These include specific versions of events as presented by courts through, for example, trial transcripts and sentences,

35 Pavlaković (n 1).

36 Croatian Parliament, 'Deklaracija o Oluji NN (Declaration on Operation Storm)' (*Narodne Novine*, 2006) art 6 <http://narodne-novine.nn.hr/clanci/sluzbeni/127530.html> accessed 16 November 2017.

37 Pavlaković (n 1) 37.

38 The exceptions are certain NGOs, members of the ethnic Serb community (although the ones interviewed in this study did use it), and certain political parties. D Jović, 'Croatia after Tudjman: The ICTY and Issues of Transitional Justice' [2009] Chaillot Paper 13, 23; Pavlaković (n 1) 39.

39 S Koren, '"Korisna prošlost"? Ratovi devetesetih u deklaracijama hrvatskog sabora' (Useful past? The wars of the nineties in the declarations of the Croatian Sabor) in T Cipek (ed) *Kultura sjećanja: 1991. Povijesni lomovi i svladanje prošlosti (Culture of memory: 1991. Historical breaks and overcoming the past)* (Disput 2011).

40 ibid.

as well as broader norms concerning the primacy of rule of law, regardless of circumstances. The justice narrative comes into conflict with the war narrative over the notion of a defensive war. ICTY convictions, such as those of Dario Kordić and Mario Čerkez, form a large part of the justice narrative and show that the Croatian state supported armed forces outside of its own territory for purposes other than the defence of the Republic of Croatia. Such convictions have the potential to undermine a narrative of defence. The notion of a joint criminal enterprise by the Croatian wartime political and military leadership held similar potential, while domestic and international trials relating to war crimes by Croatian military personnel undermine the notion that crimes could not be committed in a defensive war.

Crimes against humanity, such as those witnessed in Croatia and the region during the 1991–1995 conflict, can express the core rule of law norm that there is no escaping law's protective force.[41] Because such offences may be committed anywhere and under any circumstances, whether during war or in peacetime, they may be subject to international adjudications and prosecution by any State as a matter of universal concern.[42] This concept, however, is not without its ambiguities. Controversies surrounding Article 98 of the International Criminal Court (ICC) and Belgium's efforts at testing universal jurisdiction are both representative of this.

Transitional justice attempts to move a society from instability to stability. This includes adoptions of human rights and general democratic principles, underpinned by the rule of law.[43] Both transitional justice and the rule of law aim to uphold peace through, among other mechanisms, the establishment and strengthening of institutions.[44] (This applies more to domestic initiatives than the ICTY, which has generally avoided claims that it is doing anything more than providing trials.) Transitional justice processes have, however, often impeded what many would classify as the establishment of the rule of law.[45] For example, adversarial trials can limit pedagogical effects and the potential for reconciliation.[46] Such trials can also constrain domestic understandings of legality and lower credibility in judicial institutions.[47]

The Serbian case study is illustrative of this. Rule of law developed via ICTY conditionality in Serbia resulted in stymied development of a culture of law.[48] And, negative attitudes of the ICTY and domestic judiciaries, which are seen as lacking independence, impeded diffuse support for these institutions.[49] Using conditionality to establish the rule of law proved difficult, since it depended on the performance of the ICTY.[50] Subordinating justice to political institutions empties law of its meaning, thereby eroding potential for reconciliation and

[41] Teitel (n 6) 853.

[42] D Luban, 'A Theory of Crimes Against Humanity' [2004] Yale Journal of International Law 124.

[43] J Sarkin, 'The Interrelationship and Interconnectness of Transitional Justice and the Rule of Law in Uganda: Pursuing Justice, Truth, Guarantees of non-repetition, Reconciliation and Reparations for Past Crimes and Human Rights Violations' [2015] Hague Journal on the Rule of Law 111, 127.

[44] ibid.

[45] P McAuliffe, 'Transitional Justice and the Rule of Law: The Perfect Couple or Awkward Bedfellows?' [2010] Hague Journal on the Rule of Law 127, 129.

[46] E Stover, *The Witnesses: War Crimes and the Promise of Justice in The Hague* (University of Pennsylvania Press 2005) 23.

[47] McAuliffe (n 45) 154.

[48] K H Brodersen, 'The ICTY's Conditionality Dilemma' [2014] European Journal of Crime, Criminal Law and Criminal Justice 219.

[49] J Hagan and S K Ivković, 'War Crimes, Democracy, and the Rule of Law in Belgrade, the Former Yugoslavia, and Beyond' [2006] The Annals of the American Academy of Political and Social Science 130.

[50] Brodersen (n 48).

stability.[51] The ICTY struggled to spread a culture of law because it was unable to effectively overcome the challenges of victim interaction, lenient sentences, ambiguous decisions, and contact with the region's publics.[52] The ICTY never symbolized justice in the region, instead it was regarded as a tool of the international community to control the region. This limited its potential to establish a rule of law norm.[53] In Serbia, despite administering fair trials, the ICTY never managed to develop a significant culture of law.[54]

The lack of diffuse support was caused by the Tribunal's poor image and inconsistencies interacting with processes of localization, where norms are contested.[55] Especially where individuals feel they have an inability to influence structures of power around them, there is a greater risk of legal cynicism arising.[56] As long as confidence in judicial independence was lacking, the ICTY was never going to be able to establish the rule of law or promote democratization to the extent it aimed to do.[57]

The justice narrative in Croatia contains this inherent dynamic between the rule of law and transitional justice. It simultaneously interacts with everyday narratives and understandings of the war and the rule of law. The local dimensions of international justice, therefore, cannot be ignored.[58] The high number of atrocities committed in the former Yugoslavia and the relatively short mandate of the ICTY required collaboration with domestic judicial institutions.[59] The ICTY's legitimacy, therefore, depended on how well it took into account local norms, understandings, and attitudes.[60] The focus group data shows that feelings of powerlessness, folk theories of law, and general factual inaccuracies played large roles in shaping attitudes to law. Respondents felt powerless in a system that was unresponsive to their priorities. Perceived corruption, inefficiency, and dissatisfaction with the government resulted in distrust of institutions, including domestic and international legal institutions. Folk theories of law guided legal reasoning. Participants claimed 'not to be lawyers', which enabled them to make statements that were not consistent with the law (which partly reflected that they are not lawyers). More important, it showed that politics, law, and emotion work together to create a general understanding of the situation. Factual inaccuracies were common in the data, but some of these idiosyncratic images, such as the *baka* (grandmother) with the rifle, have a broader implication because they also justify narratives. The image of the *baka* portrays civilians as guilty and consequently justifies and permits crimes against them.

The justice narrative and war narrative sometimes work in concert. For example, the justice narrative calls for all war crimes to be investigated and processed, and Croatian authorities have been more than happy to do so when dealing with Serbian perpetrators. Both

[51] Subotić (n 1).
[52] Brodersen (n 48) 27.
[53] Brodersen (n 48); M Spoerri and A Freyberg-Inan, 'From Prosecution to Persecution: Perceptions of the International Criminal Tribunal for the Former Yugoslavia (ICTY) in Serbian Domestic Politics' [2008] Journal of International Relations and Development 350.
[54] Brodersen (n 48) 248.
[55] Hagan and Ivković (n 49) 131.
[56] R J Sampson and D J Bartusch, 'Legal Cynicism and (Subcultural?) Tolerance of Deviance: The Neighborhood Context of Racial Differences' [1998] Law & Society Review 777, 783.
[57] Hagan and Ivković (n 49) 135.
[58] A-M Slaughter, *A New World Order* (Princeton University Press 2004).
[59] Hagan and Ivković (n 49) 51.
[60] H Arendt, *Eichmann in Jerusalem: A Report on the Banality of Evil* (Penguin 2006); Hagan and Ivković (n 49) 81.

narratives stress the importance of fact finding, although one in a more universal sense than the other. ICTY decisions can conflict with or support the war narrative. The final verdicts in the Operation Storm case supported the war narrative: that the operation was legitimate and that no joint criminal enterprise occurred.[61] The dominant national narrative is continuously contested by both external and internal sources.[62] This resulted in the fierce rejection of war crimes processes, when they were deemed to question official war narrative, while at other times the processes fit into or were modelled to fit into official narratives about the past.[63] In Croatia, the everyday reproduction of the war narrative makes it difficult for the justice narrative to take hold and for associated norms to spread. Attitudes and perceptions towards the rule of law, as well as general understandings of the law, remain negatively affected in Croatian society. The result is that some people think that certain crimes are acceptable in specific situations.

23.6 Defining and Relativizing War Crimes

Participants generally discussed what war crimes are not, rather than what they are, because they mostly focused on alleged Croatian crimes. Crimes during the war (real or hypothesized) were discussed in three categories: those that were war crimes; those that were war crimes but were understandable or forgivable; and those that were not war crimes at all (if they were crimes, then they were 'ordinary' crimes). The most common narratives fit into the latter two categories: forgivable war crimes and 'ordinary' crimes. The foundation for this was an understanding that crimes of passion or revenge were not war crimes:

NU.P.1—A colleague once told me that he saw them kill his whole family. He should not have gone there. And later he did that. When they later returned, he also killed them all. As a kind of revenge.

All agree

NU.P.1—He experienced a breakdown. He had no purpose in his life, he had nothing.

NU.P.4—His only real goal was revenge.[64]

ZG.V.2—In war someone can commit a crime of passion. This a crime in war. Or in the situation, when someone for example in Vukovar lost five or ten family members, who were massacred. And he finds himself, as a man, in a different region, defending a different part of Croatia, and in a certain moment it can happen that a person he comes across there, and maybe this person is not even armed, but they provoke him. In that moment he is not conscious, he is controlled by emotions. If someone at a certain moment says 'We will repeat Ovčara!', and his family were all killed at Ovčara, he may shoot and kill the person. According to me, this is not a war crime. This is a crime in war.

[61] This concerns only the individuals on trial in this case (Ante Gotovina, Ivan Čermak, and Mladen Markač). Other individuals implicated in the joint criminal enterprise died before any potential processes were held.

[62] T K Ashplant, G Dawson, and M Roper, *The Politics of War Memory and Commemoration* (Routledge 2000) 16.

[63] K Ristić, *Imaginary Trials: War Crime Trials and Memory in Former Yugoslavia* (Leipziger Universitätsverlag 2014) 96.

[64] Focus group with non-urban pensioners, Sokolić (n 26).

ZG.V.3 agrees
ZG.V.2—What was targeted, consciously, be it rape, murder, massacres, liquidation, destruction of culture, that is a war crime.
ZG.V.1 agrees.[65]

This highlights the perceived difference between individual acts and acts carried out in response to policy or orders, thereby distinguishing crimes by individual soldiers that do not implicate the army. Underpinning this view is an apologetic attitude towards crimes committed as crimes of revenge or passion and a broader tolerance of deviance. Croatian war crimes were discussed in the context of a defensive war and consisted of two categories: war crimes considered possible in a defensive war (but that they were sporadic) and war crimes considered not possible in that context (but individuals did commit 'crimes in war'). These results have been replicated in numerous longitudinal studies. A 2001 survey found that a large majority of the public did not consider the Croatian army (74 per cent) or volunteers (69 per cent) responsible for war crimes;[66] a 2011 study found that 44.9 per cent of respondents did not believe it was possible for Croatian forces to commit a war crime in a defensive war, versus 29.8 per cent who did.[67]

There was consensus in all groups that international law or the Geneva Conventions defined war crimes. For example, participants expressed an understanding that: medical personnel were protected under the Geneva Conventions (focus group with non-urban war veterans Banovina); prisoners of war had special rights (focus group with non-urban pensioners); the conventions were taught to officers in Yugoslavia (focus group with Sisak pensioners); and, international human rights constituted a universal standard of some kind (focus group with Zadar teachers and dyad with Zagreb teachers). These resulted in folk theories of law that created contraditions in participants' understandings; participants were aware of generally implicit norms of behaviour and laws, but they still showed a tolerance for transgression.

Some individuals expressed that they felt war crimes were obvious and apparent to all, before the war or the existence of the ICTY. For example, war crimes were 'that which could happen in any war, to come to something inhuman'.[68] It was 'any act in war, on any side, that is not in line with moral, human laws. Any actions outside of what we consider to be civilised behaviour'.[69] This again highlights folk theories of law or a type of *lex non scripta*. Transgressions of human rights were intrinsically understood, but their transgression was still tolerated.

Croatian crimes were seen as sporadic, individual, and unplanned; Serbian crimes were considered to have been premeditated, planned, and committed by the whole group. This comparison was often expressed directly:

Moderator—What is your opinion about the claim that the Croatian state was responsible for ethnic cleansing during the war?

[65] Focus groups with Zagreb war veterans, Sokolić (n 26).

[66] Caritas Croatia and the Franciscan Institute for the Culture, *Peace in Croatia: Results of Research* (CROPAX 2001).

[67] P Kolstø, *Strategies of Symbolic Nation-building in West Balkan States: Intents and Results* (University of Oslo 2011) <http://www.hf.uio.no/ilos/english/research/projects/nation-w-balkan/> accessed 16 November 2016.

[68] Interview with Zagreb pensioner, Sokolić (n 26).

[69] Interview with non-urban teacher, Sokolić (n 26).

ZA.T.1—I think to a far lesser degree than on the Serbian side. That is undeniable.

ZA.T.2 agrees—I am aware that the concept of ethnic cleansing was created as a euphemism for the genocide that the Serb side did at the beginning. However, it is difficult to accuse Croatia of ethnic cleansing because realistically, in many parts of Croatia that were far away from the conflict zones, there was a similar number of Serbs and it did not change much. In areas where conflict did occur, as a rule the flight of the population was prepared by the authorities of the para-state.

ZA.T.1—Yes.

ZA.T.2—They would often say themselves that they would either be in Serbia or that they would not stay here.

ZA.T.3—Many left willingly.

ZA.T.1—Willingly.[70]

The most striking juxtaposition with Serbian crimes was, however, the narrative of the *baka* with the rifle and other similar narratives of armed civilians. It was used to relativize Croatian actions in the war and featured many of the most common elements of the Croatian war narrative. For example, the Zadar pensioners below first relativize using figures, then portray Serbs as universally and inherently armed (from children to old people), and finally contrast this with the image of Christ, a victim, speaking the truth, as Croats now must do:

ZA.P.3—Here they mobilised, I think about 50,000–100,000 of them. There was not a peasant that did not have a weapon. And today we talk about this and that. This is why Tuđman pardoned them, because he would otherwise have to punish even the simplest of peasants because the *JNA* armed them all.

ZA.P.2—From children to old people.

ZA.P.3—That is right. Today we avoid this in discussion and in politics and so on. But this is a tragedy. As Christ said, the truth will set you free. And we have to speak the truth and only the truth.[71]

Operation Storm is representative of the Croatian public's view of war crimes, since it contains the narrative of revenge and of sporadic crimes, rather than organized ones. In numerous groups the questions 'can war crimes be committed in a defensive war?' and 'what do you think about the claim that the Croatian state was responsible for ethnic cleansing during the war?' led to an immediate response about Operation Storm. This is not surprising given how the trial of Gotovina captured the attention of the public for so many years and the emotional attachment much of the public has to it, since it was seen as holding the potential to delegitimize the Croatian state. This is best captured by the response of a Sisak war veteran, who threatened to remove herself from the group if the moderator did not stop focusing solely on Operation Storm, even though the moderator had not mentioned the theme and the conversation at the time was about the crimes and trials in Bosnia. Across all groups, there was a feeling that Croatia did

[70] Focus groups with Zadar teachers, Sokolić (n 26).

[71] Focus group with Zadar pensioners, Sokolić (n 26).

not commit any organized war crimes during the war generally and during Operation Storm specifically. The juxtaposition between Croats and Serbs results in legal understanding being defined by the difference in playing fields for the two ethnicities and on emotional grounds.

Command responsibility, also a key feature of the Gotovina trial, was regarded with disbelief and confusion. Participants readily confessed they were confused about the concept, although there was consensus across groups that it was not correct to try commanders, since it was too much to expect them to exercise complete control over their soldiers in the unorganized context of the Croatian defence, mixed with the inherent difficulty in controlling vengeful individuals. Here, again, folk theories of law play a large role in legal reasoning. Participants first admitted to not understanding a concept, then outlined the premise for their definition of the concept, before arguing for why they believed Croatian generals were not guilty of command responsibility. They constructed their understanding of the situation through a mixture of law, politics, and emotion:

NU.T.2—It is difficult to talk about command responsibility in 1995 in the Croatian Army, when a man after five years liberates his house and kills someone he found inside it. Of course he is guilty for that war crime and for the murder of a civilian, but it is hard to control him.[72]

NU.P.1— [Norac] was a young boy thrown into huge responsibility, to lead those people there. He could not, so young, command those types of people in the army. Those were mainly people from that region, from that place. What we just discussed, revenge. Here the Medak Pocket and all of that happened. He was tried mainly for that and sentenced. What did they call it? A massacre. Compared to Čavoglave, what they did there, this is not normal, it is not even comparable.[73]

23.7 The ICTY—Unjust, Unfair, and Unhurried

The ICTY was above all considered inefficient and all groups spent some time discussing this topic. Survey research has reflected this: 69 per cent of respondents in a 2011 study felt trials were needlessly long, as opposed to 25 per cent who felt that trial complexity justified this.[74] Given the crimes it was dealing with and the emotional nature of the memories involved, it is debatable if it could have ever been seen as efficient since justice may never seem swift enough. Participants felt the Tribunal was poorly implemented from its original design, which led to inefficiency:

ZA.V.4—This Tribunal is not even a shadow of what it was meant to be.
ZA.V.3—The idea was good.[75]
Moderator—Do you think it was a mistake to establish The Hague tribunal?

72 Interview with non-urban teacher, Sokolić (n 26).

73 Follow-up dyad with non-urban pensioners, Sokolić (n 26).

74 *Informisanost i stavovi građana Hrvatske prema Haškom tribunalu i suđenjima za ratne zločine pred sudovima u Hrvatskoj* [*Knowledge and Attitudes of the Citizens of Croatia Towards The Hague Tribunal and War Crimes Trials in Croatian Courts*] (Belgrade Human Rights Centre 2011).

75 Focus group with Zadar war veterans, Sokolić (n 26).

SI.T.2—No.
SI.T.3—No, it was established with a different intention.
SI.T.1—As an idea it was good.
SI.T.2—As an international court of justice.
SI.T.1—However, what kind of court of justice is it if the Americans do not recognise it?
SI.T.3—That they do not respect.
SI.T.1—This is an international criminal court for the second division. For those clubs who play county level matches. This is not a court for the top division, for the Security Council. Who would they prosecute on the Security Council, when they have the right to veto. No one. This is for us small ones. To give us some sense of justice and truth.
SI.T.2—Of international justice.
SI.T.1—International justice, because we are fooled by terminology. International.
SI.T.3—To show that we are not forgotten, that they are thinking of us.[76]

Vukovar was considered emblematic of ICTY inefficiency and unjustness. The view that no one had been sentenced sufficiently, if at all, for war crimes in the city was expressed in varying degrees across all groups:

ZA.V.3—Has anyone been sentenced for Srebrenica and Vukovar?
ZA.V.4—No one.
ZA.V.3—What are we talking about here? This was a war crime, genocide was committed there.
ZA.V.2—A hard to believe genocide in the 21st century.
ZA.V.3—And no one has been indicted for that.
ZA.V.2—If you tell your children, they cannot believe you. My grandchildren cry when they hear about the genocide against the Jews, not to mention if I speak about the Homeland War. Too horrific.
ZA.V.5—That city was levelled to the ground. It is too horrific.[77]

Much of the above passage is factually incorrect (a number of individuals have been sentenced for crimes in both Srebrenica and Vukovar), but it does show how powerful this symbol of Vukovar is and how emotional it is. Other than factual inaccuracy being employed to support the war narrative, this dichotomy points to a lack of Outreach or press coverage, since trials did take place (although it is debatable how happy the Croatian public is with their outcomes).

The ICTY was seen as biased against Croats and Croatia because it was attempting to equalize guilt, especially between Croats and Serbs. In a 2012 study, 47.5 per cent agreed that this was the aim of the Tribunal, only 11.8 per cent disagreed.[78] Equalization of guilt could undermine the Croatian war narrative, because it risks portraying the Homeland War as a civil war with no exclusively Serbian aggression, no exclusively Croatian defence and no unique Croatian victimhood. Participants felt this disparaged victims, and falsified Croatian history. For example, a teacher claimed that 'as soon as the stories started that

[76] Focus group with Sisak teachers, Sokolić (n 26).
[77] Focus group with Zadar war veterans, Sokolić (n 26).
[78] Izbori 2011 *(Elections 2011)* (Ipsos Puls 2012).

Croatia committed some kind of crime and was being equalised with the aggressor, I immediately stopped following [the ICTY]'.[79] This illustrates the link between expressivist aspects of courts and their legal performance; legal decisions can be perceived as unjust, thereby delegitimizing expressivist messages, but disagreement with the expressivist message (often based on emotion) also delegitimizes legal rulings.

This is connected to views that the ICTY was politically motivated and controlled by big power politics; partly the result of political bargaining between Croatian governments and the EU, NATO, and ICTY over accession conditionality. The transfer of individuals to the ICTY was viewed as a political process, instead of a judicial one, primarily due to Tuđman's bargaining with the ICTY.[80] This tarnished the ICTY and resulted in the Croatian government being seen as only transferring individuals who lacked political connections with the government. Such a high degree of reporting occurred around the transfer of individuals that these events held more potential than others to influence public opinion. Conversely, so did judgments, such as the appeals decision in the Gotovina trial, which had the potential to make the ICTY look fairer in Croatian eyes. Trials, indictments, and verdicts were all regarded as politically motivated and the ICTY was therefore not considered to be independent.

> ZA.T.2—I had this feeling as if Croatia was rewarded for admission to NATO and the EU by releasing the Generals. If that is true, then this is truly an embarrassment for the court and for international law.
> ZA.T.1—It looks like politicisation and no one can deny that.
> All agree.[81]

This leaves the impression that the ICTY is an institution created by big powers to dictate politics in the inferior Balkan region. This factor, possibly more than any other, contributes to the general distrust of the ICTY. Together with all the other factors in this process, it helps create a widespread feeling of powerlessness, which respondents frequently expressed. Despite a range of critiques against it, the ICTY did attract a certain level of praise. Pensioners and teachers, although no war veterans, believed its establishment was not a mistake. They believed that it did help Croatia, if not the region, and that it did punish crimes that ought to have been punished:

> Moderator—Do you think it was a mistake to establish the ICTY?
> ZA.P.1—Maybe not. Because who knows when the war would have ended or how. The Americans got involved, and then the court came, so that it somehow ended up like this.[82]
> Moderator—Do you think it was a mistake to establish the ICTY?
> ZG.T.1—No.
> ZG.T.2—Perhaps it was not, I do not know, a mistake.
> ZG.T.1—A war crime has to be punished.

[79] Focus group with Zadar teachers, Sokolić (n 26).
[80] Lamont (n 13).
[81] Focus group with Zadar teachers, Sokolić (n 26).
[82] Focus group with Zadar pensioners, Sokolić (n 26).

ZG.T.2—Yes, in that light it definitely was not a mistake.[83]

The trial of Gotovina has come to represent (i) ICTY bias in that it indicted Gotovina; (ii) inefficiency in that it had two wholly different verdicts; but also (iii) correctness, since it did find him, and seemingly the foundation of the Croatian state, to be innocent. ICTY verdicts did have an effect on participants. The final Gotovina verdict can reinforce the war narrative, but the guilty verdict for Kordić on the other hand had the potential to undermine the war narrative and, therefore, erode trust in the ICTY. Teachers and some pensioners believed ICTY verdicts were correct and consequently viewed Kordić as guilty. These sequences show there is acknowledgment of guilt, but that political implications are more important than legal ones. The theme is ignored and participants tried not to discuss it at length.

ZA.T.2—Given he was sentenced, I suppose he was guilty. I do not think it is such a big problem not to agree with the verdict, maybe he is innocent but I do not know, but what was problematic was his reception when he returned as a positive individual, despite that he was sentenced. This can be compared to the reception of Gotovina, who was found innocent. It is not fair to Gotovina, or to the victims.
ZA.T.1—I agree.
ZA.T.3—Bosnia is quite a complex theme. I would not like to add much.[84]
ZG.P.4—I do not think it was fair that the Church went to welcome him and kiss him. He has served his sentence, so it was proven through a court decision. There is nothing else to consider. He should not have been welcomed like that.[85]

The above passage shows that ICTY verdicts can be significant to individuals that some believe that war criminals ought not to be accepted back into society. This guilty verdict resulted in some kind of debate over how convicted war criminals should participate in society. Despite the ICTY's huge unpopularity, it does hold some legitimacy in the eyes of the public and despite much criticism levelled at it, its verdicts do hold some meaning for the public.

23.8 Conclusion

Understandings of war crimes in post-conflict societies are in great part defined by understandings of the conflict that took place. In the case of Croatia, where the dominant narrative of the conflict paints Croats as victims and Serbs as aggressors, the result is an apologetic attitude towards war crimes committed by Croats. These crimes are seen as mitigated acts of passionate revenge or as justified self-defence against armed Serb civilians. Folk theories of law and factual inaccuracies construct images, such as the *baka* with a rifle, that are used as a mitigating circumstance and lead to an acceptance of Croat crimes. Croat war crimes were seen as unexceptional crimes in war (to be punished more leniently), while Serb crimes are

[83] Dyad with Zagreb teachers, Sokolić (n 26).
[84] Focus group with Zadar teachers, Sokolić (n 26).
[85] Follow-up interview with Zagreb pensioner, Sokolić (n 26).

seen as exceptional war crimes (to be punished more harshly). War crimes were defined by the dominant war narrative, which resulted in a tolerance for deviance.

Localized complexities and normative expectations direct the course of transitional justice processes. Attempts to instil a rule of law norm in the public have to take these into account as part of their work and transitional justice institutions operate in this type of environment. In Croatia the consequence was that all institutions—domestic and international, legal or otherwise—were seen as corrupt and inefficient. They were distrusted. As a result, people felt powerless in an unresponsive system where justice was imposed from above.

In order to be at its most effective, law needs to work in concert with social norms that govern behaviour, including norms against disorder that may give rise to crimes.[86] A potent mixture of institutional distrust and a dominant war narrative resulted in significant cynicism directed at the transitional justice process in Croatia. Within such a context, the ICTY struggled to develop understandings of law that mirrored the legally sound judgments it handed down. Pedagogical effects of trials are only possible if they take into account localized normative processes. The focus group data, however, are not exclusively pessimistic. Teachers, the youngest group in the study, had a far more optimistic view of the ICTY. This hints at a generational dimension to transitional justice's effects and that rule of law norms may take much longer to instil.

[86] T L Meares and D M Kahan, 'Law and (Norms of) Order in the Inner City' [1998] Law & Society Review 805.

24

The Legacy of the ICTY

The Three-tiered Approach to Justice in Bosnia-Herzegovina and Benchmarks for Measuring Success

Jennifer Trahan and Iva Vukušić**, ****

24.1 Introduction

The International Tribunal for the Prosecution of Persons Responsible for Serious Violations of International Humanitarian Law Committed in the Territory of the former Yugoslavia since 1991, more commonly referred to as the International Criminal Tribunal for the former Yugoslavia (ICTY or Tribunal), has made significant contributions to justice (prosecuting key perpetrators), peace, and security (marginalizing key actors through indictments and prosecutions), and creating an historical record. Yet, it has also given us something greater—namely, a robust model for adjudicating large-scale atrocity crimes through its three-tiered approach to justice. While the ICTY also assisted local trials in Croatia and Serbia, this chapter will focus on Bosnia-Herzegovina (BiH) where the ICTY's impact on local proceedings was the most significant and two different levels of local prosecutions existed.

For crimes perpetrated in BiH, there have been trials at the ICTY, by the hybrid War Crimes Chamber of the Court of Bosnia and Herzegovina in Sarajevo (State Court), and by local cantonal and district courts. Despite some controversial acquittals at the ICTY, and uneven accomplishments at the local trial levels, this three-tiered approach has provided a model for the future of international justice. While there were also multiple levels of justice for Axis crimes perpetrated during the Second World War (some tried, most famously, before the International Military Tribunal at Nuremberg),[1] as well as those in Rwanda,[2] for various reasons, the ICTY provides our strongest model of multi-levelled prosecutions. These three tiers could, of course, be further complemented by a robust approach to other transitional justice tools (over and above prosecutions) for example, truth commissions, reparations, institutional reform, and memorialization, but, for many reasons, not all of these tools are presently being utilized, or are being utilized selectively in the region. In evaluating this three-tiered approach, however, one is reminded of the importance of setting

* Jennifer Trahan is a Clinical Professor, The Center for Global Affairs, NYU-SPS.
** Iva Vukušić is a Visiting Research Fellow, War Studies Department, King's College London.
*** Erin Lovall and Heather Craig provided research assistance.

[1] For the London Charter creating the International Military Tribunal at Nuremberg (IMT), see Charter of the International Military Tribunal (1945) <http://avalon.law.yale.edu/imt/imtconst.asp> accessed July 2018.

[2] For crimes perpetrated in Rwanda, there were trials at the International Criminal Tribunal for Rwanda (ICTR), domestic courts within Rwanda, and an estimated 1.9 million cases before 'Gacaca courts'. See National Service of Gacaca Courts 'Administrative Report of the National Service of Gacaca Courts' (June 2012) <http://cnlg.gov.rw/fileadmin/templates/documents/GACACA_COURTS_IN_RWANDA.pdf> accessed July 2018.

Jennifer Trahan and Iva Vukušić, *The Legacy of the ICTY* In: *Legacies of the International Criminal Tribunal for the Former Yugoslavia.* Edited by: Carsten Stahn, Carmel Agius, Serge Brammertz, Colleen Rohan, Oxford University Press (2020). © The Several Contributors
DOI: 10.1093/oso/9780198862956.003.0025

reasonable expectations for what an adjudicative mechanism can accomplish. Despite the ICTY's noteworthy achievements, not every case will be tried (even when complemented by local trials), there is still denial or partial denial of crimes (and it was unreasonable to think a tribunal could halt this), and it is unrealistic to think that tribunals can create reconciliation—although a tribunal's work can set the indispensable foundation upon which it may be built, in the future. Also, it is local actors who will need to implement these transitional justice mechanisms. When measured against more traditional justice-related goals, we see that the three-tiered approach has achieved a variety of successes, with the ICTY being the most successful institution. When measured against more society-wide, long-terms goals—which arguably are not even appropriate goals for tribunals—one actually sees some contributions made as well.

This chapter provides an overview of the accomplishments of the three tiers of justice, examines the benchmarks by which to measure this work, and evaluates the extent to which the ICTY, complemented by local courts, has satisfied these benchmarks. It simultaneously acknowledges that goals such as reconciliation and silencing denial of crimes by political leadership must be left to locally-owned initiatives and the eventual transformation of the political scene through a new generation of political leadership. The chapter will conclude that the ICTY has been our most successful tribunal to date and is, therefore, a model for the future—including in this three-tiered approach to justice in BiH.

24.2 Overview of the Three Tiers of Justice in BiH

24.2.1 The ICTY

While there are ICTY detractors, and particularly victim communities are often dissatisfied with the time it took for convictions,[3] the existence of acquittals, and the limited number ultimately tried, it cannot be disputed that the ICTY is in fact the international tribunal that has prosecuted the greatest number of individuals from any one conflict, with 161 indicted and 111 tried.[4] The International Criminal Tribunal for Rwanda (ICTR), by contrast, indicted ninety-three and tried seventy-eight.[5] Many hybrid tribunals such as the Special Court for Sierra Leone (SCSL) and the Extraordinary Chambers in the Courts of Cambodia (ECCC) have prosecuted, or are prosecuting, far more limited numbers of individuals.[6] The International Criminal Court (ICC) also prosecutes only a limited number of individuals from each situation country.[7]

[3] International prosecutions of large-scale atrocity crimes, prosecuted systematically, with due process rigorously observed, do not produce expeditious trials. In fact, a rapid trial can be indicative of due process violations.

[4] ICTY, 'Key Figures of the Cases' <http://www.icty.org/en/cases/key-figures-cases> accessed February 2020. The 111 includes ninety sentenced, eighteen acquitted, and two being retried and one on appeal before the Mechanism for International Criminal Tribunals (MICT).

[5] ICTR, 'The ICTR in Brief' <http://unictr.unmict.org/en/tribunal> accessed July 2018. The seventy-eight includes sixty-two sentenced, fourteen acquitted, and two deceased prior to judgment.

[6] The Special Court for Sierra Leone indicted thirteen, but only prosecuted ten individuals, with judgments entered against nine. It also prosecuted a number of contempt cases. See War Crimes Research Group 'The Special Court for Sierra Leone: Outreach, Legacy and Impact' Department of War Studies, Kings College, London (February 2008) 5 <http://www.rscsl.org/Resources.html> accessed July 2018. The ECCC has to date prosecuted three individuals in cases 001 and 002. ECCC, 'Who has been prosecuted?' <https://www.eccc.gov.kh/en/who-has-been-prosecuted> accessed July 2018.

[7] See ICC, 'Cases' <https://www.icc-cpi.int/Pages/cases.aspx> accessed July 2018.

Despite some early indictments that were later withdrawn, and the Tribunal starting with a relatively low-level case against Duško Tadić, the ICTY eventually made its way up to key perpetrators, such as Slobodan Milošević, Radovan Karadžić, and Ratko Mladić. Prosecution of Croatian General Ante Gotovina, as well as that of former commander in the Kosovo Liberation Army (KLA), Ramush Haradinaj, of course, ended in controversial acquittals.[8] Another controversial acquittal at the trial level was that of Serbian radical politician Vojislav Šešelj, although on appeal he was ultimately convicted for crimes against humanity and sentenced to ten years.[9] Nonetheless, ultimately, the Tribunal has prosecuted persons from all sides of the conflict,[10] and achieved a 100 per cent success rate on arrests, with no fugitives from its main cases at large.[11]

It has meanwhile also set many significant jurisprudential 'firsts'—here, only briefly highlighted—including prosecuting sexual violence crimes, such as the running of a notorious rape camp in Foča.[12] Rape has been held to constitute a crime against humanity,[13] war crime,[14] and form of torture.[15] Significantly, of course, the ICTY also adjudicated the massacres in and around Srebrenica to constitute genocide in *Krstić*,[16] as well as in other decisions. The ICTY has also reminded us that women too can perpetrate atrocity crimes, by charging and accepting the guilty plea of former President of Republika Srpska Biljana Plavšić, for persecution as a crime against humanity.[17] Throughout their rulings, the judges have produced a wealth of generally well-reasoned and impressive jurisprudence on the parameters of the crimes of genocide, war crimes, and crimes against humanity, as well as individual and command responsibility, and procedural and other substantive law.[18]

[8] *Prosecutor v Gotovina* (Appeals Chamber Judgment) ICTY–IT-06-90-A (16 November 2012); *Prosecutor v Haradinaj* (Judgment) ICTY-IT-04-84-T (3 April 2008). The Perišić case also resulted in an unfortunate and not-well-reasoned acquittal. See J Trahan and E Lovall, 'The ICTY Appellate Chamber's Acquittal of Momčilo Perišić: The Specific Direction Element of Aiding and Abetting Should be Rejected or Modified to Explicitly Include a "Reasonable Person" Due Diligence Standard' (2015) 40 Brooklyn Journal of International Law 171.

[9] In accordance with Rule 125 (c) of the Rules of Procedure and Evidence, the ten-year sentence was viewed as served due to Šešelj's detention in ICTY custody from 14 February 2003 to 6 November 2014. *Prosecutor v Šešelj* (Appeals Chamber Judgment) MICT-16-99-A (11 April 2018) para 181.

[10] See ICTY, 'ICTY Case List' <https://www.icty.org/en/cases> accessed July 2018.

[11] See ICTY, 'Infographic: ICTY Facts & Figures' <http://www.icty.org/en/content/infographic-icty-facts-figures> accessed July 2018. By 'main cases' the authors mean cases involving genocide, crimes against humanity, and/or war crimes, and not contempt cases. The ICTY's success on arrests was achieved through a policy of 'conditionality', whereby the US conditioned financial assistance to countries in the region, and the European Union (EU) conditioned progress towards EU accession, on cooperation by countries in the region with the ICTY, particularly as to arrests and surrenders. See J Kim, *Balkan Cooperation on War Crimes Issues* (US Cong Research Serv, RS 22097, 2008); S Woehrel, *Conditions on US Aid to Serbia* (US Cong Research Serv, RS 21686, 2008). There are, however, two at large from the MICT, Petar Jojić and Vjerica Radeta, accused of contempt of court.

[12] *Prosecutor v Kunarac* (Trial Chamber Judgment) ICTY–IT-96-23 and 23/1 (22 February 2001).

[13] *Prosecutor v Kunarac* (Appeals Chamber Judgment) ICTY–IT-96-23 and 23/1A (12 June 2002) paras 127–29 (hereinafter Kunarac Appeals Chamber Judgment); *Prosecutor v Kvočka* (Trial Chamber Judgment) ICTY–IT-98-30/1 (2 November 2001) paras 175, 180–83; *aff'd on appeal* (Appeals Chamber Judgment) ICTY-IT-98-30/1-A (28 February 2005).

[14] *Prosecutor v Kvočka* (Appeals Chamber Judgment) ICTY–IT-98-30/1A (28 February 2005) para 395; Kunarac Appeals Chamber Judgment (n 13) paras 127–29.

[15] Kunarac Appeals Chamber Judgment (n 13) paras 150–51.

[16] *Prosecutor v Krstić* (Trial Chamber Judgment) ICTY–IT-98-33 (2 August 2001) (hereinafter Krstić Trial Chamber Judgment); *aff'd on appeal* (Appeals Chamber Judgment) ICTY-IT-98-33-A (19 April 2004).

[17] *Prosecutor v Plavšić* (Trial Chamber Judgment) ICTY–IT-0039 and 40/1 (27 February 2003) (case not appealed).

[18] For a compilation of the case law, see J Trahan, *Genocide, War Crimes and Crimes Against Humanity: A Topical Digest of the Caselaw of the International Criminal Tribunal for the Former Yugoslavia* (Human Rights Watch 2006).

24.2.2 The Court of Bosnia and Herzegovina in Sarajevo

The ICTY also significantly helped in the creation of, and support for, the State Court in Sarajevo. Particularly, when the ICTY was facing the 'Completion Strategy' and transferring lower-level cases back to courts in the region under Rule 11*bis*,[19] it worked to establish this unique model of a hybrid court.

The State Court's innovative design has involved a timed phase-out of its hybridization.[20] For the first years of operation, trial panels consisted of two international judges and one national judge.[21] For the second phase of operation, trial chambers consisted of one international judge and two national judges.[22] Finally, all international staff were phased out. This model has shown the advantage of creating a hybrid tribunal that phases out to become a national court, rather than the hybrid simply terminating its work after a set number of years, as have all other hybrid tribunals to date.[23] It leaves behind an ongoing judicial institution that hopefully benefitted from its hybrid phase, with national staff working alongside international staff. On the other hand, by setting rigid time-lines for phasing out hybridization, without regard to how that phase-out would impact prosecutions, the State Court has been less successful. By all accounts, the Court's work has suffered after the final phase out of international staff, which perhaps occurred too soon.[24]

Despite concerns about its current functioning,[25] and a phase earlier on, when it was 'anonymizing' judgments,[26] the State Court has prosecuted individuals belonging to all three of the main Bosnian ethnicities: Bosnian Muslims, Bosnian Croats, and Bosnian Serbs. It has indicted a total of 606,[27] and over 100 verdicts have been pronounced.[28] It currently has several cases ongoing against alleged perpetrators that belonged to various belligerent

19 Rules of Procedure and Evidence of the International Criminal Tribunal for the Former Yugoslavia, IT/32/Rev 50 (8 July 2015) <http://www.icty.org/x/file/Legal%20Library/Rules_procedure_evidence/IT032Rev50_en.pdf> accessed July 2018.

20 See B Ivanišević, 'The War Crimes Chamber in Bosnia and Herzegovina: From Hybrid to Domestic Court' (2008) International Center for Transitional Justice 39–43.

21 'Until 2008 each of the five trial panels and the appellate panel included two international members and one national member. The balance of composition [then] reversed.... [T]he panels [then] included two nationals and one international'. ibid 7.

22 ibid.

23 The Special Court for Sierra Leone operated for a number of years and then closed, leaving behind a small residual mechanism. See 'Residual Special Court for Sierra Leone' <http://rscsl.org> accessed July 2018. The ECCC is also scheduled to end after it completes case 002/02 (currently on appeal) and after any remaining work on cases 003 and 004, which prosecutions the Cambodian government has attempted to block. For background, see Open Society Justice Initiative, *Performance and Perception: The Impact of the Extraordinary Chambers in the Courts of Cambodia*, <https://www.opensocietyfoundations.org/sites/default/files/performance-perception-eccc-20160211.pdf> accessed July 2018.

24 For criticism of the recent work of the State Court, see Judge J Korner, 'Processing of War Crimes at the State Level in Bosnia and Herzegovina' (*OSCE*, June 2016) <http://www.osce.org/bih/247221?download=true> accessed July 2018. A more positive, earlier, assessment can be found at Ivaniševič (n 20) 13 ('From a comparative perspective, the [State Court] has demonstrated a reasonably high degree of professionalism and efficiency in the conduct of its trials to date').

25 For criticism of the work of the State Court, see Korner (n 24).

26 Trahan Interview with Judge Patricia Whalen (on file with author).

27 The Prosecutor's Office of Bosnia and Herzegovina (Department 1, Special Department for War Crimes) <http://www.tuzilastvobih.gov.ba/?opcija=sadrzaj&kat=2&id=4&jezik=e> accessed July 2018.

28 Balkan Investigative Reporting Network (BIRN) War Crimes Verdict Map (launched September 2016) <http://www.balkaninsight.com/en/page/war-crimes-verdict-map#content12_2710> accessed July 2018; BIRN 'BIRN Launches Interactive War Crimes Verdict Map' (*Balkan Insight*, 22 September 2016) <http://www.balkaninsight.com/en/article/birn-launches-interactive-war-crimes-verdict-map-09-20-2016> accessed July 2018. BIRN's figures were last updated in August 2016 so the actual figures now are undoubtedly higher.

parties, involving both military and civilians, low-level to mid-ranking accused, as well as female accused.[29]

While the State Court also has a significant backlog of cases,[30] it is an unfortunate reality that there are simply too many cases for all perpetrators to be prosecuted and the State Court has had to cope with a massive caseload.[31] At least there has been prioritization of cases through the National Strategy for Processing of War Crimes Cases (National War Crimes Strategy) adopted in 2008,[32] which emphasized the need to process the most complex and highest priority cases within seven years, and other war crimes cases within fifteen years—trying the most responsible perpetrators at the State Court.[33] Unfortunately, however, such deadlines have proven impossible to meet, and there has been insufficient support for the strategy's implementation.[34] Thus, although there have been flaws, at least the design of the State Court leaves an innovative legacy for future hybrid tribunals.[35]

24.2.3 Local District and Cantonal Courts

The third level of prosecutions in BiH is occurring before cantonal courts in the Federation, district courts in Republika Srpska, and one court in the Brčko District.[36] Observer reports suggest that local war crimes prosecutions vary significantly in quality. For instance, as of 2008, Human Rights Watch reported:

> The obstacles include that prosecutors' offices lack sufficient staff and generally do not specialize in one type of crime. Cooperation between prosecutors and police and between police across entity lines continues to be problematic. Witness protection measures are rarely, if ever, employed, and witness support services are generally not available. Prosecutors often fail to make use of available sources of evidence and do not take steps necessary to

[29] Court of BiH official case docket, available at <http://www.sudbih.gov.ba/stranica/40/pregled>, accessed 17 May 2018.

[30] For instance, as of June 2015, there was a backlog of 725 cases involving 5,205 suspects. Korner (n 24) 34 para 101.

[31] Ivanišević (n 20) 8–44.

[32] For background on the War Crimes Strategy, see Ministry of Justice of Bosnia and Herzegovina, *National Strategy for Processing of War Crimes Cases Adopted*, available at <http://www.mpr.gov.ba/aktuelnosti/vijesti/default.aspx?id=573&langTag=en-US> accessed 19 March 2017.

[33] At least the Special War Crimes Department in the Prosecutor's Office of Bosnia and Herzegovina made prioritization choices under the then-leadership of Prosecutor David Schwendiman. See D Schwendiman, 'Prosecuting Atrocity Crimes In National Courts: Looking Back On 2009 In Bosnia And Herzegovina' (2010) 8 Northwestern Journal of International Human Rights 269, 293 (discussing practice directions and a variety of criteria used to select and prioritize cases, including how existing cases and files were utilized to make determinations as to prioritization). Today it is less clear what the basis is for case selection and prioritization.

[34] See Korner (n 24); see also OSCE Mission to Bosnia and Herzegovina, *Delivering Justice in Bosnia and Herzegovina* (2011) 8 ('[T]he BiH Prosecutor's Office and the court of BIH have not effectively realized the objective indicated in the National Strategy that requires them to focus on the trial of the "most responsible perpetrators" as a priority'.).

[35] See also Ivanišević (n 20) 2 ('As part of a national court the [State Court] offers a promising model in terms of legacy').

[36] Human Rights Watch, 'Bosnia and Herzegovina: Local Courts Face Obstacles in War Crimes Trials' (*Human Rights Watch*, 2008) <https://www.hrw.org/news/2008/07/10/bosnia-and-herzegovina-local-courts-face-obstacles-war-crimes-trials> accessed 19 March 2017 ('It is estimated that several thousand unresolved case files involving very serious crimes committed during the 1992–95 war remain that may be tried before the cantonal courts in the Federation of Bosnia and Herzegovina and district courts in Republika Srpska').

secure suspect attendance at trial. Defense attorneys generally lack access to training in relevant areas of law and are often inadequately, or not at all, compensated for their work.[37]

There also remain a large number of unresolved case files at the local level;[38] as noted already, even with three tiers of justice, it may not be possible to prosecute all the perpetrators. Yet, the 2016 Annual Report of the Prosecutor's Office of BiH confirms that cooperation between the State Prosecutor's Office and the local entity courts in BiH continues, and cases have been sent from Sarajevo to Bihać, Goražde, Mostar, East Sarajevo, Bijeljina, and other towns and cities.[39] In total, twenty-five cases focusing on seventy-two individuals were sent to these lower-level offices in 2016.[40] Since 2010, Banja Luka received forty-one cases, Bijeljina twenty-eight, East Sarajevo thirty-six, Mostar ninety-one, Bihać sixty-two.[41] In total, 450 cases have been transferred from the State Prosecution to the lower-level courts since 2010.[42] What this report and the local authorities generally do not make clear are the profiles of the cases, the ranks of the accused, and the complexity of the cases. The process of prioritization and selection is thus not transparent. Nevertheless, prosecutions do continue, as do exhumations,[43] even if at times at a slow pace.

In addition to the prosecutions in BiH, local level trials in Croatia have been conducted in the largest district courts.[44] In Serbia, war crimes prosecutions occur at the Belgrade Higher Court's War Crimes Department.[45] KLA crimes are also set to be prosecuted before a hybrid tribunal established in The Hague, the Kosovo Specialist Chambers.[46] Montenegro has also conducted war crimes trials.[47] All told, more than 650 individuals have been convicted across the region,[48] with the most prosecutions occurring in BiH. Given that the violence

[37] ibid.

[38] See OSCE, *Delivering Justice* (n 34) 21–22 (reporting as of April 2010 'an approximate 1,381 war crimes case files pertaining to some 8,240 suspects distributed among the 17 jurisdictions dealing with war crimes cases').

[39] Prosecutor's Office of Bosnia and Herzegovina, 'Annual Report for the Year 2016' (2016) 26–27 <http://www.tuzilastvobih.gov.ba/files/docs/Informacija_2016-bosanski-_Finalno.pdf> (in BCS) accessed July 2018.

[40] ibid.

[41] ibid.

[42] ibid.

[43] Exhumation in the village of Berkovići, Bosnia and Herzegovina, conducted at the order of the State Prosecutor's Office. See also International Commission for Missing Persons (ICMP) Daily Digest (10 May 2018) <https://www.icmp.int/2018/> accessed July 2018.

[44] *Behind a Wall of Silence: Prosecution of War Crimes in Croatia* (Amnesty International Publications 2010), <https://www.amnesty.org/en/documents/eur64/003/2010/en> accessed July 2018. Croatia is conducting the fewest number of prosecutions of BiH, Serbia, and Croatia, although arguably did have fewer crimes to prosecute.

[45] B Ivanišević, 'Against the Current—War Crimes Prosecutions in Serbia' (2007) International Center for Transitional Justice15, <https://www.ictj.org/publication/against-current-war-crimes-prosecutions-serbia-0> accessed July 2018. That there are war crimes prosecutions ongoing in Serbia is certainly positive; yet, they are generally of lower-level and paramilitary members, rather than higher-level and regular armed forces or Serbian police units. See Humanitarian Law Center, 'Ten Years of War Crimes Prosecutions in Serbia: Contours of Justice' (2014) 21 <http://www.hlc-rdc.org/wp-content/uploads/2014/10/Analiza_2004-2013_eng.pdf> accessed July 2018 (quoting OSCE former legal adviser Ivan Jovanović, 'After a number of years one can conclude, since this is an objective fact, that persons occupying middle- and higher-ranking levels of responsibility are not being indicted. In 2004, 2005 and 2006 this could only have been an assumption, but now it is a conclusion').

[46] The Kosovo Specialist Chambers and Specialist Prosecutor's Office has jurisdiction over crimes against humanity, war crimes, and other crimes under Kosovo law, and is attached to the court system in Kosovo, but sits in The Hague. The Chambers and Prosecutor's Office are staffed with international judges, prosecutors, and officers. 'Kosovo Specialist Chambers & Specialist Prosecutor's Office' <https://www.scp-ks.org/en/background> accessed July 2018.

[47] See Human Rights Action, *IZVJEŠTAJ: Suđenja za Ratne Zločine u Crnoj Gori* <http://www.hraction.org/wp-content/uploads/20-maj-2013-Sudjenja-za-ratne-zlocine.pdf> accessed July 2018.

[48] BIRN War Crimes Verdict Map (n 28). This figure is undoubtedly low, as the breakdown does not include cantonal and district courts in BiH, which were not included in BIRN's figures.

there lasted longest, included particularly brutal victimization, and that the country saw significant foreign and donor involvement, this is no surprise. In addition to the over 100 judgments by the State Court, there have been approximately one 150 judgments pronounced by the district and cantonal courts.[49]

All in all, this shows an impressive three-tiered, if imperfect, approach to justice for crimes committed in BiH, as well as additional mechanisms prosecuting crimes in the region. Progress, however, is not guaranteed. For example, Serbia at one point lacked a war crimes prosecutor for over a year, and one wonders if the entire endeavour of local war crimes trials is truly sustainable, or risks falling off the agenda absent pressure from the international community.

24.3 Benchmarks for Measuring the Justice Accomplished

The measure of justice cannot of course simply be the number of cases prosecuted or number of persons apprehended, although those figures are relevant. One might also, for instance, examine: (1) whether fair trial protections were rigorously observed; (2) whether the higher-level perpetrators and cases involving the gravest crimes were prosecuted or at least prioritized for prosecution; (3) whether previously under-reported and under-prosecuted crimes were prosecuted and thereby highlighted; and (4) whether witnesses and victims have felt sufficiently protected by witness protection mechanisms to come forward and testify.[50] If we measure the work of these three tiers of justice in BiH by these standards we see mixed success, with the ICTY being the most successful institution.

24.3.1 Fair Trials

While defence counsel at the ICTY would no doubt have some complaints to lodge, it cannot be disputed that the ICTY has a broad panoply of fair trial protections in its Statute[51] and that they have been rigorously observed.[52] The same appears fairly true of the State Court[53]—with more rigour to prosecutions seen in its earlier hybridized phase.[54] As noted, prosecutions at the local cantonal and district court level in BiH vary widely in terms of rigour and quality.[55]

[49] BIRN has compiled data about local prosecutions from the courts themselves; these figures were supplied by Denis Džidić. Iva Vukušić email correspondence with Denis Džidić (21 May 2018) (on file with author).

[50] For a more comprehensive examination of what should be the criteria by which to evaluate the ICTY's work, see J Trahan, 'Examining the Benchmarks by which to Evaluate the ICTY's Legacy', in M Sterio and M P Scharf (eds), *The Legacy of* Ad Hoc *Tribunals in International Criminal Law: Assessing the ICTY's and the ICTR's Most Significant Legal Accomplishments* (Cambridge University Press 2019).

[51] See Updated Statute of the International Criminal Tribunal for the Former Yugoslavia (September 2009) art 20 (conduct of trials); art 21 (rights of the accused).

[52] See Trahan, 2006 (n 18) 335–417 (discussing cases on fair trial rights).

[53] See OSCE, *Delivering Justice* (n 34) 45 (the State Court has 'by and large succeeded in ensuring that serious war crimes are prosecuted in an efficient manner compliant with human rights standards').

[54] See Korner (n 24) (criticizing recent work).

[55] See Human Rights Watch, *Bosnia and Herzegovina* (n 36); OSCE, *Delivering Justice* (n 34) 9 (the OSCE Mission to Bosnia and Herzegovina has also identified 'concerns with regard to ... fair trial standards at both the state and entity level').

24.3.2 Case Prioritization

While the ICTY's mandate was not only to prosecute those who bore the 'greatest responsibility' and a number of lower- and mid-level perpetrators were prosecuted, a fair number of higher-level perpetrators certainly were tried, with the earlier trials contributing to building higher-level cases. At the State level, the idea of the 'National War Crimes Strategy' was to prioritize cases to ensure higher-level and more complex cases occur before the State Court. Such prioritization was designed to ensure more expeditious prosecution of the most serious cases before a court with witness protection mechanisms. Thus, while much work remains to be accomplished at the local level,[56] this prioritization is a significantly helpful step.[57]

24.3.3 Prosecuting Underreported and Under-prosecuted Crimes

While gravity of crimes and focusing on higher-level perpetrators are clearly relevant factors in case prioritization, another consideration is whether there are particular crimes that have historically been underreported and/or under-prosecuted and which deserve to be highlighted. The ICTY gets high marks in its focus on sexual and gender-based violence prosecutions.[58] While it is a sad testament to how war is perpetrated that these crimes need to be prosecuted, they historically have been largely overlooked[59] and are classically underreported. Thus, prosecuting rape as a war crime, crime against humanity, and form of torture[60] has not only highlighted the horrific way that sexual violence was utilized during the wars in the former Yugoslavia, it has helped bring international criminal law jurisprudence into the modern era, and set important precedent, perhaps conveying a message of deterrence to future would-be perpetrators. Sexual violence cases are also being prosecuted at the State and entity levels.[61]

[56] See (n 30) (case backlog).

[57] There are also times when a grave crime was committed, but due to insufficient evidence or the death of the suspected perpetrator, the investigation terminates without prosecution, leaving victims feeling deeply dissatisfied.

[58] For a comprehensive discussion of the ICTY's sexual and gender-based violence prosecutions, see S Brammertz and M Jarvis (eds), *Prosecuting Conflict-Related Sexual Violence* (Oxford University Press 2016).

[59] While the IMT at Nuremberg heard evidence of rape, the crime was missing from the IMT's Charter. The International Military Tribunal for the Far East (IMTFE) did prosecute two Japanese officials for failing to prevent rape as a crime against humanity. See *Facing History and Ourselves*, 'Rape as a Weapon of War' <https://www.facinghistory.org/nanjing-atrocities/judgment-memory-legacy/rape-weapon-war> accessed July 2018.

[60] See *Prosecutor v Kunarac* (n 12); *Prosecutor v Kvočka* (n 13); *Kunarac* and *Kvočka* Appeals Judgment (n 14).

[61] See OSCE, 'Combating Impunity for Conflict-Related Sexual Violence in Bosnia and Herzegovina: Progress and Challenges' (2014) <http://www.osce.org/bih/171906> accessed July 2018 (finding 'genuine commitment' to prosecute and 'notable achievements' made, while also making recommendations for improvement). It is also important that courts in Bosnia have started awarding compensation to victims of sexual violence. See J Borger 'Bosnia Rape Victims May Claim Compensation for First Time' (*The Guardian*, 30 June 2015) <https://www.theguardian.com/world/2015/jun/30/bosnia-victims-compensation-landmark-ruling> accessed July 2018. See also TRIAL International, 'BiH: Reducing Wartime Sexual Violence Survivors' Stigmatization During Criminal Proceedings' (17 January 2018) <https://trialinternational.org/latest-post/bih-reducing-wartime-sexual-violence-survivors-stigmatization-during-criminal-proceedings> accessed July 2018. For a discussion of male victims of sexual violence, see J N Clark, 'Masculinity and Male Survivors of Wartime Sexual Violence: A Bosnian Case Study' (2017) 17 Journal of Conflict, Security and Development 287—finding 'little attention has been given to the men who suffered diverse forms of sexual violence during the conflict'. See M G Djurdjevic, 'Wartime Rapes of Men Remains Taboo in Bosnia' (*Balkan Insight*, 18 May 2017) <http://www.balkaninsight.com/en/article/male-victims-of-war-related-sexual-abuse-shunned-in-bosnia-05-18-2017-1> accessed 3 June 2018. The number of male rape victims is listed as 3,000.

24.3.4 Effective Witness Protection

The ICTY has had a robust witness protection programme, with over a quarter of the 4,650 witnesses who testified, as of mid-2015, using some form of protective measure.[62] Protective measures included image distortion, voice distortion, assigning of a pseudonym, and allowing the witness to testify in closed session or via video link,[63] although the accused still had the right to confront witnesses, so knew the identity even of a protected witness. After trial, the ICTY also relocated witnesses and/or their families and/or provided them with new identities. Later on, in the ICTY's work, some formerly protected witnesses became willing to testify under their full names. It has also become clear that being a relocated witness can prove quite a difficult experience for the individual.[64] A report to the Council of Europe, however, also suggests some flaws in the implementation of the ICTY's witness protection mechanisms.[65] The same report suggests that while the State Court is perfectly equipped to protect witnesses during trials, actual witness protection has often been inconsistent.[66] At the local level, only the cantonal and municipal courts of Sarajevo were reported to have technical facilities for witness protection, with other local courts lacking such mechanisms.[67] That report concluded there were 'profound problems at the entity level where witnesses are not afforded adequate protection'.[68] Furthermore, protecting witnesses in small, tight-knit communities presents a challenge in any event, as it may not escape notice that someone from the community is meeting with outsiders or leaving on a trip to testify; if outsiders travel to a small village to conduct interviews, individuals in the community will notice, so that it is sometimes extremely difficult to ensure absolutely effective protection in such circumstances.

24.3.5 Regional Cooperation

While, as noted, the ICTY has achieved 100 per cent success on arrests in its main cases,[69] at the local level, the picture is different. Accused often have multiple passports, and despite

[62] See ICTY, 'Witness Statistics' (2015) <http://www.icty.org/en/about/registry/witnesses/statistics> accessed 16 May 2018. This includes charts of which measures were used by percentages.

[63] See Rules of Procedure and Evidence (n 19) Rules 75, 79.

[64] See M Simons, 'Witness in War Crimes Court Tallies Cost of a Decade in Hiding' (*The New York Times*, 15 August 2014) <https://www.nytimes.com/2014/08/16/world/europe/war-crimes-yugoslavia-serbia-slobodan-milosevic-hague.html> accessed July 2018 (about Witness B-129, relocated after testifying to Serbia's complicity with the paramilitary group known as 'Arkan's Tigers').

[65] See Council of Europe, Parliamentary Assembly, *The Protection of Witnesses as a Cornerstone for Justice and Reconciliation in the Balkans* (Doc 12440 rev 12 January 2011) paras 25–39. ('The protection of witnesses as a cornerstone for justice and reconciliation in the Balkans'.) For a more positive assessment, see University of North Texas and ICTY Registry Victims and Witnesses Section (VWS), *Echoes of Testimony: A Pilot Study into the Long-Term Impact of Bearing Witness Before the ICTY* <http://www.icty.org/x/file/About/Registry/Witnesses/Echoes-Exec-Summary_EN.pdf> accessed July 2018.

[66] See Council of Europe, *The Protection of Witnesses* (n 65) para 55.

[67] ibid para 63. There is also witness protection available at the Banja Luka District Court, 'Banja Luka Witness Protection Office' (*Pink TV Reports*, 22 February 2011) <https://vimeo.com/20278369> accessed July 2018. Another source states that in BiH 'the Witness Protection Department has provided different forms of protection to over 1000 witnesses who testified before the [State Court] and entity courts'. State Investigation and Protection Agency (SIPA), *BiH Witness Protection Department* <http://www.sipa.gov.ba/en/about-us/structure/organisational-structure/witness-protection-department> accessed July 2018.

[68] Council of Europe, *The Protection of Witnesses* (n 65) para 60.

[69] ICTY (n 11) (two are at large on contempt charges and defining 'main cases').

cooperation agreements by countries in the region, States still do not extradite for war crimes, leaving suspects sitting abroad, and courts in the region unable to reach them. Thus, while there were agreements signed on regional cooperation and exchange of evidence, and some cooperation has taken place, overall there is still much mistrust and politicization hampering such transfers.[70]

24.4 Benchmarks for Measuring Broader Societal Goals

On the other hand, if one seeks to accomplish broader, societal goals through prosecutions, such as (1) contributing to the maintenance of international peace and security; (2) establishing a single accepted historical narrative and combatting denial of crimes; (3) contributing to the development of the rule of law; (4) deterring future crimes either in the region or more globally, and/or; (5) achieving reconciliation—then one is perhaps asking too much from tribunals. Perhaps because the ICTY was the first international tribunal established since the Nuremberg and Tokyo Tribunals after the Second World War,[71] such lofty (and unrealistic) expectations were placed on its shoulders—sometimes with ICTY officials themselves making such grandiose claims.[72] For instance, the resolution creating the ICTY recites that the ICTY will bring 'justice', 'contribute to the restoration and maintenance of peace', and 'will contribute to ensuring that such violations are halted'.[73] The sister ICTR Tribunal's resolution also cites that it will create 'reconciliation'.[74] By now, however, at least some who work in the field of international justice are more cautious about making grandiose claims, and realize that first and foremost, tribunals are simply that—judicial institutions. Their core task is to render justice. To the extent one seeks for tribunals to accomplish these broader, societal goals (which one should not necessarily), the ICTY has in fact made some contributions in some of these areas.

24.4.1 Contributing to Peace and Security

While the recitation in the resolution establishing the ICTY that it would 'contribute to the restoration and maintenance of peace' was no doubt drafted into the resolution to establish

[70] According to the International Center for Transitional Justice (ICTJ): 'The Bosnian chief prosecutor has signed protocols on cooperation with his counterparts in Croatia and Serbia, in January and July 2005, respectively. However, lingering legal obstacles negatively affect the course of justice in the region. BiH pays the highest price when large numbers of victims and evidence remain in Bosnia while suspects across the border are protected from extradition'. Ivanišević (n 20) 27. The authors have not included measuring victim satisfaction as a benchmark. Although an important goal, victim satisfaction does not measure a tribunal's *actual* accomplishment, but perceptions, and depends on expectations which may be unrealistic.

[71] The Nuremberg and Tokyo Tribunals were not in fact truly international tribunals, as the IMT at Nuremberg was created by the four Allied Powers, and the IMTFE, while having judges from eleven nations, was predominately US-created. See Tokyo Charter of the International Military Tribunal for the Far East, 19 January 1946, issued by special proclamation of General Douglas MacArthur.

[72] UNGA UNSC 'Seventh Annual Report of the President of the ICTY' (7 August 2000) UN Doc AI55/273-S/20001777 para 217 ('the Tribunal works as an agency of reconciliation in southeastern Europe ...').

[73] UNSC Res 827 (25 May 1993) UN Doc S/RES/827.

[74] UNSC Res 955 (8 November 1994) UN Doc S/RES/955 ('*Convinced* that in the particular circumstances of Rwanda, the prosecution of persons responsible for serious violations of international humanitarian law would ... contribute to the process of national reconciliation').

that the UN Security Council had met the UN Charter, Article 39 trigger for utilizing its Chapter VII powers, that language nonetheless exists, and appears to have created expectations in this regard.

Here, in fact, the ICTY appears to have made such a contribution. By their indictments eventually driving Karadžić and Mladić off the political and military stages, respectively, the ICTY marginalized Karadžić and Mladić from positions of influence in Republika Srpska, with Karadžić living under the assumed name of Dragan Dabić and posing as a new-age healer, and Mladić moving from location to location for many years, in hiding.[75] By marginalizing such actors, the ICTY, likely did contribute to peace and security in the region,[76] although, it is essentially impossible to prove exactly how much contribution was made and precisely how it was made. The impossibility of precise quantification of such a contribution does not, however, mean it did not occur.

24.4.2 Narrowing the Space for Denial

Whereas it is not the task of a tribunal to create one accepted historical narrative (even if such a concept exists),[77] it can contribute to combatting denial. Here, the ICTY has helped solidify an evidence-based historical narrative by hearing more than 4,650 witnesses,[78] creating an impressive database of evidence, including forensic materials, and, based on all of this, producing well-written judgments that provide in-depth background on both the conflict and crimes at issue.[79] Additionally, expert reports have provided an extensive contribution to understanding details regarding the conflicts, such as the nature and role of local civilian and military institutions, the human (demographic) losses in the conflicts, and various military operations (such as the operation to take over Srebrenica). The ICTY has also attempted to convey its work to the public in the region through its outreach programmes, including one in BiH, where Outreach staff have gone from high-school to high-school, informing younger generations about the ICTY's work.[80]

Yet, despite, the ICTY's adjudication that the Srebrenica massacre constituted genocide and the International Court of Justice endorsing this holding,[81] there are still those who

[75] See J Borger, *The Butcher's Trail: How the Search for Balkan War Criminal Became the World's Most Successful Manhunt* (Other Press 2016).

[76] '[F]ormer ICTY Prosecutor Justice Richard Goldstone has argued that the [indictment of Karadžić and Mladić] was essential to peace because Karadžić and Mladić's subsequent exclusion from the negotiations of the historic Dayton peace accords facilitated the participation of Bosnia's Muslim-led government in those talks'. ICTJ, *Pursuing Justice in Ongoing Conflict: A Discussion of Current Practice* (Paper Prepared for Nuremberg Conference, June 2007) 3 <http://ictj.org/sites/default/files/ICTJ-Global-Justice-Conflict-2007-English.pdf> accessed July 2018.

[77] While it is frequently lamented that the former Yugoslavia lacks such a 'shared narrative', and, indeed, it does (with each country having multiple narratives), that raises the question whether any country, or region, really has a 'shared narrative' of its history. For instance, the US probably has quite a divergent number of narratives regarding slavery, its legacy, and the impact on modern society.

[78] ICTY, 'Witness Statistics' (2015) <http://www.icty.org/en/about/registry/witnesses/statistics> accessed July 2018.

[79] On history in war crimes trials, see R A Wilson, *Writing History in International Criminal Trials* (Cambridge University Press 2011); J Armatta, 'Historical Revelations from the Milošević Trial' (2012) 36 Southeastern Europe 10–38. On ICTY archives in particular, see I Vukušić, 'The Archives of the International Criminal Tribunal for the Former Yugoslavia' (2013) 98 History 623–35.

[80] Almir Alić, the ICTY's Outreach representative in Sarajevo, faced challenges simply obtaining permission to enter certain high schools. Trahan Interview with Almir Alić (June 2014) (on file with author).

[81] Application of the Convention on the Prevention and Punishment of the Crime of Genocide (Bosnia and Herzegovina v Serbia and Montenegro) (Judgment) 2007 ICJ Rep 43. The Muslim member of Bosnia's tripartite

partly deny the crimes at Srebrenica—often admitting that crimes occurred but arguing they were not genocide.[82] This is, at least, an improvement on earlier full denial, that no crimes occurred.[83] Unfortunately, no amount of outreach will silence such denial, nor was it reasonable to expect that a tribunal could achieve this.[84] Yet, the ICTY has made important contributions by establishing its evidence-based historical narrative that narrows the space for denial and gives civil society actors in the region and others the tools to help change the minds of future generations. Crucially, what judicial institutions need to do to limit manipulative attempts to politicize their work and to gain the trust of their primary constituents, that is, the affected populations, is to communicate clearly, frequently, and effectively.[85]

24.4.3 Contributing the Rule of Law

While a tribunal sitting in The Hague and not its situation country may seem ill-positioned to work on rule of law development, in fact, the ICTY has significantly contributed to the development of the rule of law in BiH (and to a lesser extent in Serbia and Croatia) by helping to create the State Court (discussed already), and sharing both evidence and expertise with Prosecutors' offices in the region.[86] Of course, some of the rule of law development in BiH was the result of intense involvement of the international community in the running of BiH in the initial years after the war; that international assistance continues today has also facilitated the funding of BiH's judicial and other institutions.[87]

presidency asked the ICJ to review the case—which held only that the Serbia failed to 'prevent' genocide but did not attribute responsibility for the genocide to Serbia—in light of newly discovered evidence; the request, however, was rejected. See M G Djurdjevic and D Kovacevic, 'Bosnia Appeal in Genocide Case Against Serbia Rejected' (*Balkan Insight*, 9 March 2017) <http://www.balkaninsight.com/en/article/bosnia-appeal-in-genocide-case-against-serbia-rejected-03-09-2017> accessed July 2018.

[82] 'Bosnian Serb Leader Denies Srebrenica Was Genocide' (*Balkan Insight*, 12 July 2010) <http://www.balkaninsight.com/en/article/bosnian-serb-leader-denies-srebrenica-was-genocide> accessed July 2018 ('Milorad Dodik, the leader of Bosnia's Serb dominated part, said Monday that the July 1995 massacre of over 8,000 Bosniak (Bosnian Muslim) men and boys by Serb troops was not a genocide . . . .').

[83] One factor helping to silence full denial was the release of the video of the Serbian paramilitary 'Scorpions' unit taking part in executions at Srebrenica. For a discussion of the video's impact see V Petrović, 'A Crack in the Wall of Denial: The Scorpions Video in and out of the Courtroom' in D Zarkov and G Marlies *Narratives of Justice In and Out of the Courtroom* (Springer Series in Transitional Justice March 2014) 89–109.

[84] To the extent the ICTY has claimed it will settle all disputes about facts and 'make it impossible for anyone to dispute' them, it was overselling its case. See M Milanović, 'The Impact of the ICTY on the Former Yugoslavia: An Anticipatory Post-Mortem' (2016) 110 American Journal of International Law 233–59. Milanović concludes that 'denialism and revisionism are not just alive and well in the former Yugoslavia—they are thriving' ibid 235. Yet, he does not blame ICTY outreach, but acknowledges 'from the moment it appeared on stage the ICTY has been the object of intense, vilifying propaganda by dominant elites, especially in the Croat and Serb ethnic communities . . . .' ibid 258.

[85] On the issue of transparency and legitimacy more broadly, see C Brants and S Karstedt (eds) *Transitional Justice and the Public Sphere: Engagement, Legitimacy and Contestation* (Bloomsbury 2017). On communication, see O Kavran, 'International Criminal Courts and the Right to Information' (2017) 15 Journal of International Criminal Justice 953–83.

[86] ICTJ notes several ways the State Court benefitted from the work of the ICTY: use of adjudicated facts established by the ICTY, reliance on ICTY jurisprudence for issues of substantive law, guidance from ICTY procedural decisions, use of ICTY evidence, and knowledge sharing. Ivanišević (n 20) 25–26.

[87] The international community has been an important donor to the BiH justice system over the years. See ICTY Press Release, 'Donors Raise 15.6 Million Euros for War Crimes Chamber of BIH Court' (30 October 2003) <http://www.icty.org/en/press/donors-raise-156-million-euros-war-crimes-chamber-bih-court> accessed July 2018. Such outside financial support continues today. European Commission, *INSTRUMENT FOR PRE-ACCESSION ASSISTANCE (IPA II) 2014–2020: BOSNIA AND HERZEGOVINA Enhanced Justice Sector and Cooperation in*

24.4.4 Deterring Future Crimes

It is notoriously difficult to prove that tribunals have a deterrent effect, and this seems particularly hard to prove in relation to the ICTY. In fact, in the early years of its existence, when the ICTY was already starting work, mass atrocities were still ongoing, including the genocide at Srebrenica. However, in the early years, it was unclear whether the ICTY would become an effective institution, so perhaps this lack of deterrence is understandable. And, possibly, there may have been some deterrence, only it is very hard to prove.[88] Yet, gradually, tribunals such as the ICTY—as well as all other international and hybrid tribunals—are creating a body of law that may eventually seep into general knowledge and potentially change behaviour. For example, as more military commanders around the world understand the concept of 'command responsibility' and realize that they, under certain circumstances, could be held responsible for crimes of their subordinates,[89] this has potential to alter their behaviour. In this way, in its rulings, the ICTY has contributed to this general global deterrence that all tribunals prosecuting core atrocity crimes are helping to form. The fact that it is very hard to measure this deterrent effect does not mean that it does not exist.[90] Yet, for deterrence to really work in any kind of universal and systematic way, the system of international justice likely requires further evolution and more rigorous implementation.[91]

24.4.5 Achieving Reconciliation

One particularly inappropriate goal sometimes sought from tribunals is 'reconciliation'—that after prosecutions, formerly antagonistic groups will be reconciled. In fact, if anything, the immediate impact of trials may be to increase ethnic tensions. In the long run, the best claim that perhaps can be made is that tribunals help set the foundation upon which reconciliation may later be built. There is little indication that trials directly 'reconcile' persons. Such work may need to be done at the grassroots level, with more modest-sounding programmes such as person-to-person interaction, such as that done by the Post-Conflict

Rule of Law, <https://ec.europa.eu/neighbourhood-enlargement/sites/near/files/pdf/bosnia_and_herzegovina/ipa/2015/ipa_2015-037888.05-bih-enhanced_justice_sector_and_cooperation_in_rule_of_law.pdf> accessed July 2018.

[88] See J R McAllister, 'Deterring Wartime Atrocities: Hard Lessons from the Yugoslav Tribunal' (2019–2020) 44 International Security 84 (concluding, based on over 200 interviews, that 'the ICTY played a key role in deterring select rebel and government forces' use of violence against civilians, particularly in the 2001 Macedonian conflict'). It is not only the ICTY that is being questioned in terms of its deterrent impact; the ICC is also facing such scrutiny. It is of course notoriously difficult to prove that institutional action contributed to crimes *not* occurring, and signs of the ICC's deterrent impact to date are sometimes anecdotal.

[89] For a compilation of the ICTY's law on command responsibility, see Trahan, 2006 (n 18) 446–505.

[90] See Human Rights Watch, 'Selling Justice Short, Why Accountability Matters for Peace' (*Human Rights Watch*, 7 July 2009) <http://www.hrw.org/en/node/84262/section/2> accessed July 2018 (citing a report that Afghan General (and current Vice President) Abdul Rashid Dostum forced more than ninety commanders to listen to a Human Rights Watch report alleging atrocities by his forces and threatened to kill any commander committing such acts). This anecdote suggests General Dostum well understood the concept of command responsibility.

[91] For a study of the future of the field of international justice, see J Trahan, 'Views of the Future of the Field of International Justice: A Scenarios Project Based on Expert Consultations' (2018) 33 American University International Law Review 837; J Trahan, 'Report of Symposium on the Future of the Field of International Justice' (*Impunity Watch, Syracuse College of Law*, 10 March 2017) <http://impunitywatch.com/report-of-symposium-on-the-future-of-the-field-of-international-justice> accessed July 2018.

Research Center in Sarajevo,[92] and the Youth Initiative for Human Rights, working with youths in Kosovo and Serbia, and those in the Federation and Republika Srpska.[93] On the other hand, vitriolic narratives perpetuated by dominant political elites (top-down narratives), can also work to undermine such grassroots (bottom-up) reconciliation work.

Thus, while the authors do not believe these kinds of lofty, society-wide transformative goals should be expected of tribunals, the ICTY has nonetheless made distinct contributions in a number of these areas.[94] There is clearly work remaining, which perhaps can be accomplished by local transitional justice actors, and perhaps a new generation of political leaders in the region, less tainted by nationalistic rhetoric than older generations. On the other hand, while such nationalistic rhetoric remains—as it does[95]—it is unclear whether new generations will indeed emerge, untainted.[96]

24.5 The Three-tiered Approach as a Model for the Future

While the three-tiered model of justice in BiH has been fairly successful, at least when one uses more traditional, justice-related benchmarks (and successful to some extent when considering broader, societal goals), what it has also accomplished is creating the precedent or model for the international community of what a robust approach to prosecuting large-scale atrocity crimes could look like, even if it has not been perfectly implemented at all levels.

As the ICC sets about prosecuting a handful of individuals in each of its situation countries, and (optimistically) States Parties to the Rome Statute[97] seem generally to leave all other prosecutions to 'complementarity' in countries where the rule of law is hardly strong—without providing the ICC funding or the mandate to work on development of complementarity—one might wonder whether the three-tiered approach in BiH is not a preferable model in some instances. The creation of the new Kosovo Specialist Chambers and a new hybrid tribunal for the Central African Republic[98] provide hope that the international community realizes that one court—the ICC—cannot 'do it all'.[99]

[92] See Post-Conflict Research Center website <http://www.p-crc.org> accessed 16 May 2018.

[93] See Youth Initiative for Human Rights website <https://www.yihr.org/ > accessed 6 March 2017.

[94] For an overview of impact in Bosnia and Herzegovina, see I Vukušić, 'Successes and Failures of Transitional Justice in BiH: The Case of the ICTY' in S Keil and V Perry (eds), *State-Building and Democratization in Bosnia and Herzegovina* (Ashgate 2015).

[95] See Press release, Office of the High Representative, 'Denial of War Crimes is Inexcusable' <http://www.ohr.int/?p=35537&print=pdf> accessed July 2018 (denouncing Republika Srpska Prime Minister Milorad Dodik for denying war crimes in Tuzla).

[96] For a more sombre assessment of the ICTY's impact in the former Yugoslavia, see Milanović (n 84).

[97] Rome Statute of the International Criminal Court (July 18 1998) UN Doc A/CONF 183/9, 2187 UNTS 90.

[98] The Government of CAR voted to establish a Special Criminal Court to be staffed by national and international judges. Peter Snyder, 'Central African Republic Government Establishes Special Criminal Court, *Jurist* (23 April 2015) <http://www.jurist.org> accessed 10 March 2017.

[99] A creative, new form of interim solution has been the General Assembly's recent creation of the International, Impartial and Independent Mechanisms (IIIM) to investigate crimes in Syria. The full name is 'The International, Impartial and Independent Mechanism to Assist in the Investigation and Prosecution of Those Responsible for the Most Serious Crimes under International Law Committed in the Syrian Arab Republic Since March 2011'. See UNGA Res 71/248 (21 December 2016) UN Doc A/Res/71/248 <http://www.un.org/en/ga/search/view_doc.asp?symbol=A/RES/71/248> accessed July 2018. The IIIM is tasked to 'collect, consolidate, preserve and analyse evidence' and 'prepare files in order to facilitate and expedite fair and independent criminal proceedings' para 4. Of course, the IIIM is needed in part because Russia and China blocked referral of the situation to the ICC. See (n 104).

Yet, one of the conditions for such a three-tiered model may be significant involvement by the international community[100]—for instance, to provide political pressure to ensuring prosecutions are undertaken, to provide funding to assist with capacity building, and to monitor trials to ensure they, inter alia, adhere to fair trial standards. It may be somewhat context-specific whether the international community is in a position to provide all of this. Undeniably, the international community played an extensive role in BiH (with the role of the Office of the High Representative essentially running the country), and, later, the role of the EU, as BiH pursued EU accession. Where there is not such extensive international involvement, it may diminish the prospects for the success of such a three-tiered approach to justice.

The three-tiered prosecutorial approach thus provides a viable model for the future as to how one might prosecute large-scale atrocity crimes—particularly where there is sufficient international assistance provided for domestic capacity building. While the ICTY itself as the 'top tier' of that model is generally disfavoured—with States roundly proclaiming there will never be another ad hoc tribunal[101] like the ICTY or ICTR due to their costs—as noted, the ICTY has in fact conducted the largest number of prosecutions of any international tribunal. Some argue that the ad hoc tribunals' high costs, actually, pale in comparison to the cost of ongoing armed conflict, which could have occurred had there been no international commitment to such trials.[102]

Going forward, when the international community seeks to prosecute large-scale atrocity crimes, such as those ongoing in Syria, it is this three-tiered approach to justice that should be the model, with a tribunal the size of the ICTY at the top tier (although perhaps not created through the UN Security Council).[103] It is admittedly presently not possible to create a tribunal for crimes perpetrated in Syria, as Russia would veto the Security Council's creation of a tribunal,[104] and the present Syrian government would never consent to creating a tribunal by agreement with the UN, because regime actors are heavily implicated in war crimes and crimes against humanity.[105] Yet, since the crimes at issue have no statutes of limitations, there could be a tribunal in the future, perhaps created by a future Syrian regime that sets more stock in the rule of law than the present one.[106] The field of international

[100] See (n 87).

[101] All hybrid tribunals are actually also 'ad hoc' in that they are created for one particular situation.

[102] Comments of Special Tribunal for Lebanon Registrar, D Mundis (NYU, 10 February 2017, 'Symposium on the Future of the Field of International Justice' (n 91)); see also Trahan Interview of Gregory Townsend (3 October 2016) (on file with the author) (noting the ICTY's contributions to peace by incapacitating key political actors and described the Tribunal's cost as 'a drop in the bucket' compared to the cost of ongoing conflict).

[103] For example, one could imagine a hybrid regional Middle Eastern tribunal created by Middle Eastern countries (not involved in the war in Syria) by agreement with the UN, under the auspices of the General Assembly acting under the Uniting for Peace resolution (see UNGA Res 377 (V) (3 November 1950) A/RES/377(V)), since the Security Council is paralysed from meaningful action due to Russia's use of the veto to protect the Assad government. See 'Russia Sides with Chemical Weapons' (*The New York Times*, 1 March 2017) <https://www.nytimes.com/2017/03/01/opinion/russia-sides-with-chemical-weapons.html> accessed July 2018.

[104] Russia and China already vetoed referral of the situation to the ICC. I Black 'Russia and China Veto UN Move to Refer Syria to International Criminal Court' (*The Guardian*, 22 May 2014) <https://www.theguardian.com/world/2014/may/22/russia-china-veto-un-draft-resolution-refer-syria-international-criminal-court> accessed July 2018.

[105] See, e.g., UNGA, 'Report of the Independent International Commission of Inquiry on the Syrian Arab Republic' (Human Rights Council 34th Session) (2 February 2017) UN Doc A/HRC/34/64 <https://documents-dds-ny.un.org/doc/UNDOC/GEN/G17/026/63/PDF/G1702663.pdf?OpenElement> accessed July 2018.

[106] The recent creation of an investigative mechanism for Syria by the UN General Assembly is an important first step. See (n 99). However, Russian military involvement in the conflict complicates the prospects of attempting to ensure justice. Russia strongly supports the Syrian government of Bashar al-Assad, including through both military assistance and direct military involvement. See 'Russia Establishing Permanent Presence at Its Syrian Bases'

justice has simply come too far for those who work in it to rest complacent while such vast atrocity crimes remain unpunished. The three-tiered model of justice for crimes committed in BiH provides a model of what this could look like when, someday, the politics allow for it.

24.6 Conclusion

Thus, in addition to its actual, substantial accomplishments, the ICTY, as well as other prosecutorial mechanisms in BiH, have given us a robust vision of what the future of the field of international justice could look like if the international community has the political will to ensure prosecution of large-scale atrocity crimes in any kind of comprehensive way. Given that the ICTY has now closed, and the the International Residual Mechanism for Criminal Tribunals (MICT) is operating at a small fraction of the staff that the ICTY once had, it remains to be seen how much of a role the MICT will continue to play locally.[107] It is also unclear how much interest the international community will continue to have in local war crimes prosecutions in BiH and the region. As former State Court and Kosovo Specialist Chambers Prosecutor David Schwendiman made clear: 'the international community… cannot afford to allow the rich legacy of the ICTY and Bosnia and Herzegovina's potential for adding to and improving on that legacy to go to waste for lack of attention, vision, or commitment'.[108] As BiH pursues EU accession, the EU *is* in a position of leverage to ensure that such prosecutions continue and to provide much needed additional support. Yet, with every passing year, the danger is that the attention of international actors will fade under the erroneous assumption that, decades after the wars, there is less need for it, when, alas, that is not the case.

(*Reuters*, 26 December 2017) <https://www.reuters.com/article/us-mideast-crisis-syria-russia-bases/russia-establishing-permanent-presence-at-its-syrian-bases-ria-idUSKBN1EK0HD> accessed 13 April 2018. Many other countries are also involved in the conflict, including Iran, the US, and Turkey.

[107] There have been, for example, numerous ICTY Office of the Prosecutor (OTP) trainings provided to OTP's within BiH. See MICT, 'Overview of Capacity Building Activities' <http://www.icty.org/en/outreach/capacity-building/overview-activities> accessed 16 May 2018. There have also been liaison prosecutors from the region working side-by-side within the ICTY's OTP. See ICTY Press Release, 'Office of the Prosecutor of the ICTY Welcomes Liaison Prosecutors from Bosnia and Herzegovina, Croatia and Serbia to the Tribunal' (1 July 2009) <http://www.icty.org/en/press/office-prosecutor-icty-welcomes-liaison-prosecutors-bosnia-and-herzegovina-croatia-and-serbia> accessed 16 May 2018.

[108] Schwendiman (n 33) 300.

25

Cooperation between Serbia and the ICTY for the Investigation and Prosecution of Violations of International Humanitarian Law

Tatjana Dawson and Ljiljana Hellman**, ****

25.1 Introduction

This chapter will look at the cooperation between the Republic of Serbia (Serbia) and the International Tribunal for the Prosecution of Persons Responsible for Serious Violations of International Humanitarian Law Committed in the Territory of the former Yugoslavia since 1991 (ICTY or Tribunal) for the investigation and prosecution of violations of International Humanitarian Law (IHL violations or IHL crimes) by Serbian authorities. It will discuss the Completion Strategy of the ICTY and how it triggered increased cooperation in many areas, such as cooperation for the reform of Serbian national law, the transfer of cases indicted or investigated by the ICTY, mutual legal assistance in the region of the former Yugoslavia, capacity building projects, and access to confidential ICTY records. The chapter will provide a brief overview of cases of IHL violations that Serbia has prosecuted to date. Through the example of the notion of command responsibility, it will highlight some of the obstacles that Serbian legal professionals face when bringing these cases to trial. The chapter concludes with thoughts on the end of the mandate of the ICTY and the future for IHL prosecutions in Serbia.

25.2 The Completion Strategy

The ICTY was established as a temporary institution and focused on investigating and prosecuting crimes committed in the former Yugoslavia since 1991. As early as 2000, the President of the ICTY, with the unanimous support of the Tribunal's judges, submitted a

* Coordinator of the Responsible Behaviour Unit at the Artsen zonder Grenzen Nederland.
** She was born in Belgrade, Serbia. She holds an LLM in International Human Rights Law from the University of Essex, as well as a Masters Law Degree from the University of Belgrade. In 1990s she worked as a Legal Analyst in the Belgrade-based NGO Humanitarian Law Center. After the fall of Milosevic's regime she joined the OSCE Mission to Serbia as a Legal Adviser and Head of the War Crimes Unit. She was Balkans Project Manager at the Dutch NGO Impunity Watch and worked as a consultant for the OSCE/ODIHR and OSCE Mission in BiH. At the ICTY she worked as a Court Officer and Legal Officer. As of 2017 she works as the Head of Judicial Records and Court Operations Unit at the IRMCT. She has been a lecturer in various courses on IHL and author, co-author and/or editor of many human rights reports and articles in the field of international law
*** At the time of writing, the authors were the current and former legal officers at the International Criminal Tribunal for the former Yugoslavia. However, the views represented in this chapter are the authors' views alone and in no manner reflect the position of the Tribunal.

Tatjana Dawson and Ljiljana Hellman, *Cooperation between Serbia and the ICTY for the Investigation and Prosecution of Violations of International Humanitarian Law* In: *Legacies of the International Criminal Tribunal for the Former Yugoslavia.* Edited by: Carsten Stahn, Carmel Agius, Serge Brammertz, Colleen Rohan, Oxford University Press (2020).
DOI: 10.1093/oso/9780198862956.003.0026

first proposal to the members of the General Assembly and the Security Council with measures to complete trials in a timely manner.[1]

With the gradual restoration of democratic institutions in the countries of the former Yugoslavia and the increasing number of arrests of persons indicted by the ICTY, in 2002, the President, Prosecutor, and Registrar—with the endorsement of the judges—jointly submitted another proposal to the Security Council that is now known as the Completion Strategy. It consisted of completing all investigations by the end of 2004, all trials by the end of 2008 and appeals by the end of 2010.[2] In order to reach these target dates, the ICTY suggested a two-pronged process of 'concentration' and 'referral'. The ICTY would concentrate on the prosecution and trial of the highest-ranking political, military, and paramilitary leaders. At the same time, the ICTY would transfer cases involving intermediary-level accused[3] to courts in Bosnia and Herzegovina (BiH) which then was the only country considered for this process.[4] This was endorsed by the Security Council and named Completion Strategy.[5]

In its proposal, the ICTY noted the conditions for the referral of cases to the region of the former Yugoslavia, BiH in particular, considering that the existing national institutions were not yet equipped to manage trials effectively and consistently with internationally recognized standards of human rights and due process. For BiH, it suggested that a special division be created within the newly established State Court. This division would have specific responsibility for cases involving serious violations of IHL and be composed of both national and international judges.[6] The ICTY also recommended adopting provisions inherent to the proper functioning of a judicial system, in particular in relation to war

1 UNGA UNSC 'Identical letters dated 7 September 2000 from the Secretary-General addressed to the President of the General Assembly and the President of the Security Council' (14 September 2000) UN Doc A/55/382-S/2000/865. The document attached another letter dated 12 May 2000, from President Judge Claude Jorda. This initial proposal involved giving more authority to senior legal officers of the Trial Chambers to take decisions regarding the conduct of the pre-trial process; creating a pool of 'judges *ad litem*', who would be assigned to supplement the existing Trial Chambers, as necessary, and to enlarge the Appeals Chambers of the ICTY and the ICTR with two judges. These recommendations were adopted by the Security Council in resolution 1329(2000), 5 December 2000, S/RES/1329(2000). In order to speed up its proceedings, the ICTY also amended its Rules of Procedure and Evidence. It created management committees and a coordination council to improve coordination between its organs and thereby allow for a more effective management of the ICTY's resources. It also established an international bar to improve legal representation before the ICTY. While these and other measures made it possible for the ICTY to run six simultaneous trials daily as of September 2001, this would still not be sufficient to end all cases in a timely manner. See UNSC 'Letter dated 17 June 2002 from the Secretary-General addressed to the President of the Security Council'(19 June 2002) UN Doc S/2002/678 ('Letter by President Jorda, dated 10 June 2002') paras 19, 20.

2 Letter by President Jorda, dated 10 June 2002 (n 1) paras 75 and 83.

3 For a discussion of the definition of this category of persons see Letter by President Jorda, dated 10 June 2002 (n 1) paras 31–32.

4 Letter by President Jorda, dated 10 June 2002 (n 1) paras 4, 83, and 84.

5 UNSC 'Statement by the President of the Security Council' (23 July 2002) UN Doc S/PRST/2002/21; UNSC Res 1503 (28 August 2003) UN Doc S/RES/1503(2003). The ICTY also proposed further reforms to enhance its effectiveness, such as the joinder of related case, the increase of the use of written evidence, limiting the number of witnesses called, and reducing the length of pre-trial and appellate proceedings. See Letter by President Jorda, dated 10 June 2002 (n 1) para 28. For a detailed description of measures taken to speed up proceedings, see ICTY, 'Completion Strategy and MICT' (ICTY, 2004–2017) <http://www.icty.org/en/documents/completion-strategy-and-mict> accessed 9 February 2018. Six-monthly reports submitted by the ICTY to the Security Council in accordance with Security Council Resolution 1534(2004) can be found on that website.

6 Letter by President Jorda, dated 10 June 2002 (n 1) paras 61–69. The War Crimes Chamber of the State Court was formally inaugurated on 9 March 2005. See UNSC 'Letter dated 25 May 2005 from the President of the International Tribunal for the Prosecution of Persons Responsible for Serious Violations of International Humanitarian Law Committed in the Territory of the Former Yugoslavia since 1991, addressed to the President of the Security Council' (25 May 2005) UN Doc S/2005/343, Annex I, para 14.

crimes and crimes against humanity.[7] With respect to the issue of command responsibility, the ICTY noted problems with the compatibility of national and ICTY law. It stated that the principles on individual criminal responsibility applicable at the ICTY were not always applied, or even recognized, in national legislation; and recommended providing for these principles in national law.[8]

In the years following adoption of the Completion Strategy, the ICTY cooperated intensely with the international community and the State authorities in BiH, Republic of Croatia (Croatia), and Serbia to prepare them for the prosecution of cases covered by the jurisdiction of the ICTY. This would subsequently allow for the transfer of cases pursuant to Rule 11*bis* ICTY Rules of Procedure and Evidence[9] and for the transfer of investigative material by the ICTY Office of the Prosecutor (OTP).[10]

25.3 Consultation and Cooperation to Enable National Prosecutions

Cooperation with the ICTY in the region, and especially Serbia, had its ups and downs. In the early years, it showed some promising signs. In 1995, BiH, Croatia, and the Federal Republic of Yugoslavia (FRY, comprised of Serbia and Montenegro) signed the Dayton Peace Agreement ending the war in BiH and, inter alia, undertook the obligation to fully cooperate in the investigation and prosecution of war crimes and other violations of IHL.[11] In 1996, Dražen Erdemović was arrested by the FRY authorities and transferred to the ICTY.[12] However, in the period that followed, the cooperation of FRY/Serbia did not progress, and finally ceased to exist with the subsequent announcement of the ICTY indictment against FRY President Slobodan Milošević.[13] Following the fall of Milošević in October 2000,[14] the new government, led by Prime Minister Zoran Đinđić, was strongly orientated towards Serbia's integration into the European Union (EU).[15] In its efforts to cut the links with the former government and move the country towards EU integration, the government re-established cooperation with the ICTY and arrested and transferred Milošević to the Tribunal in June 2001.[16] The assassination of Prime Minister Zoran Đinđić in March

[7] Letter by President Jorda, dated 10 June 2002 (n 1) paras 70–72.

[8] ibid paras 56, 73.

[9] ICTY Rules of Procedure and Evidence of the (ICTY Rules) ICTY Doc IT/32/Rev 50 (2015) <http://www.icty.org/x/file/Legal%20Library/Rules_procedure_evidence/IT032Rev50_en.pdf> accessed 9 February 2018.

[10] See UNSC 'Letter dated 21 May 2004 from the President of the International Tribunal for the Prosecution of Persons Responsible for Serious Violations of International Humanitarian Law Committed in the Territory of the Former Yugoslavia since 1991, addressed to the President of the Security Council' (24 May 2004) UN Doc S/2004/420, paras 23 to 29; UNSC 'Letter dated 23 November 2004 from the President of the International Tribunal for the Prosecution of Persons Responsible for Serious Violations of International Humanitarian Law Committed in the Territory of the Former Yugoslavia since 1991, addressed to the President of the Security Council' (23 November 2004) UN Doc S/2004/897, Annex I, paras 6 to 10; see also the assessment by the Prosecutor in 'Letter dated 25 May 2005 from the President of the International Tribunal for the Prosecution of Persons Responsible for Serious Violations of International Humanitarian Law Committed in the Territory of the Former Yugoslavia since 1991, addressed to the President of the Security Council' (25 May 2005) UN Doc S/2005/343 Annex II paras 9–15.

[11] 'The General Framework Agreement for Peace in Bosnia and Herzegovina' (Legal Tools, 1995) <https://www.legal-tools.org/doc/ebc784/pdf/> accessed 9 February 2018, art IX.

[12] *Prosecutor v Dražen Erdemović* (Sentencing Judgment) ICTY-IT-96-22-T*bis* (5 March 1998) para 2.

[13] ICTY, Case Information Sheet, 'Kosovo, Croatia & Bosnia' (IT-02-54) Slobodan Milošević (ICTY) <http://www.icty.org/x/cases/slobodan_milosevic/cis/en/cis_milosevic_slobodan_en.pdf> accessed 19 October 2017.

[14] B Barlovac, 'The Bulldozer Revolution' (*Balkan Insight*, 5 October 2010) <http://www.balkaninsight.com/en/article/timeline-the-bulldozer-revolution> accessed 19 October 2017.

[15] T Mabry et al (eds), *Divided Nations and European Integration* (University of Pennsylvania Press 2013) 236.

[16] Information Sheet, 'Kosovo, Croatia & Bosnia' (n 13).

2003[17] created a new era of inconsistency in Serbia's cooperation with the ICTY. Although the fugitives of that time have since been arrested and transferred to the ICTY,[18] some concerns over cooperation remain to date. In the pending contempt case of *Prosecutor v Jojić* et al, Serbia has failed to execute the arrest warrants for the indictees.[19]

The cooperation of Serbia/FRY with the international community regarding the development of a national legal framework for the prosecution of IHL violations followed the general trends of cooperation with the ICTY. However, it should be noted that legal professionals such as judges, prosecutors, and defence lawyers were frequently open to cooperate with international actors regardless of the political trends, either because they believed in the national prosecutions, or were motivated by professional curiosity.

25.3.1 Cooperation in the Review of the National Legal Framework

The ICTY Completion Strategy prompted a new approach in the Tribunal's relationship with Serbia and other countries of the region. The ICTY actively started looking for avenues of engagement with national authorities with a view to strengthening their capacity for the investigation and prosecution of IHL crimes. The following section will describe ICTY's engagement in the review of the Serbian national legal framework, the transfer of cases pursuant to Rule 11*bis* of the ICTY Rules, support to inter-State cooperation, capacity building projects, and enabling access to confidential material pursuant to Rule 75(H) of the ICTY Rules.

Between 2001 and 2005, the ICTY initiated and assisted with a series of specialist seminars and debates in the region of the former Yugoslavia. The goal of these events was to exchange knowledge and experience, as well as identify and bridge differences between the ICTY's and national legal frameworks.[20]

ICTY representatives were engaged in the consultation process for the drafting of the Law on Organisation.[21] This consultation process was organized by the Serbian State authorities, the Organization for Security and Co-operation in Europe (OSCE) and the International Bar Association.[22] The Law on Organisation transferred jurisdiction over the investigation and prosecution of IHL crimes in Serbia to the Office of the War Crimes Prosecutor (WCPO),[23] the War Crimes Chamber of the Higher Court in Belgrade (War

[17] The Guardian, 'Death of a Balkan Hero' (*The Guardian*, 16 March 2003) <https://www.theguardian.com/world/2003/mar/16/balkans> accessed 19 October 2017.

[18] ICTY, 'The Fugitives' (About the ICTY, 2011) <http://www.icty.org/en/about/office-of-the-prosecutor/the-fugitives> accessed 19 October 2017.

[19] UNGA UNSC 'Twenty-fourth and final annual report of the International Tribunal for the Prosecution of Persons Responsible for Serious Violations of International Humanitarian Law Committed in the Territory of the Former Yugoslavia' (1 August 2017) UN Doc A/72/266–S/2017/662.

[20] See ICTY 'Outreach activities archive' (About the Outreach Programme, 1999–2017) <http://www.icty.org/en/outreach/activities-archive> accessed 9 February 2018, in particular: Specialist Seminars, August–November 2001 in Palić and Belgrade; 23–24 May 2003, Belgrade, Serbia, and Montenegro, Conference on command responsibility—part one; 13–14 June 2003, Zagreb, Croatia, Conference on command responsibility—part two; 27–28 March 2004, Belgrade, Serbia, and Montenegro, Conference on command responsibility; 22–24 March 2001, Trakošćane, Croatia, Conference on command responsibility.

[21] Law on the Organisation and Competences of the Government Authorities in War Crimes Proceedings, Official Gazette of the Republic of Serbia No 67/2003, 135/2004, 61/2005, 101/2007, and 104/2009 ('Law on Organisation').

[22] M Ellis, 'Coming to Terms with Its Past—Serbia's New Court for the Prosecution of War Crimes' (2004) 22 Berkeley Journal of International Law 165, 189.

[23] Law on Organisation (n 21) arts 4–7.

Crimes Chamber),[24] the War Crimes Chamber of the Court of Appeal in Belgrade (War Crimes Appeals Chamber),[25] the War Crimes Investigation Unit,[26] the Special Detention Unit,[27] and the Witness Assistance and Support Unit[28] (together referred to as Specialised Institutions) and provided for specific procedural rules.[29] In its amended form, it provides that the jurisdiction of the Specialised Institutions includes crimes in violation of the Serbian Criminal Code[30] as subsequently amended,[31] crimes under the ICTY Statute,[32] and the criminal offence of 'Accessory after the fact' under the Serbian Criminal Code[33] if committed in relation to any of these criminal offences. It was hoped that the concentration of jurisdiction for IHL crimes in the Specialised Institutions would render the investigation and prosecution of these crimes effective and efficient.

In 2003, with the support of various international partners, intensified discussions began in Serbia regarding proposals for the adoption of a new criminal code, which ultimately led to its adoption in 2005.[34] This new law not only took into account existing ICTY jurisprudence regarding the interpretation of international law, but also the entry into force of the Rome Statute of the International Criminal Court on 1 July 2002.[35] It was intended to harmonize Serbian law with the Rome Statute.[36]

25.3.2 Transfer of Cases Under Rule 11*bis* of the ICTY Rules

The transfer of cases to the former Yugoslavia constitutes another crucial point of cooperation between national authorities and the ICTY, in particular the OTP. There are two main categories of cases that the ICTY has transferred. The first concerns cases for which the ICTY issued an indictment, the so-called 11*bis* cases. The second category describes cases for which the ICTY OTP led investigations, but did not issue indictments in view of the Completion Strategy and the concentration on high-level accused (Category II Cases).[37]

[24] ibid arts 9–11.
[25] ibid arts 9–11.
[26] ibid art 8.
[27] ibid art 12.
[28] ibid art 11.
[29] ibid arts 13–16.
[30] The initial text referred to the criminal code in force at that time.
[31] The Criminal Code of Serbia, Official Gazette of Serbia, No 85/2005, 88/2005, 107/2005, 72/2009, 111/2009 ('Serbian Criminal Code').
[32] UNSC, 'Statute of the International Criminal Tribunal for the Former Yugoslavia' (25 May 1993) UN Doc S/RES/827.
[33] Serbian Criminal Code (n 31) art 333.
[34] ibid.
[35] Rome Statute of the International Criminal Court (Adopted 17 July 1998, entered in force 1 July 2002) UN Doc A/CONF 183/9; 37 ILM 1002 (1998); 2187 UNTS 90. The FRY signed the Rome Statute on 19 December 2000. Serbia and Montenegro deposited their instrument of ratification of the Rome Statute on 6 September 2001. See International Criminal Court, 'Serbia' (States Parties to the Rome Statute, 2003) <https://asp.icc-cpi.int/en_menus/asp/states%20parties/eastern%20european%20states/Pages/serbia.aspx> accessed 9 February 2018.
[36] Humanitarian Law Center, *Command responsibility in international and national law* (*Komandna odgovornost u međunarodnom i domaćem pravu*), (HLC, Belgrade, 2004, available only in Srpski) <http://www.hlc-rdc.org/?p=13175&lang=de> accessed 17 February 2018, 91–95. It includes a presentation on draft amendments to the legal framework for prosecution of IHL crimes in Serbia and Montenegro given by Mr Saša Obradović, Legal Adviser at the Ministry of Foreign Affairs of Serbia and Montenegro. This publication provides the transcript of the two-part conference on command responsibility co-organized by the HLC and ICTY Outreach Programme in 2003, see Outreach Activities Archive (n 20).
[37] See section 25.4.2.

Rule 11*bis* in its amended version allows for the referral of a case for which an indictment has been confirmed by the ICTY and prior to the commencement of trial, to any State having jurisdiction and being willing and adequately prepared to accept such a case. The referral decision is taken by a bench of three judges, after having given the Prosecutor and, where applicable, the accused the opportunity to be heard and after being satisfied that the accused will receive a fair trial and that the death penalty will not be imposed or carried out. Rule 11*bis* refers explicitly to Security Council Resolution 1534(2004) when stating that the decision to refer a case considers the gravity of the crimes charged and the level of responsibility of the accused. This reflects the principle that only intermediary-level or lower-level accused would be referred under this provision. Rule 11*bis* also provides for protective measures for witnesses to remain in force, for the handover of material supporting the indictment, and for monitoring of the cases by observers. Both the accused and the ICTY Prosecutor have the right to appeal the referral decision. The referral bench has the power to revoke its decision at any time before the final verdict by the national court.

On the basis of Rule 11*bis* the ICTY referred eight cases, involving a total of thirteen accused, to BiH, Croatia, and Serbia. No further cases qualified for transfer.[38]

Following the necessary amendments to the national legal framework and the establishment of the WCPO, in 2006, the ICTY transferred the *Kovačević* case to Serbia.[39]

In the *Kovačević* case, the Referral Bench analysed whether the Serbian legal framework met the requirements for transfer of cases under Rule 11*bis*. It held that it must be satisfied that if a case were to be referred to Serbia, there would exist an adequate legal framework which would permit the prosecution and trial, but also the appropriate punishment of the accused for offences of the type charged before the ICTY.[40] It stressed that it was not the competent authority to decide which national law would apply. Rather, it saw its task to consider each of the possibly applicable legal provisions in order to determine whether there was any significant deficiency which would impede or prevent the prosecution, trial and, if appropriate, punishment of the accused for the alleged criminal conduct charged in the indictment.[41]

In its analysis of Serbian law, the Referral Bench also addressed the issue of whether the notion of command responsibility, as defined in ICTY law, was part of the different legal frameworks that might apply to the *Kovačević* case. It found that the Socialist Federal Republic of Yugoslavia (SFRY) Criminal Code[42] 'appear[ed] to address parts of the field covered by Article 7(3)' and that the Serbian Criminal Code 'contain[ed] provisions which

[38] For an overview and discussion of Rule 11*bis* and the referral of these cases, see T Blumenstock and W Pittman, 'The Transfer of Cases Before the International Criminal Tribunal for the former Yugoslavia to Competent National Jurisdictions' (2008) 21 Journal of International Law of Peace and Armed Conflict 2008. For information on the status of these cases, see ICTY, 'Status of Transferred Cases' (Legacy website for the ICTY/TPIY/MKSJ) <http://www.icty.org/en/cases/transfer-of-cases/status-of-transferred-cases> accessed 9 February 2018.

[39] *Prosecutor v Vladimir Kovačević* (Decision on Referral of Case Pursuant to Rule 11*bis*) ICTY-IT-01-42/2-I (17 November 2006) para 25. Rule 11*bis* was first adopted in 1998, but was only applied later, in its current amended version. The first referral decision (to BiH) was issued in 2005: *Prosecutor v Radovan Stanković* (Decision on Referral of Case under Rule 11*bis)* ICTY-IT-96-23/2-PT (17 May 2005).

[40] *Kovačević*, Decision on Referral (n 39) para 25.

[41] ibid paras 25, 31.

[42] The Criminal Code of the SFRY, Official Gazette SFRY, No 44/76-1329, 36/77-1478, 34/84-895, 37/84-933, 74/87-1743, 57/89-1441, 3/90-63, 38/90-1217, 45/90-1340, 54/90-1773 ('SFRY Criminal Code').

appear[ed] to address most of the field covered specifically by Article 7(3) of the Statute concerning command responsibility'.[43] While it did not exclude the possibility that the competent Serbian court might decide not to apply this mode of liability, it did not consider this as an obstacle to the referral, since all charges against the accused were also based on Article 7(1) of the Statute.[44] Unfortunately, this case has not gone to trial due to the ill health of the accused. While the Serbian judiciary has therefore not pronounced itself on the issue of command responsibility in the context of this case, it has had other opportunities to do so, as discussed further.[45]

25.3.3 Mutual Legal Assistance Between National Jurisdictions

The ICTY, and the OTP in particular, have also supported regional cooperation to allow for joint investigations across State borders, the exchange of information, the appearance of witnesses, and the extradition of accused persons. In November 2004, in the Serbian town of Palić, the OSCE initiated a series of meetings between representatives from the judiciary and the administration from the countries of the former Yugoslavia, known as the 'Palić Process'. This process aimed at enhancing inter-State judicial cooperation in IHL crimes proceedings. ICTY officials participated in each of the meetings, contributing to the process with their experience and expertise.[46]

The results of this process remain relevant to this day.[47] For example, according to the WCPO's statistics website, based on eighty-six requests, the office has exchanged 537 pieces of case-related information and evidence with other countries in the region, with the European Union Rule of Law Mission in Kosovo and the United Nations Interim Administration Mission in Kosovo.[48]

[43] *Kovačević*, Decision on Referral (n 39) paras 43 and 44.

[44] ibid para 46.

[45] See section 25.5.4.

[46] OSCE Office in Zagreb, 'The Palić Process' (*The Courier*, No 137, Zagreb, 2008) <http://www.osce.org/zagreb/32648?download=true> accessed 9 February 2018, 1–2.

[47] As a result of this process the countries in the region signed a series of bilateral and multilateral agreements such as 'Memorandum on Agreement on Regionalization and Promotion of Co-operation in Fighting All Forms of Grave Crimes', signed between the Serbian and the Croatian Prosecutor's Offices on 5 February 2005; 'Memorandum on Agreement on Regionalization and Promotion of Co-operation in Fighting All Forms of Grave Crimes', signed between the Serbian and the BiH Prosecutor's Offices on 1 July 2005; Agreement on Co-operation in Prosecution of Perpetrators of Criminal Offences of War Crimes, Crimes Against Humanity and Genocide, signed between the Serbian and the Croatian Prosecutor's Offices on 13 October 2006; Agreement on Cooperation in Prosecuting Perpetrators of Criminal Offences against Humanity and Other Assets Protected by International Law between the WCPO and the State Prosecutor's Office of Montenegro on 31 October 2007. On 31 January 2013 the WCPO and the Prosecutor's Office of BiH signed in Brussels the Protocol for the exchange of evidence and information in war crimes cases; see WCPO, Statistics, Regional Cooperation <http://www.tuzilastvorz.org.rs/en/cases/statistics> accessed 9 February 2018; ICTY, 'OTP welcomes signing of protocol on war crimes cases cooperation between Prosecutor's Offices of BiH and Serbia' (Legacy website of the ICTY/TPIY/MKSJ, 31 January 2013) <http://www.icty.org/en/press/otp-welcomes-signing-protocol-war-crimes-cases-cooperation-between-prosecutor's-offices-bih> accessed 9 February 2018; OSCE-ODIHR, ICTY, and UNICRI, *Report: Supporting the Transition Process: Lessons Learned and Best Practices in Knowledge Transfer*, OSCE/ODIHR (2009) 21; Impunity Watch, *Dealing with Impunity in Serbia—Options and Obstacles*, (Impunity Watch, Utrecht, 2008) 47.

[48] D Rupel, 'The "Palić Process"—A Success Story in Judicial Interstate Co-operation' (*OSCE*, 2005) <http://www.osce.si/docs/2005-12-00-pravda-u-tranziciji-the-palic-process-success-story.pdf> accessed 10 February 2017; WCPO Statistics (n 47).

25.3.4 Capacity Building Projects

25.3.4.1 The 'War Crimes Justice Project'

In order to allow for the effective investigation and prosecution of IHL crimes in the region, the ICTY also supported various capacity-building events, as well as access to its public court records and records held in the evidence collection of the OTP. One of the major projects in this regard was the 'War Crimes Justice Project' funded by the EU and implemented from May 2010 to October 2011 by the OSCE ODIHR, UNICRI, and the ICTY.

The design of the Project was informed by the findings and recommendations of a needs assessment report published in September 2009.[49] It included the development of training curricula and materials for members of the judiciary in the region; consultations, peer-to-peer meetings, and working visits designed to facilitate the professional development of legal professionals working on IHL cases in the region; trainings for access to the ICTY case records and evidence collected by the OTP; the production of transcripts of the most relevant ICTY proceedings in local languages, and bolstering staffing capacity in key areas such as prosecutorial analysis and legal research by embedding thirty-two support staff in justice institutions in the region.[50]

25.3.4.2 The Liaison Prosecutors and Visiting Young Professionals Programme

In 2009, the OTP initiated two projects funded by the EU and designed to enhance the capacity of national judiciaries in prosecuting IHL crimes—the Liaison Prosecutors and Visiting Young Professionals Programme.[51]

In June 2009, three prosecutors from the region designated by their respective public prosecution services, started working in The Hague as liaison prosecutors. They worked together with their OTP colleagues in collecting material for the purpose of national IHL crime investigations and cases. Through their work they exchanged knowledge and experience with their OTP colleagues.[52]

The main purpose of the Visiting Young Professionals Programme was to support the education and training of young professionals from the region of the former Yugoslavia, in relation to the investigation and prosecution of IHL crimes as an investment in the future capacity of these countries.[53]

25.3.5 Requests for Access to Confidential Evidence

Rule 75(H) of the ICTY Rules provides another important vehicle for cooperation between the ICTY and the former Yugoslavia. Under certain conditions, it allows judges and parties in national proceedings to access confidential information which has been introduced

[49] OSCE-ODIHR Report (n 47).

[50] OSCE-ODIHR, *War Crimes Justice Project* (OSCE) <https://www.osce.org/odihr/84406?download=true> accessed 10 February 2018.

[51] R Steinberg (ed), *Assessing the Legacy of the ICTY* (Martinus Nijhoff Publishers 2011) 31–32.

[52] ICTY, 'Office of the Prosecutor of the ICTY Welcomes Liaison Prosecutors from BiH, Croatia and Serbia to the Tribunal' (*OTP/OK/PR1324e Press Release*, 1 July 2009) <http://www.icty.org/en/press/office-prosecutor-icty-welcomes-liaison-prosecutors-bosnia-and-herzegovina-croatia-and-serbia> accessed 10 February 2018.

[53] ICTY, 'ICTY Weekly Press Briefing—20 August 2009' (Legacy website of the ICTY/TPIY/MKSJ, 2009) <http://www.icty.org/en/press/icty-weekly-press-briefing-20-august-2009> accessed 10 February 2018.

as evidence in cases before the ICTY. The rule has been amended several times to reflect the increase in national prosecutions and ensuing need for access to protected witnesses, transcripts of their testimony before the ICTY, and related exhibits. Requests for assistance under this rule present a significant workload for the ICTY and this is likely to continue even after its closure.[54] By the end of 2017, the ICTY had opened nearly 2,000 cases following requests submitted pursuant to Rules 75(H) and 75(F).[55]

25.4 Investigation and Prosecution of IHL Crimes in Serbia to Date

The history of the prosecution and trial of IHL crimes committed in the 1990s can be divided into two phases, based on the legal and organizational framework in which they were conducted. The dividing point—a major milestone—was the entry into force of the Law on Organisation.[56]

25.4.1 Cases Before the Entry into Force of the Law on Organisation

Before the entry into force of the Law on Organisation, the jurisdiction over IHL cases resided with both civilian courts of general jurisdiction and military courts. During this period, Serbia conducted eight trials for IHL crimes against sixteen individuals.[57] These cases were generally prosecuted under Article 142 'War crimes against the civilian population' of the SFRY/FRY Criminal Code.[58] Sentences varied between five to twenty years of imprisonment.[59]

The first trial was conducted in 1996 before the District Court of Šabac against two members of the Serbian paramilitary formation 'Yellow Wasps', who were sentenced for war crimes against Bosniak civilians in Zvornik, BiH.[60] In 2000, the former Niš Military court

[54] Rule 86(H) of the Rules of Procedure and Evidence of the Mechanism for International Criminal Tribunals closely resembles Rule 75(H) of the ICTY Rules.

[55] These numbers have been extrapolated with the help of the ICTY Judicial Database, which is an internal database. Most filings pursuant to Rule 75(H) are confidential and *ex parte* and therefore not available to the public.

[56] Law on Organisation (n 21).

[57] D Brkovic et al, *War Crimes Proceedings in Serbia (2003–2014) An Analysis of the OSCE Mission to Serbia's Monitoring Results* (OSCE Mission to Serbia 2015) 21; OSCE Mission to Serbia and Montenegro, *War Crimes Before Domestic Courts OSCE Monitoring and Empowering of the Domestic Courts to Deal with War Crimes* (OSCE 2003)7–11.

[58] SFRY Criminal Code (n 42); The Criminal Code of the FRY, Official Gazette SFRY, No 44/76-1329, 36/77-1478, 34/84-895, 37/84-933, 74/87-1743, 57/89-1441, 3/90-63, 38/90-1217, 45/90-1340, 54/90-1773 and Official Gazette FRY, No 35/92-651, 37/93-816, 24/94-273, 61/01 ('FRY Criminal Code'); HLC, 'Zvornik Verdict in accordance with Evidence' (Criminal Justice, 23 June 2008) <http://www.hlc-rdc.org/?p= 12932&lang=de> accessed 14 February 2018; HLC, 'Prokuplje Court Hands Down Sentence for War Crime' (War Crimes, 12 July 2002) <http://www.hlc-rdc.org/?p=12837&lang=de> accessed 14 February 2018.

[59] The penalty for IHL violations provided by the applicable law at the time was between five to twenty years of imprisonment or death penalty. After the abolition of the death penalty in 2002, the applicable sentence was five years to forty years of imprisonment. The abolition of the death penalty and the increase in the length of the longest possible sentence of imprisonment raised a debate as to whether the sentence of forty years of imprisonment could be issued for crimes committed before 2002 in light of the requirement under Serbian law that the law more favourable for the accused must be applied. One of the most recent Appeals Judgments on the issue held that the maximum of forty years imprisonment could be applied to crimes committed before 2002. See Supreme Court of Serbia, Ibarska Magistrala Case (*Radomir Marković* et al) Appeals Judgment, 19 June 2008. The crime prosecuted in that process was committed on 3 October 1999.

[60] HLC, Zvornik Verdict in accordance with Evidence (Criminal Justice, 23 June 2008) <http://www.hlc-rdc.org/?p= 12932&lang=de> accessed 14 February 2018; OSCE Monitoring Report (n 57) 8.

found a captain and two Yugoslav Army solders guilty of crimes committed against Kosovo Albanian civilians.[61] In the so-called 'Orahovac Case' before the Pozarevac court in 2000, one member of the Serbian police was found guilty and one acquitted for war crimes against Kosovo Albanian civilians.[62] In a trial held before the Prokuplje District court in 2002, a former Yugoslav Army soldier was found guilty of war crimes against Kosovo Albanian civilians.[63] Four Yugoslav Army members were sentenced in 2002 for killings of Kosovo Albanian civilians in Kosovo in 1999.[64]

Two cases started before the entry into force of the Law on Organisation but were finalized after its entry into force. In 2006 the Serbian Supreme Court confirmed the judgment sentencing four members of the Unit 'Osvetnici' (Avengers) for a war crime against the Bosniak civilians from Sjeverin, Serbia, concluding the case that had started in 2003.[65] In 2005, the Supreme Court confirmed the Prokuplje court's judgment sentencing a 'Scorpion' unit member for crimes against Albanian civilians in Podujevo, concluding the case that had started in 2002.[66]

25.4.2 Cases After the Entry into Force of the Law on Organisation

The Specialised Institutions[67] had, as of 20 October 2017, completed forty-five cases with seventy-three persons sentenced and thirty-seven acquitted. Six cases are pending their appeals judgment, thirteen are on trial.[68] This includes twenty-six cases related to crimes committed in BiH, twenty-two cases related to crimes committed in Croatia, and sixteen cases related to crimes committed in Kosovo.

Out of the twenty-six BiH cases and the twenty-two Croatia cases, seventeen and thirteen, respectively, were transferred to the WCPO by the authorities of BiH or Croatia or resulted from other forms of regional cooperation based on bilateral agreements.[69] One case related to crimes committed in Croatia was transferred to the WCPO by the ICTY pursuant to Rule 11*bis* ICTY Rules,[70] and one case related to crimes committed in BiH was transferred by the OTP as a Category II Case.[71]

[61] Human Rights Watch, *Under Orders: War Crimes in Kosovo* (HRW 2001) 484; OSCE Monitoring Report (n 57) 8–9.

[62] HLC, *Izmenjena optužnica—19.02.2003* (ORAHOVAC (Boban Petković i Đorđe Simić) 19 February 2003) <http://www.hlc-rdc.org/Transkripti/orahovac.html> accessed 14 February 2018; OSCE Monitoring Report (n 57) 9.

[63] HLC, 'Prokuplje Court Hands Down Sentence for War Crime' (*Criminal Justice*, 12 July 2002) <http://www.hlc-rdc.org/?p=12837&lang=de> accessed 25 April 2017; OSCE Monitoring Report (n 57) 8.

[64] HLC, *'Predmet: KUŠNIN/KUSHNIN (Zlatan Mančić i dr.)'* (19 July 2002) <http://www.hlc-rdc.org/Transkripti/kusnin.html?lang=de> accessed 14 February 2018; OSCE Monitoring Report (n 57) 9.

[65] HLC, *Drugostepena presuda 13.04.2006* (Sjeverin (Milan Lukić i dr.) 29 November 2011) <http://www.hlc-rdc.org/Transkripti/sjeverin.html>, accessed 14 February 2018; OSCE Monitoring Report (n 57) 9–11.

[66] HLC, *Podujevo 1999—Beyond Reasonable Doubt* (Humanitarian Law Series, 11 July 2006); OSCE Monitoring Report (n 57) 9.

[67] OSCE Monitoring Report (n 57) 5.

[68] WCPO Statistics (n 47).

[69] WCPO, '*Cases*' <http://www.tuzilastvorz.org.rs/en/cases/cases-> accessed 14 February 2018.

[70] WCPO, '*Case name: Dubrovnik (Vladimir Kovačević)*' (Cases) <http://www.tuzilastvorz.org.rs/en/cases/dubrovnik-vladimir-kovačević> accessed 14 February 2018.

[71] WCPO, '*Zvornik I* (*Slavković* et al)' (Cases) <http://www.tuzilastvorz.org.rs/en/cases/cases-/case-name-zvornik-i-slavkovi%C4%87-et-al> accessed 14 February 2018; which subsequently lead to *Zvornik II* (*Grujić and Popović*) case no KTP3 17/04, <http://www.tuzilastvorz.org.rs/sr/predmeti/ zvornik-ii-grujić-i-popović> accessed 25 April 2017; and WCPO, 'Case name: Zvornik III (Savić et al)' (Cases) <http://www.tuzilastvorz.org.rs/sr/predmeti/zvornik-iii-savić-i-ostali> accessed 14 February 2018.

Almost all cases were charged pursuant to the FRY Criminal Code as the successor of the SFRY Criminal Code, and only a few cases were based on the SFRY Criminal Code. Almost 80 per cent of the cases were charged under Article 142 of the FRY Criminal Code, 'War crimes against the civilian population', and several cases under Article 144 'Crimes against prisoners of war'. A few cases were also charged pursuant to Article 148 (2) 'Making use of forbidden means of warfare' of the SFRY Criminal Code.[72]

Articles 142 and 144 list a number of crimes committed against the civilian population (Article 142) or prisoners of war (Article 144) and provide that whoever orders or commits such crimes 'in violation of rules of international law effective at the time of war, armed conflict or occupation' is criminally responsible and shall be punished with not less than five years of imprisonment.

In practice, cases prosecuted under Article 142 and 144 are prosecuted in connection with different Articles of the Geneva Conventions and the Additional Protocols. The prosecution of crimes under Articles 142 and 144 is frequently linked to the modes of liability of 'complicity' under Article 22 or 'aiding' under Article 24.[73]

25.5 The Controversy Surrounding Command Responsibility

This section will look at the discussions surrounding the notion of command responsibility and highlight how cooperation between international and national legal professionals contributed to a better understanding of its elements. It will first give an overview of command responsibility in the jurisprudence of the ICTY, then look at its existence in Serbian law at the time of commission of the crimes in the 1990s, and finally provide an overview of any existing Serbian case law of relevance.

25.5.1 The Notion of Command Responsibility in the Jurisprudence of the ICTY

The concept of command responsibility is anchored in Articles 86 and 87 of Additional Protocol I to the Geneva Conventions, and is spelt out in Article 7(3) of the ICTY Statute.[74] As held by the Trial Chamber in the *Čelebići* case, it formed part of customary international law at the time of commission of crimes in the former Yugoslavia in the 1990s.[75] In its analysis in this regard, the Trial Chamber specifically held that the principle of command responsibility was recognized by the law applicable in the former Yugoslavia.[76]

72 SFRY Criminal Code (n 42), art 148; WCPO Cases (n 69).

73 SFRY Criminal Code (n 42); FRY Criminal Code (n 58); WCPO Cases (n 69).

74 ICTY Statute (n 32).

75 For a detailed analysis of the legal character of command responsibility and its status under customary international law see *The Prosecutor v Mucić* et al (Trial Chamber Judgment) ICTY-IT-96-21 (16 November 1998) para 333 (*Čelebići* Trial Judgment).

76 *Čelebići* Trial Judgment (n 75) para 340: 'Nonetheless, there can be no doubt that the concept of the individual criminal responsibility of superiors for failure to act is today firmly placed within the corpus of international humanitarian law. Through the adoption of Additional Protocol I, the principle has now been codified and given a clear expression in international conventional law. Thus, article 87 of the Protocol gives expression to the duty of commanders to control the acts of their subordinates and to prevent or, where necessary, to repress violations of the Geneva Conventions or the Protocol. The concomitant principle under which a superior may be held criminally responsible for the crimes committed by his subordinates where the superior has failed to properly exercise

According to Article 7(3) of the ICTY Statute a superior is responsible for crimes committed by his subordinates if he fails to prevent the commission of the crimes or fails to punish crimes already committed. Three elements have to be met.

The first element requires the existence of a superior-subordinate relationship. In this sense, there has to exist an effective control over the subordinates who committed crimes.[77]

The second element concerns the *mens rea* of the superior. ICTY jurisprudence has held that command responsibility is not a strict form of liability. The superior is only responsible pursuant to Article 7(3) if he either knew or had reason to know that a criminal act was about to be committed or had been committed and failed to carry out his duties. Regarding the definition of 'knowledge', the jurisprudence has held that actual knowledge of the superior cannot be assumed but has to be positively established. It has referred to a list of indicia that may be taken into account to establish knowledge.[78]

The definition of the second alternative for *mens rea*—'had reason to know'—has given rise to much legal debate. In the *Čelebići* case, the Prosecution argued for a broad interpretation of this element. It submitted that a superior would already be responsible if he omitted to keep himself informed of the state of discipline of his troops.

The Defence, on the other hand, argued for a narrow interpretation. It tried to persuade the Chamber that a superior could only be held responsible if he possessed specific information enabling him to conclude the commission of the crimes. It based its interpretation on differences in the English and French versions of Article 86 Additional Protocol I and the principle *nullum crimen sine lege*. While the English text states that superiors may be responsible for crimes committed by subordinates 'if they knew, or had information which **should have** enabled them to conclude in the circumstances at the time' that crimes were being committed; the French text translated literally is narrower and only holds supervisors responsible 'if they knew or had information **enabling** them to conclude' the same.[79]

The Trial Chamber in its analysis of the state of customary international law at the time of the commission of the crimes followed neither the Prosecution nor the Defence.

this duty is formulated in article 86 of the Protocol. A survey of the *travaux préparatoires* of these provisions reveals that, while their inclusion was not uncontested during the drafting of the Protocol, a number of delegations clearly expressed the view that the principles expressed therein were in conformity with pre-existing law. Thus, the Swedish delegate declared that these articles reaffirmed the principles of international penal responsibility that were developed after the Second World War. **Similarly, the Yugoslav delegate expressed the view that the article on the duty of commanders contained provisions which had already been accepted in "military codes of all countries".** (Emphasis added and citations omitted.) See also at para 341: '**Certainly, such a provision existed in the regulations concerning the application of the international law of war to the armed forces of the SFRY,** which, under the heading "Responsibility for the acts of subordinates", provided as follows: The commander is personally responsible for violations of the law of war if he knew or could have known that his subordinate units or individuals are preparing to violate the law, and he does not take measures to prevent violations of the law of war. The commander who knows that the violations of the law of war took place and did not charge those responsible for the violations is personally responsible. In case he is not authorized to charge them, and he did not report them to the authorized military commander, he would also be personally responsible. A military commander is responsible as a participant or an instigator if, by not taking measures against subordinates who violate the law of war, he allows his subordinate units to continue to commit the acts.' (Emphasis added and citations omitted.)

[77] *Čelebići* Trial Judgment (n 75) para 378; *The Prosecutor v Mucić* et al (Appeals Chamber Judgment) ICTY-IT-96-21-A (20 February 2001) ('*Čelebići* Appeal Judgment') paras 196, 197, and 256; *The Prosecutor v Enver Hadžihasanović and Amir Kubura* (Appeals Chamber Judgment) ICTY-IT-01-47 (22 April 2008) ('*Hadžihasanović and Kubura Appeal Judgment*') paras 20, 21.

[78] *Čelebići* Trial Judgment (n 75) para 386.

[79] 'Des informations leur permettant de conclure' rather than 'des informations qui auraient dû leur permettre de conclure'. Translation made by the author.

It found that the superior was criminally responsible if he possessed specific information which would provide notice of offences committed by his subordinates. This information did not have to be by itself sufficient to compel the conclusion of the existence of such crimes.[80] The Trial Chamber did not consider the discrepancy in language to be one of substance, since the delegates involved in the drafting of Article 86 had not considered so.[81]

The Appeals Chamber upheld the view of the Trial Chamber and found that both post-Second World War case law and Article 86 of Additional Protocol I required the superior to possess information that would put him on notice of the possibility that crimes were being committed.[82]

Finally, the third element required is that the superior failed to take the necessary and reasonable measures to prevent the criminal acts of his subordinates or punish them for those actions. A commander is responsible for failing to take such measures that are within his powers, or in other words within his material possibility.[83] According to the jurisprudence, this ability has to be determined in light of the facts of each particular situation.[84]

A question debated in the context of sentencing for responsibility under Article 7(3) of the ICTY Statute was whether the superior is responsible for his omission to properly supervise or for the actual crimes committed by his subordinates. This issue arose at the sentencing stage in case against Enver Hadžihasanović and Amir Kubura who were charged and found guilty only on the basis of Article 7(3). The Trial Chamber stated explicitly that it was not convicting the accused for the crimes committed by their subordinates, but for failing in their obligation to prevent the crimes or punish the perpetrators.[85] It then held that it was appropriate to apply a different sentencing scale than in cases where an accused was also convicted on the basis of Article 7(1).[86]

Unfortunately, neither the Trial Chamber nor the Appeals Chamber clarified how the sentencing scale differed. In response to the Prosecution's appeal the Appeals Chamber simply reiterated that when assessing the gravity of a crime in the context of a conviction

80 *Čelebići* Trial Judgment (n 75) para 393: 'It was sufficient that the superior was put on further inquiry by the information, or, in other words, that it indicated the need for additional investigation in order to ascertain whether offences were being committed or about to be committed by his subordinates.'

81 ibid para 392.

82 *Čelebići* Appeal Judgment (n 77) para 233: 'The phrase "had information", as used in Article 86(2) of Additional Protocol I, presents little difficulty for interpretation. It means that, at the critical time, the commander had in his possession such information that should have put him on notice of the fact that an unlawful act was being, or about to be, committed by a subordinate. As observed by the Trial Chamber, the apparent discrepancy between the French version, which reads 'des informations leur permettant de conclure' (literally: information enabling them to conclude), and the English version of Article 86(2) does not undermine this interpretation. This is a reference to information, which, if at hand, would oblige the commander to obtain more information (i.e. conduct further inquiry), and he therefore "had reason to know".' See also para 238: 'This information does not need to provide specific information about unlawful acts committed or about to be committed. For instance, a military commander who has received information that some of the soldiers under his command have a violent or unstable character, or have been drinking prior to being sent on a mission, may be considered as having the required knowledge.'

83 *Čelebići* Trial Judgment (n 75) para 395.

84 ibid para 394; *Prosecutor v Popović* et al (Appeals Chamber Judgment) ICTY IT-05-88-A (30 January 2015) para 1927, with further references.

85 *Prosecutor v Enver Hadžihasanović and Amir Kubura* (Trial Chamber Judgment) ICTY IT-01-47 (15 March 2006) ('*Hadžihasanović and Kubura Trial Judgment*') para 2075: 'The Accused will not be convicted for crimes committed by his subordinates but for failing in his obligation to prevent the crimes or punish the perpetrators.'

86 ibid paras 2075–76.

under Article 7(3), both the gravity of the underlying crime and the gravity of the superior's failure to act must be taken into account.[87]

ICTY jurisprudence has held in some cases that the superior was responsible for the underlying crimes of the subordinates.[88] In more recent jurisprudence, it insisted that the superior was only responsible for his failure to act and described this mode of liability as liability *sui generis*.[89] However, this debate was not decisive for sentencing, since no accused other than Enver Hadžihasanović and Amir Kubura has been found guilty on the basis of Article 7(3) ICTY Statute alone.

25.5.2 Issues Raised During Consultations in 2003

As expectations for national prosecutions of IHL cases rose in parallel with the development of the ICTY Completion Strategy, increasing attention was paid to differences between the ICTY Statute and criminal legislation in the countries of the former Yugoslavia. Through consultations with their international colleagues, national legal professionals identified several concepts that were not clearly present in their national legal frameworks, such as crimes against humanity, joint criminal enterprise, and command responsibility.[90] Peer-to-peer meetings, consultations, and training seminars organized or co-organized by the ICTY in the region focused specifically on some of these topics, command responsibility in particular.

Legal professionals from Serbia and other States in the region raised a wide range of issues and concerns related to the notion of command responsibility. However, after lengthy debates, the focus of discussions concentrated on two main issues: (1) retroactivity—whether the principle of command responsibility was part of the Serbian legal system applicable to crimes committed during the conflicts in former Yugoslavia in the 1990s; and (2) the definition of the *mens rea* requirement of command responsibility.

25.5.2.1 Retroactivity

A frequently raised question was whether the principle of command responsibility existed in the legal system of the former Yugoslavia during the 1990s. Some legal professionals argued that absent the existence of national law penalizing the acts underlying command responsibility, no other law was sufficiently specific to meet the constitutional requirement that a person may only be punished for acts that were proscribed by law at the time of

[87] *Hadžihasanović and Kubura Appeal Judgment* (n 77) para 313: 'The Appeals Chamber reiterates that, when assessing the gravity of a crime in the context of a conviction under Article 7(3) of the Statute, two matters must be taken into account: (1) the gravity of the underlying crime committed by the convicted person's subordinate; and (2) the gravity of the convicted person's own conduct in failing to prevent or punish the underlying crimes. Thus, in the context of a conviction under Article 7(3) of the Statute, the gravity of a subordinate's crime remains, contrary to Hadžihasanović's assertion, an "essential consideration" in assessing the gravity of the superior's own conduct at sentencing' (with further references to *Čelebići* Appeal Judgment, para 741).

[88] See *Čelebići* Trial Judgment (n 75) para 333 and *Čelebići* Appeal Judgment (n 77) para 198, which saw the commander responsible for the commission of the crimes.

[89] In addition to the *Prosecutor v Hadžihasanović and Kubura* (n 77), see *Prosecutor v Sefer Halilović* (Trial Chamber Judgment) ICTY-IT-01-48-T (16 November 2005) ('*Halilović* Trial Judgment'), paras 53–54 and 78, where the Trial Chamber held that command responsibility was a *sui generis* form of liability; see also *Prosecutor v Naser Orić* (Trial Chamber Judgment) ICTY-IT-03-68-T (30 June 2006) paras 292–93, with references to the *Halilović* Trial Judgment.

[90] Command Responsibility Consultations (n 36).

commission.[91] They held the view that Articles 86 and 87 of Additional Protocol I to the Geneva Conventions, to which the former Yugoslavia was a party, were not sufficient to qualify as a 'law' since they did not contain provisions on the possible punishment of the commander.[92]

Members of the military judiciary, however, did recognize the concept of command responsibility as it resembled principles accepted in the military legal system. As of 1988 command responsibility was explicitly incorporated into the military legal framework.[93]

Through discussions on the development of the notion in international jurisprudence, including that of the ICTY, even the critics began to adjust their view. While they maintained that international instruments were not sufficiently specific, they accepted that the notion of command responsibility could be deduced from other modes of liability present in the SFRY/FRY Criminal Code, such as aiding and abetting, the commission of crimes by omission, or the failure to report criminal offences. Some of these legal professionals recommended the adoption of interpretive norms in relation to the provisions of criminal law applicable in the 1990s. They did not consider such measures to violate the *nullum crimes sine lege* principle.[94] This suggestion was not adopted, however.

25.5.2.2 Strict Liability

Some considered that liability under the command responsibility's 'should have known' requirement represented a form of strict liability and was alien to the Serbian national legal system.[95]

The debate initially focused on the Yamashita case.[96] However, the familiarization of national legal professionals with the ICTY's jurisprudence and particularly the *Čelebići* Appeal Judgment,[97] which was provided as working material during the consultations, cast a different light on this issue.[98] Many considered it a ground-breaking moment when

[91] Constitution of the SFRY, *Official Gazette of SFRY* 9/74, Belgrade 1974 ('SFRY Constitution'), art 181: 'No one shall be punished for any act which before its commission was not defined as a punishable offence by statute or a legal provision based on statute, or for which no penalty vas threatened.

Criminal offences and criminal-law sanctions may only be established by statute.'

Constitution of the FRY, *Official Gazette of FRY* 1/92, Belgrade 1992 ('FRY Constitution') art 27: 'No one may be punished for an act which did not constitute a penal offense under law or by-law at the time it was committed, nor may punishment be inflicted which was not envisaged for the offense in question. Criminal offenses and criminal sanctions shall be determined by statute'.

[92] Sead Spahovic, Serbian State Public Attorney in Command Responsibility Consultations (n 36) paras 96–100; Danas, 'Da li je moguće u Srbiji suditi za komandnu odgovornost?' (Društvo, 22 September 2014) <https://www.danas.rs/drustvo/da-li-je-moguce-u-srbiji-suditi-za-komandnu-odgovornost/> accessed 17 February 2018.

[93] Art 21 of the Instructions on the Application of Rules of International Laws and Customs of War in the Armed Forces of SFRY, adopted in 1988; <<<REFO:JART>>>I Aleksandar, 'Komandna odgovornost u teoriji i praksi međunarodnog krivičnog prava' (2002) 54 Vojno delo 92–112<<<REFC>>>; Presentation on Command responsibility from a military perspective by Aleksandar Ignjatović in Command Responsibility Consultations (n 36) 38–44.

[94] See S Spahovic, Serbian State Public Attorney in Command Responsibility Consultations (n 36) 96–100;

[95] See presentation on draft amendments to the legal framework for prosecution of IHL crimes in Serbia and Montenegro given by Mr Saša Obradović, Legal Adviser at the Ministry of Foreign Affairs of Serbia and Montenegro; Ms Zlata Đurđević, Zagreb Law Faculty; and Mr Jovan Ćirić, Belgrade Comparative Law Institute, all in Command Responsibility Consultations (n 36) 44–45 and 50–51.

[96] Supreme Court, US, *In re Yamashita* 317 US 1; 66 S 340, Judgment, 4 February 1946.

[97] *Čelebići* Trial Judgment (n 75). See for a discussion of this case, section 21.5.1.

[98] See Presentation on ICTY investigations and prosecutions pursuant to command responsibility by Andrew Cayley of OTP, and presentation on jurisprudence based on arts 7(1) and 7(3) of the ICTY Statute by Reinhold Gallmetzer of ICTY Chambers, both in Command Responsibility Consultations (n 36) 59–77 and 80–89.

Mr Sead Spahović, Serbian State Public Attorney, stated that *Yamashita might not be as innocent as he seems to be.*[99]

25.5.3 Position of the WCPO

The first Serbian War Crimes Prosecutor, Mr Vladimir Vukčević, explained on numerous occasions that the position of the WCPO was that the notion of command responsibility had existed in the former Yugoslavia at the time of the armed conflicts in the 1990s.[100] He based this view on the fact that the former Yugoslavia had ratified the Geneva Conventions and Additional Protocols I and II; that the SFRY and FRY Constitutions[101] provided that ratified international treaties formed part of national law and had primacy over national legislation, and that the Military Code explicitly introduced command responsibility in 1988.[102] Prosecutor Vukčević also believed that the notion of command responsibility, although not explicitly defined, existed through other elements of the criminal codes applicable in the 1990s.[103]

Mr Vukčević held the position of Serbian War Crimes Prosecutor from 2003 until 2015. However, to date, the WCPO has not raised any indictment based explicitly on this mode of liability.[104] Out of the 184 persons indicted by the WCPO, the vast majority were charged as direct perpetrators with no command authority. The rare examples of intermediary-level accused were charged either for ordering crimes, for committing crimes personally, or both.[105]

Nevertheless, at least two of the indictments concerning intermediary-level accused have elements of command responsibility, as will be discussed further.[106]

25.5.4 Serbian Prosecutions for Command Responsibility

25.5.4.1 Zvornik II Case

The indictment was based on evidence transferred by the OTP in 2004. The Serbian War Crimes Investigation Service created a joint investigation team with the war crimes investigation services of BiH. This team finalized the investigation in 2005, and the WCPO issued

[99] See S Spahović, Serbian State Public Attorney in Command Responsibility Consultations (n 36) 123.

[100] Report of the War Crimes Prosecutor Vladimir Vukčević, Issues of Command Responsibility of Superiors for Serious Violations of International Law—Command Responsibility, 2004; War Crimes Prosecutor Vladimir Vukčević, speech given at the conference: Facing the Past in former Yugoslavia—Influence of the ICTY on the process of establishment of responsibility, 30 September 2004; War Crimes Prosecutor Vladimir Vukčević, speech, Creation of conditions for transfer of jurisdiction in cases initiated before the ICTY pursuant to Rule 11*bis*, 5 February 2005.

[101] SFRY Constitution (n 91); FRY Constitution (n 91).

[102] Report of the War Crimes Prosecutor Vladimir Vukčević (n 100); War Crimes Prosecutor Vladimir Vukčević 2004 (n 100); War Crimes Prosecutor Vladimir Vukčević, Speech 2005 (n 100).

[103] ibid.

[104] WCPO, FOUNDATION (About Us) <http://www.tuzilastvorz.org.rs/en/about-us/foundation> accessed 17 February 2018.

[105] WCPO, Cases (n 69).

[106] WCPO, *Zvornik II (Grujić and Popović) procedural remarks* (Cases) <http://www.tuzilastvorz.org.rs/upload/Indictment/Documents__sr/2016-05/o_2008_10_22_lat.pdf> accessed 17 February 2018.

a first indictment against seven accused in the so-called Zvornik I case.[107] Two of the accused were intermediary-level commanders, Branko Grujić and Branko Popović. In 2008, the Court granted the WCPO's request to separate the case against Grujić and Popović and include additional evidence based on their responsibility as superiors.[108] The new indictment initiated the so-called Zvornik II case.[109]

Branko Grujić had held the presidential offices in the Zvornik Municipality Crisis Headquarters in the provisional Government and in the War Headquarters of Zvornik Municipality. Branko Popović had been the Commander of the Territorial Defence Staff, Member of the War Staff in Zvornik, BiH, and head of the Military Territory Command.[110]

The indictment asserted that the accused failed to protect hostages under their control from crimes committed by Territorial Defence members.[111] They were found guilty by the War Crimes Chamber in its Judgment issued in 2010[112] and confirmed by the War Crimes Appeals Chamber in 2011.[113]

The War Crimes Chamber found Grujić and Popović guilty of war crimes committed against the civilian population under Article 142 of the FRY Criminal Code, in combination with Article 3(1) of the IV Geneva Convention and Articles 4(1), 4(2), and 5 of Additional Protocol II; applying the modes of liability of complicity under Article 22. Additionally, for Popović only, aiding and abetting under Article 24 of the FRY Criminal Code was applied.

Both accused were found guilty of having ordered the taking of hostages and the forcible displacement of the civilian population. The Chamber also found that both accused had failed to take measures to ensure that the hostages were properly cared for. It, therefore, found the two accused guilty of inhuman treatment of hostages, committed in complicity through omission.[114] Popović was further found guilty of aiding the killing of hostages and causing their bodily harm. The Chamber found that even after receiving information that some of his subordinates were entering the detention centre during the night and killing or causing bodily harm, Popović had not taken any steps to prevent this from happening and had thereby accepted the consequences of the acts of his subordinates.

When establishing the knowledge of the Accused Popović, the Chamber held that the existence of knowledge of activities related to crimes committed by subordinates can be established through direct or circumstantial evidence. In this regard, the Judgment refers to international customary law.[115]

This Judgment was seen by many as an example of the application of the notion of command responsibility.[116] It should be noted, however, that the decision discusses the need

[107] WCPO, *Zvornik I (Slavkivić* et al*)* (Cases, Indictment, 12 August 2005) <http://www.tuzilastvorz.org.rs/en/cases/cases-/case-name-zvornik-i-slavkovi%C4%87-et-al> accessed 21 February 2018.

[108] *Zvornik II* Procedural Remarks (n 106).

[109] ibid.

[110] WCPO, *Zvornik II (Grujić and Popović)* Case no KTP3 17/04, Indictment, 22 October 2008.

[111] ibid.

[112] War Crimes Chamber, *Zvornik II (Grujić and Popović)*, Case no 28/2010, Judgment, 22 November 2010 ('Zvornik II Trial Judgment').

[113] War Crimes Appeals Chamber, *Zvornik II (Grujić and Popović)*, Case no 6/11, Appeals Judgment, 3 October 2011.

[114] Zvornik II Trial Judgment (n 112) 298.

[115] ibid 238.

[116] The WCPO Deputy Prosecutor Bruno Vekarić believes that the Zvornik II case is the prime example of the use of the provisions that were present in the SFRY/FRY Criminal Code during the 1990s to 'reconstruct' command responsibility without referring to it explicitly. Bruno Vekarić 'Specific treatment of war crimes in international and national criminal law' (PhD Thesis, Union University, Law Faculty, February 2016) <http://union.edu.rs/wp-content/uploads/2016/07/BRUNO-VEKARI%C4%86-DOKTORAT-mart-2016.pdf> accessed 17 February

for a nexus between the acts of the superior and the crimes committed, as well as the *mens rea* of the accused in relation to the crimes. This would speak more for liability for aiding and abetting through omission, which the ICTY would try under Article 7(1) of the ICTY Statute.

25.5.4.2 Ćuška, Pavljan, Zahač, Ljubenić (Miladinović et al) Case

A second case, against commander Toplica Miladinović and ten 'Šakali' unit members, charged Toplica Miladinović for crimes against the civilian population under Article 142 in combination with Articles 3(1), 33(2), and Article 49 of IV Geneva Convention, as well as Articles 51, 52, 75, and Article 85(3) and (4) of Additional Protocol I; and Article 4, Article 13(2), and Article 17(2) of Additional Protocol II; applying the mode of liability of complicity under Article 22. The indictment states that Toplica Miladinović was a military commander who in 1999 ordered his subordinates to search villages in the Peć municipality for armed members of the Kosovo Liberation Army and to seize their weapons. The indictment states that Miladinović 'was aware that the execution of his order would result in the commission of a criminal offense by this unit as he was familiar with its behaviour in the field, its members having previously committed criminal offences of plundering and robbing civilian property, individual or mass killings of civilians'.[117] The indictment further states that he kept 'direct contact with the commander of this unit [and therefore he] was or could have been familiar with the immediate events and the way in which the given order would be implemented'.[118]

The indictment states that Miladinović's order resulted in acts of intimidation and terror against the civilian population as well as the mass murder of civilians, and concludes that by issuing this order the Accused agreed to such consequences.[119]

The War Crimes Appeals Chamber has ordered the re-trial of this case.[120]

25.5.5 Conclusion

The example of command responsibility shows how discussions between international and national legal experts and greater exposure to international jurisprudence contributed to the recognition of the existence of this mode of liability in national law. While its actual application has been sparse, this is largely due to the level of responsibility held by perpetrators tried in Serbia. Most of these perpetrators are direct perpetrators or can be found liable for

2018, not available in English; M Ostojić, *Between Justice and Stability—The Politics of War Crimes Prosecutions in Post-Milošević Serbia* (Routledge 2014) 190; S Weill, *The Role of National Courts in Applying International Humanitarian Law* (OUP 2014) 61; HRW Unfinished Business—Serbia's War Crimes Chamber (HRW 2007) 29; Amnesty International, Serbia—Ending Impunity for Crimes Under International Law (Amnesty International, London, 2014) 22.

[117] WCPO, *Optužnica Ćuška, Pavljan, Zahač, Ljubenić (Miladinović i ostali)* (Početna, 10 September 2010) <http://www.tuzilastvorz.org.rs/upload/Indictment/Documents__sr/2016-05/o_2010_09_10_lat.pdf> accessed 14 February 2018 Translation from Serbian to English by L Hellman.

[118] ibid.

[119] ibid 2.

[120] *Ćuška, Pavljan, Zahač, Ljubenić* (*Miladinović* et al*)* Case no 6/14, War Crimes Appeals Chamber's Order, 26 February 2015.

commission through omission. There is no official estimate of the number of future cases that Serbia might lead against persons for having failed in their duties as commanders.

25.6 Prospects for the Prosecution of War Crimes in Serbia

Initial targets for the ICTY's Completion Strategy had to be adjusted several times due to, among other factors, the lack of State cooperation for the arrest and transfer of accused persons and the ill health of several accused. The Prosecutor issued her last indictment for violations of IHL in 2004, bringing the total number of persons accused by the ICTY to 161. At the end of November 2017, the ICTY issued its last two trial judgments in the cases against Prlić et al and Ratko Mladić. Possible appeals in four cases, comprising a total of five accused, would be heard by the Mechanism for International Criminal Tribunals (MICT), the successor to the ICTY and ICTR.

In light of the imminent closure of the ICTY, national prosecutions become all the more important. It is now entirely for national authorities to ensure that there is no impunity with regards to IHL crimes.

Unfortunately, developments over the last two years have not been very promising. After the end of Mr Vukčević's mandate on 31 December 2015, the position of War Crimes Prosecutor remained open for seventeen months. The new Prosecutor Snežana Stanojković took up office in May 2017.[121] The absence of a War Crimes Prosecutor for a period of seventeen months created a number of difficulties for the WCPO. Following a complaint by the defendants, the Appellate Court dismissed the Srebrenica case indictment for lack of an appointed War Crimes Prosecutor. Following her appointment in May 2017, the new Prosecutor filed a motion before the Belgrade Higher Court's War Crimes Department seeking continuation of the proceedings. While the Higher Court initially ordered for a new indictment to be filed, in October 2017, the Appellate Court overturned this decision and allowed the continuation of the proceedings in the Srebrenica case based on the initial indictment issued in 2016.[122] It reasoned that with the appointment of the new Prosecutor, the case could go ahead.

In addition, Mr Vukčević's work had faced strong opposition from Serbian legal professionals. In January 2017, the Belgrade Bar Association refused to register Mr Vukčević in the lawyer's directory.[123] Slobodan Šoškić, President of the Belgrade Bar Association stated that a majority of the members of the Association considered that Mr Vukčević's work as War Crimes Prosecutor had been unprofessional as he did not conduct his function 'patriotically'. He was accused of having only prosecuted crimes committed by Serbian

[121] WCPO, 'Snežana Stanojković takes office as Serbian War Crimes Prosecutor' (Announcements, 31 May 2017) <http://www.tuzilastvorz.org.rs/en/news-and-announcements/announcements/snežana-stanojković-takes-office-as-serbian-war-crimes-prosecutor> accessed 17 February 2018.

[122] WCPO, 'In Srebrenica (K Po2 8/15) Court orders trial continuation upon original Indictment' (Announcements, 4 October 2017) <http://www.tuzilastvorz.org.rs/en/news-and-announcements/announcements/in-srebrenica-k-po2-815-court-orders-trial-continuation-upon-original-indictment> accessed 17 February 2018; WCPO, 'Prosecutor files motion to continue Srebrenica proceedings' (Announcements, 19 July 2017) <http://www.tuzilastvorz.org.rs/en/news-and-announcements/announcements/prosecutor-files-motion-to-continue-srebrenica-proceedings> accessed 17 February 2018.

[123] M Zivanovic, 'Serbia's Ex-War Crimes Prosecutor "Barred from Working"' (*Balkan Insight*, 25 January 2017) <http://www.balkaninsight.com/en/article/serbia-s-ex-war-crimes-prosecutor-barred-from-working--01-25-2017> accessed 17 February 2018.

perpetrators and not those committed by other members of other ethnicities against Serbs.[124] Consequently, he is currently not allowed to practice law in Serbia.[125]

As for the investigation and prosecution of future IHL crimes, Serbia has signed and ratified the Rome Statute and has amended its legislation to meet the requirements of the complementarity principle. In its Article 384, the Serbian Criminal Code now contains an explicit provision on command responsibility. However, Article 384 only penalizes the failure to prevent the commission of crimes, not the failure to punish. What is more, it prescribes different sentencing scales depending on whether the superior had actual knowledge of the crimes[126] or acted negligently.[127] Whereas in the first case the superior is punished by the penalty prescribed for the underlying crime, in the second case he faces a penalty of six months to five years imprisonment. This would seem to contradict the recently issued Judgment in the ICC's Bemba trial, where the Chamber held that the superior was responsible for crimes within the jurisdiction of the Court committed by his or her subordinates.[128]

Based on the experience with the ICTY, any investigation and prosecution by Serbian authorities of crimes within the jurisdiction of the ICC would benefit from their close cooperation. It is only through consultations that any existing gaps or inconsistencies in the two frameworks can be identified and ultimately closed.

[124] D 'Vukčević: Netačno je da nisam procesuirao zločine nad Srbima' ('Vukčević: It is not true that I did not prosecute crimes committed against Serbs') (Društvo, 21 January 2017)<http://www.danas.rs/drustvo.55.html?news_id=336923&title=Vuk%C4%8Devi%C4%87%3A+Neta%C4%8Dno+je+da+nisam+procesuirao+zlo%C4%8Dine+nad+Srbima> accessed 17 February 2018.

[125] M Zivanovic (n 123).

[126] Art 384(1).

[127] Art 384(3).

[128] *Prosecutor v Jean-Pierre Bemba Gombo* (Trial Chamber Judgment) ICC-01/05-01/08 (21 March 2016) paras 171–74.

26

'We Learnt that from The Hague'

How the ICTY Influenced the Fairness of Criminal Trials in the Former Yugoslavia

*Kei Hannah Brodersen**

26.1 Introduction

The International Criminal Tribunal for the former Yugoslavia (hereinafter: ICTY or Tribunal) was established by the United Nations Security Council in 1993 in the middle of the Balkan wars. After a bumpy start, it has become the—so far—most successful international criminal court, having initiated proceedings against 161 defendants, with 156 proceedings concluded at the time of writing.[1] The (almost) completed trial work is the Tribunal's most important achievement.[2]

Next to that, the ICTY has had several—at first—unintended, or at least unforeseen, 'side effects'.[3] For instance, it has been frequently claimed that the ICTY 'instill[s]',[4] 'reestablish[es]',[5] 'advance[s]',[6] 'enhance[s]',[7] 'strengthen[s]',[8] 'improve[s]',[9] 'shap[es]',[10] 'embrace[s]',[11] or

* PhD Candidate, Department of Criminal Law and Criminology, Faculty of Law, Maastricht University (hannah.brodersen@maastrichtuniversity.nl).

1 ICTY, 'Key Figures of the Cases' <http://www.icty.org/en/cases/key-figures-cases> accessed February 2018; 5 ICTY cases ongoing at the Mechanism for International Criminal Tribunals, see <http://www.unmict.org/en/cases> accessed February 2018.

2 Appeals and other 'essential functions' will be continued by the Mechanism for International Criminal Tribunals; cf United Nations Mechanism for International Criminal Tribunals, 'About the MICT' <http://www.unmict.org/en/about> accessed 14 April 2017.

3 The term 'side effects' has been chosen because it illustrates that these effects are not within the core mandate of the ICTY, and possibly not even amongst its main goals. Side effects are somewhat unintended, maybe even unforeseen, and at least not explicitly considered or pursued.

4 P Akhavan, 'Justice in The Hague, Peace in the Former Yugoslavia? A Commentary on the United Nationals War Crimes Tribunal' (1998) 20 Human Rights Quarterly 737, 749.

5 UNSG, 'The Rule of Law and Transitional Justice in Conflict and Post-Conflict Societies: Report of the Secretary-General' (2004) UN Doc S/2004/616, 13.

6 J Hagan and S K Ivković, 'War Crimes, Democracy, and the Rule of Law in Belgrade, the Former Yugoslavia, and Beyond' (2006) 605 The ANNALS of the American Academy of Political and Social Science 129, 130.

7 J Stromseth, 'Justice on the Ground: Can International Criminal Courts Strengthen Domestic Rule of Law in Post-Conflict Societies?' (2009) 1 Hague Journal on the Rule of Law 87, 88.

8 For instance: President of the Mechanism for International Criminal Tribunals (MICT), Judge Theodor Meron, on the occasion of updating the UN Security Council on the Mechanism's activities; Mechanism for International Criminal Tribunals, 'President Meron addresses the UN Security Council', press release 3 June 2015 <http://www.unmict.org/en/news/president-meron-addresses-un-security-council-2> accessed February 2018; ICTY, 'Achievements' <http://www.icty.org/sid/324> accessed February 2018; or D Orentlicher, *Shrinking the Space for Denial: The Impact of the ICTY in Serbia* (Open Society Justice Initiative 2008) 62ff.

9 P McMahon and J Miller, 'From Adjudication to Aftermath: Assessing the ICTY's Goals beyond Prosecution' (2012) 13 Human Rights Review 421, 42f.

10 E Simpson, 'Stop to The Hague: Internal versus External Factors Suppressing the Advancement of the Rule of Law in Serbia' (2004) 36 Georgetown Journal of International Law 1255, 1257.

11 Stromseth (n 7) 87.

Kei Hannah Brodersen, *'We Learnt that from The Hague'* In: *Legacies of the International Criminal Tribunal for the Former Yugoslavia.* Edited by: Carsten Stahn, Carmel Agius, Serge Brammertz, Colleen Rohan, Oxford University Press (2020). © The Several Contributors
DOI: 10.1093/oso/9780198862956.003.0027

'promot[es]'[12] (this list could go on for pages) the rule of law. For many, this claim refers to the idea that the ICTY contributed to a world in which violating the law is not accepted and will be addressed through criminal trials. It thus alludes to the enforcement of universally accepted rules. The international *law* rules—as opposed to lawlessness. Some, however, assert that the ICTY's influence went beyond that and that it affected the rule of law at the national level, in the countries under its jurisdiction. Within that context, at the very least, the ICTY would have prompted national justice systems to prosecute violations of the law. Yet, at best, influence on the domestic rule of law would imply contributions to the integrity, solidity, and competence of a national justice system.[13]

The research that will be summarized in this contribution started off with the question whether the ICTY not only prompted national war crimes trials, but also contributed to their success—and in particular, whether it strengthened the fairness of national criminal proceedings in the countries of the former Yugoslavia. The underlying interest was to find out whether the Tribunal left a 'footprint' in the national justice systems that will outlast its existence. To be sure, at the time the ICTY was established, its founders did certainly not plan for the Tribunal's side-effects—its core business was big enough of a challenge. However, this has changed at least since the initiation of the ICTY's Completion Strategy,[14] as is illustrated by the words of its then-President, who preferred to call it the 'continuation strategy'[15]:

> it is not so much a strategy to 'complete' the work of the ICTY as it is a strategy designed to allow continuation by local actors of those activities that were initially 'kicked off' by the ICTY under the mandate of the Security Council.[16]

To allow 'continuation', the Tribunal had put in place different mechanisms and initiated several partnership programmes that would, on the one hand, encourage national justice systems to take up and continue the ICTY's work, and on the other hand assist them in doing so. Arguably, the Tribunal thereby began to work on its legacy which it wanted to go beyond the 'mere' completion of the remaining trials. In the words of its last Prosecutor:

> [T]he completion of the Tribunal's mandate is not the end of war crimes justice, but the beginning of the next chapter. [...] [U]ltimately, I believe that the ICTY's legacy is not simply measured by our own work, but by whether the countries of the former Yugoslavia build

[12] L Barria and S Roper, 'Judicial Capacity Building in Bosnia and Herzegovina: Understanding Legal Reform Beyond the Completion Strategy of the ICTY' (2008) 9 Human Rights Review 317, 319.

[13] There are numerous definitions of the rule of law. Most authors categorize them into a minimalist–maximalist continuum, with minimalist conceptions referring to the idea that the 'rule of law' means that the law rules, and maximalist conceptions incorporating a number of formal and substantive rules a political system has to comply with in order to qualify for the label 'under the rule of law'. See for a comprehensive overview: B Tamanaha, *On the Rule of Law—History, Politics, Theory* (Cambridge University Press 2004).

[14] The Completion Strategy is commonly understood as the Tribunal's plan to wind down its trial and appellate activities. For further information on the Completion Strategy, see ICTY, 'Completion Strategy' <http://www.icty.org/en/sid/10016> accessed February 2018.

[15] See F Pocar, 'Completion or Continuation Strategy? Appraising Problems and Possible Developments in Building the Legacy of the ICTY' (2008) 6 Journal of International Criminal Justice 655.

[16] ibid.

> the rule of law and demonstrate they can secure meaningful justice for the victims of serious crimes during the conflicts.[17]

The present contribution will show that the ICTY had only scarce effects on fairness of national war crimes[18] proceedings, or national criminal proceedings in general (section 26.2). This will be exemplified with the help of two case studies: Bosnia and Herzegovina (hereinafter: Bosnia or BiH) and the Republic of Serbia (hereinafter: Serbia). The greatest impact can still be observed in Bosnia and Herzegovina, and it is almost absent in Serbia. The difference will subsequently be explained by relying on theories that originally stem from the research field of international relations:[19] the 'norm cascade model' and the 'spiral model' aim at describing how a norm (for instance, in this case: fairness in criminal trials) 'cascades' from the international level (here: from the ICTY) into the national justice system (section 26.3.1). It is interesting to note that this process played out quite differently in Bosnia and Serbia. It will be claimed that the reason for this difference is twofold: first, a much higher involvement of the Tribunal in the rebuilding of the Bosnian justice system, than in the Serbian—surely caused by the fact that most of the Tribunal's own trial work related to crimes that happened in Bosnia and are hence now prosecuted in Bosnia. Second, the Tribunal enjoyed much lower rates of legitimacy in Serbia than in Bosnia, not only amongst the Serbian population,[20] but also amongst the country's political elite.[21] The most important dynamics at play that either supported or impeded the cascade of fairness from the ICTY to the national justice systems will be explained in sections 26.3.2 and 26.3.3. Eventually, it will be shown that the ICTY's permanent presence in Bosnia and large absence in Serbia were the most decisive factors when it comes to convincing national counterparts to follow ICTY jurisprudence and practice.[22] Although the dynamics that will be described also explain the impact of the ICTY in other areas of war crimes proceedings, its influence on fairness has been chosen as the defendant's access to fundamental fair trial

[17] S Brammertz, ICTY Press Release, '#ICTY24: Commemoration held at United Nations Headquarters' (5 December 2017) <http://www.icty.org/en/press/icty24-commemoration-held-at-united-nations-headquarters> accessed February 2018.

[18] This generic term is used to refer to the prosecution of all so-called international crimes (namely, those commonly found in the statutes of international criminal courts and tribunals).

[19] Both models have initially been developed in the context of State compliance with international human rights law; cf M Finnemore and K Sikkink, 'International Norm Dynamics and Political Change' (1998) 52 International Organization 887; T Risse and K Sikkink, 'The Socialization of International Human Rights Norms into Domestic Practices: Introduction' in T Risse, S Ropp, and K Sikkink (eds), *The Power of Human Rights International Norms and Domestic Change* (Cambridge University Press 1999). In her most recent comprehensive contribution, Kathryn Sikkink further applies the model to show that notion of justice has in fact trickled down to the domestic level, demonstrated by the fact that the great bulk of enforcement of core human rights norms now occurs in domestic courts using a combination of domestic criminal law and international human rights law; cf K Sikkink, *The Justice Cascade: How Human Rights Prosecutions Are Changing World Politics* (W. W. Norton 2011).

[20] The OSCE's findings of continuously negative attitudes of the Serbian public towards the ICTY have become notorious. OSCE 'Views on war crimes, the ICTY, and the national war crimes judiciary' (April 2009) <http://www.osce.org/serbia/40751?download=true> accessed February 2018; OSCE 'Attitudes towards war crimes issues, ICTY and the national judiciary' (October 2011) <http://www.osce.org/serbia/90422?download=true> accessed February 2018.

[21] For a description of the difficult cooperation between the Tribunal and Serbia, see K Michaeli, 'The Impact of the International Criminal Tribunal for Yugoslavia on War Crime Investigations and Prosecutions in Serbia' (DOMAC, Reykjavik University, Reykjavik 2011) 13.

[22] It must be noted that while this contribution focuses on the ICTY's impact on fairness of national *war crimes trials*, it has sometimes been pointed out in interviews conducted in the region that this impact goes beyond this limited field. Rather, some changes that were triggered by the ICTY are generally applicable to criminal trials as they caused a general revision of criminal procedure or practice.

rights is a key indicator of equitability in any system of criminal justice, as proceedings lose their credibility and integrity without the consistent application of due process standards.[23] Fairness is thus indicative of the overall quality of the trials.

'Fairness', 'respect for fair trial rights' or for the 'rights of the defendant' will be used interchangeably. Fundamentally, this notion refers to the rights enshrined in Article 6 of the European Convention for Human Rights and Articles 9 and 14 of the International Covenant for Civil and Political Rights. However, 'fairness' goes even beyond that: 'fairness' cannot always be translated with 'respect' for certain clearly defined rights. The blackletter respect for certain rights—or the absence of their violation—does not automatically render proceedings 'fair'. What is essential, although as such not mentioned in the human rights treaties, but considered to be an 'inherent feature of a fair trial', is equality of arms between the defence and the prosecution. It requires that a fair balance be struck between the parties within criminal proceedings. As such, the specific rights mentioned in paragraph 3 of Article 6 of the European Convention of Human Rights (ECHR) are constituent elements of a fair trial, but the principle of equality of arms goes beyond these minimum rights.[24] Whether the defendant is put on an equal footing with the prosecution is often not only a question of respect for codified rights. It rather depends on often small everyday decisions taken in the courtroom and as such is also a matter of judges' and prosecutors' mindset.

This research is based on an analysis of primary documents, secondary literature, case analysis, and—most importantly—forty-five in-depth interviews with practitioners within the Bosnian and Serbian justice systems, as well as ICTY actors, conducted in The Hague, Berlin, London, Sarajevo, and Belgrade in November 2016 through to February 2017.[25] Large parts of this contribution will be based on models and language that political scientists are familiar with. Other parts might be better understandable for jurists. This is necessary, as the analysis of the role of the law within a society is only possible from an interdisciplinary perspective.

26.2 The ICTY's Impact on Fairness of National War Crimes Trials

The national justice systems of both, Bosnia and Herzegovina and Serbia, have considerably changed since the Yugoslav conflict ended and democratic regimes have started working properly in the early 2000s. While the Yugoslav substantive and procedural criminal law was generally viewed as complying with international standards,[26] in the post-war period,

[23] cf W Schomburg, 'The Role of International Criminal Tribunals in Promoting Respect for Fair Trial Rights' (2009) 8 Northwestern Journal of International Human Rights 1, 1.

[24] European Court of Human Rights, 'Guide on Article 6 of the European Convention on Human Rights: Right to a fair trial (criminal limb)' (Strasbourg 2014) 21.

[25] This research was complicated by the fact that only the jurisprudence of the Bosnian State Court is available online; see A Trapani, 'Assessing the Impact of the International Ad-Hoc Tribunals on the Domestic Courts of the Former Yugoslavia' (DOMAC, Reykjavik University, Reykjavik 2011) [11] 9.

[26] See for instance the ICTY Referral Bench's assessment of the legal framework applicable to war crimes cases in BiH: *Prosecutor v Stanković* (Decision on Rule 11*bis* Referral) ICTY-IT-96-23/2-PT (1 September 2005) para 32ff; the same for Serbia: *Prosecutor v Vladimir Kovačević* (Decision on referral of case pursuant to rule 11bis with confidential and partly exparte annexes) ICTY-IT-01-42/2-I (17 November 2006) para 25ff; interview with a defence counsel at the ICTY (ICTY, The Hague, The Netherlands, 25 November 2016).

both countries' criminal justice systems were considered inadequately prepared to conduct genuine war crimes trials.[27]

Bosnia experienced an overhaul of its criminal justice system in 2003, when both a new criminal code and a new code of criminal procedure were enacted.[28] The new criminal code codified, amongst others, the international crimes of genocide,[29] crimes against humanity,[30] and war crimes,[31] as defined in the Rome Statute of the International Criminal Court. It also enshrined new modes of liability, most prominently command responsibility, and reformed the sentencing regime. Interestingly, the newly established war crimes chamber in the State Court of Bosnia and Herzegovina (hereinafter: State Court or SCBiH) has subsequently interpreted these new legal provisions in light of the ICTY's jurisprudence and practice. In fact, this holds true not only for the new provisions—the chamber streamlined its jurisprudence with the ICTY's interpretations on virtually all issues of substantive international criminal law.[32] Hence, although it is not in any way bound by the ICTY's case law, the Tribunal has always guided the interpretation of the new Bosnian provisions.[33]

Although the inquisitorial model of criminal procedure was firmly entrenched in Bosnia's criminal justice system, the new code of criminal procedure of 2003 incorporated a number of adversarial elements.[34] Most importantly, investigative judges were abolished and the responsibility of the investigation now solely lies with the prosecution. Some say, this new hybrid procedural model was—at the very least—inspired by the ICTY's procedural model.[35] As one Bosnian legal practitioner stated: 'The adversarial or mixed model had been in front of our eyes for years. We needed a new model [of criminal procedure]. It was the obvious one to pick. We just had to copy paste.'[36] At the same time, the code was updated and henceforth incorporated international standards of protection of the rights of the

[27] cf C Jorda, 'Report on the Judicial Status of the International Criminal Tribunal for the former Yugoslavia and the Prospects for Referring Certain Cases to National Courts', annexed to the 'Letter dated 10 June 2002 from the President of the International Criminal Tribunal for the former Yugoslavia addressed to the Secretary General', annexed to the 'Letter dated 17 June 2002 from the Secretary-General addressed to the President of the Security Council' (19 June 2002) UN Doc S/2002/678 18ff.

[28] For efficiency reasons, this contribution only addresses developments at the State level of Bosnia and Herzegovina and disregards those at the entity level (in the Federation of BiH, the Republika Srpska, and the Brčko District).

[29] Art 171 Criminal Code of Bosnia and Herzegovina (CC BiH).

[30] Art 172 CC BiH.

[31] Arts 173–75, 177–79 CC BiH.

[32] Randomly selected examples out of virtually thousands of references to ICTY jurisprudence: relying on the ICTY's interpretation of a 'widespread or systematic attack', see SCBiH, *Prosecutor v Krešo Lučić* (Appeals Judgment) X-KRŽ-06/298 (16 December 2008) para 13; of enforced disappearances as other inhumane acts as a crime against humanity, see SCBiH, *Prosecutor v Boban Šimšić* (Appeals Judgment) X-KRŽ-05/04 (7 August 2007) para 46; of joint criminal enterprise as a mode of liability, see SCBiH, *Prosecutor v Mitar* Rašević (Appeals Judgment) X-KRŽ-06/275 (6 November 2008) para 25; or to justify the dismissal of the *tu quoque* principle as a complete defence, see SCBiH *Prosecutor v Krešo Lučić* (Appeals Judgment) X-KRŽ-06/298 (16 December 2008) para 14.

[33] On these legislative changes and how they have been inspired by the ICTY jurisprudence, see Y Ronen, 'The Impact of the ICTY on Atrocity-Related Prosecutions in the Courts of Bosnia and Herzegovina' (2014) 3 Penn State Journal of Law and International Affairs 113.

[34] Silvia Borelli, 'The Impact of the European Convention of Human Rights in the Context of War Crimes Trials in Bosnia and Herzegovina' (DOMAC, Reykjavik University, Reykjavik 2009) [5] 15.

[35] As Rüedi put it: 'many of the procedural rules from the ICTY have migrated into the domestic legal system and changed the course of criminal proceedings significantly'; cf L Rüedi, *War Crimes Trials in Bosnia and Herzegovina: Selected Aspects of Transitional Justice Mechanisms* (International Criminal Law Völkerstrafrecht und internationales Strafrecht, DIKE 2015) 182 and 78.

[36] Interview with a defence counsel at Sarajevo (Sarajevo, Bosnia and Herzegovina, 31 January 2017); similar claims were made by a former official of an international organization operating in the countries of the former Yugoslavia (Belgrade, Serbia, 27 January 2017).

accused, as provided for in the ECHR, and interpreted by the European Court of Human Rights (ECtHR).[37] ICTY influence is visible in the SCBiH case law with respect to a number of procedural norms.[38] For example, the war crimes chamber has relied on the ICTY when ruling on the admissibility of illegally obtained evidence,[39] or on the credibility of witness testimony.[40] Also when it comes to legal issues relevant for the fairness of proceedings and the respect for fair trial rights—such as the right of the defendant to be informed on his/her rights,[41] the obligations of the prosecutor to disclose exculpatory evidence,[42] the powers of the chamber to appoint *ex officio* defence counsel for equality of arms reasons,[43] or the chamber's obligation to weigh the right of the defendant to get a fair trial and the need for expediency and efficiency,[44] to name but a few—the war crimes chamber has been inspired by ICTY practice and jurisprudence. Bosnian legal practitioners have explained that the chamber, as well as the Bosnian State prosecutor's office, or even defence counsel use ICTY practice and jurisprudence in order to fill gaps in the criminal procedure law, or to solve inconsistencies.[45] So, they resort to ICTY practice when national law or jurisprudence gives no clear guidance. As one SCBiH judge put it: 'If the ICTY has already dealt with this issue, the solution is there. Why should we re-invent the wheel if another court has already solved the issue?'[46]

Serbia adopted a new criminal code in 2006 and a new code of criminal procedure in 2011. Similar to the developments in Bosnia, the latter incorporates adversarial elements, in particular, the strengthening of the prosecution as a party to the criminal trial, who is responsible for the investigation. This mirrors the ICTY procedure, which is an integration

[37] The code was amended through Law on Amendments to the Criminal Procedure Code of Bosnia and Herzegovina (Official Gazette of BiH, 58/08) in 2008. Many of the modifications appear to have been intended to remedy problems which had arisen in the course of the first proceedings governed by the new CPC and to ensure that the code fully reflected the fair trial standards contained in the European Convention. An example is the amendment to art 14 CPC, relating to the general principle of equality of arms, or provisions designed to remove problems relating to the presumption of innocence and/or the privilege against self-incrimination; cf Borelli (n 34) 17.

[38] It should not go unmentioned that in 373 decisions that are available on the website of the State Court of Bosnia and Herzegovina (<http://www.sudbih.gov.ba> accessed February 2018) the ICTY is mentioned 8,983 times. Most references relate to established facts, many to interpretation of substantive law, and several to procedural issues. This is a purely quantitative observation. The overwhelming presence of the ICTY in the minds of all actors involved in proceedings at the SCBiH, however, can well be retraced through these numbers.

[39] *Prosecutor v Zijad Kurtović* (Trial Judgment) X-KR-06/299 (30 April 2008) para 23, referring to the *Kordić and Čerkez* case and the ICTY, Decision on the Defence 'Objection to Intercept Evidence', *Prosecutor v Radoslav Brđanin* (Decision on the Defence 'Objection to Intercept Evidence' ICTY-IT-99-36-T (3 October 2003).

[40] *Prosecutor's Office of Bosnia and Herzegovina v Dragan Šekarić* (Appeals Judgment) S1 1 K 014550 15 Krž 8 (30 September 2015) para 47.

[41] *Prosecutor's Office of Bosnia and Herzegovina v Milorad Trbić* (Appeals Judgment) Case No X-KRŽ-07/386 (21 October 2010) para 11ff, referring to the ICTY Rules of Procedure and Evidence (RPE).

[42] *Prosecutor's Office of Bosnia and Herzegovina v Veselin Vlahović* (Appeals Judgment) S1 1 K 004659 13 Krž 15 (5 February 2014) para 17ff, referring to the 'ICTY case law' that is based on the ICTY RPE.

[43] *Prosecutor's Office of Bosnia and Herzegovina v Radovan Stanković* (Appeals Judgment) X-KR–05/70 (28 March 2007) para 10ff, referring to ICTY, Decision following Registrar's Notification of Radovan Stanković's Request for Self-Representation, *Prosecutor v Gojko Janković and Radovan Stanković* (Decision following Registrar's notification of Radovan Stanković's request for self-representation) ICTY-IT-96-23/2-PT (19 August 2005).

[44] *Prosecutor's Office of Bosnia and Herzegovina v Milorad Trbić* (Appeals Judgment) X-KRŽ-07/386 (21 October 2010) para 35f, referring to ICTY, Judgment, *Prosecutor v Dragoljub Kunarac* et al (Appeals Judgment) ICTY-IT-96-23 and ICTY-IT-96-23/1-A (12 June 2002) para 43.

[45] Interview with a SCBiH judge, Sarajevo (Sarajevo, Bosnia and Herzegovina, 1 February 2017); interview with prosecutor of the Bosnian state prosecutor's office (Sarajevo, Bosnia and Herzegovina, 9 February 2017); three defence counsel interviewed have expressed the same views: interviews conducted in Sarajevo on 31 January 2017, 6 February 2017, and on 9 February 2017.

[46] Interview with a SCBiH judge (Sarajevo, Bosnia and Herzegovina, 1 February 2017).

between continental and adversarial systems. This new code was applied in war crimes and organized crimes trials first, and became applicable to all criminal trials only in 2013.

The ICTY's impact on Serbian legislation and practice in the realm of war crimes has been much more limited than in Bosnia.[47] The 2006 criminal code maintained previous legal structures, while incorporating thereto some of the provisions of the International Criminal Court (ICC) Statute.[48] Furthermore, in line with the judicial conservatism which has characterized domestic war crimes law, the criminal code does not incorporate the doctrine of joint criminal enterprise and only partially incorporates command responsibility as formulated by the ICTY.[49] In addition, Serbian case law on war crimes has made little use of ICTY jurisprudence in interpreting the criminal law applicable to the offences committed during the Yugoslav wars;[50] that is the 1976 criminal code of the Socialist Federal Republic of Yugoslavia (SFRY) and the 1992 Serbian criminal code.[51] Only several years into Serbian war crimes proceedings, this has slightly begun to change, although ICTY jurisprudence has still only been used to the extent that ICTY cases support existing interpretations of laws.[52]

With respect to criminal procedure law, only some provisions reflect lessons from the ICTY experience. By way of example, consider the possibility to testify via video link which has been implemented in Serbian criminal proceedings. The ICTY procedures allowed video link to facilitate witnesses and victims that were unwilling or unable to be present at trial.[53] In addition, the prohibition of plea agreements with defendants charged with offenses which are punishable by over twelve years was lifted, first within the procedure governing war crimes trials, and then generally.[54]

Determining the impact of the ICTY on the fairness of national war crimes proceedings is difficult for two reasons: firstly, the relevant material is not accessible to researchers. It would be necessary to trace back discussions conducted in court and within the chamber to see whether, and if so in what context, ICTY practice and jurisprudence was consulted, and eventually used. As for now, it must suffice that virtually all my interview partners in Bosnia and Herzegovina have confirmed that the ICTY has played a role in how fair trials rights were generally understood, accepted, and respected. The SCBiH's case law seems to confirm this view, as in many instances, previously unresolved legal problems were addressed with the help of ICTY practice. In contrast, such claims have not once been made in Serbia. Secondly, the question for influence cannot be more than a counterfactual one: the Tribunal's impact can certainly not be isolated or even quantified.[55] But what if the ICTY

[47] cf Michaeli (n 21) 71.

[48] For instance, genocide is codified in art 370, crimes against humanity in art 371, and war crimes in 372–74, 376–83, and 385 Serbian Criminal Code.

[49] Command responsibility can be found in art 384 CC Serbia. It does not cover civilian superiors, only military commanders and *de facto*-commanders. The commander is liable for the offence committed by his/her subordinates and 'shall be punished by the penalty prescribed for such offence'. In cases of acting out of negligence, however, a much lower sentence (between six months and five years) is applicable.

[50] Most references to the ICTY in Serbian case law relate to evidence or facts established at the ICTY and as such recognized in national proceedings; cf Michaeli (n 21) 74.

[51] Note that Serbian war crimes jurisprudence is not available online, and only partially accessible on the spot, which renders research on this topic very difficult. The outcome of this research is thus largely based on a literature review and—more importantly—on interviews with relevant actors of the Serbian criminal justice system.

[52] Michaeli (n 21) 72.

[53] ibid 80.

[54] ibid 80f, see art 304ff Serbia Code of Criminal Procedure.

[55] Of course, it must be acknowledged that within a societal context, multiple actors determine the course of events. For the present research question, this means that the influence of the ICTY on fairness of criminal

had not been there? Would national war crimes proceedings have been considerably less just, less fair, more often violating fair trial rights? At least for Bosnia, ICTY jurisprudence is one more element in the toolkit of defence counsel that they use in order to push for respect for fair trial rights. It is one more source for inspiration. For the prosecution and the war crimes chamber, it provides guidance in their decision making. The answer must therefore be that the Tribunal, at least, facilitates sound and just proceedings at the national level.

What is striking about the ICTY's influence on national war crimes proceedings, however, is not so much whether it exists or not—but rather the significant difference between Serbia and Bosnia and Herzegovina. Possible factors will be stipulated in the following section. In doing so, I will borrow models of influence initially developed within the field of international relations. These models will first be explained in the abstract and then applied to the question of how an international criminal tribunal could promote the norm of fairness in criminal proceedings in a way that the norm becomes firmly entrenched in the national realm.

26.3 Explain Dynamics of Impact: The 'Norm Cascade' and the 'Spiral Model'

26.3.1 Conceptual Background

In explaining how the norm of fairness penetrates into a domestic justice system, working its influence through the filter of domestic structures and domestic norms,[56] Martha Finnemore and Kathryn Sikkink's model of the 'norm cascade' will be followed.[57] Although this is clearly a constructivist approach, based on persuasion, it offers the opportunity to also take into account push and pull factors that would otherwise appear more in consequentialist models. These push and pull factors will largely be borrowed from the 'spiral model'.

The basic idea of the 'norm cascade' is that national actors appeal to an international rule or norm in an effort to further certain objectives in the national arena. Through such appeals, international rules and norms can become incorporated into the policy debate,

proceedings can't be separately determined from other influences, from, for instance, international organizations or other foreign actors, through experience or training, or the individual convictions of legal practitioners. In Bosnia and Herzegovina, for instance, the Office of the High Representative (OHR), which exercises civilian oversight over the country, was a major actor. Nevertheless, during interviews, the role of the ICTY was stressed even more than the one of the OHR: the OHR is the actor that often makes and enacts legislation, and the ICTY facilitated its interpretation and application, thanks to its role model function.

[56] Finnemore and Sikkink (n 19) 893.

[57] For a conceptual critique of Sikkink's model, see B Leebaw, 'Review of Kathryn Sikkink's The Justice Cascade: How Human Rights Prosecutions Are Changing World Politics' (2012) 11 Journal of Human Rights 301; P McAuliffe, 'The Roots of Transitional Accountability: Interrogating the "Justice Cascade"' (2013) 9 International Journal of Law in Context 106; for a more empirical critique, see J Subotic, 'Review of Kathryn Sikkink's The Justice Cascade: How Human Rights Prosecutions Are Changing World Politics' (2012) 11 Journal of Human Rights 296; L Vinjamuri, 'Review of Kathryn Sikkink's The Justice Cascade: How Human Rights Prosecutions Are Changing World Politics' (2012) 11 Journal of Human Rights 283; or K Rodman, 'Intervention and the 'Justice Cascade': Lessons from the Special Court for Sierra Leone on Prosecution and Civil War' (2015) 16 Human Rights Review 39.

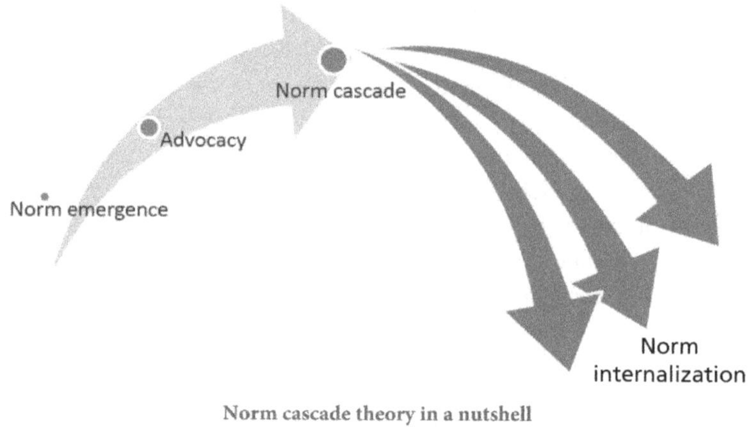

Figure 26.1 Norm cascade theory in a nutshell

and, under some conditions, may ultimately affect national policy choice.[58] Finnemore and Sikkink argue that norm influence at the domestic level is a three-stage process:[59] the first stage is 'norm emergence', the second stage involves broad norm acceptance and is called 'norm cascade', and the third stage entails internalization of the norm.[60] The point in time between the first and the second stage is described as a 'tipping' point, at which a critical mass of relevant national actors adopt the norm and it consequently cascades through the society (see Figure 26.1).[61]

Different logics of action may be involved at different stages of the life cycle of a norm.[62] The first stage ('norm emergence') is characterized by persuasion by 'norm entrepreneurs'[63] who convince a critical mass of actors to embrace the new norm.[64] Burke-White, following Finnemore and Sikkink, calls this 'norm leadership'.[65] These entrepreneurs act out of altruism, empathy, and ideational commitment: they believe in the ideals and values embodied in the norms.[66] Norm entrepreneurs work within organizational platforms[67] in what others have called 'advocacy networks'.[68] These networks can include States, international and local non-governmental organizations (NGOs), and other relevant actors 'working internationally on an issue, who are bound together by shared values, a common discourse,

[58] A similar idea is advocated in: A Cortell and J Davis, 'How Do International Institutions Matter? The Domestic Impact of International Rules and Norms' (1996) 40 International Studies Quarterly 451.

[59] Finnemore and Sikkink's theory was indeed developed in the context of international relations. In that sense, the norm is at first one that would emerge at the international, hence inter-State level, and then further diffuse amongst States and then into each State's society.

[60] Finnemore and Sikkink (n 19) 895; Koh's model of norm internalization works similarly; cf H Koh, 'How Is International Human Rights Law Enforced' (1998) 74 Indiana Law Journal 1397, 1399.

[61] Finnemore and Sikkink (n 19) 895.

[62] ibid.

[63] Term also used by Koh: Koh (n 60) 1409f.

[64] Finnemore and Sikkink (n 19) 895.

[65] W Burke-White, 'The Domestic Influence of International Criminal Tribunals: The International Criminal Tribunal for the Former Yugoslavia and the Creation of the State Court of Bosnia & Herzegovina' (2007) 46 Columbia Journal of Transnational Law 279, 306.

[66] Finnemore and Sikkink (n 19) 898.

[67] ibid 899f.

[68] For instance J Turner, 'Transnational Networks and International Criminal Justice' (2006) 105 Michigan Law Review 985; Risse and Sikkink (n 19).

and dense exchanges of information and services'.[69] The 'tipping point' is reached once the norm entrepreneurs have persuaded a critical mass of actors to adopt the norm. A 'critical mass' refers to both a certain quantity and who the convinced actors are (for instance their standing as important role models).[70]

At the second stage ('norm cascade'), a dynamic of imitation governs, as the 'norm leaders' (those who have already adopted the new norm) attempt to socialize other actors to become norm followers.[71] The primary mechanism for promoting norm cascades is thus an active process of socialization intended to induce norm breakers to become norm followers.[72] Here, a combination of pressure for conformity, desire to enhance international legitimation, and the desire of state leaders to enhance their self-esteem facilitate norm cascades.[73] Socialization is thus the dominant mechanism of a norm cascade—the mechanism through which norm leaders persuade others to adhere.[74] What happens at the tipping point is that enough actors and enough *critical* actors endorse the new norm to redefine appropriate behaviour for actors of their identity or position. Consequently, norm followers embrace the norms out of the desire for legitimacy, reputation, and self-esteem:[75] they become part of a group of 'peers' and comply with that group's norms to demonstrate that they have adapted to the social environment that they now belong to.[76]

At the very end, norm internalization occurs where norms acquire a taken-for-granted quality and are no longer a matter of broad public debate.[77] Internalized or cascading norms may eventually become the prevailing standard of appropriateness against which new norms emerge and compete for support.[78] Norms are regarded as internalized in domestic practices, when actors comply with them irrespective of individual beliefs about their validity,[79] norm compliance is 'depersonalised'.[80] They become 'standard operating procedures of domestic institutions',[81] actors follow the norm, because 'it is the normal thing to do'.[82] At the internalization stage, actors' primary motive is simple conformity.[83]

The model proposed by Thomas Risse and Kathryn Sikkink, who ask under what conditions international human rights norms are internalized in domestic practices and what accounts for the variation in the degree to which they are implemented in different states,[84] is somewhat more complex. In proposing the 'spiral model' of norm diffusion,[85] they present a theory of the stages and mechanisms through which international norms can lead to changes in behaviour.[86] Most importantly, to the purely constructivist logics stipulated in the 'norm cascade model', they add three types of causal mechanisms which are necessary

[69] Risse and Sikkink (n 19) 18.
[70] Finnemore and Sikkink (n 19) 901.
[71] ibid 902.
[72] ibid.
[73] ibid 895.
[74] ibid 902.
[75] ibid 902 and 898.
[76] ibid 903.
[77] ibid 895.
[78] ibid.
[79] Risse and Sikkink (n 19) 16.
[80] ibid 17.
[81] ibid.
[82] ibid.
[83] Finnemore and Sikkink (n 19) 898.
[84] Risse and Sikkink (n 19) 1.
[85] ibid 3.
[86] ibid 2.

for the enduring internationalization of norms: firstly, processes of instrumental adaptation and strategic bargaining; secondly, processes of moral consciousness-raising, argumentation, dialogue, and persuasion; and thirdly, processes of institutionalization and habitualization.[87] It is thus clear that the theory presented by Risse and Sikkink also draws on social constructivism,[88] but incorporates rational choice elements.[89] In particular, the spiral model tries to specify the transition points between the logic of instrumental rationality and strategic behaviour, on the one hand, and of argumentative rationality, moral discourse, and the like, on the other.[90]

26.3.2 Mechanisms to Impact the Fairness of the National War Crimes Trial

In the following, these models of norm internalization are applied to the present context, in order to explain the dynamics that influence the ICTY's impact on fairness of national war crimes proceedings and the respect for the rights of the defendant.

As the present context is different than the one for which the 'norm cascade model' and the 'spiral model' were initially developed, they should first be adapted. It is stipulated here that the models can explain how an international criminal tribunal can promote fairness in national criminal proceedings. The question is, how the norm of 'fairness' in criminal proceedings becomes internalized by national actors who have the power to decide over it, namely judges and prosecutors—and to some extent, defence counsel. As explained already, norm influence is a three-stage process; the first stage being the 'norm emergence', the second stage is when the norm 'cascades' into the national system, and the third stage marking the internalization of the norm.[91] In our context, the norm of fairness first emerges at the ICTY, which means that practice is developed to implement the rule that a defendant should get a fair trial. This includes legislative work, namely the development of the Tribunal's Statute, its Rules of Procedure and Evidence (RPE), as well as jurisprudence that interprets the applicable law and fills gaps in the rules. The 'tipping point' between the emergence of the norm and the norm cascade is reached through different dynamics. These dynamics can be based on passive role-modelling, persuasion, or even pressure. Persuasion as well as pressure is exerted by so-called 'norm advocacy networks'. Here, that is most importantly the ICTY and its actors itself, as well as 'like-minded' actors, such as former ICTY staff, non-governmental organizations, or international actors including international organizations (the Organization for Security and Co-operation in Europe (OSCE), the European Union (EU), or the like) or States. Once national actors (national judges, prosecutors, and defence counsel) are convinced, they would follow the Tribunal in the endeavour to provide criminal proceedings that adhere to high standards of fairness. It eventually becomes the prevailing standard of appropriateness. At this stage, conformity with the new standard

[87] ibid 5.
[88] ibid 8.
[89] ibid 12.
[90] cf T Risse and S Ropp, 'International Human Rights Norms and Domestic Change: Conclusions' in T Risse, S Ropp, and K Sikkink (eds), *The Power of Human Rights International Norms and Domestic Change* (Cambridge University Press 1999) 273.
[91] Finnemore and Sikkink (n 19) 895.

becomes the rule. The main interest must thus be to find out which dynamics are most effective in reaching the tipping point as of which the norm of fairness cascades into the national system.

26.3.3 Norm Advocacy: Capacity Building and Demonstration Effects

For international criminal courts, it has been brought forward that their domestic impact depends on two effects: firstly, on its 'demonstration effects',[92] and secondly, on its 'capacity building effects'.[93] In other words, what matters is not only *what* the court does, but also *how* it does it. 'Capacity building effects' refers to a court's ability to foster capacity to deliver justice within the national legal system.[94] 'Demonstration effects' refer to the character and credibility of the proceedings (*how* it does it),[95] and whether they are viewed as 'legitimate'.[96]

Combining the 'norm cascade model' with the theory on 'demonstration and capacity building effects', it is stipulated here that capacity-building activities as well as how much the court serves as a role model are decisive in achieving the tipping point of the norm cascade. In the following, the ICTY's most important capacity building and demonstration effects will briefly be recapped.

[92] Stromseth (n 7) 91; Ryngaert uses the same term: C Ryngaert, 'Transitional Justice and the Rule of Law: Atrocity Trials in Domestic Criminal Courts' (*Leuven Centre for Global Governance Studies*, 2010) 14 <https://ghum.kuleuven.be/ggs/publications/working_papers/2010/40Ryngaert> accessed February 2018.

[93] A similar statement is made by Fletcher and Weinstein when they advocate for linking criminal trials with capacity-building efforts; L E Fletcher and H M Weinstein, 'Violence and Social Repair: Rethinking the Contribution of Justice to Reconciliation' (2002) 24 Human Rights Quarterly 573, 580; P McAuliffe, *Transitional Justice and Rule of Law Reconstruction: A Contentious Relationship* (Routledge 2013) 88. Also, the United Nations Secretary General stresses the need for capacity building in order to strengthen the rule of law; cf Secretary-General, 3. Others have equally stressed the importance of capacity building, not only for criminal courts, but more generally, relating to the ability of local actors to comply with international standards set by international courts. See for instance: L Helfer and A M Slaughter, 'Toward a Theory of Effective Supranational Adjudication' (1997) 107 Yale Law Journal 273, 287; A Chayes and A Chayes, *The New Sovereignty: Compliance with International Regulatory Agreements* (Harvard University Press 1995) 22–28.

[94] Stromseth (n 7) 91; her theory is based on the claim that war crimes courts need a 'domestic impact strategy'. This entails three components: firstly, the court needs to understand the local terrain of the countries under its jurisdiction 'deeply and fully'. Secondly, it is necessary to be aware of the court's demonstration effects and use them effectively. Thirdly and lastly, it needs to be proactive about capacity building—capacity to deliver justice within the national legal system. For the implementation of its capacity-building efforts, the respective court might need to search for synergies with other international or national organizations; cf Stromseth, ibid 90f. Arguably, this goes beyond the classical mandate of war crimes courts that focuses solely on pursuing accountability for past atrocities and thereby deterring future atrocities. The classical model, which assumes that the mere existence of accountability mechanisms leads to a change in social behaviour and thus to the implementation of the rule of law, has been proven ineffective. It would be over simplistic to say that there is a 'linear causal link between the introduction of formal legal mechanisms and changes in social behavior'. Hence, the mere establishment of law enforcement mechanisms (such as tribunals) doesn't lead to a cultural change towards respecting the law; cf V Hussain, 'Sustaining Judicial Rescues: The Role of Outreach and Capacity Building Efforts in War Crimes Tribunals' (2005) 45 Virginia Journal of International Law 547, 555ff. Hussain hence similarly holds that war crimes courts need to focus on other goals than pursuing accountability and deterrence as well, in order to link up their work with the domestic legal system. She points out that capacity building in particular would contribute to promoting a rule of law culture in the country. In noting the establishment of hybrid tribunals, she welcomes a shift towards greater commitment to building a domestic rule of law; cf Hussain, ibid 551f. She explains that something like a proactive 'impact strategy', proposed by Stromseth, is thus important.

[95] J Stromseth, 'Pursuing Accountability for Atrocities After Conflict: What Impact on Building the Rule of Law?' (2006) 38 Georgetown Journal of International Law 251, 263.

[96] Helfer and Slaughter (n 93) 287; T Franck, *The Power of Legitimacy Among Nations* (Oxford University Press 1990) 24.

26.4 Reaching the Tipping Point: Dynamics in Bosnia and Serbia

26.4.1 Building Institutions

In 2002, when the ICTY judges proposed the Completion Strategy, they endorsed the Prosecutor's view that BiH would be the only country that would receive cases from the ICTY.[97] At the same time, the judges considered that the 'judicial systems in Bosnia and Herzegovina exhibit a number of serious shortcomings'[98] in respect of the ability of courts to handle referred cases effectively and in accordance with international standards. In an endeavour to address these shortcomings, the judges recommended a number of reforms to be carried out in BiH, namely to incorporate all international crimes into the country's substantive penal law, to strengthen fair trial rights,[99] to improve detention conditions, to abolish the death penalty, to ensure the independence and impartiality of the judiciary, and to adopt a code of professional conduct for the judiciary.[100] At the same time, they recommended the establishment of a specialized war crimes chamber within the State Court of Bosnia and Herzegovina, suggested that international judges should serve within that State Court, that actors of the national judiciary are trained in international criminal law, and that the national substantive and procedural criminal law be aligned with international standards.[101] Until 2005, trials for war-related crimes were held only in the courts of the entities, the Federation of Bosnia and Herzegovina and the Republika Srpska. Since 2005, war-related crimes have also been tried at the BiH state level. The suggested war crimes chamber began operating within the State Court of BiH on 9 March 2005.[102]

Overall, local actors report an overwhelming involvement of the ICTY in the establishment of these war crimes institutions in Bosnia. For instance, ICTY officials had participated in many working group sessions allowing the Tribunal to perform an important role with regard to the future work of the BiH State Court.[103] It is clear that the Tribunal not only provided expertise in establishing these institutions, but also exerted some pressure.[104] This, most importantly for our context, applies also to the so-called Criminal Defence Section, that was initially part of the SCBiH's registry and is now incorporated in the Bosnian Ministry of Justice, which provides practical and legal assistance to defence counsel.[105] It

[97] ICTY, 'Report on the Judicial Status of the ICTY and the Prospects for Referring Cases to National Courts' (June 2002) 18 <http://www.icty.org/x/file/About/Reports%20and%20Publications/CompletionStrategy/judicial_status_report_june2002_en.pdf> accessed February 2018; in view of its case load and the limited mandate, the ICTY quickly developed a strategy for how to terminate its case work timely. Referring cases was one of the measures.

[98] ibid 2.

[99] In particular that public proceedings must be guaranteed, that the accused must be tried within a reasonable time, that the principle of the presumption of innocence and the equality of arms must be respected and that the victims and witnesses must be duly protected; ibid 25.

[100] ibid 18 and 25.

[101] ibid 25.

[102] Ronen (n 33) 35.

[103] W W Burke-White, 'The Domestic Influence of International Criminal Tribunals: The International Criminal Tribunal for the Former Yugoslavia and the Creation of the State Court of Bosnia & Herzegovina' (2007) 46 Columbia Journal of Transnational Law 279, 336.

[104] ibid 60ff; Interview with a representative of the OHR official, Sarajevo, (Sarajevo, Bosnia and Herzegovina, 8 February 2017).

[105] For more information see the Criminal Defence Section's website <http://www.okobih.ba> accessed February 2018.

also holds a list of defence counsel who are qualified to defend war crimes cases, and provides them with regular mandatory trainings.[106]

Between 1991 and 2003, only a limited number of war crimes trials took place in Serbia. Serious concerns as to the proper conduct and fairness of these trials has been raised.[107] This has considerably changed with the establishment of specialized organs within the judicial system in 2003.[108] With the Law on War Crimes[109] specialized institutions within the Police, Prosecution, and Courts were established, with exclusive jurisdiction to investigate, prosecute, and adjudicate war crimes cases. These institutions include the War Crimes Prosecutor's Office, the War Crimes Department within the Belgrade High Court, and the War Crimes Investigation Service.[110] The advantage of specialized institutions is mostly that they permit to concentrate resources and expertise.[111] Especially in the field of adjudication of international crimes, which are complex to handle, both for their underlying substantive law and also in terms of procedure, this can be a decisive factor when it comes to fairness. War crimes trials pose a specific set of challenges, management of which is easier and more professional within specialized institutions. High standards of proof concerning the chapeau elements of crimes and certain modes of liability, coupled with the—at times—large amount of evidence, mostly consisting of witness statements, which is, at the same time, the least reliable type of evidence, are a significant challenge for judges. They must manage the trial in a way that these challenges don't become detrimental to the defendant's rights to an expeditious trial or presumption of innocence, as well as to the principle of equality of arms.

Contrary to the situation in Bosnia, in Croatia and Serbia the establishment of specialized institutions were not instigated or brought about directly by the ICTY, but rather by regime changes and external coercion.[112] It has been suggested that the prospect of receiving cases from the ICTY under the Rule 11*bis* procedure gave further support to the idea of a specialized war crimes system. Serbia was of course conscious of such a possibility in 2003–2004, but such prospects did not exist in 2002, when the drafting of the law on these specialized organs began, which points to the fact that the ICTY was not the primary motivation for the creation of the war crimes system.[113] Rather, this seemed to have been an independent initiative of the Zoran Đinđić government as early as 2002. However, prominent ICTY staff members, including President Cassese and Prosecutor Goldstone, participated in the expert group that assisted the Serbian government (at the instigation of the International Bar Association and the OSCE) in the drafting of the Law on War Crimes. Some of the group's

[106] Interview with OKO officials, Sarajevo (Sarajevo, Bosnia and Herzegovina, 8 February 2017).

[107] OSCE, 'War Crimes Proceedings in Serbia (2003–2014) An analysis of the OSCE Mission to Serbia's monitoring results' (Belgrade 2015) 21.

[108] Michaeli (n 21) 59.

[109] The Law on Organization and Competences of Government Authorities in War Crimes Proceedings, Official Gazette of the Republic of Serbia no 67/2003, and subsequent amendments.

[110] For more information on the war crimes prosecution office, see <http://www.tuzilastvorz.org.rs/sr/> accessed February 2018, and on the war crimes department, see <https://www.bg.vi.sud.rs/tekst/323/sudska-odeljenja.php/> accessed 2 February 2020.

[111] On advantages of specialized institutions and the Serbian experience, see M Majić and D Ignatović, 'Deset smerica zasnovanih na iskustvu Srbije vezanom za pitanja ratnih zločina' (2012) FICHL Policy Brief Series.

[112] Michaeli (n 21) 59; coercion was exerted most notably through the European Union with its conditionality policy. I have elaborated on the EU's conditionality policy elsewhere: K H Brodersen, 'The ICTY's Conditionality Dilemma' (2014) 22 European Journal of Crime, Criminal Law and Criminal Justice 219.

[113] Michaeli (n 21) 67.

recommendations found their way into it—for instance to better utilize the limited resources of the Serbian judiciary and establish specialized war crimes institutions.[114]

It has also been explained that the mindset of ICTY judges, prosecutors, and administrators was not geared towards assisting Serbia, especially when the latter was not properly cooperating with the Tribunal. The same applied to the mindset of the Serbian government. The fact that one (albeit not the most prominent) reason for the enactment of the Law on War Crimes was the hope of the Serbian government to receive cases from The Hague, or at the very least keep some cases at the national level, was not sufficient to prompt Serbia to involve the Tribunal in creating the system that would process the very same cases.[115]

26.4.2 Case Referrals, Monitoring, and Tailor-made Training

Although the idea of terminating the Tribunal's mandate was first contemplated in the early 2000s,[116] it took some time until the idea materialized into a real plan. The state of the judicial systems in the former Yugoslavia presented the greatest obstacle for the Completion Strategy.[117] As late as May 2004, ICTY President Theodor Meron was of the opinion that the Tribunal cannot 'be sure that international human rights and fair trial standards are fully satisfied'[118] in the courts of the States of the former Yugoslavia. Nevertheless, the initiative eventually received endorsement by the UN Security Council in August 2003 and the principal elements of the Completion Strategy were outlined in Resolution 1503 and subsequent resolutions. One of these elements was the transfer of cases to domestic courts,[119] which had been prepared through amendments of Rule 11*bis* of the ICTY's RPE.[120] Provided that a number of criteria were met, the Tribunal could now, upon decision of the Referral Bench, refer a case to a national judicial system. Most notably, the referral was conditioned on a determination that the accused will receive a fair trial and that the death penalty will not be imposed.[121] In addition, the Tribunal has provided professional advice on reforming relevant legislation, especially in areas such as command responsibility and witness protection, so that these cases could be properly adjudicated.[122] From the beginning, the Completion Strategy was directly related to the Tribunal's desire to strengthen the domestic justice systems in the former Yugoslavia.[123] It was believed that transferring cases would work as a 'catalyst for the strengthening of competent national judicial systems'.[124] In total, the

[114] ibid 86.
[115] ibid 87.
[116] ibid 50.
[117] ibid.
[118] T Meron, 'Assessments and report of Judge Theodor Meron, President of the International Criminal Tribunal for the Former Yugoslavia, provided to the Security Council pursuant to paragraph 6 of Security Council resolution 1534 (2004)', annexed to the 'Letter dated 21 May 2004 from the President of the International Tribunal for the Prosecution of Persons Responsible for Serious Violations of International Humanitarian Law Committed in the Territory of the Former Yugoslavia since 1991, addressed to the President of the Security Council' (24 May 2004) 8.
[119] United Nations Security Council Resolution 1534 (2004) para 4.
[120] For a chronology of amendments of Rule 11*bis*, see M Bohlander, 'Referring an Indictment from the ICTY and ICTR to Another Court—Rule 11bis and the Consequences for the Law of Extradition' (2006) 55 International and Comparative Law Quarterly 219.
[121] Rule 11*bis* (B) ICTY RPE.
[122] ICTY, 'Completion Strategy' <http://www.icty.org/en/sid/10016> accessed February 2018.
[123] ibid; UNSC Res 1503 (28 August 2003) UN Doc S/RES/1503 paras 3 and 5; see also Barria and Roper (n 12) 318.
[124] ICTY, 'Completion Strategy' (n 122).

ICTY has transferred eight cases involving thirteen accused to the countries of the former Yugoslavia:[125] ten to Bosnia and Herzegovina, two to Croatia, and one to Serbia.

An evaluation of whether the human rights of the defendant are respected if a case is handed over to the national level has occupied a prominent place in all referral cases. Hereby, different aspects are emphasized, depending on the specific characteristics of the case. Most importantly, the Referral Bench examined whether the accused would face the death penalty and whether s/he would receive a fair trial—but also whether national law provides for decent detention conditions. In its assessment, the Referral Bench strictly limited itself to what is required by the Statute and its Rules of Procedure and Evidence. It has held that assessing the available legislation is 'all [the Referral Bench is] required to do pursuant to Rule 11*bis*'.[126] For the Referral Bench, it sufficed to assure itself that the domestic law, in place in a certain State, is in line with the highest human rights standards, namely Article 14 of the International Covenant on Civil and Political Rights, Article 21 ICTY Statute and Article 6 of the European Convention on Human Rights. Further: '[i]t is not for the Referral Bench to determine *how* these provisions will be applied'.[127] It hence did not engage in an evaluation of the national *practice* in respecting human rights. Instead, it often simply referred to the fact that the Prosecution is required to monitor the proceedings at the national level and to provide regular reports.[128] Thereby, the Bench deferred the 'practice-check' to a later point in time and arguably outsourced the responsibility for safeguarding human rights. The monitoring practice has therefore been called a 'safety net',[129] which allowed the Bench to dismiss some of the defence's arguments, give the benefit of the doubt to the national authorities receiving the case, and therefore 'side in favour of'[130] them.[131] This practice was maintained also in later referral decisions, although monitoring reports, prepared by the OSCE on behalf of the Office of the Prosecutor, were already available when they were rendered.[132] This practice has been heavily criticized, as it appears that the conditions set out in Rule 11*bis* (B) do not in fact guarantee fair trials.[133]

Although Serbia strived for receiving cases from the ICTY,[134] only one case was referred to Serbia under Rule 11*bis*.[135] While the Bench declared it was satisfied that the

125 ICTY, 'Transfer of Cases' <http://www.icty.org/en/cases/transfer-cases> accessed February 2018.

126 *Prosecutor v Mitar Rašević and Savo Todović* (Decision on Savo Todović's Appeal Against Decisions on Referral under Rule 11*bis*) ICTY-IT-97-25/1-PT (4 September 2006) para 56.

127 *Prosecutor v Mitar Rašević and Savo Todović* (Decision on Referral of Case under Rule 11*bis* with Confidential Annexes I and II) ICTY-IT-97-25/1-PT (8 July 2005) para 60, emphasis added.

128 On the basis of Rule 11*bis* (D) (iv): *Prosecutor v Gojko Janković* (Decision on Rule 11*bis* referral) ICTY-IT-96-23/2-PT (15 November 2005) para 55; *Prosecutor v Stanković* (Decision on Rule 11*bis* Referral) ICTY-IT-96-23/2-PT (1 September 2005) para 52; *Rašević and Savo Todović* (n 127) para 83.

129 A Canter, '"For these Reasons, the Chamber: Denies the Prosecutor's Request for Referral": The False Hope of Rule 11 *bis*' (2008) 32 Fordham International Law Journal 1614, 1638.

130 ibid.

131 ibid; this was argued in relation to referrals by the ICTR to Rwanda, but is equally applicable with regard to the ICTY as the same monitoring practice was developed there.

132 For instance in *Rašević and Todović* (n 127) para 112ff; *Lukić and Lukić* even a whole judgment of the State Court of BiH on a previously referred case (*Janković*) was already available that could have given more precise insight on how the Bosnian court handles cases. However, the Referral Bench did not consider neither the OSCE reports nor the judgment for its assessment of referral: *Prosecutor v Milan Lukić and Sredoje Lukić* (Decision on referral of case pursuant to rule 11 bis with confidential annex a and annex b) ICTY-IT-98-32/1-PT (5 April 2007) para 57.

133 See for instance J Dieckmann and C Kerll, 'UN Ad Hoc Tribunals Under Time Pressure: Completion Strategy and Referral Practice of the ICTY and ICTR from the Perspective of the Defence' (2008) 8 International Criminal Law Review 87; and S Williams, 'ICTY Referrals to National Jurisdictions: A Fair Trial or a Fair Price?' (2006) 17 Criminal Law Forum 177.

134 Michaeli (n 21) 67.

135 ICTY, 'Vladimir Kovacevic Declared Unfit to Stand Trial' (press release, 12 April 2006) <http://www.icty.org/en/press/vladimir-kovacevic-declared-unfit-stand-trial> accessed February 2018.

Serbian legal system met the fair trial requirement, the fact that the *Kovačević* case was the only one referred to Serbia was not a source of pride considering the opposite conclusion reached by the Bench one year prior: in the *Mrkšić* case (the *Vukovar Three* case), Serbia's bid for referral was rejected (just as Croatia's) by the Referral Bench on the grounds of fair trial concerns.[136] Serbia was also denied referral of the *Mejakić* case in April 2006.[137]

Overall, the process of Rule 11*bis* case referrals is viewed as very positive amongst actors in The Hague.[138] They especially emphasize the threat of taking back the case if it is not dealt with properly—and the OSCE monitoring would provide proof for that—would have made national actors to be particularly cautious in handling these cases. As such, they were a very useful learning terrain. Knowledge and expertise was gained that could later be used also in other cases. In Bosnia, however, the enthusiasm over the impact of Rule 11*bis* cases is split. While some agree that the referred cases had the catalyst effect the ICTY was hoping for,[139] others maintain that too few cases were referred, and the threat to revoke the referral was too unrealistic to actually make a difference.[140] More decisive were in fact two other factors: firstly, the presence of foreign judges and prosecutors during the first years of the Bosnian specialized institutions, some of whom had ICTY experience. The international presence within the SCBiH and the BiH State Prosecution included judges and prosecutors, defence counsel, experts in witness protection and support, as well as other officials engaged in providing substantive and administrative support. The goal has been to build on the existing expertise of international professionals within the justice sector in order to ensure a sustainable domestic capacity to address war crimes cases after international involvement has ceased. One of the positive attributes of involving international judges and prosecutors in the work of the domestic judiciary has been its contribution to deflecting the suspicion and mistrust of the domestic public towards the judiciary, which was seen as unprofessional, corrupt, and biased against members of the 'other' side. Foreign prosecutors and judges have also been reported to be more familiar with international crimes and jurisprudence and with applying international standards of due process.[141] At the same time, the policy to incorporate internationals within the national institutions was partly motivated by the need for expertise to handle the cases referred to the SCBiH under Rule 11*bis*.[142] Many of my interlocutors emphasized the great role the on-the-job-training and mentoring between foreigners and locals has played.[143] The second decisive factor was tailor-made

[136] *Prosecutor v Mile Mrkšić, Miroslav Radić, Veselin Šljivančanin* (Decision on Prosecutor's Motion to Withdraw Motion and Request for Referral of Indictment Under Rule 11*bis*) ICTY-IT-95-13/1-PT (30 June 2005).

[137] Albeit on grounds that BiH possessed a stronger nexus with the case; cf *Prosecutor v Mejakić* et al (Decision on Joint Defence Appeal against Decision on Referral under Rule 11*bis*) ICTY-IT-02-65 (7 April 2006).

[138] Interview with a representative of the ICTY Office of the Prosecutor (The Hague, The Netherlands, 25 November 2016); interview with ICTY judge (The Hague, The Netherlands, 2 December 2016).

[139] Interview with former international prosecutor in the Bosnian State Prosecution (The Hague, The Netherlands, 7 December 2016); interview with prosecutor of the Bosnian state prosecutor's office (Sarajevo, Bosnia and Herzegovina, 9 February 2017); interview with SCBiH judge (Sarajevo, Bosnia and Herzegovina, 1 February 2017).

[140] Interview with Bosnian defence counsel (Sarajevo, Bosnia and Herzegovina, 31 January 2017); interview with representative of an international organization (Sarajevo, Bosnia and Herzegovina, 2 February 2017).

[141] Ronen (n 33) 68.

[142] ibid 67.

[143] Interview with prosecutor of the Bosnian state prosecutor's office (Sarajevo, Bosnia and Herzegovina, 9 February 2017); interview with a SCBiH judge (Sarajevo, Bosnia and Herzegovina, 1 February 2017); interviews with officials of international organizations (Sarajevo, Bosnia and Herzegovina, 2 and 3 February 2017); interview

training provided, organized or financed by the OSCE, that directly addressed the needs of the local judiciary, observed in the OSCE's trial monitoring which was initially established in the realm of Rule 11*bis* referrals.[144] However, what is for sure is that the international community, the ICTY included, was watching how Bosnia dealt with the Rule 11*bis* referrals. People who were involved at the time told me that everyone was really doing their best to 'do it right'.[145]

Contrary to the mixed picture in Bosnia and Herzegovina, that one case that was referred to Serbia, as well as the cases in which referral was eventually refused, the practice did not seem to play any role whatsoever for the development of the Serbian judiciary.

26.4.3 Contact Between ICTY and Domestic Actors

In 1999, the Tribunal's Outreach Programme was initiated by ICTY President Gabrielle Kirk McDonald. Since then, ICTY materials began to be regularly translated into BCS,[146] a website in BCS was launched and live broadcasting of the proceedings on the internet commenced. Since 2000, offices have been opened in Belgrade, Priština, Sarajevo, and Zagreb, charged with communicating with the media, the legal community, governmental and non-governmental organizations, victims' associations and diplomatic representatives.[147]

Yet, interaction between ICTY judges and their local counterparts was very difficult in the beginning, especially with Serbia. Apart from the political conditions which made such interaction difficult, the mutual mistrust between the judiciaries and the prevailing opinion amongst ICTY judges that this was not part of the mandate of the Tribunal contributed to the professional disconnect between the two systems.[148] Once the ICTY began to realize the necessity of identifying local needs of the Serbian judicial system and to cultivate a positive working relationship with Serbian institutions entrusted with war crimes prosecutions, it has managed to export expertise—as well as evidence—thereby enhancing and complementing the limited Serbian capacity to process war crimes.[149]

Since the beginning of the implementation of the Completion Strategy, the ICTY's Outreach Programme extended the scope of its activities designed to introduce legal professionals from the region to the work of the ICTY.[150] ICTY staff attended conferences, round tables, and meetings with members of the legal community, the media, ministries, university and high-school students, NGOs, and so on. In 2008, the Tribunal began developing a programme on its legacy which put special emphasis on enhancing the capacity

with a Bosnian defence counsel (Sarajevo, Bosnia and Herzegovina, 6 February 2017); for a more critical account, see J Korner, 'Processing of War Crimes at the State Level of Bosnia and Herzegovina' (OSCE, 2016).

144 Interview with OSCE officials (Sarajevo, Bosnia and Herzegovina, 2 February 2017); interview with SCBiH judge (Sarajevo, Bosnia and Herzegovina, 2 February 2017).

145 Interview with a former staff member of the Bosnian State Prosecution, 2 February 2017; interview with a former international prosecutor at the Bosnian State Prosecution (The Hague, The Netherlands, 7 December 2017).

146 This is the abbreviation (meaning Bosnian/Croatian/Serbian) commonly used at the ICTY to refer to the language spoken in BiH, Croatia and Serbia, also known as Serbo-Croatian.

147 At the time of writing, only the offices in Belgrade and Sarajevo were still operating.

148 Michaeli (n 21) 49f.

149 ibid 5.

150 For an overview on the Outreach Programme, see ICTY, 'Outreach Programme' <http://www.icty.org/en/outreach/outreach-programme> accessed February 2015.

of domestic systems in the region. Consequently, the Tribunal intensified the interaction between itself and the local judiciaries, studied their needs and responded to them directly. Efforts at transferring knowledge and expertise shifted from a more academic paradigm to direct interactions between ICTY staff and its counterparts in the region.[151]

Upon close assessment, however, the contact between the ICTY and the Bosnian judiciary was much more regular and intensive than with actors from the Serbian judiciary, especially within the realm of the War Crimes Justice Project.[152] But more importantly, everyday contact between the Tribunal—which mostly relates to sharing evidence and witness protection—and the local judiciaries was much more intense with Bosnia than with Serbia.[153] This was largely due to the fact that most of the cases that were dealt with at the ICTY related to crimes committed in Bosnia and hence, the crime base was often the same at ICTY trials and trials conducted at the SCBiH.[154] The same evidence can be used, and if the same witnesses testify, witness protection has to be coordinated between the two courts. All in all, virtually all interviewees in Bosnia underlined the great presence the ICTY had in Bosnia and the close contacts between local and ICTY actors.

In Serbia, where contact was much more limited (albeit respectful and professional),[155] the ICTY and its proceedings play almost no role at all in the work and minds of the local judicial actors. Whereas in Bosnia, proceedings seem to be almost intertwined, trials in Serbia seem to have nothing to do with the ICTY. As one prosecutor put it: 'The ICTY was supposed to prosecute the high-level accused. And we are now conducting trials against the mid- and low-level accused. Every institution does its job. We are independent.'[156]

26.4.4 Demonstration Effects

The idea of demonstration effects is linked to the notion that justice must also *be seen to be done*: a war crimes court is a 'role model'[157] for national justice systems;[158] it sets an

[151] Michaeli (n 21) 57; an overview on the activities can be found under ICTY, 'Overview of Capacity Building Activities' <http://www.icty.org/en/outreach/capacity-building/overview-activities> accessed February 2018.

[152] See, amongst others, the project's calendar of activities under OSCE, 'War Crimes Justice Project—Calender of activities'(2011) <http://www.icty.org/x/file/Outreach/capacity_building/wcjp_activity_calendar.pdf> accessed February 2018.

[153] This has been pointed out in almost all my interviews, most importantly with a representative of the ICTY Office of the Prosecutor (The Hague, The Netherlands, 25 November 2016).

[154] Also under the so-called Rules of the Road programme, under which the ICTY OTP would review indictments issued by national authorities before the suspect would be arrested, attention seemed to have been limited to Bosnia and Herzegovina. Under this programme, the prosecutors in The Hague reviewed 1,419 files involving 4,985 suspects—approval to proceed was granted for 848 persons; see ICTY 'Working with the Region' <http://www.icty.org/en/about/office-of-the-prosecutor/working-with-the-region> accessed February 2018.

[155] Michaeli (n 21) 55f. This has been confirmed in interviews with a representative of the ICTY OTP (The Hague, The Netherlands, 25 November 2016); and national prosecutors (Belgrade, Serbia, 19 January 2017 and Sarajevo, Bosnia and Herzegovina, 9 February 2017).

[156] Interview with Serbian prosecutor (Belgrade, Serbia, 19 January 2017).

[157] Several authors use this term without explicitly referring to demonstration effects (but the idea is still the same). Amongst others: Y Shany, 'How Can International Criminal Courts Have a Greater Impact on National Criminal Proceedings: Lessons from the First Two Decades of International Criminal Justice in Operation' (2013) 46 Israel Law Review 431, 440; or J Snyder and L Vinjamuri, 'Trials and Errors: Principle and Pragmatism in Strategies of International Justice' (2003) 28 International Security 5, 15. This view has also been expressed by many interviewees. In one interview, the concept of demonstration effects has been paraphrased as 'to just do it right'; interview with a former ICTY judge (Berlin, Germany, 16 December 2017).

[158] Stromseth however warns that demonstration effects can also be negative, depending on the performance of the court; cf Stromseth (n 7) 92.

example of a suitable response to international crimes; it *demonstrates* how justice can be done. Applied to the context of the ICTY's impact on Bosnia and Serbia, the hope is that the Tribunal is a role model for national courts and it develops standards that national judges, prosecutors, and defence counsel deem worth striving for. In that sense, the impact of an international criminal court through demonstration effects is indirect: without being in any way bound to follow them, the domestic justice system draws inspiration from the court's practices.[159]

How do international crimes courts become a role model? Legal and social psychologists as well as political and social scientists have argued that this is linked to the perceived legitimacy of the war crimes court.[160] Target audiences must perceive transitional justice mechanisms as legitimate before they will internalize the norms these mechanisms represent.[161] The theoretical basis for this emphasis on perceived legitimacy is provided by numerous studies by legal psychologists and sociologists which found that legitimacy is important to political and legal institutions because individuals are more likely to voluntarily adopt the norms of such institutions to regulate their own conduct when the institutions are perceived as legitimate.[162] Such legitimacy is achieved when the relevant public regards the institution as justified, appropriate, or otherwise deserving support, for reasons beyond fear of sanctions or mere hope for personal reward.[163] Ramji-Nogales posits that in order to increase institutional legitimacy, three components matter: the source of the institution, the procedure it applies,[164] and the substance of the rules the court uses.[165] Others add that the perceived legitimacy also depends on the court's institutional structure.[166] Generally

[159] E Kristjánsdóttir, A Nollkaemper, and C Ryngaert, 'Importing International Law in Post-Conflict States: The Role of Domestic Courts' (2011) Amsterdam Law School Legal Studies Research Paper 19; and E Kristjánsdóttir, A Nollkaemper, and C Ryngaert, 'Concluding Observations' in E Kristjánsdóttir, A Nollkaemper, and C Ryngaert (eds), *International Law in Domestic Courts: Rule of Law Reform in Post-Conflict States* (Intersentia 2012) 321 (stating that this inspiration might trigger legal reform).

[160] Max Weber made a distinction between sociological and legal legitimacy, the latter assuming that what is lawful is legitimate. Sociological legitimacy is connected to ethically normative beliefs which are beliefs to which people attribute a certain type of value and which, by virtue of these beliefs, they treat as a valid norm governing their action; M Weber, *Economy and Society* (University of California Press 1978) 36.

[161] Arguing in that direction, amongst others: J Ramji-Nogales, 'Designing Bespoke Transitional Justice: A Pluralist Process Approach' (2010) 32 Michigan Journal of International Law 1, 3f; and L Dickinson, 'The Promise of Hybrid Courts' (2003) 97 American Journal of International Law 295, 301ff; W Burke-White, 'Regionalization of International Criminal Law Enforcement: A Preliminary Exploration' (2003) 38 Texas International Law Journal 729, 736f; E Higonnet, 'Restructuring Hybrid Courts: Local Empowerment and National Criminal Justice Reform' (2006) 23 Arizona Journal of International and Comparative Law 347, 359ff; Stromseth (n 95) 251, 260, 268f, 281; S Nouwen, 'Hybrid Courts: The Hybrid Category of a New Type of International Criminal Courts' (2006) 2 Utrecht Law Review 180, 191; or J Cockayne, 'The Fraying Shoestring: Rethinking Hybrid War Crimes Tribunals' (2004) 28 Fordham International Law Journal 616, 638. Also many interviewees support this view. They say that through the authority and respect war crimes courts gain, they become a role model that is worth copying.

[162] See T Tyler, 'Psychological Perspectives on Legitimacy and Legitimation' (2006) 57 Annual Review of Psychology 375, 376ff (providing an overview of psychological research relating to legitimacy); similar claim: Shany (n 157) 450.

[163] R Fallon Jr, 'Legitimacy and the Constitution' (2005) 118 Harvard Law Review 1787, 1795.

[164] This element stems from procedural justice theories, repeatedly replicated (for an overview, see Jason Colquitt et al 'Justice at the Millennium: A Meta-analytic Review of 25 Years of Organizational Justice Research' (2001) 86 Journal of Applied Psychology 425, 435). These theories are based on the assumption that authorities and institutions are viewed as more legitimate and, therefore their decisions and rules are more willingly accepted, when they exercise their authority through procedures that people experience as fair ('fair process effect', see S Ford, 'A Social Psychology Model of the Perceived Legitimacy of International Criminal Courts: Implications for the Success of Transitional Justice Mechanisms' (2012) 45 Vanderbilt Journal of Transnational Law 405, 456); cf Tyler (n 162) 379.

[165] Ramji-Nogales (n 161) 4; and I Hurd, 'Legitimacy and Authority in International Politics' (1999) 53 International Organization 379, 381.

[166] Dickinson (n 161) 303; see generally Ramji-Nogales (n 161) concerning the legal bases, applicable procedure and substantive law of courts.

speaking, many authors seem to advocate for solutions in which these court characteristics are as close as possible to what is known and appreciated in their target societies. For instance, many claim that physical proximity of the court to its target society is advantageous for its perceived legitimacy,[167] or that similar procedures as within the relevant domestic legal systems should be applied and that local personnel should get involved.[168]

At first sight, this might seem intuitive: if the ICTY had been established with the involvement of local communities, if it had been geographically closer to the region, and if it had applied procedure that is known to national actors and generally perceived as just, it would have enjoyed great legitimacy amongst local actors. However, this assumption cannot account for the different views among Bosniaks and Serbs on the ICTY: the ICTY was as far away (both geographically and procedurally) from Bosnia and Herzegovina as from Serbia. Trials at the ICTY were conducted according to the same procedural rules, and yet, Bosniaks largely deem the ICTY as fair and Serbs as unfair.[169] Likewise, these hypotheses do not seem quite applicable to the professional context: judges, prosecutors, and even defence counsel in Serbia do not disrespect the ICTY; quite to the contrary. However, their respect does not go as far as that it would translate into being inspired by the ICTY jurisprudence and practice, or would trigger them to look for solutions within ICTY jurisprudence in cases of unresolved problems in the national law or procedure. In Bosnia and Herzegovina, this perceived legitimacy is strong enough for national actors to be willing to learn from the Tribunal. The explanation people in Bosnia gave is as trivial as important: the presence of the ICTY in the judges, prosecutors', and defence counsels' everyday life, the permanent contact, the close exchange on substantive and procedural issues between The Hague and Sarajevo enhanced perceived legitimacy. In the end, it seems to be more a matter of quantity (of contact) than of quality (of the proceedings at the ICTY) as to why the ICTY was persuasive in the eyes of local actors. One Bosnian prosecutor told me, when asked about the fairness of the Bosnian war crimes trials, that 'we learnt all of this from The Hague'.[170]

26.5 Conclusion: Explain the Difference in Impact in Bosnia and Serbia

The present contribution has demonstrated that an international criminal tribunal's demonstration and capacity-building effects shape its impact on the national criminal justice system. Much has been written on the ICTY's institution and capacity-building efforts as well as on its perception amongst local audiences. Here, these topics were presented in a different context and it has been shown that both capacity-building and demonstration effects created the climate, or even the momentum, for national judges to resort to ICTY practice in order to enhance fairness of war crimes proceedings. As such, the ICTY was clearly a role model for national judges, prosecutors, and even defence counsel, not only for interpreting substantive international criminal law, but also for procedural issues.

[167] Dickinson (n 161) 303; Higonnet (n 161) 361ff; Stromseth (n 95) 260ff; Shany (n 157) 450.
[168] cf Dickinson (n 161) 303; Shany (n 157) 450.
[169] This remark has been made in Ford (n 164) 456ff.
[170] Interview with prosecutor of the Bosnian state prosecutor's office (Sarajevo, Bosnia and Herzegovina, 8 February 2017).

However, this largely only applies to Bosnia and Herzegovina, not to Serbia. To come back to the 'norm cascade model', it must first be noted that—despite all the legitimate criticism—the ICTY is today largely praised for its fair proceedings and its high standards. The norm of 'fairness' has thus 'emerged' at the international level. The dynamics at play that determined whether the tipping point at which 'fairness' would be propagated to the national level are quite different in Bosnia and Serbia. To begin with, in Serbia, there were no real 'advocacy networks'. Apart from NGOs that were—and continue—to press for fair war crimes trials, and the OSCE, there are no 'like-minded' actors—and not even the ICTY is very present in Serbia. National war crimes proceedings operate thus in a largely detached manner from the ICTY.[171] The norm cascade is thus not even triggered.

In contrast, in Bosnia, very intense institution building, capacity building, and outreach efforts have created much occasion for ICTY and local actors to meet, to collaborate, and to exchange views on a formal and also on an informal basis.[172] This is socialization at its best. In addition, thanks to the ICTY's authority amongst the international community and its power to exert some pressure on Bosnia, coupled with a certain leverage on the national judiciary through the Rule 11*bis* procedure and monitoring of war crimes trials, more coercive dynamics supported the socialization and persuasion efforts. In addition, the on-the-job-training could provide for the opportunity to immediately implement innovative practices that were inspired by ICTY practices. The continuous presence and collaboration significantly improved the image national actors had of the ICTY. In the end, the positive perception of the Tribunal was certainly the trigger for their readiness to resort to ICTY practice when useful or necessary. This was certainly conducive to the overall fairness of Bosnian war crimes proceedings. In a way, the ICTY has thus contributed to the fairness of criminal proceedings in Bosnia and Herzegovina.

[171] This is not to say that this is good or bad. It is just an observation that is relevant when one wants to assess the ICTY's impact. Furthermore, this does not mean that Serbian war crimes proceedings are unfair. It is quite possible that national actors derive their inspiration and training from elsewhere.

[172] I have presented but a few here. A full picture on all ICTY–Bosnian contacts would have been beyond the scope of this contribution.

PART VIII

SOCIETAL IMPACT, RECEPTION, AND GAPS

27

The Peace versus Justice Debate Revisited

The ICTY's Impact on the Bosnian Peace Process

*Jacqueline R. McAllister**, **

'The United States wanted to use the weapons of the ICTY . . . '[1]

—M. Cherif Bassiouni

27.1 Introduction

The United Nations Security Council (UNSC) established the International Criminal Tribunal for the former Yugoslavia (ICTY) on 25 May 1993. The ICTY's Statute expressed the hope that by prosecuting 'serious violations of international humanitarian law committed in the territory of the former Yugoslavia', the Tribunal might 'contribute to the restoration and maintenance of peace'.[2] The ICTY's early proponents echoed this Statute, heralding the new war crimes tribunal as a 'historic' opportunity to achieve peace through the advancement of justice.[3] As Eric Stover—then Executive Director for Physicians for Human Rights—explained, 'to have a lasting peace in the former Yugoslavia, you're going to have to have justice'.[4] Some officials, however, expressed concerns that the ICTY might 'jeopardize' tenuous peace efforts.[5] For instance, once the ICTY was operational, UN Secretary-General Boutros Boutros-Ghali confided to Chief Prosecutor Goldstone that he would have preferred to hold off on indicting top leaders until after hostilities had ended.[6] Numerous officials from London, Paris, and the US were also concerned that the pursuit of war criminals would place a political solution in danger.[7]

* Assistant Professor of Political Science, Kenyon College, email: mcallisterj@kenyon.edu.
** I thank Karen Alter, Kirstin Hasler Brathwaite, Albert Chao, James Meernik, Alyssa Prorok, William Reno, Hendrik Spruyt, colleagues at Kenyon College and PluriCourts, as well as participants in the Journeys in World Politics Workshop for valuable suggestions and feedback. All remaining errors are my own. This work was partly supported by the Research Council of Norway through its Centres of Excellence funding scheme, project number 223274, as well as a National Science Foundation Doctoral Dissertation Research grant, project number 1160364.

1 Pierre Hazan, interview with author (19 July 2013).
2 UN Security Council Res 827 (25 May 1993) UN Doc S/RES/827.
3 UNSC Res 808 (22 February 1993) UN Doc S/RES/808.
4 J S Landay, 'Opening the Docket: Trials of a War Tribunal' *Christian Science Monitor* (16 November 1994) <https://www.csmonitor.com/1994/1116/16072.html> accessed 10 February 2020.
5 UN Official, interview with author (19 July 2013). For more details on tensions between the ICTY and international officials within BiH, see L Nettelfield, *Courting Democracy in Bosnia and Herzegovina: The Hague Tribunal's Impact in a Postwar State* (Cambridge University Press 2010).
6 R Goldstone, *For Humanity: Reflections of a War Crimes Investigator* (Yale University Press 2000) 218.
7 P Hazan, *Justice in a Time of War: the True Story Behind the International Criminal Tribunal for the Former Yugoslavia* (1st edn, Texas A & M University Press 2004) 24; John Shattuck, interview with author (30 July 2015); J Shattuck, *Freedom on Fire: Human Rights Wars and America's Response* (Harvard University Press 2003) 124.

Jacqueline R. McAllister, *The Peace versus Justice Debate Revisited* In: *Legacies of the International Criminal Tribunal for the Former Yugoslavia*. Edited by: Carsten Stahn, Carmel Agius, Serge Brammertz, Colleen Rohan, Oxford University Press (2020). © The Several Contributors DOI: 10.1093/oso/9780198862956.003.0028

Such views touch directly on the peace versus justice debate, which continues to animate scholarly and policy discussions almost twenty-five years after the ICTY's establishment. Essentially, those who rally the 'justice' perspective argue that there can be no peace without justice.[8] 'Peace' proponents, on the other hand, maintain that the pursuit of justice, particularly amidst active conflicts, threatens peace.[9] Scholars have only just begun to systematically test both sets of claims.[10] Thus far, their studies have primarily focused on how wartime International Criminal Tribunals (ICTs)—particularly the International Criminal Court (ICC)—might undermine or facilitate peace efforts.

This chapter engages in the ongoing debate over the impact of prosecutions on peace processes. It specifically focuses on how the ICTY—as the first wartime ICT—affected peace negotiations during the Bosnian War. Scholars and policy-makers have suggested that the ICTY could well have facilitated peace efforts in Bosnia.[11] Thus, it represents an ideal case for beginning to think through how ICTs might facilitate, versus undermine, negotiations to end civil conflicts.[12] Moreover, existing studies on the ICTY tend to focus on how it affected peace after fighting had stopped.[13] Thus, there is a need for further research

[8] See P Akhavan, 'Justice in the Hague, Peace in the Former Yugoslavia? A Commentary on the United Nations War Crimes Tribunal' (1998) 20 Human Rights Quarterly 737; M C Bassiouni, 'Justice and Peace: The Importance of Choosing Accountability Over Realpolitik' (2003) 35 Case Western Reserve Journal of International Law 191; H Durham and T L H McCormack, *The Changing Face of Conflict and the Efficacy of International Humanitarian Law* (M. Nijhoff Publishers 1999); M S Ellis, 'Combating Impunity and Enforcing Accountability as a Way to Promote Peace and Stability: the Role of International War Crimes Tribunals' (2006) 2 Journal of National Security Law and Policy 111; D McGoldrick, 'The Legal and Political Significance of the Permanent International Criminal Court' in D McGoldrick, P Rowe, and E Donnelly (eds), *The Permanent International Criminal Court* (Hart Publishing 2004); T Meron, 'The Case for War Crimes Trials in Yugoslavia' (1993) 72 Foreign Affairs 122; D Orentlicher, 'Settling Accounts: the Duty to Prosecute Human Rights Violations of a Prior Regime' (1991) 100 Yale Law Journal 2537.

[9] See H Cobban, 'Think Again: International Courts' (*Foreign Policy*, 20 October 2009); J R Crawford, *The Internationalization of Criminal Law, Remarks. Proceedings of the American Society of International Law* (Proceedings of the American Society of International Law 1995); A D'Amato, 'Peace vs. Accountability in Bosnia' (1994) 88 The American Journal of International Law 500.

[10] See A K Prorok, 'The (In)compatibility of Peace and Justice? The International Criminal Court and Civil Conflict Termination' (2017) 71 International Organisation 213; B Simmons and A Danner, 'Credible Commitments and the International Criminal Court' (2010) 64 International Organization 225; M Kersten, *Justice in Conflict* (Oxford University Press 2016); G Dancy and E Wiebelhaus-Brahm, 'The Impact of Criminal Prosecutions During Intrastate Conflict' (2018) Journal of Peace Research 47; G Dancy, 'Deals with the Devil? Conflict Amnesties, Civil War, and Sustainable Peace' (2018) 55 International Organization 387; J R McAllister, 'The Extraordinary Gamble: How the Yugoslav Tribunal's Indictments of Slobodan Milosevic During the Kosovo War Affected Peace Efforts' (2019) XXVI(I) Brown Journal of World Affairs 201; J R McAllister, *On Knife's Edge: The International Criminal Tribunal for the former Yugoslavia's Impact on Violence Against Civilians (Doctoral Dissertation)* (ProQuest Dissertations and Theses 2014).

[11] J Neu, 'Pursuing Justice in the Midst of War: The International Criminal Tribunal for the Former Yugoslavia' (2012) 5 Negotiation and Conflict Management Research 72; G J Bass, 'Settling with the Enemy: The Dicey Politics of Negotiating Peace in the Balkans with Accused War Criminals' (*Washington Post*, 29 October 1995); G J Bass, *Stay the Hand of Vengeance: The Politics of War Crimes Tribunals* (Princeton University Press 2000); Human Rights Watch, *Selling Justice Short: Why Accountability Matters for Peace* (Human Rights Watch 2009).

[12] '… in the early stages of a research program, selection on the dependent variable [e.g. the 'facilitation of peace efforts'] can serve the heuristic purpose of identifying the potential causal paths and variables leading to the dependent variable of interest. Later, the resulting causal model can be tested against cases in which there is variation on the dependent variable.' A L George and A Bennett, *Case Studies and Theory Development in the Social Sciences* (MIT Press 2005) 23.

[13] See J Meernik, 'Justice and Peace? How the International Criminal Tribunal Affects Societal Peace in Bosnia' (2005) 42 Journal of Peace Research 271; J Meernik, A Nichols, and K L King, 'The Impact of International Tribunals and Domestic Trials on Peace and Human Rights After Civil War' (2010) 11 International Studies Perspectives 309; L J Nettelfield, *Courting Democracy in Bosnia and Herzegovina: the Hague Tribunal's Impact in a Postwar State* (Cambridge University Press 2010); R Kerr, 'Peace through Justice? The International Criminal Tribunal for the Former Yugoslavia' (2007) 7 Southeast European and Black Sea Studies 373; J Hagan and S K Ivković, *Reclaiming Justice: The International Tribunal for the Former Yugoslavia and Local Courts* (Oxford University Press 2011).

on the Tribunal's wartime impact. Drawing on over 100 interviews with key stakeholders from the Bosnian peace process, along with recently declassified data from the Clinton administration, the chapter finds that the ICTY played a key role in facilitating peace efforts. In particular, the ICTY's indictments provided political cover for mediators to ensure that only key combatant leaders participated in talks. Moreover, by vetting entity-level indictments through the Rules of the Road programme, the ICTY helped reassure parties that they would not be subject to post-conflict victor's justice.

This chapter is organized as follows. It begins by reviewing the debate over the impact of prosecutions on peace efforts. The second section then draws on various political science literatures to develop some working hypotheses concerning how the ICTY might have facilitated, versus undermined, negotiations to end the Bosnian War. The third section provides a brief overview of the Bosnian Wars, before presenting the chapter's findings. A conclusion discussing the study's implications follows.

27.2 Existing Research on ICT's Impact on Peace Process

Two distinct perspectives—stemming from the 'peace versus justice' debate—dominate existing research on ICTs' impact on peace processes and mediation.[14] Scholars and policymakers associated with the justice perspective maintain that there can be 'no peace without justice'.[15] The assumption underlying this perspective is that the pursuit of justice addresses the underlying causes of violence by, among other things, ending impunity,[16] preventing future crimes,[17] and marginalizing or removing parties that might destabilize peace agreements.[18] During peace negotiations, the threat of criminal prosecution and marginalization or removal of disruptive leaders might prove especially useful for mediators.[19] However,

[14] The peace versus justice debate is quite broad. Due to space constraints, I specifically focus on aspects of the debate that specifically relate to ICTs' impact on peace processes amidst active armed conflicts. For a more comprehensive overview of the peace versus justice debate, please refer to L Vinjamuri and J Snyder, 'Law and Politics in Transitional Justice' (2015) 18 Annual Review of Political Science 303; T D Olsen, L A Payne, and A G Reiter, *Transitional Justice in Balance: Comparing Processes, Weighing Efficacy* (United States Institute of Peace 2010).

[15] M S Ellis, 'Combating Impunity and Enforcing Accountability as a Way to Promote Peace and Stability—The Role of International War Crimes Tribunals' (2006) 2 Journal of National Security Law and Policy 111.

[16] E L Lutz, 'Transitional Justice: Lessons Learned and the Road Ahead' in N Roht-Arriaza and J Mariezcurrena (eds), *Transitional Justice in the Twenty-First Century: Beyond Truth versus Justice* (Cambridge University Press 2006); R Goldstone, 'Justice as a Tool for Peace-Making: Truth Commissions and International Criminal Tribunals' (1996) 28 New York University Journal of International Law and Politics 485; N J Kritz, 'Coming to Terms with Atrocities: a Review of Accountability Mechanisms for Mass Violations of Human Rights (Accountability for International Crime and Serious Violations of Fundamental Human Rights)' (1997) 59 Law and Contemporary Problems 127; M Ignatieff, *The Warrior's Honour: Ethnic War and the Modern Conscienc* (Vintage 1999).

[17] See D Wippman, 'Atrocities, Deterrence, and the Limits of International Justice' (1999) 23 Fordham International Law Journal 473; P Akhavan, 'Justice in the Hague, Peace in the Former Yugoslavia? A Commentary on the United Nations War Crimes Tribunal' (1998) 20 Human Rights Quarterly 737; McAllister(n 10); K Cronin-Furman, 'Managing Expectations: International Criminal Trials and the Prospects for Deterrence of Mass Atrocity' (2013) 7 The International Journal of Transitional Justice 434;H Jo and B A Simmons, 'Can the International Criminal Court Deter Atrocity?' (2016) International Organization 1; J R McAllister, 'Deterring Wartime Atrocities: Hard Lessons from the Yugoslav Tribunal' (2019/20) 44 International Security 84.

[18] R Thakur, *The United Nations, Peace and Security: From Collective Security to the Responsibility to Protect* (Cambridge University Press 2006); Human Rights Watch, *Selling Justice Short: Why Accountability Matters for Peace* (Human Rights Watch 2009); E P Mendes, *Peace and Justice at the International Criminal Court: a Court of Last Resort* (Edward Elgar 2010); A De Waal and G H Stanton, 'Should President Omar al-Bashir of Sudan Be Charged and Arrested by the International Criminal Court?: An Exchange of Views' (2009) 4 Genocide Studies and Prevention 329.

[19] Human Rights Watch, *Selling Justice Short: Why Accountability Matters for Peace* (Human Rights Watch 2009); P Akhavan, 'Justice in the Hague, Peace in the Former Yugoslavia? A Commentary on the United Nations

justice advocates have yet to fully clarify when the marginalization or removal of leaders might facilitate, versus undermine, peace processes. For instance, targeted leaders might have more of a reason to constructively participate in peace talks, or they might lash out at civilians in retaliation.[20] Moreover, the leaders who replace the indicted party might not necessarily be 'moderate' and/or positively contribute to peace.[21] However, recent large-N analyses point to some other ways that ICTs might facilitate peace efforts. In particular, work by Beth Simmons and Allison Danner indicates that governments can credibly signal their commitment to de-escalate violence by ratifying the Rome Statute. In so doing, States might convince weaker rebel opponents to take 'tentative steps towards peacekeeping'.[22] Geoff Dancy and Eric Wiebelhau-Brahm also find that criminal prosecutions can facilitate conflict termination when trials focus on rebels. They speculate that rebel trials might compel rebels to discountinue fighting.[23] Finally, another large-N study by Geoff Dancy finds that amnesties for serious rights violations do not result in pacifying effects in civil wars.[24] While these quantitative studies have all pointed to important trends in how ICTs might positively affect peace efforts, they have yet to fully elucidate *why* ICTs might specifically have these effects. In short, there is a need for additional research into the causal forces at work.

The 'peace' side of the debate contends that there can be 'no justice without peace'.[25] Such views maintain that trials tend to undermine tenuous peace processes.[26] As J.R. Crawford summarizes, 'when you create an ad hoc tribunal, the tribunal itself becomes part of the dispute'.[27] Specifically, the threat of criminal prosecution might alienate key stakeholders from reaching an agreement unless they also secure amnesty.[28] Several empirical studies find conditional evidence of this effect.[29] Jack Snyder and Leslie Vinjamuri use a medium-N analysis on the role of international and transitional justice in thirty-two civil wars between 1989 and 2003. They find that trials do more harm than good when spoiler groups are

War Crimes Tribunal' (1998) 20 Human Rights Quarterly 737; G J Bass, *Stay the Hand of Vengeance: The Politics of War Crimes Tribunals* (Princeton University Press 2000).

[20] M Kersten, *Justice in Conflict* (Oxford University Press 2016); J Goldsmith, 'The Self-Defeating International Criminal Court' (2003) 70 The University of Chicago Law Review 89; J Goldsmith and S D Krasner, 'The Limits of Idealism' (2003) 132 Daedalus 47.

[21] L Vinjamuri, 'Deterrence, Democracy, and the Pursuit of International Justice' (2010) 24 Ethics & International Affairs 191.

[22] Simmons and Danner (n 10) 253.

[23] Dancy and Wiebelhaus-Brahm (n 10).

[24] Dancy (n 10).

[25] S Chesterman, 'No Justice without Peace? International Criminal Law and the Decision to Prosecute' in S Chesterman (ed), *Civilians in War* (Lynne Reiner 2001).

[26] See Cobban (n 9); Crawford (n 9); D'Amato (n 9); F Mégret, 'Three Dangers for the International Criminal Court: A Critical Look at a Consensual Project' (2001) XII Finnish Yearbook of International Law 193.

[27] Durham and McCormack (n 8); P Akhavan, 'Current Developments: The International Criminal Tribunal for Rwanda: The Politics and Pragmatics of Punishment' (1996) 90 American Journal of International Law 501.

[28] K A Rodman, 'Is Peace in the Interests of Justice? The Case for Broad Prosecutorial Discretion at the International Criminal Court' (2009) 22 Leiden Journal of International Law 99, 108; Goldsmith and Krasner (n 20); D Keen, *Complex Political Emergencies* (Polity Press 2008); B Leebaw, *Judging State-sponsored Violence, Imagining Political Change* (Cambridge University Press 2011); S Vandeginste and C L Sriram, 'Power Sharing and Transitional Justice: A Clash of Paradigms?' (2011) 17 Global Governance: A Review of Multilateralism and International Organizations 489.

[29] See also A Branch, 'Uganda's Civil War and the Politics of ICC Intervention' (2007) 21 Ethics & International Affairs 179; P S Wegner, *The International Criminal Court in Ongoing Intrastate Conflicts: Navigating the Peace-Justice Divide* (Cambridge University Press 2015).

strong.[30] Moreover, in a large-N analysis, Alyssa Prorok finds that when the ICC intervenes in civil conflicts where the domestic threat of punishment is low, ICC actions can generate incentives for leaders to continue fighting as a way to avoid capture, transfer to The Hague, and prosecution.[31] In addition, Mark Kersten indicates that ICC involvement complicated peace efforts in both Uganda and Libya by, among other things, reinforcing harmful conflict narratives and parties' incentives to continue fighting.[32] He argues that the Office of the Prosecutor's (OTP) efforts to balance its institutional interests and political constraints are crucial for disentangling such effects.[33]

Increasingly, scholars and policy-makers acknowledge that ICTs likely have mixed effects on peace processes, meaning there is merit to both sides of the peace versus justice debate.[34] However, while recent empirical research has been quite successful in uncovering the ways that ICTs might undermine peace efforts, it has yet to fully evaluate how ICTs might also facilitate such initiatives. In short, there is still much to learn about ICTs' impact on peace.[35] As one scholar summarized, 'the question of how the pursuit of justice has been treated at the negotiating table and how it has affected peace negotiations remains unclear'.[36]

27.3 How the ICTY Might Have Facilitated Negotiations to End the Bosnian War: Some Working Hypotheses

How might the ICTY have facilitated efforts to negotiate an end to the Bosnian War? Three distinct literatures shed preliminary insight into this question. Political scientists studying the judicialization of world politics indicate that ICTs play a unique enforcement role.[37] Specifically, ICTs are designed to assess compliance with international criminal law (ICL), as well as name ICL violations. In so doing, they can 'increase the costs of noncompliance' by, among other things, creating opportunities for compliance constituencies to leverage

[30] J Snyder and L Vinjamuri, 'Trials and Errors: Principle and Pragmatism in Strategies of International Justice' 28 International Security 5.

[31] A K Prorok, 'The (In)compatibility of Peace and Justice? The International Criminal Court and Civil Conflict Termination' (2017) 71 International Organisation 213.

[32] For more details on the ICC's impact in Libya, refer to C Hillebrecht, 'The Deterrent Effects of the International Criminal Court: Evidence from Libya' (2016) 42 International Interactions 616; C Stahn, 'Libya, the International Criminal Court and Complementarity—A Test for "Shared Responsibility"' (2012)10 Journal of International Criminal Justice 325.

[33] M Kersten, *Justice in Conflict* (Oxford University Press 2016).

[34] ibid; Vandeginste and Sriram (n 28); M Broache, 'Irrelevance, Instigation and Prevention: The Mixed Effects of International Criminal Court Prosecutions in Atrocities in the CNDP/M23 Case' (2016) 10 International Journal of Transitional Justice 388; Dancy and Wiebelhaus-Brahm (n 10).

[35] J N Clark, 'Peace, Justice and the International Criminal Court' (2011) 9 Journal of International Criminal Justice 521; A K Prorok, 'The (In)compatibility of Peace and Justice? The International Criminal Court and Civil Conflict Termination' (2017) 71 International Organisation 213; M Kersten, *Justice in Conflict* (Oxford University Press 2016).

[36] M Kersten, *Justice in Conflict* (Oxford University Press 2016) 30. See also A K Prorok, 'The (In)compatibility of Peace and Justice? The International Criminal Court and Civil Conflict Termination' (2017) 71 International Organisation 213.

[37] See, for instance, K Alter, 'Agents or Trustees? International Courts in their Political Context' (2008) 14 European Journal of International Relations 33; K Alter, *The New Terrain of International Law: Courts, Politics, Rights* (Princeton University Press 2014); K Sikkink, *The Justice Cascade: How Human Rights Prosecutions Are Changing World Politics* (W. W. Norton & Company 2011); B Simmons, *Mobilizing for Human Rights: International Law in Domestic Politics* (Cambridge University Press 2009).

the threat of criminal prosecution and implement political costs for actors that fail to comply with ICL.[38]

The conflict resolution and civil wars literatures help to clarify how various actors might specifically leverage the threat of criminal prosecution as part of a negotiation effort. First, mediators might use the threat of criminal prosecution to ensure that only key combatant leaders participate in peace talks. Combatant leaders are 'key' when they represent factions that have the capacity to continue fighting if they are unsatisfied with an agreement. They must also be able to ensure their faction's compliance with any agreement. [39] Civil war scholars have demonstrated that these leaders' involvement in a mediation effort is crucial.[40] However, it is not only hard to identify them, but the more of them that participate in talks, the harder a peace deal becomes.[41] Thus, a crucial task for mediators is to both identify and reduce the total number of key combatant leaders involved in negotiations. ICTY indictments could well have provided mediators with a tool for accomplishing both tasks. Specifically, indictments could have given mediators a basis for refusing to deal with implicated leaders. As a result, these leaders' factions—assuming they wanted to continue with a peace process—would have had to resolve questions of who would speak for them moving forward. These deliberations could well have provided mediators with more information about who was and was not actually a key combatant leader.

Hypothesis 1: ICTY indictments might have facilitated mediation efforts by providing mediators with a basis for ensuring that only key combatant leaders participated in negotiations.

A second way that the ICTY might have facilitated negotiations is by agreeing to monitor and oversee post-war prosecutions. Civil wars are asymmetric conflicts, meaning rebels generally confront much stronger government forces. Moreover, they can only end when rebels disband and cede their territory to a newly constituted central government, which they will not necessarily control.[42] Rebels, in other words, are especially vulnerable to surprise attacks or political exploitation, including victor's justice (or, excessive or unfair post-war prosecutions). Consequently, in order for rebels to commit to a peace deal, they need reassurances that government officials will actually follow through on a peace agreement.[43] To help parties overcome concerns of post-war victor's justice, mediators could potentially

[38] K Alter, *The New Terrain of International Law: Courts, Politics, Rights* (Princeton University Press 2014) 15.

[39] Political scientists refer to these leaders and factions as 'veto players'. 'Veto players' have: (1) slightly distinct preferences from other belligerents; (2) an internally cohesive organization; and (3) the capacity to withstand an assault from other parties in the conflict if they were to reach an accord. Veto players can include a range of actors from combatant groups, factions within armed groups, to external States. See D E Cunningham, *Barriers to Peace in Civil War* (Cambridge University Press 2011) 29. Political scientists might also refer to some of the aforementioned leaders and factions as 'spoilers', which are essentially a type of veto player. Specifically, spoilers are 'leaders and parties who believe that peace emerging from negotiations threatens their power, worldview, and interests, and use violence to undermine attempts to achieve it'. S J Stedman, 'Spoiler Problems in Peace Processes' (1997) 22 International Security 5, 36.

[40] D Nilsson and M S Kovacs, 'Revisiting an Elusive Concept: A Review of the Debate on Spoilers in Peace Processes' (2011) 13 International Studies Review 606; Stedman (n 39); K M Greenhill and S Major, 'The Perils of Profiling Civil War Spoilers and the Collapse of Intrastate Peace Accords' (2006) 31 International Security 7; Cunningham (n 39).

[41] See, in particular, Greenhill and Major (n 40).

[42] B Walter, 'Civil Wars, Conflict Resolution, and Bargaining Theory' in W Carlsnaes, T Risse, and B A Simmons (eds), *Handbook of International Relations: Civil Wars, Conflict Resolution, and Bargaining Theory* (SAGE Publications Ltd 2013) 661.

[43] Political scientists refer to such dilemmas as 'commitment problems'.

turn to ICTs to monitor and vet post-war prosecutions. In the event that ICTs agree to do so, ICTs can play a role in facilitating credible commitments between rebel and government forces.

Hypothesis 2: By monitoring and vetting post-war prosecutions, the ICTY might have facilitated peace efforts by reassuring belligerents that post-war prosecutions would occur, albeit in a less partial way than in domestic legal systems.

In the next section, I provide a brief overview of the Bosnian War before evaluating these hypotheses by process tracing the ICTY's impact on efforts to end the Bosnian War.[44]

27.4 Evaluating the ICTY's Impact on Peace Negotiations During the Bosnian War

27.4.1 Pre-Negotiation State: Late July–November 1995

Without the ICTY's initial indictment of Karadžić and Mladić,[45] Holbrooke and his team would have had a more challenging time ensuring that only key combatant leaders participated in talks. Specifically, the ICTY's indictments played directly into Holbrooke's efforts to implement the crucial 'Milošević Strategy'. Recognizing that the Bosnian Serbs were definite hurdles to securing a peace agreement[46] and that Milošević might be more open to peace, the Clinton administration started focusing its diplomatic efforts on the Serbian president in early 1995. However, by early August, the policy had not worked. Top National Security Council (NSC) leaders and even Secretary of State Warren Christopher wanted a change-up, arguing that the Administration would have to deal directly with the Bosnian Serbs. President Clinton sided with proponents of the direct approach, believing that diplomatic progress would be impossible without having Bosnian Serbs at the negotiating table. He only delayed a full change-up in policy at this stage because of the ICTY's indictments of Republika Srpska's President and top military leader.[47]

Holbrooke used the time the ICTY's indictment of Karadžić and Mladić bought him in order to double down on the Milošević Strategy, which he identified as crucial to restarting peace negotiations. In mid-August, Holbrooke's team indicated that they would only deal with Milošević. Moreover, before returning to Belgrade in late August, Holbrooke reiterated that he would not cut any deal regarding the post-war fate of indictees.[48] The team's efforts produced results: by the end of August, Milošević and Patriarch Pavle pressured the Bosnian Serbs to agree to a six-member delegation (which originally included Karadžić and Mladić) with Milošević at its head. The agreement, known as the 'Patriarch Paper'

44 Process tracing is a means for identifying steps in a causal process that produce a particular outcome. See A L George and A Bennett, *Case Studies and Theory Development in the Social Sciences* (MIT Press 2005) 176.

45 The OTP announced a second indictment against both Karadžić and Mladić on 16 November 1995, which included charges of genocide for crimes in the area of Srebrenica. ICTY, *Case Information Sheet: Radovan Karadzic*, IT-95-5/18.

46 Prior to 1995, they had thwarted two major peace plans: the Vance-Owen Plan in 1993 and then the Contact Group Plan in 1994.

47 I H Daalder, *Getting to Dayton: The Making of America's Bosnia Policy* (Brookings Institute Press 2000) 128.

48 R Holbrooke, *To End a War* (Random House 1998) 5.

constituted an important breakthrough in talks. In his memoirs, Holbrooke explains his reaction upon receiving the Patriarch Paper from Milošević during his late August shuttle to Belgrade:

> For a moment I did not dare believe it. For sixteen months, the Contact Group had argued fruitlessly with Milošević over how to get the Bosnian Serbs to participate in negotiations under the Contact Group plan. Now we had the answer to the question we had asked for those sixteen months: who would speak for Pale? And the answer was: Slobodan Milošević. Washington's decision to negotiate with Belgrade and try to isolate Pale had produced its first success—only a procedural one, to be sure, but a real breakthrough. Genuine negotiations were about to begin.[49]

James Pardew, who was also at the meeting, reported to the Pentagon, 'I've put down the hammer I was using to beat down my optimism. This may work'.[50]

As his late August talks with Milošević continued to unfold, Holbrooke underscored that the US would not negotiate on the ICTY, nor would it refrain from arresting Karadžić and Mladić should they show up for international negotiations. When Milošević objected that the US 'needed Karadžić and Mladić to make peace', Holbrooke replied:

> That is your problem. Karadžić and Mladić cannot go to an international conference. They will be arrested if they set foot in any European country. In fact, if they come to the United States, I would gladly meet them at the airport and assist in their arrest. You have just shown us a piece of paper giving you the power to negotiate for them. It's your problem.[51]

In the subsequent week, as negotiations unfolded with regional leaders, Holbrooke publicly and repeatedly reiterated that the US would hold firm in its commitment to ensure that either leader would be arrested should they attend negotiations, which would in all likelihood take place in the West. In his contribution to the *Dayton History Project*, O'Brien explains that the 'point' concerning the use of the ICTY as a 'tool' to undercut 'people who would be obstacles to peace. [...] never had penetrated in the policy world until late August, when Holbrooke just announced on NPR [National Public Radio] one day that Karadžić and Mladić could not attend any of the negotiations. They'd be arrested and set aside'.[52] Holbrooke's NPR interview hit the airwaves on 1 September as he was meeting with Milošević in Belgrade:

> If they leave the country and go to the United States or any of the European countries that are bound by agreements, they will be arrested and turned over to the international tribunal, as they should be. We are not discussing this issue. It is not a negotiating issue. The

[49] ibid.

[50] D Chollet and R Holbrooke, *The Road to the Dayton Accords: A Study of American Statecraft* (Palgrave Macmillan 2005) 65.

[51] Holbrooke (n 48) 107.

[52] R Holbrooke and D Owen, 'Dayton History Project: Interview', in DECLASSIFIED and RELEASED IN FULL, *2013* (US Department of State, 18 June 1996).

> War Crimes Tribunal will move forward on its own merits. I don't see how they can come out of the country to participate in talks.[53]

In the months ahead, the Milošević Strategy—buttressed by the ICTY's indictment—proved critical to advancing negotiations. Doubts persisted concerning whether Milošević could deliver the Bosnian Serbs. For instance, on 1 September, the North Atlantic Treaty Organization (NATO) halted its bombing of Bosnian Serb positions in order to negotiate the terms to end their siege of Sarajevo. The Bosnian Serb Army, however, took advantage of the pause in order to move their weapons around, rather than away from Sarajevo. Jim Pardew reported to Washington, '[the] bombing pause affair has made clear that Milošević cannot deliver Mladić, and Mladić is who counts among the Bosnian Serbs. [. . .] is there not a risk we are negotiating [sic] Milošević on a deal that Mladić won't buy, and that will then serve as the starting point for concessions to Mladić?'[54] Nonetheless, the Administration continued to deal with Milošević, who ultimately delivered: first, on an agreement related to constitutional principles signed in Geneva in early September; second, on a ceasefire agreement that ended the siege of Sarajevo in mid-September; third, on negotiations in New York related to draft principles for subsequent negotiations; fourth, on a ceasefire agreement in early October; and finally, on a final agreement at Dayton. Bosnian Serb leaders consistently opposed any and all compromises that Holbrooke's team negotiated between Zagreb–Sarajevo–Belgrade during their shuttles in the run-up to Dayton. However, just when it appeared that an agreement was about to fall through, Milošević would rein his colleagues in.

Ambassador David Scheffer has speculated that the US position on refusing to negotiate with indictees made it easier for Milošević to strong-arm his subsidiaries into holding true to the Patriarch agreement. In particular, he explains:

> The American diplomat [Richard Holbrooke] held firm with Milošević that there would be no immunity for either Karadžić or Mladić if they set foot in the United States or any nation of the European Union. The indictments were nonnegotiable. In some respects this situation would prove useful to Milošević, as it gave him the upper hand with respect to his indicted colleagues in representing Serb interests during the negotiations.[55]

Indeed, by refusing to work with indictees, Holbrooke and his team forced Milošević to step up and thereby demonstrate just how much control he exercised over his Bosnian Serb counterparts. In other words, the indictments strengthened the mediators' hand in identifying key combatant leaders. One example stands out. Holbrooke's team only ever met with Karadžić and Mladić once after they were indicted, and only under strict conditions. On 13 September, Milošević sprung both men on Holbrooke's team, which while shocked, had prepared for such a potentiality. The team specified three conditions for meeting with the indictees: first, that Milošević be confirmed as the head of their delegation; second, that the Bosnian Serbs demonstrate a commitment to 'serious discussions' (rather than historical

[53] 'Holbrooke and Milosevic Begin Serious Negotiations' interview on *National Public Radio, Morning Edition* with S Poggioli.

[54] Chollet and Holbrooke (n 50) 73.

[55] D Scheffer, *All the Missing Souls: A Personal History of the War Crimes Tribunals* (Princeton University Press 2012) 105.

diatribes); and third, that Milošević secure their consent to both terms before they met with them, which he did. When General Wesley Clark—a member of Holbrooke's team—presented the Serbs with terms for ending the bombing, Mladić and Karadžić burst into a furious tirade. Holbrooke subsequently conveyed to Milošević: 'We had an agreement. This behavior is clearly not consistent with it. If your "friends" do not wish to have a serious discussion, we will leave now.'[56] Milošević quickly reasserted control over his counterparts. US officials then secured a deal that ended the siege of Sarajevo.

After Holbrooke's team succeeded in getting Milošević to negotiate for all Serb forces, it subsequently managed to get Bosnian, Croatian, and Federal Republic of Yugoslavia (FRY) officials to agree to a broad framework for a comprehensive settlement. Shortly thereafter, in early October, US officials brokered a ceasefire, as well as secured an agreement for a formal peace conference. Once again, the ICTY's indictment of Karadžić and Mladić facilitated Holbrooke's efforts to ensure that key combatant leaders participated in negotiations. Specifically, available evidence suggests that Karadžić's participation in a formal peace conference would have made it much harder for Bosnian President Alija Izetbegović to attend. By the autumn of 1995, the tide had turned in favour of the Federation of Bosnia and Herzegovina (FBiH) after it scored a number of key victories, thanks in part to NATO air strikes against Bosnian Serb positions. Consequently, a number of top Bosnian generals—including Generals Atif Dudaković (5th Corps) and Mehmed Alagić (7th Corps)—were convinced that they should keep fighting.[57] Indeed, in late August, the Director of Central Intelligence Interagency Balkan Task Force predicted that the Bosnian government would be 'the problem' in terms of realizing a peace agreement by year's end.[58]

While negotiating with Milošević was not particularly enviable (a fact that US officials similarly underscored),[59] Izetbegović acknowledged that someone needed to speak for the Serbs. However, it would have been even more difficult to deal with Radovan Karadžić and Ratko Mladić, both of whom were then recognized as architects of the Srebrenica massacre, which took place only a month before in July 1995. Thus, by threatening to arrest Karadžić and Mladić if they attended formal talks in Europe or the US, the US was able to facilitate President Izetbegović's inclusion in talks. Indeed, Foreign Minister Sacribey later confided to ICTY Prosecutor Richard Goldstone that his government would not have attended any peace negotiations with Karadžić. Goldstone recalls, 'Some months after Dayton, during an address in New York ... To my surprise Sacirbey was in the audience and confirmed that President Izetbegović would not have considered attending any meeting at which Karadžić was present'.[60] Bosnian Croat leader Stjepan Kljuić and the Bosnian government's chief counsel in The Hague—Vasvija Vidović—similarly confirmed that Bosnian officials would not have participated in an international peace conference that Karadžić attended after Srebrenica.[61] Vidović explained:

[56] Chollet and Holbrooke (n 50) 88; Holbrooke (n 48) 147.

[57] M A Hoare, *How Bosnia Armed* (Saqi Books and the Bosnian Institute 2004) 102.

[58] 'Principles' Committee Meeting on Bosnia' in Central Intelligence Agency et al (eds), *Bosnian War (1992–1995): Bosnia, Intelligence, and Clinton's Presidency (declassified October 2013)* (BACM Research 22 August 1995) <http://www.paperlessarchives.com/bosnian-war-cia-files.html> accessed 22 November 2017.

[59] See, for instance, Holbrooke (n 48) 147; J Shattuck, *Freedom on Fire: Human Rights Wars and America's Response* (Harvard University Press 2005) 206.

[60] Goldstone (n 6) 220.

[61] Stjepan Kljuić, interview with author (17 July 2013); Stjepan Kljuić, interview with author (20 July 2013).

> I spoke about that [the exclusion of Karadžić and Mladić from international peace negotiations after their indictment] with President Izetbegović on several occasions. Before events in Srebrenica, he participated many times in peace talks in Geneva along with Karadžić. However, after the events in Srebrenica, neither President Izetbegović, Doctor Siljadžić [Bosnia's Prime Minister at the time], nor any other politician in Bosnia wanted to participate in the negotiations if the indicted persons were present at the same table.[62]

In sum, the ICTY's indictment of Karadžić and Mladić proved invaluable for advocates of the Milošević Strategy. In particular, it helped them to convince President Clinton, the NSC, and even Secretary of State Christopher to give the Strategy a bit more time to work. Moreover, by threatening to arrest Karadžić and Mladić, Holbrooke and his team were able to facilitate Bosnian President Alija Izetbegović's participation in formal talks. Thus, the evidence lends support to Hypothesis 1: the ICTY's efforts facilitated mediators' efforts to ensure that only key combatant leaders participated in negotiations.

27.4.2 Negotiation State: November–December 1995

From 1–21 November, parties convened at Wright-Patterson Air Force Base in Dayton, Ohio for formal talks. The opening of formal talks was notable both for who was and was not in attendance. In particular, despite much resistance, the Bosnian delegation—headed by President Izetbegović, Prime Minister Haris Siljadžić, and Foreign Minister Sacribey—attended. However, Bosnian Serb President Karadžić and Colonel General Ratko Mladić—both of whom had signed the Patriarch Paper, which specified that they, along with Assembly Speaker Momčilo Krajišnik, would represent Republika Srpska's negotiating delegation—were absent, and remained so for the duration of the conference. Granted, as Holbrooke recounts in his memoirs, Krajišnik's views were 'hard to distinguish ... from those of his close friend Radovan Karadžić'.[63] However, by this point his involvement mattered little: Milošević had repeatedly proven he could deliver the Bosnian Serbs on any arrangement he agreed to.

Indeed, at Dayton, Milošević relegated the Bosnian Serbs to the sidelines. He would not let them have access to either the delegation's only fax, or phones in their room. Secretary of State Christopher described to Clinton that the Bosnian Serbs were 'present but quite invisible'.[64] In, perhaps, the most dramatic display of just how much authority Milošević had over his peers in Pale, he basically conceded all the territory that the Bosnian Serbs wanted—especially Sarajevo—to the Bosnian government. Holbrooke believed he did so 'to break the back of the Pale Serbs', by undercutting one of their key promises to Bosnian Serbs that they would maintain Sarajevo.[65] The concession of Sarajevo was especially troubling to the US delegation, which believed Milošević might lose control of the Bosnian Serbs for doing so. FRY Foreign Minister Milutinović indicated that they did go 'completely crazy'. However, Milošević simply had Milutinović initial the agreement in their place. This made

[62] Vasvija Vidović, interview with author (13 August 2013).
[63] Holbrooke (n 48) 255.
[64] W Christopher, 'Christopher to Clinton: Night Note' in D Chollet and R Holbrooke (eds), *The Road to the Dayton Accords: A Study of American Statecraft* (Palgrave Macmillan 2005) 163.
[65] Holbrooke (n 48) 293.

US officials uncomfortable, so they demanded that Milošević sign a letter saying that he would deliver the Pale signatures within ten days of the conference. Milošević laughed at the request, mocking it as completely unnecessary. He told Holbrooke: 'I guarantee you that I will have the signatures within twenty-four hours of my return to Belgrade.' He was right, and even had Karadžić sign for good measure.[66] In short, at Dayton, Milošević was firmly in control of his Bosnian Serb peers thanks in part to the US' refusal to negotiate with indicted leaders.

Unfortunately, US support for the ICTY waned once formal talks were under way. In his memoirs, then-US Secretary of State for Democracy, Human Rights, and Labor John Shattuck explains why:

> ... another point of view on war crimes surfaced at Dayton. In many ways it symbolized the underlying weakness and fragmentation of the coalition behind the entire peace process. On a philosophical level, opponents of the tribunal argued that peace can only be built on compromise, and that the way to get people to stop killing each other is to focus their attention on the future, not the past. On a practical level, they argued that the threat of criminal prosecution would drive parties away from the negotiating table. It would prevent the lifting of sanctions and the resumption of normal economic relations. It would require international soldiers to act as police ... These objections revealed a deep split in the coalition over how to finish the job of making peace.[67]

The Bosnian delegation, ICTY Chief Prosecutor Goldstone, and the Tribunal's advocates in the Clinton Administration pushed for a number of agreements to facilitate the ICTY's post-conflict role. They achieved some successes. In particular, there was no amnesty clause. Additionally, the final General Framework Agreement specified,

> No person who is serving a sentence imposed by the International Tribunal, and no person who is under indictment by the Tribunal and who has failed to comply with an order to appear before the Tribunal, may stand as a candidate or hold any appointive, elective, or other public office in the territory of Bosnia and Herzegovina.[68]

It also required parties within Bosnia to 'cooperate' with the Tribunal.[69] If they failed to do so, the UNSC had the authority to renew sanctions. Moreover, the US and Bosnian delegations were able to wrangle access for US officials—and subsequently ICTY investigators post-conflict—to such sites as Banja Luka, a Bosnian Serb stronghold.

However, the General Framework Agreement was weak in terms of ensuring cooperation with the ICTY. The military annex to the agreement was silent on whether NATO's new Implementation Force (IFOR) could arrest indictees. Rather, parties opted to grant IFOR the implicit authority to arrest indictees. However, as Holbrooke recalled, 'the meaning would not be determined until the commanders on the ground decided how to use their "authority".'[70] The first batch of IFOR commanders subsequently decided that it

[66] ibid.
[67] Shattuck (n 59) 208.
[68] OSCE, *General Framework Agreement for Peace in Bosnia and Herzegovina* (OSCE, initialled in Dayton, 21 November 1995) Annex 4.
[69] ibid.
[70] Holbrooke (n 48) 220.

was not in their authority to arrest ICTY suspects. Moreover, language in the Framework Agreement associated with regional leaders' obligation to cooperate with the Tribunal was watered down. In particular, the military annex of the Framework Agreement, which only applies *within Bosnia*, required each of the *Bosnian* parties to 'comply with any order or request of the International Tribunal for the former Yugoslavia for the arrest, detention, surrender, or access to persons ... who are accused of violations within the jurisdiction of the tribunal'.[71] At Milošević's insistence, negotiators deleted a clause that would have assured *regional* leaders' cooperation with the ICTY.[72] Both Serbia and Croatia would subsequently use the vague language as a basis to justify their lack of cooperation with the Tribunal's orders. The open mandate of IFOR to arrest ICTY suspects and the responsibilities of regional leaders to cooperate with the ICTY's orders created a number of obstacles for the Tribunal post-conflict.

However, in terms of facilitating an end to the Bosnian War, the ICTY was able to play a role in the run-up to Dayton. On 1 December, parties formally signed the Dayton agreement in Paris, which ultimately put an end to the egregious violence that civilians in the region had endured for years. The ICTY's indictment of top Bosnian Serb leaders helped pave the way to Dayton and then Paris. The reason why the ICTY was able to play a role at this stage in the Bosnian War was because it maintained the backing of the US at a critical juncture. Throughout hostilities, the US—thanks in large part to the efforts of a handful of ardent advocates of the ICTY—had done a great deal to support the Tribunal. Nonetheless, until late summer 1995, the US took a back seat in efforts aimed at resolving the Bosnian War. Those from Europe that took the lead until then frequently did not share the US' view on the Tribunal as a tool for facilitating an end to hostilities. By rebooting its commitment to ending the Bosnian War, the US became just the sort of actor whose cooperation the ICTY needed. In particular, because the US was able to dictate the terms of negotiations and was in a position to apprehend indictees, the ICTY's indictment of Karadžić and Mladić became vital tools for sidelining both men from talks, shoring up Milošević's authority to negotiate on their behalf, and bringing the Bosnian Government on board. As James O'Brien recalled, when the Clinton administration held firm in its commitment to enforce the Tribunal's efforts: 'Suddenly now the War Crimes Tribunal was in the center of possibilities', for realizing an end to hostilities.[73]

27.4.3 Initial Implementation State: January–March 1996

Available evidence likewise suggests that the ICTY helped Holbrooke's team overcome a key crisis in the immediate aftermath of talks.[74] The Dayton Accords recognized the sovereign Republic of Bosnia and Herzegovina (RBiH) as consisting of two autonomous entities: the FBiH and the Republika Srpska (RS). As soon as the war ended, former opponents used their entity-level legal systems to target former wartime opponents. According to Mark

[71] Dayton Agreement (n 68) Annex 1A.
[72] Shattuck (n 59) 212, 352 fn 9.
[73] US Department of State, Declassified—Dayton History Project: interview with Richard Holbrooke and Roberts Owen (US Department of State 18 June 1996).
[74] Due to space constraints, the analysis is necessarily limited to the immediate post-war period. For a more comprehensive analysis of the ICTY's impact on the implementation of the Dayton Accords, please refer to (n 13).

Ellis, 'Bosnian Serbs, Muslims, and Croats … waged, within their respective territories, an intense campaign to bring individuals suspected of committing war crimes to justice. Each of the three parties has maintained exhaustive, if not accurate files on persons among the "other" group whom they "know" to be war criminals.'[75] A high-level United Nations official likewise observed:

> What we … saw in January 1996 was a large number of arbitrary arrests, usually men of military age who were thrown into prison and accused of war crimes. In every case, there were no charges or formal processes. These men were held on the basis of 'we heard he was with that brigade at that time when a war crime happened.' These arbitrary arrests had the potential to grind the slow movement of people back home to a halt.[76]

The race to prosecute opponents reached a turning point on 6 February 1996 when Bosnian authorities arrested two senior Serb officers, General Djordje Djukic and Colonel Aleksa Krsmanovic after they inadvertently strayed into Federation territory near Sarajevo.[77] Bosnian forces viewed the arrest as an opportunity to begin holding suspected war criminals accountable and began working with Chief Prosecutor Goldstone to transfer both men to The Hague. Bosnian Serbs, however, viewed the arrests as an affront that had the potential to reignite hostilities.[78] Moreover, the arrests had the potential to threaten the freedom of movement clauses in the Dayton Accords.

Realizing that the entity-level arrests threatened peace, Holbrooke acted quickly. He met with the top leaders of each faction to establish clear rules regarding arrests. The arrest rules were finalized at the first review conference of the Dayton Accords later in February. In particular, parties agreed to the Rules of the Road programme, which essentially granted the ICTY an oversight mechanism. The Rules of the Road provision of the Rome Agreement specified:

> Persons, other than those already indicted by the International Tribunal, may be arrested and detained for serious violations of international humanitarian law only pursuant to a previously issued order, warrant, or indictment that has been reviewed and deemed consistent with international legal standards by the International Tribunal. Procedures will be developed for expeditious decisions by the Tribunal and will be effective immediately upon such action.[79]

Thus, entity officials could only arrest parties on the basis of an ICTY, or ICTY-vetted entity-level indictment. The Rules of the Road programme subsequently dissipated tensions surrounding post-war arrests.[80] An ICTY official underscored that the Rules of the Road programme 'worked': it 'stopped arbitrary arrests, ensuring that people could travel without censure. Several thousand cases were reviewed over the next few years, and the

[75] M S Ellis, 'Bringing Justice to an Embattled Region—Creating and Implementing the Rules of the Road for Bosnia-Herzegovina' (1999) 17 Berkeley Journal of International Law 1, 6.

[76] Anonymous ICTY official, interview with author (27 March 2012).

[77] M Corder, 'Yugoslavia-War Crimes' (*Associated Press*, 3 March 1996).

[78] Ellis (n 75).

[79] Office of the High Representative, 'Agreed Measures, Rome Agreement' (18 February 1996) <http://www.nato.int/ifor/rome/rome2.htm> accessed 15 March 2016.

[80] Holbrooke (n 48); Ellis (n 75); James Pardew, interview with author (18 June 2015).

program resulted in the arrests of many people'.[81] Thus, available evidence lends support to Hypothesis 2: by monitoring and overseeing post-war prosecutions through the Rules of the Road programme, the ICTY facilitated peace efforts by reassuring belligerents that fair post-war prosecutions would occur.

27.5 Conclusion: Insights About Peace versus Justice from the ICTY

This chapter has examined how the ICTY affected negotiations to end the Bosnian War. The analysis yielded three main findings concerning the impact of prosecutions on peace efforts. First, the ICTY did in fact facilitate peace efforts. Second, the ICTY did so by providing US mediators with leverage for ensuring that only key leaders participated in talks, a finding that is consistent with Hypothesis 1. Specifically, Holbrooke's team was able to use the indictments of Bosnian Serb President Karadžić and General Mladić to pressure Serb forces to speak with one voice. Moreover, by threatening to arrest the architects of the Srebrenica massacre if they attended talks in Europe and then the US, mediators were able to pave the way for Bosnian President Izetbegović to participate at a time when a number of officials in his government did not wish to do so. Third, consistent with Hypothesis 2, the ICTY also facilitated US-mediation efforts by agreeing to monitor and vet entity-level indictments through the Rules of the Road programme. In so doing, the ICTY helped to de-escalate a major post-Dayton crisis by effectively reassuring former belligerents that they would not be subject to victor's justice.

Before turning to the study's implications, two caveats related to its findings are in order. First and foremost, there is an array of factors that can influence peace efforts. Consequently, to attribute a successful peace effort solely to the ICTY would be misleading. The results of this study suggest that the ICTY facilitated, versus determined, peace efforts. Second, this chapter provides only a snapshot of one wartime ICT's impact on peace efforts. It is therefore important to exercise caution in extrapolating the findings to other contexts. Nonetheless, this study's findings can provide a basis for the inductive development of testable hypotheses concerning the impact of other wartime ICTs on efforts to end civil conflicts.

In this vein, it is helpful to briefly consider *why* the ICTY might have facilitated, versus undermined, peace efforts. In order for ICTs to increase the costs of noncompliance with ICL, and thereby generate leverage for mediators, they need to be able to conduct legal proceedings. However, unlike the Nuremberg and Tokyo Tribunals, modern ICTs lack an occupying military force capable of carrying out their orders. Thus, ICT officials must negotiate with a range of parties to effectively conduct investigations, secure apprehensions, and hold trials. In short, ICTs require prosecutorial support. Prosecutorial support for ICTs has steadily increased ever since the ICTY's establishment. Indeed, the Tribunal's own successes in eventually apprehending an array of high-level suspects—including Slobodan Milošević—are indicative of this trend, as are the ICC's recent victories in apprehending a number of high-level suspects.[82] Political scientist Kathyrn Sikkink points to such developments as evidence of a 'justice cascade', or 'a fundamental shift legitimacy of the norm of individual criminal accountability for human rights violations and an increase in criminal

[81] Anonymous ICTY official.
[82] As of 2019, the ICC has forty-five Defendants. Fifteen Defendants are at large.

prosecutions on behalf of that norm'.[83] Thus, it is now harder—especially for the top combatant leaders who are at the centre of the ICC's efforts—to dodge criminal prosecution.[84]

However, recent research suggests that greater prosecutorial support, combined with the ICC's focus on high-level suspects, can actually make the process of negotiating peace far more difficult. For instance, Alyssa Prorok finds that both factors have made it more difficult for top leaders facing possible prosecution to attend talks for fear they might be arrested and transferred to The Hague. In addition, because amnesty is off the table, it is more challenging to negotiate a settlement.[85] The situation was quite different for the ICTY during the Yugoslav wars. The Tribunal had an immensely challenging time securing prosecutorial support, especially early on.[86] Indeed, during peace talks on Bosnia the US was one of the few actors that not only expressed a willingness to potentially arrest suspects, but also had the capacity to do so.[87] At the same time, however, the OTP was reluctant to pursue indictments against top leaders unless it could build a strong evidentiary case against them. For instance, OTP officials liked to quote a proverb: 'If you're going to strike at the king, make sure you kill him.'[88] Some OTP staffers also expressed concerns about how high-level indictments might affect the peace process. For example, when questioned about potentially indicting Serbian President Slobodan Milošević, one staffer indicated that, 'I think there'll be hesitation from the prosecutor. Politically, you don't want to dislocate someone from the political process'.[89] Consequently, the OTP did not end up targeting many top leaders until after peace negotiations had concluded.[90] This suggests that regional leaders potentially had much less to fear than their contemporary counterparts in other civil conflicts, assuming they did not run afoul of the ICTY's then-main enforcement partner: the US. Thus, the ICTY perhaps facilitated, versus undermined, peace efforts both because it was cautious in indicting top leaders and because lead mediators effectively exercised discretion over suspect arrests and transfers. At this stage, however, these conjectures are unproven hypotheses that require further testing.

Ultimately, the ICTY's record in Bosnia helps to shed insight into the positive effects that wartime ICTs can have on efforts to end civil conflict. Future research can build on this study to explore when wartime ICTs are most likely to facilitate, versus undermine, bargaining to end civil wars.

[83] Sikkink (n 37) 5.

[84] Prorok (n 31); D Krcmaric, *The Justice Dilemma: International Criminal Accountability, Mass Atrocities, and Civil Conflict (Doctoral Dissertation)* (Duke University 2015); Jo and Simmons (n 17); Sikkink (n 37).

[85] Prorok (n 31); The Rome Statute does not feature any direct mention of amnesty provisions. See M P Scharf, 'The Amnesty Exception to the Jurisdiction of the International Criminal Court' (1999) 32 Cornell International Law Journal 507; L Keller, 'Achieving Peace with Justice: The International Criminal Court and Ugandan Alternative Justice Mechanisms' (2007) 23 Connecticut Journal of International Law 209.

[86] J R McAllister, 'Bending the Arc: How to Achieve Justice at the International Criminal Court' Foreign Affairs online publication Office of the Prosecutor ICTY, 'History' <https://www.foreignaffairs.com/articles/2015-08-03/bending-arc> accessed 25 November 2017; B Reid, interview, The Hague, The Netherlands (20 March 2012); R Goldstone, interview with author (21 June 2013).

[87] McAllister (n 10) 111.

[88] Bass (n 19) 228.

[89] ibid.

[90] During the Bosnian War, the only top leaders that the ICTY indicted were Bosnian Serb President Karadžić and Colonel General Mladić. During the Kosovo War, the ICTY indicted FRY President Milošević, as well as his top deputies. For more details on the ICTY's prosecutorial strategy, refer to Goldstone (n 6); McAllister (n 17) 151.

28

Croatia's Homeland War, the Battles Over Victor's Justice, and the Legacy of the ICTY

*Victor Peskin**

28.1 Introduction

28.1.1 'A Second Nuremberg' and the Re-emergence of International Criminal Justice

Less than a year into the devastating Bosnian war, US Secretary of State Lawrence Eagleburger pointed to the re-emergence of international justice on the near horizon. During a December 1992 peace conference in Geneva, Eagleburger warned of the inevitability of Serbs winding up in the international dock for their violent pursuit of 'the suicidal dream of a Greater Serbia'. [1]

The Serbian people need 'to understand that a second Nuremberg awaits the practitioners of ethnic cleansing, and that the judgment and opprobrium of history awaits the people in whose name their crimes were committed',[2] said Eagleburger, who went on to name ten Serb and Croat political and military leaders who might face international indictment.

The looming shadow of international criminal prosecution of individuals did little to impress the Serbian electorate to abandon their nationalist leader, Slobodan Milošević, on the eve of a crucial presidential election. Milošević single-handedly won another term in office. Nor did Eagleburger's warning ameliorate the behaviour of Milošević or Bosnian Serb leaders Radovan Karadžić and Ratko Mladić, all of whom were singled out by Eagleburger as alleged war criminals. However, Eagleburger's prediction did prove correct on an important score. In May 1993, the Security Council authorized the establishment of the first ever United Nations criminal tribunal[3] and the first international war crimes court since post-Second World War, Allied-run, military tribunals at Nuremberg and Tokyo.

From the moment of its creation, the International Criminal Tribunal for the Former Yugoslavia (ICTY) was seen by many human rights advocates as the long-delayed offspring of Nuremberg. Moreover, the new court was perceived as an opportunity not only to breathe new life into the dormant principle, first established at Nuremberg, of holding leaders individually responsible for mass atrocities but also to reinvigorate the global justice

* Associate Professor, School of Politics and Global Studies, Arizona State University.

[1] E Sciolino, 'U.S. Names Figures it Wants Charged with War Crimes' (*New York Times*, 17 December 1992) <http://www.nytimes.com/1992/12/17/world/us-names-figures-it-wants-charged-with-war-crimes.html?pagewanted=all> accessed 21 February 2018.

[2] ibid.

[3] UNSC Res 877 (1993) UN Doc S/RES/877.

Victor Peskin, *Croatia's Homeland War, the Battles Over Victor's Justice, and the Legacy of the ICTY* In: *Legacies of the International Criminal Tribunal for the Former Yugoslavia.* Edited by: Carsten Stahn, Carmel Agius, Serge Brammertz, Colleen Rohan, Oxford University Press (2020). © The Several Contributors DOI: 10.1093/oso/9780198862956.003.0029

and human rights movement.[4] With the emergence of the ICTY and the UN International Criminal Tribunal for Rwanda (ICTR) in late 1994, practitioners, diplomats, and scholars came to rediscover the Nuremberg inheritance. Some scholars, like Edward M. Wise, praised Nuremberg for sparking 'the beginning of the great movement of our times to protect individuals against oppression by their governments'.[5] Others, like Gary Bass, heralded the extraordinary legal precedent that Nuremberg created for the ICTY and other contemporary tribunals.[6] Rather than carry out summary executions of captured Nazi officers, as both Stalin and Churchill initially favoured, the august legal proceedings in Nuremberg's Palace of Justice anchored the principle that all suspects, including those implicated in aggressive war and extermination, were legally innocent until proven guilty and, therefore, deserved trials with ample due process guarantees.[7] But even as it would build upon the jurisprudential foundation of Nuremberg, the new ICTY would repudiate other aspects of that famous Second World War era tribunal. Indeed, the establishment of the ICTY marked both the affirmation and negation of Nuremberg.

For better and for worse, Eagleburger's 'second Nuremberg' hardly resembled the original one. This particularly rang true when comparing the old and new tribunals on two key dimensions: (1) their capacity to deliver timely and effective justice free of State interference; and (2) their commitment to deliver justice universally by prosecuting the victors as well as the vanquished. When it came to these crucial dimensions, the Allied-run Nuremberg Tribunal and the UN-run ICTY were practically opposites.

Nuremberg scored high on the first dimension, delivering timely and effective justice in a ten-month long trial that ended in verdicts against twenty-two of the twenty-four senior Nazis charged by Allied prosecutors. But Nuremberg scored low on the second dimension, delivering one-sided justice that focused exclusively on the losers rather than seeking a more comprehensive or universal justice that scrutinized the winners as well. The ICTY, on the other hand, scored low on the first dimension insofar as it initially struggled to obtain custody of suspects and hold trials of high-level defendants because, in sharp contrast to Nuremberg, the contemporary tribunal lacked enforcement powers. Belatedly though, the ICTY would enjoy remarkable success in obtaining custody of scores of fugitives and holding many trials which, in turn, would become one of the most important legacies of this Hague-based court. By mid-2011, there was no longer a need for the ubiquitous ICTY 'wanted' posters that had been crowded with the mug shots of so many Balkan fugitives, since by that point there were no longer any ICTY suspects at large. Most suspects had either voluntarily surrendered or had been arrested and then transferred to the Tribunal, though some had died as fugitives and others had had their indictments withdrawn. Despite this belated success in arrests, the early failure to obtain custody of numerous suspects meant that verdicts in important cases—notably the one that sentenced Bosnian Serb General Ratko Mladić to a life term for genocide, crimes against humanity, and war crimes in November

[4] D Bosco, *Rough Justice: The International Criminal Court in a World of Power Politics* (Oxford University Press 2014) 36.

[5] E M Wise, 'The Significance of Nuremberg' in B Cooper (ed), *War Crimes: The Legacy of Nuremberg* (TV Books 1999) 59.

[6] G J Bass, *Stay the Hand of Vengeance: The Politics of War Crimes Tribunals* (Princeton University Press 2002) 205.

[7] ibid 205.

2017[8]—were long delayed. The ICTY, however, scored high on the second dimension mentioned, given that its prosecutorial practice eschewed victor's justice by targeting suspects from all combatant groups from the former Yugoslavia.

The Nuremberg Tribunal's ability to dispense justice effectively is directly attributable to the high level of enforcement capacity it possessed as the legal arm of the Allied occupation.[9] This endowed Allied prosecutors with the means to quickly obtain custody of suspects, secure incriminating evidence, locate and safeguard witnesses, and accomplish a range of other tasks that paved the way for the timely prosecution of indicted Nazi war criminals. The Allied dragnet in occupied Germany did have gaping holes, however. Many Nazis fled the country and the European continent via 'ratlines' that took them to South America while countless others stayed in Germany where they hid in plain sight for decades. Adolph Hitler, Heinrich Himmler, and other notorious Nazis evaded the reach of justice by their own hand while another Nazi leader, Hermann Goring, avoided punishment, though not judgment, by taking a cyanide pill hours before his scheduled execution.[10] This act of defiance would be mirrored seven decades later when the Bosnian Croat defendant Slobodan Praljak drank poison during a November 2017 ICTY courtroom hearing in which the Appeals Chamber upheld his conviction for war crimes and crimes against humanity.[11] These individual acts of defiance notwithstanding, the Allied destruction of the Nazi State prevented the possibility of German State obstruction of justice.

At Nuremberg, military triumph fostered justice. Yet, victory also facilitated impunity. Allied prosecutors, as we know, focused exclusively on the far greater crimes of Nazi Germany. This fact was not denied or downplayed, but was an explicit attribute of postwar justice at Nuremberg, as well as Tokyo.[12] Jurisdictional constraints barred prosecutors from what in any case would have been unthinkable at the time—scrutinizing the Allied bombing campaign of German cities, such as the firebombing of Dresden,[13] as well as the wave of revenge attacks and wide-scale expulsions of ethnic Germans in the wake of the war.[14] At the Tokyo Tribunal, the fire-bombing of Tokyo and the nuclear incineration of Hiroshima and Nagasaki were off limits as well.

The ICTY and its institutional successors seemed well poised to 'distance' themselves from what Matthew R. Brubacher calls 'the haunting legacies of victor's justice and impunity'.[15] Indeed, the new contemporary international tribunals have been centrally concerned with ensuring that the partisan justice of the Nuremberg and Tokyo tribunals that immunized the winners of war remained a political relic of a bygone era.

8 *Prosecutor v Ratko Mladić* (Trial Chamber Judgment) ICTY-IT-09-92-T (22 November 2017) para 2473. The case was initiated in 1995, but the arrest and transfer happened in 2011; see ICTY, 'Case Information Sheet' (The Cases) <http://www.icty.org/x/cases/mladic/cis/en/cis_mladic_en.pdf> accessed 21 February 2018.

9 Bass (n 6) 147–205.

10 On the arrest of high-level Nazis, see E Stover, V Peskin, and A Koenig, *Hiding in Plain Sight: The Pursuit of War Criminals from Nuremberg to the War on Terror* (University of California Press 2016).

11 ICTY, 'Statement on passing of Slobodan Praljak' (Press Releases, 29 November 2017) <http://www.icty.org/en/press/statement-on-passing-of-slobodan-praljak> accessed 21 February 2018.

12 Bosco (n 4) 28.

13 C S Maier, 'Targeting the City: Debates and Silences about the Aerial Bombing of World War II' (2005) 87 International Review of the Red Cross 429; W A Schabas, *Unimaginable Atrocities: Justice, Politics, and Rights at the War Crimes Tribunals* (Oxford University Press 2012) 72.

14 K Lowe, *Savage Continent: Europe in the Aftermath of World War II* (Picador 2012) 230–48.

15 M R Brubacher, 'Prosecutorial Discretion within the International Criminal Court' (2004) 2 Journal of International Criminal Justice 72.

28.1.2 Key Questions and Central Issues

The primary aim of this chapter is to determine whether and the extent to which the ICTY has moved beyond the inured practice of immunizing the winners of armed conflict witnessed at Nuremberg and Tokyo. A contemporary international tribunal, in my view, has transcended victor's justice if it has robustly held to account suspects from the victorious States or rebel groups involved in the armed conflicts under the tribunal's jurisdiction. What does it mean to robustly hold suspects to account in a contemporary international court of law? In the views of the author, an international tribunal has robustly held the victors to account if (1) its chief prosecutor has moved beyond a rhetorical embrace of the principle of justice for all by indicting suspects from the victorious as well as the losing sides of an armed conflict implicated in serious violations of international humanitarian law; and (2) its chief prosecutor and the tribunal have proved capable of overcoming obstruction of justice that is aimed at insulating the victorious State or rebel group from accountability. Overcoming such obstruction does not necessarily entail the elimination of State non-compliance altogether. Nor does it mean that the prosecution must necessarily prevail at trial or the appeals stages. Rather, it means that a tribunal has rendered timely and effective accountability—not only by obtaining custody of indicted suspects, but also by running trials devoid of the type of pervasive State interference that can sorely undermine and doom the viability of a prosecution's case and the integrity of the legal process.

This chapter examines the ICTY's battles with the Croatian government over victor's justice. Section 28.2 explains why a universal vision of accountability is so central to the mission of the ICTY and the other contemporary tribunals. The section goes on to explain why the ICTY, which initially seemed poised to receive ample global support to move beyond one-sided justice, confronted formidable resistance from the Security Council and from the winners of the Yugoslav wars of succession. This section also explains how state non-compliance can tempt some chief prosecutors at some international tribunals to soft pedal the pursuit of suspects from powerful States, especially suspects from those States that have emerged as the winners of war. The ICTY chief prosecutors, however, did not succumb to this temptation. Yet, as Section 28.3 shows, the prosecution's commitment to move beyond victor's justice in Croatia did not necessarily ensure success. Section 28.3 examines the dynamics and outcomes of the chief prosecutors' battles over victor's justice that ensued with Croatia, the decisive winner of the 1991–95 war against Serb forces. Section 28.4 concludes the chapter by arguing that despite the fact that ICTY prosecutors did not end up sustaining any convictions of Croatian generals, the Tribunal nevertheless won the larger war over victor's justice vis-à-vis the Croatian State.

28.2 Beyond Victor's Justice in the Hague

28.2.1 The ICTY and the Universal Vision of International Justice

The ICTY emerged in a post-Cold War normative climate that extolled the idea of an impartial international war crimes chief prosecutor that would vigorously pursue suspects from all sides of armed conflict. One-sided justice may have been legitimate at Nuremberg and Tokyo, but not for a contemporary international tribunal inspired by the principle of universal human rights. In fact, discomfort with the Nuremberg legacy came to the fore long before the re-emergence of the global justice movement in the early 1990s. 'There is no moral or legal basis for immunizing the victorious nations from scrutiny. The laws of war are not a one-way street', wrote Telford Taylor, an American prosecutor at Nuremberg, in the conclusion of his account of the trials.[16] Even during the Nuremberg proceedings, at least one lead prosecutor questioned a judicial process that targeted German suspects for some of the same conduct in which the Allies themselves were implicated. '[The Allies] have done or are doing some of the very things we are prosecuting Germans for', noted Robert Jackson, the lead American prosecutor at Nuremberg, in an October 1945 letter to President Harry Truman. 'We are prosecuting plunder and our allies are practicing it. We say aggressive war is a crime and one of our allies assert sovereignty over the Baltic States based on no title except conquest'.[17]

The ICTY appeared to possess the structural attributes essential for moving beyond victor's justice. First, the Tribunal had a jurisdictional framework that allowed the prosecution of anyone implicated in serious violations of international humanitarian law (IHL) in the territory of the former Yugoslavia from the start of the Balkan wars in 1991, until a date subsequently decided by the Security Council.[18] Second, the Tribunal's chief prosecutor had apparently been given the independence necessary to insulate investigation and indictment decisions from the pressures and influences of victorious States and powerful international political actors interested in immunizing these states. Third, whereas Nuremberg had been established by a coalition of victorious States intent on using law selectively to settle accounts with their vanquished enemies, the ICTY was established by the international community, in the name of humanity, and with a mission to achieve a cosmopolitan vision of justice that would not exclude the suffering of any ethnic, religious, or national group.[19]

Importantly, not only human rights activists and international prosecutors celebrated the Tribunal's mission to ensure that suspects from all sides of the Balkan wars would face accountability. The Security Council founders did as well, as illustrated by the pledge made by Madeleine Albright, the then US ambassador to the UN, on the day the Council voted to authorize the establishment of the Tribunal in May 1993. The Tribunal, Albright vowed, 'will be no victor's tribunal. The only victor that will prevail in this endeavor will be the truth'.[20] If all went well, the new tribunal would advance truth, justice, and peace in the Balkans and catalyse a new system of global criminal accountability free of the taint of one-sided justice that, from the vantage point of the early 1990s, had retrospectively tarnished the Nuremberg legacy.

28.2.2 The Security Council and the False Promise of Enforcement

In unanimously voting to establish the ICTY, the Security Council had, in effect, sworn to back up its rhetorical support for this universal vision of justice with legal authority,

[16] T Taylor, *The Anatomy of the Nuremberg Trials: A Personal Memoir* (Alfred A. Knopf 1992) 641.
[17] Bosco (n 4) 28–29.
[18] UNSC Res 827 (1993) UN Doc S/Res/827.
[19] Schabas (n 13) 76.
[20] M Scharf, *Balkan Justice: The Story Behind the First International War Crimes Tribunal Since Nuremberg* (Carolina University Press 1997) 54.

political power, and even military muscle. To aid the Tribunal in realizing its quest to hold suspects from all sides of the Yugoslav wars of succession to account, the Council equipped The Hague-based court with an impressive degree of legal authority, vis-à-vis the States in the region, regardless of whether they ended up winners, losers, or somewhere in between in their armed conflicts. All of the States of the former Yugoslavia—and any other UN Member State, including the major powers on the Council—had an international binding legal obligation to provide full and immediate cooperation to the Tribunal in providing evidence, facilitating tribunal investigations, safeguarding witnesses, and arresting and transferring suspects for trial. By law, then, all States of the former Yugoslavia implicated in wartime atrocities had to assist the Tribunal in bringing suspects from their own ethnic group to trial.[21]

Despite their binding legal obligation to cooperate with the ICTY, it soon became apparent that Slobodan Milošević's Serbia (which would become the main loser of the Yugoslav wars of succession) and Franjo Tuđjman's Croatia (which would become one of the main winners) would try their best to sabotage international justice. The spectre of non-cooperation did not disappear when democratic governments swept aside the authoritarian Milošević and Tuđjman regimes in 2000. As it turned out, even the democratic governments in Belgrade and Zagreb excelled at obstruction of justice. When the States of the former Yugoslavia obstructed justice, the Security Council had the legal authority to intervene to protect the Tribunal's global standing. State defiance of the ICTY would not only constitute State defiance of international justice, but also of the world's supreme political body because the Tribunal had been created pursuant to a Council resolution. If the Council chose to safeguard its own authority—as it made sense it would want to in order to ensure the success of its costly investment in international justice—it had a tool kit of punitive actions to use against non-compliant States. The UN could impose a range of political and economic sanctions. Pursuant to its Chapter VII powers, the Council could also mobilize military force in the form of a rapid reaction arrest team to capture notorious fugitives enjoying the protection of complicit regimes. If sticks proved ineffective, carrots might do the trick. The Security Council—or any State on the Council or any regional organization like the European Union (EU) or North Atlantic Treaty Organization (NATO)—could offer incentives to recalcitrant targeted States to induce them to abide by their legal obligation to the Tribunal.

On paper, at least, the nascent ICTY seemed the image of perfection. The Tribunal was positioned to advance a vision of universal justice that spurned *de jure* or *de facto* impunity for suspects from all State or combatant groups in the former Yugoslavia. The Tribunal also could turn to a higher power—the UN Security Council—to ensure that the winners as well as the losers would end up in the dock. The binding legal obligation on all UN Member States to cooperate combined with the Council's implicit promise to stand up for its fledgling institutional offspring, seemingly brightened the ICTY's prospects of surpassing the Nuremberg legacy by simultaneously delivering effective and equitable accountability in The Hague.

In this optimistic forecast, the Security Council would be the enforcement arm of the new tribunal, just as the Allied occupying armies in Germany served as the enforcement

[21] UNSC 'Statute of the International Criminal Tribunal for the Former Yugoslavia' (as amended 7 July 2009 by Resolution 1877), 25 May 1993, appended to UN Doc S/RES/877, arts 1 and 29.

arm of the Nuremberg tribunal. But in reality, the ICTY could not rely upon the Council to enforce States' compliance obligations and ensure that the winners and the losers of the Balkan wars would be held accountable. In fact, the Council frequently abdicated its responsibility to its judicial offspring by dealing weakly with State obstruction in the former Yugoslavia.[22] Soon after authorizing the Tribunal's establishment, the Council grew deeply ambivalent about expanding military force or much political or economic capital on behalf of the ICTY. Why then had the UN created the Tribunal if it was not prepared to ensure its success? Commentators surmised that the Council had triggered international judicial intervention not out of a genuine desire to see justice done, but as a fig leaf for its inaction in using military force to halt the bloodshed in Bosnia.[23]

A lack of international political will was not the only obstacle that stood in the way of the delivery of timely trials in The Hague. The Security Council did not possess a high level of enforcement capacity to ensure the effectiveness of the ICTY. During the Bosnian and Croatian wars, the UN deployed peacekeepers, but primarily with a humanitarian mandate. After the Dayton Accords, NATO sent 60,000 heavily armed peacekeepers to secure the fragile peace, though not initially with a mandate to apprehend tribunal suspects out of fear that arrest raids would incur troop casualties.[24] NATO troops, in sharp contrast to the Allied conquerors in post-war Germany, were hesitant occupiers wary of undermining a fragile peace. For the ICTY, obtaining custody of suspects posed an even greater challenge when it came to trying to persuade Serbia and Croatia, fully sovereign States that had no international peacekeepers present on their territories, to arrest suspects hailed at home as war heroes.

In the absence of robust UN enforcement and in the presence of a strong determination of targeted States in the Balkan wars to evade accountability, it became apparent that the fledgling ICTY might flail and ultimately fail. In a worst-case scenario, the Tribunal would not only succumb to victor's justice—by failing to obtain custody and being prevented from prosecuting suspects from the winning sides of the Balkan wars—but also fall victim to loser's justice—by failing to obtain custody of and being prevented from prosecuting suspects from the losing side. However, the absence of strong Security Council enforcement would not necessarily trigger such a worst-case scenario. As we will see in section 28.3, the ICTY would seek out the US and the EU to act as strong surrogate enforcers, ultimately compelling the recalcitrant governments in Belgrade and Zagreb to provide far-ranging, if long-delayed, cooperation.

28.2.3 The Spectre of State Non-compliance and the Logic of Prosecutorial Concessions

The well-founded fear of State non-compliance and even institutional failure has, at some international tribunals, fostered a pragmatic logic of concessions in indictment decisions geared towards ensuring the delivery of a half a loaf of justice rather than no loaf at all.

[22] For examples of Security Council passivity vis-à-vis the States of the former Yugoslavia, See V Peskin, *International Justice in Rwanda and the Balkans: Virtual Trials and the Struggle for State Cooperation* (Cambridge University Press 2008).

[23] Bass (n 6).

[24] Bass (n 6) 239–43.

At the ICTR, Chief Prosecutor Carla Del Ponte promised to indict suspects from the victorious Tutsi-led Rwandan Patriotic Front (RPF) government, implicated in widespread and systematic violations of IHL against Hutu civilians. This never materialized, amid two key developments: (1) the RPF's successful effort in Summer 2002 to halt the trials of Hutu genocide defendants by preventing Tutsi survivors from testifying at the Arusha-based court; and (2) the Security Council's 2003 decision to acquiesce to the RPF's campaign to replace Del Ponte with a compliant chief prosecutor.[25] At the International Criminal Court (ICC), a similar contemporary version of victor's justice has so far prevailed in a majority of the court's African country situations. In Uganda, Libya, Côte d'Ivoire, Central African Republic, and Mali, the ICC prosecution has effectively pursued one-sided justice, only charging suspects from defeated and despised rebel groups or deposed regimes.[26] All of today's international tribunals are highly dependent on States for cooperation. But this dependence is heightened at certain tribunals. The ICTR, for instance, found itself particularly vulnerable to Rwandan obstruction because the government could essentially shut down tribunal operations by blocking the travel of prosecution witnesses to the Tribunal. The ICC's dependence on States is pronounced because the court, in addition to needing the cooperation of targeted States in ongoing cases, also seeks to garner universal State membership and thereby live up to its aspiration to be a truly global institution.

The contemporary tribunals' lack of enforcement powers can have far reaching implications, at times creating a temptation for chief prosecutors not to alienate or anger external actors. The imperative to obtain and maintain cooperation can prompt a chief prosecutor to carefully read the tea leaves of domestic and geo-politics to surmise how best to avoid damaging interference. A chief prosecutor too anxious to risk State backlash and provoke the 'withdrawal of affection'[27] from international actors might find it more strategic to avoid enmeshing the tribunal in conflict by foregoing rigorous investigations and indictments of suspects from victorious States—or from suspects from other types of powerful States or non-State actors—from whom the tribunal relies upon to deliver accountability. It is in this scenario that an international tribunal ostensibly created to act above politics and reject *de jure* victor's justice might end up delivering *de facto* victor's justice instead.

The winners of armed conflict, such as the RPF government in Rwanda, often possess considerable leverage vis-à-vis the international community. Emerging as a winner of an intra-State or interstate war can foster a dynamic of international community dependence that in time can lead to acquiescence to the victorious post-war government. Deference to the victors can advance a range of international interests vis-à-vis the victor State. These interests can include persuading the victor State to protect vulnerable minorities, to undertake democratic reforms, to avoid meddling in neighbouring countries, to facilitate refugee return, to enter into military alliances, and to welcome foreign economic investment.

The greater the international dependence on the victor State the more likely that State will feel emboldened to withhold cooperation from an international tribunal without fear of significant international political censure. If a victorious State is particularly bold, it will try to persuade key regional and international actors to intervene on its behalf against an

[25] Peskin (n 22).
[26] Bosco (n 4).
[27] Louise Arbour as quoted in C Trueheart, 'A New Kind of Justice' (*The Atlantic*, April 2000) <https://www.theatlantic.com/magazine/archive/2000/04/a-new-kind-of-justice/305709/> accessed 21 February 2018.

international tribunal, thereby hoping that such actors will act as 'surrogate obstructors' rather than as 'surrogate enforcers' of international justice.[28] The propensity of powerful international actors to intervene on behalf of victorious States or rebel groups may be enhanced when these actors have cemented a close alliance with the victors either during war—as in the NATO–Kosovo Liberation Army (KLA) partnership during the Kosovo war—or in the aftermath of war—as in the US and British political alliance with the Tutsi-led RPF after the Rwandan genocide and civil war.

The logic of providing de facto impunity to the victors can exert a stronger or weaker pull on a chief prosecutor depending on (1) the extent to which he or she can rely upon surrogate enforcers to support their indictment decisions; (2) the leverage that a victorious State possesses vis- à-vis a tribunal and the international community; and (3) the degree to which the international diplomatic and press corps scrutinize the crimes of the victors. In regard to these three factors, the ICTY, in contrast to the ICC and ICTR, was often in a more favourable position to move beyond victor's justice. Beyond these structural factors, the ICTY chief prosecutors—Richard Goldstone, Louse Arbour, Carla Del Ponte, and Serge Brammertz—stand out for their tenacity in waging a comprehensive fight against impunity—not only targeting the losers of armed conflict, but the winners as well.

28.2.4 Engaging the Battle Against Victor's Justice at the ICTY: Inspired by Principle, Facilitated by Politics

From an early point, the ICTY Office of the Prosecutor (OTP) scrutinized suspects from all sides of the Balkan wars, even as they trained most attention on Serb suspects. In doing so, the early chief prosecutors were wary of fostering a notion of ethnic quotas or of distributing indictments among different ethnic groups, as Richard Goldstone once remarked, 'for the sake of . . . saying what an even-handed chap I am'.[29] Prosecuting suspects from all combatant groups just to be seen as impartial, remarked Louise Arbour, would be 'playing the game of holding a mirror to the former Yugoslavia about its ethnic pathologies' and seeing everything through the lens of ethnicity.[30] But leaving serious violations of IHL unpunished by foregoing indictments of non-Serbs would be even more problematic.

The ICTY's equal-opportunity approach to war crimes investigations was inspired by principle, anchored in evidence, and ultimately facilitated by politics. The successive ICTY chief prosecutors and their deputies embraced the universalistic vision of contemporary global justice that, after all, was meant to distinguish this new experiment in international law from its Second World War era predecessors. Wisely, though, ICTY prosecutors did not target each combatant group in equal numbers, given the substantial atrocity differential that existed between the greater overall crimes of Serb forces, on the one hand, and the lesser overall crimes of non-Serb forces, on the other.[31]

[28] Peskin (n 22) 12.

[29] Author interview with former ICTY Chief Prosecutor Richard Goldstone, Pasadena, CA, April 2003.

[30] Author interview with former ICTY Chief Prosecutor Louise Arbour, Brussels, May 2011.

[31] R Cohen, 'C.I.A. Report on Bosnia Blames Serbs for 90% of the War Crimes' (*New York Times*, 9 March 1995) <https://www.nytimes.com/1995/03/09/world/cia-report-on-bosnia-blames-serbs-for-90-of-the-war-crimes.html> accessed 21 April 2018.

The prosecution's decision to investigate suspects from all sides of the Balkan wars—including those from a victorious state (Croatia) and a victorious rebel group (the KLA)—was fostered by a relatively conducive political climate. During the Bosnian war, international diplomatic and media scrutiny paid significant attention to atrocities committed by all combatant groups.[32] Particularly in the early part of the war, Western diplomats blamed Serbs, Croats, and Bosnian Muslims in almost equal measure, a cynical move deployed to temper international calls for military intervention against massive Serbian ethnic cleansing attacks.[33] By the end of 1992, however, the US had singled out Serb forces as the main culprits in Bosnia, as underscored by Eagleburger's blistering 'naming names' speech. Even so, Eagleburger's list of ten potential suspects also included ethnic Croats.[34] This 'all sides are to blame' narrative raised awareness that all armed groups were implicated in atrocities. In this context, it would have been difficult for the ICTY chief prosecutors not to seek accountability for victims from all ethnic groups in the Balkans because it had already been well established globally that all sides were implicated in serious wartime crimes. Moreover, ignoring Belgrade's vocal calls to see justice delivered for crimes against Serbs would neither have been principled nor prudent, given the significance of these crimes and the importance of countering the engrained Serbian narrative that cast the ICTY as a victimizer of the Serbian people for mostly indicting Serb suspects.

Prosecuting suspects from all sides of the Balkan wars also made strategic sense for the chief prosecutors' overall campaign to garner State cooperation, and to thereby mitigate the damage wrought by Serbian defiance during the Milošević years. To be sure, targeting ethnic Croats, Bosnian Muslims, and later Kosovar Albanians risked rendering the ICTY unpopular with all groups. Indeed, until the ICTY's very last day, Croatian leaders, mirroring the long-running strategy of their Serbian counterparts, lambasted the Tribunal for supposedly casting collective guilt on their respective nations. This despite the *raison d'etre* of the contemporary international tribunals to determine *individual* criminal responsibility. Witness Croatian Prime Minister Andrej Plenković's withering criticism of the ICTY following the courtroom suicide of convicted Bosnian Croat war criminal Slobodan Praljak during a November 2017 ICTY Appeals Chamber. Praljak's life-ending decision to drink potassium cyanide to protest his conviction, remarked Plenković, 'speaks most of a deep moral injustice towards six indicted Croats from Bosnia and the Croatian people'.[35]

Croatia's longstanding anger with the ICTY notwithstanding the prosecution's comprehensive indictment approach had two strategic advantages. First, it somewhat blunted the sting of Serbian accusations of tribunal bias which Serbian authorities repeatedly deployed as a pretext for non-compliance. Second, it created more opportunities for State cooperation by increasing the number of different States or 'theatres' to which the ICTY could turn. This diversified prosecutorial approach to State cooperation prevented any one State in the former Yugoslavia from thwarting the Tribunal altogether—a scenario which loomed over the ICTR, given the RPF government's move to halt trials by blocking genocide survivors from travelling to the Arusha-based tribunal and testifying for the prosecution.

[32] S Power, *'A Problem From Hell' America and the Age of Genocide* (Harper Perennial 2002) 268–69.
[33] ibid.
[34] Sciolino (n 1).
[35] 'Praljak: Bosnian Croat War Criminal Dies After Taking Poison in Court' (*BBC News*, 29 November 2017) <http://www.bbc.com/news/world-europe-42163613> accessed 21 April 2004.

In stark contrast to Serbia during the Milošević era, Croatia during the Tuđjman era proved relatively amenable to concerted Western pressure to cooperate as seen in a wave of early voluntary surrenders of Bosnian Croats. Tuđjman detested the ICTY no less than his nationalist counterpart in Belgrade. But the ICTY's surrogate enforcers in Washington and Brussels possessed considerably greater leverage over the authoritarian Croatian leader, given his ardent desire to remain in the good graces of the West to secure membership in NATO and European institutions.[36] By opening a range of different investigations in different countries and against suspects from different sides of the conflict—including against those who fought for the victorious Croatian military and the KLA—the ICTY chief prosecutors prevented any one State from bringing the Tribunal to its knees. In this regard, targeting the victors, while certainly controversial in Croatia and Kosovo, paid an important justice dividend for the Tribunal by advancing its larger quest for State cooperation in the former Yugoslavia.

The strategic advantages of pursuing the winners did not mean the Tribunal would have an easy time holding the victors to account, however. In Croatia, as well as in Kosovo, the ICTY had to contend with targeted States whose public vows of cooperation were often belied by a campaign of delay and defiance. The ICTY faced distinct challenges in its battles over cooperation with the winners of the Balkan wars. In Croatia, the main challenge revolved around obtaining custody of Croatian fugitives hailed at home as national heroes. The arrest challenge was rendered more difficult because Croatia, unlike Bosnia or Kosovo, was a fully sovereign State without international peacekeepers on its territory to apprehend suspects. In Kosovo, the central challenge in overcoming victor's justice did not involve the matter of arrests, but rather the unprecedented witness intimidation that undermined the prosecution of KLA defendants.[37] Occurring in the shadows, the threats and harm inflicted on Kosovar Albanian prosecution witnesses proved extremely difficult to monitor and bring to an end.

28.3 The Battles Over Victor's Justice: Croatia and the ICTY

28.3.1 Of Victory and Atrocity: The Crimes of Operation Storm

It is not uncommon for combatant groups to try to score propaganda coups by claiming the mantle of victory (and victimhood). In some wars—such as the one in Bosnia which split the country and froze the conflict indefinitely—no side wins. But in other conflicts—such as the ones in Croatia and Kosovo—an undisputed winner emerges.

The Croatian army's victory in its August 1995 Operation Storm was both 'a dramatic gamble' and 'a complete success' in the estimation of US diplomat Richard Holbrooke.[38] Washington and London had warned Zagreb that Belgrade might intervene on behalf of the Croatian Serbs and repel a Croatian military attack.[39] But Milošević did not end up

[36] J Borger, *The Butcher's Trail, How the Search for Balkan War Criminals Became the World's Most Successful Manhunt* (Other Press 2016) 107.

[37] E Behar, *Tell it to the World: International Justice and the Secret Campaign to Hide Mass Murder in Kosovo* (Dundurn 2014) 214–15.

[38] R Holbrooke, *To End a War* (Random House 1998) 72.

[39] ibid 72.

lifting a finger and, as Misha Glenny observed, the Croatian Serbs 'collapsed like a pack of cards'.[40] Tuđjman's military victory forced an exodus of between 150,000 and 200,000 ethnic Serbs from Croatia,[41] placed nearly all of the country's territory under the control of the central government in Zagreb, and brought a triumphant conclusion to Croatia's war of independence.

What a difference four years can make. In the aftermath of Croatia's June 1991 independence declaration, the fledgling nation and its rag tag army had been thrust on the defensive by the superior Serbian-dominated Yugoslav National Army. By the end of the year, Serb forces had captured a third of Croatian territory, bombarded the Adriatic walled city of Dubrovnik, and laid waste to Vukovar before a UN-brokered cease-fire suspended the conflict. Over the next few years, the Croatian army, with training from an American military contractor run by former US generals, prepared to win back the disputed Krajina territory.[42] The Croatian bid to retake the Krajina included a 1993 military operation in the Medak Pocket area and Operation Storm, the culminating military campaign of the so-called Homeland War.

Some US diplomats, notably Holbrooke, were rooting for a Croatian military victory as a means to the end of weakening Serbian military prowess in neighbouring Bosnia. Given the reluctance of Washington and NATO to intervene with decisive military power to end that war, Croatia emerged as Washington's 'junkyard dogs'.[43] Croatia's victory in Operation Storm, according to Holbrooke, 'began to change the balance of power in the region'. It did so in part by revealing that Milošević, as he had with the Croatian Serbs, might similarly abandon the Bosnian Serbs in the face of an offense by a recently-formed Bosnian–Croat military alliance.[44] The Croatian victory, in the view of former US diplomat Warren Zimmermann, also 'transformed the balance of forces in Bosnia', by depriving Bosnian Serb forces of men and supplies from the Krajina.[45] This development, in turn, helped Bosnian Croat and Bosnian Muslim forces deal a blow to Serb forces on the battlefield, thereby advancing the growing American imperative to press Milošević into signing a peace agreement to end the Bosnian war.

Despite the positive strategic outcomes of a Serbian defeat in Croatia, numerous European and some American diplomats remained wary of an impending Croatian offensive to retake the Krajina, given the new cycles of bloodshed it might unleash and the encouragement it might give to Milošević to one day ethnically cleanse Kosovo.[46] In his memoirs, Zimmermann, the last American ambassador to the then Yugoslavia, characterized Operation Storm as an illegal and ruthless military operation that resulted in 'routing virtually the entire Serbian population, some of whose ancestors had lived there since before the time of the Habsburg Empress Maria Theresa' in the eighteenth century.[47] Indeed, Storm led to the single biggest exodus of refugees on the European continent since the end

[40] M Glenny, *The Balkans: Nationalism, War, and The Great Powers, 1804–1999* (Penguin Books 2001) 650.

[41] ibid; E Gordy, *Guilt, Responsibility, and Denial, The Past at Stake in Post-Milosevic Serbia* (University of Pennsylvania Press 2013) 6.

[42] Borger (n 36) 107.

[43] This appraisal was offered by US diplomat Bob Frasure to Richard Holbrooke. See Holbrooke (n 38) 73.

[44] ibid.

[45] W Zimmermann, *Origins of a Catastrophe: Yugoslavia and its Destroyers: America's Last Ambassador Tells What Happened and Why* (Times Books 1996) 232.

[46] Holbrooke (n 38); Glenny (n 40) 650.

[47] Zimmermann (n 45) 231–32.

of the Second World War.[48] Diplomats certainly understood that Croatia's war plans could result in a humanitarian disaster for the Serbs of the Krajina. US diplomat Bob Frasure conveyed to Holbrooke in the aftermath of Storm, that while 'we need to try to "control" [Tuđjman and his Croatian forces] this is no time to get squeamish about things'.[49]

US officials advised Zagreb to keep Storm short and clean. But not surprisingly, Washington's attempt to balance realpolitik with humanitarianism failed. Surely, US diplomats like Holbrooke should have anticipated Tuđjman's likely intention to forcibly remove the Serb population from the contested Krajina region and the jeopardy that such an ethnic cleansing campaign would pose for those Serbs who stayed behind.[50] There had been ample reason to anticipate a brutal Croatian military campaign in the summer of 1995. Senior American diplomats had recognized that Tuđjman was a 'fanatic ... nationalist'[51] determined to bring about an ethnically pure Croatian nation and to carve out territory in Bosnia to create a Greater Croatia.[52] This could have been inferred from studying Tuđjman's role earlier during the Bosnian war in directing Bosnian Croat militias—and the likes of Slobodan Praljak and more than a dozen other Bosnian Croats who would later face ICTY indictment—to destroy Bosnian Muslim and Bosnian Serb communities.[53]

In the end, Storm, which lasted less than 100 hours, was short, but not clean. The mass exodus of Croatian Serbs and the brutal 'mopping-up' operations after battle—which resulted in the killings of some 400 ethnic Serb civilians, many of whom were elderly and unable to flee the military assault—raised red flags of serious violations of international humanitarian law.[54]

28.3.2 A 'Bad Habit of Dying Most Inconveniently': Tuđjman Escapes Indictment

The ICTY OTP would later probe whether Croatian political and military leaders were responsible for war crimes and crimes against humanity during and after Operation Storm. Key to the prosecution's probe of individual suspects was to ascertain whether at the heart the Croatian military's battle plan lay a criminal intent to empty the Krajina of ethnic Serbs. Tuđjman's elation at seeing so many Serbs flee Croatia suggested as much. 'They were gone in a few days as if they had never been here', said the gleeful Croatian president. 'They did not even have time to collect their rotten money and dirty underwear'.[55] The subsequent release of the Brioni transcripts—revealing a Tuđjman-inspired scheme to use the cover of war to oust the Croatian Serbs—underscored the importance of the Tribunal's investigations of the winners of the Homeland War.

48 Glenny (n 40) 650.
49 Holbrooke (n 38) 73.
50 L Silber and A Little, *Yugoslavia: Death of a Nation* (Penguin Books 1997) 360.
51 Zimmermann (n 45) ix.
52 M Albright, *Madame Secretary: A Memoir* (Miramax Books 2003) 338–39.
53 M A Sells, *The Bridge Betrayed: Religion and Genocide in Bosnia* (University of California Press 1998) 94–98; Borger (n 36) 103.
54 E Pond, *Endgame in the Balkans: Regime Change, European Style* (Brookings Institution Press 2006) 122; Borger (n 36) 102.
55 E Stover, V Peskin, and A Koenig, *Hiding in Plain Sight: The Pursuit of War Criminals from Nuremberg to the War on Terror* (University of California Press 2016) 147.

Tuđjman and his defense minister, Gojko Šušak, died before the ICTY could indict them, in connection with Zagreb's role in the ethnic cleansing that occurred in Bosnia as well as in Croatia's victorious Homeland War. The prevailing assumption is that both men would have been charged had they lived longer. Some analysts believe ICTY prosecutors would have had a strong case against the Croatian president. 'There was no shortage of material to pack Tuđjman's burgeoning dossier in The Hague',[56] observed Julian Borger of *The Guardian*. Louise Arbour confirmed that her office had been investigating Tuđjman as part of her policy 'to get to the top as quickly as possible' to determine which suspects on all sides of the Balkan wars bore greatest criminal responsibility.[57] But Arbour and her prosecutors did not complete their investigations of Tuđjman and Šušak in time. 'These guys have this bad habit of dying most inconveniently',[58] she remarked sardonically in a 2011 interview. Arbour's successor, Carla Del Ponte, blamed Tuđjman for mounting 'an organized, covert effort to obstruct the Tribunal's' investigations of the Homeland War and Croatia's role in Bosnian atrocities by withholding incriminating documents and seeking to expose prosecution witnesses.[59]

Had he been indicted, Tuđjman might have 'become an albatross for Croats',[60] opined Elizabeth Pond. State resistance to sending him to The Hague, she added, would likely have kept 'the holy grail of membership in the European Union' beyond reach.[61] In this regard, as Pond argues, his death freed Croatia from its dark past and helped pave the way to the bright future of Europe.[62] Yet, Tuđjman's death raised the spectre of victor's justice at the ICTY; the alleged architect of the crimes of the Homeland War had escaped prosecution by using the machinery of the Croatian state to obstruct international justice. In time, however, ICTY prosecutors would bring indictments against half a dozen Croatian generals.

28.3.3 Nationalist Narratives and the Legitimation of Obstruction of Justice

In mid-2001, Del Ponte issued the first indictments of Croatian generals for war crimes and crimes against humanity pertaining to Operation Storm.[63] In early July, Del Ponte travelled to Zagreb to press government officials to arrest two high-level suspects. In June, the Tribunal handed over sealed indictments naming two Croatian generals in the hopes that the government would use the element of surprise to quickly make arrests. One indictment named Rahim Ademi, an ethnic Albanian who had served as a general for the Croatian army during the Homeland War. The other indictment targeted Ante Gotovina, the charismatic retired general and national war hero who led the army's victorious assault in the southern theatre of the Krajina during Storm.

[56] Borger (n 36) 105.
[57] Author interview with former ICTY Chief Prosecutor Louise Arbour, Brussels, May 2011.
[58] ibid.
[59] C Del Ponte with C Sudetic, *Madame Prosecutor: Confrontations with Humanity's Worst Criminals and The Culture of Impunity* (Other Press 2008) 245.
[60] Pond (n 54) 122.
[61] ibid 121–22.
[62] ibid 122.
[63] ICTY, 'Statement by the Prosecutor Concerning the Gotovina and Ademi Cases,' (Press Release, 26 July 2001).

If the indictments of Bosnian Croats in the mid and late 1990s were controversial, then the ICTY's targeting of Croatian army generals for crimes committed in the celebrated war of independence, including in the climactic Operation Storm, proved explosive. In all, six Croatian generals faced tribunal charges related to the Homeland War, including former army chief of staff Janko Bobetko. The indictment of Ante Gotovina, who would grow into a national icon during his years as a fugitive, proved to be the most controversial of all.

For international justice activists, the Gotovina and Ademi indictments were precedent-setting, signalling that the emerging system of global criminal accountability would not be tainted by a de facto immunity for the winners of war. But for Croatian nationalists, the ICTY's attempt to move beyond victor's justice undermined the nation by sullying the valiant image of Storm as an honourable battle of liberation waged against a brutal and unscrupulous foe. Nationalists pushed back against the emerging global norm of universal justice, insisting that the victors of war—and especially the victors of an independence war—should enjoy exemption from prosecution. 'There is no court on earth to have tried an army which defended and liberated its country, nor will there ever be' thundered Bobetko, the retired Croatian army chief of staff who faced tribunal indictment in 2002 for alleged crimes by Croatian forces during 1993 Medak Pocket military operation.[64]

During and after the Tuđjman era, Croatian nationalists insisted that any ICTY indictment of ethnic Croats would create an unfair moral equivalence between the lesser alleged crimes of Croats and the far greater crimes of Serbian forces. When Serbian forces destroyed Vukovar in late 1991—and then massacred 261 wounded Croatian soldiers—Croatia emerged internationally as the main victim of the conflict and called for the establishment of a UN tribunal.[65] But during the Bosnian war and then again in Operation Storm, the victims, in effect, became victimizers. The bottom line was that Zagreb was deeply ambivalent about the ICTY, given the potential of high-profile trials to bring attention to Croatian victims on the one hand, but to condemn Croatian perpetrators and highlight the criminality of the Croatian State, on the other hand.

Understanding the depth of societal distaste for the ICTY is key to explaining the enormous challenge in moving beyond victor's justice in Croatia. The prospect of the government handing over national war heroes who might then face a lifetime behind bars was unpopular in Croatia, to say the very least. Nationalists devised a string of pseudo-legal arguments to bolster Croatia's claim for impunity. These arguments largely centred on the proclaimed exceptional and exalted nature of the Croatian independence war. Yet, nationalists erroneously argued that their claims of *jus ad bellum*—the body of law that delineates the legitimate reasons for going to war—trumped the Tribunal's accusations of Croatian violations of *jus in bello*—the body of law that details criminal conduct during war.

In an important respect, the ICTY indictments of Gotovina and the five other generals were more controversial in Croatia than the indictments of many high-level Serb suspects were in Serbia.[66] The volatile nature of the Homeland War-related indictments stemmed from the perceived threat—that, in turn, were inflamed by nationalists for domestic political gain—that these cases posed to the dominant Croatian narrative of the war. The ICTY

[64] Peskin (n 22) 132.

[65] Government of the Republic of Croatia, *The White Paper on Cooperation with the International Tribunal* (September 1999) 4.

[66] Gordy (n 41) 46–47.

indictments were assailed as an assault on the legitimacy of the Croatian military victory and thus as an attack on the nation's epic realization of its 'thousand-year-old dream' of Statehood.[67] Therein lies the distinctively controversial nature of the ICTY Homeland War cases. 'Recognition of the guilt of people who committed crimes', Eric Gordy writes in reference to Croatia, 'risks calling into question the wars that were fought and the independence that was gained through them'.[68]

Pro-tribunal optimists hoped that Croatia's democratic transition in early 2000—following the death of Tuđjman, the electoral defeat of his nationalist party, and the emergence of a centre-left government—constituted a perfect political storm that would usher in a new era of State cooperation with The Hague. But even as established and transitional democratic States are presumed to embrace the rule of law, the political imperative to evade accountability for State-sponsored crimes can take precedence. In Croatia, the democratic transition did not diminish the outsized influence of the anti-tribunal nationalists—now in opposition, but still a political force to be reckoned with. Nor did regime change moderate the emotive politics of memory in a newly independent nation fiercely defensive of a national narrative of a just war of liberation and still intoxicated by its military triumph on the battlefields of the Krajina.

28.3.4 Hiding at Home, Fleeing Abroad: Croatia's Delayed Cooperation and the EU as Surrogate Enforcer

It was in this turbulent post-war domestic political context that the centre-left governing coalition, led by Ivica Račan, faced intense pressure not to succumb to The Hague. At the same time, Prime Minister Račan faced growing pressure from Del Ponte not to give in to the nationalists. The UN Security Council largely stood on the sidelines. Crucially, however, Brussels and Washington assumed the role of 'surrogate enforcer', often, though not always, pressing Zagreb to make arrests and comply with other Tribunal requests to advance the Homeland War cases.

In the early 2000s, Brussels began to make it abundantly clear that Croatia's quest for 'the holy grail' of EU membership—which would allow the country to exit the Balkan periphery and finally win acceptance as a European nation—was conditional on how well it fulfilled its legal obligations to the Tribunal. The EU conditionality policy would become the decisive factor in giving the ICTY the upper hand in its battles over victor's justice with the Croatian government.[69] We may live in an era that embraces the norm of justice for all. Yet, whether an international tribunal can actually move beyond victor's justice depends on the willingness of targeted States to abide by their legal obligations and the resolve of external actors like the EU to act as effective surrogate enforcers in the face of State non-compliance.

Buffeted by pressure from nationalists at home and surrogate enforcers abroad, Račan sought a middle path aimed at holding together his tenuous governing coalition, maintaining electoral support, and keeping Croatia firmly on the path towards the EU. This meant that Račan—and his centre-right successor, Ivo Sanader—would try their best to

[67] M Tanner, *Croatia: A Nation Forged in War* (Yale University Press 1997) 275.
[68] Gordy (n 41) 46–47.
[69] Pond (54) 136.

present an accommodating posture towards the ICTY while actually delaying cooperation for as long as possible and then minimizing the amount of cooperation eventually provided.

Račan's middle-path strategy was a multi-pronged one. It involved pledges of forthcoming arrests, meant to placate Del Ponte and Western diplomats, with strident condemnations of the ICTY, meant to assuage nationalists and portray the centre-left government as a strong defender of the memory of Croatia's revered military victory. Catering to the nationalists' anti-tribunal narrative would made it more difficult for Račan to cultivate the domestic support needed to legitimize the arrest and transfer of army generals when Western pressure grew too intense to ignore. President Stjepan Mesić remained an outlier among Croatian politicians, given his principled calls for State cooperation and his articulate defense of the ICTY's mission of individualizing criminal responsibility.

When international pressure did mount for arrests, Račan responded with inaction and delay. He claimed that the lack of arrests—rather than a sign of wilful non-compliance—was due to circumstances beyond the government's control—such as the poor health of the elderly Bobetko or the supposed lack of State capacity to track down Gotovina. The government portrayed Gotovina as an elusive fugitive who had fled Croatia and was therefore supposedly no longer its responsibility. Moreover, both Račan and Sanader prodded European diplomats to soften their conditionality policy and, in the absence of arrests, not to punish Croatia by slowing or stopping its progress towards EU membership.[70]

During the Tuđjman years and the democratic era, Croatian government officials excelled at playing a double-game, cloaking non-compliance in a veneer of cooperation. Richard Goldstone dryly observed that Croatian officials were 'more shrewd and more ... devious' than their Serbian counterparts who were forthright in their obstruction of justice. Croatian officials 'were happy to cooperate when it suited them, but if it got close to home they would shut up like clams', Goldstone recalled.[71] Del Ponte made a similar observation. The Croatian authorities would 'resort to stealth and deception and attack from behind' in their dealings with the ICTY.[72] Such cunning posed a serious challenge to the ICTY's bid to move beyond victor's justice.

If Croatian authorities approached the politics of State cooperation strategically, then so did the ICTY chief prosecutor, albeit in the interests of justice. Del Ponte timed her early July 2001 visit to Zagreb, to press for the arrests of Gotovina and Ademi only after Serbian leader Slobodan Milošević had been transferred to The Hague in late June. Milošević's impending trial seemingly strengthened Del Ponte's hand during her Zagreb visit. It did so by potentially neutralizing Croatian anger at the ICTY because the country's long-time nemesis was now finally in tribunal custody. With Milošević behind bars, Del Ponte had ample proof of her commitment to seek justice for Croatian suffering at the hands of Milošević. Timing her arrival in Zagreb in early July 2001 to follow Milošević's arrival in The Hague and keeping the Gotovina and Ademi indictments under seal were smart moves. But this was no guarantee the Račan government would arrest the two men. As it turned out, a leak within the Croatian government revealed the targets of the sealed indictments, sabotaging the chances of arresting Gotovina in Croatia.

70 Peskin (n 22) 119–48.
71 Author interview with former ICTY Chief Prosecutor Richard Goldstone, Pasadena, CA, April 2003.
72 Del Ponte with Sudetic (n 59) 242.

Once the Gotovina and Ademi indictments became public, they triggered a firestorm of protest, fomenting a crisis in Račan's governing coalition over whether the government should arrest the generals. Following Del Ponte's visit and after heated debate, Račan's cabinet announced a decision to comply with the government's legal obligations. In the wake of this announcement, four cabinet ministers resigned in protest, nationalists threatened unrest, and the prime minister publicly stated his fear of instability.[73]

In the West, the government's declaration of forthcoming cooperation won accolades. But actions would speak louder than words. After the cabinet decision, Račan remained intently focused on shoring up support for a mid-July vote of confidence in parliament prompted by the controversy over the ICTY indictments. Consequently, he prevaricated on arresting Gotovina. Ademi, who was charged with crimes that occurred during the 1993 Medak Pocket operation, voluntarily surrendered to the ICTY in late July.

Gotovina, who had learned of his indictment with the media leak, absconded. He would remain on the run for four and a half years. The Račan government disavowed responsibility for the leak and pled for lenient EU treatment over the failure to apprehend Gotovina. Zagreb's skill at obfuscation and obstruction would again be on display following the ICTY's September 2002 indictment of Janko Bobetko. When it came to tribunal requests to arrest the ailing eighty-three-year-old former army chief of state, Račan played the politics of delay with finesse until Bobetko died in late April 2003. When it came to Croatia's obligation to facilitate the handover of two of the three Homeland War generals indicted during his term in office, Račan largely outmanoeuvred Del Ponte, even as the government provided substantial cooperation in opening up incriminating State archives to tribunal investigators.[74] In June 2003, the Račan government made its only arrest, apprehending Ivica Rajić, a Bosnian Croat suspect who had been a fugitive since the late 1990s, and then transferring him to The Hague.

The ICTY would finally gain the upper hand in its battles over victor's justice with the Croatian government following the November 2003 election of Ivo Sanader. Initially, however, Sanader's election seemed a harbinger for increasing Croatian resistance. Some observers predicted that State cooperation would take a turn for the worse under Sanader, given that the centre-right prime minister was a nationalist and led the same party founded by Tudjman. That predication would most likely have come true if not for the decisive role played by the Tribunal's surrogate enforcers in Brussels.

In a boon for the ICTY, the EU held firm to its conditionality policy, thereby incentivizing the Sanader government to facilitate the handovers of ten suspects. These included four Croatian generals indicted for Homeland War crimes in Croatia—including Ante Gotovina—and six Bosnian Croats—including Slobodan Praljak—indicted for crimes in Bosnia. With Croatia at a crucial stage in its negotiations with Brussels over its EU membership bid, Del Ponte possessed the leverage necessary to induce Zagreb to facilitate surrenders. Soon after their March 2004 indictments, the Croatian generals Mladen Markač and Ivan Čermak, both implicated in Operation Storm-related crimes, surrendered. In July, Mirko Norac, a general indicted for crimes in the Medak Pocket operation, was transferred to The Hague. At the time, Norac had been imprisoned in Croatia in connection with a domestic conviction for wartime crimes.

[73] Peskin (n 22) 128.
[74] Del Ponte with Sudetic (n 59) 247.

For the Croatian political establishment, the political, economic, and cultural benefits of EU membership trumped the nationalist imperative of defying international justice. It is for this reason that Sanader ultimately acted to ensure the surrender of Markač and Čermak, arrange Norac's transfer, and belatedly assist international efforts to locate and arrest Gotovina. Yet when it came to Gotovina, Sanader, like Račan before him, played the politics of delay for as long as possible.

With the exception of Gotovina and Norac, Sanader managed to get the suspects to hand themselves in, avoiding the politically damaging image of Croatian law enforcement slapping handcuffs on its wartime heroes and sending them off to a reviled international court. And when it came to Gotovina, Croatia's most beloved indicted war criminal, the Spanish authorities, rather than the Croatian law enforcement, ended up making the arrest. No Croatian leader relished seeing their countrymen in The Hague. But it didn't end up so badly for Sanader. First, in the eyes of Brussels, the government had provided crucial cooperation and could now be rewarded with being advanced closer to EU membership. Second, in the eyes of key domestic audiences, the government could maintain its nationalist *bonafides* by plausibly denying that it had betrayed the Homeland War heroes in light of their own surrenders. To burnish its nationalist credentials, the Sanader government footed the legal bills of the suspects-turned-defendants and staunchly refused to confront the dark side of its victory in the Homeland War.

Sanader hoped that the EU's 2004 decision to designate Croatia as a candidate for Union membership and the string of surrenders that year meant that the country was well on its way to joining the EU and could therefore drag its feet on the international manhunt to track down Gotovina. But the prime minister badly miscalculated. The EU's resolve as a strong surrogate enforcer made all the difference for the ICTY. Zagreb's lack of State cooperation on Gotovina led the EU to call off the membership talks with Croatia, the day before their scheduled start in March 2005. This 'catastrophic blow'[75] to its quest for an early entry into Europe ended, once and for all, Croatia's say-one-thing, but-do-another approach on the matter of fugitives. Within months, Croatian authorities finally got to work monitoring Gotovina's overseas telephone calls to his family, a course of action that diplomats had long urged Zagreb to do. Intercepted calls revealed that the globe-trotting fugitive was enjoying life on the Canary Islands. In December 2005, Spanish authorities arrested Gotovina there.

28.4 Conclusion: Losing the Courtroom Battle, but Winning the War Over Victor's Justice

With Gotovina's long-delayed arrival in The Hague, the last and most important piece of the victor's justice puzzle pertaining to Croatia had fallen into place. The battle over victor's justice now shifted from the political realm—where The Hague, Brussels, and Zagreb had duelled over the latter's obligation to cooperate—to the legal arena where the battle over Gotovina's alleged guilt would be waged.

In the end, the strategic acumen of the ICTY chief prosecutors and the surrogate enforcership of the EU enabled the trial of all but one of the six suspects indicted in

[75] M Glenny, 'Backsliding in the Balkans' (11 April 2005) The Nation 27.

connection with Croatia's victorious war of independence. The indicted former army chief of staff Janko Bobetko and the unindicted President Tuđjman and Defense Minister Šušak all died before they could face justice in The Hague. In the courtroom, however, the prosecution lost the battle over victor's justice, given the Appeals Chamber's highly controversial and narrow 3–2 reversal of the Trial Chamber's conviction of Gotovina and Markač.[76] Čermak had been acquitted at trial. The ICTY never actually handed down a single conviction for the victors' alleged crimes in the Homeland War, though a number of ethnic Croats were convicted at the Tribunal for atrocities in Bosnia. To speed the closure of the ICTY, tribunal judges sent the Ademi and Norac case to the Zagreb District Court. Ademi won an acquittal, while Norac was convicted and sentenced to seven years.

Despite their disappointment in the final verdicts, the ICTY OTP, in targeting and vigorously pursuing the Croatian winners, helped establish the Tribunal's legacy by giving meaning to the principle of prosecutorial impartiality. When assessing whether an international tribunal has overcome victor's justice, one should, therefore, not examine courtroom verdicts alone. To render a comprehensive assessment of an international tribunal's confrontation with victor's justice it is important to examine whether and the extent to which its chief prosecutors have sought to hold suspects from all victor States and combatant groups accountable. Thus, a follow-up to this chapter should assess the OTP's political and courtroom confrontation with KLA defendants as well as the Office's handling of its decision not to pursue indictments in regard to the NATO air war during the Kosovo conflict.

The key to safeguarding the integrity of contemporary international justice is to ensure that high-level suspects from the winning sides of an intra-State or interstate war—as well as suspects from other States and combatant groups—undergo a comprehensive and complete investigation and, where evidence exists, face a robust international courtroom reckoning that is neither preempted by prosecutorial acquiescence to actual or anticipated external pressure nor corrupted or sabotaged by State or international obstruction. By this measure, the ICTY chief prosecutors may have lost the courtroom battle with the Croatian generals and the Croatian State, but nevertheless won the larger war over victor's justice by holding the winners to account. In so doing, one hopes that the OTP and the ICTY as a whole have bequeathed a lasting legacy for the future of global criminal justice.

[76] ICTY, 'Appeals chamber acquits and orders release of Ante Gotovina and Mladen Markač' (Press Release, 16 November 2012).

29

The (Lack of) Impact of the ICTY on the Public Memory of the War in Bosnia and Herzegovina

*Jovana Mihajlović Trbovc**, **

29.1 Introduction

The International Criminal Tribunal for the former Yugoslavia (ICTY) was grounded in an underlying assumption that it would make a range of extra-legal social impacts in the region of the former Yugoslavia, that are often subsumed under the vague notion of 'reconciliation'. Whatever the concept of reconciliation may mean,[1] the majority of scholars agree that inter-ethnic and intra-communal reconciliation, includes a range of social, psychological, and political factors that go vastly beyond the reckoning with the past that a court of law may provide.[2] Nevertheless, the idea behind these various conceptions of reconciliation, and the various notions of how exactly the ICTY would contribute to it, is that the ICTY would somehow (positively) influence the way the local communities understand and remember the traumatic events that took place during the Yugoslav wars.

The anticipated influence of the ICTY on the hearts and minds of the local population (and their political representatives) has been analysed from various angles by scholars. Studies, focused on the intra-communal relations in the post-war societies, showed that the ICTY's processes did not manage to shift deeply rooted beliefs about what happened during the wars, in the communities immediately targeted by the armed conflicts, such as Vukovar, Prijedor, Mostar, and Ahmići, to name a few.[3] The ingrained mistrust in the ICTY, such as in the case of Serbia, contributed to the rejection of factual findings of the court as untruthful.[4] Similarly, the Croatian public opinion swung from positive

* Political scientist dealing with political issues from the perspective of culture studies. Her research field is the politics of the past and public memory of the crimes which happened during the dissolution of Yugoslavia and during the Second World War. She is especially focused on the impact of the International Criminal Tribunal for the former Yugoslavia (ICTY) on the post-Yugoslav States, as well as the reproduction of the historical narratives in the school textbooks.

** The author acknowledges financial support from the Slovenian Research Agency research programme Historical Interpretations of the 20th Century (P6-0347).

[1] Definitions of reconciliation vary significantly. A R Chapman, 'Approaches to Studying Reconciliation' in H van der Merwe et al (eds), *Assessing the Impact of Transitional Justice: Challenges for Empirical Research* (United States Institute for Peace Press 2009).

[2] L E Fletcher and H M Weinstein, 'Violence and Social Repair: Rethinking the Contribution of Justice to Reconciliation' (2002) 24 Human Rights Quarterly 573. J N Clark, *International Trials and Reconciliation: Assessing the Impact of the International Criminal Tribunal for the Former Yugoslavia* (Routledge 2014) ch 2.

[3] D Corkalo et al, 'Neighbors Again? Intercommunity Relations after Ethnic Cleansing' in E Stover and Ha M Weinstein (eds), *My Neighbor, My Enemy: Justice and Community in the Aftermath of Mass Atrocity* (Cambridge University Press 2004). Clark (n 2) ch 3–7; L J Nettelfield, *Courting Democracy in Bosnia and Herzegovina: The Hague Tribunal's Impact in a Postwar State* (Cambridge University Press 2010) ch 6.

[4] J Obradovic, *Ethnic Conflict and War Crimes in the Balkans: The Narratives of Denial in Post-Conflict Serbia* (IB Taurus 2009); E Gordy, *Guilt, Responsibility, and Denial: The Past at Stake in Post-Milošević Serbia* (University of Pennsylvania Press 2013).

Jovana Mihajlović Trbovc, *The (Lack of) Impact of the ICTY on the Public Memory of the War in Bosnia and Herzegovina* In: *Legacies of the International Criminal Tribunal for the Former Yugoslavia*. Edited by: Carsten Stahn, Carmel Agius, Serge Brammertz, Colleen Rohan, Oxford University Press (2020). © The Several Contributors DOI: 10.1093/oso/9780198862956.003.0030

to negative (and back), depending on the outcome of the ICTY verdict, rather than the historical facts established in the judgments.[5] Studies, informed by social psychology, elucidated the cognitive biases that hindered target audiences in the former Yugoslavia from accepting and internalizing the ICTY's factual findings.[6] Part of the explanation scholars found was the way in which local media transmitted, framed, and distorted information about the court's operation to local audiences.[7] The most significant impediment to the ICTY making the anticipated influence is attributed to the local political elites, who interacted with the court as a political body, led by political pragmatism,[8] and thus misused the justice process for their own political gains.[9] This chapter contributes to the cohort of these studies, by shedding light on the process of reproduction of public memory[10] about the war in Bosnia and Herzegovina (BiH) and the way it was impacted by the relevant ICTY judgments.

In order to examine how exactly this problem unfolds, the research project behind this chapter followed the development of the public memory about the war over time, intersecting it with the relevant ICTY jurisprudence, with an aim to detect potential change in the dominant narratives. For that, the chapter focuses on the four main points of divergence between leading Bosniak, Croatian, and Serbian historical narratives: whether the war was a product of Serbian aggression or a civil war among the political actors within Bosnia; whether 'ethnic cleansing' was pre-planned by the Serbian side or an inevitable consequence of the war; whether genocide was the overall aim of the Serbian side or whether it took place only in Srebrenica in July 1995; and whether the Croatian side was a defender of, or aggressor in BiH.

For each of these case-studies I analysed relevant ICTY judgments, distilling the narrative created by the court. I further analysed how local media reported on the trials and judgments, in order to see which part of the court narrative penetrates the local public sphere. Finally, taking commemorations and public holidays as stages for the reproduction of dominant narratives about the last war, the chapter reconstructs their evolution over time, precisely in the period before and after the relating ICTY decisions and judgments.

[5] I Vukušić, 'Judging Their Hero: Perceptions of the International Criminal Tribunal for the Former Yugoslavia in Croatia' in J Gow, R Kerr, and Z Pajić (eds), *Prosecuting War Crimes: Lessons and legacies of the International Criminal Tribunal for the Former Yugoslavia* (Routledge 2014).

[6] M Milanović, 'Establishing the Facts about Mass Atrocities: Accounting for the Failure of the ICTY to Persuade Target Audiences' (2016) 47 Georgetown Journal of International Law 1321.

[7] M Klarin, 'The Impact of the ICTY Trials on Public Opinion in the Former Yugoslavia' (2009) 7 Journal of International Criminal Justice 89; A Džihana and Z Volčič (eds), *Media and National Ideologies: Analysis of Reporting on War Crime Trials in the Former Yugoslavia* (Mediacentar Sarajevo 2011); K Ristić, *Imaginary Trials: War Crime Trials and Memory in Former Yugoslavia* (Leipziger Universitätsverlag 2014).

[8] C K Lamont, *International Criminal Justice and the Politics of Compliance* (Ashgate 2010); M Ostojić, *Between Justice and Stability: The Politics of War Crimes Prosecutions in Post-Milošević Serbia* (Ashgate 2014).

[9] J Subotić, *Hijacked Justice: Dealing with the Past in the Balkans* (Cornell University Press 2009).

[10] Public memory 'refers to the circulation of recollections among members of a given community'; M Houdek and K R Phillips, 'Public Memory' (*Oxford Research Encyclopedias: Communication*, 25 January 2017) <http://communication.oxfordre.com/view/10.1093/acrefore/9780190228613.001.0001/acrefore-9780190228613-e-181> accessed 23 January 2018.

29.2 How it Came to be Expected that the ICTY Would Shape Public Memory

The institution of the ICTY was established against the backdrop of two prominent, and mutually interconnected, approaches to thinking about the social role of war crimes trials. The first originates from the vigorous debate on the question of whether the courts should 'write history'. While some argued that the court should only render justice,[11] others have demonstrated that 'history' cannot be expelled from courtrooms that deal with wars.[12] It seems that the founders of the ICTY embraced a third stream of argument which regards war crimes trials as inherently historical events: under the limelight of public attention, the courts create an authoritative historical account that shapes collective memory about the events being adjudicated.[13] This position of 'judicial romanticism'[14] presupposes that the creation of an authoritative account of the war would refute attempts to deny the criminal events—a position also named as 'authoritative narrative theory'.[15] This position gained prominence in the context of deep divisions among post-Yugoslav political elites, who shared a common tendency to deny responsibility for committed crimes and reluctance to acknowledge victims' suffering.[16]

The other approach to thinking about war crimes trials stems from an expanded notion of justice, developed within the transitional justice (TJ) discipline.[17] It goes beyond mere retribution and seeks to achieve *social justice* after deep strife. The founders of the ICTY embraced this understanding by attributing the court with several functions outside the legal scope of trying individuals for their criminal responsibility (e.g. 'bringing the sense of justice to the victims'). The most prominent (and most debated) extra-legal role is the expectation that the ICTY 'would contribute to the maintenance of the peace'.[18] Precisely in the spirit of TJ discipline, this 'restoration and maintenance of the peace' has been understood as a reconciliation on a general social level. The presupposition that the findings of the Tribunal would lead to reconciliation rests on the assumptions that firstly, a court is able to create an authoritative account which will refute attempts to deny the criminal events and secondly, that denial is obstructing reconciliation.

[11] H Arendt, *Eichmann in Jerusalem: A Report on the Banality of Evil* (The Viking Press 1965); T Todorov, *Hope and Memory: Reflections on the Twentieth Century* (Atlantic Books 2003).

[12] L Douglas, *The Memory of Judgment: Making Law and History in the Trials of the Holocaust* (Yale University Press 2001); R A Wilson, *Writing History in International Criminal Trials* (Cambridge University Press 2011).

[13] M Osiel, *Mass Atrocity, Collective Memory, and the Law* (Transaction Publishers 2000); R G Teitel, *Transitional Justice* (Oxford University Press 2002).

[14] P C McMahon and D P Forsythe, 'ICTY Impact on Serbia: Judicial Romanticism Meets Network Politics' (2008) 30 Human Rights Quarterly 412.

[15] T W Waters, 'Vital Signs: The Milošević Trial and Its Context—A Foundational Primer' in T W Waters (ed), *The Milošević Trial: An Autopsy* (Oxford University Press 2013).

[16] A Cassese, 'On the Current Trends towards Criminal Prosecution and Punishment of Breaches of International Humanitarian Law' (1998) 9 European Journal of International Law 2; P Akhavan, 'Beyond Impunity: Can International Criminal Justice Prevent Future Atrocities?' (2001) 95 American Journal of International Law 7; R J Goldstone, 'The Role of the International Criminal Court' in R I Rotberg (ed), *Mass Atrocity Crimes: Preventing Future Outrages* (Brookings Institution Press 2010).

[17] The concept of TJ refers to a range of legal and political mechanisms applied in societies transforming from authoritarianism to democracy, and from violent conflict to post-conflict peace building. See Teitel (n 13). This hybrid concept reflects the social, political, and legal need to address violations of human rights and/or war crimes that occurred in the recent past, with the main goal of (re)establishing a just, democratic, and reconciled society.

[18] UN Security Council, 'Resolution 827, UN Doc S/RES/827 (25 May 1993).

Therefore, the romantic belief in the court's ability to influence society by creating an objective historical account, as well as the trust in the TJ paradigm in its transformative effect on truth-telling, both rest on the underlying assumption that once the 'truth' is publicly presented, it becomes a part of public memory. This chapter challenges this expectation by examining whether the war crime trials before the ICTY have changed narratives about the 1992–95 war that dominate public life in BiH.

29.3 Serbian Responsibility for the War

The first major fault line between the dominant historical narratives revolves around the question of whether the war was a product of Serbian aggression or a civil war among the political actors within Bosnia. These two frames of interpretation ('aggression' and 'civil war') imply much larger historical narratives relating to the causes of the conflict. Since the interpretations of the origin of the Bosnian war depend on the overall interpretation of the dissolution of Yugoslavia, I examined the trial of Slobodan Milošević because of his prominent role in the disintegration process. However, this trial never came to an end, due to Milošević's death, and there is no judgment from which I could deduce the court's narrative about the war.

Looking beyond this particular case, it would be untrue to claim that the ICTY created a comprehensive narrative about the disintegration of Yugoslavia and the causes of the war in BiH.[19] Technically, complete coherence is impossible since each trial deals with the criminal responsibility of an individual, and this is inherently a particularistic perspective. The Prosecution in the trial of Slobodan Milošević tried to turn this case into a podium for creating such a comprehensive historical narrative and was, in turn, criticized by many observers and scholars for doing so.[20] The Prosecution's narrative contained four main elements: there was a master plan behind the Serbian conduct; that master plan was to create Greater Serbia; in order to create Greater Serbia genocide against Bosniaks was planned; and leadership in Belgrade had a tight control over the Bosnian Serb leadership.

Even though the case was built on the notion of Greater Serbia[21] as the final aim that guided conduct of the Serbian leadership during Yugoslav dissolution and the Bosnian war, the inability to tie Milošević personally to advocating the creation of Greater Serbia, led to the fogging of the concept over the course of the trial. It would be hard to describe precisely how the Prosecution understood the idea of Greater Serbia, since it is not clearly defined in the Indictment or in the Prosecution's Opening Statement. Furthermore, the exact phrase 'Greater Serbia' is mentioned in the Indictment of Milošević only as part of a description of the extreme-nationalist Serbian politician Vojislav Šešelj, an alleged participant in the joint criminal enterprise (JCE),[22] while in the Opening Statement the

[19] Wilson (n 12).

[20] G Boas, *The Milošević Trial: Lessons for the Conduct of Complex International Criminal Proceedings* (Cambridge University Press 2007); Wilson (n 12); H van der Wilt, 'The Spider and the System: Milošević and Joint Criminal Enterprise' in T W Waters (ed), *The Milošević Trial: An Autopsy* (Oxford University Press 2013).

[21] The idea of Greater Serbia is usually understood as 'a plan to expand the Serbian state into all [adjacent] territories inhabited by Serbs', or in other words to unite 'all Serbs in one state', as the nationalistic slogan exclaimed in the early 1990s. For the former see Wilson (n 12) 101. For the latter see M Živković, *Serbian Dreambook: National Imaginary in the Time of Milošević* (Indiana University Press 2011).

[22] *Prosecutor v Slobodan Milošević* (Amended Indictment) ICTY IT-02-54-T (22 November 2002) para 22.

Prosecution admitted: 'We don't particularly associate ["Greater Serbia"] as a title with the approach of the accused.'[23] Throughout the trial of Milošević, no document was presented which would directly 'incriminate' him for planning or envisioning a Greater Serbia. Nevertheless, the Prosecution referred to the idea when explaining the motivations and aims of those participating in the JCE, including Milošević himself.

During the trial, the judges in the *Milošević* case conceded that the aim of the JCE of the Serbian leadership was to create a 'Serbian state'; however, it remained unclear whether this referred to a 'Serbian state in Bosnia' or an 'enlarged Serbia' that would incorporate parts of BiH and Croatia. This was not crucial for rendering Milošević's individual criminal responsibility, since his participation in the JCE was inferred from his political cooperation with the Bosnian Serb leadership and the massive logistical and financial support to the Army of Republika Srpska. In the historical record created by the court, the agency of the Bosnian Serb leadership emerges much more clearly—they had a clear plan to create an exclusively Serb State from particular Bosnian municipalities (thus eradicating non-Serbs from that territory) with the prospect of joining it to Serbia proper.[24] However, the murkiness about the motives of the regime in Belgrade leaves room for speculations, further enabling quite contradictory historical interpretations.

Though in subsequent case studies I took commemorative events as sites of reproduction of dominant narratives about the past, for the topic of overall interpretation of the Bosnian war, I decided to use history textbooks since they presented the three ethnic narratives most coherently. I regard and analyse history textbooks as the most representative vehicle of what should be regarded as an 'official narrative' of each ethnic group, since the educational system in BiH is ethnically segregated. Under the idea of providing cultural autonomy to the communities, and on the basis of the Dayton constitution of obligatory ascribed ethnic categorization of school children, the educational system is administratively organized along ethnic division lines, producing segregation of students and curricula.[25] In order to obtain longitudinal temporal dimension, I traced and examined all history textbooks used in BiH since the start of the war until now. Therefore, I analysed both how historical narratives in textbooks created for the three ethnic groups differ among themselves, and how each of the narratives modified over time.

Bosniak and Croatian textbooks present very similar master-narratives about the Yugoslav dissolution, which is again coherent with the argument of the Prosecution in the *Milošević* case. This master-narrative blames 'Greater-Serbian hegemonism' for breaking up Yugoslavia and generally ascribes to the Serbs the motive of creating Greater Serbia, which led them to instigate the wars. On the other hand, Serbian textbooks concur with the main argument of Milošević's defence: that Serbs wanted to preserve

23 *Prosecutor v Slobodan Milošević* (Transcript) ICTY IT-02-54 (12 February 2002) 1-113 Prosecution Opening Statement 50.

24 This plan is laid out in the document, colloquially known as 'Six Strategic Goals', which was presenting the official war aims proposed by the President of the Republika Srpska, Radovan Karadžić, and approved at the sixteenth session of the RS Assembly (in Banja Luka) on 12 May 1992. These Goals clearly outline the borders of the envisioned Serb State on the territory of BiH. Their imperative is to secure geographical continuity with Serbia, by controlling Semberija (in North-East Bosnia) and the Drina Valley (which is the natural border to Serbia), as well as with the territories in Croatia at that point controlled by Serbs (*Republika Srpska Krajina*—RSK), by controlling the North-West of Bosnia (Bosnian Krajina).

25 P Torsti, *Divergent Stories, Convergent Attitudes: A Study on the Presence of History, History Textbooks and the Thinking of Youth in Post-War Bosnia and Herzegovina* (Taifuuni 2003); A P Kreso, 'The War and Post-War Impact on the Educational System of Bosnia and Herzegovina' (2008) 54 International Review of Education 353, 360–62.

Yugoslavia and that this was their legitimate and sovereign right as a nation (understood in ethnic terms).

These two opposing master-narratives are embedded in drastically different understandings of what the 'Yugoslav problem' was in the first place. The Croat and Bosniak perspective regarded Yugoslavia as being possible only as a federal State, with a system of extensive autonomies, which were guaranteed by the Constitution of 1974. The Serbian perspective, taken from its position as the largest ethnic community in Yugoslavia, favoured a centralist State and regarded the Constitution of 1974 as 'injustice to the Serbian people'. Though ethnic understandings of nation permeate all three narratives, the Croatian and Bosniak ones perceive the seceding *Republics* as the only level of political organization (polity) that has the legitimacy to decide on the future of the political community (independence or remaining in Yugoslavia), while the Serbian narrative perceives *ethnic groups* (particularly the Serb ethnicity) as the truly legitimate polity instead. In other words, the former position regards the Republics as sovereign, the latter sees ethnicities (ethnic groups) as bearers of sovereignty. Consequentially, the former position perceives that the majority of inhabitants of BiH had the right to decide on the independence of the Republic of BiH, while the latter position holds that the majority of members of (Serbian) ethnicity had the right to decide on the independence of the Serbian population (and territories they occupied) from the Republic of BiH, and joining the rump Yugoslavia—two positions that inherently conflict with each other. This observation is not new and has been vastly debated in the context of international recognition of post-Yugoslav States and beyond.[26] The ICTY adopted the criteria of the international community when recognizing the independence of the newly emerging States, which led them to adjudicate the war as international.

Here we should bear in mind that the issue of the internationality of a conflict is legally not the same as deciding whether that conflict was an 'act of aggression' or a 'civil war', and that 'the crime of waging a war of aggression'[27] was not put in the ICTY mandate defined by the Statute. As one of the early Judgments states 'the International Tribunal is a criminal judicial body, established to prosecute and punish individuals for violations of international humanitarian law, and not to determine State responsibility for acts of aggression or unlawful intervention'.[28] However, the Tribunal had to deal with the issue of aggression indirectly due to Article 2 of the Statute which stipulates Grave breaches of the Geneva Conventions of 1949. Since one of the Geneva Conventions protects civilian persons (and property) who 'find themselves, in case of a conflict or occupation, in the hands of a Party to the conflict or Occupying Power of which they are not nationals', the Convention may be applied only in the case of an *international* conflict.[29] Therefore each judgment that dealt with the crimes from Article 2 of the ICTY Statute, had to decide on the question whether the conflict was international.

[26] M M Kovács, 'Standards of Self-Determination and Standards of Minority-Rights in the Post-Communist Era: A Historical Perspective' (2003) 9 Nations and Nationalism 433.

[27] For instance this crime was part of the mandate of the International Military Tribunal in Nuremberg. R Overy, 'The Nuremberg Trials: International Law in the Making' in P Sands (ed), *From Nuremberg to The Hague: The Future of International Criminal Justice* (Cambridge University Press 2003).

[28] *Prosecutor v Mucić* et al. *'Čelebići'* (Trial Judgment) ICTY IT-96-21-T (16 November 1998) para 230.

[29] *Geneva Convention (IV) Relative to the Protection of Civilian Persons in Time of War* (1949) art 4 <http://www.icrc.org/ihl.nsf/385ec082b509e76c41256739003e636d/6756482d86146898c125641e004aa3c5> accessed August 2018.

Taking into account all of the judgments issued by the ICTY, one could conclude that the court generally regarded Serbian forces as hostile and intruding on the territory of the internationally recognized State of BiH. Nevertheless, the fusion between the Army of Republika Srpska and the forces coming from Serbia, coupled with the unclear motives of the Belgrade regime, leaves room for the Serbian popular narrative to claim that the war in Bosnia was fought between local 'ethnic' armies, hence it was a civil war. Therefore, the ICTY judgments did not solve the main dispute about the nature and origin of the Bosnian war, which remains profoundly conflicted, and continues to be reproduced through the Bosnian educational system, with slight modifications.

29.4 Ethnic Cleansing Plan

The case study of Prijedor provided insight into the ways the ICTY, as well as the perpetrators' and victims' communities, developed narratives about ethnic cleansing. It should be noted, 'ethnic cleansing' is not defined as a legal category; instead, what we colloquially understand by that term encompasses a combination of various crimes against humanity.

The first judgment (of Duško Tadić) framed the Serbian forces committing ethnic cleansing as being motivated by the desire to create a Greater Serbia. Later judgments (e.g. that of Radoslav Brđanin), presented the aim as creating an ethnically pure Serbian State within Bosnia. The judgments broadly cohere in their description of the events. The court's narrative presents the Serbian takeover of Prijedor municipality as candidly planned well in advance, starting with the exclusion of non-Serbs from all public posts. After the takeover, the non-Serb population was systematically discriminated against and persecuted, and the situation was aggravated after the attempts of local Bosnian Muslims to mount resistance. Given that the court regarded the Serbian takeover as an illegitimate disruption of a democratically elected local government, the Bosnian Muslims' acts are understood as self-defence. Finally, the persecutory campaign culminated with the establishment of the Omarska, Keraterm, and Trnopolje camps where civilians were held under most inhumane conditions, regularly tortured and often killed. The whole system of persecution and the camps had the clear aim of eradicating non-Serbs from Prijedor municipality, the narrative of the judgments concludes.

Immediately after the war, the media reported on the trials in a contrasting manner. Initially, the Serbian media silenced the crimes, and *Glas srpski* in particular framed the ICTY as part of an international conspiracy against the Serbs. Later, Serbian newspapers started quoting the charges and gave dry, short descriptions of the crimes in the Prijedor camps (*Nezavisne novine* in 1998 and *Glas srpski* in 2001). However, even when reporting extensively about the crimes, *Nezavisne* avoided the use of the emotionally potent term 'ethnic cleansing' and kept silent about the campaign of persecution against non-Serbs, that started with the Serbian takeover of the municipality. On the other hand, the Bosniak media presented these trials as the process of legal confirmation of a belief the Bosniak audience already shared—that events in Prijedor constituted a pre-planned and well-organized campaign of ethnic cleansing. Though the unlawful Serbian takeover of the municipality was not a central frame in reporting, it was treated as an indisputable underlying fact. I noted that the frame of Greater Serbia as the political aim for ethnic cleansing was present only in the early reporting, but vanished later on as the concept per se ceased being mentioned in the trials. Through its reporting on all trials the Bosniak media promoted the frame of 'genocide', even when the accused was not indicted for it or when the judgments dismissed this charge. This frame was further supported with the framing of places of unlawful detention in Prijedor as 'concentration camps', thus making a symbolic parallel between Nazism and the Serbian nationalism of the 1990s.

Precisely the frame of the Prijedor camps as places of extermination was the red line in the victims' narrative, as reproduced through their commemorations. In their discourse, the terms 'ethnic cleansing' and 'genocide' are often used interchangeably. However, the insistence that the persecution of non-Serbs in the Prijedor municipality constitutes genocide gained momentum only in recent years, after the narrative of the local Serb officials made yet another interpretative turn. Specifically, the local Serbian narrative initially glorified the Serbian takeover of the municipality, celebrating it as a public holiday. Under the pressure of Bosniak returnees to the municipality, this official holiday had to be annulled. Simultaneously, the less nationalistic local Serb officials (at least formally) recognized that the camps were a place of mass crimes, through participation in public discussions about the creation of a memorial on the site of the Omarska camp. However, this first tiny step towards acknowledgement was soon exposed as dishonest since the local Serb officials started commemorating the day of Prijedor's 'defence from the Muslim attack'—an event that the ICTY recognized as a rightful resistance of non-Serbs against systematic persecution. The new Serbian commemoration symbolically substituted the previous one, thus identifying a slight shift in the Serbian narrative—from presenting the takeover as a Serbian victory to framing it as a necessary defence.

Regardless of this shift, the official Serbian narrative is consistently trying to obliterate the persecutory campaign against non-Serbs from public memory, while presenting the crimes in the camps as isolated events. It seems that precisely this constant denial of the systematic nature of the persecution of non-Serbs provoked the victims' organization to enter the public space of Prijedor town, through 'white armbands' public performances, thus drawing attention to the fascist and genocidal nature of Serbian war-time rule.

29.5 Micro and Macro Genocide

Indisputably the ICTY created a detailed narrative about the genocide of Bosniaks in Srebrenica in July 1995. Though the killings targeted 'only' approximately 8,000 men, the combination of summarily indiscriminate execution of men and boys, deportation of the rest of the civilians, and the strategic spot of Srebrenica near the Serbian border, all pointed to the genocidal nature of the attack on Bosniaks. Both the *Krstić* and *Orić* Judgments described the Bosniak forces' raids in Serbian villages surrounding the 'safe area' of Srebrenica prior to 1995, which were framed as desperate searches for food that also involved the unwarranted destruction of Serb property. However, no judgment framed these raids as in any way justifying the subsequent massacre of Bosniaks in July 1995.

The media reporting on the *Orić* trial revealed the deeper layers in Serbian collective memory about Srebrenica. Ignoring the fact that the local Bosniak leader Naser Orić was not indicted for any killings during the raids, Serbian media framed him as guilty of a series of (alleged) massacres on Serb civilians, most notably the one in Kravica on Orthodox Christmas of 1993. At the same time, almost all Serbian media were silent on the dire situation within the Srebrenica enclave which forced the Bosniak population into raids in the first place. The eventual acquittal of Orić fortified the framing of ICTY bias against Serbs, in the Serbian media. The Bosniak media viewed Orić as a hero who had tried to defend Bosniaks from genocide (although he was charged with crimes that took place in the years *before* and the trial did not deal with the events of 1995). Such a point of observation left no room for reflection on the crimes (maltreatment and killing of a few Serb prisoners in the enclave) and wrongdoings (unwarranted destruction of Serbian villages) on the part of the Bosniak side prior to the genocide.

The *Krstić* Trial Judgment of 2001 gained surprisingly little attention, bearing in mind that this was the first conviction of genocide by the ICTY. Though the Serbian media reported about the Judgment, they marginalized the word 'genocide' in the reporting. The Judgment gained in importance only subsequently as a pretext for ordering the Government of the Republika Srpska (RS) to investigate the fate of the missing Bosniaks.

The RS Government's Srebrenica Commission revealed several previously unknown mass graves, but added nothing to the narrative about genocide, created by the ICTY. The true purpose of this TJ mechanism was not truth-finding, but truth-acknowledgement. Though the President and Government of the RS formally apologized for the crime, they avoided calling it genocide. The media reporting on the Srebrenica Commissions reveals that both Bosniak and Serbian media framed it as resulting from international pressure, hence the acknowledgement effect that this TJ mechanism could have had was absent.

The Serbian narrative, which framed the events of July 1995 as a 'revenge' for previous Bosniak atrocities in the region of Srebrenica, was salient since the end of the war. However, in the light of the international support for Bosniak commemorations in Potočari, the Serbian narrative shifted from celebrating the 'liberation of Srebrenica' to commemorating Serbian victims from 1992 and 1993. As the Bosniak commemorations gained prominence and an international spotlight, the Serbian commemorations in Bratunac took on the role of amassing all Serbian grievances and constructing a continuum of Serbian victimization, from the Second World War to the conflict of the 1990s. Even when the Serbian media gradually started reporting on the Potočari commemorations, they were largely framed as competition between Bosniak and Serbian victimhood. The controversial 'competitive' character of the Bratunac commemoration not only led to Bosniak media (and officials) ignoring them, but also enabled a complete lack of recognition of any Serbian victims (from the Podrinje region) by the Bosniak public.

On the other hand, the Bosniak narrative, in light of continual Serbian denial and due to strong international support, increasingly framed Srebrenica as a symbol of overall Bosniak victimization during the war. Though the Srebrenica genocide was in many ways an exceptional event of the war, the Bosniak officials (as well as many international stakeholders) used the Srebrenica commemoration as a stage for claiming that the genocidal plan was an overall motivation of the Serbian side in the conflict. As some other researchers noted 'focus on genocide profoundly shaped the [Bosniak] narrative about the past',[30] and led Bosniak victims from other regions to claim and demand to be regarded as victims of genocide as well (even in the absence of an adequate ICTY judgment).[31] Eventually, such 'macro'

[30] Subotić (n 9) 154.

[31] C A Nielsen, 'Surmounting the Myopic Focus on Genocide: The Case of the War in Bosnia and Herzegovina' (2013) 15 Journal of Genocide Research 21.

interpretation of genocide (as opposed to 'micro' genocide in Srebrenica) was employed by Bosniak officials in order to claim that the RS is a 'genocidal creation', and hence illegitimate, prompting calls for its annulment.

The Serbian narrative's framing of Srebrenica, in terms of local Bosniak–Serbian fighting, facilitated not only the avoidance of calling the massacre of July 1995 genocide, but also enabled the Serbian narrative to negate the genocidal nature of its overall war-time conduct. The link that the Bosniak narrative created between the genocide in Srebrenica and the legitimacy of the RS pushed the RS officials even further from acknowledging the crime.

29.6 Croatian Forces as Both Aggressor and Defender of BiH

The ICTY judgments of the Croatian Defence Council (HVO) leaders created a coherent narrative which described the ethnic cleansing campaign, conducted by the HVO against the Bosniak population of central Bosnia, within which the massacre in Ahmići was the most notorious event. These judgments in fact framed the President of the Republic of Croatia, Franjo Tuđman, as devising a plan to partition Bosnia and clandestinely supporting ethnic cleansing. However, Tuđman never faced trial since his death in 1999 came before the ICTY had finished collecting the evidence against him.

Though the Croatian media coverage of the trials never directly negated the crimes, they tended to present the Bosnian Croat war conduct as self-defence. The voice of the Croatian veterans was given abundant space to claim that, regardless of possible crimes committed, the HVO was a legitimate army that sought to protect the Croatian population within BiH, and thus protect BiH as a country. For the Bosniak media, the crimes undoubtedly proved the criminal conduct of the HVO during the Bosniak–Croatian conflict, which could not be exculpated by their alliance with the Army of the Republic of Bosnia and Herzegovina (ARBiH) at the beginning and during the latter part of the Bosnian war. Bosniak media also emphasized that the support the Tuđman's regime gave to Bosnian Croats proved that Bosnia was a victim of Croatian aggression. On the other hand, the Croatian media, while acknowledging the control Zagreb exercised over the HVO, placed the blame on a close circle of Tuđman's associates and avoided using the term 'aggression'.

The distancing of the post-Tuđman Croatian leadership from the policy of its predecessor, which started with the transfer of classified documents to the Tribunal, culminated in the act of apology by the incumbent President of Croatia, Ivo Josipović. He condemned the policy of Croatia from the 1990s which acted aggressively towards the State of BiH, but did not openly admit responsibility of the Croatian State for the crime in Ahmići. His act was further undermined by the dissenting opinion of the incumbent and former Croatian Prime Ministers, who denied that Croatia committed aggression against BiH. Furthermore, no Bosnian Croat politicians have made such an acknowledgement nor did they subsequently attend the Ahmići commemoration. Simultaneously, Bosnian Croat politicians continually commemorate HVO fallen soldiers and reproduce the narrative that the HVO participation in the defence of BiH gives legitimacy to contemporary political claims of Croatian representatives in BiH.

Even less acknowledgement could be found in Croatian history textbooks, which all present the HVO as a legitimate army that participated in the defence of BiH from Serbian aggression, with the particular aim of protecting the Croatian population. They portray

Croatia as a benevolent ally, and none of them mention crimes committed by the Bosnian Croat forces. Though some of them mention the Croat Bosniak conflict in negative terms, none of them provide a clear explanation of the conflict's causes, and ignore Tuđman's plan to partition BiH.

29.7 Conclusion

My research has revealed that local media reporting on the TJ processes are not of sufficiently poor quality to justify such a widespread lack of acknowledgement of the crimes committed in BiH. Though the quality of reporting about the ICTY trials improved over time, the media still 'speak' from predominantly ethnic perspectives by emphasizing claims of innocence of their 'own defendants' and favouring the victims from the ethnic group that the media outlet targets. Nevertheless, the media do transmit the court's findings with considerable accuracy. Therefore, the adjudicated facts are available in the local public sphere(s) but are not shaping public memory. Instead of media reports from the courtroom, collective memory is created at memorial sites, on memorial dates, and is reproduced through history textbooks.

Generally, I found no significant changes in the public narrative about the war, at least not in the ways expected by the TJ literature. On few occasions when a change occurred, it was not a result of the ICTY judgments, but emerged due to mutual contestations of victims' and perpetrators' narratives, or due to a political decision to acknowledge a particular crime. Similarly, changes in history textbooks are the result of pressures from international institutions rather than a consequence of the process of 'dealing with the past'. However, the TJ mechanisms do influence public narratives, though not in line with expectations of TJ literature. The findings of the judgments (and the investigative commission) impact public debates about the past, in the sense that they set the parameters for these debates (disabling complete denial that certain criminal events took place) and define critical notions or concepts (such as meaning of internationality of the conflict, ethnic cleansing, genocide) around which the public debates evolve. However, this chapter refutes the underlying assumption of TJ literature, which claims a direct link between establishing and disclosing facts about crimes and their public acknowledgement.

This research offers the assertion that the perception of the past is rather a matter of attitude; not knowledge. For political representatives in particular, the reproduction of the past is guided not by what one knows, but by what one wants to perform in public. Therefore, the acting out of certain historical interpretations sends a particular political message or serves a certain social function.

Furthermore, collective memory is a constitutive element of a community, while for an individual, participation in public reproduction of memory is *being* part of a community.[32] If the communities of memory are defined by ethnicity, so too will their narratives about the past. This is visible when comparing different types of commemorative events. Commemorations organized, or strongly supported, by officials seem to be focused more on building a certain political identity (ethnic identity and/or Statehood project) rather

[32] E Zerubavel, *Time Maps: Collective Memory and the Social Shape of the Past* (The University of Chicago Press 2003).

than memorializing a particular event that is being commemorated. This kind of memorialization is markedly different from the grass-roots commemorations organized by victims' communities, which are focused on reproducing a particular narrative of the events and are not burdened with an ethno-national pretext.

In the deeply ethnified political, educational, and media systems each ethno-national elite employs the hegemonic power within its reach to promote its own interpretation of the war and builds its legitimacy upon this. The three ethno-national political elites obtain a position of sufficient social hegemony to embark on nation-building. In such a situation, historical narratives function as ethnic markers—the promotion of a certain historical interpretation implies the ethnicity of the promoter—or vice-versa—belonging to a certain ethnicity implies the adoption of a certain historical narrative. An individual who rejects the narrative dominant within his/her own ethnic community may be considered, by members of that community, to be renouncing their ethnic identity. Historical narratives as ethnic markers intrinsically tie the perception of the past with the sense of national identity, while rendering rejection of the narrative equal to self-excommunication from the national group.

In addition, the Dayton Peace Agreement froze the divisions from the war-time situation by trying to forge a compromise between conflicting Statehood projects: that of a unitary BiH, that of the RS as a proto-State, and the project of a BiH State that would have assigned territory to the Croatian community. Elements of these projects were incorporated into the post-war constitution, thus gaining legitimacy and continuing to flourish. The memory-making conducted by the ethno-political elites serves to fortify these conflicting Statehood projects. Hence, the conflict continued in the field of the *interpretation* of the war. The combat battleground was substituted by the memorial one.

It seems that as long as the interpretations of the war bear direct consequences in the field of everyday politics; dominant narratives will be kept under tight control of political stakeholders, regardless of the findings of TJ mechanisms. This chapter refutes the underlying assumption of the field of transitional justice, that the disclosing of the truth about the troubling past directly leads to a change of collective memory in the targeted societies, which would prevent denial of war crimes and human rights violations. My research in BiH demonstrates that the perception of the past is crafted by the memory-making endeavours of the dominant ethno-national elites, rather than by the TJ processes.

30

The Broken Path to Reconciliation in Bosnia and Herzegovina

A Field Study of Memories

*Rosa Aloisi**

30.1 Introduction

Set on a hill, east of the municipality of Visegrad, in the Republika Srepska of Bosnia and Herzegovina (BiH), the Straziste Muslim Bosnian cemetery is a reminder of the atrocities perpetrated against Bosniaks during the war of 1992–1995. The dates on the graves tell us of the ethnic cleansing campaign, which occurred in a matter of months between May and July 1992. During that time, Bosniaks were the object of unspeakable violence which, in the words of Judge Robinson 'at the close of the 20th century, a century marked by war and bloodshed on a colossal scale ... remain imprinted on the memory ... '.[1] During the years of 1992–1995 about 3,000 Bosniaks were killed, and the municipality, once a Muslim Bosnian dominated town, became a Bosnian Serb village.

Yet, as the International Criminal Tribunal for the former Yugoslavia (ICTY) was finally establishing the legal responsibility and historical truth about the events surrounding the crimes committed in Visegrad, mounting tensions were ripping the community apart as a memorial plaque in the Straziste cemetery erected in memory of Bosniaks killed during the war became the object of contested versions of collective memories. The plaque, erected in 2012, read 'To all killed and missing Bosniaks, children, women and men victims of genocide in Visegrad'.[2] But, on 23 January 2014, Bosnian Serb officials removed the word 'genocide' from the plaque contesting the legal account established by the ICTY. By erasing the historical remembrance engraved on the stone which aimed at building a collective memory, this act clearly contradicted years of judicial investigations and evidence that proved, beyond any reasonable doubt, atrocities had been committed in the region.

Travelling through some of the areas known as sites where the atrocities were perpetrated we found that the Visegrad cemetery represents only one of the many examples in which the established historical record is denied by local authorities. It has been erased through the construction of a truth which stands in stark contrast with the countless pages representing the judicial archive produced by the ICTY in the last two decades. The actions undertaken by local authorities speak of a willingness to build a collective representation of

* Associate Professor in the Department of Political Science, Trinity University.

[1] *Prosecutor v Milan Lukić and Sredoje Lukić* (Trial Chamber Judgment) ICTY-IT-98-32/1-T (20 July 2009) para 740.

[2] Translation by Maria Protic, Trinity University student.

Rosa Aloisi, *The Broken Path to Reconciliation in Bosnia and Herzegovina* In: *Legacies of the International Criminal Tribunal for the Former Yugoslavia.* Edited by: Carsten Stahn, Carmel Agius, Serge Brammertz, Colleen Rohan, Oxford University Press (2020).
 DOI: 10.1093/oso/9780198862956.003.0031

the events incompatible with the ascertained past. As cogently pointed out by Cohen,[3] travelling through BiH shows that while the war among the factions might have ended, there is a war over memories that is fought between local officials and victims of the crimes which creates a sense of fragility in the peace and reconciliation process of the region.

The reconciliation process of opposing factions in the region is far from being accomplished; the construction of collective memory is contested; travelling through BiH leaves a sense of 'interpersonal' insecurity,[4] as if the work of the Tribunal has had little impact on the reconciliation process of opposing ethnic factions.

This work suggests that the efforts of local authorities to cover up sites of atrocities and negate the evidence collected by the ICTY, incites the sentiment of mistrust and the sense of injustice felt by the families of the victims and survivors of the atrocities. We suggest that, while international justice aims at establishing accountability, a full reconciliation is only possible when the communities come back together in acknowledging the occurrence of atrocities and the right of victims to visit these places to mourn and remember. True reconciliation can only happen when the legal truth is espoused by the local communities and perpetrators do not disseminate a politics of denial which only increases the fear that the crimes committed will be perpetrated again. We suggest that the mandate with which the ICTY has been created, one that promotes, among other goals, peace and security for the region, can only come to full fruition if the 'memorial of words' left by the judges in their final judgments is reflected in the social narrative. Thus, we want to assess whether the judicial legacy of the ICTY has shaped the historical memory of the events that occurred in BiH.

This chapter begins with a brief assessment of the connection between international justice and the memorialization process, and how they are both complementary and essential to achieve true reconciliation. The chapter assesses why memorialization has become a tool of reconciliation and how the construction of collective memories helps a community, healing from the wounds of war, and the victims to regain a sense of agency and trust. On this point, we contend that international tribunals might be insufficient to reconcile communities where there are constant reminders of the violence suffered and a daily attempt at denial by local officials. We offer a comparative examination of the status of some of the sites of atrocities visited and the corresponding judicial record of the ICTY, by looking at findings in judgments and evidence related to those sites. In doing this, we try to assess the effectiveness of the judicial mechanism in affecting the societal narrative of the crimes committed.

30.2 International Justice and Memorialization

When the United Nations Security Council (UNSC) created the ICTY with Resolution 808,[5] it gave the tribunal the core mandate of 'prosecuting the persons responsible for the violations of international humanitarian law committed in the territory of the former Yugoslavia

[3] L B Cohen, 'Finding Global Justice Locally at Sites of Atrocity: The Case for the Srebrenica-Potočari Memorial Center and Cemetery' in S W Murray (ed), *Understanding Atrocities: Remembering, Representing and Teaching Genocide* (Calgary University Press 2017) 49.

[4] J Halpern and H M Weinstein, 'Rehumanizing the Other: Empathy and Reconciliation' (2004) 26 Human Rights Quarterly 561, 562.

[5] UNSC Res 808 (22 February 1993) UN Doc S/RES/808 (1993).

since 1991'.[6] Albeit not expressly mentioned in the mandate bestowed upon the ICTY, it soon became very clear that the long-term goal of restoration of peace and security in the region, one in which victims and perpetrators would share the same spaces, could only be achieved if individual accountability for the commission of crimes functioned as a form of national reconciliation. The mandate of the Tribunal to punish the perpetrators of crimes and identify the guilty was intended to limit the 'wider moral responsibility' of the national community.[7] It provided the first step towards reconciliation through the condemnation of the prior government's 'political project'[8] while establishing, at the same time, a historical record of the pain and suffering of victims and survivors. Accountability was considered the major tool towards reconciliation. International trials were justified on the basis that recognition of individual responsibility helped the victims move forward and assigned the liability for the disruption of interethnic relationships to specific individuals and not to entire societies.[9]

Yet, as we assess the impact of the ICTY legacy on the region's reconciliation process, we recognize that a tension exists between the record established by the Tribunal and the social representation of the legal truth; the battleground of the interethnic relations has become the construction of collective memories at the sites of mass atrocities described by the records of the international Tribunal. Rather than becoming a source of reconciliation, the historical findings of the ICTY's judgments are being questioned; the sites of mass atrocities and the attempts at making those sites places of national dialogue and remembrance are becoming widely contested and 'used to further entrench mutually incompatible versions of the past [...] contribut[ing] to a renew of mistrust, untruth and injustice'.[10]

We believe that, at its core, reconciliation is something that cannot only be achieved through individual accountability and that, in a way, individual liability should be complemented by a national collective effort, beyond legal responsibility, to recognize the obligations of a society. We suggest that the function of memorialization is twofold. On one side, memorialization speaks of a society which is accepting its troubled past. On the other, it validates the pain and suffering of the victims, it gives names and identity to those who have died, and it offers an additional reassurance that those crimes will not be perpetrated again.

For the collectivity, reconciliation means healing the divisions of a society, the scars suffered during violence; rebuilding the trust broken by the war, 'glue back together' the broken pieces of interethnic pre-war friendly and familial relationships. This type of reconciliation is an extension of that achieved through accountability; reconciliation demands that the words written by judges in their judgments come out of those pages and are set in places where they can foster dialogue among ethnic groups and empathy among individuals in a public space, while recognizing the victims' suffering and their ability to publicly mourn and commemorate.

6 UNSC 'Report of the Secretary General Pursuant to Paragraph 2 of Security Council Resolution 808' (1993) UN Doc S/25704.

7 M Humphrey, 'International Intervention, Justice and National Reconciliation: the Role of the ICTY and ICTR in Bosnia and Rwanda' (2010) 2 Journal of Human Rights 495, 500.

8 ibid.

9 L Fletcher and H M Weinstein, 'Violence and Social Repair: Rethink the Contribution of Justice to Reconciliation' (2002) 24 Human Rights Quarterly 573, 598 and fn 87.

10 J Subotic, 'Political Memory as an Obstacle to Justice in Serbia Croatia and Bosnia and Herzegovina' in M Fischer and O Simic (eds), *Transitional Justice and Reconciliation: Lessons from the Balkans* (Routledge 2015) 121.

In this manner, memorialization becomes an extension of the truth established by the ICTY. The memorialization of the atrocities described by the Tribunal, especially at the sites where the crimes were committed, can become a reminder that we all bear a collective responsibility for the events that have destroyed the region. While international criminal justice addresses the individual accountability, memorialization can become a reminder that the crimes committed bears on the collectivity and society.[11] As cogently stated by Gustafson, 'A Hitler—like a Stalin, a Karadzic, a Tudjman, a Mao—is only as strong as the power of mass obedience and support'[12] and the collectivity carries the moral burden as well as the brunt of the crimes committed. The recognition and acknowledgement through the construction of memorials that those crimes were committed, especially at the sites where crimes were perpetrated, are meant to build a stronger society in which the rule of law is restored. It sends a message that there is a culture of *collective* moral indignation against irrational hatred and ethnic violence.[13] What we think can be achieved through memorialization, beyond the legacy of the Tribunal, is a change in collective attitudes. Beyond the trials' 'established consensus on the events as they unfolded',[14] memorials can provide places of 'mourning to restore some sense of agency. There must be public acknowledgment of the losses that people have experienced and recognition of the victimization that many feel'.[15]

The most important aspect of memorialization is the ability to remind us that, beyond a courtroom, a criminal legal definition, and a punishment, there are memories to pass on to future generations so as to avoid the repetition of the horrors. As stated by Megret, 'Monuments stand as an implicit condemnation of the faults of past regimes. They act as a reminder to future generations of certain dangers and places through which contemporary dreams of national future are imagined'.[16] In this regard, what is most important is that the memorialization of sites of atrocities become part of a collective memory of the people that can stop society's aberrations and reinforce the protection of individuals. We think that memorialization of sites of atrocity might just be that signal that the society at large is accepting the troubled past, is recognizing that crimes were committed, and is allowing victims and survivors to publicly display their sorrow and the need to mourn.

For the victims, memorialization of the sites of atrocities increases the value of the sentence handed by the ICTY. Indeed, delivering a meaningful sense of justice, one that speaks of the pain and suffering of the victims of the heinous crimes committed during times of wars, is probably the most problematic aspect in addressing societal peace after war. After all, what is the right punishment for those who have killed, raped, and tortured thousands of individuals? How can victims and survivors of those killed believe in just desert and move forward towards reconciliation, when the punishment handed down by international

[11] R Dudai, 'Rescuers for Humanity: Rescuers, Mass Atrocities, and Transitional Justice' (2012) 34 Human Rights Quarterly 1.

[12] C Gustafson, 'International Criminal Courts: some Dissident Views on the Continuation of War by Penal Means' (1998) 21 Houston Journal of International Law 51.

[13] R Aloisi and J D Meernik, *Judgement Day—Judicial Decision Making at the International Tribunal* (Cambridge University Press 2017).

[14] Fletcher and Weinstein (n 9) 625.

[15] ibid 626.

[16] F Mégret, 'Of Shrines, Museums, and Memorials—Using the International Criminal Court's Victims Reparation and Assistance Regime to Promote International Justice' (2003) 16 Buffalo Human Rights Law Review 1, 22.

courts is something short of life in prison? Scholars[17] have indicated how the judgments of the Tribunal might not fully speak to the emotional needs of victims and, after all, in the legalist framework within which the ICTY has operated, one created for the punishment of the guilty, the specific needs of victims are not necessarily the goal to be pursued. However, as rightly stated by Schabas:

> For the victims, and for the public in general, the thirst for justice may be better satisfied by *society's condemnation* of anti-social behavior than by the actual punishment of the offenders. What is desired is a judgment, *a declaration by society*, and the identification and stigmatization of the perpetrator. This alone is often sufficient redress. What is actually done to the offender as a result of conviction may be far less important.[18]

Nonetheless, the ICTY represents the first international tribunal in which the voices of the witnesses and victims were given ample space in the judgments and during the proceedings. Emblematic in the memory of all, remains the testimony of witness DD in the case of *The Prosecutor v Radislav Kristić*,[19] recalling how her son had been snatched away from her and begging the judicial bench to ask Kristić whether he knew of her son's whereabouts. Yet, once witness DD left the courtroom, as many other witnesses did, she might have returned to a community where public officials are constantly covering the sites of crimes, unmarking mass graves, and rewriting the history of the conflict. Once again, the reported details of this testimony seemingly aimed at giving an identity to a child whose name is unknown and whose suffering can only be recounted by those who briefly met him, do not find a comparable account within the local community. Memorialization of sites of atrocities reinforce and validate the suffering of victims and witnesses. They add to the accounting of events whose record populates thousands of pages of the ICTY judgments, a vivid description of the images and of the deep fear and desperation of victims. They can become the most emblematic depiction of the campaign of terror during the Bosnian genocide and a clear example of the 'ultimate suffering' of the population. More than any punishment, the sites of atrocity stand out as universal reminders of the horrors committed during the war. We might be reading in the future the names of those who have committed the atrocities during the Balkans war, but memorials stand out because they represent the living memories of those whose names or existence might be easily forgotten; the children, the women, and men who became the object of international crimes.

There are several voices among scholars warning against memorialization as a source of national reconciliation. Memorials can perpetuate the images of old wrongs, reigniting conflicts, and affecting the present and future relations of interethnic relations.[20] Memories and memorials can also become the tool of political propaganda, as we noted during our travels through BiH, where memorials and statues honouring the memory of fallen Serb soldiers are strategically located in places where Bosniak civilians suffered torture and

[17] L Moffett, *Realising Justice for Victims before the International Criminal Court* (International Crimes Database 2014) <http://www.internationalcrimesdatabase.org/upload/documents/20140916T170017-ICD%20Brief%20-%20Moffett.pdf> accessed 12 December 2017.

[18] W A Schabas, 'Sentencing by International Tribunals: A Human Rights Approach' (1997) 7 Duke Journal of Comparative and International Law 461, 502. Emphasis added.

[19] *Prosecutor v Radislav Kristić* (Trial Chamber Judgment) ICTY–IT-98-33-T (2 August 2001) para 93.

[20] D Bloomfield, T Barnes, and L Huyse (eds), *Reconciliation after Violent Conflict: A Handbook* (International Idea 2003).

death. However, we contend that this is indeed that form of unilateral historical interpretation through memorialization, which leaves little space for a public space of dialogue and imposes a political will over moral considerations. It is what memorialization should not be—namely the furtherance of a political atmosphere of terror and persecution.

30.3 Comparing Judgments and Memorialization

Before delving into the evidence collected during our visit to some of the sites of atrocity, it is necessary to make some premises about the current political division of BiH. Bosnia and Herzegovina comprises two entities: The Federation of Bosnia and Herzegovina, and Republika Srpska. These autonomous political entities were created following the Dayton Accords in late 1995 which tried to put an end to the bloodshed that had been perpetrated since 1992. The Accords, signed when there was yet no evidence of the magnitude of the crimes committed in some of the areas of the region, geographically partitioned the territory by freezing the location of the different ethnicities within specifically territorial boundaries. We conducted our gathering of evidence at some of the sites of the most infamous crimes perpetrated, such as Kravica Warehouse, Srebrenica and the Potočari Memorial, Foča, Višegrad, and Prijedor, including the latter's surrounding areas of Kozarac, Tomasica mass grave and the concentration camps of Keraterm, Omarska, and Trnopolje. Of those areas, only the Potocari Memorial is assigned as a special site under the administration of the authorities of The Federation of Bosnia and Herzegovina, while all the other municipalities we visited are in areas under the control of the Republika Srpska. As we travelled through the region, it became immediately evident that the ethnic divisions are still very much in place and the tension about how historical truth is recounted clashes along the same ethnic lines that brought about the collapse of the former Yugoslavia. We provide a preliminary analysis of some of the sites visited.

30.3.1 Kravica Warehouse

While driving to Srebrenica from Sarajevo, you pass through some of the villages, such as Goglova and Bratunac, which still carry the signs of the war. The route takes you through beautiful mountains and forests where people running small cafes greet you with a welcoming smile and ask the reasons of your travel. Some are still very reluctant to speak about the war to a professor from the US, while others may tell you more about their personal experience, especially if they have lost family members. As the drive winds down from the mountains, you find yourself on a two-way road with some rebuilt houses and farms on the side of the street.

Our first stop was very sudden as our driver[21] had to make a quick turnaround since, while speaking about his experience during the war, he had missed one of the places we wanted to visit. The Kravica Warehouse is hardly visible from the street; it is covered by trees and a fence not higher than 150 cm. The Kravica Warehouse massacre became sadly

[21] Our driver was a former soldier of the Bosnia Army and a current member of the Federal Commission for Missing Persons.

notorious as one of the most heinous steps towards the perpetration of genocide. Evidence collected by the Tribunal not only provided a vivid description of the seizing and execution of Bosnian Muslim males, but it also showed the images of mounds of bodies placed right in front of the entrance of the warehouse. In the words of a witness, recalling the night of the massacre:

> there was firing everywhere. There was so much dust. There was so much firing; you didn't know where the shots were coming from. I couldn't see anything. That was just full of noise. Next to me was sitting a man from Vlasenica called Salko Redzić. He was killed there in the warehouse. We just sat down and put our heads next to each other. And he died.[22]

According to the evidence collected by the ICTY:

> During July 1995, believed to lie within the grave [found near to the Kravica Warehouse], had been a part of a group who had walked the mountain route from Potocari and Srebrenica toward Tuzla […]. Upon arrest, some of these men were held within the confine of the building known as the Kravica Warehouse. […] It was further alleged that they had lost their lives at that location by means of gunshot wounds, explosion and shrapnel injuries from ordnance fired and thrown into the building in which they were confined.[23]

In the case of *Prosecutor v Blagojevic and Jokic*, the Trial Chamber found:

> sufficient testimonial, documentary and forensic evidence to support a finding beyond reasonable doubt that on 13 July, over 1,000 men were detained in large warehouse in Kravica and summarily executed with automatic weapons, hand grenades and other weapons.[24]

Furthermore, in the case of *Prosecutor v Popovic* et al, the Appeals Chamber established that

> in the afternoon of 13 July 1995, the killings began and that by nightfall, over 1,000 Bosnian Muslim males had been executed. To support this finding, it referred to the killings at: (1) the Kravica Warehouse where at least 1,000 Bosnian Muslim men were killed[.][25]

Yet, on the day we approached the warehouse, it looked like a regular deposit for agricultural machinery with some chained dogs barking at us. The only recognizable marks of the crimes were the bullet holes on the concrete walls inside one of the rooms of the warehouse and on the walls in front of the building. There was no sign of commemoration and no indication that the warehouse was used to kill hundreds of individuals in a matter of hours; that Muslim men were summarily executed and buried close to the farm as a part of a genocidal campaign. Ironically, right in front of the fences we crossed to enter the area of the

[22] *Prosecutor v Vidoje Blagojevic and Dragan Jokic* (Trial Chamber Judgment) ICTY-IT-02-60-T (15 January 2005) para 297.

[23] M J Hedley, 'A Report of the Examination of Recovery and Evidence from Kravica Warehouse—Bosnia and Herzegovina' (September/October 2000) <http://icr.icty.org/LegalRef/CMSDocStore/Public/English/Exhibit/NotIndexable/IT-05-88/ACE74659R0000272245.pdf> accessed 12 December 2017, 3.

[24] *Prosecutor v Vidoje Blagojevic and Dragan Jokic* (Trial Chamber Judgment) ICTY-IT-02-60-T1 (17 January 2005) para 567(d).

[25] *Prosecutor v Popovic* et al (Appeals Chamber Judgment) ICTY-IT-05-88-A (30 January 2015) para 864.

warehouse there was a small plaque commemorating a young boy who had died in a traffic accident.

30.3.1.1 Foča

Foča is a municipality in BiH on the Drina River, in the Republika Srpska entity. The town was the theatre of some of the most heinous crimes perpetrated against Muslim women. Mass rapes and enslavements of women, held captive in several of the buildings around the town, became part of the genocidal campaign against the Muslim population. The ICTY collected extensive documentation and witness testimony of the crimes. In the case of *The Prosecutor v Kunarac, Kovac, and Vukovic,* the first case to come to the Tribunal in which sexual violence was the only charge, the Appeals Chamber established that:

> From April 1992 until at least February 1993, there was an armed conflict between Bosnian Serbs and Bosnian Muslims in the area of Foca. Non-Serb civilians were killed, raped or otherwise abused as a direct result of the armed conflict.[26]
>
> One specific target of the attack was Muslim women, who were detained in intolerably unhygienic conditions in places like the Kalinovik School, Foca High School and the Partizan Sports Hall, where they were mistreated in many ways, including being raped repeatedly.[27]

One of the women who bravely came forward to testify in front of the ICTY recounted how Kunarac repeatedly raped her and when he was done with her suggested that he 'could have done much more with her if she were not the same age as his daughter'.[28] The Prosecutors and the Judges sitting on the case spoke of a widespread and systematic campaign of rape and enslavement. Almost 100 women were detained in what was called the 'rape house' and they were raped repeatedly for more than seventy days. It is difficult to imagine the anguish and humiliation suffered by the women and children, some as young as twelve years old, during those days and, while the witness testimony might have given some of these women a venue to face their perpetrators and establish a juridical truth of the crimes committed, the community within which those acts were perpetrated does not acknowledge any of the evidence collected by the ICTY. As we drove to leave Fоća, we encountered only one monument; it is a monument to commemorate the Serb soldiers who lost their lives during the war.

30.3.1.2 Visegrad

On 20 July 2009, Judge Patrick Robinson, the presiding judge in the case of *Prosecutor v Milan Lukić and Sredoje Lukić,* who were standing trial at the ICTY accused of crimes against humanity and violations of laws or customs of war, pronounced these words in front of an audience who had listened for more than thirty minutes to a short, but vivid, description of the crimes for which the accused stood trial:

[26] *Prosecutor v Kunarac, Kovav, and Vukovic* (Appeals Chamber Judgment) ICTY-IT-96-23 and IT-96-23/1-A (12 June 2002) para 12.

[27] ibid 3.

[28] ICTY, Victims 50 (ICTY public record, 2000) <http://www.icty.org/en/sid/188> accessed 20 April 2018.

> In the all too long, sad and wretched history of man's inhumanity to man, the Pionirska Street and Bikavac fires must rank high. At the close of the 20th century, a century marked by war and bloodshed on a colossal scale, these horrific events remain imprinted on the memory for the viciousness of the incendiary attack, for the obvious premeditation and calculation that defined it, for the sheer callousness, monstrosity and brutality of herding, trapping and locking the victims in the two houses, thereby rendering them helpless in the ensuing inferno and for the degree of pain and suffering inflicted on the victims as they were burnt alive.[29]

As we entered Visegrad, we were immediately caught by the striking beauty of the town on the Drina River. The Ottoman Bridge connecting the two sides of the river offers a panoramic view of Visegrad on one side, and the mountains of Bikavac on the other. On the day we visited, there was almost a surreal feeling. As we were looking for the places where the crimes described by Judge Robinson took place, the town was celebrating a local holiday and music could be heard throughout the town. The lightness of life unfolding on that day speaks of a community at peace; a peace however that is not that of the survivors or families of the victims, a peace that has been built by forgetting the past, a peace that is ultimately very fragile.

We started our walk up to the valley where Bikavac is located and found the first house where, according to the ICTY, on 27 June 1992:

> Milan and Sredoje Lukić forced approximately 70 Bosnian Muslim people into a house in the Bikavac quarter of Višegrad, blocked the exits, and activated several incendiary devices. Only one person survived. The list of the known victims which is attached to the indictment, included the names of two babies, a five-year-old girl, and three children between eight and eleven years of age.[30]

We did not find the remains of the house, we found a new house that was being built and the owner of the house was working inside. He kindly agreed to talk to us. He really did not know what will happen to the house; he mentioned that it might be turned into a place housing an office for the search of missing persons; and the only thing he was almost certain about was that a plaque commemorating the victims will be placed on the front of the house.

We left Bikavac to go to Visegrad and walked over to Pionirska Street. As we approached the area, we could not see anything that would speak of the crimes committed. The Tribunal found the Lukić cousins responsible for:

> forc[ing] approximately 65 Bosnian Muslim women, children, and elderly men into a house on Pionirska Street in a neighborhood of Višegrad known as Nova Mahala. Once these people were barricaded inside, the house was set afire and Milan and Sredoje Lukić fired automatic weapons at persons trying to save themselves by climbing out the windows

[29] *Prosecutor v Milan Lukić and Sredoje Lukić* (Trial Chamber Judgment) ICTY-IT-98-32/1-T (20 July 2009) para 740. See also (n 13).

[30] ICTY Outreach office, 'View from The Hague, "Horror Film" in Visegrad' (2004) <http://www.icty.org/x/file/Outreach/view_from_hague/balkan_040428_en.pdf> accessed 12 December 2017, 1.

> of the burning building. The indictment alleges that they killed almost all of the persons locked in the house during the incident, including seventeen children who were between the ages of two days and fourteen years.[31]

The view of the house is blocked from the street by a narrow entrance. Like the house in Bikavac, the house on Pionirska Street has gone through considerable remodelling, but only of the top floors. However, in order for us to reach the basement, where there are still signs of the fire, we had to go through high grass. Once there, we noticed that the only way we could read the plaque commemorating the victims was to go into a ditch covered by high grass, which was difficult to navigate. The evidence of the crimes committed is concealed from the view of those who pass by and the plaque is placed on the side of the building.

We spoke of Visegrad, as a community that seems at peace, but where no signs of commemoration of the sites of atrocity are visible. We did wonder whether the joyous town was indeed at peace with its troubled past and questioned whether, after all, commemoration of the sites of atrocity might not necessarily be one of the paths to reconciliation. However, our visit to the cemetery close to Pionirska Street, where the word 'genocide' was carefully chiselled out by Bosnian Serb police, speaks of underlying tensions among the ethnic groups and of efforts to deny the factual findings of the international Tribunal.

30.3.1.3 Omarska, Keraterm, and Trnopolje

In Prijedor we were surprised to find a town where neighbourhoods have been rebuilt with big and colourful houses. As we drove through the town accompanied by Sudbin Music, a survivor of the Trnopolje concentration camp, we noticed that most of the houses were empty. Perfectly rebuilt buildings surrounded by gardens whose windows were tightly closed. Sudbin told us that the 'community is dead'. Those who fled the threat of genocide only came back to reclaim their property; faced with ethnic discrimination they decided to live in some other place. Prijedor is the town where some of the biggest concentration camps were created during the war. These were the Omarska, Keraterm, and Trnopolje concentration camps. According to the ICTY in the case of the *Prosecutor v Kvocka* et al:

> in Omarska camp, evidence of abuses could be seen by observing the bloodied, bruised, and injured bodies of detainees, by observing heaps of dead bodies lying in piles around the camp, and noticing the emaciated and poor condition of detainees, as well as by observing the cramped facilities or the bloodstained walls. Evidence of abuses could be heard from the screams of pain and cries of suffering, from the sounds of the detainees begging for food and water and beseeching their tormentors not to beat or kill them, and from the gunshots heard everywhere in the camp. Evidence of the abusive conditions in the camp could also be smelled as a result of the deteriorating corpses, the urine and feces soiling the detainees' clothes, the broken and overflowing toilets, the dysentery afflicting the detainees, and the inability of detainees to wash or bathe for weeks or months.[32]

[31] ibid.
[32] *Prosecutor v Kvocka* et al (Trial Chamber Judgment) ICTY-IT-98-30/1-T (2 November 2001) para 324.

These types of events were systematic and spread out in the three concentration camps.[33] Witness testimony at the Trial Chamber and documental evidence, show emaciated and beaten men dying in Trnopolje. Yet, the Omarska concentration camp is not visible from the street. It is currently used as a factory and a strategically placed mound of dirt has been piled in front of the building to hide it from those driving by. Keraterm, on the other hand, is very visible from the street, but like Omarska, has gone back to being a factory with no sign of commemoration of those who perished at the site. The only concentration camp we could approach was Trnopolje. A white building where Sudbin described for us how men, women, and children were unloaded from buses and forced to move to the back of the building, where their fate would be decided. Of those events, nothing remains to remind the collectivity that those crimes happened. Ironically, once again, right in front of the concentration camp there is a monument commemorating a Serb soldier who perished during the war.

30.4 Conclusion

In a post-war society, one characterized by ethnic hatred and divisions, the factions still sharing the same territory face insurmountable obstacles in moving forward and rebuilding a society that has come unglued under the pressure of political demagogy. Remembering that not too long ago the villages ravaged by violence were peaceful places where neighbours had 'the keys to each other's doors'[34] has become impossible because of the viciousness of the crimes committed and the ensuing denial that those crimes did indeed occur.

The memorialization of sites of atrocity can become a tool for fighting denial and a constant reminder of the crimes committed; one reminder that not only speaks to those living in the region, but to the whole of humanity. Memorialization of sites where the crimes were committed provides historical validation for the victims and recognizes their right to mourn publicly. There is no international judgment that can ever resonate with the same power as the commemoration of the places where those crimes have happened. The perception of personal loss and tragedy is felt by the community and can become a symbol, offered by the political structure of a country, of sincere remorse and truthful effort

[33] In the case of *The Prosecutor v Sikirica* et al, the Trial Chamber, describing the conditions of the Keraterm Camp in paras 62–103, established that beatings and killings took place regularly during the night. Those who were not beaten directly had to witness the mistreatment of others, which caused an atmosphere of intimidation and fear. The Trial Chamber further established that on the afternoon of 24 July 1992, a massacre occurred in what was called Room 3 of the camp. The description of the Trial Chamber through the words of a survivor of the massacre once again evokes images of unimaginable pain and suffering: 'A machine-gun was placed on a desk or table in front of Room 3 sometime before the massacre took place. At around 3 or 4 p.m., the Room 3 detainees were put back in the room and the doors were locked. Soon thereafter, some gas was thrown into the room. Some of the prisoners attempted to break down the door and it was then that the soldiers responded with a burst of gunfire.' According to several witnesses who survived the Room 3 massacre, there were repeated bursts of gunfire. Several people ahead of Witness N, who was near the door in Room 3, were hit with bullets and three or four of them fell on top of him. As Witness N put it: 'Misfortune was my luck, because these bullets—they were absorbing these bullets that were being fired from outside. They were bouncing from the bullets that were hitting them. It was horrible. It was like being in hell, a night in hell.' The bullets entered the room through the glass windows and the door, ricocheting around the room. In addition to these accounts of the massacre, there was abundant evidence from witnesses who were detained elsewhere in the camp that night. The dead and wounded, approximately 160 to 200 men in total, were taken away in a truck. None of those whose bodies were removed that morning were ever seen again. *Prosecutor v Sikirica* et al (Sentencing Judgment) ICTY-IT-95-8-S (13 November 2001) paras 101–02.

[34] E Neuffer, *The Key to My Neighbor's House: Seeking Justice in Bosnia and Rwanda* (Picador 2015).

towards reconciliation. Where international justice cannot capture the pain and suffering of individuals, memorials can become a place of dialogue, acceptance of responsibility, and reconciliation.

What we have unfortunately assessed in this preliminary study of the sites of atrocity is the lack of memorialization and the denial that some events described by the ICTY judgments have taken place. As we mentioned, of the places visited only the Potocari memorial has been built as a symbol of the genocide. We have not discussed the history behind the memorial in Potocari. However, we would like to briefly mention that during our visit one of the curators and survivors of the Srebrenica genocide told us that, despite the efforts of the international community to build the memorial, the current political climate in Srebrenica seems not conducive to reconciliation. Mladen Grujičić, a Serb nationalist who has denied that the massacre in Sebrenica was a genocide, has become the new mayor of the town and this has increased the fears of Bosnian Muslims living in the area and of those travelling to the memorial every July to commemorate the victims of genocide. In the words of some of the survivors, they are fearful that commemoration will be stopped and signs of denial will refuel hatred and violence.

31

The ICTY, Truth, and Reconciliation

A Meta Reconceptualization

*Janine Natalya Clark**

Truth is not a highway. It is a trail hacked through snake-infested undergrowth.[1]

31.1 Introduction

This chapter reflects on the relationship between truth and reconciliation. More particularly, it discusses whether the factual truths documented by the International Criminal Tribunal for the former Yugoslavia (ICTY) constitute a basis for inter-ethnic reconciliation. Demonstrating, empirically and conceptually, that these truths are often deeply contested on the ground, it maintains that the ICTY did not contribute to reconciliation. What the chapter also seeks to demonstrate, however, is that while the Tribunal has now completed its mandate, the legacy of its work can potentially contribute to reconciliation indirectly. The realization of this potential requires a partial reconfiguration of transitional justice through an emphasis on higher-level truths. Crucially, the Tribunal established broader meta-normative truths about the conflicts in the former Yugoslavia and the crimes therein committed. The moral wrongs of rape, of targeting civilians, of destroying childhoods, of attacking a people's cultural heritage, are truths that constitute a basis on which to build broad-based cross-ethnic agreement. Just as some types of food are more easily digestible than others, so too are some types of truth.

Meta-normative truths have a greater degree of 'processing fluency'[2] than factual truths, and this is a key reason why they are more conducive to fostering reconciliation. This is not to suggest that factual truths are unimportant. Indeed, developing a consensus around meta-normative truths can help to increase the social penetrability of factual truths. Ultimately, therefore, this chapter argues that more attention should be given, within the former Yugoslavia, to the meta-normative truths associated with the ICTY's work over two and a half decades. The first part, section 31.2, examines the contestability of some of the factual truths established by the Tribunal, using the examples of Prijedor and Ahmići in Bosnia-Herzegovina (BiH). The second part, section 31.3, offers a conceptual explanation

* Professor of Gender, Transitional Justice and International Criminal Law, Birmingham Law School.

[1] D Bolinger, 'Truth is a Linguistic Question' (1973) 4 Language 539, 547.

[2] A Dechêne et al, 'The Truth about the Truth: A Meta-Analytic Review of the Truth Effect' (2010) 14 Personality and Social Psychology Review 238, 238.

Janine Natalya Clark, *The ICTY, Truth, and Reconciliation* In: *Legacies of the International Criminal Tribunal for the Former Yugoslavia*. Edited by: Carsten Stahn, Carmel Agius, Serge Brammertz, Colleen Rohan, Oxford University Press (2020). © The Several Contributors
DOI: 10.1093/oso/9780198862956.003.0032

for the persistence of contested truths, drawing on Goldin's work on 'meta-affective context'.[3] The final part, section 31.4, introduces and operationalizes the notion of meta-normative truths, focusing in particular on defendants' guilty pleas at the ICTY.

31.2 The Problem of Contested Truths

In December 2010, the United Nations (UN) Security Council created the UN International Mechanism for Criminal Tribunals (the Mechanism),[4] to carry out a number of vital functions previously undertaken by the ICTY and its sister tribunal, the International Criminal Tribunal for Rwanda (ICTR). One of these functions relates to the preservation and management of the Tribunals' extensive archives. According to the Mechanism's website, these archives constitute 'one of the most complete collections of eyewitness testimonies of some of the greatest violations of international humanitarian law to have occurred since World War II'.[5] Yet, while the ICTY unquestionably established a rich documentary record of facts, some of the claims that it made regarding the *impact* of these facts are deeply problematic.

The Tribunal often implicitly adopted the so-called correspondence theory of truth, according to which 'truth is correspondence to fact'.[6] According to its website, for example, the ICTY's judgments 'contributed to creating a historical record, combatting denial and preventing attempts at revisionism ... '.[7] However, such an assertion critically neglects the pivotal issue of how these judgments—and the facts that they contain—have been received on the ground. Further highlighting this is the Tribunal's claim that it 'established *beyond a reasonable doubt* crucial facts related to crimes committed in the former Yugoslavia'.[8] As Milanović pertinently notes, 'The facts in the cases before the ICTY were certainly established to the satisfaction of the Tribunal's judges, but even they would not say that they are the only audience that matters'.[9] Characteristically, facts established 'beyond reasonable doubt' in The Hague have often encountered deep resistance and hostility from local communities in the former Yugoslavia, thus disrupting any 'correspondence' between facts and truth. The facts determined in the ICTY's courtrooms, in short, have always competed with on-the-ground ethnic 'truths'. This point can be illustrated using the example of Prijedor.

31.2.1 Prijedor

The ICTY extensively documented the heinous crimes that occurred in the Omarska, Keraterm, and Trnopolje camps in the municipality of Prijedor in north-west BiH. In the trial of *Kvočka* et al, for example, the Trial Chamber found that ' ... the non-Serbs detained in these camps were subjected to a series of atrocities... Extreme brutality was systematic

[3] G A Goldin, 'Affect, Meta-Affect and Mathematical Belief Structures' in G C Leder, E Pehkonen, and G Törner (eds), *Beliefs: A Hidden Variable in Mathematics Education?* (Kluwer Academic Publishers 2002).
[4] UNSC Res 1966 (22 December 2010) UN Doc S/RES/1966.
[5] UN MICT, 'Archives' <http://www.unmict.org/en/about/functions/archives> accessed 5 May 2017.
[6] D Lewis, 'Forget about the "Correspondence Theory of Truth"' (2001) 61 Analysis 275, 275.
[7] See ICTY, 'Achievements' <http://www.icty.org/en/about/tribunal/achievements> accessed 30 May 2017.
[8] ibid emphasis added.
[9] M Milanović, 'The Impact of the ICTY on the Former Yugoslavia: An Anticipatory Postmortem' (2016) 110 American Journal of International Law 233, 235.

in the camps and utilized as a tool to terrorize the Muslims, Croats, and other non-Serbs imprisoned therein'.[10] In the *Stakić* judgment, the Trial Chamber emphasized that 'killings occurred frequently in the Omarska, Keraterm and Trnopolje camps ... The thousands of persons who were detained in the camps were subjected to inhuman and degrading treatment, including routine beatings'.[11] Rapes and sexual assaults also took place.[12] I conducted extensive fieldwork in BiH between 2008 and 2013,[13] and in Prijedor I was repeatedly told that the camps were simply 'collective centres' in which non-Serbs were temporarily held before being transferred to Bosnian army-held territory. These 'collective centres', moreover, were necessary to protect non-Serbs from marauding groups on the outside. While some locals did acknowledge that crimes occurred, particularly within Omarska, they viewed them as isolated incidents attributable to a few wayward individuals.[14] As Hodžić has argued, 'The denial of crimes committed in Prijedor remains deeply entrenched within the Serb community, especially in these areas where the worst crimes occurred'.[15]

The ICTY was not working with a tabula rasa. Communities in the former Yugoslavia have their own 'truths' about the wars and the crimes therein committed, and the resultant 'axiological holism'[16] creates a critical contextual framework that necessarily shaped popular reactions to the Tribunal's work. According to de Souza, axiological holism 'stipulates that we do not apprehend value in discrete units, but only in the light of a complex of factors that transcend individual experience'.[17] In other words, the facts established by the ICTY are not viewed in isolation but in relation to how they fit and converge with emic ethnic narratives. As Hodžić remarks with specific reference to Prijedor, '... the long-term impact of any judicial attempt to address the legacy of mass atrocities will be severely curtailed if it runs counter to the dominant narrative of the past created and fostered by the government, local intelligentsia and the media loyal to it'.[18]

Returning to the aforementioned *Stakić* judgement, this offers some useful insights into the dominant Serb narrative in Prijedor. The judgement notes, for example, that Stakić – a local politician – referred to Omarska, Keraterm and Trnopolje as 'reception centres'.[19] He also claimed, inter alia, that 'those in the Omarska camp who appeared to be injured or wounded had incurred such injuries before entering the camp in the course of combat operations'; and that '... the official stand of the authorities was that there must not be any

[10] *Prosecutor v Miroslav Kvočka, Milojica Kos, Mlađo Radić, Zoran Žigić, and Dragoljub Prcać* (Trial Chamber Judgment) ICTY-IT-98-30/1-T (2 November 2001) para 117.

[11] *Prosecutor v Milomir Stakić* (Trial Judgment) ICTY-IT-97-24-T (31 July 2003) para 544.

[12] ibid.

[13] I conducted this fieldwork as part of a comparative research project, partly funded by the Leverhulme Trust, which sought to empirically assess whether the ICTY's work has contributed to inter-ethnic reconciliation in BiH, Croatia, and Kosovo. See J N Clark, *International Trials and Reconciliation: Assessing the Impact of the International Criminal Tribunal for the Former Yugoslavia* (Routledge 2014, 2015). In total, I conducted 372 semi-structured interviews over a five-year period between 2008 and 2013. The largest number of interviews took place in BiH, where I interviewed 135 men and seventy-five women (from all ethnic groups). Of the 210 interviewees in BiH, 157(ninety-six men and sixty-one women)were ordinary people (as opposed to elites). They included families of killed and missing persons, former camp detainees, survivors of rape and sexual violence, and ex-combatants.

[14] See, for example, J N Clark, 'The Impact Question: The ICTY and the Restoration and Maintenance of Peace' in B Swart, Ar Zahar, and G Sluiter (eds), *The Legacy of the International Criminal Tribunal for the Former Yugoslavia* (Oxford University Press 2011) 74; Clark (n 13) 92–95.

[15] R Hodžić, 'Living the Legacy of Mass Atrocities: Victims' Perspectives on War Crimes Trials' (2010) 8 International Journal of Transitional Justice 113, 130.

[16] R de Souza, 'Emotional Truth' (2002) 76 Proceedings of the Aristotelian Society 247, 255.

[17] ibid.

[18] *Hodžić* (n 15) 135.

[19] *Stakić* (n 11) para 378.

maltreatment'.[20] The judgement additionally cites a number of reports, including one compiled by Simo Drljača, the commander of the Public Security Station in Prijedor. According to this,

> although the Muslim extremists put up a fierce resistance, ruthlessly settling scores with members of their own people who refused to fight against the Serbian forces, the local government, the army and the police were not ready for this development of events, believing to the end in a peaceful and civilised agreement between the peoples. This created a problem of the quartering, guarding and treatment of captured people. It was in this kind of situation that the Crisis Staff of the municipality of Prijedor decided to use the premises of the Keraterm RO/work organisation/ in Prijedor to accommodate captured persons under the supervision of the employees of the SJB [Public Security Station] and the Military Police of Prijedor.[21]

In other words, the local elite in Prijedor propagated a particular version of events surrounding the camps and their establishment. The resulting narrative, in turn, can be described as a stability narrative. According to Sonenshein, 'Stability narratives can be a means of reducing uncertainty by constructing meaning that is familiar'.[22] In Prijedor, the dominant Serb narrative created stability by offering a story—or a set of compass points—that the Serb community could use to make sense of what was happening on the ground. The facts established by the ICTY have necessarily disrupted this stability narrative, which helps to explain why they have often failed to penetrate and gain acceptance. The problem, moreover, is specific neither to Prijedor nor to Serb communities. As Milanović underlines, '... each ethnic group in the former Yugoslavia is still firmly attached to its own version of reality'.[23] Bosnian Croat denial vis-à-vis the 1993 massacre in Ahmići offers a poignant illustration.

31.2.2 Ahmići

Around 05.30 on the morning of 16 April 1993, Bosnian Croat forces attacked a number of areas in the Lašva Valley in Central BiH, including the villages of Ahmići, Šantići, Nadioci, and Pirići. The military assault on Ahmići resulted in the deaths of over 100 Bosniaks. The ICTY has stated that 'A clearer example of "ethnic cleansing" would be difficult to find'.[24] During my fieldwork in BiH between 2008 and 2013, and specifically my fieldwork in Ahmići and Vitez in 2008 and 2009, Bosnian Croat interviewees frequently spoke about the attack on Ahmići in a way that significantly minimized or detracted from the crimes committed.

[20] ibid para 392.

[21] ibid para 384.

[22] S Sonenshein, 'We're Changing—Or Are We? Untangling the Role of Progressive, Regressive and Stability Narratives during Strategic Change Implementation' (2010) 53 Academy of Management Journal 477, 499.

[23] Milanović (n 9) para 257.

[24] *Prosecutor v Miroslav Bralo* (Trial Chamber Sentencing Judgment) ICTY-IT-95-17-T (7 December 2005) para 30.

A common argument put forward was that the offensive was militarily justified because the Bosniaks were proving increasingly troublesome. On 15 April 1993, for example, a commander from the Bosnian Croat Army (HVO), General Totić, was abducted in nearby Zenica,[25] and there were concerns that the Bosnian Army (ABiH) was planning to regain control of the strategically important road linking the towns of Busovača and Vitez.[26] While the ICTY initially rejected the idea that the attack on Ahmići had a military justification,[27] the Appeals Chamber ultimately took a different view. Tihomir Blaškić was the HVO commander in the Central Bosnian Operative Zone, which included Ahmići. Part of Blaškić's appeal against his forty-five-year sentence, handed down by the Trial Chamber in 2000, centred on a military order (D269) that he had issued on 16 April 1993 at 01.30. According to the Trial Chamber, this was 'very clearly an order to attack'.[28] The Appeals Chamber, however, maintained that there was a 'military justification' for Blaškić to issue order D269[29]—and hence it was a 'lawful' order.[30] It noted, in particular, that 'additional evidence admitted on appeal shows that there was a Muslim military presence in Ahmići and the neighbouring villages, and that the Appellant had reason to believe that the ABiH intended to launch an attack along the Ahmići-Šantići-Dubravica axis'.[31]

If the operation itself was militarily justified, the crimes committed during the attack were not.[32] In the *Kordić* trial, for example, the Trial Chamber emphasized that 'The HVO did not restrict themselves to shooting the men of military age. They also shot women and children'.[33] Indeed, two of the Bosniak men whom I interviewed in Ahmići both lost their mothers in the attack; and a thirteen-year-old boy who subsequently testified at the ICTY witnessed the killing of his parents and eleven-year-old sister.[34] Yet, Bosnian Croat interviewees in Ahmići and Vitez often glossed over these crimes. Embracing a strongly defensive narrative, they insisted that only armed men were targeted in the attack on Ahmići.[35]

Some interviewees, nevertheless, did acknowledge that heinous crimes were committed in Ahmići and they expressed their deep regret. However, they consistently distanced local Bosnian Croat forces from these crimes and instead blamed either 'outsiders'—typically from Herzegovina—or a few lone individuals.[36] It is the case that some prisoners were

25 *Prosecutor v Tihomir Blaškić* (Trial Chamber Judgment) ICTY-IT-95-14-T (3 March 2000) para 402.

26 ibid.

27 According to the *Kordić* judgment, for example, 'The assertion that this attack was justified strategically, defensively, or in any other way, is wholly without foundation: such defenders as were available were taken completely by surprise and any defence put up thereafter was rudimentary, as the results of the day show'. *Prosecutor v Dario Kordić and Mario Čerkez* (Trial Chamber Judgment) ICTY-IT-95-14/2-T (26 February 2001) para 642. Similarly, in the *Kupreškić* case, the Trial Chamber was 'satisfied, on the evidence before it in this case, that this was not a combat operation. Rather, it was a well-planned and well-organised killing of civilian members of an ethnic group, the Muslims, by the military of another ethnic group, the Croats'. *Prosecutor v Zoran Kupreškić, Mirjan Kupreškić, Vlatko Kupreškić, Drago Josipović, Dragan Papić, and Vladimir Šantić* (Trial Chamber Judgment) ICTY-IT-95-16-T (14 January 2000) para 749.

28 *Blaškić* (n 25) para 437.

29 *Prosecutor v Tihomir Blaškić* (Appeals Chamber Judgment) ICTY-IT-95-14-A (29 July 2004) para 333.

30 ibid para 335.

31 ibid para 333.

32 ibid 438.

33 *Kordić* (n 27) para 633.

34 *Bralo* (n 24) para 37.

35 This narrative, moreover, resonated beyond the Lašva Valley. In Stolac and Široki Brijeg in Herzegovina, for example, five male interviewees who had fought in the HVO similarly maintained that no innocents were killed in the attack on Ahmići.

36 Clark (n 13) 101.

released from the Kaonik prison to take part in the attack.[37] What they participated in, however, was a highly organized and co-ordinated military operation[38] that extended far beyond individuals and went to the top of the military hierarchy.[39] As to the idea that those involved were outsiders, the Appeals Chamber in *Blaškić* found that the crimes committed in Ahmići were carried out by members of the 4th Military Police Battalion and the '*Džokeri*' (Jokers), the Battalion's anti-terrorist sub-group.[40] Both formations were established and operated within the Central Bosnian Operative Zone.

Further problematizing the 'outsiders thesis', the Appeals Chamber in *Kordić* decided that 'a reasonable trier of fact could have concluded beyond reasonable doubt that Kordić, as the responsible regional politician, planned, instigated and ordered the crimes which occurred in Ahmići on 16 April 1993 and its associated hamlets ... '.[41] Despite this, Bosnian Croat interviewees widely praised Kordić (and Blaškić) as a war hero who was defending his people. Indeed, when Kordić was granted early release in 2012, a crowd of several hundred well-wishers were waiting to welcome him at Zagreb airport. Among these supporters were church leaders and politicians,[42] including Zdravko Tomac and Zvonimir Šaparović.[43] Five days later, Tomac—who served as Deputy Prime Minister of Croatia between August 1991 and June 1992—described Kordić as the 'biggest victim of these persecutions and trials [at the ICTY]'.[44] Kordić was not a war criminal, he insisted, but rather an innocent man who had heroically accepted his victimhood and become a 'stronger believer', sending 'messages of peace and love' from his prison cell.[45] This is the reason, he claimed, that so many people came to greet Kordić at Zagreb airport. Strongly emphasizing the suffering of Bosnian Croats in Central BiH, Tomac accused the ICTY of issuing false indictments against only one side—the Croatian nation—and he lambasted 'fake anti-fascists' who speak only about crimes committed by Croats.[46]

Four years earlier, in 2010, the then Croatian President, Ivo Josipović, travelled to Sarajevo and apologized for Croatia's wartime policies.[47] Significantly, he also visited Ahmići and paid tribute to the victims. His actions, however, provoked a harsh response

[37] According to the *Bralo* judgment, Mirsolav Bralo was released from the Kaonik prison on 15 April 1993, 'on the condition that he agreed to participate in an attack on the village of Ahmići to be carried out the following day by forces of the Croatian Defence Council ("HVO"). Upon his release, he was taken to a building known as the "bungalow" that was being used as the headquarters of the "Jokers" ... He thereupon became a member of the "Jokers" and was given weapons and a uniform'. Bralo (n 24) para 10.

[38] Blaškić himself conceded that the attack must have been organized. *Blaškić* (n 25) para 431. The Appeals Chamber noted that: 'the Appellant argues that the pertinent issue is not *whether* the crimes in question were planned and ordered, but rather *who* planned and ordered them, and that no evidence at trial allowed the Trial Chamber to conclude beyond reasonable doubt that he planned and ordered the crimes'. *Blaškić* (n 29) para 311.

[39] *Blaškić* (n 25) para 393.

[40] *Blaškić* (n 29) para 374.

[41] *Prosecutor v Dario Kordić and Mario Čerkez* (Appeals Chamber Judgment) ICTY-IT-95-14/2-A (17 December 2004) para 700.

[42] D Anastasijević, 'Requiem for a Transition' (*ICTJ*, 18 June 2014) <https://www.ictj.org/debate/article/requiem-transition> accessed 2 June 2017.

[43] M G, 'Dario Kordić stigao u Zagreb: Policija privela osobu koja mu je vikala da je ubojica i sotona' (6 June 2014) <http://dnevnik.hr/vijesti/svijet/dario-kordic-danas-izlazi-na-slobodu-nakon-vise-od-16-godina-zatvora---339187.html> accessed 31 May 2017.

[44] Z Tomac, 'Dario Kordić je nevin bio u zatvoru' (13 June 2014) <https://www.hrvatski-fokus.hr/index.php/unutarnja-politika/10997-dario-kordic-je-nevin-bio-u-zatvoru> accessed 30 January 2020.

[45] ibid.

[46] ibid.

[47] S Arslanagić, 'Josipović Delivers Unprecedented Apology to Bosnia' (*Balkan Transitional Justice*, 14 April 2010) <http://www.balkaninsight.com/en/article/josipovic-delivers-unprecedented-apology-to-bosnia> accessed 17 May 2017.

from the right-wing Croatian Democratic Union (HDZ), which is once again in power. The then Croatian Prime Minister, Jadranka Kosor, stressed that Croatia was 'never the aggressor' and only fought a defensive war.[48] The former Prime Minister, Hrvoje Šarinić, echoed this.[49] In short, notwithstanding the ICTY's important work and judgments, 'defence narratives' remain strong and intact. To reiterate, moreover, such narratives are not confined to only one ethnic group. As the ICTY Prosecutor, Serge Brammertz, underlined in a speech in Mostar in July 2016, politicians and public figures across the former Yugoslavia 'repeat nationalist slogans of the past, treat war criminals as heroes, and deny atrocities for political gain'.[50]

The examples of Prijedor and Ahmići illustrate this chapter's central argument, namely that factual truths alone rarely provide a sound basis for reconciliation. When the subject of the past remains a deeply divisive subject, any 'facts' established will necessarily be open to contestation and challenge. The next section conceptually develops this argument, as a starting point for re-thinking the relationship between truth and reconciliation.

31.3 A Conceptual Perspective on Truth Contestation

Some images evoke 'multi-stable perception'. This occurs 'when sensory information is ambiguous and consistent with two or more mutually exclusive interpretations'.[51] The classic example of Rubin's Vase—developed by the Danish psychologist Edgar Rubin in the early twentieth century—highlights this. Looking at the image, our perception repeatedly oscillates between two particular interpretations; we alternately see a vase and two faces in silhouette.[52] Relatedly, when dissimilar images are shown to each eye, this can result in 'binocular rivalry', whereby 'one eye's view dominates for several seconds, only to be replaced in conscious awareness by the other eye's view'.[53] If a single pair of eyes may struggle to decipher exactly what they have seen, another layer of complexity is introduced when multiple pairs of eyes are involved. The concept of the inverted spectrum is helpful for illustrating this point. Commonly attributed to John Locke, the inverted spectrum is quintessentially about multi-perspectival seeing.[54] Often used in relation to colour, it emphasizes that

[48] I Bancroft, 'The Dynamics of Apology and Forgiveness in the Balkans' (*RFE/RL*, 27 April 2010) <https://www.rferl.org/a/The_Dynamics_Of_Apology_And_Forgiveness_In_The_Balkans/2025889.html> accessed 4 May 2017.

[49] ibid; these criticisms led Josipović to backtrack and claim that he had not apologized but had simply expressed regret about the war. Balkan Transitional Justice, 'Josipović Faces Criticism for Bosnia Speech' (*Balkan Transitional Justice*, 16 April 2010) <http://www.balkaninsight.com/en/article/josipovic-faces-criticism-for-bosnia-speech/1460/23> accessed 30 April 2017.

[50] S Brammertz, 'Statement 2016 Mostar Connection Peace Award' (23 July 2016) <http://www.icty.org/x/file/Press/Statements%20and%20Speeches/Prosecutor/160725_prosecutor_brammertz_mostar.pdf> accessed 1 May 2017.

[51] P Sterzer, A Kleinschmidt, and G Rees, 'The Neural Bases of Multistable Perception' (2009) 13 Trends in Cognitive Science 310, 310.

[52] See T Owoseye, 'The Dress, Rubin's Vase, Young Lady and Old Lady and Other Famous Illusions' (*International Business Times*, 27 February 2015) <http://www.ibtimes.co.uk/thedress-rubins-vase-young-lady-old-lady-other-famous-optical-illusions-1489764> accessed 28 May 2017.

[53] A Polonsky, R Blake, J Braun, and D J Heeger, 'Neuronal Activity in Human Primary Visual Cortex Correlates with Perception during Binocular Rivalry' (2000) 3 Nature Neuroscience 1153, 1153.

[54] In his *Treatise on Human Understanding*, for example, Locke considered the possibility that 'the same object should produce in several men's minds different ideas at the same time; e.g. if the idea that a violet produced in one man's mind by his eyes were the same that a marigold produced in another man's, and vice versa'. Cited in J Verdi, *Fat Wednesday: Wittenstein on Aspects* (Philadelphia 2010) 272. See (n 27).

individuals can perceive colour in very different ways. As Harman notes, '... it is conceivable that two people should have similarly functioning visual systems despite the fact that things that look red to one person look green to the other, things that look orange to the first person look blue to the second, and so forth'.[55]

By analogy, 'facts' and 'truth' can similarly take on different shades and hues depending on who is looking at them—and, more particularly, depending on which ethnic group is looking at them. During my fieldwork in Vukovar in eastern Croatia in 2011, for example, Serb interviewees repeatedly referred to the events of 1991 as a 'civil war' (*građanski rat*), while Croat interviewees always used the terminology of 'Serb aggression'.[56] Similarly, while Croat interviewees focused on the siege of Vukovar (August–November 1991), Serb interviewees wanted to speak about events leading up to it—including the threats that they had endured and the pressures that they had faced to leave Vukovar.[57] During my work in Kosovo in 2012 and 2013, ethnic Albanian interviewees frequently referred to the killing of their ethnic kin in Raçak/Račak, on 15 January 1999, as one of the clearest examples of Serb aggression during the war in Kosovo.[58] Kosovo Serb interviewees, in contrast, maintained that the 'massacre' was a set-up, cynically orchestrated to give the North Atlantic Treaty Organization (NATO) a pretext to bomb Serbia.[59] Fundamentally, 'facts' about the past are open to interpretation, and interpretation necessarily occurs within—and is informed by—a wider social context.

This social context can be viewed, in part, as a highly fragmented 'memory landscape' in which rival memory narratives—constructed by 'memory entrepreneurs'—compete and jostle for space.[60] These narratives, moreover, often assume a physical form. Morrisey and Gaffikin emphasize that '... in contested places, space can be, in part, a canvas inscribed with recurrent chapters of rival narratives and grievance ...'.[61] The use of political murals in Northern Ireland—with images conveying Catholic/Republican narratives and Protestant/Loyalist narratives respectively—is a case in point.[62] In the former Yugoslavia, the co-option of space for the purpose of memory politics is particularly evident in BiH. In the centre of Ahmići, a simple white memorial in front of the donja džamija (lower mosque) lists the names of those who were killed in the attack on the village on 16 April 1993. A short walk away, in front of the Catholic church, a large brown cross stands in memory of the '653 Croats' who were killed during the 'Muslim siege of Vitez'.[63] In eastern BiH, the Potočari

55 G Harman, 'The Intrinsic Quality of Experience' (1990) 4 Philosophical Perspectives 31, 33.

56 J N Clark, 'The ICTY and Reconciliation in Croatia: A Case Study of Vukovar' (2012) 10 Journal of International Criminal Justice 397, 413.

57 ibid. See also E Stover, *The Witnesses: War Crimes and the Promise of Justice in The Hague* (University of Pennsylvania Press 2007) 146.

58 In the ICTY's first instance judgment against Vlastimir Đorđević—the former Assistant Minister of the Serbian Ministry of Internal Affairs—the Trial Chamber found that '... not less than 45 Kosovo Albanians were killed in Račak/Raçak on 15 January 1999, including a woman and a child. At least one victim had been decapitated. Most of those killed were over 50 years of age. Many had been shot in the head apparently at close range. Those killed were wearing civilian clothes when killed'. *Prosecutor v Vlastimir Đorđević* (Trial Chamber Judgment) ICTY-IT-05-87/1 (23 February 2011) para 416.

59 Clark (n 13) 168.

60 N Moll, 'Fragmented Memories in a Fragmented Country: Memory Competition and Political Identity-Building in Today's Bosnia and Herzegovina' (2013) 41 Nationalities Papers 910, 912.

61 M Morrissey and F Gaffikin, 'Planning for Peace in Contested Space' (2006) 30 International Journal of Urban and Regional Research 873, 875.

62 B Rolston, 'The War of the Walls: Political Murals in Northern Ireland' (2004) 56 Museum International 38.

63 J N Clark, 'Reflections on Trust and Reconciliation: A Case Study of a Central Bosnian Village' (2012) 16 International Journal of Human Rights 239, 246.

Memorial Centre visually conveys the scale of the Srebrenica genocide in July 1995. The white gravestones of the dead extend as far as the eye can see; the length of the huge wall of names is overwhelming. In the nearby Serb village of Kravica, a counter-memorial commemorates 'Serb victims of the civil war'.[64] Local Serbs honour their own war dead on 12 July, one day after the official annual commemorations to the victims of Srebrenica. As Dimova notes, this creates a situation of 'divided memories and separate narratives in two neighbouring villages ... '.[65]

Memorials can be seen as physical impediments to the social penetration of factual truths established by the ICTY. Behind these physical impediments, however, are more ideational barriers. Particularly useful for exploring the ideational context in which the ICTY's work has been viewed and assessed on the ground is the concept of meta-affect. To illustrate the idea of meta-affect—or affect about affect—Goldin uses the example of fear. While fear is most obviously a negative state, in certain circumstances it can bring pleasure. For example, 'People flock to horror movies. They enjoy amusement park rides, where the more terrifying the roller coaster experience, the more exhilarating and "fun" it is'.[66] Fear and enjoyment closely overlap in these situations, Goldin suggests, because there is no real danger. Individuals on the rollercoaster know that they are safe, and this '*permits the fear to occur in a meta-affective context of excitement and joy.* The more afraid the rider feels, the more wonderful she feels *about* her fear'.[67] If, however, something goes wrong and the roller coaster riders are left dangling in the air for several hours, the sense of fear changes. In short, 'This fear feels entirely different, because the *meta-affect* has changed. Even if the person is really in no danger, the removal of the *belief* that she is safe changes the nature of the affective state—no longer does it feel wonderful to feel so afraid'.[68] Emotions are thus affected and influenced by the meta-affective context. This context, in turn, operates in close symbiosis with beliefs.

Goldin uses the term 'belief structure' to refer to 'a set of mutually consistent, mutually reinforcing, or mutually supportive beliefs and warrants ... in the individual, mainly cognitive but often incorporating supportive affect'.[69] While he distinguishes these belief structures from what he calls 'belief systems'—that is to say 'an elaborate or extensive belief structure that is socially or culturally shared'[70]—the two are intermeshed. Highlighting this is the fact that within the former Yugoslavia, individual beliefs about the wars, about the crimes committed, about who did what to whom, exist within—and are shaped by—wider belief systems. Ethnic narratives form a critical part of these belief systems and they typically have a blocking function; they block and obstruct any rival narratives that challenge them. In other words, they are 'constraining narratives',[71] and they set the parameters

[64] P B Miller, 'Contested Memories: The Bosnian Genocide in Serb and Muslim Minds' (2006) 8 Journal of Genocide Research 311, 321.

[65] R Dimova, 'Memory in Peril: Srebrenica as a "Commemorative Arena"' in A von Oswald, A Schmelz, and T Lenuweit (eds), *Erinnerungen in Kuktur und Kunst: Reflexionen über Krieg, Flucht und Vertreibung in Europa* (Verlag 2009) 103.

[66] Goldin (n 3) 62.

[67] ibid.

[68] ibid.

[69] ibid 64.

[70] ibid.

[71] M R Hill and V Thomas, 'Strategies for Racial Identity Development: Narratives of Black and White Women in Interracial Partner Relationships' (2000) 49 Family Relations: Interdisciplinary Journal of Applied Family Studies 193, 196.

for individual beliefs. Every year on 5 August, for example, thousands of Croats celebrate Operation 'Storm' (*Oluja*), a military operation that liberated swathes of Croatian territory seized by Serb forces in 1991. This led to a mass exodus of Krajina Serbs from Croatia.[72] Moreover, numerous crimes—including murder and inhumane acts—were committed against members of the Serb population.[73] The annual celebrations of the Croatian army's military victory, however, completely gloss over these crimes, which have no place in the dominant political narrative. Speaking in Knin on 5 August 2016, for example, Croatian President Kolinda Grabar Kitarović proudly declared that: '"Storm" was a politically justified, ethically pure and brilliant military operation that completed the liberation of Croatian national territory. It was an honourable victory for a just cause'.[74] If a country's leaders expound a glorified and air-brushed version of events, the space for alternative beliefs and interpretations is necessarily narrowed.

Significantly, beliefs, according to Goldin, 'establish *metaaffective contexts* for the experience of emotion connected to the beliefs'.[75] In the former Yugoslavia, commonly-held beliefs about the war establish a meta-affective context wherein people feel that they are right to adhere to those beliefs. Like the aforementioned Zdravko Tomac, they feel that they are showing their patriotism, loyalty to the nation, and support for 'war heroes' who have been unjustly convicted. When the former Bosnian Serb leader Momčilo Krajišnik returned home to BiH in 2013, for example, several thousand Serbs were waiting to welcome him in Pale.[76] Miodrag Kovačević, the president of the municipal committee of the Serb Democratic Party (SDS) in Pale, insisted that 'Krajišnik was "dungeoned" in The Hague and England [where Krajišnik served his sentence] because of Republika Srpska, not because of himself'.[77] Not only is Krajišnik thus depicted as a victim who has been deeply wronged, but Kovačević's reference to Republika Srpska detracts from Krajišnik's individual wrongdoing and cements the idea that the Tribunal punishes entire ethnic groups.[78] Discourse around the collectivization of guilt, in turn, has contributed to fuelling negative beliefs about the Tribunal, thereby strengthening the broader meta-affect. According to Goldin, meta-affect

[72] See *Prosecutor v Ante Gotovina, Ivan Čermak, and Mladen Markač* (Trial Chamber Judgment) ICTY-IT-06-90-T (15 April 2011) vol II, para 1712.

[73] Ante Gotovina (the overall operational commander of southern Krajina during Operation Storm), Mladen Markač (the commander of the Special Police of the Ministry of the Interior of the Republic of Croatia), and Ivan Čermak (the commander of the Knin Garrison) stood trial for these crimes. The Trial Chamber sentenced Gotovina and Markač to prison terms of twenty-four years and eighteen years respectively (Čermak was acquitted). Although the Appeals Chamber ultimately overturned these convictions, it did not say that crimes against Serbs were not committed. Rather, it held that the appellants were not responsible for them. It underlined, for example, that 'in order to link Markač to the crimes of persecution, murder, inhumane acts, plunder of public and private property, wanton destruction, or cruel treatment, his relationship to the Special Police must be established'. *Prosecutor v Ante Gotovina and Mladen Markač* (ICTY Appeals Chamber Judgment) ICTY-IT-06-90-A (16 November 2012) 147.

[74] S Milekić, 'Croatian Politicians Celebrate Operation Storm Victory' (*Balkan Transitional Justice*, 5 August 2016) <http://www.balkaninsight.com/en/article/croatian-politicians-praise-operation-storm-victory-08-05-2016> accessed 30 April 2017.

[75] Goldin (n 3) 69.

[76] Krajišnik was sentenced to twenty-seven years' imprisonment in 2006 for crimes against humanity (reduced on appeal to twenty years in 2009). *Prosecutor v Momčilo Krajišnik* (Appeals Chamber Judgment) ICTY-IT-00-39-A (17 March 2009) para 818–19.

[77] E M Jukić, 'Bosnian Serbs Welcome Home Freed Wartime Politician' (2 September 2013) <http://www.balkaninsight.com/en/article/pale-prepares-to-welcome-momcilo-krajisnik> accessed 5 May 2017.

[78] As Touquet and Vermeersch argue, '... the view that individualization [of guilt] is a straight-forward instrument to achieve reconciliation among ethnic collectives ignores the social and political reality surrounding the individual cases ... '. H Touquet and P Vermeersch, 'Changing Frames of Reconciliation: The Politics of Peace-Building in the Former Yugoslavia' (2016) 30 East European Politics and Societies 55, 59.

'can be strong enough to ensure that even careful, intelligent, rational believers will find warrants to retain their beliefs in the face of apparently contravening evidence or experience'.[79] Hence, meta-affect—and the persistence of constraining ethnic narratives that feed the meta-affective context—has been a serious impediment to the facts established by the ICTY. That these facts remain fiercely contested necessarily has broader implications for reconciliation.

If the ICTY's trials have had little positive impact on inter-ethnic reconciliation in the former Yugoslavia,[80] this chapter maintains that the long-term legacy of its work can potentially aid the process indirectly. For this to happen, what is crucial is an altering of the meta-affective context, thereby diluting the power of competing ethnic narratives. This is far from straightforward. As DeBellis and Goldin underline, meta-affect is 'usually powerful and stable'.[81] In particular, meta-affect stabilizes belief structures, which in turn suggests that the simple presentation of new facts is unlikely to weaken those beliefs. Accordingly, it is necessary to look beyond factual truths. Meernik and Guerrero maintain that:

> The legal and historical truths that emerge in the judicial record can help advance reconciliation because they begin a process of allowing victims to achieve closure through an officially sanctioned effort to ascertain who was responsible for their suffering.[82]

This chapter, in contrast, posits that it is meta-normative truths that present the strongest challenge to meta-affective context and provide the most solid basis for reconciliation.

31.4 Meta-normative Truths and Reconciliation

'Reconciliation' is a widely-used term in transitional justice and post-conflict societies, yet it is not always clear what exactly the process of reconciliation involves. According to Taylor et al, reconciliation is 'the dynamic process of reconstructing the torn social fabric that results from protracted conflict'.[83] Such a definition, however, is overly broad. What does it mean to reconstruct the 'torn social fabric'? How do we reconstruct it? The definition that Méndez proposes is similarly wide. He understands reconciliation to mean 'the long-term setting aside of disputes between factions that have divided a nation'.[84] While he further explains that reconciliation should not be 'a strained and hypocritical truce between victimizers and victims',[85] this still leaves us asking major questions about the essence of reconciliation. Where Méndez is more definitive is on the point that truth does not inevitably lead to reconciliation. For him, the challenge is to ascertain 'which elements of truth, justice, and

[79] Goldin (n 3) 69.

[80] Clark (n 13).

[81] V A DeBellis and G A Goldin, 'Affect and Meta-Affect in Mathematical Problem Solving: A Representational Perspective' (2006) 63 Educational Studies in Mathematics 131, 136.

[82] J Meernik and J R Guerrero, 'Can International Criminal Justice Advance Ethnic Reconciliation? The ICTY and Ethnic Relations in Bosnia-Herzegovina' (2014) 14 Southeast European and Black Sea Studies 383, 390.

[83] L K Taylor, M Nilsson, and B Amezquita-Castro, 'Reconstructing the Social Fabric Amid Ongoing Violence: Attitudes Toward Reconciliation and Structural Transformation in Colombia' (2016) 4 Peacebuilding 83, 84.

[84] J E Méndez, 'National Reconciliation, Transnational Justice and the International Criminal Court' (2001) 15 Ethics and International Affairs 25, 28.

[85] ibid.

clemency measures are compatible with one another ... and with the search for reconciliation.'[86] He makes clear that the relationship between these elements depends on situational variables. If, therefore, reconciliation is, at least in part, a contextual concept, it follows that it cannot be easily pinned down and labelled.

One label that is often used in relation to reconciliation, however, is the label of 'thick' and 'thin'. According to Meernik et al, 'There are what we might term "thicker" definitions and meanings of reconciliation that entail active work on the part of all concerned to forge new relationships, tolerate and accept the presence of others, and accept truths of the past.'[87] In contrast, 'Thinner definitions might involve individuals merely getting along and avoiding violence.'[88] I have always leaned towards 'thicker' conceptualizations of reconciliation. Specifically, I have defined reconciliation as the repair and restoration of relationships and the re-building of trust.[89] Such a definition can itself only take us so far. It is necessary to ask a more elemental question, namely what does reconciliation look like? More concretely, what are the visible signs of reconciliation and how do we know when it exists? Reconciliation is partly an internal process. As Bar-Siman-Tov maintains, reconciliation 'asks for deep cognitive change, a real change of beliefs, ideology and emotions ... '.[90] The internal dynamics of reconciliation, however, are exteriorized and expressed in more outward ways. Speaking in The Hague on 11 July 2016, for example, the ICTY President, Judge Carmel Agius, stressed that justice is not sufficient for reconciliation. For him:

> Equally important are the processes of coming together – all three ethnicities of this country [BiH] – and acknowledging the past; grieving together; communicating with open hearts and minds; engaging in real dialogue; looking to the future; and committing yourselves to ensuring that what happened here 21 years ago will never happen again.[91]

This idea of 'coming together' is an intrinsic part of reconciliation in a 'thick' sense. Reconciliation, thus understood, is integrally about creating a shared space that enables former enemies—or people from opposing conflict groups—to come together and ultimately realize that they have something in common with each other. The armed conflict in Colombia, for example, has persisted for more than fifty years. In November 2016, the Colombian government signed a revised peace agreement[92] with the Revolutionary Armed Forces of Colombia (FARC). Long before the signing of this peace accord, however, some erstwhile adversaries had made peace with each other. At the El Cielo restaurants in Bogotá and Medellín, ex-combatants from different sides in the conflict work together.[93] A former

[86] ibid 29.

[87] J Meernik, N Golčevski, M McKay, A Feinberg, K King, and R Krastev, 'Truth, Justice and Education: Towards Reconciliation in the Former Yugoslavia' (2016) 16 Southeast European and Black Sea Studies 413, 416.

[88] ibid.

[89] Clark (n 63) 240; Clark (n 13) 6; J N Clark, 'Reconciliation through Remembrance? War Memorials and the Victims of Vukovar' (2013) 7 International Journal of Transitional Justice 116, 118.

[90] Y Bar-Siman-Tov, 'Introduction: Why Reconciliation?' in Y Bar-Siman-Tov (ed), *From Conflict Resolution to Reconciliation* (Oxford University Press 2004) 4.

[91] ICTY, 'Judge Carmel Agius President U.N. International Criminal Tribunal for the Former Yugoslavia' (11 July 2016) <http://www.icty.org/x/file/Press/Statements%20and%20Speeches/President/160711_president_agius_srebrenica_en.pdf> accessed 28 April 2017.

[92] The first agreement was rejected in a referendum held on 2 October 2016.

[93] A S Peláez, 'Chef Juan Manuel Barrientos: Creating Dishes, and Peace, in Colombia' (*NBC News*, 20 June 2016) <http://www.nbcnews.com/news/latino/chef-juan-manuel-barrientos-concocting-dishes-peace-colombia-n593736> accessed 16 May 2017.

soldier from the Colombian army, Rubén Darío Romero, lost his eye and part of his leg due to a landmine planted by the FARC. He now works alongside a former female FARC guerrilla, and this has helped to change his views of FARC members and the crimes that they committed. In Romero's words, 'Many have been obligated to join up, others because they wanted to. But I know that I can forgive, and we can work together to create a friendship from that point on'.[94] The El Cielo restaurants, in short, have created valuable opportunities for former enemies to humanize each other, to get to know each other, and to develop understanding for each other.

To use an example from the African continent, the genocide in Rwanda in 1994 devastated the country's economy. Victims and perpetrators have therefore needed to work together in pursuit of the common goal of making ends meet. Rwanda's developing speciality coffee industry is a case in point. As Boudreaux notes:

> In the post-genocide environment, [coffee] farmers did not have the luxury of working only with members of their ethnic group ... Only by working together with those who were left could these small-scale farmers take advantage of economies of scale, improve their chances of getting funding to build washing stations, and attract the attention of foreign buyers interested in the speciality coffee market. By working together, farmers found they were better able to target the increasingly lucrative 'speciality' market for coffee.[95]

Cooperation itself is a 'thin' form of reconciliation. However, it provides a basis on which to build 'thicker' forms. If people have similar interests and goals, cooperation can potentially bring them to the realization that more fundamental similarities between them also exist, such as family or moral values. The recognition of shared commonalities and the development of these commonalities are integral parts of any reconciliation process. In the powerful Second World War story of *The Boy in the Striped Pyjamas*, the fact that nine-year-old Bruno is German necessarily makes him different from Shmuel, a Jewish boy of the same age. Accentuating this difference is the fact that a barbed wire fence (the perimeters of the extermination camp in which Shmuel is held) permanently separates them. When Bruno ultimately climbs under the fence and dons a pair of the 'striped pyjamas' that Shmuel and all of the other Jews in the camp are wearing, the artificially-created differences between them disappear; 'If it wasn't for the fact that Bruno was nowhere near as skinny as the boys on this side of the fence, and not quite so pale either, it would have been difficult to tell them apart. It was almost (Shmuel thought) as if they were all exactly the same really'.[96] While this is not an example of reconciliation per se, the important point is that once the two boys are on the same side of the fence, they are in a new shared space where they can see their similarities.

If reconciliation is about the creation of shared spaces and enabling people to find commonalities, this raises the key question of whether truth can foster reconciliation. This chapter has argued that factual truths by themselves are not readily conducive to reconciliation because they are deeply divisive. As Chapman and Ball accentuate:

[94] V Colectivo, 'A Colombian Recipe for Peace and Reconciliation' (*Americas Quarterly*, 2015) <http://www.americasquarterly.org/content/colombian-recipe-peace-and-reconciliation> accessed 16 May 2017.

[95] K Boudreaux, 'The Business of Reconciliation: Entrepreneurship and Commercial Activity in Post-Conflict Rwanda' (2011) 27 Economic Affairs 6, 11.

[96] J Boyne, *The Boy in the Striped Pyjamas* (Definitions 2008) 206.

> At the least, facts may be 'loaded' with different meaning when considered from divergent perspectives. An event leading to fundamental abuses of human rights may be recollected and interpreted quite differently by various victims . . . let alone by a victim and a perpetrator.[97]

If factual truths are thus problematic, it is argued that there should be a greater emphasis within transitional justice on meta-normative truths—or higher-level truths—about morality and war. Such truths provide the strongest basis for reconciliation because they are most likely to foster cross-ethnic consensus and agreement. A crucial reason for this lies in 'processing fluency', a concept that is typically discussed in a linguistic context.

According to Dechêne et al, 'Processing fluency is defined as the metacognitive experience of ease during information processing; it may be elicited, for example, by linguistic ease, perceptual ease, semantic priming, or retrieval ease'.[98] Some information can be processed more easily than others. As one illustration, 'watching a film at the cinema is more visually fluent than watching the same film on a small black and white television from the far end of a large room'.[99] Higher levels of processing fluency can be associated with meta-normative truths as opposed to factual truths. This is because the former, unlike the latter, transcend ethnic belonging. Meta-normative truths are not about who did what to whom, but about human suffering and the (im)morality of particular behaviours and conduct in war. The cognitive task of processing these truths is therefore closer to the 'effortless' end of the continuum than the 'highly effortful' end.[100] This, in turn, has wider implications for reconciliation. If, as Dechêne et al maintain, 'A statement that is processed more fluently is typically more likely to be judged true',[101] this means that meta-normative truths have greater potential to bring people together than to divide them.

Following its creation in 1993, the ICTY established numerous factual truths. Judicial processes, however, are not only exercises in fact-finding. They also have an important normative dimension, and what has been critically neglected to date are the vital spaces for normative discussions about the conflicts in the former Yugoslavia that the ICTY's work opened. This point can be illustrated using the example of guilty pleas. In total, twenty defendants pleaded guilty at the ICTY,[102] and these admissions have often been seen as factually significant. According to the Tribunal's website, for example, guilty pleas 'greatly contributed to the establishment of facts', and the statements that have often accompanied these pleas 'corroborate the evidence collected by the Tribunal's investigators to contribute to an irrefutable account of some of the events that occurred in the wars of the 1990s'.[103] On the ground, in contrast, guilty pleas have often proven controversial. Negative examples—most notably the case of Biljana Plavšić[104]—have helped to cement

97 A R Chapman and P Ball, 'The Truth of Truth Commissions: Comparative Lessons from Haiti, South Africa and Guatemala' (2011) 23 Human Rights Quarterly (2011) 1, 6.

98 Dechêne et al (n 2) 240.

99 A L Alter and D M Oppenheimer, 'Uniting the Tribes of Fluency to Form a Metacognitive Nation' (2009) 13 Personality and Social Psychology Review 219, 220.

100 ibid.

101 Dechêne et al (n 2) 240.

102 ICTY, 'Guilty Pleas' <http://www.icty.org/en/cases/guilty-pleas> accessed 28 May 2017.

103 ICTY (n 7).

104 Plavšić, one of the wartime Bosnian Serb leaders, pleaded guilty in 2002 to persecutions on political, racial, and religious grounds (crimes against humanity). She was sentenced to eleven years' imprisonment. Subotić notes that 'A few years after her confession, however, Plavšić retracted her most significant admissions, and in a two

the idea that defendants' expressions of remorse and regret are self-interested rather than genuine.[105]

Debates regarding the use of plea bargains, however, should not reductively focus only on defendants' motives for pleading guilty, or on the factual utility of such pleas. Defendants' guilty statements raise broader questions for discussion and thereby create a basis for the development of consensual meta-normative truths. In July 2005, for example, Miroslav Bralo—a member of the aforementioned 'Jokers' in the Lašva Valley area of Central BiH—pleaded guilty to crimes against humanity, grave breaches of the 1949 Geneva Conventions and violations of the laws or customs of war.[106] In his guilty statement, Bralo reflected:

> I tried to be proud of my actions and to think they were the actions of a successful soldier. Today I am ashamed of all of that, ashamed of my conduct and ashamed how I behaved. No, these were not the actions of the soldier I once wanted to be. I was present when women and children were gunned down in front of me, and at that moment the good soldier in me was gone, silent.[107]

Regardless of whether or not Bralo's words were sincere, his statement raises important questions that merit attention. In particular, what constitutes a 'successful' and 'good' soldier in war? What are the actions and behaviours that soldiers can be justly proud of? Such questions can be discussed and debated in the context of 'a higher-order impartiality'[108] that exists over and above ethnic and nationalist politics. The point is not to inculpate particular individuals or groups, but rather to reach a cross-ethnic consensus that certain actions—such as the gunning down of women and children—are morally indefensible regardless of who commits them.

Dragan Obrenović was the chief of staff and deputy commander of the 1st Zvornik Infantry Brigade of the Drina Corps of the Bosnian Serb Army (VRS). In May 2003, he pleaded guilty to crimes against humanity in Srebrenica.[109] In his guilty statement, he emphasized how the war destroyed relations between neighbours. In his words:

> At the beginning of the war, it seemed as if the war and all it brought with it was impossible, that this wasn't really happening to us, and that everything would be resolved within a few days, and that finally our generation would have a chance. We didn't even notice how we were drawn into the vortex of inter-ethnic hatred and how neighbours were no longer able

volume memoir published in 2005, made a series of claims that not only directly contradicted her ICTY confession, but reiterated a particularly hard-line, nationalist worldview that showed little, if any, rehabilitation and political change'. J Subotić, 'The Cruelty of False Remorse: Biljana Plavšić at The Hague' (2012) 36 Southeastern Europe 39, 40.

105 Clark (n 13) 65–67.

106 Bralo was sentenced to twenty years' imprisonment. *Prosecutor v Miroslav Bralo,* (Appeals Chamber Judgment on Sentencing Appeal) ICTY-IT-95-17-A (2 April 2007).

107 ICTY, 'Miroslav Bralo' (7 October 2005) <http://www.icty.org/en/content/miroslav-bralo> accessed 29 April 2017.

108 T Nagel, 'Moral Conflict and Political Legitimacy' (1987) 16 Philosophy and Public Affairs 215, 216.

109 In December 2003, Obrenović was sentenced to a prison term of seventeen years. See *Prosecutor v Dragan Obrenović* (Sentencing Judgment) ICTY-IT-02-060/2-S (10 December 2003).

> to live beside each other, how death moved into the vicinity, and we didn't even notice that we had got used to it. Death became our reality.[110]

What strongly emerges from this is that the concept of 'neighbourliness' in pre-war BiH was 'thicker' than simply peaceful co-existence. In Obrenović's words, 'In Bosnia, a neighbour means more than a relative. In Bosnia, having coffee with your neighbour is a ritual, and this is what we trampled on and forgot'.[111] Obrenović's statement thus invites deeper reflection on the notion of neighbourliness and on what it means to be a good neighbour. The restoration of neighbourliness—and of shared neighbourhood spaces—is potentially a step towards the restoration of deeper inter-ethnic (and intra-ethnic) relations.[112]

The late Milan Babić was the president of the Republic of Serbian Krajina in northeastern Croatia. After pleading guilty to crimes against humanity in January 2004, he committed suicide two years later.[113] In his powerful statement of guilt, he underlined that:

> [T]he fact that we all belong to the same human race is more important than any differences, and I have come to understand that only through friendship and confidence we can live together in peace and friendship, and thus make it possible for our children to live in a better world.[114]

These words powerfully convey a deep meta-normative truth with which few could disagree, namely that children should grow up and live in a world free of hatred and war. One of the many ICTY judgments that has reinforced this meta-normative truth is the *Tolimir* Trial Chamber judgment, which details, inter alia, the suffering of women, children, and the elderly who were forcibly displaced from Srebrenica in July 1995. It stresses that 'Some of the children have been unable to process what has happened'.[115] The *Karadžić* judgment describes how in Rogatica, in eastern BiH, 'girls as young as seven, as well as a thirteen-year-old boy, were taken out of the classrooms [in the Veljko Vlahović Secondary School] almost every night for a period of two and a half months and raped by the police and soldiers who guarded the camp'.[116]

Fundamentally, the Tribunal's work has opened a vital space for important debates focused around meta-normative truths. These 'truths about truths' go beyond the facts of what happened. Rather, they are broader, higher-level truths; and precisely because they operate at this meta level, they can potentially influence the aforementioned meta-affective context. It will be recalled that meta-affective context is about the emotions connected with beliefs. For example, if a community continues to support a defendant who has been convicted of committing/ordering rape, this will generate a particular meta-affective context that entrenches the collective view of that individual as a victim. If, however, the same

110 ICTY, 'Dragan Obrenović' (30 October 2003) <http://www.icty.org/en/content/dragan-obrenovi%C4%87> accessed 29 April 2017.

111 ibid.

112 C Sorabji, 'Bosnian Neighbourhoods Revisited: Tolerance, Commitment and Komšiluk in Sarajevo' in F Pine and J de Pina-Cabral (eds), *On the Margins of Religion* (Berghahn Books 2008) 108.

113 Babić was sentenced to eleven years' imprisonment. See *Prosecutor v Milan Babić* (Judgment on Sentencing Appeal) ICTY-IT-03-72-A (18 July 2005).

114 ICTY, 'Milan Babić' (27 January 2004) <http://www.icty.org/en/sid/208> accessed 29 April 2017.

115 *Prosecutor v Zdravko Tolimir* (Trial Chamber Judgment) ICTY-IT-05-88/2 (12 December 2012) para 757.

116 *Prosecutor v Radovan Karadžić* (Trial Chamber Judgment) ICTY-IT-95-5-5/18 (24 March 2016) para 990.

community is encouraged to focus on the broader meta-normative truth, and to agree that rape is a heinous crime that should never be tolerated, this could help to positively alter the meta-affective context. It is not the case, therefore, that meta-normative truths are more important than factual truths. The crucial point, rather, is that meta-normative truths can facilitate the social penetration of factual truths.

As part of its long-lasting legacy, the ICTY has laid the foundations for the development of meta-normative truths around which broad-based cross-ethnic agreement and consensus might be reached. To the extent that such truths constitute an 'ideological cohesive',[117] they have significant potential—which remains strikingly under-explored—to aid and foster processes of reconciliation. The Tribunal's Outreach Section engaged, to some extent, with local communities, most notably through its 'Bridging the Gap' series;[118] and it also worked directly with young people through its Youth Outreach Programme.[119] While this valuable work primarily focused on the crimes committed in specific communities and the prosecution of these crimes, a crucial extension of these outreach activities would have been—and could still be—the organization of wider public debates and discussions, aimed at generating constructive inter-ethnic dialogue around the pertinent normative questions and meta-normative truths that have naturally emerged from the Tribunal's work. Politicians, academics, non-governmental organizations, victims' associations, and journalists have a key role to play in initiating and facilitating these debates, and thereby developing the Tribunal's legacy in a promising new direction.

31.5 Conclusion

According to Méndez, 'Spelled out in more positive terms, a policy to deal with the past is necessary, if not sufficient, to obtain reconciliation ... It is not so much that the policy, to be successful, should settle once and for all conflicting interpretations of history; it should establish a basis of facts that cannot be honestly denied'.[120] Meernik and Guerrero have similarly underlined the importance of facts. Their working assumption is that the Tribunal has 'contributed to improving attitudes about reconciliation through its roles in delivering legal and historical truths regarding who did what to whom in the Balkan wars ... '.[121] They do also acknowledge, however, that the existence of these truth-reconciliation linkages cannot be stated 'with absolute conviction'.[122] This chapter, in contrast, has sought to question and challenge the idea that facts provide a sound basis for reconciliation. Emphasizing the contestability of factual truths, and exploring this idea both empirically and conceptually, it has focused on the notion of meta-normative truths. One step removed from the political controversies and 'messiness' of who did what to whom, meta-normative truths can be

[117] R A Wilson, *The Politics of Truth and Reconciliation in South Africa: Legitimizing the Post-Apartheid State* (Cambridge University Press 2001) xv.

[118] ICTY, 'Bridging the Gap with Local Communities' <http://www.icty.org/en/outreach/bridging-the-gap-with-local-communities> accessed 2 May 2017.

[119] N Jelačić, 'Building a Legacy: The Youth Outreach Program at the ICTY' in C Ramírez-Barat and R Duthie (eds), *Transitional Justice and Education: Learning Peace* (Social Science Research Council 2017) 261–89. See also ICTY, 'Youth Outreach' <http://www.icty.org/en/outreach/youth-outreach> accessed 3 May 2017.

[120] Méndez (n 84) 33.

[121] Meernik and Guerrero (n 82) 403.

[122] ibid.

viewed as a form of 'truth analytics'. If, as Gandomi and Haider argue, 'Text analytics (text mining) refers to techniques that extract information from textual data';[123] 'truth analytics' is quintessentially about extracting higher-level normative truths from the judicial record. This chapter has argued that important meta-normative truths can be extracted from the ICTY's work and used as a starting point for creating shared discursive spaces. As part of its long-term legacy, thus, there is still scope for the Tribunal to contribute, indirectly, to reconciliation if the meta-normative truths implicit in its work are given more attention and actively utilized in reconciliation efforts on the ground. More broadly, the significance of meta-normative truths necessarily extends beyond the ICTY. Extracting these truths from wider processes of dealing with the past, and examining their potential to bring divided communities together, represent important new directions for transitional justice scholarship and practice.

[123] A Gandomi and M Haider, 'Beyond the Hype: Big Data Concepts, Methods and Analytics' (2015) 35 International Journal of Information Management 137, 140.

Name Index

Note: *For the benefit of digital users, indexed terms that span two pages (e.g., 52–53) may, on occasion, appear on only one of those pages.*
Tables are indicated by *t* following the page number

Subject Index

Note: *For the benefit of digital users, indexed terms that span two pages (e.g., 52–53) may, on occasion, appear on only one of those pages.*
Tables and figures are indicated by *t* and *f* following the page number